The WORLD

Combined Volume

A HISTORY

Felipe Fernández-Armesto

TUFTS UNIVERSITY

PEARSON

Prentice Hall

MAPS BY

DORLING KINDERSLEY

Upper Saddle River, NJ 07458

Library of Congress Cataloging-in-Publication Data

Fernández-Armesto, Felipe
  The world: a history / Felipe Fernández-Armesto.
    p. cm.
  "Combined volume"
  Includes bibliographical references and index.
  ISBN 0-13-113499-X
    1. Civilization—History. 2. Human ecology. I. Title.
CB151.F48 2007
909—dc22

2006010708

Editorial Director: Charlyce Jones Owen

Executive Editor: Charles Cavaliere

Editorial Assistant: Maureen Diana

Editor in Chief, Development: Rochelle Diogenes

Senior Development Editor: Gerald Lombardi

Development Intern: Jaya Bharne

Senior Media Editor: Deborah O'Connell

Director of Marketing: Brandy Dawson

Senior Marketing Manager: Emily Cleary

Regional Campaign Manager: Halee Dinsey

Marketing Assistant: Jennifer Lang

VP/Director of Production and Manufacturing: Barbara Kittle

Senior Managing Editor: Joanne Riker

Production Project Manager: Kathy Sleys

Production Assistants: Marlene Gassler, Barbara Silver, Kristen Sleys

Manufacturing Manager: Nick Sklitsis

Manufacturing Buyer: Ben Smith

Creative Design Director: Leslie Osher

Cover Design: Leslie Osher/Kathy Mrozek

Interior Design: Kathy Mrozek, Ilse Lemesis

Map Program Management: Gail Cocker-Bogusz, Scott Garrison

Cover Illustration: Corrin Skidds

Director, Image Resource Center: Melinda Reo Patelli

Manager, Rights and Permissions: Zina Arabia

Manager Visual Research & Permissions: Karen Sanatar

Image Permission Coordinator: Craig A. Jones

Photo Researcher: Emma Brown

Composition/Full-Service Project Management: Caterina Melara, Prepare, Inc.

Printer/Binder: Courier Companies, Inc.

Cover Printer: Phoenix Color Corporation

About the Cover The two globes that grace the covers of *The World*—one depicting the eastern hemisphere, the second showing the western—are comprised of hundreds of details from historical images spanning human history from the first global migrations to iPods.

Though the story of *The World* is a human story, it is also the story of people's close interaction with their environment, the climates that shape their cultures, and other life-forms that depend on or compete with men and women. The mosaic of images on each globe—with each image roughly corresponding to its region of origin—is intended to show these relationships in action. In addition, each of the book's volumes only feature images that generally match up with the time span covered.

We hope that these covers are just the beginning of your deeper exploration of *The World*. To learn more about the cover images, please visit **www.prenhall.com/armesto.**

Maps designed and produced by DK Education, a division of Dorling Kindersley Limited, 80 Strand London WC2R 0RL. DK and the DK logo are registered trademarks of Dorling Kindersley Limited.

Credits and acknowledgments borrowed from other sources and reproduced, with permission, in this textbook appear on appropriate page within text or on page C-1.

Pearson Education Ltd.
Pearson Education Australia PTY, Ltd.
Pearson Education Singapore, Pte. Ltd.
Pearson Education North Asia Ltd.

Pearson Education, Canada, Ltd.
Pearson Educación de Mexico, S.A. de C.V.
Pearson Education–Japan
Pearson Education Malaysia, Pte. Ltd.

10 9 8 7 6 5 4 3 2
ISBN 0-13-113499-X

BRIEF CONTENTS

iii

CONTENTS

PART 2 Farmers and Builders, 5000 to 500 B.C.E. 60

3

Interactions matter. Societies learn from each other, compete with each other, and exchange culture. Isolation retards. 90

The Great River Valleys: Accelerating Change and Developing States 62

PART 3   The Axial Age, from 500 B.C.E. to 100 C.E.   156

6

66 The thought of the modern world has a familiar ring to a student of the axial age. It seems astonishing that today, after all the technological and material progress of the last 2,000 years, we remain so dependent on the thought of such a distant era and have added so little to it. 99   187

The Great Schools   158

7

66 Routes of commerce are the lifelines of empires: pumping them with resources, equipping them with new ideas and technologies, laying down tracks for their armies to follow. 99   193

The Great Empires   190

PART 4 Fitful Transitions, from the Third Century to the Tenth Century   230

After battlefield victories, cultural conflicts usually follow. Even where the so-called barbarians defeated the empires, they tended to get conquered in their turn by the cultures of their victims.   265

Postimperial Worlds: Problems of Empires in Eurasia and Africa, ca. 200 C.E. to ca. 700 C.E.   232

9

❝ *Even as they changed the societies in which they triumphed, the new religions changed in their turn, compromising with vested interests, modifying their messages to suit mighty patrons, serving the needs of warriors and kings, even becoming organs of the state, instruments of government, means of training bureaucrats, and communicating with subjects.* ❞ *293*

The Rise of World Religions: Christianity, Islam, and Buddhism   268

10

    ❝ *History is like climate, in which numerous cycles of varying duration all seem to be going on all the time, and where random or almost random changes frequently intervene.* ❞ *329*

Remaking the World: Innovation and Renewal on Environmental Frontiers in the Late First Millennium   298

PART 5   Contacts and Conflicts, 1000 C.E. to 1200 C.E.   336

11

    ❝ *In the pre-industrial world, the size of states and the scope of economies were functions of time as well as distance. Messages, armies, revenues, and cargoes took a long time to travel across broken country or, by sea, through variable winds.* ❞ *370*

Contending with Isolation: ca. 1000–1200   338

12

❝ The hostility of nomads and farmers arose, perhaps, less from conflicts of interest than from mutual misunderstanding: a clash of cultures, incompatible ways of seeing and coping with the world. ❞ 401

The Nomadic Frontiers: The Islamic World, Byzantium, and China ca. 1000–1200   372

13

❝ Without the Mongol peace, it is hard to imagine any of the rest of world history working out quite as it did, for these were the roads that carried Chinese ideas and transmitted technology westward and opened up European minds to the vastness of the world. ❞ 435

The World the Mongols Made   410

14

66 *Climate and microbes belong to two rebellious realms of nature that resist human power.* 99 *442*

The Revenge of Nature: Plague, Cold, and the Limits of Disaster in the Fourteenth Century   440

15

66 *An age of expansion really did begin, but the phenomenon was of an expanding world, not as some historians say, of European expansion. The world did not wait passively for European outreach to transform it, as if touched by a magic wand. Other societies were already working magic of their own, turning states into empires and cultures into civilizations.* 99 *483*

Expanding Worlds: Recovery in the Late Fourteenth and Fifteenth Centuries   480

CONTENTS

16

❝ *We recoil from the idea that any political community should be subject to another: it seems to go against our respect for principles we call "freedom" or "self-determination." But in the period from the sixteenth century to the eighteenth, when the unprecedented growth of empires was one of the most dramatic features of the history of the world, empires spread as much by collaboration as by conquest. . .* ❞ *531*

17

❝ *What historians call "the Columbian Exchange",—the transfer of plants, animals, and microbes among the Americas, Eurasia, and Africa—ought to be regarded as the biggest revolution ever effected on Earth by human agency.* ❞ *566*

18

It would be wrong to speak of the rise of science at the expense of religion. There is no necessary conflict between the two, and no one in the sixteenth or seventeenth centuries, so far as we know, even suspected that there could be. 629

Mental Revolutions: Religion and Science in the Sixteenth and Seventeenth Centuries   598

19

Slavery kept black and white people in mutual fear and loathing, driving black rebels to horrific or despairing acts to find refuge or gain revenge, and trapping colonial governments in inhuman policies of rage and repression. 662

States and Societies: Political and Social Change in the Sixteenth and Seventeenth Centuries   634

PART 8 Global Enlightenments, 1700–1800   672

20

The New World made the West big. A culture crammed, for most of its history, into a small, remote, and beleaguered corner of Eurasia now had much of the western hemisphere, the Pacific, and Africa at its disposal. 700

Driven by Growth: The Global Economy in the Eighteenth Century   674

21

Painstakingly recruited, thinly spread, colonists began to extend the limits of the inhabited world. At the edges of empires to which they belonged, where they reached out to touch the outposts of other expanding peoples, they helped to mesh the world together. 705

The Age of Global Interaction: Expansion and Intersection of Eighteenth-Century Empires   702

22

Like all topics in the history of thought, the Enlightenment is complex and elusive. We had better begin by admitting that and relishing the challenge. 738

The Exchange of Enlightenments: Eighteenth-Century Thought   736

PART 9   The Frustrations of Progress to ca. 1900   768

24

Technology widened a wealth gap between the regions that supplied commodities and those that turned them into manufactured goods. These worldwide inequalities were hugely bigger, and would prove more enduring for the future, than the internal class differences that divided industrializing societies. 839

The Social Mold: Work and Society in the Nineteenth Century 808

25

European world dominance was, by the standards of world history, a brief phenomenon. In the twentieth century, European empires would collapse as spectacularly and as quickly as they had arisen. Meanwhile, even under imperialism, people continued to make their own history. 873

Western Dominance in the Nineteenth Century: The Westward Shift of Power and the Rise of Global Empires 842

28

Freedom is ill equipped to cope with extremism because it allows its own enemies to organize and agitate and because it hesitates to proclaim its own authority as absolute. Fanatics have the appeal of certainty in an uncertain world. 966

29

It is tempting to characterize the twentieth century as a century of paradox. Frustrated hopes coincided with unprecedented progress. Utopias nourished moral sickness, suicide, and crime. The century of democracy was the century of dictators. 1022

30

❝ What are we going to do with our world? It is, so far, the only we have to live in. ❞ 1050

The Embattled Biosphere: The Twentieth-Century Environment 1024

FUEL RESOURCES **1029**

FOOD OUTPUT **1031**

URBANIZATION **1036**

THE CRISIS OF CONSERVATION **1038**

THE UNMANAGEABLE ENVIRONMENT: CLIMATE AND DISEASE **1041**

■ IN PERSPECTIVE: The Environmental Dilemma **1046**

GOING TO THE SOURCE
Rival Black Voices in the Twentieth Century **1052**

MAPS

A CLOSER LOOK

GOING TO THE SOURCE

Dear Reader,

History is stories. There are hundreds of tales in this book about real, flesh-and-blood people—commoners and kings, sons and mothers, heroes and villains, the famous and the failed. I try to combine them in two narratives that criss-cross throughout the book. One is the story of how people connect and separate, as cultures take shape and influence and change one another. Alongside this story, there is another one of how humans interact with the rest of nature—other species, the unstable natural environment, the dynamic planet.

History is global. The whole world stays in view in almost every chapter. Readers can compare and connect what was happening in every region and every continent in every period—like observers from another galaxy, gazing at the world from outer space and seeing it whole.

History is universal. This book tries to say something about every sphere of life—including science and art and thought and suffering and pleasure and imagination.

History is a problem-posing discipline. This book is full of provocations, contested claims, debated speculations, open horizons, and questions too complex and too interesting to answer easily. I wield facts not just for their own sake but also to make my readers—and myself—think.

History is evidence. Readers of this book confront the sources on every page—the words, images, and objects people really used in the past—to reveal vivid pictures of what history looked like and what it felt like to live in the past.

History enhances life. I've written believing that a textbook can be entertaining, even amusing, as well as instructive and accessible; challenging without being hostile; friendly.

History isn't over. This book is about how the world got to be the way it is, confronting present problems and perspectives for the future—which is, after all, only the past that hasn't yet happened.

A text that gives students the whole story

The World is a new kind of history text. Not just a collection of facts and figures, *The World* offers a truly holistic narrative of the world, from human beginnings to the present. All aspects of the text—from the exceptionally clear narrative that always places the story in time, to the unparalleled map program, to the focused pedagogical features—support the story. Because of the author's breadth of vision, students will come away with a deep understanding of the fundamental interrelationships—among peoples and their environments—that make up the world's story.

discovered at Wuyang (woo-yahng) in China, which are thousands of years older, bear marks that we can only explain as part of a system of symbolic representation.

Instead of restricting our definition of writing, we ought to feel awe at the adventure of combining isolated symbols to tell stories and make arguments. But familiarity disperses awe. Some cultures may have taken thousands of years to make this leap, even while they used writing systems for other purposes, such as labels, oracles, bureaucracy, and magic charms.

CHRONOLOGY
(All dates are approximate)

5000–2000 B.C.E.	Four Great River Valley civilizations develop: Middle and Lower Nile, Egypt; Indus and Saraswati Rivers; Tigris and Euphrates Rivers, Mesopotamia; Yellow River, China
4000 B.C.E.	Shaduf invented in Egypt
3000 B.C.E.	Menes unites Upper and Lower Egypt
2500 B.C.E.	Cities of Harappa and Mohenjodaro flourish; Sargon of Akkad conquers Sumer
2250–2000 B.C.E.	Ziggurat of Ur built
2000–1000 B.C.E.	Shang dynasty, China
1800 B.C.E.	*Epic of Gilgamesh* written down
1700 B.C.E.	Law code of Hammurabi

IN PERSPECTIVE: What Made the Great River Valleys Different?

Still, the fact remains that, thanks in part to their use of writing, the civilizations of the four great river valleys—or, at least, the three whose writings we can decipher—are, to us, the best-known of their time. For that reason, not because of their supposed influence on other peoples, they fairly occupy so much space in books like this one. Studying their written works helps us identify at least two reasons for the cultural divergence of the era, of which they are extreme examples. First, in part, divergence was environmentally conditioned. That is, the greater or more diverse the resource base, the bigger and more durable the society it feeds. The great river valleys were large, continuous areas of fertile, easily worked soil, and for farming societies, exploitable land is the most basic resource of all. Environmental diversity gave the river valley peoples extra resources, compared with civilizations in less privileged regions. Egypt had the Nile delta at hand. In the Yellow River and Yangtze valleys, China had two complementary ecological systems. Mesopotamia had a hinterland of pastures, and Mesopotamia and Harappa had access to each other by sea.

Second, interactions matter. Societies learn from each other, compete with each other, and exchange culture with each other. The more societies are in touch with other societies, the more these activities occur. By contrast, isolation retards. Egypt was in touch with Mesopotamia and Mesopotamia with Harappa. China's relative isolation perhaps helps explain its late start in some of the common processes of change that these societies all experienced. All these societies enclosed, within their own bounds, relatively large zones of exchange. But all were remarkably self-contained. As we shall see in the next chapter, however, travel and trade were increasingly important. These were the means of communicating the cultures from the great river valleys to other regions, some of which were less environmentally fortunate. Invasions and migrations, too, were—and still are—effective forms of interaction because they shift many people around, and people carry their culture with them.

The grandeur of the great river valley civilizations raises questions about their sustainability. Their wealth and productivity excited envy from outsiders and invited attack. Continued population growth demanded ever more intensive exploitation of the environment. At the same time, climates and ecosystems continued to change. The vast collective efforts required for irrigation, storage, and monumental building left huge classes of people oppressed and resentful of elites. As a result of these and other stresses, beginning around 1500 B.C.E., transformation or collapse threatened all these societies. Meanwhile, peoples in less easily exploitable environments found the will and means to reproduce, challenge, or exceed the achievements of these four civilizations. The question of how well they succeeded is the focus of the next chapter.

"Instructors are constantly on the lookout for textbooks that show that history is not about facts and dates but about fitting those facts into persuasive interpretations. Fernández-Armesto's *The World* is perhaps the one textbook that makes this aspect of the discipline of History most explicit."
—*Jorge Cañizares-Esguerra, University of Texas—Austin*

"I particularly like the emphasis on total history because it indicates the commonality of human beings—an aspect of human history that is lost in the usual focus on national or civilizational histories."
—*Alison Games, Georgetown University*

"This text marks a new generation of world history texts that challenge older models of world history to produce an integrative analysis of exchanges between and within cultures."
—*Sharlene Sayegh, California State University— Long Beach*

"The global perspective shows up especially strong… This is a smart, innovative text in its approach and writing."
—*Stephen Morillo, Wabash College*

A unified narrative built around a clear chronology

An integrated approach to history permeates *The World*, beginning with the chronological table of contents. Organized into ten parts and thirty chapters, the text provides a clear and unified narrative of world history.

CONTENTS

"This text not only treats the appropriate issues of a comparative, global approach to world history, it does so in a style that is convincing, clearly structured, and a pleasure to read."
—*Donald R. Abbott, San Diego Mesa College*

"This is a very intelligent text that will finally take world history courses beyond the old 'civilization of the week' approaches."
—*Donald Leech, University of Minnesota*

"*The World* has a lively writing style, is truly global, and integrates environmental and cultural history. As far as textbooks go, I very much liked this one and look forward to using it in my class."
—*David M. Kalivas, Middlesex Community College*

"I like his organization… He told great stories."
—*Student, California State University—Long Beach*

"I liked how he put chapters into chronological order."
—*Student, California State University—Sonoma*

"… I found it very easy to read the chapters because it grouped them by subject matter."
—*Student, Pennsylvania State University*

A master historian and storyteller

The World presents the compelling story of humankind with remarkable clarity and vision. Perhaps the most striking feature of *The World* is the distinct voice of author Felipe Fernández-Armesto. A renowned writer and thinker, Fernández-Armesto's dynamic voice comes through in every line of text, chapter title, and photo caption. His prose is clear and eloquent, his arguments logical, and his writing passionate. Fernández-Armesto emphasizes asking the right questions over providing set-in-stone answers. His writing brings history to life through richly nuanced stories and sparkling details that will stay with students long after they've turned the pages.

A street in Melbourne, Australia, has restaurants representing a vast range of world cuisines. Here, without turning a corner, one can experience the importance of tomatoes in the meals of Bengal in northern India and of peanuts in Malay cooking. Within a few doors' space, diners can confirm that hot chillies are prominent in the food of Thailand and Chinese Sichuan, and cassava in that of parts of West Africa. A few paces, farther on, you find how potatoes are essential at table in Ireland or northern Europe, while chocolate and vanilla are vital in French pastry. Yet before the sixteenth century, no one had ever tasted any of these ingredients in the lands that became their adopted homes. All originated in the Americas and were unknown in Europe or Asia before the sixteenth century. Indispensable items on an Italian menu are gnocchi and polenta—made from native American plants: respectively potatoes and maize (or "corn" in everyday American usage). Jerusalem artichokes originated in North America, not Jerusalem. The turkey was first recorded in Mexico, not Turkey. The pineapple was unknown in Europe until Columbus encountered and described it during his first transatlantic journey.

Fernández-Armesto opens every chapter with a vignette that encapsulates a main theme of the chapter.

Moreover, the Englightenment was global in its inspiration, as well as its effects. A great deal of debate among historians has focused on the problem of where the Enlightenment started. England, Scotland, France, and the Netherlands all have their partisans. In some ways, we can trace its origins all over northern and Western Europe. This debate misses the more fundamental contribution made by the interaction of Western European thought with ideas from overseas, and, in particular, from China. Like all topics in the history of thought, the Enlightenment is complex and elusive. We had better begin by admitting that and relishing the challenge it presents.

The best way to approach the Enlightenment may be by first telling a story that expresses its character better than any attempt at a dictionary-style definition. We can then look at the global exchange of influences that surrounded enlightened ideas, the key texts that encoded them in Europe, and the changes that overtook and—ultimately—transformed the Enlightenment during the eighteenth century.

The author frequently challenges traditional ways of looking at world history, drawing comparisons between cultures across the world, and encouraging discussion.

José Rizal (1861–1896), for instance, the great spokesman of Filipino national-ismin the late nineteenth century, was the best student in Greek at Madrid University in Spain in his day. He was also competent or excellent in Latin, French, English, German, Italian, Dutch, Swedish, and Portuguese, as well as his native Malay and Chinese. He dressed and conversed like a typical upper-class Spaniard. La Solidaridad—one of the cells from which the nationalist movement in the Philippines was formed—was founded in Barcelona in Spain among Filipino students in 1888. Rizal crammed his writings with allusions to classical, Spanish, English, and German literature, but he also searched for inspiration in the poetic traditions of his homeland. He was a hybrid of Europe and Asia—a misfit wherever he went, known in Hong Kong as "the Spanish doctor"and labeled in the Philippines as a "Chinese half-breed." Spanish observers noticed Rizal's patriotic poetry as early as 1879 and identified him as "a man who bears watching, a rare and new kind of man...for whom the mother country is the Philippines, not Spain." He spent his last years in exile, charged with conspiring with other nationalists to make the Philippines independent. The experience only deepened his sense of rootedness in his own country. When he returned to Manila and was shot by the Spaniards as a rebel, he struck out the words "Chinese half-breed" on his death warrant and wrote "pure native" instead.

Fernández-Armesto makes history come alive by weaving the stories of people into the fabric of each chapter.

East meets West. This traveling altarpiece symbolizes Jesuit success in spreading Catholicism in Japan in the late sixteenth century. Imported European sacred paintings like this Madonna inspired Japanese imitators and attracted converts. The altarpiece is lacquered and gilded in Japanese style.
Photograph courtesy Peabody Essex Museum

Forested eastern slopes

Dry coastal river

Grassy plain 13,000 ft. above sea level
Uplands: 10,500–12,500 ft. above sea level
Frost-free valleys 7,500–10,000 ft. above sea level
Lower slopes of mountains: 2,400–7,000 ft. above sea level
Dry coastal region: 2,400 ft. above sea level

FIGURE 4.1 THE ANDEAN ENVIRONMENT packs tremendous ecological diversity into a small space, with various climatic zones at different altitudes, contrasting micro-climates in the valleys, and tropical forest and the ocean close to hand. Maize grows on low slopes, coca and sweet potatoes above it, and potatoes at higher altitudes. The high grassland called puna provides grazing for llamas and their kin.

The author's lively and detailed captions do more than inform—they integrate the text's visual program with the main narrative.

"Felipe Fernández-Armesto is truly a master historian."
—*Alfred J. Andrea, University of Vermont (Emeritus)*

"A fascinating, beautifully written account of the history of the world. It comes close to being the Holy Grail for world history teachers.
—*Patricia Seed, University of California—Irvine*

"The lively, engaging writing style, from beginning to end, succeeds in speaking directly to students and is one of the highlights of the book."
—*Stephen Gosch (Class Tester), University of Wisconsin—Eau Claire*

"The quality of the writing and the intellectual [caliber] of the author is far above the norm for even the best textbooks. It hits just the right mark in being challenging, while also remaining accessible."
—*William Morison, Grand Valley State University*

"[The World] has tremendous strengths, it is very well written, and the author has a good sense of telling anecdotes and human-interest stories. At the same time he has a good sense of thematic understructures that keeps the book moving and allows readers to see that chapters unfold with a purpose."
—*John Thornton, Boston University*

"The author was extremely effective in his explanations, and it almost seemed as if he were explaining something to a friend."
—*Student, Pennsylvania State University*

"...makes me feel like I'm reading an interesting novel or watching a documentary unfold before me."
—*Student, California State University—Long Beach*

"His engaging style was easy to read and made me want to know more."
—*Student, University of Wisconsin—Eau Claire*

"It was almost like reading a novel."
—*Student, Pennsylvania State University*

An unparalleled map program

The World's extensive and integrated map program reinforces the text's unified treatment of world history in both utility and design. Dorling Kindersley, one of the world's most respected cartographic publishers, designed each of the over 200 maps, which were rigorously reviewed for accuracy and clarity. The maps employ innovative perspectives, focus on interaction and change, and pinpoint key places in the narrative.

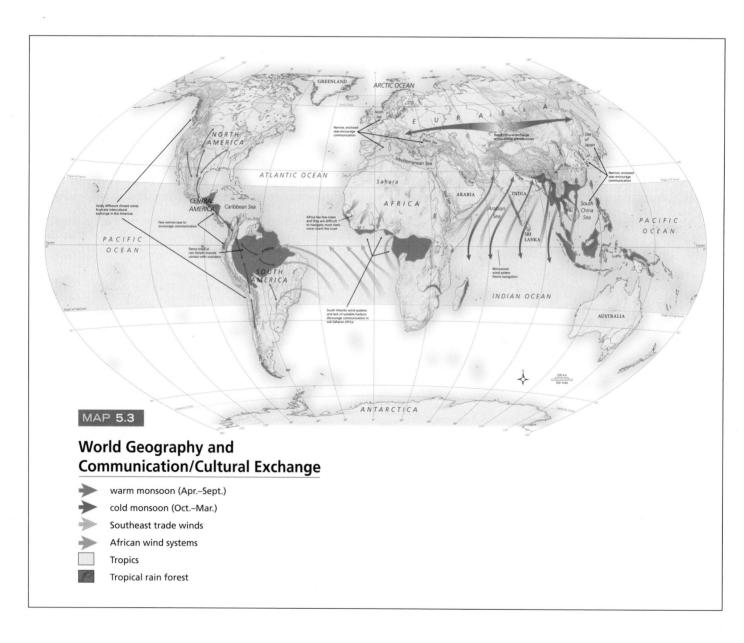

MAP 5.3

World Geography and Communication/Cultural Exchange

➤ warm monsoon (Apr.–Sept.)
➤ cold monsoon (Oct.–Mar.)
➤ Southeast trade winds
➤ African wind systems
▢ Tropics
▨ Tropical rain forest

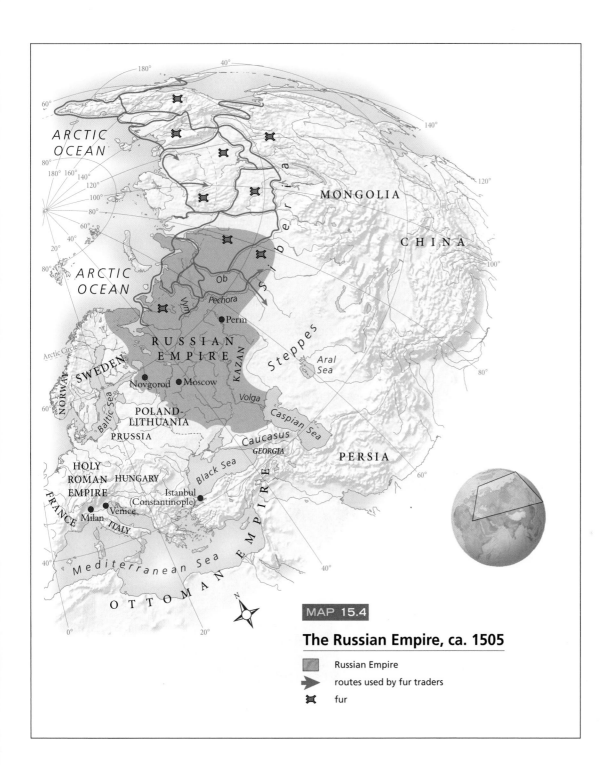

MAP 15.4

The Russian Empire, ca. 1505

▨ Russian Empire

➤ routes used by fur traders

✖ fur

"The maps in *The World* are vastly better than maps in most other textbooks. They have more interesting perspectives, more emphasis on trade routes and connections, and more space devoted to them. The two-page thematic maps are particularly well done."

—Stephen Morillo, Wabash College

"The maps are simply gorgeous! You clearly didn't scrimp on them, and, for me, attractive, provocative maps are a real selling point when I'm considering a text."

—Matthew Redinger, Montana State University—Billings

"The maps are wonderful!"

—Mary Halavais, Sonoma State University

Pedagogy that focuses and enriches

The pedagogical features in *The World* help students engage with the narrative, provide reinforcement for learning, and enrich their study of world history.

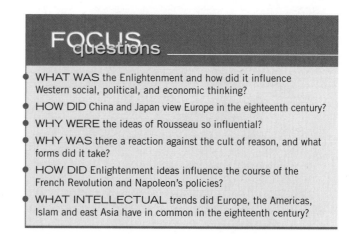

Focus Questions open each chapter and encourage students to think critically while they read. These questions set the stage for the material to come and help students focus on the key concepts of each chapter.

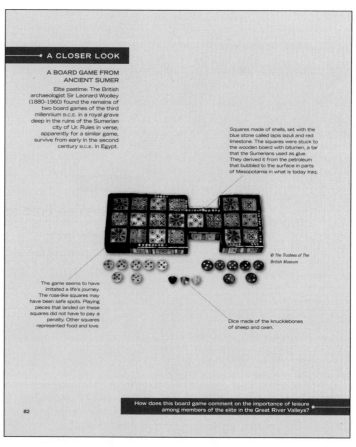

A Closer Look provides in-depth visual analysis of a specific cultural artifact. Detailed notes draw the viewer into close contact with the object, presenting opportunities to pose larger questions.

bolic importance. Nino's location on the south wall, directly opposite Tamar, forms a visual axis between the two women. Any consideration of Tamar's image must take into account its relationship with Nino.

Like Tamar, Nino had to overcome objections to her sex. As the apostolic saint who brought Christianity to the kingdom in the fourth century (see Chapter 9), Nino embodies Georgian Christianity. She is a patriotic figure, beyond the limitations of gender. Her portrait (not shown here) placed opposite Tamar's further deemphasizes Tamar's sex and strengthens Tamar's claim to rule. The ideals of nationhood that Nino represents associate themselves with Tamar, rendering Tamar's femininity irrelevant.

Although the image of Tamar, and that of Nino nearby, stress masculine and gender neutral aspects of royal power, they do not deny Tamar's femininity. Indeed, the depiction of Tamar's face embodies idealized notions of feminine beauty that prevailed in Georgia at that time (Photo 5). Her skin is pale, especially compared to her father's ruddy complexion. Most striking, however, is the smooth oval face and the distinctly oriental shape of her eyes, which are unlike those found on any figure in the church, such as the image of St. Katherine, dressed like Tamar, in Byzantine imperial costume. Katherine's angular face and broad eyes differ sharply from Tamar's (Photo 6).

Thus, in contrast to the Western Christian adornments—Byzantine robe, crown, scepter—that masculinize her power, Tamar's physical beauty derives from Eastern, non–Christian models. Her conspicuously oval face and eyes conform to Persian ideals of feminine beauty, as evidenced by a Seljuk bowl showing a queen from twelfth–century Iran (Photo 7). So, though Tamar's power as ruler is masculine (or defeminized) and Western, her role as an ideal female is Eastern. In a Christian kingdom that straddled the cultural divide between East and West, it was necessary to depict royal power in Christian terms, but it was also acceptable to portray feminine beauty in a non-Christian way. Considered together, Tamar is both king and ideal woman. The nobles who viewed the image of Tamar at Vardzia would have understood the message.

Photo 5 Tamar

MAKING CONNECTIONS

FORAGERS AND FARMERS COMPARED

FORAGERS	FARMERS
Food procurers: Hunt and gather	**Food producers:** Husbandry (breed animals, cultivate crops)
Fit into nature: Little environmental impact	**Change nature:** Herders : some environmental impact Tillers : massive environment impact
Manage the landscape	**Nature remade and reimagined**
Dependence on wild animals and plants	**Interdependence between humans, plants, and animals:** Animals and plants exploited and domesticated
Stable food supply: Nomadic foragers move in response to environmental change; sedentary foragers vulnerable to changes of climate	**Unstable food supply:** Small range of farmed foods increases vulnerability to ecological disasters
Stable population • relatively little labor needed • population control avalable, mainly by managed lactation	**Expanding population** • Breeding livestock and cultivating plants leads to increased food supply • Increased population • Concentrations of domesticated animals spread disease
Stable society • kinship and age fix individual's place in society • sexes usually share labor by specializing in different economic tasks	**Radically changed, unstable society** • Need to control labor and food distribution leads to social inequalities • Work shared between the sexes, increased reliance on female labor • Strong states develop with powerful elites, complex technologies

Going to the Source features at the end of each part examine a key problem in world history using visual and textual primary source documents. Perfect for classroom discussion or assignment, these features are often comparative, allowing students to analyze cultural encounters and exchanges.

Making Connections features throughout the text offer visual summaries of important content. Instead of simply listing facts, these tools help students see the connections that have occurred throughout history.

Cupisnique (koo-pees-nee-keh) gorge. Though the environment was similar, the physical remains suggest a different culture and different politics. Huaca de los Reyes (WA-kah deh los RAY-ess), for instance, had dozens of stucco-fronted buildings and colonnades of fat pillars, each up to 6.5 feet thick, guarded by huge, saber-toothed heads in clay. At Pampa de Caña Cruz (PAM-pah deh KAN-yah krooss), a gigantic mosaic, 170 feet long, made of thousands of fragments of colored rock, represented a similar head. It was embedded in the earth, so that a viewer could only appreciate its shape from a great height—a height the humans who made it could not reach, but their gods, perhaps, could. These regions traded with the nearby highlands, where building on a monumental scale followed soon afterward in the Cajamarca (kah-ha-MAR-kah) valley and the Upper Huallaga (wa-YAH-gah) valley. These sites constitute evidence of extraordinary cultural diversity among connected communities within a fairly small space.

Most Andean experiments in civilization were short lived. With modest technologies, they struggled to survive in unstable environments. **El Niño** (el NEEN-yo)—the periodic reversal of the normal flow of Pacific currents—was always a looming threat. At irregular intervals, usually once or twice a decade, El Niño drenches the region in torrential rain and kills or diverts the

In-Text Pronunciation Guides provide phonetic spellings embedded directly in the narrative that enhance students' ability to verbally discuss unfamiliar material. **Key terms** are defined in a glossary and set in boldfaced type in the text.

"I like the *Going to the Source* sections and can see myself using these very effectively for group and class discussion."
—Linda Bregstein Scherr, Mercer County Community College

"I really like the *A Closer Look* layout... I could see trying to tie those into my lectures and maybe even expanding on some of them."
—David Atwill, Pennsylvania State University

"I liked the layout of each chapter—starting off with good *Focus Questions* and interesting introductions."
—Student, California State University—Long Beach

A compelling visual record

The World provides a compelling visual record of our global history, from mammoth-bone cave huts at the end of the Ice Age to satellite images of the world in the twenty-first century. The illustrations are often part of the narrative, providing a tightly coordinated ensemble of text and visuals. The text's photo researchers searched the archives of the world to find an array of visual evidence never before assembled in a textbook. Experts from across the globe provided assistance on translations and historical context.

The author's image captions offer great detail, reveal fascinating insight, and shed light on problems and parallels in human history.

Astrolabe. The Syrian instrument maker, al-Sarraj engraved his signature on this fine astrolabe in 1230–1231. The purpose of the astrolabe is to assist in astronomy—one of the many sciences in which the Islamic world excelled at the time. By suspending the instrument at eye level and swiveling a narrow central bar until it aligned with any observed star, the user could read the star's elevation above the horizon, as well as such additional information as the latitude, the date, and even the time of day from the engraved discs.
© National Maritime Museum Picture Library, London, England. Neg. #E5555-3

Don Francisco and his sons, leaders of the maroon kingdom of Esmeraldas, who submitted to the Spanish crown by treaty in 1599. A government official commissioned the painting for presentation to King Philip III. The mixed culture of this community of runaway slaves is reflected in the appearance of its leaders:their black faces, their rich clothing in the style of Spanish noblemen, the costly ear and nose ornaments borrowed from Native American tradition.

Chocolate. In this canvas of about 1640—presumably intended to adorn a dining room—the Spanish painter Juan de Zurbarán (1620–1649) exalts chocolate, raising it on a silver pedestal and placing it center stage as if he were painting its portrait. In the seventeenth century, rich Europeans consumed chocolate the way the Aztec elite had—as a luxury beverage. Zurbarán here depicts a truly global experience in conspicuous consumption: expensive chocolate imported to Spain from Mexico is to be drunk in even more costly porcelain cups imported from China.

Gandhi as he wished to be seen. He squats in a traditional position for Indian mystics, working calmly in a scholarly, reflective manner. His gaunt body, modest loincloth, and simply furnished home proclaim his selflessness and asceticism. He adopted a spinning wheel as the symbol of his movement for Indian independence to signify tradition, patience, constructiveness, self-sufficiency, and peace.

An extensive teaching and learning package

The supplements package has been carefully crafted to enhance the instructor's classroom teaching experience and to provide students with resources that enrich the learning process.

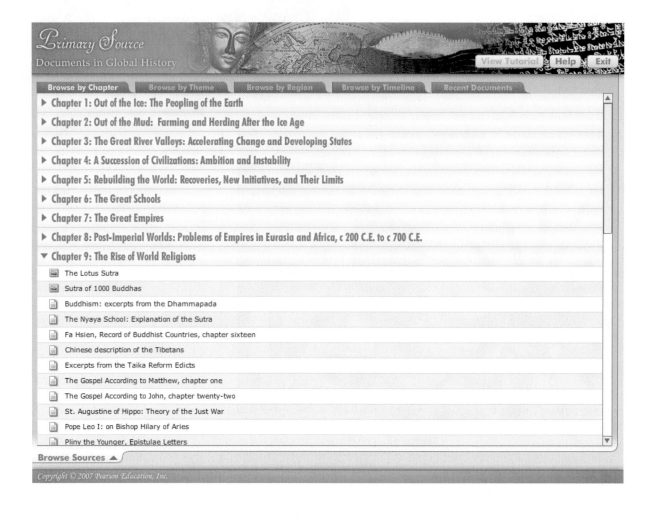

A breakthrough in the use of sources in the world history classroom, the **Primary Source: Documents in Global History CD-ROM** is both an immense collection of textual and visual documents in world history and an indispensable tool for working with sources. Extensively developed with the guidance of historians and teachers, *Primary Source* provides over 300 sources in global history and over 400 visual sources. Many of the visual sources come from the Rare Books Division of the Library of Congress and are available for the first time in published form. All sources—visual and textual—are accompanied by head-notes and focus questions and are searchable by topic, region, time period, or textbook in use. In addition, an interactive tutorial guides students through the process of working with documents. (0-13-134406-4)

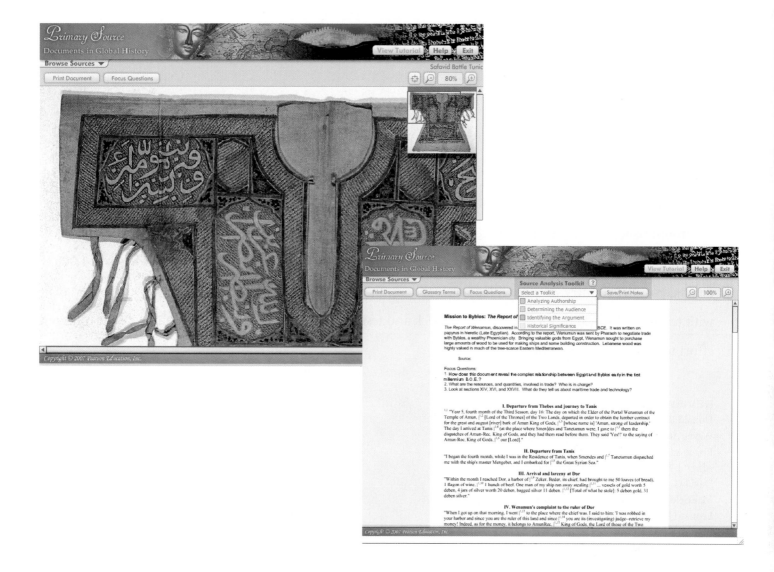

A set of **Transparencies** includes all the maps and figures included in the text, as well as many of the text's photos, for easy projection in the classroom. (0-13-198505-1)

Comprehensive Web Resources (at www.prenhall.com/ armesto) offer access to various online tools for instructors and students that are compatible with CourseCompass, BlackBoard, and WebCT course management systems.

History Notes, Volumes I and II, provide a comprehensive study guide for students, including practice tests, essay questions, and map exercises to help reinforce key concepts. (Volume I, 0-13-173929-8; Volume II , 0-13-228203-8)

The **Instructor's Guide to Teaching The World** provides everything instructors need to incorporate The World into their courses. An extensive Test Item File incorporates feedback and test questions from instructors who class-tested the materials. Sample syllabi, articles on teaching global history from the World History Association (WHA), transition notes, and other resources make teaching The World easy. Organized according to the Focus Questions from the text, the Instructor's Guide includes teaching notes authored by David Ringrose, University of California at San Diego. (0-13-198502-7)

An **Instructor's Resource CD-ROM** offers class presentation resources, including all of the maps and many of the illustrations from the text, PowerPoint presentations, and video clips. (0-13-174204-3)

Developing *The World*

Developing a project like *The World* required the input and counsel of hundreds of individuals. David Ringrose, an experienced world historian from the University of California at San Diego, served as *The World's* editorial consultant, closely reading and commenting on every draft of the book. His experience and understanding of classroom issues were invaluable to the development of *The World*. Nearly 100 reviewers critiqued portions of the manuscript from the first to the final draft. In addition, the manuscript was class-tested with over 1,000 students across the country who provided invaluable feedback and advice. Additionally, ten focus groups were held with teachers of world history to gather feedback and test ideas. We thank all those who shared their time and effort to make *The World* a better book.

REVIEWERS

Donald R. Abbott, San Diego Mesa College
Wayne Ackerson, Salisbury University
Roger Adelson, Arizona State University
Alfred J. Andrea, University of Vermont (Emeritus)
David G. Atwill, Pennsylvania State University
Mauricio Borrero, St. John's University
Leonard Blussé, Harvard University
John Brackett, University of Cincinnati
Gayle K. Brunelle, California State University—Fullerton
Fred Burkhard, Maryland University College
Antoinette Burton, University of Illinois
Jorge Cañizares-Esguerra, University of Texas—Austin
Elaine Carey, St. John's University
Tim Carmichael, College of Charleston
Douglas Chambers, University of Southern Mississippi
Nupur Chaudhuri, Texas Southern University
David Christian, San Diego State University
Duane Corpis, Georgia State University
Dale Crandall-Bear, Solano Community College
Touraj Daryaee, California State University—Fullerton
Jeffrey M. Diamond, College of Charleston
Brian Fagan, University of California—Santa Barbara
Nancy Fitch, California State University—Fullerton
Alison Fletcher, Kent State University
Patricia Gajda, The University of Texas at Tyler
Richard Golden, University of North Texas
Stephen S. Gosch, University of Wisconsin—Eau Claire
Jonathan Grant, Florida State University
Mary Halavais, Sonoma State University
Shah M. Hanifi, James Madison University

Russell A. Hart, Hawaii Pacific University
Phyllis G. Jestice, University of Southern Mississippi
Amy J. Johnson, Berry College
Deborah Smith Johnston, Lexington High School
Eric A. Jones, Northern Illinois University
Ravi Kalia, City College of New York
David M. Kalivas, Middlesex Community College
Frank Karpiel, College of Charleston
David Kenley, Marshall University
Andrew J. Kirkendall, Texas A&M University
Dennis Laumann, The University of Memphis
Donald Leech, University of Minnesota
Jennifer M. Lloyd, SUNY—Brockport
Aran MacKinnon, University of West Georgia
Moria Maguire, University of Arkansas—Little Rock
Susan Maneck, Jackson State University
Anthony Martin, Wellesley College
Dorothea Martin, Appalachian State University
Adam McKeown, Columbia University
Ian McNeely, University of Oregon
Margaret E. Menninger, Texas State University—San Marcos
Stephen Morillo, Wabash University
William Morison, Grand Valley State University
Laura Neitzel, New York University
Kenneth J. Orosz, University of Maine—Farmington
Michael Pavkovic, Hawaii Pacific University
Kenneth Pomeranz, University of California—Irvine
Phyllis E. Pobst, Arkansas State University
Sara B. Pritchard, Montana State University
Norman Raiford, Greenville Technical College
Stephen Rapp, Georgia State University

Vera Blinn Reber, Shippensburg University
Matthew Redinger, Montana State University—Billings
Matthew Restall, Pennsylvania State University
Jonathan Reynolds, Arkansas State University
Richard Rice, University of Tennessee—Chattanooga
Peter Rietbergen, Catholic University (Nijmegen)
David Ringrose, University of California—San Diego
Patricia Romero, Towson University
Morris Rossabi, Queens College
David G. Rowley, University of Wisconsin—Platteville
Sharlene Sayegh, California State University—Long Beach
William Schell, Murray State University
Linda Bregstein Scherr, Mercer County Community College
Patricia Seed, Rice University
Lawrence Sondhaus, University of Indianapolis
Richard Steigmann-Gall, Kent State University
John Thornton, Boston University
Ann Tschetter, University of Nebraska—Lincoln
Deborah Vess, Georgia College & State University
Stephen Vinson, SUNY—New Paltz
Joanna Waley-Cohen, New York University
Anne M. Will, Skagit Valley College
John Wills, University of Southern California
Theodore Jun Yoo, University of Hawaii—Manoa

CLASS TESTERS
Donald R. Abbott, San Diego Mesa College
Robert Anzalone, St. John's University
David Atwill, Pennsylvania State University
Elaine Carey, St. John's University
Stephen Gosch, University of Wisconsin—Eau-Claire
Mary Halavais, Sonoma State University
David M. Kalivas, Middlesex Community College
Tim Milford, St. John's University
Stephen Rapp, Georgia State University
Dan Ringrose, Minot State University
Sharlene Sayegh, California State University—Long Beach
Patricia Seed, University of California—Irvine
Robert Tomes, St. John's University
David Rowley, University of Wisconsin—Platteville

FOCUS GROUP PARTICIPANTS
Wayne Ackerson, Salisbury University
Babtunde Agiri, Norfolk State University
Robin Anderson, Arkansas State University
Robert Anzalone, St. John's University
Robert Arias, East Los Angeles College
Florence Baker, El Camino College
Chris Bierwirth, Murray State University
Mauricio Borrero, St. John's University
Fred Burkhard, University of Maryland—University College
Terri M. Calabrese, Timber Creek High School
Elaine Carey, St. John's University
Cathleen Carroll, Christian Brothers Academy
Chris Chekuri, San Francisco State University
Weikun Cheng, California State University—Chico
Duane Corpis, Georgia State University

Francis Curran, St. John's University
Ernie D'Albero, Red Bank Regional High School
Jim Davis, Mt. San Jacinto College
Thomas W. Davis, Virginia Military Institute
Edward C. de Briffault, St. John's University
George J. Dehner, Northeastern University
Patricia Lopes Don, California State University—San Jose
Gloria Emeagwali, Central Connecticut State University
Stephen Englehart, California State Polytechnic University—Pomona
Bruce Esposito, University of Hartford
Sue Gronewold, Kean State University
Gerald Herman, Northeastern University
Richard Horowitz, California State University—Northridge
Nicole Howard, California State University—East Bay
Aiqun Hu, Northeastern University
Deborah Smith Johnston, Lexington High School
Theodore Kallman, San Joaquin Delta College
Dennis Laumann, University of Memphis
Margot Lovett, Saddleback College
Martiere Lopez, Northeastern University
Kirk Larsen, George Washington University
John Maddox, Los Angeles Valley College
Mary Ann Mahony, Central Connecticut State University
Anupama Mande, Fullerton College
Dorothea Martin, Appalachian State University
Maxim Matusevich , Seton Hall University
Adam McKeown, Columbia University
Timothy Milford, St. John's University
Nathaniel Millett, California State University—Fresno
Eva Mo, Modesto Junior College
Gerard Morin, Northern Essex Community College
Tom Mounkhall, SUNY
Aimee Myers, Sierra College
Jeremy Neill, Northeastern University
Mary A. O'Donnell, St. John's University
Jeanne M. Ostrowski, Brookdale Community College
Chris Padgett, American River College
Charles Perrin, Georgia State University
Sanjeev Rao, Brookdale Community College
Robert Rook, Towson University
Clifford Rosenberg, City College—CUNY
William Seay, J. Sargeant Reynolds Community College
Michael Seth, James Madison University
Bradley Shope, St. John's University
Shumet Sishagne, Christopher Newport University
Itai Sneh, CUNY—John Jay College of Criminal Justice
James Sowerwine, Kutztown University
Mark Spicka, Shippensburg University
George Sussman, CUNY—La Guardia Community College
Rosemary Thurston, New Jersey City University
Robert Tomes, St. John's University
Tiffany Trimmer, Northeastern University
Bridget Turnbach, Freehold Regional High School
Charles Wheeler, University of California—Irvine
Peter Winn, Tufts University
Eloy Zarate, Pasadena City College

About Felipe Fernández-Armesto

Felipe Fernández-Armesto holds the Principe de Asturias chair of Spanish Civilization at Tufts University where he also directs the Pearson Prentice Hall Seminar Series in Global History. Fernández-Armesto is a member of the faculty of history at Queen Mary College, University of London, and is on the editorial board of the History of Cartography for the University of Chicago Press, the editorial committee of Studies in Overseas History (Leiden University), and the *Journal of Global History*.
He also serves on the Council of the Hakluyt Society and the English Committee of PEN. Recent awards include a Premio Nacional de Investigación (Sociedad Geográfica Española) in 2003, a fellowship at the Netherlands Institute of Advanced Study in the Humanities and Social Sciences, and a Union Pacific Visiting Professorship at the University of Minnesota (1999–2000). He won the Caird Medal of the National Maritime Museum in 1995 and the John Carter Brown Medal in 1999.

The author, coauthor, or editor of over 25 books and numerous papers and scholarly articles, Fernández-Armesto's work has been translated into 22 languages. His books include *Before Columbus; The Times Illustrated History of Europe; Columbus; Millennium: A History of the Last Thousand Years* (the subject of a ten-part series on CNN); *Civilizations: Culture, Ambition, and the Transformation of Nature; Near a Thousand Tables; The Americas; Humankind: A Brief History; Ideas that Changed the World; The Times Atlas of World Exploration;* and *The Times Guide to the Peoples of Europe.* Two forthcoming works are *Amerigo: The Man Who Gave His Name to America* and *The Pathfinders: A Global History of Exploration.*

By the standards of astronauts, say, or science fiction writers, historians seem timid, unadventurous creatures who are only interested in one puny species—our species, the human species—on one tiny planet—our planet, Earth. But Earth is special. So far, we know of nowhere else in the cosmos where so much has happened and is happening today. By galactic standards, global history is a small story—but it's a good one.

Humans, moreover, compared with other animals, seem outward looking. Our concerns range over the universe and beyond it, to unseen worlds, vividly imagined or mysteriously revealed. Not just everything we do but also everything that occurs to our minds is part of our history and, therefore, part of this book, including science and art, fun and philosophy, speculations and dreams. We continually generate stories—new stories—at an amazing rate.

But the present passes instantly into the past. The present is always over, transformed into history. And the past is always with us, tugging at our memories, shaping our thoughts, launching and limiting our lives. So human history may seem narrowly self-interested, but it focuses on an undeniably riveting subject that is also our favorite subject—ourselves.

THE WAY OF HUMANKIND

Though the story of this book is a human story, it can never be merely human because, in isolation humankind does not make perfect sense. Humans are animals, and to understand ourselves thoroughly and to know what, if anything, makes us unique, we have to compare ourselves with other animals. As with other animals, we are best studied in our habitats. We cannot begin to comprehend our own history except in context. Our story is inseparable from the climates where it takes place and the other life-forms that we depend on or compete with. We lord it over other species, but we remain linked to them by the food chain. We transform our environment, but we can never escape from it. We differentiate ourselves from nature—we speak loosely, for instance, of nature as if we were not natural creatures ourselves. We distance ourselves from our fellow-animals by adopting what we think are unnatural behaviors—wearing clothes, for instance, cooking food, replacing nature with culture. In short, we do what is natural to us, and all the elaborate culture we produce generates new, intimate relationships with the environment we refashion and the life-forms we exploit.

We are exceptionally ambitious compared to other animals, consciously remodeling environments to suit our own purposes. We carve out fields, turn prairies into wheat lands, deserts into gardens, and gardens into deserts. We fell forests where we find them and plant them where none exist; we dam rivers, wall seas, cultivate plants, breed creatures, extinguish some species, and call others into being by selection and hybridization. Sometimes we smother terrain with environments we build for ourselves. Yet none of these practices liberates us from nature. As we shall see, one of the paradoxes of the human story is that the more we change the environment, the more vulnerable we become to ecological lurches and unpredictable disasters. Failure to establish the right balance between exploitation and conservation has often left civilizations in ruins. History becomes a path picked across the wreckage. This does not mean that the environment determines our behavior or our lives, but it does set the framework in which we act.

We are an exceptionally successful species in terms of our ability to survive in a wide range of diverse climates and landscapes—more so than just about any other creatures, except for the microbes we carry around with us. But even we are still explorers of our planet, engaged in an ongoing effort to change it. Indeed, we have barely begun to change planet Earth, though, as we shall see, some human societies have devoted the last ten thousand years to trying to do it. We call ourselves lords, or, more modestly, caretakers of creation, but about 90 percent of the biosphere is too far underwater or too deep below the Earth for us to inhabit with the technology we have at present: These are environments that humans have only recently begun to invade and that we still do not dominate.

If we humans are peculiarly ambitious creatures, who are always intruding in the life of the planet, we are also odd compared to other animals in the way we generate change among ourselves. We are an unpredictable, unstable species. Lots of other animals live social lives and construct societies. But those societies are remarkably stable compared to ours. As far as we know, ants and elephants have the same lifeways and the same kinds of relationships that they have had since their species first appeared. That is not to say animals never change their cultures. One of the fascinating discoveries in primatology is that apes and monkeys develop cultural differences from one another, even between groups living in similar and sometimes adjacent environments. In one forest region of Gabon in West Africa, chimpanzees have developed a termite-catching technology. They "fish" with stripped branches that they plunge into termite nests but do not use tools to break open nuts. Chimps in a neighboring region ignore the termites but are experts in nut cracking, using rocks like hammers and anvils. In Sumatra in Indonesia, orangutans play a game—jumping from falling tress—that is unknown to their cousins in nearby Borneo. In Ethiopia in East Africa, males in some baboon groups control harems while others nearby have one mate after another. In some chimpanzee societies, hunting and meat eating seem to have increased dramatically in recent times.

These are amazing facts, but the societies of nonhuman animals still change little compared with ours. So, alongside the theme of human interaction with the rest of nature is another great theme of our history: the ways our societies have changed, grown apart from one another, reestablished contact, and influenced one another in their turn.

THE WAY OF THIS BOOK

This book, then, interweaves two stories—of our interactions with nature and with each other. The environment-centered story is about humans distancing themselves from the rest of nature and searching for a relationship that strikes a balance between constructive and destructive exploitation. The culture-centered story is of how human cultures have become mutually influential and yet mutually differentiating. Both stories have been going on for thousands of years. We do not know whether they will end in triumph or disaster.

There is no prospect of covering all of world history in one book. Rather, the fabric of this book is woven from carefully selected strands. Readers will see these at every turn, twisted together into yarn, stretched into stories. Human-focused historical ecology—the environmental theme—will drive readers back, again and again, to the same concepts: sustenance, shelter, disease, energy, technology, art. (The last is a vital category for historians, not only because it is part of our interface with the rest of the world, but also because it forms a record of how we see reality and of how the way we see it changes.) In the global story of human interactions—the cultural theme—we return constantly to the ways people make contact with each another: migration, trade, war, imperialism, pilgrimage, gift exchange, diplomacy, travel—and to their social frameworks: the economic and political arenas, the human groups and groupings, the states and civilizations, the sexes and generations, the classes and clusters of identity.

The stories that stretch before us are full of human experience. "The stork feeds on snakes," said the ancient Greek sage, Agathon, "the pig on acorns, and history on human lives." The only way to build up our picture of human societies and ecosystems of the past is to start with the evidence people have left. Then we reassemble it bit by bit, with the help of imagination disciplined by the sources. Anyone reading a history book needs to bear in mind that interpreting evidence is a challenge—half burden and half opportunity. The subject matter of history is not the past directly because the past is never available to our senses. We have only the evidence about it. This makes history an art, not a science, a disciplined art like that of poetry disciplined by rhyme and meter, or a novel disciplined by conventions, or a play disciplined by the limitations of stagecraft.

For a book like this, the sources set the limits of my imagination. Sometimes, these are concrete clues to what people really did—footprints of their wanderings, debris of their meals, fragments of their technologies, wreckage of their homes, traces of diseases in their bones. Usually, however, the sources reflect at best, not the way things were but the way people wished to represent them in their arts and crafts and writings. Most sources—in short—are evidence of what happened only in the minds of those who made them. This means, in turn, that our picture of what went on in the world beyond human minds is always tentative and open to reinterpretation. The historian's job is not—cannot be—to say what the past was like, but rather, what it felt like to live in it, because that is what the evidence tends to reveal.

One of the most admirable historians of the twentieth century, R. G. Collingwood, who was also a professor of history at Oxford, said that "all history is intellectual history." He was right. History—even the environmental and cultural history that is the subject of this book—is largely about what people perceived rather than what they really saw, what they thought or felt rather than what happened outwardly, what they represented rather than what was real. The nineteenth-century philosopher Arthur Schopenhauer, one of the most pessimistic thinkers ever, who drew on Hindu and Buddhist writings for his inspiration, said that history's only subject was "humankind's oppressive, muddlesome dream." He thought that made history pointless. I think that makes it intriguing.

Because the evidence is always incomplete, history is not so much a matter of describing or narrating or question-answering as it is a matter of problem-posing. No one reading this book should expect to be instructed in straightforward facts or to acquire proven knowledge. The thrill of history is asking the right question, not getting the right answer. Most of the time, the most we can hope for is to identify interesting problems that stimulate debate. And we have to accept that the debate is worthwhile for its own sake, even if we have insufficient knowledge to reach conclusions.

There is no agreement among historians even about what are the right sorts of questions to ask. Some—including me—are interested in huge philosophical questions, such as how does history happen? What makes change? Is it random or subject to scientific laws? Do impersonal forces beyond human control—environmental factors or economics or some world force called fate or evolution or God or progress—determine it? Or is change the externalization of ideas, which arise in minds and are projected onto the world through human action? And if it's a mixture, what's the balance?

At a slightly lower level of analysis, some historians ask questions about how human societies function. How and why do societies grow and fragment and take different forms? How do some people get power over others? How and why do revolutions happen and states and civilizations rise and fall?

Other historians like to pose problems about the present. How did we get into the mess we're in? Can we trace the causes of present dilemmas back into the past and, if so, how far? Why do we have a globally connected world without global governance? Why is peace always precarious? Why does ecological overkill menace our global environment? Having accounted—or failed to account—for the present, some historians like to focus on the future. They demand lessons from history about how to change our behavior or cope with recurrences of past difficulties. Others, again, search to make sense of the past, to find an overall way of characterizing it or narrating it that makes us feel we understand it.

Yet others—the majority, in the current state of historical fashion, and again including me—like to study the past for its own sake and try to identify the questions that mattered to people at the time they were first asked them. This does not mean that the sort of history found in this book is useless (although I do not necessarily think it would be a bad thing if it were). For to penetrate the minds of people of the past—especially the remote past of cultures other than your own—you have to make a supreme effort of understanding. But such effort has dividends for the individual who practices it. It enhances life by sharpening responses to the streetscapes and landscapes, art and artifacts, laws and letters we have inherited from the past. And understanding is what we need most today in our multicultural societies and multicivilizational world.

HOW THIS BOOK IS ARRANGED

After finding the time, accumulating the knowledge, posing the questions, stiffening the sinews, and summoning the blood, the big problem for the writer of a global history textbook is organizing the material. The big problem for the reader is navigating it. It is tempting to divide the world up into regions or cultures or even—as I did in a previous book—into biomes and devote successive chapters to each. You could call that "world history," if you genuinely managed to cover the world. But "global history" is different: an attempt to see the planet whole, as if from an immense, astral height, and discern themes that truly transcend geographical and cultural boundaries. In this book, therefore, I try to look at every continent in just about every chapter (there are a couple of chapters which, for reasons described in their place, focus only on part of the world). Each chapter concentrates on themes from the two great global stories: how human societies diverge and converge, and how they interact with the rest of nature.

Because history is a story, in which the order of events matters, the chapters are grouped into ten parts, arranged chronologically. There are thirty chapters—one for each week in a typical U.S. academic year (though of course, every reader or group of readers will go at their own pace)—and ten parts. I hope there is plenty to surprise readers without making the parts perversely defiant of the "periods" historians conventionally speak of. Part I runs from roughly 150,000 to roughly 20,000 years ago, and, on the whole, the periods covered get shorter as sources accumulate, cultures diverge, data multiply, and readers' interests quicken. Of course, no one should be misled into thinking the parts are more than devices of convenience. Events that happened in, say, 1850, are in a different part of this book from those that happened in, say 1750. But the story is continuous, and the parts could equally well be recrafted to start and end at different moments.

At every stage, some parts of the world are more prominent than others, because they are more influential, more populous, more world-shaping. For great stretches of the book, China occupies relatively more space; this is not for reasons of political correctness, but because China has, for much of the past, been immensely rich in globally influential initiatives. In the coverage of the last couple of hundred years, Europe and the United States get a lot of attention: this is not "Eurocentrism" or "Westocentrism" (if there is such a word), but an honest reflection of how history happened. But I have tried not to neglect the peoples and parts of the world that historians usually undervalue: poor and peripheral communities sometimes have a stunning impact on the world. The margins and frontiers of the world are often where world-changing events happen—the fault lines of civilizations, which radiate seismic effects.

ACKNOWLEDGMENTS

Without being intrusive, I have tried not to suppress my presence—my voice, my views—in the text, because no book is objective, other than by pretense, and the reader is entitled to get to know the writer's foibles and failures. In overcoming mine, I have had a lot of help (though there are sure still to be errors and shortcomings through my fault alone). Textbooks are teamwork, and I have learned an immense amount from my friends and helpers at Pearson Prentice Hall, especially my editors, Charles Cavaliere and Gerald Lombardi, whose indefatigability and forbearance made the book better at every turn. I also thank my editorial guide Harriett Prentiss, the picture researcher Emma Brown, and the members of the production and cartographic sections of the team who performed Herculean labors: Joanne Riker, managing editor; Kathleen Sleys, production project manager; Caterina Melara, production editor; Gail Cocker-Bogusz, map project manager; David Roberts, cartographer; Scott Garrison, map coordinator; Benjamin Smith, print buyer; Kathy Mrozek, designer; Leslie Osher, creative design director; Deborah O'Connell, media editor and Maureen Diana, editorial assistant. Finally, Emily Cleary has crafted a superb marketing campaign.

I also owe a debt of gratitude to the senior management team at Pearson Prentice Hall who supported this endeavor every step of the way: Tim Bozik, president of Prentice Hall; Yolanda de Rooy; president of the Humanities and Social Sciences division; Charlyce Jones Owen, editorial director; Rochelle Diogenes, editor-in-chief for development; Brandy Dawson, director of marketing; and Barbara Kittle, director of production and manufacturing.

I could not have gotten through the work without the help and support of my wonderful colleagues at Queen Mary, University of London; the Institute of Historical Research, University of London; and the History Department of Tufts University. I owe special thanks to the many scholars who share and still share their knowledge of global history at the Pearson Prentice Hall Seminar Series in Global History, which now meets at Tufts University. David Ringrose of University of California, San Diego, was a constant guide, whose interest never flagged and whose wisdom never failed. Many colleagues and counterparts advised me on their fields of expertise or performed heroic self-sacrifice in putting all of the many pieces of the book together: Natia Chakvetadze, Shannon Corliss, Maria Guarascio, Anita Castro, Conchita Ordonez, Sandra Garcia, Maria Garcia, Ernest Tucker (United States Naval Academy), David Way (British Library), Antony Eastmond (Courtland Institute), Morris Rossabi (Columbia University), David Atwill and Jade Atwill (Pennsylvania State University), Stephen Morillo (Wabash College), Peter Carey (Oxford University), Jim Mallory (Queens University, Belfast), Matthew Restall (Pennsylvania State University), Roderick Whitfield (School of Oriental and African Studies, University of London), Barry Powell (University of Wisconsin), Leonard Blussé (Harvard University), Guolong Lai (University of Florida), Frank Karpiel (College of Charleston), George Kosar (Tufts University), and Jai Kabaranda my former graduate student at Queen Mary, as well as the many good people whose assistance I may have failed to acknowledge.

Felipe Fernández-Armesto
Tufts University
Summer, 2006

The WORLD

A HISTORY

Foragers and Farmers, to 5,000 B.C.E.

Early art? Early science? Or both? In 2001, the discovery in South Africa of a stone carved 70,000 years ago showed that humans have used symbols for at least that long. These shapes, engraved in ocher, a soft reddish-brown stone that was a valuable, magical substance at the time, have been interpreted as a device to aid in counting or a kind of calendar.

1.75 million to 1.25 million years ago
Homo erectus migrations out of East Africa

ENVIRONMENT

6 million years ago
Evolution of hominids/early humans

CULTURE

since 3 million years ago
Stone tools

160,000 to 20,000 years ago
Most recent Ice Age

since 20,000
Global warming

since ca. 10,000
Agriculture

since ca. 150,000 years ago
Homo sapiens

150,000 years ago
Fire, fire hardened wood spears

since at least 100,000 year ago
Art, ritual, religion; first migrations out of Africa

since 40,000 years ago
Bow and arrow

Out of the Ice:
Peopling the Earth

The Spanish painter Francisco Goya painted these nightmare-visions in the mid-1820s on slivers of ivory, with novel techniques, burying the background in lamp-black, scratching the ivory to produce strange effects of light. He captured the fascinated unease with which human beings eye each other.
Francisco Goya y Lucientes, Spanish, 1746–1828. Boy Staring at an Apparition *(1824–1825) Carbon Black and watercolor on ivory (Black wash heightened with vermilion and brown) 6.03 x 6.03cm (2 3/8 x 2 3/8 in.) Museum of Fine Arts, Boston. Gift of Eleanor I. Arxiu Mas.*

n exile in France in the 1820s, in the last years of his tortured, haunted life, one of the most admired painters of all time etched his own nightmares—frightening faces stripped of every sane and civilized quality. In the most abstract of the images, a little boy, half bewildered, half fascinated, stares up at the face of a man. But the man's face is indistinct—a baffling blur. Like so many nightmares and so many artists' visions, Francisco Goya's (1746–1828) captured a profound truth about how we understand human nature. Like the little boy, we recognize it because it inspires us with distinctive emotions: attraction, empathy, unease. But we see it unclearly. We all think we know what it means to be human, but if anyone asks us to define humankind, we cannot do it. Or at least we cannot do it satisfactorily.

FRANCE

SO YOU THINK YOU'RE HUMAN

We can call humankind a species, but species are just convenient categories for grouping together closely related life forms. The boundaries between species are fuzzy and subject to change. There is no standard of how closely related you have to be to a fellow creature to be classed in the same species, or among species of the same sort, or, as biologists say, "genus." DNA evidence reveals that all the people we now recognize as human had a common ancestor who lived in Africa, probably more than 150,000 years ago. If we go back 5 to 7 million years, we share ancestors with chimpanzees. Double the length of time, and the fossils reveal ancestors whom we share with other great apes. Further back, the flow of evolution erodes the differences between our ancestors and other creatures. The differences are only matters of degree. If we accept the theory of **evolution**—and, in outline, it does present a true account of how life forms change—we cannot find any transforming moment in the past when humankind began. Species so like ourselves preceded us in the evolutionary record that, if we were to meet members of them today, we should probably embrace some of them as fellow humans, and puzzle over how to treat others.

Even today, there are nonhuman species—especially among the apes—whose humanlike qualities so impress people who work and live with them that they seem morally indistinguishable from humans and should, according to some biologists and philosophers, be included in the same genus and even the same moral community as

FOCUS questions

- WHERE IN the evolutionary record do humans begin?
- WHAT CAUSED the rapid population growth of *Homo sapiens*?
- WHY WAS the Ice Age a time of abundance?
- WHAT DOES its art tell us about Ice-Age society?
- WHEN DID *Homo sapiens* migrate to North and South America?
- HOW DID human life change when the Ice Age ended?

ourselves, with similar rights. In terms of the sort of cultures they have, emotions they reveal, societies they form, and behaviors they adopt, chimpanzees share many characteristics with the fellow apes we call humans. To a lesser extent, gorillas and orangutans are also like us. All of us apes use tools, learn from each other, practice altruism and deceit, like to play, detest boredom, and seem self-aware. Our bodies and our behaviors are so like those of chimpanzees that the physiologist and historian Jared Diamond has suggested we reclassify our species as a kind of chimp. Our relationship with other animals could come full circle. In the often-filmed story of *The Island of Dr. Moreau*, the British novelist H. G. Wells (1866–1946) fantasized about a scientist who strove to produce perfect creatures by surgically combining human characteristics with those of other animals. Today, in theory, genetic engineering can actually produce such hybrids, prompting us to wonder at what point a hybrid would become human. The first big question for this chapter, then, is where in the evolutionary record does it make sense to talk about humans? When does the story of humankind begin?

Human Evolution

Paleoanthropologists—the specialists responsible for answering or, at least, asking the question about which species are human—give conflicting responses to this question. The usual place to look is among creatures sufficiently like us to be classified, according to the present consensus, in the same genus as ourselves: the genus called "Homo" from the Latin word that means "human." A creature known as *Homo habilis* ("handy"), about two and a half million years ago, chipped hand axes from stones. In calling this species the first humans, scholars defined humans as toolmakers—a now old-fashioned, indeed, discredited concept. *Habilis* also had a larger brain than earlier predecessors, but this is a matter of degree and of doubtful significance. Ours is not the biggest-brained species in the evolutionary record. At one time, anthropologists backed a slightly later species, *Homo erectus* ("standing upright"), of about 1.5 million years ago, as the first human, largely because they admired the symmetrical flints for tools and weapons that species carved. From finds over 800,000 years ago, a variant (or, perhaps, a different species) called *Homo ergaster* ("workman") appeared who later—at one site at least—stacked the bones of the dead. But reverence for the dead is not a uniquely human trait, either. All these creatures, and others like them, have had champions who have claimed them as the first humans. Clearly, these instances of backing one set of ancestors over another reflect subjective criteria: supposed resemblance to ourselves. We are like the bereaved of some horrible disaster, scanning the remains of the dead for signs to prompt our recognition.

Species that occurred earlier than those we class under the heading "Homo," or who resembled us less, have tended to get labeled with names that sound less human. Anthropologists used to call them "pithecanthropoi"—literally, ape-men. Current terminology favors "**australopithecines**,"

Chimp painting. It's painting, but is it art? Works by Congo, the most famous chimpanzee painter, and others of his kind, sell for thousands of dollars. Chimps often label their work in sign language but their paintings never represent images in ways recognizable to humans. Their minds are both like and unlike ours. They seem to see the world differently from the way we do.

("southern ape-like creatures"), or "paranthropoi" ("next to humans"), as if they were identifiably nonhuman or prehuman. But in 1974, the archaeologist Dan Johansen made a discovery that blew away all notion of a clear dividing line. He spotted the bones of an australopithecine sticking out of the mud in Hadar in Ethiopia in East Africa. He dug her up and called her "Lucy" after the title of a song on a Beatles record he happened to play that night in camp. Lucy had died over 3 million years ago. She was only about three feet tall, but she and her kind turned out to have characteristics that were thought to belong exclusively to later species of *Homo*. They walked on two legs and lived in family groups. Johansen discovered tools 2.5 million years old near the site the following year and, in 1977, he found bipedal* footprints, dating back 3.7 million years. Finds with similar characteristics may date as far back as 6 million years ago.

As evolution slowly grinds out species, who's human? Who's to say? It is tempting to try to settle the issues by reserving the term *human* for ourselves—members of the species we call **Homo sapiens**. Literally, the term *sapiens* means "wise," a grandiose name that betrays the foolishness of self-ascribed wisdom. For other species also have embarrassingly strong claims to "wisdom." One example is *Homo neanderthalensis*, who vanished only 30,000 years ago. The name means "of the Neander Valley"—the spot in northern Germany where remains of this species were found in 1856. We can be fairly certain that no one living today has a **Neanderthal** ancestor since there are no certain cases of interbreeding between Neanderthals and our own ancestors. But *Homo neanderthalensis* and *Homo sapiens* coexisted for something like a hundred thousand years. Neanderthals had distinctive vocal tracts, so it is unlikely that they and our ancestors could speak each others' languages. They could have used nonverbal communication, however, just as we do today to talk with apes and even with humans whose spoken language we do not understand.

In most other respects, the two species of *Homo* were alike. Neanderthals were as big as *sapiens* and had a similar appearance; the brains were also similar but, on average, the Neanderthal brain was slightly larger. They followed the same hunting, foraging ways of life in overlapping habitats. They made the same kinds of tools our ancestors made, lived in the same types of society, ate the same foods, and had many of the same customs and rites. They cared for their old and sick and buried their dead with signs of honor that suggest a sense of religion. They also seem to have expected an afterlife, burying bears' jaws with their dead, as if to protect them and perhaps—though the evidence is uncertain on this point—strewing fragrant flowers on some graves as if to help, honor, or adorn the deceased. Yet some paleoanthropologists seem determined to deny Neanderthals the name of humans—using arguments startlingly, frighteningly reminiscent of those that nineteenth-century scientific racism employed in an attempt to deny full humanity to black people: claiming, for instance, that they were inferior and doomed to extinction in competition for "the survival of the fittest." Typical anti-Neanderthal arguments are that their physiques were poorly

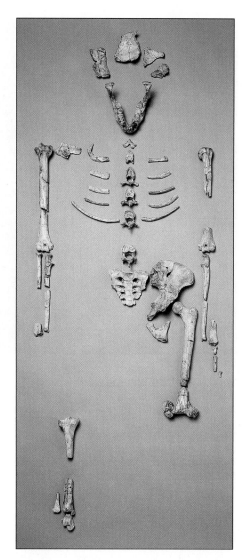

Lucy. The bones shown here aren't connected to each other, but modern imaginations have reconstructed the three-million-year-old skeleton known as "Lucy," as human or nearly so. Lucy walked on two legs and was closer to humans, in evolutionary terms, than any non-human creature that exists today.

Hybrid human. The British actor Charles Laughton in the role of Dr. Moreau gives orders to one of his hybrid creatures in the 1933 movie *The Island of Lost Souls*, based on H.G. Wells' 1896 novel, *The Island of Dr. Moreau*. Moreau engineers his islanders by surgically combining human and animal body parts. "Are we not men?" the suffering creatures ask. Like Moreau, our inability to answer that question is a reminder of our own uncertainty about what it means to be human.

*Bipedal: walking on two feet

(a)

(b)

The changing image of the Neanderthal. Gradually, over the last 30 years or so, the old imge of a bestial, inhuman creature (b) has given way to a more sympathetic vision that acknowledges how like Neanderthals we are (a). An important conflict underpins the rival images: if we classify Neanderthals as human, where and how can we set the boundaries of humankind?

adapted, that their efforts to articulate must have sounded like grunts, and that they had no art that we can recognize. Meanwhile, the evidence of their attainments is explained away. The assemblages of ritual objects found at their graves, detractors say, must be "tricks of evidence," deposited accidently by streams or winds or animals.

Paleoanthropologists continue to dig up specimens that challenge believers in human uniqueness. In October 2004, excavators published news of a stunning find in southeast Asia on the island of Flores in Indonesia, which included the remains of a woman whose teeth, when they found her, were mashed to pulp, her bones rotted and soggy. She died 18,000 years ago. She was dwarfishly tiny. Her brain was barely as big as a chimpanzee's. But she had the power to subvert anthropological orthodoxy. *Homo floresiensis*, as her finders called her and her relatives whose bones lay alongside hers, proved that big brains do not make their possessors superior to other creatures. To judge from adjacent finds, these "hobbits," as the press dubbed them, had tools typical of early *Homo sapiens*, despite chimp-sized brains in imp-sized bodies. *Floresiensis* almost certainly made those tools. In known cases where nonhuman creatures lie alongside *sapiens*-made tools, *sapiens* ate them. But the remains of *floresiensis* showed no signs of butchering.

OUT OF AFRICA

Since no clear-cut line separates human from nonhuman species, we might rationally start our story with our last common ancestor, roughly 150,000 years ago. All of us today—as far as we can tell without actually testing everyone alive today— have a chemical component in our cells that a mother in East Africa passed on to her daughters at about that time. We nickname her Eve after the first woman in the biblical Book of Genesis, but of course she was not our first ancestor nor the only woman of her day. By the best available estimates, there were perhaps 20,000 individuals of the species *Homo sapiens* at the time, all living in the same region. She may, however, have lived relatively early in the history of our species. No undisputed examples of *Homo sapiens* occur much earlier. We are therefore a young species, by the standards of evolution, with only a couple of hundred thousand years on the planet. In 2003, archaeological evidence of Eve's world turned up in Herto, in Ethiopia. Three skulls—a child's and two adults'— dated to about 154,000 to 160,000 years ago, look similar to skulls of humans today, except that they are larger than what is now average. The remains of a butchered hippopotamus lay nearby. The skulls had been stripped of flesh and polished after death, which suggests that the culture they belonged to practiced some death-linked ritual. We can begin to picture not only the appearance of the African Eve—we can do that by looking in a mirror—but also something of her way of life or, at least, life at a time close to her own.

Eve's homeland of mixed grassland and woodland was no Eden, but it was suitable for the creatures into which our ancestor and her offspring had evolved. In this environment they could make up for their deficiency as climbers by standing erect to look out around them. Here, too, they could use fire to manage the grazing of the animals they hunted and could find materials to fashion into weapons and tools. They made fire-hardened spears to kill game and sharpened stones to butcher the carcasses. They could exploit their modest physical advantages over competitor species. Humans are poorly equipped physically, with inferior senses of sight, smell, and hearing, slow movements, unthreatening teeth and nails, poor digestions, and weak bodies that confine us to the ground. But we can sweat profusely over our hairless skins to keep cool during long chases, and we can ward off rival predators with our relatively accurate throwing-arms and well-coordinated eye–arm movements. In short, like most creatures, we are physically well equipped to a particular kind of habitat.

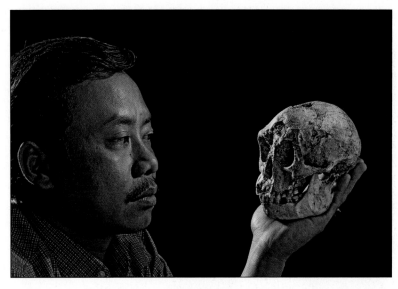

Homo floresiensis. The skull of *Homo floresiensis* is smaller than a chimpanzee's. Yet it held a brain with the same toolkit as our own species. So does size matter? Not, it seems, in brains. And the more discoveries we make about other species, the less special *Homo sapiens* seems.

Peopling the Old World

From their beginnings in East Africa, Eve's descendants spread over the world (see Map 1.1). The first great problems these migrants pose for us are why they

Paleoanthropologists have long used stone tool-making technologies to classify hominid cultures, because these artifacts have survived in relatively large numbers. The chopper on the left, of a pattern that dates from over two million years ago, was made by striking cobblestones against each other. Chimpanzees can be taught to make similar tools. The more elegant axe-blade in the center is of a kind that predominated over much of the world between about 1.5 million and 150,000 years ago. Though the size, shape, and presumably function of these tools varied, as the examples on the right show, the technology was surprisingly uniform around the world. No bone tools, for example, from the period survive.

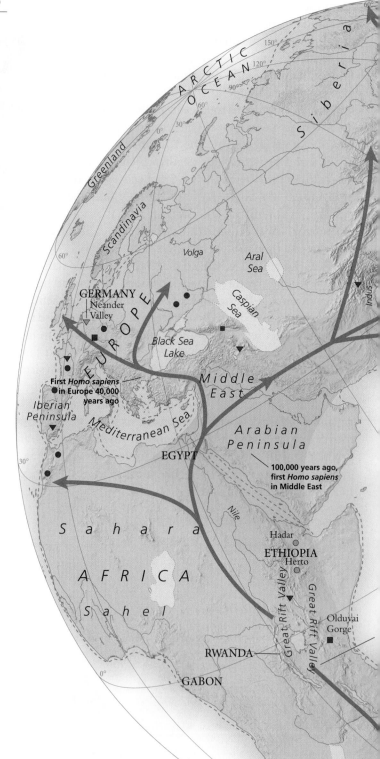

MAP 1.1

Early Human Migration 150,000–40,000 years ago

Homo erectus migration, 1.75–1.25 million years ago

Homo sapiens migration, 150,000–40,000 years ago

■ *Homo erectus* site described on page 14

● *Homo sapiens* site described on pages 7–9

▼ Neanderthal site descirbed on pages 7–8

▲ *Homo Floresiensis* site

■●▼ other *Homo erectus, Homo sapiens,* and Neanderthal
sites, 150,000–40,000 years ago

GABON modern-day country mentioned on pages 7–15

--- ancient coastline

ancient lake

150,000 years ago: earliest evidence of *Homo sapiens* in East Africa

60,000 years ago: reestablishment of *Homo sapiens* in Middle East

50,000 years ago: first *Homo sapiens* in Australia

120,000 y.a.

90,000 y.a.

60,000 y.a.

30,000 y.a

100,000 years ago: first *Homo sapiens* migrate out of Africa

67,000 years ago: first *Homo sapiens* in China

40,000 years ago: first *Homo sapiens* in Europe

PACIFIC OCEAN

Japan

Zhoukhoudian

67,000 years ago— earliest evidence of *Homo sapiens* in China

Yellow River

Yangtze

CHINA

Philippine Islands

New Guinea

Southeast Asia

Mekong

Borneo

Flores

Sumatra

INDONESIA

First colonizers in Australia 50,000 years ago

Australia

dia

INDIAN OCEAN

Scale varies with perspective

13,340 km (8290 miles)

20,040 km (12,450 miles)

11

wanted to move, and what made them so adaptable to different environments. These are big, perplexing problems because most species stay in the environments where they are best adapted. Even human populations rarely, if ever, seek new environments willingly or adjust easily. When migrants move, they try to re-create the feel of home in their adopted country, carrying with them what the twentieth-century French historian Fernand Braudel called the "heavy baggage" of their culture. They transport familiar animals and transplant familiar crops, which usually means finding a new area similar to the one they left. Many of the early English settlers in America, for instance, were pioneers and refugees, but they called the place they chose New England and tried to re-create the landscapes and streetscapes, diet, houses, and ways of life of the land they had left.

Yet when groups of *Homo sapiens* migrated out of Africa to people the world, about 100,000 years ago, they often relocated in challengingly different environments: deep forests, where grassland habits were of limited use; cold climates, to which they were physically ill suited; deserts and seas, which demanded technologies they had not yet developed. These new habitats bred unfamiliar diseases. Yet people kept on moving, through them and into them. We are still struggling to understand how it happened.

Such migration had happened before—or something like it had. Between about 1.75 and 1.25 million years ago, before *Homo sapiens* set out, *Homo erectus*, migrated from a similar region in East Africa and spread over most of what are now Africa and Eurasia. But this was a much slower and more selective peopling of the Earth, and its circumstances are too obscure to cast much light on our present problem. We can, however, look at other species that have crossed environments slowly and selectively. For example, the mountain gorillas of Rwanda in Central Africa moved into their present high, relatively cold habitat to escape the competitive environment of the tropical forest lowlands. Now, probably because food sources are relatively scarce in their new homeland, these exclusively vegetarian creatures are smaller and weaker than other gorillas. Nonetheless, they have forged a viable way of life.

We can reconstruct where and when *Homo sapiens* traveled while peopling the Earth, even though the archaeological evidence is patchy. One way is to measure differences in blood type, genetic makeup, and language among populations in different parts of the world (see Figure 1.1). The greater the differences, the longer the ancestors of the people concerned are likely to have been out of touch with the rest of humankind. This is inexact science, because people are rarely isolated for long. Over most of Eurasia and Africa, populations have moved about tremendously in recorded history. Groups of people have frequently been mixed and restirred.

There are, moreover, no agreed ways to measure the differences among languages. Still, for what it is worth, the best-informed research puts *Homo sapiens* in the Middle East by about 100,000 years ago. The colony failed, but new migrants reestablished it about 60,000 years ago. Settlement then proceeded along the coasts of Africa and Asia, probably by sea. The earliest agreed-upon archaeological evidence of *Homo sapiens* in China is about 67,000 years old (although some digs have yielded puzzlingly earlier dates for remains that seem like those of *Homo sapiens*).

It may seem surprising that humans developed nautical technology so early. Yet the first colonizers of Australia arrived over 50,000 years ago and must have used boats, because at that time, water already separated what are now Australia and New Guinea from Asia. *Homo sapiens* reached Europe only a little later. Northern Asia and

Early Human Migration

(All dates are approximate)	
150,000 years ago	Hypothetical African Eve (*H. sapiens*)
100,000 years ago	*H. sapiens* migrates out of Africa to Middle East
67,000 years ago	*H. sapiens* in China
60,000 years ago	*H. sapiens* reestablishes colony in Middle East
50,000 years ago	*H. sapiens* in Australia
40,000 years ago	*H. sapiens* in Europe
15,000 years ago	*H. sapiens* in the Americas

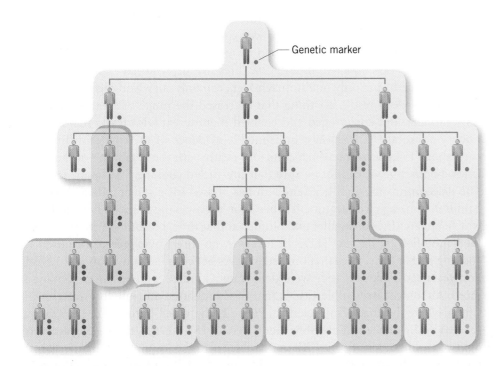
— Genetic marker

FIGURE 1.1 GENETIC DIVERSITY. Since genetic markers are inherited and are passed down from one generation to the next, they can be traced backward in time. Even through with each succesive generation, new combinations of genetic markers are created, they all descend from one ancestor. The exact shape of this evolutionary tree is affected by other evolutionary forces, such as natural selection and migration. *National Geographic Genographic Project. Reprinted by permission.*

America—isolated by impenetrable screens of cold climate—were probably colonized much later. The most generally accepted archaeological evidence indicates the New World was settled no earlier than about 15,000 years ago.

If these dates are correct, the expansion of *Homo sapiens* implies an astonishing rate of population growth. Though, we have no idea—beyond guesswork—of the actual numbers that migrated, we can estimate a figure in millions by the end of the process. A handful of Eve's children had multiplied to the point where they could colonize most of the habitable Old World in less than 100,000 years. But was the increase in population cause or effect of the migrations? And how did it relate to the other changes migration brought? Migrating groups were doubly dynamic: not just mobile, but also subject to huge social changes—divisive and violent, but also with constructive ways of organizing their lives.

Migration, Population, and Social Change

Migration changed people's relationships with each other, the size and organization of their groups, the way they saw the world, and the way they interacted with other species—including those they competed with, preyed on, and outlasted. As far as we know, everyone at the time lived by foraging and moved on foot. Because mothers cannot easily carry more than one or two infants, large numbers of children are unsuited to foraging life. Consequently, foragers usually limit their families, either by strictly regulating who can mate with whom (to reduce the numbers of breeding couples) or by practicing other forms of population control. Their main contraceptive method is a long period of lactation. Breast-feeding mothers are relatively infertile. The demographic growth that peopled the Earth is surprising, therefore, because it breaks the normal pattern of population stability in foraging communities. So how can we explain it?

Cooking with fire probably helped to make population growth possible, because it made food easier to digest. Creatures like us, who have short guts, weak jaws, blunt teeth, and only one stomach each, can only chew and digest limited energy sources. As a result, anything that increased the range of foods available to early humans and encouraged and enabled them to eat a lot was a major evolutionary advantage. The earliest indisputable evidence of cooking with fire dates back about 150,000 years, which coincides neatly with the beginning of the population boom, but we cannot be sure that fire-fueled cooking first happened then. The paleoanthropologist R. Wrangham has argued for a starting date more than 2 million years ago. His argument is based on the evolving shape of hominid teeth, which, apparently, got smaller and blunter at that time, presumably in response to food modified by flames. There is, however, no direct evidence of fire used for cooking at that time. Fires that burned in caves between half a million and 1.5 million years ago look as if they were deliberately kindled, perhaps with cooking in mind. An almost irresistible case is that of Zhoukhoudian (joh-coh-dee-ehn), in China, where the great Jesuit scientist, Pierre Teilhard de Chardin (1881–1955), excavated the evidence and the Abbé Henri Breuil (1877–1961), the leading archaeologist of the day, identified it. "It's impossible," said the Jesuit, thinking the site was too early for the controlled use of fire, "it comes from Zhoukhoudian," "I don't care where it comes from," the Abbé replied. "It was made by a human, and that human knew the use of fire." We are similarly uncertain about when other technologies started that might have improved diet by improving hunting, such as making driving lanes and corrals to herd animals for killing, but the earliest known examples of fire-hardened spears are only 150,000 years or so old—again taking us back to a date near the start of the migrations.

Whether or not new technologies did empower humans to migrate, perhaps new stresses drove them on. Food shortages or ecological disasters might explain the necessity, but no evidence supports this or fits with the evidence of rising population. In every other case we know of, in all species, population falls when food sources shrink. Another possible source of stress is warfare. Among the four horsemen of the Apocalypse—war, plague, famine, and natural disaster in the book of visions with which the Bible closes—war is the odd one out. The other three tend to inhibit human action, whereas war spurs us to new responses.

One of the most fascinating problems of history is how and when war started. According to one school of thought, war is natural to humankind. The commander of British forces in Europe in the Second World War, Bernard Montgomery (1887–1976), referred people who asked how he justified war to a book on *The Life of the Ant*. A number of distinguished anthropologists agree, arguing that evolution implanted aggressive and violent instincts in humans as it did in other animals. Romantics defend the opposite point of view. Human nature is essentially peaceful until competition corrupts it. War, according to Margaret Mead, the great liberal anthropologist of the 1920s and 1930s, was an invention, not a biological necessity.

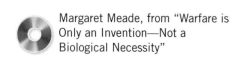
Margaret Meade, from "Warfare is Only an Invention—Not a Biological Necessity"

At first, the evidence seemed divided. The earliest archaeological proof we have of large-scale warfare is a battle fought at Jebel Sahaba (JAH-bahl sa-HAH-bah), near the modern border of Egypt and Sudan, about 11,000 years ago. The victims included women and children. Many were savaged by multiple wounds. One female was stabbed twenty-two times. At the time, agriculture was in its infancy. Today, peoples who practice the simplest agriculture as well as those who supposedly represent modernity and civilization massacre others. These facts have encouraged speculation that warfare began—or, at least, entered a new, more systematic phase—when settled communities started to fight one another to control land and resources.

Yet it seems that organized warfare must really be much older. In the 1970s, the primatologist Jane Goodall observed warfare among chimpanzee communities in the forests of Gabon in West Africa. When chimpanzee splinter groups secede from their societies, their former fellows try to kill them. Similar conflicts may have made early human splinter groups migrate to safety. It is an intriguing speculation, but, even if it were to prove correct, it poses other problems. What stresses could have caused people to divide and fight each other a hundred thousand years ago? Rising population again? Or are we driven back to more speculation about increasing competition for supposedly diminishing food stocks, or even to assertions about innate animal aggression?

In societies of increasing violence, men have enhanced roles. This is because, among all primates, including humans, greater competitiveness in mating makes males, on average, bigger and stronger than females. In consequence, alpha males rule, or at least boss, most ape societies. Human males usually seem to bond more closely with each other, or form more or stronger alliances, than females. This, too, is useful in competitive circumstances, such as those of war and politics. Yet women are, in at least one respect, more valuable in most societies than men. A society can dispense with most of its men and still reproduce itself. That is why societies more commonly risk men in war than women. Women, moreover, are more easily mistaken as sacred because of the obvious correspondences between the cycles of their bodies and the rhythms of the heavens. Menstruation and the cycle of female fertility match the phases of the moon.

So how did male domination come to be normal in human societies? One theory ascribes it to a deliberate, collective power-seeking strategy by males, inspired by dislike of women or resentment or envy or a desire to get control of the most elementary of resources—the means of reproducing the species. By analogy with chimpanzees, a rival theory suggests that male dominance is a consequence of hunting, which, in the few chimpanzee groups known to practice it, is an almost exclusively male activity. Hunting increases male dominance in chimpanzee society because the hunters distribute the meat, in almost ritual fashion. Females line up and, in effect, beg for morsels. Female chimps often exchange sex for food, espe-

Chimp agression. Humans obviously share aggressive individual tendencies with other apes. The American naturalist Jane Goodall discovered that chimpanzees organize conflicts with other groups of chimpanzees: they practice warfare, in other words. This seems to support what some philosophers and psychologists long suspected: that war is a "natural" activity, or, if it is an effect of culture, that it arose early in the history of culture.

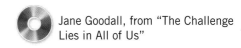
Jane Goodall, from "The Challenge Lies in All of Us"

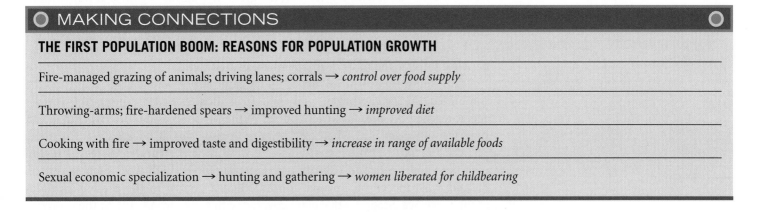

MAKING CONNECTIONS

THE FIRST POPULATION BOOM: REASONS FOR POPULATION GROWTH

Fire-managed grazing of animals; driving lanes; corrals → *control over food supply*

Throwing-arms; fire-hardened spears → improved hunting → *improved diet*

Cooking with fire → improved taste and digestibility → *increase in range of available foods*

Sexual economic specialization → hunting and gathering → *women liberated for childbearing*

cially meat. By contrast, among bonobos, who are like chimps but are strictly plant eating, both sexes share foraging, and females tend to be socially equal or even dominant. Hunting, however, seems to be a recent development in chimpanzee society and to have followed and strengthened male dominance—not caused it.

Without evidence to the contrary, it is unwise to assume that early in the migration period either sex monopolized political power. Still, migrating groups must have developed ways of liberating more women for childbirth, or increasing the fertile period of women's lives. Given the practical limitations on the number of children a woman can carry around with her, population can only have increased that way. Improved nutrition helped. Was there also some redistribution of economic activities, with men taking on more food-supplying roles?

As far as we know, in the earliest kind of sexual economic specialization, men did most of the hunting, while women did most of the gathering. Women's work seems to have been more productive in terms of calorific value per unit of energy expended. But we do not know when this specialization started or how rigid or widespread it was. In any case, the balance between hunted and gathered foods in the diets of the migrants varied according to the environment. In known cases, hunters supplied about a third of the nutrition. The migrations, and the accompanying demographic changes, would not have been possible without both hunting and gathering.

The peopling of the Earth was such a long-lasting phenomenon that we can safely presume it had multiple causes operating in different combinations in different places and at different times. Then, too, some migrations were surely one-of-a-kind events. We can imagine, for instance, the first boat people who colonized Australia as the drop-outs of more than 50,000 years ago, opting out of a changing world to settle a new continent, where they could maintain a traditional way of life. In general, if people moved into new environments, they must have been drawn by an abundance of new resources elsewhere, not driven by a shortage of resources in their old homes. The era of opportunity coincided with, and was perhaps caused by, new trends in global climate.

THE LAST GREAT ICE AGE

Whatever caused it, the peopling of the world spanned the most convulsive period of climatic change that *Homo sapiens* experienced before our own times. The cooling and warming phases of the planet are regular occurrences, and one or the other is always going on. Every 100,000 years or so, a distortion in the Earth's orbit tugs the Northern Hemisphere away from the sun. On more frequent cycles, the Earth tilts and wobbles on its axis. When these phenomena coincide, temperatures change dramatically. Ice ages set in. A great cooling began about 150,000 years ago. Roughly coinciding with the Ice Age, the great migrations began, as if humans did not just welcome the cold, but actively sought it. We think of global warming as a current phenomenon, and indeed it is. The world only began to emerge from the last Ice Age about 15,000 to 20,000 years ago. The intensive global warming we experience today is the most dramatic phase of that trend.

This is how the world we inhabit today came about. As the Earth tilted and the sun blazed, the ice cap began to shrink. At its most extensive, about 20,000 years ago, it reached the present lower courses of the Missouri and Ohio rivers in North America and deep into what are now the British Isles. It covered what is today Scandinavia. Most of the rest of what is now Europe was **tundra**, a treeless region with permanently frozen subsoil, or coniferous forest, with trees such as spruce, fir, and pine. In central Eurasia, tundra reached almost to the present latitudes of the Black Sea. **Steppe**—dry plain covered with scrub grass—licked the shores of the Mediterranean. In the New World, tundra and coniferous forest extended to where Virginia is today (see Map 1.2).

Warming started about 18,000 years ago. Not long after, between about 16,000 and 8,000 years ago, the geological record shows enormous regional fluctuations in temperature. Melting ice meant cooling seas and temporary reversals of warming in affected latitudes. As the fluctuations subsided, temperatures leaped. Glaciers retreated worldwide. Seas flooded and spilled over land, until—broadly speaking—the world map as we know it today took shape.

Ice-Age Hunters

The severity of the Ice Age is unimaginable, but it was not an entirely hostile world. For the hunters who inhabited the vast tundra that covered much of Eurasia, the edge of the ice was the best place to be. Over thousands of years of cold, a lot of mammals had adapted by efficiently storing their own body fat—and that was the hunters' target. Dietary fat has a bad reputation today, but for most of history, most people have eagerly sought it. Relatively speaking, animal fat is the world's most energy-abundant source of food.

In some of the vast Ice-Age tundra, concentrations of small, easily trapped arctic hare could supply human populations. More commonly, however, hunters favored species they could kill in large numbers by driving them over cliffs or into bogs or lakes. The cave art of the time depicts the controlled use of fire and funnel-shaped drive lanes. The bones of 10,000 Ice-Age horses lie at the foot of a cliff near Solutré in France, and remains of a hundred mammoths have turned up in pits at a site in the Czech Republic in Central Europe. About 20,000 years ago, the invention of the bow and arrow revolutionized killing technology. For the hunted species, such as the Old World's largest elephants and numerous kinds of deer, the new weapon hastened extinction, though climate change had perhaps already condemned them. But for the killers, while stocks lasted, the result was a fat bonanza, achieved with a relatively modest expenditure of effort.

It is rash to suppose that Ice-Age communities were small, limited to thirty or fifty people, like modern hunter–gatherers. Today, hunter–gatherers survive only in regions of great scarcity, where the modern world has driven them. Back then, community size varied according to the available resources; we can rarely put a figure to a group because only partial traces of Ice-Age dwellings have survived.

For Ice-Age artists, fat was beautiful. One of the oldest artworks in the world is the Venus of Willendorf—a plump little carving of a fat female, 30,000 years old and named for the place in Germany where she was found. Critics have interpreted her as a goddess, ruler, or since she could be pregnant, a fertility fetish.* However, her slightly more recent look-alike, the Venus of Laussel, carved on a cave wall in France, evidently got fat the way most of us do: by enjoyment and indulgence. She raises a horn, which must surely contain food or drink.

The remains of Ice-Age people reveal that, on average, they were better nourished than most later populations. Only modern industrialized societies surpass

Venus of Laussel. An image of a woman carved in relief on a cave wall in central France more than 20,000 years ago reveals much about Ice-Age life: esteem for big hips and body fat, the love of revelry suggested by the uplifted drinking-horn, the involvement of women in presumably sacred activity, and the existence of accomplished, specialized artists.

*Fetish: an object believed to have magical properties

The Ice Age

(All dates are approximate)	
150,000 years ago	Earth cools; last great Ice Age begins
18,000 years ago	Peak of Ice Age—farthest extent of ice cap
18,000 years ago	Warming of the Earth begins
16,000–8,000 years ago	Temperatures fluctuate; glaciers retreat; coastlines form
15,000–20,000 years ago	World emerges from Ice Age

PACIFIC
OCEAN

Kenniff Cave

Arnhem
Land

A U S T R A L I A

Tropic of Capricorn

Equator

Siberia

Arctic Circle

Yellow
Sea

Yellow

Yangtze

South
China
Sea

Mekong

SOUTHEAST
ASIA

A S I A

Himalayas

Ganges

Bay of
Bengal

Caspian Sea

Black Sea

Anatolia

Indus

Euphrates

Tigris

Sea

Arabian
Sea

INDIAN
OCEAN

1,000 km
1,000 miles
scale varies with perspective

N

R

A

Nile

I C A

Madagascar

Kahari
esert

Lion Cave

LESOTHO

TH AFRICA

MAP 1.2

The Ice Age

	extent of ice cover 20,000 years ago
	extent of ice cover 12,000 years ago
	tundra
	tundra and coniferous forests
	steppe
○	modern-city
◇	foraging settlement described on page 26
◆	places described on pages 17–26
San	native people
- - -	ancient coastlines
	ancient lake

The Flintstones—the TV and movie "modern stone-age family" imagined by cartoonists William Hanna and Joseph Barbera—inspired childish fantasy and slapstick comedy. But the more we know of the humans of over 20,000 years ago, the more "modern" they seem, with arts, ambitions, religions, social forums, political practices, and mental and physical capacities recognizably like those of our own.

Marshall Sahlins, "The Original Affluent Society," from *Stone-Age Economics*

their intake of 3,000 calories a day. In some Ice-Age communities, people ate about five pounds of food a day. The nature of the plant foods they gathered—few starchy grains, relatively large amounts of fruit and wild tubers*—and the high ascorbic acid content of animal organ meats provided five times the average intake of vitamin C of an American today. Abundant game guaranteed **Ice-Age affluence**. High levels of nutrition and long days of leisure, unequalled in most subsequent societies, meant people had time to observe nature and think about what they saw. The art of the era shows the sublime results. Like all good jokes, *The Flintstones*—the popular television cartoon series about a modern Stone-Age family—contains a kernel of truth. Cave people really were like us, with the same kinds of minds and many of the same kinds of thoughts.

Ice-Age Art

In the depths of the Ice Age, a stunningly resourceful way of life took shape. We know most about the period in Europe, where extensive art has survived because it was made in deep caves evidently chosen because they were inaccessible. Only now are the effects of tourism, too many respiratory systems, too many camera flashes, damaging these works in their once-secret caverns. Most prehistoric art has been found in northern Spain and southwest France (see "Going to the Source: Chauvet Cave," pages 56–59). About fifty cave complexes contain thousands of paintings, mostly of animals, and hundreds of smaller works. Examples of sculptures, carvings, and other art objects are also scattered across Europe, from Britain and the Atlantic in the west, to the Oder River and Carpathian Mountains in the east, and beyond, to Ukraine, and the Ural Mountains, which divide Europe and Asia.

What was the art for? It surely told stories and had magical, ritual uses. Some animal images are slashed or punctured many times over, as if in symbolic sacrifice. Where early artists used stenciling (tracing around a pattern), it seems believable that footprints and handprints inspired it. A good case has been made for seeing the cave paintings as aids to track prey. The shapes of hooves, the tracks, dung, seasonal habits, and favorite foods of the beasts are among the artists' standard stock of images.

The technology that made the cave art was simple: a palette mixed from three different colors of the mineral ochre (OH-ker)—red, brown, yellow—and animal fat, applied with wood, bone, and animal hair. Yet even the earliest works appeal instantly to modern sensibilities. The looks and litheness of the animal portraits spring from the rock walls, products of practiced, specialized hands and of learning accumulated over generations. Carvings from the same period exhibit similar elegance—ivory sculptures of 30,000-year-old arched-necked horses from Vogelherd in south Germany; female portraits from Brassempouy in France and Dolní Věstonice in Moravia, over 20,000 years old. Clay models of bears, dogs, and women were fired 27,000 years ago at Dolní Věstonice and at Maininskaya in what is now Russia.

Outside Europe, what little we know of the peoples of the time suggests that they created equally skillful work. Four painted rock slabs from Namibia in southwest Africa are about 26,000 years old, almost as old as any art in Europe, and bear similar

---

*Tubers: plants with fleshy stems, often underground

animal images. The earliest paintings that decorate the rocks of Arnhem Land in northernmost Australia show faint traces of long-extinct giant kangaroos and scary snakes. A clue to the very idea of representing life in art fades today from a rock face in Kenniff, Australia, where stencils of human hands and tools were made 20,000 years ago. But most of the evidence has been lost, weathered away on exposed rock faces, perished with the bodies or hides on which it was painted, or scattered by wind from the earth where it was scratched.

Ice-Age Culture and Society

The discovery of so much comparable art, of comparable age, in such widely separated parts of the world suggests an important and often overlooked fact. The Ice Age was the last great era of what we would now call a kind of **globalization**. That is, key elements of culture were the same all over the inhabited world. People practiced the same hunter–gatherer economy with similar kinds of technology, ate similar kinds of food, enjoyed similar levels of material culture, and—as far as we can tell—had similar religious practices.

The **material culture**—concrete objects people create—that many archeological digs yield offers clues to what goes on in the mind. A simple test establishes that fact. We can make informed inferences about people's religion, or politics, or their attitudes toward nature and society, or their values in general, by looking at what they eat, how they dress, and how they decorate their homes. For instance, the people who hunted mammoths to extinction 20,000 years ago on the Ice-Age steppes of what is now southern Russia built dome-shaped dwellings of mammoth bones on a circular plan twelve or fifteen feet in diameter that seem sublime triumphs of the imagination. They are reconstructions of mammoth nature, humanly reimagined, perhaps to acquire the beast's strength or to magically assume power over the species. In fact, ordinary, everyday activities went on inside these extraordinary dwellings—sleeping, eating, and all the routines of family life—in communities, on average, of fewer than a hundred people. But no dwelling is purely practical. Your house reflects your ideas about your place in the world.

Thanks to the clues material culture yields, we can make some confident assertions about other aspects of Ice-Age people's lives: their symbolic systems, their magic, and the kind of social and political units they lived in. Although Ice-Age people had nothing we recognize as writing, they did have highly expressive symbols, which we can only struggle to translate. Realistic drawings made 20,000 to 30,000 years ago show recurring gestures and postures. Moreover, they often include what seem to be numbers, signified by dots and notches. Other marks, which we can no long interpret, are undeniably systematic. One widely occurring mark that looks like a P may be a symbol for female because it resembles the curves of a woman's body. What looks as if it might be a calendar was made 30,000 years ago in the Dordogne region in France. It is a flat bone inscribed with crescents and circles that may record phases of the moon.

Clues to the spiritual life of the time appear in traces of red ochre, the earliest substance that seems to have had a role in ritual. The oldest known ochre mine in the world, about 42,000 years old, is at Lion Cave in what is now Lesotho in southern Africa. The vivid, lurid color was applied in burials, perhaps as a precious

Cave art. Until they died out—victims of competition with and exploitation by settler communities—in the early twentieth century, the Southern Bushmen of South Africa made cave paintings similar to those their ancestors made more than 20,000 years ago. On rock surfaces and cave walls, shamans painted their visions of the creatures of the spirit-world, glimpsed in states of ecstasy on imaginary journeys beyond the ordinarily accessible world.

MAMMOTH HUT

Between 40,000 and 16,000 years ago, on what are now the Russian and Ukranian steppe, people built dwellings made out of the bones of woolly mammoths and other creatures. The biggest surviving dwelling at Mezhirich (Ukraine) has 385 bones from about 100 different beasts that, when alive, weighed over 46,000 pounds in all.

Ninety-five jawbones with the chins facing down form a decorative outer wall that is lined with skulls and other bones.

Wooden roof covered with hides

Tusks form the porch

Generations of ancient steppe dwellers collected bones and stored them in pits. Some buildings used bones that were 8,000 years old when the buildings were constructed.

Central hearth or shrine, ornamented by an erect mammoth skull painted with ocher (a reddish brown clay) carved with zigzag designs.

Right femur (male)

The floor area is between 13 and 23 feet wide. Extensive finds of ash, charcoal, and ochre suggest that rituals took place at these sites. Skulls, jaws, and shoulder blades form the foundations of the dwellings.

How does this Ice-Age dwelling demonstrate the close connection between environment and culture?

22

offering, perhaps to imitate blood and reinvest the dead with life. The speculation that people might also have used ochre to paint their living bodies is hard to resist.

Ice-Age people also used symbols and substances such as ochre in magic, and those who controlled them wielded power. In paintings and carvings, we can glimpse the Ice-Age elite, people considered special and set apart from the group. In figures wearing animal masks—antlered or lionlike—the wearer is transformed. From anthropological studies of the recent past, we know such disguises are normally efforts to communicate with the dead or with the gods. Bringing messages from other worlds is the role of a **shaman** (SHAH-mehn), someone who acts as an intermediary between humans and spirits or gods. The shaman may seek a state of ecstasy induced by drugs or dancing or drumming, to see and hear realms normally inaccessible to the senses. He becomes the medium through which spirits talk to this world. Among the Chukchi hunters of northern Siberia, whose way of life and environment are similar to Ice-Age peoples', the shaman's experience is represented as a journey to consult the spirits in a realm that only the dead can normally enter. The shaman may adopt an animal disguise to acquire the animal's speed or strength or identify with an animal ancestor. The shaman's role can be an awesome source of authority. Shamans can challenge alpha males. Like other religions, shamanism involves spiritual insight, which people of both sexes, various levels of intellect, and all kinds of physique can acquire. It can replace the strong with the seer and the sage. By choosing elites who had the gift of communicating with spirits, Ice-Age societies could escape the oppression of the physically powerful or those privileged by birth.

Although we cannot be sure about the nature of the Ice-Age power class, we know it existed because of glaring inequalities in the way Ice-Age people were buried. In a cemetery at Sunghir (SOON-geer), near Moscow, dated about 24,000 years ago, the highest-status person seems, at first glance, to have been an elderly man. His burial goods include a cap sewn with fox's teeth and about twenty ivory bracelets. Nearby, however, two boys of about eight or ten years old have even more spectacular ornaments. As well as ivory bracelets and necklaces and fox-tooth buttons, the boys have animal carvings and beautifully wrought weapons, including spears of mammoth ivory, each over six feet long. About 3,500 finely worked ivory beads had been drizzled over the head, torso, and limbs of each boy. Here was a society that marked leaders for greatness from boyhood and therefore, perhaps, from birth.

In our attempt to understand where power lay in Ice-Age societies, the final bits of evidence are crumbs from rich people's tables, fragments of feasts. Archaeologists have found ashes from large-scale cooking and the calcified debris of food at sites in northern Spain, perhaps from as long as 23,000 years ago. The tally sticks that survive from the same region in the same period may also have been records of expenditure on feasts. What were such feasts for? By analogy with modern hunting peoples, the most likely reason was alliance-making between communities. They were probably not male-bonding occasions, as some scholars think, because they are close to major dwelling sites where women and children would be present. Instead, from the moment of its emergence, the idea of the feast had practical consequences: to build and strengthen societies and enhance the power of those who organized the feasts and controlled the food (for more discussion of feasting, see "Going to the Source: Feasting," pages 152–155).

Peopling the New World

The New World was the last part of the planet *Homo sapiens* peopled. We can be sure of that much, but it is not easy to say exactly when or by whom. According to the formerly dominant theory, a gap opened between glaciers toward the end of the Ice Age. A race of hunters crossed the land link between North America and

Shaman. In many societies, communication with the spirit-world remains the responsibility of the specialists whom anthropologists call shamans. Typically, they garb and paint or disguise themselves to resemble spirits, or the animals deemed to have privileged access to realms beyond human sense. The shamans then "journey" to the spirits or ancestors in trances induced by dancing, drumming, or drugs. Shamans often acquire social influence and political authority as healers, prophets, and arbitrators.

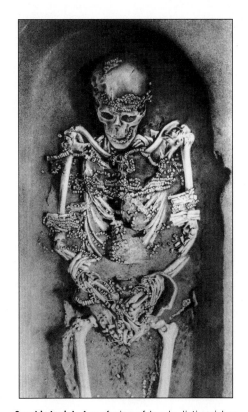
Sunghir burial. A profusion of beads distinguishes the graves of people of high status at Sunghir in Russia, from about 24,000 years ago. The distribution of signs of wealth in burials suggests that even in the Ice Age inequalities were rife and that status could be inherited.

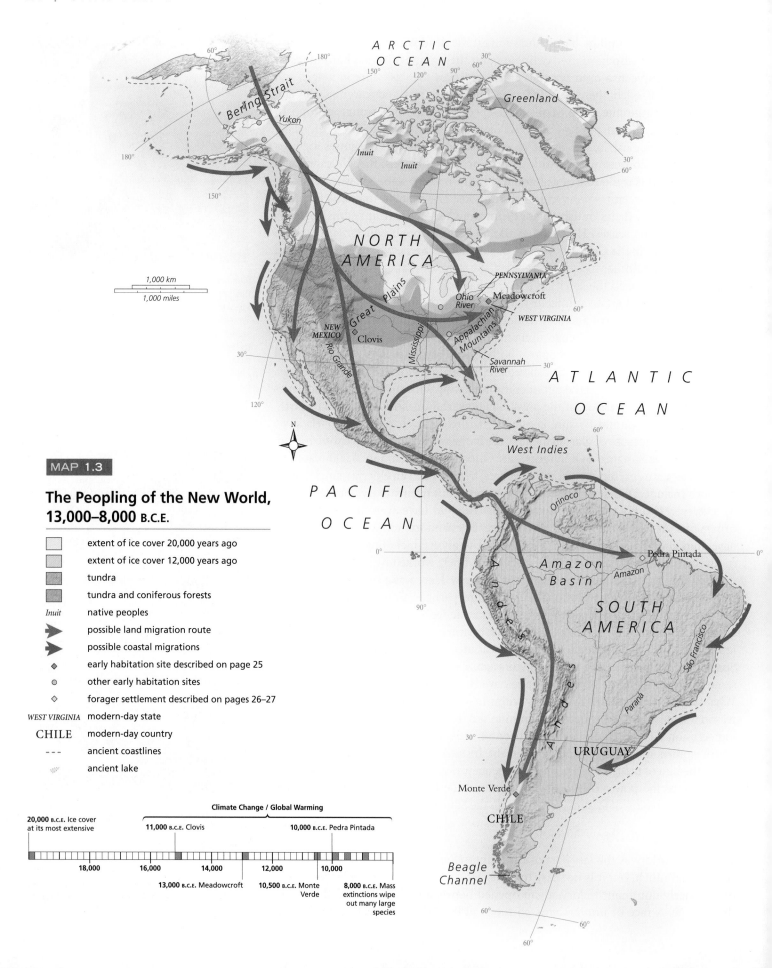

MAP 1.3

The Peopling of the New World, 13,000–8,000 B.C.E.

- extent of ice cover 20,000 years ago
- extent of ice cover 12,000 years ago
- tundra
- tundra and coniferous forests

Inuit   native peoples

➤   possible land migration route

➤   possible coastal migrations

◆   early habitation site described on page 25

◎   other early habitation sites

◇   forager settlement described on pages 26–27

WEST VIRGINIA   modern-day state

CHILE   modern-day country

- - -   ancient coastlines

   ancient lake

Climate Change / Global Warming

20,000 B.C.E. Ice cover at its most extensive

11,000 B.C.E. Clovis

10,000 B.C.E. Pedra Pintada

| 18,000 | 16,000 | 14,000 | 12,000 | 10,000 |

13,000 B.C.E. Meadowcroft

10,500 B.C.E. Monte Verde

8,000 B.C.E. Mass extinctions wipe out many large species

Asia, where the Bering Strait now flows, to enter a paradise where no human hunter had ever trod before. The abundance was so great and the animals so unwary, that the invaders ate enormously and multiplied greatly. They spread rapidly over the hemisphere, hunting the great game to extinction as they went. The story appealed to an unsophisticated form of U.S. patriotism. The Clovis people, as these hunters were dubbed after an early archaeological site in New Mexico, seemed to resemble modern American pioneers. They exhibited quick-fire locomotion, hustle and bustle, technical prowess, big appetites, irrepressible strength, enormous cultural reach, and a talent for reforging the environment.

By comparison, the truth about the peopling of the hemisphere is disappointingly undramatic. These first great American superheroes—like most of their successors—did not really exist. Although archeologists have excavated too few sites for a complete and reliable picture to emerge, a new theory dominates. We have evidence of early human settlement scattered from the Yukon to Uruguay and from near the Bering Strait to the edge of the Beagle Channel—that is, from the waterway that divides North America and Asia, to the southern limits of the South American mainland. This evidence is so widespread, over so long a period, in so many different geological layers, and with such a vast range of cultural diversity that one conclusion is inescapable—colonists came at different times, bringing different cultures with them.

No generally accepted evidence dates any inhabited sites in the American hemisphere earlier than about 13,000 B.C.E. (see Map 1.3). The first arrivals came during a time when glaciers covered much of North America. They stuck close to the cold, where the game was fattest. They followed corridors between walls of ice or along narrow shores away from glaciers. Other arrivals came by sea and continued to come after the land bridge was submerged. Around 10,000 years ago, a catastrophic cluster of extinctions wiped out the mammoth, mastodon, horse, giant sloth, saber-toothed tiger, and at least thirty-five other large species in the Americas. New hunting techniques and perhaps new hunting peoples were probably partly responsible. But we can only explain the events in the context of vast climatic changes that affected habitats and the whole ecology on which these animals depended.

Many supposedly early sites of human habitation have proved to be delusions of overenthusiastic archaeologists—false, or, at best, unconvincing. A few sites, however, offer strong evidence of the antiquity and range of settlement. Most are in the eastern United States—a long way from Asia. It must have taken a long time for these people to get there from the vicinity of the modern Bering Strait. In the mid-1970s, 15,000-year-old basketwork and tools made with fine flints emerged from deep under the discarded beer cans that topped a dig at Meadowcroft, on the Ohio River, near the border of Pennsylvania and West Virginia. Archaeologists are investigating similar sites between the Ohio and Savannah Rivers. Later in the 1970s, excavations at Monte Verde (MON-teh VER-deh) in southern Chile revealed a twenty-foot long, wooden, hide-covered dwelling preserved in a peat bog for about 12,500 years. Nearby were a big mastodon-butchery and a space devoted to making tools. The inhabitants brought salt and seaweed from the coast, forty miles away, and medicinal herbs from mountains equally far in the opposite direction. Half-chewed lumps of seaweed show the eaters' dental bites; a boy's footprints survive in the clay lining of a pit. If Meadowcroft is a long way from the colonizers' entry point near the Bering Strait, southern Chile is a world away again—almost as far as you can get in the Western Hemisphere. How long would it have taken the settlers of Monte Verde to cross the hemisphere, over vast distances and through many different kinds of environments, each demanding new forms of adaptation? Most specialists think it must have taken thousands of years. The question of the date of the first peopling of the New World therefore remains open.

Clovis Points

Monte Verde. About 12,000 years ago, a young person trod in fresh clay that lined a hearth in Monte Verde, Chile. Peat sealed and preserved the footprint to be rediscovered by archaeologists in the 1970s. Excavations at Monte Verde revealed a village of mammoth hunters so old that it made previous theories about when people arrived in the Americas questionable or even untenable.

SURVIVAL OF THE FORAGERS

As the ice cap retreated and the great herds shifted with it, many human communities opted to follow them. Archeology has unearthed traces of their routes. Along the way, in what is now northern Germany, about 12,000 years ago, people sacrificed reindeer by deliberately weighting them with stones sewn into their stomachs and drowning them in a lake. About 1,000 years later, hunters as far north as Yorkshire in England, who left a well-preserved camp at Starr Carr, found an environment as abundant as the cave artists's had, been. Not only was it filled with tundra-loving species such as red deer, elk, and aurochs (OW-roks)—huge, shaggy wild cattle—but also with wild boar in surroundings that were becoming patchily wooded.

At Skateholm in Sweden, about 8,000 years ago, hunters founded the largest known settlement of the era. It was a winter camp in an area where the eighty-seven different animal species roamed that the inhabitants ate: trapping river-fish, netting sea-birds, harpooning seals and dolphin, sticking pigs, and driving deer into pits or ponds. In summer, the people must have moved farther north. They lie today in graves decorated with beads and ochre and filled with the spoils of their careers, including antlers and boar's tusks. Their dogs are buried nearby. These burly, wolflike companions are sometimes interred with more signs of honor than humans were given. Dogs were full members of societies where hunting prowess and skill in war determined status. Many of the human dead bear wounds from man-made weapons. Here, too, is evidence of sexual specialization. Women have only a third as many wounds as the men.

The most persistently faithful followers of the ice were the Inuit (IN-yoo-it) of North America. About 4,000 years ago, they invented the blubber-filled soapstone lamp. Now they could follow big game beyond the tundra and into the darkness of an arctic winter. They could track the musk ox to the shore of the ocean and the caribou on its winter migrations, when its fur is thickest and its fat most plentiful. This way of life persisted until the late twentieth century, although the people who first practiced it have disappeared. Migrants from the Arctic Ocean replaced them 1,000 years ago.

Climate change trapped other foraging peoples in environments where they had to develop new ways of life. Some of these environments offered new kinds of abundance. Here were broad-leaved forests, rich in acorns (which make nutritious food for any humans who have enough time to fine-grind them), and lakes and rivers full of aquatic life. New World prairies held apparently inexhaustible stocks of bison (though the largest bison species was rapidly hunted to extinction). Between the unstable periods of climate change around 12,000 years ago, foragers even colonized dense, tropical forests in southeast Asia and in the New World at Pedra Pintada in Brazil where the Amazon River now flows. This is a region where foragers today have to struggle to find foods they can digest, but it seems to have been more environmentally diverse toward the end of the Ice Age.

Some societies perpetuated their foraging life in hot, arid deserts, as different from the best hunting grounds of the Ice Age as it is possible to imagine. This required two forms of adaptation. First, the thinly dispersed populations had to create collaborative networks. Such interdependence explains why peoples who live in ecologically shaky homelands often require people to marry outside the group (a practice known as exogamy) and why they regard hospitality to strangers as a sacred obligation. Second, poor environments demanded that inhabitants develop what we might call orally transmitted science. For only with accurate and extensive knowledge of their habitat can people survive in harsh environments.

The San or Bushmen of southern Africa's Kalahari Desert illustrate the difficulties and solutions. Their domain has shrunk in the last few centuries, as Bantu farmers, Khoi herdsmen, and white invaders have overrun much of their former territory. But their heartland was already dry at the time of the San's first occupancy, about 14,000 years ago. The increased rainfall that usually followed the retreat of the ice hardly fell here. There are underground rivers but few permanent water holes. The people watch for rare signs of rain and hurry to gather the vegetation that accompanies it. The scrubland plant foods, including water-bearing tubers and a kind of cactus, supply 30 percent of their sustenance. The rest comes from game, which grazes on tough desert shrubs that humans cannot digest.

Laurens van der Post, a South African adventurer who has written about the Bushmen, once accompanied a band of San hunters in search of their favorite food, eland, a type of antelope. One morning just after sunrise, they found the tracks of a herd. By three in the afternoon, after nonstop pursuit at a trot, they came on the herd and took aim. To kill large game is almost impossible with a Bushman's bow. He wounds the beast with a poisoned barb and follows it until it drops from exhaustion and the effects of the drug, before making the kill. On this occasion, the hunters ran for twelve miles without stopping "and the final mile was an all-out sprint." The next time they made contact with the herd, one bull was seen to be tiring. It still took another full hour of pursuit until he fell. Then "without pause or break for rest they were fresh enough at the end to plunge straight away into the formidable task of skinning and cutting up the heavy animal."[1] Bushmen who persist with this demanding way of life to this day are obviously pursuing a commitment that has grown out of generations of invested emotion. As difficult as it may be for us to understand, the San would find it heart-wrenching to change a way of life for the mere sake of efficiency, convenience, or material gain.

In one sense, the world's food supply still depends on foraging. The amount of food from hunting actually increased in the twentieth century, which may go down in history not only as the last age of hunting but as the greatest. World-over today, we practice a highly specialized, mechanized, and unusual form of hunting—deep-sea trawling. Fish farming is likely to replace it in the future, but in any case, deep-sea fishing is a historical throwback.

Bushmen. Though now obliged to adopt a mixed economy, supported in part by farming and donations of food, the San or Bushmen of southern Africa have been among the most conservative of the world's peoples. They maintained their foraging way of life, essentially unchanged, for millennia—despite neighbors' attempts to exterminate them. This record of survival contrasts with the rapid turnover of more ambitious civilizations that radically modify their environments, usually with disastrous results.

IN PERSPECTIVE: After the Ice

In the post–Ice-Age world, little by little, over thousands of years, most societies abandoned foraging and adopted farming or herding as the way to get their food. Among peoples who still live close to the ice cap, the Inuit remain faithful to their hunting tradition in North America. Most of their Old World counterparts, however, have long abandoned it. In Eurasia, though some hunting cultures still cling to the old ways at the eastern end of Siberia, the peoples on the western Arctic rim—the Sami (or Lapplanders) of Scandinavia and their neighbors, the Karelia, Samoyeds, and Nenets—adopted reindeer herding over a thousand years ago. The Ice-Age way of life, if not over, is drawing to a close. Hunting is now thought of

CHRONOLOGY
(All dates are approximate)

Over 3 million years ago	Lucy
2–1 million years ago	*Homo erectus* migrates from East Africa to Africa and Eurasia
100,000 years ago	*Homo sapiens* migrates out of Africa
67,000 years ago	*Homo sapiens* in Asia
50,000 years ago	*Homo sapiens* colonizes Australia and New Guinea
	Homo sapiens reaches Europe
30,000 years ago	Last Neanderthals vanish
20,000– 15,000 B.C.E.	World emerges from the Ice Age
20,000 B.C.E.	Invention of the bow and arrow
13,000 B.C.E.	*Homo sapiens* in the Americas

as a primitive way to get food, long abandoned except as an aristocratic indulgence in some countries or as a supposedly manly sport in others.

The disappearance of foraging lifeways seems a remarkable turnaround for a predator-species such as *Homo sapiens*. There was a time before hunting, when our ancestors were scavengers, but for hundreds of thousands, perhaps millions, of years, foraging was reliable and rewarding. It fed people through every change of climate. Its practitioners spread over the world and adapted successfully to every kind of habitat. *Homo sapiens* dominated every ecosystem they became part of and competed successfully with most other species. They achieved startling increases in their numbers, which we struggle to explain. They founded more varied societies than any other species (though the differences among these societies were slight compared to later periods). They had art-rich cultures with traditions of learning and symbolic systems to record information. They had their own social elites, political customs, ambitious magic, and practical methods to exploit their environment.

Our next task is to ask why, after the achievements recounted in this chapter, did people abandon the foraging life? Renouncing the hunt and pursuing new ways of life after the Ice Age are among the most far-reaching and mysterious transformations of the human past. If the puzzle of why *Homo sapiens* spread over the Earth is the first great question in our history, the problem of why foragers became farmers is the second.

PROBLEMS AND PARALLELS

1. When does the story of humankind begin? Is it possible to define what it means to be human? What characteristics do we share with chimpanzees and other apes?

2. How do Neanderthals and *Homo floresiensis* challenge commonly held definitions of *Homo sapiens*?

3. Why did *Homo sapiens* migrate out of Africa? How did migration change people's relationships with each other and with their environment?

4. What were the factors behind the rapid population growth of *Homo sapiens?*

5. Which stresses could have caused early peoples to divide and fight each other? Which theories have been put forward for how war started?

6. How did male domination come to be normal in human societies? What impact did sexual economic specialization have on early societies?

7. Why was the Ice Age a time of affluence? What role did shamans play in Ice-Age society? What insights into Ice-Age societies can we glean from its art and the remains of ancient feasts?

8. How did some societies perpetuate the foraging life after the Ice Age? How has the foraging life persisted today?

DOCUMENTS IN GLOBAL HISTORY

- Margaret Meade, from "Warfare is Only an Invention—Not a Biological Necessity"
- Jane Goodall, from "The Challenge Lies in All of Us"
- Marshall Sahlins, "The Original Affluent Society," from *Stone-Age Economics*
- Clovis Points

Please see the Primary Source CD-ROM for additional sources related to this chapter.

READ ON

F. Fernández-Armesto, *Humankind: A Brief History* (2004) traces debates over the boundaries of the concept of humankind. Jared Diamond's book on the human overlap with apes is *The Third Chimpanzee* (1992). The works of F. de Waal, especially *The Ape and the Sushi Master* (2001), and those of J. Goodall, especially *The Chimpanzees of Gombe* (1986), are fundamental for understanding the issues. B. Sykes, *The Seven Daughters of Eve* (2001), is the best introduction to the use of DNA in paleoanthropology. C. Stringer and C. Gamble, *In Search of the Neanderthals* (1995), is an interesting review of human engagement with Neanderthal remains. The classic novel by W. Golding, *The Inheritors* (1963), is an imaginative attempt to envisage Neanderthal life.

Good general introductions to human evolution include R. G. Klein, *The Human Career* (1999), and I. Tattersall, *The Fossil Trail* (1997). C. Gamble, *Timewalkers: The Prehistory of Global Colonization* (1994), is an excellent account of the migrations. On fire, J. Goudsblom, *Fire and Civilization* (1993), is a classic, which the author has kept up to date in recent editions. R. Wrangham's views appeared in "The Raw and the Stolen," *Current Anthropology*, vol: xl (1999), 567–594. On war, K. Lorenz, *On Aggression* (1966), and R. Ardrey, *The Territorial Imperative* (1997), are controversial classics. J. Haas, ed., *The Anthropology of War* (1990) and L. H. Keeley, *War Before Civilization* (1997), survey the evidence.

On sex roles, G. Lerner, *The Creation of Patriarchy* (1987), and E. Martin, *The Woman in the Body: A Cultural Analysis of Reproduction* (1992), set the terms of debate. J. Peterson, *Sexual Revolutions* (2002), is an invaluable short survey.

On the conditions of Ice-Age life, M. D. Sahlins, *Stone Age Economics* (1972), is a stimulating classic. T. D. Price and J. A. Brown, eds, *Prehistoric Hunter-Gatherers* (1985) is an important collection of studies. On the art, the most illuminating works include S. J. Mithen, *Thoughtful Foragers* (1990), and J. D. Lewis-Williams, *Discovering Southern African Rock Art* (1990).

On the peopling of the New World, the challenging and readable work of J. Adovasio, *Before America* (2004), makes a stimulating starting point. S. Mithen, *After the Ice* (2004) is an engaging and imaginative introduction to the post–Ice-Age world.

The material on L. van der Post comes from his now much maligned classic, *The Lost World of the Kalahari* (1977). For up-to-date studies see L. Marshall, *The !Kung of Nyae Nyae* (1976), and E. Wilmsen, *Land Filled with Flies* (1989).

CHAPTER 2

Out of the Mud: Farming and Herding After the Ice Age

In environments that have no plants that humans can digest, herding is a life-giving option: Animals and humans live in mutual dependence. Humans protect the flocks from predators; their livestock convert grasses and shrubs into meat and milk. But, as with the Somali herdsmen pictured here, herders' lives are often precarious in marginal environments, because domesticated animals host disease-bearing organisms that can infect humans. Typically, herding cultures cope with restricted diets by developing a tolerance to digest dairy foods after infancy.

n August 1770, the British navigator Captain James Cook reached the north coast of Australia, on the first of his spectacular voyages of exploration that charted the lands and limits of the Pacific Ocean. Near Cape York, he paused at an island he named Possession Island. For although his stated purpose was scientific, he was also an officer of the Royal Navy with orders to extend the British Empire. To Cook's mind, the island, though inhabited, was waiting to be grabbed. The natives could not be said to possess it because they had left no marks of possession on its soil. A wealth of plants that they could have domesticated—"fruits proper for the support of man"—was growing wild. Yet, Cook wrote, the people "know nothing of cultivation. . . . It seems strange." He was puzzling over one of the most perplexing problems of history—the difference between foragers and farmers, food procurers and food producers.

● ● ● ● ●

Food is the most precious of resources. Nothing can happen without it. To most people, in most societies, for most of the time, food is and always has been the most important thing in the world. Changes in how we get food and whether we get it are among history's big changes. During the global warming that followed the Ice Age, **husbandry**—breeding animals and cultivating crops—began to replace hunting and gathering and introduced the biggest change of all.

THE PROBLEM OF AGRICULTURE

Husbandry happened in two distinct ways, involving different types of environments and different levels of environmental intervention. In some environments, people could exploit creatures that had a herd instinct by managing the herds, rather than by hunting them. Breeding enhanced qualities that evolution did not necessarily favor, such as docility; size; and yield of meat, milk, eggs, and fat. On the negative side, close contact between humans and animals often allowed disease-bearing organisms to thrive, threatening human lives and health and sometimes unleashing plagues. Otherwise, however, animal husbandry barely affected the environment. Herds, on the whole, kept to their traditional patterns of migration, and people continued to accompany them—driving the beasts, now, rather than following them. Domesticated animals remained recognizably the heirs of their wild ancestors, and the landscapes through which they traveled did not change much, except that the herds' feeding and manure probably

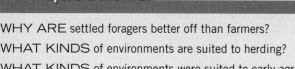

FOCUS questions

- WHY ARE settled foragers better off than farmers?
- WHAT KINDS of environments are suited to herding?
- WHAT KINDS of environments were suited to early agriculture?
- WHERE DID farming start, and what were the first crops?
- GIVEN THE disadvantages, why did people farm?

encouraged the grasses they ate to flourish at the expense of other plant species.

In other environments, however, plant husbandry involved massive human intervention. In the long run, tillage of the soil changed the world more than any previous innovation by *Homo sapiens*. From postglacial mud, people coaxed what we now call "**civilization**"—a way of life based on radically modifying the environment. Instead of merely trying to manage the landscape nature provided, farmers recarved it with fields and boundaries, ditches and irrigation canals. They stamped the land with a new look, a geometrical order. Agriculture enabled humans to see the world in a new way—to imagine that magic and science had the power to change nature. Such power, in turn, changed people's sense of where they fit into the panorama of life on Earth. Now they could become lords or, in more modest moments or cultures, stewards of creation.

Together, farming and herding revolutionized humans' place in their ecosystems. Instead of merely depending on other life forms to sustain us, we forged a new relationship of interdependence with those species we eat. We rely on them for food; they rely on us for their reproduction. Domesticated animals would not exist without humans. Husbandry was the first human challenge to evolution. Instead of evolving species through **natural selection**, farming and herding proceed by what might be called unnatural selection—sorting and selecting by human hands, for human needs, according to human agendas. In other words, we breed livestock and cultivate plants.

Herding and tilling also changed human societies. By feeding people on a vastly greater scale, agriculture allowed societies to get hugely bigger than ever before. We can only guess at the absolute figures, but in areas where farming has replaced foraging in modern times, population has increased fifty- or even a hundredfold. Larger populations demanded new forms of control of labor and food distribution, which, in turn, nurtured strong states and powerful elites. Society became more volatile and, apparently, less stable.

In almost every case, for reasons we still do not understand, when people begin to practice agriculture, the pace of change quickens immeasurably and cumulatively. States and civilizations do not seem to last for long. Societies that we think of as being most evolved turn out to be least fitted for survival. Compared with the relative stability of forager communities, societies that depend on agriculture are prone to lurch and collapse. History becomes a path picked among their ruins.

Still, for Captain Cook, and for most people who have thought about it ever since, it was indeed strange that people who had the opportunity to practice agriculture should not take advantage of it. The advantages of agriculture seem so obvious. The farmer can select the best specimens of edible crops and creatures, collect them in the most convenient places and pastures, crossbreed the livestock, and hybridize the plants to improve size, yield, or flavor. By these methods, small farming societies grow into communities and build up large populations. Usually they go on to create cities and develop ever more complex technologies. To Cook and his contemporaries in Europe, who believed that progress was inevitable and that the same kind of changes are bound to happen everywhere, peoples who clung to foraging seemed baffling.

The rice fields of Bali in Indonesia are among the most productive in the world, using varieties of rice and techniques for farming it that are about 1,000 years old. Irrigation channels, maintained and administered by farmers' cooperatives, distribute water evenly among the terraces. Though originally a lowland crop, favoring swampy conditions, rice adapts perfectly to upland environments and to terrace farming.

A Case in Point: Aboriginal Australians

Cook and others at the time saw only two explanations for why foragers, such as the **aborigines** (AB-eh-rihj-ih-neez) in Australia, would reject agriculture: They were either stupid or subhuman. Indeed, early European painters in Australia depicted aborigines as apelike creatures, grimacing oddly and crawling in trees. The colonists simply ignored the natives, or, when they got in the way, often hunted them down— as they would beasts. But not only did the native Australians reject agriculture, in some areas, they appeared to shun every technical convenience. On the island of Tasmania, in the extreme south of Australia, where the natives became extinct soon after European settlement began, they seemed to have forgotten every art of their ancestors: bows, boats, even how to kindle fire. In Arnhem Land, in the extreme north, they used boomerangs to make music but no longer as weapons for the hunt. Progress, which the European discoverers of Australia believed in fervently, seemed to have gone into reverse. Australia was not only on the exact opposite side of the world from England, it was a topsy-turvy place where everything was upside down.

We can, however, be certain that if aborigines rejected agriculture or other practices Europeans considered progressive, it must have been for good reasons. The aborigines did not lack the knowledge necessary to switch from foraging to farming had they so wished. When they gathered wild yams or the root known as nardoo, they ensured that enough of the plant remained in the ground to grow back. In many regions, too, they used fire to control the grazing grounds of kangaroos and concentrate them for hunting, a common technique among herders to manage pasture and among tillers to renew the soil. Along the Murray and Darling Rivers, aborigines even watered and weeded wild crops and policed their boundaries against human and animal predators (see Map 2.1).

The aboriginal Australians could also have systematically planted and irrigated crops, farmed the grubs they liked to eat, penned kangaroos, and even tried to domesticate them. (Kangaroos are cantankerous creatures, but people do make pets of them. Breeding selected specimens would probably produce a domestic strain in a few generations.) In the far north of Australia, aboriginal communities traded with the farming cultures of New Guinea. So, even if they hadn't developed agriculture on their own, they could have learned it from outsiders. If the aborigines did not farm, it must have been because they did not want to. In short, they were doing well without it. Similar cases all over the world support this conclusion. Where wild foods are abundant, there is no incentive to domesticate them. Of course, people often adopt practices that do them no good. We can concede this general principle, but, case by case, we still want to know why.

 James Cook, from *Captain Cook's Journal During his First Voyage Round the World*

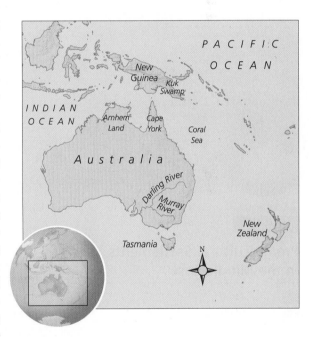

MAP 2.1 **Australia**

Preagricultural Settlements

Under some conditions, people can settle in one place without the trouble of farming. Archaeological evidence in the region we now call the Middle East shows this. After the Ice Age ended about 15,000 B.C.E., a frontier zone between forest and grassland stretched across the eastern shore of the Mediterranean and what are now Iran, eastern Turkey, and Iraq (see Map 2.2). The forests were full of acorns, pistachios, and almonds, which gatherers ground into flour and paste. The grasslands bred vast quantities of wild grass with edible seeds. These foods could all be

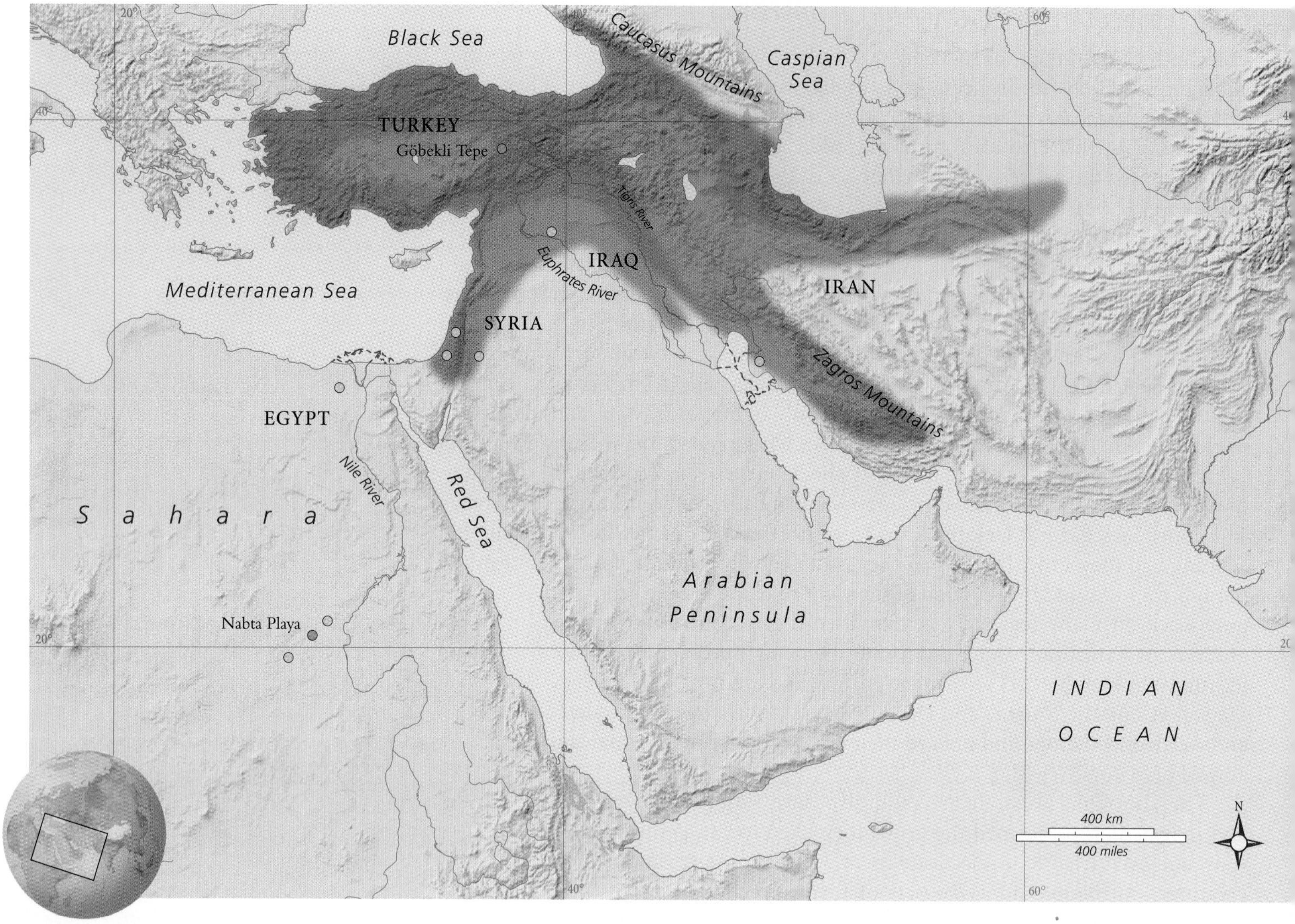

MAP 2.2

Preagricultural Settlements in the Middle East

▨	forest
▨	grassland
TURKEY	modern-day country
●	preagricultural settlement described on page 35
○	other preagricultural settlements
----	ancient coastlines

warehoused between harvests and had the additional advantage of maturing at different times. Dense herds of gazelle in the grasslands provided more nutrition for hunters to bring home. Food was so plentiful that foragers did not have to move around much to find it.

By about 14,000 to 15,000 years ago, permanent settlements arose throughout the region: clusters of dwellings with stone walls, or those made of wood on stone foundations, or cut from soft stone and roofed with reeds. The foragers who lived in these sedentary communities apparently kept to themselves. Villages had distinctive identities and habits, which almost amounted to badges of identity. Some favored gazelle toe bones for jewelry; some preferred fox teeth and partridge legs. These people married within their own communities (a practice known as endogamy), judging from the evidence of inherited physical characteristics. For example, in some villages, people were relatively short, while in others, they had distinctive dental patterns. These settlers cut what look like plans of their fields on limestone slabs, which suggests that they were territorial—that they had a sense of possession that Captain Cook would have recognized.

In sum, the lives of preagricultural settlers were so much like the lives of the early farmers who succeeded them that when archaeologists first found the foragers' villages in the 1930s, they assumed the inhabitants were farmers. But the settled foragers were actually better off than farmers. Their remains, on the whole, show better health and nourishment than the farming peoples who followed later in the same region. A diet rich in seeds and nuts had ground down their teeth, but—unlike the farmers—they have none of the streaked tooth-enamel common among people who suffer from food shortages.

Similar evidence of preagricultural settlements exists in other places. Take a few conspicuous examples. The Jomon (JOHM-mehn) people of central Honshu Island in Japan lived in permanent villages 13,000 years ago, feeding themselves by fishing and gathering acorns and chestnuts. They made pots for display, in elaborate shapes, modeled on flames and serpents and lacquered them with tree sap. Their potters were, in a sense, magicians, transforming clay into objects of prestige and ritual. In the Egyptian Sahara, at Nabta Playa, about forty plant species, including sorghum, a type of cereal grass, grew alongside hearths and pit ovens, evidence of settled life from about 10,000 years ago. In other parts of central Sahara in the same period that had plenty of water and a cooler climate than now, foragers found sorghum and millet, another cereal grass. At Göbekli Tepe (goh-BEHK-lee TEH-peh), a hilltop site in southeast Turkey, contemporaries who lived mainly by gathering wild wheat hewed seven-ton pillars from limestone. They reerected them in a sunken chamber in their village and decorated them with carvings of snakes, boar, gazelles, cranes, and symbols that look suspiciously like writing.

What was life like in these earliest settlements? Small, permanent houses suggest that nuclear families—parents and children—predominated, though some sites clearly have communal work areas for grinding seeds and nuts. As for who did the work, the most stunning finding of recent archaeology in the Middle East suggests that work was probably shared between the sexes. The way skeletons are muscled suggests that women did slightly more kneeling (and therefore slightly more grinding) than men, and men did more throwing (and therefore more hunting) than women. But both sexes did both activities. Male and female bodies began to reconverge after a long period during which they had evolved to look differently. As food production replaced hunting and gathering, war and child rearing became the main sex-specific jobs in society. The convergence between the physical features of men and women seems still to be in progress today. Indeed, it seems to be accelerating as men and women share more and more tasks, and the need for heavily muscled or big-framed bodies diminishes along with physically demanding jobs in much of the world.

The Disadvantages of Farming

Prefarming communities do not simply progress to farming. If foraging produces abundance and security, it does not necessarily follow that farming can deliver more of the same. The consequences of adopting agriculture are by no means all positive. In the early stages of moving from foraging to farming, the food supply actually becomes less reliable because people depend on a relatively small range of farmed foods or even on a single species. As a result, a community becomes vulnerable to ecological disasters. Famine becomes more likely as diet narrows. Moreover, when people have to plant and grow food as well as gather it, they have to use up more energy to get the same amount of nourishment. (Although domesticated foods, once harvested, tend to be easier to process for eating.) The need to

Jomon pottery. Ten thousand years ago, the Jomon potters of Japan produced the world's earliest known earthenware vessels. Other pottery-making peoples also practiced farming, but the Jomon people were sedentary foragers—living in permanent or long-term settlements, but managing the environment in minimal ways and relying on abundant wild foods, including nuts, seeds, acorns, some 70 marine animal species, and land mammals—eating not just boar, deer, and hare, but also wolves, wildcats, flying squirrels, and monkeys.

Overuse deforms bones. Archaeology can reconstruct how ancient people behaved by measuring the deformities in their skeletons. The woman whose toe this was lived in a community of early sedentary foragers in what is now Syria. She evidently spent much of her time kneeling, presumably to grind the acorns and kernels of wild wheat on which her people relied for food.

Early Forager Settlements

(All dates are approximate)	
15,000 years ago	World emerges from the Ice Age
14,000–15,000 years ago	Permanent settlements appear in Middle East
13,000 years ago	Honshu Island, Japan
10,000 years ago	Nabta Playa, Egypt; Göbekli Tepe, Turkey

Jack Harlan, from *Crops and Man*

organize labor encourages inequalities and exploitation. Concentrations of domesticated animals spread disease, such as smallpox, measles, rubella, chicken pox, influenza, and tuberculosis.

So the problem is really the opposite of what Cook supposed. It is farmers' behavior not foragers' that is strange. Husbandry is not a step along a march of improvement because in some ways, it makes life worse. No one has put the problem better than the historian of agronomy, Jack L. Harlan:

> ... people who do not farm do about everything that farmers do, but they do not work as hard. ... They understand the life cycles of plants, know the seasons of the year, and when and where the natural plant food resources can be harvested in great abundance with the least effort. There is evidence that the diet of gathering peoples was better than that of cultivators, that starvation was rare, ... that there was a lower incidence of chronic disease and not nearly so many cavities in their teeth.
>
> The question must be raised: Why farm? ... Why work harder for food less nutritious and a supply more capricious? Why invite famine, plague, pestilence and crowded living conditions?[1]

HUSBANDRY IN DIFFERENT ENVIRONMENTS

Part of what is surprising about agriculture is that it is so common. Not only has almost the entire human world adopted it, many peoples came to it independently of one another. Scholars used to suppose that it was so extraordinary it must have begun in some particular spot and that **diffusion** spread it from there—carried by migrants or conquerors, or transmitted by trade, or imitated. The last 40 years of research have shown, on the contrary, that the transition to food production happened over and over again, in a range of regions and a variety of environments, with different foodstuffs and different techniques. The most obvious contrast in environments is between **herders** and **tillers**. Herding develops where plants are too sparse or indigestible to sustain human life, but animals can convert these plants into meat—an energy source that people can access by eating the animals. Tilling develops where the soil is suitable or enough ecological diversity exists to sustain plant husbandry or mixed farming of plants and animals.

Chukchi herder. The choice between hunting and herding often depends on local and historical circumstances. Reindeer-herding is an ancient practice in much of northern Eurasia, whereas in North America, the caribou have remained wild. In extreme northeast Asia, close to America, the Chukchi long resisted the example of neighboring people and preferred hunting to herding. In the last two or three centuries, however, they have adopted the herdsman's vocation shown here.

Herders' Environments

In three regions of the Earth—tundra, the evergreen forests of northern Eurasia, and great grasslands—it is not possible to grow enough humanly digestible plant foods to keep large numbers of people alive. In the tundra and evergreen forests, average temperatures are too low, the growing season too short, the surface soil too vulnerable to frost, and the subsoil, in some areas, too frozen. In these environments, there are only two options. People can remain foragers—and primarily hunters, seeking the fat-rich species typical of such zones. The Inuit in the North American Arctic, for example, hunt seal and walrus. Or people can become herders, like the Sami and Samoyeds of northern Europe and northwest Asia, who live off reindeer.

○ MAKING CONNECTIONS

FORAGERS AND FARMERS COMPARED

FORAGERS	FARMERS
Food procurers	**Food producers**
hunt and gather	husbandry (breed animals, cultivate crops)
Fit into nature	**Change nature**
little environmental impact	herders: some environmental impact tillers: massive environment impact
Manage the landscape	**Nature remade and reimagined**
Dependence on wild animals and plants	**Interdependence between humans, plants, and animals**
	animals and plants exploited and domesticated
Stable food supply	**Unstable food supply**
nomadic foragers move in response to environmental change; sedentary foragers vulnerable to changes of climate	small range of farmed foods increases vulnerability to ecological disasters
Stable population	**Expanding population**
relatively little labor needed population control avalable, mainly by managed lactation	breeding livestock and cultivating plants leads to increased food supply increased population concentrations of domesticated animals spread disease
Stable society	**Radically changed, unstable society**
kinship and age fix individual's place in society sexes usually share labor by specializing in different economic tasks	need to control labor and food distribution leads to social inequalities work shared between the sexes, increased reliance on female labor strong states develop with powerful elites, complex technologies

Similarly, the soils of the world's vast grasslands—known as prairie in North America, pampa in South America, steppe in Eurasia, and the **Sahel** (sah-HEHL) in Africa—have, for most of history, been unfavorable for tillage (see Map 2.3). The sod is mostly too difficult to turn without a steel plow. Except for patches of exceptionally favorable soil, herding has been the only possible form of husbandry in these areas. The peoples of the Eurasian and African grasslands were probably herding by about 5000 B.C.E. Native American grassland dwellers of the New World, on the other hand, retained a foraging way of life because available species—bison, various types of antelope—were, for the most part, more abundant for the hunt and less suitable for herding.

For those who choose it, herding has three special consequences. First, it imposes a mobile way of life. The proportion of the population who follow the herds—and, in some cases, it is the entire population—cannot settle into permanent

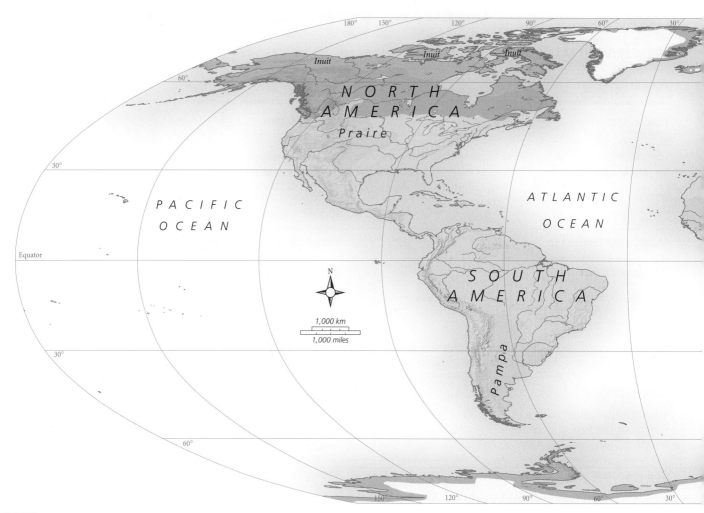

MAP 2.3

Herders' Environments

	tundra
	evergreen forests
	grasslands
Sami	hunters and herders described on pages 36–38
KENYA	modern-day country

MAP EXPLORATION

www.prenhall.com/armesto_maps

villages. Herder peoples are not unwilling or unable to build permanently or on a large scale. The Scythians, for instance, people of the western Asian steppe who first domesticated the horse and invented the wheel and axle about 6,000 to 7,000 years ago, built impressive stone structures. But these were underground tombs, dwellings for the dead, while the living inhabited temporary camps. Some herding societies in Asia and Africa have become rich enough to found cities for elites or for specialists working outside of food production, such as craftsmen or miners. Indeed, as we shall see (Chapter 13), in the thirteenth century C.E., a city of this type, Karakorum in Mongolia, was one of the most admired cities in the world. On the whole, however, herding does not favor the development of cities or the kind of culture that cities nourish, such as monumental buildings, large-scale institutions for education and the arts, and industrial technology.

Second, since herders breed from animals that naturally share their grassland habitats, their herds consist of such creatures as cattle, sheep, horses, goats—milk-yielding stock. To get the full benefit from their animals, herding peoples have to eat dairy products. To modern, milk-fed Americans, this may sound perfectly normal. But it required a modification of human evolution. Most people, in most parts of the world, do not naturally produce lactase, the substance that enables them to digest milk, after infancy. They respond to dairy products with distaste or even intolerance. The Masai of Kenya in East Africa get 80 percent of their energy

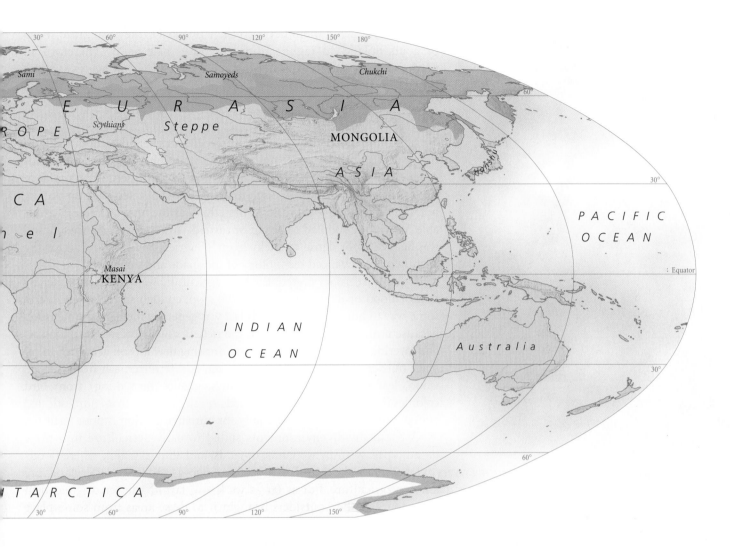

intake from milk. Their Kikuyu neighbors, who are tillers, detest the stuff. People from the steppes of Eurasia invented an amazing variety of milk products, including butter, yoghurt, and cheese.

Third, the herders' diet, relying heavily on meat, milk, and blood, lacks variety compared to diets of people in more ecologically diverse environments. This does not mean that the herders' diet is nutritionally deficient. If you eat organ meats, drink animal blood, and prepare dairy products in a variety of ways to harness beneficial bacteria, you can get everything the human body needs, including adequate vitamin C. But this does not mean that herding peoples, although they often express contempt for farmers, despise the crops farmers grow. On the contrary, herders highly prize cultivated plants and import them at great cost or take them as tribute or booty. The same goes for the products of the sedentary industries that only farming folk have land or leisure for, or which are possible only in tree-rich environments, such as wood products, silk, linen, and cotton.

Violence between herders and farmers was common until about 300 years ago or so, when the war technology of sedentary societies left herding societies unable to compete. Conflict arose not from herders' hatred of farmers' culture but from a desire to share its benefits. On the other hand, farmers have not normally had to depend on herding cultures for meat or dairy products. Typically, they can farm their own animals, feeding them on the waste or surplus of their

Masai. Humans need vitamin C, but the meat and dairy products from herds do not supply much of it. So people in herding cultures eat half-digested plants from animals' stomachs and organ meats, such as the liver, in which vitamin C tends to get concentrated. Fresh blood—drawn here from the veins of a calf by Masai women in Kenya—is also a useful source of the vitamin. Drinking blood confers an added advantage: nomads can draw it from their animals "on the hoof," without slaughtering them or halting the migrations of their flocks.

crops or by grazing them between their tillage. Or they can graze sheep or goats upland, at higher altitudes above their fields. Therefore, in herder–settler warfare, the herders have typically been aggressive and the settlers defensive.

Tillers' Environments

In the tundra, northern Eurasian evergreen forests, and great grasslands, tilling isn't an option. Husbandry is restricted to herding. But numerous other environments are suited to farming. The first essential prerequisite for farming was soil loose enough for a dibble—a pointed stick for poking holes in the ground—to work. At first, this was the only technology available. Where the sod had to be cut or turned—where, for instance, the soil was heavy clay or dense or sticky loam*—agriculture had to wait for the slightly more advanced technology of the spade and the plow.

Equally necessary prerequisites for agriculture were sufficient water, by rain or flood or irrigation, to grow the crop; enough sun to ripen it; and some way to nourish the soil. This last was generally the hardest to ensure, because farming can exhaust even the richest soils fairly rapidly. Flooding and layering with silt or dredging and dressing new topsoil is needed to replace nutrients. Alternatively, farmers can add fertilizer: ash from burned wood, leaf mold from forest clearings, guano (bird dung) from bird colonies if there are any nearby, mined potash,† manure from domesticated animals, or night soil, if all else fails, for human excretion is poor fertilizer.

We can divide environments suited to early agriculture into three broad types: swampy wetlands, uplands, and alluvial plains, where flooding rivers or lakes renew the topsoil. (Cleared woodlands and irrigated drylands are also suitable for agriculture, but as far as we know, farming never originated in these environments. Rather, outsiders brought it to these areas from some place else.) Each of the three types developed with peculiar characteristics and specialized crops. It is worth looking at each in turn (see Map 2.4 on pages 48–49).

SWAMPLAND Swamp is no longer much in demand for farming. Nowadays, in the Western world, if we want to turn bog into farmland we drain it. But it had advantages early on. Swamp soil is rich, moist, and easy to work with simple technology. At least one staple grows well in waterlogged land—*rice*. We still do not know where or when rice was first cultivated, or even whether any of these wetland varieties preceded the dryland rice that has gradually become more popular around the world. Most evidence, however, suggests that people were producing rice at sites on the lower Ganges River in India and in parts of southeast Asia some 8,000 years ago, and in paddies in the Yangtze River valley in China not long afterward.

Where rice is unavailable, swampland cultivators can adapt the land for other crops by dredging earth—which they can do by hand in suitable conditions—and by building up mounds. Not only can they plant the mounds, they can also farm water-dwelling creatures and plants in the ditches between mounds. In the western highlands of New Guinea, the first agriculture we know of started fully 9,000 years ago in the boggy valley bottoms. Drains, ditches, and mounds still exist in the Kuk swamp there. More extensive earthworks were in place by 6000 B.C.E. The crops

---

*Loam: a mixture of sand, clay, silt, and organic matter.
†Potash: various compounds containing potassium.

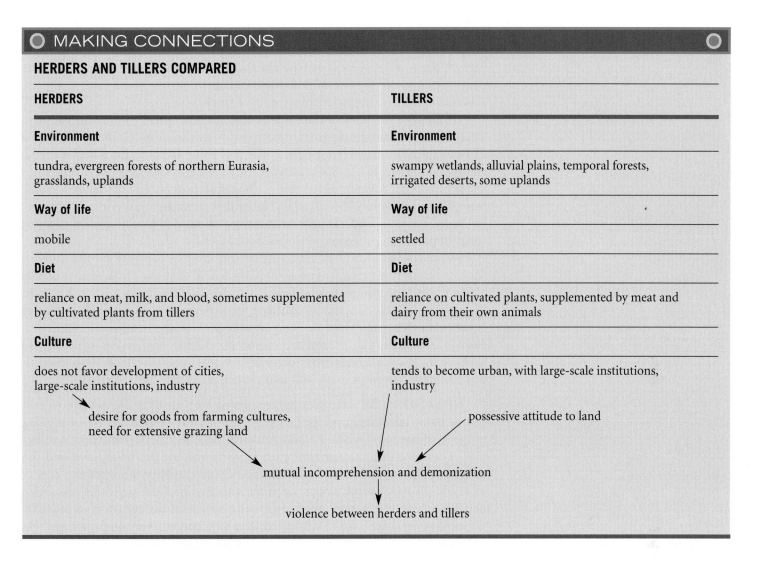

● MAKING CONNECTIONS

HERDERS AND TILLERS COMPARED

HERDERS	TILLERS
Environment	**Environment**
tundra, evergreen forests of northern Eurasia, grasslands, uplands	swampy wetlands, alluvial plains, temporal forests, irrigated deserts, some uplands
Way of life	**Way of life**
mobile	settled
Diet	**Diet**
reliance on meat, milk, and blood, sometimes supplemented by cultivated plants from tillers	reliance on cultivated plants, supplemented by meat and dairy from their own animals
Culture	**Culture**
does not favor development of cities, large-scale institutions, industry	tends to become urban, with large-scale institutions, industry

desire for goods from farming cultures, need for extensive grazing land

possessive attitude to land

mutual incomprehension and demonization

violence between herders and tillers

have vanished—biodegraded into nothingness—but the first farmers probably planted *taro*, the most easily cultivated, indigenous native root. Modern varieties of taro exhibit signs of long domestication. A diverse group of plants—native bananas, yams and other tubers, the sago palm, and *pandanus** nuts—was probably added early. At some point, pigs arrived on the island. However, a fierce and, on present evidence, unresolvable scholarly controversy rages over when that was.

Having a variety of crops made New Guinea's agriculture exceptionally sustainable. Variety may also help explain why farming has remained a small-scale enterprise there that numerous, politically independent villages, and not a large, centralized state, conduct. New Guinea never generated the big states and cities that grew up where the range of available crops was narrower and agriculture more fragile. It may sound paradoxical that the most advantageous crop range produces the most modest results, but it makes sense. One of the pressures that drives farming peoples to expand their territory is fear that a crop will fail. The more territory you control, the more surplus you can warehouse, the more manpower you command, and the more productive your fields. Moreover, if you farm an environment

---

*Pandanus: palm-like tree or shrub.

with a narrow range of food sources, you can diversify only by conquering other people's habitats. The history of New Guinea has been as violent as that of other parts of the world, but its wars have always been local and the resulting territorial adjustments small. Empire-building was unknown on the island until European colonizers got there in the late nineteenth century.

We know of no other swamps that people adapted so early, but many later civilizations arose from similar sorts of ooze. We do not know much about the origins of **Bantu** agriculture in West Africa, but it is more likely to have begun in the swamp than in the forest. Swampland is suited to the native *yams* on which Bantu farming first relied. Waterlogged land is also the favorite habitat of the other mainstay of Bantu tradition, the *oil palm*. The earliest archaeological evidence of farming based on yams and oil palms dates from about 5,000 years ago in swampy valley bottoms of Cameroon, above the forest level.

Swampland also contributed to the agriculture that began along the Amazon River in South America 4,000 or 5,000 years ago. At first, the crops were probably richly diverse, supplemented by farming turtles and mollusks.* Later, however, from about 500 C.E., farmers increasingly focused on *bitter manioc*, also known as cassava or yucca, which has the great advantage of being poisonous to predators. Human consumers can process the poison out. Olmec civilization, which, as we shall see in Chapter 3, was enormously influential in the history of **Mesoamerica**, was founded in swamps thick with mangrove trees about 3,000 years ago.

UPLANDS Like swamplands, regions of high altitude are not places that people today consider good for farming. Farmers have usually left these regions to the herdsmen and native upland creatures, such as sheep, goats, yaks, and llamas. There are three reasons for this: First, as altitude increases, cold and the scorching effects of solar radiation in the thin atmosphere diminish the variety of viable plants. Second, slopes are subject to erosion (although this has a secondary benefit because relatively rich soils collect in valley bottoms). Finally, slopes in general are hard to work once you have come to rely on plows, but this does not stop people who do not use plows from farming them. Nonetheless, in highlands suitable for plant foods—and not for livestock—plant husbandry or mixed farming did develop.

The Andes Highlands usually contain many different microclimates at various altitudes and in valleys where sun and rain can vary tremendously within a short space. Some of the world's earliest farming, therefore, happened at surprisingly high altitudes. Evidence of mixed farming survives from between about 12,000 and 7,000 years ago near Lake Titicaca (tee-tee-kah-kah), elevation 13,000 feet in the Andes of South America. Here, in the cave of Pachamachay, bones of domesticated llamas cover those of hunted *vicuñas* (vee-KOON-yahs) and *guanaco* (gwa-NAH-koh).[†] The domesticated animals fed on *quinoa* (kee-NOH-ah), an extremely hardy grainlike food that resembles some kinds of grass. It grows at high altitudes thanks to a bitter, soapy coating that cuts out solar radiation. The llamas ingested the leafy part and deposited the seeds in their manure. Their corrals therefore became nurseries for a food fit for humans to grow and eat.

The earliest known experiments in domesticating the *potato* probably occurred at about the same time in the same area—between 12,000 and 7,000 years ago. Potatoes were ideal for mountain agriculture. Not only were some naturally

---

*Mollusks: various invertebrates, such as mussels, clams, snails, and oysters.

[†]*Vicuña and guanaco*: animals related to the llama.

occurring varieties of potato hardy enough to grow at altitudes of up to 14,000 feet, they also provided total nutrition. Eaten in sufficient quantities, potatoes provide everything the human body needs to survive. Moreover, the high-altitude varieties have a hidden advantage. Whereas wild kinds of lowland potatoes are poisonous and need careful processing to become edible, the concentration of poison in potatoes diminishes the higher you climb. There is an obvious evolutionary reason for this. The poison is there to deter predators, which are most numerous at low altitudes.

The potato gave Andean mountain dwellers the same capacity to support large populations as peoples of the valleys and plains, where a parallel story began in the central coastal region of what is now Peru. There, around 10,000 years ago, farmers grew *sweet potato* tubers similar to modern varieties. If agriculture did indeed produce sweet potatoes, they would have to be counted as the New World's earliest farmed crop. Once both regions had the capacity to feed dense populations, Andean history became a story of highland–lowland warfare, punctuated by the rise and fall of mountain-based empires.

The valley of Cuzco, Peru, the homeland of the Inca (Chapter 15). Potatoes—which were first cultivated in the Andes at least 7,000 years ago and spread from there to the rest of the world—remain a staple in this region. They are the only food that—if eaten in sufficient quantities—contains all the nutrients necessary to sustain life. Suitable varieties of potatoes flourish at over 13,000 feet above sea level. In mountain climates, they can be freeze-dried for year-round nutrition.

Mesoamerica The Mesoamerican highlands, which stretch from central Mexico to Central America and are less high and less steep than those of the Andes, produced their own kind of highland-adapted food: a trinity of *maize*, *beans*, and *squash*. This combination grows well together and when eaten together provides almost complete nutrition. The earliest surviving specimens of cultivated maize are 6,000 years old. People in Mesoamerica developed maize from a wild grass known as teosinte (TEE-eh-SIN-tee), which is still found in the state of Oaxaca (wah-HAH-kah) in central Mexico, along with the wild ancestors of modern domesticated beans (see Figure 2.1). By working out how long it would take wild species to mutate, botanists estimate that people domesticated beans about 9,000 years ago. The earliest domesticated squashes date from about same period and are found at the same site as teosinte and wild beans, at Guilá Naquitz (wee-LAH nah-KEETS), in Oaxaca. The fact that their wild ancestors have disappeared suggests that farming here might have started with squashes when gatherers of wild beans and grains needed to provide food for times of drought. Squash grows well during arid spells severe enough to wither teosinte and blight beans, so it would have provided a food reserve that people did not need to store.

The Old World The Old World had no potatoes, quinoa, or even maize for highland farmers to work with. The hardiest staples available in most of Eurasia and Africa were *rye* and *barley*. Surprisingly, however, people in lowlands first domesticated both of them in what are now Jordan and Syria, probably about 10,000 years ago. Rye germinates at just a couple degrees above freezing, but its drawbacks made it more popular as a winter crop in wheat-growing lowlands than as a mountain staple. Its yield is lower, and it is less nutritious than other grains. Rye is also extremely vulnerable to fungus infection. Barley did not fulfill its potential to be an Old World equivalent of quinoa or potatoes until the sixth century C.E., when it became the staple food of a farming society in Tibet (Chapter 10).

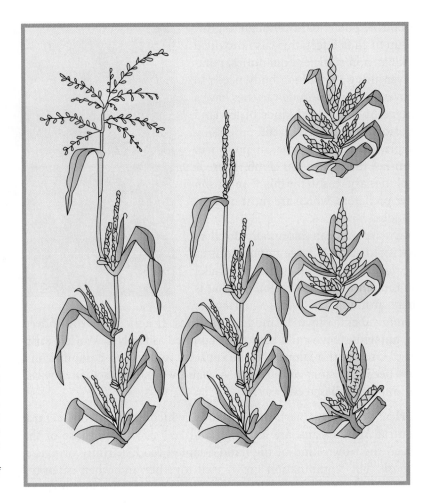

FIGURE 2.1 TEOSINTE AND MAIZE. The form of teosinte from which early farmers in Mesoamerica developed maize no longer exists. But the diagram illustrates the stages through which Mesoamericans may have bred teosinte into maize, until they developed the characteristic thick, densely packed cobs familiar today. Unlike teosinte, maize cannot germinate without human help.
Permission of The University of Michigan Museum of Anthropology.

The only other Old World grain with similar potential was Ethiopia's indigenous grass called *teff*. Though its tiny grains make teff laborious to cultivate and process, it was suited to the region's fertile soil and temperate climate above 7,200 feet. Although farmers in Ethiopia cultivated teff at least 5,000 years ago, they never had to rely on it absolutely. Some varieties of *millet*—the name of a huge range of grasses whose seeds humans can digest—had superior yields. Over time, millet displaced teff, which never became a major staple outside Ethiopia.

ALLUVIAL PLAINS Although swamps and rain-fed highlands have produced spectacularly successful agriculture, farmers get the best help from nature in **alluvial plains**, flat lands where river-borne or lake-borne mud renews the topsoil. If people can channel the floods to keep crops from being swept away on these plains, alluvium (sediment and other organic matter) restores nutrients and compensates for lack of rain. Alluvial soils in arid climates sustained, as we shall see in the next chapter, some of the world's most productive economies until late in the second millennium B.C.E. *Wheat* and barley grew in the black earth that lines Egypt's Nile, the floodplains of the lower Tigris and Euphrates Rivers in what is now Iraq, and the Indus River in what is now Pakistan. People first farmed millet on alluvial soils in a somewhat cooler, moister climate in China, in the crook of the Yellow River and the Guanzhong (gwang-joe) basin around 7,000 years ago. And in the warm, moist climate of Indochina in what is now Cambodia, three crops of rice a year could grow on soil that the annual counter flow of the Mekong River created. The Mekong becomes so torrential that the delta—where the river enters the sea—cannot funnel its flow, and water is forced back upriver.

Smaller patches of alluvium, deposited by floods, nourished the world's earliest known fully farming economies. Among the first was Jericho on the river Jordan in modern Israel. Today, the Jordan valley looks inhospitable: desert crusted with salt and sodium. Ten thousand years ago, however, Jericho overlooked an alluvial fan that trickling streams washed down from the Judaean hills, filling the river as it crept south from the Sea of Galilee. The river Jordan was thick with silt. The banks it deposited formed the biblical "jungle of Jericho," from where lions padded to raid the sheepfolds. Here, stood rich wheat fields, creating the landscape said in the Bible to resemble "the garden of the Lord." Desert people, such as the Israelites led by Joshua, were excluded and were tempted to conquer it.

In Jericho, the ritual focus of life was a cult of skulls, which were cut from bodies exhumed after burial, reenfleshed with plaster, and given eyes of cowrie shells from the Red Sea. This cult was part of a way of life Jericho shared with similar settlements dotted around the region. At Jerf al Ahmar (jehrf ahl-AH-mahr), 300 miles to the northeast, lies a farming settlement of the same era with a building used both to store grain and for ritually decapitating corpses.

In much the same period, between about 9,000 and 11,000 years ago, farming towns also appeared in Anatolia in Turkey. Çatalhüyük (chah-tahl-hoo-YOOK), the most spectacular of them, stood on an alluvial plain that the river Çarsamba flooded. Nourished by wheat and beans, the people filled an urban area of thirty-two acres. Walkways across flat roofs, not streets as we define them, linked a honeycomb of dwellings. The houses, built of mud bricks, were identical (see Figure 2.2). The wall panels, doorways, hearths, ovens, and even the bricks were a standard shape and size. You can still see where the occupants swept their rubbish—chips of bone and shiny, black flakes of volcanic glass called obsidian—into their hearths.

Çatalhüyük was not an isolated phenomenon. A wall painting there depicts what may be another, similar urban settlement. Even earlier sites, smaller than Çatalhüyük but on the same order, communicated with the Jordan valley—villages like Çayonu (CHEYE-oh-noo), which builders of skull piles who performed sacrifices on polished stone slabs inhabited. By exchanging craft products—weapons, metalwork, and pots—for primary materials such as cowrie shells from the Red Sea, timber from the Taurus Mountains in Anatolia, and copper from beyond the Tigris, the inhabitants of Çatalhüyük became rich by the standards of the time. Archeologists have unearthed such treasures as fine blades and mirrors made from local obsidian and products

Teff—the staple grain of early Ethiopian civilization—remains unique to the region, where it is still harvested regularly. But, as the picture shows, it more closely resembles wild grasses than modern high-yielding food grains. The starchy ears are tiny and require much labor to mill. So, like many traditional staples, teff faces the threat of extinction today from the competition of commercial hybrids or genetically modified varieties, promoted by powerful corporations.

Jericho Skull No one knows why people in Jericho, in the eighth millennium B.C.E., kept skulls, painted them with plaster, and inserted cowrie shells into the eye sockets. But these decorated skulls have, in a sense, helped the dead to survive. Some of the skulls even show traces of painted hair and mustaches. *Ashmolean Museum, Oxford, England, U.K.*

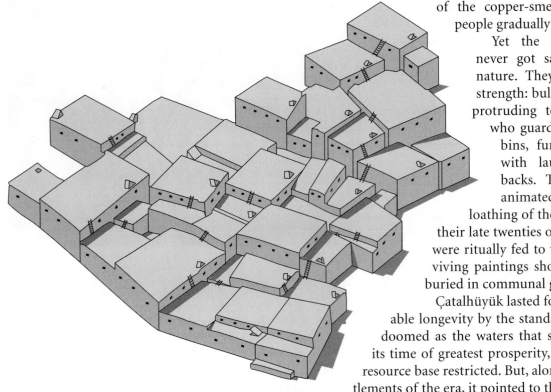

FIGURE 2.2 ÇATALHÜYÜK The houses of Çatalhüyük were linked not by streets as we know them, but by rooftop walkways, from which people presumably used ladders to reach different levels. The diagram reconstructs part of Çatalhüyük on the basis of archaeological findings. Wall paintings there show that other settlements in the region were constructed on similar principles.
Schematic reconstruction of houses and shrines from Level VI at Catalhoyuk by James Mellaart. Reprinted by permission of the Catalhoyuk Resrearch Project.

of the copper-smelting technology that these people gradually developed.

Yet the inhabitants of Çatalhüyük never got safely beyond the mercy of nature. They worshipped images of its strength: bulls with monstrous horns and protruding tongues, crouching leopards who guard goddesses leaning on grain bins, fuming volcanoes, giant boar with laughing jaws and bristling backs. This is surely farmer's art, animated by fear of the wild and loathing of the savage. Most people died in their late twenties or early thirties. Their corpses were ritually fed to vultures and jackals—as surviving paintings show—before their bones were buried in communal graves.

Çatalhüyük lasted for nearly 2,000 years, remarkable longevity by the standards of later cities. It became doomed as the waters that supplied it dried up. Even in its time of greatest prosperity, its space was limited and its resource base restricted. But, along with Jericho and other settlements of the era, it pointed to the future, showing how farming, despite all its short-term disadvantages and the sacrifices it demanded, could sustain life through hard times.

THE SPREAD OF AGRICULTURE

The development of food production in diverse environments with different foods and different techniques points to an important conclusion: It was not a unique occurrence—a one-of-a-kind accident or a stroke of genius. Rather, farming was an ordinary and fairly frequent process that could therefore be open to a variety of explanations.

Where we can be sure agriculture developed independently, we can see that early food producers focused on what they could grow or raise most easily in their particular environment. Examples include livestock herds in central Eurasia; wheat and barley in the Middle East; sweet potatoes, quinoa, and potatoes in the Andean region; the squash-maize-beans trinity in Mesoamerica; millet in China; and rice in southeast Asia. In New Guinea agriculture was based on taro, in Ethiopia on teff, and in West Africa on yams and oil palms. Nevertheless, connections between neighboring regions were unquestionably important in spreading husbandry. Some crops were undoubtedly transferred from the places they originated to other regions (see Map 2.4).

Europe

It seems likely (though the evidence is slight and subject to reinterpretation) that migrants from Asia colonized Europe. They brought their farming materials and knowledge with them, as well as their **Indo-European languages**, from which most of Europe's present languages descend. Colonization was a gradual process, beginning about 6,000 years ago. Early farmers may have cleared some land, but probably did not undertake large-scale deforestation. Later, well-documented cases from

Her seated position and uptilted head seem to suggest authority, as do the predatory felines that guard the throne, as if in obedience to someone able to command nature.

Her bulbous breasts and exaggerated sex organs suggest the importance of fertility to the society in which this image was crafted.

THE FERTILITY GODDESS OF ÇATALHÜYÜK

In recent times, the so-called "fertility goddess" or "Earth Mother" of Çatalhüyük has become a cult-object for feminists, who make pilgrimages to the site. But what her image was for, and what it represents, are unknown.

The folds of fat around her joints suggest a degree of obesity amounting to clinical pathology or physical deformity. Most human societies, for most of history, have admired body fat on both men and women.

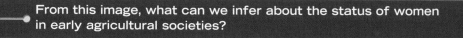

From this image, what can we infer about the status of women in early agricultural societies?

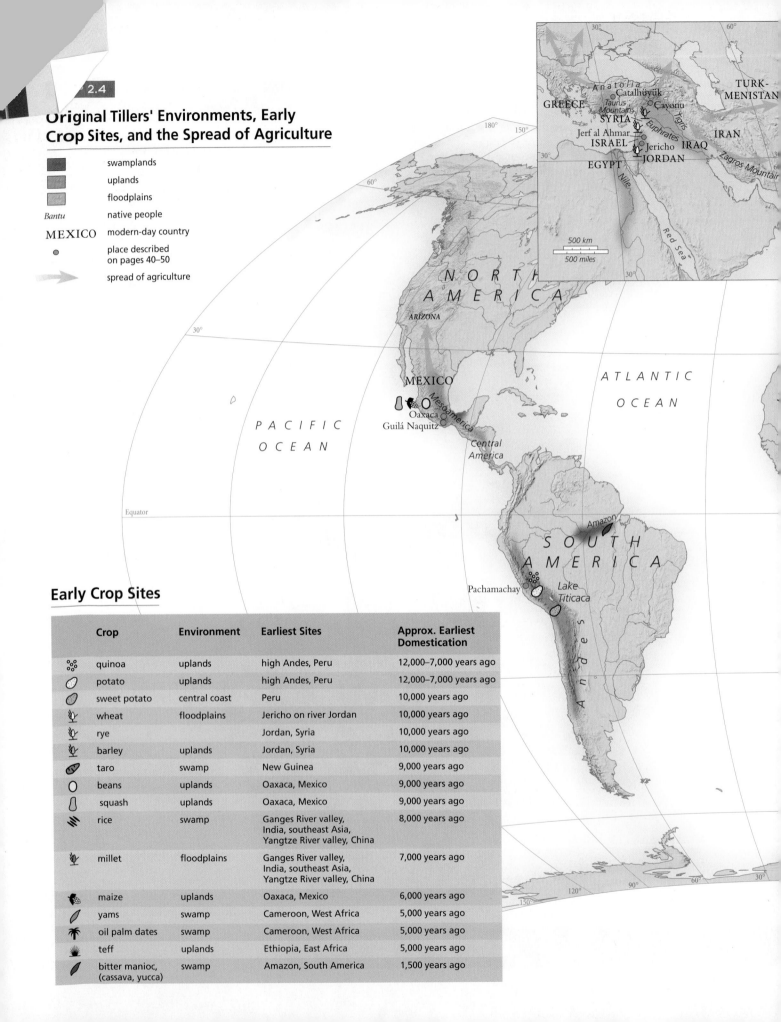

2.4

Original Tillers' Environments, Early Crop Sites, and the Spread of Agriculture

- swamplands
- uplands
- floodplains

Bantu — native people

MEXICO — modern-day country

• — place described on pages 40–50

→ — spread of agriculture

Early Crop Sites

	Crop	Environment	Earliest Sites	Approx. Earliest Domestication
	quinoa	uplands	high Andes, Peru	12,000–7,000 years ago
	potato	uplands	high Andes, Peru	12,000–7,000 years ago
	sweet potato	central coast	Peru	10,000 years ago
	wheat	floodplains	Jericho on river Jordan	10,000 years ago
	rye		Jordan, Syria	10,000 years ago
	barley	uplands	Jordan, Syria	10,000 years ago
	taro	swamp	New Guinea	9,000 years ago
	beans	uplands	Oaxaca, Mexico	9,000 years ago
	squash	uplands	Oaxaca, Mexico	9,000 years ago
	rice	swamp	Ganges River valley, India, southeast Asia, Yangtze River valley, China	8,000 years ago
	millet	floodplains	Ganges River valley, India, southeast Asia, Yangtze River valley, China	7,000 years ago
	maize	uplands	Oaxaca, Mexico	6,000 years ago
	yams	swamp	Cameroon, West Africa	5,000 years ago
	oil palm dates	swamp	Cameroon, West Africa	5,000 years ago
	teff	uplands	Ethiopia, East Africa	5,000 years ago
	bitter manioc, (cassava, yucca)	swamp	Amazon, South America	1,500 years ago

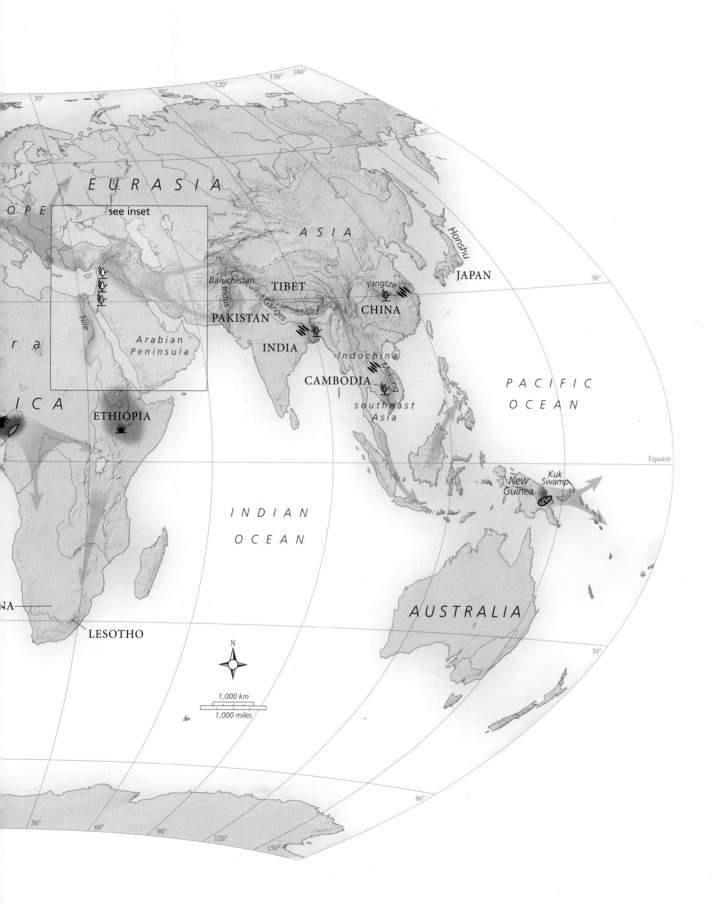

EURASIA

OPE

see inset

ra

Nile

Arabian
Peninsula

ICA

ETHIOPIA

LESOTHO

ASIA

Baluchistan

Indus

Ganges

TIBET

PAKISTAN

INDIA

CAMBODIA

Indochina

southeast
Asia

Yangtze

CHINA

Mekong

Honshu

JAPAN

PACIFIC

OCEAN

INDIAN

OCEAN

New
Guinea

Kuk
Swamp

Equator

AUSTRALIA

N

1,000 km
1,000 miles

30°

60°

90°

120°

150°

180°

60°

30°

Equator

30°

60°

30°

60°

90°

120°

150°

NA

other forest environments suggest that early agriculturists in Europe found trees useful and even revered them. So large-scale deforestation more likely occurred naturally, perhaps through tree diseases. Between 4,500 and 5,000 years ago, for instance, in northern Europe, the broad-leaved forest receded, creating areas that were well suited to farming. When the woodland grew back after a few hundred years, farmers unquestionably cut it back.

Asia

Similar migrations probably spread farming to parts of Central Asia south of the steppeland. The farming that developed in alluvial environments in Anatolia and the Jordan valley colonized or converted every viable part of the region by 8,000 or 9,000 years ago. At altitudes above 1,800 feet, inhabitants of sites east of the Zagros Mountains (in what is now Iran) replaced their wild grains with cultivated varieties. Then, too, by about 6,000 years ago, comprehensive irrigation systems for farming crisscrossed the oases in southern Turkmenistan, which had a moister climate than it has now.

In the Indian subcontinent, the sudden emergence of well-built villages in the same period was probably the result of outside influence. No intermediate phase between foraging and farming occurred, no period when foragers led settled lives. We can trace the spread of farming from southwest Asia by way of Baluchistan (southern Pakistan). Here, remnants of domestic barley and wheat in mud bricks and the bones of domestic goats confirm the presence of agriculture about 9,000 years ago. This is also the site of the world's earliest surviving cotton thread, strung through a copper bead about 7,500 years ago.

The Americas

In much of North America, the spread of maize northwards from its birthplace in central Mexico marked the transmission of agriculture. It was a process that took thousands of years and demanded the development of new varieties as the crop crossed climate zones on its northward route. The best estimate puts maize farming in the southwestern United States about 3,000 years ago. Meanwhile, some North American peoples began to farm sunflowers and sumpweed for their edible seeds and roots. In South America, the idea of agriculture spread from, or across, the high Andes, through the upper Amazon basin.

Africa

How agriculture spread in Africa is less clear than in other regions. People began to cultivate similar plant foods in the Egyptian Sahara and in the Nile valley about 9,000 years ago. It therefore looks as if one region might have influenced the other. A little later, wheat cultivation along the Nile followed developments of a similar kind in the Jordan valley. Between 4,500 and 5,000 years ago, agriculture spread southward from West Africa along with Bantu languages We can trace the path from what are now Cameroon and Nigeria in West Africa, southward and then eastwards across the expanding Sahara to the Nile valley, before turning south again (see Map 2.5).

The Pacific Islands

Scholars debate when agriculture originated in the Pacific Islands. In particular, we do not know how or when the sweet potato—which, together with the pig, is the basis of food production in most of the region—got there. The most widely

MAP 2.5

The Spread of Bantu Languages

respected theory sees agriculture as the result of diffusion from New Guinea. It was a slow process requiring many adaptations as it spread across the ocean with seaborne migrants.

SO WHY DID FARMING START?

Knowing or guessing about how food production started does not tell us why it started. Why, despite the short-term difficulties, did some peoples originate farming and others adopt it? Though scholars ferociously advocate rival explanations, we do not have to choose among them. Different explanations, or different combinations of the same explanations, may have applied in different places. Nor do we have to go through all the theories. We can group them under seven manageable headings.

Population Pressure

The first group of theories explains agriculture as a response to stress from population growth and overexploitation of wild foods. Examples include hunting game to extinction and overgathering plants, grubs, and mollusks. Logically, population should not grow if resources are getting scarce. But anthropological studies of contemporary cultures making the transition to agriculture in Botswana and Lesotho in southern Africa support the theory. Apparently, once farming starts, people cannot abandon it without catastrophe. A ratchet effect makes it impossible, while population rises, to go back to less intensive ways of getting food. As an explanation, however, for why agriculture arose in the first place, population pressure does not match the facts of chronology. Populations certainly grew in the most dedicated farming cultures, but, in most places, growth was more probably a consequence of agriculture than a cause.

The Outcome of Abundance

A group of theories has arisen in direct opposition to stress theory. These claim that husbandry was a result of abundance. Farming, it is said, was a by-product of the leisure of fishermen in southeast Asia who devoted their spare time to experimenting with plants. Or hill dwellers in northern Iraq, whose habitat was peculiarly rich in easily domesticated grasses and grazing herds, invented it. Or it was the natural result of concentrations of pockets of abundance in Central Asia in the post–Ice-Age era of global warming. As temperatures rose, oases opened up where different species congregated peacefully. Humans discovered they could domesticate animals that would otherwise be rivals, enemies, or prey. Abundance theory is a convincing description for why agriculture developed in some key areas, but it does not explain why, in good times, people would want to change how they got their food and take on extra work.

The Power of Politics

Stress theory and abundance theory may apply to why agriculture arose in different areas, but they cannot be true simultaneously. Therefore, beyond the food supply, it is worth considering possible political or social or religious influences on food strategies. After all, food is for more than nourishment. Food not only sustains the body, it also confers power and prestige. It can symbolize identity and generate rituals. In hierarchically organized societies, elites nearly always demand more food than they can eat, not just to ensure their security but also to show off their wealth by squandering their waste.

The Spread of Agriculture

(All dates are approximate)

9,000 years ago	Evidence of agriculture in Indian subcontinent; farming spreads by diffusion in the Egyptian Sahara and Nile valley
8,000–9,000 years ago	Farming spreads from Jordan valley and Anatolia to central Asia, south of the steppe
6,000 years ago	Migrants from Asia bring farming materials and knowledge with them to Europe
4,500–5,000 years ago	Bantu expansion spreads farming from West Africa southward
3,000 years ago	Maize moves northward from Mexico to southwestern United States

In a society where leaders buy allegiance with food, competitive feasting can generate huge increases in demand, even if population is static and supplies are secure. Societies bound by feasting will always favor intensive agriculture and massive storage. Even in societies with looser forms of leadership or with collective decision making, feasting can be a powerful incentive to boost food production and storage, by force if necessary. Feasting can celebrate collective identity or cement relations with other communities. Then, too, people could process most of the early domesticated plants into intoxicating drinks. If farming began as a way to generate surpluses for feasts, alcohol must have had a special role.

Cult Agriculture

Religion may well have been the inspiration for farming. Planting may have originated as a fertility rite, or irrigation as libation (a liquid offering to the spirits or gods), or enclosure as an act of reverence for a sacred plant. To plow or dibble and sow and irrigate can carry profound meaning. They can be understood as rites of birth and nurture of the god on whom you are going to feed. In exchange for labor—a kind of sacrifice—the god provides nourishment. Most cultures have considered the power to make food grow to be a divine gift or curse or a secret that a hero stole from the gods. People have domesticated animals for use in sacrifice and prophecy as well as for food. Many societies cultivate plants that play a part at the altar rather than at the table. Examples include incense, ecstatic or hallucinatory drugs, the sacrificial corn of some high Andean communities, and wheat, which, in orthodox Christian traditions, is the only permitted grain for the Eucharist. And if religion inspired agriculture, alcohol as a drink that can induce ecstasy might have had a special appeal. In short, where crops are gods, farming is worship.

Climatic Instability

Global warming, as we saw in Chapter 1, presented some foragers with thousands of years of abundance. But warming is unpredictable. Sometimes it intensifies, causing spells of drought; sometimes it goes into temporary reverse, causing little ice ages. Its effects are uneven. In the agrarian heartland of the Middle East, for example, warming squeezed the environment of nut-bearing trees but favored some kinds of grasses. The forest receded dramatically as the climate got drier and hotter between about 13,000 and 11,000 years ago. The new conditions encouraged people to rely more and more on grains for food and perhaps try to find ways to increase the amount of edible wheat. Gatherers who knew the habits of their plants tended them ever more carefully. It was, perhaps, a conservative, even a conservationist strategy: a way to keep old food stocks and lifestyles going under the impact of climate change.

Agriculture by Accident

In the nineteenth century, the most popular theory of how farming started attributed it to accident. One can hardly open a nineteenth-century book on the subject without encountering the myth of the primitive forager, usually a woman, discovering agriculture by observing how seeds, dropped by accident, germinated on fertilized soil. The father of the theory of evolution Charles Darwin (1809–1882; see Chapter 25), himself, thought something similar:

> The savage inhabitants of each land, having found out by many and hard trials what plants were useful . . . would after a time take the first step in cultivation by planting them near their usual abodes. . . . The next step in cultivation, and this would require but little forethought, would be to sow the seeds of useful plants; and as the soil near

Cult agriculture. Chimú goldsmiths (Chapter 14) produced this ceremonial dish, which depicts the succession of the seasons, presided over by the central figure of the maize god, and offerings of the characteristic starches of the Peruvian lowlands—maize, cassava, sweet potatoes. By the time this object was made, however, around 1200 C.E., maize varieties had been adapted for varied environments, including uplands and temperate climates.

the hovels of the natives would often be in some degree manured, improved varieties would sooner or later arise. Or a wild and unusually good variety of a native plant might attract the attention of some wise old savage; and he would transplant it or sow its seed. . . . Transplanting any superior variety, or sowing its seeds, hardly implies more forethought than might be expected at an early and rude period of civilisation.[2]

Darwin's reconstruction is plausible: He makes accident interact with human action. But this model leaves some unsolved problems. Historians are never satisfied to fall back on what would or might have happened (though this may be necessary to help understand remote or poorly documented periods). We want to know—and it is the historian's job to try to tell us—what really did happen. Assuming that anything a "savage" does requires "little forethought" does not fit with what we now know of human nature. Cleverness occurs at every period of history and in every type of society—in New Guinea as well as in New York, in antiquity as well as in modernity.

Charles Darwin, "Cultivated plants: Cereal and Culinary Plants," from *The Variation of Plants and Animals under Domestication*

Production As an Outgrowth of Procurement

Still, the accident theory may be right in one respect. Early practitioners may not have consciously thought of food production as different strategy from foraging. It makes sense, for instance, to see herding as a natural development of some hunting techniques, such as improving a species by culling weak or old animals, managing grazing by setting fires, driving herds down lanes to a place of slaughter, or corralling them for the kill. Similarly, farming and gathering might have been parts of a single continuous attempt to manage food sources. It is hard to tell where one leaves off and the other begins. "Even the simplest hunter–gatherer society," as archaeologist Brian Fagan has said, "knows full well that seeds germinate when planted." The Papago Native Americans of the Sonora Desert of Arizona drift in and out of an agrarian way of life as the weather permits, using patches of surface water to grow fast-maturing varieties of beans.

The archaeological evidence has begun to yield clues to how gatherer communities of southwestern Asia transformed themselves into farming communities after the Ice Age. Grasses on the whole are naturally too indigestible to be human food. But the region produced wild barley and two kinds of wheat—einkorn (EYEN-korn) and emmer (EH-mehr). We know people ate them because archaeologists have found actual remains that grinders of these grains processed from 14,000 to 15,000 years ago. Kernels of these wheats are hard to free from their tough, inedible covering, so people who ate large amounts of them may have had an incentive to try to breed varieties that were easier to process. At first, the gatherers beat sheaves of wheat with sticks where they grew and collected edible seeds in baskets as they fell. Increasingly, as time went on, they cut stalks with flint sickles, which meant that fewer seeds fell when the wheat was harvested. This new method suggests that people were selecting preferred seeds for replanting. Modern experiments show that this process could produce a self-propagating species within twenty years. Alternatively, the new method itself might have encouraged changes in the species because heavier, larger seeds would be more likely to fall to the ground at the point of harvesting. Eventually, new varieties would emerge, but the process would be much slower.

Even earlier, humans used a similar process with snails and other mollusks. They are an efficient food, self-packaged in a shell for carrying and cooking. Compared with the large four-legged beasts that are usually claimed as the first domesticated animal food sources, mollusks are readily managed. People can gather marine varieties, such as mussels and clams, in a natural rock pool. It is possible to isolate land

Einkorn is one of the few wild grasses that yield kernels that human stomachs can digest. It was a principal food source for the early sedentary foraging cultures of the Middle East, and one of the first species farmers adopted. But its grains are hard to separate from their tough husks, which helps explain why farmers strove to produce new varieties of grain by selection and hybridization.

Snails and other shell-dwelling mollusks are nature's "fast foods"—easily gathered and conveniently packaged. Discarded shells—heaps that are found all over the world, make a convenient record for archaeologists to study. In Frankthi cave in Greece, shown here, snail eaters piled huge residues nearly 13,000 years ago. Many ancient mollusks were bigger than modern species, which suggests that people were already selecting and encouraging large varieties.

mollusks by enclosing a snail-rich spot with a ditch. Moreover, snails are grazers and do not need to be fed with foods that humans would otherwise eat themselves. They can be herded without the use of fire, any special equipment, personal danger, or the need to train leashed animals or dogs to help. By culling small or undesirable types by hand, the early snail farmers could soon enjoy the benefits of selective breeding. Shell mounds from the late Ice Age or soon thereafter contain varieties of snails that are bigger on average than today's, so it looks as if the snail eaters were already selecting for size. Sometimes large-scale consumption of mollusks preceded that of foods that the more elaborate technologies of the hunt obtained. At Frankthi Cave in southern Greece, a huge dump of snail shells nearly 13,000 years old was topped first by red deer bones with some snail shells, and then, nearly 4,000 years later, by tuna bones.

IN PERSPECTIVE: Seeking Stability

So gathering, hunting, herding, and tillage, which our conventional chronologies usually place one after the other, were in fact complementary techniques to obtain food. They developed together, over thousands of years, in a period of relatively intense climatic change. The warming, drying effects of the post–Ice-Age world multiplied the opportunities and incentives for people to experiment with food strategies in changing environments. Foragers turned to farming and herding by slow stages and one case at a time, as relationships between people and other species changed and accumulated little by little. The naturalist David Rindos described early farming as a case of human–plant symbiosis, in which species developed together in mutual dependence, and—in part at least—evolved together: an unconscious relationship. Eventually, foodstuffs developed that needed human involvement to survive and reproduce. For instance, emerging kinds of edible grasses, maize, for example, would not survive because their seeds would not fall to the ground unless a person took them out of their husks.

The continuities in the worlds of the food procurers and early food producers are in many ways more impressive than the differences. The settled way of life, the art, the religious cults, even the kinds of foods (although obtained by different means) are often of the same order. The similarities suggest a new way to look at the transition to agriculture. We can see it as an attempt to stabilize a world convulsed by climatic instability—a way to cope with environmental change that was happening too fast and to preserve ancient traditions. In other words, the peoples who switched to herding or farming and those who clung to hunting and gathering shared a common, conservative mentality. Both wanted to keep what they had.

Perhaps, then, we should stop thinking of the beginnings of food production as a revolution, the overthrow of an existing state of affairs and its replacement by an entirely different one. Rather, we should think of it as a **climacteric** (kleye-MAK-tehr-ihk)—a long period of critical change in a world poised between different possi-

CHRONOLOGY

(All dates are approximate)

15,000 B.C.E.	End of Ice Age
13,000–14,000 B.C.E.	First permanent settlements in Middle East
11,000 B.C.E.	Appearance of Jomon culture, Japan
10,000–5000 B.C.E.	Mixed farming and potato cultivation develop (South America)
9000–7000 B.C.E.	Farming towns appear in Anatolia and Egypt
8000 B.C.E.	Rye and barley cultivation in Jordan and Syria; farming spreads from Jordan and Anatolia to Central Asia
7000 B.C.E.	"Trinity" of maize, beans, and squash develops in Andes; farming spreads in Egyptian Sahara and Nile valley; evidence of agriculture in Indian subcontinent; earliest evidence of agriculture in New Guinea
6000 B.C.E.	Rice cultivation in India, southeast Asia, and China
4000 B.C.E.	Scythians domesticate the horse and invent wheel and axle; Indo-European languages spread as migrants from Asia colonize Europe; millet farmed in Yellow River valley, China
5000–2000 B.C.E.	River valley civilizations flourish
3000 B.C.E.	Teff cultivated in Ethiopia; Bantu languages and agriculture begin to spread southward from West Africa; earliest specimens of cultivated maize (Mexico)
1000 B.C.E.	Maize cultivation moves northward from Mexico to southwestern United States

ble outcomes. Indeed, the concept of climacteric can be a useful way to understand change. It is worth keeping it in mind throughout the rest of this book as we confront other so-called revolutions that were really uncertain, slow, and sometimes unconscious transitions. Yet if early farmers' motivations were indeed conservative, in most cases they failed to maintain the status quo. On the contrary, they inaugurated the spectacular changes and challenges that are the subject of the next chapter.

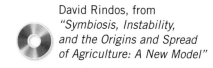

David Rindos, from *"Symbiosis, Instability, and the Origins and Spread of Agriculture: A New Model"*

PROBLEMS AND PARALLELS

1. How was husbandry, with its emphasis on "unnatural selection," the first human challenge to evolution?

2. Why would some societies (such as the aborigines of Australia), with the ability to engage in agriculture, continue to live a hunter–gatherer lifestyle? What are the disadvantages of farming compared to foraging?

3. What was life like in preagricultural settlements? How did agriculture affect the pace of change in human society? Why were agricultural settlements less stable than foraging communities?

4. Why was husbandry the first human challenge to evolution? What are the relative benefits of farming and herding? Why was violence between farmers and herders common until recently?

5. What were the prerequisites for early agriculture? Why were alluvial plains the most hospitable environment for early agricultural communities?

6. Why did farming start at different places and at different times around the world? What are some of the rival theories advocated by scholars?

7. Why is the beginning of food production more of a climacteric than a revolution?

DOCUMENTS IN GLOBAL HISTORY

- James Cook, from *Captain Cook's Journal During his First Round the World*
- Jack Harlan, from *Crops and Man*

- Charles Darwin, "Cultivated Plants: Cereal and Culinary Plants," from *The Variation of Animals and Plants under Domestication*
- David Rindos, from "Symbiosis, Instability, and the Origins and Spread of Agriculture: A New Model"

Please see the Primary Source CD-ROM for additional sources related to this chapter.

READ ON

The lines of the argument are laid down in F. Fernández-Armesto, *Near a Thousand Tables* (2002). The method of classifying events in environmental categories comes from F. Fernández-Armesto, *Civilizations* (2001). Indispensable for the study of the origins of the agriculture are J. R. Harlan, *Crops and Man* (1992); B. D. Smith, *The Emergence of Agriculture* (1998); D. Rindos, *The Origins of Agriculture* (1987); and D. R. Harris, ed., *The Origins and Spread of Agriculture and Pastoralism in Eurasia* (1996). K. F. Kiple and K. C. Ornelas, eds., *The Cambridge World History of Food* (2000) is an enormous compendium.

I. G. Simmons, *Changing the face of the earth: culture, environment, history* (1989) is a superb introduction to global environmental history, as is B. De Vries and J. Goudsblom, eds., *Mappae Mundi: humans and their habitats in a long-term socio-ecological perspective* (2004).

The quotation from Darwin comes from his work of 1868, *The Variation of Animals and Plants under Domestication*.

On feasts, M. Dietler and B. Hayden, *Feasts: archaeological and ethnographic perspective on food, politics, and power* (2001) is an important collection of essays.

O. Bar-Yosef and A. Gopher, eds. (1991), *The Natufian Culture in the Levant* is outstanding. On Çatalhüyük, up-to-date informations is in M. Özdogan and N. Basgelen, eds. (1999), *The Neolithic in Turkey: The Cradle of Civilization*, and I. Hodder, *Towards a Reflexive Method in Archaeology* (2000); but the classic J. Mellaart, *Çatal Huyuk* (1967) is more accessible. On Jericho, the classic work is by Kenyon, *Digging up Jericho; the results of Jericho excavations* (1957).

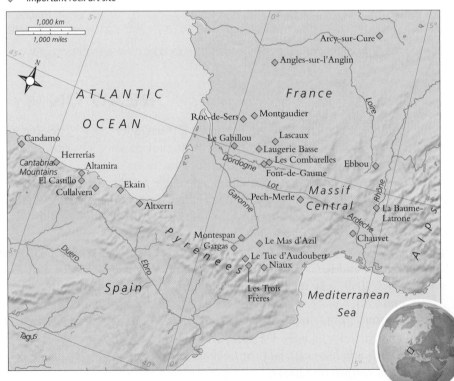

Chauvet Cave

In 1994, three cave explorers spent the Christmas holiday in the gorges of the Ardèche region in southeastern France. In the area, explorers had already discovered numerous caves that Ice-Age people had decorated between about 14,000 and 21,000 years ago. But nothing already known about the region prepared the team for the breathtaking find that awaited them. Sensing a draft from within a rock fall, they dug through earth and stones to create a gap wide enough for the thinnest of them to crawl through. When she realized there was a corridor ahead, she called the others. They shouted into the darkness to get an echo, which would give them a sense of the cave's dimensions. The noise seemed lost in vast emptiness. When they returned with full equipment, they found that the corridor led to the biggest cavern ever discovered in this part of France. Yet more astounding was their discovery in an adjoining chamber: a portrait in red ochre of a bear, rearing over 3 feet high—preserved for who knew how many thousands of years?

● ● ● ● ●

It soon became apparent that the Chauvet (shaw–VAY) cave—as the explorers named it, after their team leader—was one of the most extensive collections of Ice-Age art in the world. Furthermore, carbon dating from many of the images led to an inescapable conclusion. These were the world's oldest known paintings, yielding three dates of over 30,000 years, and none less than 23,000.

Sculpture of comparable antiquity had been discovered before. Paintings, however, that yielded such early dates by carbon dating had been too few to provide consistent, convincing evidence of their age, and too fragmentary to disclose anything about the minds

Painted Caves and Rock Art in Southern France and Northern Spain

◆ important rock art site

that made them. Now, suddenly a huge gallery of data had been added to the sources.

If the age and extent of the discovery weren't astonishing enough, Chauvet held one more surprise: These paintings subverted everything previously thought about Ice-Age art. Scholarship had assumed that Ice-Age art had evolved in style from "primitive" sketches by the earliest artists to the sublime images painted toward the end of the era in the caves of Altamira in Spain and Lascaux in France. The Chauvet paintings exhibit individual stylistic traits that can be linked to particular painters, but in technique and skill, the work is equal to paintings done in similar environments 10,000 or 15,000 years later. If Lascaux painters had seen them, they might have been as astonished as we are by the similarity to their own style.

The Chauvet finds fit with a number of other recent discoveries that, taken together, reveal a remarkably continuous sequence from the earliest discoveries to the latest.

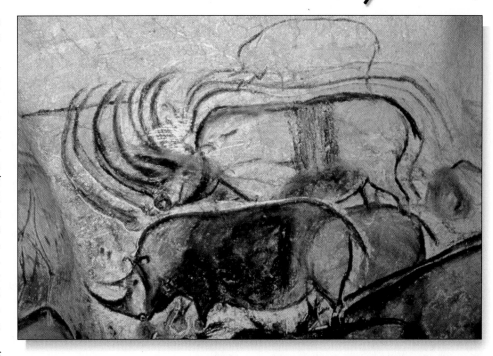

Rhinoceroses from Chauvet

Despite the similarities with later prehistoric art, the Chauvet paintings are puzzling in one regard: subject matter. Some scenes could be transferred to late Ice-Age settings without appearing out of place. There are storming bison and aurochs, stampeding horses, grazing or gazing reindeer, running ibex, creatures fleeing the hunt or falling victim to it. The Chauvet painters' favorite subjects, however, were rhinoceroses, which hardly figure in the later period (there is only one in Lascaux). They are followed by lions—often shown stalking, like fellow hunters—and mammoths, both of which are relatively rare subjects in the later period.

On the other hand, human figures are as rare as at other sites. Not until the ice began

Lions from Chauvet

receding, around 16,000 B.C.E., did human figures multiply considerably. The main exceptions are disembodied sexual organs. As at later sites, the organs seem to be used to give certain scenes a gendered or at least a sexual significance. Interestingly, a shamanlike figure—half human, half bison—of the same age has also recently come to light. Does this suggest that shamanistic religion was already part of the world of Ice-Age people 30,000 years ago, and has endured, in effect, ever since?

The evidence we have, such as it is, suggests that the Chauvet caves served the same function as the later examples. There is no sign of habitation. These caves were reserved for special activities, not for providing housing or places where the people of the time ate their meals or buried their dead. The only surviving footprints are—again as at later sites—barefoot and, in disproportionate numbers, childishly small.

Dots from Chauvet

In one respect, the images in the Chauvet caves seem somewhat less mature than their successors in southwest France and northeast Spain. There are numerous "signs" in the form of lines, dots, and stylized sexual organs. The conventional symbols of the late Ice Age—squares, rectangles, and triangles—are not present.

The Chauvet finds revolutionized the kinds of questions we ask about life in the Ice Age. They reveal a society—already in place nearly 30,000 years ago—with specialized groups of artists and perhaps of shamans. Their world and minds teemed with the animals they hunted or competed with in the hunt. Their culture was in some respects remarkably stable. Artists in the same region maintained the same outlook, saw much the same images, and painted them in much the same way for thousands of years. Radical changes of style and subject matter occurred only when climate change was refashioning the environment and challenging longstanding ways of organizing life. Similarly, by continuing the hunters' way of life in suitable environments, some human societies have managed to remain relatively stable ever since.

Although Western Europe is unique for its concentrations of cave art, there is surviving Ice-Age art in other parts of the world. This suggests that as well as being long enduring, the culture of the painters was also very widespread. People all over the world had a similar economy (based on hunting), a similar way of life (in temporarily occupied camps), and similar technologies (designed for the common activities we know about, such as hunting, cooking, and painting). They also had a similar religious life, in which shamans seem to have played a role as mediators of the magical or sacred. And they had imaginations similarly dominated by the animals of the hunt. In a sense, this Ice-Age world was an era of what we would now call globalization—of the widespread, even world-widespread—prevalence of a single cultural system. The big difference from twenty-first-century globalization is that the interdependence and intercommunication that connect today's communities were absent then.

A cave painting from approximately 12,000 years ago from Chamberlain Gorge in Western Australia depicting "Wondjina"—cloud and rain spirits.

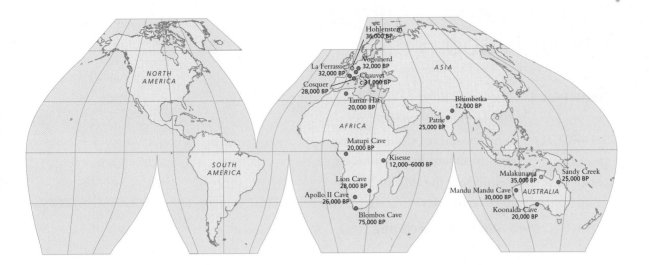

Cave 55,000—26,000 Years Ago

Early art sites

- 55,000–36,000 years ago
- 35,000–26,000 years ago

Questions to Consider

1. What can cave paintings from over 30,000 years ago tell us about the people who made them? What purpose did Ice-Age art serve?

2. Cave paintings are one type of material evidence we have from prehistoric times. Why is material evidence of a culture so important?

3. Can we speak of continuities of culture over a period of 15,000 years—from Chauvet to Lascaux? What elements of culture might be continuous? How could they survive over such a long period?

4. If the work of individual artists can be identified despite shared style and techniques, what does that imply about Ice–Age society values?

5. Why would artists choose to paint animals rather than humans? What might account for the shift to humans at the end of the Ice Age?

6. How does the half-human, half-animal portrayal reflect the role of the shaman in society? What does the existence of shaman tell us about magic, religion, and power in Ice-Age society?

7. What might the caves and the paintings have been for? Do the images support rival theories, such as that the caves were used for rituals or as schools for hunters?

8. What might the "signs" be for? What kind of information might Ice-Age people be recording in this way? Can we call it writing?

9. Based on the subject matter—a hunter-gatherer economy, technology, food, religion— does prehistoric art reveal the Ice-Age as the last era of globalization?

Sources

Chauvet, Jean-Marie. *Dawn of Art: The Chauvet Cave.* New York, 1996.

Clottes, Jean. *Return to Chauvet Cave: Excavating the Birthplace of Art*, London, 2003.

One of the World's Earliest Surviving Paintings on plaster ▶ was found at Tel-Eilat Ghasuul in Jordan. It dates to about 4500 B.C.E., but the meaning of most of the images it depicts—veiled faces, a gazelle and other creatures, a hand apparently emerging from a sleeve—are too faded and fragmentary to decipher. The star-shaped diagram, however, seems to depict a vision of the Earth or the universe. The colors, markings, and forms are geometrically arranged to suggest an ordered array of mountains, plains, skies, and waters, within an enclosed world, from which alternating light and darkness radiate.

ENVIRONMENT

ca. 4500 B.C.E.
Irrigation

ca. 3500 B.C.E.
Horses domesticated

since 5000 B.C.E.
● Intensive agriculture, bronze metallurgy: Tigris-Euphrates, Nile, Indus, Yellow Rivers

CULTURE

since ca. 3500 B.C.E.
Complex, hierarchical societies and states

Nebamun's tomb from the fourteenth century B.C.E. shows the Egyptian vizier hunting in the lush Nile delta, abundant in fish below his reed-built boat, prolific in the bird- and insect-life flushed from the blue thickets at his approach. He grabs birds by the handful and wields a snake like a whip.
© Copyright The British Museum

GREAT RIVER
VALLEYS

Witnesses in court swear to tell "the whole truth." This would be a risky oath for a historian to take because we see the past only in glimpses and patches, darkened with blind spots that our particular points of view distort. Aspects get blanked out. Sometimes-contrasting, sometimes-contradictory sources confuse or distract us. To get close to the whole picture, we have to shift perspective, change our angle of observation, dodge and slip between rival viewpoints, look at the world the way others see it and saw it. With every shift, we get a bit more of the picture—like glimpsing a scene in a forest, between the leaves and the trees.

The boldest possible perspective shift is imaginary, to envision history from a viewpoint outside it—perhaps from an enormous distance of time and space, and ask how it might look to a visitor from a remote future in another world. Galactic observers would have an enviable advantage: objectivity, which we, who are entangled in our history, can never attain. They could see that the main theme of our past, since the beginning of agriculture, has been cultural divergence. Once agriculture started, human societies became increasingly and at an ever faster pace different from one another. Today, globalization is just beginning to reverse the process, and uniform ways of life are spreading across the world.

Intensified agriculture widened the gaps among three already radically different types of economy: foraging, herding, and tillage (see Chapter 2). More spectacular, however, were the differences that separated farming cultures from each other. The societies of herders and tillers generated much more change of all kinds than those of foragers. Some of these herder and tiller societies came to occupy vast zones, to feed huge populations, and to sustain spectacular material achievements—including cities, monumental arts, and world-changing technologies. Other societies remained relatively small and static. This does not mean they were backward or primitive. Their modest scale and relative isolation kept them stable. These were peoples who succeeded in adapting to climate change without subjecting their societies to social and political convulsions, which were often part of the price other peoples paid for material achievements that seem impressive to us. The big problem we need to look at in this chapter, then, is what made the difference?

It is also worth asking whether within these diverse societies we can detect any common patterns. This is a long-standing quest for historians and, especially, for sociologists, who look for models that they can use to describe and predict how societies change. At a simple level, intensified agriculture clearly unlocks a potential pattern. More food makes it possible to sustain larger populations, to concentrate them in bigger settlements, and to divert more manpower into nonagricultural activities. But intensification also requires organization, and, broadly speaking, the more intensive the farming, the more organized it has to be. Someone with power, such as a landowner, ruler, or priest, or some group of such people has to divide the land,

FOCUS questions

- WHY DID intensified agriculture lead to cultural differences?
- WHERE DID the first great river valley civilizations develop?
- HOW CAN we account for the similarities and differences in political institutions, social structure, and ways of life in the four great river valleys?
- HOW DID the river valley states expand?
- IS WRITING a defining characteristic of civilization?
- WHY IS cultural divergence one of the main themes of human history since the beginning of agriculture?

marshal labor, regulate the distribution of water and—if necessary—fertilizers, and, finally, store and guard surplus production so that people can use it if crops fail or natural disasters strike. A more or less specialized legal elite is needed to resolve the frequent disputes that arise in thickly settled communities, where people have to compete for access to resources. So, intensively farmed areas tend to develop similar political institutions. Ruling groups in these areas must be able to command obedience and allegiance widely and deeply, which requires professional administrators and legal specialists.

We can see these changes in society and political organization that come with intensified farming in the history of many places, but especially from about 5000 B.C.E. in four regions with common environmental features. The "great river valleys," as they are traditionally called, in what are now Egypt, Iraq, Pakistan, and China, are the focus of this chapter, and their similarities and differences are among its principal themes. The next chapter follows their fortunes in the crises, catastrophes, and transformations they faced, in most cases toward the end of the second millennium B.C.E. Chapter 5 covers the recovery or renewal of ambitious states and cultural experiments after the crises had passed.

GROWING COMMUNITIES, DIVERGENT CULTURES

Most of the communities that early agriculture fed resembled the forager settlements that preceded them. They were small and did not change much over time. Lack of evidence means that we mostly have to infer what we think we know about them. So with no reason to think otherwise, we assume that early farming societies in New Guinea, North America, along the Amazon River in South America, and among the Bantu people in West Africa were like those in most of the rest of the world. They were extended family businesses where everyone in the community felt tied to everyone else by kinship. Elsewhere, owing to greater resources or to the enlivening effects of cross-cultural contacts through migration or trade, different patterns prevailed. Communities became territorially defined. Economic obligations, not kinship, shaped allegiance. Chiefs or economic elites monopolized or largely controlled the distribution of food.

Traditionally, scholars have tried to divide subsequent change in societies of this type into sequences or stages of growth—chiefdoms become states, towns become cities. But these are relative terms, and no hard-and-fast lines divide them. Nor do they have any mutually distinguishing characteristics. At most, differences are a matter of degree. For instance, we think of chiefdoms as having fewer institutions of government than states. In chiefdoms, the chief and a small group of counselors handle all the business of government. In a state, those functions get split among groups of specialists in, say, administering justice, handling revenue, or conducting war. In practice, however, we know of no community that does not delegate at least some power, or any state where the responsibilities of different government departments do not merge or overlap.

Similarly, no quality absolutely distinguishes some kinds of settlement from others. The difference between a small city and a big town or a small town and a big village is a matter of judgment. Some of the characteristics we traditionally associate with particular lifeways turn out, in the light of present knowledge, to provide little or no help for defining the societies in which they occur. We cannot, for instance, go on defining cities—or even towns or villages—as environments that promote the development of certain kinds of technology. Metallurgy, for example, exists among herding and nomadic peoples. Indeed, some of these peoples devised the earliest techniques of smelting and metalworking we know about and remained outstandingly proficient in them for most of history. Nor was weaving exclusive to settled communities. The Ice-Age creators of clay figurines understood the technique of making pottery artifacts, as we saw in Chapter 1. The earliest pottery vessels we know of come from the foragers' settlements of Jomon in Japan, as we saw in Chapter 2.

However, where many people settle together, predictable changes usually follow. As markets grow, communities and settlements acquire more craftsmen, who engage in more specialized trades and who organize into more and larger units. As they get bigger, settlements and politically linked or united groups of settlements also expand the number of government functions. Where once there was just a chief and his counselors, now there are aides, advisers, officials, and administrators.

Densely settled communities also tend to divide their populations into more categories. This usually happens in two ways. On the one hand, as society gets bigger, people seek groups within it, of manageable size, with whom to identify and to whom to appeal for help in times of need. On the other hand, rulers organize subjects into categories according to the needs of the state, which include collective labor, taxation, and war. The categories get more numerous and varied as opportunities for economic specialization multiply and as more districts or quarters appear in growing settlements. In some cases, these categories resemble what, in our society, we call classes, that is, groups arrayed horizontally, one above or below another according to power, privilege, or prosperity. For most of history, however, it is misleading to speak of classes. Societies were more usually organized vertically into groups of people of widely varying rank and wealth, linked by some form of common allegiance. They might feel bound by a place of origin, or a locality or neighborhood, or a common ancestor, or a god, or a rite, or a family, or a sense of identity arising from shared belief in some myth (see Figure 3.1).

So, if we want to try to trace the early history of cultural divergence, we should look for certain sorts of changes, namely, intensified settlement, population concentrated in relatively large settlements, multiplying social categories and functions of government, emergence of chiefs and fledgling states, and increasingly diversified and specialized economic activity. Between 5000 and 3000 B.C.E., we can detect these changes in widely separated places around the world. We can take a few examples in a selective tour through cultures launched into divergent futures.

Intensified Settlement and Its Effects

In the New World (see Chapter 1), Mesoamerica and Central America remained a region of small villages. We can document monumental cities and large states there only from about 2000 B.C.E. In North America, agriculture barely appeared. By contrast, at the base of the high Andes in South America, archaeology has unearthed early evidence of many different social rankings, economic specializations, and grossly unequal concentrations of wealth and power.

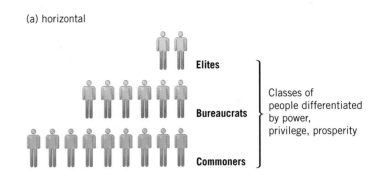

(a) horizontal

Elites

Bureaucrats

Commoners

Classes of people differentiated by power, privilege, prosperity

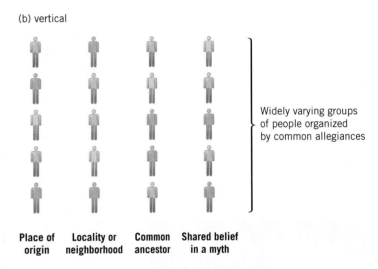

(b) vertical

Place of origin | Locality or neighborhood | Common ancestor | Shared belief in a myth

Widely varying groups of people organized by common allegiances

FIGURE 3.1 HORIZONTAL AND VERTICAL ORGANIZATIONS OF SOCIETY

Five and a half thousand years ago—about 3500 B.C.E.—large farming settlements began to appear on alluvial plains in coastal Peru, in the region north of present-day Lima, and especially in the Supe Valley, which has over 30 archaeological sites. The most impressive was Aspero, where by the mid–third millennium B.C.E. 17 mounds supported half a dozen platforms and various terraces, with large, complex dwellings and storehouses. The platforms were built up with loads of rubble in uniform containers, which suggests that a system existed to measure the labor of different groups of workers. An infant's grave gives us a glimpse into the society and perhaps the politics of the time. Under a grinding stone he lies painted with red ochre, wrapped in textiles, and scattered with hundreds of beads. This is evidence of heritable wealth and, perhaps, power in an economy dependent on grain where a flour-making tool literally marked the difference between life and death.

Covering over 32 acres, Aspero must have had a big population—uniquely big by the standards of the Americas at the time. There were, however, many settlements of between two and three thousand people. They were trading centers where people exchanged the products of different ecosystems—marine shells, mountain foods, and featherwork made from the brightly colored birds that lived in the forests east of the Andes.

Comparable developments occurred across Eurasia (see Map 3.1). In parts of eastern Europe, for instance, innovations in technology and government emerged, without, as far as we know, any influence from outside the region. These settlements were of a scale we think of as villages rather than cities. In the shadow of the Carpathian Mountains, Europe's oldest copper mine at Rudna Glava, above the middle Danube River in modern Serbia, made the region a center of early metallurgy. In Tisza in what is now Hungary, over 7,000 years ago, smelters worked copper into beads and small tools—magic that made smiths powerful figures of myth. To the people who left offerings, the mines were the dwellings of gods.

In Bulgaria of the same period, trenches and palisades surrounded settlements, with gateways exactly aligned at the points of the compass, like in later Roman army camps. Here prospectors in metal-rich hills traded gold for the products of agriculture. No place in prehistoric Europe gleams more astonishingly than Varna on the Black Sea, where a chief was buried clutching a gold-handled axe, with his penis sheathed in gold, and nearly a thousand gold ornaments, including hundreds of discs that must have spangled a dazzling coat. This single grave contained more than three pounds of fine gold. Other graves were symbolic, containing earthenware masks without human remains. At Tartaria in Romania, markings on clay tablets look uncannily like writing.

A little to the east, also around 5000 B.C.E., at Sredny Stog, on the middle Dnieper River in what is now Ukraine, the earliest known domesticators of horses filled their garbage dumps with horse bones. In graves of about 3500 B.C.E., lie covered wagons, arched with hoops and designed to be pulled by oxen, rumbling on vast wheels of solid wood. These wagons were buried as if for use in an afterlife, evidence that rich and powerful chiefdoms could carry out ambitious building projects despite a herding way of life that required constant mobility. Few other societies in the world were rich enough to bury objects of such size and value. Central Eurasia became a birthplace for early transportation technology. For instance, the earliest recognizable chariot dates from early 2000 B.C.E. in the southern Ural Mountains that divide Europe from Asia.

Meanwhile, monumental building projects, on a scale only agriculture could sustain and only a state could organize, were underway in the Mediterranean. The remains of the first large stone dwellings known anywhere in the world are on the island of Malta, which lies between Sicily and North Africa. Here, at least

Trade enriches. Gold-laden graves in a 6,000-year-old cemetery at Varna, Bulgaria lie by an inlet beside a wood-built village that is quite different from mud-walled settlements in the interior, where the graves are under the houses. The Varna culture vanished—overwhelmed perhaps by horse-tamers from the nearby steppes.

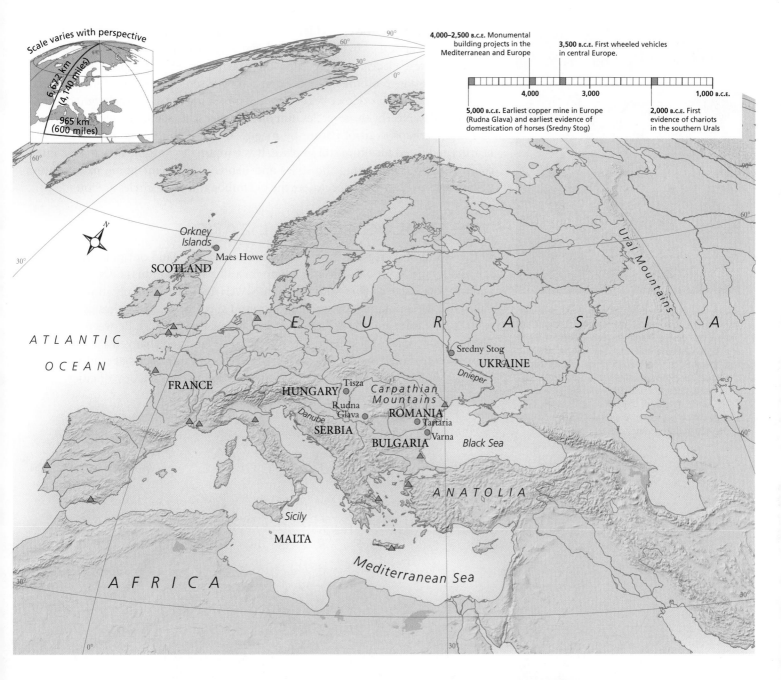

4,000–2,500 B.C.E. Monumental building projects in the Mediterranean and Europe

3,500 B.C.E. First wheeled vehicles in central Europe.

4,000   3,000   1,000 B.C.E.

5,000 B.C.E. Earliest copper mine in Europe (Rudna Glava) and earliest evidence of domestication of horses (Sredny Stog)

2,000 B.C.E. First evidence of chariots in the southern Urals

Orkney Islands
Maes Howe
SCOTLAND

E U R A S I A

Ural Mountains

ATLANTIC OCEAN

FRANCE

HUNGARY   Tisza
Rudna Glava
SERBIA

Carpathian Mountains
ROMANIA
Tartaria

Sredny Stog
UKRAINE
Dnieper

Danube

BULGARIA   Varna

Black Sea

ANATOLIA

Sicily

MALTA

Mediterranean Sea

AFRICA

half a dozen temple complexes arose in the fourth and third millennia B.C.E. They were built of limestone around spacious courts shaped like clover leaves. The biggest temple is almost 70-feet wide under a 30-foot wall. Inside one building was a colossal, big-hipped goddess attended by sleeping beauties—small female models scattered around her. There were altars and wall carvings—some in spirals, some with deer and bulls—and thousands of bodies piled in communal graves. We wonder how Malta's soil, so poor and dry, could sustain a population large and leisured enough to build so lavishly.

Even on Europe's Atlantic edge, in the fourth millennium B.C.E., luxury objects could find a market and monumental buildings arose. Some of the earliest signs of the slow-grinding social changes lie among the bones of aristocrats in individual graves with the possessions that defined their status and suggest their way of life— weapons of war and drinking cups that once held liquor or poured offerings to the

MAP 3.1

Intensified Settlements in Western Eurasia, 5,000–2,000 B.C.E.

●   Places described on pages 66–68

▲   other important archeological sites

MALTA   modern day country mentioned on pages 66–68

Malta. The world's oldest monumental stone buildings are temple complexes of the late fourth millennium B.C.E. on the Mediterranean islands of Malta and Gozo. All resemble this example at Mnajdra, with central corridors connecting kidney-shaped chambers, enclosed by fine-faced limestone, polished with stone tools. Inside, animals were sacrificed, and images of corpulent goddesses were stored. We do not know where the wealth that sustained the builders came from.

gods. Then come the graves of chiefs, buried under enormous standing stones (called megaliths), near stone circles probably designed to resemble the rings of trees, surrounding forest glades that preceded them as places of worship. In the Orkney Islands, for instance, off the north coast of Scotland, settled about 5,500 years ago, an elaborate tomb at Maes Howe lies close to a temple building, filled with light on midsummer's day. Nearby stone circles hint on a smaller scale at attempts to monitor the Sun and, perhaps, control nature by magic. A stone-built village to the west has hearths and fitted furniture still in place. It is tempting to imagine this as a far-flung colonial station, preserving the styles and habits of a distant home in southwest Britain and northwest France, where the big tombs and stone circles are found.

THE ECOLOGY OF CIVILIZATION

In this world of increasing diversification, four regions stand out in terms of scale: the middle and lower Nile River in Egypt; the valleys of the Indus (EEN-doos) River and the now dried-up Saraswati (sah-rah-SWAH-tee) River (mainly in what is now Pakistan); Mesopotamia, between and around the Tigris and Euphrates Rivers in what is now Iraq; and the Yellow River in China (see Map 3.2). Between 5000 and 2000 B.C.E., people in these regions exploited more land and changed at a faster pace than other regions. Change was measured in terms of intensified agriculture, technological innovation, development of state power, and construction of cities.

In recent times, these valleys have occupied disproportionate space in our history books and a privileged place in our store of images and memories. Their ruins and relics still inspire movie makers, advertisers, artists, toy makers, and writers of computer games. They shape our ideas of what civilizations ought to be. When we hear the word civilization, we picture Egyptian pyramids, sphinxes, and mummies; Chinese bronzes, jades, and clays; Mesopotamian ziggurats—tall, tapering, steplike temples—and writing tablets smothered with ancient wedge-shaped letter forms. Or we conjure the windblown wrecks of almost-vanished cities in landscapes turning to desert. We even call these seminal—or nursery—civilizations, as if they were seed plots from which civilized achievements spread around the world. Or we call them great civilizations, and begin our conventional histories of civilization by describing them.

Civilization is now a discredited word. People have abused it as a name for societies they approve of, which usually means societies that resemble their own. They have also denied the term to cultures they deem alien or lacking in material culture or institutions similar to their own. Or they have misapplied it as the name

MAP 3.2

The Great River Valleys

■ Great River Valley

● place described on page 66

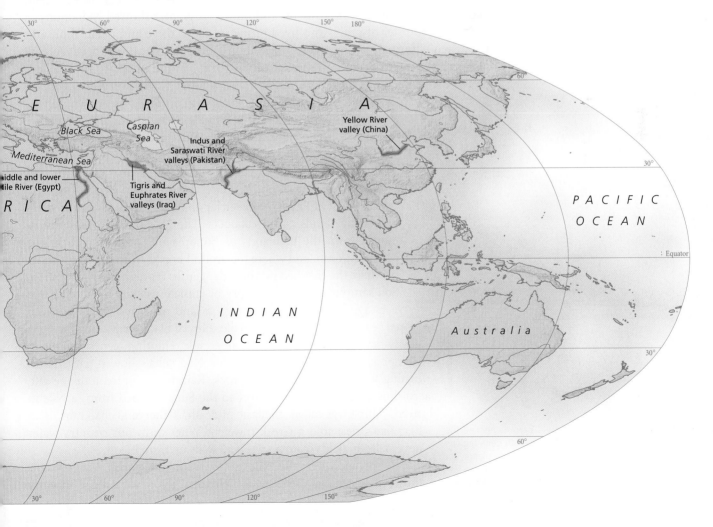

of a supposedly universal stage of social development, even though we have no evidence that societies follow any universal course of development. We can, however, understand a civilization simply as a society that, for good or ill, engages ambitiously with its environment, seeking to remodel the rest of nature to suit human purposes. That is, we can speak of the **ecology of civilization**, the interaction of people with their environment. In this sense of the word, the four river valleys housed societies more civilized than earlier cases we know of. They modified the landscape with fields and irrigation works or smothered it with monumental buildings on a scale that no people before attained or, perhaps, even conceived.

THE GREAT FLOODPLAINS

The four river valleys shared certain environmental features: a gradually warming and drying climate; relatively dry soils; and a reliance on seasonally flooding rivers and, therefore, on irrigation. If we consider them, together, however, we can see how relentless divergence opened cultural chasms inside this common ecological framework.

The Ecology of Egypt

In the north, where the lower Nile empties into the Mediterranean, Egypt had the advantage of a different kind of environment. Here, in the delta region, food sources and useful plants complemented what farmers could grow in the irrigated lands to the south. In the delta's teeming marshlands, birds, animals, fish, and plants clustered for the gatherer and hunter. A painter showed Nebamun—a scribe and counter of grain who lived probably about three and a half thousand years ago—hunting among reeds and bulrushes. Lotus and papyrus plants inspired carvers to decorate pillars. Contemporary praise of a city built in the delta paints the environment in lush colors, "full of everything good— its ponds with fish and its lakes with birds. Its meadows are verdant; its banks bear dates; its melons are abundant." The same source lists onions and leeks, lettuces, pomegranates, apples, olives, figs, sweet vines, and "red fish which feed on lotus-flowers." Thickets of rushes and papyrus provided rope and writing paper.

Most of Egypt, however, lay above the delta, as far upriver as the rocky rapids called cataracts. The Nile flows from south to north, from the highlands of Ethiopia in Central Africa to the Mediterranean, and where the ground breaks from higher altitudes or where the riverbed narrows, dangerous rapids hinder navigation. Soil samples reveal the history of climate change. By about 4,000 years ago, the valley was already a land of "black" earth between "red" earths. Floods fed the fertile, alluvial black strip along the Nile; slowly drying red desert lay on either side. Hunting scenes painted at Memphis, Egypt's first capital, in the Nile delta, showed game lands turning to scrub, sand, and bare rock. Rain became rare, a divine gift, according to a pious king's prayer to the Sun, dropped from "a Nile in heaven." Thirst was called "the taste of death." Other lands had rain, as an Egyptian priest told a Greek traveler, "Whereas in our country water never falls on fields from above, it all wells up from below."

In spring, when the Nile is low, rain in Central Africa swells the feed waters of the Nile, which turn green with algae in early

Environmental diversity nourishes civilization. Egypt combined the grainlands of Upper Egypt with the moist, game-rich delta regions of Lower Egypt, with its wealth of aquatic animals and plants. On the tomb walls of Nebamun in the fourteenth century B.C.E., an irrigated garden appears, reproducing the lush look of the Nile delta.

Making bread. Some of the activities portrayed in ancient Egyptian tomb-offerings seem humdrum. Beer-making or—as in this example, nearly 3,000 years old—bread-making, are among the most common scenes. But these were magical activities that turned barely edible grains into mind-expanding drinks and a life-sustaining staple food.

Food aid. Egypt exported surplus food across the Red Sea in exchange for the luxury aromatics, especially incense, of the land of Punt, whose queen, depicted in a painting perhaps 3,500 years old, appears comically—or realistically?—obese. Like modern Westerners, but unlike most people in most cultures, the Egyptians esteemed thin body shapes.

summer, then red with tropical earth in August. In September and October, if all goes well, the river floods and spreads the dark, rich silt thinly over the earth. If the flood is too high, the land drowns. If the level of the river falls below about 18 feet, drought follows. In one of the oldest surviving documents of Egyptian history, probably of about 2500 B.C.E., a king reveals a dream. The river failed to flood because the people neglected the gods who ruled beyond the cataracts, where the waters came from. Still, compared to the other river valleys of the period, the Nile flood waters were—and still are—exceptionally regular and, therefore, easy to exploit.

Irrigation created little microclimates, like the paintings of orchards and gardens that adorn tombs in the city of Thebes, the second capital city of Egypt. From streams filled with water lilies, a gardener with a dog at his feet swings a bucket on a pole, called a *shaduf,* that a single operator can dip, hoist, reposition, and spill over the soil. It is an invention of maybe 6,000 years ago. Strips of cattle-raising grasslands lay between floodplain and desert. But the silt the water brought was vital because the nitrogen content of the soil decreases by two-thirds in the top six inches between floods. The annually renewed topsoil grew some of the densest concentrations of wheat in the ancient world.

The economy was dedicated to a cult of **everyday abundance.** That is, it guaranteed basic nutrition for a large population, not individual abundance. Most people lived on bread and beer (a much grainier, more nutritious brew than modern beer), in amounts only modestly above subsistence level. A surplus gathered and guarded against hard times was at the disposal of the state and priests. Eaters who relied

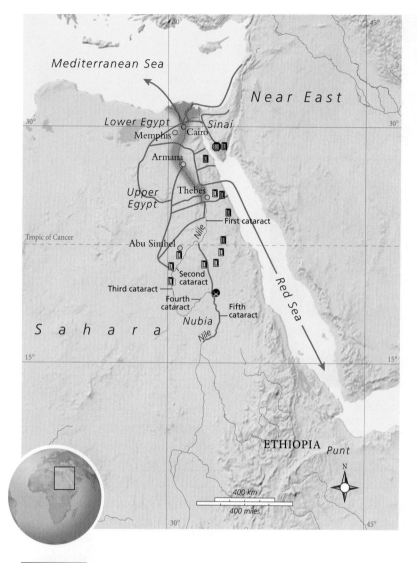

MAP 3.3

Ancient Egypt

○   modern-day city

→   trade route

Trade Goods

▯   gold

▯   copper

◑   turquoise

✕   ivory

exclusively on the wheat and barley of the irrigated dry lands were vulnerable to routine malnutrition and to famine in years of drought. Normally, however, there were greater quantities of the basic products of the economy than Egyptians could eat. The surplus generated trade, which made up for the country's lack of timber and aromatic plants for perfumes and incense. The wall carvings of a memorial to Queen Hatshepsut, a female monarch of perhaps about 3,500 years ago, reveal the nature of Egyptian "food aid." Vast stores of grain and live cattle are unloaded in the land of Punt, at the far end of the Red Sea in East Africa, in exchange for scented trees to grace a temple garden and exotic animals for the Egyptian royal zoo. Most of the courtly luxuries that today's Western museum goers see in exhibits on ancient Egypt came from trade, raids, and conquest. Gold and ivory, for example, came from Nubia, an African kingdom beyond the cataracts, and copper and turquoise came from Sinai, a region of desert uplands that link Egypt to the Near East (see Map 3.3).

Shifting Rivers of the Indus Valley

In the Indus valley, the sparse remains of the society called Harappan after Harappa (hah-RAH-pah), one of its earliest excavated cities, lie frustratingly beyond historians' reach. The rising water table has drowned evidence of the earliest phases, and the literate period is obscure because scholars have not been able to decipher the writing system. Here the Indus and Saraswati Rivers were more powerful and capricious than the Nile, changing course and cutting new channels that might deprive settlements of water supplies. Ultimately, perhaps, they were fatally unpredictable, for Egypt lasted thousands of years longer. When, the Indus altered course and the Saraswati dried up, Harappan cities dwindled to faint traces in the dust.

But three to five thousand years ago, the Indus floodplain was broader than the Nile's. The Indus and Saraswati flooded twice a year—first with the spring snowmelt when the rivers rose, and then in summer when warm air, rising in Central Asia, sucks moisture in from the sea. As a result, farmers here could grow two crops annually. The basic patterns were the same as in Egypt. Wheat and barley grew on rainless, irrigated soil, and cattle—mainly humped-back zebu, in Harappa—grazed on marginal grassland. No region was as rich as the Nile delta, but Harappa had a coastal outpost at the seaport of Lothal, on the Gulf of Cambay on the Indian Ocean, in a land of rice and millet (see Map 3.4).

The Harappan heartland had few valuables of its own. Again, as in Egypt, the basis of its wealth was the surplus of its agriculture. Around 2000 B.C.E., the Harappan-culture area was the biggest in the world, stretching over half a million square miles. This was, perhaps, evidence of weakness rather than strength. Territorial expansion was the Harrapan solution to feeding its increasingly dense population in the heartland, and no society can keep expanding forever.

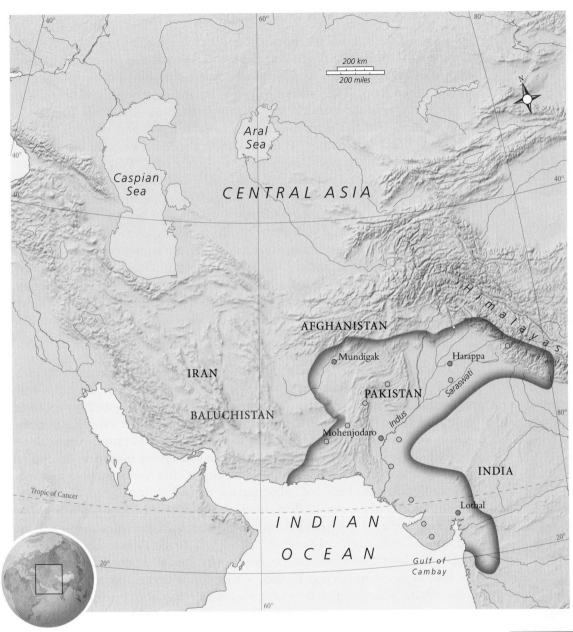

MAP **3.4**

Harappan Civilization

▬	extent of Harappan culture
●	place described on pages 72–86
○	other important Harappan site
INDIA	modern-day country

Most surviving Harappan art is engraved on seals used to mark trading goods. These little masterpieces capture how people of the time saw their world. Some show naturalistic representations of animals, especially bearded zebus, feasting tigers, and elegant, humpless bulls, that are sniffing, it seems, at an object that looks like an incense burner. Violations of realism, however, are more characteristic and include jokey elephants and rhinoceroses. Perplexing scenes, probably from Harappan mythology, include magical transformations of human into tiger, starfish into unicorn, horned serpent into flourishing tree. In one case, a human is transforming into a tree after sex with a rampant bull. A common motif shows an apelike figure defending a tree against a tiger; both creatures wear horns.

Harappan seals. In the last couple of centuries, scholarly code-crackers have worked out how to read most of the world's ancient scripts. But the writing on Harappan seals remains elusive. The seals to depict visions and monsters—but the messages they conveyed were probably of routine merchants, data-stock-taking and prices. In most cases that we know of, writing was first devised to record information too uninteresting for people to confide to memory.

Fierce Nature in Early Mesopotamia

The waters of the Nile and the Indus spill and recede according to a reasonably predictable rhythm, but the Tigris and Euphrates flood at any time, washing away dikes, overflowing ditches. At other times, desert sandstorms choke the farmers and bury their crops. The writers of Mesopotamian literature—the earliest imaginative literature in the world to survive in written form—described an environment more violent and more hostile than those of Egypt and Harappa. Gods of storm and flood dominate, or, at least, shadow, the Mesopotamian world. In the wind, according to the poets, earth shattered "like a pot." "Will new seed grow?" asked a proverb. "We do not know. Will old seed grow? We do not know."

In lower Mesopotamia, where the first big cities sprang up around 3000 B.C.E., the rivers fell through a parched landscape from a distant land of rain, like trickles across a windowpane. Even with irrigation, the summers were too harsh and dry to produce food for the early cities, which had to rely on winter crops of wheat and barley, onions, chickpeas, and sesame. Rain fell more often then than it does today, but it was largely confined to winter when ferocious storms made the sky flare with sheet lightning. "Ordered by the storm-god in hate," according to a poet, "it wears away the country." The floods that created the life-giving alluvial soils were also life-threateningly capricious. Unleashed in early summer by mountain rains, rivers could swell and sweep away crops.

Meanwhile, earth and water, the benign forces that combined to create the alluvial soil, were also celebrated in verse. The goddess Nintu personified Earth—zealous, jealous mother, yielding nourishment, suckling infants, guarding embryos. Water, to awaken the land's fertility, was a male god, Enki, empowered "to clear the pure mouths of the Tigris and Euphrates, to make greenery plentiful, to make dense the clouds, to grant water in abundance to all ploughlands, to make corn lift its head in furrows and to make pasture abound in the desert." But Nintu and Enki were subordinate deities, at the beck and call of storm and flood.

The ferocity of the climate demanded hardy plants, so Mesopotamia produced much more barley than wheat. Exhausting digging raised dwellings above the flood and diverted and conserved water. By 5000 B.C.E., farmers throughout the region were using plows drawn by oxen. The people who lived along the lower stretches of the river depicted themselves in their art as dome-headed, potbellied lovers of music, feasts, and war. But they were necessarily resourceful people who made ships in a country with no timber, worked masterpieces in bronze in a part of the world where no metal could be found, built fabulous cities without stone by baking mud into bricks, and dammed rivers as the Marsh Arabs of southern Iraq do to this day—with brushwood, reeds, and earth.

The Good Earth of Early China

Mesopotamia and Harappa certainly traded with each other. Mesopotamia and Egypt were close to each other and in constant touch. The map shows, however, that China's Yellow River valley was relatively isolated by long distances and physical barriers—mountains, deserts, ocean (see Map 3.5). Nevertheless, perhaps in part because the environment was similar, developments here unfolded in familiar ways.

The Yellow River collects rain in the mountains of Shaanxi province, where rapid thaws bring torrents of water. Where it disgorges, the stream broadens suddenly and periodically overflows. Here the climate has been getting steadily drier for thousands of years. The region today is torrid in summer, icy in winter, stung by chill, gritty winds, and rasped by rivers full of ice. The winds blow dust from the

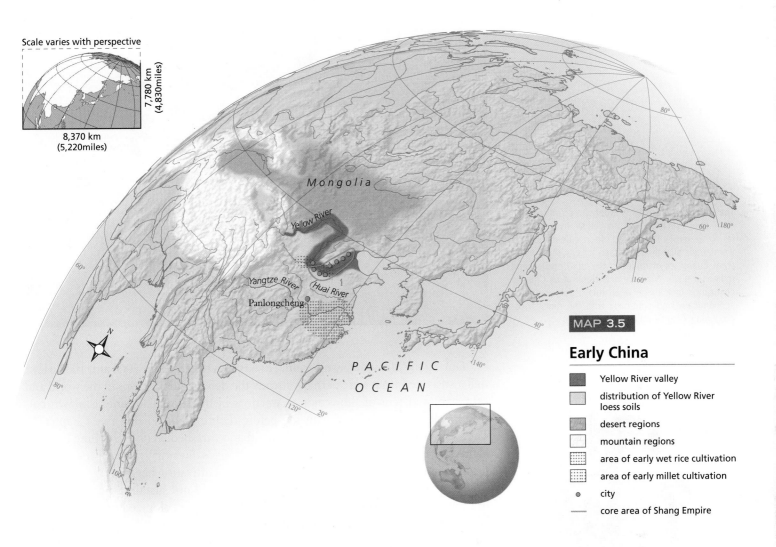

Scale varies with perspective

7,780 km (4,830 miles)

8,370 km (5,220miles)

MAP 3.5

Early China

- Yellow River valley
- distribution of Yellow River loess soils
- desert regions
- mountain regions
- area of early wet rice cultivation
- area of early millet cultivation
- • city
- core area of Shang Empire

Mongolian desert over the land, creating the crumbly, yellow earth that gives the river its name. This soil, called *loess* (loh-ehs) is almost sterile if it is not watered, but the flood coaxes it into amazing fertility. Because of its ferocity and unpredictability, the river needs careful management, with dikes to stem the flood, ditches to channel it, and artificial basins to conserve water against drought.

When farmers first began to till them, these lands were a sort of savanna, where grasslands mixed with woodland. Three or four thousand years ago, water buffalo were still plentiful, together with other creatures of marsh and forest, such as the small deer known as the elaphure, water deer, wild boar, silver pheasants, bamboo rats, and the occasional rhinoceros. In the *Shi Jing* (sher-jeeng), a collection of ancient songs, poets rhapsodize about the toil of clearing weeds, brush, and roots. "Why in days of old did they do this task? So that we might plant our grain, our millet, so that our millet might be abundant." The legendary ancestor of the most successful lineage of the time was called Hou Ji (hoh jee), "the Ruler of Millet." In folk memory, when he planted the grain,

It was heavy, it was tall,
it sprouted, it eared . . .
it nodded, it hung . . .
Indeed the lucky grains were sent down to us,
The black millet, the double-kernelled,
millet pink-sprouted and white.

 excerpt from the *Shi Jing*

The Yellow River. The powdery, wind-blown soil from inner Asia that gives the Yellow River its name is highly fertile if irrigated. In a climate slightly warmer and slightly wetter than today's, it produced great quantities of millet in the third and second millennia B.C.E. What we now think of as Chinese civilization took shape when this region combined economically and politically with the moist, rice-producing Yangtze valley to the south.

King Gudea (2141–2122 B.C.E.) of Lagash in Sumeria, was one of ancient Mesopotamia's most determined propagandists, distributing dozens of statues of himself to other rulers. This example is typical, with his head bound by his characteristic lamb's fleece fillet, his overflowing oil flagon (signifying abundance under his rule), and the self-glorifying inscription that covers his robe. But the propaganda may have been born of despair. After his reign, Lagash vanishes from the historical record.

During the Shang (shawng) ruling dynasty, between about 3000 and 1000 B.C.E., millet sustained what were perhaps already the densest populations in the world and kept armies of tens of thousands of warriors in the field. The earliest known cultivators cleared the ground with fire before dibbling and sowing (see Chapter 2). They harvested each cluster of ears by hand and threshed seeds by rubbing between hands and feet. Crop rotation secured the best yields. Eventually soya beans provided the alternating crop, but it is not clear when soya cultivation began.

Even at its wettest, the Yellow River valley could not sustain a rice-eating civilization. Rice could only become a staple when people colonized new areas. Some later poets recalled expansion from the Yellow River southward as a process of conquest, grasping at the Yangtze River. But conquest makes more interesting myths than colonization does. Colonists and conquerors probably combined with other communities, where similar changes were already in progress, in a slow process of expansion on many levels, beginning more than 3,500 years ago.

CONFIGURATIONS OF SOCIETY

All four of the great river valleys faced the same problem—population was growing denser and society becoming more complex, both of which demanded a strengthened state. Yet they adopted contrasting solutions.

Patterns of Settlement and Labor

We do not know how many people lived in the great river-valley civilizations, but they surely numbered millions, and their numbers tended to grow, crowding their heartlands. In Egypt, instead of great cities, the people were spread fairly uniformly throughout the narrow floodplain of the Nile. Cities were strewn through the other three valleys.

By 3000 B.C.E., Sumer (SOO-mehr), as lower Mesopotamia (the part nearer the Persian Gulf) was called, was already a land of cities (see Map 3.6). Each city was sacred to the deity it housed, and a king who organized war against his neighbors ruled each city. The most famous city was one of the smallest. Ur (oor), Abraham's home in the Bible story, had royal tombs of staggering wealth and towering ziggurats,

○ MAKING CONNECTIONS ○

THE ECOLOGY OF CIVILIZATIONS

REGION →	ENVIRONMENTAL DIVERSITY →	PRIMARY MODIFICATIONS →	ECONOMIC CONSEQUENCES
Egypt (Nile River)	Delta: marshlands, ponds, lakes; Upriver: "black earth," alluvial plain created from regular floods from central African headwaters; bordered by Sahara Desert, with scattered oasis	Exploitation of lush delta (*shaduf*); flooded alluvial plain with irrigation; microclimates with orchards, gardens	Everyday abundance of basic commodities (wheat, barley, cattle) leads to population increase, regional trade
Indus (Indus, Saraswati Rivers)	Wide alluvial floodplain, frequent changing river courses, varied climate—coastal outposts, hot interior, upriver Himalayan headwaters; flooding twice a year from spring snowmelt and monsoon rains	Widespread irrigation of rainless upriver regions; grazing on grasslands, marsh areas	Agricultural surplus with two harvests a year; rapid population growth, urbanization
Mesopotamia (Tigris, Euphrates Rivers)	Delta: marshlands, ponds, lakes, waterways; upriver alluvial plains flooded irregularly; harsh summer sandstorms, intense heat; winter floods, rainstorms; lack of forests, stone	Irrigation; dependence on winter crops: barley, wheat, onions, chickpeas; intensive plowing; digging of dikes and ditches to divert and store water	Widespread cultivation of grains leads to regional trade; use of mud brick for housing, temples
China (Yellow River)	Unpredictable river floods surrounding areas creating *loess* soil—basis of agriculture; probably more rainfall than the other three regions	Dikes, irrigation canals control flooding; creation of basins to conserve water; early exploitation of savanna grasslands, buffalo, and other animals; farming based on millet, later supplanted by soya	Gradual expansion/colonization southward toward rice-growing region of Yangtze River

built over 4,000 years ago. They were so impressive that centuries later, people venerated the biggest of them as a work of gods. In 2004, French archaeologists reported the discovery of the structures that seem to have inspired the ziggurats in what is now Iran, over an extensive area stretching from the Zagros Mountains eastward to Baluchistan. People at Susa, for instance, built a terraced mound of mud bricks more than 240 feet square and 34 feet high, nearly 1,000 years before the earliest Mesopotamian ziggurats. From a slightly later date, the same excavations have yielded cylinders of colorful stone, carved with the facades of many-windowed buildings. So it looks as if the culture of Mesopotamian cities developed in part as a result of cultural exchanges with this previously unknown civilization.

By the beginning of the second millennium B.C.E., 1,000 years later, China, too, was a consciously urban culture. New frontier towns—modest places like Panlongcheng (pan-lung-chung), or Curled Dragon Town, in the northern province of Hubei (who-bay)—marked the growth of the kingdom. Its nearly one and a half acres provided for a governor's house surrounded by a colonnade of 43 pillars.

In any Harappan city of the same era, a citizen would have felt as at home as in any other. The streetscapes—the layouts of residential and administrative zones—

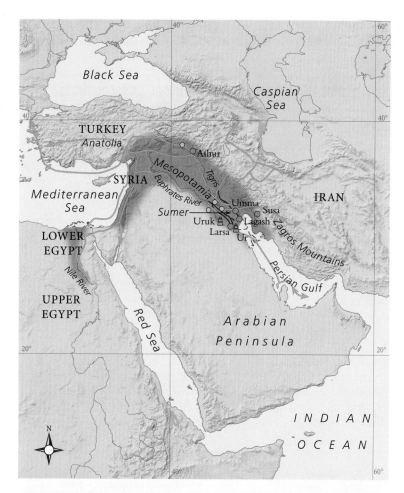

were always much the same, as were the houses. Every brick was uniform—sometimes kiln baked, sometimes pan dried. Mohenjodaro (moh-hehn-joh-DAH-roh) was big enough to house perhaps 50,000 or 60,000 people and Harappa, over 30,000. No other settlements were anything as big, but there were plenty of them—at least 1,500 are known to archaeology.

In all these valleys, population density made specialization possible. People could devote themselves exclusively to particular crafts and trades. Although the evidence is deficient, each sex undoubtedly specialized in certain occupations, and women tended to be subordinated to men. There are several clues. First, there seemed to be a shift from matrilineal to patrilineal descent—systems, that is, inheriting status from the father rather than the mother. Then birth rates rose rapidly, which might have tied women to child rearing. About the same time—whether cause or result—art depicted women in servile roles. For instance, pouting, languid bronze dancing girls—or are they temple prostitutes?—figure among the few art works excavated from Harappan cities of the second millennium B.C.E. To judge from surviving Mesopotamian law codes and Chinese texts, women's talents became increasingly focused on the family home and

The ziggurat of Ur. Typically, farming in any climate demands large-scale, highly disciplined labor, and generates seasonal manpower surpluses. Elites therefore have both the means and need to build on a monumental scale. This temple stairway at Ur in Mesopotamia is representative of the results: towering dimensions and precisely geometrical forms seem calculated to defy nature, symbolize order, and project triumphs of human imaginations.

child rearing. This is understandable because population increase created more strictly domestic work, while increasingly ambitious agriculture and construction were more efficiently entrusted to males.

So, along with other kinds of social differentiation, women seem to have been collectively disadvantaged, and men collectively privileged. Even at the most modest social levels, men had authority over women in their own households. Yet outside the home, urban life created new opportunities for specialized female labor. Women and children, for instance, were the textile workers in Ashur, a large city in northern Mesopotamia, and probably wove cotton in Harappan cities. Moreover, women were not necessarily excluded from power. These societies employed them as rulers, prophetesses, and priestesses and included them as subjects of art. Concentrating on domestic life also gave women opportunities to exercise informal power. Surviving texts show some of the consequences. Women had the right to initiate divorce, to recover their property, and, sometimes, to win additional compensation on divorce. A wife, says the Egyptian *Book of Instructions*, "is a profitable field. Do not contend with her at law and keep her from gaining control."

Politics

All four river valley societies shared, in one respect, a type of environment suited to tyranny, or, at least, to strong states exercising minute control over their subjects' lives. Indeed, for people living on the banks of silt-bearing, flood-prone rivers, intensified agriculture could have been a consequence—not a cause—of the political changes that accompanied it. That is, instead of an increased food supply requiring more political organization, a tyrannical leader may have forced people to farm more land to produce a surplus for trade, war, or feasts. Even without agriculture, people could have no security of life without collective action to manage the floods. Even foragers would need ditches and dikes to protect wild foodstuffs and defend dwellings. The mace head of an Egyptian king of the fourth millennium B.C.E. shows him digging a canal. Proverbially, a just judge was "a dam for the sufferer, guarding lest he drown," a corrupt one "a flowing lake." The importance of collectively managing the floods helps account for the obvious resemblances between the political systems of all these regions. All practiced divine or sacral kingship; all had rigid social hierarchies; all placed the lives and labor of the inhabitants at the disposal of the state.

We can see how one irrigation system worked, in Larsa in Mesopotamia, from the archive of a contractor named Lu-igisa, which has survived from around 2000 B.C.E. His job was to survey land for canal building, organize the laborers and their pay and provisions, and supervise the digging and the dredging of accumulated silt. Procuring labor was the key task—5,400 workers to dig a canal and 1,800 on one occasion for emergency repairs. In return, he had the potentially profitable job of controlling the opening and closing of the locks that released or shut off the water supplies. He was bound by oaths that were enforced by threat of loss. "What is my sin," he complained to a higher official when he lost control of a canal, "that the king took my canal from me and gave it to Etellum?"

The Egyptian State

It is tempting to attribute the loss of freedom in a forager society to the rise of a strong leader, but the one does not necessarily have to follow from the other. In ancient Egypt, the most common image of the state was of a flock the king tended like a herdsman. The comparison probably reflects the political ideas of earlier herder communities because farming as a way of life involves more competition for space than herding does. Disputes and wars over land strengthen rulership. Increased war and wealth would also shift patriarchs and elders out of supreme office in favor of stronger and wiser leaders.

In societies that rely on a single crop or a narrow range of crops, food shortages are a routine hazard. When normal weather patterns fail and reserves are inadequate, widespread famine can strike. As it is, shortages often occur annually in the unproductive season before the harvest. These problems are even worse for societies, like those of antiquity that cannot procure food through long-range trade. For

Dancing girl. One of a collection of bronze figures known as "dancing girls" unearthed at Mohenjo-daro. Their sinuous shapes, sensual appeal, and provocative poses suggest to some scholars that they may portray temple prostitutes. They are modeled with a freedom that contrasts with the formality and rigidity of the handful of representations of male figures that survive from the same civilization. *Dancing girl. Bronze statuette from Mohenjo Daro. Indus Valley Civilization. National Museum, New Delhi, India. Borromeo/Art Resource, NY*

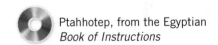

Ptahhotep, from the Egyptian *Book of Instructions*

Weighing the soul. About 4,500 years ago, Egyptian sensibilities changed. Instead of showing the afterlife as a prolongation of life in this world, tomb-painters began to concentrate on morally symbolic scenes, in which gods interrogate the dead and weigh their good against their evil deeds.

excerpts from *The Amarna Letters*

these reasons, in Egypt—a scorching environment that floods periodically douse—defying nature meant more than refashioning the landscape. Above all, it meant stockpiling against disaster, to safeguard humans from the invisible forces that let loose the floods. The temple built at Abu Simbel to house the body of Rameses II, who probably ruled around 1300 B.C.E. (nothing in ancient Egyptian chronology is certain), had storehouses big enough to feed 20,000 people for a year. The taxation yields proudly painted on the walls of a high official's tomb are an illustrated menu for feeding an empire: sacks of barley, piles of cakes and nuts, hundreds of head of livestock. The state as stockpiler existed, it seems, not to redistribute goods but for famine relief.

Methods of collecting and storing grain were as vital as the systems of flood control, precisely because the extent of the flood could vary from one year to the next. The biblical story of Joseph, an Israelite who became a pharaoh's chief official and saved Egypt from starvation, recalls "seven lean years" at one stretch. Such bad times were part of folk memories, as were spells when "every man ate his children." A tomb scene from the city of Amarna (ah-MAHR-nah) shows a storehouse with only six rows of stacked victuals, including grain sacks and heaps of dried fish, laid on shelves supported on brick pillars. A strong state was an inseparable part of this kind of farsightedness. Grain had to be taxed under compulsion, transported under guard, and kept under watch.

If pharaohs were highly glorified storekeepers, what did the Egyptians mean when they said their king was a god? Furthermore, how could pharaohs bear the names and exercise the functions of many gods, each with a separate identity? A possible aid to understanding is the Egyptian habit of making images and erecting shrines as places where the gods could manifest themselves. The image "was" the god only when the god inhabited the image. The pharaoh's person could provide a similar opportunity for a god to take up residence. For example, the goddess Isis, in some characterizations, was her deified throne.

The idea of the god-king gave birth to royal power. In the collection of ancient Egyptian diplomatic correspondence known as the Amarna letters, the ruler of a city in Palestine around 1350 B.C.E. wrote, "To the king my lord and my Sun-god, I am Lab'ayu thy servant and the dirt whereon thou dost tread. At the feet of my king and my Sun-god seven times and seven times I fall." Some 400 years earlier, a father, Sehetep-ib-Re, wrote advice to his children—"a counsel of eternity and a manner of living aright." The king is the Sun-god, but he is more. "He illumines Egypt more than the sun, he makes the land greener than does the Nile."

In Egypt the law remained in the mouth of the divine pharaoh, and the need to put it in writing was never strong. Instead, religion defined a moral code that the state could not easily modify or subvert. The evidence comes from Egyptian tombs. Early grave goods include the cherished possessions and everyday belongings of this world, suggesting that the next world would reproduce the inequalities and lifestyles of this one. At an uncertain date, however, a new idea of the afterlife emerged. This world was called into existence to correct the imbalances of the one we know. It is particularly well documented in ancient Egyptian sources that most of the elite seem to have changed their attitude to the afterlife around 2000 B.C.E. Earlier tombs are antechambers to a life for which the world was practical training. Tombs built later are places of interrogation after a moral preparation for the next life.

Wall paintings from the later tombs show the gods weighing the souls of the dead. Typically, the deceased's heart lies in one scale, and a feather symbolizing truth lies in the other. The jackal-headed god of the underworld, Anubis, supervises the scales. The examined soul renounces a long list of sins that concentrate on three areas: sacrilege, sexual perversion, and the abuse of power against the weak. Then the good deeds appear: obedience to human laws and divine will, acts of mercy, offerings to the gods and the spirits of ancestors, bread to the hungry, clothing to the naked, "and a ferry for him who was marooned." The reward of the good is a new life in the company of Osiris, the sometime ruler of the universe. For those who fail the test, the punishment is extinction.

Statecraft in Mesopotamia

Unlike Egypt, a single state under a single ruler, Mesopotamia was divided into numerous small rival kingdoms called city-states because each was based on a single city. In Mesopotamia, kings were not gods, which is probably why the earliest known law codes come from there. The codes of Ur from the third millennium B.C.E. are fragmentary—essentially, lists of fines. But the code of King Lipit-Ishtar of Sumer and Akkad (ah-KAHD), around 2000 B.C.E., is clearly an attempt to regulate the entire society. It explains that the laws were divinely inspired and ordained "in accordance with the word of Enlil," the supreme god. Their purpose was to make "children support the father and the father children, . . . abolish enmity and rebellion, cast out weeping and lamentation . . . bring righteousness and truth and give well-being to Sumer and Akkad."

The Code of Lipit-Ishtar

Hammurabi, ruler of Babylon in the first half of the 1700s B.C.E., gets undue credit because his code happens to survive intact, having been carried off as a war trophy to Persia. It is engraved in stone and shows the king receiving the text from the hands of a god. It was clearly intended to substitute for the physical presence and utterance of the ruler. "Let any oppressed man who has a cause come into the presence of the statue of me, the king of justice, and then read carefully my inscribed stone, and give heed to my precious words. May my stone make his case clear to him." These were not laws as we know them, handed down by tradition or enacted to restrain the ruler's power. Rather, they were means to perpetuate royal commands. Obedience was severely enforced in Mesopotamia—to the vizier in the fields, the father in the household, the king in everything. "The king's word is right," says a representative text, "his word, like a god's, cannot be changed."

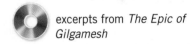

excerpts from *The Epic of Gilgamesh*

Even if we had no written evidence to confirm it, royal power would gleam from the luxurious artifacts that filled rulers' tombs, evidence of the realm's wealth: a gilded harp carved in the form of a ram; dice and gaming boards of inlaid shell and polished stone; lively animals sculpted in gold and silver with eyes of shell and lapis lazuli (a blue stone); tapering vessels of gold, and golden cups modeled on ostrich eggs. The stunning collections of jewelry seem to have religious themes, as if each had a distinct ritual function.

In Mesopotamian carvings, the king is commonly the biggest figure in any scene that includes him. He drinks. He receives supplicants who petition his help and citizens and ambassadors who pay him tribute. He presides over armies and processions of chariots drawn by wild asses. He carries bricks to build cities and temples, purifying them with fire and consecrating them with oil. To form the first brick from the mud was the king's exclusive right, and bricks from the state kilns were stamped with royal names. Royal seals make plain why this was. They show gods building the world up

A BOARD GAME FROM ANCIENT SUMER

Elite pastime: The British archaeologist Sir Leonard Woolley (1880–1960) found the remains of two board games of the third millennium B.C.E. in a royal grave deep in the ruins of the Sumerian city of Ur. Rules in verse, apparently for a similar game, survive from early in the second century B.C.E. in Egypt.

Squares made of shells, set with the blue stone called lapis lazuli and red limestone. The squares were stuck to the wooden board with bitumen, a tar that the Sumerians used as glue. They derived it from the petroleum that bubbled to the surface in parts of Mesopotamia in what is today Iraq.

The game seems to have imitated a life's journey. The rose-like squares may have been safe spots. Playing pieces that landed on these squares did not have to pay a penalty. Other squares represented food and love.

Dice made of the knucklebones of sheep and oxen.

How does this board game comment on the importance of leisure among members of the elite in the Great River Valleys?

out of mud. They mix it, carry it up ladders, and fling mud bricks up to the men who set them layer by layer. The transformation of mud into city was royal magic.

Oracles—means of supposed access to knowing the future—told kings what to do. Augurers were the hereditary interpreters of oracles. They read the will of the gods in the livers of sacrificed sheep, the drift of incense, and, above all, in the movements of heavenly bodies. Their predictions of royal victory, danger, anger, and recovery from sickness fill surviving records. Religion, however, did not necessarily limit royal power. Normally, kings firmly controlled the oracles. Kings themselves sometimes slept in temples to induce prophetic dreams, especially during a crisis, such as the failure of the floods. Of course, the predictions they reported may have merely legitimated the policies they had already decided to follow.

Yet these absolute rulers were there to serve the people: to mediate with the gods on behalf of the whole society, to organize the collective effort of tillage and irrigation, to warehouse food against hard times, and to redistribute it for the common good. A comic dialogue from Akkad illustrates the delicate politics and economics of control of the food supply in the second millennium B.C.E. "Servant, obey me," the master begins.

Gilgamesh, king of Uruk, hero of the world's earliest known work of imaginative literature, shown in a relief more than 3,000 years old, kills the Bull of Heaven. The bull was a personification of drought. It was part of a king's job to mastermind irrigation. *Royal Museums of Art and History, Brussels, Belgium. Copyright IRPA–KIK, Brussels, Belgium.*

> I shall give food to our country.
> Give it, my lord, give it. The man who gives food to his country keeps his own barley and gets rich on the interest other people pay him.
> No, my servant, I shall not give food to my country.
> Do not give, my lord, do not give. Giving is like loving . . . or like having a son. . . . They will curse you. They will eat your barley and destroy you.

The most famous relic of ancient Mesopotamian literature, the epic of *Gilgamesh*, sheds further light on the nature of leadership or, at least of heroism, on which leadership is modeled. In the surviving versions, written down, perhaps about 1800 B.C.E., the same natural forces that molded the Mesopotamian environment shaped the story. When Gilgamesh, the hero of the poem, confronts a monster who breathes fire and plague, the gods blind the attacker with a scorching wind. When Gilgamesh explores the Ocean of Death to find the secret of immortality, he encounters the only family to have survived a primeval flood. The disaster, wrought by divine whim, had destroyed the rest of the human race and even left the gods themselves "cowering like dogs crouched against a wall."

The character of Gilgamesh is a poetic invention, embroidered onto the stuff of legends. But there was a real Gilgamesh, too, or at least a king of that name in historical sources. The poem quotes a proverbial saying about the historical Gilgamesh: "Who has ever ruled with power like his?" He was the fifth king recorded in the city of Uruk around 2700 B.C.E. (according to the most widely favored chronology). Some of the genuine wonders of the city appear during his reign—its walls, its gardens, the pillared hall where the deity was housed at the heart of the city.

The First Documented Chinese State

The earliest recorded kingship traditions of China resemble those of Egypt and Mesopotamia. They show the same connection between royal status and the management of water resources and the distribution of food. The legendary engineer–emperor Yu the Great was praised for having "mastered the waters and caused them to flow in great channels." Early folk poetry describes a period of city building after his time, so fast "that the drums could not keep pace." The legendary ruler Tan-fu "summoned the Master of Works,"

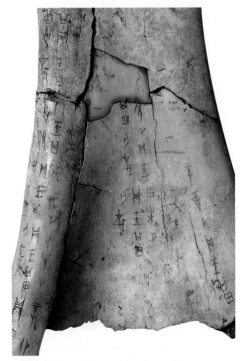

Oracle bones in China in the second millennium B.C.E. were heated until they cracked. Specialist diviners—shamans at first, later royal appointees—read the future along the lines of the cracks, scratching their interpretations into the bone. Most predictions were formal and even banal. This example says characteristically, "If the king hunts, there will be no disaster."

Tan-fu the Duke, from the *Shi Jing*

Bronze drinking vessel. The art of the bronze makers of the late second millennium B.C.E. in China has never been surpassed. Most of the bronzes, like this eleventh-century B.C.E. example in the form of a stylized tiger, were ritual drinking vessels, typically filled with grain alcohol to be offered to the spirits. Their symmetrical decoration suggests the influence of Daoism (see Chapter 6). Many have survived because they were buried as grave goods, for the use of ancestors in the afterlife.
Dagli Orti/PICTURE DESK KOBAL COLLECTION ART.

He called the Master of Multitudes,
He made them build houses.
Their plumb-lines were straight.
They lashed the boards and erected the frames
They made the temple in careful order.

The earliest China we know of was a unitary state. The dynasty known as Shang dominated the Yellow River valley for most of the second millennium B.C.E. Vital evidence about the nature of the Shang state is inscribed on oracle bones, animal bones and turtle shells used to foretell the future. Diviners, whose job was to detect the oracles' messages, heated them to breaking point and read the gods' answers to questions along the lines of the cracks. Scribes transcribed the answers onto the fragments, so the bones tell of the lives and duties of kings. The court treasury held millet, turtle shells, and oracle bones paid in tribute. The king was most often engaged in war and sometimes in diplomacy. Marriage was part of it; later emperors called it "extending my favor." To their soldiers, "our prince's own concerns" rolled them "from misery to misery" and gave them homes "like tigers and buffaloes . . . in desolate wilds."

Above all, the king was a mediator with the gods, performing sacrifices, preparing for and conducting oracle readings, breaking the soil, praying for rain, founding towns. He spent half his time hunting—presumably as a way to entertain counselors and ambassadors, train horsemen, and supplement the table. Scholars claim to detect an increasingly businesslike tone in the oracles. References to dreams and sickness diminish as time goes on, the style becomes more terse, and the tone more optimistic. Sometimes the bones reveal revolutions in the conduct of rites from reign to reign, evidence that kings fought tradition and tried to give the world a stamp of their own. Tsu Jia, for instance, a king of the late second millennium B.C.E., discontinued sacrifices to mythical ancestors, mountains, and rivers and increased those to historical figures. Beyond reasonable doubt, he was modifying the practices of the longest-lived and most renowned of his dynasty, Wu Ding (woo-ding).

The chronology is uncertain, but Wu Ding must have ruled about 1400 B.C.E. He was remembered 1,000 years later as a conqueror who ruled his empire as easily "as rolling it on his palm." He was a glorious hunter, whose oracles predicted, on one occasion, a bag of "tigers, one; deer, forty; foxes, one hundred and sixty-four; hornless deer, one hundred and fifty-nine; and so forth." One of his 64 consorts was buried in the richest known tomb of the period, with her human servants, dogs, horses, hundreds of bronzes and jades, and thousands of cowrie shells, which were used as money. Although there is room for confusion because of the court habit of calling different people by the same name, court records probably identify her correctly. Wu Ding repeatedly consulted the oracles about her childbeds and sickbeds. She was one of his three principal wives and not only wife and mother, but active participant in politics. She had a domain of her own, including a walled town, and could mobilize 3,000 warriors on command.

As mediator with the gods, the king was a substitute for the shaman, as the person who normally fulfills that role in society is called (see Chapter 1). A shaman is the intermediary—the middleman—between humans and gods. He elicits the "sharp-eared, keen-eyed" wisdom of ghosts and spirits and restores contact with heaven after disordered times. By taking over the divination of bones and turtle shells, the king transferred the most important political functions of magic and religion—foretelling the future and interpreting the will of the spirits—to the state. No longer in the hands of diviners, recording and preserving the results of divination became a secular—or nonreligious—function. The king became the guardian of a secular bureaucracy—a slowly developing corps of court historians, who could acquire experience on which predictions could be based more reliably than on the shamans' supposed insights.

At this stage, the Chinese viewed kingship in practical terms—how well the ruler looked after his subjects' well-being. Shang rulers claimed to have come to power as executors of divine justice against an earlier—doubtless mythical—dynasty, the Xia (SHEE-ah), whose last representative had forfeited his right to rule by "neglecting husbandry": failing, that is, in his duty to look after the realm as a farmer cares for his fields. The earliest scholars' texts that describe the emergence of China probably reflect traditional propaganda fairly accurately. They depict kind, generous rulers who fostered the arts of peace. The Yellow Emperor, a mythical figure, was credited with inventing the carriage, the boat, the bronze mirror, the cooking pot, the crossbow, "and a kind of football." Poems and popular legends, however, reveal more of the bloody business of kingship, which inherited ancient clan leaders' rights of life and death. An axe engraved with the emblems of the executioner—hungry smiles and devouring teeth—signified the original term for rulership. "Bring your tongues under the rule of law," says a late Shang ruler in an approving poet's lines, "lest punishment come upon you when repentance will be of no avail."

Wealth and warfare were inseparable essentials of kingship. Tombs of Shang rulers around 1500 B.C.E. display the nature of their power: thousands of strings of cowrie shells, bronze axes and chariots, lacquer ware, and hundreds of intricately carved treasures of jade and bone. The greatest treasures were bronzes of unparalleled quality, cast in ceramic molds. Bronze making was the supreme art of Shang China, and its products were a privilege of rank. Thousands of human sacrifices, buried with kings to serve them in the next world or to sanctify their tombs were—to those who buried them—among the cheapest sacrifices.

Ruling the Harappan World

In the Harappan world, the extraordinary consistency in urban layout and building design did not necessarily arise from political unity. Hierarchically ordered dwelling spaces hint at a class or even a more rigid caste structure. In a class system, individuals can rise or fall through the ranks of society. In a caste system they are stuck with the status with which they are born. In Harappan cities, the extensive communal quarters must have had something to do with the organization of manpower—soldiers, perhaps, or slaves, or scholars. Huge warehouses suggest a system to distribute food. The waste-disposal system looks like a masterpiece of urban planning, with clay pipes laid under the streets. The uniform bricks must have come from state kilns and pans. The imposing citadels or fortresses enclosed spaces that might have had an elite function, like the spacious bathing tank at Mohenjodaro (see Map 3.7). Harappan sites, however, have no rich graves, and the absence of kingly quarters or regal furnishings tempts us to imagine Harappan societies as republics or theocracies, god-centered governments that priests ran.

The Great River Valleys

(All dates are approximate)	
5000 B.C.E.	Beginning of intense agriculture in Great River Valleys; use of plows widespread in Mesopotamia
4000 B.C.E.	Shaduf invented in Egypt
3000 B.C.E.	Menes unites Upper and Lower Egypt; large cities appear in lower Mesopotamia (Sumer)
2500 B.C.E.	Sargon of Akkad conquers Sumer; cities of Harappa and Mohenjodaro flourish
2000–1000 B.C.E.	Shang dynasty (China)
2250–2000 B.C.E.	Ziggurat of Ur
2000 B.C.E.	Law code of Lipit-Ishtar (Mesopotamia); concept of afterlife becomes more moralistic in Egypt
1800 B.C.E.	Epic of *Gilgamesh* written down
1700 B.C.E.	Law code of Hammurabi
1500 B.C.E.	Reading of oracle bones becomes secularized in China; beginning of gradual expansion of Yellow River valley southward toward Yangtze

MAP 3.7 ## The Citadel at Mohenjodaro

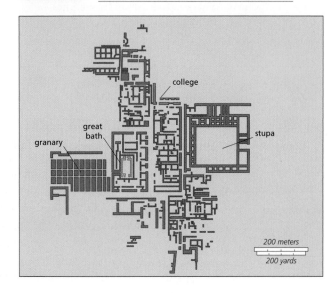

Harappan elite. Society and politics of ancient Harappa remain mysterious because little art survives as a clue to what went on, and we do not know how to decipher Harappan writings. A few sculptures, like this one from Mohenjodaro, depict members of an elite. The embroidered robe, jeweled crown, combed beard, and grave face all imply power—but is it priestly power, political power, or both?

Andy Crawford © Dorling Kindersley, Courtesy of the National Museum, New Delhi

Normally, for a society like Harappa's, whose writings we cannot read, archaeological evidence tells us what little we know. In particular, we would hope to learn something from works of art. But no pictorial art has survived, and Harappan artists seem to have produced little sculpture, except on a small scale in clay and sometimes bronze. One extraordinary figure from Mohenjodaro, of great seriousness, with almond eyes and rigidly fluted beard, wears a headband with what looks like the setting for a gem. He has a rich garment slung over one shoulder and extends what is left of his arm in what must surely have been a symbolic or ritual gesture. He has been called a priest-king or a philosopher-king, but these romantic terms are valueless. Since we know so little about Harappan politics, religion, and life, we have no context for interpreting him. We can only describe him.

The Politics of Expansion

Although just about everything in Harappan politics remains mysterious, the reach of the culture seems so vast it is hard to imagine how it can have spread so far, into a range of different environments, except by force of arms. A sense of what the Harappan frontier was like—expanding and violent—grips you when you see the garrisons that reached toward the interior of Asia, in unirrigatable deserts and siltless hills. In what is now northern Afghanistan, lapis lazuli and copper were traded at oasis settlements that reached westward toward the Caspian Sea. Mundigak, a fortified trading center, was equipped to house entire caravans. Today, behind formidable walls with square bastions, the wreck of a great citadel lunges over the landscape, baring rows of deep, round columns at its flank, like the ribs of a huge, squat beast crouched to guard the routes of commerce.

In Egypt, Mesopotamia, and China, the sources are ample enough to reveal how states grew by conquest. In Egypt, the Nile was the spine that supported a unitary state. More than the source of life-giving mud, the river was a highway

MAKING CONNECTIONS

POLITICS AND STATE POWER IN GREAT RIVER VALLEY SOCIETIES

STATE →	LEADER & SYMBOLIC ROLE →	METHOD OF UNIFICATION →	RULER'S MEANS OF CONTROL →
Egypt	Pharaoh (herdsman) sometimes functions as god	Organizing labor to manage floods; distributing food; use of Nile River as highway to unify, control	Pharaoh's commands, policies function as law, regarded as divine
Mesopotamia city-states	Kings/Royals meditate, lead worship, receive oracles	Organizing labor; distributing food; competition with other city-states	Earliest law codes; rituals performed by oracles guide decision making
China	Emperor/engineer, builder, hunter, takes on shamans' role in receiving prophecies	Organizing dike building, irrigation; use of Yellow River as highway to unify and control	Ritual divination using oracle bones—foretelling future, interpreting will of spirits
Harappa	Uncertain if singular ruler or priests dominated ruling class	Harnessing river, irrigation; distributing food; engineering and construction of complex urban systems	Unknown; widespread standardization of measurements and trade point to coordination/leadership

through a long, thin land. Culture and trade could flow freely from the coast to the cataracts. When the owner of a fleet died, his ships were illustrated on the walls of his tomb, like that of the royal chancellor Merket-ra at Thebes, painted over 3,000 years ago, with yachts, barges, and fishing boats. Models and paintings of river craft are among the most common decorations of tombs. At Thebes, you can still see painted scenes of grain-laden barges, and others with oil jars and bundles of fodder, docking by the marketplace.

The river was politically unifying, too. Pharoahs took the river route for inspection tours of the kingdom, mooring at royal docks with brick shrines and exercise yards for chariots. Egypt was an empire shaped like the fans Egyptians used to rake and beat their wheat—the long staff of the Nile linked to the spread of the delta where the river meets the Mediterranean. Mythology preserved the memory of a prehistoric Egypt divided into two realms: an upriver South Kingdom, or Upper Egypt, and Lower Egypt, occupying the delta region. Pharaohs wore a double crown to recall this past. Egypt's traditional lists of dynasties began with Menes, the culture hero who supposedly conquered the delta from his own kingdom in the south around 3000 B.C.E. He united the kingdoms and founded Memphis, his capital, at the point on the Nile where Upper and Lower Egypt joined, a little to the south of modern Cairo.

Conveyance by river was one of the features this world had in common with heaven. To accompany the immortals as they were ferried across the sky, the pharaoh Cheops was provided with transport. In one pit adjoining his pyramid lies the barge that carried his body to the burial place. Egyptologists are currently excavating an adjoining pit, where his celestial boat is buried. In this sailing vessel, he would navigate the darkness, joining the fleet that bore the Sun back to life every night.

In retrospect, the unity of Egypt seems "natural"—river shaped. Mesopotamia was not so easy to unify. Competition was probably the driving force behind Mesopotamian city-states. Inscriptions addressed to their cities' patron gods are full of victories against rivals, each one's propaganda bewilderingly contradicting the others. Around 2000 B.C.E., the most boastful author of inscriptions, Lugal Zagesi, king of the city of Umma in Sumer, claimed more. The supreme god, Enlil, "put all the lands at his feet and from east to west made them subject to him" from the Persian Gulf to the Mediterranean.

This was almost certainly just a boast. Left to themselves, the warring Sumerian city-states could never have united for long. Around 2500 B.C.E., however, invaders from northern Mesopotamia forced political change. The conquering king, Sargon of Akkad, was one of the great empire builders of antiquity. His armies poured downriver and made him King of Sumer and Akkad. "Mighty mountains with axes of bronze I conquered," he declared in a surviving chronicle fragment and dared kings who came after him to do the same. His armies were said to have reached Syria and Iran.

Such a vast empire could not last. After a century or two, native Sumerian forces expelled Sargon's successors. Nevertheless, Sargon's achievement set a new pattern—an imperial direction—for the political history of the region. City-states sought to expand by conquering each other. For a time, Lagash, a northern neighbor of Ur, dominated Sumer. One of its kings was the subject of 27 surviving images. We have no better index of any ruler's power. But around 2100 B.C.E., Ur displaced Lagash. The new capital began to acquire the look for which it is renowned, with showy ziggurats and daunting walls. Within a few years more, tribute, recorded on clay tablets, was reaching Ur from as far away as the Iranian highlands and the Lebanese coast. A 4,000-year-old box—the soundbox of a harp, perhaps—gorgeously depicts the cycle of royal life in imperial Ur—victory, tribute-gathering, and celebration (see "Going to the Source: Feasting," page 152). Thereafter, leadership in the region shifted among rival centers, but it always remained in the south.

In China, itineraries for royal travel dating around 1500 B.C.E. reveal a different political geography. Kings constantly rattled up and down the great vertical artery of the realm, the eastern arm of the Yellow River, and frenziedly did the round of towns and estates to the south, as far as the river Huai. Occasionally, they touched the northernmost reach of the Yangtze River. This was a telltale sign. Shang civilization was expanding south from its heartlands on the middle Yellow River, growing into a regionally dominant superstate. Gradually, the worlds of Chinese culture and politics absorbed the Yangtze valley. The result was a unique state containing complementary environments: the millet-growing lands of the Yellow River, the rice fields of the Yangtze. The new ecology of China helped protect it against ecological disaster in either zone. It also formed the basis of the astonishingly resilient and productive state seen in subsequent Chinese history. The consequences will be apparent throughout the remainder of this book. For most of the rest of our story, China wields disproportionate power and influence.

Moreover, the broadening of China's frontiers stimulated rulers' ambitions. They became boundless. Religion and philosophy conspired. The sky was a compelling deity: vast and pregnant with gifts—of light and warmth and rain—and bristling with threats of storm and fire and flood. A state that touched its limits would fulfill a kind of "manifest destiny"—a reflection of divine order. Comparing the state to the cosmos prompted rulers to seek a dominion as boundless as the sky's. The Chinese came to see imperial rule over the world as divinely ordained. Emperors treated the whole world as rightfully or potentially subject to them. By the time of the Zhou, the dynasty that succeeded the Shang, the phrase **mandate of heaven** came into use to express these doctrines.

The concept of the mandate of heaven spread to neighboring peoples. On the Eurasian steppes, the immense flatlands and vast skies encouraged similar thinking. We have no documentation for the ambitions of the steppe dynasties until much later. But, as we shall see, steppelanders with conquest in mind repeatedly challenged empires around the edges of Eurasia in the first millennium B.C.E. It is probably fair to say that for hundreds, perhaps thousands of years, the concept of a right to rule the world drove imperialism in Eurasia.

Literate Culture

It used to be thought—some people still think—that one reason the early Egyptians, Mesopotamians, Chinese, and Harappans qualified as "civilized" was because they were the first to use symbolic methods to record information and pass it on to future generations.

Mesopotamians devised the wedge shapes of the writing known as **cuneiform** to be easily incised, or cut, in the clay tablets used to keep records. The hieroglyphs of the earliest Egyptian texts and the symbols carved on Chinese oracle bones were **logograms**, stylized pictures that provoked mental associations with ideas they were intended to represent or with the sounds of their spoken names (see figure 3.2). We can understand the writing from Mesopotamia, Egypt, and China, but scholarship has not yet cracked the code for Harappan writing. The surviving Harappan texts are on clay seals, which suggests they served commercial purposes. Though we cannot decipher them, they clearly mark the cord or sacks of merchants' goods. Archaeologists have retrieved many of them from heaps of discarded produce.

So, these civilizations did indeed all develop writing systems of great usefulness and perhaps great expressiveness. For three reasons, however, we can no longer

Early writing. In almost all known cases, writing was devised to record neither wisdom nor art, but only tedious data, such as prices and tax returns. This clay tablet from a collection at the Library of Congress is written in Sumerian and concerns the wages paid to named supervisors of day laborers. It dates to 2039 B.C.E.

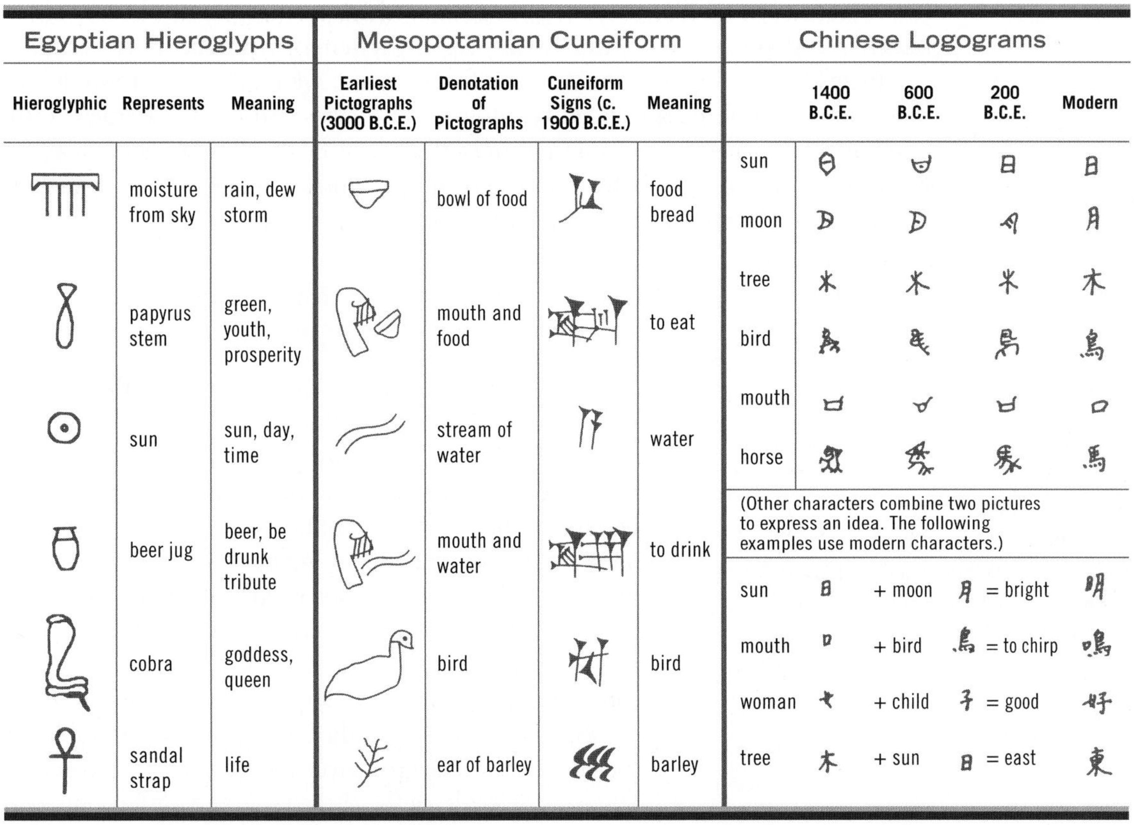

Egyptian Hieroglyphs			Mesopotamian Cuneiform				Chinese Logograms					
Hieroglyphic	Represents	Meaning	Earliest Pictographs (3000 B.C.E.)	Denotation of Pictographs	Cuneiform Signs (c. 1900 B.C.E.)	Meaning		1400 B.C.E.	600 B.C.E.	200 B.C.E.	Modern	
ⵉⵉⵉⵉ	moisture from sky	rain, dew storm	▽	bowl of food	〜	food bread	sun					
							moon					
ⵊ	papyrus stem	green, youth, prosperity		mouth and food		to eat	tree					
							bird					
⊙	sun	sun, day, time	〜	stream of water		water	mouth					
							horse					
🝮	beer jug	beer, be drunk tribute		mouth and water		to drink	(Other characters combine two pictures to express an idea. The following examples use modern characters.)					
							sun	日 + moon	月 = bright	明		
🐍	cobra	goddess, queen		bird		bird	mouth	口 + bird	鳥 = to chirp	鳴		
							woman	女 + child	子 = good	好		
⚲	sandal strap	life		ear of barley		barley	tree	木 + sun	日 = east	東		

FIGURE 3.2 ANCIENT WRITING SYSTEMS COMPARED

claim that writing was a special and defining feature that made these the first civilizations. First, writing systems originated independently in widely separated parts of the world and were far more varied than traditional scholarship has supposed. Notched sticks and knotted strings can be forms of writing as much as letters on a page or in an inscription. Some writing systems were much older than the civilizations of the river valleys. We have already seen evidence of earlier symbolic-notation systems in Ice-Age cave paintings (see Going to the Source: Chauvet Cave). Thanks to recent scholarship, our knowledge of early writing systems has grown so rapidly that the chronology and definition of writing are in turmoil.

Second, it is not clear why we should consider writing special compared to information-retrieval systems based on memory. The earliest writing systems were usually employed for trivia—merchants' price lists, tax collectors' memoranda, potters' marks, and similar jottings. Real art—the great creative poems and myths, like *Gilgamesh*—were too sacred for writing to taint and too memorable for such a crude method of transmission. Instead, for centuries, people memorized them and transmitted them orally from one generation to the next.

Finally, how much information does a system have to be able to convey before we can call it writing? Will knotted strings or notched sticks do? Surviving Shang oracle bones of the second millennium B.C.E. bear the ancestral language of modern Chinese. Yet a symbolic system of recording information seems undeniably represented on pottery more than 2,000 years older from Banpo in the Yellow River region. The symbols might be numerals and potters' marks. They do not seem to be connected sentences because the symbols are simple and used one at a time. So is this writing or something else unworthy of the name? Turtle shells recently discovered at Wuyang (woo-yahng) in China, which are thousands of years older, bear marks that we can only explain as part of a system of symbolic representation.

Instead of restricting our definition of writing, we ought to feel awe at the adventure of combining isolated symbols to tell stories and make arguments. But familiarity disperses awe. Some cultures may have taken thousands of years to make this leap, even while they used writing systems for other purposes, such as labels, oracles, bureaucracy, and magic charms.

CHRONOLOGY

(All dates are approximate)

5000–2000 B.C.E.	Four Great River Valley civilizations develop: Middle and Lower Nile, Egypt; Indus and Saraswati Rivers; Tigris and Euphrates Rivers, Mesopotamia; Yellow River, China
4000 B.C.E.	Shaduf invented in Egypt
3000 B.C.E.	Menes unites Upper and Lower Egypt
2500 B.C.E.	Cities of Harappa and Mohenjodaro flourish; Sargon of Akkad conquers Sumer
2250–2000 B.C.E.	Ziggurat of Ur built
2000–1000 B.C.E.	Shang dynasty, China
1800 B.C.E.	*Epic of Gilgamesh* written down
1700 B.C.E.	Law code of Hammurabi

IN PERSPECTIVE: What Made the Great River Valleys Different?

Still, the fact remains that, thanks in part to their use of writing, the civilizations of the four great river valleys—or, at least, the three whose writings we can decipher—are, to us, the best-known of their time. For that reason, not because of their supposed influence on other peoples, they fairly occupy so much space in books like this one. Studying their written works helps us identify at least two reasons for the cultural divergence of the era, of which they are extreme examples. First, in part, divergence was environmentally conditioned. That is, the greater or more diverse the resource base, the bigger and more durable the society it feeds. The great river valleys were large, continuous areas of fertile, easily worked soil, and for farming societies, exploitable land is the most basic resource of all. Environmental diversity gave the river valley peoples extra resources, compared with civilizations in less privileged regions. Egypt had the Nile delta at hand. In the Yellow River and Yangtze valleys, China had two complementary ecological systems. Mesopotamia had a hinterland of pastures, and Mesopotamia and Harappa had access to each other by sea.

Second, interactions matter. Societies learn from each other, compete with each other, and exchange culture with each other. The more societies are in touch with other societies, the more these activities occur. By contrast, isolation retards. Egypt was in touch with Mesopotamia and Mesopotamia with Harappa. China's relative isolation perhaps helps explain its late start in some of the common processes of change that these societies all experienced. All these societies enclosed, within their own bounds, relatively large zones of exchange. But all were remarkably self-contained. As we shall see in the next chapter, however, travel and trade were increasingly important. These were the means of communicating the cultures from the great river valleys to other regions, some of which were less environmentally fortunate. Invasions and migrations, too, were—and still are—effective forms of interaction because they shift many people around, and people carry their culture with them.

The grandeur of the great river valley civilizations raises questions about their sustainability. Their wealth and productivity excited envy from outsiders and invited attack. Continued population growth demanded ever more intensive exploitation of the environment. At the same time, climates and ecosystems continued to change. The vast collective efforts required for irrigation, storage, and monumental building left huge classes of people oppressed and resentful of elites. As a result of these and other stresses, beginning around 1500 B.C.E., transformation or collapse threatened all these societies. Meanwhile, peoples in less easily exploitable environments found the will and means to reproduce, challenge, or exceed the achievements of these four civilizations. The question of how well they succeeded is the focus of the next chapter.

Because they all made fairly extensive use of bronze, nineteenth-century archaeology—classifying societies according to their characteristic technology—called the era of the great river valley civilizations the Bronze Age. In the late second millennium B.C.E., the crises that afflicted them seemed to herald transition to an "Iron Age." Such labels no longer seem appropriate. Though there were bronze-using and iron-making societies, there was never an "age" of either. Some societies in Africa (see Chapter 5) never used bronze at all. Many societies never took up the use of iron. Where they did, they did not generally employ iron in ways that profoundly affected society—that is, to make tools and weapons—until well into the first millennium B.C.E. Although bronze making came to have an important place in the economies and art of many Eurasian peoples during the second millennium B.C.E., other societies achieved similar standards of material culture and developed comparable states without it. In any case, there are aspects of civilization—ways of thinking and feeling and behaving— more deeply influential than technology, "more lasting"—as a Roman poet said of his poems—"than bronze," and therefore more worthy of attention.

PROBLEMS AND PARALLELS

1. How did the distinctive ecological differences of the four River Valleys affect their economic activity?
2. How did environmental transformations caused by humans (such as irrigation) affect the great river valley civilizations, both positively and negatively?
3. How did the role of leaders differ in the great river valleys? Which civilization had the most effective/long-lasting leadership structure? Why?
4. What was the connection between religion and political leadership in Egypt, Mesopotamia, and China? What is the evidence for these relationships?
5. What methods did rulers use to expand their ancient states in China, Mesopotamia, Indus Valley, and Egypt? How did each area's environment affect this expansion?
6. What do the individual writing systems of China, Mesopotamia, Indus valley, and Egypt tell us about each society, in terms of politics, religion, and their economies?
7. Why are the ways a civilization thought, felt, and behaved not adequately conveyed by labels such as "Bronze Age"?

DOCUMENTS IN GLOBAL HISTORY

- Excerpts from the *Shi Jing*
- Ptahhotep, from the Egyptian *Book of Instructions*
- Excerpts from the *Amarna Letters*
- *The Code of Lipit-Ishtar*
- Excerpts from the *Epic of Gilgamesh*
- Tan-fu the Duke, from the *Shi Jing*

Please see the Primary Source CD-ROM for additional sources related to this chapter.

READ ON

R. L. Burger, *Chavin and the Origins of Andean Civilization* (1993) is an excellent introduction to the Peruvian material. H. Silverman, ed., *Andean Archaeology* (2004) contains some important recent research.

L. Nikolova, *The Balkans in Later Prehistory* (1999) is authoritative on the southeastern European sites. C. Renfrew, ed., *Problems in European Prehistory* (1979) includes some vital contributions. D. V. Clarke, *Skara Brae* (1983) is a useful pamphlet on those of the Orkneys. For the vexed question of the "rise" of "civilization" K. Wittfogel, *Oriental Despotism* (1967) is the now almost universally repudiated classic on the subject.

K. W. Butzer, *Early Hydraulic Civilization in Egypt* (1976) is a pioneering classic on the ecological dimensions. B. J. Kemp, *Ancient Egypt* (1989) is an excellent introduction.

G. Algaze, *The Uruk World System* (1993) is an important study of the origins of Mesopotamian civilization.

K. C. Chang, *Art, Myth and Ritual* (1983) and *Shang Civilization* (1980) are indispensable on China. E. L. Shaughnessy, *Sources of Western Zhou History* (1992) is immeasurably illuminating.

B. and R. Allchin, *The Rise of Civilization in India and Pakistan* (1982) is particularly useful for Harappa, on which the studies collected by G. Possehl, ed., *Harappan Civilization* (1993) are an important supplement.

A Succession of Civilizations: Ambition and Instability

One measure of the influence of the Hittites is the durability of their art. This relief, from Carchemish in Phoenicia, dates from at least two centuries after the Hittite empire collapsed, but continues to reflect Hittite conventions and values. The winged sun was a symbol other regional empires adopted.

HATTI

For a moment, the scribe thought the king was already dead. Called to the royal bedside to record the king's last words, he ruled a line under his notes.

They formed a grim, faltering record of an old man's incoherent regrets: his hatred of his treacherous sister—"a serpent" who "bellows like an ox"; the faithlessness of his adopted heir—"an abomination . . . without compassion"; the disloyalty of relatives "heedless of the word of the king . . . No member of my family has obeyed me." The dying monarch railed against his daughter, too, whom rebels first kidnapped, then recruited. "She incited the whole land to rebellion." Rebels taunted him, "There is no son for your father's throne. A servant will sit on it. A servant will become king."

With his last bit of strength, Hattusili, the great king of the Hittites, ruler of the land of Hatti, south of the Black Sea, and of an empire that touched upper Mesopotamia and the Mediterranean, sought to keep a grasp on power from beyond the grave. With no suitable adult to succeed him, he decided that his infant grandson must be the next king. The administrators of the kingdom must protect the child and prepare him for manhood, reading to him every month his grandfather's testament, with its warnings against disloyalty in the realm and its exhortations to mercy, piety, and forgiveness.

Around the deathbed in the city of Kussara, in a room gleaming with lapis lazuli and gold, the assembled warriors and officials—"lords of the watch-towers," "supervisors of the messengers," "keepers of the storehouses"—contemplated an insecure future. But the king was not yet dead. He stirred, striving to speak. The scribe hastily picked up his stylus and, straining to catch the royal words, scratched hurried characters onto his clay tablet. A woman's name fell from the king's lips: Hastayar. Who was she? Wife or concubine, sorceress or daughter? No one now knows. But she was at the bedside, consulting with the old women who were the court's official prophetesses, even as the king's life ebbed. With Hattusili's last breath came these final words: "Is she even now interrogating the soothsayers? . . . Do not forsake me. Interrogate me! I will give you words as a sign. Wash me well. Hold me to your breast. Keep me from the earth."

FOCUS questions

- WHY WERE the Hittite, Cretan, and Mycenean states more fragile than the great river valley civilizations?
- WHAT FUNDAMENTAL problems to their survival did all large ancient civilizations face?
- WHY DID Harappan civilization disappear?
- WHAT WERE the continuities between the Shang and the Zhou in China?
- WHERE DID the first states arise in the New World?
- WHY WAS Egypt able to survive when other ancient civilizations collapsed around 1000 B.C.E.?

Hattusili dictated this deathbed testament—in about 1600 B.C.E. It is the most intimate and lively document to survive from its time, our only glimpse of a king with his guard down, disclosing his own personality. It also reveals the nature and problems of a state at this time: the all-importance of the person of a king, the sacred nature of his word, the ill-defined rules of succession, the power and jealousies of military and administrative elites, an intelligence system that relied on soothsayers, and an atmosphere of danger and insecurity. In short, it was a political environment made to be volatile.

In the Hittite kingdom, we see the great themes of the second millennium B.C.E. First, features that characterized the great river valley civilizations of the previous chapter began to emerge in other environments. These features included intensive agriculture, densely distributed populations, stratified societies (with higher and lower classes), large cities, and states often seeking to build empires. Second, the number of complex states—those with large-scale systems to organize production, control distribution, and regulate life—rapidly increased. These new states also developed a great variety of political institutions and ways to structure society and organize economic activity. Finally, accelerating change claimed victims. By about 1000 B.C.E., war, natural disaster, environmental overexploitation, and social and political disintegration had strained or shattered most of the big states and civilizations that had emerged from the transition to agriculture.

Students of history often dislike this period, with its bewildering succession of empires and civilizations that rise and fall, sometimes with baffling speed. Text-book pages resemble a bad TV soap opera—crowded with action, empty of explanation, with too many characters and too few insights into their behavior. If we are to try to make sense of the millennium between 2000 and 1000 B.C.E., we need to understand the problems associated with accelerating change. This was a period of climacteric: an era of extended and critical change that extinguished some civilizations, changed others, and might have wiped all of them out. The question for this chapter, then, is, why were some ambitions in the world of around 3,000 years ago realized and others were not? What made the difference between success and failure for states and civilizations?

THE CASE OF THE HITTITE KINGDOM

Compared with the vast alluvial plains we discussed in the last chapter, the Anatolian (an-a-TOH-lee-ahn) plateau in what is today Turkey, where Hattusili's kingdom took shape, seems an unlikely place to found a large state. It had its patches of alluvium where small but spectacular towns like Çatalhüyük had flourished around 8000 to 7000 B.C.E., in a more favorable climate (see Chapter 2). But the environment had grown warmer and drier since then. Çatalhüyük's river had shifted and shrunk. By 2000 B.C.E., most of the plateau suffered alternating seasonal extremes that scorched and froze crops. Rainfall was, and still is, less than 20 inches a year. (The temperate zones of western Europe and North America receive two or three times more rain than that.) Desert tracts stretched between cultivatable patches.

Yet from the central part of this region, between about 1800 and 1500 B.C.E., the people who called themselves children of Hatti—Hittites—drew thousands of such patches and millions of people into a single network of production and distribution, under a common allegiance. They went on to build a state we can fairly call an empire. It had palace complexes, storehouses, towns, and—to take the example that the Hittites themselves would probably put at the top of the list—armies. And all were comparable in scale with those of the river-valley peoples of the last chapter. Egyptian pharaohs treated Hittite kings as equals. When one pharaoh died without heirs, his widow sent to the king of Hatti for "one of your sons to be my husband, for I will never take a servant of mine and make him my husband." We can picture the Hittites with the help of images they have left us of themselves: hook-nosed, short-headed, and—more often than not—arrayed for war. But how did their state and empire happen in such a hostile environment?

The Importance of Trade

Hatti became a regional power through enrichment by trade. In the second millennium B.C.E., new potential trading partners arose in nearby regions, as, for unknown reasons, the economic center of gravity in Mesopotamia gradually shifted upriver. Changes in the course of the Tigris and Euphrates Rivers stranded formerly important cities. Accumulations of silt kept merchants offshore. Wars at the far end of the Persian Gulf and the disappearance of some of the great cities of the Indus valley probably disrupted commerce in the Arabian Sea and Persian Gulf. New opportunities, meanwhile, arose in the north as economic development created new markets, or expanded old ones, in Syria, the Iranian highlands, and Anatolia (see Map 4.1).

Ebla's palace walls in the mid-third millennium B.C.E. were 40 or 50 feet high. The ceremonial court in the foreground was 165 feet long. The holes show where pillars supported the roof. Akkadian invaders destroyed the palace around 2300 B.C.E., but left intact the precious archives that recorded the range of trade with Mesopotamia, Anatolia, and Egypt.

For instance, the archives of Ebla, an independent city-state in Syria, bear witness to its importance as a trading center, as well as to its cultural links with Mesopotamia. Its commerce was a state monopoly. Its merchants were ambassadors. A dozen foreign cities delivered gold, silver, copper, and textiles to its markets and treasury. Ebla was a center of textile production and metallurgy in gold, silver, and bronze. Not only was it a trading center, its fertile lands made it self-sufficient to overflowing. Its royal granary stored enough food for 18 million meals. The most complete surviving record of a tour of inspection of the state warehouses names 12 kinds of wheat, abundant wine and cooking oil, and more than 80,000 sheep. The city's manufactured products— ceramic seals, ivory figurines, metalsmith work—reached the courts of chiefs in central Anatolia.

With the shift of economic activity from Lower to Upper Mesopotamia and beyond, networks of traders spread to the east and north from growing upriver cities such as Ashur on the Tigris and Mari on the Euphrates. Thousands of documents—16,000 in Ebla,

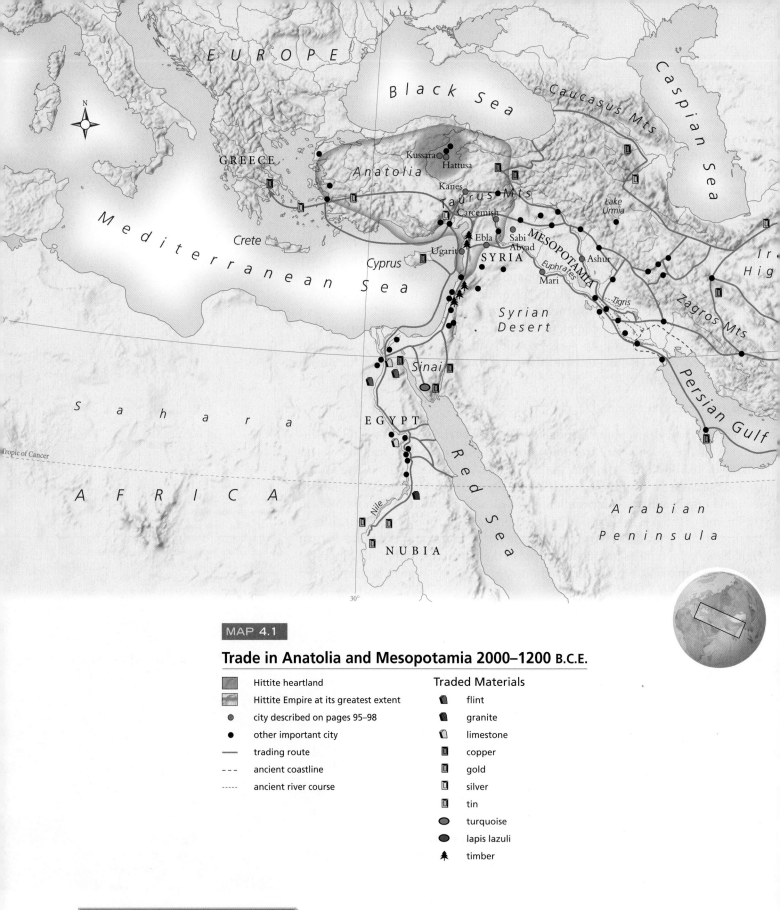

MAP 4.1

Trade in Anatolia and Mesopotamia 2000–1200 B.C.E.

Hittite heartland
Hittite Empire at its greatest extent
● city described on pages 95–98
● other important city
— trading route
--- ancient coastline
····· ancient river course

Traded Materials
flint
granite
limestone
copper
gold
silver
tin
turquoise
lapis lazuli
timber

MAP EXPLORATION
www.prenhall.com/armesto_maps

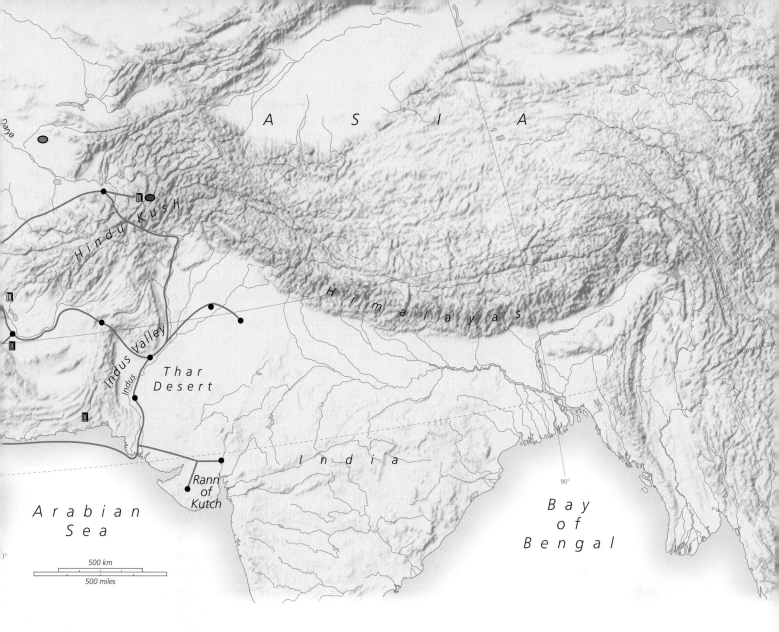

17,000 in Mari—describe these traders, from wealthy private merchants under-written by the state to stateless middlemen who served as deal makers. Trade is not just economic exchange. It also forges social obligations, establishes new relationships of power and legitimates old ones, and spreads culture. Some trade of the time was gift giving between palaces, carried by merchant-diplomats. The king of the city of Ugarit rewarded an official called Tamkaru for this kind of work with a grant of land in the mid-1200s B.C.E. On its new frontiers, trade generated unprecedented concentrations of wealth. Leaders who accumulated imported luxuries or who were tough enough to tax passing trade could reinvest in more goods or buy the allegiance of other chiefs. They might build palace centers like those of Mesopotamia and Egypt to redistribute goods.

Early in the second millennium B.C.E.—say, roughly 1800 B.C.E.—colonists from Ashur penetrated Anatolia and founded a new city at Kanes, 930 miles to the northwest. Thousands of clay tablets detail its imports of tin and textiles, its exports of gold and silver. Yet there was a human side of business then as now.

The royal family of Ashur had a state farm at Sabi Abyad, which was also a frontier trading post on the routes to Anatolia and states along the eastern coast of the Mediterranean. Over 1,000 people lived there—migrants from Ashur, exiled foreigners, prisoners of war. The steward, permanently frustrated by impractical orders, frustrated the king in turn, who wrote: "What is this, that whatever I tell you, you fail to do as I say?" The supply of beer and tableware to entertain passing embassies provoked many quarrels. So did the problems of enforcing tolls on luxuries. The king berated the steward:

> Formerly I ordered you, "Caravans that come to me from Carcemish must not pass without your leave and you must stamp all goods with your seal." Now I have heard that caravans are on their way and I repeat: any caravan that comes my way, whether it belongs to [the governor] or princesses or nobles, every one must be sealed. I have also heard that they carry balsam. If any is missing, you will be executed.

Anitta, king of Kanes, early in the second millennium had "a throne of iron and a sceptre of iron." This is a revealing remark because iron was new, originating in this region but still rare. Soft iron, smelted at a temperature only slightly higher than that required for copper, was useless for weapons and plows. The technique of combining it with carbon to make it hard was difficult at the time and too unreliable to persuade investors to develop the technology. But the appearance of iron pointed to a future more durable than bronze, which remained the metal of choice for weapons and agricultural tools. One of the towns Anitta saw as a rival was Kussara, the home town of the dynasty that later founded the kingdom of Hatti. According to one of his inscriptions, he demolished the place, sowed it with salt, and cursed it, so that it might never arise again. The curse failed. His example, however, inspired the Hittites and showed them how trade and conquest could build a state.

Hittite Society and Politics

The strength of the Hittite kingdom was that it brought farmers and herders into a single state and economic system. This was how to make the most of the rugged Anatolian environment, with its small concentrations of cultivatable soil surrounded by marginal grazing land. The wool production of specialized herders combined with the food production of small farmers. Such mixed farming by independent peasants—not bonded or enslaved workers or wage earners—was of the highest importance. Livestock produce fertilizer, which can raise (or sustain) productivity and feed growing populations. Milk-rich diets, moreover, can provide the calories and nutrients that improve human fertility. Overall, the consequences are positive: more opportunity for economic specialization, urbanization, and the mobilization of manpower for war.

Hittite Land Deed

The surviving inventory of the estate of a typical Hittite peasant, Tiwapatara, lists one house for his family of five, three dozen head of livestock, one acre of pasture, and three and a half acres of vineyard, with 42 pomegranate and 40 apple trees. The pasture must have been for his eight precious oxen. His goats, hardier animals, presumably foraged where they could. Farmers like Tiwapatara were the manpower that, for a time, made Hatti invincible. Children such as his worked the farms during military campaigns, which usually coincided with sowing and harvest. He and his kind were willing, presumably, to support the state that in turn protected them, for Hittite law laid down harsh penalties for theft or trespassing on private property. We do not know the total productivity of the economy but a single grain silo excavated in the major city, Hattusa, held enough grain for 32,000 people for a year.

Hatti developed its own political system, perhaps with some borrowings from Mesopotamia and Egypt. The king was the sun god's earthly deputy. Subjects called him, "My sun," as modern monarchs are called, "Your Majesty." His responsibilities were war, justice, and relations with the gods. Hardly any case at law was too trivial to be referred to the king, although, in practice, professional clerks dealt with most of them on his behalf. A vast household surrounded him: "the Palace servants, the Bodyguard, the Men of the Golden Spear, the Cupbearers, the Table-men, the Cooks, the Heralds, the Stable boys, the Captains of the Thousand." It was a bureaucratic court, where writing perpetuated the king's commands and conveyed them to subordinates, commanders, viceroys, and subject kings. The court was vast, too, because it had to house a huge harem. Royal concubines were rivets of the kingdom. The size and origins of the ruler's harem reflected his political reach. Moreover, he had to engender many daughters to contribute to the harems of allies and tributaries.

To judge from surviving law codes, Hittites observed many apparently arbitrary sexual taboos. Intercourse with pigs or sheep was punishable by death, but not cases involving horses or mules. Hittites evidently measured the civilization of other societies by the severity of their incest laws. Their own code forbade intercourse between siblings or cousins. Any sexual act, however, was polluting in some degree and had to be cleansed by bathing before prayer. If we knew more about Hittite religion, we might understand their morality better. Strong sexual taboos are usually found in "dualist" religions, alongside belief in the eternal struggle of forces of good and evil or spirit and matter. Hittite attitudes toward sex contrast with those in Mesopotamia, where—in what seems to have been a more typical pattern—sex was in some sense sacred, and temples employed prostitutes.

In some ways, Hatti was a man's world, with the masculine attitudes and values typical of a war state. The oath army officers took indicates this:

 Hittite Soldiers' Oath

> Do you see here a woman's garments? We have them for the oath. Whoever breaks these oaths and does the king harm, let the oaths change him from a man to a woman! Let them change his soldiers into women, and let them dress in the fashion of women and cover their heads with a length of cloth! Let them break the bows, arrows and clubs in their hands and let them take up instead the distaff and the looking-glass!

Women, however, exercised power. Old women acted as diviners at court. Others, lower down the social scale, were curers, waving sacrificial piglets over the victims of curses, with the cry, "Just as this pig shall not see the sky nor the other piglets again, so let the curse not see the sacrificers!"

Fragility and Fall: The End of Hatti

The Hittite state was formidable in war. It had to be. Its domestic economy was fragile and its homeland poor in key resources. It needed to grow. Conquests were, in extreme circumstances, the only way to guarantee supplies of food for an increasing population and of tin to make bronze weapons. But even successful conflicts can weaken a state by overextending its power and disrupting its trade. In other words, growth is paradoxical. For many states, it is both a means of survival and an obstacle to survival. It butts against immovable limits. In Hatti's case, those limits were the frontiers of Egypt and Mesopotamia.

The Hittites

(All dates are approximate)	
1800-1500 B.C.E.	Hatti develops into an empire
1800 B.C.E.	City of Kanes founded
1800 B.C.E.	Iron in use
1300 B.C.E.	Plague strikes Hatti
1210 B.C.E.	Last recorded mention of Hatti

The Hittite kingdom suffered from other weaknesses. As with all communities that made the transition to agriculture, it was vulnerable to famine and disease. Around 1300 B.C.E., King Mursili II reproached the gods for a plague: "Now no one reaps or sows your fields, for all are dead! The mill-women who used to make the bread of the gods are dead!" A couple of generations later, there was reputedly "no grain in Hatti," when Puduhepa—a formidable royal spouse—wrote to Egypt demanding some as part of the dowry of her daughter. For one of the last Hittite kings, Tudhaliya IV, an order not to detain a grain ship bound for his country was "a matter of life and death." Nomadic prowlers from the hinterlands were another common hazard. People the Hittites called *Kaska* invaded repeatedly to grab booty or extort protection. On at least one of their raids, they robbed the royal court.

In the last few decades of the 1300s B.C.E., the Hittite state was in obvious decline. Hatti lost southern provinces and (by Tudhaliya's own admission in a letter scolding a negligent subordinate) at least one major battle to an expanding kingdom in Upper Mesopotamia. The oaths the king demanded from his subordinates have an air of desperation: "if nobody is left to yoke the horses and the king has not even one house in which to enter, you must show even more support. . . . If . . . the chariot-driver jumps down from the chariot, and the valet flees the chamber, and not even a dog is left, and if I do not even find an arrow to shoot against the enemy, your support for your king must be all the greater." Among the last documents the court issued are complaints that formerly subject kings were neglecting tribute or diplomatic courtesies. After 1210 B.C.E., the Hittite kingdom simply disappeared from the record.

INSTABILITY AND COLLAPSE IN THE AEGEAN

The Hittite story is a case study of the problems of global history in the second millennium B.C.E. It demonstrates how agrarian communities became consolidated into states, elevated into empires, and how most of them failed to survive past 1000 B.C.E. Echoes, parallels, and connected cases occurred in many regions near the experiments in civilization building that we discussed in the last chapter. We will examine some of these cases before trying to explain the failures of the second millennium.

Knossos. Aquatic subjects abound in paintings on the palace walls of Knossos, Crete, from the mid-second millennium B.C.E. Dolphins were favored as food for elite feasts. The palace—at once an elite dwelling and a storehouse and distribution center for food—was rebuilt many times between destructions by earthquakes and, perhaps, invasions.

The civilization scholars call Minoan or Cretan, for instance, took shape in the second millennium on the large Mediterranean island of Crete, which lies between what are now Greece and Turkey (see Map 4.2). Nearby in the southern Peloponnese, the peninsula that forms the southern part of Greece, the civilization we call Mycenean emerged. Both have inspired Western imaginations. Europeans and Americans view Crete and Mycenae as part of their history, assuming that they can trace the civilization of classical Greece—and therefore of the Western world—to these glamorous, spendthrift cultures of three and a half thousand years ago, about 1500 B.C.E. That now seems a doubtful assumption. By the time Plato and Aristotle formulated classical Greek philosophy in the fourth century B.C.E., the last cities of Mycenae had been ruins for a thousand years. Crete and Mycenae were subjects of myth—civilizations almost as mysterious to the Greeks as they are to us, and almost as remote. Still, they are worth studying for their own sake and the light they cast on their own times.

Cretan Civilization

Crete is 3,200 square miles, big enough to be self-sustaining, but mountains cover two-thirds of it leaving little land to cultivate. In the minds of mainlanders who live nearby today, it is an impossible island, a land of devastating droughts and earthquakes. But looking today at the wall paintings from around 2000 B.C.E., when the first palace-storehouses arose there, ancient Crete was a paradise of plenty. Fields of grain and vines; orchards of olives, almonds, and quince; forests of honey and venison surround gardens of lilies and iris, gladioli and crocuses. The seas seem full of dolphin and octopus, under skies where partridge and brightly colored birds fly.

This lavish world was painfully carved from a tough environment, harsh soil, and dangerous seas. And it depended on two despotic methods to control an unpredictable food supply: organized agriculture, embracing, as in Hatti, both farming and herding, and state-regulated trade. The function of the palace as storehouse was a vital part of how the system worked. The greatest palace complex on the island, Knossos, covers more than 40,000 square feet. When it lay in ruins, visitors from Greece who saw its galleries and corridors imagined an enormous maze, built to house a monster who fed on human sacrifices. In fact, the labyrinth was an immense storage area for clay jars, 12 feet high, filled with wine, cooking oil, and grain, some still in place. The wool of 80,000 sheep was collected here.

Stone chests, lined with lead to protect the foodstuffs they contained, were like strongboxes in a central bank waiting to be distributed or traded. The Cretans were such skilled sailors that the Greeks said Cretan ships knew their own way through the water. Trade brought exotic luxuries to the elites. Ivory tusks and ostrich eggs can still be found at another palace complex at Zakros. Palace walls depict blue baboons from Egypt. Craft workshops inside the palaces added value to imports by spinning and weaving fine garments, delicately painting stone jars, and hammering gold and bronze into jewels and chariots. Palace records suggest a staff of 4,300 people.

Yet Knossos and buildings like it were also genuine palaces—dwellings of an elite who lived in luxury. Majestic stairwells rose to the noble floors, supported on squat columns with tops like fat pumpkins. These pillars, and those supporting the principal chambers, were lacquered red, and the wall paintings glowed with a wonderful sky blue—scenes of feasting, gossiping, playing, and bull leaping. At Zakros, a site that was never plundered, you can see marble-veined chalices, stone storage jars, and a box of cosmetic ointment with an elegant little handle in the form of a reclining greyhound.

Lesser dwellings, grouped in towns, were tiny imitations of the palace. Many had columns, balconies, and upper-storey galleries. In the houses of more prosperous inhabitants, colorful pottery, that was as thin as porcelain, elaborate stone vases ground into seductively sinuous shapes, and elaborately painted groundstone baths survive in large numbers. Yet at lower levels of society there was little surplus for luxury or time for leisure. Few people lived beyond their early forties. If the purpose of the state was to recycle food, its efficiency was limited. Skeletons show that the common people lived near the margin of malnutrition.

The cities' environment was potentially destructive and, in combination with war, doomed the cities to eventual abandonment and the palaces to ruin. On the nearby island of Thera, which a volcanic eruption blew apart around 1500 B.C.E., the lavish city of Akrotiri was buried under layers of ash and rock. Knossos and similar palaces along the coasts of Crete at Phaistos, Mallia, and Zakros were all rebuilt once or twice on an increasingly generous scale, after unknown causes, possibly earthquakes, destroyed them.

Crystal vase. Under the elite apartments, Cretan palaces contained workshops where craftsmen made luxuries for elite consumption and for export, such as this crystal vase, about 3,500 years old, from the palace of Zakros, and the unguents and perfumes that vessels like these contained.

The walls of Mycenae in southern Greece, built over 3,000 years ago, when warlike city-states arose in this region of modest agricultural productivity, apparently on the profits of the manufacture and export of luxuries for markets in Egypt and Anatolia. In the second half of the second millennium B.C.E., the language of Mycenae replaced that of Crete in official Cretan records, suggesting a change in political mastery.

The way the palaces were reconstructed suggests there was another hazard—internal warfare. Fortifications began to appear. Some of the elite from the eastern and southern ends of the island apparently moved to villas near Knossos about the time the palaces were rebuilt. There may have been a political takeover. At the time of the last rebuilding of Knossos, generally dated around 1400 B.C.E., a major change in culture occurred. The archives began to be written in an early form of Greek. As a result, we can now read them. The language previously in use is unknown and its records undecipherable. By this time, the fate of Crete seems to have become closely entangled with another Aegean civilization—the Mycenean.

Mycenean Civilization

The fortified cities and gold-rich royal tombs of the Mycenean civilization began to appear early in the 1500s B.C.E. States in the region already had kings who made war and hunted lions, shortly before these creatures became extinct in Europe. The kings' courts were centered in palace-storehouses similar to those of Crete. At Pylos, one of the largest Mycenean palaces, clay tablets list the vital and tiresome routines of numerous palace officials: levying taxes, checking that the landowner class observed its social obligations, mobilizing resources for public works, and gathering raw materials for manufacture and trade. In the palace of Pylos, workshops turned out bronzeware and perfumed oils for export to Egypt and the Hittite empire.

MAP 4.2

The Eastern Mediterranean, ca. 2000-1200 B.C.E.

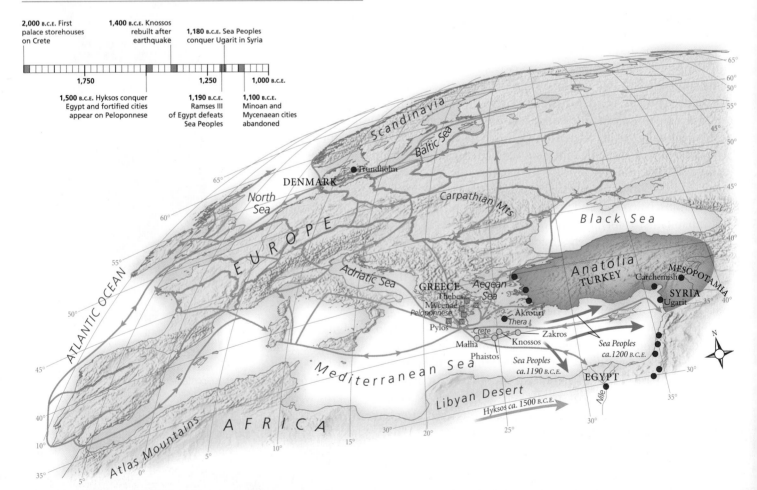

A SUN CHARIOT FROM TRUNDHOLM

The Trundholm bog in Denmark has preserved many objects and the remains of humans who were sacrificed in antiquity. The most elaborate find is a bronze and gold model of the sun, made in the mid-second millennium B.C.E. A horse draws the sun back and forth across the heavens, displaying a bright face by day and a dark side by night.

The disc, about ten inches wide, is gilded with gold on one side only.

The use of precious bronze and gold to represent the sun suggests the veneration that the source of warmth and light attracted in cold, dark northern Europe.

The sun's golden face bears intricate concentric designs.

The bronze horse, modeled around a clay core, is mounted on bronze wheels, which suggests that the object was designed for use in religious rituals or astronomical demonstrations.

How does this object testify to the sophistication of Scandinavian culture in the middle of the second millennium B.C.E.?

Mycenean traders reached across northern Europe as far as Scandinavia (see Map 4.2). Unlike the minutely recorded trade transactions that helped spread civilization north from Mesopotamia, this commerce was not documented. Yet we know that eastern Mediterranean elites craved Baltic amber for glowing jewels. Scandinavia lacked tin for bronze making, which meant its craftsmen had to try to imitate Mediterranean dagger designs in flint. Trade changed Scandinavian society. The evidence was laid in graves, carved on rocks, and, above all, preserved in peat bogs. The most abundant of these natural archives are the bogs at Trundholm in Denmark, which mercilessly preserved corpses, some still with their hats on and their faces composed or contorted in death. The elite emerge from the peat, as they appear in engravings on the rocks in their tasseled garments and horned helmets. They had a taste for serpentine lines, displayed in the curving prows of engraved ships that curl like antlers, and sinuous bronze trumpets.

The volume of trade with Scandinavia was too small or perhaps too remote from state control to be included in Mycenean records. The essential duty of the palace bureaucrats was to equip their rulers for almost constant warfare. Unlike Cretan sites, the mainland palaces were heavily and cleverly fortified. As well as fighting each other, the kingdoms felt the threat of the barbarian hinterland, which may, in the end, have overwhelmed them. Paintings on the walls of Pylos show warriors, in the boar's-head helmets also worn on Crete and Thera, in battle with skin-clad savages.

Stunned by earthquakes, strained by wars, Mycenean cities followed those of Crete into abandonment by 1100 B.C.E. What is surprising is not, perhaps, that they should ultimately have perished, but that their fragile economies, sustained by elaborate and expensive methods of collecting, storing, and redistributing food, should have managed to feed the cities and support the elite culture for so long.

Crete and Mycenae

(All dates are approximate)	
2000 B.C.E.	First palace-storehouses on Crete
1500 B.C.E.	Fortified cities appear on the Peloponnese (Greece)
1400 B.C.E.	Knossos (Crete) rebuilt after earthquake; early Greek language used at Knossos
1100 B.C.E.	Cretan (Minoan) and Mycenaean cities abandoned

A GENERAL CRISIS IN THE EASTERN MEDITERRANEAN WORLD?

Although we could explain the extinction of Crete, Mycenae, and Hatti in terms of local political failures or ecological disasters, it is tempting to try to relate them to a general crisis in the eastern Mediterranean. For, not only was the grandeur of the Aegean civilizations blotted out and the Hittite empire of Anatolia overwhelmed, nearby states also reported fatal or near-fatal convulsions. The Egyptians almost succumbed to unidentified **Sea Peoples**, who exterminated numerous states and cities in the region. Meanwhile, in Upper Mesopotamia, an anguished king of Ashur prayed to Assur (AHS-soor), the city's god, "Darkness without sunshine awaits the evildoers who stretch out threatening hands to scatter the armies of Assur. Wickedly, they conspire against their benefactor."

The Egyptian Experience

Egypt had survived invasion before the Sea Peoples. Perhaps toward 1500 B.C.E., the Hyksos (HIHK-sohs) arrived, sweating from the Libyan desert, to overwhelm the land and commission carvings of a sphinx seizing an Egyptian by the ears. Like so many nomadic conquerors of sedentary cultures around the world, the Hyksos adopted Egyptian culture and became Egyptianized before they were expelled. For their part, Egyptians considered all foreigners barbarians and viewed them with contempt.

But the narrowness of the Black Land, as Egyptians called the fertile Nile valley, was a cause of unease, and Egyptians alternated between arrogance and insecurity. On the one hand, desert and sea constituted protection against barbarian attack. Egypt was flanked by almost uninhabitable spaces, difficult to cross, whereas civilizations, like those of Mesopotamia and Harappa, with more attractive environments at their frontiers were under constant threat from marauders and invaders. On the other hand, sea and desert were the realm of Seth, the god of chaos who threatened to overwhelm the cosmic order of life along the Nile.

Exposure to invasion continued. The descent of the Sea Peoples—about 1190 B.C.E.—is well documented because the pharaoh who defeated them, Ramses III, devoted a long inscription to his achievement. It is glaring propaganda, a celebration of the pharaoh's power and preparation: "Barbarians," it says vaguely, "conspired in their islands . . . No land could withstand their arms." A list of victims follows, including Hatti and a string of cities in southern Anatolia and along the eastern Mediterranean. "They were heading for Egypt, while we prepared flame before them . . . They laid their hands on the land as far as the edges of the Earth, their hearts confident and trusting, 'We will succeed!'" The Nile delta, however, "made like a strong wall with warships . . . I was the valiant war-god, standing fast at their head. Those who came forward together on the sea, the full flame was in front of them at the river mouths, while a stockade of lances surrounded them on the shore. They were dragged in, enclosed, and prostrated on the beach, killed and made into heaps."

Sea Peoples. "Now the northern peoples in their isles were quivering in their bodies," says the inscription that accompanies a ship-borne battle-scene of the reign of Ramses III. "They penetrated the channels of the mouths of the Nile. . . . They are capsized and overwhelmed where they stand. . . . Their weapons are scattered on the sea." Pharaohs' propaganda tended to lie or exaggerate, but the "Sea Peoples" really existed, and Egypt really escaped conquest or colonization by them.

The Roots of Instability

Yet even after unpicking the propaganda, we can be confident that the pharaoh's boasts reflect real events. Other documents confirm the existence of the Sea Peoples. For example, when the city of Ugarit (OO-gah-riht) in Syria fell, probably early in the twelfth century B.C.E., never to be reoccupied, messages begging for seaborne reinforcements were left unfinished. The reply from the governor of Carchemish (KAHR-keh-mihsh), an inland trading center on the way to Hatti and Mesopotamia, was typical—too little, too late: "as for what you have written me, 'Ships of the enemy have been seen at sea.' Well, you must remain firm. . . . Surround your towns with ramparts. Have your troops and chariots enter there, and await the enemy with great resolution."

The image of a general crisis brought about by barbarian invasions has had an almost irresistible romantic appeal for Western historians influenced by a familiar episode of their own past: the decline and fall of the Roman Empire. A general crisis also fits with a popular conception of the past as a battlefield of barbarism versus civilization. However, such an idea is, at best, a gross oversimplification because both barbarism and civilization are relative, subjective terms. In any case, the difference between barbarism and civilization that became glaring in a later age was by no means always apparent to people at the time. Cultural divergence was in its infancy, and cultural gaps seemed bridgeable. As we have seen, the gap between herders and tillers was closed, and combined wool and grain production became the economic base for Hatti, Crete, and other societies with limited

 Ramses III, "The War Against the Sea Peoples"

Instability in the Eastern Mediterranean

(All dates are approximate)	
1500 B.C.E.	Hyksos conquer Egypt
1200 B.C.E.	Sea Peoples attack Mesopotamia and Anatolia
1190 B.C.E.	Ramses III defeats Sea Peoples
1180 B.C.E.	Sea Peoples conquer Ugarit in Syria

The walled mounds of Mohenjodaro, a Harappan city abandoned in the late second millennium B.C.E. The walls were a defense against floods, not invaders. None of the "massacre victims" identified by archaeologists in the 1940s died by violence. Rather, a slow decline of population, a gradual impoverishment of material culture, and a relentless increase in disease set in as the river Saraswati dried up.

farming land. Furthermore, there is no evidence, as some historians claim, that barbarian invaders enjoyed a technological advantage because they had iron weapons or a tactical advantage because they used massed infantry against chariots.

We can best understand the violent arrival of the Sea Peoples as a symptom of a broader phenomenon of the period: the widespread instability of populations driven by hunger and land shortages. Egyptian carvings show desperate migrations, would-be invaders with ox carts full of women and children. From Mesopotamia and Anatolia comes evidence of savage marauders in the late thirteenth century B.C.E. But migrants probably did not cause the decline of the states they ravaged. Rather, they were among its consequences. Environmental and economic historians have scoured the evidence for some sign of a deeper trauma, such as earthquakes or droughts or commercial failures that might explain grain shortages and disrupted trade. But they have found nothing of the sort at the time of the migrants' invasions.

The causes of the crisis lay in common structural problems of the states that faltered or failed, namely, their ecological fragility and unstable, competitive politics. In this respect, the crisis was even more general, not just confined to the civilizations around the eastern Mediterranean where the Sea People roamed. If we turn to trace the fate of communities elsewhere in Asia, and even to some examples in the New World, we can detect similar strains and comparable effects.

THE EXTINCTION OF HARAPPAN CIVILIZATION

In the Indus valley, city life and intensive agriculture were in danger of collapse even when they were at their most productive. Many sites were occupied only for a few centuries. Some sites were abandoned by about 1800 B.C.E., and by 1000 B.C.E., all had dwindled to ruins. Meanwhile, in Turkmenia, on the northern flank of the Iranian plateau, relatively young but flourishing fortified settlements on the Oxus (AHK-suhs) River, such as Namazga and Altin, shrank to the dimensions of villages. We know little about these places, and what brought about their end—or Harappan's—has provoked furious debate among scholars. Some believe in a sudden and violent invasion, while others think the end was the result of a gradual ecological disaster.

The Evidence of the *Rig Veda*

Evidence for the theory that invaders destroyed Harappan civilization comes from a collection of hymns and poems called the **Rig Veda** (rihg VEH-dah). The people who created this literature of destruction were a sedentary people living in what is now the Punjab, the area north of the Indus valley where northern India and Pakistan meet. They spoke an Indo-European language and had probably been living there from about 1500 B.C.E. They were not newcomers or nomads. When poets wrote down the *Rig Veda*, some time around 800 B.C.E., after centuries of oral transmission, it still had the power to carry hearers and readers back to a lost age of heroes.

The hymns tell of a people who wanted a world of fat and opulence, basted with butter, flowing with milk, dripping with honey. Their strength in horses and chariots is not incompatible with a settled way of life. Elites of many essentially sedentary peoples have relied on horses in warfare. They valued boasting and drinking. Their rites of fire included burning down their enemies' dwellings. Their favorite god, Indra, was a "breaker of cities," but this was part of his generally destructive role, which included mountain smashing and serpent crushing.

Can these people have sacked the cities of the Indus and left corpses in Mohenjodaro buried in ash? Some of the cities seem already to have been in ruins when the *Rig Veda* poets beheld them. It would be surprising if invaders or rebels or neighbors or some combination of the three had not attacked these cities at some point in their history. But excavators who claimed that they could read such traumatic events at Mohenjodaro, in the bones of massacre victims and scorch marks on the walls, seem to have been wrong. Few of the supposed massacre victims have any wounds. Instead of a single violent event, the more likely explanation speaks of a gradual decline—a climacteric, a point at which Harappan civilization collapsed, and its cities were abandoned (see Map 4.3).

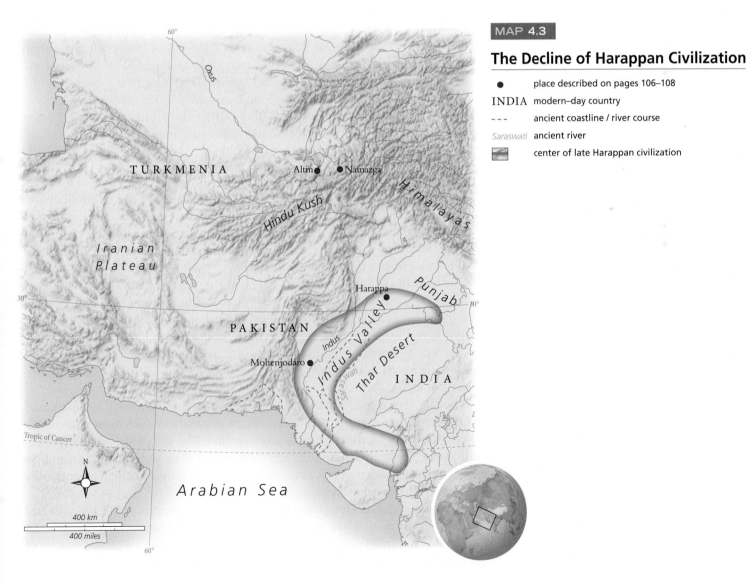

MAP 4.3

The Decline of Harappan Civilization

●   place described on pages 106–108

INDIA   modern–day country

- - -   ancient coastline / river course

Saraswati   ancient river

    center of late Harappan civilization

Selections from the *Rig Veda*

The Collapse of Harappan Civilization

(All dates are approximate)	
1800 B.C.E.	Some Harappan cities abandoned
1000 B.C.E.	All Harappan cities in ruins
800 B.C.E.	*Rig Veda* written down

The Environment of Stress

The climate was getting drier in the Indus valley, and earthquakes may have shifted riverbeds. Unlike the crisis in the eastern Mediterranean, events in the Indus valley seem to fit with the chronology of environmental disaster. The Saraswati River, along which settlements were once densely clustered, disappeared into the advancing Thar Desert. Yet not even the loss of a river adequately explains the abandonment of the cities. The Indus River is still disgorging its wonderful silt, year by year, over vast, shining fields, which would have been sufficient to maintain the urban populations. Presumably, something happened to the food supply that was connected with the drying climate or human mismanagement of environmental resources—the cattle and hinterland products that supplemented the wheat and barley of the fields.

In addition—or instead—the inhabitants apparently fled from some plague more deadly than the malaria that anthropologists have detected in buried bones. In an environment where irrigation demands standing water, mosquitos can breed. Malaria is inevitable. The people left, "expelled by the fire-god," as the *Rig Veda* says, and "migrated to a new land." This is probably an exaggeration. People stayed on or squatted in the decaying cities, inhabiting the ruins for generations. But the fall of Harappan civilization remains the most dramatic case of large-scale failure in the second millennium B.C.E. In broad terms, Harappa suffered essentially the same fate as the Hittite and eastern Mediterranean civilizations: The food distribution system outran the resource base. And when networks of power began to break down, invaders broke in.

CONFLICT ON THE YELLOW RIVER

China experienced different problems toward the end of the second millennium B.C.E. from those of Egypt or Harappan. China suffered no large-scale population loss, no wholesale abandonment of regions, or wreck of cities. Nonetheless, what the Chinese of the period experienced was in some ways similar to other peoples in what looks increasingly like a global pattern.

The basis of the Shang (shawng) state had always been shaky. War, rituals, and oracles are all gamblers' means of power, vulnerable to the lurches of luck. Manipulating the weather, the rains, the harvests, for instance, was a big part of the king's job, but in reality, of course, it was not one he could accomplish. Failure was built into his job description. It was a common problem for monarchs of the time, exposing pharaohs to blame for natural disasters, driving Hittite kings to depend on soothsayers.

The late Shang state was shrinking. Beginning about 1100 B.C.E., the names of subject, tribute-paying, and allied states gradually vanish from the oracle bones. The king's hunting grounds grow smaller. The king took on greater personal responsibility, becoming the sole diviner and army general, as the numbers of courtiers and commanders at his disposal fell. Whether through opportunity or necessity, former allies became enemies.

Meanwhile, just as Mesopotamian culture had been exported to Anatolia and Cretan ways of life to Mycenae, so Shang was exported beyond the Shang state, and its effects were becoming obvious. For one, new chiefdoms were developing in less favorable environments under the influence of trade. As far away as northern

Vietnam and Thailand, bronze making techniques similar to those of China, appeared at the courts of chiefs who delighted in personal ornaments, spittoons, and, in Vietnam, heavily decorated drums. More ominously and closer to home, right on the Shang border, a state arose in imitation and, increasingly, in rivalry: Zhou (jaow).

The Rise of Zhou

The earliest Zhou sites—of the 1100s B.C.E.—are burials in the Liang (lee-ahng) mountains above the Wei (way) River in western China. This was probably not the Zhou heartland, but the area they had migrated to from grazing country farther to the north. Their own legends recalled time spent "living among the barbarians." Muye (moo-yeh)—the name of the battlefield where they reportedly overthrew the Shang—means "Shepherd's Wild." The Zhou were highland herders, an upland, upriver menace to the Shang just as Akkad was to Sumer in Mesopotamia (see Map 4.4).

Except for the material culture visible in their graves, we know nothing of the Zhou before they attacked and conquered the Shang—not their origin, or their economic or political systems, or even their language. We know them after they had fallen under the Shang's spell, imitating Shang culture and, presumably, envying its wealth. They had also learned the Shang's most accomplished art: bronze casting.

According to chronicle evidence, Shang-style turtleshell oracles had inspired the Zhou to conquest, and later Zhou rulers upheld that tradition. Chronicles composed in the third century B.C.E. tell the same story as texts hundreds of years older. If they can be believed, the Zhou "captured"—as they put it—the Shang state in a single battle in 1045 B.C.E. at Muye. They annexed it as a kind of colony and established garrisons all along the lower Yellow River to the coast. Archaeological evidence shows that they shifted the center of the empire, north, to the hilly Shaanxi (shawn-shee) region, west of where the Yellow River turns toward the sea.

The Zhou Political System

Inscriptions on bronze loving cups are the only contemporary written sources to survive from the period of Zhou supremacy, which lasted from about 1000 through the 700s B.C.E. Those who could afford them—and, of course, few could—recorded their inheritances, their legacies to their families, and, above all, the key moments in their family's relationships with the imperial house. Documenting the family's achievements was related to a belief in inherited virtue. Indeed, as Shao Gong, uncle and adviser to an early Zhou king, put it: "there is nothing—neither wisdom nor power—that is not present at a son's birth."

The inscriptions tend to be long and give lots of detailed but unimportant information, perhaps in an effort to legitimize what they describe. Shortly before 1000 B.C.E., for instance, a king's nephew recorded how he had been made ruler of the colony of Xing (shing). He tells us first of the royal decision to make the appointment. Then we get the circumstances: The nominee performs a sacrificial libation—a drink offering—of gratitude. He accompanies the king on a lake hunt in a ship with a red banner. The king bags a goose and gives the nominee a black axe. "In the evening, the lord was awarded many axe-men as vassals, two

Bronze drum. This intricate geometric design on the face of a Vietnamese drum shows a sunburst at the center, surrounded by humans and birds. Rulers often displayed these impressive bronze drums as emblems of their royal status.

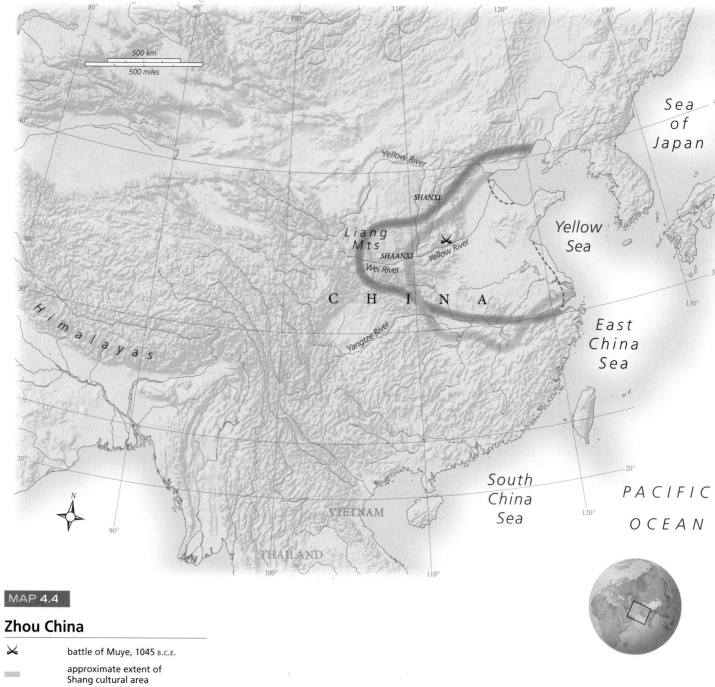

MAP 4.4

Zhou China

✕   battle of Muye, 1045 B.C.E.

▬   approximate extent of
Shang cultural area

▬   approximate extent of Zhou state

VIETNAM   modern-day country

---   ancient coastline

hundred families, and was offered the use of a chariot-team in which the king rode; bronze harness-trappings, an overcoat, a robe, cloth and slippers." The gifts apparently mattered a great deal because all such inscriptions mention them. The special clothes conferred status. The newly ennobled lord then commissioned a commemorative cup, which bore the inscription. "With sons and grandsons, may he use it for ever to confer virtue, invoke blessings, and recall the order to colonize Xing."

Once the Zhou conquered the Shang, they did not continue all Shang traditions. Indeed, despite pious declarations, they gradually abandoned the most sacred Shang rite: divination by bone oracles. Although the Zhou extended China's cultural frontiers before their own state dissolved in its turn in the eighth century B.C.E., their leaders were not universal emperors in the mold of the Shang, ruling all the world that mattered to them. Rival states multiplied around them, and their own power tended to erode and fragment. But they originated the ideology of the **mandate of heaven**, which "raised up our little land of Zhou." All subsequent Chinese states inherited the same notion that the emperor was divinely chosen. Furthermore, all subsequent changes in rule appealed to the same claim that heaven transferred power from a decayed dynasty to one of greater virtue. The Zhou created an effective myth of the unity and continuity of China that dominated the way the Chinese came to think of themselves. This myth has been passed on and is now the standard Western view of China, too, as a monolithic state—massive, with a uniform culture of exceptional durability, and a tendency to claim dominion over all the world.

Zhou China	
1100 B.C.E.	Shang state in decline
1045 B.C.E.	Zhou overthrow Shang at Battle of Muye
1045–700 B.C.E.	Zhou supremacy

STATE-BUILDING IN THE AMERICAS

On a relatively smaller scale and over a longer time span, communities in parts of the New World experimented with some of the same processes of state-building and civilization that we have seen in the Old World. People in two areas—parts of the Andean region of South America and in Mesoamerica were particularly ambitious in modifying their environments.

Andean Examples

About 3,500 years ago, experiments in civilization spread from alluvial areas on the Peruvian coast to a variety of less obviously favorable environments (see Map 4.5). In Cerro Sechín (SER-roh se-CHEEN), only about 300 feet higher than the Supe (SOO-peh) valley in north-central Peru (see Chapter 2), an astounding settlement existed in about 1500 B.C.E. It occupied a site of about 12 acres dominated by a stone platform 170 feet square. Rites of victory seem to have been celebrated here. Hundreds of carved warrior images slash their victims in two, exposing their entrails, or slicing off their heads. By about 1200 B.C.E., nearby Sechín Alto (se-CHEEN al-toh) was one of the world's great ceremonial complexes, with gigantic mounds erected to perform rituals, and monumental buildings arrayed along two boulevardlike spaces, each more than a mile long, at its heart. The biggest mound covers 30 square miles and is almost 140 feet tall.

These places, and others like them, suggest new experiments to manage the environment and coordinate food production in numerous small, hilly areas, each irrigated by a gravity canal and organized from a central seat of power. The violent carvings of Cerro Sechín show the price paid in blood to defend or enlarge them.

In the same period—in the last three centuries or so of the second millennium B.C.E.—farther up the coast, new settlements took shape around the

Cerro Sechín. As urban life and monumental building spread upland from the river valleys of coastal central Peru in the second millennium B.C.E., warfare and rites of human sacrifice spread with them. Walls at Cerro Sechín are carved with scenes of warriors overseeing the severed heads and cleft bodies of their victims.

MAP 4.5

State-Building in the Americas, ca. 1500–1000 B.C.E

Olmec cultural area		Olmec sculptural site
Chavín cultural area		PERU	modern-day country
normal flow of Pacific Ocean current		TABASCO	state province
El Niño current			

Cupisnique (koo-pees-nee-keh) gorge. Though the environment was similar, the physical remains suggest a different culture and different politics. Huaca de los Reyes (WA-kah deh los RAY-ess), for instance, had dozens of stucco-fronted buildings and colonnades of fat pillars, each up to 6.5 feet thick, guarded by huge, saber-toothed heads in clay. At Pampa de Caña Cruz (PAM-pah deh KAN-yah krooss), a gigantic mosaic, 170 feet long, made of thousands of fragments of colored rock, represented a similar head. It was embedded in the earth, so that a viewer could only appreciate its shape from a great height—a height the humans who made it could not reach, but their gods, perhaps, could. These regions traded with the nearby highlands, where building on a monumental scale followed soon afterward in the Cajamarca (kah-ha-MAR-kah) valley and the Upper Huallaga (wa-YAH-gah) valley. These sites constitute evidence of extraordinary cultural diversity among connected communities within a fairly small space.

Most Andean experiments in civilization were short lived. With modest technologies, they struggled to survive in unstable environments. **El Niño** (el NEEN-yo)—the periodic reversal of the normal flow of Pacific currents—was always a looming threat. At irregular intervals, usually once or twice a decade, El Niño drenches the region in torrential rain and kills or diverts the usually ample supply of ocean fish. Andean civilizations also faced crises their own success caused when population levels outgrew food supplies, or overexploitation impoverished the soil, or envious neighbors unleashed wars. Their traditions, however, lasted and spread to a great variety of environments, notably Chavín de Huantar (cha-VEEN deh wan-tar).

The city of Chavín de Huantar began to emerge about 1000 B.C.E., over 3,300 feet up in the Andes, on the Mosna River. Chavín demonstrates how people could achieve prosperity and magnificence at middling altitudes. The essential prerequisites were command of trade routes and the availability of diverse foodstuffs that grow in the microclimates of mountain environments like Chavín's (see Figure 4.1). Gold-working technology, which was already at least a thousand years old in the highlands, provided objects for luxury trade, and forest products from east of the mountains were also in demand in the lowland cities. Chavín was in the middle of these trades, acting as a distribution center.

Even in the impressive world of early Andean civilizations, the sheer workmanship of Chavín stands out in architecture, water management, engineering, metalwork, and ceramics. People from all over the central Andes and lowlands admired and imitated Chavín and its arts. The many ceremonial spaces, storehouses, and barracklike dwellings have inspired much speculation about how this society was organized and ruled. The best clues, however, are probably in the sculptures. They are full of forest creatures: jaguars, anacondas, and the small crocodiles called caymans. But humans half-transformed into jaguars are dominant, often with traces of drug-induced ecstasy. Nausea and bulging eyes contort their faces; their nostrils stream with mucus. Here is the evidence of a society ruled by shamans—the go-betweens who rise above the level of their subjects by drug-induced ecstasies. Proof of their power lay in the messages they brought back from the gods and the spirit world.

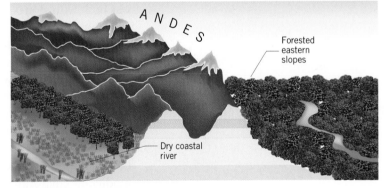

Forested eastern slopes

Dry coastal river

◻ Grassy plain 13,000 ft. above sea level
◻ Uplands: 10,500–12,500 ft. above sea level
◻ Frost-free valleys 7,500–10,000 ft. above sea level
◻ Lower slopes of mountains: 2,400–7,000 ft. above sea level
◻ Dry coastal region: 2,400 ft. above sea level

FIGURE 4.1 THE ANDEAN ENVIRONMENT packs tremendous ecological diversity into a small space, with various climatic zones at different altitudes, contrasting microclimates in the valleys, and tropical forest and the ocean close to hand. Maize grows on low slopes, coca and sweet potatoes above it, and potatoes at higher altitudes. The high grassland called puna provides grazing for llamas and their kin.

Shaman. Masks, music, and dance often play roles in bringing about shamanic ecstasy. This ceramic flute-player from Chavín de Huántar in the Peruvian Andes, of the mid-first millennium B.C.E., wears a jaguar mask, with the bulging eyes and dilated nostrils typical of a visionary trance.

Developments in Mesoamerica

States developed in the Andes the same way they developed in the Old World—as responses to the stimulation of trade. Both followed the model described in Chapter 3: beginning with intensified agriculture, leading to population density, economic specialization, growing markets, and trade. In the Andes, the model emerged from the soil of Aspero in the Supe valley and climaxed in Chavín. In Mesoamerica, however, stunning experiments in civilization began, as far as we know, without the benefit of trade.

The culture we loosely call Olmec (OL-mek) arose in what is now the province of Tabasco in southern Mexico in the second millennium B.C.E. (see Map 4.5). We can picture the Olmecs with the help of portraits they left: huge sculpted heads, carved from stones and columns of basalt, each of up to 40 tons, toted or dragged over distances of up to a hundred miles. Some have jaguarlike masks or squat heads with almond eyes, parted lips, and sneers of cold command. Perhaps they, too, are shaman-rulers with the power of divine self-transformation, though they are never as thoroughly transformed as the coca-crazed shamans of Chavín.

The swamps of Tabasco had supported agriculture for at least a thousand years before the first monumental art and ceremonial centers in the Olmec tradition appeared. The Olmec chose settlement sites near mangrove swamps and rain forest, close to beach and ocean, where they could exploit a variety of environments. Marshy lakes, full of aquatic prey, were alluring to settlers. They dredged mounds for farming from the swamp, and between the mounds, coaxed canals into a grid for raising fish, turtles, and perhaps caymans.

The agricultural mounds became the model for ceremonial platforms. The earliest known ceremonial center was built on a rise above the river Coatzalcos (kwa-TSAL-kos) around 1200 B.C.E. Two large centers soon followed, at La Venta, deep among the mangrove swamps on the Tonalá (to-nah-LAH) River, and at nearby San Lorenzo in what is now the state of Vera Cruz in Mexico. By about 1000 B.C.E., San Lorenzo had substantial reservoirs and drainage systems, integrated into a plan of causeways, plazas, platforms, and mounds. At La Venta, there are early examples of the ritual spaces that fitted into these gridworks. The center was built with stones toted and rolled from more than 60 miles away. The focus of La Venta is a mound over a hundred feet tall—evidently a setting for the most important rituals. One of the ceremonial courts has a mosaic pavement that resembles a jaguar mask that its creators appear to have deliberately buried. Similar buried offerings were placed under other buildings, perhaps the way some Christians bury relics from saints in the foundations and altars of churches. Although the stone buildings—those that survive—were designed for ritual life, these were cities: dense settlements clustered around the ceremonial centers.

Two unsolved problems exist in connection with the Olmecs: How and why did intensive food production begin? And how and why did ambitious attempts to modify the environment begin? Monumental building requires ample food supplies to support manpower and generate spare energy. Many scholars still believe that the Olmecs could have produced sufficient food by slashing forest clearings, setting fire to the stumps, and planting seeds directly in the ash. But this theory is unconvincing because, as far as we know, no society using such methods ever prospered the way the Olmecs did. It is more likely that the transition to city-building began when the Olmecs started farming high-yielding varieties of maize. With beans and squash, maize provided complete nourishment. The three plants together were so important to Olmec life that they depicted them on gods' and chieftains' headgear.

It is risky to make inferences on the basis of such scanty evidence, but it looks as if a determined, visionary leadership energized by shamanism drove Olmec civilization forward. An exquisite scene of what seems to be a ceremony in progress suggests the seemingly pivotal role of shamanism. Archaeologists found it buried in sand, perhaps as an offering. Carved figures with misshapen heads, suggesting that the skull was deliberately deformed, stand in a rough circle of upright stone slabs. They wear nothing but loincloths and ear ornaments. Their mouths are open, their postures relaxed. Similar figures include a *were-jaguar*—a small creature, half jaguar, half human. Others carry torches on phallic staffs. Or else they kneel or sit in a restless posture, as if ready to be transformed from shaman into jaguar, as other works depict. For the rites these figures suggest, the Olmecs built stepped platforms—forerunners, perhaps, or maybe just early examples of the angular mounds and pyramids typical of later New World civilizations.

Rulers were buried in the sort of disguises they wore for ritual performances. They became fantastic creatures with a cayman's body and nose, a jaguar's eyes and mouth, and feathered eyebrows that evoke raised hands. They lay in pillared chambers with bloodletting tools of jade or stingray spine beside them. We can still see their images carved on benchlike thrones of basalt, where they sat to shed blood—their own and their captives'. One of these carvings shows a throne with a submissive figure roped to a majestic character in an eagle headdress, who leans outward as if to address an audience.

Believers in the diffusionist theory of civilization have often hailed the Olmecs as the mother civilization of the Americas. Diffusionism states, in brief, that civilization is such an extraordinary achievement that we can credit only a few gifted peoples with creating it. It then diffused—or spread by example and instruction—to other less inventive peoples. This theory is almost certainly false. Rather, several civilizations probably emerged independently, in widely separated places. The Olmec civilization was one among many, including the Egyptian, Mesopotamian, Harappan, and Chinese.

Nevertheless, Olmec influence seems to have spread widely in Mesoamerica and perhaps beyond. Numerous aspects of Olmec life became characteristic of later New World civilizations: mound building; a tendency to seek balance and symmetry in art and architecture; ambitious urban planning around angular temples and plazas; specialized elites, including chieftains commemorated in monumental art; rites of rulership involving bloodletting and human sacrifice; a religion rooted in shamanism with bloody rites of sacrifice and ecstatic performances by kings and priests; agriculture based on maize, beans, and squash.

ASSESSING THE DAMAGE

By 1000 B.C.E., failed states littered the landscape. Some of the world's most spectacular empires broke up, and mysterious catastrophes cut short the histories of many of its most complex cultures. Food distribution centers controlled from palace labyrinths shut down. Trade was disrupted. Settlements and monuments were abandoned. The Harappan civilization vanished, as did the Cretan and Mycenean. Hatti was obliterated.

In Mesopotamia, Akkadian armies spread their own language along the length of the Tigris and Euphrates. Sumerian speech slowly dwindled from everyday use

State-Building in the Americas

(All dates are approximate)	
1500 B.C.E.	Cerro Sechín (Peru)
1200 B.C.E.	Sechín Alto (Peru)
1000 B.C.E.	Chavín civilization emerges
1000 B.C.E.	Olmec cities of San Lorenzo and La Venta flourishing
500 B.C.E.	End of Chavín civilization
300 B.C.E.	Olmec civilization in decline

Olmec head. The Olmec carving known to archaeologists as Head No. 1, in San Lorenzo, Veracruz, in Mexico, where nine such sculptures, each over six feet high, are concentrated. San Lorenzo is far from the source of the basalt from which the heads were carved. Their close-fitting helmets have inspired the fantasy that they were representations of space men. Their thick-lipped faces have induced almost equally incredible speculations about prehistoric arrivals from Africa. More probably—like later monumental portraits in Mesoamerica—they represent stylized images of rulers.

Wall painting in the tomb of the vizir Rekhmire—one of hundreds of Egyptian nobles buried in sumptuous graves in Thebes around the mid–second millennium B.C.E. Part of Rekhmire's job was to receive "tribute" or, in effect, trade samples from foreign lands. Items depicted here include copper ingots with handles from the eastern or northern shores of the Mediterranean and exotic products from the Nubian frontier—ivory, apes, a giraffe.

MAP 4.6 **Egypt and Nubia, ca. 1500 B.C.E.**

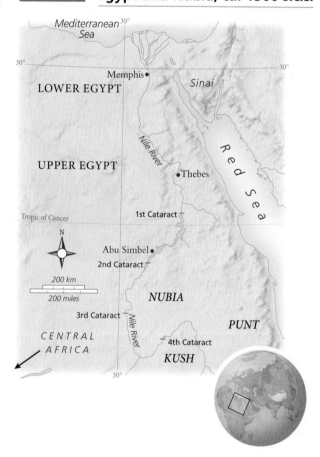

to become—like Latin in the Western world today—a purely ceremonial language. The cities of Sumer crumbled. Their memory was preserved chiefly in the titles that invaders from uplands and deserts used to dignify the rule of their own kings. Ur declined to a cult center and tourist resort.

Something similar occurred in China, which succumbed to a new ruling elite of conquerors, the Zhou, from neighboring uplands. Aspects of the civilization survived, but its center of gravity was shunted upriver. As we shall see in a later chapter, when numerous competing kingdoms in turn succeeded Zhou in the 700s B.C.E., continuity was not broken. Society and everyday life remained essentially intact. This was a pattern often repeated in Chinese history. In the New World, meanwhile, Mesoamerica and the Andean region undertook environmentally ambitious initiatives, but none showed much staying power.

The Survival of Egypt

Though there were more losers than winners after the climacteric of the second millennium B.C.E., the outstanding case of endurance, as we saw in the last chapter, was Egypt. Invasions in the late second millennium failed, and the basic productivity of the agrarian system remained intact. But even Egypt was reined in.

Nubia (NOO-bee-ah)—the region upriver of the cataracts, what is now Sudan—disappeared from Egyptian records by 1000 B.C.E. This was a major reversal because extending its empire along the Nile had been one of Egypt's most constant objectives. The abundant ivory, the mercenaries that Nubia supplied, and the river trade that made gold in Egypt "as plentiful as the sand of the sea" had long drawn Egypt southward. Egypt originally became interested in Central Africa when the explorer Harkhuf made three expeditions around 2500 B.C.E. He brought back "incense, ebony, scented oil, tusks, arms, and all fine produce." Harkhuf's captive pygmy, "who dances divine dances from the land of the spirits. . ." fascinated the boy pharaoh Pepi. Writing to the explorer, the pharaoh commanded the utmost care in guarding him: "inspect him ten times a night. For my Majesty wishes to see this pygmy more than all the products of Sinai and Punt."

Contact and commerce led to the formation of a Nubian state in imitation of Egypt, beyond the second cataract (see Map 4.6). From about 2000 B.C.E. on, Egypt tried to influence or control this state, sometimes by erecting fortifications, sometimes by invasion, sometimes by pushing its own frontier southward to beyond the third cataract. Pharoahs' inscriptions piled curses on the Nubians as the latter became more powerful and more difficult to handle. Eventually, around 1500 B.C.E., Pharoah Tut-mose I launched a campaign beyond the fourth cataract, conquering the kingdom of Kush and making Nubia a colonial territory. Egypt studded Nubia with forts and temples. The last temple, to Ramses II, at Abu Simbel, was the most crushingly monumental that Egyptians had built for 2,000 years. It has remained a symbol of power ever

⦿ MAKING CONNECTIONS

INSTABILITY: CONDITIONS LEADING TO DOWNFALL OF KINGDOMS 2000–1000 B.C.E.

KINGDOM AND REGION →	PRIMARY PROBLEMS →	CONSEQUENCES
Egypt	Exposure to invasion; limited areas of soil fertility; occasional grain shortages	Famines, land shortages, and sizable migrations; invasion by Sea Peoples exploits instability
Hatti—Northern Anatolia	Growth overlaps with frontiers of Egypt, Mesopotamia; overextension of power; disruption of trade through warfare; vulnerability to famine and disease in early stages of agriculture	Nomadic prowlers attack during weak periods, conquered subjects revolt
Crete—Aegean Sea	Uneven organization of labor; distribution of food; competition with other city-states; destruction of environment; little fertile soil; dangerous seas	Social inequality, internal warfare combine with nearby volcanic activity and earthquakes to force abandonment of cities, palaces
Mycenaean Civilization	Barbarian raiders from north attracted by wealth of palaces; earthquakes; social inequality; internal warfare	Social inequality, internal warfare combine with nearby volcanic activity and earthquakes to force abandonment of cities, palaces
Harappa and Mohenjodaro: Indus River	Gradually drying climate; evidence of earthquakes, shifting riverbeds, disease; overuse of environmental resources	Gradual collapse of food distribution system; political control; cities and towns abandoned
Shang and Zhou Dynasties—China	Overdependence of Shang leaders on rituals, oracles, war, conquest to manipulate harvest, weather	Collapse of Shang rule; rise of Zhou state; shifting center of empire; lessened dependence on divination by bone oracles

since. But during the reigns of his immediate successors, disastrously little flooding of the Nile, on which the success of Egyptian agriculture depended, was recorded. This was the era, toward the end of the thirteenth century B.C.E., when Egypt came closer to collapse than at any time since the invasion of the Hyksos. To abandon Nubia in the late second millennium B.C.E., after investing so much effort and emotion, shows how severe Egypt's need for retrenchment must have been.

IN PERSPECTIVE: The Fatal Flaws

The causes of instability in the four great river valleys and the smaller states that arose later were much more general than any general crisis theory suggests. If Harappan society was unsustainable in the silt-rich Indus valley, how realistic were the Hittite or Olmec or Cretan or Andean ambitions in much less favorable environments?

Paradox racked the most ambitious states of the era. They were committed to population growth, which imposed unsustainable goals of expansion as conquered territory became farther and farther away from the center. They were

CHRONOLOGY

(All dates are approximate)

2500 B.C.E.	Egypt expands southward
2000–1000 B.C.E.	Climacteric: critical and accelerating change; state-building in Hatti, Crete, Egypt; Shang China, the Andes, and Mesoamerica
2000 B.C.E.	Nubian state formed, emulating Egypt, Cretan civilization emerges
1800–1500 B.C.E.	Hittite kingdom flourishes
1500 B.C.E.	Mycenae civilization appears; Cerro Sechín flourishes in Andes (Peru)
1210 B.C.E.	Last record of Hatti
1190 B.C.E.	Ramses III defeats Sea Peoples
1000 B.C.E.	Cretan and Mycenaean cities abandoned; Shang state in decline; Harappan cites in ruin; Chavín civilization emerges; Nubia disappears from Egyptian records
300 B.C.E.	Olmec civilization declines (Mesoamerica)

founded on intensified methods of production, which drove them to overexploit the environment. They concentrated large populations in an area, making them more vulnerable to famine and disease. Enemies surrounded them, jealous of their wealth and resentful of their power. They created more enemies for themselves by inspiring rivals and imitators in their hinterlands. When their food-distribution programs failed, disruptive migrations resulted. Their rulers condemned themselves to failure and rebellion because they lived a lie, manipulating unreliable oracles, negotiating with heedless gods, bargaining with hostile nature.

In some cases, the traditions that failed or faltered during the great climacteric simply got displaced, to reemerge elsewhere. In others, dark ages of varying duration—periods of diminished achievement, about which we have little evidence—followed the climacteric. Chavín survived for about 500 years, until about 500 B.C.E., but during the following several centuries, people in the Andes attempted nothing on a comparable scale. After the Olmec stopped building on a large scale, probably in the 300s B.C.E., they had no successors for many centuries. Squatters occupied the cities of Harappa and Mycenae. The literacy of these civilizations was lost, their writing systems forgotten. When writing resumed in these regions hundreds of years later, the inhabitants had to invent new alphabets.

Our next problem is to penetrate that darkness and trace the displaced traditions from failed states. We want to examine the context that would produce a different world after the climacteric, post-1000 B.C.E. In the last millennium B.C.E.—thanks to an extraordinary blossoming of intellectual and spiritual life—the world was literally rethought.

PROBLEMS AND PARALLELS

1. How did the features that characterized the great river-valley civilization begin to emerge in other environments in the second millennium B.C.E.?
2. Why did the number of complex states rapidly increase during this period?
3. Why did the Hittite Kingdom fall? Why did Cretan and Mycenean civilization collapse and disappear in this period, while Egypt survived?

4. What factors might account for the long-term survival of Chinese civilization and the collapse and disappearance of Harrapan/Indus Valley civilization?
5. Why is the period between 2000 and 1000 B.C.E. a climacteric in global history?

DOCUMENTS IN GLOBAL HISTORY

- Hittite Land Deed
- Hittite Soldiers' Oath

- Ramses III, "The War Against the Sea Peoples"
- Selections from the *Rig Veda*

Please see the Primary Source CD-ROM for additional sources related to this chapter.

READ ON

T. Bryce, *Life and Society in the Hittite World* (2002) is incomparable in its field. To understand the nature and importance of trade, the books of M. W. Helms, *Ulysses' Sail* (1988) and *Craft and the Kingly Ideal* (1993) are of great help. M. Heltzer, *Goods, Prices and the Organisation of Trade in Ugarit* (1978), and E. H. Cline, *Sailing the Wine-Dark Sea* (1994) are valuable studies of particular trade routes.

The classic work on Malta is J. Evans, *Prehistoric Antiquities of the Maltese Islands* (1971). The best book on Crete is now O. Dickinson, *The Aegean Bronze Age* (1994). E. D. Oren, ed., *The Sea Peoples and Their World* (2000) is an important collection.

Leading works on the so-called Indo-Europeans are J. P. Mallory, *In Search of the Indo-Europeans* (1989), and C. Renfrew, *Archaeology and Language* (1987). The books listed for Chapter 3 by Shaghnessy, Posspehl, and Bulger remain important for this chapter.

Especially useful on the Olmecs are M. D. Coe, ed., *The Olmec World: Ritual and Rulership* (1996), and E. Benson and B. de la Fuente, eds., *Olmec Art of Ancient Mexico* (1996). D. O'Connor, *Ancient Nubia* (1994) is a good introductory work.

CHAPTER 5

Rebuilding the World: Recoveries, New Initiatives, and Their Limits

The elephant wall of Anuradhapura, the city in northern Sri Lanka that became a courtly center in the second half of the first millennium B.C.E., when kings endowed it with great irrigation cisterns, monumental trees, and sites of sacrifice, pilgrimage, and monastic life. The elephants guard a stupa—a dome-like spiritual dwelling place for the Buddha—built in the second century B.C.E. (See pp. 140–141.)

T he time was high summer, a little over 3,000 years ago; the place, the eastern Mediterranean. "Guided," he says, "only by the light of the stars," Wenamun, an Egyptian ambassador, was on his way to the city-state of Byblos (BEEB-lohs), in Phoenicia, on the shore of what is now Lebanon. His mission: to procure timber for the Egyptian fleet from the mountain forests the king of Byblos controlled. The mission was important because Egypt had no timber of its own.

PHOENICIA

On arrival he found a place to stay and set up an altar to Egypt's chief god, Amun. At first, King Zeker Baal refused to see him, preferring, he claimed, to reserve his forests for his own purposes. He kept Wenamun waiting for weeks. Then the king suddenly summoned the ambassador in the dead of night. Presumably, the summons was a negotiating ploy. Wenamun, however, reported it as a dramatic change of heart that Amun had brought about. "I found him," says Wenamun of the king, "squatting in his high chamber, and when he turned his back against the window, the waves of the Great Syrian Sea [the Mediterranean] were breaking against the rear of his head." The ambassador recorded the dialogue that followed—doctored, no doubt, but still highly revealing.

"I have come," Wenamun began, "after the timber contract for the great and august ship of Amun, king of gods." He reminded Zeker Baal that his father and grandfather had sent timber to Egypt, but the king resented the implication that timber was due as tribute.

"They did so by way of trade," he replied. "When you pay me I shall do it." The two men bickered over the price, and each threatened to call off, the negotiations. "I call loudly to the Lebanon which makes the heavens open," claimed Zeker Baal, "and the wood is delivered to the sea."

"Wrong!" retorted Wenamun. "There is no ship which does not belong to Amun. His also is the sea. And his is the Lebanon of which you say, 'It is mine.' Do his bidding and you will have life and health."

It was an impressive speech, but in the end, the Egyptians had to pay Zeker Baal's price: four jars of gold and five of silver, unspecified amounts of linen, 500 ox hides, 500 ropes, 20 sacks of lentils, 20 baskets of fish. Wenamun wrote: "And the

FOCUS questions

- WHY WAS the Phoenician alphabet so significant in world history?
- WHAT WERE the political and economic foundations of the Assyrian Empire?
- WHAT ROLES did colonization and trade play in Greek and Phoenician cultures?
- WHY DID the Zhou state decline in China?
- HOW WAS civilization built anew in India and Sri Lanka?
- HOW DID geography influence the transmission of culture in the Americas and Africa?

Mission to Byblos: *The Report of Wenamun*

ruler was pleased and he supplied 300 men and 300 oxen. And they felled the timber, and they spent the winter at it and hauled it to the sea."

• • • • •

The Egyptian ambassador's document is vivid and dramatic, a true story better than fiction. But its value goes deeper. It opens a window into a world recovering from the crises and climacteric of the late second millennium B.C.E. The confidence of a small city-state like Byblos in the face of demands from a giant like Egypt seems astounding. But new opportunities that were opening up, thanks to increasing trade and cultural exchange in Eurasia, justified it.

The question for this chapter, then, is what happened between 1000 and 500 B.C.E. that led some places to recover from the failures of the second millennium? Investigating the nature and extent of those recoveries will equip us to approach a far bigger problem in the next part of this book: How do we explain the vitality and influence—the intellectual and spiritual achievements—of some groups and centers in Eurasia in the period that followed, beginning about 500 B.C.E.?

Equally important in its way is the problem of why new initiatives were so rare, late, and slow beyond Eurasia. In particular, why did the promising initiatives in parts of the Americas and sub-Saharan Africa wither instead of grow and thrive in this period? Why, for example, was Greece's dark age after the fall of Mycenae so much shorter than the dark ages of the Andes after Chavín or Mesoamerica after the Olmecs? Why did big states and monumental cities appear later in sub-Saharan Africa than in China, say, or India, or the Mediterranean? And why did so much historical initiative—the power of some human groups to influence others—become so concentrated in a few regions?

The best way to approach these questions is to look first at the regions that recovered from the disrupted traditions and overthrown states of the late second millennium. Recovery came about in the Middle East, where Hatti had vanished and Lower Mesopotamia—Sumer—declined; in the Mediterranean, where Crete and Mycenae were in ruins; in China, where Zhou had replaced Shang; and in India, where the Harappan cities disappeared. We will then look at the history of Africa and the Americas to see how isolation frustrated and slowed down certain changes.

TRADE AND RECOVERY IN THE MIDDLE EAST

Byblos was one of the largest city-states of Phoenicia (foh-NEE-see-ah), a maritime culture along the eastern coast of the Mediterranean (see Map 5.1). The name "Phoenicia" expresses Phoenicians' chief interest—trade—for the word almost certainly means "suppliers of purple dye." Tyre, an even bigger port near Byblos, developed a deep, rich purple from the crushed shells of sea mollusks that became Western antiquity's favorite and most expensive color. Beginning early in the first millennium B.C.E., Phoenician traders and colonists spread around the Mediterranean. Meanwhile, however, new, land-based empires arose that grew rich as much by conquest as by trade, threatening Phoenicia and, eventually, engulfing it.

The Phoenician Experience

In front of them, Phoenicians had waters accessible through excellent harbors. Behind them, they had mountains with forests of cedar and fir for shipbuilding and timber exports. What they did not have was much land to farm. They turned, therefore, to industry and trade. Their craftsmanship was the stuff of other peoples' stories. In legend, at least, Phoenician ships brought gold for King Solomon from distant Ophir, a mythical or lost kingdom. Timber from Tyre built the Temple of Solomon in Jerusalem, in exchange for food and oil. Phoenician cities stood, as the biblical prophet Ezekiel said of Tyre, "at the entry of the sea . . . a trader for the people of many isles. Their ports ring with precious metals, exude aromas of spice, and swirl with dye-steeped textiles. But the basis of everything is shipbuilding: the timbers from Lebanon, the oak for the oars, benches of ivory, sails of Egyptian linen, and mariners and builders from the Phoenician coast."

This was a period when the only way to trade with a region that did not have its own merchant class or tradition of long-distance commerce was to colonize it. According to legend, the Phoenicians' earliest colonies were in what is now Tunisia in North Africa and at Cadiz in Spain. Phoenicians founded the city of Carthage near modern Tunis around 800 B.C.E., and colonized the Mediterranean islands of Malta and Sardinia by 700 B.C.E. From these bases, Phoenician navigators broke into the Atlantic and established a trading post as far away as Mogador on the northwest coast of Africa. Roman sources even credit them, probably mistakenly, with sailing around Arabia and Africa.

Where they built cities, the Phoenicians were agents of cultural exchange, borrowing from all over the eastern Mediterranean, while introducing clay-lined beehives, glass blowers' techniques and their own vats for mixing Tyrian dye. They also exported some of their religious cults. In Carthage, newborn babies rolled from the arms of statues of their gods, Baal and Tanit, as sacrifices into sacred flames.

The colonies remained, even when the cities of Phoenicia fell to foreign raiders or rulers. In 868 B.C.E. the king of Assur (see Chapter 4) "washed his weapons in the Great Syrian Sea," and his successors continued to grab tribute from Phoenicia for over a century. Egyptian and Babylonian rulers—and by the early sixth century, conquerors from Persia—then preyed on the region in their turn. By 500 B.C.E., Carthage aspired to be an imperial capital of its own, fighting to control Mediterranean trade—first with Greek cities, then with Rome. It had a fine harbor just where a lot of shipping needed it—in the center of the Mediterranean—and a fertile hinterland of flocks, wheat fields, irrigated gardens of pomegranates and figs, and vineyards. Its aspirations seemed justified. The city's worst enemy, the Roman statesman, Cato the Elder (234–149 B.C.E.), preached, to the Roman Senate, "Carthage must be destroyed." To show why, he displayed plump, fresh figs, a delicate fruit that spoils quickly, newly imported from there. With this single gesture, he conveyed that the land was fertile, the city was rich and strong—and Rome was within its easy reach.

A Roman poet later recalled Phoenicians as "a clever people who prospered in war and peace. They excelled in writing and literature and the other arts, as well as in seamanship, naval warfare, and ruling over an empire." Their records might illuminate for us the dark age of lack of sources after the fall of Mycenae, but the Romans, who defeated Carthage in three wars and destroyed the city in 146 B.C.E., were too thorough in victory. The Phoenician language gradually yielded in North

Byblos—King Zeker Baal's city—on the shore of Lebanon. Baal, the god for whom the king was named, supposedly lived far away on the crest of the forested mountains. Byblos' ability to deliver timber to traders on the coast therefore demonstrated a divine relationship. Zeker Baal boasted that he could induce Baal to 'fling trees down on the shore.'

Atlantic
Ocean

FRANCE

A l p s

SLOVENIA
● Race

ILLYRIA

ETRURIA

Adriatic Sea

Elba

ITALY

Tarquinii ●
Caere ● ● Rome

Corsica

see inset

Aegean Sea

GREECE

Sardinia

● Croton

Ionian
Sea

● Rio Tinto

S P A I N

Balearic Islands

M e d i t e r r a n e a n   S e a   (G r e a t   S y r i

Sicily

● Elche

P O R T U G A L

Tartessos ●
Cadiz ●

Malta

Carthage ●
(Tunis)

TUNISIA

Pillars of
Hercules

N O R T H

● Mogador

A F R I C A

L I B Y A

FEZZAN

GARAMANTES

S a h a r

MACEDONIA

T H R A C E

P H R Y G I A

A n a t o l i a

● Troy

L Y D I A

Aegean
Sea

GREECE

Euboea

I O N I A

Phocaea ○

Delphi ●

Eretria ●
● Athens

Samos ○ ○ Miletus

L Y C I A

Corinth ●
Mycenae ●

Peloponnese

Helicon ●

Crete

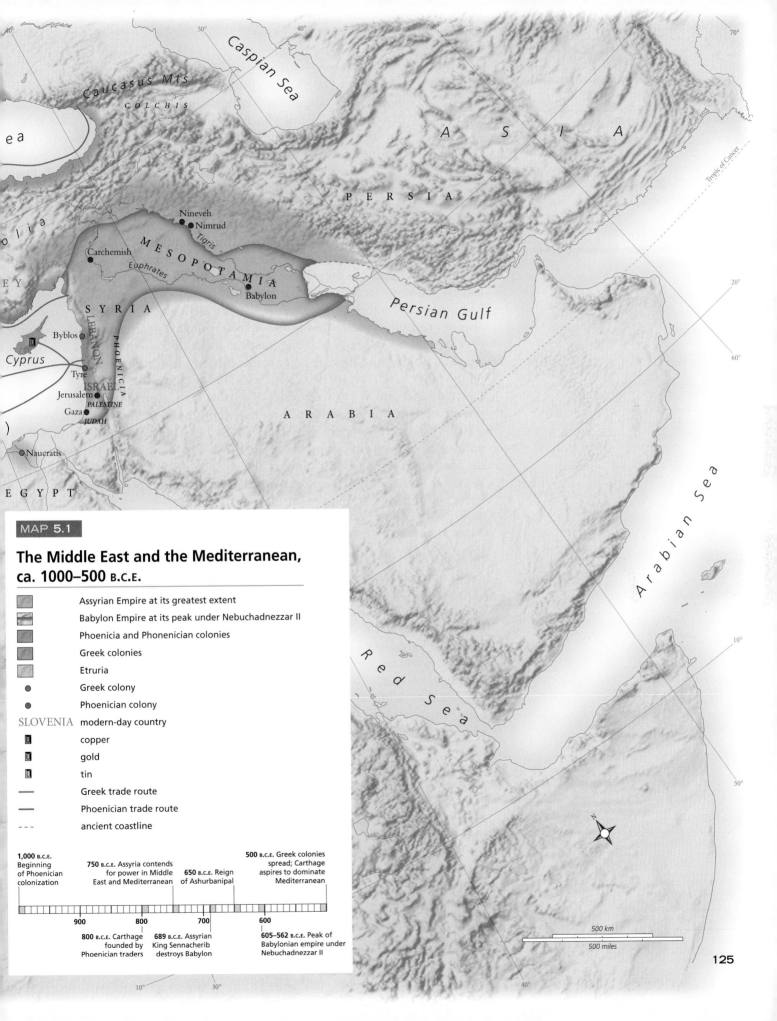

Caspian Sea

Caucasus Mts

COLCHIS

ea

A S I A

Tropic of Cancer

P E R S I A

Nineveh
Nimrud

M E S O P O T A M I A

Tigris

Carchemish

Euphrates

Babylon

Persian Gulf

Byblos

olia

S Y R I A

Cyprus

Tyre

P H O E N I C I A

L E B A N O N

ISRAEL

Jerusalem

PALESTINE

Gaza

JUDAH

A R A B I A

Naucratis

E G Y P T

Arabian Sea

Red Sea

The Middle East and the Mediterranean, ca. 1000–500 B.C.E.

- Assyrian Empire at its greatest extent
- Babylon Empire at its peak under Nebuchadnezzar II
- Phoenicia and Phonenician colonies
- Greek colonies
- Etruria
- Greek colony
- Phoenician colony
- SLOVENIA modern-day country
- copper
- gold
- tin
- Greek trade route
- Phoenician trade route
- ancient coastline

1,000 B.C.E. Beginning of Phoenician colonization

750 B.C.E. Assyria contends for power in Middle East and Mediterranean

650 B.C.E. Reign of Ashurbanipal

500 B.C.E. Greek colonies spread; Carthage aspires to dominate Mediterranean

900

800

700

600

800 B.C.E. Carthage founded by Phoenician traders

689 B.C.E. Assyrian King Sennacherib destroys Babylon

605–562 B.C.E. Peak of Babylonian empire under Nebuchadnezzar II

500 km

500 miles

Phoenicia

(All dates are approximate)	
1000 B.C.E.	Phoenicia trades and colonizes in the Mediterranean
800 B.C.E.	Carthage founded as a colony
700 B.C.E.	Malta and Sardinia colonized
500 B.C.E.	Carthage seeks control of Mediterranean trade
146 B.C.E.	Carthage destroyed by the Romans

Africa and Phoenicia itself to Latin and Greek—the languages the Romans introduced for administrative and literary purposes—and almost the whole of Phoenician literature disappeared. Only fragments of stone inscriptions survive, along with the Phoenicians' unique gift to the world, the alphabet.

All writing systems, as far as we know, except those indebted to the Phoenician, are based on syllables, logograms, or some combination of both. In the former, each sign represents a syllable, usually composed of one vowel sound and one consonant. In the second type, a sign stands for an entire word. Both methods require the user to know a large number of signs—typically, dozens in the syllabic system and hundreds or even thousands in a logographic one. But both methods have their advantages. Since only the leisured had time to learn them, they were secrets of a well-educated elite. They should also, in principle, consume less time and fewer valuable writing materials—stone or clay tablets, monuments, papyrus, or costly hides—than a system that demands at least one sign for every sound. Systems in the Phoenician tradition, on the other hand, suit societies with wide literacy and cheap writing materials. Easy to master and to use, these kinds of writing systems encourage learning and make it easier to do the kinds of business—both political and commercial—in which written records are helpful. The simpler the writing system, the greater the number of people who can master it and use it. The Greeks seem to have gotten the idea of an alphabet and some of the symbols from the Phoenicians. From there, the idea spread to the Romans and other European peoples who, in turn, later transmitted it around the world.

The Assyrian Empire

By 1000 B.C.E., Hatti's extinction was Assur's opportunity (see Chapter 4). Kings of Assur, who were already wide-scale raiders, forged a state along the Upper Tigris (TEYE-grihs), in the hills where enough rain fell to make agriculture possible without irrigation. By about 750 B.C.E., Assyrian (ahs-SEE-ree-ahn) rulers considered themselves successful enough to contend for more than regional power (see Map 5.1). King Tiglath-pilaser III adopted the title of King of the Four Quarters, or, as we would say, King of the World.

Close to home, within Upper (northern) Mesopotamia, Assyrian might reduced the traditional local rulers to purely ceremonial roles. To exercise real power in their place, the Assyrian kings appointed governors to run provinces, which were too small to mount successful rebellions. Beyond this core, Assyrian supremacy was looser, exercised by more varied means, adjusted according to local feeling and custom. In Babylon, for instance, the king of Assyria performed the annual rite of allegiance to the city god; in the city of Gaza, near the border between modern Israel and Egypt, he was enrolled among local divinities. Elsewhere, he destroyed temples and statues of gods to demonstrate his power and then restored them to show his generosity.

Fear was the cement of Assyria's empire. An ideology of domination is obvious in the remnants of Assyria that archaeologists have dug up: in the crushing weight of palace gates, the gigantic scale of the royal beasts that guard them, and the monumental sculptures, with their endless portrayals of battles and processions of tribute bearers. Colossal winged bulls carved for the palace at Nimrud were so heavy they sank the rafts when they were first transported. But, reported the governor, "Although it cost me a great deal of trouble, I have hauled them out again." The king was not divine, but heroic and intimate with gods. In portraits he kills bulls and lions and consults heaven, while winged spirits attend him. He literally entertained gods in his bedchamber: Attendants brought the statues of gods in and offered them food and libations.

Inscriptions from the reign of King Ashurbanipal (ah-shoor-BAH-nee-pahl) in the mid-seventh century B.C.E. best capture the character of the Assyrian state. He was probably the most self-celebrated monarch in the history of the Mesopotamian world. While never dethroning war as the Assyrians' priority, he made a cult of literacy, looting the learning of Babylon for his library at Nineveh (NIH-neh-veh). He was proud of the canals dug and the wine pressed in his reign, the 120 layers of bricks in the foundations of his palace, the offerings he made "of first fruits to [the god] Assur, my lord, and the temples of my land." We can picture him in his pleasure gardens, where pomegranates clustered as thick as grapes and "I, Ashurbanipal, pick fruit like a squirrel." A portrait survives of him picnicking with his wife under a vine; but dangling from it is the head of a captured enemy.

To celebrate a new palace and flaunt the wealth of his realm, Ashurbanipal held a banquet for 16,000 citizens, 5,000 visiting dignitaries, 1,500 palace officials, and 47,074 workmen "summoned from all over the kingdom." They consumed history's biggest meal: 10,000 jugs of beer; 10,000 skins of wine; 30,000 quarts each of figs, dates, and shelled pistachios; 1,000 each of lambs and fat oxen; 14,000 sheep; 20,000 pigeons; 10,000 eggs; 10,000 desert rats; and hundreds of deer. "For ten days I gave them food, I gave them drink, I had them bathed, I had them anointed. I honored them and sent them back to their lands in peace and joy." Palace-building, evidently, was politically functional, bringing subjects and tributaries together in a common enterprise. This, perhaps, was why Assyrian kings built so many of them.

But instability lay at the heart of the monarchy. Like Egyptian and Chinese rulers, the Assyrian kings sought to enhance their power by claiming to communicate with forces in Nature—a doomed enterprise. When their supposed magic failed, they lost power, and competing factions arose. Some Assyrian monarchs asserted their legitimacy so vigorously as to make us doubt it. Ashurbanipal's father tried to secure the succession against rebellion with 150 lines of oaths and curses:

> Just as the noise of doves is persistent, so may you, your women, your sons, your daughters have no rest or sleep. Just as the inside of a hole is empty, may your inside be empty. Just as gall is bitter, so may you, your women, your sons, your daughters, be bitter towards each other. Just as the water of a slit waterskin runs out, so may your waterskin break in a place of thirst and famine, so that you die of thirst.

In the background of internal conflicts, was a harem of ambitious women with time to conspire in favor of their own sons. In the early eighth century B.C.E., Sammuramat was one such woman who effectively ruled the empire and accompanied her son on military campaigns. Naqia was another. She was virtual coruler with her

Winged bull. "May the guardian bull, the guardian genius, who protects the strength of my throne, always preserve my name in joy and honor until his feet move themselves from this place." An inscription left by King Esarhaddon, son of Sennacherib, explains the function of the winged bulls—usually carved with the portrait heads of kings—that guarded Assyrian gates and throne rooms.
Human-headed winged bull and winged lion (lamassu). Alabaster (gypsum); Gateway support from the Palace of AshurnasirpalII (ruled 883–859 B.C.E.). Limestone. H: 10' 3/1/2". L: 9' 1". W: 2' 1/2". The Metropolitan Museum of Art, Gift of John D. Rockefeller, Jr., 1932. (32.143.2) Photography (c) 1981 The Metropolitan Museum of Art.

King Ashurbanipal II reclines to feast with his queen in the garden of his palace at Nineveh. Servants whisk flies and bring refreshments. In parts of the relief not shown here, birds sing, harpists play, and the head of the king of conquered Elam decorates a tree. The picnic is perhaps a victory celebration. Success in war bought Assyria's luxuries.

husband, Sennacherib (seh-NAH-keh-rihb), the Assyrian monarch famed for descending on the Hebrew holy city of Jerusalem "like a wolf on the fold." She did everything kings did, from dedicating inscriptions to building a palace, and receiving important war dispatches.

The Babylonian Revival

As the old cities of Lower (southern) Mesopotamia declined and trade shifted upriver, the city of Babylon became the heir of Sumer—the resting place of all the learning and much of the remaining wealth. To the Assyrians, Babylon was always the great prize, and it became part of their expanding empire. But Babylonians never forgot their independence and frequently tried to reclaim it. In 689 B.C.E., Sennacherib, attempted a definitive solution. He massacred or dispersed the population, razed buildings to the ground, threw the debris into the river, and dug channels across the site of the city, with the deliberate aim of turning it into a swamp. His son relented and set to rebuilding the city, but in the next generation Ashurbanipal resumed the policy of vengeance.

In 649 B.C.E., Ashurbanipal was said to have deported half a million people from their homes to prevent anyone from stealing back to Babylon, "and those still living," he announced, "I sacrificed as an offering to the spirit of my grandfather, Sennacherib." Yet the name of Babylon still retained mythic power as a rallying point for native resistance to Assyria, and a reversal of fortunes was at hand. Overextended along the Euphrates River, Assyria succumbed to enemies on other fronts. In the late seventh century B.C.E., Nabopolassar—"the son of nobody," as his inscriptions admit—masterminded a Babylonian revival. His boast was that he "defeated Assyria, which, from olden days had made people of the land bear its heavy yoke."

Assyria and Babylon

(All dates are approximate)	
750 B.C.E.	Assyria is an empire under Tiglath-pilaser III
689 B.C.E.	Sennacherib destroys city of Babylon
620s B.C.E.	Assyrian empire falls; Ashurbanipal is last king
605–562 B.C.E.	Peak of Babylonian empire under Nebuchadnezzar II

○ MAKING CONNECTIONS ○

CONDITIONS LEADING TO RECOVERY IN MIDDLE EAST AND MEDITERRANEAN

STATE →	TYPE OF LEADERSHIP AND INITIATIVES →	EFFECTS
Phoenician city-states	Merchant elites; economy based on trade and proximity to forest, mineral, metal resources; colonization of Mediterranean	Spread of Phoenician technical knowledge, culture, and alphabet throughout Mediterranean
Assyrian Empire	Powerful king with provincial governors; cult of personality combined with ideology of domination; palace-building, other monumental architecture	Imperial state based on upper Tigris River spreads to lower Mesopotamia, Mediterranean coast
Babylonian Empire	Strong city-state asserts independence, becomes imperial center after decline of Assyrians; large-scale building projects; monumental architecture	Large metropolis becomes regional political/trade/cultural center; Babylon and Egypt battle for control of regional resources

Babylon now became once more an imperial metropolis, exploiting the vacuum Assyria's collapse left. Babylon's fame peaked during the long reign (605–562 B.C.E.) of Nebuchadnezzar (neh-boo-kahd-NEH-zahr) II, whose campaigns the Bible describes. He attacked the kingdom of Judah, destroyed King Solomon's temple at Jerusalem, and deported the Jews into exile. He fought off the Egyptians at Carchemish in Palestine. His building projects, however, made a more worthy monument. Ancient Greek guidebooks attributed two of the proverbial wonders of the world to him: the terraced "hanging" gardens of Babylon, supposedly built to please a concubine, and city walls broad enough to race four chariots abreast. Nebuchadnezzar was a master of theatrical gestures, a genius at attracting esteem. He cultivated an image of himself as the restorer of ancient glories by rebuilding ziggurats and city walls all over Mesopotamia. On what survives of his showy works, bulls, lions, and dragons strut elegantly in glazed brick.

Whether because Nebuchadnezzar overreached himself or because his dynasty could produce no more dynamic leaders, his was Babylon's last era of greatness. In effect, Babylon and Egypt fought each other to exhaustion in their efforts to replace Assyria. Five centuries later, the Greek geographer Strabo reflected that Babylon had been "turned to waste" by the blows of invaders and the indifference of rulers. "The great city has become a great desert."

GREECE AND BEYOND

In the late second millennium B.C.E., when the Sea Peoples and other displaced communities disrupted the eastern Mediterranean and threatened Egypt (see Chapter 4), a similar upheaval took place on land. Migrants from the north swept into southern Greece, eradicating literate culture. Refugees streamed across the Aegean and Ionian Seas to Italy, Anatolia, and islands in the eastern and central Mediterranean.

Babylon. No king of Babylon built more grandly than Nebuchadnezzar II (r. 604–562 B.C.E.) who gave the city center a gate, shown here in reconstruction, dedicated to the goddess Ishtar. Precious lapis lazuli colored the tiles that smother the gate. Guardian bulls and dragons adorn it.

Olive harvest. The export of olive oil was vital to Greece's recovery from the so-called "dark ages" that followed the fall of Mycenaean cities. Greece's poor soils and hot climate could not produce much else that was salable abroad. Solon, the legendary law-giver, supposedly compelled the Athenians to grow olives. Scenes of laborious techniques to harvest olives from their trees decorate this vase by the most prolific Athenian artist of the late sixth century B.C.E., known as the Antimenes Painter.

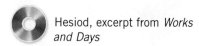

Hesiod, excerpt from *Works and Days*

The Greek Environment

By early in the first millennium B.C.E., the massive Mycenaean palace centers were in ruins. The only stone or rubble buildings from this period that we know of in Greece were in the city of Eretria, on the island of Euboea. Few iron tools were available for farming. Barley was the staple crop, laboriously cultivated in Greek soil, where bones of rock poked through the emaciated earth. (The image is the Greek philosopher Plato's.) Most Greeks lived by goat farming and in thatched huts.

Industry and trade were ways to escape rural poverty. In the tenth century B.C.E. Athens, Corinth, and a few other centers exported finely decorated pots and pressed olives—the only surplus farm product—for their oil. Neighboring peoples considered the Greeks' barley unfit to eat. But olive oil was exportable and came from a crop with advantages. Its care was seasonal and left plenty of time for seafaring. It would grow in ground that grains disdained. It permitted farming at remarkably high altitudes, over 2,000 feet. It had many uses. It added badly needed fat and flavor to the diet, could be burned as fuel in lamps, and, in a world without soap, could be used to clean the body by providing a lubricant for scraping off sweat and grime. Olive processers became rich and invested wealth in promoting more trade. Commercial enterprise soon lined the Aegean and Ionian Seas with cities; then, from the mid–eighth century B.C.E. onward, spread all over the Mediterranean and the Black Sea. The Greeks lived, they said, "around a sea, like frogs around a pond."

The Greek poet Hesiod recorded a conversation that evokes the way Greece took to the sea. Perses, his younger brother, was lolling around their humble farm in the annoying manner younger brothers sometimes have, while Hesiod sweated at the plow. "Greece and poverty are sisters," Perses began, "How can I make money easily?" Hesiod recommended work on the land. But Perses insisted, "I want to avoid toil, Hesiod. You know me!"

"Get a house first," said the elder brother, "and a woman and a plowing ox—a slave woman, not a wife—a woman who can take her turn following the ox." But Perses was the type of person who asks for advice only because he wants to confirm his own opinion. He revealed what he really wanted: "to buy and sell in distant markets."

"Please don't be a fool," rejoined Hesiod. "Our father tried that. He came here in his black ship, fleeing from the evil poverty with which God punished us men. And where did he end up? In this miserable dump, bad in winter, hard in summer. . . . "

"But that's why my heart is set on escape. . . . "

"Not now. . . . Till the soil as I tell you, and wait for the sailing season and then haul your ship to the wine-dark sea and stuff it with cargo."

"What do you know about sailing? You've only been over the sea once, to Euboea, for the poetry contest . . . "

" . . . Where I was victorious and carried off the prize. . . . But just as God taught me the secrets of composition, so shall he tell me the secrets of navigation for me to confide to you."

Hesiod went into the trancelike state poets of the time affected when composing. He revealed detailed sailing directions to his brother, along with typically Greek moral advice. "Money may be all you want in life, but it is not worth the risk of drowning. . . . Be moderate, my brother. Moderation is best in everything."

All over Greece, however, men like Perses won the arguments. Greek writers included merchants and explorers among their heroes, something unthinkable, for example, in China of the time, which valued only farmers, warriors, and scholars. In the 500s B.C.E., trade was growing so rapidly that some Greek states introduced their own coinage and designed and built new, larger types of ships.

Greek Colonialism

By Hesiod's time, iron tools improved agriculture and increased food production, which in turn led to an increase in population. But more people meant more demands on food and land. Now, not only were the Greeks a trading people, they also became colonizers (see Map 5.1). Their settlements extended to wheat-growing areas in Sicily, southern Italy, the north shore of the Black Sea, and then to rich markets in what are now France and Spain. Greek experience echoed that of Phoenicia: city-communities at home, outreach by sea, colonies abroad.

The Greeks founded colonies on the advice of gods who spoke through oracles, especially the one at Delphi, a cave in central Greece where smoke rose from deep crevices in the earth. Here, a priestess sat on a three-legged throne that was cast in the form of writhing serpents and uttered divine pronouncements. The oracle recommended colonization in a baffling array of cases. One supplicant went to the shrine to find a remedy for childlessness, with no thought of starting a colony, and received orders to found Croton in southern Italy. More understandably, others were told to colonize to escape famine. Founding colonies became so much a part of the Greek way of life that a comic playwright speculated on the chances of founding one in the sky. "Not that we hate our city," the would-be colonists protest, "for it is a prosperous mighty city, free for all to spend their wealth in, paying fines and fees." That is a Greek joke. Grasping humor across chasms of time and culture is one of the pleasures of studying the past.

Most colonists were outcasts, exiles, and criminals—frontiersmen forging a new society. But from nostalgia, need, and lack of imagination they clung to familiar ties and patterns. Wherever they went, they reproduced Greek ways of life. At Naucratis in the Nile delta, for example, colonists dedicated shrines to cults from their home towns—the goddess Hera of Samos and the Sun-god Apollo of Miletus. In the sixth- and fifth-centuries B.C.E., offerings to Aphrodite, goddess of love, show a steady stream of Greek sex-tourists to the lively local brothels. Such sober travelers as Solon, the great lawgiver of Athens, also visited Naucratis. They came to Egypt on business or on a grand tour in search of enlightenment from a great civilization.

Meanwhile, growing contacts inspired Greek artists and thinkers at home. The sea washed new cultural influences back toward Greece. The most striking example is the creation of a writing system, loosely based on Phoenician models. Unlike so many of the earlier systems that were developed to catalog merchandise or record trade transactions, the Greek alphabet was rapidly used to record creative literature and preserve epic poems that bards once recited at warriors' drinking parties. Poems attributed to the bard Homer, for instance, were written down in their surviving versions probably toward the end of the second century B.C.E. They have been revered—and imitated—ever since in the West for the brilliance with which they evoke war and seafaring. The *Iliad* tells a story of the interplay of gods and mortals during a military expedition from Mycenae to the city of Troy in what is now Turkey. The *Odyssey* recounts the wanderings of one of the heroes of the same war on his way home. The *Iliad* bristles with ships' masts. The *Odyssey* is loud with waves. Greek literature rarely strayed far from the sea.

Paestum. Around 600 B.C.E., Greek colonists founded the city now called Paestum in southern Italy. This view of the ruins of the Temple of Hera, queen of the gods, shows how faithfully the builders reproduced the style and feel of home. An upper gallery is visible on the left. No more perfect example of Greek architecture of the early sixth century survives in Greece itself.

Early Greek Society

Greeks had a remarkably uniform set of ideas about themselves—"our community of blood and language and religion and ways of life." Some of their notions were mythical, and Western tradition has multiplied the myths. We have idealized the Greeks as originators of our civilization and embodiments of all our values. However, scholars have been revising almost everything that has traditionally been said about them. We now know that the pure white marble Greek buildings and statues we saw as chaste specimens of classical taste were painted in gaudy colors in their day. The Greek gods appear no longer as personifications of virtues and vices, but as unpredictable and often demonic manipulators. Their world—and the imagination of most Greeks who shared it—was run not by reason but by weird and bloody rites, goat dances, orgiastic worship, sacrifices, signs, and omens.

The Greeks formed two kinds of community, which they called *ethne* (EHTH-nay) and *poleis* (POH-lihs), usually translated as "tribes" and "cities." Debate about what these terms really meant distracts us from the important point: what they had in common. Greeks lived in relatively small communities of citizens who saw themselves living together out of choice. Political institutions took many different forms, including hereditary and elected monarchies and states with ruling elites, defined by blood or wealth. Until recently, people in the West hailed the Greeks as originators of democracy. The Greeks certainly coined the word *demokrateia* to mean a state where supreme power belonged to an assembly of all citizens. But most Greeks disapproved of such an arrangement. The Greeks counted only privileged males as citizens, and normally only if both their paternal and maternal grandfathers had also been citizens. Women were excluded. So were slaves, who made up 40 percent of the population in fifth-century B.C.E. Athens. In some Greek states, citizens used bits of broken pottery as ballots on which to scrawl their votes to exile unpopular leaders. When we look at them now, we see fragments of an oppressive system that made slaves of captives, victims of women, battle fodder of men, and scapegoats of failures.

Families—groups based on monogamous couples and their descendants—were the basis of society in Greek communities. When Aristotle, the greatest of Greek scholars, speculated in the fourth century B.C.E. about the origins of the state, he assumed that it arose from the voluntary alliance of families. In Athens, some of the earliest group burials known to archaeologists are in family plots. Typically, girls married at age fourteen or fifteen to men twice their age. So men dominated. "The Greeks," said a writer of the fourth century B.C.E., "expect their daughters to keep quiet and do wool-work."

Myth eliminated women from Athenian origins—the founders of the community supposedly sprang from the soil. Wives and daughters did not normally inherit property, unless their menfolk specifically said they could. They rarely appeared in public, except as extravagantly emotional mourners or as priestesses in particular religious cults. In art of the first half of the millennium, men are shown

Aristophanes, excerpt from
The Birds

Greek women. Women collecting water from a fountain was a common subject for Greek painters of water pots. This example from the Greek colony of Vulci in Italy, where the native population esteemed women more highly than the Greeks did, follows a standard Greek pattern. It shows the women in profile, forming a line at a fountain with a lion's-head spout under a roof supported by slender columns.

more and more in the company of only other men, women with only other women. Women's function was to serve the community by bearing and raising children and thereby increasing manpower for production and war. In the city-state of Sparta—which Greeks always regarded as "utterly different" from other Greek states—all women had to train for motherhood, and women who died in childbirth were commemorated in the same way as heroic warriors killed in battle.

Scholars used to infer Greek values and morality from philosophical writings, but now we also look to popular plays and satires and find that the average Greek's social attitudes were different from the philosophers'. Athenian elites, for instance, tended to idealize homosexual relationships between older men and boys, but the playwrights' audiences despised them. At times, Plato (see Chapter 6) called for women to be men's equal partners, but popular literature almost always presented women as despicable creatures. Even women who were intellectually superior to men were portrayed as dangerous or vulgar.

One of the discredited notions is of Greek "purity"—the idea that the Greeks were a self-made civilization, owing almost nothing to other cultures. To some extent, this was one of their myths of themselves: a way of differentiating themselves from foreigners, whom the Greeks equated with barbarians. Indeed, the Greeks went beyond mere imitation when they received influences, whether from abroad or from an antiquity that they saw as their own. But they were heavily indebted to what they called Asia, which to them, included Egypt, and, especially, to Lydia, Lycia, Phrygia in Anatolia and to the Ionian islands in the Aegean. Here—as we shall see in the next chapter—the learning we call Greek first appeared. Helicon (the mountain sacred to the Muses, the nine goddesses who presided over the arts and learning) had, as scholars now say, an east face. Greece was not merely Greek. It was a land open to the eastern Mediterranean, and influences from around the sea's rim fashioned Greek culture.

The Spread of State-Building and City-Building

Phoenician and Greek colonization and trade made the Mediterranean a highway of cultural exchange. Around and across its peninsulas lay a thick crust of peoples who could build up a large surplus of resources, strong states, monumental cities, literate culture, and vibrant art (see Map 5.1). Most of them tend to get left out of books on global history, because they are ill known or underrated. But they help us see the Phoenicians and Greeks in context. They also help us understand the later role of the region in the world—what made the Mediterranean a potential forge of empires and fount of influence for the future. A tour is in order.

THE THRACIANS The lands of the Thracians lay along the Aegean Sea, north and east of Greece. Thracian history has to be felt and inferred, for their written works have perished. Perhaps this is because they chose odd materials, like the mushroom on which the last Thracian ruler wrote a message to a Roman emperor in the first century C.E. Scholars have not been able to decipher the only surviving Thracian inscription, even though it was written in Greek letters. But archaeology gives us inklings of their culture.

Because Thrace was close to the trading centers of the eastern Mediterranean, its chiefs made an early start accumulating wealth and state-building. They practiced rites of fire, commemorated in spiraling incisons that swirled on their hearths. A fine example imitates a shimmering Sun. A horseback hero

A CLOSER LOOK

THRACIAN HORSEBACK HERO

Pre-Christian fragments of Thracian art sometimes survive because Christians recycled them as building material for churches. This heroic figure on a horse was a favorite subject for Thracian artists. Goldsmiths had depicted a similar figure, known to historians as "The Master of the Animals," for centuries.

Dominating a rearing horse and calmly feeding a lion, the hero has powers of control over sometimes unconquerable and savage forces of nature. The posture of the horse has signified command in Western art and imagery ever since.

The hero's servant contributes to mastery of the horse by pulling its tail. Perhaps in an attempt to represent Alexander the Great (r. 336–323 B.C.E.) as divine, later artists copied this feature in their depictions of him.

Two women are often onlookers in pre-Christian sacred scenes from Thrace.

How does this image shed light on state-building and cultural exchange in the Mediterranean world around 500 B.C.E.?

134

dominated their art, and defaced images at early Christian shrines leave no doubt that he was worshipped. In surviving examples he hunts with hounds, wrestles a three-headed monster, leads a bear in triumph, and does battle among severed heads.

Around 500 B.C.E., energetic rulers unified the Thracian city-states into a kingdom and sought to expand their domain. These were flesh-and-blood figures whom we know from Greek sources, not mythic heroes. In 429, the Thracian King Sitalkes invaded Macedonia in northern Greece with an army said to number 150,000. There he built a palace-city of 12.5 acres, mostly of mud bricks and painted stucco. His failure to build a permanent empire marks a new period, when Thracian states squirmed to survive alongside mightier neighbors.

THE ILLYRIANS AND GARAMANTES On both shores of the central Mediterranean were thriving civilizations about which we now know little because few sources from them have survived. To the Thracians' west, along the coast of the Adriatic Sea around 500 B.C.E., lay Illyria, whose rulers and elites were buried with hoards of gold and silver and sacrifices of oxen and wild boar. The most famous object they are known to have left—an urn found at Vace in present-day Slovenia—depicts the luxurious life of an Illyrian court. Warriors parade. Hawkers and deer hunters stalk. Dignitaries display their authority with double-headed scepters or play on pipes. Voluptuous, long-haired women feed them.

Across the Mediterranean in North Africa, in the ferociously hot and dry region of Libya called the Fezzan (feh-ZAN), lived the Garamantes. They dug nearly a thousand miles of irrigation tunnels under the Sahara desert, carving out the limestone that lies between the water table and the sand. On all sides, desert surrounded their cities, of which, according to Roman reports, there were fourteen. The Garamantes grew wheat where they could and barley elsewhere. No records of their own survive, but early Greek descriptions call them a slave-trading elite, driving four-horse chariots. Romans depicted their tattooed and ritually scarred faces under ostrich-plume helmets.

THE ETRUSCANS On the north shore of the Mediterranean, stretching like a garter across central Italy, was Etruria, the land of the Etruscans. Their "loamy, fat and stoneless" soil had to be plowed nine times to make a furrow, so they needed the iron mines of Elba, a nearby island, and the most up-to-date smelting technology. Much of the region, however, lay under malarial marshes that the Etruscans drained. Their language, which their neighbors could not understand, became a soothsayers' tongue in Roman times, and was then forgotten. So we cannot decipher their inscriptions.

We can, however, glimpse Etruscan culture through their arts. Theater was their specialty. They gave the Romans their word for actor: *hister*. After acting, soothsaying was the skill they esteemed most, reading omens from sheep's livers and the flight of birds. These were borrowed techniques. Sheep's livers, for example, were called "tablets of the gods" in ancient Mesopotamia. Like the Phoenicians (and perhaps thanks to trade with them), Etruscan culture drew from all over the Mediterranean.

Etruscan cities were the earliest in Italy. Caere covered 150 acres and Tarquinii 135. Each could have accommodated 20,000 inhabitants. The layout of their tombs imitated their houses, as if to prepare for an afterlife. In a tomb at Caere, a warrior lies alongside two chariots, with shields and arrows nailed to the

Soothsayer. A diviner between earth and heaven. The legendary Greek soothsayer, Chalcas, whose name is clearly legible in the inscription, sprouts wings in this late fifth-century B.C.E. bronze mirror, as he peers at the liver of a sacrificed animal, searching for auguries.

A ceramic sarcophagus from a richly painted Etruscan burial chamber of the sixth century B.C.E. at Cerveteri in central Italy. The couple is shown together, hospitably sitting up as if to entertain visitors. They appear in death as they might have in life—reclining together at a dinner party, exchanging affection with vivid realism. The scene would be unimaginable in Greece at the time, where women were confined to subordinate roles. *Sarcophagus of a married couple on a funeral bed. Etruscan, from Cerveteri, 6th BCE. Terracotta. Lewandowski/Ojeda. Musee Louvre, Paris France. RMN Reunion Des Musees Nationeaux/Art Resource, NY*

walls. It is tempting to identify him as a king of Caere whom Roman sources reviled for having "mocked the gods" with cruelty to his captives. But the grave was not made for him. The tomb's best chamber houses a heavily bejeweled woman. Strewn around her, objects of gold, silver, and ivory are marked with her name: Larthia.

Among the Etruscans, women had freedom Greeks and Romans of the time mistook for immodesty. They could go out of their homes, attend games, dine with men. In Greek art, the only women who did such things were prostitutes, but Etruscan wives routinely dined with their husbands. In one tomb, a married couple was buried under a portrait showing them reclining as companions, side by side on a couch, in the way Mediterranean elites of the time typically ate dinner. With easy affection, he draws her close, as she offers him a garland of flowers. Since mirrors and combs often display inscriptions, we can assume upper-class Etruscan women were literate.

In Greek and Roman eyes, Etruscans spent too much time on grooming and dress, like characters in ads on television, and wantonly displayed their bodies, like beach cultists in modern California. Accusations that Etruscans performed sexual acts in public may be only slight exaggerations. On the wall of one tomb, a half-naked couple shares a bed. Depictions of banquets show nude serving boys, as in Greece—but this may have been normal attire, or lack of it, for the young.

SPAIN In the mid-millennium, Greeks said, "The god of riches dwells in Spain." Treasures of Spain survive. From a western Spanish province comes a belt decorated with a hero in combat with a lion and a huge funeral monument depicting a banquet of monsters—one with two heads, one with a forked tongue—feeding on wild boar. In another scene, a hero challenges a fire-breathing monster. The region evidently had an elite with the resources to build on a large scale and the power to inspire heroic and terrible images of authority.

From eastern Spain comes an imposing female sculpture—startling in its realism—called the Lady of Elche. Originally, she was probably enthroned in a tomb. A hollow space in her back may have held an offering to the gods or the ashes or bones of a human fellow occupant. Her luxurious dress, elaborate hairstyle, grand headdress, and enormous jewels, which bulge like Hollywood costume pieces, leave no doubt of her social status or the wealth of the society that produced her.

FROM THE MEDITERRANEAN TO THE ATLANTIC
From deep inside the steamship age, it is hard to imagine how inhibiting was the strength of the eight-knot current—the "rapacious wave," a Greek poet called it—that stoppered the Atlantic entrance to the Mediterranean. Here, according to myth, the divine hero Hercules erected his pillars as a warning against the monster-haunted "sea of darkness" beyond. But Greek and Phoenician traders braved them. Tartessos, their first destination,

Greece and the Mediterranean

(All dates are approximate)	
1000–900 B.C.E.	End of Greek dark ages
750 B.C.E.	Trade expands and Greek cities line the Mediterranean
500s B.C.E.	Greek colonies spread
500 B.C.E.	Thracian city-states united
500 B.C.E.	Illyrian, Garamantine, Etruscan, and Spanish civilizations thrive
100 B.C.E.	*Iliad* and the *Odyssey* probably written down

was the Eldorado of its day. At its heart, lay the iron pyrites belt—an area in southern Portugal and Spain, rich in iron, copper, silver, gold. The banks of the Rio Tinto are blotched with the flow of copper-bearing ores. Miners dug deep underground galleries, drained with siphons.

Greek tales help us reconstruct Tartessos' history. Early stories are of a shepherd king, Geryon, followed by Theron, a conqueror so powerful it took the strength of Hercules to halt him. Then, in the mid-first millennium B.C.E., King Arganthonios was said to have subsidized the city walls that protected the marketplace of Phocaea at the other end of the Mediterranean. For a transition of this kind, from pastoralism to plutocracy, trading partners were essential. But Tartessos belongs to a long tradition of civilization-building in Spain, dimly detectable in even earlier treasure hordes. Native cultures, given the resources, were capable of spontaneous economic growth.

EMPIRES AND RECOVERY IN CHINA AND SOUTH ASIA

Summaries nearly always distort. But it is probably fair to say that the story of this chapter so far is one of formerly marginal regions becoming—at least for a while—rich and powerful, like Phoenicia and Greece, Assyria and Babylon, and parts of the western and central Mediterranean, as if to replace the old centers of power and wealth in Lower Mesopotamia, Hatti, and Crete. This suggests problems to bear in mind when confronting what happened in China and South Asia in the same period: Were the traditions of the Shang and Zhou, in China, and of Harappa in India passed on to successors in new places? Or was the continuity of history ruptured, and a new beginning made in new locations?

Lady of Elche. The limestone sculpture known as the Lady of Elche evokes the splendor of Iberian civilization in the first millennium B.C.E. Carved with startling realism, she was originally enthroned and housed in a tomb, with offerings concealed in a hollow in her back. Her luxurious dress, elaborate hairdo, and bulging jewels were glamorously painted.

The Zhou Decline

When the Zhou conquered the Shang, they explained their victory as a mandate from heaven—they were divinely chosen to rule the world because they were more virtuous than the Shang (see Chapter 4). This was all well and good, but as Zhou supremacy spread, the realm became increasingly decentralized. Moreover, the impossibility of using magic to manage the state undermined royal authority. Zhou rituals to appease the gods became ever more elaborate: The vessels got bigger, the ceremonies larger scale, the hymns of praise to Zhou ancestors more extravagant. "Heaven's mandate is unending," intoned the court poets and congregations, with evident unease. A poet in the provinces disagreed: "Drought has become so severe, ... glowing, burning. ... The great mandate is about to end."

King Li (LEE) ascended the throne in 857 B.C.E. Chroniclers portrayed him as a failure—self-indulgent and heedless of advice. After all, if he had been virtuous, he would not have lost the mandate of heaven. A bronze inscription preserves Li's own version: "Although I am but a young boy, I have no leisure day or night," sacrificing to ancestors, elevating "eminent warriors" and well-recommended sages. But there was more urgent business than these ceremonial acts. In 842 B.C.E., rebels drove him from his capital, eventually installing the young heir, Xuan (shoo-ehn). For a reign of 46 years, Xuan held off the main external threat, the western barbarians, while trying to confront natural disasters with magic.

When he died in 782 B.C.E.—reputedly murdered by the ghost of a subordinate he had unjustly executed—an earthquake hit. "The hundred rivers bubble and jump, the mountains and mounds crumble and fall." Following tradition, the poet blamed the disaster on the government's shortcomings. But the problems went much deeper. As wealth from Zhou trickled outward from trade, outlying states grew more powerful and insubordinate. In 771 B.C.E., people whom the Zhou called "Dog barbarians" drove them from their ancestral lands forever.

The Zhou moved east, to a region much changed since its glorious era under the Shang. Zhou garrisons had colonized it and divided it among 148 *fiefs* that Zhou relatives or nominees ruled. Consolidation and reconfiguration gradually reduced the number, and by the sixth century B.C.E., the former empire had been transformed into jostling states (see Map 5.2). Leadership among them was usually determined by war—and, within states, by assassination and massacre. In 541 B.C.E., at one of the periodic summits of rulers, Zhao Yang (jaow yahng), the leading minister of the largest state north of the Yellow River, summed up what Chinese historians came to call the "Warring States Period":

> Ever since the time when there has not been a true king, rulers of states have competed to preside at the inter-state conferences, which therefore rotate among the rulers. Is there a constant leader? . . . Which presiding state can pass judgment?

The kind of instability that Yang described seems bound to inhibit cultural and economic development and unleash violence. Yet the consequences were, in some respects, the opposite. As we shall see in the next chapter, the vibrant era of thinking and learning from the sixth century B.C.E. onward mainly coincided

MAP 5.2

China and South Asia ca. 750 B.C.E.

China during Warring States Period

barbarian incursions

Ganges River Valley

Sinhalese cultural area

with the failures or absence of imperial initiatives. Politically fragmented environments fostered intellectual endeavor. Indeed, well before the turn of the mid-millennium, this fact was evident in the new initiatives and new thinking in South Asia.

South Asia: Relocated Centers of Culture

After the erosion and disappearance of the Harappan cities, Indian history differed in an important respect from other regions of large-scale state-building and city-building. In Europe, Mesopotamia, Phoenicia, and China, as we have seen, people tried to cope with the instabilities of the late second millennium in various ways. All depended on the survival or revival of previous traditions or on stimulation by outside influences. But India provides clear proof that such conditions were not necessary.

Historical orthodoxy has long insisted that something of the Harappan past—some migrants, some aspects of culture—must have survived. Indian civilization seems to deserve a pedigree as old as the Indus cities, and those cities, in turn, deserve to have left lasting traditions. But written and archaeological sources are few, and we have no evidence of real continuities or unmistakable transmissions of culture across the dark, undocumented centuries of Indian history. When civilization did reemerge in South Asia in the first millennium B.C.E., it was in two areas. One was the Ganges valley and the other was the island of Sri Lanka, which was once known as Ceylon.

The Ganges Valley

After a lapse of centuries, iron axes cleared the way for farming in the Ganges valley, a different environment from the hot, dry floodplains of the Indus valley. It was a region of abundant rain and rich forests. We have no knowledge that the Ganges received colonists from Harappa at the time. The only artifacts from the region during this period are fine copperware, which no one has found in the art of the Indus people, although some decorative designs may be similar.

Later Indian cultural history does not exhibit strong evidence that Harappan culture was transplanted to the Ganges, either. Only pottery fragments exist, with glazes similar to Harappan wares. Moreover, the first urban sites and fortifications in the Ganges valley have none of the tell-tale signs of Harappan order: no seals, no weights and measures, no uniform bricks. This makes it hard to believe that the Ganges civilization could be the Harappan civilization transplanted. On the contrary, the lack of material evidence makes early Indian civilization seem even more distant from the Harappan than Greek civilization was from the Cretan and Mycenaean. In only one respect does the world of the Ganges clearly resemble that of Harappa—we know all but nothing about its political and social life.

The literature of its sages, however, survives in abundance. It is impossible to find evidence for traditional claims that the earliest texts originate from orally transmitted traditions from deep in the previous millennium. But surviving versions could have begun to be written down early in the first millennium B.C.E. The theoretical sections of these texts, the **Upanishads** (oo-PAH-nee-shahdz), show the recollection of a time when teaching passed from one generation to another by word of mouth. The very name "Upanishad" means something like "the seat close to the master."

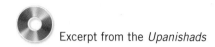

Excerpt from the *Upanishads*

One of the earliest Upanishads tells how the powers of nature rebelled against nature itself—how the lesser gods challenged the supreme god **Brahman** (BRAH-mahn) and failed. "But the fire could not burn straw without Brahman. The wind could not blow the straw away without Brahman." On its own, the story might suggest no more than a doctrine of divine omnipotence, similar to the doctrines Jews, Christians, and Muslims hold. But in the context of the other Upanishads, it seems part of a more general, mystical belief in the oneness of the universe, infinite and eternal. Such a "theory of everything" does not appear in the thought of earlier civilizations.

Sages of the time proclaimed two more stunningly new ideas. The first was that matter is an illusion. The world is Brahman's dream; the creation of the world was like a falling asleep. Sense organs can tell us nothing that is true. Speech is illusory since it relies on lips and tongues. Thought is illusory, since it happens in—or at least passes through—the body. Most feelings are illusory because our nerves and guts register them. We can glimpse truth only in purely spiritual visions or certain kinds of feeling, like selfless love and unspecific sadness, which do not arise from particular physical stimuli. Second, the Upanishads describe a cycle of reincarnation or rebirth. Through a series of lives virtuously lived, the soul can advance toward perfection, at which time its identity is submerged in the divine "soul of the world" known as Brahman.

These profound ideas are so startling and innovative that we want to know how they occurred. And who were the patrons and pupils of the sages who uttered them? Why did society value such sublimely unworldly—such apparently useless—speculations? We have no evidence on which to base answers to these questions. But these ideas are glimmerings of a new era of unprecedented and intense intellectual activity. Ideas from this period—from about the sixth century B.C.E. to about the first century C.E.—are antiquity's most influential legacy to us and the subject of our next chapter. They still inform the questions that confront our religions and philosophies and still mold the way we think about them.

Building Anew in Sri Lanka

South Asia's other nursery of large-scale cities and states was in Sri Lanka, off the southern tip of India, in the Indian Ocean (see Map 5.2). Here, the *Mahavamsa* (ma-ha-VAHM-sah), chronicles of the long-lived "Lion Kingdom," are deceptive documents. In surviving versions, they were written down in what Westerners think of as the sixth century C.E., to serve a partisan political purpose: to justify the ruling *Sinhalese* (sihn-hah-LEEZ) people, sanctify their ground, legitimize their conquests. Their account of the early history of the kingdom features a prince born of a lion who battles with amorous female demons. The founders of the realm are characters in a familiar moral fable of the sea: storm-driven exiles, redeemed from sins bemoaned but never described. The chronicles begin the history of the kingdom with a credible event: colonization by seafarers from the Indian Ocean Gulf of Cambay, on the edge of the Harappan culture area. But the *Sinhalese* had no known connection with the Harappans. They became large-scale builders and irrigators but produced nothing to rival the logic, creative literature, mathematics, and speculative science written down along the Ganges about 2,500 years ago.

The heartland of the early kingdom was in the relatively dry northern plateau, where annual rainfall is heavy—about 60 inches a year—but painfully long dry spells are common. In summer, droughts crack the earth, shrivel the scrub, and scatter dust everywhere. Nowadays in the dry zone, rice cultivation relies on village reservoir tanks dug out of seasonal streams, dammed with earth. There is not always enough water for annual crops of rice. Even if we allow for changes in the climate, the *Sinhalese* colonists could not have built great cities without considerable feats of hydraulic ingenuity. At Maduru Oya, for instance, watertight valves dammed the flow of water from artificial lakes six miles long. Even before the adoption of Buddhism, which tradition dates to the third century B.C.E., Anuradhapura (an-uh-rad-POO-ra) was a large and splendid capital, with the largest artificial reservoir in the world (see chapter-opening illustration).

The new initiatives in the Ganges valley and in Sri Lanka exhibit so little connection to earlier civilizations or to others of this era that we have to acknowledge that civilizations can arise without the help either of recovered traditions or stimulation from outside influences. Yet the question remains, why didn't what happened in India occur in most of the rest of the world? If people in the Ganges valley and Sri Lanka could build states and cities without traditions from the past or influences from outside, why did something similar not occur in the Americas and most of Africa? Why were these vast regions relatively dormant for so long, despite the promising starts described in earlier chapters?

India and Sri Lanka

(All dates are approximate)	
1000 B.C.E.	Civilization emerging in Ganges valley
800 B.C.E.	Upanishads probably written down
? B.C.E.	*Sinhalese* colonize Sri Lanka
500 C.E.	*Mahavamsa* probably written down

THE FRUSTRATIONS OF ISOLATION

In discussing developments in the Americas and Africa, we have to allow for a trick of the evidence. The cultures of Eurasia churned out huge amounts of documents and literature, much of which we can read today. This alone accounts for their dominant place in historical tradition, compared with cultures that employed other, less accessible ways to record events and ideas. In the West, prejudice also favors Eurasian cultures over others. That is, we pay more attention to history that seems to anticipate the way we live now. Sometimes we read into that history the origins of our own societies. Conversely, we overlook or fail to recognize history that appears too different from our own.

Compared to Eurasia, the geography of the Americas and sub-Saharan Africa discourages communication and cultural exchange (see Map 5.3). Much of Africa and Central and South America lies in the tropics, where dense rain forests make it difficult and unhealthy for any outsider attempting to cross them. Africa has relatively few rivers, and for the most part, they do not allow long-range navigation. In Eurasia, cultural exchange was rapid. It happened across zones of similar climate, with no need for either the people or the food plants and livestock they brought with them to adapt. Cultural transmission in Africa and the Americas, on the other hand, had to cross vast chasms of climate from north to south and south to north, calling for different survival strategies along the way.

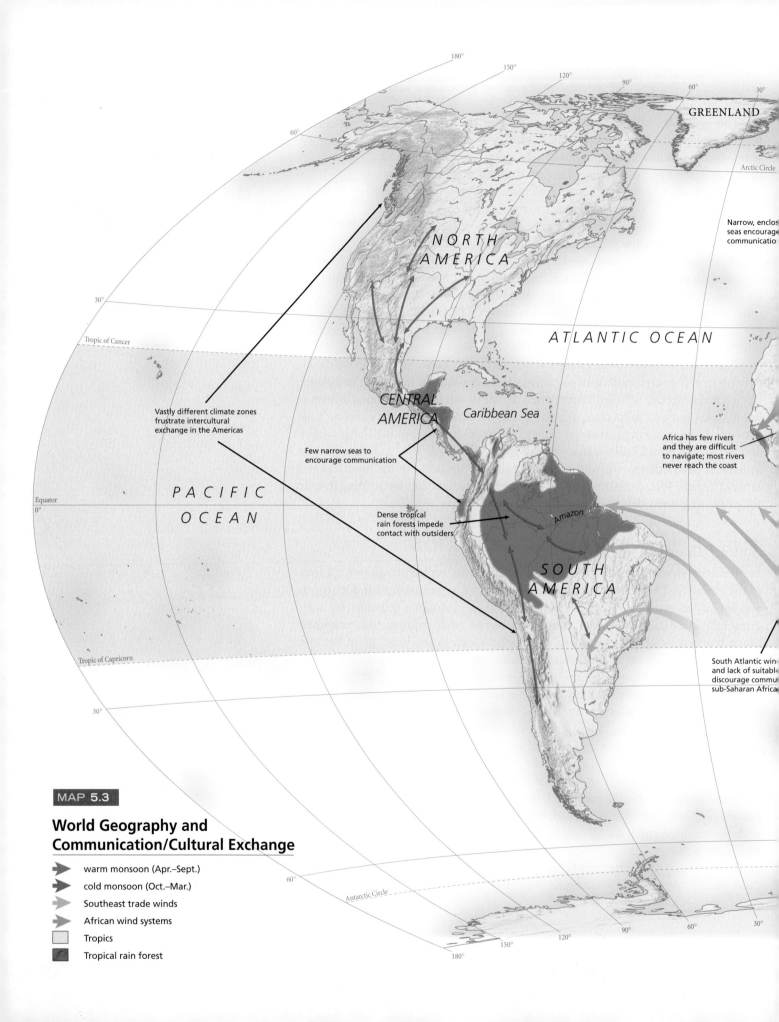

GREENLAND

Arctic Circle

NORTH
AMERICA

Narrow, enclos
seas encourag
communicatio

60°

30°

Tropic of Cancer

ATLANTIC OCEAN

CENTRAL
AMERICA   *Caribbean Sea*

Vastly different climate zones
frustrate intercultural
exchange in the Americas

Africa has few rivers
and they are difficult
to navigate; most rivers
never reach the coast

Few narrow seas to
encourage communication

Equator
0°

PACIFIC
OCEAN

Dense tropical
rain forests impede
contact with outsiders

Amazon

SOUTH
AMERICA

South Atlantic win
and lack of suitabl
discourage commu
sub-Saharan Africa

Tropic of Capricorn

30°

Antarctic Circle

60°

MAP 5.3

World Geography and
Communication/Cultural Exchange

- warm monsoon (Apr.–Sept.)
- cold monsoon (Oct.–Mar.)
- Southeast trade winds
- African wind systems
- Tropics
- Tropical rain forest

Rapid cultural exchange
across similar climate zones

Narrow, enclosed
seas encourage
communication

Monsoonal
wind system
favors navigation

Black Sea

Mediterranean Sea

Persian Gulf

Red Sea

Nile

ARABIA

Arabian
Sea

INDIA

Ganges

SRI
LANKA

Yellow River

Yangtze River

Yellow Sea

Sea
of
Japan

Mekong

South
China
Sea

E U R A S I A

OCEAN

RICA

PACIFIC
OCEAN

INDIAN OCEAN

AUSTRALIA

TICA

Arctic Circle

Tropic of Cancer

Equator

Tropic of Capricorn

Antarctic Circle

N

500 km

500 miles

North America

Civilizations developing between 1000 and 500 B.C.E.

Dorset culture—Northwest Canada to the Arctic

Poverty Point—Gulf of Mississippi

Foraging communities—Ohio River valley

San Juan and Tucson basins—Southwest United States

Monsoonal wind systems in much of maritime Asia and relatively stable weather in the Mediterranean favor navigation. By contrast, lee* shores and hostile winds enclose and hem in much of sub-Saharan Africa. Except in the Caribbean, the Americas have none of the narrow seas and with which parts of Europe and Asia are relatively well endowed that encourage communication. Even the civilizations of the Ganges and Sri Lanka, though they originated independently, could take advantage of the communications systems of maritime Asia and trans-Eurasian trade routes early in their histories, linking up with China and southwest Asia by land and sea.

Developments in North America

In any case, there were plenty of developments in the world beyond Eurasia between 1000 and 500 B.C.E., and they tend to get left out of the global story, overshadowed by more spectacular changes in Eurasia. In the American far north, for instance, the Dorset culture, transformed life. People there began to build semisubterranean longhouses and stone alleys for driving caribou into lakes. Their art realistically depicted all the species that shared their environment.

The critical new technology was the blubber-fueled soapstone lamp, which enabled the Dorset people to colonize deserts of ice. Now hunters could go far from home in the Arctic darkness, tracking the musk ox to graveyards on the shore of the Arctic, devouring its entrails, boiled and dressed with seal oil. They could pursue the caribou to remote salt licks. For the caribou cannot be hunted at the hunter's pleasure. You have to wait until the beginning of winter, when its hair is thick enough to make the warmest clothing. No longer limited to the forest, the users of oil lamps could hunt on the ice, where abundant fat game waited without competitors and where the climate preserved carcasses. People of the Dorset culture speared seals and harpooned walruses from kayaks on the open sea. Now that their prey was too fat to be felled by arrows, they abandoned the bow for the barbed harpoon. Ingenious notched blades stayed in the victim's flesh, until it was so tired that it could be hauled in, butchered, and sped home on hand-drawn sleds with runners of walrus ivory.

Equally dramatic new ways of life developed in the same period—between the late second and mid-first millennia B.C.E.—on the lower Mississippi River and the coast of the Gulf of Mexico (see Map 5.4). The culture—inappropriately called Poverty Point after the location of its biggest site in Louisiana—worked in copper and manufactured fine tools and jewelry of colorful stones. Trade goods arrived along the Mississippi, Red, and Tennessee Rivers. More than a hundred sites, grouped around ten major centers, appear to be forager settlements comparable to settlements in the Middle East (see Chapter 2). The biggest covers a square mile and is divided by a series of semicircular earth work ridges. Alongside is a mound almost 70 feet high, which appears oriented to the spring and autumn equinox. The mound is a ceremonial center utterly unlike anything seen earlier in Mesoamerica and therefore likely to have grown up independently.

Poverty Point in Louisiana is the oldest and one of the most impressive of the mound-builders' sites of the lower Mississippi valley. The plaza shown in this drawing was in place by about 1000 B.C.E. The mound on the edge of the concentric ridges is 70 feet high.

Drawing by Jon L. Gibson

---

*Lee: the side away from the direction from which the wind blows.

ARCTIC
OCEAN

GREENLAND

ARCTIC
OCEAN

Dorset Culture

A R C T I C

NORTH

AMERICA

Mississippi

ATLANTIC
OCEAN

San Juan
Basin

Ohio River
Ohio River Valley
Tennessee River

SOUTHWEST

PACIFIC
OCEAN

ARIZONA

Tucson
Basin

Tucson

Red River
Poverty Point

LOUISIANA

Mississippi

Tropic of Cancer

Gulf
of
Mexico

Caribbean
Sea

MAP 5.4

Tropic of Cancer

MESOAMERICA

MEXICO

North America, ca. 1000–500 B.C.E

	Dorset cultural area
	mound-building culture of Ohio River valley
	cultures of American Southwest
ARIZONA	modern-day state
squash
maize
beans
grains
sunflower
burial mounds
musk
aquatic mammals

Olmecs

N

Equator

500 km

500 miles

Meanwhile, burial mounds in the Ohio River valley provide evidence of new social patterns and perhaps chiefdoms. Here, settled foragers planted grains and sunflowers to supplement the food they gathered and hunted, painted their dead in lively colors, and buried them with ornaments of copper and shell.

In the same period, contact with Mesoamerica brought about changes in parts of the North American Southwest. In the San Juan and Tucson basins in Arizona, people developed a new variety of maize that matured in 120 days. They could now cultivate maize in dryer areas where squash also grew. From around 500 B.C.E., the number of sites with traces of beans greatly increased. Farmers in the region were working their way toward the same complete system of nutrition—maize, squash, beans—that the Olmecs had developed in Mexico (see Chapter 4).

New Initiatives in Africa

As in North America, change between 1000 and 500 B.C.E. in Africa was slow and localized compared to the most dynamic parts of Eurasia. Nonetheless, events set a direction for the future. Four developments in particular are worth mentioning (see Map 5.5). First, around 750 B.C.E., Egypt weakened, and a Nubian state reemerged on the Upper Nile (see Chapter 4), with its chief cities at Napata (na-PAY-tuh) and Meroe (MEHR-oh-ee). Ever since Egypt had first colonized Nubia, Egyptian culture had heavily influenced it. Late in the millennium, however, the language of the Nubian royal court changed from Egyptian to an indigenous Nubian tongue. Scholars today have difficulty reading the distinctive script in which this language was written. This change shows that Nubia was becoming less Egyptian and more Sudanic, or, as some scholars like to say, more African.

Second, Africans developed hard-iron technology. This was almost certainly an independent discovery. African smiths had smelted soft iron and copper for centuries. The first iron foundries emerged along the Niger (NEYE-jurh) River in West Africa around 500 B.C.E., and again, perhaps independently, in Central Africa's Great Lakes region soon after. Natural drafts fanned the furnaces that melted the iron ore through long clay tubes. The people who made the tubes also left clay heads—wide-eyed, open-mouthed, partly shaved, with decoratively scarred foreheads. The use of fired clay suggests how Africans may have made the breakthrough in iron forging. These were people who knew the seemingly magical uses of fire—how fire turns hard what is soft and helps make art out of mud. Forging iron was a further stage in the process of exploring the potential of fire.

Third, Bantu languages continued their slow spread south (see Chapter 1), reaching the Great Lakes of Central Africa by about 1000 B.C.E. In this region, farmers could grow grains as well as yams, a major improvement in nutrition. Surplus production of food made trade with Nubia possible. Trade was part of a broader shift to new ways of life. At about this time, too, round dwellings with conical roofs replaced rectangular ones with ridged roofs. By the end of the first millennium B.C.E., thanks, perhaps, to improved tools made of iron, Bantu farmers reached what are now Kenya in East Africa and South Africa.

Finally, the growth of trade was pregnant with consequences for the future. The slaving activities of the Garamantes from what is today Libya suggest that one of the major routes to tropical Africa was already developing across the Sahara from the Mediterranean. The other great potential link was across the Indian

Heads sculpted from coarse-grained clay, in what is now central Nigeria, in the second half of the first millennium B.C.E., are not just fine works of art—as this example of the first century B.C.E. shows. They are also evidence of the technical accomplishments of the craftsmen who made clay tubing for the forges in which iron tools were made.

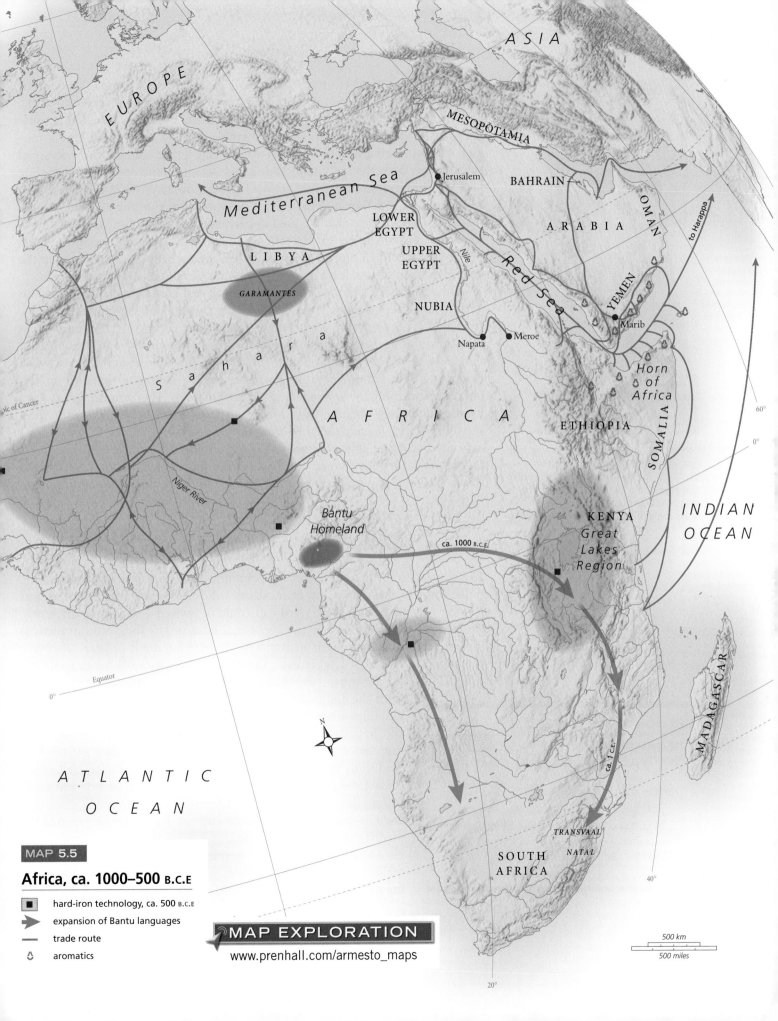

ASIA

EUROPE

Mediterranean Sea

MESOPOTAMIA

Jerusalem

BAHRAIN

LOWER
EGYPT

ARABIA

OMAN

to Harappa

LIBYA

UPPER
EGYPT

Nile

Red Sea

GARAMANTES

YEMEN

Marib

Sahara

NUBIA

Napata

Meroe

Horn
of
Africa

Tropic of Cancer

A F R I C A

60°

ETHIOPIA

SOMALIA

0°

Niger River

Bantu
Homeland

ca. 1000 B.C.E.

KENYA
Great
Lakes
Region

INDIAN
OCEAN

Equator

0°

ca. 1000 B.C.E.

MADAGASCAR

N

ca. 1 C.E.

ATLANTIC

OCEAN

TRANSVAAL

NATAL

SOUTH
AFRICA

40°

MAP 5.5

Africa, ca. 1000–500 B.C.E

■ hard-iron technology, ca. 500 B.C.E

➤ expansion of Bantu languages

— trade route

♨ aromatics

MAP EXPLORATION

www.prenhall.com/armesto_maps

500 km

500 miles

20°

Incense burner. An alabaster incense burner from Saba in southern Arabia, made in the third century B.C.E. The inscription records the name of the donor who gave it to a temple. The camel rider is carrying a pod of incense.
The Trustees of the British Museum.

Ocean from Asia to the Horn of Africa in what is today Somalia and Ethiopia. This link was at least as important for the history of civilization in East Africa as the link to the Mediterranean was to Europe. We do not know when this route opened, but developments in southern Arabia provide clues about how it may have begun. Southern and southeast Arabia has fertile valleys, where seasonal streams flow from the mountains before they soak into the desert and evaporate into the air. Here, the areas that are now Oman (oh-MAN) and Bahrain forged copper goods, and Yemen (YEH-mehn) produced frankincense and myrrh, aromatic resins from trees that are used in perfumes and, as biblical accounts show, were much in demand for religious rituals. Some of these goods reached Mesopotamia and Harappan cities. But when those civilizations collapsed in the second millennium B.C.E., so did most economic development in this region.

Only Saba (SAH-bah), a state in the southwest corner of Arabia, closest to Africa, continued to grow. This was where the Queen of Sheba supposedly came from to King Solomon in Jerusalem in the tenth century B.C.E., if we can trust traditional biblical chronology. Numerous inscriptions survive from soon after that time. A temple outside Marib (MA-rihb), the Sabaeans' chief city, bears bronze plaques commemorating victories—grisly scenes of warriors in triumph, brandishing the severed hands of their victims. This same temple houses bronze sculptures—tribute from kings and landowners, some, evidently, personal likenesses. Piecing together the inscriptions, we see how the Sabaean state expanded at its neighbors' expense. Understanding what happened in Saba is the best way to study one of the most intriguing problems in the next part of this book—the growth of great states, great buildings, and great ambitions in East Africa.

IN PERSPECTIVE: The Framework of Recovery

The climacteric of the late second millennium B.C.E. damaged and changed the frameworks of civilization but in most cases did not break them. Recovery was possible because traditions survived—or could be revived—or because there were stimulating outside influences. In Greece and India, people forgot the art of writing, and they had to reinvent it from scratch after hundreds of years. Recovery sometimes happened in new places and among new peoples. After the extinction of the Harappan world, civilization gradually emerged in India, far from the Indus. In Sri Lanka, monumental irrigation works and buildings arose. In Mesopotamia and China, the centers of activity and initiative were relocated, but, again, the continuities of tradition, which are the foundations of progress, were never entirely lost. Traditions spread through neighboring regions. Greek civilization crystallized on the edges of the Greek world, in islands and small colonies around the Ionian and Aegean Seas. Fertilized by Phoenicia and Greece, a ring of ambitious cities and states formed around the Mediterranean and Black Seas.

Gradually, fitfully, and despite reversals, people continued to make ambitious attempts to modify the environment, transforming new areas. In some parts of Eurasia, the pace of state-building

Africa/Southwest Arabia

(All dates are approximate)	
1000s B.C.E.	Bantu languages expanding southward
900s B.C.E.	Sabaean empire grows
750 B.C.E.	Nubian kingdom reemerges
500 B.C.E.	First iron foundries along Niger River
100s B.C.E.	Bantu languages reach South Africa

○ MAKING CONNECTIONS ○

AMERICAS, AFRICA, AND EURASIAN CIVILIZATIONS: 1000–500 B.C.E.

REGION →	MEANS OF CULTURAL, ECONOMIC, POLITICAL DEVELOPMENT →	DISTINCTIVE ACHIEVEMENTS
Greece	Seaborne trade; colonization of Mediterranean basin; extensive cultural exchange	New forms of government (*demokrateia*) and communities (*poleis, ethne*); colonial autonomy; highly developed written literature
Zhou Dynasty/ Warring States Period (China)	Centralized rule; elaborate court rituals; ancestor worship; trade and taxation; constant threat from barbarians	Political instability fosters intellectual endeavors
Ganges Valley	Highly developed spiritual literature (Vedas, Upanishads); agriculture with iron tools; little understanding of political, economic policies	First philosophies focused on doctrine of reincarnation, *maya* (matter as illusion), large-scale urban settlements, fortifications
Sri Lanka	Sophisticated water-management systems combined with urbanization	Large-scale cities, early adoption of Buddhism from neighboring India
North America	In the far north: decentralized communities, simple technologies, group hunting techniques; South/ Midwest: widespread trade networks connecting to Mesoamerica, settlements	Northern regions: long-term adaptation to hostile environments, gradual depletion of wildlife; South/Midwest: forager settlements, mound building, mixed agriculture/hunting–gathering culture
Sub-Saharan Africa/Southwest Arabia	Widespread trade, cultural exchange with hard-iron technology accelerating tool and weapon making, spread of Bantu language	Growth of Nubian state south of Egypt; sophisticated art, industry in Niger region; building and farming techniques spread with Bantu speakers; trade and state-building in southwest Arabia (Saba)

and economic expansion not only resumed, it quickened. The imperial experiments between 1000 and 500 B.C.E. failed to take hold, but efforts to expand borders and dominate other states became a typical feature of regions where change was accelerating. Political instability among competing states may seem unfavorable, but it stimulated technological change: hotter furnaces, more iron. It also, perhaps, multiplies the opportunities of patronage for artists and intellectuals. An "age of sages" was detectable in India and would soon be apparent in other parts of Eurasia.

In the Mediterranean and what we think of as the Middle East, between 1000 and 500 B.C.E., state-building and growing trade led to imperial ambitions that eventually failed. Elsewhere, imperial projects ran out of steam or into trouble—as in China—or simply did not happen. Was this because the contenders were too well matched? Or was it because the economic environment was too undeveloped

CHRONOLOGY

(All dates are approximate)

1000–500 B.C.E.	Traditions and states of the late second millenium recover; dorset culture in American far north thrives; peoples of lower Mississippi and Gulf of Mexico develop new ways of life
1000 B.C.E.	Civilization reemerges in Ganges valley; bantu languages continue slow spread southward
800 B.C.E.	Phoenicians colonize the Mediterranean
771 B.C.E.	Zhou driven eastward from their ancestral lands
750–500 B.C.E.	Rapid expansion of Greek trading and colonization
750 B.C.E.	Egypt declines and Nubian state reemerges
605–562 B.C.E.	Peak of Babylonian empire
500 B.C.E.	Carthage seeks control of Mediterranean trade until defeated by Romans in 146 B.C.E.; West Africans develop and spread hard-iron technology southward
100s B.C.E.	Bantu languages reach present-day South Africa

or the ecological environment too fragile? Or was it because no conqueror had found an enduring formula, or a means to solidify states that were prone to failure? Whatever the problems that frustrated imperial ambitions in the first half of the millennium, states soon found ways to overcome them. The second half of the millennium was not only remarkable as an age of sages in Eurasia, but also as an age of robust empires. A zone of connected, communicating cultures began to take shape across Eurasia and the Mediterranean, from the Pacific to the Atlantic. They nourished each other. Faint links were beginning to put parts of this central zone in touch with northern Europe and parts of Africa. In the rest of the world, isolated cultures, still organized in kinship groups or chiefdoms or small states, were able, at best, to develop regional networks on a relatively small scale.

As a result, the focus of the next part of this book is on Eurasia and, in particular, the regions where sages founded well-rooted intellectual traditions that have continued, ever since, to shape the way we think: in China, India, southwest Asia, and Greece. These were homelands of huge ambitions to understand the world, change it, or—in some cases—conquer it. Their stories occupy the next chapters.

PROBLEMS AND PARALLELS

1. Why was the ruler of the city-state of Byblos able to stand up to a giant nation-state like Egypt?

2. Why did the Phoenician writing system play such an important role in the "recovery" of the Mediterranean world?

3. How did rulers such as Ashurbanipal and Nebuchadnezzar II enhance and extend their imperial states?

4. Why was Greek cultural influence so important for the Mediterranean world?

5. What evidence for the continuity of Harrapan/Indus valley culture exists in the civilizations of South Asia in the first millennium B.C.E.?

6. How did the interplay of cultures in the Mediterranean and Indian Ocean basins in the first millennium B.C.E. affect the development of civilizations in those areas? How did the isolation characteristic of cultures in the Americas affect the development of civilizations there?

DOCUMENTS IN GLOBAL HISTORY

- Mission to Byblos: *The Report of Wenamun*
- Hesiod, excerpt from *Works and Days*
- Aristophanes, excerpt from *The Birds*
- Excerpt from the *Upanishads*

Please see the Primary Source CD-ROM for additional sources related to this chapter.

READ ON

H. Goedicke, ed., *The Report of Wenamun* (1975) is a first-rate edition of the text. S. Moscati, ed., *The Phoenicians* (1968), and M. A. Aubet, *Phoenicians and the West* (1993) introduce the Phoenicians and their colonies. The standard works by H. W. F. Saggs, *The Might that was Assyria* (1984), and *The Greatness that was Babylon* (1962) are still valuable introductions, as is J. Oates, *Babylon* (1979). J. and D. Oates, *Nimrud* (2001) describes the palace.

S. Hornblower, *Greek World* (1983), and O. Taplin, *Greek Fire* (1989) make exciting introductions to the Greeks. J. Boardman, *The Greeks Overseas* (1964) covers Greek colonization admirably. C. Morgan, *Athletes and Oracles* (1990) is a splendid study. S. B. Pomeroy, *Goddesses, Whores, Wives, and Slaves: Women in classical antiquity* (1995); C. B. Patterson, *The Family in Greek History* (1998); and L. Foxhall and J. Salman, eds., *When Men Were Men* (1998), deal with women. The long quotation from Hesiod on page 130 is from I. Morris and B. Powell, *The Greeks* (2006).

R. F. Hoddinott, *The Thracians* (1981); J. Wilks, *The Illyrians* (1992); C. M. Daniels, *The Garamantes of Southern Libya* (1970), and R. Harrison, *Spain at the Dawn of History* (1988) are outstanding on their respective subjects.

For the Zhou see page 110 above. On the Upanishads, J. Mascaro, *The Upanishads* (1965) is the best edition in translation; N. S. Subrahmanian, *Encyclopedia of the Upanishads* (1985) is a valuable companion.

On North America, B. Trigger and W. E. Washburn, *The Cambridge History of the Peoples of North America* (1996–2000) is an invaluable guide. B. Fagan, *Ancient North America: The Archaeology of a Continent* (1991) is a helpful introduction.

For Bantu languages in particular and the African background in general, J. Ki-Zerbo, ed., *The UNESCO General History of Africa*, i, (1993) is of great value.

Feasting

Feasting is a major topic of interest and controversy in archaeology today. Such questions as *When and why did people begin to gather to consume large amounts of food and drink?* are important for three reasons. First, feasting is a way to measure the success of a society's ability to produce, store, and distribute food. Second, and this is what makes the topic controversial, feasting may reveal facts about origins of political authority, such as chieftainship and kingship. Feasts are not just for enjoyment. They create obligations of gratitude that the feasters owe to the host. To have a feast, some person or persons must be in charge of collecting, storing, and distributing the food. Third, and this is even more controversial, feasting may help us understand how and why human societies began to turn from gathering wild food to producing their own food—from being foragers to being herders and farmers. Could feasting have been the idea or project of leaders who got their authority because they were able to organize feasts?

● ● ● ● ●

HAMBLEDON HILL

MESOPOTAMIA

One revealing archaeological site is Hambledon Hill in southwest England. Here, a complex of ceremonial enclosures surrounded by possible defensive earthworks, was constructed between around 3700 and 3300 B.C.E. by a population scattered over a wide area. Those who gathered at the hill brought with them cattle, pigs, deer, and sheep; wheat and barley that had already been cleaned of chaff; and wild plant foods, especially hazelnuts. Fragments found at the site show that the emphasis was on eating the food rather than producing it—there are a lot of small cups and bowls, suitable for eating and drinking but few large vessels for storing food. The community used the animals it raised for both meat and milk, and the day-to-day diets of the people (or at least those whose remains were buried at the

Pig and cattle bone

Deer antler

Dig from Hambledon Hill

site) were varied. Analysis of human skeletons shows that, while most people in the area obtained the bulk of their protein from animal sources (meat or milk), a minority ate mostly vegetable foods.

Beyond the enclosures on the hill itself, animals were slaughtered and consumed on a large scale. Around the middle period of the site's use, two or three cattle were sometimes butchered and eaten in a single event, each of them yielding some 600 pounds of meat, organ meats, and fat. These quantities must reflect the gathering of hundreds, possibly thousands, of people. The beef may even have been washed down with wine, since archaeologists have found the remains of grapes and grape vines at the site.

It is remarkable that such a large-scale event, bringing together so many eaters at a single meal, took place only a few centuries after agriculture was adopted in this part of the world. Unlike the centrally organized feasts of more complex societies, the feasting at Hambledon Hill may have sprung from the old way of life of the participants' hunter–gatherer ancestors. Once they kill a large animal like a deer or even a wild ox, hunters have to eat the meat quickly in communal meals before it rots.

Meanwhile, in the fully agrarian world of Sumer in Mesopotamia, from early in the third millennium B.C.E., roughly at the time of the Hambledon feast, pictorial sources begin to supplement the archaeological evidence. Pictures of Sumerian kings and queens eating and drinking with other people are among the earliest surviving scenes of royal life. The diners are often seated facing one another, which suggests that the meals were social occasions, rather than, or as well as, offerings made to gods. In any case, they were clearly important, and perhaps symbolic, events, worthy of commemoration.

Typically, the feasts were recorded on clay moldings, the purpose of which seems to have been to make multiple reproductions of the depicted scenes on clay tablets, or on textiles. The aim is unlikely to have been purely decorative because Sumerian kings used clay tablets to make records, write letters, and exchange messages with one another.

Drinking was a common activity, and persons are often shown raising a goblet. Sometimes the drinkers suck the liquid through strawlike tubes—to filter out the grains that often floated on the surface of ancient beer (see Figure 1). Musicians and dancers are sometimes in attendance. The settings include gardens and boats.

Figure 1

Strawlike tube

Gods seem to be present at some banquets—note the horned figure, for instance, in Figure 2. So some feasts may represent the afterlife or funeral rites. Sumerians called death "the invitation of the gods." In the *Epic of Gilgamesh,* the hero Enkidu found that in the underworld, royalty feasted on roast meat, bread, and fresh water.

The biggest banquet scene of the Sumerian period, however, displays a different and celebratory function. The feast shown in the "Standard of Ur" has an obviously political

Horned Figure

Figure 2

meaning. Large amounts of tribute arrive at the royal court, and the rulers consume part of it. The king is the kilted, seated figure near the top left-hand corner of the composition, faced by his guests, all of whom are male. The reverse side of the panel shows the king inspecting prisoners after a victory.

The Standard of Ur, "Peace" panel

Questions to Consider

1 Are there any common threads that underlie the functions of the feasts at Hambeldon and Sumer?

2 How does the evidence from Hambledon and Sumer support the theory that one of the primary purposes of kings and elites was to redistribute food resources?

3 From the evidence we have from Hambledon and Sumer, what can we infer about the role of feasts in fostering group cohesion in ancient societies?

4 How does the function of feasting today compare with the way it was practiced in antiquity?

Sources

Hambledon

Healy, F. 2004. "Hambledon Hill and its implications." In *Monuments and Material Culture. Papers in Honour of an Avebury Archaeologist: Isobel Smith,* edited by R. Cleal and J. Pollard, 15–38. East Knoyle: Hobnob Press.

Jones, G. and Legge, A. 1987. The grape *(Vitis vinifera L.)* in the Neolithic of Britain. *Antiquity* 61, 452–5.

Jones, G. and Legge, A. J. Evaluating the Role of Cereal Cultivation in the Neolithic: Charred Plant Remains from Hambledon Hill. In *Hambledon Hill, Dorset, England. Excavation and Survey of a Neolithic Monument Complex and its Surrounding Landscape,* edited by R. Mercer and F. Healy. English Heritage Archaeological Report, forthcoming.

Sumer

Dentzer, J. M. *Le motif du banquet couche dans le Proche-Orient et le monde grec du VIIe au IVe siecle avant J.-C* (Rome, 1982).

Babylonian World Map The world as seen ▶ from Babylon in the mid-first millennium B.C.E. The circle represents the ocean. The towers of Babylon can be seen just inside the ring. Other cities are indicated by circles, and the Tigris and Euphrates Rivers by lines. *British Museum, London, UK/Bridgeman Art Library*

ENVIRONMENT

since 800 B.C.E.
Trans-Mediterranean trade

since 3000 B.C.E.
Steppe pastoralism

CULTURE

650–550 B.C.E.
Zoroaster

ca. 623–543 B.C.E.
Buddha

551–479 B.C.E.
Confucius

since 300 B.C.E.
Silk Roads;
Monsoon driven Indian
Ocean trade

since 100 B.C.E.
Mediterranean–Atlantic trade

ca. 550–334 B.C.E.
Persian Empire

427–347 B.C.E.
Plato

334–323 B.C.E.
Alexander's
Empire

ca. 300–223 B.C.E.
Mauryan Empire

240 B.C.E.–**400s** C.E.
Roman Empire

221 B.C.E.–
220s C.E.
Han Empire

ca. 3–33 C.E.
Jesus Christ

The Buddha's first sermon, depicted here in a Kushanese relief of the late second or early third century C.E. The Buddha squats under a lotus tree, on a pedestal decorated with a prayer wheel. The attentive figures who stand on small pedestals among the onlookers who surround him are probably the patrons who commissioned this sculpture. Kushanese art—from the mountainous northwest of the Indian subcontinent and Afghanistan—combines influences from India, Persia, Greece, and China, demonstrating the vitality of cultural exchange across Eurasia.
Scenes from the Life of Buddha, late 2nd-early 3rd century, Kushan dynasty, Stone. Courtesy of the Freer Gallery of Art, Smithsonian Institution, Washington, D.C.

J ust over halfway through the first millennium B.C.E., a frustrated administrator in the police service set out from the small Chinese state of Lu (loo), south of the Yellow River, on a journey in search of a worthy master. Conflicting traditions claim him as the descendent of kings and the child of a humble home. By what is said to be his own account, he was a studious child, who worked his way through his education, learning menial jobs, including grain counting and bookkeeping. He could never get ahead in the bureaucracy of Lu, perhaps because he was openly disgusted with the immorality of its politics. A book later published under his name recounts the history of his times in deadpan fashion, listing the violence and injustice of the kings and aristocrats, without any apparent moralizing. The effect heightens the reader's revulsion.

China had fragmented into the warring kingdoms described in the last chapter. It was a time of heightened warfare, in which ruthlessness replaced ritual combat. Thanks to the growth of populations, increasingly wealthy kingdoms mustered ever-larger armies of mass infantry, instead of relying on the more restrained battlefield traditions of professional soldiers and warrior aristocrats. There were plenty of rulers' courts where a sharp-witted official could try his luck in search of employment. But, far as the exile from Lu wandered, he never found the ideal ruler he sought. Instead, he lived by attracting pupils and left a body of thought that still influences ideas on the conduct of politics and the duties and opportunities of daily life. For him—and for most other thinkers in an era disfigured by the disintegration of China—loyalty was the key virtue: loyalty to God, to the state, to one's family, and to the true meanings of the words one uses. Most of the world knows him today by a name that is a corruption of his honorific title: "Master Kong"—Kong Fuzi (koong foo-tzeh) in Chinese, "Confucius" in the West.

● ● ● ● ●

The importance of Confucius is a reminder of how much the world of our own day owes to the world of his—how thinkers of the time anticipated and influenced the way we think now. Heroic teachers gathered disciples and handed down traditions. Typically, followers treated the founders with awestruck reverence, recast them as supermen or even gods, and clouded our knowledge of them with legends and lore. We can unpick enough evidence, however, to get tentative pictures of outstanding examples of some of them—some we even know by name—and some impression of what they taught.

FOCUS questions

- WHAT DO historians mean by the term *axial age*?
- WHAT WERE the main areas of axial-age thinking in Eurasia?
- WHAT WERE the most important religious ideas that developed during the axial age?
- WHAT SIMILARITIES developed among Chinese, Greek, and Indian science and medicine during the axial age?
- HOW DID political pessimists differ from optimists in their ideas about human nature and the role of government?
- WHY WAS the axial age confined to such a limited area of the world?

Between them, these sages came up with ideas so influential as to justify a term that has become popular with scholars: the *axial age*. Different writers assign different meanings to this term. In this chapter and the next, it designates the 500 years or so, roughly up to the beginning of the Christian era. The image of an axis suits the period, for three reasons. First, as a glance at the map shows, the areas in which the thought of the sages and their schools unfolded stretched, axislike, across Eurasia, in regions that more or less bordered on and influenced each other (see Map 6.1). Second, the thought of the period has remained central to, and supporting of, so much later thought—not just in the lands where it originated, but all over the world, as its influence spread with developments described throughout the rest of this book. The religious leaders of the time founded traditions of such power that they have huge followings. The secular thinkers ran out, as if with their fingernails, grooves of logic and science in which people still think. They raised the problems of human nature—and of how we can devise appropriate social and political solutions to these problems—that still preoccupy us. And because disciples wrote down much of their teaching, a body of texts has survived to become reference points for later study.

No one should try to study this material expecting it to be easy. Part of the fun, part of the excitement, is engaging with minds active long ago, but still—with a bit of effort—intelligible to us today and with ideas we can still recognize. We could dodge the difficulties by talking about the personalities instead of the problems of the axial age. But this chapter is designed to concentrate on what the axial-age sages thought and why they thought it—not on their own lives and characters. So, after first briefly outlining who the sages were and where they operated, we shall turn to the common content of their minds: the religious, political, and scientific ideas that characterized the age and made it "axial"—the shared features, which for students of global history are the most interesting.

Finally, we examine the big problem that arises: Why was there an axial age at all? Why did so much thinking—so much enduring thinking, so much thinking that has shaped the world ever since—happen in such a relatively concentrated period? We will try to answer this question, toward the end of the chapter, by investigating the networks to which the sages and their disciples belonged. The way those networks operated is inseparable, of course, from the political and economic history of the age: The last chapter sketched the context from which axial-age thinking arose; the next chapter describes the political world that axial-age thinking formed, and the empires that surrounded, nourished, and transmitted it across the centuries to us.

China, India, Greece, and southwest Asia, as we shall see, were the linked locations in which axial thinking happened. So we also have to keep in mind the problem of why other parts of the world seem to have experienced nothing similar. If Africa, or the Americas, or the Pacific world, or western or northern Europe, or northern or Central Asia had comparable sages and schools, they left no record, and we know nothing of them. But of course, people who lived in those areas did initiate traditions of thought that had local or regional influence, inviting us to try to understand why evidence of those other traditions has not survived and to make comparisons between the Eurasian arena of the axial age and other parts of the world.

THE THINKERS OF THE AXIAL AGE

As we saw in the last chapter, the work of thinkers of great depth and complexity was recorded earlier in India. But that does not necessarily mean that it had happened nowhere else. The idea of writing down thoughts as profound, as precious, or as sacred as those of the sages took hold little by little. To the sages' early disciples, it seemed sacrilege to confide their secrets to writing. Gradually, however, evidence emerged that issues similar to those the Indian Upanishads raised (see Chapter 5) were also attracting attention—whether independently, or as a result of contacts with India, we cannot say—in other parts of Asia.

In the region of southwest Asia, for instance, that we now call Iran, the influential sage usually known as Zoroaster (zoh-roh-AHS-tehr) is rather insecurely dated to the late seventh and early sixth centuries B.C.E. Texts ascribed to him are so partial, corrupt, and obscure that we cannot reconstruct them with confidence. As practiced by his followers, however, and twisted by tradition, Zoroastrianism assumed that conflicting forces of good and evil shaped the world The single good deity, Ahura Mazda (ah-HOO-rah MAHZ-dah), was present in fire and light; the rites of his worshippers were connected with dawn and fire-kindling, while night and darkness were the province of Ahriman, the god of evil. This **dualist** way of making sense of the world, as an arena of conflict between opposing principles of good and evil, dominated mainstream thinking in Iran for 1,000 years. By influence or coincidence, it has appeared in the ideas of other Eurasian religions. Zoroastrian communities are still scattered around the world. For reasons we shall come to, however, Zoroaster had no comparable successor in his homeland.

In India, meanwhile, around the middle of the millennium, texts of the Veda multiplied. In particular, teachings about Brahman, handed down in the early Upanishads and described in Chapter 5 were a focus of study, and began to be written down. Alongside this defining—as we might call it—of Brahmanism in written texts, new thinking explored the moral implications of religious life, in a world of competing states comparable to that of China. Vardhamana Jnatrputra, for instance, whose life is traditionally assigned to the sixth or early fifth century B.C.E., is universally known as "Mahavira" (ma-ha-VEE-rah)—"the great hero." He founded **Jainism**, a way of life designed to free the soul from evil by ascetic practices: chastity, detachment, truth, selflessness—and charity so complete that a religious Jain (JAH-een) should accept only what is freely given, preferring starvation to ungenerous life. Jainism, though it attracted lay followers, is so demanding that it could only be practiced with full rigor in monasteries and religious communities. It never drew a following outside India.

Gautama Siddharta (GAW-teh-mah sihd-AHRTH-ah), however, who probably lived between the mid–sixth and early fourth centuries B.C.E., founded in India a religion of potentially universal appeal. Or perhaps the tradition he launched is better described as a code of life than as a religion, since Gautama himself seems never to have made any assertions about God. Rather, he prescribed practices that would liberate devotees from the troubles of this world. Gautama, whose followers called him "the Buddha" or "Enlightened One," taught that a combination of meditation, prayer, and unselfish behavior, of varying degrees of intensity for different individuals according to their vocations in life, could achieve happiness. The object was escape from desire—the cause of unhappiness. For the most privileged practitioners of what came to be called *Buddhism*, the aim was the ultimate extinction of all sense of self in a mystical state, called **nirvana** or "extinction of the flame." Devotees gathered in monasteries to help guide each other toward this end—but individuals in worldly settings could also achieve it. Many early Buddhist stories of

Zoroastrians. Though persecuted almost to extinction in Iran, the land of its birth, Zoroastrianism survives among exiled communities, especially in India, the U.S., and Western Europe. Here Zoroastrian priests in London mark the New Year by kindling sacred light.

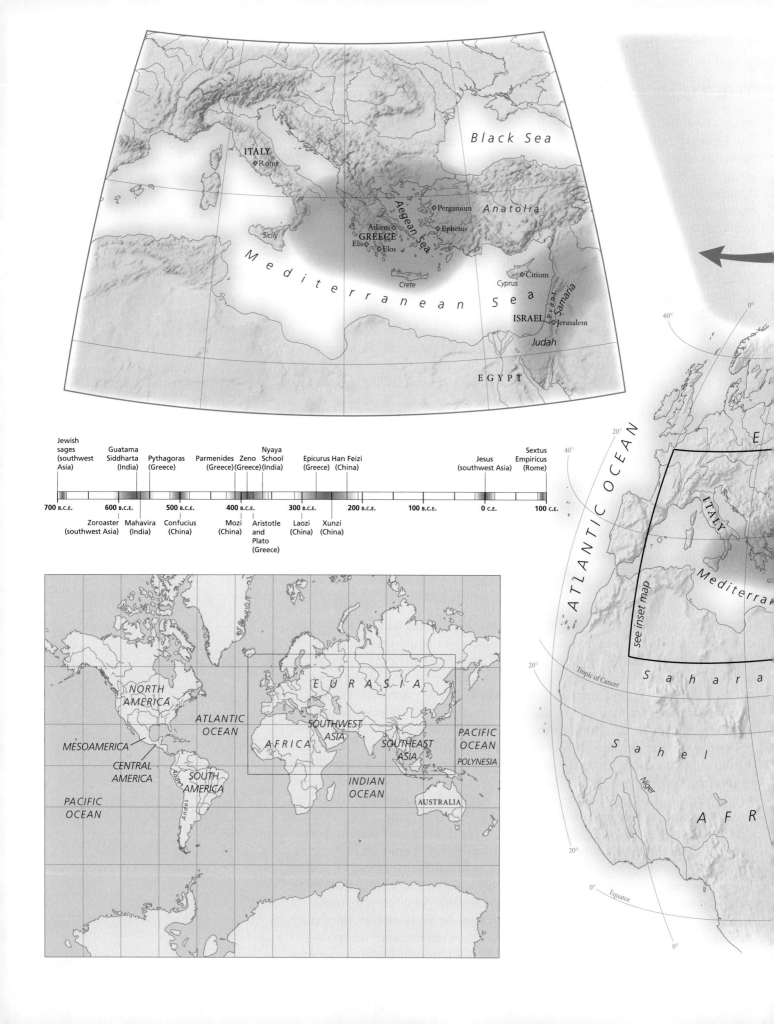

Black Sea

ITALY
◇Rome

Anatolia

◇Pergamum

Aegean Sea

Athens◇ ◇Ephesus
GREECE
Elis◇
◇Elos

Sicily

M e d i t e r r a n e a n   S e a

Crete

Cyprus ◇Citium

Levant

Samaria

ISRAEL
◇Jerusalem

Judah

EGYPT

Timeline

Jewish sages (southwest Asia)

Guatama Siddharta (India)

Pythagoras (Greece)

Parmenides (Greece)

Zeno (Greece)

Nyaya School (India)

Epicurus (Greece)

Han Feizi (China)

Jesus (southwest Asia)

Sextus Empiricus (Rome)

700 B.C.E. — 600 B.C.E. — 500 B.C.E. — 400 B.C.E. — 300 B.C.E. — 200 B.C.E. — 100 B.C.E. — 0 C.E. — 100 C.E.

Zoroaster (southwest Asia)

Mahavira (India)

Confucius (China)

Mozi (China)

Aristotle and Plato (Greece)

Laozi (China)

Xunzi (China)

World map

NORTH AMERICA

EURASIA

ATLANTIC OCEAN

MESOAMERICA

CENTRAL AMERICA

SOUTH AMERICA

Andes

SOUTHWEST ASIA

AFRICA

SOUTHEAST ASIA

PACIFIC OCEAN

POLYNESIA

PACIFIC OCEAN

INDIAN OCEAN

AUSTRALIA

Inset map

ATLANTIC OCEAN

0°

60°

40°

20°

ITALY

E

Mediterr

see inset map

Sahara

20°

Tropic of Cancer

Sahel

Niger

AFR

20°

0°   Equator

0°

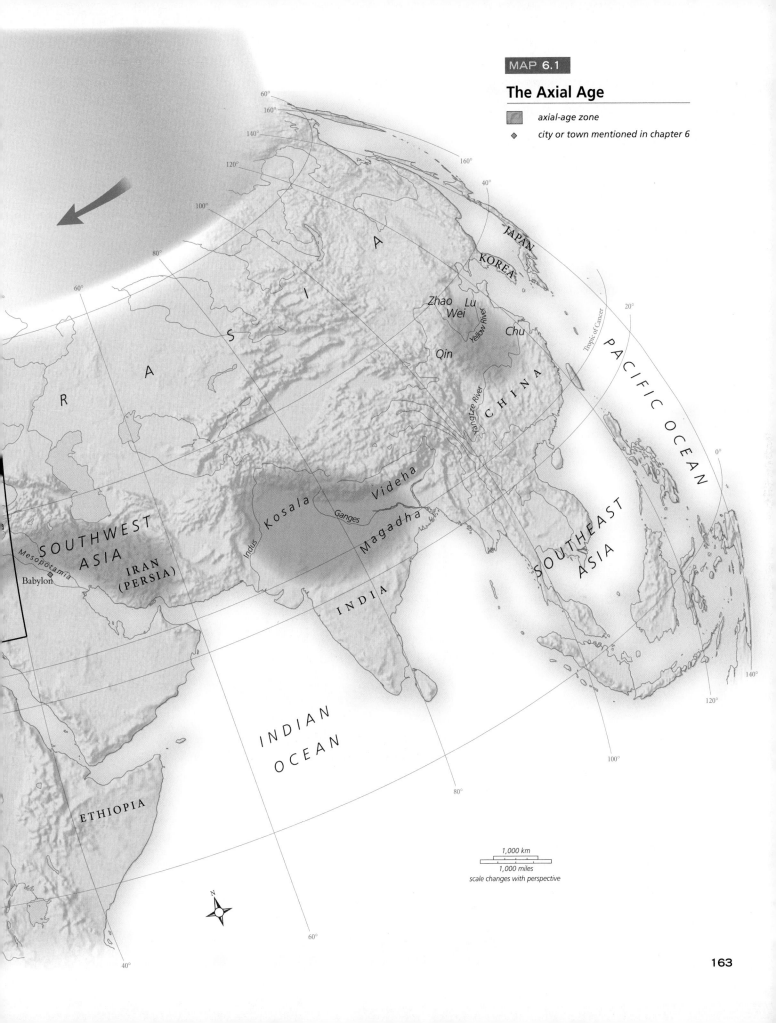

JAPAN

KOREA

Zhao Lu
Wei

Chu

Qin

Yellow River

CHINA

Yangtze River

A S I A

PACIFIC OCEAN

Tropic of Cancer

R

A

SOUTHWEST
ASIA

IRAN
(PERSIA)

Mesopotamia

Babylon

Indus

Kosala

Ganges

Videha

Magadha

INDIA

SOUTHEAST
ASIA

ETHIOPIA

INDIAN
OCEAN

1,000 km

1,000 miles

scale changes with perspective

N

THE BUDDHA'S FOOTPRINTS

This carved slab formed part of a Buddhist shrine in India. It depicts the Buddhapada, or footprints of the Buddha. Tradition holds that the Buddha's feet were imprinted with 108 auspicious symbols. Elaborate cults developed around the Buddhapada, particularly in south and southeast Asia.

The makara, a mythological sea monster with an elephant's trunk and a fish's tail, acts as a protector for the Buddha's footprints here.

The central wheel is symbolic of the Buddha's teachings, which set the wheel of dharma in motion.

One of the 32 marks of a "superman" in Buddhist tradition is that his toes are long and straight.

This three-pointed symbol represents the triple jewel, or triratna. The three jewels are the Buddha, his teachings (dharma), and the community of monks (sagha), who preserve and transmit those teachings.

A lotus blossom joins the triratna symbol. Because the lotus has its roots in mud, but flowers into pure open space, it symbolizes both the doctrine of the Buddha and the state of enlightenment that a person can reach through that doctrine.

The swastika is a traditional Indian symbol of good fortune, usually found on depictions of the palms of the Buddha's hands and the soles of his feet.

How does this carving symbolize the teachings of the Buddha?

the attainment of enlightenment concern people in everyday occupations, including merchants and rulers. This helped create powerful constituencies for the religion. To liberate the soul from the world, either by individual self-refinement or by losing oneself in selflessness, was likely to be a long job. In the meantime, the soul could expect to be recycled by reincarnation. The distinctive element in the Buddhist view of this process was that it was ethical. A principle of justice—or at least of retribution—would govern the fate of the soul, which would be assigned a "higher" or "lower" body in each successive life according to how virtuous its deeds had been in its previous incarnation.

Critics sometimes claim that these new religions were really forms of old magic: that the desire to "escape the world" or "extinguish the self" or achieve "union with Brahman" was, in effect, a bid for immortality, and that mystical practice was a kind of alternative medicine designed to prolong or enhance life. Or else such practices as prayer and self-denial could be seen as a bid for the charismatic power of self-transformation of the shaman (see Chapter 1), obtained without using mind-bending drugs. These analyses may have some validity. The Buddha called himself healer as well as teacher. Many legends of the era associate miracles of therapy with founders of religions. The identification of detachment from the world with the pursuit of immortality is explicit, for instance, in writings attributed to Laozi (low-tzeh), probably a fourth-century B.C.E. figure, who founded **Daoism** (daow-ihzm) in China. His doctrine was obviously a response to the insecurities of life among the warring states described in the last chapter. Disengagement would give the Daoist power over suffering—power like that of water, which erodes even when it seems to yield: "There is nothing more soft and weak; for attacking the hard and strong there is nothing better."

Yet, however much the new religions owed to traditional magic, they were genuinely new. They upheld the effectiveness of moral practice, alongside formal rituals, as ways to adjust humans' relationship with nature or with whatever was divine: not just sacrificing prescribed offerings fittingly to God or gods, but modifying the way people behaved toward each other. They attracted followers with programs of individual moral progress, rather than with rites to appease nature. In other words, they were emerging as religions of salvation, not just of survival. They promised the perfection of the human capacity for goodness, or "deliverance from evil"—attainable in this world or, if not, by transfer to another world after death, or by a total transformation of this world at the end of time.

Siddhartha Gautama: *Identity and Nonidentity*

Laozi, from the *Tao Te Ching*

Nature worship. This rare Daoist scroll, from about 1150 C.E. only a portion of which is reproduced here, depicts some of the feats of the "Eight Immortals," the most famous characters in Daoist folklore. The serene landscape is typical of Daoist painting.

Traditions developed during the axial age among Jews also showed a drift in this direction. This relatively small and politically insignificant people of southwest Asia's Mediterranean coastal region, or Levant (leh-VAHNT), demands attention because of the enormous long-term influence of some Jewish religious thinking. The Jews inhabited the war zone described in the last chapter, among Mesopotamia, Egypt, and the Mediterranean Levant. We cannot satisfactorily reconstruct their early history, though they were self-consciously a people of pastoral origins, as the biblical story of Cain and Abel shows. The blood sacrifice of Abel, the herdsman, was more "acceptable" to God than were the crops that his brother Cain, the "tiller of soil," offered. Traditionally, in the attempt to retrieve the facts of early Jewish history, scholars have relied on supposedly historical narratives in the Bible, the sacred writings of the Jews. But archaeological investigation has made this history increasingly difficult to confirm. So any account has to be tentative.

Like most people, and in common with other peoples of their region, the Jews seem to have started with a religion tailored toward worldly ends, worshipping a tribal deity who promised material success, prosperity, and victory. Their sacred writings, however, tell a moving story of disillusionment: of defeats and dispossessions by their enemies. From the eighth century B.C.E., Egyptian, Assyrian, and Babylonian inscriptions confirm essential features of the story. Jews inhabited two kingdoms they called Israel and Judah, which fought each other and fell victim to the wars of neighboring empires. Large-scale deportations—including a massive forced migration to Babylon after the fall of the Jews' holy city of Jerusalem in the 580s—incited a "diaspora mentality": exiles' sense of loss, resignation, nostalgia, defeat, and hope. "By the waters of Babylon," as psalmists put it, "we lay down and wept. . . . If I ever forget Jerusalem, let my tongue cleave to the roof of my mouth."

Exile of the Jews. "The king of Assyria carried the Israelites away to Assyria." This relief from the palace of the invading king seems to illustrate the scene described in the biblical Book of Kings (II.18:11), as soldiers take prisoners from the fortress of Lachish, which the Assyrians captured in 701 B.C.E. The Bible says that the Hebrew king then "stripped the gold from the doors of the Temple of the Lord" in an attempt to buy off the invaders.
Relief, Israel, 10th-6th Century: Judean exiles carrying provisions. Detail of the Assyrian conquest of the Jewish fortified town of Lachish (battle 701 BC). Part of a relief from the palace of Sennacherib at Niniveh, Mesopotamia (Iraq). Erich Lessing/Art Resource, N.Y.

During traumas of conquest, dispersal, return to Jerusalem, and submission to foreign rule, in the period from the seventh century to the fifth B.C.E., the Jews defined their sense of identity—expressed in writings now generally called the Old or Hebrew Testament. Instead of turning the Jews against their deity, their disasters inspired them to reevaluate their relationship with him, and to see him not just as superior to the gods of other peoples, but even as the only true God, beside whom all other gods were false. Sufferings were trials of faith and punishments for sin—especially, for failures to acknowledge God's uniqueness. By means of a **covenant**, God promised deliverance, if not in this life, then in the afterlife, or at the end of history, or, at best, in a remote future, as a reward for present fidelity. Jews signified that fidelity by adhering to prescribed rituals and rules of life, known as "the Law." Jews differed among themselves about what deliverance would mean. For some, it would be individual immortality; for some, relief from a sense of sinfulness; for some, the elimination of evil from the world; for some, national independence; for some, an empire of their own over their enemies.

The last great teacher of the age—the greatest, in terms of the scale of his influence—was the Jew we usually call Jesus, who died in or about 33 C.E. Scholars have questioned traditions concerning his life, on the grounds that his own followers were virtually the only ones who collected and wrote down the sources, and that we have almost no independent confirmation that he even existed. Actually, however, we are much better informed about him than we are about most other figures of his time or type. Collections of stories and sayings were written down within 30 or 40 years of his death. The brevity of this interval makes them unusually reliable by the standards of most such sources for ancient history.

To the secular historian, Jesus is best understood as an independent-minded Jewish rabbi, with a radical message. Indeed, some of his followers saw him as the culmination of Jewish tradition, embodying, renewing, and even replacing it. The name *Christ*, which his followers gave him, is a corruption of a Greek attempt to translate the Hebrew term *ha-mashiad*, or **Messiah**, meaning "the anointed," which Jews used to designate the king they hoped for at the end of history to bring heaven to earth. Jesus' message was uncompromising. The Jewish priesthood should be purged of corruption, the temple at Jerusalem "cleansed" of money-making practices. Even more controversially, some of his followers understood him to claim that humans could not gain divine favor by appealing to a kind of bargain with God—the "covenant" of Jewish tradition. God freely gave or withheld his favor, or grace. According to Jewish doctrine, God responded to obedience to laws and rules. But Jesus' followers preferred to think that, however righteously we behave, we remain dependent on God's grace. No subsequent figure was so influential until Muhammad (moo-HA-mahd), the founder of Islam (ihs-LAM), who died six centuries later, and none thereafter for at least 1,000 years.

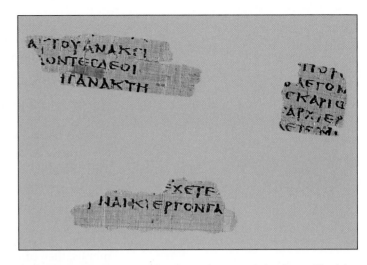

The Magdalen papyrus. These fragments of papyrus belonging to Magdalen College, University of Oxford, echo the story of the death of Jesus of Nazareth as the Gospel according to Matthew records it. Though of disputed date, it tends, together with other early documents, to suggest that traditions about Jesus circulated among his followers soon after he is supposed to have died.

The religious teachings of the sages of the axial age were highlights in a world teeming with other new religions, most of which have not survived. In a period when no one recognized a hard-and-fast distinction between religion and secular life, spiritual ferment stimulated all kinds of intellectual innovation. It is still hard to say, for instance, whether Confucius founded a religion. After all, he ordered rites of veneration of gods and ancestors, but disclaimed interest in worlds other than our own. The other schools of the axial age in China—so numerous that they were called the Hundred Schools—shared similar priorities, but mixed what we would now think of as secular and religious thinking. Confucius's opponent, Mozi (moh-tzeh), is a case in point. He taught a philosophy of **universal love**, on secular grounds, 400 years before Jesus' religious version (see "Going to the Source: Mozi and Jesus on Universal Love").

Some other innovators of the age, however, formulated ideas that belong without doubt in the realm of what we would now classify as secular thought. Greek sages, for instance, whose work overlapped with that of the founders of new religions in Asia, taught techniques for telling good from evil and truth from falsehood that we still use. The towering figures were two teachers of the fourth century B.C.E.: Aristotle, a physician's son from northern Greece, who was, perhaps, the most purely secular thinker of the age, and his teacher, the Athenian aristocrat, Plato. Aristotle left a body of work on science, logic, politics, and literature that had no equal in the West for centuries. It is commonly said that the whole of Western philosophy since the classical age of Athens in the fourth century B.C.E. has been "footnotes to Plato." Logicians and scientific observers and experimenters who belonged to the Hundred Schools in China and thinkers in India of the school known as Nyaya paralleled these achievements. We can only reconstruct the teachings of the

Nyaya school, uncertainly, from later or, in some cases, hostile texts, because few original sources have survived. But together with logicians of the era in Greece and China, the Nyaya school shared confidence in reason and the urge to analyze it, resolving arguments step by step.

THE THOUGHTS OF THE AXIAL AGE

There is no easy way to analyze the thinking of the axial age. Textbook writers usually divide the subject by regions, because scholars tend to specialize in regions. This method, however, conceals the fact that an almost continuous zone across Eurasia stretching from China, through India, southwest Asia, and the Mediterranean Levant, to Greece linked these regions together (see Map 6.1).

A thematic approach, of the kind we will attempt over the next few pages, helps to reveal the connections and contrasts, under the headings, first, of religion and morals, then of politics, and finally of reason and science. Of course, no such classification is watertight. No sage saw these headings as separate from each other. But between them, these categories cover the most explosive new ideas of the axial age. We start with religious ideas, bearing in mind the now-familiar warning that religion and secular life were overlapping categories for most thinkers at the time.

Religious Thinking

Of new thoughts of God formulated or developed in the axial age, three proved especially influential in global history: the idea of a divine creator, responsible for everything else in the universe; the idea of a single God, uniquely divine, or divine in a unique way; and the idea of an involved God, actively engaged in the life of the world.

CREATION Gods and spirits are hard to imagine. It is even harder to imagine nothing: an idea, beyond experience, at the uttermost limits of thought. The idea of nothing enabled thinkers to understand the order of nature in a new way. For, once you have got your head around the concept of nothing, you can imagine creation from nothing. This is the key to a tradition of thought that is crucial to most modern people's religions. How did it come about?

Before the axial age, creation narratives, as far as we know, were not really about creation, but were explanations of how the universe came to be the way it is. Ancient Egyptian creation myths, for instance, tell of a creator transforming chaos into a world endowed with time: but the chaos was there for him to mold. The big bang theory—today's favorite explanation of how the universe began to expand from an almost infinitesimally small core—resembles many early creation myths: Matter was already there when the bang redistributed it in space.

Some of the masters of the early Upanishads in India certainly had a notion of nothing, which they called "the void." We know this because they poured scorn on it. "How could it be so," sneered one text, "that being was produced from non-being?" The eternal being whom early Indian writings call Brahman created the world out of himself, "as a spider spins its web." In Greece in the fifth century B.C.E., Leucippus (who is credited with devising **atomic theory**—the theory that matter is not a continuous whole, but is composed of tiny particles) raised an apparently invincible logical objection: "the void is a non-being; and no part of what is can be a non-being, for whatever is, is absolutely." Plato's creator-god did not start from nothing, but rearranged what was already there.

Some ancient Greek poetry, however, described a world-beginning without prior matter. Emotion or thought was the prime mover of the universe. Indeed, feeling and thought can be defined in terms of each other. Feeling is thought unformulated, thought is feeling expressed in communicable ways. This Greek idea informed the mysterious notion of a world spawned by an intellectual act. As the Gospel according to John put it in the late first century C.E., "In the beginning was the logos"—literally, the thought, which English translations usually render as "the word." Of all the early Christian accounts of Jesus' life, John's was the gospel Greek thought influenced most heavily. Most other Christian accounts relied heavily on traditions peculiar to Jesus' own people, the Jews.

For the most challenging account of creation from nothing arose among the Jews, who brought an unusual philosophical twist to divine thinking: the idea of a creator who always existed but who made everything else out of nothing. Conclusions followed. The creator was unique, for nothing else could precede creation; he was purely spiritual, since there was no matter until he made it; he was eternal—he existed, that is, outside time—since he was not himself a product of creation; he was therefore unchanging; nothing greater than he could be conceived: His power had no limits.

Since its conception, the idea of creation from nothing has gradually convinced most people who have thought about it and has become the unthinking assumption of most who have not. It seems problematical, but so does the idea of eternal matter: If matter is eternal, how come it changes?

MONOTHEISM The idea of a unique God, who monopolizes power over nature, is now so familiar, at least in the West, that we can no longer sense how strange it is. Yet, until the first millennium B.C.E., as far as we know, most people who imagined an invisible world—beyond nature and controlling it—supposed that it was diverse: crowded with gods, the way creatures crammed nature. To systematize the world of the gods in the axial age, Greeks arrayed gods in order. Persians reduced them to two—one good, one evil. In Indian *henotheism*, a multiplicity of gods collectively represented divine unity.

Once again, the most powerful formula developed in the sacred writings of the Jews. Yahweh (YAH-weh), their tribal deity, was, or became, their only God. The chronology is insecure, and we do not know whether the Jewish creation theory was cause or consequence of this development. Their writings called him "jealous"—unwilling to allow divine status to any rival. Fierce enforcement of his sole right to worship was part of the covenant in which Yahweh's favor was exchanged for obedience and veneration. "I am Yahweh your God. . . . You shall have no other gods to rival me."

Jews were not obliged to impose the Yahweh cult on others. On the contrary, for most of history, they treated it as a treasure too precious to share with non-Jews. Elsewhere, monotheism seemed unappealing. Buddhism dispensed with the need for a creator by upholding that the universe was itself infinite and everlasting. When asked about the existence of God, Buddha, in the recollection of his disciples, always answered evasively. In India, China, and Greece, the idea of a unique creator left options for polytheism: If one being inhabited eternity, why—in strict logic—might not others? Other uniqueness can be divided: You can shatter a rock, parse a statement, refract light. So maybe the uniqueness of God is of this kind. Alternatively, it could be a kind of comprehensiveness, like that of "Nature," "the Earth," or the sum of everything. God is one—any good Brahmanist would acknowledge—in the sense that everything is one. In any case, if God's power is without limits, surely he can create other gods.

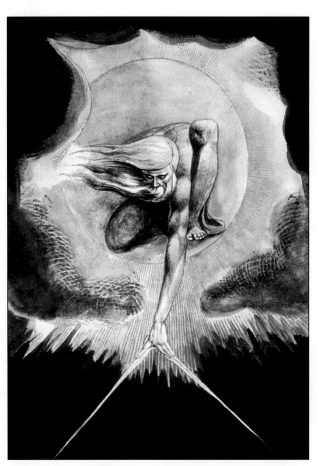

The Creator. The British poet and artist William Blake (1757–1827) was explicit; he painted visions. His version of the Creation—probably now the most famous in the world—is certainly visionary, but has obvious sources. It calls the Bible to mind, as God measures "a world without form, and void." The use of rushing wind to suggest the Holy Spirit, and of sun rays to signify Jesus, are among the oldest conventions of Christian art. God's stooped posture and his dividers, flashing like lightning, recall medieval paintings of God as the architect of the cosmos (see Chapter 13).

Despite these arguments, three developments have conspired, in the long run, to make the God of the Jews the favorite God of much of the world. First, the Jews' own "sacred" history of sacrifices and sufferings gave a compelling example of faith. Second, a Jewish splinter group, which recognized Jesus as—so to speak—the human face of God, opened its ranks to non-Jews. Christianity built up a vigorous and sometimes aggressive tradition of trying to convert non-Christians everywhere. Thanks in part to a message that has been adaptable to all sorts of cultural environments, it became, over a period of nearly 2,000 years, the world's most widely diffused religion. Finally, early in the seventh century C.E., the prophet Muhammad studied Judaism and Christianity, and incorporated the Jewish understanding of God in Islam, the rival religion he founded. In its turn—in many of the places where it was preached and spread—Islam became at least as appealing as Christianity. By the end of the second millennium C.E., it had attracted almost as many followers. Well over a third of the present world's population belongs to this so-called Abrahamic tradition (named after Abraham, the biblical father of the Jewish people), which includes Jewish, Christian, and Muslim monotheism (see Figure 6.1).

DIVINE LOVE Having created, did God remain interested in creation? Most Greek thinkers of the era ignored or repudiated the suggestion. Aristotle's description of God is of a perfect being: therefore one who needs nothing else, who has no uncompleted purposes, and who feels neither sensibility nor suffering. "The benevolence of heaven" was a phrase much used in China around the midpoint of the millennium, but this seems a long way short of love. Mozi, as even his philosophical adversaries admitted, "would wear out his whole being for the benefit of humankind." But his vision of humankind bound by love was not theologically inspired. Rather, he had a romantic vision of a golden age of "Great Togetherness" in the primitive past.

Contrasting systems inspired similar ethics of unselfishness, even in different contexts. We have seen unselfishness recommended in Brahmanism, for instance, where the world is illusory, or in some Greek thought, where the world is divine, or in Confucianism, where it is morally neutral, or in Zoroastrianism, where it is actually evil, or Christianity, where it is good, or in Buddhism, where it is transient. Indeed, Buddhism's teachings of universal sympathy are so like those ascribed to Jesus that scholars have often suspected Buddhist influence on the making of Christianity.

The Abrahamic Tradition

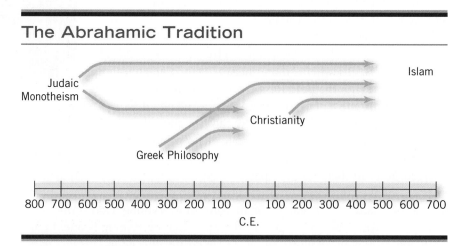

FIGURE 6.1 THE ABRAHAMIC TRADITION

For humans, the claim that God's interest is specially focused on them seems suspiciously self-centered. Gradually, however, axial-age thinking made it believable by insisting that humankind was special—higher than other animals. There were dissenting traditions. Philosophers in southern Italy in the late sixth century B.C.E. taught "All things that are born with life in them should be treated as kindred." Religious Jains' reverence for animals' souls was—and still is—so intense that they swept the ground to avoid walking on insects. But the biblical God makes "man in His own image" as the last word in creation and gives humans dominion over all other animals.

In the second half of the millennium, thinkers in other traditions formulated similar ideas. In the mid–fourth century B.C.E., Aristotle developed a hierarchy of living souls, in which the human soul was superior to those of plants and animals, because it had rational as well as "vegetative" and "sensitive" faculties. The Chinese formula was similar, as, for example, by Xunzi (shoon-tzeh) put it early in the next century: "Man has spirits, life, and perception, and in addition the sense of justice; therefore he is the noblest of earthly beings." Humans could exploit stronger creatures because they were able to form societies and act collaboratively. Buddhism ranked humans as higher creatures than others for purposes of reincarnation.

These new thoughts on humans' place in creation left open the question of whether they were its lords or its stewards. But humankind now occupied a special relationship to God. Late in the axial age, some Jews began to use the image of **divine love** to express this relationship—perhaps to cope with the frustrations of their history, in which they had never recovered political independence. Jesus and his followers seized on the identification of God with love. It was emotionally satisfying, for love is a universal emotion. By making God's love embrace all humans—rather than favoring a chosen race or a righteous minority—Christianity acquired universal appeal. Creation became an act of love consistent with God's nature. This solved a lot of problems, though it raised another—why does a loving God permit evil and suffering?

New Political Thinking

The evidence was glaringly ambiguous: Were misdeeds the result of corrupted goodness or inherent evil? Were human beings by their very nature good or bad? "The nature of man is evil—his goodness is only acquired by training," said Xunzi, for instance, in the mid–third century B.C.E. He believed that the original state of humankind was a grim swamp of violence, from which progress painfully raised people. "Hence," he continued, "the civilizing influence of teachers and laws, the guidance of rites and justice. Then courtesy appears, cultured behavior is observed and good government is the consequence." Confucius, on the other hand, thought, "Man is born for uprightness. If he lose it and yet live, it is merely luck." Since the axial age, political solutions to the problem of human nature have always been of two contrasting kinds: those that emphasize freedom, to release human goodness, and those that emphasize discipline, to restrain human wickedness. Either way, in liberating goodness or impeding evil, for axial-age thinkers, the state was an agent for virtue.

The biblical account of the creation of humans, in the book of Genesis, contained the most widely favored compromise. God made humans good and free. The abuse of freedom made people bad. Logically, this was unpersuasive. If Adam was good, how could he use freedom for evil? To escape this trap, Genesis added a diabolical device. The serpent (or other devilish agents in other traditions) corrupted goodness from outside. This has left politics with a difficult balancing act to perform, which no system has ever adequately accomplished, between freedom

Divine love. "I am the good shepherd," said Jesus, according to the Gospel of John (10:14), "and I lay down my life for my sheep." During the persecutions that punctuated the first 300 years of the history of the Church, Christian artists interpreted the New Testament's many texts about "straying" and "lost" sheep as metaphors for the souls of martyrs, whom Jesus gathered into his fold. This third-century example shows how Christians continued the heroic and aesthetic conventions of classical sculpture.
"The Good Shepherd," marble, height: as restored 99 cm, as perserved 55 cm, head 15.5 cm. Late 3rd century A. D. Vatican Musuems, Pio-Christian Museum, Inv. 28590. Courtesy of the Vatican Museums.

and force. In consequence, we can categorize most of the rest of the history of political thought as a debate between those who are pessimistic about human evil, and those who are hopeful of human goodness.

POLITICAL PESSIMISM For pessimists, the way to overcome human deficiencies was to strengthen the state. Plato was a member of an Athenian gang of rich, well-educated intellectuals and aristocrats, who felt qualified for power and therefore resented democracy. His rules for the ideal state were harsh, reactionary, and illiberal. The many objectionable features—censorship, repression, militarism, regimentation, extreme communism, and collectivism, selective breeding of superior human beings, austerity, rigid class structure, active deception of the people by the state—all had a distressful influence. The key idea was that political power should be concentrated in a self-electing class of philosopher-rulers called **Guardians**.

Their qualification for office would be intellectual superiority, guaranteed by a mixture of heredity and education, which would make them selfless in their private lives and godlike in their ability to see what was good for the citizens. They would achieve Plato's declared "objective in the construction of the state: the greatest happiness of the whole, and not that of any one class." He wrote so brilliantly and so persuasively that this reasoning has continued to appeal to state builders ever since. "There will be no end to the troubles of states, or indeed, of humanity," he claimed, "until philosophers become kings in this world, or till those we now call kings and rulers really and truly become philosophers." His Guardians, however, became the inspiration and the intellectual ancestors of elites, aristocracies, party hacks, and self-appointed supermen whose justification for tyrannizing others has always been that they know best.

Chinese counterparts exceeded the severity even of Plato's thinking. For most of the time, they were in the minority: The consensus among the sages was that the ruler should be bound by law (a point in which Aristotle, at the other end of Eurasia, agreed). Confucius even said that ethics should override obedience to the law. The age-old tension between rules and rights showed, however, that law could function without any respect for ethics. In the fourth century B.C.E., a school of thought in China known as the **Legalists** made a virtue—or pretended virtue—of this deficiency. Their basic principle was that "goodness" was meaningless. Society required only obedience. What the law actually said was irrelevant. All that really mattered was that it should be obeyed. Morality was nonsense. The only good was the good of the state. Law and order was worth tyranny and injustice. Ethics was a "gnawing worm" that would destroy the state.

This was a remarkable new twist in the history of thinking about law. All previous schools had tried to make human law more moral by aligning it with divine

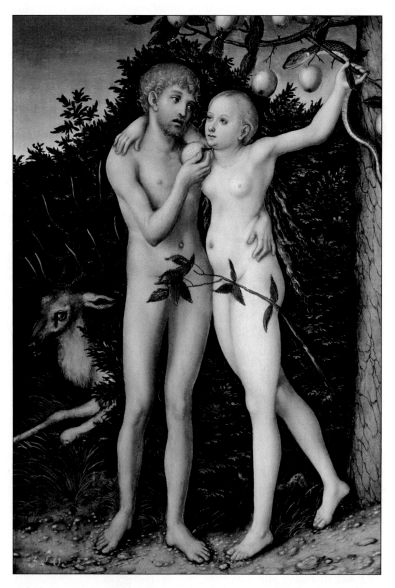

Original sin. "For better, for worse." The embrace of Adam and Eve suggests sanctified love. Their unashamed nakedness (concealed later by an over-painter) signifies innocence. But the serpent is stroking Eve's hand, and sin and death are about to enter the world. This is one of at least 30 depictions of the scene by Lucas Cranach (1427–1553), one of the first Protestant painters, who longed to reverse humankind's self-alienation from God.

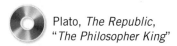

Plato, *The Republic*, "*The Philosopher King*"

or natural law. The explanation lies in the terror of the times. Legalist doctrine was born in a time of great civil disaster and has tended to resurface in bad times ever since. The Chinese Legalists were reacting against generations of disastrous feuding among the "Warring States." The ethics-based thinking of the Confucians and Daoists had done nothing to prevent this feuding. The legalists laughed off earlier sages' belief in the innate goodness of people. The best penalties were the most severe: cutting off people's heads, slicing people in half, pulling their bodies apart with chariots, boring a hole in their skulls, roasting them alive, or cutting out a wrongdoer's ribs. As well as in the worship of order, ancient Chinese Legalism anticipated modern fascism, for instance, in advocating and glorifying war, recommending economic self-sufficiency for the state, denouncing capitalism, praising agriculture, and insisting on the need to suppress individualism in the interests of state unity.

POLITICAL OPTIMISM But by a big majority, the sages of the axial age were optimists. They thought human nature was essentially good. Hence, the political doctrines of Confucianism, which demanded that the state should liberate subjects to fulfill their potential. Hence, too, the democracy some Greek sages advocated, which entrusted citizens (though not, of course, excluded groups, such as women or slaves) with a voice in affairs of state, even if the citizens were poor or badly educated. The citizens and their participation in the governing of the state were ends in themselves, according to the underlying ideology, and, though to serve rulers or support society was an inescapable duty, it was not the purpose of life.

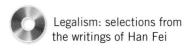

Legalism: selections from the writings of Han Fei

The Great Wall of China. Legend assigns the Great Wall of China to the Warring States period in the third century B.C.E. In fact, it took centuries to build and was often rebuilt thereafter. Little of the surviving workmanship, which stretches for some 4,000 miles, is more than 500 years old. Chinese culture now extends way beyond it, but it has an important place in the formation of Chinese identity—defining the supposed boundary of the non-Chinese world, displaying the ambition and achievement of Chinese civilization.

Chinese thinkers applied similarly individualistic doctrines, which gathered strength during the axial age, to the state. But they did not go on to question the role of monarchy. The state, after all was meant to reflect the universe. Its unity could not be compromised. All that could be expected was that the ruler should consult the people's interests and views and should face, in case of tyranny, the subject's right to rebel. In Daoist political thought, the ruler's job is to enforce virtue. Confucius advocated a return to a golden age supposedly located at the foundation of the Zhou dynasty (see Chapter 4). He called aristocracy and subordinate kings to an allegiance ordained by heaven. "Heaven sees according as the People see," said Mencius, Confucianism's outstanding spokesman. "Heaven hears according as the people hear." This was a reminder to the ruler, not a recipe for republicanism. Nor does Indian literature of the time mention popular institutions. But some Indian states did have elites hundreds strong—perhaps thousands in some cases—that ruled as a group, electing leaders for fixed terms among themselves.

Meanwhile, in Greece, sages considered states to be purely practical mechanisms to be tinkered with at need. An enormous variety of political experiments unfolded, including republican or aristocratic systems, and even democratic ones. Aristotle made a masterly survey of them in the fourth century B.C.E. He thought monarchy was the best system in theory, but not in practice, because it was impossible to ensure that the best man would always be the ruler. More practical was aristocratic government, in which a manageable number of superior men administered the state. But it tended to generate into the self-interested rule of the wealthy (oligarchy) or permanent power for an hereditary clique. Democracy, in which all the citizens shared, sustained—as we saw in Chapter 5—a long, if fluctuating, record of success in Athens. From early in the sixth century B.C.E., Athenian lawmakers appealed to the body of citizens to legitimate the laws. "Being master of the vote the people became master of the constitution." Aristotle denounced this system because it could lead to demagogues and mob rule. The best system was a carefully crafted mixture in which aristocracy predominated, under the rule of law. Broadly speaking, this was embodied in the Roman state of the second half of the millennium (see Chapter 8), which became, in turn, the model for most republican survivals and revivals in Western history. Even when, toward the end of the axial age, Rome abandoned republican government and restored what was in effect a monarchical system, Romans still spoke of their state as a republic and the emperor as merely the chief magistrate.

In politics, Jesus preached a subtle sort of subversion. A new commandment to "love one another," he claimed, could replace virtually all laws. The Kingdom of Heaven was more important than the empire of Rome. In one of history's great ironic jokes, Jesus advised fellow Jews, in effect, to despise or even ignore the state: "Render unto Caesar that which is Caesar's and unto God that which is God's." All Jews at the time would have understood what this meant, for everything, to them, was God's.

For society at large, Jesus was equally dangerous, welcoming social outcasts—prostitutes, tax collectors, "sinners," and people from Samaria, whom Jews despised as both sinners and heretics. He favored the weak against the strong: children, women, the lame, the blind, and beggars—the "meek," who, he promised, "shall inherit the earth." In view of the radical nature of this bias, it is unsurprising that Jewish and Roman authorities combined to put him to death. His followers then turned from political activism to spiritual preparation for personal salvation.

Challenging Illusion

New thinking about reason and reality, and the relationship between them, flourished alongside or within the work of the religious leaders. Perhaps the most startling feature that united the thought of the axial age across Eurasia was the sages' struggle against illusion—their effort to see beyond appearances to underlying realities. "Behold," for instance, "people dwelling in a cavern," said Plato. "Like us, they see only their own shadows, or each other's shadows, which the fire throws onto the wall of their cave." Our senses deceive. We are mental cave dwellers. How can we see out of our cave? For convenience, we can group the novelties this quest inspired under the headings of mathematics, reason, and science (from which we can separate medicine as a distinct category). After reviewing the axial ages' achievements in those fields, we can turn to skepticism—mistrust of all of them and, in general, of human capacity to achieve more than practical happiness, a trend of thought that was, in some ways, an outcome of the others.

Math

Evidence of the previously unperceived complexity of reality accumulated during the axial age. Indian sages, building on their early speculations about the possibility of nothing and of infinity, discovered in numbers a genuinely limitless universe. Jain speculators about the age of the cosmos involved the concept of mind-boggling big numbers, partly to demonstrate how impossible it was to attain the infinite. Workers in arithmetic discovered unreachable numbers: ratios that could never be exactly determined, yet which seemed to underpin the universe—π, for instance ($22 \div 7$), which determined the size of a circle, or the complex ratio that Greek mathematicians called "the Golden Number" (roughly 1.618), and which seemed to represent perfection of proportion. The invention of geometry showed how the mind can reach realities that the senses obscure or warp: a perfect circle, a line without magnitude. Reality can be invisible, untouchable, and yet accessible to reason.

A figure of enormous importance in unfolding these mysteries (for that is what they were to people at the time) was Pythagoras. His life spanned the Greek world. He was born on an island in the Aegean, around the mid–sixth century B.C.E., but spent most of his teaching life in a Greek colony in southern Italy. He attracted stories—he communed with the gods; he had a golden thighbone; he was not a mere man but a unique being, between human and divine.

He is most famous today for two relatively trivial insights: that musical harmonies can be expressed as arithmetical ratios; and that consistent ratios characterize the lengths of the sides of right-angled triangles. His importance goes much deeper. He was the first thinker, as far as we know, to formulate the idea that numbers are real. They are obviously ways we have of classifying objects—two flowers, five flies. But Pythagoras thought there was more to it than that—that two and five really exist, quite apart from the objects they enumerate. They would still exist, even if there were nothing else to count. He went further still. Numbers are the basis on which the cosmos is constructed. "All things are numbers," was his way of putting it. Numbers determine shapes and structures—we still speak of "squares" and "cubes"—and numerical proportions underlie all relationships. Geometry, Pythagoras thought, is the architecture of the universe.

Not everyone was equally enthusiastic about the cult of numbers. "I sought the truth in measures and numbers," said Confucius in a text, which, though he probably did not really write it, reflects the prejudices of the third-century B.C.E. Daoist

Render unto Caesar. If the coin the Pharisees showed Jesus was up to date, it showed the head of Tiberius Caesar (r. 14–37 C.E.). "Render unto Caesar that which is Caesar's," said Jesus. Later ages misinterpreted him to mean, "Pay taxes." But he was probably making an ironic, rabbinical joke, and really meant the opposite—that nothing was Caesar's because everything belonged to God.

who compiled it, "but after five years I still hadn't found it." Still, the exploration of numbers was a widespread interest among axial-age sages. **Rationalism**—the doctrine that unaided reason can elicit truth and solve the world's problems—was among the results.

Reason

The first pure rationalist we know by name was Parmenides, who was from a Greek colony of southern Italy in the early fifth century B.C.E. He started with the geometry Pythagoras had taught. If you believe geometrical figures are real, you believe in the truth of a super-sensible world—for a perfect triangle, for instance, is like God: No one has ever seen one, though crude manmade approximations are commonplace. "It is natural," as Bertrand Russell—reputedly one of the twentieth century's clearest thinkers—said, "to go further and to argue that . . . the objects of thought are more real than sense-perception." The only triangles we know about are those in our thoughts. Parmenides therefore suggested that the same might be true of trees—and of everything else.

In some ways, the consequences are impressive. If, say, a pink rose is real by virtue of being a thought rather than a sensible object, then a black rose is equally real. The nonexistence of anything is an incoherent concept. Few of Parmenides's followers were willing to go that far, but reason did seem able to open secret caverns in the mind, where truths lay. "Fire is not hot. Eyes do not see": These were the numbing, blinding paradoxes of the fourth-century B.C.E. Chinese philosopher Hui Shih (hway-sheh)—who wrote five cartloads of books. They show that data act directly on the mind, which processes them before they become sensations. Thought needs no objects outside itself. It can make up its own. It is pure. It does not have to arise from experience. For a true rationalist, the best laboratory is the mind, and the best experiments are thoughts.

In partial consequence, rationalism became an escapist's alternative to reality. Parmenides, for instance, thought he could prove that change was illusory and differences deceptive, and that only the unchanging and eternal were real. One of his successors, Zeno of Elea, invented famous paradoxes to demonstrate this: An arrow in flight always occupies a space equal to its size, therefore it is always at rest. You can never complete a journey because you always have to cross half the remaining distance first. Matter is indivisible because "if a rod is shortened every day by half its length, it will still have something left after ten thousand generations" (see Figure 6.2).

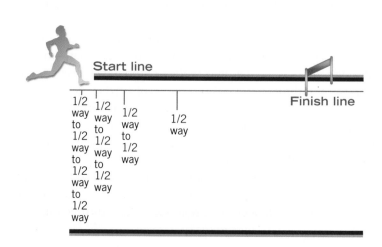

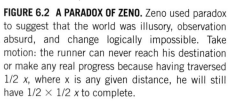

FIGURE 6.2 A PARADOX OF ZENO. Zeno used paradox to suggest that the world was illusory, observation absurd, and change logically impossible. Take motion: the runner can never reach his destination or make any real progress because having traversed 1/2 x, where x is any given distance, he will still have 1/2 × 1/2 x to complete.

Baird, Forrest E., Philosophic Classics Volume I: Ancient Philosophy *4th edition, © 2003. Electronically reproduced by permission of Pearson Education, Inc., Upper Saddle River, New Jersey.*

Despite these rationalists' excesses, reason has helped to temper or restrain rival approaches to regulating the world—systems founded on dogma or charisma or emotion or naked power or lies. Philosophers have often dangled the tempting hope that reason could do more. It could reshape the world, formulate laws, and construct society. In practice, chapters on an "Age of Reason" in history books usually turn out to be about something else. Reason has never had much appeal outside elites and has only rarely ruled entire societies. It did, however, give axial-age thinkers a systematic way of organizing thoughts.

Early in the second half of the millennium, teachers in India, Greece, and China showed intense interest in proposing rules for the correct use of reason. Practical issues probably underpinned these movements. For pleading in courts, arguing between embassies, persuading enemies and praising rulers, it was important to make arguments watertight. Logic was a fascinating by-product of these practical needs.

The most rigorous and systematic exposition was Aristotle's, strapping common sense into intelligible rules. If we think we understand him, it is because he taught us how to think. To this day, even people who have barely heard of him use the techniques he taught, which have seeped into mental habits through the channels of tradition. He was the best-ever analyst of how reason works, in as much as it works at all. According to Aristotle, we can break valid arguments down into phases, called **syllogisms**, in which we can infer a necessary conclusion from two premises that prior demonstration or agreement have established to be true. If the premises are, "All men are mortal" and "Socrates is a man," it follows that "Socrates is mortal."

At roughly the same time in India, the Nyaya school of commentators on ancient texts analyzed logical processes in five-stage breakdowns that resembled syllogisms. Their conception, however, was in one fundamental way different from Aristotle's. They claimed reason was a kind of extraordinary perception that God conferred. Nor were they strictly rationalists, for they believed meaning did not arise in the mind. God, tradition, or consensus conferred it on the object of thought.

 The Nyaya school

Science

Meanwhile, another route through the thought of the axial age led to science. As with the exploration of reason, the starting point was distrust of the senses. As the Daoist text, the *Lü Shi Chong Qiu* (lew-sheh-chuhng-chee-oh) of the third century B.C.E., points out, some metals may seem soft but can be combined to form harder ones; lacquer feels liquid but can be made dry by the application of another liquid; herbs taste poisonous but can be mixed to make medicine. First appearances are deceptive. "You cannot know the properties of a thing merely by knowing those of its components." The science of the axial age sought to penetrate the veil and expose underlying truths. Greeks agreed. "Truth," said Democritus around the turn of the fifth and fourth centuries B.C.E., "lies in the depths." Although no strictly scientific texts from India survive from this period, the Upanishads contain similar warnings about the unreliability of appearances (see Chapter 5).

The idea of a distinction between what is natural and what is supernatural was, as far as we can tell, new. Previously, the two realms seemed so thoroughly interpenetrated that science seemed essentially sacred, medicine magical. The earliest clear evidence of a shift in thinking is Chinese. In 679 B.C.E. the sage Shen Xu (shehn-shoo) is said to have taught that ghosts were just the products of the fears and guilt of those who see them. Confucius deterred followers from thinking "about the dead until you know the living" and defined wisdom as aloof respect for gods and demons. Confucians professed interest in human affairs—politics and practical morality—and

 Confucius, selections from *The Analects*

indifference to the rest of nature. But as far as they did delve into nature studies, it was in an effort to dig out what they regarded as superstition: the claim that inanimate substances had feelings and wills, the notion that spirits inhabit all matter, the claim—advanced sometimes even by sophisticated thinkers on grounds of cosmic interconnectedness—that the natural world is responsive to human sin or goodness. "If one does not know causes, it is as if one knew nothing," says a Confucian text of about 239 B.C. "The fact that water leaves the mountains is not due to any dislike on the part of the water but is the effect of height. The wheat has no desire to grow or be gathered into granaries. Therefore the sage does not enquire about goodness or badness but about reasons." Thus "natural" causes displaced magic.

In Greece, the origins of science are inseparable from a background of magic, nature worship, and shamanistic attempts to penetrate the mysteries of unseen worlds by rites and ecstasies. Most ancient Greeks, indeed, probably never escaped belief in the supernatural. From the late sixth century B.C.E., however, nature worship was beginning to encourage naturalistic explanations of curious phenomena. Texts, for instance, denounce attempts to understand omens or to foretell the future through magic as useless or delusive, and use observed data as the basis of speculations about the material nature of the universe. But for science to thrive in a world that, in most people's minds, gods and sprites and demons still ruled, a method was needed to observe nature systematically, order the information, and test the resulting hypotheses. Aristotle was the best representative of Greek science in its maturity. "We must have facts," he said and proceeded to gather them in enormous quantities. Like the perfect example of a "nutty professor," he prowled around his lecture room, dissected flies, and noted every stage in the incubation of birds' eggs. Other highlights of Greek science of the period included Archimedes's discovery of the mechanics of leverage in the mid–third century B.C.E., and, slightly later, the work of Eratosthenes, who produced an almost exactly accurate calculation of the size of the planet (see Map 6.2).

Chinese practical science—systematic investigation of nature through observation and experiment—probably arose, in parallel with that of Greece, from Daoist doctrines of nature. Habits of observation and experiment developed from magical and omen-seeking practices of early Daoism. The only Daoist word ever used for a "temple" means *watchtower*—a platform from which to observe the natural world and launch naturalistic explanations of its phenomena. Daoism has, in Confucian eyes, a reputation for magical mumbo-jumbo because its priests practice strange ceremonies, many of which seem indebted in their origins to the magical fallacy that nature responds to human ritual. But Daoism also teaches that Nature—to the one who would control it—is like any other beast to be tamed or foe to be dominated—she must be known first.

Aristotle, excerpts from *Physics* and *Posterior Analytics*

Delphi. Around Mount Parnassus, north of Athens, Greeks found or founded many shrines consecrated to Earth and Nature, as well as the most famous oracular site, at Delphi, where priestesses uttered obscure prophecies, supposedly under the influence of hallucinogenic fumes that rose from a fissure in the ground. Nearby, the circular sanctum known as the Tholos was built in the fourth century B.C.E., at or near the place where the Greeks' predecessors had located the navel of the Mother-Goddess or, as we might now say, the center of the Earth.

MAP 6.2

The World According to Eratosthenes

Eratosthenes of Alexandria (ca. 275–195 B.C.E.) was a Hellenistic geographer. His map, reconstructed here, was remarkably accurate for its time. The world was divided here by lines of "latitude" and "longitude," thus anticipating our global divisions today.

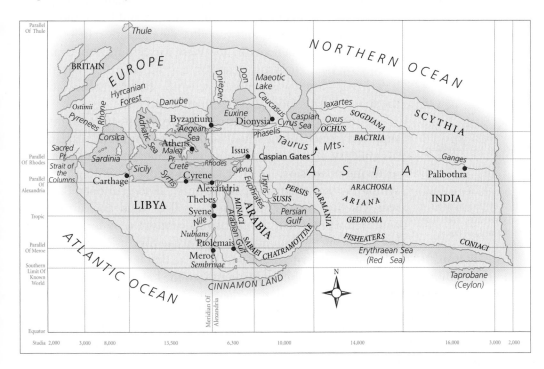

Part of the result is that Daoism encouraged the beginnings of scientific practice: observation, description, classification, and experiment. In second-century B.C.E. China, for instance, the Daoist legend told of Yi (YEE) the archer, who on sage advice sought the medicine of immortality away in the west, when the weed that would confer it was growing outside his door. Daoist texts often have amusing dialogues between craftsmen who know their work and rationalists who persuade them to do it in a different way, with ruinous results. Grand theory is discouraged as an intrusion of reason into the workings of wisdom, which can be attained only by gaining knowledge. Chinese science has always been weak on theory, strong on technology.

Medicine

Controversy followed between magic and medicine—or was it just between rival forms of magic? Illness, like any abnormal state, including madness, could be the result of possession or infestation by a spirit, a "demon"—to recycle a commonly used word for it. Or some diseases could have material causes, others spiritual. Or all could be a mixture of the two. Or sickness could be a divine affliction earned by sin.

In an incident in China, attributed to 540 B.C.E. by the chronicle that recorded it, an official told his prince to rely on diet, work, and personal morale for bodily health, not on the spirits of rivers, mountains, and stars. Officials, however, usually

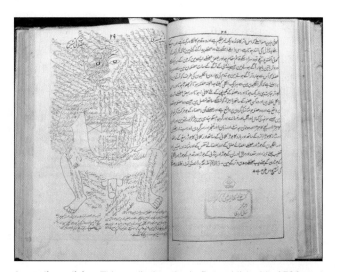

Ayurvedic medicine. This medical textbook, first published in 1593, and based on *The Canon of Medicine* written by the great Muslim scholar Avicenna early in the eleventh century, is still used by students at the Unani Medical College in Hyderabad, India. Ayurvedic treatments are usually herbal, although diet and exercise are also important remedies. The illustration and text shown here concern the muscles of the human body.

command little prestige as physicians. The controversy that mattered occurred within the ranks of professional healers. In Greece in the late fifth century B.C.E., a secular school known as the Hippocratics tried to monopolize the medical profession, at the expense of rival healers who were attached to temples. The Hippocratics thought that health was essentially a state of balance among four substances in human bodies: blood, phlegm, and black and yellow bile. Adjust the balance, and you alter the patient's state of health. This condemned patients in the West for centuries to treatment mainly by diet, vomiting, laxatives, and bloodletting. The theory was wrong—but it was genuinely scientific, based on observation of the substances the body expels in pain or sickness.

A treatise sometimes attributed to Hippocrates himself—supposed founder of the school—advocates a naturalistic explanation for epilepsy, which many people at the time assumed to be a form of divine possession. The test is: Find a goat exhibiting the same symptoms that a human epileptic does. "If you cut open the head, you will find that the brain is ... full of fluid and smells foul, convincing proof that the disease and not the deity is harming the body." The method sounds bizarre, but the conclusion is impressive. "Personally," the Hippocratic writer went on, "I believe that human bodies cannot be polluted by a god." A similar shift of business into the hands of secular medical specialists occurred in China. Xunzi, who died in 235 B.C.E., scorned a man who "having got rheumatism from dampness beats a drum and boils a suckling pig as an offering to the spirits." Result: "a worn-out drum and a lost pig, but he will not have the happiness of recovering from sickness." Religious explanations of disease remained. But the Hippocratics and their Chinese counterparts started a presumption that has gained ground ever since: that nothing needs to be explained in divine terms. The physical world is all there is.

These changes had close parallels in India. In the earliest known Indian work of medicine, the Arthaveda (ahr-thah-VEH-dah), which dates from the early first millennium B.C.E., diseases and demons are more or less identical and are treated with charms or drugs. From the sixth century B.C.E. onward, however, we see evidence of professional medical training and literature. Work largely complete by the second century C.E. summarizes these medical teachings. Writings attributed to Susutra, who probably lived in the sixth century B.C.E., concern surgery; writings attributed to Charaka (which may be the name of a school rather than a person) concentrate exclusively on diet and drugs. A saying attributed to Charaka is strikingly similar to the morals of the Greek Hippocrates: "If you want your treatment to succeed, to earn wealth, to gain fame, and to win heaven hereafter ... seek the good of all living creatures, strive with your whole heart to cure the sick." The similarities among Indian, Greek, and Chinese axial-age medicine are so remarkable that historians often assume that they influenced each other. There is, however, no direct evidence for this influence.

Skepticism

A consequence of the rise of a scientific point of view was the suspicion that the world is purposeless. In particular, this line of thinking raised an idea that challenged another axial-age orthodoxy: If the world was purposeless, it was not made for man, who was reduced to insignificance. The idea Aristotle called the "Final Cause"—the purpose of a thing, which explains its nature—becomes incoherent. The world is a random event.

In around 200 B.C.E., this was such a dangerous idea that a skeptical Chinese treatise, the *Liezi* (lee-ay-tzeh), avoided direct advocacy of it by putting it into the mouth of a small boy, who challenged a pious host for praising the divine bounty that provided good things for his table. "Mosquitoes suck human blood, wolves devour human flesh but we do not therefore assert that Heaven created man for their benefit." The greatest-ever exponent of a purposeless cosmos was the Chinese philosopher of the first century C.E., Wangchong (wahng chohng). Humans, he said, live "like lice in the folds of a garment. When fleas buzz in your ear, you do not hear them: How could God even hear men, let alone concede their wishes?" Some materialist thinkers still take pride in asserting that the whole notion of purpose is superstitious and that asking why the world exists or why it is as it is is pointless.

In a world without purpose, there is no need for God. The name of the Greek philosopher Epicurus, who died in 270 B.C.E., has become unfairly associated with the pursuit of physical pleasure—which he certainly recommended, albeit with restraint. A far more important element of his thought was his interpretation of the atomic theory. In a world of atoms and voids, there is no room for "spirits." Since atoms are subject to "random swerves," there can be no fate. Since they are perishable, and everything is composed of them, there can be no immortal soul. Gods, if they can be said to exist at all, inhabit an imaginary world from which "we have nothing to hope and nothing to fear." Epicurus's arguments were formidable, and materialists and atheists kept returning to them. At about the end of the first century C.E., the Roman writer Sextus Empiricus suggested, like a modern Marxist, that "some shrewd man invented fear of the gods" as a means of social control. The doctrines of an all-powerful and all-knowing god were devised to suppress freedom of conscience. "If they say that God controls everything, they make him the author of evil," he concluded. "We express no belief and avoid the evil of the dogmatisers."

In revulsion from the big, unanswerable questions about the nature of reality, skeptical thinkers and their schools refocused philosophy on practical issues. One of the great anecdote-inspiring characters of ancient Greece was Pyrrho of Elis, who accompanied Alexander the Great's invasion of India in 327–324 B.C.E. (see Chapter 7) and imitated the indifference of the naked sages he met there. On board ship on the way home, he admired and shared the calm response of a pig to a storm. He was absent minded and accident prone, which made him seem unworldly, but his deepest indifference was to reason. The achievements of the Greek rationalists of the previous hundred years left him cold. Since, he argued, you can find equally good reasons on both sides of any argument, the only wise course is to stop thinking and judge by appearances. More effective was the argument that all reasoning starts from assumptions; so none of it is secure. Mozi had developed a similar insight in China around the beginning of the fourth century B.C.E. Most problems were matters of doubt. "As for what we now know, is it not mostly derived from past experience?"

Later Greek philosophy focused on systems that concerned the best practical choices for personal happiness or for the good of society. **Stoicism**, for instance, is the outstanding example, both for the coherence of stoic ideas and for the scale of their influence. Stoicism appealed to the Roman elite and through them had an enormous effect on Christianity. First taught in the school that Zeno of Citium

Axial-Age Science and Medicine

Sixth century B.C.E.	Susutra (India)
Late fifth century B.C.E.	Hippocrates (Greece)
ca. 250 B.C.E.	Archimedes (Greece)
d. 235 B.C.E.	Xunzi (China)
ca. 200 B.C.E.	Eratosthenes (Greece)

Skeptics and Stoics

Fourth century B.C.E.	Pyrrho of Elis (Greece)
Late fourth century B.C.E.	Zeno of Citium (Greece)
d. 270 B.C.E.	Epicurus (Greece)
First century C.E.	Wangchong (China)
First century C.E.	Sextus Empiricus (Rome)

founded in Athens in the late fourth century B.C.E., stoicism started from the insight that nature is morally neutral—only human acts are good or evil. The wise man therefore achieves happiness by accepting misfortune. Further stoic prescriptions—fatalism and indifference as remedies for pain—were similar to teachings preached at about the same period at the far end of Eurasia, especially by Buddha and his followers, or Laozi and his. People have sought the "happiness priority" in so many contrasting ways that it is hard to generalize about its overall effect on the history of the world. Stoicism, however, was certainly its most effective manifestation in the West. It has supplied, in effect, the source of the guiding principles of the ethics of most western elites ever since it emerged.

AXIAL AGE–AXIAL AREA: THE STRUCTURES OF THE AXIAL AGE

Monotheism, republicanism, Legalism, rationalism, logic, science (including scientific medicine), skepticism, the most enduring religions and ethical systems—the tally of new thinking in the axial age looks impressive by any standards, but especially because of its legacy to us. We have to confront the problems of why this period was so productive and why—though widely dispersed in Eurasia—it was confined, by global standards, to so few societies around the globe.

Clearly, the structures that underpinned the work of the axial-age thinkers were important for making it happen. The schools and sages formed four obvious and sometimes overlapping categories. First, there were professional intellectuals, who sold their services as teachers, usually to candidates for professional or public office, but perhaps also to those who sought happiness or immortality or, at least, health. A second class sought the patronage of rulers or positions as political advisers. Many sages belonged to both these groups: Aristotle, for instance, taught in Athens but also served as a royal tutor to the prince who later became Alexander the Great (see Chapter 7). Confucius eked out life as a teacher, but not for want of a calling to serve states. A third category was made up of prophets or holy men, who emerged from ascetic lives with inspired messages for society; a fourth was composed of charismatic leaders with visions to share with and, if possible, impose on their peoples.

Most sages fitted into networks. Though lonely, hermitlike existence was an ideal that many of them recommended, affected, and even sought, there were few, if any, genuinely isolated thinkers among these sages. Those, at least, who founded schools or established enduring influence depended on contacts to make and spread their reputations. Networks also stimulated innovation. They nourished competition, fertilized ideas through discussion and debate, and gave innovators emotional support. Plato wrote all his works in the form of dialogues and conversa-

The Academy of Athens. Romans continued to admire the philosophy of classical Greece. The Acropolis of Athens is recognizable in the background of this mosaic, preserved in the ruins of Pompeii. The columns and gardens recall what the setting of Plato's Academy at Athens was really like.

tions—which make the function of the network visible. The Confucian Mencius, the Daoist Zhuangzi (Jwahng-tzeh), and Hui Shi, the analyst of language, were contemporaries. Competition and debate probably sharpened their views and helped make them famous. Similarly, Plato's teacher Socrates was probably the most famous sage of Greece in the early fourth century B.C.E. and was in contact and conflict with all the Greek schools of his day, attacking those known as Sophists for allegedly putting the elegance of an argument as more important than its truth. Epicurus and Zeno of Citium established schools in Athens within a few years of each other toward the end of the fourth century B.C.E. (see Map 6.3).

Formal institutions of education played their part in defining networks and stimulating competition. We know little of how they functioned, but the Academy of Athens, founded in 380 B.C.E., had a garden and lodgings for students, which Plato purchased. Members took meals in common and contributed to costs according to their means. Master–pupil relationships created tradition or what we might call cross-generational networks. Socrates taught Plato, who taught Aristotle. Traditions of this sort can get rigid, but clever pupils often innovate by reacting against their masters' teaching (something all textbook writers should bear in mind) and set up chains of revisionism from one generation to the next. Confucius was a critic of the establishment of his day. Mohists, similarly, opposed Confucians. A succession of masters as well as a series of conflicts linked Mozi to Confucius. Han Feizi (hawn-fay-tzeh), a Confucian pupil, founded the Legalist school in reaction to his teacher, Xunzi (see Figure 6.3).

MAP 6.3

Philosophical Schools in the Mediterranean Region, 600 B.C.E.–100 C.E.

● Schools mentioned or described on pages 181–185

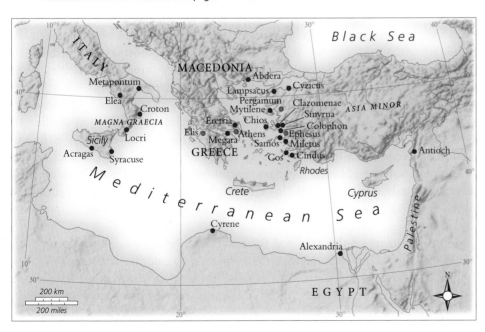

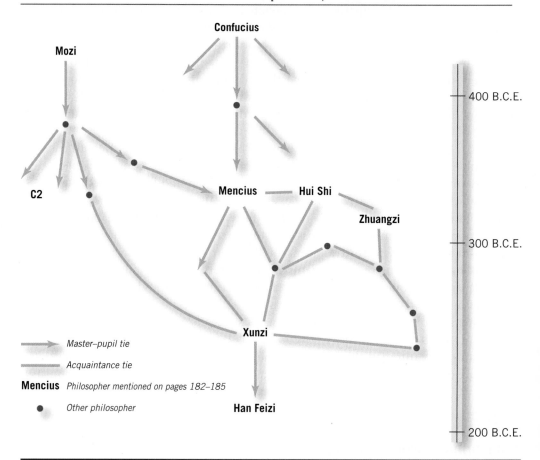

Network of Chinese Philosophers, 400–200 B.C.E.

Master–pupil tie

Acquaintance tie

Mencius *Philosopher mentioned on pages 182–185*

● *Other philosopher*

FIGURE 6.3 NETWORK OF CHINESE PHILOSOPHERS, 400–200 B.C.E.

Adapted from R. Collins, The Sociology of Philosophers *(Cambridge, MA: Belknap Press, 1998) p. 55.*

Disciples and pupils confided masters' works to writing. Literacy is not necessary for great thinking, but it helps. Many sages were hostile or indifferent to writing. The Upanishads were probably transmitted orally before they were finally written down. Socrates wrote nothing. Jesus wrote nothing himself that has survived—only, as far as we know, a few words scratched in the dust. Buddha's teachings were too sacred—his first disciples thought—to confide to writing and had eventually to be retrieved from memories when it was finally decided to write them down. Does this mean that the axial age is a trick of the evidence? That the ideas of its sages became so influential only because they were eventually written down? Not entirely, but it does mean that its thoughts have come down to us in a way that other regions and other periods did not have or did not use.

Some thinkers of the axial age were rich men. Plato was an aristocrat who could endow his own school with his own money. Buddha and Mahavira, the founder of Jainism, were princes. Usually, however, intellectuals need patrons or employers to survive. The politically fragmented worlds of axial-age Greece,

China, and India, had plenty of potential patrons. A wandering scholar like Confucius might not retain a patron for long—but he could turn to others. This made for independence of thought and liberated political philosophy to criticize rulers. Every subsequent age has successfully adapted Confucius's message, but he addressed it to his own time. Hence his emphasis on the renewal of tradition, the resumption of sacred rites, the restoration of land and property to their rightful owners. Of course, royal patrons are rarely disinterested. In mid–fourth century B.C.E. China, Mencius found his patron, the King of Wei, interested only in schemes to improve military efficiency. Also at the court of Wei, Hui Shi turned his talent for argument to negotiations with other states.

To patronize sages became, in itself, a source of princely prestige. In China the prince of Zhao allegedly had 1000 scholars at his court toward the mid–third century B.C.E. Intellectual wars paralleled interstate bloodshed. The Chinese state of Chu supported the followers of Mozi against the Confucians. Qin, supposedly a "barbarian" kingdom on the edge of the Chinese culture area, was home to thousands of scholars. When its ruler burned books in the 220s B.C.E., it was less perhaps an act against learning than a gesture of partisanship on behalf of thinkers he favored.

In India, too, among the twelve or sixteen states that shared the Ganges valley in the period, similar rivalries and opportunities existed. The Veda contains fragments of sages' dialogues with kings, in which the kings sometimes out-argued the sages. Buddhism relied on rulers' patronage in the kingdoms of Kosala and Magadha. Mahavira was related to the rulers of Videha, where his doctrines enjoyed official favor. His followers debated with Buddhists for supremacy in Magadha. As we shall see in the next chapter, political unification and large-scale imperialism did not promote intellectual productivity. One of the reasons why Zoroaster had no comparably influential successors in Persia is probably because, as we shall see in the next chapter, Persia rapidly became an imperial power. In China, India, and Greece the axial age waned as empires grew at the expense of small states, even though the empires themselves spread axial-age ideas.

In some places, alongside state patronage, public values and popular support may have nourished the intellectuals. The sage and holy man are most useful to the public in times of political dissolution. Their wisdom and objectivity make them sought after to arbitrate between neighbors or to take the place of absent justice. Public interest is apparent in the multiplicity of schools and the willingness of pupils to seek the benefit of masters' expertise. Learned writings attracted readers. Democritus, an exponent of atomic theory in the early fourth century B.C.E., was credited with 60 books. Heraclitus, one of the first generation of Greek sages around the beginning of the sixth century B.C.E., was a notorious loner who refused to take on pupils. But he nonetheless deposited his writings in the famous temple of the goddess Artemis at Ephesus on the western coast of Anatolia—in effect, his local public library.

IN PERSPECTIVE: The Reach of the Sages

Although the new thinking of the axial age was confined to parts of Asia and Europe, it was a worldwide story because of the way axial-age thinking later spread and shaped thoughts and feelings in every clime and continent. Empires

○ MAKING CONNECTIONS ○

THINKERS AND THOUGHTS OF THE AXIAL AGE

REGION →	SAGE/THINKER AND TIME PERIOD →	PHILOSOPHY/RELIGION →	DISTINCTIVE IDEAS
Southwest Asia	Jewish sages, ca. 700–500 B.C.E.	Judaism	Monotheism; trials of faith; punishments for sin; covenant with God
Southwest Asia	Zoroaster, ca. 600 B.C.E.	Zoroastrianism	Eternal conflict between good and evil (dualism)
India	Gautama Siddharta, ca. 560 B.C.E.	Buddhism	Meditation; karma; Four Noble Truths; escaping desire
India	Mahavira, ca. 559 B.C.E.	Jainism	Sanctity of life; nonviolence (*ahimsa*)
Greece	Pythagoras, ca. 550 B.C.E.	Mathematics	Geometrical and mathematical ideas; ratios; ideas that numbers are real
China	Conficius, ca. 500 B.C.E.	Secular philosophy	Loyalty to God, state, and family; importance of ethics and right conduct
Greece	Parmenides, ca. 425 B.C.E.	Rationalism	Objects of thought are more real than sense perception
China	Mozi, ca. 400 B.C.E.	Secular philosophy	Universal love
Greece	Zeno, ca. 390 B.C.E.	Stoicism	Nature is morally neutral; happiness achieved by accepting misfortune
Greece	Aristotle and Plato, ca. 380 B.C.E.	Secular philosophy	Logic; science; political thought
India	Nyaya school, 350 B.C.E.	Rationalism	Logic; reason as an extraordinary perception conferred by God
China	Laozi, ca. 300 B.C.E.	Daoism	Detachment from world; quest for immortality
Greece	Epicurus, ca. 280 B.C.E.	Skepticism	Centrality of matter; soul is not immortal; if God exists he is indifferent to human affairs
China	Xunzi, ca. 250 B.C.E.	Secular philosophy	Human goodness can be attained through progress and freedom
China	Han Feizi, ca. 225 B.C.E.	Legalism	Only good is the good of the state; law and order more important than tyranny and injustice
Southwest Asia	Jesus, ca. 30 C.E.	Christianity	Importance of faith, divine love

that are the subject of the next chapter helped to spread it. Trade and colonization, which can be traced at intervals throughout the rest of this book, took axial thought further, until it had spread across the planet. The Roman Empire carried Greek science and philosophy into western Europe. Buddhism became a state ideology in the first empire to cover almost all of India. The Chinese Empire became a growing arena in which Buddhism, as well as native Chinese thought, spread within and across China's widening borders. Japan and Korea fell under Chinese cultural influence and their intellectual traditions developed from Chinese-inspired starting points. Migration and trade bore Indian thinking into parts of southeast Asia. Christianity fused Jewish and Greek intellectual traditions and spread them—ultimately—all over the world. Islam shared much of the same heritage and spread it almost as far. Buddhism is the third, in terms of numbers of followers, of the three World Religions of today. Alongside Christianity and Islam, both of which developed after the axial age, it has spread over many different countries and cultures, whereas most religions tend to remain specific to their cultures of origin. We do not fully understand the reasons for Buddhist success in this respect, but we shall trace its history, at appropriate intervals, in this book. But the scale of demands Buddhism makes on its followers is well suited to a variety of walks of life.

As a result of the spread of the work of the sages and their schools, the thought of the modern world has a familiar ring to a student of the axial age. It seems astonishing that today, after all the technical and material progress of the last 2,000 years, we should remain so dependent on the thought of such a distant era and have added so little to it. We debate the same issues about the nature of reality, using the same tools of logic and science. We struggle with the same problems about the relationship of this world to others, and most of us still follow religious traditions founded by axial-age sages. We search for a balance between the same kinds of optimistic and pessimistic assessments of human nature that people of the axial age identified, and we seek resolutions of similar conflicts of political ideas that arise as a result. To a remarkable extent, we express ourselves in terms the ancient sages taught.

Although the sages and schools of the axial age were confined to Eurasia, comparisons with other parts of the world help us understand how cultural contacts shape and spread what people think and believe. Over and over again, readers of this book will see and will have seen, for example, how ways of thought and life and worship radiated outward from kernel regions: from Mesoamerica, for example, into North and Central America; or from parts of the Andes along the coasts and mountain chains of South America and across the Amazon valley; or from the Ethiopian highlands into surrounding areas; or from centers on the Niger River in West Africa into the Sahel and the forest; or

Temple of Artemis. In Heraclitus's day, the Temple of Artemis at Ephesus, in what is today Turkey, served as a repository of books which citizens could consult. Early in the second century C.E., however, Ephesus acquired the Library of Celsus, erected in memory of a Roman governor, specifically to house the city's collection of books. The facade—the only surviving part of the library—is modeled not on a temple but on a Greek theater, where knowledge, wisdom, intellect, and virtue played like characters in a drama.

CHRONOLOGY

(All dates are approximate)

600 B.C.E.–100 C.E.	Teachers and their disciples influence thinking all across Eurasia
	Spread of Zoroastrianism for next 1,000 years primarily in present-day Iran
	Teachings about Brahman begin to be written down; Buddhism develops in India
	Confucianism, Daoism, and Legalism spread in China
	Legacy of Plato and Aristotle to Western philosophy
	Proponents of Secular Medicine (Susutra in India, Hippocrates in Greece, and Xunzi in China)
580 B.C.E.	Forced migration of Jews from Jerusalem to Babylon creates a "diaspora mentality," influential up to present times
33 C.E.	Jesus and spread of Christianity over the next two millennia

(as we shall see in later chapters) from western Polynesia deep into the Pacific. But the relatively isolating geography of the Americas, sub-Saharan Africa, and the Pacific worked against the kinds of comparatively intense exchange that were possible across Eurasia.

It is impossible to trace to their outer limits the networks that bound the axial-age sages. But the similarities between their thoughts across Eurasia suggest that long-range cultural exchanges must have been going on among them. This was perhaps the critical difference that made Eurasian societies relatively prolific in a period when we know of no comparable achievements in intellectual life anywhere else in the world. Our next task is therefore to look not only at the changing political frameworks of the axial age, but also at the evidence of the spread and strength of long-range cultural contacts in the world of the time.

PROBLEMS AND PARALLELS

1. What were the similarities among the ideas of the great sages of the axial age? How do they influence the way we think now?

2. How did the concept of nothing enable thinkers to understand the order of nature in a new way?

3. How did the idea of divine love alter humankind's relationship with God and the world?

4. How did religious ideas affect political thought in the axial age? Why were most axial sages optimists rather than pessimists?

5. How did axial-age science investigate nature? How did axial-age medicine distinguish itself from magic?

6. What roles did networks, schools, and patrons play in spreading axial-age thinking?

7. What comparisons can be made between the axial age and the way culture radiates outward from kernel regions in other parts of the world?

DOCUMENTS IN GLOBAL HISTORY

- Siddhartha Gautama: *Identity and Nonidentity*
- Laozi, from the *Tao Te Ching*
- Plato, *the Republic*, "*The Philosopher King*"
- Legalism, selections from the writings of Han Fei
- The Nyaya school
- Confucius, selections from the *Analects*
- Aristotle, excerpts from *Physics* and *Posterior Analytics*

Please see the Primary Source CD-ROM for additional sources related to this chapter.

READ ON

The Analects of Confucius is the best work with which to begin study of the sage. Many editions are available: R. Dawson, *Confucius* (1982) is perhaps the best general introductory account of the subject. E. L. Shaughnessy, *Before Confucius* (1997) gives the background to the thought of the period of the Hundred Schools. T. De Bary, ed., *Sources of Chinese Tradition* (2000) is an excellent introductory anthology of extracts

from key texts. J. Needham, *Science and Civilisation in China* (1961), i and ii, with vol. vii by C. Habsmeier, set Chinese thought—not only on science—in global context, stressing the priority of Chinese achievement in antiquity and the middle ages. N. Sivin, *Medicine, Philosophy and Religion in Ancient China* (1996) collects essays on the links between Tao and science. For Chinese political thought, see S. DeGrazia, *Masters of*

Chinese Political Thought (1973) for a selection of texts and B. I. Schwartz, *The World of Thought in Ancient China* (1985), for a critical guide.

R. Zaehner, *The Dawn and Twilight of Zoroastrianism* (2003) is an unsurpassed classic. R. Gotshalk, *The Beginnings of Philosophy in India* (1998) can be recommended on the Upanishads; for texts, E. Deutsch, *A Source Book of Vedanta* (1971) has a good selection. A. T. Embree, ed., *Sources of Indian Tradition* (1988) collects some useful texts. R. Gombrich, ed., *The World of Buddhism* (1991) is a superb introduction to its subject, especially good on Buddhist monasticism. K. H. Potter, ed., *Encyclopedia of Indian Philosophies* (1994) 6 vols, is a comprehensive guide to Indian thought.

On the Jewish and Jesusian concept of God, K. Armstrong, *A History of God* (1993), and J. Miles, *God: A Biography* (1995) are suggestive and instructive; the revisionist M. S. Smith, *Origins of Biblical Monotheism* (2001) can also be recommended. C. S. Lewis, *The Four Loves* is a classic work contrasting the Jesusian notion of divine love with other traditions. The version in *The New Jerusalem Bible* is the most reliable modern translation of the gospels and has manage-able and instructive notes. On Jesus, G. Vermes, *Jesus the Jew* (1973) is provocative, enlightening, and gripping. C. P. Thiede and M. D'ancona, *The Jesus Papyrus* (1997) too, offers an invigorating challenge to conventional thinking. M. Staniforth, trans., *Early Jesusian Writings* (1968) collects some of the texts that did not make it into the Bible.

W. K. C. Guthrie, *A History of Greek Philosophy* (1962) is a model of scholarship; the sixth and last volume, *Aristotle: An Encounter* is also an intensely personal and fascinating study of the single most important thinker in the history of Western thought. A. A. Long, *Hellenistic Philosophy* (1974) takes up the story where Guthrie leaves off. The classic work by E. R. Dodds, *The Greeks and the Irrational* (1957) remains a valuable corrective to conventional thinking. O. Taplin, *Greek Fire* (1990) is an accessible and up-to-date study of ancient Greek thought. M. L. West, *The East Face of Helicon* (1997) settles the controversy about where Greek ideas "originally" came from. R. Collins, *The Sociology of Philosophies* (1998) makes an important contribution to tracing the connections that made schools of thinkers and forged the contacts between them.

CHAPTER 7

The Great Empires

China and Rome on the Silk Roads. A face with Caucasian features on a woolen weaving from the first or second century C.E. is evidence that the Chinese and the Romans were linked by trade. The cloth was discovered in a grave on the Silk Roads in Xinjiang. The face was stitched into a pair of pants and woven in a style not used by the Chinese.

I n about 33 B.C.E., Maecenas, one of the Roman Empire's leading ministers, gave a small farm to a penniless poet. It was a gift in appreciation of the brilliant satirical verses the poet—whose name was Horace—wrote as evening entertainment for Roman intellectuals and elites. The farm was just what Horace wanted. For the rest of his days, he devoted much of his best poetry—some of the cleverest, loveliest work any wordsmith has ever forged—to celebrating the simple, rural life and praising his patrons. In one poem, he imagined Maecenas worrying over what the Chinese might be plotting. In others, Horace pictured Augustus, the Roman emperor, intimidating them with his power and fathering a future conqueror of China. This was outrageous flattery, since there was no likelihood of the Roman and Chinese empires having much contact of any kind, let alone going to war. In 97 C.E., China did send an envoy, Gan Ying (gahn-yeeng), to Rome, but he turned back at the Black Sea, deterred by warnings from local enemies of Rome, who did not want the mission to succeed. They said to Gan, "If the ambassador is willing to forget his family and home, he can embark." So Gan sent home a favorable report on the Romans: "The people have an air comparable to those of China. . . . They trade with India and Persia by sea."

That was as close as the Roman and Chinese Empires ever came to direct mutual dealings. But that Horace was aware of China, and realized that events at the far end of Eurasia could affect Roman interests, shows how the world was changing. It was, as we say now, getting smaller.

● ● ● ● ●

The world began shrinking during the period known as the axial age, from about 500 B.C.E. to 100 C.E., for three main reasons. First, land trade routes opened communications across Eurasia. Second, traffic grew along the existing maritime routes of the Indian Ocean. And, finally, sea travel began to connect the Mediterranean with northern Europe's Atlantic shores. The trade routes of the Phoenician and Greek trailblazers described in Chapter 5 led north from the Strait of Gibralter to the tin-producing British Isles. Their colonies were staging posts in the making of a new economy—helping goods, people, and ideas cross or get around the sharply divisive watershed that separates Mediterranean from Atlantic Europe.

ROME

FOCUS questions

- WHY WERE trade routes so important to axial-age empires?
- HOW DID the Persian Empire benefit its inhabitants?
- HOW WAS Rome able to conquer and rule a vast empire?
- HOW DID Asoka seek to unify his empire?
- WHAT WAS the significance of the Han dynasty for China?
- WHERE DID the first potentially imperial states arise in the Americas?

Not only did travelers and trade expand communications, but the need for big armies and the growth of commerce created a demand for stronger, bigger states. The axial age became an age of empires, with states of unprecedented size, including within their borders many political communities in common allegiance to a single source of authority. The new empires of the period took shape first in southwest Asia, then around the Mediterranean, and finally in China and India. They established common frontiers or frontier zones of conflict and culture exchange. Around the axes of travel, chiefs, enriched by trade, turned into kings.

The empires spilled some of their people, technology, and means of life into frontier areas that had been little populated. Cultivated crops and domesticated livestock transformed previously undisturbed ecosystems. At an increasing rate, neighbors who had lived by hunting and foraging for wild plants adopted agriculture, following the empires' example. They developed or adapted varieties and species of plants and animals for their own environments. Those who continued to resist change were cast as enemies and savages. In the great grasslands, the steppes of central Eurasia, where tilling the soil was impossible, empires formed with a different sort of economy, based on herding livestock. A pattern began that lasted for some 2,000 years, of violence between these nomad empires that lived by herding and the sedentary farmers who lived near them.

Meanwhile, beyond the routes that connected Eurasian empires, people still had the option of remaining foragers and small-scale farmers. They could minimize risk by minimizing change. Most of them took this option. In parts of the New World, however, experiments in embracing change and attempting to control it continued. Large-scale interventions in the environment and imaginative adaptations of human society took forms that were familiar from Eurasia. Agriculture led to urbanization, long-range commerce, and eventually imperialism. Seen from today's perspective, the Americas seemed to be reliving the history of the Old World.

ROUTES THAT DREW THE OLD WORLD TOGETHER

As a general rule in history, bigger states mean more exchange over longer distances. In part, this is simply because they facilitate trade and travel within their own expanding borders; in part, because they generate increasing contacts with each other by way of commerce, diplomacy, and war. To understand the cultural exchanges of the period—

⊙ MAKING CONNECTIONS

THE DYNAMICS OF EMPIRE

ENVIRONMENT →	SOCIETY →	ECONOMY →	COMMERCE →	POLITICS →
Cultivated crops and livestock transform ecosystems across Eurasia	Foragers adopt agriculture	Urbanization leads to increased trade over longer distances	Increased contact between regions leads to conflict, war, diplomacy, and cultural exchanges	Increased commerce, conflicts, numerous routes of communication provide opportunities for stronger, bigger states that can manage many political communities more efficiently

how and why they happened and to what extent—we therefore have to understand the political framework: where and how new states formed; how their horizons broadened; what were the new institutions—the mechanisms for conveying commands and exacting obedience—that enabled them to function over unprecedented distances.

State-building and the development of communications are mutually dependent processes. Routes of commerce are the lifelines of empires: pumping them with resources, equipping them with new ideas and technologies, laying down tracks for their armies to follow. Eurasia would have had no great empires—or, at least, empires would have been smaller—if new or developing avenues of communication had not become available. Indeed, this is a large part of the reason why Eurasian empires in this period were bigger, and exercised more power over their subject-peoples, than those elsewhere in the world, where no comparable long-range routes emerged. We must begin, therefore, by drawing in the long-range causeways of the period: the sea lanes and land routes that crossed Eurasia, making possible the cultural exchanges of the axial age and the new political developments in the empires the routes linked (see Map 7.1).

The Sea Routes of the Indian Ocean

The world maps Indian geographers of the axial age drew look like the product of stay-at-home minds. Four—then, from the second century B.C.E. onward, seven—continents radiate from a mountainous core. Around concentric rings of rock flow seven seas, made up respectively, of salt, sugarcane juice, wine, ghee (butter), curds, milk, and water. One should not suppose on the basis of this formal, sacred image of the world that Indians of the time were ignorant of geography. That would be like inferring from the stylized subway map that New Yorkers could not build railways.

We can detect real observations under the metaphors of the maps. The world is grouped around the great Himalaya Mountains, and the triangular, petal-like form of India, with the island of Sri Lanka falling from it like a dewdrop. The ocean is divided into separate seas, some imaginary or little known, but others representing real routes to frequented destinations and commercial centers. The Sea of Milk, for instance, corresponds roughly to what we now call the Arabian Sea, and led to Arabia and Persia. The Sea of Butter led to Ethiopia.

Stories of Indian seafaring from late in the first millennium B.C.E. appear in the *Jatakas*, collected tales of Buddhahood—guides to how to become enlightened. Here, piloting a ship "by knowledge of the stars" is a godlike gift. The Buddha saves sailors from cannibalistic goblin-seductresses in Sri Lanka. He puts together an unsinkable vessel for a pious explorer. A merchant from the city of Benares (beh-NAH-rehs), following the advice of an enlightened sage, buys a ship on credit and sells the cargo at a profit of 200,000 gold pieces. Mani-mekhala (MAH-nee may-KHAH-lah), a guardian-deity, saves shipwreck victims who have combined commerce with pilgrimage "or are endowed with virtue or worship their parents." These are legends, but the surviving tales contain so many practical details that they only make sense against a background of real navigation. Similar legends appear in Persian sources, like the story of Jamshid (jahm-SHEED), a hero who is both king and shipbuilder and who crosses oceans "from region to region with great speed."

Accounts of real voyages back these stories. Toward the end of the sixth century B.C.E., Darius I—an emperor enthusiastic for exploration—ruled Persia. He ordered a reconnaissance of the Indian Ocean from the northern tip of the Red Sea, around Arabia, to the mouth of the Indus River in northern India. This venture no doubt extended the range of navigation in the region, since the Red Sea, with its concealed rocks and dangerous currents, was notoriously hard to navigate.

An Indian globe of the early eighteenth century depicts a traditional view of the world. The island of Sri Lanka is the central dot located on the equator. A squat representation of India, reminiscent of the shape of the subcontinent in most earlier Arab and European maps, occupies most of the space to the north. The small blue arc represents the Himalaya Mountains.

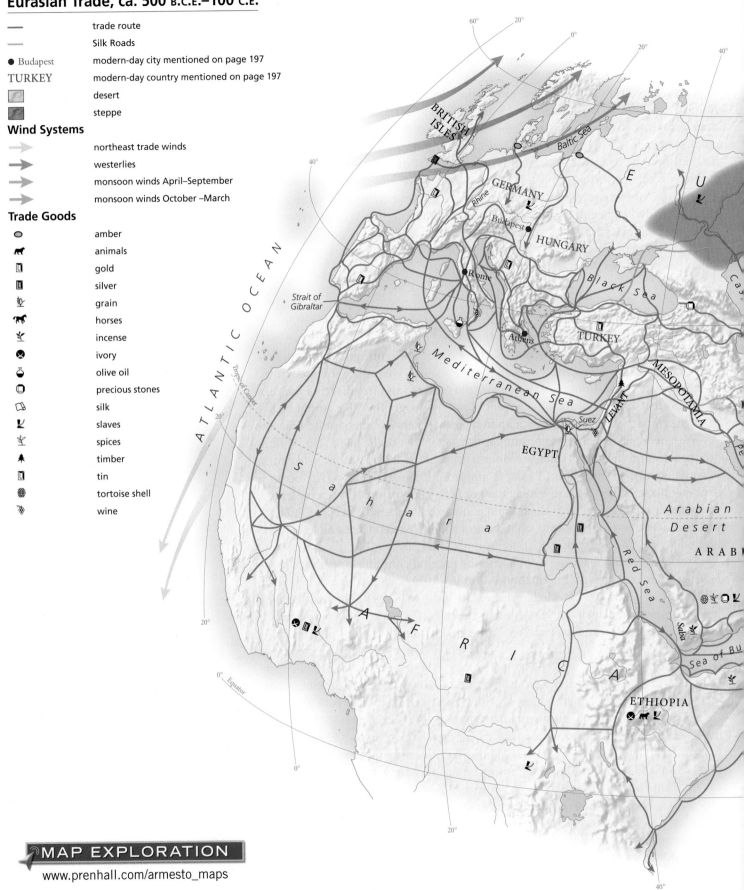

MAP 7.1

Eurasian Trade, ca. 500 B.C.E.–100 C.E.

——		trade route
——		Silk Roads
● Budapest		modern-day city mentioned on page 197
TURKEY		modern-day country mentioned on page 197
▨		desert
▨		steppe

Wind Systems

→	northeast trade winds
→	westerlies
→	monsoon winds April–September
→	monsoon winds October –March

Trade Goods

⬭	amber
▰	animals
▯	gold
▮	silver
⚘	grain
⚞	horses
⚘	incense
⬤	ivory
⬤	olive oil
⬤	precious stones
⬙	silk
⚒	slaves
⚘	spices
🌲	timber
▯	tin
⬤	tortoise shell
⚘	wine

MAP EXPLORATION

www.prenhall.com/armesto_maps

ASIA

FERGHANA

Oxus

SOGDIANA

Pamirs

BACTRIA

AFGHANISTAN

Indus

Taklamakan Desert

Dunhuang

Yellow River

CHINA

Yangtze

H i m a l a y a s

Ganges

Benares

Tropic of Cancer

20°

PACIFIC OCEAN

I N D I A

Bay of
Bengal

Arabian
Sea

Sea of Milk

(Erythraean Sea)

SRI LANKA
(Ceylon)

S
o
u
t
h
S
e
a
I
s
l
a
n
d
s

Equator

0°

INDIAN OCEAN

N

1,000 km

1,000 miles

60°

80°

100°

120°

140°

Among the consequences were penal colonies on islands of the Persian Gulf. A canal built from Suez on the Red Sea to the Nile indicates there must have been traffic for it to serve, traffic that the canal increased.

What Indian mapmakers called the Seas of Milk and Butter were, to Greek merchants, "the Erythraean Sea," from which traders brought back aromatics—especially frankincense and myrrh—and an Arabian cinnamon substitute called cassia. Many important ports for long-range trade lined Arabia's shores. At Gerrha, for instance, merchants unloaded Indian manufactures. Nearby, Thaj also served as a good place to warehouse imports, protected by stone walls more than a mile and a half in circumference and 15 feet thick. From Ma'in (ma-EEN), one of the south Arabian states Saba conquered (see Chapter 5), a merchant supplied Egyptian temples with incense in the third century B.C.E. We know this because he died in Egypt, and the story of his life is engraved on his stone coffin.

The reason for the long seafaring, sea-daring tradition of the Indian Ocean lies in the regularity of the monsoonal wind system. Above the equator, northeasterlies prevail in winter; but when winter ends, the direction of the winds is reversed. For most of the rest of the year, the winds blow steadily from the south and west, sucked toward the Asian landmass as air warms and rises over the continent. By timing voyages to take advantage of the predictable changes in the direction of the wind, navigators could set sail, confident of a fair wind out and a fair wind home.

Agatharchides of Kindos describes Saba

It is a fact not often appreciated that, overwhelmingly, the history of maritime exploration has been made into the wind, presumably because it was at least as important to get home as to get to anywhere new. This was how the Phoenicians and Greeks opened the Mediterranean to long-range commerce and colonization (see Chapter 5). The same strategy enabled South Sea Island navigators of this period to explore and colonize islands of the Pacific (see Chapter 10). The monsoonal wind system in the Indian Ocean freed navigators from such constraints. One must try to imagine what it would be like, feeling the wind, year after year, alternately in one's face and at one's back. Gradually, would-be seafarers realized how the changes of wind made outward ventures viable. They knew the wind would change, and so could risk an outward voyage without fearing that they might be cut off from the chance of returning home.

Still, the Indian Ocean has many hazards. Storms wrack it, especially in the Arabian Sea, the Bay of Bengal, and the deadly belt of bad weather that stretches across the Ocean below about ten degrees south of the equator. But the predictability of a homeward wind made this the world's most benign environment for long-range voyaging. The fixed-wind systems of the Atlantic and Pacific were almost impossible to cross with ancient technology. We know of no round trips across them. Even compared with other navigable seas, the reliability of the monsoon season offered other advantages. No reliable sources record the length of voyages in this period, but, to judge from later statistics, a trans-Mediterranean journey from east to west, against the wind, would take 50 to 70 days. With the monsoon, a ship could cross the entire Erythraean Sea, between India and a port on the Persian Gulf or near the Red Sea, in three or four weeks in either direction.

Land Routes: The Silk Roads

In the long run, sea routes were more important for global history than land routes. They carried a greater variety of goods faster, more economically, and in greater amounts. Nevertheless, in the early stages, most Eurasian long-range trade was small scale—in goods of high value and limited bulk. It relied on **emporium trading**—goods moved through a series of markets and middlemen, rather than an expedition across entire oceans and continents. In the axial age, the land routes that linked Eurasia were as important as the sea routes in establishing cultural contacts: bringing people from different cultures together, facilitating the flow of the ideas of the axial-age sages, transmitting the works of art that changed taste and the goods that influenced lifestyles.

Bit by bit, the evidence helps us see where and how these routes emerged, as a result of a mixture of economic and political initiatives, and what extremities they connected. From around the middle of the first millennium B.C.E., Chinese silks appeared here and there across Europe—in Athens, and at the site of present-day Budapest in Hungary, and in a series of south German and Rhineland burials. By the end of the millennium, we can trace the flow of Chinese manufactured goods from the southern Caspian to the northern Black Sea, and into what were then gold-rich kingdoms in the southwest stretches of the Eurasian steppe. Meanwhile, roads that kings built and maintained crossed what are now Turkey and Iran, penetrated Egypt and Mesopotamia, reached the Persian Gulf, and, at their easternmost ends, touched the Pamir (pah-MEER) Mountains in Afghanistan and crossed the Indus River.

Merchants could also use these routes. The first written evidence of presumed commerce across Eurasia appears in a report from Zhang Qian (jwhang-chee-en), a Chinese ambassador who set out for Bactria, one of the Greek-ruled kingdoms established in Central Asia in the wake of Alexander the Great—in ca. 139 B.C.E. His main objectives were, first, to recruit allies against the aggressive steppeland dwellers on China's northern borders and, second, to obtain horses for the Chinese army from the best breeders, deep in Central Asia (see Map 7.1).

Zhang Qian, *Hon Shu*, "Descriptions of the Western Regions"

His mission was one of the great adventures of history. Captured en route, he remained a hostage with the steppelanders for ten years. He escaped and continued across the Pamir Mountains and the River Oxus. He was captured again, escaped again, and finally reached home, with a steppeland wife in tow, after an absence of 12 years. He never encountered potential allies, but from a commercial point of view, his reports were highly favorable. The kingdoms beyond the Pamir Mountains had "cities, houses and mansions as in China." In Ferghana (fehr-GAH-nah) in what is today Central Asia, the horses "sweat blood and come from the stock of the heavenly horses." Zhang Qian saw Chinese cloth in Bactria. "When he asked how they obtained these things, the people told him their merchants bought them in India, which is a country several hundred li south-east [a li was about one-third of a mile]." From the time of his mission, "specimens of strange things began to arrive" in China "from every direction."

In 111 B.C.E., a Chinese garrison founded the outpost of Dunhuang (doon-hwang)—the name means "blazing beacon"—beyond China's western borders. It was a desolate region of desert and mountains. Here, according to a poem inscribed in one of the caves where travelers sheltered, was "the throat of Asia," where "the roads to the western ocean" converged like veins in the neck. We now call them the **Silk Roads**. They led to the markets of Central Asia—in the trading states of Bactria, and Ferghana and neighboring Sogdiana—and linked up with other routes: those that branched off into Tibet, or doubled back from beyond the Pamir Mountains toward India, or continued westward across the Iranian plateau toward Anatolia, Arabia, the Levant, and, ultimately, the Mediterranean.

From the neighborhood of Dunhuang, the Silk Roads skirted the Taklamakan (tahk-lah-mah-KAHN) Desert, under the mountains, to the north and south. It was a terrible journey, haunted, in Chinese accounts, by screaming demon drummers—personifications of the ferocious winds. But the desert was so demanding that it deterred even bandits, and the mountains offered some protection from the predatory nomads

Heavenly horse. Chinese artists have favored horses as subjects in almost every period, but never more than during the Han Dynasty (206 B.C.E.–220 C.E.), when an intense effort to import fine horses from Central Asia enriched China's equine bloodstock. More than for their utility, horses inspired artists—as in this example from Wuwei (Gansu province) of the second century C.E.—as symbols of the fleeting, ever-changing nature of human life.
The Art Archive/Picture Desk, Inc./Kobal Collection

China and the Silk Road

ca. 500 B.C.E.	Chinese silks appear in Europe
ca. 139 B.C.E.	Zhang Qian sets out for Bactria
111 B.C.E.	Chinese found Dunhuang
102 B.C.E.	Chinese invade Ferghana

who lived beyond them. The Taklamakan took 30 days to cross—clinging to the edges, where water drains from the surrounding mountains.

A few years after the founding of Dunhuang, a Chinese army, reputedly of 60,000 men, traveled to secure the mountain passes at the western end and to force the horse breeders of Ferghana to trade. A painted cave shows the general, Wudi (woo-dee), kneeling before the "golden men"—idols taken, or perhaps mistaken, for Buddhas—that Chinese forces seized. In ca. 102 B.C.E., the Chinese invaded Ferghana, diverted a river, and obtained 30,000 horses in tribute. Meanwhile, caravans from China reached Persia and Chinese trade goods became common along the eastern Mediterranean.

Trade across Eurasia exposed great disparities in wealth between East and West. These differences helped to shape the history of that region over the next 2,000 years. Already in the first century C.E., the Roman geographer, Pliny, worried about it. The Roman world produced little that its trading partners wanted, whereas the silks of China and the spices and incense of Arabia and the Indian Ocean were much in demand in Rome. The only way people in Europe could pay for them was in cash—gold or, more commonly, silver. Nowadays, we would call

○ MAKING CONNECTIONS ○

TRADE ROUTES AND THEIR CONNECTIONS

LONG-RANGE ROUTES →	ADVANTAGES →	GEOGRAPHICAL SCOPE →	COMMERCE AND EXCHANGE →	POLITICAL SYSTEMS
Sea Route: Indian Ocean	Changeable, predictable monsoon winds lead to reliable schedules; great variety and amount of goods can be carried via ship (emporium trading); seaborne trade usually faster than land routes	East Africa, Arabia, India, southeast Asia; canal between Red Sea and Nile River eventually connects to Mediterranean	Aromatics (incense), spices, gold, and "thousands of other things" (including wild animals)	African kingdoms, Indian empires and kingdoms, Arabian tribal chiefdoms, Mediterranean empires
Land Route: Silk Roads across Eurasia	Less investment needed to embark on small-scale trading expeditions; more cultural contacts between vastly different peoples; widespread trade of high-value items	China, Bactria, Sogdiana, Persia, Mesopotamia, Anatolia, Caspian/Black Sea, Mediterranean	Spices, silk, gold, silver, cloth, horses, aromatics	Imperial China, Central Asian kingdoms, Egypt, nomadic tribes of Middle East, Persian Empire, Roman Empire, Mediterranean city-states
Sea Route: Mediterranean	Relatively high population densities along the coastal Mediterranean provides more opportunities for trade, numerous ports; shorter distances, calmer waters than vast Indian Ocean routes	Europe, North Africa, southwest Asia, Black Sea, with Red Sea–Nile canal connections to Arabia, Indian Ocean route	Grain, wine, olive oil, timber, metals	Greek city-states/colonies, Egypt, North African city-states, Roman Empire

this an adverse **balance of trade**—the value of Europe's imports from Asia far surpassed the value of its exports. The problems of financing it, by finding enough silver, and ultimately of overcoming and reversing it, by finding and supplying goods Asians wanted to buy, became a major theme of the history of the West and, in the long run, as we shall see, of the world.

THE FIRST EURASIAN EMPIRE: PERSIA

A glance at the map shows how the region we know today as Iran commanded a central position in the developing trade across Eurasia, linking Central Asian markets to those of southwest Asia and the Mediterranean. So—in view of the way trade and empire are mutually nourishing—it is not surprising that the first of the great empires of the axial age originated here.

In earlier periods, Akkadians and Assyrians had carried the traditions of lowland Mesopotamia north into their hills, like booty. Now conquerors from the adjoining and even higher tableland used the same traditions to create a new state. This state became the biggest the world had yet known: the Persian Empire (see Map 7.2).

The Persian Heartland

The heartland of the Persian Empire in what is today Iran consisted of scatterings of good soil and precious water in a vast, arid plateau. Ragae, with its brackish streams and sweet wells overlooked the Zagros (ZAH-grohs) Mountains. Hamadan lay in a valley watered with springs, known for good fruit and inferior wheat. The Kur Valley of Fars (fahrs) was the richest area in ancient times. Water

General Wudi worships the Buddha. In the early second century B.C.E., shortly after the founding of Dunhuang, the Chinese General Wudi invaded Central Asia along the Silk Roads in search of horses. "Two golden men" were among the other booty he captured. Buddhist painters at Dunhuang assumed that these statues were Buddhas and depicted Wudi worshipping them.

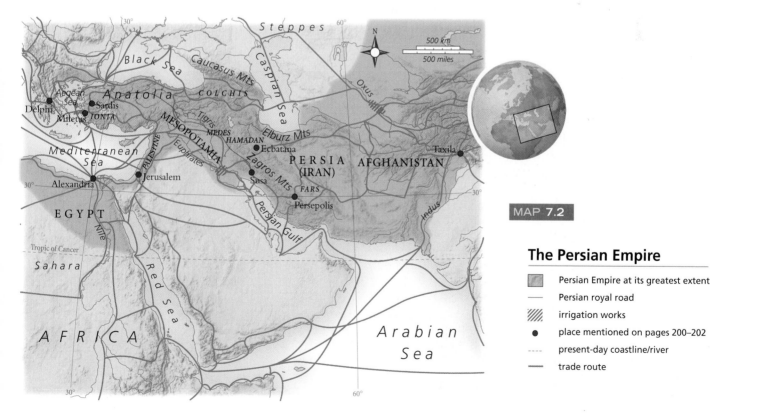

MAP 7.2

The Persian Empire

- ▨ Persian Empire at its greatest extent
- — Persian royal road
- ▨ irrigation works
- ● place mentioned on pages 200–202
- ---- present-day coastline/river
- — trade route

from the Zayinda Rud—a modest stream much glorified in poetry—enriched the plain of Isfahan (IHS-fah-hahn), where the inhabitants used pigeon droppings for fertilizer. Rivers—including the Tigris and Euphrates—laced the southwest. Here, at the old trading city of Susa (SOO-sah), on the border of the Mesopotamian world, the Persians established the capital of their state. Generally, between mountains and deserts, lay narrow strips of good pasture and land, watered by seasonal streams that could be irrigated for farming. Like the old Hittite Empire (see Chapter 4), Persia was another alliance of farmers and flocks. Hymns, that are among the earliest sources for Iranian history, praise herders and husbandmen as followers of truth and pronounce their nomadic enemies "adherents of lies, who uproot crops and waste livestock," which would be better employed fertilizing farmland. Farming communities' depictions of bull sacrifice show spurting blood transformed into sprouting wheat.

The founding of the Persian Empire is traditionally credited to Cyrus (SEYE-rus) the Great, a general from the province of Fars. Toward the mid–sixth century B.C.E., he launched a coup to take over one of the biggest successor-states of Assyria, the kingdom of the Medes (meedz). His subsequent campaigns stretched from Palestine to Afghanistan. His power reached almost the farthest limits the Persian Empire would ever attain. Legends credited him with dreams foretelling the conquest of Europe and Asia. This seems doubtful. His inscriptions call him simply, "I, Cyrus, the Achaemenid" (eh-KEE-meh-nihd)—the name of a proud but previously provincial family to which he belonged. But he headed a conquest state, poor in resources, with a need to keep growing. The Persian Empire gradually adopted the old world–conquering ambitions of Sargon of Akkad (see Chapter 3) and the Assyrians but with a difference: The Persians put these ambitions into practice.

The empire joined two regions—Mesopotamian and Persian—that mountains had formerly divided. At its greatest extent, it encompassed Greek cities on the Aegean coast, Egypt, and the Indian city of Taxila beyond the Indus River. It was an

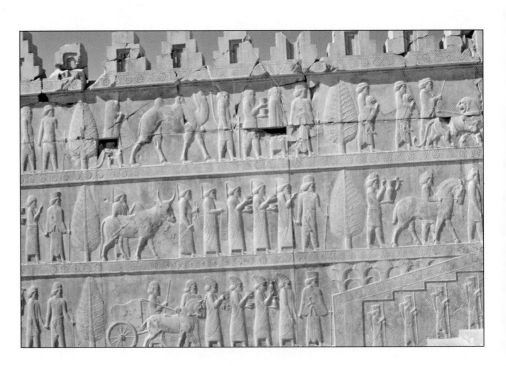

Persepolis. Reliefs that line the approach to the audience chamber of the ruler of Persia at Persepolis show exactly what went on there: reception of tribute, submission of ambassadors. The figures look uniform at first, but their various styles of beards, headgear, and robes indicate the diversity of the lands from which they came and, therefore, the range of the Great King's power.

empire of unprecedented scale that relied on long-range trade and, therefore, needed to invest in communications. By early in the fifth century B.C.E., nearly 1700 miles of road crossed the empire from Susa to Sardis in western Anatolia. Royal armies tramped them at a rate of 19 miles a day, and "Nothing mortal," it was said, "travels as fast as the royal messengers." The road was also a channel for tribute. Carvings at the imperial city of Persepolis (puhr-SEH-poh-lees), founded deep inside Iran around the end of the sixth century B.C.E., show ivory, gold, and exotic animals arriving at the court of the ruler of Persia, the "Great King."

Persian Government

Persia was more than a robber empire. Persian rule gave good value to subjects in remote regions. The empire provided a canal linking the Nile to the Red Sea and irrigation works on the Oxus and the Karun Rivers. Forts beyond the Caucasus (KAW-kah-suhs) Mountains kept steppe nomads at bay. At Jerusalem, Cyrus the Great undertook to rebuild the temple that symbolized the city's sanctity for the Jews, whom the Babylonians had deported to Mesopotamia (see Chapter 6). Cyrus's gesture was typical of the way Persian rulers conciliated the subjects they acquired. In gratitude, the biblical prophet Isaiah hailed Cyrus as God's anointed.

Greeks accused Persians of treating their kings like gods, in the Egyptian manner, because Persians had to prostrate themselves before the king, but this charge was unjust. Persian kings were not gods, but their right to rule was god given. Many inscriptions describe Ahura Mazda, god of light, as investing the king with power. The court religion—which was, effectively, for much of the time, the state religion—was the cult of fire and light that Zoroaster supposedly founded (see Chapter 6).

The other Persian practices that Greeks found peculiar were the Persian love of luxury—a criticism excused, perhaps, by envy—and their respect for women. Surviving Achaemenid ration lists—the records of wages and payments in kind that court personnel received—assign professions by sex. These show that royal attendants could be of either sex and that women could supervise mixed groups of men and women and earn higher wages than men. It was not, however, a society of sexual equality. Scribes had to be male, while servers of rations—the lowest category by pay—had to be female. Mothers got extra rations for the birth of boys. Nevertheless, women could hold property in their own right. This gave them a political role as what, in modern American politics, would be called "campaign funders"—backers and patrons of men who sought power. Greek sources, exaggerating the amount of power women enjoyed as a result, blamed every lurch of palace politics on female willfulness. For Greeks, who barred women from political life in their own communities, saw them as dangerous agents of chaos in other cultures' states.

The Persian-Greek Wars

Greeks who lived on and beyond the western edge of the Persian Empire were in a giant's shadow. They needed to find ways to cope with insecurity and defeat fear. In about 500 B.C.E., the ruler of Miletus, a Greek colony on the Ionian shore of western Anatolia, showed a map of the world to the rulers of Sparta, a city in mainland Greece with a great reputation in war (see Map 7.3). Engraved on a bronze tablet, the map showed two roughly equal areas—an exaggeratedly large Europe at the top, like a protruding lip over Asia and Africa crammed into the lower half.

The image was unrealistic, but the agenda was clear. Asia was reduced to a manageable conquest. The Miletian proposed an alliance against Persia.

Was the map a sign of confidence or bravado? It looked brash, but it concealed unease. Some combined raids by Greeks states followed Miletus's initiative, but they ended in failure. The Persian Empire had already conquered the mainland north of Ionia and launched into the sea, controlling Samos and all islands to the north. Rumors claimed that the Persians wanted to conquer Europe because "its trees were too fine for anyone but the Great King to possess." More likely, the empire was committed to expanding because it needed tribute from subject-lands to support it. In any event, the Greeks saw the Persians as a threat, but did not feel threatened enough to stop feuding with each other even when the Persians prepared to invade Greece.

The Greek world was in panic—but the panic was not strong enough to make Greeks unite. The oracle of Delphi (Chapter 5) even advised submitting to Persian rule, with its reputation for efficiency, generosity, and respect for trade. In the wars that followed, intermittently, throughout the fifth century and into the fourth, Greek unity was sporadic, occurring only in dire moments of Persian invasion. Persia, after testing the difficulties of conquering Greece in unsuccessful invasions in 490 and 480 B.C.E., was generally content to keep these enemies divided, while prioritizing Persian rule over rich, soft Egypt.

The sea became the effective frontier between the Greek and Persian worlds. A Persian decree of 387 B.C.E. sums it up: the king "deems it right that the cities in Asia be his. . . . The other Greek cities, both small and great, shall be independent," while most of the Greek colonies on the islands of the Aegean were divided between Persia and Athens. This was an indication that Athens—best resourced of the Greek cities because it controlled silver mines—had imperial ambitions of its own, which many Greek states found more menacing than those of Persia.

MAP 7.3

The World According to Hecataeus

In 500 B.C.E., the ruler of Miletus, a Greek city on the coast of Anatolia, commissioned a world map in bronze to encourage a Greek alliance against Persia. The map showed a big Europe dominating Asia and Africa and probably resembled this reconstruction.

The Empire of Alexander the Great

Not even Athens could assert long-term hegemony in Greece. Macedon, however, could. Macedon is an example of a now familiar fact: On the edges of civilizations, chiefdoms developed into states. This northern kingdom had what to southern Greeks was a barbarian background, but Greece profoundly influenced its culture. Increasingly, in the fourth century B.C.E., Macedonians saw themselves as Greeks. Aristotle (see Chapter 6) served as a tutor to the royal court.

In 338 B.C.E., King Philip of Macedon imposed unity by force on the Greeks and revived the idea of conquering Persia. When he was assassinated—allegedly by a Persian-backed conspiracy—two years later, his 19-year-old son, Alexander, inherited his father's ambitions. For Philip, attacking Persia was probably intended to focus his uneasily united realm on an external enemy. Alexander's motivation, however, has baffled historians. Was he seeking to vindicate his dead father? Or to reenact legendary romances of Greek campaigns in Asia, which filled his head from his boyhood reading? Or was he full of insatiable ambition to leave "no world unconquered" as some early biographers claimed? Did he have humdrum economic aims? He certainly showed interest in opening up Indian Ocean trade or seizing control of its routes. He ordered reconnaissance by sea of the routes between India, Persia, and Arabia, and began, just before his death, to plan the conquest of Arabia.

Probably, his ambitions grew with his success. Alexander destroyed the Persian Empire at lightning speed in three years' campaigns from 334 B.C.E. (see Map 7.4). When the last Persian emperor died at his own officers' hands, perhaps because he had decided to abandon resistance, Alexander proclaimed himself "Great King." His success seems inexplicable except in terms of the interconnected skill and luck of the battlefield. The Persian Empire was essentially strong, well run, and easily governed. Alexander took it over intact, maintained its methods of control, and divided it at will among his subordinates.

Success and flattering omens convinced him that he enjoyed divine favor—perhaps, even, that he was divine. His methods became increasingly arbitrary, his character increasingly unpredictable. He dealt with disloyalty first by judicial murder, then assassination, then slaughter by his own hand, then arbitrary executions. In the last years of his life, his control slipped. He failed to impose Persian rituals of homage on his Greek and Macedonian followers who felt that it was demeaning to prostrate themselves before a mere mortal, even if he was a king. He sought conquests beyond Persia's frontiers, but his troops became insubordinate, and he had to halt his invasion of India, shortly after crossing the Indus. Characteristically, Alexander saved face by pretending he had submitted not to the demands of his men, but to warnings from the gods. He had just set the conquest of Arabia as his next objective when he fell dead at age 32, from unknown causes, during a drinking bout—the favorite Macedonian form of excess.

It was what modern publicists might call "a great career move." He became the world's most written-about hero. Epic romancers embroidered his life with wonder stories of his uncontainable prowess. They credited him with exploring the depths of the ocean and ascending to heaven in a chariot drawn by ravens. An epic poem celebrated him in Malay. Kings in India, Ethiopia, and Scotland named themselves after him.

Rise and Fall of the Persian Empire

Sixth century B.C.E.	Cyrus the Great founds Achaemenid dynasty
Early fifth century B.C.E.	Completion of royal road from Susa to Sardis
490 and 480 B.C.E.	Unsuccessful efforts to conquer Greece
334 B.C.E.	Alexander conquers Persian Empire

MAP 7.4

The Empire of Alexander the Great

Empire of Alexander at its greatest extent

route of Alexander the Great

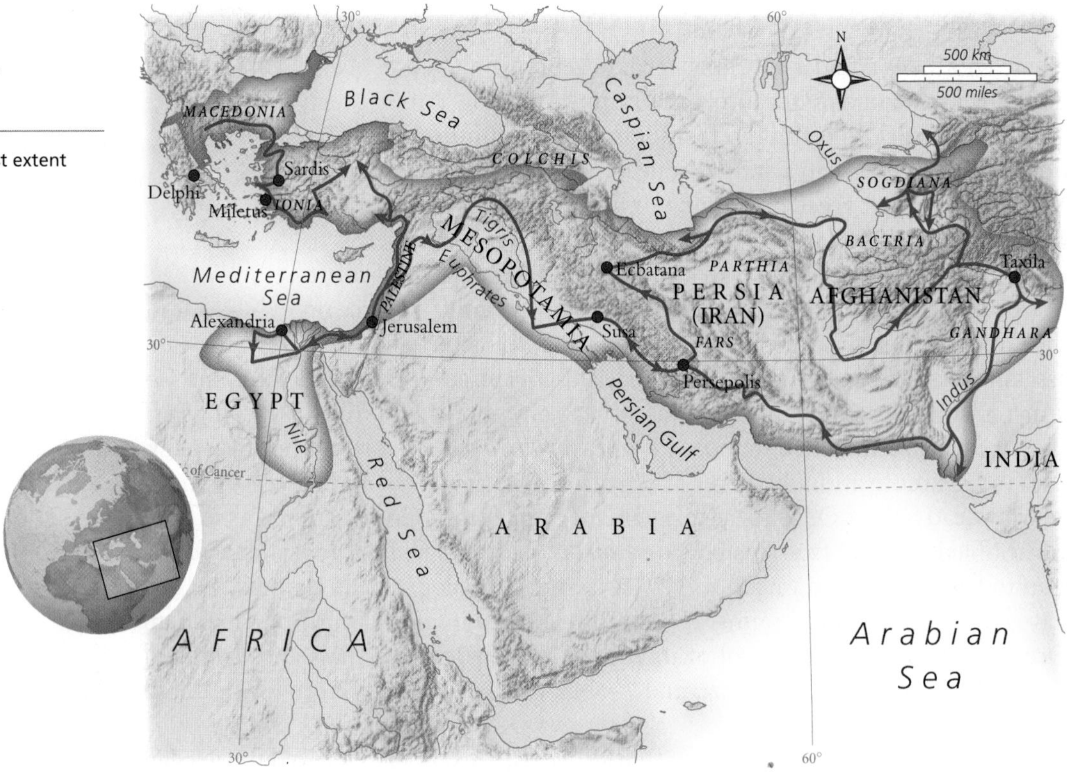

MACEDONIA
Black Sea
Caspian Sea
COLCHIS
Delphi
Sardis
Miletus
IONIA
Mediterranean Sea
Alexandria
Jerusalem
PALESTINE
MESOPOTAMIA
Tigris
Euphrates
Ecbatana
PARTHIA
PERSIA (IRAN)
Susa
FARS
Persepolis
Persian Gulf
Oxus
SOGDIANA
BACTRIA
AFGHANISTAN
Taxila
GANDHARA
Indus
INDIA
EGYPT
Nile
Red Sea
ARABIA
AFRICA
Arabian Sea
500 km
500 miles
N
30°
60°

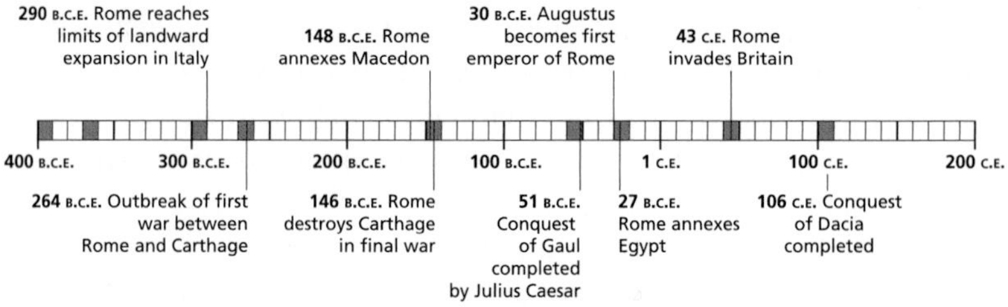

290 B.C.E. Rome reaches limits of landward expansion in Italy
148 B.C.E. Rome annexes Macedon
30 B.C.E. Augustus becomes first emperor of Rome
43 C.E. Rome invades Britain
400 B.C.E.
300 B.C.E.
200 B.C.E.
100 B.C.E.
1 C.E.
100 C.E.
200 C.E.
264 B.C.E. Outbreak of first war between Rome and Carthage
146 B.C.E. Rome destroys Carthage in final war
51 B.C.E. Conquest of Gaul completed by Julius Caesar
27 B.C.E. Rome annexes Egypt
106 C.E. Conquest of Dacia completed

His material legacy was surprisingly meager. His empire did not outlast him. But long-term, long-range cultural exchanges throve in the states among which it fragmented. On the frontiers of India, the kingdom of Gandhara (gahn-DAH-rah) combined Buddhist religion and Greek-style art. In Alexandria, the city Alexander founded at the Nile Delta, Greek and Egyptian traditions fused. Through the kingdoms of Bactria and Sogdiana, the trade of the Silk Roads funneled. A Persian rump state, Parthia (PAHR-thee-ah), arose in the Iranian heartland and soon conquered Mesopotamia, but the defeat of Persia's empire and the collapse of Alexander's left a power vacuum in the eastern Mediterranean that none of Alexander's many imitators could fill. The eventual beneficiary was Rome.

THE RISE OF ROME

One of the great unsolved puzzles of history is how a small city-state of obscure origins and limited manpower conquered the Mediterranean, extended its frontiers to the Atlantic and North Sea, and transformed almost every culture it touched. The

Romans started as a community of peasants, huddling for defense in an unstrategic spot. The site of Rome had poor soil, no metals, and no outlet to the sea. Its inhabitants became warlike by necessity. They had no way to gain wealth except at their neighbors' expense.

The Romans organized their society for war, and made victory their supreme value. Roman citizens owed the state at least 16 years of military service. They learned—to quote Horace again—that "to die for the fatherland is sweet and fitting." Their generals celebrated victories in triumphal public parades, showing off booty and prisoners. Roman education emphasized the virtues of patience and endurance. As a result, Rome was exceptionally well equipped to tough out defeats. Like those other great imperialists, the nineteenth-century British, they could "lose battles but win wars."

Gandharan sculpture. Soldiers of Alexander the Great (r. 336–323 B.C.E.) founded the kingdom of Gandhara. Greek influence is unmistakable in its art: in the realistic modeling, the sculptural plasticity, the deep reliefs. Buddhist piety dominates the subject matter. Here the artist illustrates the legend of how King Sibi became a Buddha by sacrificing his eyes and flesh to save the life of a pigeon while gods look on.
Copyright The British Museum.

This was particularly evident in the Punic Wars the Romans fought against Carthage (see Chapter 5) for domination of the western Mediterranean and adjoining regions. The background against which they began is clear enough. In the late third century B.C.E., Roman armies reached the limits of landward expansion in Italy. They were therefore tempted further afield. First, they turned their aggression westward, toward the wealth of Sardinia, Sicily, and Spain. They were not, however, the only imperialists drawn toward those lands. Carthage, the most formidable naval empire of the western Mediterranean, already had colonies, allies, and subject-communities there. Reluctantly, the Romans took to the sea to fight the Carthaginians. This was remarkable, as the Romans hated the sea. "Whoever first dared to float a ship," wrote Horace in about 30 B.C.E., "must have had a heart of oak covered with a triple layer of bronze." Carthage recovered from every defeat, until in 146 B.C.E. Rome finally destroyed it and turned the western Mediterranean into a zone free of rivals. Historians generally regard these wars as the crucial episode in the ascent of Rome.

 Horace, "Dulce et Decorum est Pro Patria Mori"

Meanwhile, on its eastern flank, Rome invaded the islands of the Adriatic Sea and then engaged the major powers of the eastern Mediterranean. Macedon was first to fall, annexed to Rome in 148 B.C.E., after 50 years of intermittent wars. The rich kingdom of Pergamum, in Anatolia, once part of the Persian Empire, was next. When its last king died, he willed his kingdom to the Roman people in 133 B.C.E. Then came Syria and Palestine. When Rome annexed Egypt in 30 B.C.E., it controlled virtually all the shores of the Mediterranean (see Map 7.5).

The Roman Frontiers

The Roman Empire was an empire of coasts, with the sea as it central axis. It therefore exposed long, vulnerable frontiers to landward. On the African and Levantine shores, Roman territory seemed protected—delusionally, as it turned out—by deserts. The European flank, however, despite a hundred years of further conquests, never seemed satisfactorily established. There was no reliable barrier against attack. An endless quest for security led beyond the Mediterranean to the

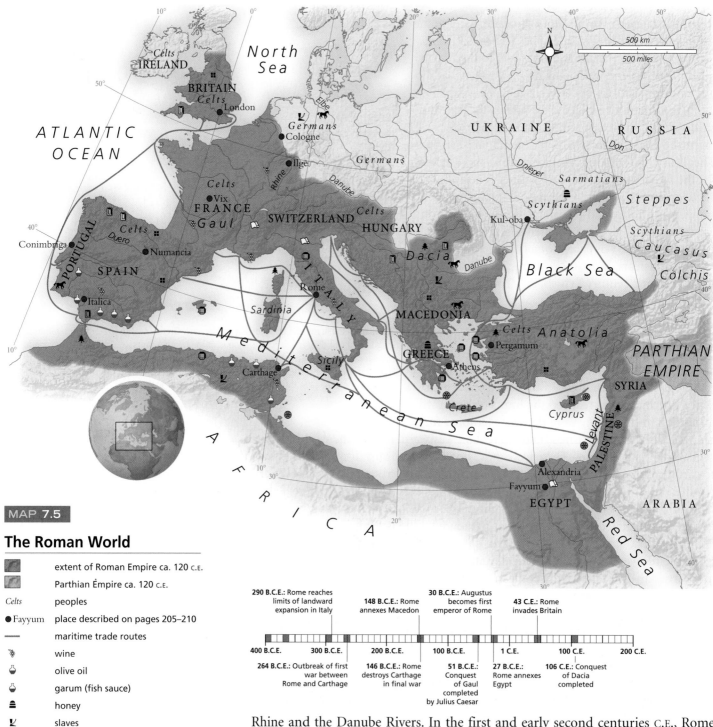

MAP **7.5**

The Roman World

	extent of Roman Empire ca. 120 C.E.
	Parthian Empire ca. 120 C.E.
Celts	peoples
●Fayyum	place described on pages 205–210
—	maritime trade routes
	wine
	olive oil
	garum (fish sauce)
	honey
	slaves
	horses
	wool
	flax/linen
	murex (purple dye)
	marble
	timber
	gold
	tin
	copper

290 B.C.E.: Rome reaches limits of landward expansion in Italy

148 B.C.E.: Rome annexes Macedon

30 B.C.E.: Augustus becomes first emperor of Rome

43 C.E.: Rome invades Britain

400 B.C.E. 300 B.C.E. 200 B.C.E. 100 B.C.E. 1 C.E. 100 C.E. 200 C.E.

264 B.C.E.: Outbreak of first war between Rome and Carthage

146 B.C.E.: Rome destroys Carthage in final war

51 B.C.E.: Conquest of Gaul completed by Julius Caesar

27 B.C.E.: Rome annexes Egypt

106 C.E.: Conquest of Dacia completed

Rhine and the Danube Rivers. In the first and early second centuries C.E., Rome lavished resources on the conquest of Dacia (modern Romania), where deadly womenfolk were said to torture prisoners, flaying them with staves, clawing them with fingernails, burning them with torches. The Romans subdued Dacia, but the result was an even longer and more irrational frontier.

Roman expeditions also tested German defenses as far east as the Elbe River, but the Germans seemed worse than the Dacians—too barbaric to absorb. They were "wild creatures" incapable of laws or civilized arts, according to Velleius, a Roman cavalry officer who fought them around 4 B.C.E. Julius Caesar (d. 44 B.C.E.), whose methodical generalship extended the empire to the Rhine, regarded that

Romans and barbarians. Presumably, the Roman general who dominates the composition—in the center, with arm outstretched—was buried inside this magnificent sarcophagus of the mid–third century C.E. Bearded Germans succumb beneath the horses' hooves of the clean-shaven Romans. In reality, the Germans were not so easy to defeat.

river as the limit of civilization. So Rome abandoned the Germans to their own devices. This was probably a mistake. Almost all speakers of Germanic languages outside those in Switzerland and the Rhineland were left outside the empire, seething with resentment and vengefulness at their exclusion from the wealth they associated with Rome. If Rome had absorbed them and the other sedentary peoples beyond its frontiers, as China did at the other end of Eurasia, the Roman Empire might have proved as durable as China's. The sedentary peoples China absorbed on its frontiers formed a formidable coalition, guarding the Chinese Empire against nomadic outsiders.

Imperial Culture and Commerce

Retired soldiers—Latin-speaking and schooled in allegiance to Rome—helped spread a common culture across the empire, settling in lands where they had been stationed and often marrying local women. On his tombstone in Cologne, in the Rhineland, the image of a retired veteran from southern Spain reclines; his wife and son serve food and wine from an elegant, claw-footed table. A tombstone in northern Britain commemorates a 16-year-old boy from Roman Syria. He died, says the inscription, "in the land of the Cimmerians"—the rainy, foggy land that the Greek poet Homer (see Chapter 5) had imagined on the way to the underworld.

Roman culture was so well known in Britain, despite the remoteness of the province, that mints in the third century C.E. could stamp coins with references to the poetry of Virgil—the epic poet who, in the reign of Augustus (r. 27 B.C.E.– 14 C.E.), celebrated Rome's foundation myth. Everywhere, the empire promoted the same classical style for buildings and urban planning: symmetrical, harmonious, regular, and based on Greek architecture. The artistic traditions of subject-peoples became provincial styles. For instance, the last monuments of the funerary

TOMBSTONE OF A ROMAN SOLDIER

The Roman Empire shifted people across vast distances. This tombstone in Cologne, Germany, records a veteran soldier, Marcus Valerius Celerinus, who married and settled locally after his legion was transferred to Germany from his home in Écija in southern Spain, late in the first century C.E.

His wife, Marcia Procula, sits in a subordinate position, ready to serve him from a basket of fruit.

Marcus reclines to dine, the way a Roman gentleman would. At his elbow is his slave. A table with wine cups and a wine jar stands beside him.

The inscription proclaims the image "from life" of Marcus, naming his tribe, his citizenship of his birthplace in Spain, and his status as a veteran of the Tenth Legion.

at does this tombstone reveal about Roman culture early in the first millennium C.E.?

art of the pharaohs are the Fayyum portraits, which stare from the surfaces of burial caskets in Roman Egypt. They are recognizably in an ancient Egyptian tradition, yet faces as realistic and sensitive as these might be found in portraits anywhere in the Roman Empire.

Engineering was the Romans' ultimate art. They discovered how to make cement, which made unprecedented feats of building possible. Everywhere the empire reached, Romans invested in infrastructure, building roads, sewers, and aqueducts. Amphitheatres, temples, city walls, public baths, and monumental gates were erected at public expense, alongside the temples that civic-minded patrons usually endowed. The buildings serviced new cities, built in Rome's image, where there were none before, or enlarged and embellished cities that already existed. The biggest courthouse in the empire was in London, the widest street in Italica, a Roman city in southwest Spain. Colonists in Conimbriga, on the coast of Portugal, where salt spray corroded the mosaic floors, demolished their town center in the first century C.E. and rebuilt it to resemble Rome's. Trade as well as war shipped elements of a common culture around the empire. Rome exported Mediterranean amenities—the building patterns of villas and cities, wine, olive oil, mosaics—to the provinces, or forced Mediterranean crops like wine grapes and olive trees to grow in unlikely climates.

As industries became geographically specialized, trade and new commercial relationships crisscrossed the entire empire. In the first century C.E., merchants from the Duero valley in Spain were buried in Hungary. Greek potters made huge jars to transport wine from Spain to southern France. In southwest Spain, huge evaporators survive from the factories where garum—the empire's favorite fish sauce—was made from the blood and entrails of tuna and mackerel. The lives of cloth merchants from northeast France are engraved on a tomb at Igel, on the frontier of Germany. They conveyed bales of cloth by road and river and sold it in elegant shops, lavishing their profits on banquets to lord it over their farming neighbors.

Of course, as the empire grew, its political institutions changed. When Rome was a small city-republic, two annually elected chief executives, called consuls, shared power between themselves, subject to checks by the assembly of nobles and notables known as the senate, and by the tribunes, representatives of the common citizens. Increasingly, however, as the state expanded, in the emergencies of war, power was confided to individuals, called dictators, who were expected to relinquish control when the emergency was over. In the second half of the first century B.C.E., this system finally broke down in a series of struggles between rival contenders for sole power. In 27 B.C.E., all parties accepted Augustus, who had emerged as victor from the civil wars, as head of state and of government for life, with the right to name his successor.

Effectively, henceforth, Rome was a monarchy, though Romans, schooled in republicanism, hated to use the word. Part of the consequence of Roman distaste for kings was that the rules of succession to supreme power were never perfectly defined. Although the hereditary principle tended to prevail, it was never fully respected. Augustus called himself *princeps*—a word roughly equivalent to "chief" in English. Gradually, however, "emperor" took over as the name people normally used to designate the ruler. The Latin term— *imperator*—originally meant an army commander, and the army, or parts of the army, often in rivalry with each other, increasingly took

Fayyum portrait. When Egypt became a Roman province in 30 B.C.E., burial practices remained the same: Mummies were encased in painted caskets. But the style of painting that depicted the deceased gradually took on Roman conventions of portraiture, as in this lovely example of a young woman from the mid–second century C.E.

Aqueduct. Nearly 3,000 feet long and rising to 115 feet high, the second-century C.E. aqueduct of Segovia, Spain, is one of the surviving marvels of Roman engineering. In laying the infrastructure of communications and supply, the Romans were not only building up their own power and their ability to shift and sustain armies, they were also demonstrating spectacularly the benefits, self-confidence, and durability of their rule for their subject and "allied" peoples.

Roman Expansion

ca. 290 B.C.E.	Rome reaches limit of expansion in Italy
146 B.C.E.	Rome destroys Carthage
148 B.C.E.	Rome annexes Macedon
133 B.C.E.	Pergamum added to Roman Empire
51 B.C.E.	Conquest of Gaul completed
30 B.C.E.	Rome annexes Egypt
43 C.E.	Rome invades Britain
106 C.E.	Conquest of Dacia completed

to itself the role of dethroning and electing emperors.

Nonetheless, unified command and sustained leadership helped to make the growing empire manageable, but the problem remained of melding such diverse and widespread peoples into a single state. Roman identity—a sense of belonging to Rome—spread with Roman ways of life, as Rome granted Roman citizenship to subject-communities. Envoys from allies on the Atlantic and Black Sea came to Rome to hang offerings in the temple of Jupiter, "greatest and best" of Rome's guardian gods. Yet this was by no means a uniform empire. It was so big that it could only work by permitting the provinces to retain their local customs and religious practices. At one level it was a federation of cities, at another a federation of peoples. Everywhere, Rome ruled with the collaboration—sometimes enforced—of established elites. Spanish notables with barbarous names followed Roman law in legal decisions that they ordered to be carved in bronze. Hebrew princes and Germanic chiefs ruled as imperial delegates. Celts were Rome's partners in the west, Greeks in the east, where Greek rather than Latin was the most widespread common tongue and served at most levels as the official language of government.

The Celts

The Celts dominated Western Europe by the mid–first millennium B.C.E. They occupied present-day France, Britain, Ireland, and most of Spain. Their settlements were widespread in Central Europe and even reached Anatolia. Everywhere they lived in numerous chiefdoms and small states. What united them was language. They all spoke mutually intelligible versions of a single tongue.

Stories about the Celts made Roman gooseflesh ripple. They hunted human heads and hung them on their saddles. They stitched sacrifice victims for burning inside wicker images of gods. They had a reputation for drunkenness. A 35-year-old Celtic hostess at Vix in central France, was buried with a Greek wine vessel so large that it had to be imported in sections and assembled on arrival. The Celts' courage was also renowned. Roman sculpture shows them dead or dying but never giving up.

Despite their fierce and undisciplined reputation, the Celts had a way of life that Romans recognized as civilized. For one thing, the Celts had a professional learned class, the Druids. They were supposedly suspicious of writing wisdom down, but many inscriptions survive, including laws, administrative records, and a calendar to foretell the future. When Julius Caesar conquered the Celts in Gaul (modern France in the 50s B.C.E.) he used captured census returns to calculate the number of men he faced.

Urbanization in Celtic lands was patchy before Roman conquest. Caractacus, for example, a captured British Celtic chief paraded in triumph in Rome, marveled that inhabitants of such a city could covet his poor huts. But there were modest Celtic towns in France and Spain. The town of Numancia, which was rich in iron, was a minor metropolis by Celtic standards. Covering almost 1,800 square feet, it was arranged in neat streets up to 21 feet wide. Here, on one terrible campaign, the Romans took 3,000 oxhides and 800 horses in booty. The dwellings of Numancia were of mud and thatch on a rubble base, but the inhabitants enjoyed freshwater supplies and sanitary drainage.

By the time Rome seriously began to wage war on them—early in the last quarter of the second century B.C.E.—the Celts of what is now France had a soci-

Celtic conspicuous consumption: this wine vessel, buried with the queen or princess to whom it belonged in the mid-first millennium B.C.E., was as tall as she was. Too big and heavy to handle, it was just for show. Like the wine it contained, it was imported from the Mediterranean. Greek soldiers and chariots decorate the rim. Serpent-haired Gorgons form handles, inside which lions climb—all symbolizing the owner's power.

ety Romans acknowledged as like their own: no longer organized along tribal lines but according to wealth, prowess, and ancestry. Nobility was measured in livestock, not land. Peasant-tenants paid their rents in calves, pigs, and grain. After ferocious initial resistance to Roman conquest, Celts usually accepted Romanization and became enthusiastic subjects of and collaborators in the Roman Empire. Generally, they welcomed the enriching economic consequences of the peace the Romans enforced.

THE BEGINNINGS OF IMPERIALISM IN INDIA

Meanwhile, beyond the eastern frontiers of Persia, in India, Alexander's threat seems to have had an immediately galvanizing effect. When one of his generals recrossed the Indus in 305 B.C.E., he found the states of the Ganges valley confederated under a leader from the delta region, Candragupta (chahn-drah-GOOP-tah). The sources are hazy, however, until the next reign, that of Asoka (ah-SHOH-kah), which began in the 260s B.C.E. The *Arthasastra* (ahr-tha-SHAS-trah), purportedly the work of a servant of Candragupta, describes the political world of Asoka. More importantly, his thoughts and deeds come to life in the many decrees and self-reflexive ruminations he had inscribed on pillars and rock faces. If it were not such an awful pun, one would say that the rock inscriptions are hard evidence.

 Excerpts from the *Arthasastra*, "The Duties of Government Superintendents"

The sources show first, the extraordinarily long reach of Asoka's power. The rock inscriptions are scattered around the Indian subcontinent, but concentrated in three areas: the Ganges valley, a frontier zone in and around the Krishna (KREESH-nah) valley, and a northwest mountain zone on the upper Indus (see Map 7.6). Second, the evidence reveals an expanding realm, constantly reforging environments. "The king shall populate the countryside," says the *Arthasastra*, "by creating villages on virgin land or by reviving abandoned village sites. Settlement can be effected either by shifting some of the population of his own country or by immigration of foreigners. . . . The villages shall be so sited as to provide mutual protection. . . . Like a barren cow, a kingdom without people yields nothing."

The same source describes two main types of environment—one rainy and the other requiring irrigation—and specifies suitable crops for both: two varieties of rice, two of millet, wheat, and barley, six sorts of beans, four types of oil seeds, various vegetables, herbs, and spices. The king is responsible for irrigation and should encourage others to irrigate by exempting them from the water tax. Pasture, mines, and forests (for obtaining war elephants) are all worthy objects of conquest. Roads are emphasized, with sign posts and wells at nine-mile intervals. Regulating trade—including coinage, weights, and measures—and processing the raw materials of royal lands are also part of the ruler's job.

Government

Methods and means of government reflected central control. Peasants paid a quarter of their produce in tax, apparently directly to the king, with no mention of any intermediate rulers. (In Lumbini, where the Buddha was born, they paid only an eighth, as a mark of the king's piety.) Army leaders received pay in cash, rather than being given a share of royal power, as was customary in later Indian states. Asoka's inscriptions portray him as what we would now call a hands-on ruler. He "received reports at all times"—in his harem or gardens, his carriage, or his barns, where he inspected his livestock. "And whatever I order by word of mouth, whether it concerns a donation or proclamation or whatever urgent matter is entrusted by my

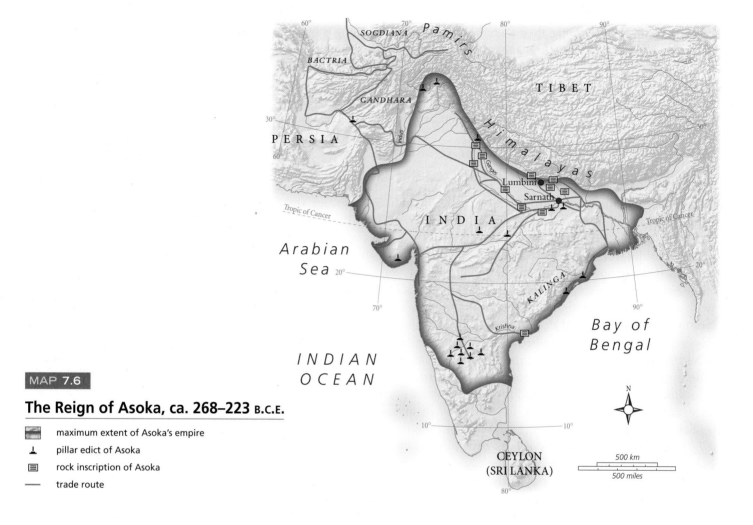

The Reign of Asoka, ca. 268–223 B.C.E.

maximum extent of Asoka's empire

pillar edict of Asoka

rock inscription of Asoka

trade route

officers, if there is any dispute or deliberation about it at the Council, it is to be reported to me immediately."

The *Arthasastra* expresses an ideology of universal rule and emphasizes the supremacy of "the king's law" and the importance of uniform justice. It is hard to know, however, what this meant in practice. India was already becoming a **caste** society, where social rank was inherited, unchangeable, and made sacred by religious sanctions. Brahmanical literature (see Chapter 5) treated women as if they were imperfectly human, though Buddhism admitted them to one form of high status as nuns. Few other occupations were open to them. There were state-run weaving shops for unmarriageable women, including retired prostitutes, the elderly, and the deformed. The king had female bodyguards, but this was because women's social exclusion made them trustworthy: They had nothing to gain by rebelling.

Asoka and His Mental World

The rock inscriptions are, in a sense, Asoka's autobiography, disclosing an extraordinary personal story of spiritual development. The first secure date in his reign is the conquest of Kalinga, a kingdom in eastern India around 260 B.C.E. In his commemorative inscription, he expresses regret for the suffering he caused: 150,000 deportees, 100,000 killed, "and many times that number who perished." He goes on "The Beloved of the gods [meaning Asoka himself] felt remorse, for, when an independent country is conquered the slaughter, death and deportation of the people is extremely grievous to the Beloved of the gods, and weighs heavily on his mind." The inscription then gets to what one suspects is the real point: "The Beloved of the gods believes that one who does wrong should be forgiven. . . . And the Beloved of the gods conciliates the forest tribes of his empire, but he warns them that he has power even in his remorse, and he asks them to repent, lest they be killed."

So, in part at least, Asoka's remorse was intended as a warning, and he could hardly have won such a large empire except by war. Still, within a few years, the repudiation of conquest became a major theme of his inscriptions. "Any sons or grandsons I may have should not think of gaining new conquests. . . . The Beloved of the gods considers victory by the teaching of the Buddha to be the foremost victory. . . . The sound of the drum has become the sound of the Buddha's doctrine, showing the people displays of heavenly chariots, elephants, balls of fire, and other divine forms." Asoka put the policy of conquest-by-conversion into practice, sending missionaries to the kingdoms that replaced the old Persian Empire and to Sri Lanka (see Chapter 5). His descendants, he hoped, would adhere to this policy "until the end of the world."

How are we to explain Asoka's extraordinary behavior? His realm was expanding into areas where city life was only starting or, in northwest India, only reviving after the disappearance of the Harappan civilization. In the absence of existing bureaucracies, Asoka had to resort to the one disciplined, literate group available: the Buddhist clergy. This was the period when Buddhist scriptures were being recorded. Asoka recruited the scribes to his service. In an early inscription, he assured them of his fidelity to the Buddha. He listed the scriptures the scribes were writing down and declared his desire that monks, nuns, and his lay subjects should hear the scriptures frequently and meditate upon them.

These words are the telltale trace of Asoka's bargain with the clergy, probably made in the tenth year of his reign, 258 B.C.E. About this time, too, he made a much-publicized pilgrimage to the scene of the Buddha's enlightenment. In a further inscription, of perhaps two and a half years later, he admitted that his personal faith had made little progress for a year, but then he "drew close to the monks and became more ardent." He had made society holy or, as he put it, he made "gods mingle with men" for the first time in India.

As the Buddhist clergy became more powerful, however, the monks' rivalry for the gifts of the pious and their disputes over matters of theology threatened the peace of the realm. So Asoka forbade them to speak ill of one another. "Concord is to be recommended, that men may hear one another's principles and obey them." Asoka's alliance with religion was the shape of things to come. As we shall see, it became a practice of kings all over the world, bringing common problems and advantages.

Buddhist ideology underlies Asoka's many decrees against unnecessary killing of animals. "Formerly in the kitchens of the Beloved of the gods many hundreds of thousands of living animals were killed daily for meat," but Asoka cut the kill rate to two peacocks and one deer per day and promised, "Even these three animals will not be killed in future." He banned outright the slaughter of particular species, including geese, queen ants, and iguanas, perhaps because these creatures were used in sorcery. He proclaimed that his duties embraced "care of man and care of animals. Medicinal herbs, useful to man or beast, have been bought and planted wherever they did not grow; similarly roots and fruit have been bought and planted wherever they did not grow. Along the roads wells have been dug and trees planted for the use of men and beasts."

The stupa of Sanchi. The Emperor Asoka (r. ca. 272–223 B.C.E.) built the first shrine at Sanchi, near Bhopal in India, to honor a place made holy by the footprints of the Buddha. Enriched by the donations of pilgrims, it was adorned by dozens of elaborate structures over thousands of years. The northern gateway, shown here, is elaborately carved with scenes of legends of the Buddha's life and with tales of exemplary charity. Note the elephants and tree spirits, in the form of dancers entwined with mango trees, who hold up the upper crossbeams.

The Reign of Asoka

ca. 268–232 B.C.E.	Reign of Asoka
260 B.C.E.	Conquest of Kalinga
258 B.C.E.	Conversion to Buddhism
ca. 200 B.C.E.	Breakup of Asoka's empire

Excerpts from *The Edicts of Asoka*

The language of Buddhism also infused Asoka's declarations of policy: "All men are my children. . . . There is no better work than promoting the welfare of the whole world. And whatever may be my great deeds, I have done them to discharge my debt to all beings. I work for their happiness in this life, that in the next they may gain heaven." The disadvantaged were specifically included—slaves and servants, women and prisoners. In the twenty-sixth year of his reign, he likened the role his administrators played for his people to the way nurses cared for children. Officials toured the empire to instruct people in Asoka's version of Buddhist ethics: family loyalty, piety for holy men, mercy toward living creatures, and personal austerity. He made such tours himself, taking more pleasure in distributing alms and consulting holy men, he said, than in all other pleasures. These activities replaced hunting, formerly a royal obligation, now banned.

Toward the end of Asoka's reign, it appeared that his enlightenment was beginning to damage the empire. He tightened laws on the treatment of animals, forbidding the slaughter of young livestock and animals that were nursing their young. "Capons [castrated roosters] must not be made." Fishless days were imposed. "Chaff, which contains living things must not be set on fire. Forests must not be burned to kill living things or without good reason. An animal must not be fed with another animal." Gelding and branding were restricted. These decrees must have caused outrage and threatened livelihoods. The emperor's pride in the 25 amnesties he granted to imprisoned criminals can hardly have endeared him to their victims. His condemnation of all rituals as trivial and useless compared with a life in accordance with Buddhist doctrine alienated ordinary people. Perhaps worst of all, his policy against conquests meant the empire could not expand and turned the violence of the military classes inward.

Only 25 years after Asoka's death in 232 B.C.E., his empire (which historians call the Mauryan Empire) broke up into separate states. But state-forming, environment-modifying habits had spread throughout India. The economic infrastructure—the routes of commerce, the enhanced range of resources—was not invulnerable. But the Mauryan infrastructure was unforgettable and it could usually be repaired or reconstructed, if necessary, after future wars and environmental disasters.

CHINESE UNITY AND IMPERIALISM

Even after 500 years of division among warring states, the ideal of imperial unity had not been forgotten in China. The Hundred Schools (see Chapter 6) kept it alive. The return of real unity, however, owed less to nostalgia than to a ruthless and innovative program of renewal, imposed by force. Of all the warring states, Qin was the most marginal, occupying relatively infertile uplands, far from the rice-growing regions. The intelligentsia of most other states considered its people imperfectly civilized.

Toward the middle of the third century B.C.E., Qin began what, in retrospect, looks like a systematic strategy of rejecting the very idea of empire. In 256 B.C.E., its ruler discontinued all imperial rites, in effect dissolving the empire. Ten years later, a new king of Qin, Shi Huangdi, (shee hwang-dee) declared that having been dismantled, the empire could be replaced. Over the next 25 years, he systematically isolated and conquered all rival kingdoms and declared himself "First Emperor" of a new monarchy.

"If," he declared, "the whole empire has suffered and has been the prey of wars and rivalry, which have destroyed peace, it is because there were nobles and kings." In other words, with himself as sole ruler, a unified China would enjoy peace and prosperity.

Our picture of his reign comes from histories compiled one or two generations later. They are distorted partly by the awe Shi Huangdi inspired and partly by revulsion from his oppressive rule. They were based not on what he actually did, but on the sometimes-unrealistic ambitions his decrees reveal. To judge by these sources, he aimed to break the aristocracy, abolish slavery, outlaw inheritance practices that concentrated wealth in noble hands, and replace the power of kings and lords with a uniform system of civil and military districts under his own appointees. He ordered the burning of hundreds of people he considered disloyal and, reputedly, of thousands of books. Only useful technical manuals and the writings of the Legalist school (see Chapter 6) were allowed. Uniformity was the keynote of the new state. Laws, coinage, measures, script, even axle lengths of carts had, by decree, to be the same all over the kingdom. Unauthorized weapons were melted down.

Even if some of his plans went unfulfilled, Shi Huangdi's demonic energy is obvious in everything he attempted. He mobilized 700,000 laborers to build a network of roads and canals. He knocked the Great Wall of China together out of a series of older fortifications, as protection against nomad attacks. When he died, he was buried with thousands of life-size clay models of soldiers and servants—each with different facial and body features—to accompany him into the next life. He was a showman of power on a huge scale—which is usually a sign of insecurity. His empire was too fragile to last, but sweeping away the warring states made it easier for his successors to rebuild an enduring Chinese Empire.

Terracotta Warriors. Though his life and reign were short, everything else about Shi Huangdi (r. 221–210 B.C.E.), the Qin ruler who conquered China, was on a monumental scale. The size and magnificence of his tomb, guarded by an army of terracotta warriors, echoes the grandeur of his engineering works and the scope of his ambitions and uncompromising reforms.

Unity Endangered and Saved

The first instinct of the rebels who overthrew his feeble son in 207 B.C.E. was to break up the empire again and restore the system of the Warring States period. The result was chaotic warfare, with one of the rebel leaders, Liu Bang (lee-oh-bahng), emerging victorious over all the others. He put in place a carefully tempered version of Shi Huangdi's system. Restored kings had small territories within military districts. Peasants owed the state two years' military service plus one month's labor a year on state projects, which must have seemed lenient compared to Shi Huangdi's enforced labor and heavy taxation.

Legalism remained the dominant political philosophy. Liu Bang put most of his former allies to death and showed contempt for Confucianism. In the long run, however, Liu Bang's policies were not sustainable. Only Confucian scholars and officials could supply the literate administrators that a growing state needed. Gradually, especially in the 50-year reign of Han Wudi (hawn woo-dee), beginning in

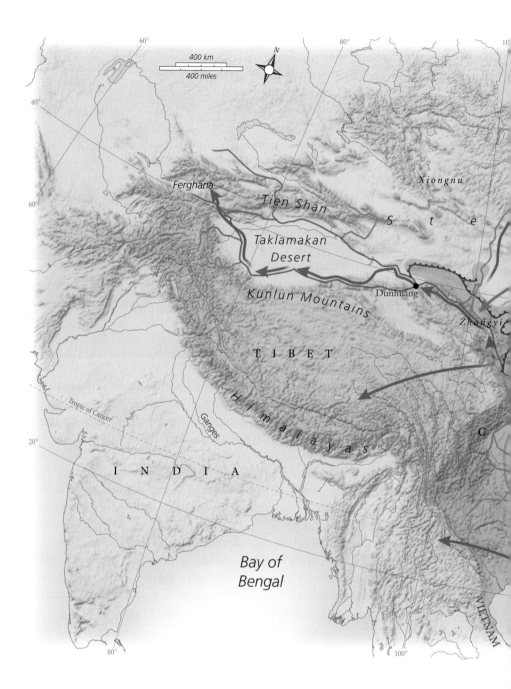

141 B.C.E., Legalism was repudiated, and Confucianism became the state ideology again. A new elite—a Confucian-educated aristocracy dedicated to serving the state—replaced the old ruling class of kings and warrior aristocrats. The new regime invoked the Confucian myth of a golden age (see Chapter 6) and claimed to be restoring ancient virtue.

Liu Bang called his dynasty "Han" after the portion of the country he received in the carving up of Shi Huangdi's realm. In the period of expansion that began in the late second century B.C.E., Han China became the essential China that we see on maps of later eras. It occupied not only the Yellow River and Yangtze basins but also the West River valley, which joins the sea at Guangzhou (gwang-joh), stretching from the Great Wall in the north to Vietnam in the south. It also occupied

MAP 7.7

China and Its Neighbors 250 B.C.E.–200 C.E.

- Qin Homeland
- Maximum extent of Qin Empire
- Han Empire, 2 C.E.
- Han expeditions
- Xiongnu incursions
- Silk Road
- Chinese imperial canals
- Great Wall
- Chinese imperial roads
- Yayoi culture
- Silla
- Paekche
- Koguryo

VIETNAM   modern country

SHAANXI   region

Xiongnu   people

northern Korea, and in the west reached toward Tibet and the Silk Roads between the Kunlun (kwuhn-lwuhn) and Tian Shan (tee-en shahn) mountains. Chinese began to call themselves Han (see Map 7.7).

The return of peaceful conditions under the Han dynasty stimulated a population explosion. The figures recorded in the bureaucracy's censuses fluctuate unconvincingly. It is likely, however, that the population of 20 million in Shi Huangdi's day tripled by the end of the millennium. In part, the huge increase was also probably a consequence of the increased size and environmental diversity of the state. Rice-growing and millet-growing regions could again exchange supplies in each other's bad times. The government coped with disasters, such as drought, famine, or earthquakes, by massive frontier colonization

The Qin and the Han

ca. 400 B.C.E.	Beginning of Warring States period
ca. 256 B.C.E.	Ruler of Qin discontinues imperial rites
ca. 247 B.C.E.	Shi Huangdi becomes ruler of Qin state; beginning of Qin expansion
214 B.C.E.	Construction of Great Wall begins
210 B.C.E.	Death of Shi Huangdi
206 B.C.E.	Beginning of Han dynasty
141 B.C.E.	Han Wudi becomes Han emperor
ca. 139 B.C.E.	Embassy of Zhang Qian to Central Asia
220 C.E.	Collapse of Han Dynasty

programs and redistributing population on a large scale. Forced migrations peopled newly conquered provinces in the southeast at the same time that settlers were encouraged to migrate south toward the Huai valley. These movements shifted the distribution of population, making the Yangtze River the main axis of China. Meanwhile, in the north in 120 B.C.E., 700,000 families were moved into a new conquest beyond the province of Shaanxi, which famine had devastated.

The Han dynasty lasted for 400 years (from 206 B.C.E. to 220 C.E.), despite a succession system that bred palace conspiracies. Succession was determined by designating a principal wife to be the mother of each emperor's heir. This gave empresses' families a unique opportunity to profit from the emperor's favor. But the advantage rarely lasted more than two generations—less, if the empress failed to produce a future emperor. Consequently, every empress's family was tempted to seize power for itself—and most tried. In these circumstances, a dynasty that survived a long time was a triumph against the odds.

The Menace from the Steppes

The other main problem China faced in this period emerged from the steppelands, north of the Great Wall and the Silk Roads. The region had a bad reputation with the Chinese. Its climate was inhospitable, its soil unworkable, its native herdsmen reputedly savage. In some ways, however, it was a good place in which to start building an empire. It bred plenty of horses and men accustomed to the saddle. Its people were voracious because they were poor. It was a vast, flat tract of land, with few geographical obstacles to the creation of a large state. Because the steppeland fringed the region of the Silk Roads, leaders of steppelander war bands could conduct raids, amass treasure, and use their wealth to build up large followings. For the steppelander chiefs who lived closest to China, among the people the Chinese called Xiongnu (shee-ohng-noo), Chinese wealth was another means to transform themselves into kings and emperors (see "Going to the Source: Chinese and Roman Perceptions of Steppelanders").

In the absence of adequate evidence, guesswork can tentatively reconstruct how the Xiongnu Empire came into being. Chinese booty, ransom, and protection money enriched war chiefs who became wealthy enough to extend their followings beyond their own kin and mobilize ever-larger forces. According to Chinese evidence, compiled much later—which is all we have—the first Xiongnu state emerged late in the third century B.C.E., under a leader who styled himself "Son of Heaven," which was a Chinese imperial title and therefore perhaps suggests Chinese influence. His warriors hunted heads—exhibiting scalps from their bridles, making the skulls of their enemies into cups. The basis of their success in war was their skill in mounted archery. Sheep, horses, cattle, and camels were the basis of their economy—guaranteeing the advantages of mixed pastoralism, with milk yields of different species of animals peaking at different times. In about 176 B.C.E., they conquered Gansu (gohn-soo), at the western end of the Great Wall, and became a serious, constant nuisance to China.

Confucian doctrine advocated what we would now call appeasement: "Your Majesty has but to manifest your virtue towards them and extend your favors to cover them, and the northern Barbarians will undoubtedly come of their own accord to pay you tribute at the wall." This policy was not as feeble as it sounds.

Many neighboring peoples genuinely felt the "peaceful attraction" of Chinese rule, and Chinese culture proved remarkably adept at absorbing huge numbers of subject-peoples. The Xiongnu, however, were unresponsive to such methods.

In the late second century B.C.E., Han efforts to recruit allies against them failed. Zhang Qian's mission, described earlier in this chapter, was part of the effort and part of the failure. But between 127 and 120 B.C.E., the Chinese General Wei Qing (way-cheeng) mounted a series of successful operations against the Xiongnu and induced some of their bands or tribes into Chinese service. The fortification of the Silk Roads followed. Xiongnu victories became infrequent. Chinese defenses prevailed. For a while around the turn of the millennium, the Xiongnu even abandoned hostilities.

Thereafter, weakened by civil wars, the Xiongnu succumbed to a series of celebrated campaigns by General Ban Zhao (ban-jaow) in the late first century C.E. He recruited nomads to fight nomads and secured victories at small cost in Chinese lives. His most daring march took him to the shores of the Caspian Sea. In the exaggerated reports of Chinese chroniclers, he slaughtered thousands of foes and captured hundreds of thousands of head of livestock. He also "cut off the right arm of the Xiongnu" when he captured their permanent court. By the time Ban Zhao retired in 102 C.E., the Xiongnu themselves had come under increasing pressure from neighbors to the north and east, who, in their turn, were beginning to move toward statehood.

BEYOND THE EMPIRES

Evidently, in the second half of the first millennium B.C.E., the edges of empires bred states. The Xiongnu were not the only example of economic and political development in China's shadow. Large-scale state formation also occurred in the same period in Japan and Korea, under Chinese influence, and at the other end of Eurasia, among the Scythians and Sarmatians, pastoral peoples whose lands bordered the Roman and Persian Empires. The proximity of empires, however, was a sufficient, but not necessary condition for new states to thrive. When, after discussing these Eurasian cases, we turn to the other side of the globe, we shall face the problem of how states formed in different contexts in Mesoamerica.

Japan and Korea

In the fourth century B.C.E., a rice-growing, bronze-using culture known to archaeologists as Yayoi emerged in Japan. It gradually developed into a state system, under the stimulus of contacts with China. In 219 B.C.E., for instance, a Chinese expedition visited Japan in search of the Isles of the Immortals, fabled in Daoist tales (see Chapter 6). According to Chinese records, in about 200 C.E., one of the Japanese states, Yamatai, conquered the others, under the rule of a female shaman. When she died, 1,000 attendants were burned at her burial. This is the first inkling we have of a unified Japanese state.

Korean states developed faster. The Chinese were in touch with three Korean states—Silla on the Naktong River, Paekche on the Kum River, and Koguryo on the Taedong River. The Chinese sources are so vague, and the archaeological evidence so scanty, that historians can

The Han and the Xiongnu

Third century B.C.E.	First Xiongnu state emerges
ca. 176 B.C.E.	Xiongnu conquers Gansu
127–120 B.C.E.	Chinese mount successful operations against the Xiongnu
78–94 C.E.	Ban Zhao leads celebrated campaigns against the Xiongnu

At the Edge of Empires

Seventh century B.C.E.	First written evidence of the Scythians
ca. 500 B.C.E.	Silla, Paekche, and Koguryo states dominate Korea
Fourth century B.C.E.	Yayoi culture emerges in Japan
ca. 200 B.C.E.	Sarmatians displace Scythians

A gold cup of the mid-first millennium B.C.E. shows why Scythian art was admired in the classical world. Despite the Scythians' fierce reputation, their goldwork usually shows peaceful images of camp life, vividly depicted, such as this scene in which one warrior binds another's leg.

say nothing reliable about the political history of these realms. But their rulers were buried in impressive tombs—usually with a wooden chamber at their core, piled with stone and earth. Grave goods reveal something of the nature of power and trade: iron weapons, fabulous gold diadems and chains, bronze ornaments that imitate Chinese work.

The Western Eurasian Steppe

Meanwhile, at the other end of the Eurasian steppe, in what is modern day Ukraine and southern Russia, states were forming among the pastoral peoples known as Scythians and Sarmatians. Scythian states formed in and around Crimea (creye-MEE-ah), a peninsula that juts into the Black Sea, where the Scythians came into contact with Greek colonies. Here was the Scythian center of Neapolis, a ruler's court covering 40 acres and surrounded by a stone wall. Evidence of Sarmatian royal courts is concentrated in an area to the east, beyond the rivers Dneiper and Don.

On one level, Greek writers sensed this pastoral, nomadic world was alien, wild, and menacing. The fifth-century B.C.E. Greek historian, Herodotus, told of a legendary traveler who undertook a mysterious, dreamlike journey to their land, beyond the river Don in modern Ukraine. He returned to tell the tale—but as a ghost. On another level, the nomads were familiar trading partners. Greek craftsmen depicted them in everyday scenes, milking ewes or stitching their cloaks of unshorn sheepskin. Greek and Celtic trade goods filled princely graves in the last half of the first millennium B.C.E.

Much of this art was produced under the patronage of Scythian and Sarmatian princes and is echoed in their own goldsmiths' work. A gold cup, for instance, from a royal tomb at Kul-Oba near, the Black Sea, shows bearded warriors in tunics and leggings at peace or, at least, between wars. They tend one another's wounds, fix their teeth, mend their bowstrings, and tell campfire tales. A Sarmatian queen of the first century C.E. stares, in Greek clothes and hairstyle, from the center of a gold crown. She looks as if she fancied herself a Greek goddess. Above her head, what look like deer feed on golden fig leaves, or, perhaps, in the steppeland tradition, the artist meant them to be magical horses, crowned with antlers. When we look at their art, we can never be sure whether these people were happy in their own traditions or envious of the sedentary empires—probably a bit of both.

Mesoamerica

Far more remarkable than these cases of state-building by peoples on the edges of existing empires, are independent but comparable developments that began in this period in Mesoamerica (see Map 7.8). As we have seen, chiefdom-formation and state-building had a long history in this region, and in other parts of the Americas, but every innovation had been blocked or frustrated. The geography and vast climate zones of the Americas discouraged communication and cultural change (see Chapter 5).

Now, at least two centers sprang into what might fairly be called a potentially imperial role. Monte Albán (MON-tay al-BAHN) in what is now the Mexican state of Oaxaca was the first. In a period of social differentiation early in the millennium, the region had deer-fed elite, buried in stone-lined graves with their jade-bead lip studs and earrings. Population growth accompanied their supremacy, with increasing exploitation of irrigation and the spread of settlement into areas of sparse rainfall. Around the middle of the millennium, ever-larger settlements appeared, with ritual mounds and the first engraved picture-writing, or glyphs. We do not know how to read this writing, and the inscriptions are all short—perhaps no more than names and dates. From about the same time and place, we have the first evidence of what the ritual platforms were for: a carving of a human sacrifice, with blood streaming from a chest sliced open to pluck out the heart.

Not long after this, Monte Albán began to draw in population from surrounding settlements. It was a natural fortress, enhanced by defensive walls. From a modest village, Monte Albán became a city of perhaps 20,000 people by about 200 B.C.E., when the population stabilized. Faded carvings proclaim its warlike values in parades of sacrifice victims. A palace and a reservoir that could have held 20,000 gallons of water suggest a familiar story: collective effort under strong rule. The main plaza contains 40 huge carved stones—probably of the second century B.C.E. These are "conquest slabs," listing the names of subject-cities from as much as 53 miles away, perhaps as much as 90, if the most daring readings are correct. The slabs record the tribute these cities had to pay.

Monte Albán casts light on the later and, in the long run, more spectacular case of Mesoamerican empire-building. Teotihuacán (tay-oh-tee-wah-KAHN), in the valley of Mexico, about 450 miles north of Albán, was destined to be a far greater metropolis. At 6,000 feet above sea level, a little higher than Monte Albán, its agriculture was based on what were by then the region's standard products: maize, beans, and squash. Around the end of the millennium, perhaps as the result of a war, a migration as sudden as Albán's shifted almost the entire population of the valley of Mexico to Teotihuacán. The building of the towering Sun Pyramid began. By about 150 C.E., 20 monumental pyramids were in place. The other buildings included some apparently for housing people from distant lowland sites: ambassadors, tribute bearers, hostages.

Monte Albán. The builders of Monte Albán (Oaxaca, Mexico) reshaped the 1,500-foot-high mound on which it stands to fit their idea of how a city should be: 50 acres of terraces supporting temples, palaces, and garrisons. This was truly an imperial metropolis, decorated with gaudy, gory slabs depicting dismembered captives.

MAP 7.8

Monte Albán and Teotihuacán

➤	Monte Albán
➤	Teotihuacán
○	settlement
●	place mentioned on pages 220–222
OAXACA	modern province
HONDURAS	modern country

The art of Teotihuacán suggests an ecologically fragile way of life, dependent on rainfall and unreliable gods to deliver fertile soil and crops. The artists imagined the sky as a serpent whose sweat fell as rain and fed the plant life of Earth, where sacrificers in serpent masks scattered blood from hands lacerated with cactus spikes or impaled human hearts on bones. Yet the city and the reach of its trade and power continued to grow for over 350 years. At its peak, Teotihuacán was big enough to house well over 100,000 people. Carvings over 625 miles away depicted its warriors, and its trade goods and tribute came from a similarly wide area. Teotihuacáno artifacts of the period have turned up in archaeological digs as far away as Alta Vista in Zacatecas to the north and what is today Honduras in the south.

Teotihuacán. Regularity, symmetry, order, monumentality: the builders and rulers of Teotihuacán in the valley of Mexico evidently thought they could improve on nature. The so-called Temple of the Sun is on the left of the central avenue, which is more than a mile long.

IN PERSPECTIVE:
The Aftermath of the Axial Age

The axial age left three legacies: a remarkably durable heritage of ideas, less secure though lengthening routes for trade and cultural exchange in Eurasia, and a fragile group of empires. In some ways, these legacies seemed interdependent. The empires did little to add to the intellectual achievements that preceded them, but they did safeguard, enshrine, and nurture them. The Roman Empire, for example, adopted and fostered Greek learning and, as we shall soon see, later did the same service for Christianity.

Persian emperors adopted Zoroastrian rites. Asoka became the patron of Buddhism in India. The Han dynasty rehabilitated Confucianism as the dominant ideology of China. And although the empires had probably been as much the effect as the cause of improved sea and land communications in Eurasia, they unquestionably helped them develop further. The road-building programs of all the empires, the Chinese effort to scout out the Silk Roads and build forts to guard them, and the interest Alexander and his Persian predecessors took in Indian Ocean navigation all demonstrate that.

The collapse of the Persian Empire and the rapid unraveling of Asoka's empire showed that the world was not yet safe for large-scale imperialism. But the pattern of state-building seems to have been irresistible. The new states that emerged on the edges of the existing Eurasian empires—and, as we shall see in the next chapter, in parts of Africa where contacts with Eurasia were multiplying—suggest

Mesoamerican representations of the world of the gods show extraordinary continuities over time and remarkable consistency between cultures. On a temple façade at Teotihuacán, for instance, the reliefs show images of the gods that remained roughly similar for more than 1,000 years and resemble those made by both the Maya and the Aztecs. The round-eyed image of a god, known as Tlaloc to the Aztecs and Chaac the Maya, alternates with the mask of Quetzal-coatl, the feathered serpent, who slinks, full length, across the facade.

CHRONOLOGY

Seventh century B.C.E.	First written evidence of the Scythians
Sixth century B.C.E.	Cyrus the Great founds Persian Empire
Fifth century B.C.E.	1,700 miles of road cross Persian Empire
	Chinese silks appear in Europe
	Silla, Paekche, and Koguryo states dominate Korea
Fourth century B.C.E.	Yayoi culture emerges in Japan
334 B.C.E.	Alexander conquers Persian Empire
Third century B.C.E.	Roman Empire expands beyond Italy
	First Xiongnu state emerges north of China
ca. 268–232 B.C.E.	Reign of Asoka (India)
206 B.C.E.	Beginning of Han dynasty in China
200 B.C.E.	Population of Monte Albán reaches 200,000 (Mesoamerica)
127–120 B.C.E.	Chinese mount successful operations against the Xiongnu
27 B.C.E.	Augustus becomes first emperor of Rome
ca. 150 C.E.	Teotihuacán at peak of its influence (Mesoamerica)
220 C.E.	Collapse of the Han dynasty

this. The New World resembled a "parallel universe," where, despite the environmental differences, histories similar to those of parts of Eurasia and Africa were beginning to unfold.

In some ways, the next part of the story is of the continuation and extension of these themes: of growing convergence, in these respects, between the New World and the Old, and of more, roughly parallel developments in parts of Africa and the Pacific island world, where previously they had been absent or undetectable in the evidence. More puzzling—and therefore worth more attention in the next few chapters—are the problems of how, and how far, the intellectual legacy and communications framework of the axial age survived the crises, collapse, or transformation of the empires that had nurtured and transmitted them.

PROBLEMS AND PARALLELS

1. How do increased travel and trade create a demand for stronger, bigger states? How do the ensuing cross-cultural contacts, larger road networks, and increased communication benefit or disadvantage states?

2. Both Rome and Persia offered their conquered peoples numerous benefits and considerable autonomy. What were the benefits and drawbacks of these policies both for the imperial power and the subject peoples?

3. What were the relative advantages and disadvantages of sea routes versus land routes for commerce and communication in the ancient world?

4. What common factors contributed to the fall of the empires discussed in this chapter?

5. How did each empire in this chapter try to meld together diverse peoples into a single state? Did they succeed or fail?

6. Beyond the great Eurasian empires, other states and societies thrived. Can they justifiably be termed *empires*? Why or why not?

DOCUMENTS IN GLOBAL HISTORY

- Agatharchides of Kindos describes Saba
- Zhang Qian, *Hon Shu*, "Descriptions of the Western Regions"
- Horace, "Dulce et Decorum est Pro Patria Mori"

- Excerpts from the *Arthasastra*, "The Duties of Government Superintendents"
- Excerpts from *The Edicts of Asoka*

Please see the Primary Source CD-ROM for additional sources related to this chapter.

READ ON

For Indian maps, J. B. Harley and D. Woodward, eds., *History of Cartography* (1987) vol. ii is fundamental. L. Feer, *A Study of the Jatakas* (1963) is a good introduction to those texts. The texts I cite on the Erythraean Sea are easy to consult in L. Casson, ed., *The Periplus of the Erythraean Sea* (1989), and S. Burstein, ed., *Agatharchides of Cnidos: On the Erythraean Sea* (1989). P. Horden and N. Purcell, *The Corrupting Sea* (2000), and D. Abulafia, ed., *The Mediterranean in History* (2003) are the best histories of the Mediterranean; for the link to the Atlantic, see B. Cunliffe, *Facing the Ocean* (2001). On the Indian Ocean, M. Pearson, *The Indian Ocean* (2003) is a masterly survey; the demanding work of K. Chaudhuri, *Asia before Europe* (1991) repays the effort it requires.

On the Silk Roads, the outstanding book is now the British Library exhibition catalog edited by S. Whitfield, *The Silk Roads* (2004). On Dunhuang, see R. Whitfield et al., eds., *Cave Temples of Dunhuang* (2000). J. Mirsky, *The Great Chinese Travelers* (1976), collects extracts from key texts, including the journey of Zhang Qian.

On the Persian empire, *The Cambridge History of Iran* (1993) is unbeatable. On women, I follow M. Brosius, *Women in Ancient Persia* (1998). On the Persian Wars, P. Green, *The Greco-Persian Wars* (1996) is authoritative. S. Hornblower, *The Athenian Empire* (2000) is a superb study. The same author's *The Greek World* (1983), provides the backdrop down to the time of Alexander, on whom R. Lane Fox, *Alexander the Great* (1973) is both scholarly and irresistibly readable. My remarks on Alexander's legacy are indebted to G. Cary, *The Medieval Alexander* (1967) which is a wonderful book.

On the Romans, T. Cornell, *The Beginnings of Rome* (1995) takes the story down to the Punic Wars. A. Goldsworthy, *The Fall of Carthage* (2004) is a history of those wars. R. Syme, *The Roman Revolution* (1939) is a classic of abiding interest and importance, centered on the rise of Augustus and

a monarchical system of government. The best study of Virgil is probably R. Jenkyns, *Virgil's Experience* (1999).

For Celtic history, N. K. Chadwick, *The Celts* (1971), remains standard. H. D. Rankin, *Celts and the Classical World* (1987) is particularly interesting on Greek and Roman images. M. J. Green, *Celtic Art* (1997) is a good introduction.

On India in this period, F. R. Allchin, ed., *The Archaeology of Early Historic South Asia* (1995) is fundamental. R. Thapar, *Asoka and the Decline of the Mauryas* (1961) is insightful and close to the sources. R. McKeon and N. A. Nikam, *The Edicts of Asoka* (1959) analyzes these important sources.

For the Qin-Han revolution D. Twitchett and M. Loewe, eds., *The Cambridge History of China* (1986) is invaluable. Li Xueqin, *Eastern Zhou and Qin Civilizations* (1985) is excellent on the background. For the Xiongnu, as for all steppeland history, the classic work of R. Grousset, *The Empire of the Steppes* (1970) remains fundamental.

For Japan and Korea, *The Cambridge History of Japan* (1993) is inescapably useful. W. Hong, *Paekche of Korea and the Origins of Yamato Japan* (1994) is helpful on the links between the two regions. K. Mizoguchi, *An Archaeological History of Japan* (2002) surveys the archaeological evidence.

The Scythians and Sarmatians have inspired much good work. Useful introductions are supplied in T. Talbot Rice, *The Scythians* (1957); E. Phillips, *The Royal Hordes* (1965); and T. Sulimirski, *The Sarmatians* (1970). On Mesoamerica, J. A. Hendon and R. A. Joyce, *Mesoamerican Archaeology* (2004) has the most up-to-date account.

For Monte Albán, R. E. Blanton, *Monte Albán* (1978) is the standard work. For Teotihuacán, important works include J. C. Berlo, ed., *Art, Ideology and the City of Teotihuacán* (1993), and R. Storey, *Life and Death in the Ancient City of Teotihuacán* (1992).

Mozi and Jesus Christ on Universal Love

The claim that all human beings form a single community, united by the mutual obligations to care for one another, is a familiar one today. Westerners know it best in the Christian moral code to love other humans as we love ourselves. But how did this doctrine originate? Was it a Christian idea? Did Jesus or his followers develop it from Jewish tradition? Or did it arise elsewhere in Eurasia, and spread along the routes of trade and cultural exchange that developed among China, Europe, India, and the Middle East during the axial age in the first millennium B.C.E.?

Most cultures, for most of history, did not even have a word for "human being." Anyone outside one's family, clan, or tribe would usually be labeled by words meaning "beast" or "demon." And the idea that we owe obligations to people we do not know, or who can do nothing for us, seems to contradict our own self-interest.

CHINA

Yet in the second millennium B.C.E., various cultures developed the concept of humankind as a large category that extended far beyond the immediate group to which a person belonged. This notion seems particularly strong in the Upanishads—the teachings of Indian sages. But, as far as we know, no one taught universal love until the fifth century B.C.E., when the Chinese sage Mozi argued that it was a practical basis for life:

INDIA

PALESTINE

• • • • •

If men were to regard the states of others as they regard their own, then who would raise up his state to attack the state of another? It would be like attacking his own. If men were to regard the cities of others as they regard their own, then who would raise up his city to attack the city of another? ... If men were to regard the families of others as they regard their own, then who would raise up his family to overthrow that of another? ... Now when states and cities ... and families and individuals do not ... injure one another, is this a harm or a benefit to the world? Surely it is a benefit.

When we inquire into the cause of such benefits, what do we find produced them? Do they come about from hating others and trying to injure them? Surely not! They come rather from loving others and trying to benefit them. And when we set out to classify and describe those men who love and benefit others, shall we say that their actions are motivated by partiality or by universality? Surely we must answer, by universality, and it is this universality in their dealing with one another that gives rise to all the great benefits in the world. Therefore Mozi has said that universality is right...

Suppose there are two men, one of them holding to partiality, the other to universality. The believer in partiality says, "How could I possibly regard my friend the same as myself, or my friend's father the same as my own?" Because he views his friend in this way, he will not feed him when he is hungry, clothe him when he is cold, nourish him when he is sick, or bury him when he dies. Such are the words of the partial man and such his actions. But the words and actions of the universal-minded man are not like these. He will say, "I have heard that the truly superior man of the world regards his friend the same as himself, and his friend's father the same as his own. Only if he does this can he be considered a truly superior man...

...Continued

And yet the men of the world continue to criticize, saying, "Such a principle may be all right as a basis in choosing among ordinary men, but it cannot be used in selecting a ruler.

Let us try considering both sides of the question. Suppose there are two rulers, one of them holding to universality, the other to partiality. The partial ruler says, "How could I possibly regard my countless subjects the same as I regard myself? That would be completely at variance with human nature! Man's life on earth is as brief as the passing of a team of horses glimpsed through a crack in the wall." Because he views his subjects in this way, he will not feed them when they are hungry, clothe them when they are cold, nourish them when they are sick, or bury them when they die. Such are the words of the partial ruler, and such his actions. But the words and actions of the universal-minded ruler are not like these. He will say, "I have heard that a truly enlightened ruler must think of his subjects in this way: he will feed them when they are hungry, clothe them when they are cold, nourish them when they are sick, and bury them when they die. Such are the words and actions of the universal-minded ruler."

Texts written down probably no later than the third century B.C.E. ascribed to the Buddha a doctrine called "Great Compassion." It differed from Mozi's teachings in at least three ways. First, it applied not just to humans but to all living beings. Second, Buddhists advocated it for the sake of the self rather than of society: Loving others brought one closer to perfect happiness. Third, love earns merit only if it is selfless—a free gift of enlightened humans to their fellow beings.

Mohist and Buddhist teachings could have influenced each other. The flow of contacts between China and India at the time means that sages in both regions were probably aware of some, at least, of each other's teachings. As we have seen, the Silk Roads were open, or became open, for business in this period.

In the first century C.E., Jesus' followers ascribed to him a doctrine similar to those earlier ascribed to Mozi and the Buddha. The writer of the Gospel according to Matthew was, like Jesus himself and most early Christians, a Jew. He tried to set Jesus' teaching against the background of Jewish tradition.

Bodhisattva
A detail from a fifth-century C.E. wall painting in Ajanta, India, showing a Bodhisattva. In Buddhist doctrine, Bodhisattvas are great beings that have achieved enlightenment but have resolved not to enter Nirvana until every last being has achieved the same state.

LOVE FOR ENEMIES

You have heard that it was said, "Love your neighbor and hate your enemy." But I tell you: Love your enemies and pray for those who persecute you, that you may be sons of your Father in heaven. ... If you love those who love you, what reward will you get? Are not even the tax collectors doing that? And if you greet only your brothers, what are you doing more than others? Do not even pagans do that? Be perfect, therefore, as your heavenly father is perfect.

(Matthew 5:43–48)

Settle matters quickly with your adversary who is taking you to court. Do it while you are still with him on the way, or he may hand you over to the judge, and the judge may hand you over to the officer, and you may be thrown into prison.

(Matthew 5:25)

AN EYE FOR AN EYE

You have heard that it was said, "Eye for eye, and tooth for tooth." But I tell you, Do not resist an evil person. If someone strikes you on the right check, turn to him the other also. And if someone wants to sue you and take your tunic, let him have your cloak as well. If someone forces you to go one mile, go with him two miles. Give to the one who asks you, and do not turn away from the one who wants to borrow from you.

(Matthew 5:33–42)

Perhaps even before the writers of the surviving Gospels got to work, traditions about Jesus' teachings were recorded in letters circulating among early Christian communities. Many of these letters were the work of Paul—a Jew converted after a career as a selfconfessed persecutor of Christians. He insisted on the divinity of Christ and on the power of God's grace to redeem even the most apparently worthless sinners. He also shared the emphasis many of the early Christian letter writers placed on the obligation to universal love and expressed it in one of the most famous early Christian texts:

Jesus and apostles

A fresco from a Roman catacomb from the third century C.E. showing Jesus Christ surrounded by his apostles.

LOVE

If I speak in the tongues of men and of angels, but have not love, I am only a re-sounding gong or a clanging cymbal. If I have the gift of prophecy and can fathom all mysteries and all knowledge, and if I have a faith that can move mountains, but have not love, I am nothing. If I give all I possess to the poor and surrender my body to the flames, but have not love, I gain nothing.

Love is patient, love is kind. It does not envy, it does not boast, it is not proud. It is not rude, it is not self-seeking, it is not easily angered, keeps no record of wrongs. Love does not delight in evil but rejoices with the truth. It always protects, always trusts, always hopes, always perseveres.

Love never fails. But where there are prophecies, they will cease; where there are tongues, they will be stilled; where there is knowledge, it will pass away....

And now these three remain; faith, hope and love. But the greatest of these is love.

(I Corinthians 13: 1–13)

Christian doctrine was certainly different from what Jewish tradition—"the law," as the Gospel writers called it—said on this subject. Jewish tradition said simply, "there is no obligation to love your enemies." By contrast, Jesus' followers clearly felt that he had given them a new commandment to love one another, which they took as a call to universal love.

Questions to Consider

1 How were the doctrines of Mozi and Jesus related to the needs of society and the state?

2 Whom or what did they intend their doctrines to benefit?

3 What arguments did they use to get people to adopt the practice of universal love?

4 What are the differences between the doctrines of Mozi and Jesus Christ?

5 Are these differences evidence that the two thinkers arrived at their views independently, or are they just different versions of a common idea?

6 Is there any evidence in the extracts that the sources of Jesus's thought were primarily Jewish?

7 How might Jesus or his followers have heard about the teachings of Mozi and the Buddha?

Sources

The extracts from the Bible are from the *New International Version.*

The extracts from Mozi are from *The Ethical and Political Works of Mo Tzu,* Translated by Yi-Pao Mei. London: Arthur Probsthain, 1929.

The World Map of Beatus of Liebana ▶
The eighth-century Spanish monk, Beatus of Liebana, illustrated his Commentary on the last book of the Bible with a world map. Almost all those who the later made copies of his work produced versions of their own maps. In this one, from 1109, the picture of Adam, Eve, and the serpent indicates the presumed location of the Garden of Eden, at the extreme limit of the East. Europe is the disproportionately large, nearly square shape at the lower left.

ENVIRONMENT

200–400
Spread of maize cultivation into North America

CULTURE

220
Breakup of Han Empire

200s and on
Spread of Buddhism to east Asia

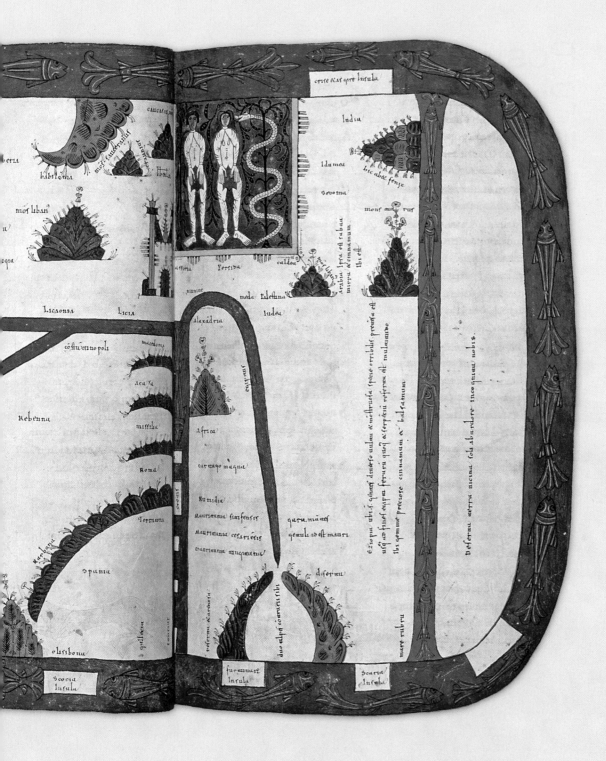

crite &at qre infula

caucaf...

Iberia

babilonia   mof caucbaruf

mof liban   minutuf Italia

...qua

Licaonia   Licia

cofttantinopoli   macedonia

Aca?a

Rebenna

miffilia

Roma

Tetracona

Rechana

Spania

olisibona

Scoria
Infula

India

Idumca

Sovotna   hic abac fenic

mof minuruf

affiria   terfida   culdeu   mof liban

Arabia fpca oft rubia
myra d'omnamum   Ibi oft

pinnine   moda   taleftina

alaxadria   Iudca

equinui

Africa

cartingo magna

Numidia

Mauricania fimfenfcf   qara mantcf
Mauritania cefarienfif   gentili ad oft mauri
mauritanna tinugitant

diferma

deferta Barbarici

duo alpof commictibi

furammait
Infula

Scaria
Infula

Ethiopa ubi eft quinq; dinerfo modio unlu d'mulitude fpecic orribilu pretiofa eft
ufq; ad finuf fupra ferrura quoq; afperfii referrui of muliendo
ibi gemme pretiofe conuenium av hoifarmm

mare rubru

Deferta terra uicina foli abardore incognitui nobis.

mid–500s
Plague in Arabia
and eastern Mediterranean

600–800
Growing trans-Saharan trade;
Polynesian diaspora

800–1000
"Internal colonization" in
China, Japan, western Europe

300s on
Spread of Christianity
in Roman world

400s
Break up of Roman Empire

630 on
Rise and spread of Islam

CHAPTER 8

Postimperial Worlds: Problems of Empires in Eurasia and Africa, ca. 200 to ca. 700 C.E.

Detail from a Mayan vase, early sixth century C.E. The color scheme of red on a gold background is characteristic of ceramics from Tikal, while the bird-like symbols with forked, blood-sucking tongues on the bottom row have similarities with glyphs from Teohituacán.

They arrived in January 378, soon after the beginning of the annual rainy season, in the moist, tropical lowlands of what is now eastern Guatemala. They came from Teotihuacán, 7,500 feet high in the mountain-ringed valley of central Mexico. The weather was unfamiliar. Teotihuacán had its rainy season in summer. They were not numerous or heavily armed, to judge from a picture an artist made of them, or travelers like them, as they completed their journey. Some of them looked and behaved like ambassadors, wearing the tasseled headresses that signified ambassadorial rank and carrying ceremonial vessels, carved or painted with mythic scenes and political messages, as diplomatic gifts. They crossed hundreds of miles of mountains and forests, or perhaps descended by sea along the coast, to the land of the Maya, whose environment, culture, and language were different from their own. The Maya called the leader of the group Siyaj K'ak (SEE-ah kah-AK), meaning "fire born." Previously, historians called him "Smoking Frog"—a literal interpretation of his name-glyph. Contemporaries in the Maya world added a nickname, "The Great Man From the West." But why had he come?

His destination was the city of Tikal (tee-KAHL), over 625 miles from his home, in the region now called the Petén, where the limestone temples and gaudily painted roof combs of the city rose above the dense forest. Tikal was one of the oldest and clearly the largest of the many city-states among which the Maya world was divided. Its population at the time was perhaps over 30,000. But if Tikal was a great city by Maya standards, Teotihuacán dwarfed it, at probably more than three times its size. Teotihuacán, moreover, was no mere city-state but the nerve center of an empire that covered the valley of Mexico and spilled into neighboring regions, now called Tlaxcala and Morelos. Teotihuacáno influence and tribute gathering probed further still. Traders from central Mexico had penetrated deep into the Maya lands for many decades. Contacts with the jade-rich highland Maya, who lived in the mountainous regions to the south and west of Tikal, were multiplying.

Relations between Tikal and Teotihuacán were important for both cities, because of the complementary ecologies of their regions (see Map 8.1). The Maya supplied Mexico with products unavailable in the highlands, including the plumage of forest birds for ornament, rubber for the ball games the elites of the region favored, cacao (which provided the elite with a mildly narcotic drink), jade for jewelry, and rare kinds of incense for rituals. But visitors like Siyaj K'ak and his Teotihuacános were rare, or even, perhaps, unprecedented. As they approached, day by day, along the river now called San Pedro Mártir, the communities they passed through recorded their passage without comment but presumably with apprehension, and handed on the news to neighbors down the line. What were the newcomers' intentions? Were they invaders or invitees? Conquerors or collaborators? Envoys or adventurers? Were they mercenaries, perhaps, or a marriage party? Had they come to arbitrate disputes or to exploit them for their own purposes?

The inscriptions that record the events are too fragmentary to answer these questions. But they tell a suggestive story. When Siyaj K'ak reached Tikal on January 31, his arrival precipitated a revolution. On that very day, if the inscriptions can be taken literally, the life of the city's ruler, Chak Tok Ich'aak (chak tok eech-AH-AK) (or "Great Jaguar Paw," as historians used to call him), came to an end. He "entered the water," as the Maya said, after a reign of 18 years, ending the supremacy of a royal line that had supplied the city with 13 kings. The monuments of his dynasty were shattered into fragments or defaced and buried: slabs of stone on which images of kings were carved, with commemorations of the wars they fought, captives they took, astronomical observations they recorded, and sacrifices they offered to the gods—sometimes of their own blood, sometimes of the lives of their captives.

To judge from the portraits his court sculptors left, the new king, whom Siyaj K'ak placed on the throne, dressed in the style of his Teotihuacáno patrons, wore adornments with images of central Mexican gods, and carried weapons of central Mexican design. His chocolate pots came from Teotihuacán or were copied from models made there. When he died early in the next century, he was buried with a carving of an underworld god, seated on a throne of human bones, holding a severed head.

Siyaj K'ak installed new rulers not only in Tikal but also in other, smaller cities in

Tikal. The roof-combs of the Maya city of Tikal—hoisted facades set over the temples like mantillas in ladies' hair—rise over the forest of the Petén in Yucatan. Gaudily painted in their day, they warned off enemies, invited trade, celebrated kings. The small stones lining the plaza bear images and records of the deeds of rulers. The great temple in the middle ground was built as a tomb for King Jasaw Chan K'awiil (682–734), who restored the city's fortunes, after a period of impoverishment and defeat, and embarked on the most ambitious building program in Tikal's history.

Dagli Orti/Picture Desk, Inc./Kobal Collection

MAP EXPLORATION

www.prenhall.com/armesto_maps

MAP 8.1

The Maya and Teotihuacán

	Maya
	Teotihaucán and directions of influence
♨	Mayan temple
▲	important Mayan site
△	important Teotihaucán site
●	obsidian mine
MEXICO	modern-day country
PETÉN	modern-day province or region
○	city described or mentioned on pages 233–237

Products Supplied from Maya to Teotihuacán

	cacao
♣	incense
	jade
	plumage
⌣	rubber

Products Supplied to Teotihaucán from Neighboring Colonies

	avocado
	cacao
	cotton
	lime

the region over the next few years. Imperfect inscriptions suggest that some, perhaps all, of the affected cities professed allegiance to a ruler whose name-glyph shows an owl with a spear-thrower. This is also an image associated with war and power at Teotihuacán, suggesting that the supremacy of Teotihuacán, or at least of Teotihuacános, was part of the new order. Moreover, a rash of new cities in the lowlands was founded from Tikal over the next few years, though they seem quickly, in most cases, to have asserted or exercised independence. It would exceed the evidence to speak of the birth of a new regional state, or the foundation of a new province of the empire of Teotihuacán. But we can confidently assert that contacts across Mesoamerica were growing, that state formation was quickening and spreading, and that a complex political pattern was emerging: jealous Maya cities, competing and combining, with elites often drawn or sponsored from central Mexico.

The influence and power of Teotihuacán were close to their maximum. Whether or not Maya cities were becoming formally dependent on Teotihuacán, they were certainly submitting to Teotihuacáno influence. In the lowlands, that influence seems rapidly to have waned. In the highlands, however, it grew for a century and a half. Meanwhile, Teotihuacános founded colonies wherever the city needed supplies. Chingú (cheen-GOO), near the later site of Tula (TOO-lah), was one, where lime was exported for Teotihuacán's gigantic building projects. San Ignacio in Morelos was another, supplying avocados, cacao, and cotton, which would not grow in the highlands but was vital for everyday clothing and—increasingly, from about this time—for the quilted armor warriors favored.

In part, pressure of population drove this expansion. Teotihuacán probably produced or attracted more people than it could contain. In any case, to sustain a growing city, Teotihuacán needed a growing empire. The basic foodstuffs the city consumed—maize and beans—were part of the ecosystem of its own region. But the concentration of population that had to be fed was enormous by the standards of preindustrial cities anywhere in the world and probably required extra supplies from farther away. The cotton and the luxuries and ritual objects on which elite life depended had to come from other climes. Teotihuacán had its own mines of obsidian—the glasslike substance of which the cutting blades of tools and weapons were made. But it had no other resources to export. It had to be a military state.

We do not know how the state was organized. Unlike the Maya, the Teotihuacános produced no art depicting kings and, as far as we know, no chronicles of royal activities. Some curious features, however, show up in the archaeological record. During the fourth century, many families were shifted from small dwellings into large, lavishly built compounds, as if the city were being divided among rival, or potentially rival, focuses of allegiance. From the mid–fifth century, there are signs of internal instability. One of the most lavish temples was demolished. Thick, high internal walls divided different quarters of the city from each other. New building of other kinds gradually ceased. Meanwhile, Teotihuacáno influence over areas far from the city withered. At an uncertain date, probably around the mid–eighth century, a traumatic event ended Teotihuacán's greatness. Fire wrecked the great temples and pyramids in the center of the city, and much of the population fled. We do not know what the state ideology was—but, whatever it was, it looks as if it was abandoned or replaced. Teotihuacán remained a city of perhaps 30,000 people, but it never again displayed imperial trappings or ambition. It is hard to resist the impression that the empire had overreached itself, committed to expansion that was increasingly hard to keep going, nurturing resentment abroad at its unparalleled power, and restlessness at home over the division of the spoils. No single city or empire of comparable dimensions replaced Teotihuacán. But people in Mesoamerica remembered it, conserved its influence, and tried to imitate it, as they entered a period of kaleidoscopic change, in which small, well-matched states fought among themselves without ever settling into an enduring pattern.

Teotihuacán was one of the world's most out-of-the-way empires—isolated from most of the others that arose in or after the axial age. Yet it was typical of its time. Other new imperial initiatives of the era—in the formative Islamic world and in Ethiopia—succumbed to remarkably similar challenges. Even the old empires struggled with similar problems. In Rome, India, China, and Persia, imperial traditions inherited from the axial age were extinguished or suffered periods of fragmentation or submersion by invaders whom the natives regarded as barbaric. And on the edges of empires in transformation, as well as within them, new states felt the effects.

In this chapter and the next two, we have to face the questions of how, if at all, these stories are connected, and why their outcomes differed. How, for instance, imperial unity revived in China but not in the other affected areas, or why Christianity and Islam, but not Buddhism, became almost monopolistic ideologies in their areas of dominance. Less pressing, perhaps, but no less interesting, is the problem of how the history of the rest of the world echoes or connects with the fates of Eurasia's empires.

The political history of the period, chiefly in Eurasia and Africa, is the subject of this chapter, as we look in turn at each major area of imperial and state development, first filling in the stories of the third, fourth, and fifth centuries C.E. before focusing on a protracted spell of critical challenges in the sixth and seventh centuries. The ascent of the Christian, Muslim, and Buddhist religions is the theme of the next chapter. The last chapter in this part of the book provides an opportunity to explore global and environmental contexts and trace the world that emerged from the transformations, in the last two or three centuries of the millennium.

THE WESTERN ROMAN EMPIRE AND ITS INVADERS

On the summit of the Capitoline, one of Rome's seven hills, sits a bronze statue of the Emperor Marcus Aurelius, victoriously horsed, carrying a globe. Since the emperor's death in 180, no image has been so often copied for rulers' portraits. For most beholders, the statue evokes Rome's peace through strength. Yet the reign of Marcus Aurelius (r. 161–180) has traditionally been regarded as the far edge of the high plateau of Roman achievement, after which decline set in, punctuated only by the lower peaks of ever more desperate recoveries.

The empire suffered from abiding problems: its sprawling size, its long, vulnerable land frontier; the unruly behavior of its politicized soldiery, with Roman armies fighting each other to make and unmake emperors; the uneasy, usually hostile relationship with rivals in Persia. Two new, growing dangers were increasingly apparent. First, for most of the elite, Christianity seemed subversive. To the pious, Rome's greatness was at the disposal of the gods. To the practical, Roman unity depended on the maintenance throughout the empire of politically charged cults: the worship of the emperor as divine, the cults of the patron gods of Rome. Second, Germanic peoples beyond the empire's borders in Europe coveted Roman wealth. The prosperity gap was like that between "North and South," on a global level, today—inspiring fear in the prosperous and envy in the poor. Increasingly, Germans from beyond the Rhine and Danube Rivers raised problems of war and diplomacy as hard to manage as those the Persians posed on the empire's eastern frontiers.

Marcus Aurelius anticipated ways in which the empire would cope with these problems for the next three centuries. He sensed the need to divide responsibility for governing the vast empire, admitting his adoptive brother to the rank of coemperor and delegating to him responsibility for guarding the eastern frontier. This sort of division of responsibility at the summit of government was to be a recurrent formula for saving the state from crisis. And Marcus Aurelius practiced stoicism—the philosophy, as we have seen, in which pagans and Christians could be reconciled (see Chapter 6). He repudiated fancy theories in favor of practical ethics—appropriate for the ruler of an empire racked by economic slumps and wars. His was a dark world, glinting with campfire light, as he fought to keep the Danube frontier secure. He snatched moments on campaign to write his *Meditations* in Greek, which was still the common language of the eastern half of the empire and still the prestige language favored for philosophy. "Renew yourself," he wrote in a memo to himself, "but keep it brief and basic."

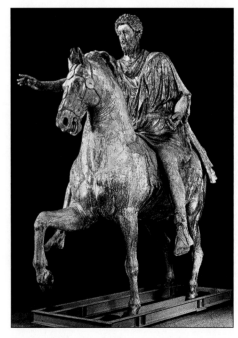

The philosopher at war. *The Meditations* of the Emperor Marcus Aurelius (r. 161–180) were written in military camps while he was campaigning against the barbarians on the empire's northern frontiers. His statue atop the Capitol at Rome has always symbolized dynamism and power, not only because of the commanding gesture of the emperor, but also because of the power his horse displays with its flared nostrils and stamping hoof.

In combination with the strain of threats from Persia and the convulsions of Roman politics, Germanic invasions in the third century almost dissolved the empire. In the late fourth century, the struggle to keep out the immigrants became hopeless. Some bands of Germans were drawn into the empire, others were driven in. Those drawn were usually relatively small, highly mobile war parties, numbering hundreds or at most a few thousand. They were composed of men detached from their traditional kinship structures by loyalty to a "ring giver"—a warlord who could buy their allegiance with the rewards of booty, protection money, ransom, extortion, or mercenary service. Trinkets of war-band service survive in burial sites: armbands set with jewels or onyx or inscribed with reminders of loyalty, rings bulging with garnets.

The biggest bands of migrants, numbering tens of thousands at a time, and traveling with women and children, were driven by stresses that arose beyond their borders, in the Eurasian steppelands. Here, the mid and late fourth century was a traumatic time, when war or hunger or plague or exceptional cold or some combination of such events induced unprecedented mobility, conflict, and confusion. The Roman historian and retired soldier, Ammianus Marcellinus, reported a conversation with some Huns, reputedly the most ferocious of the steppeland peoples of the time (see "Going to the Source: Chinese and Roman Perceptions of Steppelanders" pages 332–335). "Ask," he said, "who they are and whence they came—and they cannot tell you." Fear of the Huns glistens between the lines of every account: fear of their monstrous appearance, which Roman writers suspected must be produced by self-deformation; fear of their relationship with their horses, which made their mounted archery deadly; fear of their merciless treatment of enemies, which cowed resistance. (Fear of their smell too, since reputedly they never bathed.) Late in the fourth century, the Huns broke out of their heartlands in the depths of Asia—perhaps on the northeast borders of China, where many scholars identify them with the people the Chinese called Xiongnu (see Chapter 7). A kind of ricochet effect set in, as peoples collided and cannoned off each other, like balls on a pool table. Or perhaps all the turbulence of peoples, Germans and steppelanders alike, was the result of common problems: cold weather, shrinking pastures; or new sources of wealth, such as trade and booty, enriching new classes and disrupting the traditional stability of the societies concerned. Whatever the reasons, in the late fourth and early fifth centuries, displaced communities lined up for admission into the enticing empires of Rome, Persia, China, and India.

The hardest part of the story to appreciate is what it felt like for those who took part. In volatile conditions, illiterate masses leave few sources. Inklings emerge from the earliest surviving poem in what is recognizably German: the *Hildebrandslied*, the story of a family split between the war bands of rival chiefs in the chaos of the fifth century. Hildebrand's wife was left "in misery"; his baby grew into his battlefield adversary. The boy, raised in ignorance of his father's identity, unwittingly rejected his present of gold and jewels, "which the King of the Huns had given him." Only the first few lines survive of the terrible climax, in which father and son fight to the death. The story obviously has origins in a standard, traditional tragic theme of conflict between the generations of a single family. But it also shows something peculiar about the predicament of Germanic peoples at the time: the chaotic, divisive effects of the migrations, the interdependence of the worlds of the Germans and the Huns.

Germans were not nomadic by nature but, according to their own earliest historian, Jordanes, who wrote in the sixth century, were "driven to wander in a prolonged search for lands to cultivate." The Ostrogoths, or Eastern Goths, for example, farmed

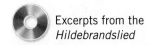

Excerpts from the *Hildebrandslied*

on the banks of the Don River in what is now Ukraine from the late second century until the 370s, when Hun invaders forced them over the Dniester River into the territory of the Visigoths or Western Goths. In 376, a reputed 200,000 Visigothic refugees were admitted into the Roman Empire. But the Romans then left them to starve, provoking a terrible revenge at the battle of Adrianople in 378 when the Goths killed a Roman emperor along with most of his army. From 395 to 418, the Visigoths undertook a destructive migration across the empire, terrorizing areas they crossed. In 410, they sacked Rome, inspiring speculations about the end of the world among shocked subjects of the empire, before settling as paid "guests" and, in effect, the masters of the local population in southern France and northern Spain. Other Germanic peoples found the Visigoths' example irresistible. Rome's frontier with the Germans was becoming indefensible (see Map 8.2).

Jordanes, *Deeds of the Goths,* Book Twenty-Six

Changes Within the Roman Empire

Meanwhile, the center of power in the dwindling empire shifted eastward into the mostly Greek-speaking zone, where barbarian incursions were more limited. Constantinople replaced Rome as the principal seat of the emperors. In 323, the Emperor Constantine elevated this dauntingly defensible small garrison town, surrounded on three sides by water and close to the threatened Danube and Persian frontiers, into an imperial capital.

From here, the emperors were able to keep invaders out of most of the eastern provinces of the empire in the fourth and fifth centuries, or limit immigration to manageable proportions or, in some places, to numbers needed for imperial defense. In the west, however, the empire could not control the incursions. In part, the greater durability of the eastern empire was the result of the direction invaders took. The Rhine River was an easily crossed frontier—especially in the cold winters of the early fifth century, when the river often froze. From there, invaders usually swung through northern France toward Spain, or turned south to reach Italy. Moreover, the eastern provinces of the empire—from Italy's Adriatic coast eastward—could be relatively easily reached, supplied, and garrisoned from Constantinople, whereas the western Mediterranean lay beyond the terrible navigational bottlenecks between Italy, Sicily, and North Africa. The extra time it took to reach the west had not mattered much when the empire was politically stable; but it mattered now. Finally, the eastern provinces—especially those east of the Adriatic—were better equipped for survival by the presence of the emperor and by the wealth of great estates in regions where mountain barriers, deserts, and seas deterred at least some invaders.

By founding Constantinople, Constantine ensured that the city of Rome would continue to stagnate. Though the Roman Senate—the assembly of noblemen

Stilicho. The late Roman Empire increasingly relied on immigrant mercenaries for its defense. The Vandal Stilicho (right) was one of the best, defending—as a Roman poet of the time said— "all within the sun's fiery orbit" in trust for the emperors of Rome. "All virtues meet in thee." He married an emperor's niece and maneuvered to make his son, Eucherius, also shown here, emperor. His daughter married an emperor. But, falsely accused of treachery, he loyally gave himself up for execution in 408 C.E. These ivory panels are examples of an art form traditionally used to commemorate Roman consuls.

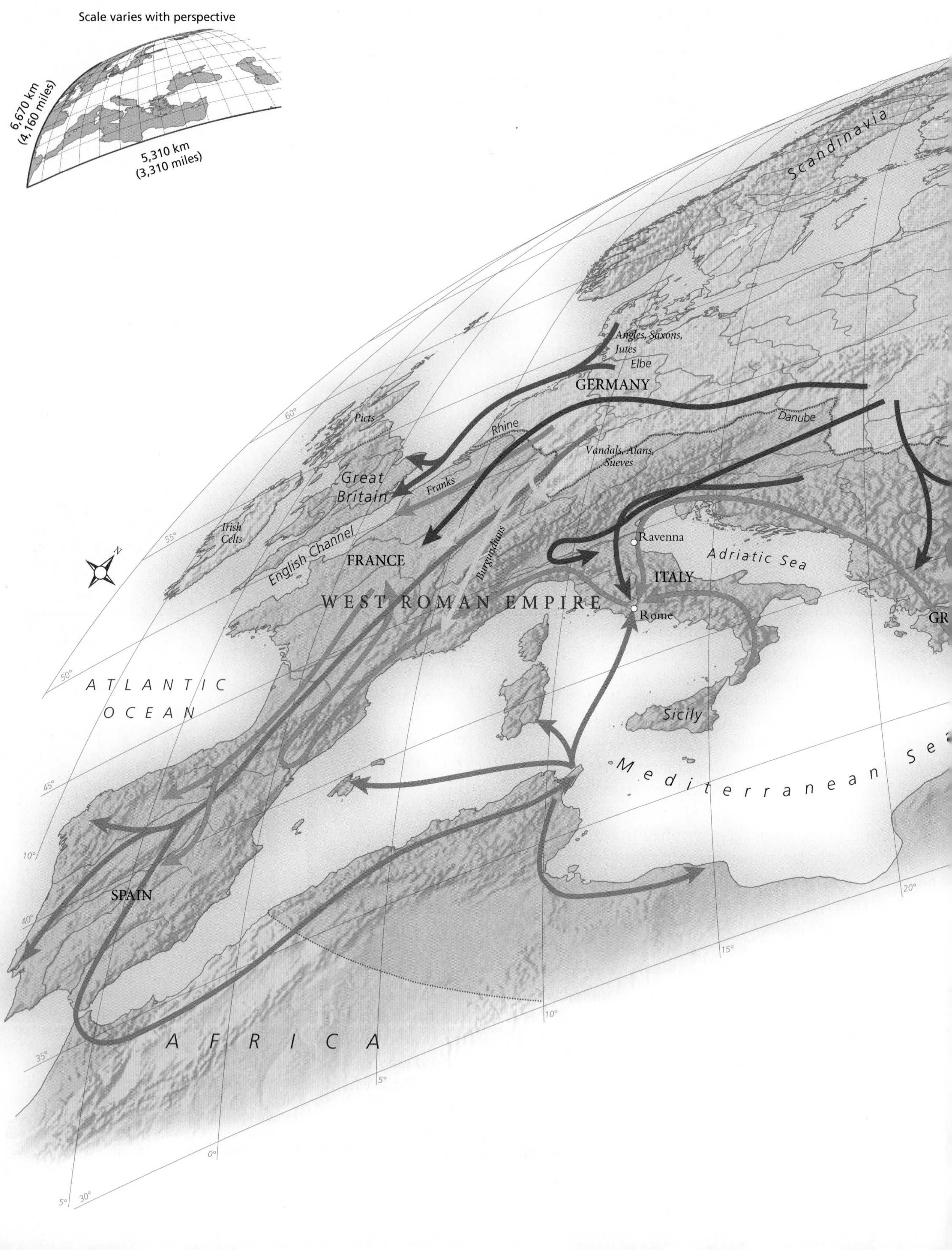

6,670 km
(4,160 miles)

5,310 km
(3,310 miles)

Scandinavia

Angles, Saxons,
Jutes
Elbe
GERMANY

Picts

Rhine

Danube

Great
Britain

Franks

Vandals, Alans,
Sueves

N

Irish
Celts

Ravenna

Adriatic Sea

English Channel

FRANCE

Burgundians

ITALY

Rome

GR

WEST ROMAN EMPIRE

ATLANTIC
OCEAN

Sicily

Mediterranean Sea

SPAIN

AFRICA

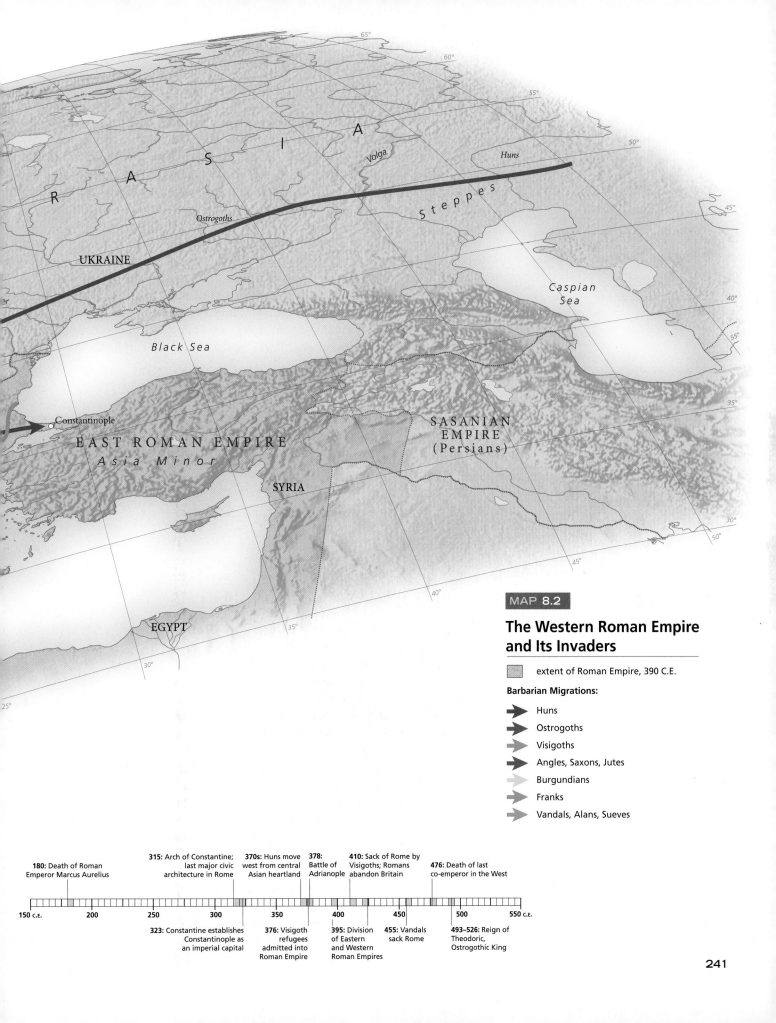

EURASIA

65°
60°
55°
50°
45°
40°
35°

Volga

Huns

Ostrogoths

Steppes

UKRAINE

Caspian
Sea

Black Sea

55°

Constantinople

SASANIAN
EMPIRE
(Persians)

EAST ROMAN EMPIRE
Asia Minor

35°

SYRIA

30°

50°

25°

EGYPT

35°

40°

30°

MAP 8.2

The Western Roman Empire and Its Invaders

extent of Roman Empire, 390 C.E.

Barbarian Migrations:

➡ Huns

➡ Ostrogoths

➡ Visigoths

➡ Angles, Saxons, Jutes

➡ Burgundians

➡ Franks

➡ Vandals, Alans, Sueves

180: Death of Roman Emperor Marcus Aurelius

315: Arch of Constantine; last major civic architecture in Rome

370s: Huns move west from central Asian heartland

378: Battle of Adrianople

410: Sack of Rome by Visigoths; Romans abandon Britain

476: Death of last co-emperor in the West

150 C.E.   200   250   300   350   400   450   500   550 C.E.

323: Constantine establishes Constantinople as an imperial capital

376: Visigoth refugees admitted into Roman Empire

395: Division of Eastern and Western Roman Empires

455: Vandals sack Rome

493–526: Reign of Theodoric, Ostrogothic King

241

and notables responsible for the government of the city—continued to meet, civic projects gradually ceased. The western empire was beset with problems. Impeded by war, long-range exchanges of personnel and commerce became increasingly impractical. Communications decayed. Aristocrats withdrew from traditional civic responsibilities—retiring to their estates, struggling to keep them going amid invasions. Bishops replaced bureaucrats. In localities from which imperial authority vanished, holy men took on the jobs of judges. Almost everywhere, barbarian experts in warfare took military commands. Garrisons withdrew from outposts of empire beyond the Rhine, the Danube, and the English Channel. After 476, there was no longer a coemperor in the west. Regional and local priorities replaced empire-wide perspectives. The most extreme form of the dissolution of authority inside the empire was the establishment of kingdoms led by foreigners, as Germans—settled as uneasy allies, entrusted with tasks of imperial defense, and quartered at the expense of their host communities—gradually usurped or accepted authority over non-Germanic populations (see Map 8.3). Where such kingdoms delivered peace and administered laws, they replaced the empire as the primary focus of people's allegiance.

The "Barbarian" West

At the time, writers of history and prophesy, peering through the twilight of the empire, could not believe Roman history was over. Rome was the last of the world monarchies the Bible foretold. Its end would mean the end of time. Everyone,

MAP 8.3 **The Barbarian West, ca. 526**

including barbarian kings, connived in pretending that the empire had survived. Germanic settlers were all, in varying degrees, susceptible to Romanization, and their kings usually showed deference to imperial institutions. A Visigothic leader, Athawulf, vowed "to extirpate the Roman name," but ended by marrying into the imperial family and collaborating with Rome. Burgundian kings in what is now eastern France continued a flattering correspondence with the emperors in Constantinople for as long as their state survived. The Franks, who occupied most of France in the late fifth and early sixth centuries, adorned their monarchs with emblems of Roman governors and consuls. No barbarians were proof against the appeal of Roman culture. Vandals, whose name has become a byword for destruction, had themselves portrayed in Roman-style mosaics. Even the Germanic settlers of Britain, most of whom had had virtually no contact with the Roman Empire, recalled the rule of Roman "giants" in their poetry.

Yet to Romans, the new rulers remained barbarians—foreigners of inferior culture. In turn, the limits of barbarian identification with Rome were of enormous importance. The notion of Roman citizenship gradually dissolved. Although the barbarians envied Roman civilization, most of them hankered after their own identities and—not surprisingly amid the dislocation of the times—clung to their roots. Many groups tried to differentiate themselves by upholding, at least for a time, unorthodox versions of Christianity. Some of their scholars and kings took almost as much interest in preserving their own traditional literature as in retaining or rescuing the works of classical and Christian writers. Law codes of barbarian kingdoms prescribed different rules for Germans and Romans.

The realm of the Ostrogothic king, Theodoric, was typically hybrid. He ruled Italy from 493 to 526. A church wall in his courtly center at Ravenna displays his palace, with throne room of gold, curtained like a sanctuary. His tomb is the burial mound of a Germanic king but is also in the style the Roman aristocracy of his era favored. Boethius, his chief minister, who was a Roman senator, not a Goth, worked hard to Romanize him. In a world of bewildering change, where traditional values vaporized and traditional institutions collapsed, Boethius clung to the old order, insisting on the continuity of the Roman Empire, reveling in his sons' election to ancient Roman offices of diminishing significance, and banking on the domestication of barbarian invaders. Imprisoned by Theodoric, he wrote *The Consolation of Philosophy*, fusing the stoical value system of happiness with the Christian tradition of deference to God. Happiness and God, Boethius argued, were identical.

The Church of San Apollinare Nuovo. Though Arians—who rejected the doctrine of the equality of the Persons of the Trinity—and other Christians denounced one another for heresy, they designed and decorated their churches in Ravenna in the early sixth century in remarkably similar ways, with processions of mosaic saints and martyrs lining the nave. Here the palace of the Arian king Theodoric, who endowed this church, is also depicted—with the skyline of Ravenna behind it, the city as if itself a sacred space.

The Collapse of Empire in the West

162–180	Reign of Emperor Marcus Aurelius, high point of Roman Empire
Third and fourth centuries	Germanic migrants enter empire in increasing numbers
323	Founding of Constantinople
378	Battle of Adrianople, Roman emperor killed
Late fourth century	Huns break out of Central Asia
410	Visigoths sack Rome
476	End of empire in the west

"A Parthian shot" now means a cutting parting remark—so-called from the tactics Parthian-mounted archers used in defending their homeland in what is now Iran and Iraq against the Romans. Retreating, or pretending to retreat, they turned in their saddles to shoot at their pursuers. Steppelander armies copied or developed this technique on their own. This 2,000-year-old Chinese design shows a Turkic warrior wielding a double-curve bow, constructed to be compact but with high tensile strength for use on horseback.

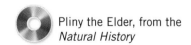

Pliny the Elder, from the
Natural History

STEPPELANDERS AND THEIR VICTIMS

Because Germanic peoples lined the zone between Rome's frontier and the Eurasian plains, steppeland peoples like the Huns made relatively few and brief forays into the Roman Empire. Empires centered in China, Persia, and India, by contrast, had to cope with the steppelanders directly (see Map 8.4). In some ways, invading herdsmen were easier to deal with than the Germans who were used to settled agriculture. Their techniques of warfare were less flexible. Reliant, in this period, on mounted archery, they were ill equipped for mountain warfare on the frontiers of Persia or India, or in the rice paddy–scored terrain of central and southern China. When successful as conquerors, the steppelanders were usually easier to wean from their cultural traditions than the Germans, assimilating to Chinese or, in some cases, to Indian ways within a few generations.

China

China's, moreover, was an empire better adapted for long-term survival than Rome's. Thanks to China's roughly round shape, centrally retained armies could get quickly to any point on its frontiers. No invaders threatened the long sea coast. China also had excellent internal communications systems, based on rivers and enhanced by canals. Chinese culture was more absorbent than Rome's. Subject-peoples tended to embrace Chinese identity with a surprising degree of commitment and even enthusiasm. *Barbarian* immigrants—the Chinese, like the Romans, used a contemptuous term for foreigners—commonly discarded their traditions and adopted Chinese customs, language, and identity. Above all, size, productivity, and technical inventiveness made China self-sufficient, if necessary. There was no adverse balance of trade, such as Rome endured, to drain wealth out of the empire—as Gaius Pliny the Elder, the nearest thing Rome had to an economist, complained in 77. China's internal market was huge—more internal trade meant more wealth.

But, like Rome in the same period, China under the Han dynasty never solved the most basic problem of imperial government: how to secure the succession of emperors. As we saw in the last chapter, factionalism and rebelliousness tended to breed in the families of imperial Chinese consorts. To offset the danger, emperors relied ever more heavily on the services of **eunuchs**, whom Roman emperors, too, regarded as perfect servants, and whose inability to father families of their own made them proof against dynastic ambitions. The long-term result was to create another faction and a new focus of resentment, as eunuchs usurped control over the succession. As in Rome, armies in China contended for the power to make and unmake emperors. Rivalry between armies and eunuchs precipitated civil war in 184, when Chang Chueh (chahng joo-ay), a wandering medic, whose plague remedy made him a popular hero, proclaimed rebellion against eunuch rule. The army emerged ascendant from nearly 40 years of war that followed.

In 220, the last Han emperor was forced to abdicate in favor of a new, army-backed dynasty, known as Jin. But the former patterns of politics resumed. Civil war became chronic, made worse by emperors' efforts to divide their responsibilities along lines similar to those Rome adopted, giving members of the imperial family

◯ MAKING CONNECTIONS ◯

CHINA AND ROME COMPARED

	CHINA	ROME
Geography	Round shape ensures that centrally located armies can get quickly to any point on frontier. Numerous rivers and canals facilitate communication	Long land frontier and narrow sea lanes impede movement of troops and information
Culture	Subject peoples embrace Chinese identity; barbarian immigrants adopt Chinese customs and language	Germanic peoples beyond empire's borders covet Roman wealth. "North–South" prosperity gap leads to envy and hostility. Limited identification by barbarians with Roman identity
Economy	Size, productivity, and technical inventiveness lead to self-sufficiency	Adverse balance of trade drains wealth out of the empire

regions to run. Steppeland migrants and marauders played increasingly important roles in the wars. In 304, contenders for the disputed succession called in rival barbarian armies. The leader of one of these armies proclaimed himself emperor, and his son, Liu Cong (lee-oh tsohng), drove the Jin south, into the Yangtze valley. The old capital, Chang'an (chahng-ahn), filled with "weeds and thorns."

Northern China became a kaleidoscope of kingdoms and self-styled empires, continually reshaken by warlords, adventurers, and new migrants, variously Turkic and Mongol. These migrants fitfully, but in the long term, irrepressibly adopted Chinese ways. Buddhist missionaries promoted it; the development of the silk routes favored it. Toward the end of the fifth century, the ruler of the ascendant barbarians, the Xianbei (shee-on bay), was deeply committed to Buddhism. Xiaowen (r. 471–499), or Toba Hung II, to give him his name in his native language, abolished traditional Xianbei rites and language in favor of Chinese practices. Aspiring to make a reality of his ancestors' claims to the mandate of heaven, he revived the state cult of Confucius the Han had established and moved to a new capital at Luoyang (lwoh-yahng). But the state he founded fragmented in its turn. The old aristocracy resisted Chinese values, while the court practiced Chinese-style cycles of factionalism, family rifts, and civil wars.

India

For the sedentary civilizations that lined Eurasia to the south, stability was impossible as long as the steppeland churned out uncontainable migrant hordes, as India's case also shows. The Huns who began to infiltrate India around 415—working their way west and south around the mountain barrier, were, presumably, part of the fallout of the same catastrophes that spilled steppelanders into the Roman and Chinese Empires. On the way, they wiped out Bactria and Gandhara, states founded in the era of Alexander the Great, which had developed distinctive cultures by blending Greek and Buddhist ideas (see Chapter 7).

Although the invasion routes into India from the steppes look formidable on the map, they were poorly guarded at the critical time (see Map 8.4). In the fourth century, a ruler of Maghada who called himself Candra Gupta (CHAHN-drah GOOP-tah),

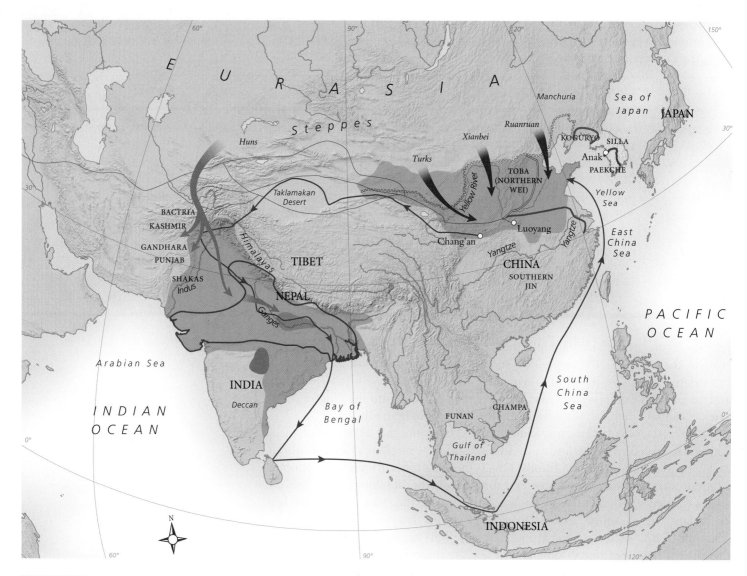

5,000 km (3,107 miles)

6,667 km (4,143 miles)

MAP 8.4

Steppelanders and Asian Kingdoms, ca. 300–700 C.E.

- farthest extent of Toba Wei, ca.500 C.E.
- kingdom of Candra Gupta I
- farthest extent of Gupta dynasty, ca.500 C.E.
- Vakataka dynasty
- — Harsha's empire, ca.650 C.E.
- → Hun invasions
- ➤ Steppeland migrants into China
- → Journey of Faxian, 405–411 C.E.

- ∿∿∿ Great Wall
- ═ Grand Canal
- — Silk Roads
- ○ city mentioned or described on pages 244–248
- *Xianbei* people

after a hero of the time of Alexander the Great, attempted to restore the unity of the Indian subcontinent. His dynasty, the Guptas (GOOP-tahs), never established as wide a dominion as that of Asoka (see Chapter 7), but they did weaken the states of India's northwest frontier, where the Huns got in. The loose-knit Gupta political system, which covered most of India as far south as the Deccan, linked many diverse layers of intermediate authority, and so it was easily overthrown.

The morale of the population also favored the invaders. Writers generally agreed that they were living in the *Kaliyuga*, the age of decline. A play written by Kalidasa—who probably lived in the fourth century—depicted alienated classes in a morally corrupt state, where corrupt officials tortured a fisherman charged with stealing the king's signet ring. In fact, the fisherman had saved the ring by catching the fish that swallowed it. He paid his torturers off with the reward the king sent him and, at their suggestion, treated them to drinks in a wine shop. It was hard for the empire's poorest subjects to identify with a system that perpetuated their poverty by making social rank inherited. According to Faxian (faw-shee-ehn), a Chinese Buddhist pilgrim in India in 405–411, the "untouchables" of the lowest caste had to sound a clapper in the street to warn against their polluting presence (see Map 8.4 for the path of Faxian's journey).

In the 450s, when the Huns broke in—"Kings of churlish spirit," who killed "women, children and cows"—their customs included reliance on flesh foods and, within the royal family, rituals in which kings sacrificed their mothers. Not surprisingly, against such a background, they persecuted Buddhists, as well as followers of native Indian traditions, who revered cows as sacred. The Gupta Empire showed little resilience. The decline of the empire is conventionally dated from 467—less than a decade before the last emperor in Rome was forced to abdicate and was pensioned off. Subsequent Gupta emperors are shadowy—barely known, except by name, from contemporary sources. Yet within another 50 years or so, the Hunnic realm seems to have become one Indian state among many. Indian unity—such as it was—dissolved among a multitude of principalities in the north and a few relatively large, unstable kingdoms in the south.

The End of Dynasties in China and India

220	Last Han emperor forced to abdicate
304	Contenders for Chinese throne call in barbarian armies
415	Huns begin to infiltrate India
ca. 467	Demise of Gupta Empire

Faxian, *Record of Buddhist Countries*, Chapter Sixteen

NEW FRONTIERS IN ASIA

For the Chinese and Gupta Empires the barbarian invasions inaugurated times of troubles, but it was a time of opportunity for developing states on their frontiers, where imperial power might otherwise have inhibited or repressed development. An early Gupta inscription mentions developing states around the frontiers: the Shaka dynasty in western India and the Vakatakas, whose daughters the Guptas took in marriage in the Deccan. The conditions favored similar effects in other parts of Asia.

Korea

Refugees from China, for instance, fled from the nomad invaders in search of tamer barbarians, to whom to offer their services as technicians or sages. Dong Shou—to take a case in point—was a scholar who escaped from the Xianbei in 337, and took refuge in neighboring Koguryo (koh-goo-ryuh), an emerging state that occupied parts of what are now southeastern Manchuria and northern Korea. After a prosperous career, he was buried at Anak, amid wall paintings that document the history of Koguryo at the time. Buddhist and Daoist emblems mingle with scenes of the life of the kingdom: proudly displayed images of prosperity and strength, including irrigation works, rice production, people and horses eating, and a procession of well-armored soldiers. While China dissolved, Koguryo expanded. A memorial of King Kwanggaet'o, erected at the time of his death in 413, credits him with the conquest of 64 walled towns and 1,400 villages. Continuing prosperity—the result of the introduction of ox-drawn plows and irrigation for rice fields—can be measured in the results of the census the Chinese took when they eventually conquered Koguryo in 667–668. The country had 176 walled cities and 697,000 families. Unlike other communities whom the Chinese considered barbarians, however, Korean states had, by then, too much self-pride and too long a history of achievement to adopt Chinese identity.

Meanwhile, similar histories unfolded in the southern Korean kingdoms of Silla (shil-lah) and Paekche (pek-jay). There, royal tombs were full of gold—spangled crowns in the shape of stylized antlers, golden belts with pendants of gold, jade, and glass. Although the iron trade contributed to the enrichment of the state, Korean states were agrarian kingdoms whose wealth was in manpower. They fought one another to gain population. Paekche paid a ransom of 1,000 households, for instance, when raiders from Koguryo occupied its capital. Silla was particularly resolute in following Chinese models of state-building. In 520, King Pophung began to give positions of power and social prestige to Confucian scholars. The kingdom, however, also had a caste system of its own. Many positions were open only to those ranked as possessing "sacred bone"—the rank of the royal family—and "true bone," the birthright of the courtly elite. (This distinction, however, disappeared after 653, when a true bone became king.) Silla unified the Korean peninsula in over a hundred years of warfare from the mid–sixth century.

Funan

Meanwhile, the turbulence of central Eurasia, which periodically disrupted the Silk Roads, favored states along the maritime route across Eurasia, beside monsoonal seas. Chinese travelers' accounts give us glimpses into their world. The land of Funan occupied a stretch of territory, wrapped around the coast of the Gulf of Thailand. Chinese officials singled it out as a possible tributary or trading partner during a surge of interest in the potential of the region in the third century. Its culture was almost certainly borrowed from India. By Chinese reports, it was a repository of learning, rich enough to levy taxes in "gold, silver, pearls and perfumes." Its success depended on its role as a middleman in Chinese trade with Indonesia and the Bay of Bengal.

THE RISE OF ETHIOPIA

The most remarkable product of growing commerce across monsoonal seas was not Funan but, unquestionably, Ethiopia, a country at the limit—almost beyond the reach—of the Indian Ocean network, a land that surrounding deserts and high mountains made hard to reach (see Map 8.5). The right balance between accessibility and isolation was the key to Ethiopia's success. High altitude made the emergent state defensible and guaranteed it a temperate climate in tropical latitudes. Axum (AHK-soom), the capital, was around 7,200 feet up, on a spur of the loftiest highlands.

Outsiders saw Axum as a trading state, where all the exotic goods of black Africa awaited: rhino horn, hippo hides, ivory and obsidian, tortoise shell, monkeys, slaves. Objects manufactured in China and Greece found their way to Axumite tombs. The frequent use of Greek in inscriptions, alongside the native Ge'ez (geh-EHZ) language, indicates a cosmopolitan community. Ethiopian products could reach the outside world through links with the Mediterranean via Roman and later Byzantine Egypt and with the Indian Ocean via the Red Sea. The highlands could dominate the long Rift valley land route to the south, to lands rich in gold, civet (the glands of civet cats were used to make perfumes), slaves, and ivory.

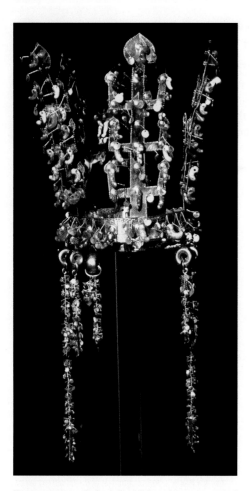

Korean crown. Before Buddhism became rooted there in the sixth century C.E., Korean rulers were buried with fabulous treasures. This crown, with antler-like ornaments, is from one of the many royal burial mounds of the kingdom of Silla. It shows the influence of Chinese and Central Asian goldsmiths' work.

The Rise of Ethiopia

340s	Spread of Christianity in Ethiopia
Early sixth century	King Kaleb begins conquest of southern Arabia
530s	Environmental crisis undermines control of south Arabia

But the corridor from the Ethiopian highlands to the port of Adulis on the Red Sea is long, and the Red Sea is hard to navigate. For the people of Axum, intent on their own agrarian way of life, trade was probably a sideline. They stamped ears of wheat on their coins. Terraces of grains sprang from valley soils, plowed with oxen and irrigated by stone dams across mountain streams. The highlands were fertile enough to produce two or three crops a year. Food mentioned in inscriptions includes wheat, beer, wine, honey, meat, butter, vegetable oils, and the world's first recorded coffee.

The material remains of the culture include finely worked ivory, metalwork, and huge, cubical tombs lined with brick arches. Axum contained an elaborate mausoleum of ten galleries opening off a central corridor. Three enormous stone pillars, each of a single slab of locally quarried granite, towered over the city. The largest was 160 feet tall and weighed nearly 500 tons—bigger than any other monolith ever made. Depictions of many-storied buildings or figures of hawks and crocodiles adorned the pillars. According to a Greek visitor's description, the central plaza of the city had a four-towered palace and thrones of pure marble, smothered with inscriptions, and statues of gold, silver, and bronze.

Inscriptions from early in the fourth century recorded what people at the time regarded as the key events of politics: numbers of captives; plunder in livestock; oaths of submission; doles of bread, meat, and wine granted to captives; their punitive relocation in distant parts of the empire; thank offerings for gods who bestowed victory—native gods at first, then, from the 340s, the Christian God. The ambitions of the kings seemed to tug across the strait to Arabia (see Chapter 5). Early in the sixth century, King Kaleb launched an expedition to conquer southern Arabia, much of which the Ethiopians occupied for most of the rest of the century.

THE CRISES OF THE SIXTH AND SEVENTH CENTURIES

Ethiopian control of south Arabia probably faltered because of an environmental crisis in the 530s. Plague played a part in the collapse of the irrigation states of southern Arabia and drove migrants northward, some seeking refuge in Roman-controlled Syria, others swelling the cities of Mecca and Medina. Twice during the Ethiopian occupation, the great dam at Marib broke. The losses of irrigation water were so traumatic that they became a major theme for poets' laments.

These disasters roughly coincided with other, more widespread catastrophes. In 535, the skies of the Northern Hemisphere darkened. A massive volcanic eruption in Indonesia split Java from Sumatra (soo-MAH-trah) and spewed ash into the atmosphere. Thanks to the diminished sunlight, temperatures fell. The new conditions suited some disease-bearing microorganisms. A plague-bearing bacillus ravaged Constantinople. A disease that resembled smallpox devastated Japan. Even Mesoamerican graves contain evidence of a severe decline in health in what is now central Mexico toward the middle of the sixth century. In the same period, the Eurasian steppes overspilled anew, impelling horseborne warbands into Europe: refugees, perhaps, from plague. Historians still debate how far these events are connected and whether a single volcanic explosion can account for them. Still, the sixth century marked a trough—a low point from which reformers, with varying fortunes, could launch revivals of endangered traditions and rally weakened states.

In India, for instance, early in the seventh century, Harsha, king of Thanesar, tried to fill in the political fissures and reconstruct an empire (see Map 8.4).

Stela of Axum. Until the rulers of Ethiopia adopted Christianity in the mid–fourth century, they invested huge amounts of capital and labor to create gigantic stelae—still the biggest structures made of single blocks of stone anywhere in the world. The largest examples—which reach well over 100 feet high—stood on ground long used for burials and probably marked important tombs. They have the skyscraper-like form of towering buildings. This art form climaxed in the early fourth century, just before Ethiopian priorities switched to church building, and the last stelae were left to topple or perhaps were never even hoisted into position.

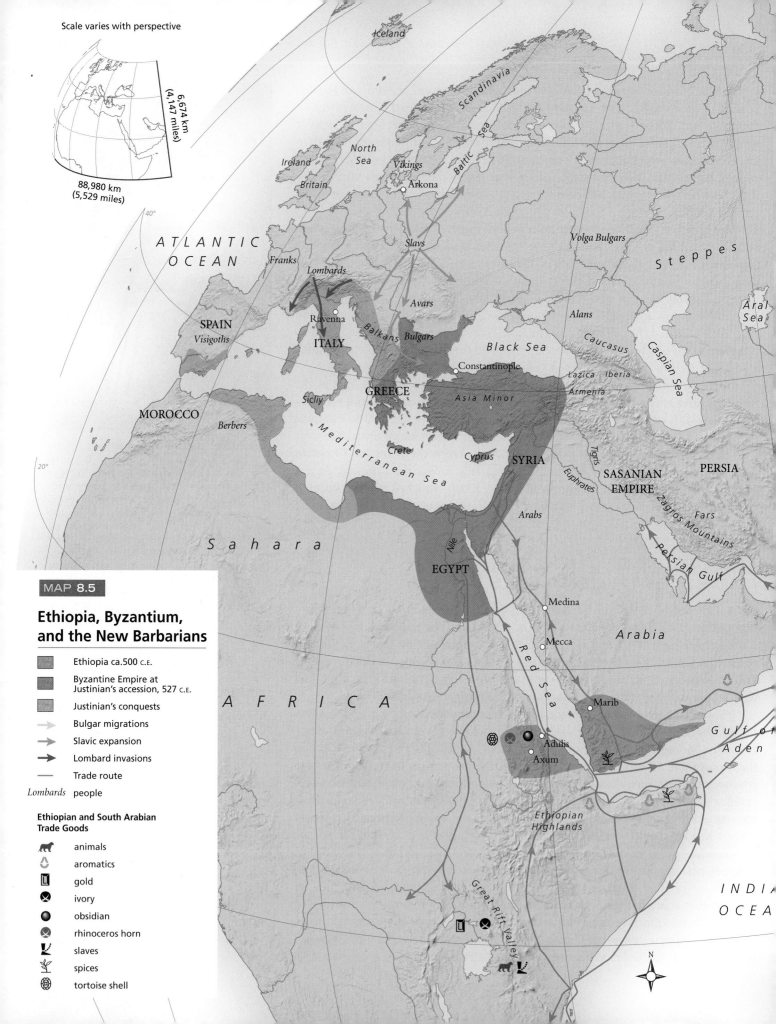

Scale varies with perspective

6,674 km
(4,147 miles)

88,980 km
(5,529 miles)

40°

20°

ATLANTIC
OCEAN

Iceland

Scandinavia

Ireland

Britain

North
Sea

Vikings

Arkona

Baltic
Sea

Franks

Lombards

Ravenna

ITALY

SPAIN

Visigoths

MOROCCO

Berbers

Sicily

GREECE

Crete

Mediterranean Sea

Cyprus

Slavs

Avars

Balkans

Bulgars

Black Sea

Constantinople

Asia Minor

Lazica Iberia

Armenia

Volga Bulgars

Steppes

Alans

Caucasus

Aral
Sea

Caspian Sea

SYRIA

Tigris

Euphrates

SASANIAN
EMPIRE

PERSIA

Fars

Zagros Mountains

Persian Gulf

Sahara

Nile

EGYPT

Arabs

AFRICA

Medina

Mecca

Arabia

Red Sea

Marib

Gulf of Aden

Great Rift Valley

Ethiopian
Highlands

INDIA
OCEAN

Adulis

Axum

N

MAP 8.5

Ethiopia, Byzantium, and the New Barbarians

- Ethiopia ca.500 C.E.
- Byzantine Empire at Justinian's accession, 527 C.E.
- Justinian's conquests
- → Bulgar migrations
- → Slavic expansion
- → Lombard invasions
- — Trade route

Lombards people

Ethiopian and South Arabian Trade Goods

- 🐾 animals
- ⌂ aromatics
- ⬜ gold
- ⊗ ivory
- ⬤ obsidian
- ⊘ rhinoceros horn
- ⚒ slaves
- ⚘ spices
- ⊕ tortoise shell

He devoted his exceptionally long reign of 41 years to the reunification of most of the Ganges basin. Rulers in Punjab, Kashmir (kahsh-MEER), and Nepal paid him tribute. He made tireless tours of his realm, collecting tribute, giving alms, dispensing judgments. But even in the biography Harsha himself commissioned, practical compromises with kingly ideals are evident. The book describes the poor, gathering fragments of grain left after the king's camp has moved on. The king's elephants trample the hovels of peasants who can defend themselves only by hurling clods of earth. Harsha's dominion was an improvised conquest, and his achievement did not survive him. He had, however, more successful counterparts in China and Rome.

JUSTINIAN AND THE EASTERN ROMAN EMPIRE

Though the eastern Roman Empire remained a single state, it, too, was transformed. In the perceptions of its leaders, it remained "Roman," even after 476, when the emperors no longer had any power in Rome itself. Nowadays, however, historians of the period tend to stop calling the empire "Roman," at least from the sixth century onward, preferring the term *Byzantine Empire*, from "Byzantium" (bih-ZAN-tee-uhm), the former name of Constantinople. From the sixth or seventh centuries onward, the use of Latin—always restricted in the eastern provinces to fairly high levels of administration—dwindled. Although most invaders were defeated, turned away, bought off, or deflected by diplomacy, and no Germanic kingdoms took shape inside the eastern provinces, migrants seeped through the frontiers, especially in the eighth century. Meanwhile, the empire effectively abandoned ambitions to reconquer the western provinces. In the late sixth and early seventh centuries, emperors concentrated on the struggle with Persia, and largely left the western provinces to the barbarians.

Justinian, emperor from 527 to 565, was the last emperor to adopt a grand strategy of imperial reunification, giving equal importance to recovery in the west and defense and expansion in the east. He aimed to be a restorer but was more suited to be a revolutionary—"a born meddler and disturber," as a chronicler who knew him called him. As the heir of a peasant-turned-soldier whom the army had elected to rule, he enjoyed thumbing his nose at established elites. At a time when the Church legitimized authority, he infuriated bishops with his attempts to reconcile conflicting theological opinions. The monarchy needed its traditional supporters, but Justinian's tax policies made the rich howl with anguish. He was a great lawgiver who had himself depicted as the biblical Moses and yet exploited his prerogative as lawmaker to break all the rules

Theodora. According to court gossip, Theodora (ca. 500–548), wife of the Roman Emperor Justinian (r. 527–565), was a former prostitute of insatiable sexual appetite. But the propagandist who portrayed her in mosaic, in the church of San Vitale at Ravenna, depicted her as a sacred figure, towering over priests and nobles and equal in stature to her husband. She approaches the altar arrayed in jewels—a convention used in the art of the time to personify the Church—bearing a gift of communion wine to be converted miraculously into the blood of Christ.

Hagia Sophia. The minarets of the mosque of Hagia Sophia in Istanbul conceal the building's origins as the greatest Christian church of its day, built at the command of the Emperor Justinian to defy time and display the largest dome in the world at the time. The dome collapsed some 20 years after its completion. So the emperor had it rebuilt on an even more ambitious scale. Daring perforations around the base of the dome—over 100 feet wide and nearly 200 feet high—bathed the sanctuary in light.

Lombard cross. Some of the finest goldsmith work of Germanic invaders of the Roman Empire went into offerings kings made to churches. This jeweled cross, made for the sixth-century Lombard King Agilulf was designed to hang in a sanctuary, catching the light from the lamps over the altar. In return for such treasures, kings expected priests to pray for victories and for God to grant them.

himself. Typically, he outraged straitlaced courtiers by choosing a notoriously dissolute actress named Theodora to be his empress. He relied on her strength and intellect. She was the counselor of every policy and the troubleshooter of every crisis. In the famous mosaic portrait of her in the church of San Vitale at Ravenna in Italy, she wears jewels of triumph and a cloak embroidered with images of kingship and wisdom.

Justinian had the ill-disciplined energy of all insomniacs as he paced the palace corridors at night, "like a ghost," as hostile courtiers said. He thought big. His projects included importing silk from China and allying with Arabs and Ethiopians against Persia. He built Hagia Sophia (AH-gee-ah soh-FEE-ah) (Holy Wisdom) in Constantinople to be the biggest church in the world and, when it fell down, built it again. His reconquests from barbarian kingdoms reunited most of the Mediterranean world (see Map 8.5). Buildings he erected stretched from Morocco to the Persian frontier. He left his partially restored empire impoverished but enlarged. The robust performance of the eastern empire under Justinian seems impressive compared with the more radical transformation of the empire in the west. In particular, the eastern empire survived the new wave of barbarian invasions that was about to overwhelm Rome's old enemy, Persia.

THE NEW BARBARIANS

For the barbarian invasions were not yet over. The next invaders of Italy, the Lombards, entered the peninsula in 568 from the north, just in time to gather the spoils of Justinian's wars, in which Romans and Goths had exhausted each other. On a plaque made to adorn the helmet of their King Agilulf, winged figures brandish drinking horns of a traditional Germanic court along with placards marked "Victory" of a kind carried in Roman triumphs. Agilulf's sumptuous cross—all Christian barbarian kings had something similar—is a wand of victory: a sign to conquer by. In the late seventh century, the Bulgars, another invader-people from the steppes, crossed the Danube and set up as the elite of a state that stretched from the northern Balkans almost to the walls of Constantinople. In his shrine at Arkona, on the Baltic, the four-headed deity of the Slavs was perhaps already developing the thirst for wine for which he later became notorious. During the seventh and eighth centuries, in an expansion almost undocumented and never explained, Slavs spread over most of eastern Europe from the Baltic to southern Greece. Meanwhile, in North Africa, the Berbers, upland pastoralists, mobilized camel-borne war bands to terrorize the southern Mediterranean shore. In Scandinavia, in the eighth century, warriors who fought on sleds with prows carved with the heads of monsters took to the sea.

THE ARABS

These all proved formidable enemies of what was left of the Roman world. But most formidable of all the loiterers on the threshold were the Arabs, or, more precisely, nomadic, Arabic-speaking peoples of central Arabia. They lived astride the trade routes of the peninsula, between Romanized communities and city-states in the north, and the maritime-oriented kingdoms of the seaboard. In the seventh century, they were transformed from a regional nuisance into a dynamic force. The preceding period in Arabia has a bad press—represented as chaotic and morally clueless, until the prophet Muhammad brought peace and justice in the 620s and early 630s. But the contrast between the periods before and after the Prophet's arrival may be too sharply drawn.

The few glimpses the sources give us suggest that Arab society was already demographically robust, militarily effective, and—at least in its poetry—artistically creative. "Poetry, horses, and numbers of people" were the standards by which different communities measured their rival merits. It is true, however, that Arabia was politically divided and riven by internal wars among tribes. The best-documented war was said to have started when the tribe of Dhubyan cheated in a horse race against the Abs. It lasted for generations, and inspired the work of Antarah ibn-Shaddad al-Absi (AHN-tah-rah ihb-ihn shad-DAD ahl-AHB-see), the most renowned poet and warrior of the age.

 Pre-Islamic Arabic poetry: "The Poem of Antar"

It is also true that the economy of the tribes had come to depend on war: raiding the Byzantine, Persian, and Arab cities that were scattered around the edges of the region and milking their trade. In one respect the transformation of these Arabs resembled that of other nomadic peoples mobilized for war by social change. As trade and banditry concentrated wealth, new styles of leadership dislocated the traditional, kinship-based structures of society and created an opportunity for a single, charismatic leader to unite an overwhelming force. In the Arabs' case, however, Muhammad's distinctive character marked him out from all other such leaders. His impact changed every aspect of life it touched. The Prophet taught a religion that was as rigorously monotheistic as Judaism, as humane and potentially as universal as Christianity, as traditional as paganism, and—for its time—more practical than any of them. More than a religion, Islam—literally "submission" to God—was also a way of life and a blueprint for society, complete with a demanding but unusually practical moral code, a set of rules of personal discipline, and the outline of a code of civil law.

Islam

A belief dear to Islamic scholars represents Muhammad as God's mouthpiece and therefore, in human terms, utterly original. His teachings crackle and snap with the noise of a break with the past, but from Arab merchant communities he picked up Jewish concepts: monotheism, providence, history ruled by God. His earliest followers regarded themselves as descendants of the biblical patriarch Abraham through Abraham's maidservant Hagar (HAY-gahr) and their son Ishmael (IHSH-mahy-ehl). The inspiration of Islam combined elements borrowed from Judaism and Christianity with a measure of respect for some of the traditional rites and teachings of pagan traditions in Arabia.

Muhammad claimed to have received his teaching from God, through the Archangel Gabriel, who revealed divine words into his ear. The resulting writings, the **Quran** (kuh-RAHN), were so persuasive and so powerful that hundreds of millions of people believe him to this day. By the time of his death, Muhammad had equipped his followers with a dynamic form of social organization, a sense of their own unique access to the truth of God, and a conviction that war against nonbelievers was not only justified but also sanctified. Warriors were promised an afterlife in a paradise where sensual pleasures were like those of this world—pleasure gardens, young women. Muhammad's legacy gave Muslims (those who "submit" to God's message) administrative and ideological advantages against potential enemies. Yet the opportunity for the Arabs to become an imperial people arose as much, perhaps, from the weakness of the Byzantine and, especially, the Persian Empires, as from the dynamics of their own society.

THE QURAN

The earliest known Arabic texts, from the fourth century C.E. onward, are inscribed in stone. Yet the earliest versions of the Quran, which date from the eighth century, are in a rounded script designed to be written with a brush. This form of written Arabic is known as Kufic—from the town of Kufa in Iraq, where it supposedly originated. Below are three lines from a Quran written in Kufic:

"This [divine writ], behold, is no less a reminder to all the worlds—and you most certainly grasp its purport after a lapse of time!" (Quran 38:87–88)

"In the name of Allah, the merciful the compassionate." (This is the *bismallah*, which begins all but one chapter of the Quran.)

"The bestowal from on high of this divine writ . . ." (Quran 39:1)

Arabic Manuscript: 30.60 Page from a Koran, 8th-9th century. Kufic script. H: 23.8 x W: 35.5 cm. Courtesy of the Freer Gallery of Art, Smithsonian Institution, Washington, D.C.: Purchase, 1930.60r

What advantages did the Quran confer on early believers in Islam?

The Arabs Against Persia and Rome

Of the old Eurasian empires, Persia's was the most successful in fending off steppeland turbulence. The Parthians, the Iranian dynasty that had come to power after the death of Alexander the Great (see Chapter 7) had favored the western regions of their empire and Mesopotamia. The Sasanians, however, who succeeded the Parthians as Persia's ruling dynasty from 226, concentrated their power in the most defensible part of the empire, building heavily in their own heartlands in the highlands of Fars and in and beyond the Zagros Mountains (see Map 8.5). A commanding position in the world, along the trade routes that linked the Mediterranean to the Indian Ocean and the Silk Roads, gave them the resources to maintain their traditional hostility to Rome—symbolized in a rock carving of 260, where the Roman emperor, Valerian, grovels at the feet of his Persian captors. Yet mutual respect tempered Persia's wars against Rome. Each empire recognized the other as civilized, while condemning all other neighbors as barbarians. In the 380s, Rome and Persia responded to the barbarian menace by making peace.

Sasanian victory. Huge rock carvings were traditional media of propaganda for Persian kings. None celebrates a more spectacular victory than that of Shapur I (r. 241–272) at the battle of Edessa in 260 C.E., when he took the Roman Emperor Valerian captive. The sculptor captured Valerian in another sense by showing him bending the knee in submission, while his cloak billows in the wind. The realism of the art enhances its symbolic significance, suggested by Shapur's huge crown, bulging physique, imperious gestures, and the stamp of his horse's hoof.

The peace lasted throughout the steppeland turbulence of the fifth century, but at the beginning of the sixth century, as other dangers seemed to recede, war between Romans and Persians resumed with deadly intent—like a fistfight between sparring partners that becomes deadly. By the time of the Arab conquests, the two giant empires had worn each other out. After more than a hundred years of almost continuous conflict, the Roman Empire was close to exhaustion and the Persian, which got the worse of the fight, was near collapse. In consequence, neither empire could deal with the sudden rise of the Arabs. Mountains had protected Persia from northern steppeland invaders—but the Arab frontier to the southwest was flat. The Muslim Arabs absorbed the Persian Empire in its entirety in a series of campaigns from the late 630s to the early 650s. The Roman provinces of Syria, Palestine, Egypt, and North Africa—Rome's wealthiest and most populous subject-areas—fell to Arab or Arab-led armies by the early eighth century.

THE MUSLIM WORLD

Most of the area comprised within these limits became, in effect, a Muslim world (see Map 8.6). In some respects, it functioned remarkably cohesively, like a single empire, gradually spreading Islam, the Arabic language, and a common Muslim identity wherever it went, and introducing more or less uniform principles of law and government. Flexibility brought success. Although Arabs and descendants of the Prophet's own tribe enjoyed social privileges, every male Muslim could share a sense of belonging to an imperial elite. Although women were repressed, they at least had some important rights: to initiate divorce (albeit under much stricter conditions than those that applied to men); to own property and retain it after

⬤ MAKING CONNECTIONS ⬤

EMPIRES IN TRANSFORMATION

EMPIRE/ REGION →	EXTERNAL ENEMIES →	INTERNAL WEAKNESSES →	STRENGTHS →	SURVIVAL STRATEGIES →	SUCCESSOR STATE
Teotihuacán/ Mesoamerica	Resentful tributary city-states	Overpopulation; reliance on imports; limited resources to export	Widely emulated culture; extensive trade network	Continual expansion to sustain population growth; installing friendly rulers in neighboring regions	——
Roman/ Mediterranean	Germanic border peoples; Huns from Eurasian steppes; Persians	Sprawling, vulnerable land frontiers; politicized military; Christian threat to paganism; internal disorder; mass migrations; uncertain succession of leadership; adverse balance of trade	Occasional strong leaders; strong military tradition; eastern provinces easily defended and supplied	Division of leadership responsibility under Marcus Aurelius (162); division of empire after Constantine (d. 337); transfer of capital to Constantinople	Byzantine Empire in east; Germanic and barbarian kingdoms in west
Han/China	Steppeland raiders and migrants	Uncertain succession of leadership; feuding imperial factions; warlords	Circular shape facilitates movement of troops and information; Chinese culture imitated by barbarians; strong internal economy	Use of eunuchs for administration; promotion of Chinese customs and language among barbarians	Jin dynasty, followed by civil war and political fragmentation
Gupta/India	Huns	Cultural pessimism (age of Kaliyuga); poor defenses; inequality fostered by caste system; corrupt bureaucracy	Several strong leaders (Candra Gupta)	Differing layers of local authority linked together	Hunnic states and other principalities; kingdom of Harsha
Sasanian/ Persia	Romans; nomadic Arabs	Exhaustion after continuous wars with Rome	Commanding geographic position; strong defenses; effective diplomacy	Concentrating power in most defensible areas; diplomacy with Rome	Islamic caliphate

divorce; to conduct business in their own right. Christians and Jews, though vulnerable to periodic persecution and compelled to pay extra taxes, were normally allowed to worship in their own way. So, at first, were the Zoroastrians of Persia, who, though despised as pagans, were too numerous to alienate. Although other forms of paganism were forbidden, many traditional shrines and pilgrimages were resanctified as suitable for Muslim devotion.

But the Islamic world was too big to remain a single empire for long. And the precepts Muhammad left his followers at his death were not intended for a large

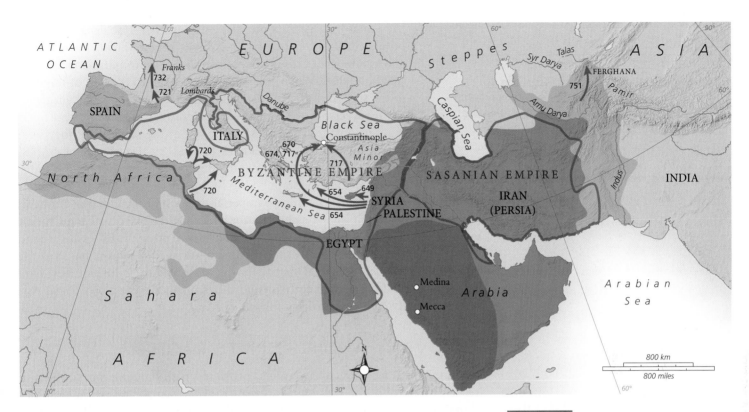

MAP 8.6

The Muslim World, ca. 756

- Muslim lands by 634
- Muslim lands by 656
- Muslim lands by 756
- → Muslim invasions, with dates
- — Byzantine Empire ca. 610
- — Sasanian Empire ca. 610

MAP EXPLORATION

www.prenhall.com/armesto_maps

Excerpts from the Quran

state. For his followers, he was both prophet and ruler. Whereas Jesus invited individuals to respond to God's grace, Muhammad, more straightforwardly, called them to obey God's laws. Whereas Moses legislated for a chosen people, the Jews, and Jesus preached a "kingdom not of this world," Muhammad aimed at a code of behavior covering every department of life. He failed, however, to leave a code that was anything like comprehensive. So schools of jurisprudence set out to fill in the gaps by inferring Muhammad's principles from such laws as he did make in his lifetime, applying them more generally and, in some cases, adding insights from reason, common sense, or custom. The **Sharia**—literally, "the camel's way to water"—was both a religious discipline and a law code for the state. The principles of law were unchangeable: revealed to the masters of the eighth and ninth centuries, whose interpretations of Muhammad's tradition were regarded as divinely guided. The reconciliation of the various schools' opinions, however, has always allowed some opportunities for development.

One consequence of the way Islam developed was that where Jesus had proclaimed a sharp distinction between the secular and the spiritual, Muslims acknowledged no difference. The supreme Islamic authority, the **caliph** (KAY-lihf)—literally, the "successor" of the Prophet—was, Christians said, both pope and emperor. The problem of identifying who was caliph split Islam between rival claimants and incompatible methods of choosing a caliph within a generation of Muhammad's death. The major division that eventually developed was between **Shia** (SHEE-ah) (meaning the "party" of Ali), which regarded the caliphate as the prerogative of Muhammad's nephew, Ali, and his heirs, and **Sunni** (SOO-nee) (meaning "tradition"), which maintained that the Muslim community could designate any member of Muhammad's tribe to hold the office. The rift has never healed, and although Sunnism became the dominant tradition in the Islamic world, the schisms multiplied and, with them, internal conflicts, rival caliphates, and secessionist states.

Islamic Expansion

570–632	Life of Muhammad
630–early 650s	Muslim conquest of Iraq, Syria, Palestine, Egypt, Persian Empire
ca. 700	Muslim conquest of North Africa
ca. 715	Muslim conquest of Spain
751	Battle of Talas; Arabs victorious against Chinese

For as long as unity prevailed, the limits of Arab expansion show both its explosive nature and its reliance on mobilizing the resources and manpower of conquered or converted communities to make further conquests. When Arab expansion began to run out of impetus, in the second decade of the eighth century, armies owing allegiance to the successors of Muhammad, under Arab generalship, were operating in northern Spain. More or less at the same time, they were destroying Zoroastrian temples beyond the Jaxartes (jahk-SAHR-teez) River in Central Asia and a Buddhist shrine in northern India. At its northeast extremity, the Arab effort even touched the outermost frontier of Chinese imperialism, west of the Pamir Mountains, where, in the first half of the eighth century, local rulers played off the Chinese against the Arabs in their efforts to maximize their own power. In 751, Chinese and Arab armies met in direct conflict for the first and last time, on the banks of the Talas River. The result was total victory for the Arabs and their Turkic allies. After this, China withdrew permanently behind the Pamirs, and most of Central Asia became securely part of the world of Islam.

RECOVERY AND ITS LIMITS IN CHINA

At home, China faced relatively familiar problems, with only internal conflicts to weaken it and only the well-known threat from the steppelands to hold at bay. China's recovery from the crisis of the sixth century started later than Rome's under Justinian but lasted longer. Toward the end of the 570s, a professional soldier, Yang Jian (yahng jhee-en), became arbiter of power in the Yellow River valley—elevated to civil command because of his outstanding record in wars that had reunited the region. In 581, he proclaimed himself emperor, put to death 59 princes of the dynasty he had formerly served, and launched a strategy to re-create the empire by conquering the Yantgze valley (see Map 8.7). It proved remarkably easy—accomplished in about seven years, perhaps because dynastic instability had undermined the loyalty of southern Chinese to their existing rulers. As a Chinese who had proved that he could master barbarians on the battlefield, Yang Jian was an attractive candidate for the throne.

Conscious of his lack of all traditional credentials except success, the new emperor looked to Buddhism to legitimize his rule and to Legalism (see Chapter 6) for practical guidance in government. Law, he said, should "suit the times." In other words, there were no sacred, everlasting, or universal principles. He vowed "to replace mercy with justice"—and demonstrated his commitment by endorsing the condemnation of his own son to death for embezzlement. He affected contempt for Confucian bookworms and controlled the court by violent displays of temper, personally beating underlings who displeased him, sometimes to death. His workaholic and frugal ways—he rationed the palace women's cosmetics—were the characteristics that most impressed observers.

His brutal, strong-arm methods were appropriate to a time of reunification by force. His successor, Yangdi (yahng-dee), who came to the throne in 605, reverted to tradition, announcing the revival of clemency, Confucian learning, and "ancient standards." The great triumph of his reign was the reintegration of the Yellow River and Yantgze valleys by an improved and extensive canal system, the Grand Canal. This was the kind of project that ought to have identified the dynasty with the "ancient virtue" Confucians prized. It was in the tradition of the great engineering emperors of legend, back to Yu the Great (see Chapter 3). Yangdi, however, forfeited this potential goodwill by the forced labor and taxes the canal-building effort demanded. From about the fourth or fifth year of his reign, moreover, he became prey to dreams of expansion. His policy of attempting the conquest of Korea at the same time as his building projects strained the finances of the empire and the loyalty of the elite. He attempted unsuccessfully to buy the alliance of the nomad states on the northern border, but China was compelled to undertake the Korean adventure unaided. The effort was ruinous and unsuccessful—the usual prelude to a political revolution.

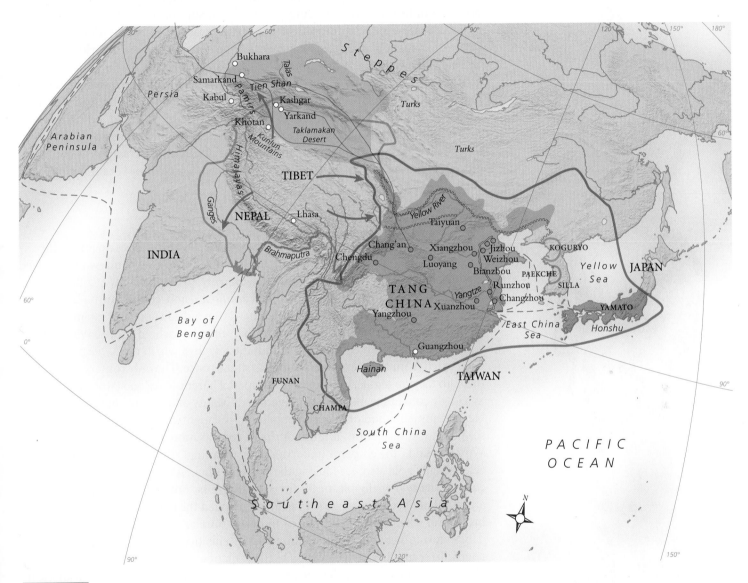

MAP 8.7

Tang China, Tibet, and Japan ca. 750 C.E.

▨ Tang Empire at its greatest extent	∿∿ Great Wall
▨ areas of temporary Tang control	═ Grand Canal
▨ Yamato state	– – maritime trade routes
─ approximate extent of Chinese cultural influence	● city with over 300,000 inhabitants
─ Tibetan Empire ca. 750 C.E.	○ other major city
→ Tibetan invasions	
─ Silk Roads	

Scale varies with perspective

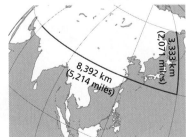

Rise of the Tang

In 617, Yangdi was deposed, but his sons could not agree on which of them should rule. Provincial armies rebelled. The most respected family in the kingdom, the Li, led a rebellion. Loyalty was not an option for the Li. Obsessed by fears of the Li's power and prophesies of their elevation to imperial status, Yangdi had attempted to exterminate their entire family. Li Yuan (lee yoo-ehn), head of the family after the massacre, was well connected in the army after having held many commands. By promises of future favor, he secured neutrality or support from the nomad princes. The reconquest of the country from rival rebels was not complete until about 624, but the exhaustion and disenchantment of the country favored a period of peace. The new dynasty, which called itself Tang (tahng), relied at first on this comfortable mood. The second emperor of the dynasty, Taizong (teye-tzong), took an interventionist, reformist line. He favored the skeptical, scientific tradition, derided omens and magic potions, and held ceremonies when he pleased, not when seers told him to. He rationalized methods of administration, cutting down the numbers of posts and administrative divisions and subdivisions, creating a new, hand-picked bureaucracy for the provinces that he selected by examination, and simplified the law codes.

Empress Wu

Taizong's reforms did much to stabilize the empire. Dynastic crises no longer threatened to dissolve the state. A grueling test occurred in 690, when a woman seized the throne. On the face of it, this was unlikely to happen. Two collections of anecdotes—the *Nüjie* (noo-jay) and *Nüchunyu* (noo-chuhn-yoo)—dominated perceptions of women. They urged women to avoid idleness and promiscuity: A virtuous woman got up early and applied herself to household chores. Women were largely excluded from education—a limitation against which the *Nüjie* protested—and barred from the examinations for the state service. The only route to power was through the dangerous, overpopulated imperial harem. Wu Zhao (woo-jow) started as a lowly concubine, but her combination of beauty and brains impressed Taizong. Her recommendation of torture, brutality, and slaughter as methods of government supposedly amused him. It arose during a conversation about horse training, but, Wu Zhao said, "the emperor understood my meaning." She sought power by a characteristically bold stroke: seducing the emperor's heir. As the former emperor's concubine, she was ineligible to be the next empress, but she maneuvered her way around that obstacle with ease. In 655, she married the heir to the throne, replacing his official wife, whom she tortured to death. Similar methods ensured her ascendancy during her husband's lifetime and as effective regent during the next two reigns. To secure her own elevation to the rank of emperor, she mustered every disaffected faction. The Buddhist clergy were her agents, proclaiming her as an incarnation of God, circulating propaganda on her behalf around the empire. Urged by 60,000 petitioners, she became emperor—literally, because she did not rule as an empress but used the masculine title emperor.

Lady-in-waiting. Though the politics of Tang China could be turbulent, they never disturbed the serenity of the arts of the imperial court. Women were frequently depicted. Many images of women as servants or, as in this example, as imperial ladies-in-waiting, have survived because they were often placed as offerings in tombs. But portraits of female artisans—especially silk-makers—poets, students, equestrians, and matriarchs are also common, showing that, in an era that produced a female emperor, many occupations and roles were open to women.
Dagli Orti/Picture Desk, Inc./Kobal Collection

Tang Decline

These extraordinary and—to most people at the time—unnatural events hardly disturbed the continuity of the Tang and provoked no serious attempts at provincial succession of the kind that had been routine under previous dynasties. Resentment accumulated, however, under the less resolute rule of Wu's successors. In the mid–eighth century, the defenses of the empire were beginning to look shaky as defeats by nomads became increasingly frequent. A frontier general, An Lushan (ahn loo-shawn), was selected as scapegoat. He had therefore little recourse except to rebel. The ensuing civil war confirmed the militarization of society, which, owing to the demands of frontier wars, was already happening anyway. 750,000 men were under arms in the 750s. Governors became virtually autonomous rulers of their provinces. About a quarter to a third of the empire was effectively outside imperial control. In the late 770s, Dugu Ji (doo-goo gee) reported that 90 percent of peasants of Shuzhou (shoo-joh) and Anhui (ahn-hway) lived "without a penny to their name."

The emperors Dezong (duh-tzong) (r. 779–805) and Xianzong (shee-ehn-tzohng) (r. 805–820) tried to restore central power. To "bring the provinces under the rule of law," was now the watchword. "Only then can proper order be restored to the realm." Tax reforms in 782 decreed a single, uniform system throughout the empire. In practice, local authorities were left to fulfill quotas. Both emperors took the initiative against the autonomous provinces and even began to restore control of provincial armed forces to the central government. But they failed to control the most wayward province, Hebei (huh-bay), which was effectively independent by 822. Meanwhile the provinces that remained supposedly subject to direct imperial control gained power at the expense of a central government that the efforts at recovery had impoverished. Governors enjoyed long tenures, levied unauthorized taxes, appointed local nominees to powerful administrative positions, and acquired ever-larger revenues and retinues. Central government recovered some taxpayers. There were two and a half million registered households in 807, five million in 839. This was still little more than half the figure attained before An Lushan's revolt. Imperial power became confined to the Yangtze valley.

Dezong, on the art of government

Recovery and Its Limits in China

581	Yang Jian proclaims himself emperor (Sui dynasty)
605	Yangdi becomes emperor
609	Grand Canal completed
617	Yangdi deposed; rebellion ensues
618	Li Yuan begins reconquest of China from rival rebels; beginning of Tang dynasty
626	Beginning of reign of Taizong, second Tang emperor
690	Wu Zhao (Empress Wu) seizes throne
755–763	Rebellion of An Lushan
822	Province of Hebei effectively independent

IN THE SHADOW OF TANG: TIBET AND JAPAN

In the shadow of Tang China, some promising states emerged. Tibet and Japan provide contrasting examples (see Map 8.7).

Tibet

At the time of the presumed beginnings of the first Tibetan state in the sixth century, the Chinese spoke of Tibetans in the conventional language used for barbarians, as pastoralists who "sleep in unclean places and never wash or comb their hair. They do not know the seasons. They have no writing and keep records only by means of knotted cords or knotched tally sticks." In the river valleys of Tibet, however, sedentary agriculture was possible. A little-understood agricultural transformation in the fifth century brought barley to these areas as a staple crop. Once a cereal food was available in large amounts, the advantages of a cold climate for storage helped to create large food surpluses. A land from which small numbers of nomads eked a precarious living now became a breeding ground of armies that could march on far campaigns with "ten thousand" sheep and horses in their supply trains.

Chinese descriptions of Tibetans

Before the seventh century, divine monarchs ruled Tibet, "descended," according to early poems, "from mid-sky, seven stories high," and aspiring to rule "all under heaven." Like other divine kings, they were liable to be sacrificed when their usefulness expired. They were given no tombs, for it was believed that they ascended back into heaven. At an unknown date in the sixth century, kings who ruled until they died a natural death replaced this system. Long reigns, with stability and continuity, were now possible. The first king known from more than fragmentary mentions was Songtsen Gampo. His reign, from about 627 to 650, marked an unprecedented leap in Tibetan power. China bought him off with a Chinese bride in 640. Preserved among a cache of documents in a cave on the Silk Road is the oath of allegiance he exacted: "Never will we disobey any command the king may give." In practice, however, in most of the communities he conquered, he simply levied tribute, rather than practicing direct rule or close supervision.

Tibetan aggression continued for most of the next 250 years. Tibetan armies conquered Nepal, and invaded Turkestan (TOOR-keh-stahn) in Central Asia. A pillar at Lhasa, the Tibetan capital, erected before 750, records campaigns deep inside China. On the western front, Tibetans collaborated with Arab forces in the conquest of Ferghana, in 715. In 821 a Chinese ambassador described the Tibetan war camp, where shamans in tiger skins banged drums before a tent "hung with gold ornaments in the form of dragons, tigers and leopards." Inside, in a turban "the color of morning clouds," the king watched as chiefs signed the treaty with China in blood.

The kings' tastes were increasingly cosmopolitan. Ten of them, including Songtsen Gampo, lie under small mounds at Phyongrgyas, where "dead companions" attended them—now no longer sacrificed but appointed to guard and tend the graves without direct contact with the outside world. Pillars in Indian, Central Asian, and Chinese styles, and a guardian lion modeled on a Persian original attest to the role of Tibet as a cultural crossroads. Their metal smiths' ingenuity was

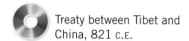
Treaty between Tibet and China, 821 C.E.

The Potala Palace, towering above the valley of Lhasa, stands on the supposed site of the palace of the kings of Tibet in the seventh and eighth centuries. The present construction, however, began to rise in the mid–seventeenth century. The building is designed to suggest mystical power—cloud-shrouded, hard of ascent, overwhelming.

famous. Mechanical toys of gold dispatched as gifts to the Chinese court included a horse with moving limbs and a tiger with roaring jaws. Tibetan chain mail had an almost magical reputation for deflecting missiles. Yet even this could not protect the Tibetans from the effects of the instability of the era of Tang decline, which must have disrupted trade, while the power of the steppelanders limited Tibetan opportunities to raid or expand. In the early ninth century, Tibet suffered a dreary sequence of defeats on all fronts. Rebellions ensued. Tibet signed its last treaty as an equal with China in 823. Its last known king was assassinated in 842.

The Rise and Decline of Tibet	
Fifth century	Barley introduced as a staple crop
627–650	Reign of Songtsen Gampo
715	Tibetan and Arab conquest of Ferghana
Early ninth century	Beginning of Tibetan decline

Japan

Better prospects of enduring experiments in statecraft existed on the remoter edges of Chinese cultural influence, in Japan, where the steppeland menace could not reach. Chinese culture began to arrive in Japan from Korea when the Buddhist monk Wani became tutor at a Japanese court in about 400. The Korean kingdom of Paekche sent scholars and Buddhist scriptures. The leading state in Japan, Yamato, was a maritime kingdom, attracted by Korean and Chinese civilization, and at least as interested in expanding onto the mainland of Asia as in growing within the Japanese islands. Around 475, Yuryaku, king of Yamato, applied to China for the rank of general and minister when he was preparing an expedition against the Korean kingdom of Koguryo. He claimed his ancestors had conquered "55 kingdoms of hairy men to the east and 65 barbarian kingdoms to the west." Crossing the sea to the north, he added, they had subjugated 95 kingdoms. "The way to govern is to maintain harmony and peace, thereby establishing order." Communications with China were still via Paekche. The advice of counselors from Korea reflects the restraining influence of Buddhist and Confucian precepts on the warlike culture of Yamato. The ruler, one of the Korean advisers suggested, should "try to make farmers prosperous. . . . After he has followed this policy for three years, food and soldiers will become plentiful." From the mid–sixth century, Japan was following this sort of program, organizing royal estates, taking censuses.

Early in the seventh century, direct contact with China opened. The first Japanese embassy to China presented greetings "from the Son of Heaven in the land where the sun rises to the Son of Heaven in the land where the sun sets." The Chinese dismissed this as impertinence. Their accounts make the queen who ruled Japan at the time say, "As barbarians living in an isolated place beyond the sea, we do not know propriety and justice." It is not clear that the Japanese really saw themselves like that. They staked a claim to equality with China—and imperial rank—that subsequent Japanese regimes never entirely abandoned.

In the 640s, the dynasty narrowly beat off a bid for the throne from a Chinese immigrant family. Reform of the administration then began in earnest. The drive to centralize by breaking up and replacing traditional power structures is reflected in a decree of 645 that blamed clan chieftains for dividing up the land, engaging in conflict, unjustly exploiting labor, and impoverishing peasants "who lack enough land to insert a needle." Landlords were forbidden "to increase, by one iota, the miseries of the weak." Indirectly, China's invasion of Korea in the 660s boosted imperial rule in Japan. One hundred Korean refugees were appointed to court rank. After victory in a civil war of 672, the ruling dynasty of Japan was unchallenged. Japan solved the problem that bedeviled the politics of other empires— devising a secure means to ensure the succession—by two means. First, women's aptitude to rule was accepted. This increased the dynasty's stock of suitable

◉ MAKING CONNECTIONS

DEVELOPING FRONTIER STATES

STATE/REGION/ PERIOD →	IMPERIAL NEIGHBOR →	RESOURCES/ ORGANIZATION →	ACHIEVEMENTS
Koguryo, Silla, Paekche/Korea ca. 300–500	China	Chinese religious influence—Buddhism and Daoism; Chinese migrants and technical knowledge	Complex irrigation system for rice cultivation; hundreds of walled towns; strong military
Funan/Indochina ca. 100–400	India, China	Indian cultural influences; commercial traders strategically located between India and China	Sophisticated culture; wealthy mercantile class; expansion around Gulf of Thailand
Ethiopia/Africa ca. 300–500	Rome, Byzantine Egypt	Accessible to Indian Ocean trade routes, isolated enough to be defensible; temperate climate; trade center connecting Africa to India, Arabia, and Mediterranean ports	Productive agriculture system—up to three crops a year; developed industry (metalwork, ivory) and large-scale urbanization
Tibet/Central Asia ca. 500–800	China, India	Development of barley as primary cereal crop for vast high-altitude plateau; food surpluses and strong military	Long-term alliance/tributary, relationship with China; stable leadership; conquest of neighboring kingdoms
Japan/East Asia ca. 400–600	China, Korea	Chinese/Korean cultural influences; strategic position for maritime trade; isolated and defensible; organization of royal estates; censuses	Long-term tributary relationship with China; gradually centralized power structure to maximize productivity; stable power structure with some women emperors

candidates for the throne. Indeed, until the 770s, when a disastrous empress inspired lasting revulsion against women rulers, most rulers were women. Second, from 749, it became normal for rulers to abdicate and watch over the transmission of power to their heirs. The system worked well until the mid–ninth century, when a single courtly family, the Fujiwara, established an effective monopoly over supply of the chief wives for successive emperors. Thereafter, in the Japanese system of government, the emperor presided over the realm, but a dynasty of court favorites or chief ministers usually did the ruler's job. The last big political development—the search for a means to harness Buddhism for state service while preserving Japan's native religion—belongs in the next chapter.

IN PERSPECTIVE: The Triumph of Barbarism?

Had Siyaj K'ak been able to continue his journey from Teotihuacán and cross the ocean to Eurasia, he might have been gratified by the contrast between the stability and growth of the empire he represented and the perils that beset the empires of the Old World. In the year of his arrival, the Visigoths challenged Roman might at Adrianople. The crises that accompanied the traumas of the Eurasian steppelands and the migrations of Germanic and steppelander peoples into neighboring empires were already beginning. One measure of the instability that ensued is particularly striking. In much of Europe and India, the fifth and sixth centuries were so chaotic that record keeping collapsed, and we can no longer reconstruct a complete outline even of the most basic facts of political history—the names and chronology of kings and dynasties. By contrast, in the same period, for the Maya world Siyaj K'ak visited, we know far more about the rulers of many city-states, whose records are inscribed in stone in meticulous detail.

Yet, despite the waves of migrants and invaders that washed over Old World empires in the half millennium or so from about 200 onward and the crises they provoked, the most remarkable feature of the period is perhaps the durability of old orders. Cultural conflicts usually follow battlefield victories. And even where the so-called barbarians defeated the empires, they tended to get conquered in their turn by the cultures of their victims. The German invaders of the Roman world were partly Romanized, while the eastern Roman empire survived, centered on Constantinople. Steppeland conquerors played havoc with the political unity of India—but the cultural transformations of India happened from within. "Barbarians" disrupted China politically but did not disturb the continuity of Chinese civilization. On the contrary, when barbarians settled within China, they adjusted to Chinese ways. Indeed, Chinese civilization overspilled China into new areas, such as Korea, Japan, southeast Asia, and Tibet. The instability of the steppes damaged the land-bound trade of Eurasia, but the commerce of the Indian Ocean continued to grow, and the development of Ethiopia was among the consequences.

Still, despite continuities that survived the barbarians, the world that emerged in the last three centuries of the first millennium C.E. was genuinely, deeply transformed. Rather than the world of empires that had dominated the densely populated belt of the axial age, it might be proper to speak of a world of civilizations. Western civilization was a hybrid—partly Germanic, partly Christian, partly Roman in heritage. The Islamic world was far more innovative, but it had, in some respects, a similar profile: with a biblical heritage, reinterpreted by Muhammad, and the learned legacies of Rome, Greece, and Persia, under an Arab elite from outside the empires, established by conquest but susceptible to the cultural influence of its victims. In both the Islamic world and Christendom, notions of universal empire survived: the caliphate, Byzantium. But neither could maintain unity in practice, and the respective regions became arenas of states contending for the imperial legacy or ignoring it. In India, political fragmentation under the impact of barbarian invasion was more thoroughgoing, in China less so. In both, however, the invaders and immigrants were like chameleons, taking on the cultural hues of their new environments. In both, moreover, the traditional culture spread into new areas and new states, such as those of south India, and China's neighbors. So nowhere, by the eighth century, except in Ethiopia, was there any longer a civilization that was confined to a single state.

Even at the end of a chapter crowded with politics, we still have not reached the deepest transformative influences on the period. One of the traditional limitations of history textbooks is that politics, which generates

CHRONOLOGY

(All dates are C.E.)

220	End of Han dynasty in China
323	Founding of Constantinople
340	Spread of Christianity in Ethiopia
Third and fourth centuries	Germanic invasions of Roman Empire; Huns break out of Central Asia
ca. 375	Teotihuacán (Mesoamerica) at peak of its influence and power
Fifth century	Introduction of barley as a staple crop in Tibet
400	Beginning of Chinese influence in Japan
410	Visigoths sack Rome
415	Huns begin to infiltrate India
467	Death of last-known Gupta emperor (India)
476	End of west Roman Empire
493–526	Reign of Theodoric, Ostrogothic king
527–565	Reign of Justinian, Byzantine emperor
ca. 535	Massive volcanic eruption in present-day Indonesia
570–632	Life of Muhammed
Seventh century	Beginning of Slav expansion in eastern Europe
609	Grand Canal completed in China
627–650	Reign of Songtsen Gampo in Tibet
630–720	Rapid Arab expansion
667–668	Chinese conquest of Koguryo (Korea)
690	Beginning of reign of Empress Wu (China)
751	Arabs defeat Chinese at battle of Talas

most of the sources, tends to dominate the foreground. But politics is full of short-term changes, while ideas and environmental influences generate the sea changes. The next two chapters explore the religious changes that made this world of civilizations distinct, in particular, from the empires that preceded them, and the discovery and development of resources that not only renewed the Old World, but also opened up new frontiers in other parts of the globe.

PROBLEMS AND PARALLELS

1. How were imperial traditions inherited from the axial age extinguished or fragmented by the year 500?

2. How does the history of Teotihuacán echo Eurasian developments in this period?

3. What were the differences between the ways that China and Rome dealt with steppeland migrants and invaders? Why was China more successful?

4. How did the Byzantine Empire and the barbarian kingdoms in Western Europe continue the traditions of Rome?

5. To what extent was Ethiopia able to achieve a balance between accessibility and isolation?

6. How did states develop on the edges of empires during this period?

7. Why were the Arabs able to conquer a vast empire in so short a time?

8. How was the world that recovered from the crises of the third through seventh centuries a world of civilizations?

DOCUMENTS IN GLOBAL HISTORY

- Excerpts from the *Hildebrandslied*
- Jordanes, *Deeds of the Goths,* Book Twenty-Six
- Pliny the Elder, from the *Natural History*
- Faxian, Record of Buddhist Countries, Chapter Sixteen

- Pre-Islamic Arabic poetry: "The Poem of Antar"
- Excerpts from the Quran
- Dezong, on the art of government
- Treaty between Tibet and China, 821 C.E.

Please see the Primary Source CD-ROM for additional sources related to this chapter.

READ ON

Helpful information on relations between Teotihuacán and the Maya is in D. Drew, *The Lost Chronicles of the Maya Kings* (1999); R. Hassig, *War and Society in Ancient Mesoamerica* (1992); and S. Martin and N. Grube, *Chronicle of the Maya Kings and Queens* (2000), which is also a lavish compendium of facts and images. G. Braswell, *The Maya and Teotihuacán* (2003) is an important revisionist study that challenges the account of Siyaj K'ak above.

On the transformation of the Roman world, Peter Brown, *The World of Late Antiquity* (1989) is the ideal introduction—sprightly and subtle. A. H. M. Jones, *The Later Roman Empire* (1964) is a classic study of undiminished interest. J. Herrin, *The Formation of Christendom* (1987) is assured, fluent, and in touch with the sources. A. Cameron et al., eds., *The Cambridge Ancient History*, xiv (2000) is forbiddingly comprehensive and magisterial. R. Collins, *Early Medieval Europe* (1991) is a vigorous, thoughtful textbook. The classic works by F. Lot, *The End of the Ancient World and the Beginning of the Middle Ages* (2000), and by H. Pirenne, cited below, can still be recommended in combination with more recent scholarship.

There are many editions of the *Meditations of Marcus Aurelius*. On Constantine, R. Macmullen, *Constantine* (1987) is standard. Sources on his conversion are collected in M. Edwards, trans., *Constantine and Christendom* (2003). D. Bowder, *The Age of Constantine and Julian* (1978) is valuable in setting the context. M. Grant, *The Emperor Constantine* (1993) is lively and readable. R. Macmullen, *Christianity and Paganism in the Fourth to Eighth Centuries* (1997) is a valuable introduction. A. Momigliano, *The Conflict of Paganism and Christianity in the Fourth Century* (1964) is a collection of classic studies. R. Lane Fox, *Pagans and Christians* (1987), and K. Hopkins, *A World Full of Gods* (1999) are also helpful. On the transformation of the city of Rome, B. R. Ward-Perkins, *From Classical Antiquity to the Middle Ages* (1985) sets the context of urban change in Italy, while P. Llewellyn, *Rome in the Dark Ages* (1993) is a graphic account of the reemergence of Rome as the pope's capital.

W. Goffart, *Barbarians and Romans* (1980) is an introductory overview. E. A. Thompson, *A History of Attila and the Huns* (1972) is a classic study, still vital. There are many editions of the *Hildebrandslied*, but I know of no substantial critical studies in English except F. Norman, *Three Essays on the Hildebrandslied* (1973). The most useful study of the Christianity of Germanic invaders of the Roman Empire is E. A. Thompson, *The Visigoths in the Time of Ulfila* (1966). J. M. Wallace-Hadrill, *The Barbarian West* (1952) is the best-possible introduction to the Germanic kingdoms; his *The Long-Haired Kings* (1962) is an absorbing collection of essays on the same subject, which should be read in conjunction with I. N. Wood, *The Merovingian Kingdoms* (1994). *The Consolation of Philosophy* is widely available in many editions. For Boethius's life and thought, J. Marenbon, *Boethius* (2003) is excellent, and H. Chadwick, *Boethius* (1981) is both authoritative and concise. S. Williams and G. Friell, *The Rome That Did Not Fall* (1999) is a helpful essay on the survival of the empire in the east. See now the revisionist, archaeologically informed survey of B. R. Ward-Perkins, *The Fall of Rome and the End of Civilization* (2005).

The steppes are covered in R. Grousset, *The Empire of the Steppes* (1970). Volume iii of *The Cambridge History of China* (1978) covers this period admirably. S. A. M. Adshead, *Tang China* (2004) provides an introduction to that dynasty. C. P. Fitzgerald, *The Empress Wu* (1955) is a captivating classic biography. R. K. Dwivdki and D. L. Vaish, *A History of the Guptas* (1985), and S. Goyal, *History and Historiography of the Age of Harsha* (1992) provide a political and cultural outline of India. W. E. Henthorn, *A History of Korea* (1971) is particularly good on this period.

On Axum, see the works of Munro-Hay and Phillison mentioned in Chapter 9.

On Justinian, *The Secret History of Procopius* (1927) is an irresistibly engaging, albeit cruelly prejudiced, source. Balanced modern studies include J. A. S. Evans, *The Age of Justinian* (1996), and R. Browning, *Justinian and Theodora* (1971). G. Greatrex, *Rome and Persia at War* (1998) admirably covers the Persian wars of this period.

For an understanding of Byzantium in this period, A. Cameron, *Changing Cultures in Early Byzantium* (1996) is an authoritative, clear, and insightful collection. M. Grant, *From Rome to Byzantium* (1998) is a readable narrative. M. Whittow, *The Making of Orthodox Byzantium* (1996) is invaluable on the development of a distinctive religious culture. A. Cameron and J. Herrin, *Constantinople in the Early Eighth Century* (1984) is helpful. M. Angold, *Byzantium* (2001) is a good overview. W. E. Kaegi, *Byzantine Military Unrest* (1981) takes an interesting approach. On eunuchs see K. Ringrose, *The Perfect Servant: Eunuchs and the Social Construction of Gender in Byzantium* (2003). On the Bulgars, O. Minaeva, *From Paganism to Christianity* (1996) wields fascinating artistic evidence. On Lombard Italy and its context, C. Wickham, *The Long Eighth Century* (2000) and *Early Medieval Italy* (1990) are excellent.

A. Hourani, *History of the Arab People* (2003) is probably the best overall survey of Arab history. M. A. Cook, *Muhammad* (1983) is a brief and brilliant introduction. Some of the same author's important essays are collected in *Studies in the Origins of Early Islamic Culture and Tradition* (2004). M. Cook and P. Crone, *Hagarism: The Making of the Islamic World* (1977) is a ground-breaking study. M. Hodgson, *The Venture of Islam*, 3 vols., (1974) is a marvelous classic. G. R. Hawting, *The First Dynasty of Islam* (2000) is an efficient narrative of the early caliphate. On the impact of the Arab conquests, all students should read—critically, of course, the classic by H. Pirenne, *Mohammed and Charlemagne* (1939).

CHAPTER 9

The Rise of World Religions: Christianity, Islam, and Buddhism

Priests, officials, and bystanders (shown prostrating themselves, on the right) greet the pilgrim Xuanzang on his return to China from India, where he had traveled to find Buddhist scriptures. Pack horses bear the 75 sacred texts he had acquired to a temple on the left. Monks at the rear carry holy relics.

n 872, Ibn Wahab (ihb-ihn wah-HAHB), a Muslim traveler from Basra in Iraq, arrived in China at the Tang court. The emperor called for a box of scrolls, which he ordered to be put before the visitor, saying, "Let him see his master."

Ibn Wahab recognized the portraits of biblical prophets and patriarchs.

"I said," his account continues, "Here is Noah with his ark, which saved him when the world was drowned . . ."
At these words, the emperor laughed and said, "You have identified Noah, but, as for the ark, we do not believe it. It did not reach China or India."
"That is Moses with his staff," I said.
"Yes," said the emperor, "but he was unimportant and his people were few."
"There," I said, "is Jesus, surrounded by his apostles."
"Yes," said the emperor. "He lived only a short time. His mission lasted only thirty months."

Then I saw the Prophet on a camel . . . and I was moved to tears. "Why do you weep?" asked the emperor. . . . "He and his people founded a glorious empire. He did not live to see it completed, but his successors have." Above each picture was an inscription which I supposed to contain an account of their history. I saw also other pictures, which I did not recognize. The interpreter told me that they were the prophets of China and India.

It would be rash to believe every word of this story. The remarks Ibn Wahab puts into the emperor's mouth seem calculated to show Islam in the best light, at the expense of Judaism and Christianity. Nevertheless, the anecdote does illustrate three important themes of the time. First, the effectiveness of communications across Eurasia is clear from Ibn Wahab's presence in China, and the extent of Chinese knowledge of Islam and the West. Second, the superiority of Chinese knowledge appears from the fact that the emperor knew a lot about the three Abrahamic faiths (Judaism, Christianity, and Islam claimed, each in its own way, to be based on the covenant between God and the biblical patriarch Abraham), while his visitor knew nothing about the Buddhist sages displayed in the same box of scrolls.

FOCUS questions

- WHY DID Buddhism, Christianity, and Islam become world religions?
- HOW DID commerce help spread religion in parts of Eurasia and Africa?
- WHY DID missionaries seek to convert rulers and elites?
- HOW DID Christian and Muslim rulers deal with religious minorities?
- WHY WAS monasticism more important for Christianity and Buddhism than for Islam?
- WHAT ROLE did women play in the consolidation and spread of world religions?
- HOW DID world religions accommodate themselves to local cultures?

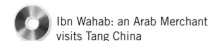

Ibn Wahab: an Arab Merchant visits Tang China

Finally, the story raises the subject of this chapter: the beginnings of the ascent of Christianity, Islam, and Buddhism to be *world religions*, with followings in all sorts of physical and cultural environments. Most religions tend to be culturally specific—they only appeal to peoples with certain cultural profiles. Usually, they do not spread beyond their cultures of origin. Christianity, Islam, and Buddhism were unusual in aspiring to be universal, and in becoming global.

● ● ● ● ●

Historians often claim to be interested in the past for its own sake. If we also want to understand our own world, and trace the emergence of its key features, we have to confront the problem of why Christianity, Islam, and Buddhism began to acquire the global acceptance they have today. So in this chapter, we have to stay in Eurasia and Africa—in the parts where these three religions had penetrated by Ibn Wahab's time—and catch up in the next chapter with changes occurring in the meantime in other parts of the world.

There has never really been an "age of faith." Of course, there are plenty of sincere individual conversions, spiritually inspired or intellectually induced. Most people, however, in most periods, experience religion only superficially. If they do undergo real conversion or spiritual rebirth, it happens sporadically and rarely lasts long. Nor should we judge the spread of religion by the extent of people's intellectual grasp of it. If you ask most Christians or Muslims or Buddhists about the doctrines of their faiths, they will usually give you, at best, a shallow account. Their religion will probably not affect their ethical behavior much as they live out their daily lives. Instead of understanding religion as belief, or spiritual experience, or doctrine, or ethics, we should treat it, for our present purposes, as cultural practice, and say that a religion has "spread" where and when people in large numbers take part in its rites and identify with their fellow worshippers as members of a community. Four processes made possible the spread of religions in this sense during the period of takeoff for Islam, Buddhism, and Christianity: war, trade, missionary activity, and elite—especially royal—sponsorship (see Map 9.1).

COMMERCE AND CONFLICT: CARRIERS OF CREEDS

Forcible conversion is—strictly speaking—no conversion at all. "There is no compulsion in religion," says the Quran. Though Christians have sometimes done it, the law of the Catholic Church forbids using force to spread faith. Buddhism, too, has no place for coercion. But it sometimes works.

In the Islamic World

The Arabic word **jihad** (jee-HAHD) literally means *striving*. Muhammad used the word in two contexts: first, to mean the inner struggle against evil that Muslims must wage for themselves; second, to denote real war, fought against the enemies of Islam. These have to be genuine enemies, who "fight against you to the death."

MAP 9.1

The Rise of World Religions to 1000 C.E.

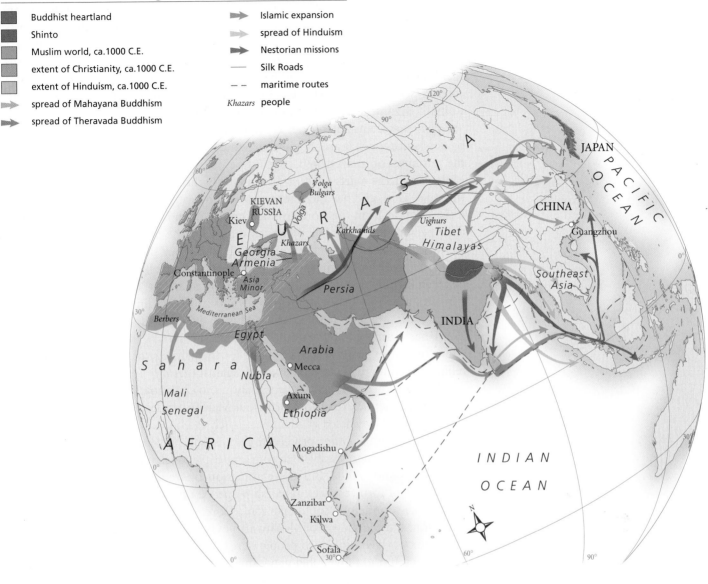

- Buddhist heartland
- Shinto
- Muslim world, ca.1000 C.E.
- extent of Christianity, ca.1000 C.E.
- extent of Hinduism, ca.1000 C.E.
- → spread of Mahayana Buddhism
- → spread of Theravada Buddhism

- ⇒ Islamic expansion
- ⇒ spread of Hinduism
- ⇒ Nestorian missions
- — Silk Roads
- -- maritime routes
- *Khazars* people

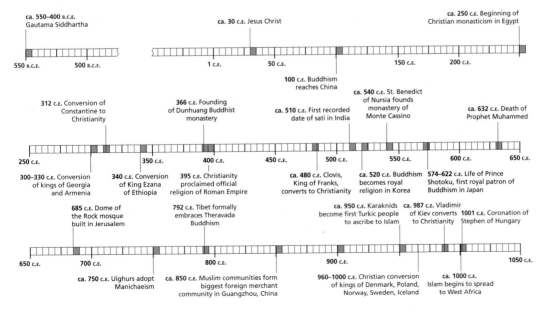

ca. 550–400 B.C.E. Gautama Siddhartha

ca. 30 C.E. Jesus Christ

ca. 250 C.E. Beginning of Christian monasticism in Egypt

550 B.C.E.   500 B.C.E.

1 C.E.   50 C.E.   150 C.E.   200 C.E.

312 C.E. Conversion of Constantine to Christianity

366 C.E. Founding of Dunhuang Buddhist monastery

100 C.E. Buddhism reaches China

ca. 540 C.E. St. Benedict of Nursia founds monastery of Monte Cassino

ca. 510 C.E. First recorded date of sati in India

ca. 632 C.E. Death of Prophet Muhammed

250 C.E.   350 C.E.   400 C.E.   450 C.E.   500 C.E.   550 C.E.   600 C.E.   650 C.E.

300–330 C.E. Conversion of kings of Georgia and Armenia

340 C.E. Conversion of King Ezana of Ethiopia

395 C.E. Christianity proclaimed official religion of Roman Empire

ca. 480 C.E. Clovis, King of Franks, converts to Christianity

ca. 520 C.E. Buddhism becomes royal religion in Korea

574–622 C.E. Life of Prince Shotoku, first royal patron of Buddhism in Japan

685 C.E. Dome of the Rock mosque built in Jerusalem

792 C.E. Tibet formally embraces Theravada Buddhism

ca. 950 C.E. Karaknids become first Turkic people to ascribe to Islam

ca. 987 C.E. Vladimir of Kiev converts to Christianity

1001 C.E. Coronation of Stephen of Hungary

650 C.E.   700 C.E.   800 C.E.   900 C.E.   1050 C.E.

ca. 750 C.E. Uighurs adopt Manichaeism

ca. 850 C.E. Muslim communities form biggest foreign merchant community in Guangzhou, China

960–1000 C.E. Christian conversion of kings of Denmark, Poland, Norway, Sweden, Iceland

ca. 1000 C.E. Islam begins to spread to West Africa

Scale varies with perspective
13,340 km (8290 miles)
20,040 km (12,450 miles)

But in Muhammad's day the community he led was almost constantly at war, and Chapter Nine of the Quran seems to legitimate war against all "polytheists" and "idolaters." After the Prophet's death, his successors turned the doctrine of jihad against the "apostates" who abandoned Islam because they considered that their obligations to Muhammad had ended when he died. It was then used to proclaim a series of successful wars of aggression against Arabian states and the Roman (Byzantine) and Persian (Sasanid) empires.

Holy war seems an appropriate translation for "jihad": an enterprise sanctified by obedience to what are thought to be the Prophet's commands and rewarded by the promise of martyrdom. According to a saying traditionally ascribed to Muhammad, the martyr goes straight to the highest rank of paradise, nearest to the throne of God, and has the right to intercede for the souls of his own loved ones. This is not far from the words of the Quran: "Allah has purchased of the believers their persons and their belongings in return for the promise that they shall have Paradise, for they fight in the cause of Allah and they slay the enemy or are slain." This is no more bloodthirsty than many passages in the Bible and needs no more to be taken literally than Paul's injunction to Christians to "fight the good fight." But it makes a handy justification for war and implies a link between war and the spread of Islam. The tenth-century Muslim jurist, al-Kayrawani (ahl keye-rah-WAH-nee), summed up the tradition as it had evolved by that time. Enemies could either submit to Islam or pay a poll tax for the privilege of persisting in their own religion. "Failing that, we will make war against them."

That was theory. Practice was not always so clear-cut. But in the first couple of centuries of Islamic expansion, victorious Muslim armies did normally aim to wipe out religions they classed as idolatrous, such as Hinduism, and to tax Christians, Jews, and, at times, other privileged groups, such as Zoroastrians in Persia. The result would not necessarily be to convert people to Islam, in the sense of changing their hearts and minds. But the elimination of traditional priesthoods and the destruction of former places of worship opened up spaces in which Islam, the religion of the conquerors, could take root. Moreover, God seemed to endorse Islam. The astonishing conquests of Muslim armies in the seventh and eighth centuries set up a framework within which people were both exposed to Islam and impressed by its victories. If traditional religion became a badge of resistance to conquest, it withered when that resistance failed. Among the pagan Berbers of northwest Africa, for instance, Muslim writers complained of the rejection of Islam during the seventh century. But when the last great Berber revolt against the Arabs failed in 703, the woman who had led it sent her sons to receive instruction in Islam.

In Christendom

So, slowly, faith followed the flag of conquest. Within the narrower limits of their lesser success, Christian conquerors also abused religion to justify war and imposed new forms of worship along with the terms of peace. In the eighth century, the Frankish king Charlemagne gave the pagan Saxons in eastern Germany a choice of baptism or death. In the ninth, Alfred the Great of England imposed baptism on defeated pagans as a condition of peace. Olaf, king of Norway in the early eleventh century, massacred, mutilated, or blinded pagans who refused Christianity. It seemed consistent with the nature of the Lord of Hosts, as the Bible frequently referred to God, to spread Christianity by war. Yet in all these cases, and others like them, however violent and arbitrary the beginnings of Christianity, the affected communities joined Christian civilization and built springboards for further missions elsewhere.

THE CATHEDRAL DOORS OF GNIEZNO

The bronze doors of the cathedral in Gniezno in Poland are both a masterpiece of the eleventh century and a document of the way political alliances spread Christianity. Boleslaus I (r. 992–1025)—the first ruler of Poland to call himself "king"—grew up at the court of the Emperor Otto III, who presented him with a relic incomparably sacred to a soldier—the lance that was supposed to have pierced Christ's side at his Crucifixion. Of almost equal importance were the relics of St. Adalbert–a Slav martyr whose body Boleslaus bought from pagans in Prussia. The doors of this cathedral tell a politicized, propaganda version of Adalbert's story.

Adalbert converts the royal house of Hungary.

Adalbert retires from the mission field in fear, but an angelic vision (in reality, orders from the pope) sends him back.

Adalbert's body is brought to Poland.

The Prussians put Adalbert to death in 997 when he tries to chop down their sacred trees.

Boleslaus presides over the baptism of pagans.

How do these cathedral doors document the relationship between missionary work and politics in spreading religion?

Dunhuang. The Silk Roads spread Buddhism as well as trade. Here—in a tenth-century example of the thousands of devotional paintings merchants endowed at the monastery of Dunhuang in Central Asia—a convert and his family pray at the feet of a Bodhisattva. Many Chinese converts to Buddhism retained the family values characteristic of Confucianism.

In the Buddhist World

Less well known is that much of the early spread of Buddhism relied on similar strategies by royal strongmen. As in Christendom, Buddhist rulers practiced remarkable intellectual contortions to justify the imposition by violence of a doctrine of peace and love. Asoka (see Chapter 7) was not alone in priding himself on conquests allegedly achieved "by **dharma**"—the teachings of Buddha. Asoka's near contemporary, Kaniska, King of Peshawar in what is today Pakistan, enforced Buddhism on his own subjects, as did King Vattagamani, whose efforts we know from inscriptions in Sri Lanka, early in the first century B.C.E. In the mid–eleventh century C.E., when King Anuruddha (ah-noo-ROOD-dah) introduced Buddhism to Burma (present-day Myanmar), he showed his piety by waging war on the neighboring Mon kingdom to gain possession of holy scriptures.

Trade

Still, even if we accept that war can spread religions, we still need wider, deeper explanations for the rise of the potential world religions of our period. After the time of Asoka, Buddhism never became the ideology of a widely successful conqueror until the sixteenth century; nor did Christianity, until European empires began to spread it around the world. Meanwhile, though enlarged by conquest on and around the edges of Christendom, Christianity had, by comparison with Islam, relatively unsuccessful champions. To achieve wide-ranging conversions, it had, like Buddhism, to spread with individual journeys beyond political frontiers. Even Islam, as a religion, spread beyond the boundaries of Muslim political expansion.

Trade was probably at least as important as war for spreading religion. The temples of Dunhuang are full of images of the role of the Silk Roads in spreading Buddhism. Merchants who rested at the monastery there on their way along the road endowed thousands of paintings that still line chambers carved from the rock. According to tradition, a Chinese monk began to hollow the caves out of the cliff face in 366, when, "traveling the wilds with his pilgrim's staff, he arrived at this mountain and had a vision of a golden radiance in the form of a thousand Buddhas." Many of the paintings portray individual merchants in acts of worship, often with their families, and sometimes in the company of their ancestors. In one image, brigands, converted by a Buddhist merchant they have captured, join him in prayer. In others, merchants ransom themselves from bandits by acts of piety. In others, famous Buddhas and sages travel roads familiar to the merchants. These works of art are metaphors of spiritual redemption that people like merchants whose business requires constant travel, with its deadly dangers and distant rewards, could easily interpret. Networks of monasteries accommodated these merchants as well as pilgrims who traveled the roads from China to visit Buddhist shrines in India and acquire sacred texts and teachings.

Manichaeanism and the Uighurs

Buddhism met rival religions along the Silk Roads. The Uighurs (OOEE-goors) were a pastoral, Turkic-speaking people who dominated the steppeland north of the roads for a hundred years from the 740s. On service as mercenaries during the

Chinese civil wars of the mid–eighth century, they picked up **Manichaeanism** (mah-nih-KEE-ahn-ih-sihm), a religion of obscure origin, probably rooted in a heretical form of Zoroastrianism (see Chapter 6). Mani (MAH-nee), its supposed founder in Persia in the third century, divided the universe into realms of spirit—which was good—and matter, which was evil. This kind of dualism, with its stark moral teaching and suspicion of sex, was an ancient and influential idea. But although Mani relentlessly sought to spread his religion, it had never previously captured the allegiance of a state. On the contrary, Zoroastrians, Christians, Muslims, and even (on at least one occasion, in China, in 732) Buddhists persecuted it. Now, however, the Uighur ruler proclaimed himself the "emanation of Mani," and Manichaean zealots became his counselors, rather as Buddhist and Christian rulers chose clergy as advisers and bureaucrats. Indeed, a Uighur bureaucracy developed, using its own language and script. According to a ninth-century inscription, Manichaeanism transformed "a barbarous country, full of the fumes of blood into a land where the people live on vegetables, from a land of killing to a land where good deeds are fostered." Uighur monarchs endowed temples in China and sponsored the collecting of Manichaean scriptures. However, Buddhism and, to a lesser extent, Christianity ultimately replaced Manichaeanism among the Uighurs, and the creed of Mani never caught on to the same extent anywhere else.

Christianity on the Silk Roads

By comparison with Buddhism and even Manichaeanism, Christianity was only moderately successful along the Silk Roads. Relatively few Christians, especially from Western Europe, engaged in long-range trade. Among Christian peoples who did have strong vocations for commerce, the Armenians kept to themselves and avoided trying to convert others so as not to invite persecution by non-Christian rulers. **Nestorians**—Christians in a tradition of fifth-century origin named after Nestorius, Bishop of Constantinople, who regarded the human Jesus as merely human, quite distinct from the divine Jesus—had a network of monasteries and communities that reached China and spread the faith among adherents who came to number millions. But the Nestorians remained a thin and patchy presence across a vast area.

Islam on Trade Routes

If Buddhism dominated much of the Silk Roads, Islam spread almost equally effectively by trade along the sea routes of maritime Asia and across the Sahara. As Muslim merchant communities dispersed, they founded their own mosques, elected or imported their own preachers, and sometimes attracted local people to join them. Muhammad's commands for peaceful conversion were at least as strong as those for jihad. "Call unto the way of thy Lord with wisdom and fair exhortation," the Quran commands. "Say to those who have received the Book and to those who are ignorant, 'Do you accept Islam?' Then . . . if they turn away, it is thy duty to convey the message." In the ninth century, the major Chinese ports acquired mosques. According to a contemporary estimate, thousands of Muslims constituted the biggest of the foreign merchant communities who perished in what is now Guangzhou (Canton) in a rebel massacre in 879. Seaborne pilgrims began to arrive at Mecca in the ninth century. In the same period, as East African ports became integrated into the trade routes of the Indian Ocean, so they developed Muslim

Xuanzang was the foremost Chinese Buddhist of the seventh century. He went along the Silk Roads on a pilgrimage to India to visit the sites where the Buddha had lived and taught and to retrieve Buddhist manuscripts. Here he is depicted, some 250 years after his death, with much of the typical items a Buddhist monk took on pilgrimage, including a censer to burn incense in worship and a rattle to attract alms from pious passersby. The tiger alludes to his visit to the spot where, according to legend, the Buddha, moved by compassion, gave his life to feed a starving tiger.
Reunion des Musees Nationaux/Art Resource, NY

Camel caravan is still the most practical way to cross the Sahara, and camels still carry part of the traditional salt trade there. Like other long-range trade routes, those across the Sahara in the middle ages were avenues for the transfer of culture, spreading Islam, for example, from North Africa to the kingdoms of the West African Sahel and the Niger valley.

War, Trade, and Religion

366	Founding of Dunhuang
Fifth century	Nestorius, bishop of Constantinople
Seventh and eighth centuries	Rapid Islamic expansion
Mid–eighth century	Uighurs adopt Manichaeanism
Ninth century	Seaborne pilgrims begin to arrive in Mecca; Muslim merchant communities thrive in major Chinese ports
Mid–eleventh century	King Anuruddha introduces Buddhism to Burma; Islam begins to penetrate East and West Africa

communities, composed at first of Arab and Persian merchants and gradually attracting local people to the new religion. Although it did not penetrate far inland, Islam was probably the most influential religion of the East African coast in the region lapped by the monsoons by the twelfth century.

In West Africa, way beyond the African frontiers of the caliphates, Arab visitors to Soninke chiefdoms and kingdoms from the ninth century noted that some people followed "the king's religion," while others were Muslims. Although Islam made little documented progress in West Africa before the eleventh century, immigration and acculturation along the Saharan trade routes prepared the way for Islamization. On this frontier, Islam lacked professional missionaries. Occasionally, however, a Muslim merchant might interest a trading partner or even a pagan ruler in Islam. A late eleventh-century Arab compiler of information about West Africa tells such a story, from Malal south of the Senegal. At a time of terrible drought, a Muslim guest advised the king that if he accepted Islam, "You would bring Allah's mercy on the people of your country, and your enemies would envy you." Rain duly fell after prayers and Quranic recitations. "Then the king ordered that the idols be broken and the sorcerers expelled. The king, together with his descendants and the nobility, became sincerely attached to Islam, but the common people remained pagans."

MONARCHS AND MISSIONARIES

Although not much practiced by Muslims in this period, conversion of kings was one of the main strategies Buddhist and Christian missionaries employed to spread their faiths. They learned to start at the top of society because religion, like other forms of culture, tends to trickle downward, encouraged by the example the power of leaders imposes.

For Christians, in particular, the strategy of targeting elites marked a profound innovation in the history of the Church. Christianity in antiquity was branded—not altogether justly—as a "religion of slaves and women." It was deliberately addressed to outcasts. It appealed to a low level of society and, at first, to those with a low-level education. In its earliest days, it was actually unwelcoming to persons of high status, like the rich young man in the Gospels whom Jesus sent away grieving, or the well-to-do for whom admission to the Kingdom of God was as if through the eye of a needle. In apostolic times, converts of respectable status were few and modest: a Roman army officer; a tax collector; the "most excellent Theophilus," who was probably a Roman official addressed at the beginning of the Gospel of Luke and the Acts of the Apostles; an Ethiopian eunuch who was a royal official. Over the next two to three centuries, the Church grew and embraced people of all classes in the towns of the empire— thanks especially to Christian women, who became the evangelizers of their own husbands and children. But Christianity remained a minority religion, unable to capture the allegiance of rulers or the institutions of states. In the first half of the fourth century, however, three spectacular conversions inaugurated an era in which efforts at conversion targeted the top. The rulers of three great states adopted Christianity: the Roman Emperor Constantine, King Ezana of Ethiopia (Axum), and King Trdat (tuhr-DAHT) of Armenia.

Constantine

Like so many future invaders and tourists from the north, Constantine, commander of the Roman army in Britain from 306, was seduced by the feel and flavor of Mediterranean culture. The standard tale of the beginning of his conversion to Christianity is not credible. In 312, he was heading south, intent on capturing the Roman throne for himself. Approaching the decisive battle of his bid for power, at Milvian Bridge, not far from Rome, he saw a vision that he later described as "a cross of light, superimposed on the sun"— perhaps like the crosslike clouds mountaineers have reported in the Alps, or perhaps an unusual grouping of planets, or perhaps just a dream. As Constantine already worshiped the Sun, the image seemed calculated to appeal to him. The priorities reflected in the accompanying message, "In this sign, conquer!" seem to have reflected Constantine's own. He was looking for a Lord of Hosts rather than a God of Love. An alternative account of the conversion may be Constantine's own. It is a stock story of revelation by grace. "I did not think that a power above could see any thoughts which I harbored in the secret places of my heart . . . but Almighty God, sitting on high, has granted what I did not deserve."

Everywhere politics was so deeply implicated in royal religion that it is hard to resist skepticism about the spirituality of royal converts and the sincerity of their conversions, just as today we prudently disbelieve politicians who claim to be "born again." Bet hedging was the usual strategy. Even for Constantine, despite the emperor's growing interest in Christianity, emperorship was an essentially pagan office. The emperor was the chief priest of the official pagan cults and was worshipped as divine. The emperor's role could not suddenly lose its traditional character. Official religion continued. Court poets and orators classified Constantine's victims in battle as divine sacrifices and his birth as a gift of the gods. (His father was also deified.) One of them constructed a framework of paganism over which the emperor's Christianity could fit:"you have secret communion with the Divine Mind, which, delegating our care to lesser gods, deigns to reveal itself to you alone." Constantine continued to personify the Unconquered Sun in official portraits. Even Christian emperors were honored and portrayed as gods. A sumptuous ivory plaque of the late fourth century in the British Museum shows winged spirits bearing an emperor up to his ancestors by way of the signs of the zodiac. The sacredness of the emperor's person, however, could now be redefined in Christian terms by calling him God's deputy on Earth and, in deserving cases, making him a saint after his death. In coins his sons issued, the hand of God guides Constantine into heaven on a chariot, like the prophet Elijah's in the Bible.

Galla Placidia. As matriarchs of households, and sometimes as powerful agents in the Roman state, women played vital roles in spreading and shaping Christianity. In the early fifth century, Galla Placidia, an emperor's daughter, depicted here on a gold coin as "Principessa Augusta," with titles normally reserved for emperors, converted her first husband, the Visigoth King Athaulf, from heresy and from opposition to Rome. She not only built churches; she also intervened in the elections of popes and bishops and tried to influence church doctrine.

Imperial patronage profoundly affected Christianity. Constantine himself became, according to his own propaganda, "like an apostle"—settling disputes between quarreling theologians, influencing the election of bishops, summoning church councils. During the fourth century, Christianity gradually began to displace the old pagan cults as the official religion of the empire. Pulpits spread imperial propaganda. The church supplied the state with a ready-made bureaucracy. Millions of subjects of the empire began to go to church—without necessarily embracing, or even understanding, Christian doctrines. More than ever, learned and aristocratic classes, who had previously despised Christianity, blended its teachings with the philosophy of classical antiquity. God became "the divine mind." Christian virtues blended with those of stoicism (see Chapter 6). Traditional Christian pacifism withered as Christians felt obliged to support the empire's wars.

Ezana

The adoption of Christianity at the court of Ethiopia at Axum in the 340s illustrates a similar dilemma for a war leader seeking to appropriate a religion of peace. The inscriptions of King Ezana were bloodthirsty documents, full of the numbers of his conquests and the tally of his captives. As his reign unfolded, they remained bloody but became increasingly high minded, full of the concept of the good of the people and service to the state. The king still waged wars but grew moralistic about justifying them. One adversary "attacked and annihilated one of our caravans, after which we took to the field." The king of neighboring Nubia (see Chapter 4) was guilty of boastfulness, raiding, violation of embassies, refusal to negotiate. "He did not listen to me," Ezana complains, "and uttered curses." The new tone reflects the growing influence of Christian clergy.

Before the 340s, Ezana described himself as "son of Mahreb"—a war god synonymous with the ancient Greek god Ares in Greek versions of the inscriptions. Suddenly, he dropped the claim and waged war in the name of "Lord of heaven and Earth" or "the Father, Son and Holy Spirit." His last monument proclaims, "I cannot speak fully of his favors, for my mouth and my spirit cannot fully express all the mercies he has done to me. . . . He has made me the guide of my kingdom through my faith in Christ." He toppled the great stone pillars of Axum or ceased to erect them and began to build churches. Fragments from his sanctuary are still visible in the Old Cathedral of St. Mary of Zion at Axum.

Trdat

To become Christian was to join the growing common culture—vertex of a triangle of Christian states, Ethiopia, Rome, Armenia. For Armenia, the evidence is too indistinct to yield a clear picture of what happened. The supposedly contemporary sources exist only in late, contradictory, and probably corrupt versions. A supposed letter King Trdat wrote in the late third century to an anti-Christian Roman emperor declares "loathing for Christians" and a promise to persecute them. His submission to baptism arose, according to the traditional story, in revulsion from the fate of 33 nuns whom he had put to death. The case of Gregory the Illuminator—Trdat's former friend, whom he imprisoned in a pit of snakes—accentuated his remorse. This looks like a theologically crafted tale of a change of heart induced by divine grace. The number of nuns was probably conventional, chosen to represent the Christian Trinity of Father, Son, and Holy Spirit and the supposed years of Jesus' life. The whole story seems loosely modeled on that of the Apostle Paul in the

Christian and pagan cultures were so similar and so mixed in the fourth-century Roman Empire that it is sometimes hard to tell them apart. Here an emperor, having ridden in life in triumph on an elephant, is hoisted skyward by the chariot of the sun, which pagans worshipped as a god and Christian artists used as an image for Christ. Winged spirits ascend with the emperor's soul, through the spheres of heaven, marked by the signs of the zodiac, top right, to the heavenly home of his ancestors. This is one of the last works of art that portrays a Roman emperor in a predominantly pagan setting.

Bible—the persecutor turned converter. The date of Trdat's conversion cannot be fixed more exactly than between 301 and 314. The latter date seems likely, as by then Constantine had begun to favor Christianity, and Trdat favored alignment with Rome against Persia.

Diplomatic Conversions

In the Caucasus Mountains near Armenia, at about the same time, tradition credits an unnamed slave woman (whom later tradition called Nino) with converting the people we now know as the Georgians. Her prayers cured a queen's illness. When the king proposed to shower the slave with rewards, "She despises gold," said the queen. "She feeds on hunger as if it were food itself. The only way we can repay her is to worship divine Christ who cured me thanks to her prayers." The story sounds made up. The invocation of a miracle cure seems contrived to make the new religion attractive. The verifiable fact, however, is that the priests who launched the Georgian state church came, by general agreement among the sources, from Constantine's empire. Christianity was a political option for small states in imperial hinterlands, striving to preserve their independence and playing Persia against Rome. It made sense to associate with Rome, which was the more distant threat.

The Georgian kingdoms of Iberia (ih-BEH-ree-ah) and Lazica (LAH-zih-kah) pried themselves free of Persian dominance, partly by opting for Roman support. By the early sixth century, a Roman ambassador to Lazica could hardly restrain his enthusiasm for a people who were "in no way barbarians, long association with the Romans having led them to adopt a civilized and law-abiding way of life." From 522, the kings of Lazica ceased to accept election by the emperors of Persia and chose to be invested by those of Rome. King Ztathius had the Roman emperor's portrait embroidered on his robes. His successor, King Gobazes, had the official rank of usher (an honored post) at the court of Constantinople.

It became normal for religious allegiances to change with political alliances. Poised between Christian and Muslim powers, the rulers of the Khazars (HAH-zahrs)—Turkic pastoralists between the Black Sea and the Caspian, who built up a state that endured for 400 years from the early seventh century—adopted, at different times, Christianity, Islam, and Judaism in their efforts to preserve their independence.

Buddhist Politics

Buddhist missionaries, like their Christian counterparts, displayed partiality for royal and imperial disciples. The Chinese emperor Ming was supposed to have introduced Buddhism as the result of a vision in the late first century. This was untrue, but it is evidence of the importance the Buddhist clergy who invented the tale attached to imperial patronage. As we saw in the last chapter, Buddhism became the favorite spiritual resource of usurpers of the Chinese throne who

The monastery church at Jvari ("the Cross") in Georgia occupies a hilltop where St. Nino, a female evangelist traditionally credited with helping to spread Christianity in Georgia in the fourth century, is said to have paused to pray. A church on the site is documented from the seventh century, but the existing building resembles Western churches of the ninth and tenth centuries. Above the entrance, angels brandish a cross from which the "living water" of Christian baptism flows.

Early Conversions to Christianity

312	Emperor Constantine of Rome
ca. 301–314	King Trdat of Armenia
ca. 325	Georgia (King Mirian and Queen Nana)
340s	King Ezana of Ethiopia

wanted to legitimize their rule and of monarchs who needed a propaganda machine. In Dunhuang paintings, pious emperors preside at debates between rival schools of Buddhism. But however personally committed to Buddhism, or reliant on Buddhist support, no Buddhist emperor ever suspended the traditional rites and sacrifices that Chinese emperors were required to perform. Only Yang Jian in the sixth century (see Chapter 8)—a skeptic contemptuous of all religion—had the nerve to do that.

So Buddhism could never monopolize the Chinese imperial court. Not only the venerability of the traditional rites, but also the strength of Confucianism and Daoism ensured that. Buddhism had, moreover, to contend with Chinese belittlement of anything foreign. Indeed, the measure of Buddhism's success is that, until "Westernization" began in the late nineteenth century, it was the only movement of foreign origin ever really to catch on in China. Sporadic bursts of imperial favor enabled Buddhists to establish an enormous network of monasteries that became magnets of piety for millions of people. The scale of Buddhism's ascent was revealed during one of the spasms of persecution of Buddhism in which emperors occasionally indulged. In the 820s through the 840s, thousands of monasteries were dissolved, and a quarter of a million monks and nuns forced back into lay life.

Korea

In the neighboring Korean kingdom of Koguryo, the beginnings of the rise of Buddhism were inseparable from the context of the late fourth century, when barbarian invasions of China enriched Koguryo with refugees. A series of fugitive Chinese monks made themselves indispensable at court and devised ways to reconcile Buddhism with royal responsibilities under the old, indigenous religion. King Kwanggaet'o dedicated one of Korea's first royally endowed temples with the inscription, "Believing in Buddhism, we seek prosperity." King Changsu, who ruled for more than three-quarters of the fifth century and died in 491, is depicted at the tomb of his predecessor at Pyongyang in what is today the capital of North Korea performing Buddhist as well as native rites. The rest of Korea resisted Buddhist intrusions at first, perhaps because of the importance of local religious rites as part of the ceremonial of kingship. The kings of Silla, for instance, derived prestige from their claim to have arisen from a dynasty of holy men. State formation in Korea was essentially a process of extending uniform religious rites to one community after another.

The launch of Buddhism as a royal religion in southern Korea is traditionally ascribed to the personal conversion of King Song in Paekche and King Pophung of Silla in the 520s or 530s. The bone ranks (nobility) opposed Pophung's choice, but the martyrdom of a young Buddhist official, Ich'adon awed them. Both the king's wives became Buddhist nuns. Monks, like the chief minister Hyeyong in the mid–550s, became useful state servants. Won'gwang, who returned from China in 602 to head the bureaucracy, adapted dharma for political purposes. Serve your lord with loyalty and "face battle without retreating" became precepts of the faith. Having adapted to one political system in the sixth century, Korean Buddhism did so again, under new political conditions, in the tenth century, when the reform of the Korean administration along Chinese lines filled the bureaucracy with men trained in the study of Confucianism. The scholar-administrator Ch'oe Sungno expressed the ensuing compromise well in 982: "Carrying out the teachings of Buddha is the basis for the cultivation of the self. Carrying out the teachings of Confucius is the source for regulating the state."

Japan

Japan was the scene of the most remarkable working compromise between a new, universal religion and kingly commitment to traditional paganism. The first image of the Buddha in Japan was said to have arrived as a diplomatic gift from Korea in 538. The pious efforts of the Soga clan—immigrants from China—supposedly spread the new religion around the end of the sixth century. Underlying the tale is a political saga. The Soga aimed to replace the ruling imperial dynasty, which claimed descent from the Sun-goddess. The Soga saw Buddhism as the path to power. The traditional "way of the gods"—**Shinto** in Japanese—was the reigning dynasty's special responsibility. The same word in Japanese meant "shrine" and "palace." The word for *government* also meant "religion."

A traditional anecdote captures the true lines of the debate that raged in the mid–sixth century. "All neighboring states to the west already honor Buddha," Soga no Iname pointed out. "Is it right that Japan alone should turn her back on this religion?" But native ministers replied, "The rulers of this country have always conducted seasonal rites in honor of the many heavenly and earthly spirits of land and grain."

The search was on for a synthesis that would harness Buddhism for the state without disturbing the traditional Shinto ideology and magic of the monarchy. Prince Shotoku (574–622), the first great royal patron of Buddhism in Japan, realized the value of the Buddhist clergy as potential servants of the state. He wrote learned commentaries on Buddhist doctrine and founded monasteries. Shotoku saw that the emperor could take on the roles and advantages of a Buddhist patron while adhering to the old Shinto rites. His injunctions include, "The emperor is heaven and his ministers are Earth. . . . So edicts handed down by the emperor must be scrupulously obeyed. If they are not obeyed, ministers will bring ruin on themselves." Endorsed from the court, Buddhism flourished. The Japanese census of 624 counted 816 monks. By 690, 3,363 monks received gifts of cloth from the throne.

A reaction set in. The traditional elite feared Buddhism as a foreign intrusion and a menace to the imperial rites. Early eighth-century law codes banned wandering monks from "speaking falsely about misfortunes or blessings based on mysterious natural phenomena," "deluding the people," and begging without permit. Various measures attempted to prevent monasteries from abusing their tax-exempt status.

The advances of Buddhism, however, were irresistible. A Buddhist scripture warned kings that "if they do not walk in the law, the holy men go away and violent calamities arise." In the 730s, the monk Gembo returned from China with 5,000 volumes of Buddhist scriptures and endeared himself by curing an empress's depression. In 747, 6,563 monks were ordained at a palace ceremony. As we shall see in the next chapter, emperors found socially useful ways to channel the dynamism of Buddhist devotion. Buddhist rituals originally intended in India to treat snakebites, poison, and disease were used

Prince Shotoku. As regent for the first reigning Japanese empress in the early seventh century, Prince Shotoku, shown here with two of his sons in a Korean painting of nearly two centuries later, used his influence to promote contacts with China, remodel the Japanese government on Chinese lines, and spread Buddhism in Japan.

The Introduction of Buddhism in Korea and Japan

Late fourth century	Chinese refugees introduce Buddhism in Koguryo
ca. 520–530	Kings of Paekche and Silla convert to Buddhism
538	First image of Buddha arrives in Japan
574–622	Life of Prince Shotoku, first great royal patron of Buddhism
Seventh century	Rapid expansion of Buddhism in Japan under royal patronage

in Japan to protect the state. The outcome was a characteristically Japanese compromise. No one in Japan, it is often said, was purely Buddhist. The traditional Shinto shrines played a part in the devotions even of monks, as they still do. Even Empress Shotoku in the 760s, whose Buddhist devotion was unsurpassed, never tried to tamper with the traditional rites.

Tibet

According to a legend crafted in Tibet about 500 years after the supposed event, a Chinese or Nepalese wife of King Songtsen Gampo brought Buddhism there in the sixth century. The true story was of long, slow monastic colonization. Though Songtsen Gampo probably patronized Buddhist monks and scholars, who frequented his court in the households of the Nepalese and Chinese princesses of his harem, he continued to represent himself as divine.

Even King Trisong Detsen in the second half of the eighth century, whom Buddhists hailed as a model of piety and whom their opponents denounced as a traitor to the traditional royal religion, depicted himself as both the divine defender of the old faith and the enlightened enthusiast of the new. In 792, he resided over a great debate between Indian and Chinese champions on the question of whose traditions better represented the Buddha's doctrine. The issue was decided in favor of the Indian traditional moral disciplines **Theravada Buddhism**, as it is usually called), by which the soul might advance to Buddhahood by tiny incremental stages of learning and goodness, lifetime after lifetime, rather than the **Mahayana Buddhism**, argued by Chinese spokesmen, who claimed that the soul could achieve Buddhahood in one lifetime. Mahayana Buddhism, which also took root in Japan, is known as the "greater vehicle" because its proponents believe that it can carry more people to salvation than Theravada Buddhism, the "lesser vehicle."

But this debate was premature. Tibet was hardly yet a Buddhist country, nor could one tradition of Buddhism be imposed in the contexts in which Buddhism spread: missionary work and monastery founding; the ebb and flow of armies, who transmitted ideas as the tide shifts pebbles; and the spread of culture, including religion, along the routes of merchant caravans.

By the time of Tibet's treaty with China in 821, Buddhism had made real progress. The treaty invoked Buddhist as well as pagan gods, and after traditional sacrifices and blood-smearing rites, the Buddhists among the treaty's negotiators withdrew for a celebration of their own. King Ralpachen was so devout that he let monks sit on his prodigiously long hair. But a reaction set in at his death in 836, and Buddhism survived in Tibet only precariously into the next century, awaiting renewal by a new wave of monastic colonization. Its main rival was not the old religion but **Bon**. Of the origins of this faith, we know nothing reliable, but it was similar and heavily indebted to Buddhism. The sayings of the great Bon-po sage, Gyerspungs, closely resembled those of Buddhist masters: Existence is like a dream. "Validity is vacuity." Truth must "transcend sounds and terms and words." The main difference lay in the sages'

Samye monastery. The first Buddhist monastery in Tibet was reputedly founded at Samye in the valley of Lhasa. It illustrates the importance of royal patronage in bringing Buddhism to Tibet. According to legend, King Trisong Detsen in the 770s invited an Indian sage into the kingdom, who consecrated the site of the monastery after a battle with the demons who infested it.

attitude to India. Buddhists acknowledged that their teaching came from there, whereas Bon-pos traced it to a legendary land in the west, and regarded their mythical founder, Shen-rab, as the original Buddha.

India

Ironically, the effort to combine Buddhism with traditional kingship failed most conspicuously in India itself, the Buddha's homeland. In the sixth century, kingdoms multiplied in India, and kings issued many grants of revenue and property to holy men to found religious establishments, in an effort to gain their support. Kings made relatively few grants, however, to Buddhists. The circumstances of the period—the conflicts with the Huns (see Chapter 8) and the crumbling of political unity—seem to have driven popular piety back to its roots in the worship of local gods, as if the troubles of the time were proof that Buddhism had failed.

Rites and practices associated with the traditions we now call **Hinduism** were taking hold. Indeed, some holy men set out to systematize them as an alternative to Buddhism. The development of the caste system—in which everyone has an unchangeable ritual rank, defined at birth, that determines one's place in society—indicates how Hinduism was spreading. The caste system was not yet fully defined, but according to the description of India in 630 through 645 by Xuanzang (shoo-en-tzang), the greatest Chinese Buddhist manuscript collector, butchers, fishermen, actors, executioners, and scavengers were ritually unclean and had to live outside city limits. Almost everyone acknowledged the superiority of the highest caste, the priestly Brahmans. The spread of blood sacrifice also shows that Buddhism was in retreat. The Guptas (see Chapter 8) sacrificed horses, in defiance of Buddhist teaching, but protected cows, which Hinduism regards as especially sacred. The first **sati**—the burning of a widow on her husband's funeral pyre—was recorded in 510. The Palas dynasty of Bengal in the eighth to the eleventh centuries was the last Buddhist reigning family in India, and their Buddhism, embodied in images of animal-shaped deities sprouting with heads and limbs, seems hardly recognizable as the doctrine of Buddha the founder. Most Indian kings preferred to stake their power on devotion to particular traditional gods rather than on Buddhism.

The Margins of Christendom

In Christendom, the *Constantinian model*, according to which conversion begins with the ruler, prevailed for most of what we think of as the Middle Ages. Almost every conversion of a nation or a people, as related in medieval sources, began with the conversion of a king. There were, of course, some exceptions or possible exceptions. Clovis, the Frankish chief who took over most of Gaul (modern France) in the 480s, gave up his claim to descent from a sea god when he converted to Christianity for the advantage of allegiance to a God who could deliver victory and equip him with administrators who could read and write. But conversion among the Frankish people preceded or accompanied Clovis's. In the traditional story, the Franks responded directly to the appeal of Bishop Remigius, not to any initiative by the king. In Iceland, where supposedly "democratic" decision making is generally supposed to have prevailed, the collective adoption of Christianity was resolved in the assembly of the people in 1000, but the law speaker who presided over the assembly, Thorgeirr Thorkelsson, withdrew to meditate or commune with the gods for a day and a night before lending his decisive influence to the debate. Of course, Christianity was also spread in undocumented or barely documented ways: movements of population, journeys of merchants and envoys. But missionary strategy remained focused on leaders as means of mobilizing peoples.

The Jelling Stone. The Norse King Harold Bluetooth adopted Christianity in 965 and had commemorative stones carved with Christian symbols in memory of his parents, to atone for their paganism. The detail here shows the Crucifixion. "This Harold," claims the inscription on the stones, "conquered all Denmark and Norway and turned the Danes to Christianity."

In northern and eastern Europe, a great sequence of royal conversions in the late tenth and early eleventh centuries more or less established the frontier of Christendom, beginning with Harold Bluetooth in the 960s in Denmark and Mieszko of Poland in 966. In Norway, an exchange of stories and attributes in the earliest chronicles between St. Olaf and his predecessor, Olaf Tryggvason has confused the outline of events, but it is clear that a year or two after Tryggvason's confirmation as a Christian in England in 995, a popular assembly in Norway endorsed the new religion. In Sweden Olof Skötkunung of the Svear began minting coins with Christian symbols on them before 1000. His reception as king established an uninterrupted sequence of Christian rulers. The coronation of Stephen of Hungary in 1001 settled the Christian destiny of that country.

Vladimir and the Rus

No case was more significant for the future than that of Vladimir, ruler of Kiev in what is today Ukraine, in 987 through 988, for his adherence ensured that Christianity would be privileged among the eastern Slavs—including the Russians, who became Europe's most numerous Slav community. Like the culture of his country, formed by the interaction of native Slavs with Scandinavian migrants who spread along the valley of the river Volga, Vladimir was the descendant of Scandinavians as well as Slavs, pagans on both sides (see Chapter 10). Like many great saints, he sinned with gusto. His harem was said to contain over 800 girls. Russians trace proverbs in praise of drunkenness to his invention. He left a reputation, in the words of a German chronicler, as "a cruel man and a fornicator on a huge scale."

Among his people, paganism was entrenched by the psychological power of terror. The horror of a human sacrifice among the Rus (roos) profoundly impressed the caliph's ambassador, Ibn Fadlan, who witnessed it in 969. The slave girl chosen to die with her master sang songs of farewell over her last cups of liquor before ritually copulating with her executioners. An old woman called the Angel of Death then wound a cord around her neck and handed the slack to men standing on either side. Warriors beat their shields to drown the victim's screams. While the cord was tightened, the Angel of Death plunged a dagger repeatedly in and out of the girl's breast. The funeral pyre, built on a ship, was then lighted, and the fire fed until it burned to ashes. "After this, on the spot where the ship had lain, when they dragged it from the river, they built something that looked like a round mound. In the middle of it, they set up a big post of birch wood, on which they wrote the name of the dead man and of the king of the Rus. Then they went away."

To replace this religion, and break the power of its priests, Vladimir needed something equally powerful. The traditional story of his emissaries' quest for a perfect religion led first to the Muslim Bulgars, who "bow down and sit, look hither and thither like men possessed, but there is no joy in them, only sorrow and a dreadful stench. Their religion is not good. Then we went to the Germans, and we saw them celebrating many services in their churches, but we saw no beauty there. Then we went to the Greeks, and they led us to the place where they worship their God [the church of Hagia Sophia that Justinian had built in Constantinople]; and we knew not whether we were in heaven or on Earth; for on Earth there is no such vision or beauty and we do not know how to describe it. We only know that there God dwells among men."

In fact, Vladimir's decision in favor of Orthodox Christianity owed more to politics than aesthetics. Conversion was the price he paid for the hand of a Byzantine princess whom he demanded with threats. (The Russians had tried to attack Constantinople several times in the ninth and tenth centuries.) Imperial Byzantine princesses were not normally permitted to marry foreign suitors, for, according to the tenth-century emperor, Constantine VII, "just as each animal mates with its own species, so it is right that each nation should also marry and cohabit not with those of other race and tongue but of the same tribe and speech." Put more bluntly, his point was that marriages between imperial princesses and foreign rulers diminished the sacred, divinely sanctioned dignity of the Byzantine monarchy and opened the way for foreign rulers to claim the Byzantine throne. Vladimir solemnly evicted the occupants of his sacred grove of idols. The golden-haired, silver-moustached thunder god, Perun, was buffeted, insulted, and dragged through the dust before being flung in a muddy river. Vladimir imposed Christianity by violence, while making it more acceptable and perhaps more intelligible by ordering that Christian liturgy be conducted in the Slavonic language the Rus spoke, rather than in Greek.

The Spread of Christianity	
ca. 500	Clovis, king of the Franks, converts to Christianity
960	Harold Bluetooth of Denmark converts
966	Conversion of King Mieszko of Poland
ca. 988	Vladmir of Kiev adopts Orthodox Christianity
ca. 997	Norway and Sweden convert to Christianity
1000	Iceland converts to Christianity
1001	Coronation of Stephen of Hungary as a Christian monarch

Islam and the Turks

The magnetism Christianity exerted on the frontiers of Christendom was paralleled in the Islamic world. Around the middle of the tenth century, the Karakhanids (kah-rah-HAHN-ihds) became the first Turkic people to subscribe to Islam—apparently as a result of the favorable impression they derived from raiding Islamic territory. This was an event pregnant with consequences for the future, because the Turks would bring to the Islamic world a vital infusion of manpower and expertise in war—"the army of God, whom I have installed in the East," according to a legendary saying of the Prophet. Islam's attraction for them is easier to express than explain. The memories they conserved of the time of their paganism reveal warlike values. Boys were not named until they had "lopped off heads in battle." A hero was judged by the number of times he could plait his moustache behind his head. Even women were war trained and "made the enemy vomit blood." Yet some of their leaders continued to see attractions or advantages in Islam. In 962, Altigin (AHL-tee-geen), a Turk who had adopted Islam while serving as a slave in Persia, founded at Ghazni (GAHZ-nee) in Afghanistan a Muslim state that was to exert great influence in the future. In about 985, a Turkic chief, Seljuk (SEHL-jook), who dreamed of "ejaculating fire in all directions" and conquering the world, ruled a small state, cobbled together by conquest, in Central Asia. His decision to become a Muslim was of enormous significance, as his descendants supplied some of the Islamic world's most effective frontiersmen.

TRICKLE DOWN: CHRISTIANIZATION AND ISLAMIZATION

When they converted rulers and conquered elites, religions trickled down to the rest of society. For Christians, for example, Constantine's patronage was an extraordinary windfall. At the time, despite the gradual—and, in some eastern provinces, formidable—accumulation of converts among the socially respectable and intellectual, Christianity had remained essentially one of many eastern cults popular in the Roman Empire. Christianity still bore the marks of its origins as a Jewish heresy, founded by a rabbi whose birth and death were, in the world's eyes,

Seljuk sultan. "Like a chess player, one has to observe the enemy's moves as well as one's own," wrote an historian of the mid-twelfth century, commenting on the war of the Seljuk Sultan Tughril II (1132–1134). This ceramic figure is inscribed with the name of "Our Lord Sultan Tughril, the just, the learned." It may have been part of a chess-set inspired by Seljuk politics.

● MAKING CONNECTIONS

FACTORS AIDING THE SPREAD OF UNIVERSAL RELIGIONS

RELIGION →	WAR →	TRADE →	MISSIONARIES →	ELITES
Buddhism	Early rulers Asoka, Kaniska, Anuruddha invoke "dharma" (teachings of Buddha) in violent conquests	Silk Roads fundamental to spreading Buddhism via traveling monks and monasteries housing merchants, pilgrims	Missionaries/pilgrims important—Xuanzang (China); conversion of kings a primary means of accelerating social acceptance	Emperor Ming (China); King Song (Korea); Prince Shotoko (Japan); Trisong Detsen (Tibet)
Christianity	Charlemagne, other rulers (Alfred the Great of England, Olaf of Norway) justify war, conquest by forcible conversion	Few long-distance Christian traders along Eurasian trade routes; Nestorians a thin and patchy presence along Silk Roads	Converting kings and elite groups a fundamental strategy	Constantine (Roman Empire); Ezana (Ethiopia); Trdat (Armenia); Vladimir (Kiev, Russia)
Islam	Jihad justifies both interior struggle and warfare against polytheists, idolaters, apostates; continual warfare against non-Islamic neighboring states	Effectively spread via land and sea routes across Africa. Dispersal of Muslim–merchant communities throughout south and southeast Asia	Traveling merchants; conversion encouraged by specific social/political policies favoring Muslims (beneficial tax system, legal codes)	Especially important in Turkic areas (Central Asia): tenth-century leaders Altigin, Seljuk

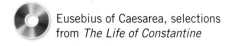

Eusebius of Caesarea, selections from *The Life of Constantine*

equally disreputable, and whom many saw as just another failed messiah or prophet. Its scriptures were, by the sophisticated standards of the Greek schools of rhetoric and philosophy, so badly written as to embarrass all educated Christians.

Now, after the conversion of Constantine, according to the fourth-century Christian historian Eusebius, who had chronicled the persecutions of previous reigns, "It felt as if we were imagining a picture of the kingdom of Christ and that what was happening was no reality but a dream." There were subsidies for the Church, exemptions from fiscal and military obligations for the clergy, jobs in the state service for Christians, and the assurance, from the emperor's own hand, that the worship of Christians benefited the empire.

The rise of the Church from persecution to predominance was completed in 395, when the emperor Theodosius proclaimed Christianity the official religion of the Roman Empire and reduced pagan traditions to the underprivileged status formerly imposed on Christians. From the late fourth century onward, nobility and sanctity converged. So many young aristocrats became monks that monasteries came to resemble "noblemen's clubs." Christianity guaranteed the best opportunities for promotion in the army and bureaucracy and for personal enrichment. Those who accepted it subscribed to a cultural package associated with success. Ethiopian sources are too meager for certainty, but in Armenia, too, the continuing progress of Christianity depended, at least until the Arab conquest in the eighth century, on royal and aristocratic initiatives.

To some extent, the same considerations applied within the Islamic world. Because the Muslim conquests were vast, and the conquerors relatively few in number, Muslim rulers could not exclude non-Muslims from positions of authority. The caliph Umar (OO-mahr) I expelled non-Muslims from Arabia in 635, but without the services of Christians and Jews in the rest of the Middle East, or of Zoroastrians in Persia, the administrations of the eighth- and ninth-century caliphates would have been understaffed. Still, by favoring Muslims, discriminating against non-Muslims, and insisting on the exclusive use of Arabic as the language of administration, rulers created a climate of prejudice in favor of Islam among elites. The caliph Abd al-Malik (ahbd al-MA-lihk) effectively proclaimed Islam's superiority to Christianity by building the Dome of the Rock and the al-Aqsa (ahl-AHK-sah) mosque in Jerusalem in the late seventh century to dwarf the Church of the Holy Sepulchre built on the site where Jesus had supposedly been buried. The new Islamic buildings symbolized the sacredness to Islam of what had been only a Christian and Jewish holy city—indeed, *the* holy city, the reputed center of the world. Even mild persecution could exert considerable pressure. The caliph Umar II (r. 717–720) tried to exclude Christians and Jews from public offices. He also forbade them to build places of worship or lift their voices in prayer. They had to wear distinctive clothing and were forbidden saddles for their horses. If a Muslim killed a Christian, his penalty was only a fine. Christians could not give valid testimony against Muslims in legal cases. Later caliphs sporadically renewed persecution. In 807, Caliph Harun al-Rashid (hah-ROON ahr-rah-SHEED) ordered all churches on the frontiers of his empire demolished and reenforced the clothing laws against Christians. In the 850s, the caliph al-Mutawakkil (ahl-moo-tah-WAH-keel) ordered that Christian and Jewish graves should be level with the ground. Converts to Islam, on the other hand, could rapidly ascend through the ranks of society. The leader of the coup that dethroned the Umayyads (oo-MEYE-yadz), the first caliphal dynasty, in 750, was a freed slave, and not even an Arab by birth, but a Persian. The second caliph of the next dynasty, the Abbasids (ah-BA-sihds), was the son of a Berber slave woman from North Africa.

For most Christian and Jewish subjects of Islamic states, the tax system—which exempted Muslims from most charges—was the focus of discrimination. Umar II declared that he would be happy to see Islam spread and revenues diminish, even if it meant he had to till the soil with his own hands. Indeed, many people proclaimed themselves Muslims simply to take advantage of reduced tax rates, until Al-Hajjaj (ahl-hah-JAHJ), the brutal governor of Iraq in the 690s and early 700s reimposed the old tax levels on supposedly phoney converts.

Partly because Islam tolerated some other religions, the conquered societies were slow to become Islamized. Indeed, substantial Christian minorities have survived in Egypt, Iraq, Syria, and, especially, Lebanon to this day. Some historians have tried to measure the rate of acceptance of Islam by calculating the numbers of people who gave their children Muslim-sounding names. This method suggested to Richard W. Bulliet, its greatest exponent, that only 2.5 percent of the population of Iran were converted to Islam in the seventh century. Not until the early ninth century was the majority of the population Muslim. The remainder were Islamized during the ninth and tenth centuries. The significance of name

The Dome of the Rock in Jerusalem marks the spot where, according to Muslim tradition, the Prophet Muhammad ascended to paradise. The Caliph Abd al-Malik had it built in the late seventh century, marking as sacred to Islam a city that Christians and Jews already revered. The splendor and scale of the building outdazzled and dwarfed the nearby Church of the Holy Sepulcher and the remains of the last Jewish Temple.

giving is broadly cultural, in most places, rather than specifically religious. But the names people were given or adopted do help to demonstrate roughly the rate at which Islam became the dominant influence on the culture of Iran. Though—strictly speaking—it tells us nothing about the personal religion or depth of conviction of the individuals who bestowed or received Islamic names, the evidence of personal names is consistent with the view that, once a new religion commands the allegiance of the elite, the rest of society can adopt the same religion without having their conversion significantly change their lives.

RELIGIOUS LIVES: THE WORLD OF MONKS AND NUNS

In Buddhism and Christianity, monasticism grew as these religions spread and, in turn, became a major cause of their continuing success.

Christian Monasticism

As a result of the triumph of Christianity as an elite religion, the Church became the great upholder of Roman standards of learning, art, and government. This is not surprising among aristocratic bishops, whose family traditions were of power. In the sixth century, Pope Gregory the Great organized the defense of Rome against the Lombards (see Chapter 8), launched missions of spiritual reconquest to parts of western Europe, such as England, that had become paganized, and reimposed on the western empire a kind of unity by the sheer range of his correspondence. In Visigothic Spain, Isidore of Seville (ca. 560–636) passed the learning of classical Greece and Rome on to future generations in the form of an encyclopedia. Martin of Braga dedicated to a Germanic king a book about virtue, based on a lost Roman work.

It was harder to domesticate the church's own barbarians—the antisocial ascetics and hermits, whose response to the problems of the world was to withdraw from them or rail at them from their caves. The monastic movement made their lives "regular," concentrating them in houses of work, study, and prayer to benefit society as a whole. There is no scholarly consensus on the origins of monasticism. Christians perhaps got it from Buddhists, or maybe it arose independently in various cultures as hermits and holy men clubbed together for mutual support. The earliest recorded Christian monastic communities emerged in Egypt in the second century, among ascetics seeking to imitate Jesus' period of self-exile in the desert. Of the many rules of life for monks written in the following centuries, the most influential rule in the western church was that of Benedict of Nursia.

The only certain date in his life is 542, when the Ostrogothic king Totila visited him at his monastery of Monte Cassino in southern Italy. He started as a typical, obsessive ascetic, in a cave, where food was lowered to him while he disciplined the lusts of the flesh in a convenient thornbush. In one of the earliest surviving illustrations of his life, the cave mouth is jagged and bloody. When he established his own community, he rededicated the pagan shrine of the Roman god Jupiter on the spot to St. Martin, the patron of poverty, who gave half his cloak to a beggar. The nearby pagan shrine of Apollo became the chapel of John Baptist, the biblical voice crying in the wilderness. These rededications disclose Benedict's program: the practice of charity in refuge from the world.

Isidore of Seville's T-O map of the World

St. Catherine's Monastery, Sinai. For almost 1,800 years, Christian monks have sought the desert, imitating Jesus and John the Baptist, who, the Bible says, both withdrew into the wilderness to think and pray. St. Catherine's monastery in Sinai in Egypt is in an oasis in a desert gorge, nearly 5,000 feet deep. Its remoteness protected it for centuries and helped to keep its collection of early Christian writings intact.

His book of rules for monks was one of many. It borrowed freely from others. Most of it was filtered out of a rambling earlier rule. But its superiority and universality were recognized almost at once, and there has hardly been a monastic movement or revival in the west since then that has not been based on or deeply influenced by it. The animating principles are the quest for salvation in common and the subordination of all individual willfulness. Benedict banned extremes of mortification in favor of steady spiritual progress, manual labor, study, and prayer in private and in common. Pope Gregory the Great showed how well he had interpreted Benedict's spirit when he dictated the last line of his biography of Benedict: "I must stop talking now for a while so that by silence I may repair my strength and be able to narrate the miracles of others." Benedict had sought a way to imitate paradise here on Earth. He had found a means to make civilization survive, for monastic study also embraced the learning of ancient Greece and Rome. Monasteries became centers for colonizing wasteland and wilderness. Monks sought "desert" frontiers to build new monasteries, and lay people followed them.

Buddhist Monks

Monasticism was even more important in Buddhism than in Christianity, since, in principle, most of the Buddhist clergy were subject to monastic discipline. In practice, however, Buddhist monasteries performed particular functions, especially in transmitting learning, that made their contributions similar to those of monasteries in Christendom. The 50,000 ancient manuscripts preserved in the library cave of Dunhuang—a precious time capsule, sealed for 800 years in the tenth century—are a measure of the importance of scholarship in Buddhist monasteries. The business of retrieving, translating, editing, and purifying the best written evidence of the Buddha's teachings turned the monks responsible for it into giants and heroes of learning. The first Chinese to be ordained as a Buddhist priest, for instance, in about 250, was Zhu Shixing (joo she-shing). He was nearly 80 years old when he made a pilgrimage to India to procure a manuscript of the Buddha. Exhausted by the journey, he handed it to his disciples to carry to China before he died. Kumarajiva, translator into Chinese of the most famous of Buddhist scriptures, the **Lotus Sutra**, in the early fifth century, was said to be able to

Buddhist nun. In this painting of 910 from the Buddhist shrines at Dunhuang, the learned nun Yanhui and her brother, an imperial Chinese chamberlain, offer lotus flowers and incense to Avalokitesvara, the Buddhist personification of compassion. "In the hope," says the inscription, "that the empire may be peaceful and that the wheel of the law may continually turn therein."
© The Trustees of the British Museum

◎ MAKING CONNECTIONS ◎

THE RELIGIOUS LIFE

RELIGION →	EXAMPLES OF RELIGIOUS COMMUNITIES →	MONASTERY FUNCTIONS/ACTIVITIES
Christianity	Egyptian monasteries, second century; Benedictine monasteries, Italy and Europe, sixth century onward	Scholarly (preservation, translation of ancient manuscripts); cultural (lay people followed monks in reclaiming desert regions); religious (Benedict's widely followed program focused on steady spiritual progress, manual labor, study, and prayer)
Buddhism	Silk Road monasteries (ca. 200–800)	Scholarly (transmission of learning; translation and preservation of texts); secular and religious education, centers of lay life (reading groups, pilgrimage sites, inns for travelers, and granaries for food storage)
Islam	Sufi monasteries, Turkey/Mideast (ninth century and after)	Mystical orders focusing on intense spiritual practices (dancing, prayer, study) organized into brotherhoods, sisterhoods

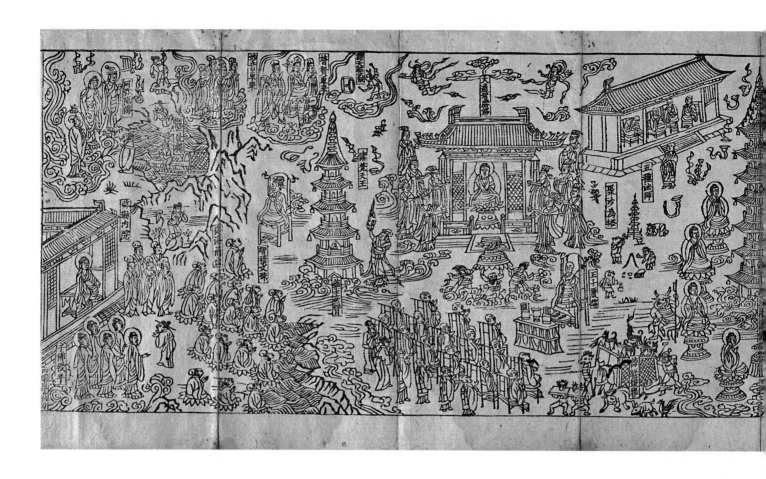

memorize 30,000 words a day. As in Christendom, Buddhist monastic libraries diversified into secular learning, imaginative literature, and administrative and historical records of life way beyond the monastery walls. They were centers of lay life, too, hosting reading clubs for believers, including groups of women, who would pay fines—such as a jug of wine or bowl of cereal—for failure to attend meetings. And monasteries functioned as objects of pilgrimage, inns for travelers, and granaries to store food against hard times.

Sufism

Strictly speaking, there should never have been anything like monasticism in Islam. The Quran warned against the asceticism of Christian monks, which Muhammad evidently regarded as blasphemous. But Christian influence was not easy to filter out of early Islam. In the early eighth century, Hasan al-Basri quoted Jesus to support his view that asceticism is God's "training ground that his servants might learn to run to him." He advocated fasting and meditation to induce a mystical sense of identity with God. When, toward the end of the same century, the female mystic, Rabia al-Adawiyya (rah-BEE-yah ahl-ah-dah-WEE-yah), experienced a vision of Muhammad, he asked her if she loved him. "My love of God has so possessed me," she replied, "that no space is left for loving or hating any but him." Groups of devotees who increasingly organized themselves into orders and sometimes founded houses of common life, or, at least, schools in which they trained in mystical techniques cultivated the tradition these thinkers established.

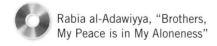

Rabia al-Adawiyya, "Brothers, My Peace is in My Aloneness"

The Lotus Sutra. Composed between the first century B.C.E. and the second century C.E., the Lotus Sutra is the most important text of Mahayana Buddhism. This printed version, from around 1000 C.E., shows the Western Paradise of the Amitabha Buddha and his court of Bodhisattvas.

Though fellow Muslims often suspected these **Sufis** (SOO-fees) of being heretical, Sufism supplied Islam with some of its supplest thinkers and most dedicated and successful missionaries.

Religious Women

In Christianity, Buddhism, and the Islamic world, women acquired new roles, inside the home as guardians of religious tradition for their children, and outside the home as members of religious orders, seeking sanctity in common with other women. Nuns played the same role as monks in prayer and scholarship. In some places, both sexes shared the same houses of religion, often under female leadership. At Whitby in seventh-century England, the formidable Abbess Hilda ruled one of the largest religious establishments of the day, with one of the highest reputations for learning. Nunneries played an important part in Buddhist life in China and Japan, often serving as nurseries and places of education for women. The empresses Shotoku of Japan (see Chapter 10) and Wu of China (see Chapter 8) were nuns before their ascent to power. In the Buddhist world, indeed, the nun's vocation was often a stage before returning to secular life, often in households where husbands had several wives and concubines. In Islam, which also allowed men to have up to four wives, there was relatively little spare woman power. So female monasticism never

Early Monasticism

ca. 250	Zhu Shixing is the first Chinese to be ordained Buddhist priest
Second century	Earliest Christian monastic communities (Egypt)
Sixth century	Life of Saint Benedict
Seventh century	Abbess Hilda rules important religious establishments
Late eighth century	Rabia al-Adawiyya, Islamic Sufi mystic

developed, and female Sufis—though often individually influential—were rare. Only exceptionally strong-minded women like Rabia al-Adawiyya could pursue their vocations in a life of renunciation of marriage.

IN PERSPECTIVE: The Triumphs of the Potential World Religions

The story of this chapter has been of cultural change, rather than religious conversion. Some cases of societies that Christianity, Islam, and Buddhism recruited happened in conditions similar to those pinpointed for individual conversions by psychological research. Violence, mass migration, enforced refugeeism, pestilence, famine, natural disaster, "culture shock," and demographic collapse constitute, on a large scale, influences comparable to the disturbing, dislocating events that often precede individual conversion. Yet, when we monitor the public progress of Christianity, Islam, and Buddhism, we glimpse, at best, shadows of individual religious experience. Instead, we see shrines multiplying; congregations growing; influence deepening on laws, rites, customs, and the arts.

By around 1000, all three religions had demonstrated their adaptability to different cultures and climates (see Map 9.2). Buddhism had big followings in China, Japan, Tibet, and southeast Asia and had spread into Central Asia along the Silk Roads. Christianity had a near monopoly in western Europe and was spreading east and north into Scandinavia and the Slav lands, while retaining the allegiance of communities scattered through Asia. Islam, dominant in southwest Asia and North Africa, spread by conquest, conversion, and migration among Turkic peoples and around the trade routes of the Indian Ocean and the Sahara. Among them, the three religions seemed to have carved up the world known to Ibn Wahab, whom we encountered at the start of this chapter discussing religion with the Chinese emperor. The bases from which all three religions would expand further, especially in the sixteenth and seventeenth centuries (see Chapter 18), to encompass even more of the world, had been laid.

Their competitive advantages with the religions they displaced were already evident. From an archaeological perspective, the decline of the old religions is as noticeable as the progress of the new. Pagan groves and temples became the sites of churches. Local deities reemerged as saints. Excavations at the shrine of the Irish saint, Gobnet, for instance, have yielded 130 anvils dedicated to the smith god, Goibhnin. In Scotland, the pagan goddess Brigid, associated with childbirth, became St. Bride. In the Islamic world, the sacred sites of paganism blended into the new religious landscape. The holiest site of Islam, the black stone of the **Kaaba** in Mecca, where Muslims have to perform pilgrimage at least once in their lifetimes, was a pagan shrine in the time of Muhammad, housing 360 deities. Muslims still perform the same rites—kissing the sacred stone, running the course of the sacred stream that flows nearby—as their pagan predecessors did. Buddhists had no difficulty incorporating local gods into the vast Buddhist pantheon, or sanctifying local shrines with relics of Buddhas.

This flexibility and adaptability made Christianity, Islam, and Buddhism suitable for projection around the world. These religions could combine local with universal appeal. This does not explain, of course, why other religions failed in this respect, or never made the attempt. The blend, which we now call Hinduism, of local Indian religions with the universally applicable philosophy of the Vedas (see Chapter 3) spread throughout India and parts of southeast Asia, but no farther. Daoism, similarly, never

The Kaaba. Promoters of new religions often had to reconsecrate pagan sites—it was easier to do that than to persuade worshippers to abandon them. Muhammad, for instance, made pilgrimage to the black rock housed in a building known as the Kaaba in Mecca compulsory for Muslims. As the picture shows, tens of thousands of pilgrims circle the site each year at the beginning of a series of annual rituals called the hajj. But the rock had already been a place of pagan pilgrimage in Arabia, and a shrine of many gods, for generations, perhaps centuries, before Muhammad's time.

reached beyond China. Nor, until migrants carried it to small colonies abroad, did Zoroastrianism penetrate beyond southwest Asia, where it struggled to compete with Islam. Traditional paganism, Manichaeanism, and the many cults that came and went, leaving little trace in the record, withered in the face of Christian, Muslim, or Buddhist competition. Some religions, such as Bon in Tibet, Shinto in Japan, and, as far as we know, the religions of sub-Saharan Africa, had no universal aspirations and were designed only for their traditional followers. To judge from later evidence, there was a good deal of exchange between the local and regional religions of Mesoamerica. Though, expressed in different languages and called by different names, the divine attributes personified in the arts of the peoples of what we now think of as Mexico and Central America were highly similar, or, at least, showed considerable overlaps, from the twelfth century to the sixteenth. We cannot say how much farther they might have spread had Christianity, arriving in the 1500s, not transformed the religious profile of the region. In the Americas, in sub-Saharan Africa, and in regions of which we know even less, such as Australia and the Pacific, the same reasons that inhibited the spread of other forms of culture also tended to limit the communicability of religions. There were no great, long-range avenues of communication, such as the Silk Roads and the monsoonal ocean. The kind of competition that Islam, Christianity, and Buddhism generated, never took effect.

Even as they changed the societies in which they triumphed, the new religions changed in their turn, compromising with vested interests, modifying their messages to suit mighty patrons, serving the needs of warriors and kings, even becoming organs of the state, instruments of government, means of training bureaucrats, and

CHRONOLOGY

(All dates are C.E.)

Second century	Earliest Christian monastic communities (Egypt)
ca. 250	Zhu Shixing becomes first Chinese to be ordained as Buddhist priest
ca. 314	King Trdat of Armenia converts to Christianity
ca. 340	King Ezana of Ethiopia converts to Christianity
366	Founding of Dunhuang monastery, western China
395	Proclamation of Christianity as official religion of Roman Empire
ca. 520	Conversion of kings of Paekche and Silla to Buddhism
538	First image of Buddha arrives in Japan
Sixth century	Life of Benedict of Nursia
Seventh and eighth centuries	Rapid expansion of Islam; spread of Buddhism in Tibet
Ninth century	Seaborne Muslim pilgrims begin to arrive in Mecca
ca. 988	Vladimir of Kiev converts to Orthodox Christianity

ICELAND

SCOTLAND

NORWAY

SWEDEN

Scandinavia

RUS

IRELAND

Whitby

DENMARK

Baltic Sea

ENGLAND

Saxons

Elbe

GERMANY

POLAND

Slavs

Kiev

UKRAINE

ATLANTIC
OCEAN

Rhine

Volga

FRANKISH
KINGDOM

HUNGARY

Dneiper

Braga

Alps

Po

Khazars

Danube

Black Sea

Caucasus

ITALY

Nursia

Rome

Monte Cassino

GEORGIA

Constantinople

Seville

Balkans

ARMENIA

Sicily

GREECE

Mediterranean Sea

North Africa

SYRIA

to Central Asia

Jerusalem

Baghdad

Alexandria

EGYPT

IRAQ

Muslim ruled
by 750 C.E.

N

Red Sea

Arabian
Peninsula

Nile

Mecca

Scale varies with perspective

4,444 km
(2,762 miles)

3,867 km
(6,228 miles)

30°

60°

MAP 9.2

The Christian World, ca.1000 C.E.

	Catholic Christianity
	Orthodox Christianity
	Christian churches believing Jesus to be wholly divine (Monophysite)
	Nestorian Christianity
	area with significant Christian minorities today

→ missions

✝ important church or monastery

Saxons people

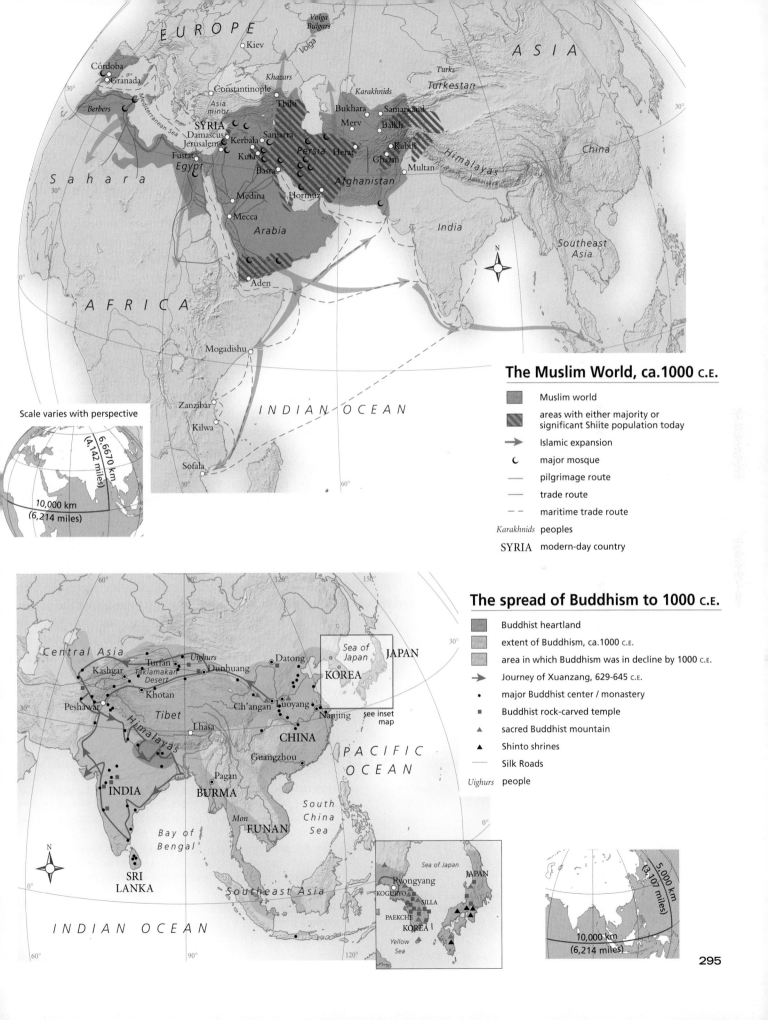

The Muslim World, ca.1000 C.E.

- ▨ Muslim world
- ▨ areas with either majority or significant Shiite population today
- → Islamic expansion
- ☾ major mosque
- — pilgrimage route
- — trade route
- --- maritime trade route
- *Karakhnids* peoples
- SYRIA modern-day country

Map labels (top)

EUROPE
ASIA
Kiev
Volga Bulgars
Volga
Córdoba
Granada
Constantinople
Khazars
Asia minor
Tbilsi
Turks
Turkestan
Karakhnids
Bukhara
Samarkand
Merv
Balkh
Berbers
Mediterranean Sea
SYRIA
Damascus
Jerusalem
Kerbala
Samarra
Persia
Herat
Kabul
Ghazni
China
Himalayas
Fustat
Egypt
Kufa
Basra
Afghanistan
Multan
Sahara
Medina
Hormuz
India
Southeast Asia
Mecca
Arabia
Africa
Aden
Mogadishu
Zanzibar
INDIAN OCEAN
Kilwa
Sofala

Scale varies with perspective
6,6670 km (4,142 miles)
10,000 km (6,214 miles)

The spread of Buddhism to 1000 C.E.

- ▨ Buddhist heartland
- ▨ extent of Buddhism, ca.1000 C.E.
- ▨ area in which Buddhism was in decline by 1000 C.E.
- → Journey of Xuanzang, 629-645 C.E.
- • major Buddhist center / monastery
- ■ Buddhist rock-carved temple
- ▲ sacred Buddhist mountain
- ▲ Shinto shrines
- — Silk Roads
- *Uighurs* people

Map labels (bottom)

Central Asia
Uighurs
Datong
Sea of Japan
JAPAN
KOREA
Kashgar
Turfan
Dunhuang
Taklamakan Desert
Khotan
Ch'angan
Luoyang
Peshawar
Nanjing
see inset map
Tibet
Lhasa
CHINA
Himalayas
INDIA
Pagan
Guangzhou
PACIFIC OCEAN
BURMA
Mon
FUNAN
South China Sea
Bay of Bengal
SRI LANKA
Southeast Asia
INDIAN OCEAN

Inset (Korea/Japan)
Sea of Japan
JAPAN
Pyongyang
KOGURYO
SILLA
PAEKCHE
KOREA
Yellow Sea

5,000 km (3,107 miles)
10,000 km (6,214 miles)

Crown of Reccesvinth. Even by the high standards of the jewel work of Germanic invaders of the Roman Empire, Visigothic goldsmiths were outstanding. Crowns like this one from Spain were made not to be worn but to hang over the altars of the churches as offerings from pious kings. The fringe of gold filigree, pearls, and crystals spells the name of the donor, King Reccesvinth (d. 672), although the initial R is lost.

communicating with subjects. A further consequence of expansion was that different traditions within each of the religions lost patience or touch with each other. Christians in different parts of the world adopted different theologies. In Ethiopia, for instance, the church believed that Jesus was wholly divine, with no distinctly human person. The Nestorian Christian communities of the Silk Roads preached the opposite doctrine: that the human Jesus was wholly human, leaving his divine nature in heaven. Theological differences gradually drove Christians in Europe apart. After 792, most congregations in western Europe followed the pope in modifying the creed, the basic statement of Christian belief, to make the Holy Spirit "proceed" from "the Father and the Son" rather than "the Father" alone. Most churches in eastern, Byzantine Europe denounced the new wording as heresy. Different Islamic states subscribed variously to Shiism and Sunnism (see Chapter 8) and to different interpretations of Islamic law. In Buddhism divisions between followers of the Theravada and Mahayana traditions were sometimes just as bitter, as rival sects multiplied.

Although all these religions had started by appealing to people of modest or marginal social position, they "took off" by converting rulers and elites. In any case of mass adhesion to a new religion, relatively few individuals experience personal conversion. Most become adherents by attraction, in imitation of converted leaders; or by compulsion, when rulers or conquerors impose the new religion by force; or by default, as the old religion withers; or by birth, as subsequent generations join a community more or less educated in the new religious self-description. More important for changing the religious profile of a whole society than promoting the new religion is banning or underprivileging the old one.

Ultimately, elites supported new religions—spiritual merits apart—because they saw advantages in doing so. The support of the church, for instance, was expensive for rulers and aristocrats. But it was worth it because it meant that God and his angels and saints became one's allies and friends. We can measure the value a typical royal convert got from the deal in the weight of gold and jewels in the votive crown that the seventh-century Spanish Visigothic king Reccesvinth hung in the sanctuary of his royal church. In return for such rich gifts, matched by comparable generosity in land, he got the prayers of the priests and monks, the services of a clerical bureaucracy, and the miraculous power of the relics of an army of martyrs. There was also a hidden advantage that no ruler could have banked on and that the next chapter must disclose. In the last three centuries of the first millennium, Islam, Buddhism, and, to a lesser extent, Christianity played vital and spectacular roles in new forms of environmental management.

PROBLEMS AND PARALLELS

1. What were the four chief ways in which world religions were spread? In which world religions did merchants play a leading role in spreading the faith?

2. What were the advantages Buddhism, Christianity, and Islam enjoyed over older religions?

3. How did rulers and elites use religion to consolidate and justify their power and control over societies?

4. Why is Japan a unique example of a world religion coexisting with a traditional native religion? Was such a working compromise possible in other areas of the world? Why or why not?

5. How did differing forms of Christianity arise on the margins of Christendom?

6. How did Christianity and Islam trickle down to the masses after the elites adopted these religions in Eurasia and Africa? How did average citizens benefit from adopting (or not adopting) these religions?

7. Why did monasticism play such a large role in the early history of Buddhism and Christianity? Why was monasticism less important in the Islamic world? What new roles did women acquire?

8. How did the triumph of Buddhism, Christianity, and Islam change the societies and cultures where they triumphed? How were they in turn changed and modified?

DOCUMENTS IN GLOBAL HISTORY

- Ibn Wahab: an Arab Merchant visits Tang China
- Eusebius of Caesarea, selections from *The Life of Constantine*
- Isidore of Seville's T-O Map of the World
- Rabia al-Adawiyya, "Brothers, My Peace is in My Aloneness"

Please see the Primary Source CD-ROM for additional sources related to this chapter.

READ ON

To understand the problems of what conversion means, A. D. Nock, *Conversion: The Old and the New in Religion from Alexander the Great to Augustine of Hippo* (1933) is an indispensable classic, and K. F. Morrison, *Understanding Conversion* (1992) is an up-to-date introduction.

On Buddhism H. Bechert and R. Gombrich, eds., *The World of Buddhism: Buddhist Monks and Nuns in Society and Culture* (1984) is a superb survey, much wider in scope than the title implies. Works which deal with the reception of Buddhism in particular cultures are E. Zürcher, *The Buddhist Conquest of China* (1959), which is a work of outstanding scholarship; K. Lal Hazra, *Royal Patronage of Buddhism in Ancient India* (1984); M. T. Kapstein, *The Tibetan Assimilation of Buddhism* (2000); and the collections of essays edited by L. R. Lancaster and C. S. Yu, *Introduction of Buddhism to Korea* (1989); *Assimilation of Buddhism in Korea* (1991); and (with K. Suh) *Buddhism in Koryo* (1996). *The Cambridge History of Japan* (1988) deals expertly with all aspects of Japanese history in the period, include the reception of Buddhism. The travels of Xuangzang and other Chinese monks in search of Buddhist learning are covered in J. Mirsky, *The Great Chinese Travelers* (1964).

On Manichaeanism, P. Mirecki and J. BeDuhn, *Emerging from Darkness: Studies in the Recovery of Manichaean Sources* (1997) is a fascinating insight into the development of current scholarship. C. Mackerras, *The Uighur Empire* (1972) is a masterly survey.

On the spread of Islam it is helpful to consult G. S. P. Freeman-Grenville, *Historical Atlas of Islam* (2002). For the Indian Ocean, K. Chaudhuri, *Asia before Europe* (1990) is again to be recommended, with a word of caution about the demanding nature of this work.

For Africa, T. Insoll, *The Archaeology of Islam in sub-Saharan Africa* (2003) is of great importance. M. Hiskett, *The Course of Islam in Africa* (1994) is a useful introduction. On East Africa, J. Trimingham, *Islam in East Africa* (1964), and M. Horton and J. Middleton, *The Swahili* (2000) (which is a good general history of the coastlands) can be recommended. For West Africa, M. Hiskett, *The Development of Islam in West Africa* (1984) and J. S. Trimingham, *A History of Islam in West Africa* (1962) are standard. For the Turks, an interesting source from the pre-Muslim period is G. Lewis, ed., *The Book of Dede Korkut* (1974). The important work I cite on Persia is R.W. Bulliet, *Conversion to Islam in the Medieval Period: An Essay in Quantitative History* (1979).

On Christianity, W. H. C. Frend, *The Rise of Christianity* (1984); R. MacMullen, *Christianizing the Roman Empire* (1984); and R. Fletcher, *The Barbarian Conversion: From Paganism to Christianity* (1997) are fundamental and between them take the story down to the late Middle Ages. Exemplary case studies can be found in H. R. Mayr-Harting, *The Coming of Christianity to Anglo-Saxon England* (1972), J. Muldoon, ed., *Varieties of Religious Conversion in the Middle Ages* (1997), and B. Sawyer et al., eds., *The Christianization of Scandinavia* (1987).

For works on Constantine, see Chapter 8.

For the rise of Christianity in Ethiopia, S. Munro-Hay, *Aksum* (1991) is vigorous and makes much use of the stela texts; D. W. Phillipson, *Ancient Ethiopia* (2002) is a superb survey based on archaeological evidence; G. W. B. Huntingford, *The Historical Geography of Ethiopia* (1989) is a basic and classic work.

For the Caucasus, N. Garsoian, *Church and Culture in Early Medieval Armenia* (1999), and *Armenia between Byzantium and the Sasanians* (1985) are collections of significant essays. C. Toumanoff, *Studies in Christian Caucasian History* (1963), and D. Braund, *Georgia in Antiquity* (1994) are also useful and important.

On Vladimir, F. Butler, *Enlightener of the Rus* (2000) is an interesting work, tracing the subject's historical reputation. The work of S. Franklin is fundamental.

On the origins of monasticism, G. Gould *The Desert Fathers on Monastic Community* (1993), and W. Harmless, *Desert Christians* (2004) are highly instructive; and M. Dunn *The Emergence of Monasticism* (2000) is a good introduction. There are many editions of *The Rule of St. Benedict*.

On Sufism, F. Meier, *Essays on Islamic Piety and Mysticism* (1999) contains many interesting pieces, while A. D. Knysh, *Islamic Mysticism* (2000) surveys the whole history of the subject efficiently. For Buddhist monasticism, the already-cited work edited by Bechert and Gombrich is excellent.

The long quotation on page 284 is from S. H. Gross and O. P. Sherbowitz, eds. *The Russian Primary Chronicle: Laurentian Text* (1953), p. 111.

CHAPTER 10
Remaking the World: Innovation and Renewal on Environmental Frontiers in the Late First Millennium

The small castle of Qusayr Amra dates from the reign of Caliph Walid I (ca. 705-715). It contains his spectacular bathhouse, lavishly decorated with paintings, including portraits of the monarchs he considered his rivals: the rulers of Byzantium, Ethiopia, Armenia, and Visigothic Spain.

One of the oddest monuments of the early Islamic world is a bathhouse at Qusayr Amra (koo-SAY-ehr AHM-rah) in the Jordanian desert. In the early eighth century, it was attached to the caliph's hunting lodge. Here the successor of the prophet Muhammad could relax, unseen. He could also relax Islamic condemnations of art that depicted human beings and animals, for Muhammad was said to have specifically exempted bathhouses from such bans.

JORDAN

ETHIOPIA

The walls and ceilings of the bathhouse are smothered with lavish mosaics depicting the human form, made by local Christian artists. The caliph could lounge in his bath, enjoying scenes of his subjects, engaged in their everyday lives. In one room, he had an image of a naked female bather before his eyes. Another wall was devoted to a different kind of satisfaction—decorated with six portraits of failed enemies of Islam. Two of the images are too decayed to be recognizable. The others show a Visigothic king from Spain, Roman and Persian monarchs, and an Ethiopian emperor, depicted as the equal of the other great rulers of the world.

● ● ● ● ●

In the eighth century, Ethiopia was not yet in the state of collapse that had overcome the Roman and Persian realms, but it was in trouble. Ethiopia had its own "barbarian" hinterlands. The infiltration of nomadic peoples from the north seems to have driven Ethiopian families to resettle southward. No coinage was being issued. Monumental building had stopped. Squatters soon began to take over abandoned mansions in Axum, the Ethiopian capital. At the port of Adulis on the Red Sea, eighth-century ash lies thickly over ruined buildings, evidence that fire had wrecked the city. By the ninth century, central political control was hard or impossible to maintain. Later writers remembered shadowy, allegedly demonic female rulers, who seized power in the tenth century and desecrated religious shrines. "God has become angry with us," wrote a fugitive king. "We have become wanderers. . . . The heavens no longer send rain and the earth no longer gives its fruits."

Environmental influences played a big part in Ethiopia's eclipse. The surviving literary evidence, authored by monks, blames bad times on pagan revivals. According to the same sources, Christian resurgence brought recovery in the twelfth century. The archaeological record tells a different story. Increasing hardship drove the royal court from Axum. Trees vanished from hills overexploited for

FOCUS questions

- HOW DID geography influence the transmission of culture in sub-Saharan Africa and the Americas?
- WHAT WERE the environmental consequences of the Islamic conquests?
- HOW DID Japan, China, and the states of southeast Asia seek to stimulate economic growth?
- HOW DID Pacific islanders succeed in colonizing the Pacific?
- WHERE DID Christendom expand in the eighth and ninth centuries?
- WHERE—if anywhere—did civilizations experience "dark ages" in this period?
- HOW WIDESPREAD during the history of this period was ecological experiment?

wood and charcoal. Intensive farming exhausted the soil. Heavy rains aggravated erosion, stripping slopes down to the stony subsoil. Mudslides buried buildings. Below the old volcanic hills, once-rich earth turned to dust. Axum never recovered its ancient greatness, but remained a frequent place of coronation for kings seeking to legitimize their rule. To renew the state and resume expansion, Ethiopians had to find new resources, new frontiers, new techniques.

From around 700 to 1000, states all over the world responded to similar problems. Slowly, uncertainly, unspectacularly, the discovery and exploitation of new resources, and the colonization of previously under-exploited lands, equipped widely dispersed societies, in parts of Eurasia, Africa, the Americas, and the Pacific, with the means to sustain bigger populations, longer-range trade, and more ambitious environmental exploitation. The effect was to stimulate recovery and renewal in some of the regions the events of Chapter 8 had disrupted, and to encourage rare or unprecedented initiatives elsewhere. Previously underrepresented parts of the world seem to leap into the historical record, because intense new activity leaves marks in the environment, and, in some cases, memorials of art, thought, and high politics.

New ways to manage the environment multiplied during these centuries. They constitute something like a global story—or at least, a story that spans most of the world. Outcomes, however, continued to vary, and in some regions, such as the Islamic world, China, and Japan, the innovations of the period proved more durable than in others. What we might call the **axial zone** of the world expanded. The densely populated central belt of Eurasia, stretching from China to Europe and North Africa—the region that had seen so many experiments in civilization for so long—got bigger, as it incorporated new frontiers within it. In the Americas, sub-Saharan Africa, and the Pacific, similar but smaller zones began to take shape but remained fragile (see Map 10.1).

ISOLATION AND INITIATIVE: SUB-SAHARAN AFRICA AND THE AMERICAS

African Geography

In sub-Saharan Africa, it is tempting to treat Ethiopia as the exception that proves the rule: the one region where developments historians usually treat as crucial—states and empires, radical modifications of the environment, the maintenance of a literate tradition—have been comparable with those in the most favored parts of Eurasia. Geography is often said to imprison sub-Saharan peoples. While great axes of communication cross-fertilize much of the Old World, the Sahara and the Indian Ocean separate most of Africa from those highways of cultural exchange. Geography also separates African peoples from each other. Except on the Mediterranean and along the coast north of the Mozambique Channel in East Africa, shores exposed to the wind—*lee shores*, as sailors call them—make communication difficult by sea. The continent's high

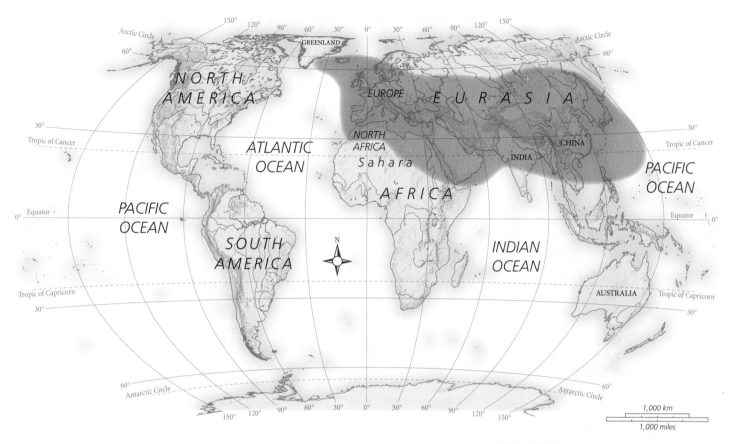

MAP 10.1

The Axial Zone, ca. 1000

Axial zone

ground has relatively abrupt breaks, so that rivers fall sharply and are hard to navigate. In any case, Africa has only five or six major river basins, widely separated. Half of Africa's river drainage never reaches the coast. Dense forest impedes communications across the heart of the continent, where malarial mosquitoes are deadly to outsiders who have not developed resistance to the disease. Some of the flows of culture that we can detect, such as the spread of farming and of Bantu languages (see Chapter 5), took centuries longer than comparable transmissions in Eurasia.

THE EMERGENCE OF GHANA AND GAO Still, it is surprising that there has never been much exchange along the obvious axis of transcontinental communication in Africa: the Sahel, the belt of grassland that links East Africa where Ethiopian civilization took shape, to another precocious region in the Niger valley in West Africa. Here, urban life, commerce, and industry show up in the archaeological record of the third century B.C.E. onward. By the first century C.E., at Jenne-Jeno, where floods fed the soil, farmers and ironworkers grew millet and rice. The population was reputedly so dense that royal proclamations could be "called out from the top of the city's walls and transmitted by criers from one village to the next."

The region was a natural crossroads, where traders from the north could deal in slaves from the south, desert salt, local copper, and gold from the mines of

Figure of a sacred king. The Oni, or king, of Ile-Ife, excavated at Ita Yemoo, Nigeria in 1957, eleventh or twelfth century C.E. The king is shown draped in beads, a symbol of royalty. The fleshy naturalism is typical of the finest of Ife works, and the proportions emphasize the king's sacred head.

Senegambia and the middle Volta River. Toward 1000, two states impressed Arab visitors: Ghana and Gao (gow). Ghana inspired particularly vivid reports (see "Going to the Source: Arab Accounts of Ghana," pages 404–407). It was located in the territory of the Soninke (son-in-KAY) people, west of the middle Niger River. Its capital at Kumbi-Saleh had houses of stone and acacia wood, and a royal compound. It was said that a sacred snake with a sensitive snout that sniffed out royal quality from among the contenders chose the king. Enriched by taxes on trade, the monarchs of Ghana and Gao attracted the reverence paid to sacred beings. At royal audiences, subjects prostrated themselves and covered their heads with dust. When the king of Gao ate, all business in the town was suspended, until shouts announced he had finished.

Sacred kingship spread along the Sahel. The Zaghawa of the Chad region in the late ninth century had "no towns," according to an Arab traveler's report, but "they worshipped their king as if he were Allah." There was a difference from the setup in Gao. To appear divine, the Zaghawan king took his meals in secret. Evidence of divine kingship—Ghana and Gao Perhaps influenced by—also begins to appear in Yoruba (YOH-roo-bah) territory on the lower Niger River from the tenth century, in the form of clay portraits of individuals—both men and women—with elaborate headgear and hairstyles. Had contacts developed across the Sahel between West African realms and Ethiopia, rather in the way that the steppeland linked Europe to China, African history might, in the long run, more closely have resembled that of Eurasia. But the West African kingdoms remained focused on relations north across the Sahara, while Ethiopia's avenues of approach to the rest of the world led every direction but westward: north to the Nile, east to the Indian Ocean, south along the Rift valley (see Map 10.2).

American Geography

It is tempting to use similar arguments about the geography of the Americas to explain why the Old World developed differently from the New. The shape of the American hemisphere slowed diffusion of new culture and new crops, which had to travel across climate zones through the narrow, central continental funnel. Most of the great rivers flow east and west from the mountain spines that run up and down North and South America, and only the Mississippi River traverses much distance from north to south.

Still, the effects of isolation could be overcome. The peoples of the Andes knew little or nothing, as far as we know, of those of Mesoamerica, until Spanish conquerors put them in touch with each other. That isolation did not prevent civilizations from developing in the Andean region, in parallel with those of Mexico and Central America, taking advantage of the different ecosystems that a world of slopes and valleys, microclimates and diverse plants and animals provided. The highlands of North America, on the other hand, housed nothing comparable. This may have been, in part, because the Andes and the Sierra Madre in Central America and Mexico are better placed than the mountains of the north: close to rain forests, seas, and swamps for maximum biological diversity. But the Rocky Mountains presented, in one respect, a more favorable environment. They provided a habitat for a large animal that could have been domesticated—the bighorn sheep—but that for unknown reasons was not—perhaps because it likes to inhabit relatively high altitudes in regions where humans have, for most of history, preferred to live at lower altitudes and exploit the abundant game, such as bison and deer.

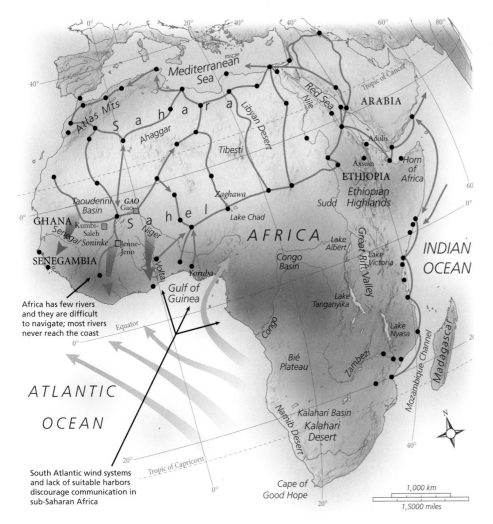

MAP 10.2

African Geography

— trade route

■ city described on pages 301–302

● other city/town/village

GAO state

Yoruba people

➤ South Atlantic trade winds

➤ African wind systems

Africa has few rivers and they are difficult to navigate; most rivers never reach the coast

South Atlantic wind systems and lack of suitable harbors discourage communication in sub-Saharan Africa

MOCHE AND NAZCA Similarly, though North and South America both have arid deserts, the effort to civilize them encountered earlier success in the south (see Map 10.3). One of the strangest deserts in the world is in northern Peru. Except when El Niño drenches the land, almost no rain falls. The region is cool, although only five degrees south of the equator, and dank with ocean fog. Little grows naturally, but modest rivers streak the flats, creating an opportunity to irrigate. The sea is at hand, with rich fishing grounds, and the mines of guano (manure from sea birds) provide rich fertilizer to turn desert dust into cultivable soil. From the third century to the eighth, the civilization known as Moche (MOH-cheh) made this desert rich with turkeys and guinea pigs, corn, squash, peppers, potatoes, and peanuts, which the people admired so much that they modeled them in gold and silver.

Under platforms, built as stages for royal rituals, their rulers' graves lie: divine impersonators in golden masks, with earspools decorated with objects of the hunt, scepters and bells with scenes of human sacrifice, necklets with models of shrunken heads in gold or copper with golden eyes, and portraits of a divine sacrificer wielding his bone knife. At San José de Moro, a woman was buried with limbs encased in

Gulf of
Mexico

Tropic of Cancer

Sierra Madre

Mesoamerica

see inset map

Caribbean Sea

CENTRAL
AMERICA

GUATEMALA   HONDURAS

▽ Tula

95°

Plat

Yucatá
Peninsu

Palenque ●

Tikal ●

Lowlands

Highlands

Cop

15°

90°

PACIFIC
OCEAN

1,000 km

1,000 miles

Andes

Amazon

Marajó
Island

0°

Ayacucho
Valley

Lake Titicaca

BOLIVIA

B R A Z I L

S O U T H
A M E R I C A

Tropic of Capricorn

Tropic

80°

70°

30°

MAP 10.3

Mesoamerica and the And
300 C.E. to 1000 C.E.

Maya cultural area

Moche cultural area

Tiahuanaco cultural area

Nazca cultural area

Huari cultural area

🌽 maize

○ beans

◡ squash

⬭ cacao

🦃 turkeys

🐹 guinea pigs

🥜 peanuts

⬭ peppers

○ potatoes

▽ irrigated river valleys

△ underground aqueduct

HONDURAS modern-day country

Moche

10°

Huari

Nazca

Tiahuanaco

ATLANTIC
OCEAN

80°

70°

60°

plates of precious metals. In 2006, archaeologists in southern Peru found another female Moche mummy who had been buried not only with gold jewelry but also with weapons. Farther south, in the same period, in the even more inhospitable desert of northern Chile, the people known as the Nazca (NAS-cah) built underground aqueducts to protect irrigation water from the sun. Above ground, they created some of the most ambitious works of art in the world: stunning representations of nature—a hurtling hummingbird, a cormorant spread for flight, sinuous fish—and bold abstract lines, triangles, and spirals, scratched in ochre deposits that film the rock. The dry air has preserved them to this day. Some of the images are 1,000-feet wide, too vast to be visible except from a height the artists could not reach, capable of permanently arousing the imagination.

Despite these achievements, the desert remained a fragile environment for such ambitious ways of life as those of the Moche and Nazca. They survived repeated droughts, which archaeologists have inferred from cores sampled from nearby mountain glaciers. El Niño events periodically drove away the fish and washed away the irrigation works. These were occurrences frequent enough for the locals to learn to live with. After the mid–eighth century, however, no mounds were built, no great artworks made, and the irrigated land dwindled. No one knows why, though most scholars speculate that the people may have overexploited their environment, or an unusually protracted drought may have defeated them.

ANDEAN DEVELOPMENTS The center of gravity of large-scale innovation shifted inland and upslope to the high Andes, though with little long-term gain in security. The city of Huari, 9,000 feet up in the Ayacucho valley in Peru, lasted, as a metropolis, only from the seventh century to the ninth. It had garrison buildings, dormitories for the elite, and communal kitchens, with a population of at least 20,000 clustered around it. It also seems to have had satellite towns dotted about the Ayacucho area.

At over 12,000 feet above sea level, potatoes fed the city of Tiahuanaco (tee-ah-wahn-AH-koh) in Bolivia because its altitude was hostile to growing grains. The city had already reached its greatest extent before Huari was founded, spreading over 40 acres. Mound agriculture could feed up to 40,000 people there. The tillers built stone platforms topped with clay and silt. They drew water from Lake Titicaca through channels to irrigate their mounds and protect them from violent changes of air temperature. Beds in this form stretched more than nine miles from the lakeside and could produce up to 30,000 tons of potatoes a year. By about 1000, building had ceased, and the site was becoming abandoned—again, for unknown reasons, but perhaps because of local overexploitation of the soil, or a regional shift in the balance of power. Tiahuanaco, as it gradually subsided into ruins, became a source of inspiration for all subsequent efforts to cultivate and build in the Andes. In short, the problem of initiating and sustaining civilization in the Americas remained acute throughout the period.

THE MAYA No case has excited more curiosity than that of the Maya. They inhabited—their descendants still inhabit—three contrasting environments: the abrupt, volcanic highlands of Guatemala, where microclimates create diverse

Nazca lines. The Nazca made the vast images for which they are famous by scraping the surface of the desert in Peru to reveal the bare rock underneath. But why did they do it? Vivid, intricate designs, such as this monkey, were too big to be fully visible except from the air. The people who made them can only have experienced them by walking the pathways the patterns made. The straight lines that accompany the images may have served as maps, perhaps indicating underground irrigation channels, but the pictorial devices themselves remain a mystery.

Mayan kings. The legitimacy that royal ancestry conferred was an important part of Maya kingship—especially, perhaps, when things were going badly. Yax Pasaj, who became king of Copán in 763, when he was still a small boy, ruled in a time of economic decline and political unrest. This may be why he had himself depicted in the company of all Copán's previous rulers, seated as if in conference around a small stone platform designed, perhaps, for the king to sit on. The kingdom dissolved shortly after Yax Pasaj's death.

eco-niches at different altitudes; the dry, gently hilly, limestone plateau of Yucatán (yoo-kah-THAN), the peninsula on Mexico's Caribbean coast, where agriculture depends on irrigation from pools and wells; and tropical lowlands in Central America with dense forests of heavy seasonal rain. There is bound to be some cultural diversity across such varied environments, and among these regions, the chronology of Maya civilization varied considerably. The lowlands experienced a Classic Age of monumental-scale building and art from about the third to about the tenth centuries, whereas the plateau "peaked" later in these respects. But Maya civilization has some surprisingly uniform features.

The Maya demonstrated, in spectacular ways, common threads of Native American civilizations seen from the Olmecs onward (see Chapter 4). Maya rulers had three areas of responsibility: war, communication with the gods and the dead, and building and embellishing monumental ceremonial centers. Royal portraits, often engraved on slabs of stone and displayed in the grand plazas where their subjects assembled, show rulers in roles similar to those of professional shamans, wearing divine disguises, or engaged in rituals of bloodletting designed to induce visions. Amazingly, we can still confront the images of many kings. At Palenque (pa-LEHN-keh), in the rain forest of southern Mexico, the seventh-century King Pacal (pa-KAL) is depicted on his tomb—dead, but refertilizing the world. A ceiba tree, sacred to the Maya, springs from his loins. In Copán (koh-PAN) in Honduras, the kings of the Macaw dynasty from the fifth century to the ninth, are shown communing together, as if at a celestial conference. At Tikal, when the sun is in the west and gilds the huge temple where he was buried, you can still pick out the vast outline of the fading image of King Jasaw Chan Kaui'il (ha-SA-oo chan kah-wee-EEL), molded onto the temple facade.

Politically, the Maya world, like that of classical Greece (see Chapter 5), was divided among city-states that sometimes engaged in territorial expansion, sometimes in close alliance, and sometimes in attempts at regional overlordship. But, in the period under consideration, they did not form large empires. They were perhaps too equally matched for imperialism to succeed. They were competitive in trade and competitive in war, which, for most of them, seems to have been almost constant. Wars were fought by terror. Boasts of captives sacrificed are common in the texts. Mayan art often depicts scenes of sacrifice—including torturing to death and dismemberment while the victim was still alive.

Everything the Maya thought important—everything on Earth that they thought worth recording—happened in and around the ceremonial centers. The countryside was there to support and sustain those centers. In these cities were monumental buildings, intended to house elites and display rites to appease the gods and promote civic solidarity. Elite dwellings were imposing and built of stone, but the facades of some of them are adorned with carvings of humble dwellings, such as the Maya peasantry still inhabit today, built of reeds and thatch with a single stone lintel. The temples, which often doubled as tombs, always evoked the mounds on which, in the lowlands, farming was practiced: structures resembling pyramids or Mesopotamian ziggurats, with vast, terracelike flights of steps, surmounted by platforms on which rituals were enacted. Typically, especially in the highlands and lowlands, they were topped by false facades jutting into the sky, decorated with molded reliefs, displaying the symbols of the city, the portraits of the kings, the records of war, and the rewards of wealth. Even today, though faded and decayed, many of these roof combs still rise gleaming over forest treetops. In their time, for travelers, traders, or would-be aggressors, they carried an unmistakable message of propaganda: an invitation to commerce, a deterrent against attack.

These monumental centers were surrounded by markets and thousands—sometimes many thousands—of peasants' flimsy dwellings, in a landscape adapted for intensive agriculture. Small fields called *milpas*, were carved into highland terraces or dredged, in the lowlands, between canals that were used for irrigation or fish farming. The fields were sown with the three Native American staples: maize, beans, and squash, supplemented with other foods according to region or locality. Or they were devoted to cash crops, like cacao, which was in high demand as the source of the luxury beverage that accompanied rituals and feasts.

The Maya possessed a singular feature—it is tempting to say, a secret ingredient—because their writing system, the most expressive and complete known in the Native American world before the arrival of Europeans, did not spread to other culture areas. Much more common in lowland regions than in the plateau and highlands, these writings were carved in stone and therefore able to withstand destruction and decay. Despite the efforts of Christian missionaries in colonial times, who labored to erase memories of paganism at the cost of destroying valuable old texts, a vast body of Mayan inscriptions survives from the cities of the classic age from about the third to about the tenth centuries. Since the 1950s, heroic scholarship has gradually deciphered it.

The Dresden codex. The Maya almanac known as the Dresden Codex contains a wealth of data on agriculture, divination, and religion. But its most remarkable contents, perhaps, are the detailed astronomical observations and predictions, especially the table recording the cycle of Venus, one page of which is shown here. The red bars and dots at bottom right are numbers, adding up to 584—the average number of days between the dates on which Venus rises with the sun. Such dates were favorable for war and sometimes foretold drought and death. The gods depicted represent from top to bottom, the Morning Star, Venus as bringer of war, and Venus demanding sacrifice.

Virtually all Maya writing falls into two categories: first, records of astronomical observations and priestly timekeeping, which was a vital area of interest in Maya efforts to communicate with the gods and appease nature; second, dynastic records—the genealogies of kings, the records of their conquests, sacrifices, and acts of communion with their ancestors. On commemorative stone slabs and altars, on the facades of buildings, and in one case, at Copán in northern Honduras, on a monumental stairway, the records of ruling dynasties are transmitted in such detail, with such a wealth of meticulous chronological and genealogical information, that we are better informed about the political history of some Maya states than many European ones of the same era. A prominent theme of the royal records is always the observation, celebration, and commemoration of the movements of stars and planets. Especially in the lowlands, astronomical computations were a Maya obsession. In that region, the Maya dated almost every recorded event, from the third century to the tenth, in at least three different ways: according to the cycle of the planet Venus, as well as of the sun, and according to the number of days since an arbitrary starting point more than 3,000 years in the past.

Of course, all the surviving written evidence is propaganda. All of it was produced under the patronage of states. The claims and counterclaims of conquests and captures are evidence not of what the kings actually did but what they thought important. The central drama of kingship—the ritual the inscriptions most often commemorate—was the spilling of royal blood. A king would use a bone needle or spike to draw blood from his penis or scatter it from his hand. A queen might perform the ceremony by dragging a knotted thong, studded with sharp bones or spines, through a perforation in her tongue. Blotted onto bark, the blood would burn with hallucinatory drugs in an open fire. Enraptured by the fumes and by loss of blood, the monarch would succumb to a vision, characteristically depicted as a serpent rising from the smoke. The serpent was the mouthpiece of the ancestors. Their message usually justified war.

Maya civilization largely abandoned the lowlands in the ninth and tenth centuries. New building in ceremonial centers ended. Inscriptions ceased. The royal cult disappeared. Evidence vanished of rich elites and professions specialized in learning and the arts. Squatters occupied the ruins of decaying ceremonial centers. Traditional scholarship has dramatized and mystified these events as the collapse of classic Maya civilization—an echo of the decline and fall of the Eurasian civilizations of the axial age. It seems more helpful to see what happened as the displacement of the centers of the Maya world from the lowlands to the plateau. Still, it is mysterious. None of the explanations scholars suggest fit the chronology or the evidence. War is unlikely to have put an end to the lowland tradition. The Maya practiced wars so constantly that warfare must have served a useful purpose in their society. Spells of severe and prolonged drought certainly overlapped with the period of decline, but do not seem to have matched it. Political revolutions—rebellions of the masses or struggles within the elite—might have overthrown the regimes. But even if there were direct evidence of such upheavals, we would still need to explain why they occurred at roughly the same time in so many states.

That elite activities ended only in one eco-zone suggests that an environmental explanation should help us understand what happened. The lowlands were always a vulnerable environment, hostile

Civilizations of the Americas, ca. 200–1100

ca. 200–900	Flourishing of Moche and Nazca civilizations
ca. 200–1100	Maya Classic Age (lowlands)
1000	Andean city of Tiahuanaco abandoned
ca. 1106–1200	Tula abandoned

The date of the ritual, shown here, was October 26, 709.

The carvings announce that the king and queen are shedding their blood.

ROYAL BLOODLETTING

The reign of Itzamnaaj B'alam ("Shield Jaguar") II of Yaxchilán (681–742), in what is today Mexico, produced some of the finest stone reliefs in which Maya rulers commemorated their performance of important rituals. The most common ritual was royal bloodletting, which was intended to provoke visions. During these bloodlettings, kings communicated with ancestors or gods.

The king wears a sacrificed captive's skull on his headdress and an emblem of the sun on his breast.

The queen draws a spiked thong through her tongue to spill her blood. A king would draw blood from his penis. Bark paper in the bowl below the monarchs absorbed the blood, which was then burned. The monarchs would inhale the smoke to induce a trance.

What does this stone relief tell us about Mayan kingship?

Bird claw. Cut from a sheet of mica, this sublime representation of the claw of a hawk or eagle was buried in a chief's grave in what is now Ross County, Ohio, in about 400 C.E. Hands and birds of prey were the symbols most often placed in the graves of the region's chieftains in this period.

to intensive agriculture and monumental building. In some ways, it is more surprising that such practices should have happened at all, and attained such impressive achievements, than that they should ultimately have failed. To sustain hundreds of cities and what were evidently densely packed populations, the Maya probably had to exploit their environment close to the limit of its possibilities.

TULA For a while, the influence and, in some degree, the power of the central Mexican empire of Teotihuacán stretched into the Maya world. For instance, on a carving at Tikal, Teotihuacáno bodyguards flank a fifth-century king. Yet, as we saw in Chapter 8, Teotihuacán itself withered, for unknown reasons, in the eighth and ninth centuries. This vast metropolis—once the center of a population that could probably be numbered in six figures—was never reoccupied, but became something like what we today would call a heritage site: revered and remembered by peoples who imitated its art and recalled its grandeur and its passing in their poetry. A new metropolis arose, well to the northwest, at Tula, the "garden of the gods," where groves of stone pillars and ceremonial enclosures, irrigated by bloodsacrifices, justified the garden name. The environment at Tula was similar to the almost rainless limestone hills the Maya favored when the center of their civilization removed from the lowlands to Yucatán—except that at Tula, rivers could supply irrigation. The region already had a history of unstable settlement and, by comparison with most earlier Maya cities or with Teotihuacán, Tula did not last long. Its site was abandoned in the twelfth century, but the ruins continued to inspire experiments in urbanization.

The Maize Frontiers

We can sum up all these New World histories of the late first millennium as efforts to open up new frontiers of exploitation for intensive agriculture, state formation, and city-building—activities of kinds formerly confined to narrowly limited areas, and vulnerable to periodic extinction. Hunter–gatherers, too, could engage with their environment in more productive ways. On the northwest coast of North America, houses got bigger as fishhooks got more plentiful and became more specialized. Along the northern edge of America, whale hunters were working their way along the Arctic coast, spreading new hunting and fishing techniques as they went, reaching Greenland by about 1000.

In other parts of the Americas, new crops and new technologies were extending farmers' frontiers, sometimes with transforming effects. Between the Missouri and Ohio River valleys, for instance, a large trading network flourished among peoples of similar material culture from about 200 to about 400. They buried their dead extravagantly, with copper earrings and breastplates, clay figures and smoking pipes, and ornaments carved from flat sheets of mica* in the shape of leaves and claws. They built tombs into mounds of astonishingly elaborate design: One in Ohio is in the shape of a long, coiling serpent—detectable as such only from a practically unattainable height, like the artworks of the Nazca in Chile. Their way of life, or, at least, of death ended sometime after 500. Lead-

---

*Mica: an aluminum-like mineral

○ MAKING CONNECTIONS ○

EXPANDING STATES OF THE AMERICAS, 200–900

REGION/CULTURE →	ENVIRONMENT →	POLITICAL ORGANIZATION →	ACHIEVEMENTS
South America Moche and Nazca	Desert; adjacent to Pacific Ocean; cool weather; little precipitation; abundant fish; small rivers	Communities governed by elites	Highly developed ceramics, gold/silver work; pottery; elaborate irrigation systems, some underground
Andean highlands (Huari)	Mountainous; glacier-fed streams and lakes; cultivable soil	Empire governing highlands and coast after decline of Moche; administrative centers; satellite towns	Intensive mound agriculture (potatoes); religious centers; road networks
Mesoamerica Maya	Contrasting environments: volcanic highlands of Guatemala; limestone plateau of Yucatán; tropical lowlands	City-states with rulers responsible for war, communication with gods; numerous ceremonial sites	Large-scale cities with monumental architecture; writing system and literature; long-distance trade networks; intensive agriculture, industry fueling population growth
Tula	Highlands with access to rivers, trade routes	City-states with ceremonial enclosures; use of blood sacrifice	Successor to Teotihuacán, largest city-state in Mesoamerica; monumental architecture; intensive irrigation
North America	Wide range of environments from mountains, to forests, deserts, open plains	Primarily chiefdoms, with larger-scale communities in Mississippi, Missouri, Ohio River valleys	As maize agriculture spreads, agricultural populations increase, displacing hunter–gatherer groups; large-scale mounds, tombs mark large population centers

ership of society changed as maize cultivation spread through the region, and population grew.

This was the period of the great extension of maize cultivation into regions of North America formerly inhabited almost exclusively by hunter–gatherers, displacing former power groups, coaxing chiefdoms into existence and existing chiefdoms toward statehood. Farmers brought maize and beans into the central plains and, in some places from the Dakotas to the Red River in Canada, built burial mounds and earthworks similar to those found earlier along the Ohio and Missouri Rivers. In some respects, this process looks like another case of a culture not extinguished, but changed and displaced from its former heartland. Maize farming reached the Great Basin of the North American plains, at sites where pottery and rock art were also made for the first time in this period. Beginning after 700, in the North American southwest, where maize had been long established (see Chapter 5), large dwellings of adobe or stone displaced the semiunderground houses in which people formerly sheltered. Villages got larger, building toward the urban network that emerged around 1000 and that is a subject for the next chapter. Meanwhile, in the southeast, the arrival of maize and, by around the year 1000, beans fed the ancestors of the large-scale builders of the early part of the next millennium.

On Marajó Island, in the mouth of the Amazon River in Brazil, although there is no evidence of new crops or techniques, people were practicing traditional agriculture with enhanced efficiency in an expanded area. Clusters of villages got denser after the middle of the first millennium, with mounds raised for ceremonies as well as for agriculture. Here, the bones of the elite, boiled of their flesh, were buried in pots with clay representations of female genitals and gifts of beads, axes, and other valuables dependent on rank. The richly decorated burial urns grant glimpses of the creatures of their myths: turtles, scorpions, snakes, lizards, alligators, and almond-eyed humans.

THE ISLAMIC WORLD AND THE ENVIRONMENT

So cultures widely scattered around the New World showed how basic tool kits or limited new crops could have profound effects. This feature of the period was paralleled in the Old World—especially, on a huge scale, in the Islamic world. Though Islamic conquests slowed in the eighth century, an even more significant kind of expansion followed it: ecological expansion, as cultivators developed new crops and introduced them to new environments (see Map 10.4). For the desert pastoralists who bore Islam abroad, every frontier was a revelation. When, for example, the followers of Muhammad captured Basra on the Persian Gulf in what is today Iraq in 637, an eyewitness reported how they found two food baskets that the retreating Persians had abandoned. They ate the basket of dates but assumed the other contained poison, until a horse ate its contents without ill effects. "And their commander said, Pronounce the name of Allah over it and eat. And they ate of it and they found it a most tasty food." It was the Arabs' first taste of rice. When they took the Persian city of Ctesiphon (suh-TEHS-ih-fahn), they mistook camphor* for salt.

They soon learned about the world that conquest spread at their feet. The outreach of Islam was a process of discovery and renaissance in which a great array of new foods was gathered, adapted, and relocated in new environments. The Islamic world extended over the Mediterranean, and touched Sahel, savanna, and tropical forests in sub-Saharan Africa, as well as monsoon lands in Yemen and northwest India, and regions of severe continental climate in Central Asia. The result was an unparalleled opportunity to exchange useful plants and animals among diverse environments.

Most of the new plants transmitted to the Middle East were exotics, reared in tropical or semitropical climates far from the areas in which they became adapted. Rulers encouraged new introductions, employing agronomists to manage their gardens, enhance their collections of medicinal plants, supply their tables, and improve their estates. Under the caliph al-Mahdi (ahl-MAH-dee), for example, between 775 and 785, Yahya ibn Khalid (YAH-yah ihb-ihn HA-lihd) led a mission to India to study medicinal

The garden of Islam. Enclosed from the world, enraptured by music, scented by flowering trees, cooled by drinks, and enlightened by conversation, the inmates of the garden of Islam inhabit an earthy paradise, in an illustration to a country romance about amorous intrigue.

*Camphor: an aromatic compound, obtained from the wood or leaves of the camphor tree and used as an insect repellent, and in medicine as an external preparation to relieve mild pain and itching

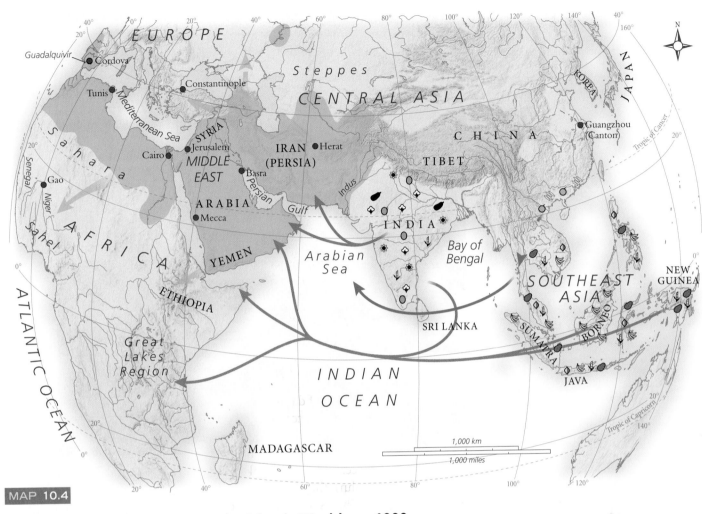

MAP 10.4

Transmission of New Crops to the Islamic World, ca. 1000

- Islamic world, ca. 1000
- spread of crops from India
- spread of crops from South and southeast Asia
- spread of crops from China (by way of southeast Asia/Indian Ocean
- Transmission of crops beyond Islamic frontier

- eggplant
- safflower
- mung bean
- cotton
- lemon/lime
- sugarcane
- bananas
- taro
- orange
- rice

drugs. Abd al-Rahman (ahbd ar-rah-MAN), ruler of Muslim Spain in the mid–eighth century, sent plant collectors to Syria. By the tenth century, Cordova his capital, had, in effect, a special garden to grow exotic plants with fields for cuttings and seeds from abroad.

Plants from the tropics made a new summer growing season possible in the Middle East. Sugarcane, for instance, originated in south or southeast Asia. From India, "a reed that produced honey without bees" had reached Persia. The Arabs extended its cultivation to the Mediterranean. Eggplant, too, was unknown in the Mediterranean or Middle East before this period. Other introductions from India included safflower, an herb pressed for cooking oil, with seeds used in cosmetics, and the Indian mung bean. The tenth-century geographer, Ibn Hawqal, tells of a landowner in northern Iraq who doubled his revenues by planting cotton and rice.

Watermill. Increased agricultural output caused demand for more and bigger mills to grind grain. Most have not survived, but a fine example of medieval watermill technology, pictured here, is on the Orontes River at Hama, Syria. Water wheels on this scale also hoisted water from riverbeds to aqueducts and irrigation channels.

Food and Plants with Arabic or Persian Word Origins

aubergine (eggplant)*
Camphor
Caraway (seeds)
Coffee (by way of Turkish)
Cotton
Henna
Lemon
Orange
Saffron
Sherbet
Spinach
Sugar
Syrup

*Italic words are of Persian origin

The most important development to improve mass nutrition was of hard durum wheat in the Middle East. Some crops were transmitted onward, beyond the frontiers of the Muslim world. West Africa got cotton, taro, bananas, plantains, sour oranges, and limes in this period, probably across the Sahara. Christian Europe, by contrast, was slow to receive the benefits of Muslim agronomy. Spinach and hard wheat were not cultivated there until the thirteenth century, rice not until the fifteenth.

Along with the new crops, technology and extended settlement increased productivity further. The new crops required watering during summer, stimulating irrigation by underground tunnels and wells, which led, in turn, to the adoption for agriculture of more previously marginal land. Forest clearance was practiced more widely and intensively than before. The use of fertilizer increased crop yields. Fertile land left uncultivated seems to have been rare in the Muslim world. Islamic law favored farmers. Landowners could use and dispose of their land as they liked. The enforcement of a free market in land meant that farms tended to fall into the hands of owners who used them most productively. Tenants acquired farms, as conquest broke up big holdings that had stagnated under the previous regimes. Tax rates in regions under the rule of the caliphs in Baghdad (bag-DAD) were low after reforms in the late eighth century—commonly a tenth of output, with summer crops often being exempted. Villages thrived. There were 12,000 villages along the Guadalquivir (gwahd-ahl-kee-BEER) River in Muslim Spain by the tenth century. Forty-eight thousand square miles were subject to land tax in seventh-century Sawad (sah-WAD) in Syria—virtually the entire cultivable area.

FRONTIER GROWTH IN JAPAN

The vast extent of the Islamic world made this rich environmental history possible. But on a smaller scale, a similar program, including the development of new foodstuffs, the exploitation of under-exploited frontiers, and the adaptation of new areas for cultivation, was possible even in relatively small and isolated Japan. Here, a sense of struggle against nature animated the most persistent and consistent effort any state of the time made to boost food resources. Bureaucrats carefully totted up the hostility of the natural world. Between 806 and 1073, official records list 653 earthquakes, 134 fires, 89 cases of damage to crops, 91 epidemics, 356 supernatural warnings (including volcanic eruptions), and 367 appearances by ghosts. They recorded only 185 favorable events in the same period. In the *Nihongi* of the early eighth century, one of the earliest native Japanese chronicles, the rise of the imperial dynasty is linked with the overthrow of Susa-no-o, a god who "brought many people to an untimely end" by "making green mountains wither" and wrecking rice fields. Japanese rulers took seriously their responsibility to regulate their subjects' relations with the natural world. Unlike their counterparts in most other cultures, they did not limit themselves to acts and sacrifices intended to appease the forces of nature. From the early eighth century, they had ambitious environmental policies.

Selection from the *Nihongi*

Some growth in the yield of agriculture would have happened even without state guidance. Rice yields improved thanks to new, labor-intensive techniques in which whole communities cooperated: growing seedlings in nurseries and transplanting them to the fields. Heavy plows arrived from Korea in the fifth century. It is doubtful, however, whether they made much impact until the ninth or tenth century because Japan had little iron to make plows from. Most cultivation was on wetlands. Dry farming, which made the heavy plow familiar, spread slowly. Evidence of the increased stabling of animals implies systematic exploitation of them as resources for power, and suggests that farmers were using more and more land to grow crops. Meanwhile, barley gradually replaced millet as the country's second most important crop after rice, with some benefits for nutrition. Although we lack reliable figures for overall population, it is obvious that it was growing. Census returns show—by global standards—exceptionally large households of an average of ten persons each. Family customs helped. Young mothers commonly spent the first 5 to 15 years of married life in their parents' home, where their husbands visited them. This spread the burden of child care.

The government drive to boost food production was under way by 711, when a decree authorized aristocrats to apply to provincial governors for permission to cultivate virgin land at their own expense. The aim, according to a proclamation of 722, was to add 2.5 million acres to the area devoted to rice production. In the following year, farmers became eligible to inherit newly cultivated fields for three generations if they irrigated those fields from new ditches or ponds. In 743, farmers acquired absolute ownership of such lands.

As well as a state-sponsored, aristocratic enterprise, the conquest of new environments was a preserve of freelance holy men. In 735, the dismay a devastating smallpox epidemic caused boosted the appeal and numbers of these zealots. Most were Buddhists. The most effective of them was the monk Gyoki. Traditionalists accused him of embezzling alms, impiously burning the bodies of the dead, and aggressively pursuing converts. But everyone approved of the way he organized his followers to perform public works—building bridges and roads, digging ponds and embankments. The state soon collaborated in this mobilization of labor and contracted Gyoki's workers to undertake official projects. In 741, 750 of Gyoki's disciples joined the Buddhist priesthood after building a bridge over the Kizu River.

Frontier expansion at the expense of the "barbarians" of Japan's northeast Honshu island increased available land. The native Emishi (eh-MEE-shee) were denounced as "hairy people," who dwelt among "evil deities in the mountains and perverse devils on the plains." They were described in terms that seem almost universal among imperial peoples who want to conquer, dispossess, or exterminate others. They were "fierce and wild," dangerous, lacking a recognizable political or legal system. Without chiefs, they "all rob each other. . . . In winter they lodge in holes, in summer they dwell in nests." By 796, the state had settled 9,000 colonists in fortified households on Honshu to cultivate conquered lands.

By the early ninth century, the state was growing more confident about its ability to manage the environment and keep disaster at bay. After performing a successful rainmaking rite, the hermit Kukai began his song of self-praise with a conventional reflection. Nature, he said, responded to human decadence. "And thus," he continued, "even though it is time for rain to fall, the four horizons are blazing with heat: the sun burns up everything, and rice and millet ears are all dry. The entire natural world dries up and hardens, and animals of fur and scale alike perish. With nothing to see but aridity in the land, court and peasants alike pour tears ceaselessly." In such circumstances, the emperor intervenes. He fasts, and orders appropriate rites in all temples. "As the venerable monks chant the sacred scriptures . . . waterfalls gush forth from high peaks and soak wild animals, while rain fills the fields enough to drown water buffaloes. . . . Peasants! Do not lament any more. . . . See the storehouses, where grain piles up like islands, like mountains."

CHINA AND SOUTHEAST ASIA

In Japan, as in the Islamic world, the human assault on the natural frontier had effective states of growing power to back it. But in the same period, similar developments occurred even in politically unstable and apparently unfavorable conditions in China and India. After the collapse of the Gupta empire (see Chapter 9), kingdoms in south India and the Deccan boosted their revenues, reach, and power by granting wasteland to priests, monks, and warriors to promote agriculture. In land grants recorded in forest areas acquired by conquest in the sixth century, monks and holy men are the biggest beneficiaries. This should not be seen merely—or perhaps at all—as evidence of kings' religious priorities but of monasteries' ability to transform the environment.

An inscription on copper, dated 753, shows what happened when a priest received a royal land grant. "We the inhabitants went to the boundaries which the headman of the district pointed out, circumambulated the village from left to right, and planted milk-bushes and placed stones around it. . . . The donee shall enjoy the wet land and the dry land included within these four boundaries, wherever the iguana runs and the tortoise crawls, and shall be permitted to dig river channels and inundation channels." The king would receive taxes on the use of these facilities. The inscription also includes a list of payments that the priest did not have to pay, revealing the full range of collective activities that community contributions supported. The settlers made and operated oil presses

Indian land grants, 753 C.E.

The Grand Canal. China's ancient canals are still useful to commerce. Here, long lines of barges sail the Grand Canal, an artificial waterway that was first built in the seventh century C.E.

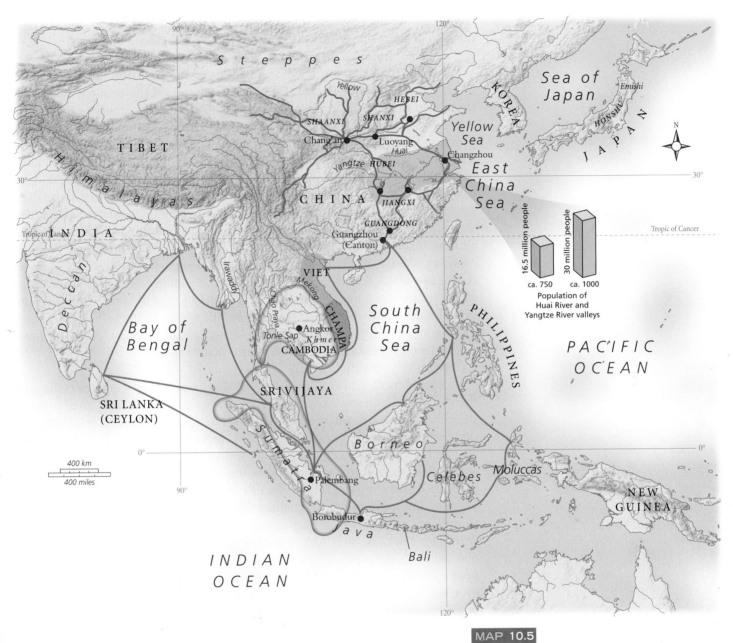

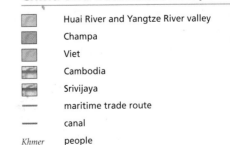

MAP 10.5

China and Southeast Asia, ca. 1000

- Huai River and Yangtze River valley
- Champa
- Viet
- Cambodia
- Srivijaya
- maritime trade route
- canal
- *Khmer* people

and looms. They dug wells. They paid taxes to support the king, the district administration, and the priestly caste out of the yield of crops, including water lilies, "the share of the potter," the price of ghee (butter) and cloth. They supplied huntsmen, messengers, dancing girls, servants, fodder, cotton, molasses, "the best cow and the best bull," and "the fourth part of the trunks of old trees," including areca palms and coconut trees, to the royal court. When fines were due from the village "to the accountant and the minister," the priest-landlord, did not have to contribute to them. Irrigation and double cropping appear in many Indian inscriptions of the following two centuries. Marginal land was coming under the plow. In a land grant of 994, in an arid region, for instance, the landlord was only entitled to a third of the water from a single well.

In China, although the emperors of the early seventh century were unable to sustain a lasting dynasty, they did contribute to the enduring infrastructure of the economy, building a canal system that crisscrossed the country. This alone stimulated the internal grain trade and therefore the productivity of the regions that grew rice and millet. The canals also improved irrigation. In 624, in Shaanxi province, imperial waterworks irrigated more than 80,000 acres. Meanwhile, large-scale land reclamation proceeded by drainage, as population growth and improving food supply stimulated each other. The policy of the Tang dynasty (see Chapter 8) was usually to break up large landholdings and distribute them among taxpayers. A major land reform of 737 divided great estates among their workers. This may have discouraged large landowners from investing in reclamation, but it encouraged cultivation because peasants farmed their holdings more intensively than large landowners did. It was part of an ideology of imperial benevolence that also established price-regulating granaries where food stocks accumulated at government expense when prices were low for redistribution at a discount when prices were high. The resulting stocks helped cushion disaster in the plague-ravaged, famine-fraught 730s through 740s. Improved rice strains, adapted from varieties of rice that Tang armies brought back from campaigns in Vietnam, helped.

Imperial policy also stimulated the southward shift of settlement, and therefore of the centers of production, into regions, far from the threat of steppeland invasion, where rice grew, with beneficial effects on nutrition and therefore on levels of population. In 730, vagrant families were ordered to be resettled in agricultural colonies under military discipline. Such proclamations often failed to produce results, but some colonies did take shape under this program, cultivating rice on the Huai River in 734. Although governments were prone to periodic bouts of hostility against Buddhism and Daoism, which Confucians tended to despise as superstitious, monasteries were generally encouraged because they were effective colonizers that could kick start development in under-exploited areas. By the mid–eighth century, a third of China's people lived in the Huai and Yangtze River valleys, and, by the eleventh century, over half did. As colonization proceeded, Chinese villages replaced aboriginal populations, which were exterminated, assimilated, or driven into marginal areas. Population figures—statistics untrustworthy anywhere at the time except in China—suggest Tang environmental policies paid off. China had about 50 million people after An Lushan's rebellion in the 750s (see Chapter 8). Its population had grown to 60 million by the year 1000.

The extension of the frontier of settlement and of rice cultivation in southern China was part of a bigger phenomenon, extending over the moist, hot, dense forests of mainland southeast Asia (see Map 10.5). In the sixth century, Chinese geographers ceased to refer to Funan (see Chapter 8) and located a state they called Chen-la in the interior of what is now Cambodia. This was the first sign we get in sources available to us of an important change under way in the region. Alongside the maritime states, founded on trade that lined the routes from China to India, agrarian kingdoms were growing up, based on rice production. For centuries

Population of China, 730–1000

730	Vagrant families ordered to resettle in agricultural colonies
734	Rice cultivation on the Huai River
750	China's population is 50 million
Mid–eighth century	One-third of China's population lives in the Huai and Yangtze valleys
1000	China's population is 60 million
Eleventh century	Half of China's population lives in the Huai and Yangtze valleys

◯ MAKING CONNECTIONS ◯

EXPANDING STATES IN EAST AND SOUTHEAST ASIA, 600–1000

REGION/CULTURE →	ENVIRONMENT →	POLITICAL ORGANIZATION →	ACHIEVEMENTS
Japan	Temperate climate; mountainous; volcanoes; relatively small areas of fertile soil	Centralized dynasty with provincial governors; high degree of social coordination	Productive rice, barley agriculture with community cooperation; creation of public infrastructure; frontier expansion to northeast island of Honshu
China and Southeast Asia Yangtze River valley	Moist, semitropical and crisscrossed with rivers	Large canal building; irrigation and drainage projects	Imperial-controlled land distribution; improved rice strains; state-controlled granaries; population increases; growth of Buddhist, Daoist monasteries
Indochina Angkor/Viet/Cham kingdoms	Coastal areas: Mekong River delta in south; Red River in north with adjacent forests; inland: mountainous areas	Small chiefdoms coalesce into single states	Combines highly productive rice agriculture and maritime trade (South China Sea); population increases; large-scale Buddhist temple complexes
Sumatra Srivijaya kingdom **Java** Sailendra dynasty	Tropical coastal regions; frequent earthquakes and volcanoes; thick forests	Chiefdoms and kingdoms with Muslim and Chinese merchants, advisors	Plentiful trade in agricultural goods, fish, wood, incense, spices; development of large-scale Buddhist and Hindu temple complexes

small chiefdoms and aspiring states had dotted the lower Mekong River valley, but in the eighth century, the people of the region, the Khmer (k-MER), began to coalesce into a single kingdom, centered at the new city of Angkor (AHNG-kor), on the north shore on the Tonle Sap—a natural reservoir of monsoonal rains. This region had no mines, no great commercial fleets, and no great industries. The wealth of the Khmer derived from a peculiar feature of the way the Mekong works. Swollen by the monsoon, the river becomes, in effect, too heavily charged to empty into the sea through its own delta. The water begins to flow backward, flooding the plain of the Tonle Sap. The soil there is so rich that, provided the waters are well managed and channeled into reservoirs, it yields three rice crops a year. Angkor was also well placed for contact with other major rice lands in the Maenam and Chao Phraya basins. In 802, it became a capital with explicitly imperial pretensions, when King Jayavarman II proclaimed himself monarch of the universe, and priests in his employ performed a ceremony nullifying all former oaths of loyalty.

Similar experiments occurred all over southeast Asia. The growth of the Viet and Cham kingdoms—the other big states that took shape in Indochina in the period—owed something to the traditional wealth of the region in ivory, rhinoceros horn, and aromatic woods, and much to the bureaucracy that arrived with Buddhism. But it was based mainly on taxes from lumber, as forests fell, and food products, as new fields replaced the forests. By the year 1000, a comparable transformation was beginning to take shape in the northwest corner of the region. Here, in the Irawaddy valley on the borders between India and Bangladesh, dry rice cultivation began to transform a near-desert where little rain fell. Meanwhile, offshore, the axis of maritime state building shifted outward, toward the Indonesian islands.

Here, in the seventh century, the realm of Srivijaya (sree-vee-JEYE-ah), on the Sumatran coast, impressed the first Chinese sources to notice it. When the pilgrim I-ching (yee-jing) stopped there in 671, the capital had a community of Buddhist monks, said to number a thousand. The court employed Hindu and Buddhist scholars. But a tradition of pagan magic fascinated Muslim observers. Magic was meant to control the sea. The maharajah (ma-ha-RAH-jah), as the sources called the king of Srivijaya, was said to have enchanted crocodiles to guard the mouth of his river. He supposedly bought the goodwill of the sea with annual gifts of gold bricks.

Srivijaya's economy relied on harbor tolls and the profits of piracy. A river-linked domain behind it supplied it with soldiers and rice, because even trading states needed their own food supplies. Srivijaya had big commercial resources in the form of spices and aromatic woods, but the inhabitants still worked to expand rice production. According to a legend of the foundation of Palembang, the fathers of the city chose its site by weighing the waters of Sumatra's various rivers for silt and finding that those of the Musi would be best for irrigating rice lands. Palembang's earliest inscription, dated 685, expresses a king's concern that "all the clearances and gardens his people made should be full, that the cattle of all species raised by them and their bondsmen should prosper."

The capital, where even the parrots spoke four languages, attracted merchants. The maritime strength of Srivijaya was concentrated in the ragged east coast of Sumatra, with its fringe of islands and mangrove swamps, its deep bays and shelters for shipping, its natural coral-reef defenses, its abundant fish and turtles. Its greatness and survival—for it was "invariably described as great," according to a Chinese administrator of its trade in the early eleventh century—depended on Chinese commerce, especially for the sandalwood and frankincense in which it established a dominant trading position.

In eighth-century Java, the Sailendra dynasty rivaled Srivijaya. They built a huge Buddhist temple, Borobodur, which seemed to proclaim their patrons' privileged access to heaven. Built of half a million blocks of stone, it arose between about 790 and 830. Buddhism was a relative newcomer. The site of Borobodur had been intended for a Hindu temple when the ruling ideology abruptly changed. Terraces lead the pilgrim upward. The climb is like a mystic's spiritual ascent toward heaven. At the top, the pinnacle of experience awaits: a representation of the central world-mountain of Buddhist belief. Carvings that depict tales from Buddhist scriptures are a stone book, reminders of the stages that prepare the soul for nirvana.

The maritime economy of Sailendra has left no archives, but comes to life in the carvings. One of the most famous depicts a legendary voyage to a promised land that Hiru, the faithful minister of the mythical monk-king Rudrayana, made. Hiru earned the goodwill of heaven by intervening with the king's wicked son and successor, who proposed, among other evil acts, to bury his father's spiritual counselor alive. Miraculously advised to flee in advance of a sandstorm that would smother the court, Hiru fled by sea in a windborne ship to a happy shore.

(a) **The temple of Borobodur** on the Indonesian island of Java began to receive pilgrims in the early ninth century. Visitors, emerging from the dense tropical forest that surrounded the site, would ascend through four galleries, where stories of virtuous Buddhists were carved in relief (and, in their day, plastered and brilliantly painted), eventually reaching the realm of Enlightenment—the circular platform, guarded by statues of Bodhisattvas.

(b) **The galleries of Borobodur** relate legends of individuals who achieved Enlightenment by practicing virtue. The story of Hiru, the royal counselor who narrowly eluded death and endured exile for urging virtue on a wicked ruler is shown in the lower of these reliefs. The realistic depiction of his wind-blown ship is a vivid reminder of the maritime culture of Java under the Sailendra kings.

He found granaries, peacocks, varied trees, and hospitable inhabitants. The artist who carved the story had seen such scenes. He knew what a ship looked like and how it worked. The kind of art he produced—evidence, too, of a kind of spirituality—could only come from a world in which travel and trade were regarded as noble, virtuous activities.

According to later inscriptions—in which we must make allowance for mythical distortions or propagandistic exaggerations—a rival kingdom to the Sailendras arose in regions of Java where forest had been newly converted to rice cultivation on the plains of the Solo and Brantas Rivers. Inscriptions credit the expulsion of the Sailendras from these regions in the mid–ninth century to Pikatan, an ascetic king who doubled as a holy man, forest clearer, and temple builder.

THE PACIFIC

Growing trade stimulated these developments in maritime southeast Asia. But an even more impressive drive to colonize new lands and exploit new resources occurred deep in the Pacific, where, as far as we know, the commerce of the monsoonal seas barely reached (see Map 10.6).

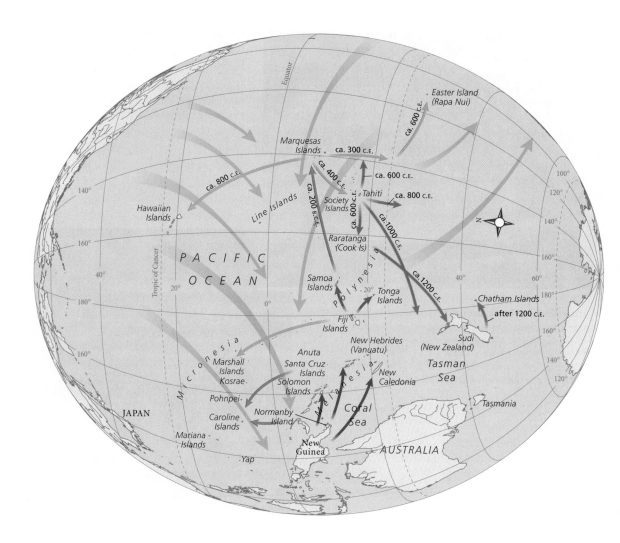

MAP 10.6

The Colonization of the Pacific to 1000 c.e.

➤ migrations before 1500 B.C.E.

➤ migrations 1500–1000 B.C.E.

➤ migrations 1000–1 B.C.E.

➤ migrations 1–500 C.E.

➤ migrations after 500 C.E.

➤ Trade Winds

To judge from the currently available archaeological evidence, the Caroline Islands in Micronesia were probably first colonized about 2,000 years ago, not from the relatively nearby Asian mainland but from the southeast, in the Solomon Islands and New Hebrides (modern-day country of Vanatu), by people who made distinctive round pots, intricately patterned by pressing tooth-shaped stamps into the clay, and whose houses were raised on stilts. The way this culture changed—relatively suddenly and at vastly different rates on different islands—awaits explanation. The most precocious island was Pohnpei, at the Carolines' eastern end. It is small—probably incapable of supporting more than 30,000 people—but it was a center of ambitious activity toward the year 1000. Large-scale labor was mobilized to carve out artificial islets with increasingly monumental ceremonial centers—for tombs and rites including turtle sacrifices and the nurture of sacred eels. On nearby Kosrae island, a similar history began soon after. Within a couple of hundred years, cities were arising around paved streets within high walls of massive construction—observed with "total bewilderment" by the French expedition that came on the city of Lelu by accident in 1824.

Beyond the Carolines, in the South Pacific, lay one of the world's most daunting frontiers: an ocean, too big to traverse with the technology of the time, where the winds blew almost without stop from the southeast, and where vast distances separate islands that can support human life. Polynesians conquered this environment mainly after 500. Polynesians are easily defined as speakers of closely related languages. It is harder to find a common cultural profile for them in other respects. Using archaeological and linguistic evidence, however, we can piece together how they lived during the early centuries of their dispersal through the Pacific. They grew taro and yams, supplemented with coconut, breadfruit, and bananas. They kept chickens and pigs. They named 150 kinds of fish, and exploited them for tools—files made of sea-urchin spines, fish hooks from oyster shells. They consumed kava, a fermented drink made from a plant whose roots have narcotic properties, to induce trances and celebrate rites. Although archaeology cannot retrieve their notions of the sacred, we can infer it from language and later evidence. **Mana**—a supernatural force—regulated the world. The mana of a net makes it catch fish; the mana of an herb makes it heal.

The Polynesians' was a frontier culture in origin. It grew up in the central Pacific, probably in the islands of Tonga and Samoa, beginning about 2,000 to 3,000 years ago. The chronology of Polynesian expansion is relentlessly debated and deeply uncertain. These people were, from their first emergence in the archaeological record, constant voyagers, venturing ever farther into the paths of the southeast trade winds, which restricted the range of navigation but which at least promised explorers a good chance of getting home. Around 600, however, there was clearly a period of "takeoff," in which archaeological finds multiply across the ocean and thousands of islands, as far as Easter Island (see Chapter 14). In further phases of expansion, Polynesians colonized northward as far as Hawaii, by about 800, and, ultimately settling New Zealand and the Chatham Islands.

To colonize so many islands, many of which seemed dauntingly far apart, was such a surprising achievement that scholars who investigated it long assumed that it must have happened by accident—as a result of seafarers or regional traders drifting off course or being blown to new lands by freak winds. But long-range navigation is part of the logic of life on small islands—a characteristic way to maximize resources, extend economic opportunities, diversify the ecosystem. The Polynesians, in common with the Caroline Islanders and other sailors of the northern and western Pacific, had

Nineteenth-century description of Lelu

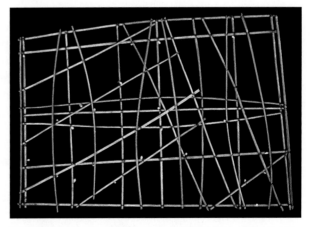

Polynesian reed map. Traditional Polynesian maps of the Pacific show routes across the ocean in the form of linked reeds between islands symbolized by small shells. The patterns of the reeds enable navigators to identify changes in the ocean swell.
© The Trustees of the British Museum

⦾ MAKING CONNECTIONS ⦾

ENVIRONMENTAL/GEOGRAPHIC OBSTACLES TO DEVELOPMENT OF STATES

REGION →	ENVIRONMENTAL/ OBSTACLES →	ADAPTIVE STRATEGIES
Sub-Saharan Africa	Isolation—desert in north and lee winds offshore impede communication; widely separated river basins; lack of navigable rivers near coasts; dense forests, malarial jungles	Exploitation of agricultural, mining resources near Sahel grassland; West Africa; trans-Sahara trade routes focusing on copper, salt, gold
North and South America	Bounded by vast oceans—Atlantic and Pacific Oceans; most rivers flow east–west preventing north–south contacts; mountainous terrain	Taking advantage of South/Mesoamerican highlands' proximity to rain forests, seas, swamps for resource exploitation; intensive development of fishing/hunting techniques in North America; introduction of new crops and technologies aided by trade networks from Mesoamerica to Mississippi River basin
Japan	Isolated geography; few navigable rivers; poor soil; earthquake prone	Labor-intensive wetland agricultural techniques; highly regulated society; systematic exploitation of animals as sources of power
Pacific	Vast and isolated region; few food crops, little cultivable soil on many islands;	Skillful development of navigational, boat-building techniques; unsurpassed knowledge of ocean and night sky; introduction of basic "tool kit" (fishhooks, taro, coconut, breadfruit, kava, banana plants, chickens, pigs) to uninhabited islands

impressive maritime technology: double-hulled canoes big enough to carry 200 people, or smaller vessels with outriggers for longer journeys, rigged with claw-shaped sails that kept the mast and rigging light. Their direction-finding techniques were the best in the world. Chants helped navigators remember the complex guidance of the stars in a hemisphere where no single polestar is available to guide voyagers, as it is north of the equator. Navigation was like "breadfruit-picking," star by star. They mapped the ocean's swells—mentally or perhaps with maps made of reeds, of which later examples survive. Eighteenth-century European observers noted that Caroline and Polynesian navigators could literally feel their way around the ocean, identifying their position by the way that waves felt on their own bodies.

By about the year 1000, the Polynesians may have gotten close to the limits of navigation accessible to them with the technology at their disposal. Oral traditions recall and presumably embellish their history. The most heroic tale is

Polynesian Expansion

3,000–2,000 years ago	Origins of Polynesian civilization
600	"Takeoff" of Polynesian expansion
ca. 800	Settlement of Hawaii
ca. 1000	Colonization of New Zealand

perhaps that of Hui-te-Rangiora, whose journey from Raratonga in the Cook Islands in the remote Pacific in the mid–eighth century took him through bare white rocks that towered over a monstrous sea, to a place of uninterrupted ice. Myths ascribe the discovery of New Zealand to the god-like Maui, who baited giant stingray with his own blood. A less shadowy figure is the indisputably human Kupe, who claimed that a vision of the supreme god Io guided him to New Zealand from Raratonga. Maybe, however, he just followed the migration of the long-tailed cuckoo birds. His sailing directions were: "Let the course be to the right hand of the setting sun, moon, or Venus in the second month of the year."

THE EXPANSION OF CHRISTENDOM

At the opposite end of Eurasia, in the eighth century, Christendom began to outgrow the frontiers of the Roman Empire (see Map 10.7). Here conquest was the main agent of change. Christendom developed no new crops or technologies. The heavy plow had long been in use. Rye and barley—the grains suitable for the frost-rimed, dense soils of northern Europe—were ancient crops.

Beyond Rome's farthest northern and western frontiers, monastic exiles took memories of antiquity into Scotland and Ireland, like the monk Columba, longing to compose his hymns "on a rocky outcrop, overlooking the coiling surface of the sea." A similar—more dangerous—enterprise flickered in Germany, where Boniface traveled from England in 719 to share the gospel with his fellow Saxons. Boniface was martyred around 754, but the task of converting the Saxons was taken up 30 years later, from inside the most dynamic spot on the frontier of Christendom: the kingdom of the Franks.

Two events transformed its ruler, Charlemagne, into the self-styled renovator of Rome. His journey to Italy in 774 opened his eyes to the ruined splendors of ancient Rome and enabled him to gather books and scholars. From the 790s, he could afford unprecedented ambitions when he captured the treasure of invading steppelanders, the Avars. Taking advantage of the fact that Irene, an empress of dubious legitimacy ruled in Constantinople, he now proclaimed himself successor of the ancient Roman emperors. Charlemagne—while remaining first and foremost a Frankish king—fancied himself in his new role. He affected what he thought was imperial Roman taste. He appeared on coins in a laurel crown. His seals were stamped with slogans of imperial revival. His court writers, who must have known what he wanted to hear, compared him to Constantine and Justinian (see Chapter 8). The manuscript painters, scribes, and ivory carvers of his palace copied ancient models.

Even before Charlemagne came to the throne, the Frankish realm had incorporated lands beyond the margins of the old empire, especially along the North Sea and in central Germany. Charlemagne's conquest of Saxony, which took eighteen years to complete, was the first annexation of a large new province in Europe by a self-consciously "Roman" empire since the Emperor Trajan had conquered Dacia in the early second century. More significant yet was the enduring nature of this conquest. Saxony, wrested—said Charlemagne's servant and first biographer—from devil worshippers, became a parade ground of Christendom, converted from an insecure frontier into an imperial heartland.

On Christendom's other exposed flanks, similar expansion made slow progress. In the early ninth century, Mojmir I established a Slav state patterned on Charlemagne's monarchy, beyond the Danube in Bohemia, in a region where the Avar Empire used to rule. In 864, the Bulgar Tsar Boris decided to accept Christianity and impose it on his people. The Bulgars rapidly became like the Franks, rival claimants to the mantle of Rome, under a ruler who called himself "emperor of all the Greeks and Bulgars." Yet if the Bulgar Empire was a threat to Constantinople, it was a bulwark for Christendom against pagan steppelanders from farther east.

Despite an isolated position and scant resources, Asturias in northern Spain in the ninth century successfully defended Christendom's frontier at the opposite end of the Mediterranean. Part of the sacred armory of its kings lies in Oviedo Cathedral—vessels of gold, ivory, and lapis lazuli, housing even more precious scraps of wood and bone from the saints that could have a magical effect on the battlefield. On a hill above the town, Ramiro I could look out on his kingdom from his summer palace, or receive ambassadors in a hall decorated with carvings molded after Persian silverwork that must have been inherited from the Roman past. By the end of the century, the kingdom ruled from here had begun to expand beyond the mountains that screened it to the south.

Exploitation of the shrine attributed to the Apostle James the Great at Compostela gave Asturias advantages over other Christian states in Spain—in pilgrim wealth, monastic colonization, and the chances of recruiting knightly manpower. But a frontier position generally was good for state-building. In the 890s, Wilfrid the Hairy, Count of Barcelona, claiming the hairy man's birthright God promised in the biblical story of Esau, conquered almost all counties around his own, south of the Pyrenees. Laborious settlement of underpopulated areas is the subject of all the documents that survive from his time. A church synod at Barcelona recalled Wilfrid's generosity a few years later: "Moved with pity for that land, the Lord made arise the most noble prince Wilfrid and his brothers, who, filling men of diverse provenance and lineage with pious love, managed to return the famous church with its dependencies to its former state." Here, and in later charters, are hints of Wilfrid's success in attracting population to the lands of his border state. Wilfrid's story was typical of the edges of Christendom. In lands reclaimed from pagan conquest on the northern frontier, in England, Alfred the Great was securing a similar reputation as a state builder by lavish generosity to monks, the custodians of the historical record. By 924, Alfred's heirs had completed their reconquest of northern and eastern England. The extension or restoration of the frontier of Christendom was pushing Europe outward.

At the same time, a secular political tradition was being spread even farther afield. Christianity, as we saw in the last chapter, was barely beginning to penetrate Scandinavia, which—in terms of the colonists it generated, the new lands it explored—was the most dynamic part of Europe. A letter from the northern Russian city of Novgorod is said to have reached a Viking prince in 862. "Our land," it read, "is great and rich. But there is no order in it. Come and rule us." In response, he founded the state that eventually became Russia. Vladimir of Kiev, whose conversion to Orthodox Christianity we discussed

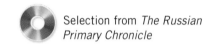

Selection from *The Russian Primary Chronicle*

Christian Conquest and Expansion

Ninth century	Growth of kingdom of Asturias
ca. 802	Charlemagne completes conquest of Saxony
ca. 860	Beginning of Scandinavian colonization of Iceland
864	Bulgar Tsar Boris accepts Christianity
884	Kiev becomes capital of Russian state
890s	Expansion of Barcelona under Wilfrid the Hairy
924	Completion of conquest of formerly pagan lands in England

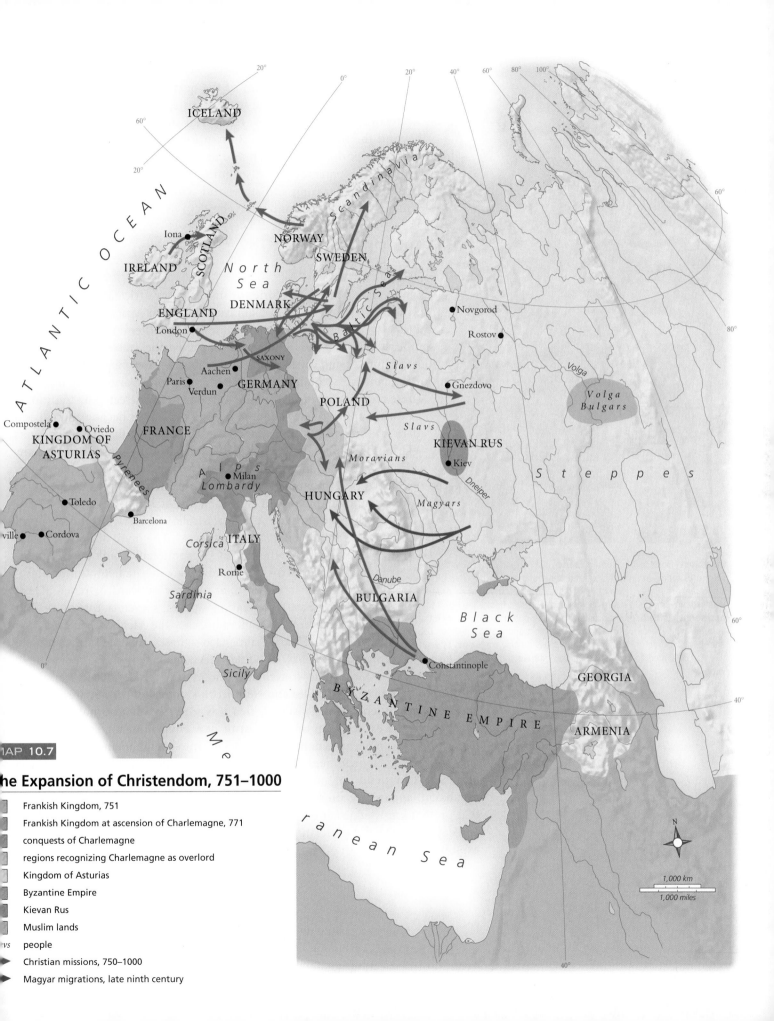

ATLANTIC OCEAN

ICELAND

60°

20°

0°

20°

40°

60°

80°

100°

60°

80°

NORWAY

Scandinavia

Iona

SCOTLAND

IRELAND

North
Sea

SWEDEN

Novgorod

Rostov

Baltic Sea

ENGLAND

DENMARK

London

SAXONY

Slavs

Gnezdovo

Volga

Volga
Bulgars

Aachen

Paris

GERMANY

POLAND

Verdun

Slavs

Steppes

Compostela

Oviedo

FRANCE

Moravians

KIEVAN RUS

KINGDOM OF
ASTURIAS

Pyrenees

Alps
Lombardy

Milan

Kiev

Dneiper

Toledo

Barcelona

HUNGARY

Magyars

ville

Cordova

Corsica

ITALY

Rome

Danube

Sardinia

BULGARIA

Black
Sea

GEORGIA

Sicily

Constantinople

BYZANTINE EMPIRE

ARMENIA

Mediterranean Sea

40°

MAP 10.7

The Expansion of Christendom, 751–1000

- Frankish Kingdom, 751
- Frankish Kingdom at ascension of Charlemagne, 771
- conquests of Charlemagne
- regions recognizing Charlemagne as overlord
- Kingdom of Asturias
- Byzantine Empire
- Kievan Rus
- Muslim lands

vs people

➤ Christian missions, 750–1000

➤ Magyar migrations, late ninth century

1,000 km
1,000 miles

N

Irish cross. Outside the Roman Empire, Christianity was slow to take root in Europe—except in Scotland and Ireland. Isolation made Irish Christian art highly distinctive. This eighth-century bronze crucifix was probably made to adorn the cover of a gospel book. The artist was apparently concerned to represent scripture authentically—hence the soldiers who pierce Jesus' side and hoist a sponge to his lips. The angels who perch on the arms of the cross display fragments of what may be intended to represent Christ's shroud, or the cloth used to wipe his face.

in Chapter 9, was a descendant of the Scandinavian founding fathers of Russian principalities. The story may have gotten oversimplified in the record, but it shows how territorial statehood was exported, far beyond the limits of the old Roman Empire, to relatively immature political worlds in northern and eastern Europe. Meanwhile, Scandinavian expansion was also going on northward, spreading the frontiers of farming and statehood within its own peninsula, and turning seaward, colonizing Iceland.

IN PERSPECTIVE: The Limits of Divergence

On the face of it, the histories of sub-Saharan Africa and the Americas seem to diverge from that of Eurasia and North Africa from the eighth century to the end of the millennium. In Christendom, Islam, China, southeast Asia, and the western and central Pacific, states came and went, but economies and civilizations were robust—extending frontiers, colonizing new areas, founding new states and empires, or reviving old ones. These regions seem to have bucked the patterns detected by traditional historiography: to have endured beyond periods of decline and fall and dark ages. At first glance, the contrast with sub-Saharan Africa looks glaring. Ethiopia's dark age really was dark, in the sense that we know virtually nothing about it. Ghana's frustration, and the absence of any evidence of comparable state-building initiatives elsewhere, confirm the traditional picture of sub-Saharan Africa in this period as a region—like far northern Asia or Australia—about which historians of the period can find almost nothing to say. The myth of Maya collapse has long dominated the way we conventionally think of the Americas in this period. This was a hemisphere in which it was more usual for civilizations to perish than to grow outward or renew themselves. This is an exaggeration—perhaps even a caricature. But there is something in it. Teotihuacán, the Moche, the Nazca, the lowland Maya, Huari, Tiahuanaco—these casualties of the era were replaced, if at all, by unstable successors.

Nevertheless, a theme that, if not quite global, genuinely embraces the Old and New Worlds underlies the apparent differences between them. Broadly stated, this was a period of unusual ecological experiment: the exploration or conquest of new environments. In some cases, new frontiers were breached by expansion into neighboring regions and already-familiar environments, like those of the Islamic world or southeast Asia or most of Christendom. In others, like the Caroline Islands or the Scandinavian expansion, apparently unprecedented adventures were launched from origins that present knowledge cannot adequately explain. In others again, as in China and Japan, internal colonization adapted and transformed previously underexploited wastelands. In others, such as the Andes, central Mexico, and the Maya world, the centers of activity were displaced to new environments—the limestone hills of Tula or Yucatán, the almost incredibly high altitude of Tiahuanaco. In others, which remain necessarily underrepresented in history books because of the absence of evidence, the business of locating resources, developing foodstuffs, and improving production techniques continued without leaving much trace in the record. In the 800s and 900s, for instance, all we have is linguistic evidence for two enormously important developments in the ecology of East Africa. An explosion of new terms shows that banana cultivation and cattle breeding spread inland from the Indian Ocean coast to the Great Lakes of Central Africa. Against this background, the history of the next three centuries, which is the subject of the next part of the book, becomes intelligible. Vibrancy and innovativeness, which became characteristic of most of these regions—and of others where the evidence only begins to mount up from this point onward—grew out of preceding, painstaking efforts to find new, more productive ways to exploit the environment.

The story of the last few centuries of the first millennium C.E. suggests an important point about how history happens. In the past, the search for patterns that help to explain it, and that make it easier to write textbooks about it, has driven historians to grotesque oversimplifications: seeing history as a continuous story of "progress" or decline; or representing it as a kind of swing between revolutions and counterrevolutions, or between decadence and dynamism, or between dark ages and rebirths. The reality, it seems, as we get to learn more about the past, is much more subtle and intriguing. At one level, the slow growth of compatible changes—what historians' jargon sometimes calls "structures"—gradually gave the world a new look. Simultaneously, and often with contradictory effect, random or short-term changes stimulate, impede, interrupt, or temporarily reverse those trends, and—sometimes—permanently deflect or end them. So both continuity and discontinuity tend to be visible in the story, pretty much all the time. A picture that omits either is almost certain to be distorted.

In these respects, history is rather like climate, in which many cycles of varying duration all seem to be going on all the time, and where random or almost-random changes frequently intervene. With increasing intensity in recent years, historians have struggled to match changes in the human record to knowledge of how these cycles and changes have interacted since the end of the Ice Age. As we are about to see, some of the most remarkable insights to have emerged from this quest illuminate worldwide changes that began—or that we can first begin to detect—around 1,000 years ago.

CHRONOLOGY

(All dates are C.E.)

200–400	Flourishing of mound-building culture in eastern North America
600	"Takeoff" of Polynesian expansion
750	China's population reaches 50 million
754	Martrydom of Boniface
Third through tenth centuries	Maya Classic Age
Seventh through tenth centuries	Ecological expansion of Islam
Eighth century	Government drive to boost food production in Japan
Eighth through ninth centuries	Decline of Ethiopia
790–830	Construction of Borobodur temple, Java
ca. 800	Settlement of Hawaii
ca. 802	Charlemagne completes conquest of Saxony
ca. 860	Scandinavians begin colonization of Iceland
884	Kiev becomes capital of Russian state
ca. 1000	Andean city of Tiahuanaco abandoned; China's population reaches 60 million
1100s	Tula abandoned

PROBLEMS AND PARALLELS

1. What were new ways of managing the environment during the late first millennium? How did societies exploit new resources and colonize new lands?

2. What role did geography play in impeding the diffusion of culture and crops in sub-Saharan Africa and the Americas?

3. What factors contributed to the flourishing of South American and Mesoamerican cultures and states?

4. What were the effects of environmental expansion under Islam?

5. What roles did monumental architecture and religious ritual play in many of the cultures discussed in this chapter? How were monks and holy men important to the conquest of new environments and the expansion of states?

6. What was the importance of ecological experiment and the conquest of new environments in Christendom, China, southeast Asia, and the Pacific in the late first millennium?

7. Why are the environmental histories of such varied regions as the Islamic world, China, Japan, and Mesoamerica so important? Are such long-ago transformations relevant or meaningful today?

DOCUMENTS IN GLOBAL HISTORY

- Selection from the *Nihongi*
- Indian land grants, 753 C.E.

- Nineteenth-century description of Lelu
- Selection from *The Russian Primary Chronicle*

Please see the Primary Source CD-ROM for additional sources related to this chapter.

READ ON

The written sources on West Africa are collected in J. F. P. Hopkins and N. Levtzion, eds., *Corpus of Early Arabic Sources for West African History* (2000).

J. Diamond, *Guns, Germs, and Steel* (2003) sets out the case for the isolating effects of American geography.

On the Moche, G. Bawden, *The Moche* (1996) is standard. For the Nazca, A. F. Aveni, *Nazca: Eighth Wonder of the World* (2000) is useful. B. Fagan, *Floods, Famines, and Emperors* (1999) is a lively romp through the history of the effects of El Niño. For Tihuanaco, A. Kolata, *Tiwanaku and its Hinterland* (1996), 2 vols., is exhaustive. R. Keatinge, ed., *Peruvian Prehistory* (1988) collects important essays on the Andean background. On the Maya, M. Coe, *The Maya* (2005), and N. Hammond, *Ancient Maya Civilization* (1982) are the most useful overviews. The exhibition catalog by L. Schele and M.

Miller, *The Blood of Kings* (1992), is important for understanding royal rituals. D. Webster, *The Fall of the Ancient Maya* (2002) is a brilliant and provocative study of the crisis of the ninth and tenth centuries. On Copán in particular, W. Fash, *Scribes, Warriors, and Kings* (1993) is a vivid and engaging study. On Tula, R. A. Diehl, *Tula* (1983) is authoritatie. On Marajó and related topics, the exhibition catalog by C. McEwan et. al., *Unknown Amazon* (2001), contains a wealth of exciting data.

For maize, see W. C. Gallinat, "Domestication and Diffusion of Maize" in R. I. Ford, ed., *Prehistoric Food Production in North America* (1985).

A. M. Watson, *Agricultural Innovation in the Early Islamic World* (1983) is the standard work on Islam's agrarian revolution in this period. K. W. Butzer, *Archaeology as*

Human Ecology (1982) is classic, and D. W. Phillipson, *African Archaeology* (1994) is a survey by the leading living expert on Ethiopia.

The Cambridge History of Japan (1993) is unsurpassed on Japanese environmental history in this period.

R. Thapar, *Early India* (2004); and B. Chattopadhyaya, *Aspects of Rural Society and Settlements in Early Medieval India* (1990), and *The Making of Early Medieval India* (1994) are the best works to consult on environmental aspects of Indian history at the time.

M. Elvin, *The Retreat of the Elephants* (2004) is a sparkling historical study of the Chinese environment, focusing on the history of deforestation, about which there is much, too, in N. K. Menzies, "Forestry," in J. Needham, ed., *Science and Civilisation in China*, vi (2000). *The Cambridge History of China*, iii (1979) is fundamental for Chinese history generally in this period.

On Angkor, the classic by G. Coedes, *Angkor, an Introduction* (1986) remains fundamental, supplemented now by the ingenious work of E. Mannika, *Angkor Wat: Time, Space, Kingship* (1996). M. D. Coe, *Angkor and the Khmer Civilization* (2005) is of special interest from a comparative point of view, as the author is a Mayanist. On southeast Asia generally, D. G. E Hall, *A History of South-East Asia* (1981) and the same author's contribution to *The Cambridge History of South-East Asia*, i (2000) are important.

On the Pacific, important contributions are collected in P. V. Kirch and T. L. Hunt, eds., *Historical Ecology in the Pacific Islands* (1997). P. V. Kirch, *On the Road of the Winds* (2001) is immeasurably helpful. P. Bellwood, *The Polynesians* (1987) is a useful introduction. The classic by B. Malinowski, *Argonauts of the Western Pacific* (1984) can still be read for pleasure and profit.

On Christendom, useful essays are collected in the forthcoming series, edited by F. Fernández-Armesto and J. Muldoon, *The Expansion of Christendom: The Middle Ages*, especially in my volume, "The Internal Frontier." C. Wickham, *The Mountains and the City* (1988), and R. Bartlett, *The Making of Europe* (1994) are fundamental.

Early Chinese and Roman Perceptions of Steppelanders

Relations between the steppelanders of the Eurasian interior and the sedentary peoples of the Eurasian rim were of enormous importance in global history. But it is impossible to say what the steppelanders in the period covered in this part of the book were really like. Steppelander archaeology is in its infancy. The steppelanders themselves wrote little. So our only substantial evidence about them comes from what their sedentary neighbors wrote. By comparing Chinese and Roman impressions we can learn something, if not about the steppelanders, at least about the Romans and Chinese. These accounts show what they feared, hated, and admired about steppeland life and some of their strategies for countering the threat from the steppes. Three sources in particular, across 500 years, enable us to chart the way these sedentary peoples felt about the steppes.

The earliest is Sima Qian, China's "Grand Historian," who probably died around 90 B.C.E. He devoted an entire chapter of his great history of China to steppelanders he called the Hsiung-nu, or Xiongnu, and to their relations with the Chinese. The extract below is from that chapter.

● ● ● ● ●

From the time of the Three Dynasties [the second millennium B.C.E.] on, the Hsiung-nu has been a source of constant worry and harm to China. The Han [the Chinese dynasty under whom Sima Qian wrote] had attempted to determine the Hsiung-nu's periods of strength and weakness so that it could adopt defensive measures or launch punitive expectations as the circumstances allow. Thus I made The Account of the Hsiung-nu....

We hear of these people, known as Mountain barbarians, Hsien-yun, or Hun-chu, living in the region of the northern barbarians and wandering from place to place pasturing their animals. They move about in search of water and pasture and have no walled cities or fixed dwellings, nor do they engage in any kind of agriculture. Their lands, however, are divided into regions under the control of various leaders. They have no writing, and even promises and agreements are only verbal. The little boys start out by learning to ride sheep and shoot birds and rats with a bow and arrow, and when they get a little older they shoot foxes and hares, which are used for food. Thus all the young men are able to use a bow and act as armed cavalry and make their lives by hunting, but in periods of crisis they take up arms and go off on plundering and marauding expeditions. This seems to be their inborn nature. For long-range weapons they use bows and arrows, and swords and spears at close range. If the battle is going well for them they will advance, but if not, they will retreat, for they do not consider it a disgrace to run away. Their only concern is self-advantage, and they know nothing of propriety or righteousness....

Ammianus Marcellinus (ca. 330–390), a former soldier who devoted himself to historical and geographical scholarship in his retirement, wrote in Rome over 400 years later in an attempt to explain the crisis of the Roman Empire: the uncontrollable inflow of immigrant peoples. His focus was on the Huns and a similar but (he claimed) less "uncivilized" steppelander people, the Alans, because he regarded their migrations as responsible for driving other "barbarians" into Roman territory. The following extract is from his *History of Rome from Constantine to Valens.*

They [the Huns] are certainly in the shape of men, however uncouth, but are so hardy that they neither require fire nor well-flavored food, but live on the roots of such herbs as they get in the fields, or on the half-raw flesh of any animal, which they merely warm rapidly by placing in between their own thighs and the back of their horses.

They never shelter themselves under roofed houses...but they wander about, roaming over the mountains and the woods, and accustom themselves to bear frost and hunger and thirst from their very cradles.

There is not a person in the whole nation who cannot remain on his horse day and night. On horseback they buy and sell, they take their meat and drink, and they recline on the narrow neck of their steed, and yield to sleep... And when any deliberation is to take place any weighty matter, they all hold their common council on horseback. They are not under the authority of a king, but are contented with the irregular government of their nobles, and under their lead they force their way through all obstacles.

None of them plough, or even touch a plough handle; for they have no settled abode, but are homeless and lawless, perpetually wandering with their wagons, which they make their homes; in fact, they seem to be people always in flight. Their wives live in these wagons, and there weave their miserable garments; and here, too, they sleep with their husbands, and bring up their children till they reach the age of puberty; nor, if asked, can any one of them tell you where he was born, as he was conceived in one place, born in another at a great distance, and brought up in another still more remote.

In truces they are treacherous and inconstant, being liable to change their minds at every breeze of every fresh hope which presents itself, giving themselves up wholly to the impulse and inclination of the moment; and, like brute beasts, they are utterly ignorant of the distinction between right and wrong. They...have no respect for any religion or superstition whatever, are immoderately covetous of gold; and are so fickle and irascible that they very often, on the same day that they quarrel with their companions without any provocation, again become reconciled to them without any mediator.

Modern Steppelanders
Modern-day steppelanders: Two Kazak horsemen gallop across a snowy plain with golden eagles used for hunting perched on their arms.

As far as we know, neither Sima Qian nor Ammianus Marcellinus ever visited the steppes or even met a steppelander. Our third author, Priscus, however, wrote from direct observation, as a member of a Roman embassy to the court of the Hunic king, Attila, toward the mid–fifth century. Attila was the most powerful monarch in the world at that time. The security of the Roman Empire—or what was left of it—depended on Rome's ability to handle him. Priscus's embassy took him to the north bank of the Danube River, the frontier of an empire that stretched deep into the steppes, which Attila had created by uniting an unprecedented coalition of peoples. The following extract recounts a banquet to which Attila invited Priscus and his entourage. Note that Priscus refers to the Huns as "Scythians," the name the Greeks and Romans gave to the ancient steppelanders who had inhabited the westernmost part of the Eurasian plain.

We proceeded to take our seats; all the chairs were ranged along the walls of the room on either side. Attila sat in the middle on a couch…The places on the right of Attila were held chief in honour, those on the left, where we sat, were only second.…The attendants of Attila first entered with a dish full of meat, and behind him came the other attendants with bread and viands for us and the barbarian guests, but Attila ate nothing but meat on a wooden trencher. In everything else, too, he showed himself temperate; his cup was of wood, while to the guests were given goblets of gold and silver. His dress, too, was quite simple, affecting only to be clean. The sword he carried at his side, the latchets of his Scythian shoes, the bridle of his horse were not adorned, like those of the other Scythians, with gold or germs or anything costly. When evening fell torches were lit, and two barbarians coming forward in front of Attila sang songs they had composed, celebrating his victories and deeds of valour in war. And of the guests, as they looked at the singers, some were pleased with the verses, others reminded of wars were excited in their souls, while yet others, whose bodies were feeble with age and spirits compelled to rest, shed tears. Attila, however, remained immovable…nor by word or act did he betray anything approaching to a smile of merriment except at the entry of Ernas, his youngest son, whom he pulled by the cheek, and gazed on with a calm look of satisfaction. I was surprised that he made so much of this son, and neglected his other children, but a barbarian who sat beside me and knew Latin, bidding me not reveal what he told, gave me to understand that prophets had forewarned Attila that his race would fall, but would be restored by this boy.

Questions to Consider

1. Do the first two extracts yield any clues about how Sima Qian and Ammianus Marcellinus knew the steppelanders and why they wrote about them?

2. What did our authors admire about the steppelanders and what did they dislike about them?

3. What do these accounts tell us about Chinese and Roman ideas of civilized life?

4. Where do our authors think the Huns and Xiongnu came from?

5. What do the extracts tell us about steppelander material culture, government, warfare, religion, and technology?

6. Do these sources give any reason for thinking that the Huns and the Xiongnu may have been the same people?

7. Is there any evidence that steppelander life changed between the second century B.C.E. and the fifth century C.E.? If so, how?

Sources

Sima Qian, *Records of the Grand Historian of China,* translated by B. Watson (2 vol., 1961, repr. 1969).

Ammianus Marcellinus: C.D. Yonge, *Ammianus Marcellinus: The Roman History*, London 1862.

Bury, J.B., *History of the Later Roman Empire*, Macmillan & Co., Ltd., 1923.

PART 5

Contacts and Conflicts, 1000 C.E. to 1200 C.E.

The World Map of Al-Idrisi, a Muslim geographer who worked in Christian-ruled Sicily in the mid-twelfth century. He tried to follow the advice of the ancient Greek geographer, Ptolemy, and constructed his map on a grid. South is at the north. The shape of Arabia is clearly recognizable to a modern eye (upper center), as is that of Spain at the extreme right.

ENVIRONMENT

1000–1300
North Atlantic warm spell

1000–1200
Transfer of crops
from south and southeast
Asia to Islamic world

CULTURE

ca. 1000
Tale of Genji (Japan)

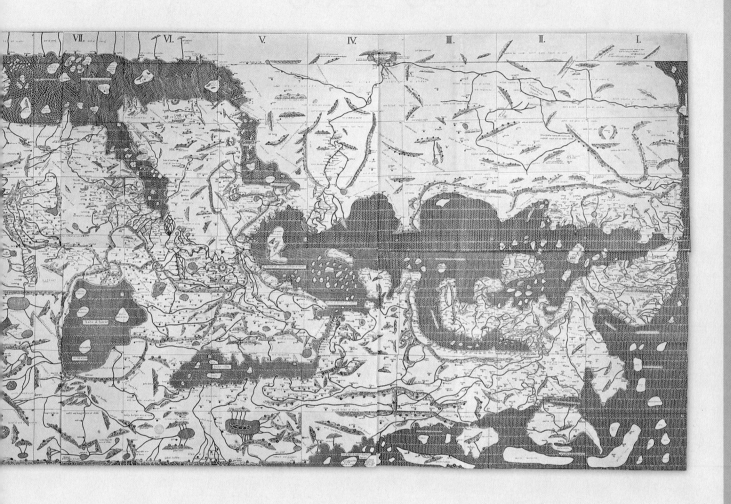

1040s–1090
Increased steppelander
migrations into Middle East

ca. 1070–1122
Chola maritime expansion

900–1200
Growing population,
especially in Europe and China

1098
First Crusade

ca. 1125
Angkor Wat

1000–1200
Spread of Islam
to West Africa

ca. 1200
Cahokia, height of Mississippian
mound building

CHAPTER 11

Contending with Isolation: ca. 1000–1200

The pilgrimages of Buddhist monks inspired Japanese stories about the ferocity of the sea. One of the most popular tales in the late twelfth and early thirteenth centuries was about Gisho, a monk who renounced the love of a beautiful woman and set sail for Korea. But in the incident depicted here, she followed him and flung herself into the sea, where, transformed into a dragon, she protected him from storms.
Tokyo National Museum, Photographer: Kanai Morio/DNP Archives.

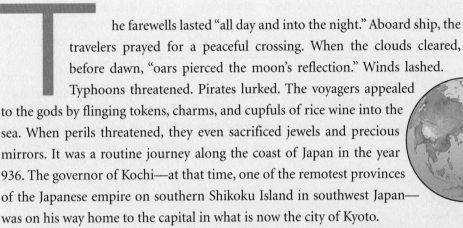

JAPAN

The farewells lasted "all day and into the night." Aboard ship, the travelers prayed for a peaceful crossing. When the clouds cleared, before dawn, "oars pierced the moon's reflection." Winds lashed. Typhoons threatened. Pirates lurked. The voyagers appealed to the gods by flinging tokens, charms, and cupfuls of rice wine into the sea. When perils threatened, they even sacrificed jewels and precious mirrors. It was a routine journey along the coast of Japan in the year 936. The governor of Kochi—at that time, one of the remotest provinces of the Japanese empire on southern Shikoku Island in southwest Japan— was on his way home to the capital in what is now the city of Kyoto.

A journal that the governor's wife supposedly wrote carefully recorded the events of the journey. Scholars have doubted whether a woman really wrote the work, which is full of ironies and has flashes of male humor—as when, for instance, the wind gets up the writer's skirts. But, soon after the date of the diary, literature in Japan became a suitable occupation for rich, intelligent women who did not have to worry about money but were barred from Japanese public life. The "Tosa lady," as the diarist is called, could have been the author. In some ways, the work is obviously a literary creation and a moral tale. The ship navigates between perils. The sea is the arena of the "gods and Buddhas." Only prayer and sacrifice can save the travelers. When clouds recede, pirates emerge. When fear turns the voyagers' hair white, "Tell us, Lord of the Islands," prays the lady to the local god, "which is whiter—the surf on the rocks or the snow on our heads?"

• • • • •

Despite these dramatizations and fictional conventions, the sailing conditions the diarist described were true to life. The coast was so strewn with dangers that sailors dared not sail at night, except to elude pirates. Persistent and unpredictable head winds kept the voyagers cowering in harbor, yearning for home, passing the time in writing poetry. The journey from Tosa to the ship's terminal in the port of Osaka can hardly have covered more than 400 miles; yet it took well over two months. Hostile seas penned in the Japanese, despite their skill in nautical technology. This fact helps to explain why, for most of their history, the Japanese have been confined in their own islands and remained in a relatively small country, despite considering themselves to be an empire.

FOCUS questions

- HOW DID geography influence the spread of culture and state-building in North America and Mesoamerica?
- WHY WAS the Indian Ocean so important for the spread of culture?
- WHY WERE the land routes across Eurasia less significant than the sea routes across the Indian Ocean?
- WHICH AREAS of India were most prosperous in the tenth and eleventh centuries and what was the basis of their prosperity?
- HOW DID their relative cultural isolation affect Japan and Western Europe during these centuries?

Kino Tsurayuki, excerpt from the *Tosa Diary*

The experiences of the Tosa Lady, moreover, highlight a startling truth about her times. In other parts of the world, long-range navigations were leaping oceans. For in the amount of time the Tosa Lady took to get to Osaka, an Indian Ocean trader, with the benefit of the reversible wind system, could get all the way from the Persian Gulf to Sumatra (in modern Indonesia): a distance of more than 5,000 miles. The lady's Persian contemporary, Buzurg ibn Shahriyar, told stories of Persian and Arab mariners in *The Book of the Wonders of India*. One Persian captain made the journey to China and back to Persia seven times. The Japanese could only imagine such journeys. Not long after the Tosa diarist wrote, a fanciful Japanese sea story told of a ship—a "hollow tree"—blown by accident nonstop all the way from Japan to Persia.

As well as by commerce, pilgrim traffic to Mecca stimulated Indian Ocean navigation, as Muslim merchant communities spread across Asia and Muslim holy men took the increasing opportunities to travel and make converts. Meanwhile, beyond the range of the monsoon, migrants from what is now Indonesia crossed the ocean across the path of the southeast trade winds and colonized Madagascar, off the east coast of Africa. Their descendents are still there, speaking the same language the navigators brought—though what inspired such an extraordinary voyage remains unknown. Meanwhile, Polynesian navigators, as we have seen, were penetrating deep into the Pacific Ocean with the aid of some of the world's most regular long-range winds (see Chapter 10). Even more remarkably, around the year 1000, Thule Inuit from the Pacific and Norse from Scandinavia crossed the Arctic and Atlantic Oceans from opposite directions and met in Greenland.

These extraordinarily long-range migrations were part of a double dynamic, as people stretched the resources available to them in one of two ways: exploring for new resources and exploiting existing opportunities in new ways. Region by region, culture by culture, in this chapter and the next, we can see people in widely separated parts of the world using similar strategies: felling forests, extending areas of cultivation and pasture, expanding into new terrain, enhancing muscle power with new technologies.

In the eleventh and twelfth centuries, these forms of expansion were widespread themes of world history; but, as we shall see, they followed divergent courses in different regions. As was so often the case, relative isolation was usually the key to the difference between long-lasting innovation and faltering, short-lived change. Cultures that exchanged information and artifacts were relatively robust. Peoples isolated from fruitful contacts found it much harder. In the Americas, therefore, as so often before, experiments in new ways of life were arrested by checks, frustrated by failures, interrupted by discontinuities. Meanwhile, however, some parts of the Old World, where long-range contacts were easier and more frequent, experienced enduring transformations.

Pilgrim ship. The monsoon helped to make the Arabian Sea a Muslim lake. The Indian pilgrim ship depicted in this Iraqi manuscript of the *Maqamaat* of al Hariri of 1238 is equipped with square sails to make the most of the winds on the outward and homebound crossings of the sea.

The new opportunities of the period arose partly from the environmental changes of the preceding centuries, described in the last chapter. To see how people responded, we can devote this chapter to a sort of world tour of some of the regions most affected—starting in the Americas, before turning to the world around the shores of the Indian Ocean, including the parts of East Africa that face that ocean, and ending with the extremities of Eurasia in Japan and Western Europe. In these parts of the world, we see societies contending with isolation with varying degrees of success.

In other regions of Africa and Eurasia—China, Central Asia, West Africa, the Byzantine Empire, and the Islamic world—the single most important source of new pressures for change arose from the stirrings of nomadic peoples. These are the subject of the next chapter.

AMERICAN DEVELOPMENTS: FROM THE ARCTIC TO MESOAMERICA

The history of the Americas in the eleventh and twelfth centuries is scattered with stories of new frontiers, developed by new migrations or new initiatives. But the effects of isolation and, sometimes, the challenges of hostile environments checked or restricted the achievements. We can start in the north and work, patchily, southward.

Greenland and the North

About 1,000 years ago, a relatively warm spell disturbed the lives of the ice hunters all along North America's Arctic edge. Taking advantage of improved conditions for hunting and navigating, migrants worked their way across the southern edge of the Arctic Ocean, following, from west to east, the line of what we now call the Northwest Passage along the northern coast of the New World in what is today the Canadian Arctic. The Thule Inuit, as archaeologists call them, traveled in vessels made of walrus hides, stretched across wooden ribs and sewn with sealskin thongs. They drew their bone needles only halfway through the hides to create waterproof seams. Their vessels were shallow, so that they could hug the shore, and light, so that the voyagers could lift them from between ice floes. When ashore, their crews could camp under the upturned hulls.

The Thule (TOO-lee) people hunted at sea for whales and polar bears. They mounted their harpoons on floats made from seal bladders, which they blew up like balloons. Game could then be towed home through the sea. Alternatively, they attacked their prey on rafts of ice, which they attached to the harpooned creatures until it was time to haul them in. On land, they hunted with dogs of a breed new to North America. Their spear-armed boatmen trapped reindeer in rivers. For warfare against human enemies, they reintroduced the bow and arrow (see Chapter 1). By about 1000 they had reached Greenland and the western extremities of North America (see Map 11.1). The navigation of the Arctic was an astonishing feat, unrepeated until the twentieth century.

At the same time, almost equally heroic migrations were under way in the opposite direction, toward the same destinations, across the North Atlantic. A series of exploitable currents helped navigators from Scandinavia cross the ocean, via Iceland, below the Arctic Circle. It seems extraordinarily daring to risk such a long journey across the open sea, but the Scandinavians knew that the prevailing winds blew from the west in the latitudes they inhabited. So they could always hope to get home if the Atlantic venture proved fruitless. Even so, it

Inuit seacraft. European technology was unable to make a ship that could sail around the Arctic coast of North America between the Atlantic and the Pacific until 1904. But the Thule Inuit accomplished the task with hide-covered craft by about 1000 C.E. Their boats were shallow enough to hug the shore, light enough to hoist onto the ice, and buoyant enough to avoid being crushed by ice floes.

MAP 11.1

Thule Inuit and Norse Migrations to ca. 1200

→ Thule Inuit migrations to ca. 1000
● Thule Inuit settlements
▢ extent of Inuit, ca. 1200
➤ assumed route of Norse settlement, late 9th century
➤ assumed route of Eric the Red, late 10th century
➤ conjectural route of Leif Eriksson, late 10th century
➤ westerlies
--➤ ocean current
CANADA modern-day country
● Norse settlement/town
● city mentioned on page 343

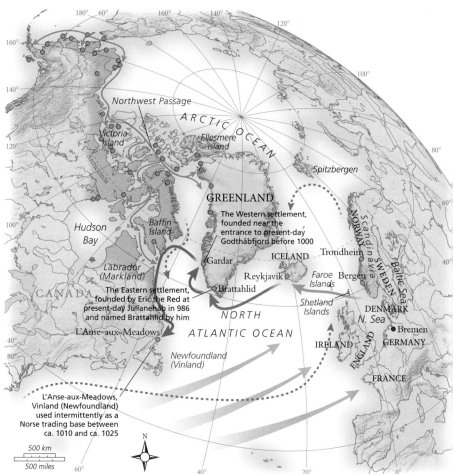

MAP EXPLORATION

www.prenhall.com/armesto_maps

Excerpt from *Speculum Principi*, "The Animal Life of Greenland and the Character of the Land in Those Regions"

The Norse and Thule Inuit

900–1100	Warm spell in Arctic
ca. 982	Erik the Red reaches Greenland
ca. 986	Founding of Brattahlid
ca. 1000	Thule Inuit reach Greenland
1189–1200	Construction of cathedral at Gardar

was remarkable to navigate so far without chart or compass. The voyagers probably steered, like the Polynesians (see Chapter 10), by now-unrecoverable techniques, judging their latitude by observing the polestar with the naked eye on cloudless nights. By day, the only technical aid they had, as far as we know, was the so-called "Sun compass"—a stump of wood with a protruding stick. The shadow it cast would tell the navigator whether his latitude had changed.

Whereas the Thule Inuit were blazing a trail of abundance, drawn by the fat-rich foods of the Arctic, the Norse—or Northmen—as the Atlantic voyagers are called, were usually escapees or exiles from poverty or restricted social opportunity. Erik the Red, traditionally celebrated as the first colonizer of Greenland, arrived there in 982, having been expelled from Iceland for murderous feuding. Most of the colonists he induced to follow him must have been extreme types—extremely desperate or extremely optimistic. "As to your enquiry what people go to seek in Greenland and why they fare thither through such great perils," said a medieval Norwegian book, the answer is "in man's threefold nature. One motive is fame, another curiosity, and the third is lust for gain."

In the early years of their settlement, the environment, harsh as it was, had a lot to offer the newcomers: plenty of fish and game, including luxury items valuable as potential exports to Europe, such as hunting falcons and walrus ivory. Greenland was not, however, a land the Norse cared to settle without changing the environment profoundly. They introduced grain and European grasses for grazing. They developed a breed of sheep whose wool was prized. The big wooden ships the Norse used, held together with iron nails, in a land with little timber or iron, must have seemed wildly extravagant to the Inuit in their skin canoes. The Norse town of Brattahlid in western Greenland—the remotest outpost of medieval Christendom—was heroically elaborate, with 17 monasteries, and churches of stone with bells of bronze. The cathedral at Gardar was built between 1189 and 1200, of red sandstone and molded soapstone, with a bell tower, glass windows, and three fireplaces. The largest farms supported an aristocratic way of life, with big halls in which to feast dependents. But it remained an extremely precarious and isolated colony. Adam of Bremen, a canon of the cathedral of that north German city and a learned geographer of the late eleventh century confided what little he knew: "Greenland is situated far out in the ocean opposite the mountains of Sweden. . . . The people there are greenish from the saltwater, whence, too, that region gets its name."

Brattahlid. The ruins of an eleventh-century Norse church at Brattahlid in Greenland show how ambitious—and, therefore, perhaps, ultimately how unsuccessful—the Norse colonists there were. Huge stone buildings, imported materials, dense settlements, ecologically revolutionary methods of agriculture, adherence to the culture of distant Europe in an environment where that culture could hardly be sustained—all these features of Norse life in Greenland made their colonies fragile.

The North American Southwest and the Mississippi Region

Beyond the colony in Greenland, the shore station that Greenlanders or Icelanders set up in Newfoundland off the east coast of Canada in about 1000 did not last. There were simply not enough wealthy or settled communities in the area with whom the Norse could establish contact, trade, and cultural exchange. A glance at the map of North America at the time shows similar cases, deep inland, of peoples struggling with isolation. The new way of life traveled along two routes: from the heartlands of maize in what is now Mexico, into the arid lands of the North American Southwest; and from the Gulf of Mexico into the wetlands of the Mississippi valley and parts of what is now the United States' Deep South. The results included the rise of cultures with unmistakable similarities to predecessors in Mesoamerica (see Chapter 4), with urban life, irrigation, elaborate ceramics and shellcraft, gold work and copper work, ball games in some cases, and unmistakable signs of statehood (see Map 11.2).

In parts, for instance, of what are now the states of Colorado, New Mexico, and Arizona, evidence of some sort of political network spread over 57,000 square miles: from high in the drainage area of the San Juan River in the north to beyond the Little Colorado River in the south, and from the Colorado River to the Rio Grande. An extraordinary system of roadways, up to 12-yards wide, radiated from a cluster of sites around the great canyon near the source of the Chaco River. Only two needs can account for such an elaborate network. Either some unknown ritual was being enacted, demanding and reinforcing close ties between the places linked; or the roads were there to move armies.

The environment is surprising: parched and—one would think—unsuitable for settled life. Apart from turquoise, which became the basis of a limited export trade, natural wealth was scarce. But the region was densely settled, at least in patches.

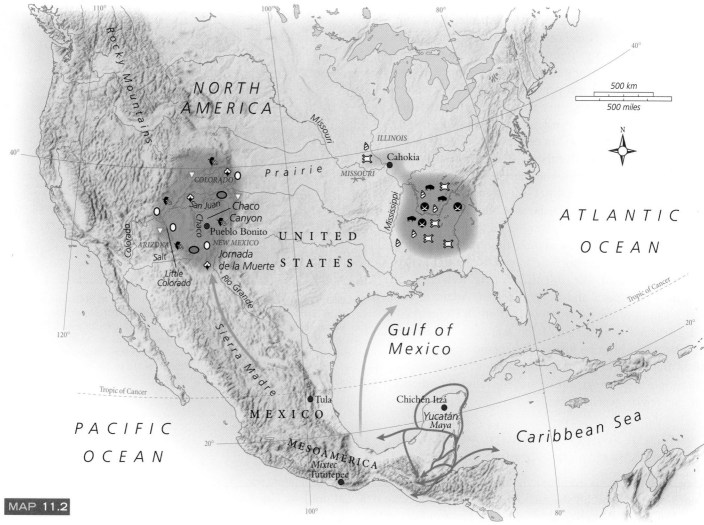

MAP 11.2

North America and Mesoamerica to ca. 1200

- ▨ canyon cultures
- ● major city or ceremonial center
- ▨ Mississippian cultures
- ◠ city associated with Mississippian peoples
- ➤ roads leading north from Mesoamerica
- ➤ sea route from Mesoamerica to Mississippi River valley
- → Mayan trade route
- *Mixtec* peoples
- ARIZONA modern-day state

Economic Basis of Canyon People

- 🌾 maize
- O beans
- ⬧ cotton
- ▽ irrigation
- ⬭ turquoise

Mississippian Trade Goods

- ◊ seashells
- ⋈ deerskins
- 🦬 bison pelts
- ☣ horn

The canyon people built ambitious cities or ceremonial centers around irregular plazas, surrounded by large, round rooms and a honeycomb of small rectangular spaces. Massive outer walls enclosed them. The main buildings were of stone, faced with fine masonry. Roofs were made of great timbers from pine forests in the hills—a dazzling show of wealth and power in a treeless desert. Two hundred thousand trees were felled to construct the ceremonial center at Chaco Canyon. We do not know what the political system was. But we know it was tough. Mass executions have left frightening piles of victims' bones, crushed, split, and picked as if at a cannibal feast.

The economic basis of this civilization was fragile. Sometimes the Chaco River would flood, though not regularly enough to create rich, silty soils. Rainfall levels are likely to have been higher than now, though irrigation was essential to help crops grow in the virtually rainless summer. If water could be delivered to the fields, cotton, maize, and beans would grow predictably, without danger from the sort of fluctuating temperatures that threatened at higher altitudes. Long irrigation canals did the job.

From the twelfth century onward, the climate got drier, which put the irrigation system under a constant strain. Faced with this kind of ecological crisis, communities usually try to adapt, at first, before giving up or moving on.

Canyon de Chelly

Canyon Culture. The adobe-built settlement of Pueblo Bonito in New Mexico enclosed large underground ceremonial spaces and storehouses for the maize painstakingly grown by irrigation in this parched region. The builders seem to have stuck to a single, coherent plan over the many generations it took to build the complex. In the twelfth century, before drought or some unknown disaster overwhelmed the place, Pueblo Bonito was a genuine imperial center, with outlying dependent pueblos built in imitation of it and a network of roads radiating from it.

The rulers of the canyon people responded by expanding into new zones, building more ambitiously, organizing labor more ferociously. But decline, punctuated by crisis, shows through a series of periodic contractions of the culture area and reorganizations of the settlements. Meanwhile, the harsh peacekeeping methods seem to have stopped working. Around the mid–twelfth century, settlements withdrew to high ground, where defense was easier, but where it was much harder to make an ample living from the fields. Revivals of a similar way of life happened frequently, but the problems of isolation defeated or limited all of them until the nineteenth century.

The canyon cultures were at least as remote from Mesoamerican civilizations as the Norse of Greenland were from Europe. Roads north from Mesoamerica led across dangerous territory. Nomadic peoples patrolled the northern edges of the Mesoamerican culture area, practicing raids and conquests, like those launched in Eurasia from the steppes into China or Europe, albeit on a smaller scale. The high road north from what is now Mexico to the nearest patch of easily cultivable soil led through a 61-mile pass known in modern times as the *Jornada de la Muerte:* the "march of death," through rock-strewn defiles and dunes where the glare was so fierce that a traveler's eyes "boiled and bulged" and seemed to burst from their sockets, and men "breathed fire and spat pitch."

It was hard to travel that road—harder still to transmit Mesoamerican crops and traditions beyond the world of Chaco Canyon. The prairie, though a flat expanse, was an ecological barrier, where few patches could sustain sedentary life. It is more likely that Mesoamerica's tool kit, food, and ways of life and thought traveled across the Gulf of Mexico, by seaborne trade, to reach the North American southeast. In parts of this region, the environment was promising. In the Mississippi valley and other riverside floodplains, natural ridges accumulated over centuries, wherever the floods dumped soil. These ridges were the nurseries of the farmers' crops and the inspiration for mounds dredged from the swamps to provide gardens. A hinterland of pools and lakes provided ideal centers for fish farming to supplement the field plants, among which maize was increasingly dominant.

In this region, between the ninth and thirteenth centuries, people laid out ceremonial centers in patterns similar to those of Mesoamerica. Platforms, topped with chambered structures, were loosely grouped around large plazas.

Cahokia. In the eleventh and twelfth centuries, Cahokia, near modern St. Louis, Missouri, was the most ambitious city north of the Rio Grande. As this reconstruction, with huge temple mounds surrounding a central plaza, suggests, Mesoamerican influence must have been at work here. Maize—a hardy northern variety developed from strains originating in Mexico—fed over 10,000 inhabitants and sustained an imperial society. The ambition of Cahokia's rulers demanded huge efforts to work the porous clay soil, exploit nearby forests, fight wars of domination, and control floods and mudslides.

A European explorer's description of Cahokia

The platform mounds grew. In generation after generation, people enlarged and enhanced them, as if to commemorate their own passage through the world. Each generation piled its structures on top of those of its predecessors.

Cahokia, east of St. Louis, is the most spectacular site. Cahokia stands almost at the northwestern limit of the reach of the culture to which it belongs. Its frontier position may have allowed it to act as a commercial gateway between zones of interrelated environments and therefore of interrelated products: shells from the Gulf, deerskins from the eastern woodlands, bison pelts and horn from the prairies. It is hard to calculate its overall size, because modern developments cover much of the area, but it probably covered five and a half square miles. Cahokia's central platform is over 100-feet high—"a stupendous pile of earth" in the opinion of one of the first explorers to record its appearance in 1810. At about 13 acres, the base of the great mound is as big as that of the biggest Egyptian pyramid.

The city first arose in the tenth century. The remains of monumental building works date from the eleventh and twelfth centuries. At its height, in about 1200, Cahokia probably had about 10,000 inhabitants in its built-up area. It was the most intensely and elaborately constructed of a great arc of mound clusters from the site of present-day St. Louis in the west to the easternmost edges of the Mississippi floodplain. Farther away, smaller, similar sites extend from the riverbanks to the uplands of Illinois and Missouri. Cahokia's size gives it the look of a focal point for this scattering of settlements. Its air of importance tempts some scholars to think of it as something like the capital of something like a state, or, at least, a cultural center from which influence radiated. The chronology of Cahokia's development is uncertain in the present state of our knowledge, but a spate of sudden growth and intensive building around the mid–eleventh century seems to have coincided with the abandonment or decline of smaller sites in the same region. This coincidence makes it tempting see the rise of Cahokia as an example of successful imperialism.

Graves at Cahokia have given up honored dead. Their treasures included tools and adornments of copper, bones, and tortoiseshell covered in copper. One grave had gold and copper masks. Thousands of seashells, from the Gulf of Mexico, must have possessed the highest imaginable status and value in this deeply inland place. As time went on, increasing numbers of finely made stone arrowheads were buried in elite graves. This is a precious clue to how Cahokian culture changed but is hard to interpret. Were the arrows trophies of success—or imputed success—in war or hunting, or simple counters of wealth? In any case, the arrows were aristocratic possessions in a society graded for status and equipped for conflict. When Cahokia lost political power in the thirteenth century, the place retained a sacred aura: its manufactures—pots, shell work, soapstone carvings, and small axe heads that presumably had a place in forgotten rites—circulated over hundreds of miles and for hundreds of years after the mound dwellers died out or dispersed.

When objects of great value are concentrated without evidence of a dwelling, grave, or warehouse, it is tempting to talk of a temple. An impressive cache of this type, found at what is now an automobile showroom, at a site somewhat to the southeast of Cahokia, contains carvings that give us glimpses into a mythic history or symbolic system that attached a high value to two themes: fertility and farming, and especially to maize and squash. One female figure tames a snake whose multiple tails are in the form of squash plants. Another female, kneeling on a mat, holds a stalk of maize. Images and fragments from other sites repeat some of these themes: female guardians of corn and serpents, some of whom also hold dishes as if offering a sacrifice.

The people who built Cahokia inaugurated a way of life that was economically successful and artistically productive for not much more than a couple of hundred years—not a bad tally for its place and time, but much shorter than the span major cities in Eurasia achieved. After a spell of stagnation or decline, their inhabitants deserted the upper Mississippi valley culture sites over a period of about four generations around the thirteenth and fourteenth centuries.

Yet culture of the kind that climaxed at Cahokia did not disappear. Rather, it was displaced and some of its more ambitious features—the huge mounds, the vast reach of trade—were abandoned. Mound building continued on a smaller scale, at sites scattered over the lower Mississippi valley and across the North American southeast. Here, traditions of burying chiefs, with rich grave goods and sometimes with large-scale sacrifices, were also maintained.

Mesoamerica

In a similar way in Mesoamerica, the collapse of the cities of the classic Maya in the ninth and tenth centuries in Central America and southern Mexico (see Chapter 10) did not put an end to Maya experiments in civilization. Although the Maya cities of the lowlands never revived, and their peculiar culture, with its heavy investment in inscriptions on stone, never reappeared in quite the same form elsewhere, Maya city life and state-building continued in a new environment on the limestone peninsula of Yucatán in eastern Mexico. Here the environment contrasted with the old lowland heartlands of the Maya. The climate was dry, and irrigation relied on pools and wells. But it was possible to reconstruct the old Maya way of life with remarkable fidelity. In Yucatán, lowland tradition met links with central Mexico, which was accessible through a mixture of seaborne and overland routes (see Map 11.2).

The greatest Yucatán city, Chichén Itzá (chee-CHEHN eet-SAH), began to arise in the tenth century, at about the time the lowland Maya culture withered. Its groves of columns resemble those of Tula (see Chapter 10), which it probably influenced. Some reliefs have undecipherable inscriptions and images that recall central Mexican art. Marked cultural continuities with the former Maya world are evident in the way the buildings are arrayed in the cities of Yucatán, in layouts that reflect an abiding interest in the observation of the movements of the stars and

North America and Mesoamerica, 10th to 13th Centuries

Tenth century	Flourishing of canyon culture in American Southwest; founding of Cahokia in Mississippi River valley; founding of Chichén Itzá in Mesoamerica
Eleventh century	Mixtec first appear in historical record
1063–1125	Life of Eight-Deer Tiger-Claw
ca. 1100	Climate in American Southwest gets progressively drier
Eleventh–twelfth centuries	Maya intensively exploit Yucatán peninsula
ca. 1150	Canyon settlements withdraw to higher ground
1200	Cahokia population reaches 10,000
ca. 1300	Decline of upper Mississippi valley culture sites

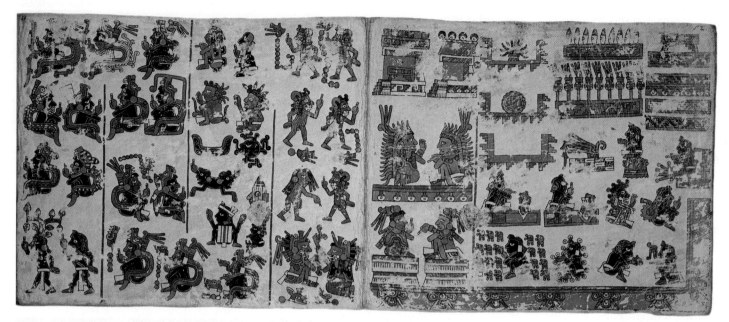

Mixtec creation myth. This Mixtec manuscript about the origins of the Earth predates the fifteenth century. Known as the Vienna Codex and painted on deerhide, it depicts Lord and Lady One-Deer, the legendary ancestors of all the Mixtec rulers, offering sacrifices to the gods of incense and tobacco.

planets, and in the huge temple facades decorated with the snouts of curl-nosed gods or the jaws of feathered serpents. The ball court of Chichén Itzá is the biggest in the Mesoamerican world, and its sides are smothered with scenes of human sacrifice. If traditions recorded later are reliable, a dynasty with imperial ambitions, the Cocom, ruled in this city, and their wars with dynasties in rival centers dominated the history of the region for centuries.

Yucatán was a new frontier for the Maya: a region of unprecedentedly intense exploitation in the eleventh and twelfth centuries. It was not the only such area in Mesoamerica. The Pacific-facing regions of Mexico, beyond the Sierra Madre, leap into the historical record in the same period. This is the region where the people known as Mixtec (MEESH-tehk) lived, in relatively small communities that one could hardly call cities but that were densely settled and famed for their specialized professions of elite craftsmen, especially in gold work and books made of bark. One of the greatest of all Mesoamerican heroes came from here: Eight-Deer Tiger-Claw. From surviving royal genealogies, we can date his life with some confidence to the years 1063 to 1125. He came from Tututepec (too-too-TEH-pehk) in the lowlands of Mexico and spent most of his career among Mixtec communities of the coastal region. His conquests have encouraged scholars to believe in an "empire of Tututepec," but we can best understand them as part of a violent power game to acquire deference, tribute, and victims for sacrifice.

Eight-Deer's wars did not necessarily lead to extensions of territorial power or of direct rule, but they did spawn a great reputation. He figures prominently in all surviving Mixtec histories. His activities show what was expected of a Mesoamerican king. He married frequently and had many children. He visited shrines, mediating between gods and men, offering sacrifices, consulting ancestors. He sent and received ambassadors, played the ball game against rival kings, negotiated peace, and—above all—made war. He died as he had lived. This model of Mesoamerican kingship was defeated, sacrificed, and dismembered by his enemies—entombed with his royal symbols in an episode vividly recorded in the genealogy of the kings of two small Mixtec towns, who wanted to be remembered as his descendants.

AROUND THE INDIAN OCEAN: ETHIOPIA, THE KHMER, AND INDIA

In the Americas, poor communications kept peoples apart and made it hard for them to exchange wealth and ideas. The Indian Ocean, by contrast, was, as we have seen, the world's great arena of exchange, crossed by trade routes and rimmed with rich societies. In the eleventh and twelfth centuries the effects increased. In East Africa and southeast Asia, the evidence of increasing wealth—and therefore the power of rulers able to harness that wealth—became more plentiful than ever, and new or renewed states and trading communities grew in size and influence. Meanwhile, in India, though political troubles convulsed many states, and their cultural influence shrank, trade across the ocean remained buoyant, prosperity survived, and some new or newly powerful kings emerged. We can continue our tour of the world by looking at each of these areas in turn.

East Africa: The Ethiopian Empire

The effects of isolation and of hostile environments, which inhibited so much long-term change in America, had also characterized the history of eastern Africa until this time (see Chapters 5 and 7). Gradually, as we have seen, links across the Indian Ocean lessened East Africa's isolation. By the twelfth century, important changes were occurring there.

Arabic-speaking geographers of that period recorded the names of places along the east African coast as far south as the Limpopo River in Mozambique and knew of Muslim communities as far away as the island of Zanzibar. Arab traders already frequented Mogadishu (moh-gah-DEE-shoo) in modern Somalia. By 1200, Muslims from the Persian Gulf—the Shirazi (shee-RAH-zee) dynasty—ruled it. Muslim geographers mentioned Mogadishu's transoceanic trade, bound for India and China, via the Maldive and Laccadive islands in the Indian Ocean. Indeed, some places in Africa occur in Chinese books on geography as early as the tenth century, and East Africa, which formed part of the Indian Ocean world, bound to the trade of the ocean by the winds that linked it to Asia is well marked on thirteenth-century Chinese maps.

The increased trade of coastal kingdoms and cities could affect state-building far inland in East Africa. This is important, not because state-building is necessarily good or progressive in itself, but because it is a measurable indicator of thoroughgoing, long-term change. In twelfth-century Ethiopia, a new dynasty recovered political unity and began a modest recovery. In this land, which had now been predominantly Christian for over 700 years (see Chapter 9), a time of internal crusade began, recorded in the lives of trailblazing frontier saints. On tireless pilgrimages, for instance, Takla Haymanyot made converts, dethroned idols, and chopped down forests, seizing "devils' trees" to build churches. An ideology of holy war seems to have taken hold. As early as the seventh century, some texts began to identify the ancient Ethiopian capital of Axum (see Chapter 9) as the "nursling of Zion" and her kings as "the children of Solomon," the biblical king of Israel. By the end of the twelfth century, kings regarded themselves as the heirs of Solomon and custodians of the Hebrew Ark of the Covenant, which had disappeared from the temple in Jerusalem centuries earlier. From Ziqwala, near Addis Ababa (ah-dees AH-bah-bah), the modern capital of Ethiopia, a monk called Gebre-Menfas-Qeddus challenged the surrounding Muslims and pagans to convert to Christianity.

On the Ethiopian frontier, the monastery churches of Lalibela began to emerge from the rocks: literally so, for they are hewn out of the ground. King Lalibela after whom their location is named, and who is credited with building most of them, is known only from semilegendary sources. His archives were lost in later wars or, as some scholars think, the next dynasty deliberately erased them. But the traditional tales are revealing. Emphasis, for instance, on the king's personal beauty "without defect from head to foot" reflects esteem for the artistic perfection of the buildings of his time. According to legend, a vision of heaven, which he then sought to realize on Earth, inspired Lalibela. After showing him what churches are like in heaven, God said to Lalibela, "It is not for the passing glory of this world that I will make you king, but that you may construct churches, like those you have seen, . . . out of the bowels of the earth." Stories of angels who worked on the buildings reflect the superiority of the craftsmanship. The monks who wrote Lalibela's life story emphasized that he used wage labor to supplement angelic work. Hatred of slavery was common in the writings of Ethiopian monks.

The Zagwe (ZAHG-way), as the kings of Lalibela's dynasty were called, were themselves frontiersmen. The metropolitan elites of the central highland region around Axum despised them for speaking a provincial language and regarded them as intruders. Nor perhaps did the Zagwe carry total conviction when they claimed to be heirs of Solomon. Everyone knew that they were upstarts who were not related to the old kings of Axum. Propaganda increasingly identified Ethiopia with the realm of the biblical Queen of Sheba, Solomon's concubine. Ethiopia was even proclaimed as "the new Israel." These claims to ancient roots favored rivals for the throne, who emerged in the second half of the thirteenth century, representing themselves as the rightful heirs of the Axumite monarchs, or calling themselves Solomids (meaning that they claimed to be descended from the biblical King Solomon). In 1270, they seized power. The state was organized for war, its court turned into an army, and its capital into an armed camp. The monasteries of Debra Hayq and Debra Libanos, the little world of religious communities on the islands of Lake Tana, became schools of missionaries whose task was to consolidate Ethiopian power in the conquered pagan lands of Shoa and Gojam.

Ethiopia remained primarily an agrarian state, not a trading center. In some degree, it was always a mountain kingdom, with an ideology of defiance against neighboring states and peoples. But the multiplication of contacts across the Indian Ocean enabled Ethiopia to struggle against the effects of isolation with increasing success.

Southeast Asia: The Khmer Kingdom

At the opposite end of that ocean in southeast Asia, the same context helps to explain the rise to fabulous wealth and power of another inland, agrarian kingdom: that of the Khmer (K-MER) in Cambodia. As we have seen (see Chapter 10), the Khmer homeland on the Mekong River, around the Tonle Sap, is ideal for rice growing. The fertility of the soil, enriched by silt from annual floods, nourishes three rice harvests a year. That productivity was the foundation of the kingdom's greatness. The rhythms of its rise, however, matched the growth of Indian Ocean trade, which opened outlets for the Khmer farmers' surplus. The ascent of the kingdom is documented in the growth and embellishment of its great city of Angkor.

The plan of the city reflects influences from India across the Bay of Bengal. Angkor was laid out to evoke the divine design of the world common to both Hindu and Buddhist beliefs: the central mountain or *Meru*, the mountains that ring it, the outer wall of rock, the seas flowing beyond in circlelike patterns. The royal palace built in the eleventh century centered on a tower that bore the characteristic inscription: "He thought the center of the universe was marked by Meru, and he thought it fitting to have a Meru in the center of his capital."

The architecture of the twelfth-century King Suryavarman II proclaims a new era. He had himself carved in the walls of his greatest foundation, the biggest temple in the world, Angkor Wat (AYNG-kor waht). Previously, monumental sculptures had only honored dead monarchs or royal ancestors. Suryavarman appears repeatedly in one of the temple galleries, surrounded by environment-defying goods: umbrellas against the sun, fans against the humidity. A dead snake dangles from his hand, perhaps in allusion to an anecdote about his accession. He seized the throne in his youth from his aged predecessor by leaping on the royal elephant and killing the king, like a god in a legend, who, "landing on the peak of a mountain, kills a serpent." Carvings he commissioned reenact the creation of the world, as if his reign were the world's renewal. They show the cosmic tug of war between good and evil gods. Scenes of the churning of the magic potion of life from the ocean suggest that the fortunate age of the world is about to begin. According to Hindu myth, peace and unity will prevail in the new age, and the various ranks of society will willingly perform their roles.

Hindu tradition predicted that this new age would last 1,728,000 years. Suryavarman's was over by 1150. But his ambitious building programs continued, especially under King Jayavarman VII later in the century. Jayavarman surrounded Angkor with shrines and palaces, way stations, and—it was said—more than 100 hospitals. A proclamation of his public health policy reads:

> He felt the afflictions of his subjects more than his own. . . . Full of deep sympathy for the good of the world, the king expresses this wish: all the souls who are plunged in the ocean of existence, may I be able to rescue them by virtue of this good work. May all the kings of Cambodia, devoted to the right, carry on my foundation, and attain for themselves and their descendants, their wives, their officials, their friends, . . . deliverance in which there will never be any sickness.[1]

The allocation of resources for the hospitals hints at both the scale and the basis of Khmer wealth. Over 80,000 tributaries provided rice, healing spices, 48,000 varieties of fever medicines, salve for hemorrhoids, and vast amounts of sugars, camphor, and other antiseptics, purgatives, and drugs. From no other realm of the time—not even China—do we have figures of this sort or on this scale.

Even amid all this medication, the favorite remedy for illness was prayer. In 1186, Jayavarman dedicated a temple to house an image of his mother as "the Perfection of Wisdom." Again the statistics recorded in surviving documents are dazzling for their precision—which reveals the participation of meticulous bureaucrats—and the sheer volume of wealth they display. The temple received tribute from over 3,000 villages. Its endowments included vessels made of a mixture of gold and silver weighing more than 1,100 pounds and a similar set in silver. The records itemize thousands of precious stones, together with imported and locally produced luxury textiles. Daily provisions for a permanent establishment of 500 residents included rice, butter, milk, molasses, oil, seeds, and honey. Worshippers at the temple required annual supplies of wax, sandalwood, camphor, and sets of clothing for the temple's 260 cult images of Buddhas. This is all ample evidence of the penetration of Cambodia by Indian Ocean trade.

Rock-cut church. Perhaps because of its relative isolation in a mountainous region, Ethiopian civilization has always shown great originality. The political and cultural revival of Ethiopia in the late twelfth and early thirteenth centuries is associated with King Lalibela, who began to build a new sacred capital in a frontier region, where masons dug churches out of the rock. Lalibela seems to have conceived this work as a place of pilgrimage, a "New Jerusalem," and an embodiment of what he claimed was a vision of heaven.

The same source adds evidence on a revolution of Jayavarman's reign: the triumph of Buddhism over Hinduism as the court religion. "Doing these good deeds," the inscription concludes,

> the king with extreme devotion to his mother, made this prayer: that because of the virtue of the good deeds I have accomplished, my mother, once delivered from the ocean of transmigration, may enjoy the state of Buddhahood.[2]

Meanwhile, in the inner chamber of the gilded tower that the king added to the city, a Buddha replaced the Hindu images of previous reigns. The triumph of Buddhism in a state deeply rooted in Hinduism is remarkable. It owed something to the piety of the queen, who sought consolation in Buddhist devotions when her husband was away on campaign. But it was also part of a broader trend. Though Buddhism dwindled in India, it showed its potential for making converts elsewhere, slowly spreading in east, southeast, and Central Asia.

India: Economy and Culture

The strength of the cultural links across the Bay of Bengal, linking India and southeast Asia, is a reminder of another problem. India had long been a fertile source of influences exerted across Eurasia: Buddhism and Hinduism; the science, logic, and technology of the Indian sages (see Chapter 6). The Indian subcontinent's central position athwart Indian Ocean trade routes guaranteed it against isolation and gave it privileged access to far-flung markets (see Map 11.3). India's long, open coasts could soak up ideas and influences from across the oceans, like the pores of a sponge.

Yet there are signs that from the eleventh century India's role in originating and recycling cultural influences began to diminish. Whereas earlier generations of Muslim scholars had looked to India as a source of useful learning, Al Biruni, who came from Persia in the 1020s, found Indian science and scholarship disappointing. He was widely regarded as the most learned man of his time, so he should have been in a position to know. Hindu science, he found, "presumed on the ignorance of the people." He found the Indian sages of his day complacent and uninterested in learning from abroad. His picture was exaggerated, and perhaps distorted by a hidden agenda: the desire to advocate the superiority of Islam over native Indian religion.

Angkor Wat. By the time of King Suryavarman II (r. 1113–1150), the great central temple of Angkor Wat, rising like the sacred mountain Hindus and Buddhists imagined at the center of the world, already dominated the skyline of Angkor. Thanks to silt deposited by the Mekong River, intensive rice cultivation generated huge food surpluses, making possible the investment of work and wealth required to build the stupendous city.

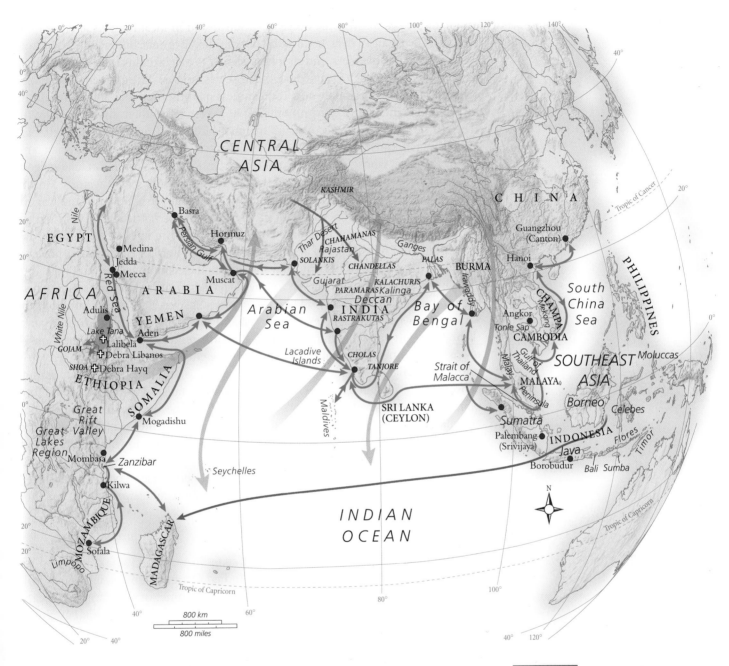

MAP 11.3

The Indian Ocean: From Ethiopia to Cambodia, ca. 1000–1200

- ▩ Zagwe dynasty, Ethiopia
- → Ethiopian expansion under the Solomids
- ✠ monastery
- → maritime trade route
- *CHOLAS* Indian dynasty, 9th–13th centuries
- → colonization route to Madagascar
- → warm monsoon (April to September)
- → cold monsoon (October to March)
- → Muslim raids into northern India, 11th century

There was, however, some truth on al Biruni's side. At least in the north—the part of India he knew—political dissolution accompanied a decline in the quality and output of works of art and learning. The large states that had filled most of the subcontinent since the early ninth century collapsed under the strain of trying to compete with each other and the impact of invaders and rebellions. Much of central and northern India was not divided among territorial states but among competing royal dynasties who found it hard to sustain the loyalties of their followers. The rich Hindu temples of northern India became the prey of Muslim raiders from Afghanistan.

Nevertheless, though states provide the peace commerce requires—and, if the rulers are wise, the infrastructures that help trade thrive—economies can sometimes function well despite political troubles. In some parts of India, the economy was booming. Records of tribute paid to the temples in Rajasthan (RAH-jahs-tahn) in northwest India reveal the range of produce sold in local markets and the lively pace of trade in sugar, dyes, textiles, salt, areca nuts, coconuts, butter, salt, sesame oil. Charcoal makers, distillers, and shopkeepers had to pay taxes in cash. A local ruler in Shikar in Rajasthan in 973 levied tribute in pearls, horses, "fine garments," weapons, camphor, betel nuts, sandalwood, "and endless quantities of gold and with spirited rutting elephants, huge like mountains, together with their mates." From the eleventh century, we can reconstruct merchant lineages from inscriptions that are astonishing, because they reveal how merchants saw themselves. The Pragvata family, for instance, whose activities extended across Rajasthan and into Gujarat (goo-jah-RAHT), considered themselves warriors in a trade war against Muslim competitors and advanced loans to rulers to fight real wars. Not only the warrior caste, says one inscription, can fight in "the shop of the battlefield." This is amazingly ambitious, arrogant language for merchants, who, in most societies of the time, would not have dared to liken themselves to the warrior elite. Clearly, however turbulent the politics of the time may have been, the economy was doing well.

The most spectacular effect was the revival of Indian cities after what seems to have been a long period of relative stagnation. This effect was particularly strong in the south, where political troubles were fewer and invasions infrequent. In Karnataka (kahr-NAH-tah-kah) in southwest India, eleventh-century inscriptions mention 78 towns—three times the number recorded for the eighth century. A grant to a temple in northern Karnataka in 1204 reveals how a city was laid out, with streets leading between white-plastered temples, many bazaars, water tanks, flower gardens, and food plots, with arterial roads at the city's edges. The grant lays the economy of the region and the wealth of the cities before us. It enumerates 24 city precincts, both residential and commercial. Merchants and manufacturers met in the town assembly, which decided how to tax produce passing through the town, including foodstuffs, common drugs and medicines, raw cotton, cloth, perfumes, and horses. Local manufacturers mentioned in the same text included clothiers, perfumers, and jewelers.

India: The Chola Kingdom

Far from the political disorder of the north, states in southern India could enjoy the increase of strength that the wealth of the Indian Ocean made possible. The Chola kingdom was the most remarkable. Like that of the Khmer or of Ethiopia, its heartland lay away from the coasts, in rice fields and pastures. The Chola kings almost invariably attached more importance to landward security and expansion than to the sea. A raid that touched the Ganges River did more for the prestige of the monarchy than the remotest seaborne adventure. The Chola labored to extend their landward frontiers and develop their landward resources by ruthless exploitation. Indeed, they felled forests on a gigantic scale. The founding myth of the dynasty concerns King Chola, who was out hunting antelope when, lured deep into the forest by a demon, he came to a place where there were no Brahmans to receive alms. So he cleared the forest and planted temples. His successors followed this pattern.

The power, wealth, and ambitions of the Chola kings fused with those of the merchant communities on the coast. In the kingdom's grand ports, gold was exchanged for pearls, coral, betel nuts, cardamom, loudly dyed cottons, ebony, amber, incense, ivory, and rhinoceros horn. Elephants were luxuriously warehoused and were stamped with the royal tiger emblem before being shipped out for export.

The merchants' vocation blended with the pirates'. Chola merchants had private armies and a reputation "like the lion's" for "springing to the kill." The imperial itch seemed strongest in kings whose relations with merchants were closest. King Kulottunga I (r. 1070–1122), who relaxed tolls paid to the crown, imagined himself—there is a pillar inscription to prove it—the hero of songs "sung on the further shore of the ocean by the young women of Persia." Most Chola seaborne "imperialism" was probably just raiding, though there were Chola footholds and garrisons on Sri Lanka and the Maldives and perhaps in Malaya (mah-LAH-yah). Its impact, however, crippled Srivijaya in Indonesia (see Chapter 10) and enriched the temples of southern India.

Hindu temples were the allies and support of the Chola kings in managing the state and the biggest beneficiaries of victories in war. While the seaward drive lasted, the registers of gifts inscribed on temple walls show its effects: a shift from livestock and produce of the soil to dazzling bestowals of exotic goods and cash, especially from about 1000 to about 1070. The treasures of the city temple of Tanjore included a crown with enough gold to buy enough oil to keep 40 lamps alight in perpetuity, and many hundreds of precious gemstones and jewels, with plenty of umbrellas and fly whisks for the comfort of the worshippers at ceremonies.

When King Rajendra (rah-JEHN-drah) (r. 1012–1042) built a new capital to commemorate his campaign on the sacred river Ganges, he gave the temples an extravagant new look. Concave, sinuous forms were meant to match the supple figures of queens and goddesses, who shimmied and sashayed in the bronzes earlier kings commissioned. Into the artificial lake, 16-miles long and 3-miles wide, Rajendra poured water drawn from the Ganges. The site of the building, according to a twelfth-century poet, could overwhelm with joy "all fourteen worlds encircled by the billowing ocean. . . . The very landscape around was made invisible."

The temples are the best evidence of the grandeur of the Chola Empire and the reach of its power and trade. But they also suggest why, ultimately, the Chola withdrew from overseas ventures. The temples invested heavily in land and in the revenues of farmers whom they supplied with capital to make agricultural improvements. In consequence, they may have contributed to a shift of priorities toward agriculture and land-based wealth, and therefore, in the long term, to weakening Chola maritime imperialism—an enfeeblement that became marked in the thirteenth century. So, although India remained as rich as ever, some forms of Indian enterprise turned inward.

EURASIA'S EXTREMITIES: JAPAN AND WESTERN EUROPE

The Indian Ocean enclosed the main routes of communication around maritime Asia and between Asia and Africa. Of secondary importance were the land roads across Central Asia and the Sahara, which are subjects for the next chapter. For travelers on both the ocean roads and the land roads, Japan and Western Europe—the regions at the easternmost and westernmost extremities of Eurasia—were hard to get to and from. They were distant from the centers of the system. Europe could not communicate directly with Asia by sea. Africa was in the way. Little of the land-based trade reached the extreme west. Trade was far more intense

The Chola Kingdom

1012–1042	Reign of Rajendra; new capital to commemorate Ganges campaign
1070–1122	Reign of Kulottunga I, proponent of seaborne imperialism
Thirteenth century	Decline of Chola

Chola temple. The great era of Chola temple building in stone began in the reign of Queen Sembiyan Mahadevi in the late tenth century. Her grandson Rajendra dwarfed her achievements with this towering example—over 200 feet high—at Tanjavur. All the villages of the kingdom had to subscribe to its upkeep.

Genji. The earliest illustrated manuscripts of *The Tale of Genji* date from the 1120s, more than 100 years after the novel was written. But they demonstrate its enduring popularity and faithfully capture its atmosphere: the leisured opulence of the imperial palace at Heian, the learning and luxury of the court ladies, and the difficulty of leading a private life—let alone conducting the complex love affairs that the story depicts—behind frail partitions that were literally paper-thin.

between the relatively rich markets concentrated in the region between Byzantium in the west, India in the south, and China in the east. As we saw at the start of the chapter, the typhoon-torn seas that plagued the Tosa Lady surrounded Japan.

Societies, therefore, threatened with isolation occupied the extremities of Eurasia. But they were placed close enough to the major communications routes to tap into the great exchanges of culture of the time. During the eleventh and twelfth centuries, both areas emerged from relative isolation. For Western Europe, as we shall see in the next chapter, the revitalization even led to ambitious attempts to make conquests from the Islamic world.

Japan

While in much of the world people struggled to overcome isolation, in Japan rulers had formerly tried to make a virtue of it. Japanese rulers were fearful of losing migrants to richer regions and apprehensive of Chinese power. They had suspended diplomacy and trade with China in 838 and with Korea nearly a century later (see Map 11.4). Permission to trade abroad was hard to obtain. Even Buddhist monks had to apply for permission to leave the country on pilgrimage. Of course, illicit trade—or "piracy" as officials called it—went on. But self-sufficiency remained the object of government policy.

The best-known Japanese literature of the tenth and eleventh centuries is focused on a narrow, closed court society in a narrow, closed country. The fiction of Murasaki Shikibu in *The Tale of Genji*, one of the earliest realistic novels ever written, unfolds in palace chambers and corridors dark enough to make her stories of mistaken identity among lovers believable. She depicts a world in which the supreme values seem to be snobbery and sensitivity. Struggles for precedence dominate court life. The emperor grants his favorite cat the privileges "of a lady of middle rank." A nurse can tell from the sound of a visitor's cough to what level of the nobility he belongs. Murasaki's male heroes are excited to love by exquisite penmanship, a girl by the "careless dexterity of a folded note." "Sometimes, people of high rank sink to the most abject positions," muses her main character, Prince Genji, "while others of common birth rise to be high officers, wear important faces, redecorate the insides of their houses, and think themselves as good as anyone." The court is everything. Even an appointment as governor of a province is a disgrace. Court literature scarcely mentions the peasants, beaten down by famine and plague, whose rice production sustained the court aristocracy through a system of grants of "public-allowance rice" or *kugeto*.

Murasaki was an acute observer, and her work portrayed the vices of a faction-ridden system. Genji was an underemployed prince demoted from the imperial family, like scores of surplus sons, for reasons of economy. She was a spokeswoman for courtiers excluded from power by the man she hated, whose amorous advances she claimed to have turned down: the all-powerful courtier, Fujiwara no Michizane, who manipulated the political system by marrying his womenfolk into the imperial family and providing an effective bureaucracy from his own household. He was the brother-in-law of two emperors, uncle and father-in-law to another, uncle to one more, and grandfather to another two. After three emperors died in factional struggles, he was left as regent of the empire in 1008. He exploited his opportunities so well that, according to one embittered critic, "not a speck of earth was left for the public domain." Emperors were so preoccupied with ritual duties that the only way they could bid for power was by abdicating and attempting to control their heirs.

Provincial rule was left to administrators supported by retinues of hired tough guys. Despised at court for their "badly powdered faces," these local leaders wielded real power and handled real wealth. Many of them, like Murasaki's Genji, were the descendants of imperial princes who had been sent to the provinces for want of employment at court, or who had opted for provincial careers to pursue autonomy, wealth, and authority of their own. Increasingly they became warriors whose authority depended on force. As the court began to lose control of the provinces, these provincial war-mongers allied in rival bands. In the early twelfth century, Taira no Tadamori was a warrior-descendent of one of the most powerful clans and the son of a provincial governor. His feats against pirates, bandits, and a rebel army of disgruntled Buddhist monks won him a reception at court, but the court aristocracy despised his provincial origins and ridiculed his efforts at poetry.

In the 1070s, however, courtiers, temples, and merchants succeeded in opening Japan to foreign trade in their own economic interests. Trade with Korea resumed for a while as a result of the initiative of Korea's energetic King Munjon (r. 1046–1083). Direct relations between Japan and China followed.

The results were dramatic: Newly rich families became players for power. The greatest profiteers were the Taira clan, who relentlessly, during the twelfth century, built up their power by acquiring provincial governorships and penetrating and, by early in the second half of the twelfth century, dominating the imperial court. In a series of civil wars, culminating in 1185, their rivals and relatives, the Minamoto clan, had replaced them as imperial "protectors" or **shoguns** (shoh-GUNS). From then on the emperors never recovered real power. The renowned monk Mongaku was an adviser to successive shoguns. Invited to pray for a new shogun in 1200, he showed just what he thought of the request: "In the dwellings of those who offend, prayer is of no avail."

As the diary of the Tosa Lady shows, it was hard to get around Japan's home islands—even that relatively small part of the islands the Japanese state occupied. Overseas contacts were genuinely difficult, the surrounding seas genuinely daunting. Yet even at its most restrictive, Japan's isolation had never shut out Chinese cultural influence. Some of Murasaki's characters showed impatience with "Chinesified" styles, appealing to the "spirit of Japan." And popular literature did depict China as strange and exotic. But educated Japanese were well aware of their dependence on China for almost all their models of learning, art, and government. Chinese was the language of the upper administration as well as of all serious literature. The elite used handbooks of quotations from Chinese classics to clinch arguments. Confucian ceremonies and Chinese poetry contests (on such subjects as "the thin, solitary voice of the first cicada" and "the freshness of mountains and streams after the sky has

Japan: Official Isolation

838	Trade and diplomacy with China suspended
ca. 1000	*The Tale of Genji* written
1070s	Opening of Japan to limited foreign trade; restoration of direct relations with China
1160	Taira clan ascendant
1185	Minamoto replaces Taira as shoguns

 Morasaki Shikibu, Selections from the *Tale of Genji*

MAP 11.4

Japan, Korea, and Northern China

A Muslim view of the world. The world, mapped by the Muslim geographer al-Istakhri in the tenth century. The map is now in the library of Leiden University in the Netherlands. Persia, the mapmaker's homeland, is in the center. Europe is the tiny triangle at the lower right. The Caspian and Aral Seas are represented as two large round blobs in the middle of Asia in the lower portion. West Africa is the landmass at the top.

cleared") were among the main occupations at court. Murasaki Shikibu, by her own account, repelled Fujiwara's unwanted attentions by capping his Chinese verses.

Western Europe: Economics and Politics

Nowhere else in the world were there long-range trade routes to match those of the Indian Ocean. But—though the subject is poorly documented in this period—the land routes across Eurasia, from Europe to China, and across the Sahara, between the Mediterranean and the Sahel, were probably carrying increasing amounts of traffic through the eleventh and twelfth centuries. Western Europe–or "Latin Christendom," where people used Latin as the language of Christian worship, government, and scholarship—lay at or just beyond the western and northern extremities of these land routes.

Its relative isolation always threatened the region with backwardness. The Atlantic clouded Europe's outlook to the west. The Sahara cut it off from access to much of Africa. Europe's frontier on the east to the great civilizations of Asia was vital but hard to keep open across plains that hostile steppelanders patrolled or forests flanked by vast marshlands obstructed. There was no direct access to the Indian Ocean. Western European merchants rarely went there—and, when they did, they had to undertake epic overland journeys via the Nile valley or across Arabia or what are now Turkey and Iraq. Unlike in Japan, no one in Western Europe wanted to stay outside the great circuits of Eurasian exchange. But isolation was hard to overcome.

In the early eleventh century, the German chronicler Radulf Glaber hoped to see the Latin church extend over the world "as once Christ and Peter trod the sea." Disillusionment, however, soon set in. The very dynamism of Latin Christendom brought its peoples into contact with other civilizations and made Europeans aware of their own insignificance in others' eyes. A Muslim geographer, al-Istakhri, contemplating the world from Persia in 950, hardly noticed Western Europe at all. In his map, the West was squeezed almost out of the picture, dangling feebly off the edge of the known world. Meanwhile, Latin Christians who looked out at the world in their own imaginations probably saw something like the version mapped at about the same time by the monks who drew the illustrations in the *Commentary on the Apocalypse* of Beatus of Liébana in northern Spain: Asia takes up most of the space, Africa most of the rest. Europe consists mainly of three peninsulas—Spain, Italy, and Greece, jutting into the Mediterranean—with a thin strip of hinterland above them. In 1095, urging fellow Christians to new efforts against the Muslims, Pope Urban II expressed the feeling of being under seige:

> The world is not evenly divided. Of its three parts, our enemies hold Asia . . . a part of the world our forefathers rightly considered equal to the other two put together. . . . Africa, too, the second part of the world, has been held by our enemies for two hundred years and more. . . . Thirdly there is Europe. . . . Of this region we Christians inhabit only a small part, for who will give the name of Christians to those barbarians who live in the remote islands and seek their living on the icy ocean as if they were whales?[3]

Otto III. The workshop of the Abbey of Reichenan in Germany was one of the finest art studios in tenth- and early eleventh-century Europe, producing the Gospel book of Emperor Otto III on gilded pages. The enthroned emperor grasps the orb of the world, stamped with the cross of Christ. He towers over clergy and aristocracy alike, while the regions of Europe, led by Rome, shuffle humbly toward him with their tribute.

Urban wanted Christendom to act together to redress what he saw as an imbalance of power. But it was hard for Christendom to function as a unit as it crumbled into competing states with no strong focus of common allegiance. It became what political scientists call a state system, with lots of interlocking territorial states, rather than an imperial system that a single state dominated or covered, as it had been in the time of the Roman Empire. From 962, the German ruler Otto I called himself—more in hope than in reality—"Roman emperor," and made a big investment to recover a sense of the lost unity. As he understood it, his empire was "holy"—serving the whole of Christendom—and the emperor's duty was to guard and extend its frontier. He arrayed his court city of Magdeburg in north central Germany, near the eastern frontier of Christendom, like a shop window of treasures and relics to lure and fascinate the pagans beyond the Elbe River. When his grandson, Otto III, looked back at the reflection of himself that stared, enthroned in power, from an illustration in his gospel book, he could see lavish images of Germany, Gaul, and the Slav lands humbly bearing their tribute toward him, led by a personification of Rome. Yet these pretensions were hollow. The empire of the Ottos was essentially a German state, covering not much more than modern Germany. Map 11.5 shows where other major states of the system took shape in the eleventh century.

The rise of the state system did not necessarily make Christendom weaker or less able to expand. On the contrary, as many theorists argue, competition between states can stimulate innovation and promote expansion. Great unitary empires, like China, are vulnerable to bad central decision making whereas, in the complexity of a system of many states, one state may fail without incapacitating the rest. Yet if we had the chance to ask medieval Europeans what they thought on this issue, even those who benefited most from the supremacy of the state—the monarchs and their ministers—would generally have expressed regret at disunity. They spoke nostalgically of Roman times, and would have admitted that, when collective action was called for in war against Islamic states, the system usually seemed unable to function effectively.

Although Latin Christendom failed to reunite, it continued to respond to the growing sense of being under attack by outsiders. As we have just seen in the case

SCOTLAND

IRELAND

ENGLAND

WALES

London

ATLANTIC
OCEAN

Bay of
Biscay

KINGDOM OF
NAVARRE

Douro

PORTUGAL

CASTILE

ARAGON

Guadelquivir

GRANADA

Granada

NORWAY

SW[

North
Sea

DENMARK

Lübeck

Elbe   Oder

Bruges

Ghent   Cologne   GERMANY   Madgeburg

Rhine

Rouen   Seine

Paris   CHAMPAGNE

Loire

FRANCE

HOLY ROMAN
EMPIRE

St. Gotthard
Pass   Brenner Pass

Rhône   Milan

Genoa   Po   Venice

Catalonia   Bologna

Florence

Adri

Mediterr

Palermo   KINGDOM O

AFRICA

200 km

200 miles

N

MAP 11.5

The Economy of Europe, ca. 1200

- region of commercially produced cereals
- region of commercially produced wine
- ○ town with population over 50,000
- Muslim frontier in Spain, ca. 1200
- predominantly pagan lands

Principal Trade Routes

- — main overland route
- — Venetian
- — Genoese
- — Catalan
- — Hanseatic
- major textile area
- silver mine
- wax
- timber
- salt
- fish
- furs
- wool

Novgorod

RUSSIAN PRINCIPALITIES

Riga

Western Dvina

BALTIC PEOPLES

LITHUANIA

Volga

Dnieper

Dniester

Danube

Black Sea

BULGARIA

Pera

TREBIZOND

BYZANTINE EMPIRE

Aegean Sea

Athens

SELJUK STATES

RUM

LITTLE ARMENIA

CYPRUS

...an Sea

30°

40°

50°

60°

50°

50°

40°

40°

30°

361

of Ethiopia, expansion does not only happen outward. There are often inward cracks and gaps to fill, slack to take up. From the eleventh to the early fourteenth centuries, a process of internal expansion, accompanied by new economic activity, was under way in Western Europe. Latin Christendom emerged as a genuinely expanding world, as it stretched between increasingly remote horizons.

New settlement and new forms of exploitation converted previously uninhabited or sparsely inhabited environments. Settlement encroached on marginal soils and headed uphill. In mountain settings, Western civilization spread up slopes formerly unoccupied or abandoned to the domain of hostile highlanders, whom their lowland neighbors despised as barbarians. The new accessibility of highlands to settlement from below is intelligible against a long background of climate change: a "warm spell" that lasted from the late tenth to the mid–thirteenth centuries.

Meanwhile, other environments were transformed and ecologies disturbed. Forests fell. Bogs were drained. Farmers moved in. Church and state grasped communities formerly isolated by forest, marsh, or mountain, whose conversion to Christianity, before this period, was sometimes sketchy and whose habitats were often blanks on the map. This was more than an economic enterprise: it was a sacred undertaking—reclaiming for God part of the terrain of paganism. The forest was stained with pagan sensuality and alive with sprites, demons, and "wild men of the woods." The pious felled trees sacred to pagans.

The most famous example is the best. Unable to sleep "on a certain night" in 1122, Abbot Suger of Saint-Denis, a monastery near Paris, rose to search the forest for 12 trees mighty enough to frame the new sanctuary he was planning for his abbey church, built—he hoped—to be full of light and "to elevate dull minds to the truth." The foresters smiled at him and wondered if the abbot was "quite ignorant of the fact that nothing of the kind could be found in the entire region"; but he found what he needed "with the courage of faith." It was a representative incident in a vast project to tame little-exploited and under-exploited environments. At about the same time, the German missionary Bishop Otto of Bamberg was struggling to hack a path through forest and marshland beyond the Polish frontier. "This wood," his chaplain noted, "had never before been crossed by mortal men—except by the King of Poland on a mission of plunder prior to the subjected conquest of the whole of Pomerania."

The Cistercians, one of the most dynamic new monastic orders of the period, directed their efforts into "deserts" where habitation was sparse and nature hostile. They disputed Suger's views on church architecture—advocating simplicity and austerity in worship—but favored building and tree felling on at least a comparable scale. They razed woodlands and "made rough places plain"—fulfilling one of the conditions the Bible specifies for the end of the world. Cistercian activity had a sense of frantic urgency. They drove flocks and ox teams into wildernesses where today, all too often, the vast abbeys lie ruined in their turn. Sometimes, in their craving to escape the greedy secular society that put their souls at risk, Cistercians actually drove existing settlers away from their lands, extending the frontiers of colonization even farther as peasants imitated Cistercian practices on even more marginal lands.

Engineering came to the aid of environmental adaptation. The word *engineer* first appears in a document of 1170, and became common in the thirteenth century, as the applications of engineering multiplied. Drainage helped extend the land on which people could dwell. In Holland, rapid population growth seems closely linked with the success of a project Count Floris V (r. 1256–1296) launched to reclaim waterlogged land. New embankments and canals made rivers easier to navigate. The impact on ecosystems was sometimes dramatic. Searching out new

Wild man. A member of the Butchers' Guild of Nuremberg, Germany, dressed as a Wild Man of the Woods for the annual procession that accompanied the slaughter of cattle in late winter during the carnival that preceded the beginning of Lent, the season of penance during which Christians were forbidden to eat meat. The victim bound to the Wild Man's tree recalls the struggle between savagery and civilization and perhaps also the human sacrifices of of pre-Christian times.

routes and building roads and bridges were urgent tasks for the common good, for which monarchs accepted some responsibility and for which—for example—Domingo de la Calzada, who built causeways and bridges for pilgrims to the shrine of St. James at Compostela in northern Spain, was made a saint. People were able to travel faster and farther. Traffic grew, and people moved peacefully in increasing numbers—as migrants, merchants, pilgrims and "wandering scholars"—along new arteries of what we would call today the infrastructure of Europe.

Behind the expanding frontiers, modest technical revolutions were boosting production. Among inventions originating in Europe at this time were windmills, ground lenses, and clocks. Others, brought there thanks to improved communications across Eurasia, were paper mills, the compass, firearms, and—a little later in the fourteenth century—the blast furnace. Large, heavy plows with curved blades bit deeply into the land, which enabled farmers to exploit the dense, wet soil of northern Europe. More effective harnesses enabled horses to pull the plows and take over a lot of hard work in the fields. More efficient windmills and water mills, more exact metallurgy and new products, especially in arms and glassware, extended the range of business and the flow of wealth. The advances in agriculture that began in the Islamic world toward the end of the previous millennium (see Chapter 10) spread hesitantly, across Western Europe, improving farming with new strains of wheat and—where it would grow—of rice. More varieties of beans improved nutrition and added nitrates to the soil.

Historians debate who was responsible for extending tillage and coaxing new wealth from the soil. Was it primarily the work of "free peasants"? Or did landowners force peasant dependants into greater productivity? There were many different patterns of landholding, which varied regionally and locally, and the drive to improve efficiency probably happened no matter what form landholding took. In any case, the colonization of new lands created opportunities of enrichment at all social levels. More food meant more people. The population of Europe may well have doubled, from about 35 million around the year 1000, while these changes took place.

As production and population increased, so did opportunities for trade. New trade routes knitted Atlantic and Mediterranean seaboards in a single economy. This was an important development, because Western Europe has two natural economic zones—formed respectively along the Mediterranean and Atlantic coasts. The Strait of Gibraltar separates them, with widely different sailing conditions along the two seaboards. Inland a chain of breakwaters splits the continent, determining the flow of rivers and, therefore, the directions of exchange. For much of Europe's history, communication between these two zones was not easy. Limited access through routes across France and the Alpine passes kept restricted forms of commerce alive, even when commercial navigation from sea to sea was abandoned.

New kinds of economic activity became possible in growing towns. In the twelfth century, German merchants unified the northern seas, linking London and Bruges in modern Belgium with the Baltic ports of Lübeck and Riga in Latvia. Lübeck, founded in 1143, was the pioneer city of what became the **Hanseatic League**—a network of allied ports along the North Sea and Baltic coasts that collaborated to promote trade. Soon after, Mediterranean craft, mainly from the Italian city of Genoa, the island of Majorca, and Spain, resumed large-scale ventures along Atlantic coasts, such as had not been recorded since the Western Roman Empire collapsed in the fifth century (see Chapter 8).

Town hall clock. The early fifteenth-century town hall clock of Prague—now capital of the Czech Republic—illuminates the growing concern among the citizens of late medieval European cities to know what time it was. Prague's clock divides the day into arbitrary hours of equal length, while also marking the passage of the hours of daylight, which varied from one day to another. Christian ideology also has its place on the clock. Every hour, the archangel Michael appears to do battle with a Muslim Turk, and the Twelve Apostles move across the clock face.

○ MAKING CONNECTIONS ○

CONTENDING WITH ISOLATION, CA. 1000–1200

REGION/ PEOPLE OR KINGDOM →	OPPORTUNITIES →	EXPLOITATION STRATEGIES
Arctic/Inuit	Change in climate: warming weather allows for navigation across Canadian Arctic; introduction of new breed of pack dogs for transportation; introduction of bow and arrow	New techniques for constructing walrus-hide boats; new uses for sealskin, other animal hides for transport, hunting, food
Greenland/Norse	Warming climate; wealth of fish and game in almost uninhabited region; availability of export items such as hunting falcons, walrus ivory	Improved navigational techniques; new understanding of prevailing winds, ocean currents to improve chances of successful voyages; introduction of European grains and grasses for grazing animals; development of new breed of sheep
North American Southwest and Mississippi region/ Native Americans	Southwest: introduction of maize from Mexico; defensible canyons with water supply; growing population Mississippi: introduction of Mesoamerican "tool kit," food, way of life, thought; expanded trade routes bring deerskin, shells, bison hides, metals, and minerals	Southwest: irrigation canals to expand agriculture; many ceremonial centers; expansion into new zones; intensive organization of labor; development of multistoried residential structures Mississippi: expansion of trade routes; new forms of agriculture with maize, beans, squash, and fish farming; larger populations lead to more intensive crafts development/industry.
Mesoamerica/Yucatán: Maya	Abundant forests, wildlife, coastal resources	New forms of irrigation, wells; new communities lead to expanded sea and land trade routes
East Africa/Ethiopia	Wider access to trade goods	Increased Indian Ocean trade with Arabs, Chinese, Indians helps equip Ethiopian dynasties to expand into new terrain
Southeast Asia: Khmer kingdom (Cambodia)	Growth of Indian Ocean trade opens outlets for Khmer rice surplus; wealth from trade and taxes funds Angkor Wat	Expansion of kingdom coincides with monumental temple complexes at Angkor, complete with expanded amenities for subjects—hospitals, shrines, etc.
India/Chola kingdom	Expansion of frontiers through inland raids brings additional natural resources (forests, agricultural land)	Landward strategy of clearing forests, planting crops and building large temples; coastal merchant communities merge with pirate expeditions sponsored by Chola kings to raid foreign ports
Japan	Provincial warriors break away from imperial court, open Japan to foreign trade; new wealth	Taira and other newly rich families, begin to dominate imperial court, develop shogunate system of government to rule more efficiently
Western Europe	Expanding settlements into marginal agricultural areas; new engineering techniques to manage rivers, build infrastructure	Intensive land management—felling forests, draining bogs combines with Christianizing efforts to "civilize" barbarian areas; increased commerce leads to economic specialization, growth of towns and communes

Exchange across vast distances made geographical specialization and genuine industrialization possible. Historians speak loosely of industrial revolutions and "economic miracles" in this period. For instance, all the industries served by the trade of Genoa depended on geographical specialization. Textiles depended on concentrating wools and dyestuffs from widely separated places of origin. Food processing relied on matching fresh foodstuffs, such as herring, with salt. Shipbuilding demanded a similar marriage of raw materials—wood, iron, sailcloth, and pitch.

The results included urbanization: the revival of old cities and the building of new cities in new lands. The best way, indeed, to measure the economic progress of the period in much of Europe is by the growth of towns—ways of organizing life, which, at the time, were prized as uniquely virtuous. "The order of mankind," according to Gerald of Wales in the 1180s, "progresses from the woods to the fields and from the fields to the towns and the gatherings of citizens." Even old, established cities might experience a renewal of civic spirit. A carving on the facade of the cathedral of Verona in northern Italy displays a typical moment in the forging of civic consciousness, when Verona's patron saint, Zeno "with a serene heart, grants to the people a standard worthy of defence." On the facade of the Church of Sant'Anastasia in the same city, Zeno presents the assembled citizens to the Holy Trinity. In Milan, the assembly point for the citizens was in front of the Church of Sant' Ambrogio, decorated with a similar, equally mythical scene of St. Ambrose calling the citizens to assembly. At times of assembly, in sight of symbols such as these, civic identity was symbolized and reinforced.

In reality, the **commune**—as the citizen body was collectively called—became an institution of civic government in most cities only in the late eleventh or early twelfth century. In what seems to have been a conscious reaching back to a Roman model, many Italian cities acquired "consuls" in this period. By the mid–twelfth century Otto of Freising regarded autonomous city governments as typical of northern Italy. Instead of deferring to some great protector—bishop, nobleman, or abbot—Italian cities became their own "lords" and even extended jurisdiction into the countryside. "Scarcely any noble or great man," Otto reported, can be found in all the surrounding territory who does not acknowledge the authority of his city. In effect, some cities were independent republics, forming alliances in defiance of, or in spite of, their supposed lords. Others tried unsuccessfully for the same status.

Self-ruling city-states were most common in Italy, where, perhaps, memories of Rome remained most alive. But similar phenomena occurred over much of Europe, as urban awareness and the numbers and size of towns grew. We can measure urban growth in the multiplication of parishes. It was exported to new areas of frontier settlement on the edges of Christendom, where planned towns were laid out with the measuring rod and peopled by wagon trains. In Spain, the granting by monarchs of founding documents to tiny new communities marked the progress of settlement on the frontier with the Islamic world. These usually gave the inhabitants some share in judicial or administrative power. All towns of the time were small by modern standards. As few as 2,000 citizens could make a town if it had walls and a charter. "Feelings," it was said, "make the town." If the people felt urban, in other words, they *were* urban. Thirty thousand inhabitants was a metropolis.

For the sake of comparison, it is worth glancing at the farther edge of Christendom, beyond the reach of the Latin church, in western Russia. Here the cities of Novgorod and Pskov contended against a hostile climate beyond the grain lands on

Technology and Growth in Europe

Late tenth century	Beginning of warm spell in climate
1000	Population of Europe approximately 35 million
1143	Founding of Lübeck; beginning of Hanseatic League
1170	First appearance of word *engineer*
ca. 1200	Introduction of new technologies: heavy plows, better harnesses, windmills, water mills, ground lenses, clocks
1300	Population of Europe approximately 79 million

which they relied for sustenance. Famine beseiged them more often than human enemies did. Yet control of the trade routes to the river Volga made Novgorod cash rich. It never had more than a few thousand inhabitants, yet its monuments record its progress: its *kremlin* (or palace-fortress) walls and five-domed cathedral in the 1040s; in the early twelfth century, a series of buildings that the ruler paid for; and in 1207, the merchants' church of St. Paraskeva in the marketplace.

From 1136, communal government prevailed in Novgorod. The revolt of that year marks the creation of a city-state on an ancient model—a republican commune like those of Italy. The prince was deposed for reasons the rebels' surviving proclamations specify. "Why did he not care for the common people? Why did he want to wage war? Why did he not fight bravely? And why did he prefer games and entertainments rather than state affairs? Why did he have so many gerfalcons and dogs?" Thereafter, the citizens' principle was, "If the prince is no good, throw him into the mud!"

Western Europe: Religion and Culture

Transformations in art, thought, and worship matched the dynamism of the economy and of political change in Europe. New forms of heresy, for instance, were among departures of enormous importance for the future of Western Christendom. If popular heresy existed in Western Europe before the eleventh century, no one noticed it. After the year 1000, however, it emerged as a threat. A French peasant named Leutard had a vision in which bees—a traditional symbol of supposedly sexless reproduction—entered his body through his penis. The vision drove him to renounce his wife, shatter the images of Jesus and the saints in the local church, and preach universal celibacy. Among fellow peasants, he attracted a following that survived his death, albeit not for long. In 1015, the first burnings of heretics in the West for over 600 years were kindled. From then on, popular heretical movements were a continuous and, on the whole, a growing feature of Western European history.

Two long, slow changes seem to underlie this phenomenon. First, this was a kind of ugliness in the beholder's eye: imperfections in lay religion that zealous clergymen detected. By the late eleventh century, a movement of Christian renewal and evangelizing fervor (known to historians as the Gregorian Reform after Pope Gregory VII [r. 1073–1085], its greatest sponsor) was demanding new and exacting standards both of clerical behavior and of lay awareness of the faith, and challenging kings and noblemen for control over appointments in the church. More than a power struggle, it was a drive to purge the church of profanity.

At the same time, the evangelical fervor of the clergy was lowering its sights to include the peasantry, to whom clerics had, up to then, paid little attention. This was the result, in part, of a long build up of dissatisfaction with the shallowness with which Christianity had penetrated popular minds. Among its effects was a new or increased emphasis in saints' lives on how saints could—in today's jargon—"relate" to ordinary people by doing menial jobs. A French count, for instance, who joined a monastery in about 990, was set first to keep the hens, then the sheep, then the pigs, and was astonished at his own delight in each successive task.

On the other hand, the rise of popular dissent bears some signs of a revolution born of prosperity. Lay people were themselves stepping

Hell's mouth. The Archangel Michael locks the gate of hell, pictured as a monster's jaws. Note that some of the tortured souls in this thirteenth-century miniature painting are monarchs and monks, with crowns and tonsures. Whatever their wealth or social position, all Christians were equally subject to God's judgment.

up the demands they made of their clergy. The really popular heresies of the eleventh and twelfth centuries were those ministered to by men of ferocious sanctity, like the preachers who called themselves "the perfect," and whose fanatical renunciation of worldly pleasures made them seem holier than the church. At the same time, the new security of life, the opportunities to gather harvests without being attacked, the leisure that increased yields from the soil gave to people, all bought time for a luxury unavailable in hard times: time to think about the Christian mysteries and to develop a desire to get involved in them. At a relatively high level of education, the church could satisfy these stirrings by providing pilgrimages, private prayers, devotional reading matter, and, ultimately, orders of chivalry for the warrior class. Spiritually minded peasants, like Leutard's enthusiasts, could not be accommodated so easily (see Map 11.6).

In the struggle to save their souls, European laymen in the Middle Ages were at a disadvantage. The religious life opened heaven's gates; the warrior's life, stained with bloodshed, distracted by the world, closed them. The religious model suggested the idea that obedience to rules—like those of monks and nuns—could sanctify the lay life. The first such rules or "codes of chivalry" in the twelfth century emphasized religious vows of chastity, poverty, and obedience, but lay virtues gathered prominence, redirected against deadly sins: generosity against greed, self-control against anger,

MAP 11.6

Pilgrim Routes and Shrines in Western Europe, ca. 1200

— pilgrim route
▨ Latin Christendom
▨ Orthodox Christianity
◆ shrine to Jesus Christ
◆ shrine to Mary
◇ shrine to saints

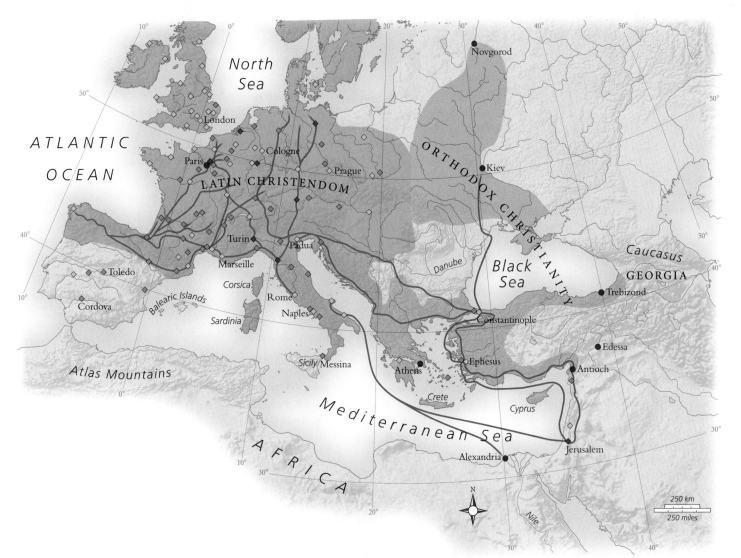

VÉZELAY

Though damaged by anti-Christian vandals in the 1790s during the French Revolution, the doorway of the monastery church of Vézelay, carved in the early thirteenth century, remains one of the masterpieces of Western art. It is a startling attempt to depict the world in all its diversity of peoples and cultures, activities, woes, and hopes.

Clouds, stormy and serene, signify the powers to pardon and condemn that Christ gave the apostles.

This is no mere "Jesus" but a divine Christ. Rays of light fly from his fingertips to empower the apostles. His garment swirls and whirls—he is clothed in the cosmos. Yet he remains human, with a face oppressed by compassion.

In the outer curve of the arch, signs of the zodiac are interspersed with depictions of workers performing the labors of the corresponding seasons. Between Aries and Taurus, for instance, a shepherd feeds kids with new buds. Between Taurus and Gemini, a naked dancer wreathes flowers.

The peoples of the Earth come to Christ— the pagan Greeks, Romans, Persians, and Scythians, and even the "monsters" of legend: dog-headed, pig-snouted, elephant-eared, stunted. Some philosophers denied that such deformed creatures could be fully human, but Christ's love includes them all.

Carved with stunning realism, the inner curve of the arch depicts ordinary people experiencing miracles of healing and conversion.

What does this portal reveal about medieval European faith?

loyalty against lies and lust. **Chivalry** became the prevailing disposition among the aristocracy of the age. It did not make warfare any more gentle or moral; nor did it make all aristocrats good. But it did widen the range of the virtues to which aristocrats aspired.

The art of the West in the eleventh and twelfth centuries reveals a sort of cult of the commoner. Images of peasants and artisans were carved alongside those of saints and angels around church doorways, engaged in the productive economic activities that paid for this art. Here were arrayed the members of a peaceful and orderly society, with everyone in their place and doing well out of it. The new mood affected the way artists showed God, the Virgin Mary, and the saints. Most people nowadays unfairly associate the art of the era with a cold and distant style of other-worldly portraits: with images of the Virgin staring, passionless, and kingly, judgmental Christs. Yet the humanization of heaven was the essence of the artists' inspiration: the evocation of piercing emotions, using everyday people in scenes that depict the kingdom of heaven. Early in the eleventh century, the painter of the gospel book of Abbess Hilda of Merschede painted a scene of Jesus asleep in a storm on the Sea of Galilee, in which the ship leaps into life and the anxiety of the apostles burdens their brows. The Jesus carved for Archbishop Gero of Cologne in Germany dates from before the end of the tenth century, but no modern master ever chiseled the face of the suffering Jesus with more exquisite agony: drawn lips, taut cheeks, nerveless lids, and a trickle of blood at the brow.

In the art, literature, and scholarship of the time, a strong sense of continuity with ancient civilization shines through. Sculptors and builders copied classical works wherever they could find them. The ideas of Abbot Suger on the beauty of light were derived from what he thought was a Greek text from the time of the Apostle Paul's visit to Athens in the early first century. The twelfth-century English historian, Geoffrey of Monmouth, claimed to be able to trace the "British" monarchy back to characters from the ancient Greek poet Homer. Poets in England and Germany tried to write like ancient Roman poets. Lectures in Paris introduced students to the logic of Aristotle. Abelard (1079–1142), the most renowned teacher of the era in Paris, gave audiences the impression that there was nothing logic could not do. In his book on logic, *Sic et Non* (*Yes and No*) of 1122, he exposed the contradictions in many treasured assumptions of the theology and philosophy of his day. The twelfth-century Archbishop of Canterbury, Anselm, too, wrote about God using reason as his only guide—suppressing references to Scripture or the tradition of the church. Indeed, Anselm sought to prove the existence of God—or at least of a real being with the perfection Christianity ascribed to God—by unaided reason. Roughly, his proof says that the most perfect being we can think of must exist, since, if he did not, we should be able to think of another, more perfect being who did.

By the twelfth century, students of nature were beginning to "stand on the shoulders of giants" of antiquity and see farther than they had. In 1092, Walcher of Malvern fixed the difference in time between Italy and England by timing an eclipse. Adelard of Bath noted that light travels faster than sound. He agreed with his younger contemporary, William of Conches, that God likes to work through nature and that miraculous explanations should never be invoked when scientific ones will do. Practical observations piled up: the heights of tides, the habits of volcanoes. Carvers of capitals on pillars in churches imitated natural forms. From this time onward, sculptors chiseled plants and flowers into monastery cloisters.

Abelard, *Sic et Non*

Romanesque art has a reputation for stylization and formality. But in this early example that Archbishop Gero of Cologne in Germany commissioned before the end of the tenth century, the artist was evidently already interested in anatomical realism and in depicting intense emotion. Instead of a remote, divine, judgmental Christ, we see the sorrow and resignation of Jesus, a suffering human being.

IN PERSPECTIVE: The Patchwork of Effects

The great leap of Latin Christendom—the renaissance or rebirth in art and thought that began after the year 1000—was possible because people in Western Christendom found ways to cope and contend with their relative isolation. Scholars in the late tenth and eleventh centuries went to Muslim centers of learning in Spain to acquire groundings in science and mathematics and to learn Arabic. Gerbert of Aurillac—the Emperor Otto III's tutor—sweated to learn mathematics in the Spanish Muslim city of Toledo. Adelard of Bath studied Arabic to get access to Arabic translations of classical Greek books, lost in the West. In the late eleventh and twelfth centuries, as we shall see in the next chapter, pilgrimages, wars, and trade took Western Europeans in unprecedented numbers eastward, to the eastern Mediterranean, and to contact with the Islamic world and Eastern Christendom at Constantinople. At the same time, the westward trickle of communications with south and east Asia probably increased along the Silk Roads.

For Japan, too, isolation might have been frustrating. But there was just enough contact with Korea and China to stoke Japanese art and learning with Chinese influences. The delicately folded poems written by Genji and his friends and real-life counterparts were all in Chinese—part of an ancient renaissance, as influential as anything Europeans wrote or sculpted in imitation of antique models.

In the preindustrial world, the size of states and the scope of economies were functions of time as well as distance. Messages, armies, revenues, and cargoes took a long time to travel across broken country or, by sea, through variable winds. Around the Indian Ocean, increased traffic brought areas in East Africa and southeast Asia out of isolation and kept India rich, despite its political troubles. Despite the heroic efforts of the Norse in the Atlantic, the Thule Inuit in the Arctic, and the Polynesians in the Pacific, the wealth-creating effects of sustained transoceanic or interoceanic commerce could not yet be reproduced outside the region of the monsoons around the Indian Ocean.

Even so, India was much less influential in world history—far less productive of ideas and movements that affected the rest of the world—after 1000 than it had been before. This is only one of many ways in which India seems to have reached a "peak" of achievement. According to the best available studies, India's population was over 200 million in 1000 and fell for the rest of what we think of as the Middle Ages. The Chola kingdom was the last Indian empire to exert major influence in southeast Asia, where Hinduism began to decline—ultimately, to survive only in patches outside India itself.

In the Americas and parts of sub-Saharan Africa, the arresting effects of isolation could not be overcome. Cultural contacts between Mesoamerica and parts of North America helped, for a while, to produce spectacular experiments in building states and modifying environments. But the networks were still too fragile and temporary for the effects to endure.

In the next century, the thirteenth, changes in the pattern of communications across Eurasia would heighten the differences between the Old and the New Worlds. To understand these events and their effects, we have to turn first to the other great theme of the history of the eleventh and twelfth centuries: the growing contacts and conflicts between sedentary and nomadic peoples in Eurasia and parts of Africa, and their effects on the interactions of surrounding regions.

CHRONOLOGY

Tenth century	Flourishing of canyon culture in American Southwest; Chichén Itzá founded
Late tenth century	Norse reach Greenland
ca. 1000	*The Tale of Genji* (Japan); Thule Inuit reach Greenland
1000–1300	Rapid population growth in Europe and development of new technologies; Maya intensively exploit Yucatán peninsula
1000–1100	Flourishing of Chola kingdom (India)
1070s	Opening of Japan to limited foreign trade; restoration of direct relations between China and Japan
Early twelfth century	Building of Angkor Wat (Cambodia) begins
1150	Canyon settlements in American Southwest withdraw to higher ground
1200	Population of Cahokia reaches 10,000
1270	Solomids seize power in Ethiopia
1300	Decline of upper Mississippi valley culture

PROBLEMS AND PARALLELS

1. How did societies around the world contend with their relative isolation between 1100 and 1200?

2. How did isolation affect Greenland and the North American cultures from 1000 to 1200?

3. What roles did Cahokia play in central North America? What evidence is there that it was influenced by the civilizations of Mesoamerica?

4. How did Buddhism and Hinduism spread throughout southeast Asia? How did these religious traditions affect parts of Asia outside India?

5. How did the lands on the extremities of Eurasia (Japan and Europe) overcome their isolation and emerge with powerful political, cultural, and economic systems?

6. How did urbanization affect religious, economic, and political life in Europe between 1000 and 1200?

7. How did increased trade across the Indian Ocean affect East Africa during the eleventh century?

8. What are the benefits and drawbacks of cultural and economic isolation?

DOCUMENTS IN GLOBAL HISTORY

- Kino Tsurayuki, excerpt from the *Tosa Diary*
- Excerpt from *Speculum Principi,* "The Animal Life of Greenland and the Character of the Land in Those Regions"
- Canyon de Chelly

- A European explorer's description of Cahokia
- Morasaki Shikibu, Selections from the *Tale of Genji*
- Abelard, *Sic et Non*

Please see the Primary Source CD-ROM for additional sources related to this chapter.

READ ON

A convenient version of the Tosa diary is printed in D. Keene, ed., *Anthology of Japanese Travel Literature* (1960). *The Book of the Wonders of India* is available in an edition by G S P Freeman-Grenville (1984). G.R. Tibbetts, *Arab Navigation in the Indian Ocean before the Coming of the Portuguese* (2002) gives the background.

On Greenland, K. Seaver, *The Frozen Echo* (1997), is a brilliant work, with contentious conclusions.

On the North American south-west, S. Lekson et al., *Great Pueblo Architecture of Chaco Canyon* (1986) is outstanding; pages in B.G. Trigger and D. Washburn, eds., *The Cambridge History of the Native Peoples of North America*, v.1, Part I, bring it up to date. The Mississippi sites are covered in T. R. Pauketat and T. E. Emerson, Cahokia: Domination and Ideology in the Mississippian World (2000); T. E. Emerson and R. B. Lewis, eds., *Cahokia and the Hinterland* (2000); and T. R. Pauketat, *The Ascent of Chiefs* (1994). On the Mixtec, R. Spores, *The Mixtec Kings* (1967) cannot be bettered.

For Ethiopia under the Zagwe, some sources appear in R. B. Pankhurst, *The Royal Chronicles of Ethiopia* (1967). On Ethiopia and Angkor the works recommended for chapter 9 are good for the period covered here.

Albiruni's *India*, ed. C. Sawyer is the classic text. M. A. Saleem Khan, *Al-Biruni's discovery of India* (2001) attempts an interpretation. The works of Chattopadhyaya and Thapar mentioned above remain fundamental for this period in India. For the Cholas, V. Dehejia, *Art of the Imperial Cholas*

(1990) is a breathtaking work; B. K. Pandeya, *Temple Economy under the Colas* (1984) is important.

V. K. Jain, *Trade and Traders in Western India* (1990) and B. Stein, Peasant, *State and Society in Medieval South India* (1994) are useful on their subjects.

There are many editions of *The Tale of Genji*. For Japan in this period, *The Cambridge History of Japan, ii* (2002) is comprehensive.

On western Europe, R. Southern, *The Making of the Middle Ages* (1961) is a classic work, unsurpassed. R. Bartlett, *The Making of Europe* (1994) is fundamental. Classic essays on some of the topics covered here are collected in F. Fernandez-Armesto, ed, *The Internal Frontier of Christendom*. A useful little collection of Cistercian sources is in P. Matarasso, ed., *The Cistercian World* (1993). Abbot Suger is best approached through E. Panofsky, ed., *Abbot Suger on the Abbey Church of St Denis and its Art Treasures* (1979). On technology, J. Gimpel, *The Medieval Machine* (1977) is superb and standard. On peasants, G. Astill and J. Langdon, eds., *Medieval Farming and Technology* (1997) provides an excellent introduction.

On heresy, M. Lambert, *Medieval Heresy* (2002) is spirited and comprehensive. A. Murray, *Reason and Society in the Middle Ages* (1978) is an ingenious work, full of insights. C. H. Haskins, *The Renaissance of the Twelfth Century* (2005) is a classic, once pioneering, now enduring. P. Lasko, *Ars Sacra* (1995) is a good introduction to the art of the period.

CHAPTER 12

The Nomadic Frontiers: The Islamic World, Byzantium, and China, ca. 1000–1200

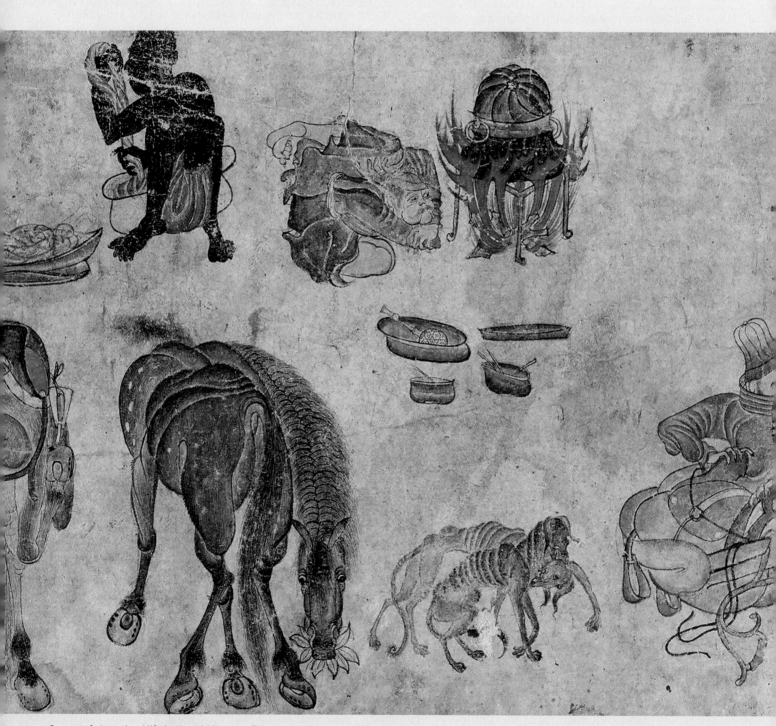

Scenes of steppeland life in the middle ages. Two warriors do their washing. A shaman wriths by the campfire. Weapons are stacked. Horses graze. Starving dogs hope for scraps. A chief mends his saddle.

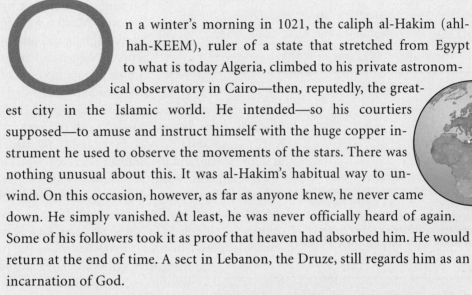

CAIRO

On a winter's morning in 1021, the caliph al-Hakim (ahl-hah-KEEM), ruler of a state that stretched from Egypt to what is today Algeria, climbed to his private astronomical observatory in Cairo—then, reputedly, the greatest city in the Islamic world. He intended—so his courtiers supposed—to amuse and instruct himself with the huge copper instrument he used to observe the movements of the stars. There was nothing unusual about this. It was al-Hakim's habitual way to unwind. On this occasion, however, as far as anyone knew, he never came down. He simply vanished. At least, he was never officially heard of again. Some of his followers took it as proof that heaven had absorbed him. He would return at the end of time. A sect in Lebanon, the Druze, still regards him as an incarnation of God.

To most observers, however, he was just mad. His "deeds were without reason," said a typical critic, "and his dreams without interpretation." Some of his actions were certainly erratic. At different times, he outlawed dogs, churches, evening traffic, canal trade, and women's shoes. He expected the end of the world—which perhaps explains his habits of personal austerity and reckless alms giving. His main defect, in his critics' eyes, was that he was a Shiite (SHEE-eye-iht) (see Chapter 9). The two chief doctrines of Shiia clearly mattered to al-Hakim. He thought that supreme power in Islam passed by heredity—through Fatima, Muhammad's daughter, and her husband, Ali to his own so-called Fatimid dynasty. And he saw himself as the fulfillment of Shiite belief in the divine appointment of an infallible **imam**, or holy ruler, to supplement Muhammad's own teaching.

For a while, it looked as if Fatimid success in war was a sign of God's favor and a prelude to the triumph of the divine imam. The conflict between rival caliphs, the Shiite in Cairo, and the Sunni in Baghdad, divided the Islamic world into roughly equal portions. To make matters worse, from the 920s, a third dynasty, with its court in Cordova in Spain, also claimed to be the caliphs. At intervals in the tenth and eleventh centuries, Shiite rebels or invaders seized Baghdad and humiliated or manipulated the Sunni caliphs. From 1090, the Shiite sect known as the Assassins occupied Alamut (AH-lah-moot)—a mountain fortress in Persia—from where they launched raids and unleashed allegedly drug-crazed fanatics to execute political murders. The word *assassin* comes from "hashish."

• • • • •

Important threads of cultural unity still linked the rival political and religious traditions in the Islamic world: veneration of the prophet Muhammad, adherence to the Quran, the use of Arabic as the language of religion and learning, the unifying force of the pilgrimage to Mecca that every Muslim was required to make once in a lifetime. Mutual obligations among Muslims were still strong, even between Shiites and Sunnis. In 1070, for instance, when a famine threatened Cairo, the Fatimid caliph sent his womenfolk to Sunni Baghdad to escape starvation. Islamic civilization was still the most widely dispersed civilization the world had ever seen. Muslims ruled a continuous band of territory from northern Spain, across North Africa and into Asia, to the Indus, the Jaxartes River (now called Syr Darya) in Central Asia, and the Arabian Sea (see Map 12.1).

Nonetheless, political disunity was strange and disturbing for Muslims. Fragmentation weakened the states it created and wasted their strength in wars against each other. The strain told. In the early eleventh century, the Spanish caliphate crumbled. In most of Iran and Kurdistan (KOOR-deh-stahn), the seizure of power by minor dynasties made the rule of the caliph in Baghdad no more than symbolic. The Fatimid caliphate had reached the limits of its expansion, and its North African provinces began to slip from its grasp after the Fatimids moved their court from Tunisia (too-NEE-zyah) to Cairo in 973. On the western frontiers of the Islamic world in Spain, southern Italy, and Anatolia, aggressive Christian states were active. Both a challenge to and the salvation of Islam came from unlikely directions: the Sahara and the steppes of Central Asia.

THE ISLAMIC WORLD AND ITS NEIGHBORS

The Islamic world was caught up in a sweeping Eurasian confrontation. Settled societies in Europe, Africa, and Asia faced warlike, nomadic, pastoral societies that had emerged in Central Asia and North Africa. Sometimes the relationship was hostile. It was always tense. In this chapter, we look in turn at the societies most affected—the Islamic world, with its western neighbors in Spain and West Africa, and then the Byzantine and Chinese Empires.

The Coming of the Steppelanders

The steppelands—home of unruly and warlike pastoral peoples—seemed more full of threat than promise to the Muslim world. The Turkic peoples of the Asian steppe, in particular, had a fearsome reputation for courage and stubbornness in battle.

Pilgrim Caravan. "I cling to journeying, I cross deserts, I loathe pride." The freedom and frequency of travel across the Muslim world are among the main themes of one of the most popular Arabic works of the thirteenth century, the *Maqamat* (or *Scales of Harmony*) of al-Hariri, which inspired some of the finest illustrated manuscripts of the time.

The *Dede Korkut* (DEH-deh kohr-KOOT)—the epic that celebrated their virtues—vividly captures the Turks' love of virility and violence (see Chapter 9). Turks had filtered into Islamic lands for centuries, usually as slaves and soldiers, as individuals or in small bands. Now Turkic peoples over-spilled the steppeland in waves of migrants and invaders. As so often with movements of peoples in the steppelands, we do not know what set them off. But once the shifts of population began, they ignited a kind of chain reaction, with some migrant groups pushing others ahead of them.

From the *Dede Korkut*

The city of Bukhara (boo-HAH-rah) in modern Uzbekistan, once "the focus of splendor" and "the horizon of the literary stars of the world," according to an account based on the childhood recollections of a palace official's son, became for a while the headquarters of the Seljuk Turks (see Chapter 9), who overran Iran between the 1030s and the 1050s. One of Seljuk's brood seized Baghdad in 1055 and turned the caliph into a client—"a parrot in a cage." Farther east, in Afghanistan, the warlord Mahmud of Ghazni (mah-MOOD of GAHZ-nee) was the self-appointed guard of Islam, whose 17 raids into India gathered so many captives that prices in the slave markets of Afghanistan tumbled. He was himself the descendant of a Turkish adventurer. Seljuk's sons and grandsons first took service with him, then turned on him. The Turkish cavalry overwhelmed Mahmud's elephants. Muslims called the Turks "the army of God"—not in approval but in fear. God had unleashed these ferocious pagans to punish Muslims' sins.

Al-Thalibi, *Recollections of Bukhara*

Turkish hostility might have shattered the Islamic world—just as the Arabs had destroyed the Persian Empire and the western barbarians had broken Rome. The Turks certainly altered the political framework of the Islamic world. After a stunning series of conquests, however, the Turks stopped, converted by the culture they had conquered. The first Turks to embrace Islam were a people of Central Asia known as the Karkhanids, whose conversion, according to traditional dating, occurred in 960. The fervor of their conversion set a precedent that almost all other Turkic peoples followed in placing themselves at the service of Islam.

Seljuk and his sons were among the next wave of converts. The effect was to change their whole way of life. The ruins of the capital they built at Konya (KOHN-yah) in Anatolia show how thoroughly they abandoned pastoralism and absorbed the urban habits of the peoples they conquered. By the end of the twelfth century, 108 towers enclosed the city. Vast market gardens stretched far into the surrounding plain, feeding a population of perhaps 30,000. Charters of charitable foundations mention a marketplace and shops of all kinds. Inns with high-arched aisles were built to accommodate traveling merchants and their camels. But the Seljuks never entirely forgot the steppe. Their coins showed hero-horsemen with stars and haloes round their heads. Their sultans lay in tombs, shaped to recall the tents in which their ancestors dwelled.

The Seljuk experience was typical of that of pastoralists in and around the Muslim world at the time. No one knows how it happened, but the Islamic world absorbed most of the Turkic invaders and transformed them into its strength

Caravanserai. In 1229, a Seljuk sultan built this imposing structure in Anatolia near Aksaney on the road to Konya as a place where caravans could halt. On either side of the gateway, which had to be big enough to admit laden camels, the slender columns are topped by capitals that still seem to be in the tradition of ancient Rome. There were over 200 such structures known as *caravanserai*, around the Seljuk realms, facilitating the movement of armies and officials as well as of merchants.

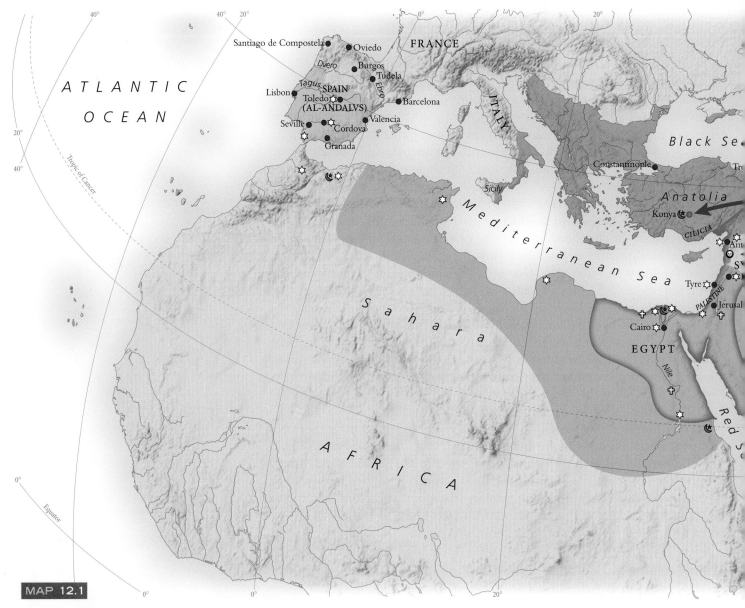

ATLANTIC
OCEAN

Tropic of Cancer

Equator

Santiago de Compostela • Oviedo

FRANCE

Duero

Burgos
Tudela

Tagus SPAIN
Lisbon • Toledo ☆
(AL-ANDALVS)
Seville • Cordova
Granada

Ebro

Barcelona

Valencia

ITALY

Sicily

M e d i t e r r a n e a n   S e a

Black Se

Constantinople •

Anatolia

Konya

CILICIA

Tyre

PALESTINE Jerusal

Ant

S

S a h a r a

A F R I C A

Cairo

EGYPT

Nile

Red S

MAP 12.1

The Middle East and the Mediterranean, ca. 900–1100

▨	extent of caliphate, ca. 900
▨	area controlled by Ghaznavids, ca.1000
➤	raids by Mahmud of Ghazni
BUWAYHIDS	Muslim dynasty with dates
➤	Seljuk conquests, ca.1040–1090
●	Seljuk capital (from 1077)
☻	assassin stronghold
UZBEKISTAN	modern-day country
▨	Byzantine Empire, ca. 1050
⚔	battle
Karkhanids	people
☆	Jewish communities
☪	Sufi shrines, ca. 1250
✚	Christian communities
▨	caliphate of Cordova
▨	Fatimid dynasty

and shield. The newly converted Turks brought badly needed strength. They turned on the enemies—or alleged enemies—of orthodox, Sunni Islam. They conquered Anatolia and Armenia from Christians, Syria and Palestine from Shiites. In India and, later, on the frontiers of Europe, they began to drive back the bounds of the dominant cultures—Hindu and Christian respectively—and advance those of Islam (see Map 12.1).

Success in attracting, converting, and domesticating pastoral peoples—and recycling their violence in Muslim service—is one of the decisive and distinctive features of the history of the Islamic world. Its importance is apparent when one compares the Islamic record with those of other settled agricultural societies in Christendom, China, India, and Africa. Christendom usually dealt with steppelander threats by trying to fight them off or buy them off. The Magyars (MAHG-yahrs) and Bulgars, who settled in Hungary and Bulgaria respectively, were the only cases in which Europe

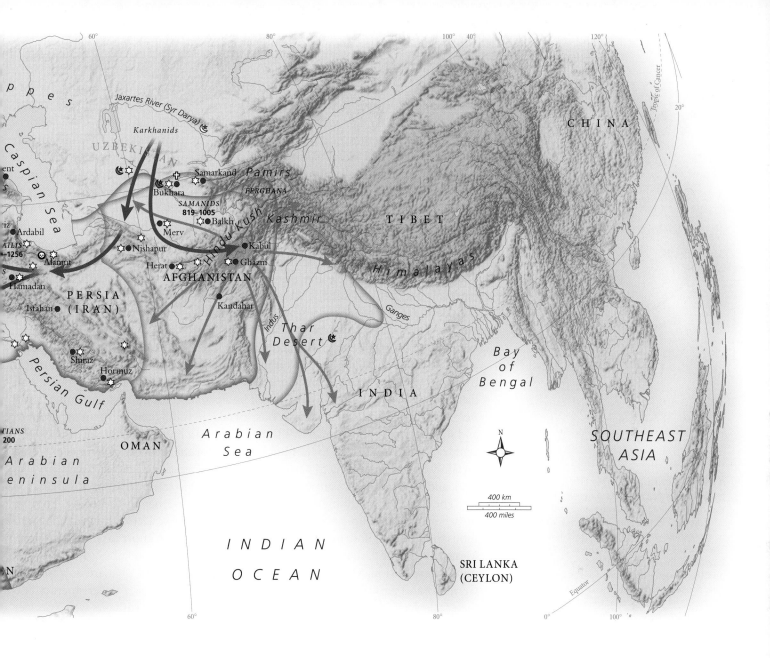

successfully absorbed steppeland invaders. China seduced steppeland conquerors to Chinese ways of life, but was unable or unwilling to turn them permanently into a favorable fighting force. In India invading pastoralists frequently became ruling elites, sometimes adopting parts of Indian culture, but usually remaining alien intruders on the Indian scene. In none of these regions did native cultures manage to harness nomad energies for wars of aggression of their own. Yet the nomads brought new energy to the Islamic world and revitalized Muslim states' capacity for war.

The Crusades

It is worth comparing the Islamic world's response to the steppeland invaders with the fate of the other intruders: the crusaders, who attacked from Christian Europe. Writers of world history usually give the Crusades a lot of attention, because the

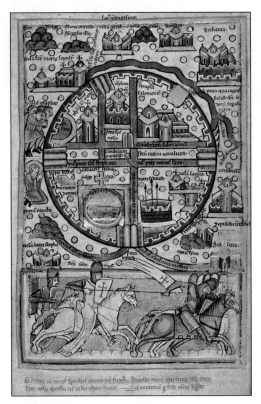

A medieval tourist-guide. This late twelfth-century guide was made to help English pilgrims find the major tourist attractions and useful spots in and around Jerusalem. The money exchange is in the center, and the food market is to its right. The Temple of Solomon occupies the upper right quarter of the city (surrounded by circular walls), and the Golden Gate "where Jesus entered sitting on a donkey" leads to it. The cross marks Golgotha where Jesus was crucified. The Holy Sepulcher where he was buried is below it.

A Muslim view of the Crusaders

Crusades seem to be early signs of the vitality of the West—the capacity of Western European peoples to reach overseas and make war way beyond their frontiers. For the Islamic world, however, the Crusades were a minor nuisance. The crusaders were few. The states they carved out on the Muslim world's eastern Mediterranean coast were small and mostly short lived. Crusaders could not be converted to Islam, but—thanks to the availability of Turkish manpower and leadership—their threat was neutralized or contained.

The Crusading movement started as an outgrowth from the tradition of pilgrimage. Increasingly in the tenth and eleventh centuries, Christians made the difficult journey to Jerusalem—and a few other destinations considered holy—as an act of penance for their sins. In the second half of the eleventh century, disorder in the Islamic world and the selective persecution of Christians by some Muslim rulers, especially the Fatimid caliphs who had taken possession of Jerusalem, made the Jerusalem pilgrimage more dangerous. Pilgrimages—which, in theory, were peaceful journeys, on which the pilgrims relied on the mercy and charity of people whose lands they crossed—became armed expeditions. Simultaneously, Christians began to adopt what had formerly been a Muslim notion: holy war. The land where Jesus' feet trod, and where so many saints' bones lay buried, sanctified those who fought and died for it. War in a holy cause could itself be a penance. Knights need no longer envy monks their easy route to salvation. Warriors could fulfill their vocation for violence and still be saved. "The blood of Muslims," declared a French poet in the early twelfth century, "washes out sins." Even if not holy, war for the recovery of Jerusalem would certainly be just, according to Christian theorists: Palestine had once been Christian land, and Muslims had "usurped" it—so it was right to try to win it back.

These trends in thought and devotion came together in the 1090s. Popular preachers whipped up a mass movement—a kind of collective hysteria that sent thousands of poor, ill-armed pilgrims to their deaths in an effort to get to Jerusalem. Meanwhile, Pope Urban II (r. 1088–1099) orchestrated a relatively well-planned military expedition. Most participants were from France and what are now western Germany and parts of Italy. They included leading members of the aristocracy and their followers and dependents. It is often claimed that the crusaders were younger sons, with inadequate inheritances, and adventurers "on the make," escaping from restricted social and economic opportunities at home. This seems false. Many crusaders were rich men with a lot to lose by going on crusade. The church is also often thought to have encouraged the Crusades, so that it could increase its own wealth. That was certainly one of the effects, as crusaders left property to monasteries and churches to look after in their absence, and, once they got to the east, made grants of conquered land and treasure to religious institutions there.

The early crusaders blundered to surprising success, capturing Jerusalem in 1099 and lining the shores of the Levant with states their own leaders ruled (see Map 12.2). Muslim divisions made these successes possible. Muslim indifference and infighting allowed most of the new states to survive for a while. The crusader kingdoms got support from Italian merchant-communities, who welcomed access to trade, and, occasionally, they received reinforcements from Europe. The newcomers from Europe, however, were often religious zealots who tended to disrupt the delicate tolerance between Christians and Muslims on which the crusader states relied for stability.

In the mid–twelfth century, Zangi (ZAN-gee)—a Turkish chief who dubbed himself "pillar of the faith"—lost patience with the chaos of what we call the Middle East. Or, at least, he saw the opportunities it presented to build an empire. He proclaimed a *jihad* against infidels and Shiites. The strategy worked. Zangi and his heirs began to reconquer the lands lost to the crusaders. Saladin (SAH-lah-deen), the Kurdish

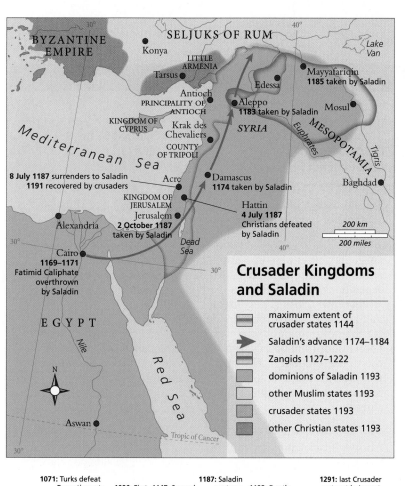

BYZANTINE EMPIRE

SELJUKS OF RUM

Konya

LITTLE ARMENIA

Tarsus

Antioch
PRINCIPALITY OF ANTIOCH

KINGDOM OF CYPRUS

Edessa

Mayyafariqin
1185 taken by Saladin

Aleppo
1183 taken by Saladin

Mosul

Lake Van

Mediterranean Sea

Krak des Chevaliers

COUNTY OF TRIPOLI

SYRIA

MESOPOTAMIA

Euphrates

Tigris

8 July 1187 surrenders to Saladin
1191 recovered by crusaders

Acre

Damascus
1174 taken by Saladin

Baghdad

KINGDOM OF JERUSALEM

Jerusalem

2 October 1187 taken by Saladin

Hattin
4 July 1187 Christians defeated by Saladin

Dead Sea

200 km
200 miles

Alexandria

Cairo
1169–1171 Fatimid Caliphate overthrown by Saladin

EGYPT

Nile

Red Sea

N

Aswan

Tropic of Cancer

Crusader Kingdoms and Saladin

	maximum extent of crusader states 1144
→	Saladin's advance 1174–1184
	Zangids 1127–1222
	dominions of Saladin 1193
	other Muslim states 1193
	crusader states 1193
	other Christian states 1193

MAP 12.2

The Crusades

	Muslim-ruled territory
	Latin Christian-ruled territory
	Orthodox Christian-ruled territory
	Armenian Christian-ruled territory
→	First Crusade, 1096–1099
→	Second Crusade, 1146–1148
→	Third Crusade, 1188–1192
✱	massacre of Jews, 1096

3,890 km (2,420 miles)

3,650 km (2,270 miles)

1071: Turks defeat Byzantines at Manzikert

1096: First Crusade

1147: Second Crusade

1187: Saladin captures Jerusalem

1193: Death of Saladin

1291: last Crusader outpost in Levant (Acre) eliminated

1000 — 1050 — 1100 — 1150 — 1200 — 1250 — 1300

1095: Byzantine emperor appeals for aid to Pope

1099: Capture of Jerusalem

1171: Saladin overthrows Fatamid Caliphate

1192: Third Crusade

1202: Fourth Crusade
1204: Crusaders sack Constantinople; divide Byzantine empire

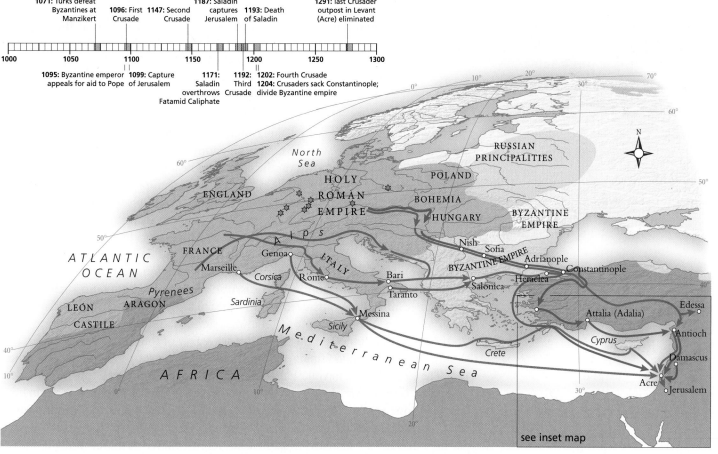

RUSSIAN PRINCIPALITIES

North Sea

ENGLAND

HOLY ROMAN EMPIRE

POLAND

BOHEMIA

HUNGARY

BYZANTINE EMPIRE

N

FRANCE

Alps

Genoa

ITALY

Nish

Sofia

Adrianople

Constantinople

ATLANTIC OCEAN

Marseille

Corsica

Rome

Bari

Taranto

BYZANTINE EMPIRE

Salonica

Heraclea

Pyrenees

ARAGON

Sardinia

Messina

Sicily

Attalia (Adalia)

Edessa

LEÓN

CASTILE

Crete

Cyprus

Antioch

Damascus

Mediterranean Sea

AFRICA

Acre

Jerusalem

see inset map

379

● MAKING CONNECTIONS

THE CRUSADES

HISTORICAL BACKGROUND →	CAUSE FOR ACTION →	EUROPEAN CONSEQUENCES →	CONSEQUENCES IN EASTERN MEDITERRANEAN
Tradition of pilgrimage—Christians go to Jerusalem	By 1050, increased danger, disorder, and occasional persecution in Middle East	Transformation of armed escorts; adoption of Islamic idea of holy war	Transformation of Holy Land into region of continual battle
Jerusalem formerly a Christian and Jewish land	Muslim population, kingdoms control the region	Religious leaders whip up mass movement—disorganized expeditions lead to disastrous results; Pope Urban II organizes a military expedition (First Crusade)	Quick capture of Jerusalem; creation of small "crusader kingdoms"
Roman Catholic church most important institution in Western Europe	Church needs land, wealth to fund its clerics, infrastructure, and religious activity; new spirituality favors annual pilgrimages as a form of penance	Local bishops and papacy help coordinate, orchestrate Crusades; crusaders left property to monasteries and churches while abroad	Conquered land and treasure often granted to church institutions
European lay aristocracy needs means of salvation	Development of chivralric ethos; founding of knightly orders	Aristocratic violence exported on Crusades	Crusades become ruling elite over large Muslim population
Defeat of Muslims by crusaders	Weak, disorganized Muslim kingdoms in eastern Mediterranean	Initial success of Crusaders; occupation of Jerusalem and Holy Land	Proclamation of *jihad* by Zangi, Turkic chief; reconquest completed by Saladin; overthrow of crusader Kingdoms

professional soldier who seized the Zangid Empire in 1170, largely completed the reconquest. He overthrew the crusader kingdom of Jerusalem in 1187, reduced the crusader states to tiny enclaves on the coast, and beat off attempts by new crusaders from Europe to recover Jerusalem. Yet that was not Saladin's greatest achievement. He sought to be remembered above all as the "reviver of the empire of the Commander of the Faithful," a restorer of Islamic unity, a torch of Sunni Islamic orthodoxy.

The defeat of the crusaders was a sideshow. More important, in the long run, for the future of the Islamic world was the success of the Zangids' main strategy: the extinction of the Fatimid caliphate in Cairo and the conquest of Egypt for Sunni Islam. Though heresy continued to disrupt Islamic uniformity, no such large or menacing Shiite state outside the Shiite heartland of Iran ever again challenged Islamic solidarity. From now on, Shiia was confined, in most of the Muslim world, to the status of a subject minority. The other legacy of the Zangids and Saladin was Islamic militancy. Jihad remained a way to legitimize upstart dynasties and regimes.

The Crusades, meanwhile, left an equally sad legacy. For most of the Middle Ages, Christian, Muslim, and Jewish communities in the Middle East, Egypt, and Spain lived alongside one another in relative peace (see Map 12.1). Christians and Muslims intermarried, exchanged culture, and, in some frontier zones, even worshipped at the same shrines. In war, Christian and Muslim states rarely behaved as if they thought of each other as natural enemies. They often made alliances against third parties, regardless of religious affiliation. The Crusades, however, fed on religious propaganda and encouraged the two traditions to demonize each other. Crusading fervor also contributed to growing hostility in Europe between Christians and Jews, since Jews were often the victims of rioting that laments over the loss of the Holy Land aroused. In most places, Jews were the only non-Christian communities the mob found to hand.

As for the common opinion that the Crusades were strategically important in demonstrating the growing power of Latin Christendom, that seems—at best—exaggerated. As we saw in the last chapter, there was a great deal of evidence of dynamism in the Western Europe of the eleventh and twelfth centuries, but most of it was expended on inward development and on expanding the frontiers. If anything, the Crusades contributed indirectly. Their failure helped alert people in Europe to the backwardness and vulnerability of their part of the world compared to the cultures of the Near East.

The Invaders from the Sahara

It was not only in Asia that the Islamic world successfully mobilized pastoralists for the jihad. On their westernmost frontier, in Spain and Portugal, Muslims badly needed new strength. Since the eighth century, Muslim rulers had held territory as far north as the Duero and Ebro River valleys. But **al-Andalus** (ahl-AHN-dah-loos), as they called the region was a sprawling state, with a structure hard to hold together and frontiers hard to defend. The original Muslim settlers—mostly Berbers from North Africa—were few in number. They were scattered in towns or strung out around the southern and eastern river valleys and coasts, uneasily holding down large subject Christian populations. Internal communications relied on roads that the Romans had built centuries earlier to link widely scattered communities. The vast region between the rivers Tagus and Duero was a frontier in depth, strewn with fortifications, protecting the Islamic world's long flank against raids from the small Christian states that huddled in the mountains of the northwest. Wealth made al-Andalus viable: wealth gathered from the huge agricultural surplus of rich soils in the south and east; wealth spent on the fabulous luxuries—ivory work, jewels, palace-building, lavish gardens—for which Spanish art of the time is renowned.

In the late tenth century, a strong-arm general, Almanzor (ahl-mahn-SOHR), kept the potentially mutinous armies and regional aristocracies of the Spanish "caliphate," as its rulers called it, busy with wars against the Christians. Almanzor died in 1002. In 1009 Berber mutineers sacked his headquarters, "wilder now than the maws of lions, bellowing the end of the world." The caliphate dissolved into numerous competing kingdoms. The Islamic world's defense in the west was divided among more and weaker hands. The Christian frontier stole and lurched southward, as the northern Christian kingdoms took advantage of the disunity in the Islamic south. By the 1080s, the Tagus valley was in Christian hands. In alarm, some of the Spanish Muslim kingdoms called on warrior ascetics from North Africa, the Almoravids (ahl-moh-RAH-vihds), for help.

In Arabic the Almoravids' name is a pun, suggesting both hermits and soldiers. They emerged as an alliance of pastoral bands from the Sahara, whom firebrand preaching aroused into self-dedication to holy war. From the mid–tenth century, reports began to cross North Africa of large alliances of nomads, belonging to the veiled Sanhaja (sahn-HA-jah) peoples whose territory covered most of the western Sahara. By the 1040s, the Sanhaja, apparently united in the cause of jihad, broke out of the desert to conquer Morocco. They were not the first such invaders. Nomads whom the Fatimids had expelled from southern Egypt had already wrought havoc in the region. The Almoravids, however, were apparently more numerous and evidently more effective.

Christian and Muslim harmony. Songs in praise of the Virgin Mary, written by King Alfonso X of Castile (r. 1252–1284), could be played and enjoyed by both Christian and Muslim musicians. Both traditions upheld—and still uphold—the virginity of Jesus' mother. Food, dress, language, and even some religious practices spanned the frontier between Christian- and Muslim-ruled areas.
A Moor and a Christian playing the lute, miniature in a book of music from the 'Cantigas' of Alfonso X 'the Wise' (1221-84). 13th Century (manuscript). Monasterio de El Escorial, El Escorial, Spain/Index/Bridgeman Art Library

A CORDOVAN IVORY JAR

Richly carved ivory jars for holding rare and costly essences, such as camphor, ambergris, and musk, show how luxurious life was in the palace of Madinat al-Zahra in Cordova in Muslim Spain in the late tenth century. This example was made for a brother of the reigning caliph.

The domed shape suggests the architecture of palaces and mosques. The missing knob would have had the form of a rich fruit, such as a pomegranate.

The inscription reads: "Blessings from God, goodwill, happiness, and prosperity to al-Mughira, son of the Commander of the Faithful, may God's mercy be upon him," with the date, 967.

The scenes depict hunters picking dates, court attendants, boys stealing eagles' eggs, and lions devouring bulls. The exact meaning of the images—if there ever was any—is lost, but all hint at royal power and well-being.

Ivory pyxis of Al–Mughira. Scene of harvesting dates. 968 CE. From Cordoba, Spain. Inv. 4068. Photo: H. Lewandowski/ Musee du Louvre/RMN Reunion des Musees Nationaux, France. Art Resource, NY.

How does this ivory jar reflect the wealth of Muslim Spain around 1000 C.E.?

When they received the summons to Spain to help its Muslim rulers fend off the Christian states, the Almoravids already had a reputation for military efficiency, having created a state that spanned the Sahara. In the tradition of many Saharan tribes, they had—at least at an early stage of their history—a surprisingly egalitarian attitude to women. A woman, Zaynab al-Nafzawiya (ZAY-nab ahn-nahf-zah-WEE-yah), dominated, for a time, Almoravid politics and nominated generals. "Some said the spirits spoke to her," said orally transmitted traditions, "others that she was a witch."

The Almoravids and Almohads

1040s	Sanhaja conquer Morocco
1076	Kumbi Saleh falls to Almoravid armies
1080s	Muslim kingdoms in al-Andalus call on Almoravids for help
1140s	Almoravid Empire falls to the Almohads

In Spain, the Almoravids drove back the Christians and preserved most of the peninsula for Islam. The Almoravids spent much of their fury, however, on the rulers of the petty Muslim kingdoms, whom they swept away, first denouncing their luxury, then seizing it for themselves. The corruption to which the Almoravids submitted in their turn became a provocation and an enticement to other religiously inspired desert pastoralists. In the 1140s the Almoravids' empire was conquered by a new ascetic alliance, the Almohads (AHL-moh-hads)—the name means "people of the oneness of God"—who again invaded Spain from North Africa and, for a while, succeeded in propping up the Islamic frontier (see Map 12.3).

These movements of desert zealots also turned south Islam's frontier with paganism in Africa. The most celebrated of Almoravid generals, Abu Bakr al-Lamtumi (AH-boo BA-kuhr ahl-lam-TOO-mee), was said to have abandoned the embraces of Zaynab herself to take up the war against the black pagans. Almoravid efforts focused on Ghana, the kingdom of the Soninke (sohn-ihn-KAY) of the upper Niger River (see Chapter 10). Ghana was enviably gold-rich, for it controlled access to the routes of trans-Saharan trade, where gold was exchanged for salt. It was also offensive to the Almoravids as the home of "sorcerers," where, according to collected reports, the people buried their dead with gifts, "made offerings of alcoholic beverages," and kept a sacred snake in a cave. Muslims—presumably traders—had their own large quarter in or near the Ghanian capital Kumbi Saleh, reportedly with a dozen mosques, but were kept apart from the royal quarter of the town. The Soninke fought off Almoravid armies with some success until 1076. In that year, Kumbi fell, and its defenders were massacred. The northerners' political hold south of the Sahara did not last, but Islam was firmly implanted in West Africa.

By the middle of the next century, Arab writers regarded Ghana as a model Islamic state, whose king revered the true caliph in Baghdad and dispensed justice with exemplary openness (see "Going to the Source: Arab Views of Ghana"). They admired his well-built palace, with its objects of art and windows of glass; the huge natural ingot of gold that was the symbol of his authority; the gold ring by which he tethered his horse; his silk clothes; his elephants and giraffes. This magnificence did not last. After a long period of stagnation or decline, pagan invaders overran the Soninke state, and destroyed Kumbi. But Islam had spread so widely by then among the warriors and traders of the Sahel that it retained its foothold south of the Sahara for the rest of the Middle Ages.

The Progress of Sufism

For all the achievements of the strong men who emerged from steppes and deserts to champion Islam, it is doubtful whether war alone could heal the divisions among Muslims and equip the Islamic world to expand. For that, inventive intellectuals were necessary—shapers of a religion that could appeal to a diversity of cultures and engage human sympathies and sensibilities without provoking conflict. Sufism

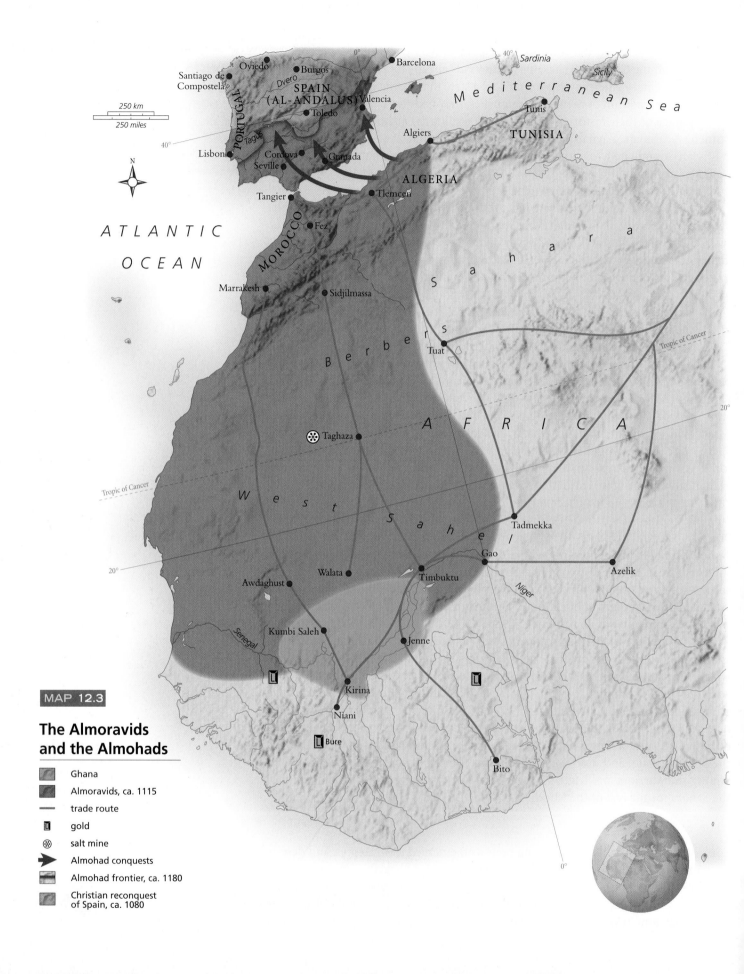

ATLANTIC
OCEAN

Mediterranean Sea

Sardinia

Sicily

**SPAIN
(AL-ANDALUS)**

Santiago de
Compostela
Oviedo
Burgos
Barcelona
Dvero
Valencia
Toledo
Lisbon
Cordova
Granada
Seville
Algiers
Tangier
TUNISIA
Tunis
ALGERIA
Tlemcen
Fez
MOROCCO
Marrakesh
Sidjilmassa

PORTUGAL
Tagus

250 km
250 miles

N

40°

40°

0°

B e r b e r s

S a h a r a

Tropic of Cancer

A F R I C A

20°

Taghaza

Tropic of Cancer

W e s t   S a h e l

Tuat

Tadmekka

Gao

Azelik

Walata

Timbuktu

Niger

20°

Awdaghust

Kumbi Saleh

Jenne

Senegal

Kirina

Niani

Bure

Bito

0°

MAP 12.3

The Almoravids
and the Almohads

Ghana

Almoravids, ca. 1115

trade route

gold

salt mine

Almohad conquests

Almohad frontier, ca. 1180

Christian reconquest
of Spain, ca. 1080

(see Chapter 9) had enormous popular appeal. But most of the Muslim elite rejected it. In the early tenth century, for instance, ordinary people revered the great spokesman of Sufism, al-Hallaj (ahl-hahl-LAJ), as a saint, but the Islamic authorities put him to death, because he claimed to have achieved self-extinction and mystical union with God. Gilani (gee-LAH-nee), his successor, who became one of the most popular preachers in mid–eleventh-century Baghdad, had a popular reputation as the "perfect man." He offered a simple morality of dependence on God—based on the rule, "Expect nothing from human beings"—as an alternative to the rigid legalism of Islamic scholars.

The divergence between legal-minded and mystic-minded Muslim theologians seemed unbridgeable until Abu Hamid Muhammad al-Ghazali (ah-boo hah-MEED moo-HA-mad ahl-ga-ZA-lee) entered the debate. He was blessed or cursed with an intellect he described as an "unquenchable thirst for investigation . . . an instinct and a temperament implanted in me by God through no choice of my own." At the height of a career as a conventional theologian in Baghdad, he experienced a sudden awareness of his ignorance of God. He became a Sufi, retired to his native Nishapur (NEE-shah-poor) in Persia, and, before his death in 1111, wrote a dazzling series of works reconciling Sufism and Sunni orthodoxy. He was a master of reason and science but demonstrated, to the satisfaction of most of his readers, that human minds could not grasp some truths without direct illumination from God. Study could tell you about God, but only a mystical experience can show you who God is. Al-Ghazali likened the effect of mysticism to the difference between knowing what health is and being healthy. He valued the faith of the poor and uneducated as highly as the learning of the officials of the mosques. Al-Ghazali's rehabilitation of Sufism was vital for the future of Islam. Because Sufis were indifferent to externals, Sufi mystics could tolerate cultural differences among Muslims and between Muslims and non-Muslims in a way the legal-minded Islamic intellectuals could not. Though most people found Sufis' mystical practices as difficult to understand as any of the doctrines of the conventionally learned, Sufis' emphasis on experience, faith, and emotions was universally accessible. Their habits of holiness satisfied ordinary people's craving for saints. They were Islam's most effective missionaries in subsequent centuries (see Map 12.1).

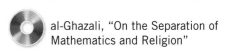 al-Ghazali, "On the Separation of Mathematics and Religion"

THE BYZANTINE EMPIRE AND ITS NEIGHBORS

If the pastoralists contributed to the salvation of the Islamic world, their attacks were disastrous for the many non-Muslim states that proved less skillful at absorbing them or deflecting their power. A dramatic case in point is that of the state—centered on Constantinople—whose rulers called it "The Roman Empire." In Western Europe, the Roman Empire was little more than a pious memory and its revival an impractical dream. But in Eastern Europe, the empire still existed—at least, in some people's perceptions. Nowadays, historians usually balk at using the word *Roman* and prefer to call it the Byzantine Empire—from Byzantium, Constantinople's ancient Greek name. The rulers, after all, had no authority at Rome and spoke Greek rather than Latin. But Byzantines claimed the exclusive right to regard themselves as heirs of ancient Rome. When ambassadors arrived in Constantinople in 968 from the "august emperor" Otto I in Germany (see Chapter 10), Byzantine officials laughed at "the audacity of it!

To style a poor barbarian creature 'Emperor of the Romans.'" And the Byzantine emperors did maintain a principle of government that went back to the emperor Constantine himself—they ruled both state and church. The kind of clergy the popes strove to give to the Latin church in the eleventh century—"purified" of lay power, privileged by its own system of appointments, laws, and courts—was unacceptable in Byzantium, where emperors appointed all bishops, and the church accepted state control.

Byzantium and the Barbarians

The Roman-ness of Byzantium dwindled by degrees. In the time of Justinian in the mid–sixth century, the government at Constantinople was actively engaged in trying to reconstruct the Roman world, and Latin was still the official language (see Chapter 8). In the early seventh century, Byzantium still ruled substantial parts of the Western Roman Empire, with enclaves as far away as Spain. But events of the seventh and eighth centuries shifted its frontiers and changed its character. The Arab expansion after the death of Muhammad (see Chapter 9) stripped away the empire's territory south of the Mediterranean—Syria, Egypt, and North Africa. Meanwhile, from the sixth century to the eighth, speakers of Slav languages slowly colonized much of the Balkans, including Greece. Arabs, Bulgars, and Russians threatened Constantinople itself.

In defense of the empire, missionaries and diplomats were as important as armies. The church virtually monopolized literacy in the areas of the Balkans and Russia where Byzantine missions were active. Missionaries invented the alphabets in which Slav languages were written. They also helped to spread statehood, legitimating strong rulers, sanctifying weak ones. Many Balkan states slipped and slid between allegiance to the Latin- and Greek-speaking churches, but for a while, thanks to missionary efforts launched from Constantinople, Moravians, Croats, and Hungarians hovered in Byzantium's orbit before finally opting for the Latin church. The greatest success for this religious diplomacy was the conversion of the rulers of much of what is now Russia (see Chapter 9). The policy was most effective when lavish gifts and the hands of Byzantine princesses, who married Bulgar khans and Russian princes, backed it. Instead of an empire like Rome's, a Byzantine "commonwealth" of Christian states was being built up—a diplomatic ring of outer defenses.

Byzantine diplomacy was exceptionally good at economizing on force by intimidating visiting barbarians with elaborate ceremonials. The early tenth-century emperor, Constantine VII, laid down rules for courtly displays that were designed to embody imperial power and, in effect, to wield it. There was even an official whose job was to bribe paupers to line the streets for imperial processions—or, perhaps, reward those who would turn out anyway. The effect designers aimed for was unashamedly theatrical. When an ambassador arrived at Constantinople in 924, the artificial roar of mechanical lions that guarded the imperial throne surprised him.

The deftness of Byzantine diplomacy, its rulers' ability to impress or intimidate surrounding "barbarians," is part of the repertoire of strategies with which all successful states managed the surge of migrations of the period. The wealth of the empire underpinned those strategies and paid for vital military backup. The Byzantine economy relied on the productivity of the peasantry of Anatolia and the trade that passed through Byzantine territory, for the empire enjoyed a privileged position, close to where great arteries of trade converged: the Silk Roads, the Volga, the Mediterranean.

Liutprand of Cremona, from *Report of his Mission to Costantinople*

The crown King Geza I of Hungary (r. 1074–1077) received from Byzantium was not a disinterested gift, but an attempt to imply that the king was a subject of the empire and dependent on Byzantium for the legitimacy of his rule. Hungary, however, remained firmly attached to the Church of Rome and to Latin culture.

Yet the system was rickety. Wealth depended on security, which was hard to guarantee. And the effectiveness of Byzantine diplomacy had its limits. While a zone of Byzantine influence took shape in the Balkans, Russia, and the Caucasus, most steppeland peoples, and the Muslims who predominated to the east and south, were indifferent to Byzantine religion and unintimidated by Byzantine methods. Caught between Bulgars and the Turks, Byzantium seemed to lie at the eye of the steppelander storm. Byzantines tended to see their predicament as a test of faith—an episode of sacred history. In 980, the miracle at Chonae first appeared in a collection of Byzantine writings: the story of how the Archangel Michael diverted a river that evil pagans had turned to threaten his church. It is tempting to read this story as an allegory for the hoped-for, prayed-for escape of the "Roman Empire" from destruction at barbarian hands.

Basil II

The longed-for savior appeared from an unlikely quarter. The emperor Basil II barely survived adolescence. Successive usurpers surprisingly allowed him to live on after his father's death until he succeeded to the throne peacefully on coming of age in 976. His image appears on a page from his surviving prayer book—heavily armed, attended by angels, while barbarians cringe at his feet. This is how he liked to see himself and wished to be remembered.

He ruled intuitively, as if coping with a constant state of emergency, enforcing his own will, administering rough justice, respecting no laws or conventions. In 996, he dealt with a landowner he saw exploiting peasants: "we had his luxurious villa razed to the ground and returned his property to the peasants, leaving him with what he had to begin with and reducing him to the peasants' level." This was an instance of a long conflict between great landowners and the throne. Emperors needed prosperous, independent peasants to provide bedrock taxes and manpower for the armies. Landowners wanted to control the peasants themselves. Aristocratic revolts and resistance to taxation were commonplace.

Basil dealt with the most troublesome of Byzantium's satellite peoples, the Bulgars, by blinding—so it was said—14,000 of their captured warriors and cowing them into submission. His nickname was Bulgaroctonus—the Bulgar-Slayer. He incorporated Bulgaria into the empire in 1018. On the southern front, he made peace with the Arabs, whom the Byzantines had fought, strenuously but successfully, for half a century under previous emperors. In consequence, he gave the empire virtually ideal borders, with frontiers on the Danube and the Euphrates Rivers, beyond which direct rule by Byzantium seemed neither practicable nor desirable. In Bulgaria he followed up his terror stroke by a policy of conciliation, cooperating with the native elite, appointing a Bulgar as the local archbishop. In Greece he relied on repression, forcing the empire's religion and language on the immigrant Slavs. In the Caucasus he attacked Georgia. In Armenia, his successors lost patience with diplomacy and reconquered the region (see Map 12.4).

Force was expensive by comparison with the waiting game, bribes, and tricks characteristic of traditional Byzantine policy. Basil paid for a professional army by heavily taxing the aristocracy. When he died in 1025, his treasury was full: bigger than any emperor's since the sixth century. The empire he left to his heirs exerted influence and drew deference from far away. Prayers cited his name in Kiev and Vladimir in Russia and in Ani in Armenia. Hungary's kings deferred to the pope on religious matters, but they still felt the pull of Constantinople. As late as the 1070s, a Hungarian king accepted a crown from Constantinople. The so-called crown of St. Stephen depicts the king reverencing the rulers of the Byzantine Empire.

Basil II. This is how the Byzantine emperor Basil II (r. 976–1025) liked to see himself. Unlike the German emperor Otto III (see Chapter 11), Basil needs no human helpers. He leans on his own sword while defeated barbarians crawl at his feet and angels crown him and invest him with a scepter. Isolated above the earth, he is perfumed with incense and adorned with a halo. Images of the saints guard him on either hand. Basil may have stressed these divine sanctions for his rule because his family had peasant origins. But the proof that God was on his side was the many victories he won against the empire's foes.

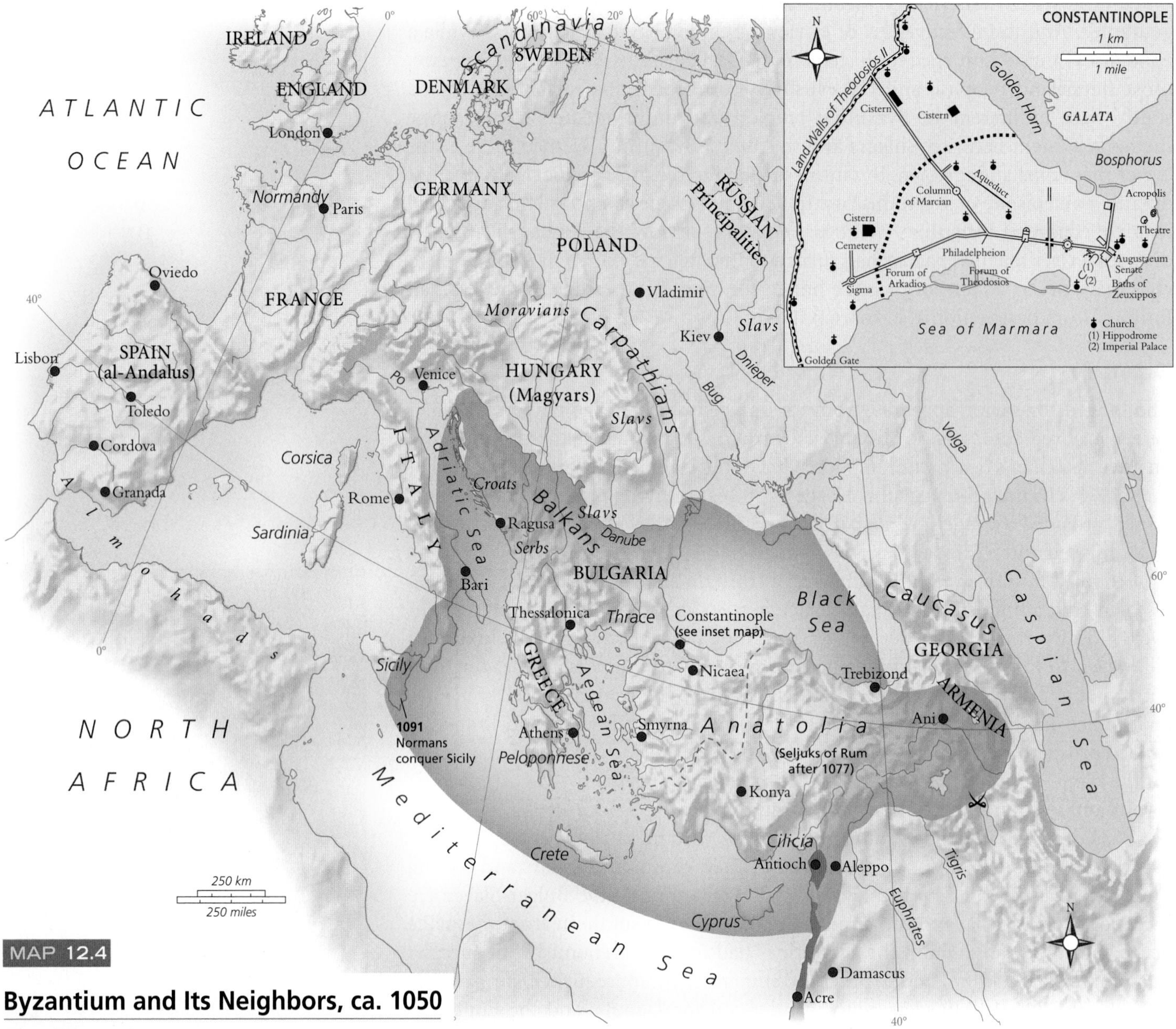

Map labels

ATLANTIC OCEAN

IRELAND
ENGLAND
London
DENMARK
SWEDEN
Scandinavia
GERMANY
Normandy
Paris
FRANCE
Oviedo
SPAIN (al-Andalus)
Lisbon
Toledo
Cordova
Granada
Almohads
Corsica
Po
Venice
Rome
Sardinia
ITALY
Adriatic Sea
Croats
Ragusa
Serbs
Bari
Balkans
Slavs
Danube
BULGARIA
Thessalonica
Thrace
Sicily
GREECE
Aegean Sea
Athens
Peloponnese
Crete
NORTH AFRICA
Mediterranean Sea
POLAND
Moravians
Carpathians
HUNGARY (Magyars)
Slavs
RUSSIAN Principalities
Vladimir
Kiev
Slavs
Dnieper
Bug
Volga
Black Sea
Constantinople (see inset map)
Nicaea
Smyrna
Anatolia
Konya
Cilicia
Antioch
Aleppo
Cyprus
Damascus
Acre
Trebizond
Caucasus
GEORGIA
ARMENIA
Ani
(Seljuks of Rum after 1077)
Caspian Sea
Tigris
Euphrates

1091 Normans conquer Sicily

250 km
250 miles

CONSTANTINOPLE
1 km
1 mile
GALATA
Golden Horn
Bosphorus
Land Walls of Theodosios II
Cistern
Cistern
Column of Marcian
Aqueduct
Acropolis
Theatre
Cistern
Cemetery
Philadelpheion
Forum of Arkadios
Forum of Theodosios
Sigma
Augusteum
Senate
Baths of Zeuxippos
(1)
(2)
Golden Gate
Sea of Marmara
✝ Church
(1) Hippodrome
(2) Imperial Palace

MAP 12.4

Byzantium and Its Neighbors, ca. 1050

- Byzantine empire, ca. 1050
- ✂ battle of Manzikert, 1071
- maximum extent of crusader kingdoms, 1144
- - - - frontier with Seljuks of Rum after 1077
- *Croats* people

The Era of Difficulties

Basil's legacy, however, was unsustainable. His methods of government were personal and arbitrary. The aristocracy could afford his taxes only while his power protected their lands from invaders. Their restiveness and rebelliousness grew even worse after his death. As Turkish migrations and invasions began to roll over Byzantine Anatolia, the revenues failed. The succession to the throne, moreover, was problematic. Basil had no children, and his brother, who succeeded him, had only daughters. These were unusual circumstances: an opportunity for strong women to come to the fore. In the background, deeper, ill-understood social changes were under way. The family—formerly, in theory, a second-best lifestyle to monastic chastity—rose in Byzantine esteem in the tenth century. Women began to be admired for fertility as well as virginity.

Anna Comnena, from the *Alexiad*

In the eyes of influential classes—clergy, landowners, courtiers—eleventh-century experiments did not seem to justify the empowerment of female rulers. Princesses spent their lives confined to the palace, and though they got the same formal education as men, they were denied the opportunity to accumulate useful experience of the world. Basil's niece, Zoe, regarded the throne as a family possession and responsibility. Her "family album" is laid in mosaic in her private enclosure in the gallery of Hagia Sophia, Constantinople's cathedral. Her third husband's portrait smothers that of her second, who murdered his predecessor, at Zoe's behest. Zoe outraged Constantinople's snobbish elite by adopting a workman's son as her heir—an upstart "pygmy playing Hercules," said the snobs. Zoe's sister Theodora ruled alone in 1055–1056, "shamefully" and "unnaturally"—according to her opponents—refusing to marry. These judgments lack objectivity, but show the outrage the sisters provoked among the elite.

Meanwhile, relations between the Latin- and Greek-speaking churches broke down. Differences had been growing over rites, doctrines, language, and discipline between the sees of Constantinople and Rome for centuries. Underlying the theological bitterness were deep cultural differences. Language was in part to blame. The Greek-speaking Byzantine Empire could not share the common culture of the Latin-speaking elites of Western and Central Europe, while few in the Latin West could speak or read Greek with fluency. Subtle theological distinctions, inexpressible in Latin, came easily in Greek.

Dogmas supposed to be universal turned out differently in the two tongues. For most people, religion is more a matter of conduct than creed. In this respect, differences between the Roman and Byzantine traditions built up over centuries of relative mutual isolation. The process began as early as the mid–sixth century, when the Eastern churches resisted or rejected the supremacy of the pope. The effects were gradual but great. From the 790s, Greek and Latin congregations recited slightly different versions of the creed, the basic statement of Christian belief. By about 1000, the pope was the supreme authority regarding doctrinal questions and liturgy and the source of patronage in the church, throughout Western Europe from the Atlantic to the river Bug and the Carpathian Mountains. The Western church still enclosed tremendous local diversity, but it was recognizably a single communion. Eastern Orthodox Christians felt no particular allegiance to the pope. In the West, moreover, the popes generally maintained, with difficulty, their own political independence. In the east, the patriarchs of Constantinople, as that city's bishops were titled, were the emperor's subjects and generally deferred to imperial power.

A moment when it might have been possible to restore Christian unity occurred in the mid–eleventh century. Constantinople and Rome faced common enemies. Norman invaders, the descendants of the Vikings, threatened the pope's political independence and the Byzantine emperor's remaining possessions in southern Italy and Sicily. On June 17, 1053, a Norman army cut the pope's German guard to pieces and, imploring the pope's forgiveness on bended knees, carried him off as a hostage.

Eventually, the papacy would win the Normans round and turn them into its sword bearers. At first, however, the pope turned to the Byzantines for help. A Byzantine cross of the period is engraved with his message: Constantine the Great, founder of Byzantium, bows before images of the patron saints of Rome, Peter, and Paul held by a pope. Meanwhile, in 1054 in Constantinople, the patriarch, who was the head of the Byzantine church, saw an opportunity to exploit

Empress Zoe. The gallery of the great church of Hagia Sophia in Constantinople functioned as a private enclosure for members of the imperial family and was decorated with portraits of rulers and their spouses in pious attitudes. The mosaic dedicated to the Empress Zoe (980–1050) betrays the questionable complexities of her sex life. The face of Constantine IX Monomachus, her third husband, shown offering gold to Christ, was remodeled to replace the likeness of her second spouse, Michael IV, whom she had first employed to murder his predecessor, then banished to a monastery in 1041 when she tired of him. The squashed lettering above Constantine's halo to the left is clear evidence of a botched job.

the pope's weakness. He closed the churches of the city's Latin-speaking congregations. The pope, teaching himself Greek, in the grip of a mortal sickness, sent an uncompromising mission to Constantinople. His representative, Cardinal Humbert, after weeks of bitter insults, served notice of excommunication on the "false patriarch, now for his abominable crimes notorious." The patriarch responded by excommunicating the pope. At the time, most people assumed this was just a political maneuver, soon to be rescinded or forgotten. In fact, relations between the Eastern and Western churches never fully recovered. A cultural fault line was opening across Europe.

The shenanigans of the imperial family and the quarrelsome habits of the church have given Byzantium a bad name as a society doomed by its own decadence. But it was not doomed. There are no irreversible trends in history. Nor, even when beset by difficulties, was the Byzantine Empire particularly decadent. On the contrary, the most unsuccessful emperor of the era was a model of energy and courage. Becoming emperor in 1068, Romanus IV Diogenes had to cope with aristocratic unrest while fighting on two fronts. In the west, the Normans threatened Byzantium's last possessions in Italy. In the east, Turks were penetrating Armenia and Anatolia, stealing the empire's vital food-producing zone. Romanus' military record made him look insuperable, but his generalship proved unequal to the task. In 1071, at the battle of Manzikert (MAHN-zih-kehrt), the Turks forced the emperor to kiss the ground before the feet of their leader, Alp Arslan (ahlp ahrs-LAHN)—a great-grandson of Seljuk's. Romanus could only raise a fifth of his ransom. He was released but deposed by a coup in Constantinople. Feuding at Constantinople between aristocratic factions paralyzed the government and allowed the Turks to overrun much of Anatolia.

Byzantium and the Crusaders

In 1097, crusaders arrived at Byzantium, ostensibly to help. But by then, the Byzantines had already begun to recover the lost ground on their own. The Byzantine princess Anna Comnena considered the newcomers more of a hindrance. Superbly educated in the classics, she was the official biographer of her father, the emperor. To her, the crusaders seemed "a race under the spell of Dionysos and Eros"—a classical way of saying they were lustful drunkards. A minority among them "undertook this journey only to worship at the Holy Sepulchre" (the tomb of Jesus at Jerusalem). Most crusaders, however, were enemies whose object was "to dethrone the emperor and capture the capital." The newcomers arrived already embittered by the religious squabbles that had divided the churches of Rome and Constantinople.

The tense cooperation between Byzantium and the crusaders, which characterized the First Crusade, broke down completely in the twelfth century. The crusaders failed to return to the empire most of the Byzantine territory they recaptured from the Muslims. Instead, they kept it for themselves. The crusaders blamed "Greek treachery" for their failures against the Muslims. The Byzantines were convinced of their own moral and cultural superiority over impious, greedy Westerners. The crusaders might have saved Byzantium, as the Turks saved the Islamic world. Instead, they undermined the empire.

Byzantium's difficulties multiplied. Agriculture was stagnant, despite the boom in other parts of Eurasia. The empire's hinterland beyond Constantinople was too insecure to prosper. In the twelfth century, in a serious reversal of earlier emperors' policy of nurturing the peasants at the landowners' expense, emperors tried to revive their rural revenues by granting control of peasant lands to great lords and encouraging monastic colonization of new lands. To some extent, this was another case of the attempt to exploit new resources, familiar in other societies of the time. The emperor Isaac II Angelus (r. 1185–1195), for instance, gave a port to a monastery that settled a site at Vera in Thrace, formerly "devoid of men and dwellings, a haunt of snakes and scorpions, just rough ground, overgrown with spreading trees." Measures like these—which so dramatically increased the farmland of Western Christendom, Ethiopia, or, as we shall see, of China at the time— were of limited usefulness in a state whose territory was much diminished. Byzantium never recovered most of inland Anatolia from the Turks.

Increasingly, the empire was obliged to look to trade and industry for its wealth. There were, as a Byzantine poet observed, "big merchants" who "for large profits disdain terrors and defy seas." Self-made upstarts coveted money "as a polecat gazes at fat." The huge city of Constantinople, crowded and riotous as it was, benefited from its uniquely favorable position for trade, where Mediterranean and trans-Asian routes met. The Jewish merchant, Benjamin of Tudela, who visited in about 1170, celebrated "a busy city" with inhabitants so rich they "they look like princes" where "merchants come from every country by sea and land." With revenues of 20,000 gold pieces a year from rents, market dues, and the tolls on passing trade, "Wealth like that of Constantinople," Benjamin wrote, "is not to be found in the whole world. Here also are men learned in all the books of the Greeks, and they eat and drink, every man under his vine and his fig tree." For William of Tyre, a Latin bishop who visited at about the same time, the city seemed equally splendid on the surface. But William was a moralist, not a merchant. He was more aware of underlying squalor and inequalities of wealth. "The wealthy overshadow the streets," he wrote—alluding to the teetering mansions of the rich—"and leave dark, dirty spaces to the poor and to travelers." William's prejudices are obvious, but, precisely because he was so keen to criticize the city, we can trust his witness to its wealth.

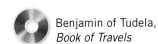

Benjamin of Tudela,
Book of Travels

A special relationship developed between Byzantium and Venice, a maritime republic near the northernmost point of the Adriatic Sea, where trade routes across the Alps converged with the main axis of north Italian commerce, the river Po. Venice's position on marshy, salty islands allowed little scope to accumulate wealth except by piracy, which Venetians practiced, mainly at the expense of Muslim shipping. In the ninth and tenth centuries, however, they began to build up enough capital to become major traders, channeling toward Europe a share of the valuable trade in silks and spices that was concentrated at Byzantium. Culturally, as well as economically, Venice was close to Byzantium. Though Venetians belonged to the Latin church and spoke a language derived from Latin, Byzantine models saturated their taste in art and buildings. It could not be otherwise. They knew Byzantium well, and so they had to admire it—and, in some measure, to covet what they saw there.

To would-be attackers, Byzantium's wealth was a magnet and its weakness a motive. Toward the end of the 1190s, in Western Europe, popular enthusiasm revived for a new effort to launch a Crusade to recapture Jerusalem. The Venetians agreed to ship the crusading army out at what was to prove an unaffordable price. While the army gathered, an embassy arrived from the pretender to the Byzantine throne, Alexius IV, proposing a detour. If the crusaders put Alexius on the throne, he would reward them with treasure and help them against the Turks. Gradually, faced with their inability to pay the Venetians' bill, most of the crusaders agreed to

Byzantium

527–565	Reign of Justinian
Sixth to eighth centuries	Colonization of Balkans by Slavs
Seventh and eighth centuries	Loss of territory as a result of Arab expansion
Ninth century	Missions to convert Balkans and Central Europe to Byzantine Christianity
1018	Bulgaria incorporated into Byzantine Empire
1054	Schism between Orthodox and Latin churches
1071	Battle of Manzikert; Byzantine army routed by Seljuk Turks
1095	First Crusade
1204	Sack of Constantinople

a diversion. The Fourth Crusade, launched in 1202 as a "pilgrimage" under arms to recapture Jerusalem, ended by shedding Christian blood in 1204 by capturing and sacking Constantinople and dividing most of what was left of the Byzantine Empire in Europe among the victors. The big gainer was Venice, which seized—in the words of the treaty that divided the empire—"one quarter and one half of one quarter" of Byzantine territory, achieving virtual monopoly rights in Byzantine trade and suddenly becoming an imperial power in the eastern Mediterranean (see Map 12.4). Meanwhile, in the remnants of the Byzantine Empire in western and coastal Anatolia, rival dynasties disputed claims to the imperial title.

Byzantine Art and Learning

Throughout the period this chapter covers, even amid the most severe difficulties of the twelfth century, Byzantium remained a beacon of learning and art. It is easy to get starry-eyed about the excellence of Byzantine culture. In 1078, Kekaumenos, a self-educated Byzantine exgeneral who took learning seriously, complained that babblers "picked passages to gossip about." The most constant and careful Byzantine work in copying and analyzing the texts of classical authors and of the fathers of the Church was probably over by the tenth century. Mystics, represented by Saint Symeon the New Theologian (as he is called), who died in 1022, proposed an alternative route to learning, through divine illumination. "Orators and philosophers" could not access the wisdom of God. Painters developed a tradition that seemed consciously unclassical, abandoning realism in favor of stylized, formal figures, usually set against abstract or sketchy backgrounds, more indebted, perhaps, to the mosaic tradition, in which Byzantine artists excelled, than to classical painting or sculpture. Most painters worked only on religious commissions and accepted the artistic vocation as a sacred obligation, aiming at work that captured the spirit of its subject and that would be revered as holy in itself. Innovation happened slowly and subtly, for artists had to treat every subject strictly in accordance with tradition and church dogma.

Nonetheless, in most arts, and in learning, Byzantium preserved the classical legacy, and more. In the eleventh and twelfth centuries, it was revived in an intellectual movement comparable with the renaissance of the same period in the West (see Chapter 11). The historian and biographer Michael Psellus (1018–1078), for instance, wrote in an antique style based on classical Greek models, interpreted the meanings of ancient art, and lectured on Plato and Aristotle (see Chapter 6). Anna Comnena's historical work was saturated in knowledge of Homer (see Chapter 5), and she commissioned commentaries on previously neglected works of Aristotle. A renaissance of classical pagan themes in art followed in the twelfth century. A famous ivory carving of that time in classical style shows Europa, a princess who in Greek mythology was abducted by the god Zeus disguised as a bull, playing with satyrs and centaurs, pouting prettily at her pursuers. In Byzantine scholarship of the late twelfth century, nothing commanded more prestige than classical research. Michael Choniates, bishop of Athens, was delighted to have the famous temple of the goddess Athena, the Parthenon, as a church to preach in and classical Greek poets to read for pleasure. Another Byzantine bishop wrote commentaries on ancient Greek poetry and searched through old manuscripts to improve the texts of classical plays.

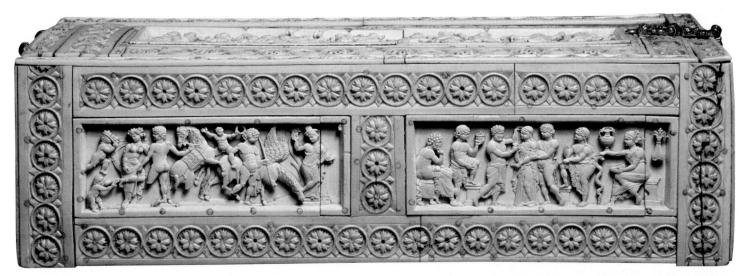

The Veroli casket. Classical stories with an erotic edge decorated Byzantine trinket boxes in the twelfth century. The panels visible in this picture of a famous example, the Veroli casket, finely carved in ivory, show Helen of Troy, Bellerophon with his winged horse, and the chaste Hippolytus on the right resisting the sexual advances of his wicked stepmother. Such were the subjects that entertained a rich lady's mind while she donned her jewels.

Rather than the title of Roman Emperor, or the claims to diminished power that rivals disputed after the collapse of 1204, this tradition of art and learning is Byzantium's most significant legacy. As in the Islamic world, texts and art works inherited from ancient Greece and Rome survived in the Byzantine portion of the former Roman Empire, while, in the West, they were lost among the far more destructive invasions that transformed the Roman world in the fifth century. The recovery of classical traditions in the West would probably have been impossible without cross-fertilization with the Islamic world and Byzantium.

CHINA AND THE NORTHERN BARBARIANS

Beyond the limits of the Turkish steppe, other steppeland peoples were even harder to deal with. Not even the Seljuks seemed able to win battles against them. Fortunately, however, for the Islamic world, none of these remoter nomads yet seemed willing to extend their conquests beyond the steppeland in the west. Their critical relationships lay to the east, with China. We thus need a brief account of what had happened in China in the ninth and tenth centuries at this point.

The End of the Tang Dynasty

Superficially, the history of China, in the 800s and 900s, looks like a series of disasters. An era of political disintegration began in the ninth century. Eunuchs controlled the succession to the imperial throne. The Xuantong (shoo-ehn-tuhng) emperor, who died in 859, never named an empress or an heir lest he be "made idle," that is, murdered. Steppelander incursions continued. In 840, in a typical incident, 10,000 Uighurs (see Chapter 9), driven from their Central Asian homeland by rival nomads, arrived on the bend of the Yellow River proposing to garrison the Chinese frontier. A new menace—or, at least, one of unprecedented scale—was the rise of banditry. In a land as densely populated as China's, every dislocation invasion, war, or natural disaster had profound environmental consequences, impoverishing many peasants and driving them to survive by any available means. In the late ninth century, bandit gangs grew into rebellious armies led by renegade members of the elite—students who had failed to pass the examinations for the civil service, Buddhist clergy forced out of monasteries the government had confiscated.

Barabarians. In the Confucian scale of values, superior wisdom outweighed superior strength. The cringing figures with their caps, furs, pelt banners, and armored horses are Uighurs, Turkic steppe nomads, whom General Guo Ziyi, unarmed and simply attired, graciously enlists in Chinese service. The scene supposedly depicts an eighth-century episode of the wars against Tibet. For the Song artist who painted it in the eleventh century, it represented emotions invested in the program, advocated by political theorists such as Ouyang Xiu, to use the barbarian world to benefit China (see p. 396).

An imperial decree of 877 complained that the bandit forces "come and go just as they please." The emperor's professed wish to "equalize food and clothing so that all might be prosperous" was an admission of weakness. His threat to apply "force without remorse" against those who refused to lay down their arms was empty. In 879, the bandit leader, Huang Chao (hwang chow), unified most of the gangs and crossed the Yangtze River with, reputedly, 600,000 men. He took Chang-an, the seat of the court, with effects described in the verses of one of the most striking poems of the time, the *Lament of Lady Qin*: rape, pillage, and bloodshed. Huang's successor, Zhu Wen (joo wehn), emerged as the most powerful man in China, effectively replacing the Tang dynasty in 907. His state fell in turn in 923 to Turkic nomads whom the Chinese had tried to use against the bandits. The Chinese Empire dissolved into "ten kingdoms."

China's situation recalls that of Western Europe, striving to maintain the ancient sense of unity and—for some rulers—even actively seeking to recover it, in times of political dissolution. The Chinese predicament also parallels those of the Islamic world and Byzantium, beset by nomadic migrants and invaders. Chinese responses, as we shall see, were also similar. They tried to fend off the "barbarians" by methods akin to those of the Byzantines: diplomacy, bribery, intimidation, displays of cultural superiority. As in the Islamic world, Chinese worked to convert invaders to their own culture, usually successfully. As in all the states we have looked at, the reexploitation of internal resources—especially by converting forest to farmland—made an important contribution.

For China, however, the outcome was different from those of other comparable regions. Throughout the period this chapter covers, the reconstruction of unity never seemed perfect or stable, but unity remained an actively pursued and—as we shall see—ultimately recoverable ideal. Divisions over religion, which deepened disunity in Christendom, or in the world of al-Hakim, had no parallel in China. China survived the invaders from the steppes but surrendered much territory to them. And, unlike the Islamic world, China never wholly succeeded in turning invading warriors into a force it could use for its own expansion.

The Rise of the Song and the Barbarian Conquests

The fight for unity after the collapse of the 920s began in 960, when a mutinous army proclaimed its general as emperor. The dynasty he founded, the Song (soong), lasted until 1279, but it always had to share China's traditional territory with steppeland invaders who created empires and dynasties of their own in parts of the north. These barbarian states adopted Chinese political ideas and bureaucratic methods and claimed the mandate of heaven—or, at least, a share in it—for themselves. But none of them were able to extend their conquests south of the Huai River, into the intricately patterned lands of rice paddies and dense population the Song retained.

First, from the early tenth to the early twelfth centuries, the Khitan state of Liao (lee-ow) loomed over China from heartlands in Mongolia and Manchuria. Under the warrior-empresses Chunjin (926–947) and Xiao (982–1009), the Liao state acquired a southern frontier across the Yellow River valley. The Khitans remained faithful to their pastoral traditions, but in the tenth century, they split their empire into two spheres, creating a Chinese-style, Chinese-speaking administration for their southern provinces. They began to build cities, following Chinese urban planning models, apparently to attract migrants. The Khitan Empire had its own civil service, selected on Confucian principles, issuing documents that scholars still do not fully understand. In a treaty of 1004, the Song conceded equality to Liao, which became known as the Northern Kingdom, alongside the Southern Kingdom of the Song. The Song paid Liao 100,000 ounces of silver and 200,000 bolts of cloth annually. This was tribute, which the Chinese disguised as "gifts" in a face-saving formula. The two dynasties affected kinship in an elaborate exchange of titles. The Liao empress mother, for instance, became the Song emperor's "junior aunt." In 1031, they jointly proclaimed "reunification of the universe," but this was a wild exaggeration. The two states lived together in uneasy equilibrium, punctuated by occasional hostilities.

Toward the end of the 1030s, a second steppeland state proclaimed itself an empire—the Tangut (tan-goot) realm of Xia (hsia). The axis of the state was a strip of grazing land, 900-miles long, squeezed between Tibet and the southern Gobi Desert. In 1044, a great Tangut victory forced another treaty out of the Song. Xia was accorded the status of a kingdom superior to all others except Song and Liao and received annual tribute from the Song of about half the value that the Song paid to the Liao. Xia, too, had its own system of writing, its own bureaucracy, and an iron coinage much used along the Silk Roads. It also had a considerable scholarly establishment, largely devoted to acquiring and commenting on Buddhist scriptures.

The last state builders to intrude into the region were the Jurchen (juhr-chehn), who from 1115 began to build up conquests that eventually included the whole Liao Empire and covered northern China as far as the Huai River (see Map 12.5). Their homeland was in the forests of northern Manchuria. Their traditional economy relied on hunting rather than herding. They were "sheer barbarians," Chinese envoys reported, "worse than wolves or tigers." On this occasion, for once, we can be reasonably confident about the events that provoked their migration. It coincided with several years' exceptional cold and rain.

The Jurchen wars forced the Chinese to acknowledge Jurchen claims to the mandate of heaven. A treaty of 1127 imposed annual tribute on the Song of 300,000 ounces of silver, 1,000,000 strings of copper cash, and 300,000 bolts of silk. Jurchen campaigns penetrated far into the south of China. In 1161, however, the invaders despaired of creating a river navy strong enough permanently to dominate the Yangtze. The Song and Jurchen states learned to live with each other.

Meanwhile, the Jurchen adopted Chinese habits and traditions more fully than even the Khitans and Tanguts had. The Jurchen emperors were uncertain about this trend. On the one hand, they were quick to adopt Chinese bureaucracy and courtly customs themselves. On the other hand, they were afraid that the Jurchen would lose their warlike strength and will to dominate. The Jurchen, after all, were few in number—perhaps a few hundred thousand—compared with their more than 50 million Chinese subjects recorded in a census of 1207. Despite legislation forbidding Jurchens to adopt Chinese language or dress, distinctive Jurchen culture largely vanished.

Chinese thinkers found it hard to adjust to a world in which "barbarians" seemed at least their equals. On the whole, the Song coped by accepting the reality of the new distribution of power and opting for coexistence and peaceful persuasion, bribing and coaxing the foreigners into remaining quiet. One of the most supple intellects of the Song era was that of the early eleventh-century palace official, Ouyang Xiu (oh-yahng shoo). Earlier barbarian attacks, he thought, had

Barbarian crown. Although the scalloped form is typical of the headgear of Central Asian nomads, this Khitan cap of the eleventh century—which is so magnificent that it must have been worn by someone of very high status—shows the influence of Buddhist religion and Chinese art. From a stylized mountain, a lotus grows upward, symbolizing the ascent of the soul to enlightenment, toward a sun-like flaming jewel—a common Buddhist symbol for wisdom. Dragons, symbolizing benevolence, reach for the same goal.
Khitan headgear with repoussé decoration of two dragons chasing a flaming jewel. Chinese, early 11th century Photograph © 2007 Museum of Fine Arts, Boston.

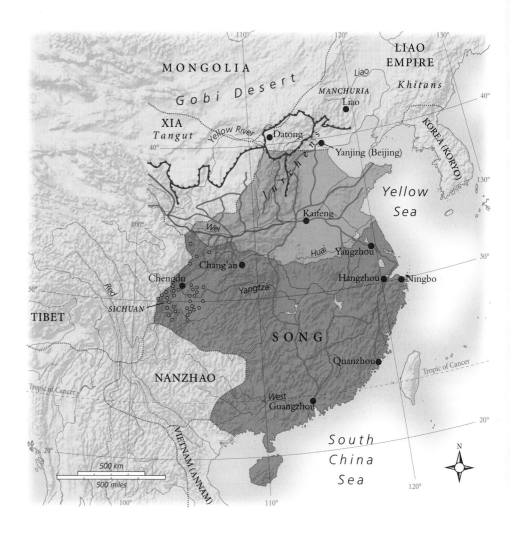

MAP 12.5

Song Empire, ca. 1150

▨	Song empire, ca.1050
▨	Song empire, 1127–1234
—	Silk Road
⊥⊤⊥	Great Wall
○	salt mine
—	imperial highways
Jurchens	people

been like "the sting of gadflies and mosquitoes." Now they were more serious and could not merely be brushed aside. He advised,

> Put away . . . armor and bows, use humble words and . . . generous gifts. . . . Send a princess to obtain friendship . . . transport goods to establish firm bonds. Although this will diminish the emperor's dignity, it could for a while end fighting. . . . Who would exhaust China's resources . . . to quarrel with serpents and swine? . . . Now is the moment for binding friendship. . . . If indeed Heaven causes the rogues to accept our humaneness and they . . . extinguish the beacons on our frontiers, which will be a great fortune to our ancestral altars.[1]

According to Ouyang Xiu, civilization would always win encounters with savagery. Barbarians might be invincible in battle, but in the long run, they could be shamed into submission. There was a lot to be said for this point of view. China always survived. Barbarian invaders always did get seduced by Chinese ways and adopt Chinese culture. But military defeats usually preceded these cultural victories, and the adoption of Chinese ways by barbarians usually followed bloody wars and costly destruction.

In their way, Ouyang Xiu's arguments simply rewrote the old script—Chinese superiority would ultimately prevail. This kind of thinking made defeat by the Jurchen even harder to bear. The traumas the victims of the wars suffered come to life in pages by the poet Li Qingzhao (lee ching-jhao): a memoir of her life with her husband, whom she had married for love when he was a student and she was a teenager. The couple played intellectual games at teatime, rivaling each other in being able to identify literary quotations. Their books were their most cherished possessions. When the Jurchen invaded in 1127, the fleeing couple "first gave up the bulky printed volumes, the albums of paintings, and the bulkiest ornaments." They still had so many books that it took 15 carts to bear them and a string of boats to ferry them across the Yangtse. Another Jurchen raid scattered more of the collection "in clouds of black smoke." When Li Qingzhao finally got beyond danger, after the couple's parting and her husband's death, only a few baskets of books were left—and most of those were later stolen.

Economy and Society Under the Song

Under pressure from the barbarian north, Song rule shrank toward the south (see Map 12.6). The Yangtze became the axis of the Song Empire. This potentially traumatic adjustment—the amputation of the ancient Yellow River heartlands, the "cradle" of Chinese civilization—was bearable because population, too, had shifted southward. About 60 percent of Chinese lived in the Yangtze valley by the last years of the tenth century. The trend continued under the impact of barbarian conquests in the north.

Away from the steppeland frontier, Chinese expansion continued. Loss of traditional territory, combined with the growth of population, stimulated colonization in new directions. The census of 1083 reported 17, 211, 713 families. By 1124, the number had grown to 20,882,258. Censuses tended to underestimate numbers, because tax evaders eluded the count. The Jurchen wars brought the growth of population to an end, but by then, Song China must have had well over a hundred million inhabitants—perhaps about half as many again as the whole of Europe. The state had the most basic resource: labor. It needed food and space.

The founder of the Song dynasty, Zhao Guangyin (jaow gwang-yeen), known as the Taizu (teye-tzoo) Emperor, realized that China's new opportunities lay in a further shift in the center of gravity of the empire, to the southwest: the vast, underpopulated region of Sichuan (seh-chwan). Colonization needed peaceful conditions. So the native tribes had to be suppressed. In a heavily forested, mountainous region, where tribal chiefs had a demonic reputation, this was not an easy task. By repute, the wildest inhabitants were the Black Bone Yi, led by a chief the Chinese called the "Demon Master" led. In 1001, the Song divided the region into two administrative units called "routes." A campaign in 1014 began the pacification. In 1036, the Demon Master became a salaried state official. The "forbidden hills" of Sichuan were stripped of forests and planted with tea and with mulberries for silk production. The salt mines became resources of the Chinese Empire. A land poets formerly praised as a romantic wilderness of "streams and grottoes" became China's "heavenly storehouse."

Alongside the colonization of new land, new methods of exploitation enriched China, in a process of internal expansion strikingly reminiscent of what was going on at the same time in many other regions, notably in Europe and Ethiopia (Chapter 11). Environmental change fed the growing population. Wetlands were drained. New varieties of rice arrived from Vietnam, adapted to local conditions by trial and error. Planting and harvesting two crops a year effectively doubled the capacity for food production in the Yangtze valley. From the 1040s, the

Rice cultivation. In the second half of the thirteenth century, Zhen Ji illustrated poems on rice cultivation in a long series of paintings, all copied—like the poems—from twelfth-century originals. His art demonstrates the continuity of Chinese agriculture. Even after revolutionary new strains of rice were introduced in China, older varieties of the crop were still cultivated in traditional ways.

MAP 12.6

Population Change in China, 742–1102

<table>
<tr><td>high density</td></tr>
<tr><td>medium density</td></tr>
<tr><td>low density</td></tr>
</table>

Population in China, 742

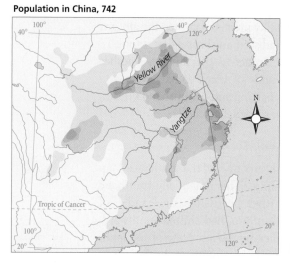

Population in China, 1102

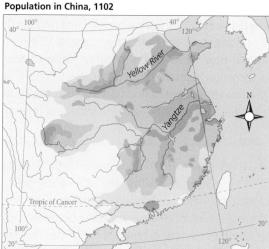

MAP EXPLORATION

www.prenhall.com/armesto_maps

Lu Yu, from *Diary of a Journey to Sichuan*

state promoted agriculture by making loans to peasants for seed grain, at favorable rates. Deforestation continued, stimulated by a tax on unharvested timber. By the end of the eleventh century, the forests around the city of Kaifeng (keye-fung) had disappeared, sacrificed to huge iron-smelting works, employing 3,000 men. In 1132, a new palace at Kaifeng was built with timber from the Qingfeng (chihng-fung) Mountains, reputedly inaccessible for centuries, like the enchanted forests of fairy tales.

Meanwhile, the money economy boomed. Song mints were always busy, always pumping out new coins—a million strings of coins a year in the early years of the century, six million in 1080—and always devaluing the currency by putting less precious metal—gold and silver—into coins. Paper money became a state monopoly from 1043. Towns grew spectacularly. Until the Jurchen captured it, Kaifeng was not just a seat of government but a thriving place of manufacture and trade. A famous twelfth-century painting by Zhang Zeduan (jwang tzeh-dwan) depicts the bustling life of the city—perhaps somewhat idealistically. On a roll more than 22-yards wide, all the life of Kaifeng at festival time unfolds—craftsmen, merchants, peddlers, entertainers, shoppers, and gawking crowds. Groaning grain ships bring the extra food. A river thick with traffic, intersects the criss-cross framework of the neat streets with buildings roofed with thatch. Zhang also shows restaurant diners enjoying their meals. Kaifeng had 72 large restaurants, each of up to five pavilions, three-storeys high, and connected by delicate bridges. In 1147, the poet Master Meng (mung) recalled in his *Dream of the Eastern Capital's Splendor* how in Kaifeng the entertainers' din "could be heard for miles . . . Wildman Zhao would eat and drink while hung upside down . . . Li Waining (lee weye-ning) would pop up puppets with explosives."

Women, however, rarely appear in Meng's verses or on Zhang's scroll. They never enjoyed the same status in China as among the pastoral cultures of the steppeland, where women were always important partners in managing the herds.

Chinese Night Revels. A female musician entertains members of the scholar-gentry in The Night Revels of Han Xizai, painted in the tenth century by Gu Hongzhong. Chinese paintings rarely show men and women together in this kind of interior setting. The elaborately laid and decorated table, the porcelain ware, and the luxury and sexual appeal of female entertainment provide an intimate glimpse of courtly life during the Song dynasty.

Increasingly, in China, women were traded as commodities, and as young girls, their feet were tightly bound with cloth, so that they became permanently deformed, in a practice perhaps originally designed to hobble them against escape. It soon, however, became a fashion that men supposedly found erotic. In the *Romance of the Western Chamber*—the sublime Chinese love classic of around 1200—feet "dainty but firm, like lotus flower buds" excite the hero's interest.

Despite the troubled relationship with the nomads and the loss of the northern provinces, the late Song Empire brimmed with wealth and inspired pride and satisfaction in its subjects. In 1170, a newly appointed official set off up the Yangtze to his job in Sichuan. He admired everything he saw: the newness of the bridges, the flourishing commerce, the boats crowded together "like the teeth of a comb." The war readiness of 700 river galleys, with their "speed like flight," excited him. He celebrated ample signs of prosperity. The province for which he was bound possessed enviable wealth. Two districts in Sichuan had between them 22 centers of population producing annual tax revenue of between 10,000 and 50,000 strings of cash—more than any other district of the Song Empire outside the lower Yangtze. The frontier had been drawn into the empire.

Song Art and Learning

The era left an enduring legacy of intellectual and artistic achievement. To the eleventh-century elite, philosophy was not an occupation of luxury or leisure, but the basis and business of government. On one side of the debate, Ouyang Xiu aimed to restore "the perfection of ancient times"—an ideal age "when rites and music reached everywhere." His writings capture the agenda and atmosphere of a sort of renaissance, a revival of ancient ethics and letters. He belonged to a type familiar in almost every great courtly society: urbane, world-weary, and with highly sophisticated sensibilities. His poems in praise of singing girls and strong drink made him vulnerable to attack by moralists. During a struggle among rival groups at court in 1067, he was disgraced in a sex scandal. Ouyang Xiu retired to what he called his "old tippler's pavilion" in the country.

Wang Anshi (wahng ahn-sheh), who led the party on the other side of the debate, thought life was like a dream and valued "dreamlike merits" equally with practical results. He carried the notion of socially responsible government to extremes and consulted "peasants and serving girls" rather than relying on Confucian principles and ancient precedents. The policies he pursued, when he was in charge of the government in the 1070s, included progressive taxation, the substitution of taxes for forced labor, cheap loans for farmers, and state-owned pawnshops. Wang mistrusted Confucian confidence in China's ability to tame the steppelanders—he introduced universal conscription. To combat banditry, and prevent the desertion of young peasants to bandit gangs, he organized village society in groups of ten families, so that each family was held responsible for the good behavior of the others.

Both parties supported reform of the examination system that produced the imperial officials with two objectives in mind: to encode in it an ethic of service to society, and to recruit the state's servants from as wide a range of social backgrounds as possible. The old examination tested only skill in composition, especially in verse, and in memorizing texts. The new test asked questions about ethical standards and about how the state could serve the people better. It was a conservative revolution.

While Wang's agenda shaped policy, Ouyang Xiu's dominated the intellectual mainstream. The dominant trend in philosophy for the rest of the Song era was the effort to reinterpret the Confucian classics for the readers' own times. The work of Zhu Xi (joo shi) (1130–1200) summarized and synthesized all previous thinking on this subject. In his own mind, he was an orthodox Confucian, but in some ways, he

Misty mountains. Chinese landscape painters under the Song dynasty celebrated the mountains and caves of newly colonized lands in southwest China. Mi Fu (1051–1107) was one of the outstanding exponents of this type of painting, developing what came to be known as the "misty mountain style." No Western artist even began to show a similar appreciation of nature before the thirteenth century, and no Westerner painted landscapes without people in them until the sixteenth century. "Mountains are rivers," says the line from Confucius that captions Mi Fu's painting, "that put forth clouds." *Pavilion of Rising Clouds, Mi Fu. Freer Gallery of Art, Smithsonian Institution, Washington, D.C.: Gift of Charles Lang Freer, F. 1908. 171*

Kaifeng. In this most famous of Song dynasty scroll-paintings, Zhang Zeduan captures the vitality of life on the Yellow River at the city of Kaifeng in the early twelfth century and the wonderful commercial opportunities that the approach of the Spring Festival brought. Hundreds of wares arrive by cart, mule, or camel train or on poles slung across peddlers' backs.
The Art Archive/Picture Desk, Inc./Kobal Collection.

was what we would now call a secular humanist. He upheld the doctrine of the natural goodness of human beings. He doubted whether "there is a man in heaven judging sin" and dismissed prayer in favor of self-examination and study of the classics. Morality, he thought, was a matter of individual responsibility, not heavenly regulation. But he did accept the tradition on which the Chinese state was based: "heaven" decreed the fortunes of society according to the merits of its rulers. So influential was Zhu's synthesis that it defined what subsequent ages called Confucianism.

The intellectual and economic environment of the Song Empire was highly favorable to the arts. There was money and enthusiasm for abundant patronage of artists. In the early twelfth century, the Huidzung (hway-dzuhng) emperor, who was an accomplished painter himself, founded a school of painting and expanded the palace gallery to exhibit paintings and ceramics. The painting of the era has always attracted special admiration, not just because it was prolific and technically excellent, but also because it specialized in scenes from the natural world. Admiration for the beauty of nature, untouched by human hands, is, perhaps, a measure of the maturity of a civilization. It is doubtful, however, whether Song artists painted nature, as modern romantics do today, for its own sake. To them, the natural world was a book of lessons about humankind and from which they could make comparisons about human nature. Every subject for a painting demanded long meditation in which the artist strove to understand the essence of what he was going to paint. Su Dongpo (soo dohng-pwoh) (1036–1101) painted virtually nothing but bamboo, because its fragility suggested human weakness. Li Longmian (lee lung-mee-en) (1049–1106) favored gnarled trees, defying weather, as symbols of the resilience of the sages. Mi Fei (mee fay) (1051–1107) perfected the representation of mist—which is the breath of nature, with power to shape the image, like the spiritual dimension of human beings. With other painters of the same era, they produced some of the world's most influential, most imitated images.

IN PERSPECTIVE: Cains and Abels

The North African Muslim Ibn Khaldun (ihb-ihn hahl-DOON), one of the world's best historians, looking back from the late fourteenth century, saw history as a story of struggle between nomads and settled people. To some extent, he based his view on his reading of the experience of his native region in the eleventh and twelfth centuries, when, as far as he could make out, pastoralist invaders wrecked the peace and prosperity of the region: first, Arab herders whom the Fatimids released or expelled from southern Egypt; then the Almoravids and Almohads from the Sahara. Modern historians have challenged his interpretation. The mutual disdain between tillers and herders was neither as deep nor destructive as Ibn Khaldun thought. But the tension he perceived was real. The biblical story of Cain and Abel traces the origins of human conflict to the mutual hatred and murderous rivalry of a tiller of the soil and a keeper of flocks.

Nomads threatened their farming neighbors in various ways. The nomadic way of life demanded immeasurably more land per head of population than the intensive agriculture that fed dense farming populations. Nomads were ill equipped for some economic activities, including mining and silk manufacture, and the production of some favored commodities, such as tea, fruit, and grain. For these things, therefore, they depended on theft, tribute, or trade from farming communities. The nomads were better equipped for war. Horsemanship made their way of life a preparation for battle. Sedentary peoples had not yet developed firearms or fortifications good enough to tilt the balance in their own favor. The nomads tended to cherish ideologies of superiority—variously of jihad or of divine election for empire—that clashed with the equal and opposite convictions of the settled peoples. Nomads could exploit farmers' lands, but agricultural communities did not yet have the technology—steel plows, mechanical harvesters—needed to turn the unyielding soils of the grasslands into productive farmland.

Yet the hostility of nomads and farmers arose less, perhaps, from conflicts of interest, than from mutual misunderstanding: a clash of cultures, incompatible ways of seeing the world and coping with it. There is no moral difference between settled and nomadic lifeways. Yet each type of community tended to see the other as morally inferior. This was probably because for followers of each way of life, those of the other came to represent all that was alien. Their mutual descriptions were full of incomprehension and even disgust.

Real differences underpinned this mutual revulsion. Pastoralist diets were, for farmers, literally stomach churning. Pastoralists relied on dairy foods, which most farmers' digestive systems rejected, because after early childhood they did not

○ MAKING CONNECTIONS ○

NOMADIC THREATS TO SEDENTARY PEOPLES

CHARACTERISTICS OF NOMADS		CONSEQUENCES
Nomadic way of life requires extensive land	➞	Constant threat of attack on sedentary peoples
Nomads ill-equipped for certain economic activities and the manufacture of favored commodities	➞	Dependence on theft and tribute from, or trade with sedentary peoples
Nomads expert horsemen	➞	Until development of firearms and fortifications, sedentary peoples at a disadvantage in war
Nomads cherish ideologies of superiority	➞	Clash between nomads and settled peoples
Nomads can easily exploit farmers' lands	➞	Until development of steel plows and mechanized harvesters, farmers could not exploit grasslands

CHRONOLOGY

907	End of Tang dynasty
960	Beginning of Song dynasty; conversion of Karkhanid Turks to Islam
1040s	Sanhaja conquer Morocco
1054	Schism between Latin and Orthodox Christianity
1071	Battle of Manzikert; end of Byzantine dominance in Anatolia
1076	Kumbi Saleh falls to Almoravid armies
1080s	Muslim kingdoms in al-Andalus call on Almoravids for help
1095	Pope Urban II calls for crusade to capture Jerusalem
1099	Jerusalem falls to crusaders
1111	Death of al-Ghazali, Sufi mystic and theologian
1140s	Almoravid Empire falls to the Almohads
1187	Crusader kingdom of Jerusalem falls to Saladin
1204	Sack of Constantinople by crusaders

naturally produce lactase—the substance that makes milk digestible. It was also normal for herders to open their animal's veins for fresh blood to drink. This practice enabled nomad armies to take nourishment without halting on the march. Nomad diets tended to be short on plant foods. So to balance their intake, nomads would usually eat the raw organ meats of dead animals. This sort of food contains relatively high levels of vitamin C, which, in other cultures, people get from fruit and vegetables. Indeed, meat processed without cooking was important in the treeless environments of the steppe and the desert, where the only cooking fuel was dried animal dung. One of the great resources of the Eurasian steppe was the fat-tailed sheep, specially bred to drag its tail—as broad as a beaver's—behind it. Its fat is wonderfully soft. Even if nomads have no time to heat this fat, or no available kindling with which to cook it, they can eat it raw and digest it quickly. These were all elements of a rational food strategy for the nomadic life, but they inspired denunciations of the "barbaric" customs of eaters of raw meat and drinkers of blood. The nomads responded with equal contempt. For them, the settled life was soft and corrupted by luxury. Farming involved grubbing and groveling in mud. Cities and rice paddies were cramped and unhealthy.

After successful conquests, the nomads could usually be absorbed and induced to adopt or tolerate settled ways of life; but the conquerors kept coming. The relative success of the Islamic world in absorbing and converting the invaders of the tenth and eleventh centuries was a decisive feature of the history of the period. Byzantium, by contrast, failed to tame the intruders, while Western Christendom could recruit no more pastoralists after the Magyars. China developed no strategy to cope with the nomads, except to retreat and wait for them to adopt Chinese ways. Unprecedented changes in the steppeland, however, were about to upset the balance between nomads and settled peoples and unleash the most formidable steppeland conquerors of all, the Mongols. The outcome would transform the history of Eurasia.

PROBLEMS AND PARALLELS

1. Was the Islamic world's disunity an inevitable outcome of its vast geographic expansion by 1000? What parallels, if any, are there to earlier empires?

2. What was the influence of steppeland invaders on the Islamic world? Why was the Islamic world more successful in absorbing nomads than was Christian Europe?

3. The European Crusades started as an outgrowth of the tradition of pilgrimage. How was a religious process transformed into a series of violent military campaigns? What were the ultimate effects of the Crusades?

4. Did the Almoravids' and Almohads' involvement in Spain in the twelfth century ultimately hinder or help Islamic power there? Why is the conversion of Ghana to Islam ultimately of more historical significance?

5. Why did most Muslim elites and clerics reject the Sufis? Why were the Sufis more popular with ordinary Muslims than with the Islamic elite?

6. Why was it important for the Byzantines to claim to be the Roman Empire? Why was it strategically important for the rulers of Constantinople to build a Byzantine "commonwealth"? What were the consequences of the rupture in relations between Latin and Orthodox Christianity?

7. How did China under the Tang deal with nomadic invaders? Were the Chinese more or less successful than their European and Muslim contemporaries?

8. Why does the hostility between pastoralists and sedentary peoples have less to do with conflicts of interest than with a clash of cultures?

— DOCUMENTS IN GLOBAL HISTORY ·—

- From the *Dede Korkut*
- Al-Thalibi, *Recollections of Bukhara*
- A Muslim view of the Crusaders
- Al-Ghazali, on "Separation of Mathematics and Religion"

- Liutprand of Cremona, from *Report of his Mission to Costantinople*
- Anna Comnena, from the *Alexiad*
- Benjamin of Tudela, *Book of Travels*
- Lu Yu, from *Diary of a Journey to Sichuan*

Please see the Primary Source CD-ROM for additional sources related to this chapter.

READ ON

B. Lewis, *The Middle East* (1997) is a broad introductory narrative. M. S. Hodgson, *The Venture of Islam* (1977) is as always fundamental for anything in Islamic history. L. Yaacov, *State and Society in Fatimid Egypt* (1991) is an important collection of studies on the background to the caliphate of al-Hakim. T. Talbot-Rice, *The Seljuks in Asia Minor* (1960) is important for understanding the assimilation of the Turks. The *Dede Korkut* (1974) is available in an excellent edition by G. Lewis.

T. Asbridge, *The First Crusade* (2005) is a vigorous, up-to-date account. H. Mayr, *The Crusades* is an efficient general introduction, as is J. Riley-Smith, *The Crusades* (2005). J. Riley-Smith, *Atlas of the Crusades* (1990) is a useful standby. K. M. Setton, ed., *A History of the Crusades* (1969) is exhaustive.

H. Kennedy, *Muslim Spain and Portugal*, (1997) and R. Fletcher, *Moorish Spain* (1993) are helpful as introductions. D. Wasserstein, *The Rise and Fall of the Party Kings* (1985) deals with the dissolution of the caliphate of Cordova and its successor states. For the Spanish background, R. Fletcher, *The Quest for El Cid* (1991) is scintillating and highly readable. E. W. R. Bovill, *The Golden Trade of the Moors*, (1992) and *Saharan Myth and Legend* are classic works which unfold the background to the Almoravids. N. Levtzion, *Ancient Ghana and Mali* (1980) is an authoritative and concise study. J. S. Trimingham, *The Sufi Orders in Islam* (1998) is the great classic treatment of its subject.

On Byzantium, as well as works recommended in earlier chapters, C. Mango, *Byzantium and its Image*, (1984) is particu-larly good on cultural aspects, and D. Obolensky, *The phoenix: The Byzantine Commonwealth*, (2000) which is particularly good on diplomacy, are helpful. B. Hill, *Imperial Women in Byzantium* (1999) is an indispensable modern study. A. J. Toynbee, *Constantine Porphyrogenitus and His World* (1973) is a timeless classic by one of the great historians of the last century. Among the texts referred to in this chapter, *The Embassy to Constantinople and Other Writings of Liutprand of Cremona*, ed. J. J. Norwich is instructive and there are many editions of the *Alexiad* of Anna Comnena and *The Itinerary of Benjamin of Tudela*. On relations with the Latin church, S. Runciman, *The Eastern Schism*, (1955) though now half a century old, is concise and readable. J. J. Norwich, *A History of Venice* (1982) is a richly detailed narrative. D. E. Queller, *The Fourth Crusade* (1999) nicely blends narrative and analysis. There are many editions of the most engaging source: G. de Villehardouin, *The Conquest of Constantinople* (2006). N. Wilson, *Scribes and Scholars* (1991) is a lively account of Byzantine learning.

On Liao, J. S. Tao, *Two Sons of Heaven* (1988) is valuable; for the Jurchen, Y. S. Tao, *The Jurchen in Twelfth-Century China* (1977) is particularly good on sinicization. R. von Glahn, *The Country of Streams and Grottoes* (1988) is scholarly and well-written, bringing the internal frontier of China to life. R. Egan, ed., *The Literary Works of Ou-yang Hsiu* (1984) is an invaluable source. J. T. C. Liu, *Reform in Sung China*, which originally appeared in the 1950s, has not been replaced as far as I know.

Muslim Accounts of Ghana

The state known as Ghana in the Middle Ages was nowhere near the modern nation of Ghana. As the map below shows, it was in the West African interior, in the grassland region known as the Sahel, on the trade routes where salt from the Sahara was exchanged for gold.

The first passage included here was written about 1094, and is by the Muslim Spanish writer al-Bakri. It is the fullest surviving account of medieval Ghana, even though al-Bakri seems never to have left his native Spain. The work of al-Zuhri follows, probably written in about 1137. Little is known about him, except that he was in Spain between 1137 and 1154. Finally, al-Idrisi, who wrote in Sicily, describes Ghana as it was around 1150.

These three authors wrote for different reasons: al-Bakri was, in part, a collector of sensational tales as well as a source of data for merchants interested in Saharan trade routes; al-Zuhri and al-Idrisi were what today we would call professional academic geographers. Muslims generally despised black Africans as pagans and slaves. The main reasons for Muslims to go to the "the lands of the blacks" were commercial, although they also went south to make war, find patronage if they were scholars or artists, and make converts to Islam.

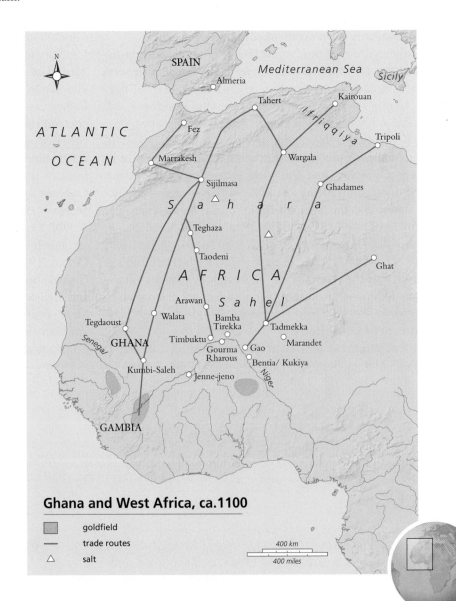

Ghana and West Africa, ca.1100

- ▢ goldfield
- — trade routes
- △ salt

400 km
400 miles

Awdaghust is a large town, populous and built on sandy ground....

In Awdaghust there is one cathedral mosque and many smaller ones, all well attended. In all the mosques there are teachers of the Koran....

The people of Awdaghust enjoy extensive benefits and huge wealth. The market there is at all times full of people, so that owing to the great crowd and the noise of voices it is almost impossible for a man to hear the words of one sitting beside him. Their transactions are in gold, and they have no silver....

Wheat, dates and raisins are imported to Awdaghust from the domains of Islam despite the great distance....

Most of the inhabitants of Awdaghust are native of Ifriqiya, but there are also a few people from other countries. There are Sudan women, good cooks, one being sold for 100 mithqals or more. They excel at cooking delicious confections such as sugared nuts, honey doughnuts, various other kinds of sweetmeats, and other delicacies. There are also pretty slave girls with white complexions, good figures, firm breasts, slim waists, fat buttocks, wide shoulders and sexual organs so narrow that one of them may be enjoyed as though she were a virgin indefinitely....

The animal from whose hides shields are made is very common around Awdaghust. Objects of worked copper and amply-cut robes dyed red and blue are sent to Awdaghust, and from there natural ambergris of excellent quality is exported, for the Atlantic is not far away; also pure gold worked into twisted threads. The gold of Awdaghust is better and purer than that of any other people on earth....

Their country adjoins the land of the Farwiyyun. This is the independent kingdom of the Farwiyyun. Among the strange things found there is a pool where water collects and in it a plant grows of which the roots are the surest means of strengthening and aiding sexual powers. The king reserves this for himself and does not allow anyone else to partake of it. He owns an enormous number of women, and when he wants to make the round of them he warns them one day before, takes the medicine, and then takes them all in turn and scarcely tires. One of the neighboring Muslim kings gave him precious gifts, requesting some of this plant in exchange. In return he gave presents of equal value and wrote a letter saying; "Muslims may lawfully wed only a few women, and I fear that if I sent you this medicine you would not be able to restrain yourself and you would commit excess which your religion makes unlawful. I am, however, sending you a herb which will enable an impotent man, if he eats it, to beget children." In the country of the Farwiyyun salt is exchanged for gold....

AL-BAKRI

What al-Bakri calls *Awdaghust* was almost certainly the northernmost trading center under Ghanaian rule in the writer's day. Ifriqiya is the region of North Africa centered on what is now Tunisia.

The *Nil* is the Niger. Like many geographers of his time, al-Bakri misidentified it as the main channel of the upper Nile.

Ghana and the Customs of Its Inhabitants

The city of Ghana consists of two towns situated on a plain. One of these towns, which is inhabited by Muslims, is large and possesses twelve mosques....The king has a palace and a number of dwellings all surrounded with an enclosure like a city wall. In the kings' town, and not far from his court of justice, is a mosque where the Muslims who arrive at his court pray. Around the king's town are domed buildings and groves and thickets where the sorcerers of these people, men in charge of the religious cult, live. In them too are their idols and the tombs of their kings....

...Continued

The king's interpreters, officials in charge of his treasury, and the majority of his ministers are Muslims. Among the people who follow the king's religion only he and his heir apparent (who is the son of his sister) may wear sewn clothes.... When the people who profess the same religion as the king approach him they fall on their knees and sprinkle dust on their heads, for this is their way of greeting him. As for the Muslims, they greet him only by clapping their hands....

On the opposite bank of the Nil is another great kingdom...called Malal, the king of which is known as al-musulmani*. He is thus called because his country became afflicted with drought one year following another; the inhabitants prayed for rain, sacrificing cattle till they had exterminated almost all of them, but the drought and the misery only increased. The king had as his guest a Muslim...To this man the king complained of the calamities that assailed him and his people. The man said: "O king, if you believed in God (who is exalted) and testified that He is One, and testified as to the prophetic mission of Muhammad (God bless him and give him peace) and if you accepted all the religious laws of Islam, I would pray for your deliverance from your plight and that God's mercy would envelop all the people of your country and that your enemies and adversaries might envy you on that account." Thus he continued to press the king until the latter accepted Islam and became a sincere Muslim. The man made him recite from the Koran some easy passages and taught him religious obligations and practices which no one may be excused from knowing. Then the Muslim made him wait till the eve of the following Friday, when he ordered him to purify himself....The two of them came out towards a mound of earth, and there the Muslim stood praying while the king, standing at is right side, imitated him. Thus they prayed for a part of the night, the Muslim reciting invocations and the king saying "Amen." The dawn had just started to break when God caused abundant rain to descend upon them. So the king ordered the idols to be broken and expelled the sorcerers from his country. He and his descendants after him as well as his nobles were sincerely attached to Islam, while the common people of his kingdom remained polytheists. Since then their rulers have been given the title of al-musulmani.*

AL-ZUHRI

Janawa (or *Ganawa*) seems to have been a Berber term for what Muslims called "the land of the blacks" or more exactly, here, Ghana and its environs.

...Its boundary on the west is the great Sea [the Atlantic Ocean] and on the east the end of the land of Waraqlan as far as the end of the land of the Almoravids. In it there is the town of Ghana. Between this town and the great Sea to the west there is eight days' traveling. It is the capital of Janawa...In former times the people of the country professed paganism....Today there are Muslims and have scholars, lawyers, and Koran readers and have become pre-eminent in these fields. Some of their chief leaders...have traveled to Mecca and made the Pilgrimage and visited the Prophet's tomb....

AL-IDRISI

Al-Idrisi's reference to Ghana straddling a river is not echoed in any other source. Wanqara is probably Bambuko in modern-day Mali

Ghana consists of two towns on both banks of the river. This is the greatest of all the towns of the Sudan in respect of area, the most populous, and with the most extensive trade. Prosperous merchants go there from all the surrounding coutries....

*al-musulmani: "the Muslim"

...Continued

Its people are Muslims, and its king...has a palace on the bank of the Nil, strongly built, and perfectly fortified. His living quarters are decorated with various drawings and paintings, and provided with glass windows.

According to what is related about him, he is the most righteous man. One of his practices in keeping close to the people and upholding justice among them is that he has a corps of army commanders who come on horsebacks to his palace every morning. Each commander has a drum, which is beaten before him. When he reaches the gate it is silenced. When all the commanders have assembled, the king mounts his horse and rides at their head through the lanes of the town and around it. Anyone who has suffered injustice or misfortune confronts him, and stays there until the wrong is remedied....

....From the town of Ghana to the beginning of the country of Wanqara is eight days' journey. This country of Wanqara is the country of the gold, famous on account of its good quality and abundance.

Most of the gold is bought by the people of Wanqara and al-Maghrib al-Aqsa who export it to the mints in their own country, where dinars are struck from it, which they use in trade. This is the greatest source of income for the Sudan, upon which both great and small rely.

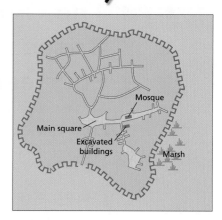

Kumbi Saleh

VISUAL SOURCES

Various sites from medieval Ghana have attracted archaeological investigation. One group of excavations, at Kumbi-Saleh, reveals a town nearly one-and a half square miles, founded in the tenth century, housing perhaps 15,000–20,000 people. This might be the merchant town, inhabited by Muslims, mentioned by al-Bakri, situated near the royal compound (see map). Note the regular plan and the evidence of large, multi-storeyed buildings, including what excavators have designated as "mansions" of up to nine rooms, and a mosque measuring 23 meters by 46 meters, begun in the tenth century and subject to periodic additions over a period of over 400 years (Photo 1). The biggest addition was made in the late eleventh century. Artifacts include glass weights for weighing gold and many finely wrought examples of metal tools, and evidence of a local form of money (see Figure 1).

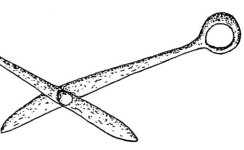

Photo 1 The Ruins of Kumbi–Saleh

Figure 1 Scissors

Questions to Consider

1 To judge from the extracts, what happened in Ghana between the times of al-Bakri and al-Idrisi?

2 Why do the writers refer to sensational tales, sex, and ritual?

3 Do the extracts help to explain how and why Islam reached Ghana?

4 What evidence do these sources provide about the nature of trade in the Sahel?

5 With the help of the map and the sources, is it possible to say why Ghana had such a privileged position and government?

Sources

Levtzion, N. *Corpus of Early Arabic Sources for West African History,* Cambridge, 1981.

Insoll, T. *The Archeology of Islam in sub-Saharan Africa, Cambridge*, 2003.

The Crucible: The Eurasian Crises of the Thirteenth and Fourteenth Centuries

This Korean World Map, from about 1402, known ▶ as the Kangnido, is the earliest known map of the world from east Asia. It is also the oldest surviving Korean map. Based on Chinese maps from the fourteenth century, the Kangnido clearly shows Africa (with an enormous lake in the middle of the continent) and Arabia on the lower left. The Indian subcontinent, however, has been merged into a gigantic landmass that represents China. The Korean peninsula, on the upper right, is shown as much bigger than it actually is, while Japan, on the lower right, is placed much farther south than where it is actually located.

1300–1800
Little Ice Age

ENVIRONMENT

since mid–1200s
Lenses and clocks in Europe

CULTURE

1206–1360s
Mongol hegemony

歷代州域博古今彊域之圖

CHAPTER 13

The World the Mongols Made

FRONT

FRONT

BACK

The Mongols arrive in Georgia. Two coins from the kingdom of Georgia, minted less than two decades apart, show that the Mongols had conquered that Caucasian state. The front of the top coin, minted by Queen Rusudan of Georgia in 1230, features a bust of a bearded Jesus Christ, draped in a mantle and backed by a cross-shaped halo. The Greek abbreviations for the words "Jesus" and "Christ" flank his right and left shoulders respectively. A Georgian inscription runs along the border. The back of the coin shows inscriptions in both Georgian and Arabic. In contrast, on the bottom coin, minted by King David in 1247, a figure on horse back has replaced the image of Jesus Christ (front), while the inscription on the back of the coin is exclusively in Arabic and identifies the king as "the slave of the Great Khan."

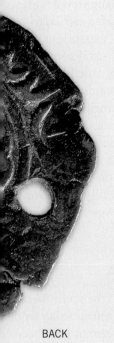

BACK

Two coins lie alongside each other in the British Museum in London. One, minted in the Caucasus Mountains, in 1230, is stamped with the name of the queen of Georgia, Rusudan (roo-soo-DAHN), and the words, "Queen of Queens, Glory of the World and Faith, Champion of the Messiah." Beside it, another Georgian coin, minted only 17 years later, shows a figure on horseback, named as "King David, slave of the empire of the Great Khan Kuyuk." A lot had happened in Georgia in a short time. The changes the coins reflect were important, not just for Georgia but for the world, for they were huge in scale, reshaping the politics, communications, and culture of Eurasia.

GEORGIA

Georgia, protected by its high mountains, had been remarkably successful in resisting the nomad armies of the eleventh and twelfth centuries. Though the Seljuk Turks (see Chapter 12) had briefly terrorized the kingdom and exacted tribute, the Georgians fought back. They refused to pay tribute, recovered their lost possessions, and extended their frontiers over parts of neighboring Armenia. In the early thirteenth century, Georgia was a formidable state, capable of imposing rulers as far afield as the Byzantine city of Trebizond (TREH-bih-zahnd) on the Black Sea and the Muslim city of Ahar in Azerbaijan (ah-zehr-bay-ZHAHN) on the Caspian. In the 1220s, James of Vitry, a Catholic bishop and historian of his own times, admired Georgian pilgrims he saw in Jerusalem, who "march into the holy city with banners displayed, without paying tribute to anyone, for the Muslims dare in no way molest them" (See "Going to the Source: Gender and Power in a Medieval Kingdom," pages 524–527.)

As James of Vitry noted, Georgia was "surrounded by infidels on all sides". That did not seem to matter. The Georgians even wrote to the pope promising assistance in a new crusade. Suddenly, however, in 1224, letters from Georgia arrived in Rome, withdrawing the promise. "A savage people of hellish aspect has invaded my realm," wrote Rusudan, "as voracious as wolves in their hunger for spoils, and as brave as lions." In the next decade, her letters got increasingly desperate. The Mongols were coming. The world would never be the same again.

FOCUS questions

- WHY WERE the Mongols able to conquer such a vast empire?
- WHAT WERE the positive and negative effects of the Mongol conquests?
- WHY DID the Mongols fail to conquer Egypt, India, and Japan?
- HOW DID Kubilai Khan's reign blend Mongol and Chinese traditions?
- WHAT TECHNOLOGIES did the West develop in the thirteenth century and what were the consequences?
- WHY DID nothing comparable to the Mongol Empire develop in Africa or the Americas?

The effects of the events of the rest of the century refashioned Eurasia, destroying old states, creating new ones, disrupting existing communications and reforging stronger, wider-ranging links. Eurasian civilizations benefited from enhanced contacts the Mongols fostered. Mongol methods were at first pitilessly bloody. They used terror and massacres to overawe their enemies. They razed cities, destroyed crops, slaughtered elites, and depleted peoples. It looked as if a safer, richer, more interconnected, more dynamic, more expanding, and more enlightened world might emerge—as if something precious were to form in an alchemist's crucible, out of conflicting ingredients, flung at random and stirred with violence. Then a century of environmental disasters arrested these changes in most of Eurasia. Catastrophes reversed the growth of populations and prosperity. But previously marginal regions began to be drawn more closely into a widening pattern of contacts and cultural exchange. Some peoples, in Africa and southeast Asia, for example, looked outward because they escaped disaster, others, especially in Europe, did so because their reverses were so enormous that there was nothing else they could do.

THE MONGOLS: RESHAPING EURASIA

The earliest records of Mongol peoples occur in Chinese annals of the seventh century. At that time, the Mongols emerged onto the steppes of the central Asian land now called Mongolia, from the forests to the north, where they seem to have been hunters and small-scale pig breeders. On the steppes they adopted a pastoral way of life. They became horse-borne nomads and sheep herders. Chinese and Khitan writers used versions of the names "Mongols" and "Tatars" (TAH-tahrs) for many different communities, with various religions and competing leaderships. One thing they had in common was that they spoke languages of common origins that were different from those of the Turks. In the early twelfth century, the bands or alliances they formed got bigger, and their raids against neighboring sedentary peoples became more menacing. In part, this was the effect of the growing preponderance of some Mongol groups over others. In part, it was the result of slow economic change.

Contact with richer neighbors gave Mongol chiefs opportunities for enrichment as mercenaries or raiders. Economic inequalities greater than the Mongols had ever known arose in a society in which blood relationships and seniority in age had formerly settled every person's position. Prowess in war enabled particular leaders to build up followers in parallel with—and sometimes in defiance of—the old social order. They called this process "crane catching"—comparing it to caging valuable birds. The most successful leaders enticed or forced rival groups into submission. The process spread to involve peoples who were not strictly Mongols, though the same name continued to be used—we use it still—for a confederation of many peoples, including many who spoke Turkic languages. In 1206, Temujin (TEH-moo-jeen), the most dynamic leader, proclaimed himself ruler (**khan**) "of all those who live in felt tents"—staking a claim to a steppe-wide empire. He was acclaimed by a title of obscure meaning, perhaps signifying "Ocean-King" and therefore, by implication, king of everything the ocean encloses. The title is traditionally rendered in the Roman alphabet as "Genghis Khan" (GEHN-gihs hahn).

We know maddeningly little about him. Today, his memory is twisted between myths. When Mongolia was a communist state between 1921 and 1990, he was an almost unmentionable figure, inconsistent with the "peace-loving" image communist Mongolians tried to project. Now he is their national hero. In his own day, he toyed with similarly contradictory images: a warlord who intimidated enemies into submission by massacre; an avenger of insults to his dynasty and tribe; an embodiment of Mongol convictions of superiority over sedentary peoples; a scourge of heaven, divinely appointed to chastise a wicked world; a lawgiver and architect of enduring empire.

In surviving documents, he addressed different audiences with conflicting messages. To Muslims, he was an instrument of God, sent to punish them for their sins. To Chinese, he was a candidate for the mandate of heaven. To Mongols, he was a giver of victory and of the treasure it brought. When he addressed monks and hermits, he stressed his own asceticism. "Heaven is weary of the inordinate luxury of China," he declared. "I have the same rags and the same food as cowherds and grooms, and I treat the soldiers as my brothers."

The violence endemic in the steppes now turned outward to challenge neighboring civilizations. Historians have been tempted to speculate about the reasons for the Mongols' expansion. One explanation is environmental. Temperatures in the steppe seem to have fallen during the relevant period. People farther west on the Russian plains complained that a cold spell in the early thirteenth century caused crops to fail. So declining pastures might have driven the Mongols to expand from the steppes. Population in the region seems to have been relatively high, and the pastoral way of life demands large amounts of grazing land to feed relatively small numbers of people. It is not a particularly energy-efficient way to provide food because it relies on animals eating plants and people eating animals, whereas farming produces humanly edible crops and cuts out animals as a wasteful intermediate stage of production. So perhaps the Mongol outthrust was a consequence of having more mouths to feed. Yet the Mongols were doing what steppelanders had always sought to do: dominate and exploit surrounding sedentary peoples. The difference was that they did it with greater ambition and greater efficiency than any of their predecessors.

Genghis Khan enforced or induced unity over almost the entire steppeland. The confederation of tribes he put together really did represent a combined effort of the steppe dwellers against the sedentary peoples who surrounded them. A single ideology came to animate, or perhaps reflect, that effort: the God-given terror-enforced right of the Mongols to conquer the world. The way events were recorded at the Mongol court in the next generation, it seemed as if from the moment of Genghis Khan's election as supreme ruler, "eternal heaven" had decreed that his conquests would encompass the world. The ruler is depicted as a constant devotee of **Tengri** (tehng-REE)—the sky, conceived as a supreme deity. The early Mongol-inspired sources constantly insist on an analogy between the over-arching unity of the sky and God's evident desire for the Earth to echo that unity through submission to one ruler.

Genghis Khan. Rashid al-Din (1247–1318) was a former Jewish rabbi, converted to Islam, who became the chief minister of the Mongol rulers of what is now Iran. His *Compendium of Chronicles* was propaganda that depicted Mongol rulers in Persian style. This is the image of Genghis Khan his successors liked to project—a lone, simple tent-dweller who was the arbitrator and lawgiver to petitioners from many nations.

"Exceptionally adaptable warmongers". This fourteenth-century Muslim painting shows the Mongols capturing Baghdad in 1258, with the help of siege craft and specialist engineers as well as their traditional cavalry. The last caliph appears behind a screen in his palace in the left background. In the center background, he emerges on a white horse to meet the Mongol leader, Hülegü. The painting seems to show the Mongols respecting the sacredness of the city and its ruler. Indeed, they showed their respect by putting the caliph to death without spilling his blood—a sign of reverence for the condemned in their culture.

It is more likely, however, that the sky cult was invented during the Mongol conquests to explain Genghis Khan's uniformly successful fortunes in war. The khan's imperial vision probably grew on him only gradually, as he felt his way from raiding, tribute gathering, and exacting ransom to constructing an empire, with permanent institutions of rule. Tradition alleges a turning point. When one of his generals proposed to exterminate ten million Chinese subjects and convert their fields into pasture for Mongol herds, Genghis Khan realized that he could profit more by sparing the peasants and taxing them to the tune of 500,000 ounces of silver, 400,000 sacks of grain, and 80,000 bolts of silk a year. The process, however, that turned him from destroyer to builder was tentative. Ghengis himself may have been only dimly aware of it.

His initially limited ambitions are clear from the oath the Mongol chiefs swore to him at his election as khan, recorded in the earliest surviving Mongol record of the events. "If you will be our khan, we will go as your vanguard against the multitude of your enemies. All the beautiful girls and married women that we capture and all the fine horses we will bring to you." The khan acquired an unequaled reputation for lust and bloodlust. "My greatest joy," he was remembered for saying, "is to shed my enemies' blood, wring tears from their womenfolk and take their daughters for bedding." Meanwhile, he made the streets of Beijing (bay-jeeng)—according to an admittedly imaginative eyewitness—"greasy with the fat of the slain." His tally of victims in Persia amounted, believably, to millions. When his army captured the city of Herat (heh-RAHT) in Afghanistan, it killed the entire population. Even after Genghis Khan had introduced more constructive policies, terror remained an instrument of empire. Mongol sieges routinely culminated in massacre. When the Mongols captured Baghdad in 1258, the last **caliph** (KAY-lihf) and his sons were trampled to death—a ritual form of death reserved for rulers, which was designed to demoralize the enemy.

Wherever the Mongol armies went, their reputation preceded them. Armenian sources warned Westerners of the approach of "precursors of Antichrist . . . of hideous aspect and without pity in their bowels, . . . who rush with joy to carnage as if to a wedding feast or orgy." Rumors piled up in Germany, France, Burgundy, Hungary, and even in Spain and England, where Mongols had never been heard of before. The invaders looked like monkeys, it was said, barked like dogs, ate raw flesh, drank their horses' urine, knew no laws, and showed no mercy. Matthew Paris, the thirteenth-century English monk who, in his day, probably knew as much about the rest of the world as any of his countrymen, summed up the Mongols' image: "They are inhuman and beastly, rather monsters than men, thirsting for and drinking blood, tearing and devouring the flesh of dogs and men. . . . And so they come, with the swiftness of lightning to the confines of Christendom, ravaging and slaughtering, striking everyone with terror and with incomparable horror."

The Rise of the Mongols

Seventh century	Earliest records of the Mongol people
Early twelfth century	Larger Mongol bands attack sedentary peoples
1206	Temujin proclaims himself khan

Mongol defeat. Japanese screen painters recorded the defeat of Mongol invaders. Though the Mongols adapted successfully to every kind of terrain, they were unable to continue their conquests overseas. The "divine winds"—kamikaze, as the Japanese called them—protected Japan by making it impossible for the Mongols adequately to supply or reinforce their task force.
Copyright Museum of Imperial Collections, Sannomaru Shozo kan. Photographs through courtesy of the International Society for Educational Information, Inc.

The Mongol conquests reached farther and lasted longer than those of any previous nomad empire (see Map 13.1). After Genghis Khan's death, the energy that the conquests generated took Mongol armies to the banks of the Elbe River in eastern Germany and the Adriatic Sea. Invasions of Syria, India, and Japan failed, and the Mongols withdrew from Europe without attempting to set up a permanent presence west of Russia. They completed the conquest of China, however, in 1279. At its fullest extent, therefore, the empire covered the region from the Volga River to the Pacific, encompassing the whole of Russia, Persia, China, the Silk Roads, and the steppes. This made it by a big margin the largest empire, in terms of territorial extent, the world had seen.

Efforts to explain this unique success appeal to Genghis Khan's military genius, the cunning with which the Mongols practiced feigned retreats only to encircle and destroy their advancing enemies, the effectiveness of their curved bows, the demoralizing psychological impact of their ruthless practices. Of course, they had the usual steppelander advantages of superior horsemanship and unrivaled mobility. It is likely that they succeeded, in part, through sheer numbers. Though we call it a Mongol army, Genghis Khan's was the widest alliance of steppelander peoples ever. And it is probable—though the sources are not good enough for certainty—that, relatively speaking, the steppeland was more populous in his day than ever before.

Above all, the Mongols were exceptionally adaptable warmongers. They triumphed not only in cavalry country, but also in environments where previous steppelander armies had failed, pressing into service huge forces of foot soldiers, mobilizing complex logistical support, organizing siege trains and fleets, appropriating the full potential of sedentary economies to finance further wars. The mountains of Georgia could not stop them. The Mongols captured the Georgian capital, Tbilisi (t-BEE-lee-see), in 1234, turning Georgia into a puppet kingdom. Nor, in the long run, could the rice paddies and rivers of southern China where the Mongols destroyed the Song dynasty in the 1270s. Toward the end of the century, when another supreme khan wanted to conquer Java and Japan, they were even willing to take to the sea. But both attempts failed.

As well as for extent, the Mongol Empire was remarkable, by steppelander standards, for longevity. As his career progressed, Genghis Khan became a visionary lawgiver, a patron of letters, an architect of enduring empire. His first steps

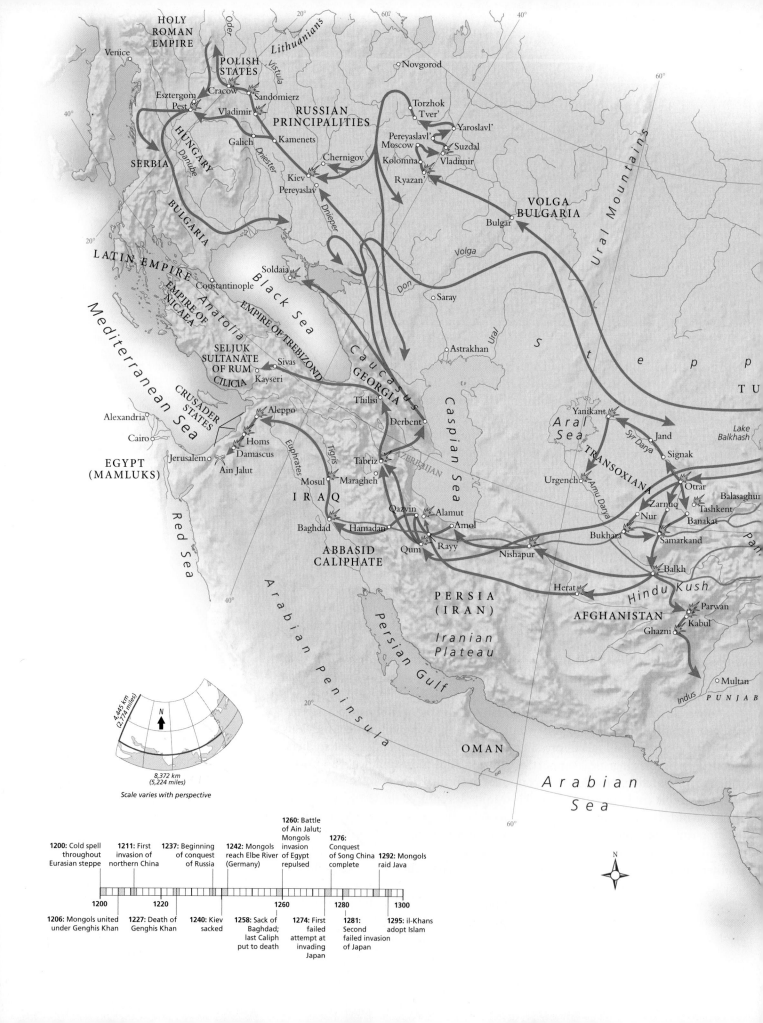

HOLY ROMAN EMPIRE
Venice
POLISH STATES
Oder
Lithuanians
Vistula
Novgorod
Esztergom
Cracow
Sandomierz
Pest
Vladimir
RUSSIAN PRINCIPALITIES
Torzhok
Tver'
HUNGARY
Galich
Kamenets
Yaroslavl'
SERBIA
Danube
Kiev
Chernigov
Pereyaslavl'
Moscow
Suzdal
Vladimir
Pereyaslav
Kolomna
Ryazan'
BULGARIA
Dnieper
VOLGA BULGARIA
LATIN EMPIRE
Soldaia
Bulgar
Constantinople
Black Sea
Don
Volga
Ural Mountains
EMPIRE OF NICAEA
Anatolia
EMPIRE OF TREBIZOND
Saray
Mediterranean Sea
SELJUK SULTANATE OF RUM
Sivas
Caucasus
GEORGIA
Astrakhan
S
t
e
p
p
Ural
CILICIA
Kayseri
Thilisi
Caspian Sea
TU
CRUSADER STATES
Aleppo
Derbent
Aral Sea
Yanikant
Lake Balkhash
Alexandria
Homs
Tabriz
AZERBAIJAN
Syr Darya
Jand
Cairo
Damascus
Euphrates
Tigris
Mosul
Maragheh
Qazvin
Alamut
Urgench
Signak
TRANSOXIANA
Jerusalem
Ain Jalut
Amol
Amu Darya
Otrar
Balasaghur
EGYPT (MAMLUKS)
IRAQ
Baghdad
Hamadan
Qum
Rayy
Nishapur
Zarnuq
Nur
Tashkent
Banakat
Bukhara
Samarkand
Pan
Red Sea
ABBASID CALIPHATE
PERSIA (IRAN)
Balkh
Herat
Hindu Kush
AFGHANISTAN
Parwan
Kabul
Arabian Peninsula
Iranian Plateau
Ghazni
Persian Gulf
Multan
Indus
PUNJAB
4,445 km
(2,774 miles)
N
OMAN
8,372 km
(5,224 miles)
Scale varies with perspective
Arabian Sea
N

1200: Cold spell throughout Eurasian steppe

1211: First invasion of northern China

1237: Beginning of conquest of Russia

1242: Mongols reach Elbe River (Germany)

1260: Battle of Ain Jalut; Mongols invasion of Egypt repulsed

1276: Conquest of Song China complete

1292: Mongols raid Java

1200

1220

1260

1280

1300

1206: Mongols united under Genghis Khan

1227: Death of Genghis Khan

1240: Kiev sacked

1258: Sack of Baghdad; last Caliph put to death

1274: First failed attempt at invading Japan

1281: Second failed invasion of Japan

1295: il-Khans adopt Islam

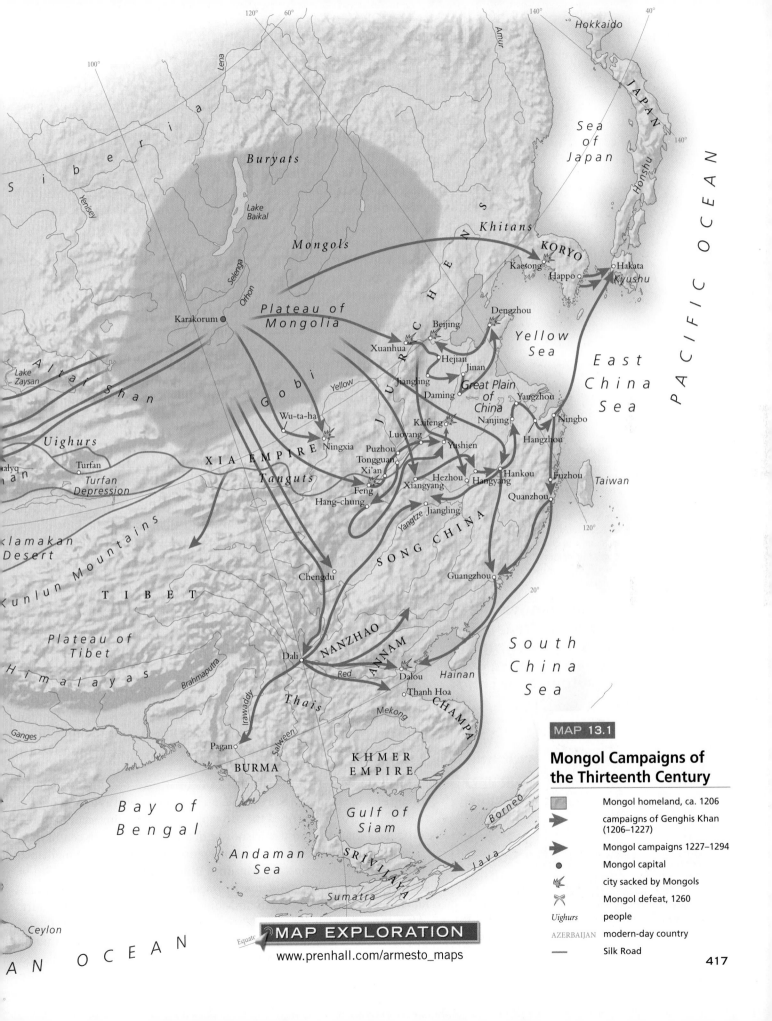

MAP 13.1

Mongol Campaigns of the Thirteenth Century

	Mongol homeland, ca. 1206
	campaigns of Genghis Khan (1206–1227)
	Mongol campaigns 1227–1294
	Mongol capital
	city sacked by Mongols
	Mongol defeat, 1260
Uighurs	people
AZERBAIJAN	modern-day country
	Silk Road

MAP EXPLORATION
www.prenhall.com/armesto_maps

toward acquiring a bureaucracy and a judicial system more or less coincided with his election as khan. He then turned to lawmaking. Gradually, a code took shape, regulating hunting, army discipline, behavior at feasts, and social relationships, with death the penalty for murder, serious theft, conspiracy, adultery, sodomy, and witchcraft. Initially, the khan relied on Uighurs (OOEE-goorz) (see Chapter 9) for his administrators and ordered the adoption of the Uighur script for the Mongols' language. But he recruited as and where he conquered, without favoritism for any community or creed. His closest ministers included Muslims, Christians, and Buddhists.

In 1219, a Chinese Daoist sage, Changchun (chahng-chwuhn), answered the khan's call for wise experts. At the age of 71, he undertook an arduous three-year journey from China to meet the khan at the foot of the Hindu Kush mountains in Afghanistan. There were sacrifices of principle he would not make. He would not travel with recruits for the imperial harem, or venture "into a land where vegetables were unavailable"—by which he meant the steppe. Yet he crossed the Gobi Desert, climbed "mountains of huge cold," and braved wildernesses where his escort smeared their horses with blood to ward off demons. Admittedly, Changchun's meeting with the khan was disappointing. The question the conqueror was most eager to put was not about the art of government, but about a potion to confer longevity on himself.

The Mongol Steppe

Still, many lettered and experienced officials from the Jurchen (juhr-CHEHN), Khitan, and Tangut (TAHN-goot) states (see Chapter 12) took service at the khan's court. The result was an exceptional, though short-lived, era in steppeland history: the **Mongol peace**. A European, who witnessed it in the 1240s, described it in an evident effort to reproach his fellow Christians with the moral superiority of their enemies: "The Mongols are the most obedient people in the world with regard to their leaders, more so even than our own clergy to their superiors. . . .

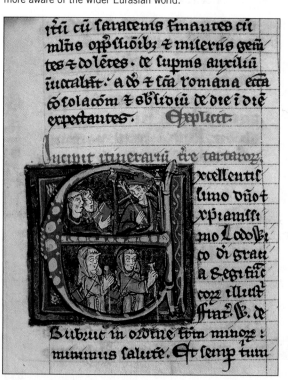

William of Rubruck. "He shall pass into the country of strange peoples. He shall try good and evil in all things." In the only surviving illumination that illustrates his report, Friar William of Rubruck looks alarmed at the instructions from King Louis IX of France to go on a mission to the Mongols. William's journey of 1253–1255 took him as far as the Mongol capital of Karakorum and generated an account full of vivid and faithful detail. The text illustrates how western Europeans were becoming more aware of the wider Eurasian world.

There are no wranglings among them, no disputes or murders." This was obviously exaggerated, but Mongol rule did make the steppeland safe for outsiders. This was new. A previously inaccessible road through the steppes opened across Eurasia north of the Silk Road. Once they had learned the benefits of peace along the steppeland road, the Mongols became its highway police. Teams of Mongol horses, for instance, took the pope's ambassador, John of Piano Carpini, 3,000 miles in 106 days in 1246. Missionaries, spies, and craftsmen in search of work at the Mongol court also made the journey in an attempt to forge friendship between the Mongols and the Christian West, or, at least, to gather intelligence (see Map 13.2).

William of Rubruck—a Franciscan envoy recorded vivid details of his mission to Genghis Khan's grandson in 1253. As well as describing the road, William also described the Mongol way of life more accurately and completely than any Western visitor until the late nineteenth century.

After taking leave of the king of France, who hoped for an alliance with the Mongols against the Muslims, William crossed the Black Sea in May and set out across the steppe by wagon, bound for Karakorum (kah-rah-KOH-ruhm), the new city in Mongolia where the khan held court. "After three days," he recorded, "we found the Mongols and I really felt as if I were entering another world." By November, he was in the middle of Transoxiana (tranz-ahk-see-YA-nah), "famished, thirsty, frozen, and

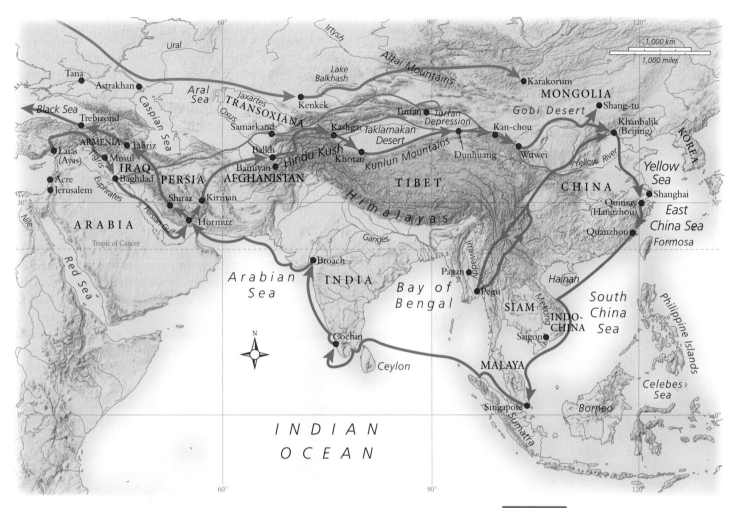

MAP 13.2

European Travellers of the Mongol Roads, 1245–1295

→ John of Piano Carpini 1245–1247 and William of Rubruck 1253–1254

→ Marco Polo 1271–1275

→ Marco Polo 1275–1295

— Silk Road

exhausted." In December, he was high in the dreaded Altai Shan (AHL-tay shahn), the mountain barrier that guarded the road to Karakorum. Here he "chanted the creed, among dreadful crags, to put the demons to flight." At last, on Palm Sunday, 1254, he entered the Mongol capital.

Friar William always insisted that he was a simple missionary, but he was treated as an ambassador and behaved like a master spy. And, indeed, he had more than one objective. The Mongols might be amenable to Christianity or at least to an alliance against common enemies in the Muslim world. On the other hand, they were potential enemies, who had already invaded the fringes of Europe and might do so again. Intelligence about them was precious. William realized that the seasonal migrations of Mongol life had a scientific basis and were calculated for military efficiency. "Every commander," he noted, "according to whether he has a greater or smaller number of men under him, is familiar with the limits of his pasture lands and where he ought to graze in summer and winter, spring and autumn."

Little useful intelligence escaped William. But he also showed interest in the culture he tried unsuccessfully to convert to Christianity. His description of a Mongol tent dwelling still holds good. The layout, social space, and way of life William saw have not changed much since his day. A frame of interlaced branches stretched between supports made of branches, converging at the top. The covering was of white felt, "and they decorate the felt with various fine designs." Up to 22 oxen hauled houses on wagons 20-feet broad.

Yurt. The shape and decoration of a Mongol tent dwelling—known as a *yurt* or *ger*—has not changed since William of Rubruck described those he saw in the thirteenth century. In the background of this photograph are the Pamir Mountains, which travelers westward on the Silk Roads had to cross when they emerged from the Taklamakan Desert.

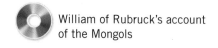

William of Rubruck's account of the Mongols

Each wife of the master of the household had her own tent, where the master had a bench facing the entrance. In an inversion of Chinese rules of precedence, the women sat on the east side, the men to the right of the master, who sat at the north end. Ancestral spirits resided in felt bags arrayed around the walls. One each hung over the heads of master and mistress, with a guardian image between them. Others hung on the women's and men's sides of the tent, adorned with the udders of a cow and a mare, symbols of the sources of life for people who relied on dairy products for their diet. The household would gather to drink fermented mare's milk in the tent of the chosen wife of the night. "I should have drawn everything for you," William assured his readers, "had I known how to draw."

Shamans' trances released the spirits from the bags that held them. Frenzied drumming, dancing, and drinking induced the shamans' ecstasies. The power of speaking with the ancestors' voices gave **shamans** enormous authority in Mongol decision making, including the opportunity to interfere in making and unmaking khans. This was a point William missed. The Mongols leaders' interest in foreign religions, and their investment in the cult of heaven, were, in part at least, strategies to offset the power of the native priests.

Outside the tent, William vividly captured the nature of the terrain—so smooth that one woman could pilot 30 wagons, linked by trailing ropes. He described a way of life that reflected steppeland ecology. The Mongols had mixed flocks of various kinds of sheep and cattle. Mixed pastoralism is essential in an environment in which no other source of food is available. Different species have different cycles of lactation and fertility. Variety therefore ensures a reliable food supply.

The horse was the dominant partner of life on the steppe. Mare's milk was the Mongols' summer food. The intestines and dried flesh of horses provided cured meat and sausages for winter. By drawing blood from the living creatures, Mongols on campaign could refresh themselves without significantly slowing the herds. This was the basis of their reputation for blood-sucking savagery among their sedentary neighbors. They made, said William, "very fine shoes from the hind part of a horse's hide." Fermented mare's milk was the favorite intoxicating drink. The Mongols revered drunkenness and hallowed it by rites: offerings sprinkled over the bags of ancestral spirits, or poured out toward the quarters of the globe. Challenges to drinking bouts were a part of nightly entertainment. To the accompaniment of singing and clapping, the victim would be seized by the ears, with a vigorous tug "to make him open his gullet."

William related in detail his conversations with the habitually drunken Möngke Khan (MOHNG-keh hahn), grandson of Genghis Khan. Despite the khan's bluster and self-righteousness, the conversations revealed some of the qualities that made the Mongols of his era great: tolerance, adaptability, respect for tradition. "We Mongols believe," Möngke said, if we can trust William's understanding of his words, "that there is but one God, in Whom we live and in Whom we die, and towards him we have an upright heart." Spreading his hand, he added, "But just as God has given different fingers to the hand, so He has given different religions to people."[1] Later in the thirteenth century, Kubilai Khan

A MONGOL PASSPORT

Although they were in use in China before the Mongols arrived, documents called *paizi*, such as the one depicted here, were used as passports to regulate communication and administration in the vast Mongol empire. Their use, the way they were designed, and the language in which they were written help us understand the massive movements of people and the rapid exchange of ideas and technology that occurred across Eurasia during the thirteenth and fourteenth centuries when Mongol rule was at its height. William of Rubruck and Marco Polo would have carried one of these passports on their return journeys from Mongol courts in Asia to Europe.

This passport is made of iron. Thick silver bands on it form characters in the script that the Tibetan monk Phagspa, a close advisor to Kubilai Khan (r. 1260–1294), devised for writing the Mongol language in 1269.

Above the inscription is a handle with a silver lion mask inlaid on it that shows the influence of Tibetan and Indian art.

Most *paizi* were circular or rectangular in shape and were either fastened on an item of clothing or suspended from the neck, so that customs officers could easily see them.

The inscription reads: "By the strength of Eternal Heaven, an edict of the Emperor [Khan]. He who has no respect shall be guilty."

The Metropolitan Museum of Art, Purchase, Bequest of Dorothy Graham Bennet, 1993 (1993.256) Photograph © The Metropolitan Museum of Art.

● What does this passport reveal about the Mongol peace?

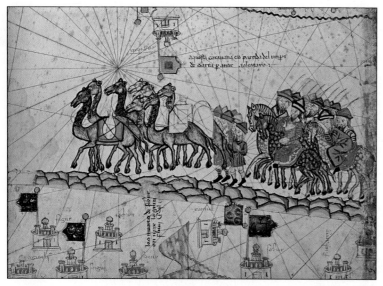

The Silk Roads. Cresques Abraham was the finest mapmaker of his day. He painted this image of a caravan on the Silk Roads in the late 1370s or early 1380s in an atlas probably commissioned for the king of France. By that date the Mongols no longer controlled the whole of the route, though the lances of an armed escort, presumably of Mongols, are visible behind the merchants. The caption says the caravan is bound for China, but it is heading in the opposite direction.

from *The Travels of Marco Polo*

(KOO-bih-la-yee hahn), another of Genghis Khan's grandsons, expressed himself to the Venetian traveler, Marco Polo, in similar terms. So this was genuinely a Mongol saying.

THE MONGOL WORLD BEYOND THE STEPPES: THE SILK ROADS, CHINA, PERSIA, AND RUSSIA

The steppeland route was ideal for horseborne travelers. Trading caravans, however, still favored the traditional **Silk Roads**, which crossed Eurasia to the south of the steppe through the Taklamakan (tahk-lah-mah-KAHN) Desert. These routes had developed over centuries, precisely because high mountains protected them from steppeland raiders. But they had never been totally secure before the Mongol peace. The new security boosted the amount of traffic the roads carried. Mongol partiality for merchants also helped. Mongols encouraged Chinese trade, uninhibited by any of the traditional Confucian prejudices against commerce as an ignoble occupation. In 1299, after the Mongol Empire had been divided among several rulers, a Persian merchant was made the ambassador of the Supreme Khan to the court of the subordinate Mongol **Il-khan** (EEL-hahn) in Persia—an elevation unthinkable under a native Chinese dynasty, which would have reserved such a post for an official educated in the Confucian classics. The khans gave low-cost loans to Chinese trading companies. Chinese goods—and with them, patterns and styles—flowed to Persian markets as never before. Chinese arts, under Mongol patronage, became more open to foreign influences.

Geography still made the Silk Roads hard to travel. Marco Polo was a young Venetian who accompanied his father and uncle on a trading mission to Mongol-ruled China in the early 1270s. "They were hard put to it to complete the journey in three and a half years," Marco Polo reported at the start of his own account, first "because of the snow and rain and flooded rivers and violent storms in the countries through which they had to pass, and because they could not ride so well in winter as in summer." The Taklamakan Desert was the great obstacle. The normal rule for caravans was the bigger the safer. But the modest water sources of the desert could not sustain many more than 50 men at a time with their beasts. The key to exploiting the desert routes was the distribution of water, which drains inland from the surrounding mountains and finds its way below the desert floor by underground channels. It was normal to go for 30 days without finding water, though there might be an occasional salt-marsh oasis or an unreliable river of shifting course, among featureless dunes. The worst danger was getting lost—"lured from the path by demon-spirits." "Yes," said Marco,

> and even by daylight men hear these spirit-voices and often you fancy you are listening to the strains of many instruments, especially drums, and the clash of arms. For this reason bands of travelers make a point of keeping very close together. Before they go to sleep they set up a sign pointing in the direction in which they have to travel. And round the necks of their beasts they fasten little bells, so that by listening to the sound they may prevent them straying off the path.[2]

As a fourteenth-century painter at Persia's Mongol court imagined, the demons were black, athletic, and ruthless, waving the dismembered limbs of horses as they danced. As Friar William had seen, the Mongols recommended warding them off by smearing a horse's neck with blood.

A fourteenth-century guide included handy tips for Italian merchants who headed for East Asia to extend the reach of the commerce of their cities. At the port of Tana (TAH-nah), on the Black Sea, you should furnish yourself with a good guide, regardless of expense. "And if the merchant likes to take a woman with him from Tana, he can do so." On departure from Tana, 25 days' supply of flour and salt fish were needed—"other things you will find in sufficiency and especially meat." The road was "safe by day and night" and protected by Mongol police. But it was important to take a close relative for company. Otherwise, should a merchant die, his property would be forfeit. The text specified rates of exchange at each stop and recommended suitable conveyances for each stage of the journey: oxcart or horse-drawn wagon to the city of Astrakhan (AHS-trah-hahn) where the Don River runs into the Caspian Sea, depending on how fast the traveler wanted to go and how much he wanted to pay. Thereafter camel train or pack mule was best, until you arrived at the river system of China. Silver was the currency of the road, but the Chinese authorities would exchange it for paper money, which—Westerners were assured—they could use throughout China.

After the deserts, the next obstacles were the mountains on their rims. The Tian Shan, which screens the Taklamakan Desert, is one of the most formidable mountain ranges in the world: 1,800 miles long, up to 300 miles wide, and rising to 24,000 feet. The extraordinary environment these mountains enclose is odder still because of the deep depressions that punctuate them. That of Turfan (toor-FAHN) drops to more than 500 feet below sea level. Farther north, the Altai Shan mountains guard the Mongolian heartlands. "Before the days of the Mongols," wrote the bishop of the missionary diocese the Franciscans had established in China, "nobody believed that the Earth was habitable beyond these mountains, . . . but by God's leave and wonderful exertion the Mongols crossed them, and . . . so did I."

Europeans frequently made the journey to China. That reflects the balance of wealth and power at the time. China was rich and productive, Europe a needy backwater. We know of only one subject of the Chinese emperor who found it worthwhile to make the journey in the opposite direction. Rabban Bar Sauma (rah-BAHN bahr SAH-oo-mah) was a Nestorian (neh-STOH-ree-yahn)—a follower, that is, of a Christian tradition that had long flourished in Central Asia but the West had regarded as heretical since the fifth century (see Chapter 9).

When making a pilgrimage to Jerusalem, Bar Sauma planned a route between Nestorian monasteries, heading initially for Maragha (ma-rah-GEH) in what is now Azerbaijan, where the most respected bishop of the Nestorian church had his see. Maragha was a suitable way station: the intellectual capital of the western Mongol world, with a library reputedly of 400,000 books and a new astronomical observatory. There, Bar Sauma took service, first with the bishop, and later with the local Mongol ruler of Persia, the Il-khan. He never completed his pilgrimage. In 1286, however, Bar Sauma did resume his travels. He was appointed the Mongols' ambassador to the kingdoms of the Christian West, to negotiate an alliance against Muslim Egypt (see Map 13.3).

Demons. In Chinese and Mongol art, images of demons personify the torments of the desert—thirst, glare, sandstorms, extremes of heat and cold, the perils of being lost or attacked. William of Rubruck sang to drive away demons. Other travelers rang bells or deterred the demons with blood. In this fourteenth-century painting produced under Mongol patronage, the demon's dance evokes the swirling, stinging desert winds.

 from *The History of the Life and Travels of Rabban Bar Sauma*

Travelers During the Mongol Peace

1245–1247	John of Piano Carpini
1253–1254	William of Rubruck
1271–1275; 1275–1295	Marco Polo
1275–1288	Rabban Bar Sauma

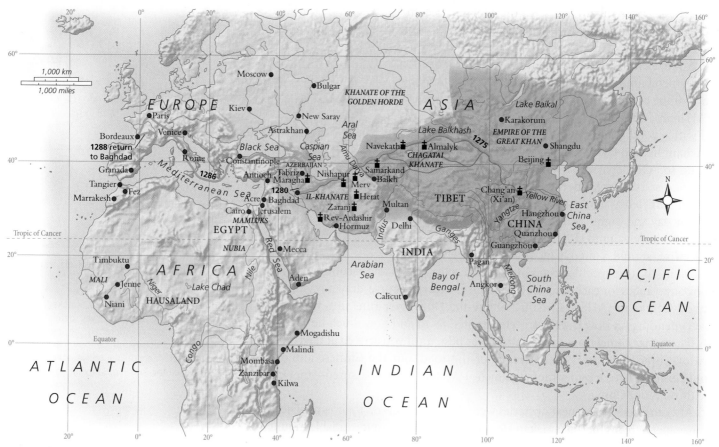

MAP 13.3

The Travels of Rabban Bar Sauma, 1275–1288

——— Silk Road

——— travels of Rabban Bar Sauma, 1275–1288

✝ Nestorian see

When he got to Rome, he was accorded a signal honor: reception by the cardinals who had assembled to elect a pope. In Paris, he recognized the university there as an intellectual powerhouse reminiscent of Maragha, with schools of mathematics, astronomy, medicine, and philosophy. Persian was the only language in which Bar Sauma could communicate with Western interpreters. From the errors he makes in describing Western manners and politics, a lot evidently got lost in translation. He mistook diplomatic evasions for assent and vague expressions of Christian fellowship for doctrinal agreement. He returned to Persia with many assurances of friendship and exhortations to the Il-khan to convert to Christianity. The fact that he completed the journey at all shows how the Mongols made it possible to cross Eurasia.

China

The Mongols never ran their dominions as a centralized state. Nor did they apply consistent methods to govern territories as vast and diverse as theirs. Three main areas of conquest beyond the steppeland—in China, Persia, and Russia—were added after Genghis Khan's death. All were exploited in different ways, specific to the Mongols' needs and the peculiarities of each region.

The conquest of Song China was long and difficult for two reasons. It was a more powerful state than any the Mongols faced elsewhere, and it was highly defensible: compact, so that its armies could maneuver on interior lines of communication, and scored by terrain inhospitable to Mongol horsemen. But, fueled by resources from the Mongols' other conquests, and pursued with unfailing tenacity, the conquest unfolded relentlessly bit by bit. Letters from the Chinese court seeped desperation as the Mongols closed in for the kill. In 1274, the Chinese empress mother, Xie Qiao (shay chow), reflected on where the blame lay.

> The empire's descent into peril is due, I regret, to the instability of our moral virtue. . . . The sound of woeful lament reverberated through the countryside, yet we failed to investigate. The pall of hunger and cold enveloped the armed forces, yet we failed to console.[3]

The real reasons for China's collapse lay in the superiority of the Mongols' war machine. Unlike previous steppelander invaders, the Mongols spared no resources to pursue all-out victory and hired the troops and equipment needed to subdue a country of cities, rice paddies, and rivers. Clearly, the size of the Mongols' existing empire helped. Persian engineers built the siege engines that helped overcome southern Chinese cities. The last battle was at Changzhao (chahng-jeeow) in 1275. The Chinese poet Yi Tinggao (yee teen-gow) was there, "smelling the acrid dust of the field," spying "the green irridescence of the dead." The human misery could be measured in the grief-stricken literature that survives: the suicide notes, the cries of longing for loved ones who disappeared in the chaos, massacred or enslaved. Years later, Ni Bozhuang (nee-bwo-chwang) bailiff of a Daoist monastery, recalled the loss of his wife: "I still do not know if you were taken because of your beauty, or if, surrounded by horses, you can still buy cosmetics." In 1276, with his advisers fleeing and his mother packed for flight, the young Song emperor wrote his abdication letter to the Mongol khan. "The **Mandate of Heaven** having shifted, your Servant chooses to change with it, . . . yet my heart is full of emotions and these cannot countenance the prospect of the abrupt annihilation of the . . . altars of my ancestors. Whether they be misguidedly abandoned or specially preserved intact rests solely with the revitalized moral virtue you bring to the throne."

For the Mongols, the conquest of China was a logical continuation of the policies of Genghis Khan and a stage in fulfilling the destiny of world conquest heaven supposedly envisaged. But it was also the personal project and passion of Kubilai Khan (1214–1294), Genghis's grandson, who became so immersed in China that he never asserted his supremacy against those Mongol leaders in the extreme west of the Mongol world who resisted his claims to supremacy. Some of his Chinese subjects resented Kubilai's foreign ways: the libations of fermented mare's milk with which he honored his gods, his barbarous banquets of meat, the officials he chose with great freedom from outside the Confucian elite and even from outside China. Marco Polo reported that all the Chinese "hated the government of the Great Khan, because he set over them steppelanders, most of whom were Muslims, and . . . it made them feel no more than slaves." In this respect, the khan indeed broke with Chinese tradition, which was to confine administrative positions to a meritocracy, whose members were selected by examination in the Confucian classics. Kubilai showed his reverence for Confucius by building a shrine in his honor, but he needed to recruit, as Genghis Khan had, from the full range of talent the Mongol Empire supplied.

Kubilai Khan. Liu Guandao was Kubilai Khan's favorite painter. So we can be fairly sure that this is how the khan would like to be remembered: not just in the traditional inert Chinese pose (which Liu also painted), but also active, dressed and horsed like a Mongol ruler, engaged in the hunt. A woman, presumably his influential consort, Chabi, is at his side. The blank silk background evokes the featurelessness of the steppe, while also highlighting the human figures.

Kubilai, indeed, remained a Mongol khan. In some respects, he flouted Chinese conventions. He showed traditional steppelander respect for the abilities of women, giving them court posts and, in one case, a provincial governorship. His wife, Chabi, was one of his closest political advisers. He introduced a separate tier of administration for Mongols, who became a privileged minority in China, ruled by their own laws, and resented for it by most Chinese. In defiance of Confucian teachings, Kubilai felt obliged to fulfill the vision of world conquest he inherited from Genghis Khan. But beyond China, he registered only fleeting success. In Java, the Mongols replaced one native prince with another, without making permanent gains. In Vietnam, the Mongols were only able to levy tribute at a rate too low to meet the cost of their campaigns there. So-called *kamikaze* winds—divine typhoons that wrecked the Mongol fleets—drove Kubilai's armies back from Japan.

While upholding Mongol traditions, Kubilai also sought, emphatically, to be a Chinese emperor, who performed the due rites, dressed in the Chinese manner, learned the language, patronized the arts, protected the traditions, and promoted the interests of his Chinese subjects. Marco Polo, who seems to have served him as a sort of professional storyteller, called him "the most powerful master of men, lands, and treasures there has been in the world from the time of Adam until today."

Persia

In Persia, meanwhile, the Mongol rulers were like chameleons, gradually taking on the hues of the culture they conquered. But, as in China, they were anxious to maintain a distinct identity and to preserve their own traditions. The court tended to stay in the north, where there was grazing for the kinds of herds their followers brought with them from the steppe. The Il-khans—"subordinate rulers," so called in deference to Kubilai Khan's nominal superiority—retained nomadic habits, migrating every summer and winter to new camps with palatial tents. At the end of the thirteenth century, Gazan Khan's tent took three years to make, and 200 men took 20 days to erect it. In southern Iran and Iraq, the Il-khans tended to entrust power to local dynasties, securing their loyalty by marriages with the ruling family or court nobility. In effect, this gave them hostages for the good conduct of provincial rulers.

Eventually in 1295, the Il-khans adopted Islam, after flirtations with Nestorianism and Buddhism. This marked an important departure from the tradition of religious pluralism Genghis Khan had begun and Kubilai upheld. From the moment the Il-khan Ghazan (r. 1295–1304) declared his conversion to Islam, the state began to take on a militantly religious character, excluding the Christians, Zoroastrians, Buddhists, and Jews formerly admitted to the khan's service. Moreover, the form of Islam the Il-khans finally adopted was Shiism, the prevailing tradition in Iran. Shiites (SHEE-eye-its) (see Chapter 9) embraced doctrines most Muslims rejected: that Muhammad's authority descended by heredity from his nephew Ali; that a divinely selected leader or imam would perfect the Prophet's message; and that in the meantime the clergy had the right to interpret Islam. The Il-khan's option for Shiism ensured that eventually Persia would remain an exceptional region in the Muslim world as the only officially Shiite state.

Indeed, the religious art of the Il-khanate is strikingly unlike that of any other Muslim country. The painters freely painted human figures, especially those of Muhammad and his nephew, and even copied Christian nativity scenes to produce

Il-Khan art. When Mongols converted to Islam, they did not necessarily accept all the beliefs and conventions of orthodox religion. In this fourteenth-century painting from what is now Iran, the white rooster symbolizes the Muslim call to prayer—but the rooster was also a traditional Zoroastrian symbol of dawn. The prophet Muhammad, moreover, is realistically depicted at bottom right—something most Muslim painters would regard as impious, even today. The other figures are of angels.

versions of the Prophet's birth. The Il-khans' Persia, however, was not isolated from neighboring states. On the contrary, as was usual in the Mongol world, the presence of rulers descended from Genghis Khan promoted trans-Eurasian contacts and exchanges of goods, personnel, and ideas. Persia supplied China, for instance, with engineers, astronomers, and mathematicians, while Persia received Chinese porcelain and paper money, which, however, did not take root in Persia before the twentieth century. Chinese designs influenced Persian weavers, and Chinese dragons appeared on the tiles with which Persian buildings of the time were decorated. Mongol rule ended in Persia in 1343 when the last Il-khan died without an heir.

Novgorod. The cathedral of St. Sophia in Novgorod in Russia would have presented essentially the same outline in the thirteenth century that it does today. At the time, it was one of relatively few buildings in that mercantile city-state built of stone rather than wood. The tallest gilded dome shows the position of the sanctuary at the heart of the church.

Russia

Meanwhile, the Mongols who remained in their central Asian heartlands continued to lead their traditional, unreconstructed way of life. So did those who formed the elite in the remaining areas the heirs of Genghis Khan inherited: in Turkestan and Kashgaria in Central Asia, and the steppes of the lower Volga River. From the last of these areas, where the Mongols were known as the Golden Horde, they exercised a form of overlordship over Russia, where they practiced a kind of imperialism different from those in China and Persia. The Mongols left the Christian Russian principalities and city-states to run their own affairs. But their rulers had to receive charters from the khan's court at Saray (sah-REYE) on the lower Volga, where they had to make regular appearances, loaded with tribute and subject to ritual humiliations. The population had to pay taxes directly to Mongol-appointed tax gatherers—though as time went on, the Mongols assigned the tax gathering to native Russian princes and civic authorities.

The Russians tolerated this situation—albeit unhappily, and with many revolts—partly because the Mongols intimidated them by terror. When the Mongols took the great city of Kiev in 1240, it was said, they left only 200 houses standing and strewed the fields "with countless heads and bones of the dead." Partly, however, the Russians were responding to a milder Mongol policy. In most of Russia, the invaders came to exploit rather than to destroy. According to one chronicler, the Mongols spared Russia's peasants to ensure that farming would continue. Ryazan, a Russian principality on the Volga, southeast of Moscow, seems to have borne the brunt of the Mongol invasion. Yet there, if the local chronicle can be believed, "the pious Grand Prince Ingvary Ingvarevitch sat on his father's throne and renewed the land and built churches and monasteries and consoled newcomers and gathered together the people. And there was joy among the Christians whom God had saved from the godless and impious khan." Many cities escaped lightly by capitulating at once. Novgorod, that hugely rich city (see Chapter 11), which the Mongols might have coveted, they bypassed altogether.[4]

Moreover, the Russian princes were even more fearful of enemies to the west, where the Swedes, Poles, and Lithuanians had constructed strong, unitary monarchies, capable of sweeping the princes away if they ever succeed in expanding into Russian territory. Equally menacing were groups of mainly German adventurers, organized into crusading "orders" of warriors, such as the Teutonic Knights and the Brothers of the Sword, who took monastic-style vows

Excerpt from the *Novgorod Chronicle*

but dedicated themselves to waging holy war against pagans and heretics. In practice, these orders were self-enriching companies of professional fighters, who built up territorial domains along the Baltic coast by conquest. In campaigns between 1242 and 1245, Russian coalitions fought off invaders on the western front, but they could not sustain war on two fronts. The experience made them submissive to the Mongols.

THE LIMITS OF CONQUEST: MAMLUK EGYPT AND MUSLIM INDIA

In the 1200s, Egypt was in chaos because of rebellions by pastoralists from the southern desert and revolt by the slaves who formed the elite fighting force. It seems counterintuitive to arm slaves. But for most of the thirteenth century, the policy worked well for the heirs of Saladin who had ruled Egypt since 1192. The rulers handpicked their slave army, or Mamluks. The slaves came overwhelmingly from Turkic peoples that Mongol rebels displaced or captured and sold. These slaves had nowhere else to go and no future except in the Egyptian sultan's service. They were acquired young. They were trained in barracks, which became their substitutes for families and the source of their pride and strong sense of comradeship. They were, from the ruler's point of view, ideally reliable: a dependent class. Increasingly, however, the Mamluks came to know their own strength. In the 1250s, they rebelled. Their own later propaganda cites the sultan's failure to reward them fairly for their services in repelling a crusader attack on Egypt, and their outrage at the promotion of a black slave to one of the highest offices in the court. The Mamluks "threw themselves upon him like the onrush of an unleashed torrent." In 1254, the Mamluks replaced the last heir of Saladin with rulers from their own ranks.

The rebels, however, while contending with internal enemies, perceived the Mongols as a greater threat and turned to face them. In September 1260, they turned back the Mongol armies at one of the decisive battles of the world at Ain Jalut (EYE-in jah-LOOT) in Syria. It was the first serious reversal the Mongols had experienced since Genghis Khan united them. And it gave the slave army's commander, Baybars (BEYE-bahrs), the chance to take over Egypt and Syria. He boasted that he could play polo in Cairo and Damascus within the space of a single week. The Mamluks mopped up the last small crusader states on the coast of Syria and Palestine between 1268 and 1291. In combination with the effects of the internal politics of the Mongol world, which inhibited armies from getting too far from the centers of power, the Mamluk victory kept the Mongols out of Africa.

Mamluk victory marked a further stage in the Islamization of Africa. The Mamluks levied tribute on the Christian kingdoms of Nubia (NOO-bee-ah) (see Chapter 9). Then, in the next century, they imposed Islam there. Cairo, as we shall see in the next chapter, became a normal stopping place on the pilgrimage route to Mecca for Muslim kings and dignitaries from West Africa. Islam percolated through the region of Lake Chad and into Hausaland (HOW-sah-land) in what is today Nigeria.

Muslim India: The Delhi Sultanate

After the disruptions the violent Turkic migrations of the twelfth century caused, it took a long time for a state in the mold of Mahmud's (mah-MOOD) to reemerge in Ghazna (GAHZ-nah) (see Chapter 12). By the 1190s, however, a Muslim Turkic dynasty

Rise of the Mamluks

1254	Mamluks depose sultan of Egypt
1260	Mamluk army victorious at the battle of Ain Jalut in Syria
1268–1291	Mamluks overthrow last of the crusader states

and people, the Ghurids (GOO-rids), had resumed the habit of raiding into Hindu India. As their victories accumulated, they began to levy fixed tribute in the Punjab and even established permanent garrisons in the Ganges (GAN-jeez) valley. One of their most far-flung outposts—and therefore one of the strongest—was at the city of Delhi in northern India. The adventurer Iltutmish (eel-TOOT-mihsh) took command there in 1211. He was a former slave who had risen to general and received his freedom from his Ghurid masters. He avoided war with Hindus—which was, in essence, his job—in favor of building up his own resources. In 1216, exhibiting to his subordinates the letters that had granted him his freedom, he effectively declared himself independent. Over the next 12 years, he played the power game with skill, exploiting the rivalries of Muslim commanders to construct a state from the Indus River to the Bay of Bengal. Meanwhile, the effects of the Mongol conquests on Central Asia protected this new realm, which became known as the Sultanate of Delhi, against outside attack (see Map 13.4). The Mongols effectively eliminated any possible invader and drove many refugees to take service with Iltutmish. As one of the early chroniclers of the sultanate said, "Rulers and governors, . . . and many administrators and notables came to Iltutmish's court from fear of the slaughter and terror of the accursed Mongol, Genghis Khan."

There was no consistent form of administration. In most of the remoter territories, the Delhi sultan was an overlord, mediating between small, autonomous states, many of which Hindus ruled. Bengal was exceptional—a forest frontier, in which governors tried to promote Muslim settlement by making land grants to pioneering holy men and religious communities. But there was a core of lands that was the sultan's personal property, exploited to benefit his treasury and run by administrators he appointed. Lands the sultan granted to warriors in exchange for military service ringed the core. For most of the rest of the century, the sultanate had a volatile history, punctuated by succession wars that were resolved at great oath-taking ceremonies, when the aristocracy of the realm—encompassing a great diversity of effectively freelance warriors and local rulers whom it was difficult or impossible for the sultan to dismiss—would make emotional but often short-lived declarations of loyalty.

Iltutmish's personal choice of successor set the tone on his deathbed in 1236. As an ex-slave, Iltutmish was no respecter of conventional ideas of hierarchy. Denouncing his sons for incompetence, he chose his daughter, Radiyya (rah-DEE-ah), as his successor. In the steppes, women often handled big jobs. In the Islamic world, a woman ruler was a form of impiety and a subversion of what was thought to be the natural order of the world. When, in 1250, a little before the Mamluks took over in Egypt, a woman had seized the throne there and applied to Baghdad for legitimation by the caliph, he is supposed to have replied that he could supply capable men, if no more existed in Egypt. Radiyya had to contend both with a brother who briefly ousted her—she had him put to death—and, what was harder, with male mistrust. Some of her coins emphasize claims to unique feminine virtues as "pillar of women." Others have modest inscriptions, in which all the glorious epithets are reserved for her father and the caliph in Baghdad. Her best strategy was to behave like a man. She dressed

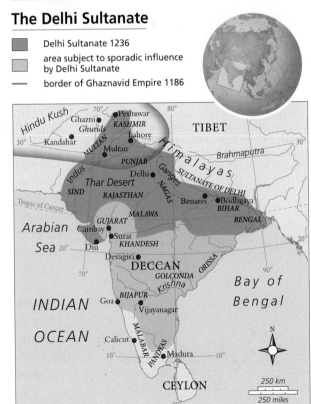

MAP 13.4

The Delhi Sultanate

- Delhi Sultanate 1236
- area subject to sporadic influence by Delhi Sultanate
- — border of Ghaznavid Empire 1186

The Qutb Minar. The founder of the Ghurid dynasty began the Qutb Minar, near Delhi, as a monument to his own prowess in battle, toward the end of the twelfth century. Successors continued the project until, by the late fourteenth century, it was the tallest tower in India—much bigger than any minaret designed to hoist the call to prayer. The ridged form and decorative use of sandstone are typical of the stylistic traditions the Ghurids brought to India from Afghanistan.

in male clothing, refused to cover her face, and, according to a slightly late source, "mounted horse like men, armed with bow and quiver." To conventional minds, these were provocations. She was ousted on grounds that—true or false—reflect male prejudices about female behavior. Accused of taking a black slave as a lover, she was deposed in 1240 in favor of a brother. Her real offense was self-assertion. Those modest coin inscriptions suggest that power brokers in the army and the court were willing to accept her, but only as a figurehead representative of her father, not as an active leader of men.

The sultanate had to cope not only with the turbulence of its own elite, but with its Hindu subjects and neighbors. Dominion by any state over the entire Indian subcontinent remained, at best, a dream. Frontier expansion was slow. Deforestation was an act of state, because, as a Muslim writer of the fourteenth century complained, "the infidels live in these forests, which for them are as good as city walls, and inside them they have their cattle and grain supplies of water collected from the rains, so that they cannot be overcome except by strong armies of men who go into these forests and cut down those reeds." In Bengal, the eastward shift of the Ganges River made Islamization easier. Charismatic **sufis**, with tax-free grants of forest land for mosques and shrines, led the way.

For most of the thirteenth century, the Mongol menace overshadowed the sultanate. The internal politics of the dynasty of Genghis Khan caused dissensions and hesitancies that protected Delhi. Mongol dynastic disputes cut short periodic invasions. Moreover, a buffer state dissident Mongols created in Delhi's western territories diminished the sultanate but also absorbed most of the khans' attacks. In the 1290s, however, the buffer collapsed. By what writers in Delhi considered a miracle, the subsequent Mongol attacks failed, faltered, or were driven off.

EUROPE

With the scare the Mongol invasions caused and the loss of the last crusader states in Syria to the Mamluks, Latin Christendom looked vulnerable. Attempts to revitalize the crusading movement were made—especially by Louis IX, the king of France (r. 1226–1270) who became a model monarch for the Western world. But they all failed. A further reverse was the loss of Constantinople by its Latin rulers to a Byzantine revival. The Mongols destroyed or dominated most of the successor states that claimed Byzantium's legacy, but at the city of Nicaea in western Anatolia, rulers who continued to call themselves "Roman emperors" maintained the court rituals and art of Byzantine greatness. In 1261, they recaptured the old capital from the crusaders "after many failures," as the ruler at the time, Michael VIII, admitted, "because God wished us to know that the possession of the city was a grace dependent on his bounty."

Nevertheless, Latin Christendom grew on other fronts, extending the frontier deep into formerly pagan worlds along the Baltic in Livonia, Estonia, Prussia, and Finland. The *Rhyming Chronicle* of the conquest of Livonia recounts with equal pleasure the destruction of native villages and the piety of forced converts. The Swedish knights led by Henry of Finland (d. ca. 1160) were said to have wept over the potential converts they slew in the twelfth century.

Between the 1220s and the 1260s, Christian kingdoms seized most of the Mediterranean seaboard of Spain and the Balearic islands from the hands of

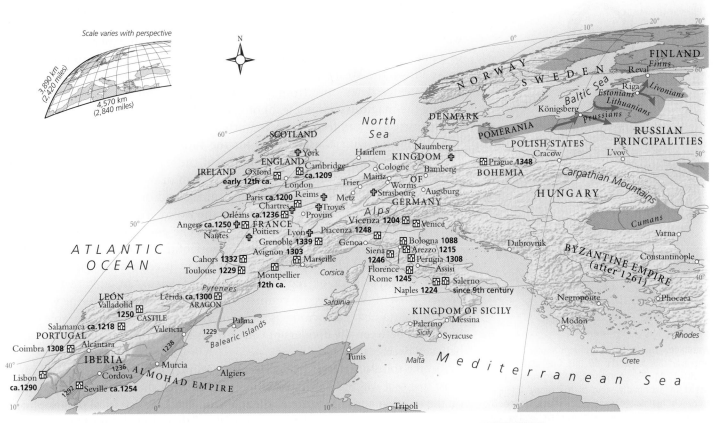

MAP 13.5

Latin Christendom, 1200–1300

predominantly pagan lands

reconquest of Spain in thirteenth century

university, with date of foundation

important churches with stained glass

campaigns of Teutonic Knights and Sword Brothers

Muslim rulers. Here the existing economy and population were not much disturbed. Conquests Castile and Portugal made over the same period in the Iberian southwest became a sort of wild west, of sparse settlements, tough frontiersmen, and vast cattle and sheep ranches. Meanwhile, traders of the western Mediterranean increased their commerce with northern Europe along the coasts the Spaniards conquered, through the Strait of Gibraltar (see Map 13.5). Toward the end of the century, as they became accustomed to Atlantic sailing conditions, some of them began to think of exploring the ocean for new routes and resources. In 1291, an expedition set off from the Italian city of Genoa to try to find "the regions of India by way of the ocean." The voyagers were never heard of again, but their voyage marked the beginning of a long, faltering effort by maritime communities of Western Europe to exploit the ocean at their feet.

The big new opportunities, however, lay eastward. The thirteenth century was the most intense period ever in trans-Eurasian communications, and European traditions were rechanneled as a result or, at least, guided more securely in directions they might have taken anyway. Paper, for instance, was a Chinese invention that had already reached the West through Arab intermediaries. Chinese technicians captured in the battle of Talas in 751 (see Chapter 9) were said to have revealed the secret of its manufacture to entrepreneurs in the central Asian city of Samarkand. Paper was manufactured as a luxury north of the Alps in the twelfth century, but only in the late thirteenth century was it adopted in Europe as a major contribution to what we would now call **information technology**. European maritime technology—a prerequisite of the prosperity borne

Astrolabe. The Syrian instrument maker, al-Sarraj engraved his signature on this fine astrolabe in 1230–1231. The purpose of the astrolabe is to assist in astronomy—one of the many sciences in which the Islamic world excelled at the time. By suspending the instrument at eye level and swiveling a narrow central bar until it aligned with any observed star, the user could read the star's elevation above the horizon, as well as such additional information as the latitude, the date, and even the time of day from the engraved discs.
© National Maritime Museum Picture Library, London, England. Neg. #E5555-3

Roger Bacon on experimental science

by long-range trade and of the reach of most long-range imperialism—was especially primitive by non-European standards up to this time. The compass was first recorded in Europe in about 1190 in a text that explained the marvels of a pin well rubbed "with an ugly brown stone that draws iron to itself." As far as we know, the West had as yet no maritime charts. The earliest reference to such a device dates only from 1270. Gunpowder and the blast furnace were among the magical-seeming technologies that first reached Europe from China in the thirteenth and fourteenth centuries.

Meanwhile, with consequences for the future that can hardly be overestimated, Western science grew more **empirical**, more reliant on the reality of sense perceptions, more committed to the observation of nature. At the University of Paris, which the Nestorian Rabban Bar Sauma so admired, scholars cultivated a genuinely scientific way of understanding the world. The end products were the marvelously comprehensive schemes of faith the encyclopedists of thirteenth-century Paris elaborated, especially in the work of the greatest intellect of the age, Thomas Aquinas (1225–1274), who arrayed in precise categories, everything known by experience or report. In northwest Spain, an unknown probably French artist of the thirteenth century depicted a similar vision of the whole cosmos in the stained glass windows of León cathedral. It was a measurable cosmos portrayed between the dividers of Christ the geometer, like a ball of fluff trapped between tweezers.

In the third quarter of the thirteenth century, Parisian teachers, of whom the most insistent was Siger of Brabant, pointed out that the doctrines of the church on the creation and the nature of the soul conflicted with classical philosophy and empirical evidence. "Every disputable question," they argued, "must be determined by rational arguments." Some thinkers took refuge in an evasive idea of "double truth," according to which things true in faith could be false in science and vice versa. The church condemned this doctrine in 1277 (along with a miscellany of magic and superstition).

Meanwhile, another professor in the thirteenth century at the University of Paris, Roger Bacon, said that excessive deference to authority—including ancestral wisdom, custom, and consensus—was a cause of ignorance. He insisted that scientific observations could help to validate holy writ and that medical experiments could increase knowledge and save life. He also claimed—citing the lenses with which Archimedes reputedly set fire to a Roman fleet during the siege of the Greek city of Syracuse in Sicily in 212 B.C.E.—that science could cow and convert infidels. It was part of a modest scientific revolution in Western Christendom. The most relentless experimenter of the age was the German emperor and King of Sicily, Frederick II (r. 1212–1250). He was said to have had two men disemboweled to show the varying effects of sleep and exercise on the digestion, and to have brought up children in silence "in order to settle the question" of what language men "naturally" speak. "But he labored in vain, for all the children died."

Bacon was a Franciscan friar, a follower of Francis of Assisi (1181–1226), and his enthusiasm for science seems to have owed something to Francis's rehabilitation of nature—because the world made God manifest, it was worth observing. Francis was a witness and maker of the new European imagination. He was a rich man's son inspired by Jesus' advice to a rich youth ("Go, sell what thou hast and give to the poor. Then take up thy cross and follow me"). He renounced riches for a life of total dependence on God. In anyone less committed and charismatic, his behavior might have been considered insane or heretical. He launched his mission by stripping naked in the public square of his native city of Assisi (ah-SEE-see) in northern Italy, as a sign that he was throwing himself, unprotected, on God's mercy. He relied for sustenance on what people gave him. He attracted a following and modeled his followers' way of life on the way he thought Christ and the apostles lived, refusing to accept property, sharing everything the brethren received by way of alms. For a church that relied on immense wealth to keep its operations going, and that reserved to the pope and the hierarchy the right to guide traditions that had, in many ways, departed from scripture, these were dangerous ideas. The very notion of a religious order unconfined in monasteries, wandering around the world without the constant discipline of common life, ran counter to everything the church had believed about monasticism for at least 500 years.

Francis, however, could be tamed. No rebel, he had enough personal humility to defer to the church's discipline, and for that very reason was allowed to stretch the hierarchy's tolerance to its limits. Bishops who met him—including the pope himself—were content to let him carry on. He made compromises with respectability, ordering his female followers into nunneries, and—in obedience to a vision in which Christ told him, "Build my Church,"—put his efforts into buildings of stone and mortar, as well as spiritual edification. Francis was suspicious of learning. It was a kind of possession—a compromise with poverty. It made men vain. But he accepted that education was part of the church's mission and that friars had to be encouraged to spend part of their lives in study to equip them to be preachers and confessors.

The Franciscans became the spearhead of the church's mission to the poor and inspired other orders of friars—clergy who combined religious vows of poverty, chastity, and obedience with work in the world. In an age of urbanization, this was a particularly important mission, because friars could establish bonds of sympathy with the rootless masses who gathered in towns and faced the problem of adjusting to life away from the familiar companionship of rural parishes. Friars were also a valuable counter force to heretics who denounced the church for worldliness, and, in particular, to the preachers who called themselves "the perfect" and who propagated the belief that the world was hopelessly evil. Friars, if they stayed true to their vocations, could match these enemies in holiness of life and in strict self-denial.

In his attitude to nature, Francis was representative of his time. Partly to rebut heretics repelled by the disorder of creation, Francis insisted on the goodness of God's creation, which was all "bright and beautiful." Even its conflicts and cruelties were there to elicit human love. He tried to enfold the whole of nature in love. He preached to ravens and called creatures, landscapes, Sun, and Moon his brothers and sisters, eventually welcoming "Sister Death." He communicated his sensibilities to his followers. As a result, Franciscans were prominent in scientific thinking in the West. Love of nature made them observe it more closely and keenly and scrutinize it for good uses.

Franciscans also became patrons of increasingly naturalistic art. The art they commissioned for their churches drew the onlooker into sacred spaces, as if in eyewitness of the lives of Jesus and the saints. The devotion of the rosary, introduced

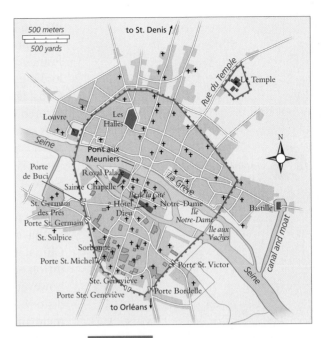

MAP 13.6

Paris ca. 1300

- university and schools
- other important building
- built-up area
- + church
- ⫟⫟ city gate
- ⟋ wall ca. 1200

The measurable cosmos. This thirteenth-century illustrator of the creation of the world shows God as a well-equipped designer, measuring creation with an architect's or mathematician's dividers. The Earth is not the center of the cosmos, but a tiny blob in the corner, surrounded by chaos and dwarfed by God.

early in the thirteenth century, encouraged the faithful to imagine sacred mysteries, while praying, with the vividness of scenes of everyday life, as if witnessed in person. Franciscan art stirred the emotions of the devout by unprecedented realism—looking at the world with eyes as unblinking as those of the new scientific thinkers. Considered from one point of view, the realism Western painting increasingly favored was a tribute to the enhanced prestige of the senses. To paint what one's eyes could see was to confer dignity on a subject not previously thought worthy of art. So art linked the science and piety of the age.

It is hard to resist the impression that the revolutionary experiences of the West at the time—the technical progress, the innovations in art, the readjustment of notions of reality through the eyes of a new kind of science—were owed in part to influences transmitted along the routes the Mongols maintained. None of this experimentation and imagination put Western science abreast of that of China, where observation and experiment had been continuous in scientific tradition since the first millennium B.C.E. (see Chapter 6). In two technologies, however—key technologies, as they later proved to be, for their influence on world history—Western Europe came to house the world's leading centers of development and production.

The first was glass making. In the thirteenth century, demand for fine glassware leaped in the West because of the growing taste for using church windows made of stained glass, penetrated by light, to illuminate sacred stories and to exhibit glowingly the wonders of creation as the windows at Chartres did.

Francis of Assisi, selection from *Admonitions*

○ MAKING CONNECTIONS

EUROPEAN TRANSFORMATIONS AND INNOVATIONS, THIRTEENTH AND EARLY FOURTEENTH CENTURIES

TRADE AND TRANSPORTATION	TECHNOLOGY AND SCIENCE	POLITICS	RELIGION
Increased communication across Eurasia leads to introduction of Chinese and Arabic technology, medicine, and inventions	Imported inventions such as paper, magnetic compasses, gunpowder, and blast furnace combine with focus on empiricism	Christian kingdoms seize Muslim lands in Spain, Mediterranean islands; revival of Crusades, extension of frontier north to the Baltics, Finland, and Scandinavia	Francis and his religious order place new emphasis on observing nature, serving the poor, and renouncing wealth; increased emphasis on sacred mysteries
↓	↓	↓	↓
Increased transportation and trade links within Europe aided by new infrastructure (roads, canals); growth of towns; economic and political stability leads to larger towns and cities; more productive industry	Better maritime technology expands range of sea voyages; demand for elaborate church windows spurs glassmaking and innovation in glass lenses; clocks provide regularized timekeeping for monasteries and cities; availability of paper multiplies books and empowers states with a medium for their messages	Bigger, richer states with more scope to communicate and enforce commands; more church–state competition and conflict	Mendicants prominent in scientific thinking in West; spearhead Church's mission to poor in growing towns

Simultaneously, glassmakers adapted their skills to meet domestic demand for glass mirrors and optical lenses. These objects were not manufactured on a significant scale anywhere else in the world, though for centuries scholars writing in Arabic had known how to make them and use them as aids to scientific observation. Now Western savants could make the same experiments themselves and even improve on them. In the thirteenth century, Robert Grosseteste, the first chancellor of the University of Oxford in England, explained the geometry of the way lenses operate. "It is obvious," he concluded, "that they can make very large objects appear very small, and contrariwise very small and remote objects as if they were large and easily discernible by sight."

Second, the West drew ahead in the technology of clockwork. Mechanical clocks had a long history in China and the Islamic world. But clockwork never caught on except in Europe. This is a hard fact to explain. Clockwork is too regular to match the movements of the heavens. It divides the day into arbitrary hours of equal length that do not match those of the Sun. But this way to organize life suited Western monasteries, where, apart from the prayers prescribed for the dawn and nightfall, the services of prayer were best arranged at regular intervals, independently of the Sun. For city churches in an age of urban growth, regular timekeeping was also convenient. Clockwork suited the rhythms of urban life. Civic authorities began to invest heavily in town clocks in the thirteenth and fourteenth centuries. This was the beginning of the still-familiar Western convention of an urban skyline dominated by the town hall clock tower.

The combination of lenses and clockwork mattered in the long run because eventually—not until the seventeenth century, when telescopes were combined with accurate chronometry—they gave Western astronomers an advantage over Muslim and Chinese competitors. This in turn gave Western scientists the respect of their counterparts and secured the patronage of rulers all over the world in societies interested in astronomy either for its own sake or—more often—because of astrology (the belief that events on Earth reflected the movements of the heavenly spheres).

Francis of Assisi. Franciscan art patronage rewarded painters like Giotto, who were interested in creating vivid versions of sacred scenes in which the actors seemed real rather than abstract. Francis preached to the birds because humans failed to heed his message—but the image suggests, too, how the Franciscans promoted awareness of the natural world. Piety and science coincided in the observation of nature.

IN PERSPECTIVE: The Uniqueness of the Mongols

In the thirteenth century, a state arose that embraced the whole of the steppe. Like most great revolutions, the episode started bloodily and became constructive. When the Mongol alliance first challenged its neighbors, it seemed to threaten civilization with destruction—slaughtering settled peoples, razing cities, despising art and learning. Yet the Mongols came to play a unique and constructive role in the history of Eurasia. First, fear of the most devastating conquerors the interior had yet bred linked the peoples beyond the steppe, from Christendom to Japan. Then a peace that those same conquerors imposed connected them. For a hundred years after the initial horror of the Mongol conquests, the steppe became a highway of fast communication, linking the extremeties of the landmass and helping transfer culture across two continents. Without the Mongol peace, it is hard to imagine any of the rest of world history working out as it did, for these

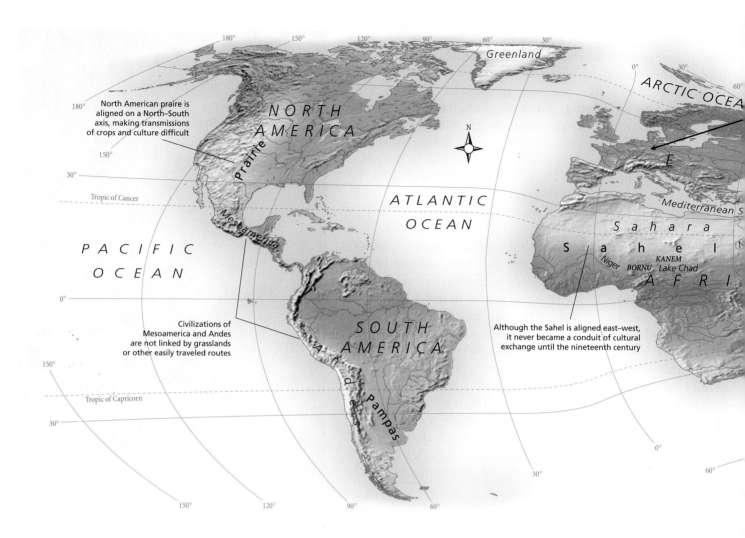

North American praire is aligned on a North–South axis, making transmissions of crops and culture difficult

Civilizations of Mesoamerica and Andes are not linked by grasslands or other easily traveled routes

Although the Sahel is aligned east–west, it never became a conduit of cultural exchange until the nineteenth century

were the roads that carried Chinese ideas and technology westward and opened up European minds to the vastness of the world. The importance of the Mongols' passage through world history does not stop at the frontiers of their empire. It resonated across Eurasia.

The Eurasian experience was unique. Why did nothing like it happen in Africa or the Americas? Cultural exchanges across the grasslands of prairie, pampa, and Sahel never spread far until the nineteenth century. None of those regions saw conquerors like the Mongols, able to unify the entire region and turn it into a causeway of civilizations, shuttling ideas and techniques across a continent.

In the Americas, geography was an inhibiting influence. The North American prairie is aligned on a north–south axis, across climatic zones, whereas the steppe stretches from east to west. Plants and animals can cross the steppe without encountering impenetrable environments. Seeds can survive the journey without perishing and without finding, at the end of the road, an environment too sunless or cold to thrive in. In North America, it took hundreds of years longer to achieve exchanges on a comparable scale. As we have seen repeatedly—almost whenever the Americas have entered our story—transmissions of culture across latitudes are much harder to effect than those that occur within latitudes, which have relatively narrow boundaries, where climate and conditions are familiar.

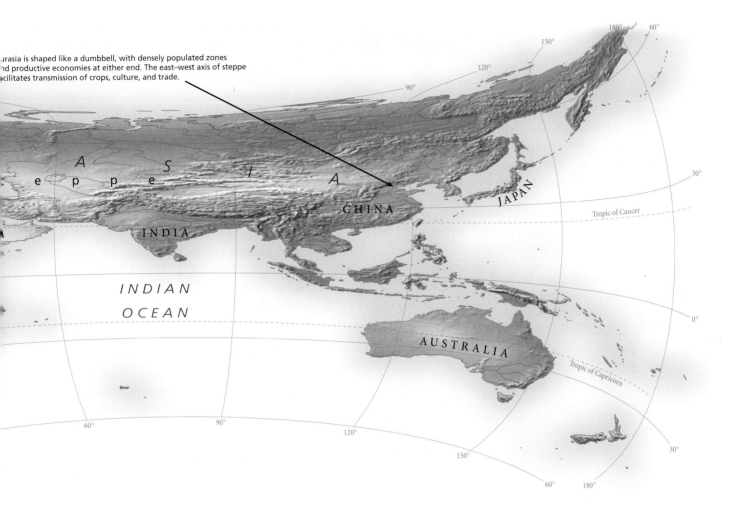

...urasia is shaped like a dumbbell, with densely populated zones
...nd productive economies at either end. The east–west axis of steppe
...cilitates transmission of crops, culture, and trade.

MAP 13.7

Grassland Environments Compared

Moreover, to function, an avenue of communications needs people at either end of it who want to be in touch. The Eurasian steppe was like a dumbbell, with densely populated zones and productive economies at either end of it (see Map 13.7). For people in Europe, southwest Asia, and North Africa, access to the products of south, southeast, and east Asia was highly desirable. For the suppliers of spices, drugs, fine textiles, and luxury products in the east, it was good to have customers who paid in silver. In the Americas, there was no chance to reproduce such relationships. The concentrations of wealth and population were in two regions—Mesoamerica and the Andes—that neither grasslands nor any other easily traveled routes linked. Though societies in other parts of the hemisphere drew lessons, models of life, technologies, and types of food from those areas, the results, as we have seen (see Chapter 11) were hard to sustain because communications between these areas and outlying regions were hard to keep up. Without the horse—extinct in the Americas for 10,000 years—the chances of an imperial people arising in the prairie or the pampa to do the sort of job the Mongols did in Europe, were virtually zero. (Much later, as we shall see in Chapter 21, when European invaders reintroduced the horse in the Americas in the 1500s, experiments in grassland imperialism by peoples such as the Sioux followed.)

In Africa, the constraints were different. The **Sahel** might have played a role similar to that of the steppes in Eurasian history. There was a viable corridor of

CHRONOLOGY

1181–1226	Life of Francis of Assisi
1190	First European recorded reference to a compass
1206	Temujin proclaims himself khan
1211–1236	Reign of Iltutmish, sultan of Delhi
1225–1274	Life of Thomas Aquinas
1234	Mongols conquer Georgia
1241–1242	Mongol armies reach Elbe River, Germany
1253–1254	Mission of William of Rubruck to Mongolian court
1258	Mongols capture Baghdad, last caliph put to death
1260	Mamluks defeat Mongols at battle of Ain Jalut
1261	Byzantine Empire regains Constantinople
1268–1291	Mamluks overthrow last crusader kingdoms
1270	Earliest European reference to maritime charts
1271–1275	Marco Polo's first journey to China
1274, 1281	Failed Mongol attempts to invade Japan
1279	Mongol conquest of China completed
1286	Rabban Bar Sauma appointed Mongol ambassador to Christian West

communication between the Nile and Niger valleys. In theory, an imperial people might have been able to open communications across the continent between the civilizations of East Africa, which were in touch with the world of the Indian Ocean, and those of West Africa, which the trade routes of the Sahara linked to the Mediterranean. But it never happened. For long-range empire building, the Sahel was, paradoxically, too rich, compared with the Eurasian steppe. The environment of the Sahel was more diverse. Agrarian or partly agrarian states had more opportunity to develop, obstructing the formation of a Sahel-wide empire. Although pastoral peoples of the western Sahel often built up powerful empires, they always tended to run into either or both of two problems. First, as we have seen, and shall see again, invaders from the desert always challenged and sometimes crushed them (see Chapter 12).

Second, while they lasted, the empires of the Sahel never reached east of the region of Lake Chad. Here states grew up, strong enough to resist conquest from outside, but not strong enough to expand to imperial dimensions themselves: states like Kanem and Bornu—which were sometimes separate, sometimes united. The accounts of early Muslim visitors reviled the region for its "reed huts . . . not towns" and people clad only in loin cloths. But by the twelfth and thirteenth centuries, Kanem and Bornu commanded respect in Arab geography. Lakeshore floodplains for agriculture enriched them, together with the gold they obtained from selling their surplus millet. According to Arab sources, the region enclosed twelve "kingdoms" around 1300.

The Mongols, after their initial bout of extreme destructiveness, brought peace, and, in the wake of that peace, wealth and learning. But with increased travel, it was not only goods and ideas that circulated with increased freedom. The steppeland also became a highway to communicate disease. The Mongol peace lasted less than 150 years. The age of plague that was now about to begin would influence the history of Eurasia, and therefore of the world, for centuries.

PROBLEMS AND PARALLELS

1. How did the Mongols transform Eurasia in the thirteenth century? What techniques did the Mongols use to rule neighboring civilizations, and how successful were they?

2. How did the steppelanders spiritual and religious life differ from that of their settled neighbors?

3. How did Mongol rule affect travel and trade along the Silk Roads?

4. How did the civilizations they conquered affect the Mongols? How did Mongol culture in turn influence the civilizations they ruled?

5. Why did Egypt and India show so much vitality in the thirteenth century?

6. How did Francis of Assisi and the Franciscan order remedy some of the social problems that medieval Europe faced?

7. What was the impact of empirical-based learning on European thinking at this time?

8. How did geography hinder the development of continent-wide empires in Africa and the Americas?

DOCUMENTS IN GLOBAL HISTORY

- William of Rubruck's account of the Mongols
- From *The Travels of Marco Polo*
- From *The History of the Life and Travels of Rabban Bar Sauma*
- Excerpt from the *Novgorod Chronicle*
- Roger Bacon on experimental science
- Francis of Assisi, selection from *Admonitions*

Please see the Primary Source CD-ROM for additional sources related to this chapter.

READ ON

D. Morgan, *The Mongols* (1986) is the best history of the Mongols: concise, readable, reliable. R. Grousset, *The Empire of the Steppes* (1970) is a translation of the unsurpassed classic history of steppeland peoples in antiquity and the middle ages. Samuel Adshead, *Central Asia in World History* (1993) is also helpful on this period.

P. Jackson, ed., *The Travels of Friar William of Rubruck* (1990) is an outstanding and informative edition of the most vivid of sources. Extracts from sources of the same kind are in I. de Rachewitz, ed., *Papal Envoys to the Great Khan* (1971) and. Dawson, ed., Mission to Asia (1980). A. Waley, ed., *The Secret History of the Mongols* (2002) collects some Mongol sources in lively translation.

M. Rossabi, *Voyager from Xanadu: Rabban Sauma and the First Journey from China to the West* (1992), and *Kubilai Khan* (1989) are the best books on their respective subjects. On the voyage of Chang Chun, J. Mirsky, *Chinese Travellers in the Middle Ages* (2000) translates the main texts.

On the Silk Roads, the exhibition catalog edited by S. Whitfield, *The Silk Roads* (2004) is the best work. R. Latham, ed., *The Travels of Marco Polo* (1958) is a convenient and accessible abridgement in translation.

On China, R. Davis, *Wind against the Mountain: the Crisis of Politics and Culture in Thirteenth-century China* (1996) is an outstanding account written with close reference to the sources. The exhibition catalog edited by M. Rossabi, *The Legacy of Genghis Khan* (1996) is the best guide to the art of the Ilkhanate and other Mongol successor-states. M. Ipsiroglu, *Painting and Culture of the Mongols* (1966) is indispensable.

J.A. Boyle, ed., *The History of the World Conqueror*, (1997) and *The Successors of Genghis Khan* (1971) translates some of the most important sources on the Ilkhanate.

On the Mamelukes, R.Irwin, *The Middle East in the Middle Ages: the Early Mamluk Sultanate* (1986) is the best account of the their rise, and R. Amitai-Preiss, *Mongols and Mamluks* (2005) is superb study of the wars against the Mongols, S.A. El-Banasi, ed., *Mamluk Art* (2001) covers a wide range of revealing objects.

P. Jackson, *The Delhi Sultanate* (2003) is a splendid introduction to the subject. The best edition of Ibn Battuta is by HWGibb and CFBeckingham for the Hakluyt Society, *The Travels of Ibn Battuta* (1956).

On the transmission of Chinese technology westward, J. Needham, *Science and Civilisation in China* (1956) is fundamental–but it is a vast work still in progress. An abridged version in two volumes–*The Shorter Science and Civilisation in China* (1980)–is available. For western science in the period, A. Crombie, *Robert Grosseteste and the Origins of Experimental Science* (1971) is controversial and stimulating. D.C. Lindberg, *The Beginnings of Western Science* (1992) gives an efficient and comprehensive account.

Of many studies of St Francis none is entirely satisfactory, but J.H.R. Moorman, *St Francis of Assisi* (1976) can be recommended, the first for its scholarship and brevity, the second for its vivacity. K.B.Wolf, *The Poverty of Riches* (2003) is good on St Francis's theology.

On glassmaking see G. Martin and A. MacFarlane, *The Glass Bathyscape* (2003) and, on clockwork, D. Landes, *Revolution in Time: Clocks and the Making of the Modern World* (1983). On the general background of the thirteenth-century West, D. Abulafia, ed., *The New Cambridge Medieval History*, vol. 5, (1999) is as close as one can get to a comprehensive guide.

CHAPTER 14

The Revenge of Nature: Plague, Cold, and the Limits of Disaster in the Fourteenth Century

City of the dead. The fourteenth-century Arab traveler Ibn Battuta described Cairo's Southern Cemetery as "a place of peculiar sanctity" that "contains the graves of innumerable scholars and pious believers." The Mamluk domes and minarets visible here form part of the Sultaniyyah tomb complex that was built around 1360, a little over ten years after the plague known as the Black Death had struck the city.

"The people of Cairo are fond of pleasure and amusement," wrote Ibn Battuta (ih-bihn bah-TOO-tah), when he first visited the Egyptian city in 1325. Wanderlust had made this Muslim pilgrim the world's most traveled man. Yet he had never seen, and would never see again, a city so big. Cairo had—so Ibn Battuta was told—12,000 water carriers, 30,000 donkey-rental businesses, and 36,000 river craft transporting food and goods. Among sources of pleasure he noted were "boys and maids with lustrous eyes" and the park and promenade along the Nile River, "containing many beautiful gardens." "Mother of cities, . . . mistress of broad provinces and fruitful lands, boundless in multitude of buildings, peerless in splendor. . . ." There seemed no end to Ibn Battuta's praise. The next time he visited Cairo, 23 years later in 1348, plague raged in the city and corpses were piled in its streets. "I was told that during the plague the number of deaths there had risen to twenty-one thousand a day. I found that all the sheikhs (shayks) I had known were dead. May God Most High have mercy upon them!"

CAIRO

● ● ● ● ●

Ibn Battuta was witnessing the most devastating natural catastrophe ever to have hit Eurasia: the so-called **Black Death**. The visitation of disease was not an isolated episode, but part of an enormous change, the consequences of which overtook the world. In the fourteenth century, Eurasia entered an age of plague (which would later spread worldwide), while the world entered an age of cold, as the climate got cooler. The combination of environmental disasters killed millions of people, disrupted states, and checked expansion. Themes of the story of global history, familiar from the last few chapters of this book, halted or were reversed as Eurasia's densely populated zone contracted. The growth of populations, trades, and states in Eurasia slowed or stopped. Cultural transmissions across the landmass diminished. Isolation from the main routes of trade and travel suddenly became, in some respects, an advantage.

Among the hardest-hit societies were the most ambitious—those with the longest and most active records in challenging their environments to suit themselves. Peoples that suffered most included those that had succeeded best in exploiting nature by turning land and energy sources to their own uses: those at and around the edges of Eurasia—in east, southwest, and south Asia; Europe; and North Africa. Their contacts with each other, which had formerly enriched them

FOCUS questions

- HOW DID the climate change globally in the fourteenth century?
- WHICH PARTS of the world suffered most from the plagues of the fourteenth century?
- WHAT WERE the social and political effects of the plague in China, the Islamic world, and Europe?
- WHY DID some parts of the world not suffer from plague?
- HOW DID the absence of plague affect Japan, Java, India, Mali, and the cultures around the Pacific Ocean?

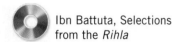

Ibn Battuta, Selections from the *Rihla*

with the benefits of cultural exchange, now communicated unprecedented deadly disease.

It was as if nature had struck back. Indeed, that was more or less how many Europeans and Muslims saw it. The weather, they thought, was a whiplash and the plague a scourge that God wielded to humble human arrogance and remind people of the unshakable power of death. One school of Muslim theologians accepted plague as God's punishment for sins, while others argued that plague, when Muslims suffered it, was "a martyrdom and a mercy from God," but "a punishment for an infidel." In China, too, conventional wisdom understood natural disasters as examples of what historian Mark Elvin calls "moral meteorology"—the corrections of heaven, unleashed to restore the balance of nature disturbed by human wickedness.

In history books human agency tends to crowd out the rest of nature. Nonhuman life gets into the picture only as a source of analogies for human behavior, or as the means of human strategies—part of an Eden or enemy to be used or abused. It is easy to forget that humans inhabit only a fraction of the biosphere, most of which is still outside our dominion. Currents in the ocean and the atmosphere change climate and shape our world, despite us. Nor do we even control the whole of the ecosystem of which we form part. Our own bodies host microorganisms that feed on us whether we like it or not, sometimes benefiting us, sometimes doing us harm. Disease bearers can change their habits and patterns of attack with bewildering speed, leaving us unsure how to respond. Viruses, for example, are a part of the ecosystem that is largely beyond our control.

Climate and microbes belong to two rebellious realms of nature that resist human power. What happens when they combine—when sudden, unpredictable changes in both realms threaten humans simultaneously? To find out, we need only look back 700 years.

The fourteenth century was exceptional in human history because, in parts of the world, climate change and disease coincided to menace or undermine human activities. The loss of life could be made up—eventually. The empires we shall see shaken and states overthrown in this chapter and the next were restored or replaced. The regions and classes that profited from disaster—for there were some, as there always are in every disaster—did not always retain their advantage for long. But the social shake-up that accompanied the changes had, for some of the people affected, irreversible effects. And it was impossible to undo the jarring psychological impact on societies that had accumulated self-confidence over a long period of expansion.

The best—or even, because of the evidence available, the only—way to approach the changes of the fourteenth century is to start in those parts of the northern hemisphere, especially in Eurasia and North Africa, where the effects of cold and plague combined. We can then turn to areas that escaped plagues, or escaped their worst consequences, in India, sub-Saharan Africa, Japan, and southeast Asia. Finally, we shall turn to far-away and out-of-touch societies in and around the Pacific to appreciate how isolation—which usually retards change—acted as a form of quarantine against disease. This should help us see some of the difference plagues made. As plagues affected some of the planet's previously most dynamic regions, other parts of the world leaped into the sight lines of global history, drawing our attention.

Readers should be aware that the distribution of material in the pages that follow reflects the distribution of sources and of scholarship. Most of what we know about the ecological disasters of the era comes from Eurasia, and, within that area, most relates to Europe. For other areas, for instance, only scattered archaeological studies help us trace the course and character of the diseases of the time. Legal records of the kinds that help us establish the social consequences of ecological change in Europe are, at present, unavailable for most other places.

CLIMATE CHANGE

In the fourteenth century, temperatures fell. Broadly speaking, over the preceding four centuries or so, global temperatures had been relatively warm. The warm spell had been a period of expansion for most societies, with much erosion of natural environments as people converted previously under-exploited land for farming or grazing (see Chapter 10). Peoples overcome by ecological disasters in the past had been victims of droughts or of their own overexploitation of the land. Now a cool period—of fluctuating but relatively low temperatures—would last for about 500 years more. During the intense phases of the cool period, a fall in average temperatures of two or three degrees could reverse expansion, forcing people to abandon high ground, remote settlements, and northerly latitudes (such as, in the fourteenth century, parts of Greenland and of what are now Norway and Finland).

Though meteorologists scour tree rings and glaciers for evidence of weather cycles, hot and cold spells seem to alternate unpredictably. If a common cause—some cosmic rhythm—underlies all of them, we do not know what it is. Short-term fluctuations are sometimes traceable to particular causes. The middle of the second decade of the fourteenth century, for instance, was a cold period all over the northern hemisphere, probably because of a sudden, localized occurrence: the explosion of Indonesian volcanoes, pumping ash into the atmosphere and clouding the sun. But the fall in temperatures was not confined to a few exceptional years. It was part of a general, long-term trend.

The trend began in the Arctic in the thirteenth century. The ice cap crept southward. Glaciers disrupted shipping. From the fourteenth century, indicators of falling temperatures in the North Atlantic and parts of Eurasia are abundant, and it is fair to suppose that the Northern Hemisphere generally was registering the effects. Mean annual temperatures in China, which had stayed above 32 degrees Fahrenheit from the seventh century to the eleventh, remained below freezing from the thirteenth century—a period of abrupt fluctuations—until late in the eighteenth. Evidence of marginal glacier growth suggests that North America, too, felt the cold in the fourteenth century. Other indicators for the same century include the persistence of pack ice in summer in the seas around Greenland and the disappearance of water-demanding plants from the hinterland of Lake Chad in Central Africa from about 1300 onward. This is important, because glacier growth affects precipitation. When water ices over, less of it evaporates, and less therefore falls as rain. Weakening winds may also have contributed to changes in rainfall patterns and to the lack of moisture in deep interior regions with continental climates.

Worldwide effects—it is worth adding—of the continuing trend are detectable in glacier levels from the sixteenth century onward. A particularly marked period of glacier growth, even in low latitudes and in the southern hemisphere, occurred in the seventeenth century. The cold therefore remained dominant, with some fluctuations, and intensified in the seventeenth century. Warming resumed gradually in the eighteenth and early nineteenth centuries, and, after a mid–nineteenth-century cold spell, has now been a constant and consistent feature of global climate probably for about the past 150 years (see Figure 14.1).

It is important to stress that the rhythms of climate change are full of fluctuating and conflicting shifts and contrasts of pace. Three levels are detectable. At one level, there is a long-term alternation between ice ages, which periodically smother great parts of the globe, and global warming, when some glacier-covered areas reemerge. We are between ice ages now. Historians, perhaps rather overdramatically, have adopted the **Little Ice Age** as a name for the protracted period of relative cold that began in the fourteenth century, but this term is misleading if it encourages readers to think of huge ice sheets spreading over the globe. All the fluctuations of the period this book covers have happened in a relatively warm era of the history of the planet.

Meanwhile, at another level, periods of a few hundred years of relative cold and warmth alternate within eras of global warming. But even within these periods, sudden changes in the winds and ocean currents can reverse the overall trend, producing spells, lasting from 10 to 50 years or so, of warmer or cooler temperatures.

Finally, there are sudden interruptions of normal conditions—occurring irregularly and, in the present state of our knowledge, unpredictably—when the normal distribution of atmospheric pressure is disturbed for unknown reasons. This produces the notorious **El Niño** effect in the tropics and the southern hemisphere (see Chapter 4). In Europe, reversals of normal patterns of atmospheric pressure in the North Atlantic produce longer spells, often of a decade or so, of extremely cold weather. And of course, above the deep and various rhythms of climate, the irregular lurches of the weather continue all the time.

Climate change is usually slow, but can become perceptible suddenly. Contemporary descriptions show that people in Europe began to feel the cold, along with other unaccustomed weather, in the early fourteenth century. Of course, people felt the cold, and it affected their lives, because temperatures were lower than previously, not because it was cold in any absolute sense. Even after the intense global warming we have experienced recently, global temperatures are probably only now getting back to where they were when the Little Ice Age began. And European summers were probably, on average, hotter in the fourteenth century than in the twentieth.

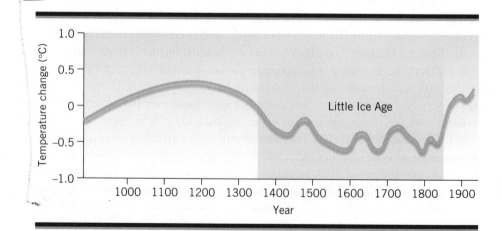

FIGURE 14.1 GLOBAL TEMPERATURE CHANGE, 1000–1900

Hidore, John E. Global Enviornment Change: It's Nature and Impact, 1ST © 1996. Electronically reproduced by permission of Pearson Education, Inc., Upper Saddle River, New Jersey.

The weather of the early fourteenth century, however, seemed hostile to people who had to endure it (see Map 14.1). In 1309–1310 the Thames (tehmz) River, which flows through London, froze and, wrote a chronicler, "bread wrapped in straw or other covering froze and could not be eaten unless it was warmed." Colder weather forced farmers to abandon formerly productive land above 1,300 feet in the southwest of England and 1,000 feet in the north. The cold was, an English poet wrote, "a new kind of affliction, . . . not known for a thousand years. . . . No horror left us e'er so like a ghost." Encroaching glaciers forced farmers into retreat in Norway.

During the prolonged cold of 1315–1316, before the icebergs grew sufficiently to disrupt rainfall, heavy rains were reported all over northern Europe, wrecking the crops, inflicting famine. "The corn [grain] could not ripen, nor had bread such power or essential virtue as it usually has," complained an English chronicler. A chronicler in Salzburg, Austria, likened the rains to Noah's flood in the Bible. Fifteen or 16 people usually died each month in the towns of Bruges and Ypres in what is today Belgium. During 1316, the figure rose to 150 in Ypres and 190 in Bruges. From May to October, while these cities ran out of food, they lost over 5 percent and 10 percent of their population respectively. Calamitous flooding and coastal erosion became common around the North Sea, culminating in the "Great Drowning" of 1362, when the sea swallowed vast areas of Holland and 60 parishes in Denmark. On the North Sea coast of England, drowned villages can still be visited offshore, victims of the rips the floods of the era tore in the coastline.

Far from the sea, cooling in the Northern Hemisphere brought droughts and famines. In Central Asia, the accumulated abundance that fueled Mongol conquests in the previous century seems to have run out. The Mongol world began to contract. According to official chronicles, China experienced exceptionally severe winters for 36 of the fourteenth century's 100 years. In partial consequence, famines struck some part of China in every year of the reign of the Shun Ti emperor (r. 1333–1368).

Though the evidence is too slight for certainty, climate change at about the same time seems to have helped to destroy an impressive regional system of agriculture and urban life deep in the North American interior, between the Gila and San Juan Rivers and in the neighborhood of present-day Phoenix, Arizona. First the Hohokam (hoh–HOH–kahm) people—as archaeologists called them—re-located, from their scattered villages and small dwellings, for closer collaboration in relatively few, dense settlements with huge multistorey adobe houses. At Paquimé they huddled in a city with all the traditional amenities of earlier indigenous civilizations (see Chapter 11): ball courts, carved facades for temples and palaces, wells and irrigation works, workshops for copper workers and jewelsmiths. There was even a macaw hatchery to produce

"The Frozen Thames," 1677. The Thames River with old London Bridge in the middle distance and Southwark Cathedral on the right. People amuse themselves on the ice. Some shoot, and others skate. The Thames no longer freezes because the arches of the modern bridges across it don't impede the flow of water.

Casa Grande. In the fourteenth century, Casa Grande—as this adobe structure is now called—stood five stories high. Massive outer walls and clusters of small dwellings surrounded it. It was part of the last phase of a long effort to raise monumental architecture and concentrate dense populations in what is now desert in Arizona, Colorado, and New Mexico.

PACIFIC
OCEAN

Lack of rainfall
leads to population
loss throughout the
American Southwest

North American
glaciers increase

Phoenix ARIZONA
Casa Grande ● ● Paquimé

Rocky Mountains

NORTH
AMERICA

Mississippi

Hudson
Bay

Greenland

Falli
force
settlem
latitudes and

Persistence of pack
ice in summer off
coast of Greenland

Iceland

Caribbean Sea

Thames River
freezes during
the winter of
1309–1310

Cold, heavy rain and
flooding destroy crops
and erode coastlines
in northern Europe

N

ENGL

London ●

Y pres

FRA

Andes

ATLANTIC
OCEAN

SPAIN

M

MOROCCO

North A

Andes

Sah

SOUTH
AMERICA

Amazon

Niger

1,000 km

1,000 miles

scale varies with perspective

Water demanding
plants disappear from
the Lake Chad region

N

PACIFIC
OCEAN

JAPAN

KOREA
Yellow Sea

Severe winters and famines
strike China throughout
the fourteenth century

MONGOLIA

Cooling in Northern
Hemisphere reduces
food abundance,
forcing Mongol world
to contract

Yellow

CHINA

South China Sea

Mekong

SOUTHEAST
ASIA

Yangtze

TIBET

Himalayas

Ganges

Bay of Bengal

Between 1310 and 1315
Indonesian volcanoes pump
ash into the atmosphere,
clouding the sun.

Caspian Sea

lack Sea

natolia

Euphrates

Tigris

PERSIA

Indus

INDIA

AUSTRALIA

INDONESIA

Arabian Sea

INDIAN
OCEAN

ARABIA

PT

Nile

ea

CA

Madagascar

MAP 14.1

Climate Change in the Fourteenth Century

⌂ ice pack

▭ polar ice pack

▲ major volcanic eruptions

➤ prevailing current, South Pacific (Humboldt Current)

➤ El Niño current

● city or town mentioned or descibed on pages 445–448

ARIZONA modern-day state or country

◯ MAKING CONNECTIONS ◯

CLIMATE CHANGE IN EURASIA, AFRICA, AND THE AMERICAS

REGION/PERIOD →	EVIDENCE AND ENVIRONMENTAL EFFECTS →	EFFECTS ON HUMAN SOCIETY
Arctic / 1200s	Polar ice cap in northern hemisphere creeps southward	Glaciers disrupt shipping
North Atlantic, Arctic Ocean / 1300s	Increased evidence of falling temperatures, glaciation	Persistence of pack ice in summer around Greenland disrupts sea voyages
Central Africa / 1300s	Disappearance of water-demanding plants near Lake Chad	Lessened rainfall reduces crop yields
Europe / 1300s	Colder climate freezes Thames River; glaciers encroach in Norway; calamitous flooding and coastal erosion occurs around North Sea coasts	Formerly productive agricultural land abandoned in England; famine and mortality increases dramatically throughout northern Europe; numerous coastal villages disappear in flooding
Central Asia, China / 1300s	More severe winters	Abundance of food that fueled Mongol advances runs out; Mongol world begins to contract; famines strike China from mid-1300s
American Southwest / 1300s	Evidence of decreasing rainfall, water supplies	Relocation of Hohokam villages in Arizona; severe population loss throughout Southwest including Arizona, New Mexico sites

the ornamental feathers the elite coveted. It was a splendid effort, but it was clearly a response to stress. Every indicator shows severe population loss throughout the North American Southwest in the thirteenth and fourteenth centuries. By around 1400, even the new settlements were abandoned. Ruins remain. Casa Grande, in Pinal County, Arizona, leaves onlookers amazed at the ambition of the builders and clueless about what befell them. Some scholars have speculated that the conditions that crushed the Hohokam may also have driven migrants southward to colonize central Mexico and found the state that later became the kernel of the Aztec world (see Chapter 15). But the only evidence for this is in later, untrustworthy legends.

THE COMING OF THE AGE OF PLAGUE

In Eurasia the cold spell coincided with the beginning of an age of plague. Starting in the 1320s, unprecedented bouts of pestilence spread over much of Eurasia, culminating, in the late 1340s, in the Eurasian disaster known to Europeans as the Black Death, which, in terms of the proportion of the population it wiped out in affected areas, was probably the most lethal event ever experienced in human history up to that time. Innumerable recurrences—less widespread and less intense—of similar or identical diseases remained common and frequent in Eurasia until the eighteenth century. The age of plague was such an unusual and significant episode that we want to know what the disease was, where it came from, what caused it, and how much damage it did. All these questions are hard to answer.

Most attempts to write the history of disease have foundered on a false assumption: that we can recognize past visitations of identifiable diseases, known to modern medical science, from symptoms historical sources describe. For two reasons, this is an unrealistic expectation.

First, people in the past looked at disease with perceptions different from ours. The symptoms they spotted would not necessarily be those an observer today would note, nor would they use the same sort of language to describe them. The signs we look for change as culture changes. From time to time, literary and scientific literature introduces new paradigms of disease and discards or displaces old ones.

Second, diseases change. They change, perhaps, more than any other aspect of history because many of the microorganisms that cause disease are subject to rapid mutations. They evolve fast because they reproduce rapidly. They respond quickly to changing environments. The plagues of the age of plague need not all have been visitations of a single disease. They could have been "cocktails" of different diseases. They may have included some diseases recognizable in today's medical handbooks. But we must be open to the likelihood—it is stronger than a possibility—that some of the diseases that devastated Eurasia in the age of plague were peculiar to that period. They did not exist previously in the same forms and have ceased to exist since. New pathogens are deadly, because they are unfamiliar. When they strike, no one has had a chance to build up immunity to them.

So what can we say about the pathology of the Black Death? Of diseases now known to medical science, bubonic plague—not, perhaps, of the same variety we know today—was most likely to have played a part in the age of plague. Bubonic plague is a rat-borne disease. Fleas that live on rats transmit it to humans. When they bite, fleas regurgitate the bacillus, ingested from rats' blood, into the bloodstream of human victims, or communicate infection by defecating into their bites. In cases of septicemic plague (a systemic disease caused by pathogens in the blood), one of the first symptoms is generally death. Otherwise, swellings appear—small like Brazil nuts or big and ridged like grapefruit—over the neck and groin or behind the ears. Jitters, vomiting, dizziness, and pain might follow, often accompanied by an inability to tolerate light.

Fourteenth-century sources describe all these symptoms, together with sudden fainting, before victims, as one observer explained, "almost sleeping and with a great stench eased into death." The trouble is that during the first hundred years of the age of plague, of all the sources that describe the symptoms, fewer than one in six lists symptoms of this kind. Moreover, almost everyone at the time was convinced that plague spread by infection or contagion. Rats—the normal agent for the spread of bubonic plague—play no part in the accounts in the sources. Finally, it seems most unlikely that the frequent epidemics reported in China from the 1320s to the 1360s can have been of bubonic plague in the form now familiar to us, which, as we shall see, hit an unimmunized China in the late eighteenth century. The suddenness and virulence of the visitations that afflicted China suggest the arrival of a new and previously unexperienced pathogen. For the Chinese, with their long experience in farming and animal domestication, enjoyed highly developed natural immunities to the familiar diseases that breed in farming environments.

Marchione di Coppo Stefani, from
The Florentine Chronicle

Plague victims. The illustrator of an early fifteenth-century German chronicle imagined the plague of Egypt—sent by God, according to the Book of Exodus in the Bible, to make Pharaoh "let my people go"—with the same symptoms as the Black Death. In the background, Moses brings plague down on Egypt by prayer. By implication, prayer and obedience to the will of God could also be remedies for plague.

Many accounts of the Black Death include a bewildering variety of symptoms that are not associated with bubonic plague: complications in the lungs, spitting blood, headaches, extremely rapid breathing, strangely colored urine. The emphasis of some sources on lung disorders suggests a mixture of bubonic and pneumonic plague, which primarily attacks the lungs. To judge from other surviving descriptions, outbreaks of typhus, smallpox, and various kinds of influenza coincided with some visitations of plague. In the Mediterranean, the plague usually struck in summer, while in northern Europe, autumn seems to have been the deadliest season. But, looked at as a whole, the plagues of the period had no seasonal pattern and no obvious connection with any particular weather systems or atmospheric conditions. This again points to the involvement of more than one pathogen.

Anthrax has been claimed as a contributing factor. This is not impossible. A form of anthrax certainly existed among cattle in Europe at the time. Whether or not anthrax was a factor, it seems likely that domestic animals were an essential part of the background—as carriers of disease, as a reservoir of infection, and even as sufferers. One of the curious features about the way some early plague victims described the disease is that they were sure that their domestic animals suffered from it, just as they did themselves. A chronicler in the city of Florence in Italy listed "dogs, cats, chickens, oxen, donkeys, and sheep" among the sufferers, with the same symptoms as humans suffered, including swellings in the groin and armpits. At the port of Salona on the Adriatic coast, the Black Death's first victims were "horses, oxen, sheep, and goats." The Egyptian chronicler, al-Maqrizi (ahl-mah-KREE-zee), who was among the most observant and thoughtful witnesses, believed that the disease started, like so many others, among animals before transferring to human hosts. It had spread from grazing flocks on the steppe in 1341, after which "the wind transmitted their stench around the world." Al-Maqrizi and other Muslim commentators thought wild animals caught it, too. If any of these sources are correct, the Black Death must have been—or included—a disease unknown today.

An unresolved question is, *How, if at all, were changes in climate and disease patterns linked?* The plague pathogens, as we have seen, were remarkably indifferent to weather, striking at different seasons and in climatically different regions of Eurasia, from the cold environment of Scandinavia and rain-drenched Western Europe to the hot, dry lands of the Middle East. The plagues were less penetrative, however, in hot, moist regions and do not seem to have gotten across the Sahara to tropical Africa, even though many potential disease carriers crossed that desert to trade. It is worth bearing in mind, however, that the plague pathogens seem to have included new arrivals in the microbial world that remained active for as long as global cooling lasted.

The Course and Impact of Plague

The nature of the plague is hard to define, but the routes by which it traveled are easier to describe (see Map 14.2). The Italian chronicler Matteo Villani said the plague came "from China and upper India," by which he meant Central Asia, for which "India" at the time was a synonym, "then through their surrounding lands and then to coastal places across the ocean." Broadly speaking, Arabic sources specify the same, or a similar, path.

The age of plague indeed seems to have started in China. But that is not the same as saying that subsequent outbreaks elsewhere were the result of communication from China, or even that they were necessarily outbreaks of the same disease or diseases. Repeated occurrences—or, perhaps, a continuous visitation—of massively lethal maladies were recorded in southwest China, and over much of central China, north of the Yangtze River, in the early 1320s. In 1331, mortality rates in parts of northeast China that had endured five reported outbreaks of plague in the previous two decades reputedly reached 90 percent. Two years later, a plague claimed 400,000 lives in the Yangtze and Huai (hway) valleys. In 1353–1354, chroniclers reported that around two-thirds of the population perished from pestilence in eight distinct Chinese districts. Most of those areas experienced repeated bouts of disease of the same sort in the late 1350s or early 1360s.

Doubt persists, however, over whether the diseases rampant in China were the cause of—or even the same as—those found farther west. From the perspective of most commentators at the time in Europe and the Middle East, plague, like the Mongols, seemed to be an invader from the steppeland. Many observers at the time noted that the Mongols transmitted plague. A lawyer in northern Italy wrote one of the most detailed and doom-laden accounts of the arrival of plague in Europe. In 1346, by his account, "countless numbers of Tatars" as he called the Mongols, and Muslims "were struck down by a mysterious illness which brought sudden death." At the time, a Mongol army was laying siege to the Genoese trading colony of Kaffa in Crimea (creye-MEE-ah) on the Black Sea, where Italian merchants made contact with two great trade routes: those of the Silk Roads and the Volga valley. "But behold!" he continued, "the whole army was affected by a disease . . . which killed thousands every day. . . . But they ordered corpses to be placed in catapults and lobbed into the city in the hope that the intolerable stench would kill everyone inside."

The besiegers' stratagem worked. The disease proved highly contagious. "As it happened," the account went on, "among those who escaped from Kaffa by boat, there were a few sailors who had been infected with the poisonous disease. Some boats were bound for Genoa, others went to Venice and to other Christian areas. When the sailors reached these places and mixed with the people there, it was as if they had brought evil spirits with them."

Of course, there were multiple points of entry, as the same author acknowledged:

> Almost everyone who had been in the East, or in the regions to the south and north, fell victim to sudden death after contracting this pestilential disease. . . . The scale of the mortality and the form which it took persuaded those who lived, weeping and lamenting, . . . the Chinese, Indians, Medes, Kurds, Armenians, Cilicians (sih-LEES-see-yahns), Georgians, Mesopotamians, Nubians, Ethiopians, Turks, Egyptians, Arabs, Saracens (SAH-rah-sehns) and Greeks (for almost all the East had been affected)—that the last judgement has come.[1]

A pandemic on this scale was unprecedented. The pathogens responsible had found an eco-niche as wide as Eurasia.

Chroniclers' estimates of mortality are notoriously unreliable. Historians have been reluctant to believe claims that the plague wiped out half or more—sometimes much more—of the population where it struck, but verifiable

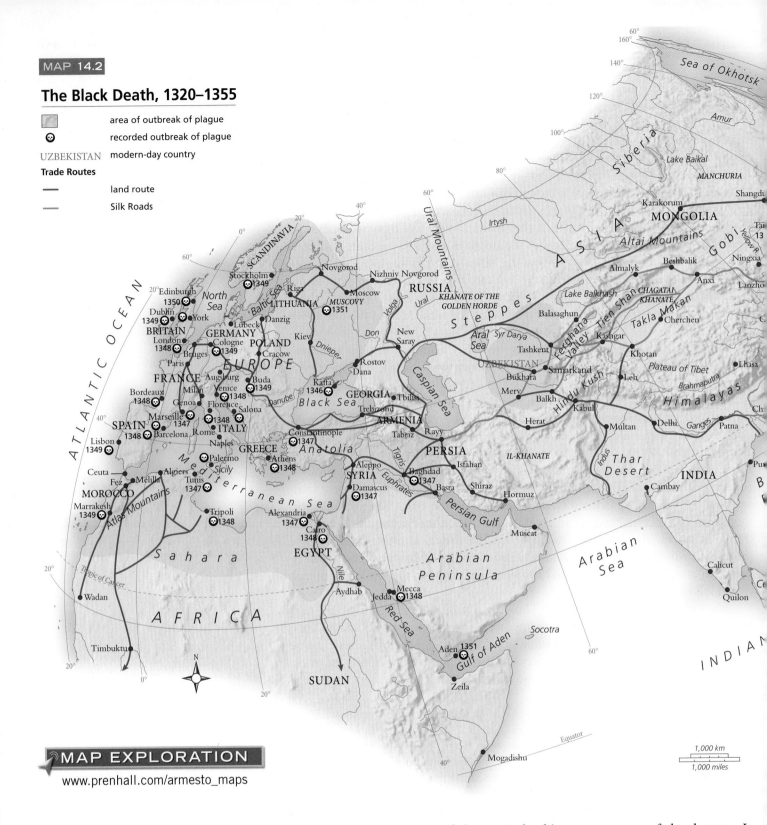

MAP 14.2

The Black Death, 1320–1355

- ▨ area of outbreak of plague
- ☺ recorded outbreak of plague
- UZBEKISTAN modern-day country

Trade Routes

- land route
- Silk Roads

MAP EXPLORATION

www.prenhall.com/armesto_maps

evidence bears out some of the most shocking assessments of the damage. In Barcelona on the Mediterranean coast of Spain, 60 percent of jobs in the church fell vacant. Clerical records of the archdiocese of York in northern England suggest the first visitation of the plague killed 40 percent of clergy there. Clergy were, perhaps, members of a high-risk profession, exceptionally exposed to infection by the need to minister to the sick. But the laity suffered just as much. In some manors in England, up to 70 percent of tenants died. Some villages in

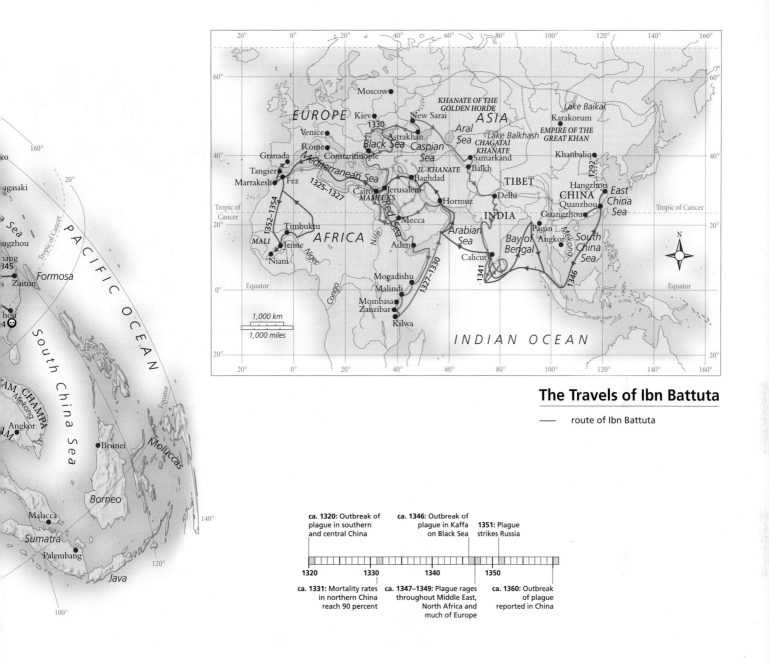

The Travels of Ibn Battuta

—— route of Ibn Battuta

ca. 1320: Outbreak of plague in southern and central China

ca. 1346: Outbreak of plague in Kaffa on Black Sea

1351: Plague strikes Russia

1320   1330   1340   1350

ca. 1331: Mortality rates in northern China reach 90 percent

ca. 1347–1349: Plague rages throughout Middle East, North Africa and much of Europe

ca. 1360: Outbreak of plague reported in China

southern France lost four-fifths of their population. Towns ran out of cemetery space. The living had to pile the dead in pits with quicklime to speed decomposition and minimize rot. Half the villages of Sicily were abandoned, as were a third of those around Rome.

When the plague reached the Middle East, the tireless traveler, Ibn Battuta, was there to observe it, on his way back to Cairo. Arriving in Syria in May 1348, he found that deaths in the city of Damascus reached 2,400 a day. In one town,

453

Flagellants. In 1349, the Black Death inspired thousands of penitents to organize processions and cults of self-flagellation across Europe in an attempt to deflect God's wrath. Like many others, the Flemish chronicler whose work is depicted here denounced the flagellants for claiming that their penance was a kind of baptism, that it could wipe out sin, and that it was a sacrifice akin to Christ's death on the cross. The king of France banned flagellation, and the pope outlawed it.

three-quarters of the public officials had died. A sheikh delayed a banquet for Ibn Battuta until a day arrived when "I did not pray over a corpse." The plague spread along the coast of North Africa, causing—so people claimed—1,000 deaths a day at its height in Tunis, and reaching Morocco, where Ibn Battuta's own mother was among the victims.

In Central Asia, where plagues bred or where microorganisms traveled between the densely populated ends of Eurasia, we can find indications of mortality despite the lack of sources. Arab sources reported that many steppeland dynasties and Mongol warriors succumbed to plague. Nestorian headstones at Chwolson in what is now Russian Central Asia refer to plague as the cause of deaths in 1338 and 1339. In 1345 and 1346, according to Russian chronicles, pestilence devastated cities in the Mongol-ruled parts of southern Russia. Uzbek villages emptied. In 1346–1347, an official in Crimea reputedly counted 85,000 corpses.

In China, too little work has been done on the demographic impact of plagues to make firm assertions. In general, there seems little doubt that the population of the empire fell in the relevant period. The census of 1393, with adjustments demographers made to compensate for the official habit of underestimating the numbers, suggests a total population of perhaps a little over 80 million—compared with about 120 million in the mid–fourteenth century. The loss of people was by no means uniform. Some regions even seem to have made slight gains.

Moral and Social Effects

Natural disasters always inspire moralizing. Although the Black Death killed people indiscriminately—the vicious and the virtuous alike—it was tempting, especially for Christians, to see it as a moral agent, even a divine instrument to call the world to repentance and make people good. The plague was a leveler, attacking all sorts and conditions. For many who experienced it, the plague was a test of faith, first eliciting selfish reactions of terror and flight, profiteering and despair, then, as Matteo Villani observed, "people without suspicion began to help one another, from whence many were cured, and people were secure in helping others." Dice makers, claimed an abbot in northern France, turned to the manufacture of rosary beads. In China, as we shall see, plague, combined with other natural disasters, helped to stir up religious movements that over spilled into political revolution (see Chapter 15). In the Islamic world, fear of plague stimulated a revival of features of popular religion the clergy normally condemned: summoning spirits, magical spells, and charms.

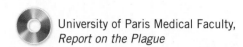
University of Paris Medical Faculty, *Report on the Plague*

As well as to prayer, penance, and superstition, plague was a stimulus to science as people searched for a cure. It was normal to speak of sin as if it were the cause of the plague. But most people did not take such talk literally. Moralistic explanations of the origins of disease were hardly more convincing in the fourteenth century than they are today, and scientific inquiry soon replaced lamentations. The University of Paris medical faculty blamed "a year of many fogs and damps . . . We must not overlook the fact that any pestilence proceeds from the divine will, . . . but this does not mean forsaking doctors." Astrologers produced fatalistic explanations. "Corrupt air" was widely blamed, perhaps originally caused by polluted wells, perhaps by earthquakes. In the Islamic world, too, religious interpretations of the origin of plague never inhibited scientific inquiry into its causes and possible cures. Muslim physicians also blamed corrupt air, caused in its turn by irregular weather, decaying matter, and astrological influences.

As for how to treat plague, practices were wildly different. In Cairo, when the Black Death broke out in 1347, healers smeared the swellings on the bodies of the afflicted with Armenian clay. In Muslim Spain, the physician Ibn Khatib (ih-bihn khah-TEEB) advised abstention from grains, cheese, mushrooms, and garlic. Barley water and syrup of basil were widely prescribed as remedies or ways to prevent becoming ill. Gentile of Foligno in central Italy, who died of the plague in 1348, recommended dried snake's flesh, at least a year old. This was not as silly as it sounds. Snakes, whose venom can be beneficial in measured quantities, had a long and honorable therapeutic record with the medical profession. Another Italian, Gabriele de' Mussis, favored bloodlettings and plasters made of mallow leaves. Turks sliced off the heads of the boils on the bodies of the sick and supposedly extracted "green glands."

The overwhelming medical consensus among both Christians and Muslims saw infection and contagion as the main threats to the population. Where the authorities responded accordingly in time by imposing quarantine, lives were spared. Quarantine worked in places as various as the great city of Milan in northern Italy and the tiny village of Eyam in England.

Where it could not be averted, plague shattered morale. A poet in Cairo, al-Sallah al-Safadi (ahs-sahl-LAH ahs-sah-FAH-dee), described the psychological effect of the disease. Those it spared were maddened. It "spread fear and misery in the hearts of women" and convinced even the mighty of their mortality. It entered houses "like bands of thieves," dispelling people's sense of security. "God has not just subdued Egypt," al-Safadi concluded, "he has made her crawl on her knees." The Florentine poet, Petrarch, felt the guilt of survival among the corpses. He saw "just one comfort: that we shall follow those who went before." He raged at his

Treating the plague. In the mid–fifteenth century, a patron who was probably a plague survivor endowed a chapel in the high Alps at Lanslevillard. The chapel was dedicated to St. Sebastian, whom plague victims adopted, perhaps because his arrow wounds resembled the pockmarks and pustules of so many diseases. The scene reproduced here shows the underarm buboes that are also a symptom of bubonic plague, the indiscriminating nature of the disease, its supposed origin as a punishment from God, and physician's efforts to cure it by lancing pustules.

fellow survivors: "Go, mortals, sweat, pant, toil, range the lands and seas to pile up riches you cannot keep. . . . The life we lead is a sleep; whatever we do, dreams. Only death breaks the sleep and wakes us from dreaming. I wish I could have woken before this."

Plague had winners and losers. In Europe, Jews were among the losers. A skeptical German Franciscan reported the common opinion that Jews started the plague by poisoning wells "and many Jews confessed as much under torture: that they had bred spiders and toads in pots and pans, and had obtained poison from overseas. . . . Throughout Germany, and in all places, they were burnt. For fear of that punishment many accepted baptism and their lives were spared." The massacres that ensued, especially in Germany, were nearly always the result of outbreaks of mob violence, which the authorities tried to restrain. In July 1348, Pope Clement VI declared the Jews innocent of the charge of well poisoning and excommunicated anyone who harmed them. In January 1349, the city council of Cologne in the Rhineland warned authorities in other cities that anti-Jewish riots could ignite popular revolt. "Accordingly we intend to forbid any harrassment of the Jews in our city because of these flying rumors, but to defend them and keep them safe, as our predecessors did—and we are convinced that you ought to do the same." Not all authorities, however, were equally vigilant, equally effective, or equally committed to the defense of the Jews, and massacres continued.

Why did some people in Europe victimize Jews? Jewish communities had existed all over the Mediterranean since Roman times (see Map 14.3). Like other migrants from the east, such as Greeks, Syrians, and Arabs, they were an urban and often a commercial people. The itinerary of the twelfth-century Jewish merchant, Benjamin of Tudela, describes their close-knit world, in which a structure of family firms and the fellow feeling of coreligionists gave Jews a commercial advantage and helped them to trade between the Christian and Muslim worlds. An isolated reference to Jews in Cologne occurs as early as 321 C.E. when the Rhineland was part of the Roman Empire, but Mediterranean communities were probably the springboard for Jewish colonization of northern European cities between the sixth and eleventh centuries.

Wherever they went, Jews were alternately privileged and persecuted: privileged, because rulers who needed productive settlers were prepared to reward them with legal immunities; persecuted, because host communities resented intruders who were given special advantages. **Anti-Semitism** has been traced to the influence of Christianity. Indeed, medieval anti-Semitism did exploit Christian prejudices. Gospel texts could be read—as they were, for example, at the time of the First Crusade (see Chapter 12)—to saddle Jews with collective responsibility for the death of Jesus. And Holy Week, when Christians prepare to commemorate Christ's death, was at best an expensive and at worst a fatal time for Jewish communities, who had to buy security from bloody reprisals.

In the Greek world, however, anti-Semitism was older than Christianity. Medieval anti-Semitism, moreover, was just one aspect of a wider phenomenon: society's antipathy for groups it could not assimilate—comparable, for instance, to the treatment of lepers, Muslims, and, later, gypsies. Outbreaks of anti-Jewish hatred are intelligible, in part, as examples of the prejudice outsiders commonly attract. At the time of the Black Death, lepers also attracted accusations of well poisoning. So did random strangers and individuals unpopular in their communities. We can find similar phenomena in almost every culture. The case of the Jews in Europe demands attention not because it is unique, but because it is surprising, given Western society's indebtedness to Jewish traditions, and to the individual genius of many Jews.

The increasing pace and intensity of persecution in the fourteenth century drove Jews to new centers. England had already expelled those Jews who did not convert to Christianity in 1290. The Jews were forced out of most of France in the early fourteenth century, and from many areas of western Germany in the early fifteenth century. (Spain and Portugal followed suit in the 1490s.) The effect was to shift Jewish settlement toward the central and eastern Mediterranean, Poland, and Lithuania (which first admitted Jews in 1321).

Though the evidence relates almost entirely to Europe, there were also people—whole groups of people—who benefited from the effects of plague. In Western Europe, propertied women were certainly among them. The aristocratic marriage market could be fatal to women who married young and faced repeated pregnancies, but it tended to leave many young widows—the last wives of aging, dying husbands. So property law had to provide for widows by ensuring them an adequate share in their dead husbands' estates and reversion of the property the women had brought to their marriages as dowries. More widows burying more husbands could shift the balance of property ownership between the sexes.

Chroniclers, insisting on Death as a leveler, often remarked that the plague carried off men and women alike. But, after the terrible devastations of 1348, contemporaries who noticed a difference in mortality rates between the sexes all saw men as the main victims. The plagues of the fourteenth century, taken as a whole, seem to have hit men harder than women, presumably because women led relatively secluded, and therefore protected, lives compared to men. Rich widows, often accumulating property from successive marriages, wielded power in their own right. To some extent, the same considerations applied lower down the ranks of society. For instance, during the period of high mortality associated with cold and famine in the second decade of the fourteenth century, more than half the weddings among the peasants of the manor of Taunton in southwest England involved rich widows. After the Black Death, the lords of the manor introduced massive license fees for anyone who wanted to make such marriages, ostensibly to protect widows from predatory Romeos. In unprecedented numbers, widows became the administrators of estates. Women of leisure, education, and power played a bigger part in Western society after this. The increased prominence of women in political, literary, and religious life from the fifteenth century onward might not have been possible without the damage plague did to men.

Burying the dead. "How come you feel no sadness when you bury a fellow-creature . . . that you remain unready for your own graves . . . that you pay no heed when warnings of death reach your ears?" The twelfth-century Muslim writer al Hariri asked this question in his *Maqamat*, a collection of moralistic stories. Al Hariri had no doubt that sickness, besides being a physical affliction, also served a moral purpose. God sent it to test human virtue and compassion. When the Black Death struck in the 1300s, many Muslims and Christians also saw the plague this way and tried to minister to the sick and dying. Yet the number of deaths could overwhelm the living, and many of the dead were dumped in mass graves.

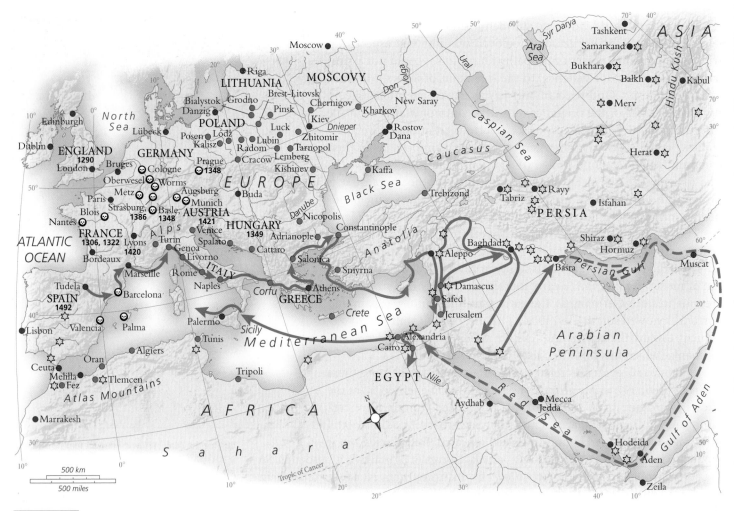

MAP 14.3

Jews in Medieval Europe and the Middle East, 1100–1400

- ● major centers of Jewish resettlement, 1200–1500
- ☻ massacres of Jews, ca. 1100–1400
- **1290** date of expulsion of Jews
- ➤ travels of Benjamin of Tuleda, ca. 1160–1173
- ▪▶ presumed route of Benjamin of Tuleda
- ☆ Jewish communities in Muslim world

In Western Europe peasants, if they survived the plague, also benefited from it. In the long run, owners could only keep great properties viable after plague had scythed the labor force by splitting the proceeds with their workers, or by breaking the estates up and letting peasants farm the parcels as tenants. Instead of taking orders from the lord's agent or bailiff, tenants paid rent and could manage their landholdings as they liked to their own best advantage. The trend toward "free" peasantries started long before the Black Death struck because in many cases it suited landowners, too. Peasants often made the land more productive. It made economic sense to allow them the initiative to improve their holdings. In England, where the royal courts encouraged peasant freedom to expand their own jurisdiction at aristocrats' expense, about half the peasants in the south of the country were already free when the plague arrived.

Lords wrote off their rights to labor services because, as a steward on an English estate admitted in 1351, "the lord's interest made it necessary." The contract peasant dependants of an English abbey renegotiated is revealing. "At the time of the mortality or pestilence which occurred in 1349, scarcely two peasants remained on the manor." They threatened to leave unless a new contract were made. Most of their former services—including plowing, weeding, carting, and preparing soil for planting—were commuted for rent "as long as it pleases the lord—and would that it might please the lord for ever," added the scribe, "since the aforesaid services were not worth very much." It is remarkable, however, that the growth of leaseholding and the relaxation of lordly controls over peasant farmers happened on a large scale in the late fourteenth and fifteenth centuries in the parts of Western Europe plague affected. In areas the Black Death bypassed—such as Poland, much of Russia, and what is now the Czech Republic and Slovakia—the opposite happened. Peasants became tied to their lords' land and subject to the landholders' jurisdiction.

Were the effects on the European peasantry duplicated in other plague-ridden lands? Certainly, the rural population became more restive and mobile in Egypt and Syria, where, in 1370, one jurist railed against the laws that obliged justices to return peasant refugees to the places from where they had fled. Villages in Egypt often had their tax burdens reduced in acknowledgment of the loss of population. The cost of labor services rose as population fell, creating opportunities for economic mobility among peasants and urban workers, and stimulating a further decline in rural population levels as peasants migrated to towns. But these changes did not disturb landowners' grip on their holdings. Peasants and landowners seem to have suffered together the effects of declining rural productivity.

Medieval Jews. Rabbis exhort Jews against eating pork in this engraving of 1475. "We Jews should all this lesson learn / How our deeds brought us to this turn." Their congregations, however, invite divine vengeance by conspicuously ignoring the prohibition.

Where peasants benefited, improved conditions took a long time to take effect. Combined with the effects of climate change, the immediate consequences of the plague disturbed, even subverted, the sense of security and stability associated with a traditional way of life. Moreover, most governments responded to the demographic disaster, loss of revenue, and loss of labor by raising taxes and trying to limit labor mobility. In previous centuries, ecological disasters and political oppression had often driven peasants into religious extremism or rebellion. Now, popular revolt took on a new agenda: revolutionary **millenarianism**—the doctrine that in an imminent, divinely contrived relaunch of history, God would empower the poor. This happened independently but in strikingly similar ways, in both Europe and China. A popular preacher who incited peasant rebels in England in 1381, expressed the doctrine of egalitarianism:

> How can the lords say or prove that they are more lords than we—save that they make us dig and till the ground so that they can squander what we produce? . . . They have beautiful residences and manors, while we have the trouble and the work, always in the fields and under the snow. But it is from us and our labor that everything comes with which they maintain their pomp. . . . Good folk, things cannot go well in England, nor ever shall until all things are in common and there is neither villein nor noble, but all of us are of one condition.[2]

The Wife of Bath. "Thanks be to God, who is for age alive / Of husbands at Church door have I had five." "The Wife of Bath" was a fictional character of about 1400—shown here in a contemporary illustration to the English writer Geoffrey Chaucer's verses about her. But, like all good satire, she was representative of the society of her times: sexually shameless, irrepressibly bossy, and determined to exert "power, during all my life" over any husband "who shall be both my debtor and my slave." *Eileen Tweedy/Picture Desk, Inc./Kobal Collection*

Prophesies helped nourish revolt. Some Franciscans (see Chapter 11) with their special vocation for the service of the poor, excited expectations that the end of the world could not be far off, and that a new age was at hand when God would release riches from the bowels of the Earth and eliminate inequality. In China, a similar doctrine from Buddhist tradition inspired peasant rebels in the 1350s. A new Buddha would arise to inaugurate a golden age and give his followers power over their oppressors (see Chapter 15). According to both movements, a divinely appointed hero would put a bloody end to the struggle of good and evil.

The next chapter describes the politics of the ensuing revolt. According to popular traditions dating from soon after the time, the leader of the rebellion, the founder of China's Ming dynasty, who claimed to be the prophesied hero, experienced the effects of ecological crisis himself. In one story, he rose to prominence by inventing a medicine that could cure a devastating new plague "which killed half the people and which no known medicine could combat." In another version, the plague and the great Yellow River flood of 1344 reduced him to beggary, and eventually he joined the rebellion that brought him to supreme power.

As well as contributing to revolution and a change of dynasty in China, and to instability in Europe, the plagues helped transform the Mongol world. The region the Mongols dominated spanned the plague's trans-Eurasian corridors of transmission. Though the evidence comes from European observers, it is a safe assumption that Mongol manpower suffered, and that population levels in some regions from which the Mongols levied recruits and collected taxes also fell. The loss of China in 1368 was, of course, the Mongols' most spectacular forfeiture of power. But the effects went further. Mongol control slackened in other dominions, and, on the Chinese front, it never recovered.

The Yellow River. This pictorial map of the Yellow River is both an artistic masterpiece and a scientific source of information. Ten famous painters representing China's northern and southern schools of art worked on it. Ordered by the first emperor of the Ming Dynasty (1368–1644), the map was drawn to an exact scale and was an invaluable tool to assess the impact of the frequently flooded Yellow River. The houses in the map indicate the population of cities, with each house representing 100 families.

In general, plague-stricken societies showed more of what we now call social mobility. The ranks of aristocracies, which were always subject to rapid turnover as families died out, thinned and refilled faster than ever. This seems to have applied as much to China's scholar elite, whose hold on power lapsed and was not fully reasserted until well into the fifteenth century, as to Western European nobilities, whose composition changed. In Western Europe, the increase in the numbers of free peasants and tenants created a form of rural capitalism. Families formerly restricted to modest social ambitions could accumulate wealth and bid for higher status, buying education or business opportunities or more land.

THE LIMITS OF DISASTER: BEYOND THE PLAGUE ZONE

How far did the plagues of the fourteenth century reach? In terms of effects, the plague was a regional phenomenon, changing the history of China, Western Europe, the Middle East, and the steppeland empires. But much of Central and Eastern Europe escaped. So did areas that ought to have been vulnerable to a disease contagion or infection spread, such as southeast Asia, and the parts of West and East Africa that were in touch, by way of the Indian Ocean or the Saharan caravan routes, with affected regions. Its relative isolation protected Japan. Apart from a pestilence in the capital Kyoto in 1342, which chroniclers were inclined to attribute to the vengeful spirit of a former emperor, there were no visitations of any disease on a scale resembling that of the Black Death. The principalities and city-states of central and northern Russia suffered relatively little and late—not before 1350, which is surprising in view of Russia's openness to the steppeland and close contact with the Mongols. India was relatively little affected—references to pestilences are not much more frequent in fourteenth-century sources than for other periods, and recorded outbreaks were localized.

Beyond the reach of the plagues—or, at least, beyond the zone of its most severe effects—the fourteenth century was an era of opportunity in Eurasia (see Map 14.4). The Mongols were now troubled giants, from whom states in India, Japan, and southeast Asia were at last safe. We can look at those regions first, before turning to others where, as far as we know, the plagues never penetrated, in sub-Saharan Africa and the Pacific.

India

In India, the sultanate of Delhi profited from the opportunity the Mongols' decline offered. Sultan Muhammad Ibn Tughluq (moo-HA-mahd ih-bihn TOOG-look), whose reign occupied the second quarter of the fourteenth century, was the driving force of a policy of conquest that almost covered the subcontinent with campaigns. Ibn Battuta, who knew the sultan well, called him "of all men the most addicted to the making of gifts and the shedding of blood. His gate is never without some poor man enriched or some living man executed." Emphasis on the sultan's generosity reflects Ibn Battuta's own priorities. He was always on the lookout for rich

Daulatabad. The Delhi Sultan Ibn Tughluq (r. 1320–1325) transferred his court to the strongest fortress in India, which he called Daulatabad or "City of Riches," near the frontier of his campaigns against Hindu kingdoms in the south. He planned to re-locate the entire population of the city of Delhi to the surrounding slopes. The steep ascent made the place defensible. A narrow gangway was the only approach to the palace complex.

patrons. But the key facts about Ibn Tughluq's methods are clear. He ran his court and army by balancing lavish gifts with intimidating displays of wrath.

His administration was a machine for recycling wealth. Ibn Battuta describes the regular arrival of revenue collectors from villages, casting gold coins into a golden basin: "These contributions amount in all to a vast sum which the sultan gives to anyone he pleases." Annually, "the daughters of the infidel kings and who have been taken as captives in war during that year" were distributed among the sultan's chief supporters, after performing a sort of audition—singing and dancing, presumably to establish which girls were the most valuable.

While praising Ibn Tughluq's sense of justice, Ibn Battuta indicts him for the use of terror, arbitrary abuses of power, and judicial murder. "The Sultan was far too free in shedding blood. . . . Every day there are brought to the audience hall hundreds of people, chained, beaten and fettered, and those who are for execution are executed, those for torture tortured, and those for beating beaten." He put one of his brothers to death on a charge of rebellion, which Ibn Battuta clearly felt was trumped up—the first of many judicial murders. On one occasion, the sultan executed 350 alleged deserters at once. A sheikh who accused him of tyranny was fed with excrement and beheaded. Twice, Ibn Tughluq dealt with suspected conspiracies in Delhi by expelling the classes of Muslim notables whom he suspected of disaffection.

Ibn Tughluq's was a personal empire. His own dynamism and reputation, and a policy of religious toleration held it together—the only policy workable for a Muslim elite in a largely Hindu country. But Ibn Tughluq's state was not built to last. It relied on conquest to fuel the system. The Turkic elite, who provided the muscle for revenue collection at home and for war on the frontiers, demanded constant rewards. When they did not get them, they seceded from the state. This began to happen on a large scale toward the end of Ibn Tughluq's life. Conquest is, in any case, a gambler's game. Military fortunes change, and military systems, even of the most crushing superiority, can fail unpredictably. Disaster struck Ibn Tughluq, for instance, when a plague devastated his army. "The provinces withdrew their allegiance," Ibn Battuta reported, "and the outer regions broke away."

Moreover, the Delhi sultans were under constant pressure from the Muslim establishment to impose Islam by force, launch holy war, and ease the tax burden on Muslims at the expense of "infidels." The discontent evident among sheikhs and some Muslim notables during Ibn Tughluq's reign owed something, no doubt, to fear of the sultan's arbitrary measures. But frustration with his policies of toleration also inspired much of it. Ibn Tughluq's successor succumbed to these pressures. He forfeited Hindu allegiance. Beyond the frontier, Hindu states adopted a counter ideology of resistance to Islam—at least at the level of rhetoric, since religion rarely took priority over politics. In southern India, a Hindu state with imperial ambitions arose at Vijayanagar. The conquest juggernaut of the sultanate of Delhi stopped rolling, and provincial elites in outlying regions in Gujarat and Bengal dropped out of the empire. Again, as so often before in Indian history, both the difficulties of and the capacity for an India-wide empire had been demonstrated. But again, the problems of maintaining such a large and diverse state were obvious. Future attempts would run into the same kinds of difficulties as those that caused the sultanate's control of the outer edges of the state to unravel and its expansion to come to a halt.

Southeast Asia

Rather as Delhi did in India, a native kingdom in Java, the main island of what is today Indonesia, exploited the opportunity the waning of the Mongol threat created. The offshore world of southeast Asia produced goods the Chinese market wanted. Some states in the region were in a position to threaten or control the passage of those goods by sea: pepper and cinnamon from southern India and Sri Lanka; sandalwood from Timor; timber and aromatic spices, nutmeg, cloves, and mace from Borneo and the Moluccas. Control of the strait between Malaya, Java, and Sumatra was strategically vital for China-bound trade, and the shipping of Java made an important contribution to the commerce of the region. That is why Kubilai Khan focused on Java when he tried to extend his empire into southeast Asia (see Chapter 15).

The establishment of a powerful state on Java, centered on the secure, inland city of Majapahit (Mah-jah-PAH-heet), was the achievement of Kertanagara, who died in 1292. Chroniclers credited him with magic powers or saintly virtues, according to their own prejudices. In fact, he seems to have balanced the rituals of Buddhist, Hindu, and indigenous religions to keep a diverse array of followers together. Kertanagara repulsed Kubilai Khan's Mongol invasion.

The king who launched Majapahit on its own imperial career in the mid–fourteenth century was Hayan Wuruk, who died in 1389. He had dazzling ambitions. We know this because his childhood playmate, who became one of his chief ministers, wrote a poem in his praise. The verses reveal how the king wanted people to think of him. The verses lovingly describe the royal palace at Majapahit. It had gates of iron and a "diamond-plastered" watchtower. Majapahit was like the

MAP 14.4

South and Southeast Asia, ca. 1350

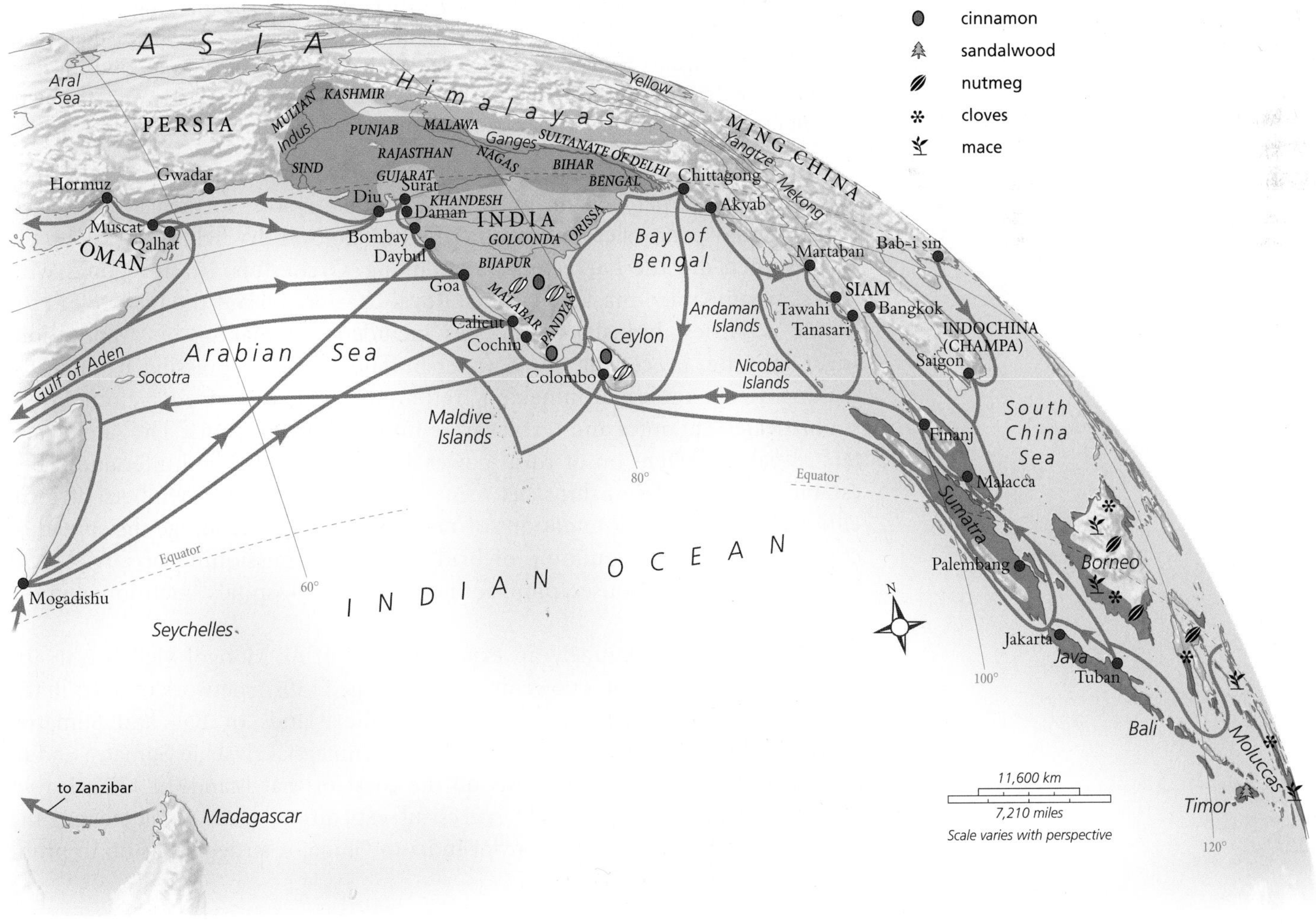

- region where Majapahit claimed tribute
- Delhi sultanate at its greatest extent, ca. 1335
- area subject to sporadic influence by Delhi Sultanate
- —— main trade route
- ● important trade centers

Traded Goods

- pepper
- cinnamon
- sandalwood
- nutmeg
- cloves
- mace

Sun and Moon, while the villages of the rest of the kingdom are "of the aspect of stars." When Hayan Wuruk traveled the country, his court filled numberless carts. Through the streets of his capital, he paraded, clad in gold, borne on a throne carved with supporting lions, to the music of lutes and drums, conches and trumpets, and singers. Ambassadors from foreign courts brought him praises in Sanskrit verse.

He was both "Buddha in the body" and "Shiva incarnate"—worshipful to Buddhist and Hindu subjects alike. He was also a master of native rituals, skilled in the theater, dance, and song. "The king's song put them under a spell," the poet assures us, "like the cries of a peacock." Hayan Wuruk's realm, according to the poet, was more famous than any country in the world except India. In reality, the kingdom occupied little more than half the island of Java. The king, however, aimed to make it bigger. The poet listed tributaries in many islands in what is today Indonesia, and "protectorates" in northern Malaya, Thailand, and Indochina. Even China and India, he claimed, defer to Hayan Wuruk. "Already the other continents," he boasts, "are getting ready to show obedience to the illustrious prince" and a state "renowned for its purifying power in the world."

That was all the exaggeration of propaganda. But a disinterested chronicler, from Samudra-Pasai, a pepper-exporting port beyond the Strait of Malacca to the west, left a description of Majapahit that confirms much of the picture:

> The empire grew prosperous. People in vast numbers thronged the city. At this time every kind of food was in great abundance. There was a ceaseless coming and going of people from the territories overseas which had submitted to the king. . . . The land of Majapahit was supporting a large population. Everywhere one went there were gongs and drums being beaten, people dancing to the strains of all kinds of loud music, entertainments of all kinds like the living theater. . . . These were the commonest sights and went on day and night in the land of Majapahit.[3]

Hayan Wuruk, from the *Nagara Kertagama*

Surviving temple reliefs show what the Java of Hayan Wuruk was like. Wooden houses, perched on pillars over stone terraces, formed neat villages. Peasants grew paddy rice, or coaxed water buffalo over dry fields to break up the soil. Women did the harvesting and cooking. Orchestras, beating gongs with sticks, accompanied masked dancers. Royal charters fill out the picture of economic activities. Industrial processes included salt making by evaporation, sugar refining, processing cured water-buffalo meat, oil pressing from seeds, making rice noodles, ironmaking, rattan weaving, and dyeing cloth. More sophisticated ceramics and textiles were imported from China. The same charters reveal the extension of royal power and impact into the hinterland. They establish direct relationships between the royal court and members of local elites. They favor the foundations of new temples and encourage the spread of communications, the building of bridges, the commissioning of ferries, and the erection of "rest houses, pious foundations, and hospitals" mentioned in the king's praise poem.

Majapahit was genuinely an expanding realm. As Mongol vigilance in the region relaxed, Majapahit's power increased. In the 1340s, a network of ports in the hands of Majapahit garrisons spread over the islands of Bali and Sumatra. Majapahit indeed seems to have annihilated commercial rivals in Sumatra and to have maintained fortified outposts on the coast of that island. In 1377, Hayan Wuruk launched an apparently successful expedition against Palembang, the major way station on the route from India to China. A struggle was on to profit from southeast Asia's trade.

Japan

Japan, like Java, was a region that the plagues spared and the Mongols failed to conquer. Here, however, security from the Mongol menace had a contrasting effect. As the threat from the Mongols receded, so did pressure to stay united and serve the state. Potential rebels could now raise armies with increasing ease. Fourteenth-century Japan began to experience unprecedented instability. Familiar patterns in politics and social life were shaken like the contents of a kaleidoscope. Since the beginning of the rule of the shoguns, the hereditary chief ministers who controlled the government (see Chapter 11), Japan had enjoyed more than a century of stability. The warrior class had been pacified—maintained by grants of estates and their revenues. Now people at all social levels were accumulating wealth. Social status, which was supposedly protected by complicated standards of eligibility for different ranks, was up for grabs. Warriors began to diversify into new occupations, to sell or break up their estate rights, and, in increasing numbers, to resort to violence as a way of life.

At the top of this volatile society, rival branches of the imperial family contested the throne. From 1318, the emperor Godaigo fought not only to exclude family competitors but also to take back the power the shoguns exercised in the emperor's name. He accused them of "drawing water from a stream and forgetting its source." Godaigo had his portrait painted showing himself with a sword—an accessory normally considered too active for an emperor, but one that signified two intentions: to recover real power, and to keep hold of the symbols of imperial authority, which included a sacred sword.

The emperor found, however, that he could not simply take up the reins of power himself. Traditional methods could no longer govern the country. Loyalty, though much talked of by writers at the time, became an unpredictable commodity, liable to change hands as circumstances changed. An oath the members of a warband took in 1336 declared, "Let there be no differences of opinion. Everything shall be discussed at a council. If some disobey this, they shall suffer the punishment of all the middling, small, and great gods of the country of Japan in Heaven, Earth and Hell." "Then was then," proclaimed a saying of the time. "Now is now: rewards are lord!"

Godaigo's army deserted in dissatisfaction over the rewards he could provide. "How," complained one of the officials who worked for Godaigo's party, "can those who tend to have the outlook of a merchant be of use to the court?" Clearly, the new disorder was, for some, a kind of social revolution: the result of violations of the proper boundaries of class and rank.

In 1335, the most powerful of the warlords, Ashikaga Takauji, seized the position of supreme power as the protector of the emperor or **shogun** in defiance of Godaigo's wishes. The Ashikaga dynasty emerged with the greatest share of authority because they promised the most rewards. They survived as shoguns almost until the end of the century by accepting the realities of the changed world, withdrawing into a role as the greatest of a number of regional powers, and attempting only modest interventions in the spheres of other major warlords. The Ashikaga also restored the old relationship between shogun and emperor, in which pieties smothered the real displacement of power into the shogun's hands. "There is heaven," declared Ashikaga Takauji in his testament of 1357, "there is the sovereign, there is the earth, and there is the minister. . . . If the joint path of sovereign and subject is reversed, then there will be neither heaven nor earth, sovereign nor subject."

A SHOGUN'S ARMOR

This armor is believed to have belonged to Ashikaga Takauji who was shogun from 1338 to 1358.

Stenciled in lacquered doeskin, an image of Fudo Myo-o—the god who personified the samurai virtues of outward ferocity and inner calm—adorns the breastplate.

The quality and costliness of the gilt copper breastplate and helmet mountings show that the armor belonged to a person of high status.

Silk ribbons of many colors, symbolizing the fleeting beauty of the rainbow, were used to tie up the skirts of the armor.

The Metropolitan Museum of Art, Gift of Bashford Dean, 1914 (14.100.121) Photograph © 1991 The Metropolitan Museum of Art

What does this armor say about the warrior class in fourteenth century Japan?

In 1336, the Ashikaga overwhelmed Godaigo's remaining supporters at the Battle of Minato River. Godaigo and his heirs, however, did not give up. Ashikaga victories confined them to a small enclave in the south of the country, but they resisted until the 1380s.

The chaos of the fourteenth century favored the rise of **Zen**, a tradition of Buddhism that valued personal extinction as a part of mystical experience. A twelfth-century Japanese text defined it: "a special transmission outside the scriptures, not founded on words or letters, which allows one to penetrate the nature of things by pointing directly to the mind." Zen made progress, partly because of the influx of monks from China, escaping from the Mongols, and partly because Zen ideas suited the warriors and warlords who now effectively ruled Japan. Discipline, self-denial, and willingness to die are martial virtues. The warriors recognized Zen monks as kindred spirits. Warrior families made Zen practitioners the custodians of their ancestral temples and tombs.

For the women of families of warrior and aristocratic rank, the changes of the period were oppressive. Women could attain responsible positions in the emperor's court. Hino Meishi, for instance, was in charge of the sacred imperial symbols in 1331, when the shogun tried to depose Godaigo. But changing marriage customs were unfavorable to women's personal independence. Until the fourteenth century, marriage in Japan was predominantly a private, essentially sexual relationship. Now it became increasingly formalized, as a union of two families. Wives moved into the homes of their husbands' families, instead of remaining in their own homes. Hino Meishi, for instance, started her experience of married life in 1333 in traditional manner, when her lover started visiting her openly. This publicly acknowledged the relationship as a permanent one. She worried, not because the arrangement was informal, but because her husband's family was of higher rank than her own. In the confused conditions of the civil war then raging, Meishi was forced to move house, but she ended up in her husband's home.

A sign of women's changed circumstances is that they stopped writing fiction and the kind of personal diaries familiar from earlier periods. Hino Meishi herself was the author of the last autobiographical memoir by a woman—which is why we know so much about her life. Self-expression was now considered inappropriate for the female sex. Wives came to be thought of as their husbands' property. In the same period, following changes in the practices of the imperial family, it became common for women aristocrats to receive a life interest in a share of family property, rather than inheriting property outright. Property rights were steered toward a single male heir. Among commoners, however, this practice failed to take hold, and women held growing amounts of property and engaged in more business in their own right.

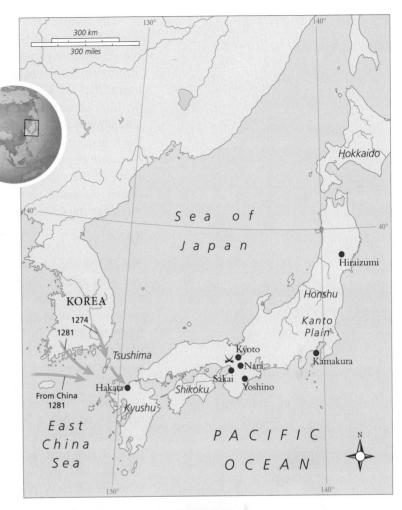

MAP 14.5

Japan, ca. 1350

→ Mongol invasion attempts

⚔ battle of Minato River

The Ashikaga Shogunate

Fourteenth century	Changing marriage customs diminish women's independence
1318	Emperor Godaigo seeks to regain imperial power
1335	Ashikaga Takauji seizes shogunate in defiance of Godaigo
1336	Last of Godaigo's supporters defeated

The changes that were transforming the warrior class do not seem to have affected peasant prosperity. On the contrary, the peasants profited. Relaxation of central authority freed villagers from intrusive legislation. They could get on with improving crop yields as they saw fit. The new regime of rewards for military service meant that the landlords were always changing—dispossessed and replaced as the fortunes of war shifted. The rapid turnover of lords, who were usually absentees, also allowed the peasants to get on with their business. There were no epidemics in the fourteenth-century countryside in Japan, and serious crop failures were rare. Nor were population growth and the extension of cultivated land interrupted. As a result of the successful exploitation of formerly marginal lands, outside the great estates, the numbers of small independent farmers multiplied, though not on anything like the scale discernible at the same time in Western Europe.

Mali

Just as Java and Japan seemed to grow in stature by comparison with the afflictions of China and the Mongols, so parts of West Africa projected an image of abundance toward the devastated Mediterranean world. A conspicuous piece of evidence for West African prosperity is the Catalan Atlas, made in the studio of the finest mapmaker in Europe, Cresques Abraham, on the Mediterranean island of Majorca (Mah–YOHR-Ka), in the 1370s or 1380s. The map is smothered with gold paint, scattered with bright images in costly pigments, like the contents of a spilled jewel box. In the part of the map devoted to West Africa a black king appears—bearded, crowned, enthroned, surrounded by depictions of rich cities of many turrets—holding a huge nugget of pure gold. "This is the richest king in all the land," says a caption.

His kingdom, Mali (MAH-lee), occupied the region of grassland and mixed savanna between the Sahara Desert and the tropical forest. The desert sealed it from the effects of plague (see Map 14.6). According to tradition, a hero known as **Sundiata** founded the kingdom in the early thirteenth century. His story has obviously mythical features. He was a cripple, mocked and exiled, who returned home as a conqueror and avenger. The strength of his army, and those of his successors, was horsemen. Terracotta sculptures show us what they were like. Helmed and armed, with round shields and breastplates over slashed leather jackets, they kept their heads haughtily tilted and their horses on short rein, with elaborately braided bridles. Their great age of conquest came in the 1260s and 1270s when, according to the Muslim historian Ibn Khaldun, "their dominions expanded and they overcame the neighboring peoples . . . and all nations of the land of the blacks stood in awe of them."

The "mansas," as the kings of Mali were titled, made pilgrimages to the Muslim holy city of Mecca via Cairo at intervals from the late thirteenth century, spreading the fame of their land. Although all Muslims are supposed to make the *hajj*, as the pigrimage to Mecca is called, at least once in their life, the mere fact that the mansas could leave their country for the year-long journey shows how stable the state must have been. In about 1324, Mansa Musa (MAHN-sah MOO-sah) stayed in Egypt for about three months on his way to Mecca. He gave 50,000 gold coins to the Mamluk sultan and distributed ingots of raw gold to officials. He endowed so many mosques and shrines that he caused inflation. By various accounts, the value of gold in Egypt fell by between 10 and 25 percent as a result of his stay. On his homeward journey, he raised loans that, it was said, he repaid at the rate of 700 coins for every 300 of the same value.

The location of West Africa's gold mines was a closely guarded commercial secret, but it was probably in Bure (BOO–ray), around the upper reaches of the Niger

Mansa. "All the peoples of the land of the Blacks stood in awe of them," wrote Ibn Khaldun of the mounted warriors of the Mansas of Mali. Many fired-clay representations of these soldiers survive from the thirteenth to the fifteenth centuries. Nearly all show the same erect posture, proudly uptilted head, and elaborate helmets and bridles.

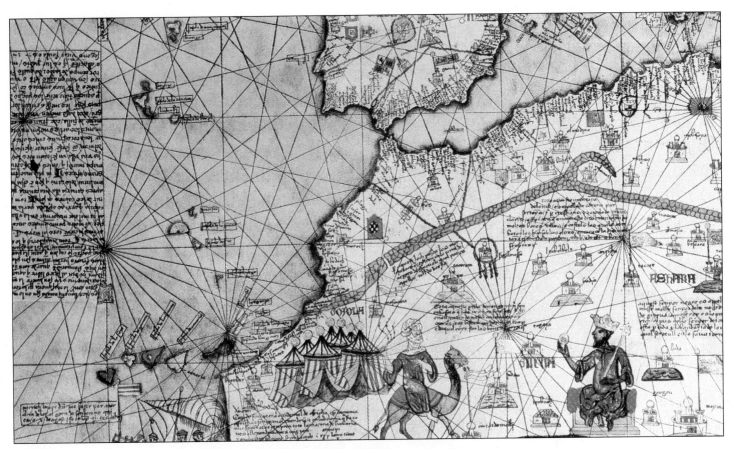

Mansa Musa. "Lord of the blacks of Guinea," reads the legend accompanying the portrait of Mansa Musa (r. ca. 1312-1327), the king of Mali in West Africa, on the fourteenth-century Catalan Atlas. "This lord is the richest and most noble lord of all this region owing to the abundance of gold which is gathered in this land." The Mansa's wealth was said to exceed that of all other kings. His European-style crown and ample beard are compliments bestowed by an artist who had not learned, as Europeans were to do in later centuries, to despise black African kingship.

River and the headwaters of the Gambia and Senegal Rivers. The Volta River valley also had some gold. The merchants of Mali handled the gold trade but never controlled its production. When they tried to take over the mines, the miners refused to work. But the gold had to pass through the mansa's lands to get to trading cities, such as Walata and Timbuktu (tihm-buhk-TOO) near the edge of the Sahara. The mansa took nuggets for tribute—hence the image on Cresques Abraham's map.

In 1352, Ibn Battuta—that relentless traveler—set off to find the kingdom of Mali. He journeyed south from his home in Morocco to Taghaza, the salt-mining desert town on the edge of the Sahara, where "houses and mosques are built with blocks of salt." There he joined one of the merchant camel caravans that regularly crossed the Sahara, trading salt for gold. Mali was so rich in gold and so short of salt that the price of salt reputedly tripled or quadrupled in the kingdom's markets. Ibn Battuta and his companions crossed the desert by night marches. They ate "desert truffles swarming with lice" in a land "haunted by demons. . . . There is no visible road or track in these parts," Ibn Battuta recorded, "nothing but sand blown hither and thither by the wind." Water sources were sparse—ten days' journey apart.

Ibn Battuta reached the frontier of Mali at Walata. "It was then," he complained, "that I repented of having come to their country because of their lack of manners and their contempt for white men." He found the food disgusting, not appreciating

 Mansa Musa of Mali

MAP 14.6

The Kingdom of Mali, ca. 1350

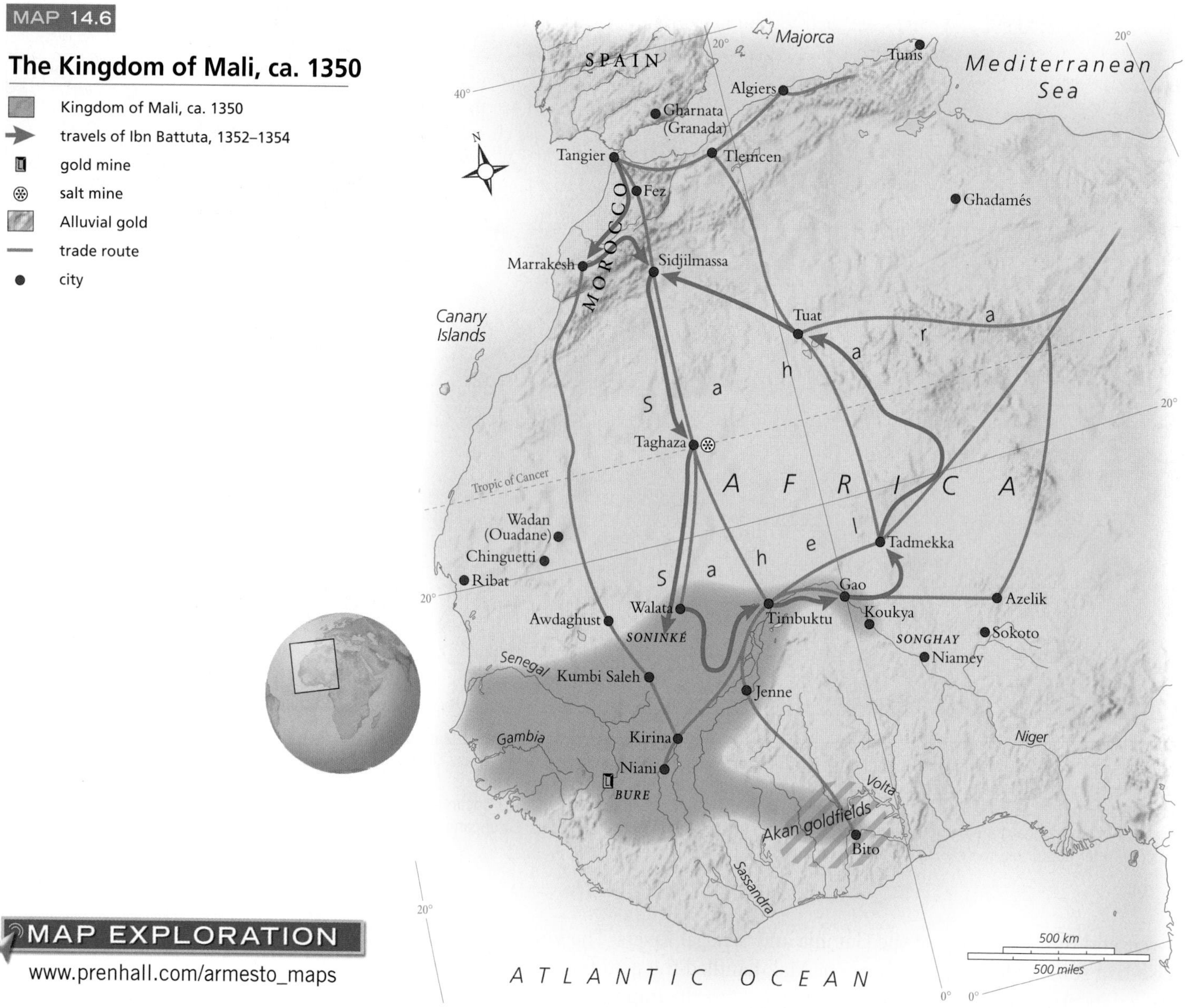

- Kingdom of Mali, ca. 1350
- → travels of Ibn Battuta, 1352–1354
- gold mine
- salt mine
- Alluvial gold
- — trade route
- • city

MAP EXPLORATION
www.prenhall.com/armesto_maps

how lucky he was to be served expensive millet at the desert's edge. Outraged to find himself watched when he relieved himself in the Niger, he failed, at first, to realize that the spectator was there to guard him from crocodiles. He found the sexual freedom of the women alarming, but approved of the way children were chained until they learned the Quran. He praised the "abhorrence of injustice" he found among the black people.

The mansa's court impressed him, as it impressed other visitors in the same period. This consensus is striking, because North African Muslim writers rarely praised black achievements. The mansa, according to Ibn Battuta, commanded more devotion from his subjects than any other ruler in the world, though most of the court ceremonial was traditional among black kingdoms in West Africa. the mansa, for instance, spoke only through an intermediary, for to raise his voice was beneath his dignity. Suppliants had to prostrate themselves and sprinkle dust on their heads as they addressed him. When his words were relayed to the people, guards strummed their bowstrings and everyone else hummed appreciatively. Sneezing in the mansa's presence was punishable by death. Hundreds of servants attended him with gilded staves. Court poets and scholars came to serve the mansa from Muslim Spain and North Africa.

Meanwhile, the gold of West Africa inspired heroic European efforts to get to its source. Western Europe produced only small amounts of silver, and its economies were permanently short of precious metals with which to trade. There was a long-standing adverse trade balance with more productive Silk-Road economies. To keep it going, this trade always needed infusions of cash. So, as Mali's reputation grew, the search for African gold obsessed European adventurers. Cresques Abraham depicted the fate of one of them, the Spaniard Jaume Ferrer, lost to shipwreck off the West African coast in 1346 in an attempt to find a sea route to Mali. The endeavor was hopeless. Mali was landlocked, and the African coasts had little gold until well into the fifteenth century.

Ibn Battuta, from *The Travels of Ibn Battuta*

THE PACIFIC: SOCIETIES OF ISOLATION

Beyond the world that escaped the Black Death lay regions contagion did not threaten. Isolation, which had arresting effects in so many cases already familiar to readers of this book, was a privilege in the fourteenth century. To understand this unaccustomed reversal of what can only be called the normal pattern of global history, we need to look at some relatively isolated societies. The vastness of the Pacific—which the technology of the time could not cross—ensured that exceptionally isolated cultures lay scattered around and about that ocean.

For instance, no part of the inhabited globe was more isolated than Easter Island, which lay, at the time, more than 2,000 miles away from any other human habitation. The island covers only 64 square miles of the Pacific Ocean, way off the usual routes of Pacific navigation and the usual course of the winds. It is hard to believe that the Polynesian navigators who first colonized the island, possibly over 1,500 years ago, would have stayed if they had been able to continue their journey or turn around and go home. Most of the soil is poor. Nowadays, there are no nearby fisheries, though native traditions recall a time when the island's elite feasted on porpoise and dolphin. Chickens and the starchy food plant called taro arrived with the first settlers. But not much that was edible was available to them when they arrived. Migrant birds were their renewable source of food. The oldest art on the island shows a birdman. Feasts of bird flesh and egg-stealing competitions greeted the annual arrival of flocks of sooty terns.

Yet despite the natural poverty of the island and its isolation from other societies, it housed, in the fourteenth century, a people at the height of their ambition. Probably late in the first millennium, they had begun to erect monumental statues called *Moais* for reasons we can no longer determine. The statues resemble those other Polynesian peoples erected: tall, elongated, stylized faces hewn of stone. They were originally adorned with red topknots—sitting hatlike on their heads—and white coral eyes, looking out with a fixed stare. The Easter Island statues are unique compared with other Polynesian works of the same sort only because they are so big and there are so many of them—878 in all, including those abandoned, incomplete, in the quarries. Some 600 finished examples survive, most of them more than 20 feet tall (see Map 14.7).

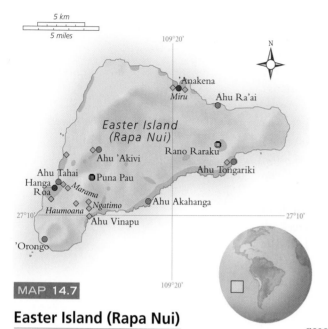

MAP 14.7

Easter Island (Rapa Nui)

	main area of statues
◇	restored statue site
◒	ceremonial center
●	settlement
◙	quarry for red topknots
◙	quarry for statues

It took real communal effort to make and erect the statues, each carved from a pillar of rock weighing between 30 and 40 tons. A single extended family—say, about 400 people—joining together to provide the labor and feed the workers, would have taken more than a year to complete the task. As time went on, the statues got bigger—a clear case of competition, driving up the costs of the culture, and, perhaps, condemning it to ultimate collapse, a century or two later. So an enterprising community could buck the effects of isolation, and even turn isolation to advantage—but, in an extreme case like that of Easter Island, the effort was evidently hard to sustain. Statue building slowed and, in the sixteenth or seventeenth century, stopped.

New Zealand was another, almost equally remote outpost of the Polynesian world, but with infinitely more resources than Easter Island, and therefore with better prospects of sustainable development. Although the date of the first settlement of New Zealand is disputed (see Chapter 11), fairly secure dates are possible for changes under way by the fourteenth century. Population increased. Hunting resources diminished in populated areas as the fur seal and the moa began to get scarce. The moa was a huge, flightless bird, with eggs as big as a hundred hen's eggs, that was among early settlers' main sources of food. Human overexploitation was almost certainly responsible for the bird's extinction. Moa meat was processed in immense butcheries. At the biggest, at the mouth of the Waitako River in South Island, up to 90,000 were butchered with blades made of obsidian, a volcanic stone that can be honed to a razor-sharp edge. The same region had over 300 smaller sites, each handling at least 5,000 moa.

As the balance of the way of life shifted from hunting toward farming, mobile colonies settled down. The kind of wear the teeth of people buried in this period shows is different from that of their predecessors: ground down by fibrous foods and gritty mollusks, showing fewer traces of the effects of a meat-rich diet. The results included stronger community identification with land and,

Moais. Monumental statue making on Easter Island was probably at its most intense in the fourteenth century. For a small population on a poorly provided and remote island, the investment of energy the practice required seems astounding. The images are similar to those of ancestor cults elsewhere in Polynesia, but they are exceptional in being carved from stone, rather than wood, huge, and numerous. Isolation apparently made Easter Island culture distinctive, but still recognizably like that of other Polynesian colonies.

therefore, more competition for cultivable resources. Part of the farming surplus was invested in war. From the fifteenth century, the number of places where weapons were made grew enormously. So did the number of fortified villages, especially in the North Island. War was only one of many forms of new or newly intensive activity that favored the power of chiefs. Farming required strong centers of power to organize collective activity and regulate the distribution of food. So did new fishing technologies with gigantic nets that needed many hands to operate them.

Meanwhile, on the Pacific rim of the New World, people experimented with contrasting responses to isolation (see Map 14.8). Good evidence has survived for two different communities. One body of evidence comes from a community of hunters in the north of the hemisphere. Exact dates are hard to assign, but probably toward the end of the fifteenth century, a mudslide at Ozette, in Washington State, buried the homes of a community of whalers and seal fishers. The mud perfectly preserved the site. Archaeologists have revealed layers of sediment that show that ways of life had not changed here significantly for centuries before the disaster. The mud of Ozette gives us a unique glimpse into the lives of a hunting culture in what we think of in European terms as the late Middle Ages.

The victims of the mudslide lived in big buildings of cedarwood, each more than 50 feet long and 30 feet wide. Each building housed about 40 people, divided typically by partitions into half a dozen smaller family units, each with its own hearth. Hanging mats helped insulate the walls. The Ozette people ate almost no vegetable matter except wild berries. Though they hunted some land animals and birds, they relied overwhelmingly on the sea as their hunting ground. Fur seals provided nearly 90 percent of their meat. For cooking, they filled watertight cedarwood boxes with hot water and boiled or steamed their food. They hunted and fished in dugouts. Whale images dominated their art, probably because the art had a ritual or magical function in bringing good fortune to the whale hunt. Carvers also made bowls in the shape of men, depicted realistically except for big cavities, where the belly should be, to hold food or offerings. Their way of life was, broadly speaking, similar to that of the Thule Inuit centuries earlier (see Chapter 11).

On the Pacific's South American edge, we can trace new activity to roughly the same period. Of course, this was not a region as isolated as New Zealand, Easter Island, or even Ozette. As we have seen many times in this book, the coasts of what are now Peru, Ecuador, and Pacific-side Colombia were always in touch with the cultures of the high Andes and, through them, with the lowlands beyond. In South America, in and around the fourteenth century, the latest experiment in state-building, intensive agriculture, and city life was under way at Chan Chan. This city was in the coastal desert region of Peru where the Moche had formerly built complex irrigation works and prosperous cities (see Chapter 10) in defiance of a hostile environment. The methods of the Chimú (chee-MOO) people of Chan Chan were different. They

Huaca del Dragón. The date of the stacked platforms of Huaca del Dragón, near the site of Chan chan in Peru, is much disputed, but the adobe reliefs—of which a recently restored section is depicted here—are probably of Chimú workmanship. Below a frieze of warriors, a divine feast is shown. A double-headed serpent, with a rainbow-like body surrounded by clouds, devours curl-nosed victims, framing similar scenes shown in profile. Food-storage areas were built into the structure, which seems to have been both temple and warehouse—a repository, perhaps, for food of the gods.

MAP 14.8

Societies of the Pacific, ca.1400

☐ area of Polynesian settlement

Economic activities and food resources

🦭 seals

🐟 fishing

🫘 taro

🦤 moa

♙ cotton

🐦 migrant birds

🦃 chickens

🐖 pigs

🥥 coconuts/breadfruit

PERU modern country or state

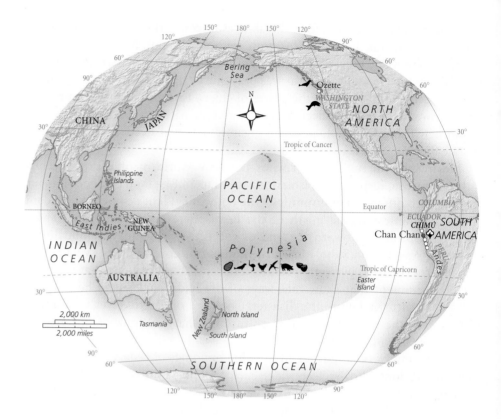

concentrated agriculture in the environs of the city, where 30,000 people lived. Hinterland population was thinly distributed and not much bigger in total than that of Chan Chan itself.

Cotton production was a major economic activity. Fishing seems to have mattered little. For protein, the Chan Chan people—or, perhaps, just the elite, relied on llamas. Pasture was limited, so the llamas were farmed in corrals in and around the city. Fodder supplemented grazing.

The city of Chan Chan covered almost seven square miles. Spaces in Chan Chan served as the tombs of kings, dwellings for elites, and warehouses to store and distribute food. The layout shows that the Chimú state was oppressive, with a security-obsessed elite. High walls, fortified gateways and dogleg corridors, designed with sharp turns to delay attackers and favor defenders, protected the rulers' quarters from their own people.

The warehouses were the most important buildings. Access to them was through chambers where costly ceremonies unfolded: sacrifices of llamas and men, deposits of precious objects. The storerooms were vital—the most vital part of the state—because El Niño periodically and unpredictably washed away the irrigation works. Stockpiling enabled the Chimú to recover when disaster struck.

The rulers' tombs were so rich that colonial-era Spaniards spoke of "mining" them. The Chimú elite favored gold for their precious ornaments and ritual objects. But gold did not occur naturally in this part of Peru. Trade or tribute must have brought it to Chimú. For Chimú was evidently an expansionist state. Perhaps it had to be to boost its resources in a difficult and depleted environment. Sites of towns built in the style of Chan Chan stretch between the Sana and Supe Rivers.

IN PERSPECTIVE: The Aftershock

Ibn Khaldun left an often-quoted but unforgettable description of the effects of the Black Death on the Muslim world:

> Civilization shrank with the decrease of mankind. Cities and buildings were bared, roads and signposts were abandoned, villages and palaces were deserted. Tribes and dynasties were expunged. It was as if the voice of existence in the world had called out for oblivion, and the world had responded to the call.[4]

But how serious and enduring were the consequences? For Latin Christendom in Western Europe, the picture looked bleak. After the achievements of the previous century, and the benefits of a long period of enhanced contacts with the Islamic world and China, the West seemed poised for a great age of expansion. Now many promising initiatives of the preceding period ended. North Atlantic navigation, which Norse seafarers had developed so heroically in previous centuries, dwindled. The last Icelandic voyage to mainland America was in 1347. The Norse Greenland colonies became increasingly isolated. When a bishop's representative sailed to the more northerly of them in the 1340s, he "found nobody," he reported, "either Christians or heathens, only some wild cattle and sheep, and they slaughtered the wild cattle for food, as much as the ships would carry, and then sailed home therewith themselves." When the Greenland colony was finally extinguished in the fifteenth century, it was by

⦿ MAKING CONNECTIONS ⦿

BEYOND THE PLAGUE ZONE

REGION →	TENTATIVE REASON FOR ABSENCE OF PLAGUE →	CONSEQUENCES
Japan	Protected by relative isolation	Protected from Mongols; new threats emerge from prosperous provincial warlords; in addition, the imperial family divides into rival factions; new dynasty emerges; Zen Buddhism expands influence
Northern Russia	Unknown—abundant interaction with Mongols should have made Russians vulnerable	Grand Duchy of Moscow begins to throw off the rule of Mongols in late 1300s
India	Unknown—although Silk Roads and sea-trade routes were adjacent	Islamic sultanate of Delhi profited from Mongols' decline, initiating policy of conquest; Turkic elite responsible for war and revenue collecting eventually secedes; problems of Hindu/Muslim relations are ever present
Southeast Asia	Unknown—trade routes from China, Europe, Africa should have made the region vulnerable	Establishment of powerful state on Java (Majapahit), to control trade with China and India, creating stable and prosperous society
Pacific	Isolation	Expansion of existing societies; new efforts at developing agricultural resources
Sub-Saharan Africa	Unclear	Control over West Africa's gold trade leads to affluence, European obsession with finding Mali

mysterious raiders of savage ferocity known to the Norse as Skraelingar—presumably, the Thule Inuit with whom the Norse had long shared the island. Exploration of other parts of the Atlantic virtually stopped at the time of the Black Death. In the half century preceding the onset of the plague, explorers from maritime communities in Western Europe had made considerable progress. Mapping of the African Atlantic had begun, with the Canary and Madeira Islands, and navigators had begun to investigate the pattern of the northeast trade winds. Jaume Ferrer's shipwreck was symbolic. Few similar voyages were recorded in the second half of the fourteenth century.

Human foes supplemented the plague, famine, and cold. In 1354, an earthquake demolished the walls of the Byzantine city of Gallipoli at the entrance to the Dardanelles, which divides Europe from Anatolia. Ottoman Turks were waiting to take over the ruins, inaugurating a history of European anxiety about the defensibility of the eastern Mediterranean frontier against the Muslims that would last, with fluctuations, for over 200 years. In the northeast, pagan Lithuanians eroded the conquests of the Teutonic Orders along the Baltic (see Chapter 13). To some extent, the gradual diffusion of Catholic faith, under Polish influence, into Lithuania made good these losses—for Christendom, if not for the Germans. Meanwhile, in the parts of Eastern Europe the plague spared, state-building continued, under rulers whose longevity helped bring stability. The period of the Black Death in Western Europe was spanned by the reigns of Charles the Great in Bohemia (r. 1333–1378), Casimir the Great in Poland (r. 1333–1370) and Louis the Great of Hungary (r. 1342–1382). On the whole, the effects of plague favored the state even in the West, because afflicted populations turned to monarchs as potential saviors and were willing to trust them with enhanced powers. Even peasant rebels tended to focus their resentments on the rest of the elite and appealed for aid directly—albeit, usually, unsuccessfully—to monarchs.

In the Mongol dominions, the case was different. Mongol expansion ceased. Russian principalities began to pry themselves free of Mongol control. The Mongol state in Persia fragmented, and the last Il-khan died in 1343. From the ruins of Mongol domination, a new state arose in Anatolia, ruled by a Turkish dynasty, known as the Ottomans, whose center of operations from 1326 was at the formerly Byzantine city of Bursa, in what is now western Turkey, from where they were able to profit from the dislocation the Black Death caused (see Map 14.9). They gradually came to dominate Byzantium, invaded the Balkans, and established a close trading relationship with the Italian city of Genoa. Toward the end of the fourteenth century, they began to construct a navy, to extend their power into the Mediterranean. In China, as we shall see in the next chapter, the strain of the ecological crisis of

CHRONOLOGY

1290	England expels Jews
Thirteenth and fourteenth centuries	Climate change in northern hemisphere
1309–1310	Thames River freezes (London)
1315–1316	Heavy rains reported all over northern Europe
1320s	Plague epidemics in southwestern and central China
1324	Mansa Musa makes *hajj* to Mecca
1325–1351	Reign of Ibn Tughluq (India)
1326	Ottoman Turks set up capital at Bursa (western Anatolia)
1330s	Mortality rates in northeast China reach 90 percent
1335	Ashikaga Tokauji seizes shogunate (Japan)
1343	Last Il-khan dies in Persia
1346	Plague reported in Crimea (Black Sea)
1347	Last Icelandic voyage to America
1347–1349	Plague rages throughout Europe, Middle East, and North Africa
1350s	Peasant rebellions spread throughout China
1351	Plague strikes southern Russia
1352	Ibn Battuta sets off for Mali
1360	Plague reported in China
1389	Death of Hayan Wuruk (Majapahit)
1400	Settlements in American Southwest abandoned

the mid–fourteenth century contributed to the dissolution of the Mongol state and its replacement by a new regime of native Chinese rulers, under the Ming dynasty.

At a deeper level than that of the rise and fall of states and political elites, the coming of the age of plagues, made worse by unpredictable changes in climate, affected the balance of population—and therefore of power—among Eurasian civilizations. Natural disasters usually do not affect population trends for long. Population can recover with surprising speed. Recovery was harder in the wake of the Black Death because, although plagues became less ferocious, and populations built up immunity, plagues affected the same regions for centuries to come, at a rate too rapid to enumerate—more than once on average every four years, for instance, in Egypt in the two centuries following the Black Death. The population of Eurasia probably remained static during the late fourteenth century and most of the fifteenth. In the long run, of the three culture areas that suffered most, it looks as if the Islamic world may have been more affected than Christendom or China, both of which seem to have recovered faster and resisted better. This can only be a tentative conclusion, because the evidence is unreliable. It does seem, however, that the population of Christendom and of China recovered to preplague levels by the end of the fifteenth century, while in Egypt, Syria and, perhaps, in other parts of the Islamic world, the recovery did not even begin until then. The increase of population thereafter was generally slower in the Islamic world than in Christendom and China until

MAP 14.9

The Ottoman State, ca. 1400

Ottoman state, ca. 1400

Byzantine Empire, ca. 1400

FIGURE 14.2 THE POPULATION OF EUROPE, CHINA, AND THE ISLAMIC WORLD COMPARED

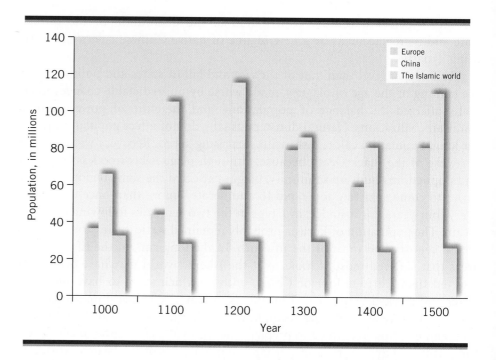

the twentieth century (see Figure 14.2). If correct, this conclusion may help to explain one of history's great shifts in wealth, power, and every kind of dynamism—away from the Islamic world. Whereas in what we call the Middle Ages, the Islamic world had contributed enormously—far more than Christendom—to cultural exchange in Eurasia, and had tended to win out in conflicts with Christendom, Muslim power dwindled over the succeeding centuries. The relative eclipse of the Islamic world and the relative ascent of Europe are major themes of the age of plague and, therefore, of the next two parts of this book.

PROBLEMS AND PARALLELS

1. How might Mongol rule have facilitated the spread of plague during the fourteenth century?

2. What were the long-term effects of the climate change and age of plagues that began during the fourteenth century?

3. What parts of the globe were most adversely affected by plague and climate change during the fourteenth century? Why were some areas of the world hit badly by these phenomena and others hardy at all?

4. Was there a relationship between climate change and plague, and if so, what was it?

5. Is it now possible to understand the medical causes of the fourteenth-century Black Death? Why or why not? Are the available historical sources reliable?

6. Who were the "winners" and "losers" in the plague years (other than the immediate survivors and victims)?

DOCUMENTS IN GLOBAL HISTORY

- Ibn Battuta, Selections from the *Rihla*
- Marchione di Coppo Stefani, from *The Florentine Chronicle*
- University of Paris Medical Faculty, *Report on the Plague*

- Hayan Wuruk, from the *Nagara Kertagama*
- Mansa Musa of Mali
- Ibn Battuta, from *The Travels of Ibn Battuta*

Please see the Primary Source CD-ROM for additional sources related to this chapter.

READ ON

H. Lamb, *Climate, History and the Modern World* (1995) is the classic work on its subject, complemented by B. Fagan's *The Little Ice Age* (2000). Classic works—now superseded on many points—on the global history of disease are H. Zinsser, *Rats, Lice, and History* (1996), and W. H. McNeill, *Plagues and Peoples* (1998). S. Cohn, *The Black Death* (2003) is indispensable for the plagues in Europe and for the epidemiology of the Black Death. N. Antor, *In the Wake of the Plague* (2001) has some interesting material on social effects. R. Horrox, *The Black Death* (1994) is a valuable anthology of source material. M. W. Dols, *The Black Death in the Middle East* (1977)—though corrected in some respects by Cohn's work—is invaluable on its subject. As so often, the edition by H. Gibb and C. Beckingham of *The Travels of Ibn Battuta* (1994) is an indispensable guide.

On China, the *Cambridge History of China* multiple volumes, is in preparation; meanwhile, vol. vi is of some help, and the collection of essays edited by P. J. Smith and R. von Glahn, *The Song-Yuan-Ming Transition in Chinese History* (2003) crackles with revisionism. For Europe, M. Jones, ed., *The New Cambridge Medieval History* vi, (2000) is a comprehensive survey. On the problems of the status of women, G. Duby and M. Perrot, eds., *A History of Women* (2000) is the leading work; particularly useful work on the subjects touched on in this chapter includes R. Smith, "Coping with Uncertainty: Women's Tenure of Customary Land in England," in J. Kermode, ed., *Enterprise and Individual in Fifteenth-Century England* (1997), and L. Mirrer, ed., *Upon My Husband's Death* (1992).

For Hohokam, the article by P. Crown, "The Hohokam of the American Southwest," *Journal of World History*, iv (1990) is a good introduction. G. J. Gumerman, ed., *Themes in Southwest Prehistory* (1994) contains some important contributions.

On the Jews, N. Cohn, *Europe's Inner Demons* (2001) is a controversial but gripping attempt to trace the origins of anti-Semitism. P. Johnson, *History of the Jews* (1988)—though superseded in its coverage of the early period—remains the best general history. L. Kochan, *The Jew and his History* (1985) is a good introduction.

On peasant millenarianism, N. Cohn, *The Pursuit of the Millennium* (1970) remains unsurpassed. On Japan, J. Mass, ed., *Origins of Japan's Medieval World* (1997) amounts to a fine history of the fourteenth century. The Delhi sultanate is covered in R. Majumdar, *The History and Culture of the Indian People*, iv (1951). On Java, T. Pigeaud, ed., *Java in the Fourteenth Century* (1960) is a marvelous edition of the poem I cite about Hayan Wuruk. D. G. Hall in N. Tarling, ed., *The Cambridge History of Southeast Asia*, i (1992). provides further help. On Mali, N. Levtzion, *Ancient Ghana and Mali* (1986) is highly accessible, and D. T. Niane covers the subject expertly in *UNESCO History of Africa*, iv (1998), but the classic work by E. W. R. Bovill, *The Golden Trade of the Moors* (1995), can still be read with pleasure. For the Pacific, J. van Tilburg, *Easter Island* (1995) is the only fully reliable work on that island. J. Belich, *Making Peoples* (2002) is insuperable on New Zealand. On Ozette, see R. Kirk and R. D. Dougherty, *Hunters of the Whale* (1998). On the Chimú, R. Keatinge, *Peruvian Prehistory* (1988) is standard.

CHAPTER 15

Expanding Worlds: Recovery in the Late Fourteenth and Fifteenth Centuries

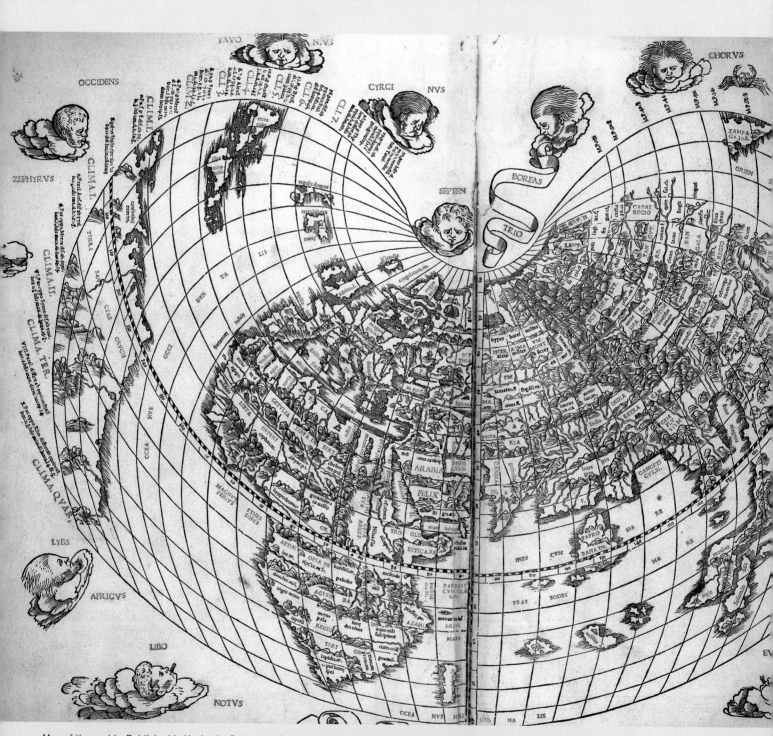

Map of the world. Published in Venice by Bernardus Sylvanus in 1511, this is the first map printed in two colors and represents the earliest period of European exploration of the New World. The islands of Cuba and Hispaniola are identified on the far left side, while Newfoundland is inaccurately shown just to the west of Ireland.

Abd-ar-Razzak (ahbd ar-rah-ZAK) was a landlubber. The stories he knew about navigation on the Indian Ocean presented the sea as God's arena, where luck changed with the wind and storms fell like divine arrows. Every story ended with a shipwreck. The thought of a voyage terrified Abd-ar-Razzak. But he had a journey to make that he could only make by sea. In 1417, he was appointed Persian ambassador to Vijayanagar (vee-jeh-yeh-NAH-gar), a powerful kingdom in southern India, and there were too many hostile kingdoms between it and Persia for him to cross by land. But his ship sailed late,

> so that the favorable time for departing by sea, that is to say the beginning or middle of the monsoon, was allowed to pass, and we came to the end of the monsoon, which is the season when tempests and attacks from pirates are to be dreaded. . . . As soon as I caught the smell of the vessel, and all the terrors of the sea presented themselves before me, I fell into so deep a faint that for three days breathing alone indicated that life remained within me. When I came a little to myself, the merchants, who were my intimate friends, cried with one voice that the time for navigation was past, and that everyone who put to sea at this season was alone responsible for his death.

Abd-ar-Razzak's predicament, however, had a positive side. The late monsoon is so fierce that ships speed before it. He made the journey in only 19 days, only about two-thirds of the time one might normally expect.

● ● ● ● ●

Abd-ar-Razzak's voyage demonstrates the crucial importance of winds in world history. Most of the planet's surface area is sea. Long-range communications have to traverse wide waters. Throughout the age of sail—that is, throughout almost the entire history of travel—winds and currents set the limits of what was possible: the routes, the rates, the mutually accessible cultures. More particularly, Abd-ar-Razzak's experience illustrates the paradox of Indian Ocean navigation in his day. The monsoon winds made travel speedy, but the Indian Ocean was stormy, unsafe, and hard to get into and out of. Access from the east was barely possible in summer, when typhoons tore into the shores. Fierce storms guarded the southern approaches. No one who knew the reputation of

FOCUS questions

- **WHY WERE** some African empires able to expand on such an impressive scale during this period?
- **WHAT ROLE** did geographic diversity play in the Inca and Aztec Empires?
- **WHAT STRONG** new empires arose on the Eurasian borderlands?
- **WHY DID** China turn away from overseas expansion in the fifteenth century?
- **WHY DID** Europe begin to reach out and cross the oceans in the late 1400s?

these waters cared to venture between about 10 and 30 degrees south and 60 or 90 degrees east during the hurricane season. Arab legends claimed the region was impassable. Many European maps of the fifteenth century depicted the Indian Ocean as landlocked—literally inaccessible by sea. Yet it was the biggest and richest zone of long-range commerce in the world.

By the end of the fifteenth century, European navigators had found a way to penetrate it. Meanwhile, the Atlantic was developing into a rival zone, with transoceanic routes ready to be exploited. Indeed, seafaring on the Atlantic would transform the world by bringing cultures that had been torn apart into contact, conflict, commerce, and cultural and ecological exchange. The divergent, isolated worlds of ancient and medieval times were coming together to form the interconnected world we inhabit today.

How did it happen? How did the world rebound from the plagues and climate changes of the fourteenth century? For one thing, populations gradually acquired immunity against plague, as susceptible people died and those who were naturally most resistant passed on their genes. As for worsening climates, survivors relocated or just got used to colder, wetter conditions. To some extent, technological advance made up for—indeed, was a response to—decreased population. As we have seen, across Eurasia, and in parts of Africa that were in contact with Eurasia, the long period of accelerated exchange in the Song and Mongol eras had equipped expanding economies with improved technology (see Chapter 13). In regions that escaped the catastrophes of the

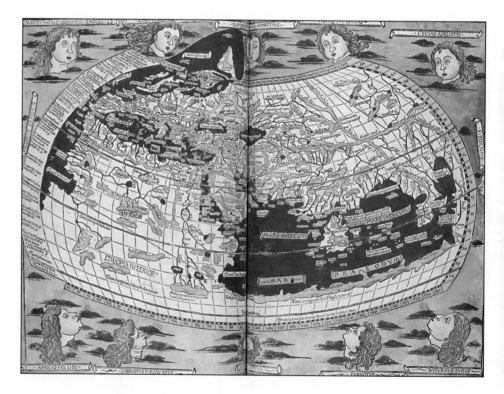

Claudius Ptolemy's *Geography*, written in Alexandria, Egypt in the second century, was still the standard source for how educated Europeans saw the world in the fifteenth century. Printed editions, like this one of 1482, usually included attempts to map the world as Ptolemy described it. Common features include a grid of lines of latitude and longitude—the system Ptolemy devised for locating places in relation to one another; the exaggerated size and prominence of Sri Lanka; locating the source of the Nile in mountains beyond large lakes deep in Africa; and showing the Indian Ocean as landlocked, which undermined navigators' confidence that they could reach India and Asia by sea.

fourteenth century, long-term population growth continued to strengthen states and economies. So it is not surprising that the world of the late fourteenth and fifteenth centuries was a world in recovery and even a world of resumed expansion.

Toward the end of the period, from about 1460 on, in states in widely separated parts of the world, expansion speeded up like springs uncoiling. An age of expansion really did begin, but the phenomenon was of an expanding world, not, as some historians say, of European expansion. The world did not wait passively for European outreach to transform it, as if touched by a magic wand. Other societies were already working magic of their own, turning states into empires and cultures into civilizations. Beyond the reach of the recurring plagues that stopped demographic growth in much of Eurasia, some of the most dynamic and rapidly expanding societies of the fifteenth century were in the Americas and sub-Saharan Africa. Indeed, in terms of territorial expansion and military effectiveness against opponents, some African and American empires outclassed any state in Western Europe until the sixteenth century.

From the *Narrative of the Journey of Abd-ar-Razzak*

As we shall see, some European communities played big and growing roles. And their expansion did have unique features—exceptional range, above all, which enabled people from parts of Western Europe to cross unprecedented distances on previously unexplored routes. But to appreciate what was special about Europe, we have to see it in global context and acknowledge that expansion was a worldwide phenomenon. If we start in Africa and approach Europe only after looking at the Americas and following Abd-ar-Razzak's route in Asia, we can begin to make sense of the peculiar features of the history of Atlantic-side European peoples who launched empires that will take up more and more space in the rest of the book.

FRAGILE EMPIRES IN AFRICA

East Africa

Ethiopia emerged relatively early from its period of quiescence following the rise and stagnation of the Solomid dynasty in the thirteenth century (see Chapter 10). In the late fourteenth century, the highland realm again began to reach beyond its mountains to dominate surrounding regions. Monasteries became schools of missionaries whose task was to consolidate Ethiopian power in the conquered pagan lands of Shoa and Gojam. Rulers, meanwhile, concentrated on reopening their ancient outlet to the Red Sea and thereby the Indian Ocean. This they accomplished by conquering the hostile lowlanders and recapturing the port of Massaweh in 1403. By then, Ethiopian rule stretched into the Great Rift valley. Trade northward along the valley was in slaves, ivory, gold, and civet*, and Ethiopia largely controlled it. The resulting wealth funded defense of the empire and fueled expansionist ambitions. European visitors multiplied, as Ethiopia's Massaweh road became a standard route to reach the Indian Ocean.

Although Ethiopia conquered no more territory after 1469, a major source for Ethiopian history in this period, saints' lives, tells of internal expansion. Wasteland was converted to farmland and settled by monks. In 1481, the Ethiopian church resumed contact with Rome, where the pope provided a church to house visiting

---

*Civet: Small cat whose scent glands are used in the manufacture of perfumes

The Reemergence of Ethiopia

Late fourteenth century	Ethiopia expands into surrounding regions
1403	Recapture of port of Massaweh
1469	End of period of conquest
1481	Ethiopian church resumes contact with Rome
1490s	First Portuguese diplomatic missions arrive in Ethiopia

Ethiopian monks. When Portuguese diplomatic missions began to arrive in Ethiopia—the first in the 1490s, a second in 1520—"men and gold and provisions like the sands of the sea and the stars in the sky" impressed them. As we shall see in the next chapter, however, they overestimated the empire's stability. Ethiopia had probably already overreached its resources.

Southward from Ethiopia, at the far end of the Rift valley, lay the gold-rich Zambezi valley and the productive plateau beyond, which stretched to the south as far as the Limpopo River, and was rich in salt, gold, and elephants. Like Ethiopia, these areas looked toward the Indian Ocean for long-range trade with the economies of maritime Asia.

Unlike Ethiopia, communities in the Zambezi valley had ready access to the ocean, but they faced a potentially more difficult problem. Their outlets to the sea lay below the reach of the monsoon system and, therefore, beyond the reach of the normal routes of trade. Still, adventurous merchants—most of them, probably, from southern Arabia—risked the voyage to bring manufactured goods from Asia in trade for gold and ivory. Some of the most vivid evidence comes from the mosque in Kilwa (Kil-WAH), in modern Tanzania, where fifteenth-century Chinese porcelain bowls line the inside of the dome.

Further evidence of the effects of trade lie inland between the Zambezi and the Limpopo Rivers, where fortified, stone-built administrative centers—called **zimbabwes**—had been common for centuries. Now, in the late fourteenth and fifteenth centuries, the zimbabwes entered their greatest age. The most famous, Great Zimbabwe, included a formidable citadel on a hill 350 feet high, but remains of other citadels are scattered over the land (see Map 15.1). Near stone buildings, the beef-fed elite were buried with gifts: gold, jewelery, jeweled ironwork, large copper

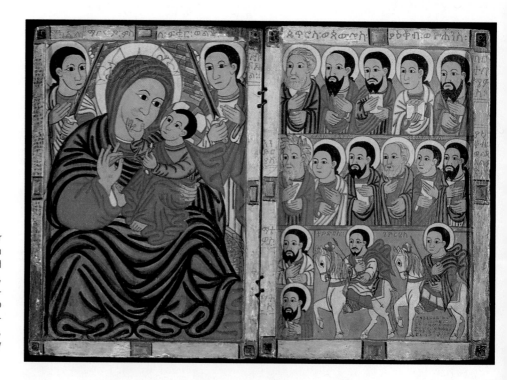

Virgin and Child. In the dynamic reign of Emperor Zara Yacob (1434–1468), Ethiopia conquered an outlet to the sea, extended and fortified its land frontier, pacified and Christianized pagan peoples, and made contact with Europe. But the enforcement of religious orthodoxy was perhaps closest to the emperor's heart. He commissioned many paintings of the Virgin and Child, often shown guarded, as here, by armed angels and worshipped by warrior saints.

The turreted walls of Great Zimbabwe surround a 350-foot high hill, crowned by a formidable citadel, which housed the elite, who ate beef and were buried with gifts of gold, copper, jewels, and Chinese porcelain. Though it was the biggest of the stone-built settlements of the period, Great Zimbabwe was typical, in style and substance, of other buildings in the region south of the Zambezi River during what we think of as the late Middle Ages.

ingots, and Chinese porcelain that Arab traders brought across the Indian Ocean to Kilwa and Sofala, another great coastal city.

In the second quarter of the fifteenth century, the center of power shifted northward to the Zambezi valley, with the expansion of a new regional power. Mwene Mutapa (MWEH-nee MOO-TAH-pah), as it was called, arose during the northward migration of bands of warriors from what are now parts of Mozambique and KwaZulu-Natal. When one of their leaders conquered the middle Zambezi valley—a land rich in cloth, salt, and elephants—he took the title Mwene Mutapa, or "lord of the tribute payers," a name that became extended to the state. From about the mid–fifteenth century, the pattern of trade routes altered as Mwene Mutapa's conquests spread eastward toward the coast. But Mwene Mutapa never reached the ocean. Native merchants, who traded at inland fairs, had no interest in a direct outlet to the sea. They did well enough using middlemen on the coast and had no incentive for or experience of ocean trade. Like Mali (see Chapter 14), Mwene Mutapa was a landlocked empire, sustained by trade in gold and salt. The colonists were drawn, not driven, northward, though a decline in the navigability of the Sabi River may have stimulated the move.

West Africa

New states emerged in West Africa, too, but here the opportunities were the result, at least in part, of the decline of the old regional power, Mali. Like many empires of promise in out-of-the-way places, Mali became a victim of its relative isolation.

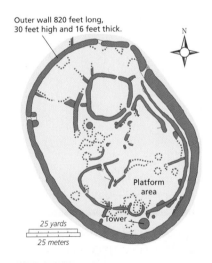

Outer wall 820 feet long, 30 feet high and 16 feet thick.

Platform area

Tower

25 yards
25 meters

MAP 15.1

Great Zimbabwe

■ stone construction

····· walls in ruin

— drain

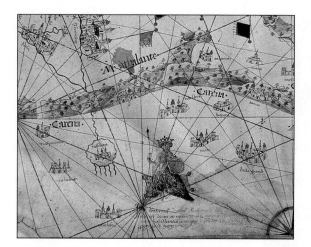

A European view of the King of Mali, ca. 1480. By the 1430s, familiarity with the West African kingdom of Mali had caused disillusionment among European visitors, who expected magnificence of the sort depicted in the previous century in the Catalan Atlas (see Chapter 14). But Mali had declined, and its ruler appeared in this map by Gabriel Vallseca of Majorca, and others of the time, as a poorly dressed and even laughable figure.

From about 1360, a power struggle pitted the descendants of Mansa Musa against those of his brother, Mansa Sulayman. At about the end of the century, the Songhay, a people from lower down the Niger River, broke away and Mali lost Gao (gow). This was disastrous for Mali, because Gao was one of the great trading cities between the rain forest and the desert. Traders could now outflank Mali's trading monopoly. Mali was further weakened in the 1430s when invaders from the Sahara seized its northernmost towns.

Two decades later, in the 1450s, when Portuguese expeditions, pushing up the river Gambia, made the first recorded European contact with Mali, the Mansa's power was virtually confined to the original heartland. The result was a tragedy for the history of the world, for the absence of a strong African state undermined Europeans view of black Africans as equals. The Portuguese expected to find a great, rich empire. Instead, they found Mali a ramshackle wreck. Their disappointment prejudiced them, and they wondered if black Africans had any capacity for political greatness. Thus, in maps, instead of the magnificent depictions of the Mansa of Mali typical of the fourteenth century—bearded and costumed in European fashion—the ruler of Mali became a figure of fun. Though some Europeans continued to treat black Africans as equals—and the Portuguese crown, in particular, maintained the affectation that black kings were fellow monarchs on a par with those of Europe—from now on, white people in Africa could nourish convictions of superiority. Although, as we shall see, other African realms or regions replaced Mali in European esteem and became famous for wealth or as places of opportunity for European adventurers, their elites never again commanded the same prestige in Europe.

Songhay (SOHNG-eye) gradually succeeded Mali as the most powerful state in the region, but it never controlled as much of the Saharan trade as Mali had. At first, isolated areas were converted to Islam, but Muhammad Touray Askia, an upstart general who used Islam to justify seizing the throne, wrenched Songhay into the Islamic mainstream in the late fifteenth century. In 1497, he undertook a pilgrimage to Mecca on a scale of magnificence calculated to echo that of Mansa Musa in 1324–1325 (see Chapter 14). Askia's ascent to power represented the triumph of Islam over the pagan magic that some of his predecessors and opponents claimed to wield. His victory also ensured that Sahelian Africa—the band of dry grasslands south of the Sahara—would be predominantly Muslim. His alliance with the Muslim intelligentsia made Songhay a state "favored by God" in the eyes of religious Muslims—the class on which the state depended for administrators. He stimulated trade by imposing peace and so increasing Saharan merchants' sense of security. He promoted a modest sort of capitalism by concentrating resources in the hands of religious foundations, which had the personnel and range of contacts to maximize their holdings' potential. New canals, wells, dikes, and reservoirs scored the land. Cultivated terrain was extended, especially for rice, which had long been known in the region but never previously farmed on a large scale.

Songhay, like Mali before it, benefited from the trade routes of the Sahara, which linked the Mediterranean coast to the Niger valley. The river Niger is navigable for almost its entire length, providing access to rich goldfields and the best national commu-

The Portuguese in West Africa and the Congo

1450s	First reported Portuguese contact with Mali
1480s	Portuguese make contact with kingdom of Kongo
1482	West African trading post of São Jorge da Mina established
1486	Senegambian chief baptized in Lisbon

nications system in Africa. At the same time, the Atlantic's adverse winds and currents limited opportunities for long-range communications by sea. The states and cultures of the tropical forest and coast in the African "bulge" were therefore limited to contending for strictly regional power and wealth. Nevertheless, they have left plenty of evidence of economic expansion and of the growing wealth and power of their kings in the fifteenth century. There are, for instance, the fortifications of the city-state of Benin and the splendid metal weapons, adornments and courtly furnishings of Benin and the Ife.

The whole African coast from Senegambia to the mouth of the Niger impressed Europeans at the time. In 1486, the Portuguese crown celebrated the baptism of a Senegambian chief in Lisbon with a lavish display. The trading post that Portugal opened at São Jorge da Mina, on the underside of the African bulge, in 1482, appeared on maps as a fantasy city. It suited the purposes of the Portuguese monarchs to exaggerate the grandeur, but their propaganda reflected the reality of a region of rich kingdoms, busy commerce, and patches of urban life.

Farther south, too, in the Congo basin, the opportunities for states to reach out by sea were limited. The Kingdom of Kongo dominated the Congo River's navigable lower reaches, probably from the mid–fourteenth century. The ambitions of its rulers became evident when Portuguese explorers established contact in the 1480s. Kongo enthusiastically adopted the religion and technology of the visitors. The kingdom became host to Portuguese missionaries, craftsmen, and mercenaries. The royal residence was rebuilt in Portuguese style. The kings issued documents in Portuguese, and members of the royal family went to Portugal for their education. One prince became an archbishop, and the kings continued to have Portuguese baptismal names for centuries thereafter. In emulating Portugal, the kings of Kongo were, of course, serving their own self-interest. Equipping their armies with European firepower, for example, gave the kings a military advantage over their neighbors. They gained territory and, more importantly, slaves, many of whom they sold to the Portuguese for export.

Although Ethiopia, Mwene Mutapa, Songhay, and Kongo were all formidable regional powers, and although many small states of the West African coast expanded commercially and territorially, little of this activity was on an unprecedented scale (see Map 15.2). Ethiopia's resumed rise was part of a sequence of rise and decline that had been going on for centuries. Songhay was the latest in a series of empires in the Sahel. Trading states had long studded the underside of the West African bulge. Mwene Mutapa was the successor state of the builders

Portuguese soldier. The court art of Benin, in the Niger Delta of West Africa, preserves precious images of Portuguese visitors, as native artists saw them in the sixteenth century. The Obas, as the rulers of Benin were called, frequently asked for Portuguese military help—sometimes offering to adopt Christianity in exchange—and this Portuguese soldier, carved in ivory, is supporting the Oba's saltcellar. Salt was a precious commodity in Benin. The soldier's short spear, feathered straw hat, and sweatband are local touches, but the rest of his clothes, his beard, his sword, and his pectoral cross were exotic emblems to the African artist who carved them.

African, Nigeria, Edo peoples, court of Benin, Saltcellar: Portuguese Figure, 15th-16th century, Ivory; H. 7–1/8 in. (18.1 cm). The Metropolitan Museum of Art, Louis V. Bell and Rogers Funds, 1972. (1972.63ab) Photograph by Stan Reis. Photograph © 1984

Equator

Tropic of Cancer

Tropic of Capricorn

EUROPE

Rome
Lisbon
Granada
Tangier · *Strait of Gibraltar* · Tunis
Fez
Marrakesh
Tripoli

Mediterranean Sea

Damascus
Alexandria · Jerusalem
Cairo

ASIA

Hormuz
Bahrain

Persian Gulf

Arabia

Arabian Sea

India

Calicut

Azores
Madeira
Canary Islands

Cape Bojador
Cape Blanc

Sahara

Taghaza

Red Sea
Nile

Jedda
Mecca

Dhofar

Walata
Senegal
Cape Verde
Timbuktu · Gao

Sahel

Massaweh
Axum · Sana
Lake Tana · Aden
GOJAM
SHOA

Cape Verde Islands

Gambia
Niger
Kano

Bissagos Island
Niani

Ife
Elmina · Benin
São Jorge de Mina

AFRICA

Mogadishu

Cape Palmas
Gulf of Guinea
Príncipe
São Tomé
Cape St. Catherine

Lake Victoria

Malindi
Mombasa

INDIAN OCEAN

ATLANTIC OCEAN

Congo

Ascension Island

Cape St. Mary (Cape Lobo)

Lake Tanganyika

Dar es Salaam
Kilwa
Cape Delgado

St. Helena

Lake Nyasa

Zambezi
Mozambique

Cape Cross
Walvis Bay

Great Zimbabwe

Limpopo
Sabi
Sofala
Cape Correntes

Madagascar

Cape da Volta (Dias Point)
Orange

KWAZULU NATAL

St. Helena Bay

Cape of Good Hope
Mossel Bay
Algoa Bay

N

1,000 km
1,000 miles

MAP 15.2

Major African States, 1400–1500

▨	Ethiopia	– – –	other African states
▨	Mwene Mutapa	➤	Indian Ocean trade route
▨	Zimbabwes	→	Trans-saharan trade route
▨	Mali	▨	extent of Portuguese exploration of West African coast up to 1487
▨	Songhay	✚	Portuguese markers erected in token of their claim to sovereignty
▨	Benin / Ife		
▨	Kongo	MOZAMBIQUE	modern country or state

of the zimbabwes. If there was something new out of the Africa at this time, it was part of a wider phenomenon. The empires grew at impressive rates and to impressive extents because they were in touch with other phenomena of commercial and political expansion: Songhay across the Sahara, Ethiopia and Mwene Mutapa across the Indian Ocean, the coastal trading cities and Kongo with Portuguese visitors. In the Americas, however, in the late fifteenth century, even states that had to contend with isolation could expand on a new scale.

ECOLOGICAL IMPERIALISM IN THE AMERICAS

Since the inventive historian, Alfred Crosby, coined the term **ecological imperialism** in 1972, historians have used it to refer to the sweeping environmental changes European imperialists introduced in regions they colonized. The term also suits Native American empires, especially in mountainous regions of Mesoamerica and the Andes, where, as we have seen, the key to success in large-scale state-building lay in combining diverse regions and exploiting the complementary products of contrasting ecosystems.

The Inca Empire

In the late fifteenth century, the world's fastest-growing empire was the Inca Empire of Peru. Inca chronology is always uncertain because until the 1530s, the Incas made records in forms that are now indecipherable. Nonetheless, evidence suggests that they built their empire within a concentrated period—all during the reigns of three rulers in the late fifteenth and early sixteenth centuries.

Probably early in the second half of the fifteenth century, the founders of the Inca state descended from the highlands to find fertile land. They occupied Cuzco in what is today Peru, which became their biggest city, and began subjugating their neighbors. Their story was typically Andean. They gathered many diverse environments into one state to facilitate exchanging and stockpiling a wide range of products. It was the story of Chavín de Huántar in 1000 B.C.E. (see Chapter 4). The Incas, however, took this well-established practice to new lengths. Theirs was one of the most environmentally diverse empires of the time. It was long and thin, with the Andes forming its spine and creating valleys and microclimates. Abrupt mountains multiplied microclimates, where sun, wind, and rain hit different slopes in different ways (see Figure 15.1). The Inca realm encompassed coastal lowlands and the fringes of the Amazonian rain forest. The tribute system was based on the

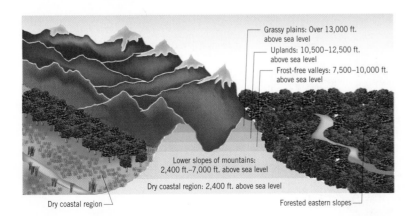

Grassy plains: Over 13,000 ft. above sea level

Uplands: 10,500–12,500 ft. above sea level

Frost-free valleys: 7,500–10,000 ft. above sea level

Lower slopes of mountains: 2,400 ft.–7,000 ft. above sea level

Dry coastal region: 2,400 ft. above sea level

Dry coastal region

Forested eastern slopes

FIGURE 15.1 MICROCLIMATES OF THE ANDES. The Andean environment packs tremendous ecological diversity into a small space, with various climatic zones at different altitudes, contrasting microclimates in the valleys, and tropical forest and the ocean close at hand.

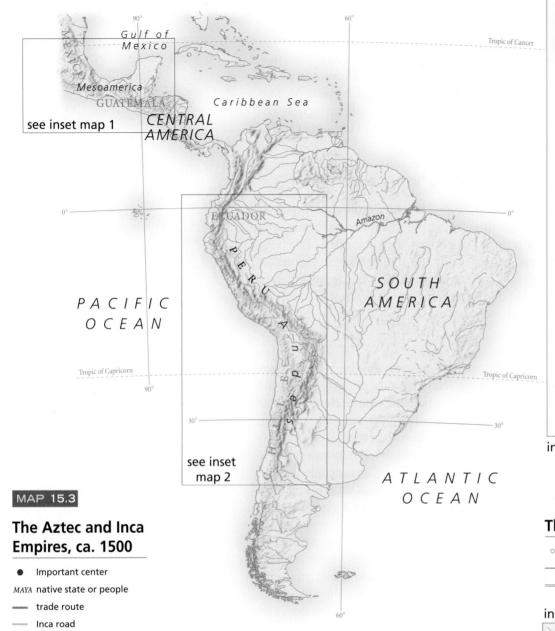

Gulf of
Mexico

Mesoamerica

GUATEMALA

Caribbean Sea

CENTRAL
AMERICA

Tropic of Cancer

see inset map 1

ECUADOR

Amazon

PERU

SOUTH
AMERICA

PACIFIC
OCEAN

Andes

0°

Tropic of Capricorn

90°

30°

see inset
map 2

ATLANTIC
OCEAN

60°

MAP 15.3

The Aztec and Inca Empires, ca. 1500

- ● Important center
- *MAYA* native state or people
- ▦▦▦ trade route
- ─── Inca road

inset map 1

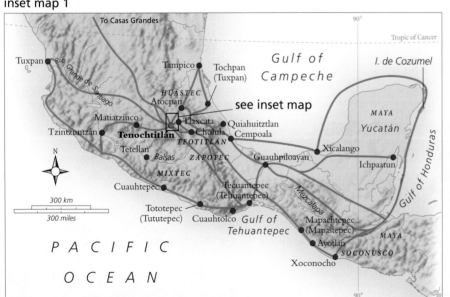

To Casas Grandes

Tropic of Cancer

Tuxpan
Rio Grande de Santiago

Tampico
Tochpan (Tuxpan)

HUASTEC
Atocpan

see inset map

Gulf of
Campeche

I. de Cozumel

MAYA
Yucatán

Matiatzinco
Tlaxcala
Cholula
Quiahuitztlan
Cempoala

Tzintzuntzán
Tenochtitlán
TEOTITLÁN

Tetellan
ZAPOTEC
Guauhpiloayan
Xicalango

Balsas
Ichpaatun

MIXTEC
Cuauhtepec

Tecuantepec (Tehuantepec)

N
Mexcalapa

Tototepec (Tututepec)
Cuauhtolco
Gulf of Tehuantepec
Mapachtepec (Mapastepec)

300 km
Ayotlan
SOCONUSCO

300 miles
Xoconocho

MAYA

PACIFIC

OCEAN

inset map 2

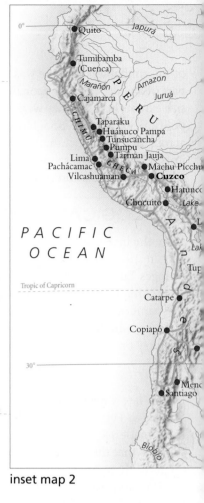

Quito
Japurá

Tumibamba (Cuenca)

Marañón
Amazon
Juruá

P
E
R
U

Cajamarca

CHIMÚ

Taparaku
Huánuco Pampa
Tunsucancha
Pumpu
Tarman Jauja

Lima
Pachácamac
CHECA
Machu Picchu
Vilcashuaman
Cuzco

Hatunco

Chucuito
Lake

PACIFIC
OCEAN

Andes

Tup

Tropic of Capricorn

Lak

Catarpe

Copiapó

30°

Meno

Santiago

Bíobío

inset map 2

The Valley of Mexico

- ○ Aztec town or city
- ─── aqueduct
- ═══ causeway
- ─── dike
- ▦ marshlan

inset map of Tenochtitlán

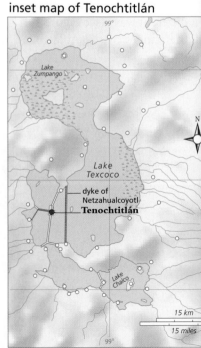

Lake
Zumpango

Lake
Texcoco

N

dyke of
Netzahualcoyotl
Tenochtitlán

Lake
Chalco

15 km

15 miles

exchange of products between contrasting zones, as a form of insurance against disaster. When the maize of the lowlands failed, for instance, potatoes from the highlands might still be abundant. The Inca uprooted populations and transferred them to new locations according to the needs of the system.

Economic security, however, came at a political price. To maintain the state, the Incas had to acquire new territories, leading to hectic and, in the long run, perhaps, unsustainable expansion. Moreover, their methods of subjugation were extreme. For example, they extinguished the coastal civilization of Chimú (see Chapter 14), razing its capital at Chan Chan almost to the ground and deporting its entire population. An Inca ruler was said to have drowned 20,000 enemy warriors when he conquered the Cañaris (kan-YAR-ees). The survivors became irreconcilable opponents. Many subject-peoples harbored grievances arising from memories of massacred warriors and forced migrations. Even the Incas' allies and elites were dissatisfied. The Checa, for instance, a people important to the Inca system of control, because their homeland straddled the route from Cuzco to the coast, never forgave the Inca for breaking his promise to perform ritual dances at their principal shrine in acknowledgment of their alliance. The Inca never seemed to have enough rewards to go around. The cults of dead leaders—who lay, mummified, in expensive shrines maintained by huge payrolls—existed to appease key Inca clans and factions, whose resources they boosted at the state's expense because tribute had to be diverted to meet the costs. Toward the end of the fifteenth century, the Inca Empire approached its greatest extent, from Quito (KEE-toh) in what is today Ecuador in the north to the river Bío-Bío in what is today Chile in the south—over 1,000 miles. But at its core, the empire was shaky.

The Aztec Empire

In the same period, rapid expansion and environmental diversity characterized Mesoamerica. Here, an exceptionally dynamic state grew from the city of Tenochtitlán (teh-noch-teet-LAHN) in the valley of Mexico (and some neighboring, allied cities). Tenochtitlán stood in the middle of a lake, some 5,000 feet above sea level. It could not grow some of the staples of Mesoamerican life or any of the luxuries elites demanded for social or ritual purposes. The ground was swampy, and there was too little cultivable soil to grow enough maize and beans to feed the city. Tenochtitlán was too high and the climate too severe for cacao (kah-KOW) and cotton. Its people, whom we have traditionally called Aztecs, had only two options: poverty or warfare. They chose the latter.

Aztec expansion, like Inca expansion, was largely a late fifteenth- and early sixteenth-century phenomenon (see Map 15.3). At its peak, the Aztec Empire stretched from the Pánuco River in the north to what is now the Mexican-Guatemalan border on the Pacific coast, covering nearly 100,000 square miles. It encompassed hundreds of tributary communities, meticulously listed in the few documents to have survived from Aztec archives or that European colonizers copied in the early colonial era.

The tribute collected demonstrated the power and reach and the ecological diversity of the regions from which the Aztecs extorted tribute. The Aztec

The Inca city of Machu Picchu in Peru is a miracle of urban engineering. It was built on a sharp 2,000-foot rise in the high Andes. Unrecorded in colonial times it was discovered early in the twentieth century when the eccentric and adventurous American archaeologist, Hiram Bingham, was searching for another lost Inca city, Vilcamba. Unknown to Bingham, however, Vilcamba was in the tropical lowlands of Peru. The vast difference in climate between the two cities is stunning evidence of the environmental diversity of the Inca world.

 The founding of Tenochtitlán

THE CODEX MENDOZA

Early colonial Spanish administrators were careful to copy tribute records from the archives of the preconquest Aztec state. The records show both the complexity of the tributary networks that linked the Aztec world and the amazing environmental diversity of the regions from which tribute flowed. This folio, from the Codex Mendoza, shows the tribute due to Tenochtitlán—the Aztec capital in central Mexico—from the "hot country" near what is now the Mexican-Guatemalan border.

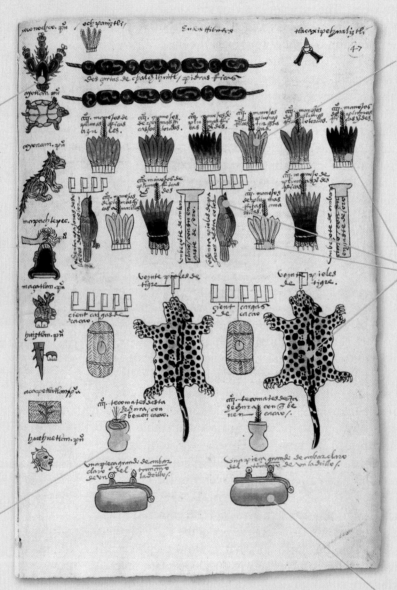

The glyph signifies 20; so 80 specimens of each kind of bird skin were one form of tribute.

The list names the communities that owed the depicted tribute. The town of Xoconochco on the Pacific coast is signified by a prickly pear ("*nochtli*" in Nahuatl, the Aztec language). It was an important center for trade with the Maya world to the south and was the most remote outpost the Aztecs garrisoned.

Rich ornamental feathers and bird skins for ceremonial headdresses and jaguar pelts to make divine disguises for Aztec warriors, priests, and ball game players.

Chocolate to make the ceremonial beverage that all the Mesoamerican elites drank.

Jade beads, amber, and gold.

How does this document reveal the environmental diversity of the Aztec empire?

bureaucracy meticulously listed and depicted it. From the "hot countries" in the south came ornamental feathers and jaguar pelts, jade, amber, and gold, rubber for ritual ball games, and resin for incense. Overlapping regions supplied cacao, the essential ingredient of the addictive, high-status drink essential at Aztec ceremonies and parties. Ornamental shells arrived from the Gulf Coast and live eagles, deerskins, and tobacco from the mountain lands that fringed the valley of Mexico. For war and for the ball game, which was a form of mock warfare and an aristocratic exercise, Aztec nobles and priests dressed as gods, So on almost every folio of the tribute roll appear magnificent ritual garments and divine disguises. The tribute system brought necessities as well as luxuries: hundreds of thousands of bushels of maize and beans every year, with hundreds of thousands of cotton garments and quilted cotton suits of armor. Finally, there was the product that best expressed Aztec power and—perhaps in Aztec minds—supplied the blood that fueled the universe: human-sacrifice victims, captured in war or tendered in tribute. In 1487, for instance, at the dedication of a temple in Tenochtitlán, thousands of captives were said to have been slaughtered at once.

The Aztec system was complex, in the sense that tributary networks linked hundreds of communities. Some communities exchanged tribute, often collecting it from some tributaries in order to pass part of it on to others. Tenochtitlán was at the summit of the system, but it left most communities to their own devices as long as they paid tribute. This was contrary to the highly interventionist politics of the Incas. According to records copied in the sixteenth century, Tenochtitlán only garrisoned or directly ruled 22 communities. The Aztecs did, however, share some of the same problems that afflicted the Incas. They relied on fragile alliances, bore the resentment of tributary peoples, and expanded so rapidly that their reach always threatened to outrun available manpower and technology.

The Aztecs and Incas saw themselves as continuing the traditions of earlier empires. They recalled ruined supremacies of the past: Tula and Teotihuacán in the Aztec case, Tiahuanaco in that of the Incas. The reach of their power seems, however, to have exceeded anything either region had witnessed before. So how did they do it? Long-range exchanges with other cultures helped to propel empires in Eurasia and Africa into expansion, but these advantages did not apply in the Americas. Indeed, the Andean and Mesoamerican worlds were so isolated that they do not even seem to have been in touch with each other. They did not benefit from new technology. Nor, as far as we know, were people in either region bouncing back from anything resembling the demographic catastrophe of parts of the Old World in the previous century. There was no momentum of recovery behind the enormous extensions of Aztec and Inca power. The most likely explanation is that demographic growth crossed a critical threshold in both areas. Probably, only imperial solutions could command the resources and compel the exchanges of goods needed to sustain the growing cities in which the Aztecs and Incas lived. In any case, both empires, as we shall see in the next chapter, were short lived. Essentially they were empires of types traditional in the region and overreached the realistic limits of their potential.

Incas and Aztecs

ca. 1325	Aztecs found city of Tenochtitlán
ca. Mid–fifteenth century	Inca begin period of conquest and expansion
ca. Late–fifteenth century	Inca Empire approaches greatest extent
ca. Early sixteenth century	Aztec Empire reaches its peak

⊙ MAKING CONNECTIONS ⊙

EXPANSION AND ITS LIMITS: AFRICA AND THE AMERICAS IN THE FIFTEENTH CENTURY

REGION/STATE OR EMPIRE →	CAUSES FOR EXPANSION →	EVIDENCE/EFFECTS OF EXPANSION →	LIMITATIONS
East Africa / Ethiopia	Access to long-range trading routes to Indian Ocean via Red Sea ports	Recapture of coastal cities in 1400s, increased trade in slaves, ivory, gold, incense; creation of main access road to Indian Ocean	Limited agricultural land; need to control mountainous and lowland areas to access trade routes; major river systems to south and east with large populations; gradually encroaching Portuguese and Muslim influence by sixteenth century
East/Central Africa / Zambezi River valley, Great Zimbabwe	Difficult access to Indian Ocean seaports; large populations with ivory, gold, metal resources	Manufactured goods from Asia (porcelain, silk, etc.) traded for gold, ivory; increasingly large administrative centers in stone, large amounts of coins, jewelry, gold, etc.	Landlocked; altered trade routes; decline in navigability of rivers
West Africa / Songhay Empire	Trade routes of the Sahara, linking Mediterranean and Niger valley; astute leadership (Muhammad Askia) and alliance with Muslim clerics, scholars	Canals, dikes, reservoirs; extension of cultivable land; rich trade with Niger valley goldfields	Limited long-range communication; adverse Atlantic winds/currents
Central Africa / Kongo	Domination of Congo River; alliance with Portuguese; abundant natural resources	Use of Western firearms, Christian religion and symbols to legitimate and maintain control; trading of slaves from conquered territories to Portuguese	Ultimate loss of control over slave trade to Portuguese leads to decline and fall
South America / Inca	Diversity of environments, resources; tribute system allows exchange of products between zones	Quick expansion and use of extreme methods of control; extensive road system; large shrines for dead leaders	Mass executions and other methods of subjugation alienate subject peoples and allies
Mesoamerica / Aztecs	Environmental diversity; hundreds of tributary communities; efficient recordkeeping; large array of natural resources	Intensive transformation of environment in/around capital (Tenochtitlán); abundance of commodities, both necessities (food, tools) and luxuries; widespread human sacrifice; monumental architecture	Loose administrative control; fragile alliances; alienation of tributary peoples; excessively rapid expansion

NEW EURASIAN EMPIRES

The expanding states of fifteenth-century Africa and the Americas were conspicuous in their day. However, they proved relatively fragile. Sixteenth-century European conquerors swallowed the Aztec and Inca states almost at a gulp. Ethiopia barely endured in the sixteenth century, eroded by Muslim invaders and waves of pagan, pastoralist immigrants. Songhay fell to invaders from Morocco in the late sixteenth century. Finally, though Mwene Mutapa survived into the seventeenth century, having fought off would-be conquerors from Europe, it then dissolved gradually and ingloriously into numerous petty states. It was the borderlands that straddle Europe and Asia that nurtured the really big, really enduring new or resumed empires of the age, those of Turks and Russians.

The Russian Empire

The rise of a powerful Russian state was without precedent. Previously, the geography of the region produced volatile and therefore, usually, short-lived empires. Its open, flat expanses of land and widely scattered populations contributed to an environment in which states could form with ease but only survive with difficulty. Most came and went quickly, vulnerable to external attack and internal rebellion.

In the fifteenth century, however, the rulers of Moscow established a state of imperial dimensions. Muscovy—as the early Russian Empire was called—has always been volatile at the edges, but it has been exceptionally enduring. One of the features that made Muscovy different was the shape of its heartland. It was based on control of the Volga River, a north–south axis of trade. Earlier empires, including the Mongol, were based on the east–west axis of the steppes, which served as highways for horse-borne armies.

The new empire's beginnings in the fourteenth century were almost imperceptible to those who experienced them or witnessed their effects. As we have seen, Russian princes could sometimes use Mongol dominance to their own advantage. Rulers of Moscow were the most adept in exploiting the Mongols to secure independence of and—increasingly—power over other Russians. Ivan I, known as Kalita or "Moneybags" (r. 1325–1340), got his nickname from his success as a tax collector for the Mongols. In 1378–1382, shortly after the collapse of Mongol rule in China, Muscovy attempted to drive the Mongols out of Russia. The challenge was premature, but Moscow's privileged relationship with the overlords survived. Mongol supremacy faded gradually.

The Russian world was expanding northward in the late fourteenth and early fifteenth centuries, as missionaries opened roads to convert people in the forests and tundra. An astonishing example of expansion by sea occurred in the 1430s. The evidence comes from a monastery on an island—bare, poor, and ice bound for much of the year—in the White Sea, on the edge of the Arctic. The monks painted their home not as it was but as they envisioned it, with a golden sanctuary and domes like candle flames. They showed the founders of their monastery rowing to the island, while whip-wielding angels expelled the original inhabitants. The paintings show merchants arriving, and monks rescuing shipwreck victims, with help from the ghosts of the monastery's saintly founders, who drive back the pack ice. Angels supply bread, cooking oil, and salt. All the ingredients of a typical story of European colonialism appear: the

Russian expansion. The monastery these Russian Orthodox monks—Zosima and Savatti—founded in the White Sea off the Arctic coast of Siberia was really a modest and precarious little community, housed in wooden buildings in an icy desert. But the monks painted it as they would like it to be—big, grand, prosperous, and frequented by commerce.

religious inspiration, the heroic voyage into a perilous environment, the ruthless treatment of the natives, the struggle to adapt and establish a viable economy, the quick arrival of commercial interests, and, finally, success through perseverance.

Muscovy's sudden take-off in the second half of the century, when territorial conquests of neighboring peoples turned it into an imperial state, overshadowed early efforts at expansion. Indeed, when Constantinople fell to the Turks in 1453, Muscovites could see their city as, potentially, the "Third Rome," replacing Constantinople as Constantinople had replaced Rome, the former capital (see Chapter 9). By the 1470s, Ivan the Great (r. 1462–1505) had absorbed most of Russia's other surviving principalities and was ready to throw off Mongol overlordship. He married a Byzantine princess, incorporated an imperial eagle into his coat of arms, forged a genealogy that traced his family back to the Roman Caesars, imported Italian technicians to fortify his palace complex, the Kremlin, and contemptuously dismissed an offer from the German emperor to invest him as king. "We have been sovereign in our land from our earliest forefathers," he replied, "and we hold our sovereignty from God."

During his reign, Ivan the Great more than trebled the territory he ruled—to over 240,000 square miles (see Map 15.4). His realm also took a new shape around most of the vast length of the Volga, stretching across the breadth of Eurasia, unit-

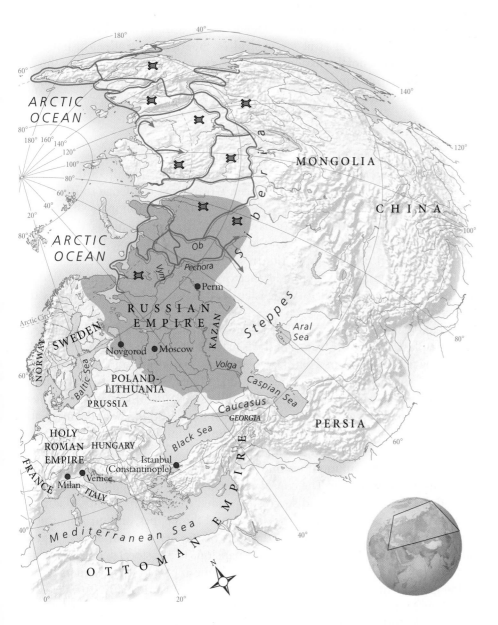

MAP 15.4

The Russian Empire, ca. 1505

Russian Empire

routes used by fur traders

fur

ing the fur-rich north and the cash-rich fringes of Asia, and reaching for the Baltic and Caspian Seas. The city of Novgorod, which Muscovy absorbed in the 1470s, formed the northern pole of the state. Fur was the "black gold" of the north, inducing Russians to conquest and colonization, just as gold and spices lured other European peoples to Africa and the East.

War parties gathered pelts as tribute along a northern route that missionaries pioneered in the late fourteenth century, by way of the Rivers Vym and Pechora. Repeatedly from 1465, Ivan sent expeditions to the rivers Perm and Ob to levy tribute. The expedition of 1499 numbered 4,000 men, equipped with sleds drawn by reindeer and dogs. They crossed the Ob in winter, returning with 1,000 captives from the forest-dwelling peoples who hunted for the furs. Ivan's ambassador to the rich Italian duchy of Milan boasted that his master received 1,000 gold ducats' worth of tribute annually in furs—five or six times an Italian nobleman's income.

In the south, Russian dominance extended over Kazan (kah-ZAHN), near the Black Sea, Russia's great rival for control of Siberia's fur trade. Muslims ruled Kazan, while in the north missionaries, seeking to convert pagans, formed the vanguard for Russian conquests. Russian expansion therefore became a conscious crusade. Rulers justified it on religious grounds.

Timurids and the Ottoman Empire

In the early fifteenth century, Turkish—and therefore Muslim—expansion resumed in southern Europe and Asia, still under the leadership of the Ottoman dynasty. The Mongol supremacy had been a traumatic challenge to Islam, shattering the reputation of Muslim armies, breaking the monopoly of Sharia or Islamic law, exposing the limitations of the clergy, and inspiring the religious minded to withdraw from the world in a spirit of resignation. The Black Death had also battered the Islamic world. In some ways, indeed, it never fully recovered. Muslims' numerical preponderance over Christians never got back to earlier levels. But, for global history, the Islamic recovery is a much bigger story than the temporary setback.

To understand recovery, we turn to one of its most brilliant Muslim observers after the Black Death, the historian Ibn Khaldun (ihb-ihn hahl-DOON). In 1377, he sat down in a village in what is now Algeria "with ideas pouring into my head like cream into a churn." His efforts produced one of the most justly admired works of all time on history and political philosophy, the *Muqaddimah*. Its theme was the counterpoint of herder and tiller, which Ibn Khaldun saw as the motivating force of historical change. He had plenty of opportunity to observe the often violent interplay of nomads and sedentarists, their periodic collaboration, the incorporation of herder communities into Islamic states, and the way they launched new empires of their own. The consequences were clear. Everywhere in Ibn Khaldun's day, Islamic survival and success depended on Muslims' ability to tame the invaders challenging them from the deserts and the steppes, and turn their power to the service of Islam. Despite the disasters of the Black Death, new manpower stoked the Islamic world's potential for expansion. The pastoral peoples of Central Asia continued to provide converts. Islam's unique appeal to steppelanders was one of the great formative influences in the late medieval world. Most Turkic peoples and many Mongols were converted into warriors for Islam. Consequently, Central Asia stayed Muslim, and the Indian Ocean linked mainly Muslim shores. In other words, the Silk Roads and maritime routes of Eurasia had to pass through Muslim-ruled territory. Equally important, human fuel renewed the Islamic world's capacity to wage war and expand its frontiers

The most conspicuous mobilizer of steppeland manpower in Muslim service in the late fourteenth and early fifteenth centuries, was the self-proclaimed "world conqueror," Timur (tee-MOOR) the Lame. Western writers, who traditionally call him Tamerlane, have tended to see him, romantically, as an embodiment of the superior virtues and simple lives of pastoral peoples. In reality, Timur was a nobly born townsman from Central Asia. Unlike most steppeland upstarts, he could justly claim to be descended from Genghis Khan (see Chapter 13). His court historian represented him as "the being nearest to perfection" and a pious devotee of holy war, but his role models were the pagans, Alexander the Great (see Chapter 5) and Genghis Khan.

When Turkic nobles rebelled against their Mongol masters in his homeland, Timur emerged as their leader. Deftly eliminating his rivals, he remained as ruler of the region by 1370. By the time he died in 1406, he had conquered Iran, halted the growth of the Ottoman Empire and captured and caged its sultan, invaded Syria and India, and planned the conquest of China (see Map 15.5). Wherever he went, he heaped up the skulls of citizens unwise enough to resist his sieges. But this destruction was for efficiency, not for its own sake. It made most conquests submit cheaply. His success was by no means uniform, but it was impressive enough and consistent enough, to seem decreed by God. He addressed enemies in terms reminiscent of Mongol tradition: "Almighty God has subjugated the world to my domination, and the will of the Creator has entrusted the countries of the Earth to my power".

The day after his death, as his heirs turned on one another, his achievements seemed transitory. Even today, Timur's impact on the Islamic world is usually seen as negative. His success against the Ottomans gave Christendom a reprieve. By humbling the Mongols, he encouraged Christians in Russia. By weakening the Muslim sultans of Delhi, he liberated millions of Hindus. These reflections, however, overlook his psychological legacy. He was a champion of Islamic orthodoxy and exerted great influence as a patron of Muslim education. He is also important as an example of the process that converted pastoralists. Having been the scourge of the Islamic world, they became its sword.

Timur was like a hurricane—his force soon spent. The Ottomans were more like a monsoon, whose armies returned and receded as each season came and went, but they constantly made new conquests. The fate of the Mongols—expelled from China, retreating from Russia—shows how hard it was for a great Eurasian Empire to survive in the aftermath of the Black Death, which jarred economies and felled manpower. Yet, falteringly in the early fifteenth century but with renewed strength thereafter, the Ottoman Empire managed to do so.

Timurid horoscope. Despite their fearsome reputation, Timurid princes—the descendents of the Muslim Turkic conqueror whom Westerners called "Tamberlane"—were great patrons of both astronomers and astrologers. This horoscope was drawn up in Shiraz, Iran, in 1411 for one of Timur's grandsons, Iskandar Sultan. The date of his birth, 1384, is given in Persian, Uighur, and Chinese.

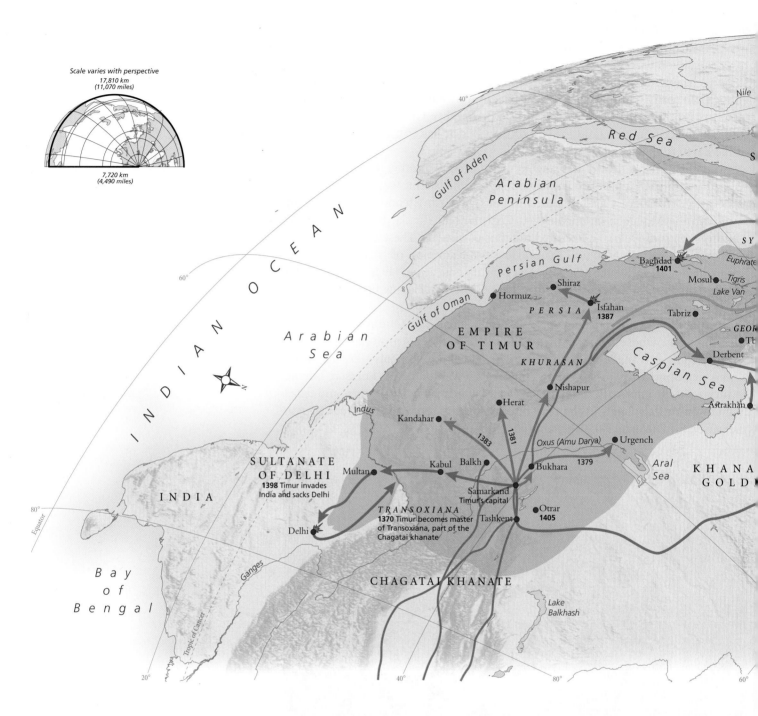

The Ottomans' great advantage was location. The heartlands of the empire were at the crossroads of some of the world's great trade routes, where the Silk Roads, the Indian Ocean routes, the Volga, the Danube, and the Mediterranean almost converged (see Map 15.5). The history of the Byzantine Empire showed the importance of this location and of holding on to it. Byzantium flourished while it occupied these lands, faltered when its control there slackened and ceased (see Chapter 12). From their own past, the Ottomans inherited the traditions of steppeland imperialism. They were content, at first, to levy tribute and allow their tributaries to govern themselves or to exist as puppet states to be manipulated according to Ottoman needs.

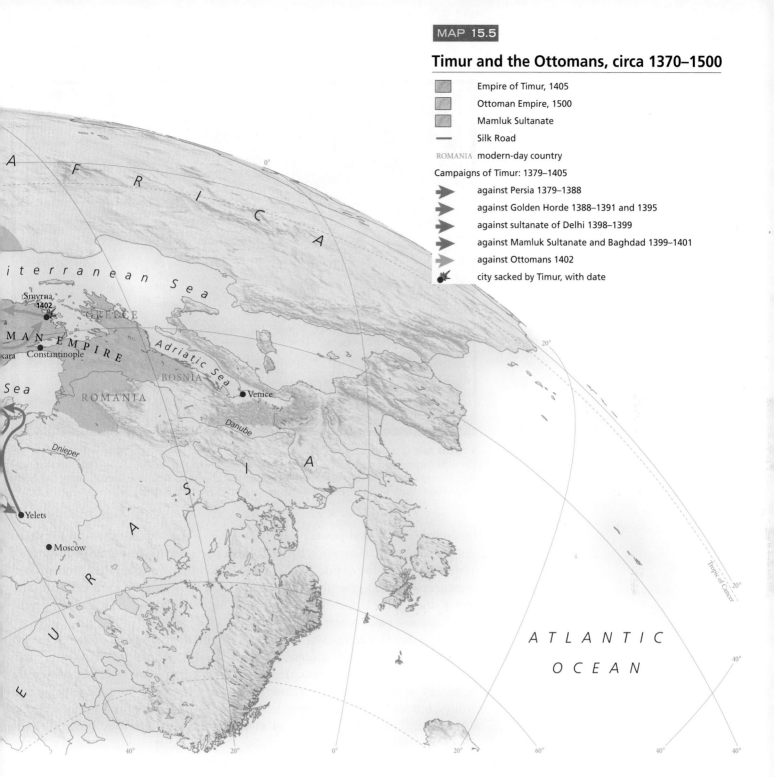

MAP 15.5

Timur and the Ottomans, circa 1370–1500

- Empire of Timur, 1405
- Ottoman Empire, 1500
- Mamluk Sultanate
- Silk Road
- ROMANIA modern-day country

Campaigns of Timur: 1379–1405

- against Persia 1379–1388
- against Golden Horde 1388–1391 and 1395
- against sultanate of Delhi 1398–1399
- against Mamluk Sultanate and Baghdad 1399–1401
- against Ottomans 1402
- city sacked by Timur, with date

Gradually, they adapted to the conditions of the environments they conquered, which were predominantly agrarian, urban, and maritime. As their conquests grew, their methods of governing became, necessarily, more bureaucratic and centralized. As their frontiers touched formidable foes, they modified their military traditions. Other empires of nomadic origins failed when required to adapt to new military technologies, but the Ottomans' readily became a gunpowder empire. Their forces could blow away cavalry or batter down city walls.

The Ottomans even took to the sea. In the 1390s, the sultans began to build permanent fleets of their own. It was a long process and hard to catch up with

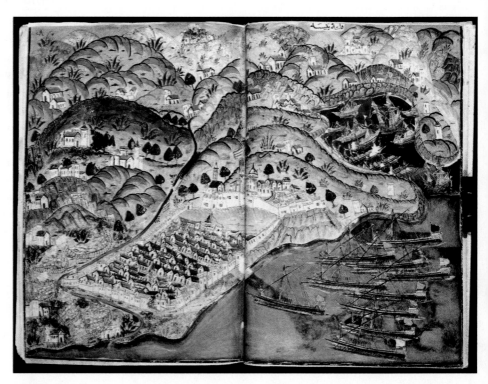

A Turkish fleet at anchor off Toulon, in southern France, in 1543, from a chronicle written to celebrate the wide-ranging campaigns of Sultan Suleiman the Magnificent (r. 1520–1566). The Ottomans were able to wage naval war in the western Mediterranean, thanks to the many harbors along the North African coast controlled by Muslim chiefs who were subjects of the sultans.

long-established naval powers. As late as 1466, a Venetian merchant in Constantinople claimed that to win a battle Turkish fleets needed to outnumber those of Venice by four or five to one. By the end of the century, however, the Ottomans had overturned the 400-year-old Christian maritime supremacy in the Mediterranean. Never since Rome defeated Carthage (see Chapter 7) had such an unlikely candidate become a naval power.

Like other imperialists of steppeland origin, the Ottomans mastered the art of keeping subjects of diverse religions loyal to them. At the same time, Ottoman leaders, as self-appointed warriors of Islam, took whatever steps were necessary to strengthen the Islamic state. They tolerated Jews, Christians, and Shiites, but had no qualms about levying punitive taxes on these minorities. On Christians, they imposed a levy of male child slaves, who were brought up as Muslims to form the **Janissaries**, an elite corps of the armed forces, and staff the ranks of the administration. The system provided servants for the state, and converts for Islam, while keeping Christian communities in submission. From the 1420s, consistently with the character of the empire as a Muslim state with people of many religions and customs, the sultan functioned as head of two linked systems of law and justice. The first consisted of secular laws and customs that the sultan's appointees administered. The second was enshrined in the Quran and the traditions of Islamic law, with a body of experts to run it, who met in the sultan's palace.

In 1451, Mehmet (MEH-meht) II became sultan at the age of 19, uninhibited by caution, committed to reform. This was a decisive step in the shift from indirect rule to centralized government. Mehmet's predecessors had prudently allowed self-rule to continue in the city of Constantinople and its few surviving dependencies—the last fragments of the Byzantine Empire that still proclaimed itself the heir of Rome. The Ottomans controlled what happened in Constantinople by manipulating political factions with threats and bribes. But some factions in the city were determined to challenge the Turks and formed an alliance with Western Christendom. Mehmet laid siege to Constantinople. He built huge forts to command the sea approaches to the city and fired the heaviest artillery ever made at its walls. He transported ships overland in pieces to get round the great chain the defenders stretched across the entrance to the harbor. In the end, the sheer weight of numbers was decisive. The attackers climbed the walls over the bodies of dead comrades. The last Byzantine emperor, Constantine XI, fell fighting—only the eagles on his purple boots identified his corpse.

With the fall of Constantinople in 1453, Mehmet II could see his empire as a continuation of Rome. He looked westward for fashions to incorporate into his court culture and chose Italians to paint his portrait, sculpt his medals, and write some of his propaganda. The direction of Ottoman conquests tilted toward Europe as Mehmet attempted to recreate the Byzantine Empire. He extended his territory into most of what are now Greece, Romania, and Bosnia, seeking to control the shores of the Adriatic and Black Seas.

THE LIMITATIONS OF CHINESE IMPERIALISM

So Ottoman imperialism in the fifteenth century resumed its former course after setbacks caused by the Black Death and the rise of Timur. An observer at the time might have predicted that China, too, would resume expansion and even anticipate the Ottomans in bidding for a maritime empire. The best way to understand why such developments seemed likely—and why they were, in fact, frustrated—is to look back at China's recovery from the mid–fourteenth-century plagues. Like so many decisive episodes of Chinese history, the story begins among the people on whose labor and manpower the empire depended: peasants.

The rhythms of peasant life sometimes seem slow and changeless, peasants' expectations low: deferring hope, shrugging off promises of improvement. Their response, in a surprisingly wide variety of cultural contexts, is to wait and pray for the millennium—a fabled future, when divine intervention will either perfect the world or end it. Often, however, in times of extreme disaster, peasant movements arise to try to trigger the millennium. One of the most explosive of all such movements began among Chinese canal workers in 1350.

Mid–fourteenth-century China, was particularly wretched. Peasants were the victims of the slow-grinding effects of economic misery and the survivors of terrible environmental disasters. The plagues that began in the 1320s kept on returning. Not until well into the 1350s did the plagues begin to lose their virulence or to encounter naturally immunized populations. In 1344, the Yellow River flooded. Persistent droughts followed. Decayed communications that prevented timely help worsened local famines. The population of the empire had fallen, by some calculations, to half what it had been at its height. In this setting, peasants were forced into labor to repair the Grand Canal, which carried essential food supplies from southern and central China to Beijing.

Sultan Mehmet II (r. 1451–1481) extended the Ottoman Empire westward into Europe, taking great interest in the culture of lands that had once belonged to the Roman Empire—especially after he captured the old Roman capital of Constantinople in 1453. Gentile Bellini, who worked at Mehmet's court and was one of the best Venetian painters of the day, painted this portrait of the sultan in the realistic style that was popular in Italy at the time. Bellini framed the sultan's image with columns decorated in the European style.

The peasants' millenarianism—their hope of deliverance in a transfigured world—was based on a Buddhist myth. The lord Maitreya, the last of the earthly Buddhas, would come to prepare the world for extinction. Now, however, given the peasants' miserable lives, the myth acquired a political edge. Maitreya would put a triumphant end to the struggle of good against evildoers and give his followers power over their oppressors. A similar movement was current at the same time in Western Europe, where the Fraticelli, a group of Franciscan friars, identified with the needs and interests of the wretched of the Earth. The Franciscans predicted that a cosmic hero would come to wrest treasures from the soil and enrich the poor. Fulfilling the biblical prophecy uttered by the mother of Jesus, which the prayers of the church repeated every day, he would put down the mighty from their seat and exalt the humble and meek.

In China, the mood was particularly dangerous. Along with their desire for deliverance, peasants harbored a folk memory of the Song dynasty (see Chapter 12) and a hankering for the good times supposed to have preceded the Mongol invasions of a century before. Peasant revolts are often revolutionary in the most literal sense of the word, wanting to turn the world back, "revolve" it full circle, to an imagined or misremembered golden age. Therefore, when the Mongol rulers executed a pretender to the throne who claimed to be the heir of the Song in 1351, a revolt broke out among his followers. They easily recruited thousands of peasants to their cause. Some members of the elite even joined in, out of resentment at the ruling dynasty's partiality for foreign advisers.

The leader who emerged from the chaos of rebellion was Zhu Yuanzhang (joo yoo-ehn-jhang), the recruiting officer of a rebel band. By the end of the 1350s, the empire in the Yangtze region had dissolved into a chaos of small states run by similar upstarts. Between 1360 and 1363, in river warfare of reckless daring, Zhu conquered his rivals. At this stage, he was careful to represent himself as a mere servant of the rebel cause. By 1368, however, he was so powerful that he proclaimed the start of a new dynasty.

Zhu cleverly managed the coalition that had brought him to power. He juggled all the rebels' conflicting ideologies while reconciling former enemies. To please the Confucian establishment, he restored ancient court ceremonies and the examinations for public service. He kept the military command structure and even dressed in some of the same ways as the previous Mongol dynasty had. He renounced the cult of Maitreya, but only after making it clear that he had fulfilled it in his own person by adopting the name "Ming" for his dynasty. The word, which means bright, was traditionally used to describe the lord Maitreya.

Zhu had the self-educated man's typical contempt for the academic establishment. "Chewing on phrases and biting on words," he said, "they have never had any practical experience. When you examine what they do, it is nothing." But he recognized that the Confucian bureaucrats had expertise he could use. His empire—vast and literate, as it was—needed a civil service that would heed a traditional code of ethics. He also needed to keep the Confucian elite under his control. He therefore kept the traditional power centers of his court in balance: the military top brass, the eunuchs who ran the imperial household, the foreign and Muslim advisers and technicians, the Buddhist and Daoist clergies, and the merchant lobby. Combined, they limited the power of the Confucian elite.

The result was a brief period when expansionist policies prevailed over Confucian caution. Zhu's son, the Yongle (yuhng-leh) emperor (r. 1402–1424) aggressively sought contact with the world beyond the empire. He meddled in the politics of China's southern neighbors in Vietnam and enticed the Japanese to trade.

From Ma Huan, *The Overall Survey of the Ocean's Shores*

The most spectacular manifestation of the new outward-looking policy was the career of the Muslim eunuch-admiral, Zheng He (jehng heh). In 1405, he led the first of a series of naval expeditions, the purpose of which has been the subject of long and unresolved scholarly debate, but which was intended in part, at least, to show China's flag all over the Indian Ocean (see Map 15.6). He replaced unacceptable rulers in Java, Sumatra, and Sri Lanka, founded a puppet state on the commercially important strait of Malacca, and gathered tribute from Bengal. He displayed Chinese power as far away as Jiddah, on the Red Sea coast of Arabia and in major ports in East Africa as far south as the island of Zanzibar. "The countries beyond the horizon," he announced with some exaggeration, "and from the ends of the Earth, have become subjects." He restocked the imperial zoo with giraffes, ostriches, zebra, and rhinoceroses—all hailed as beasts bringing good luck—and brought Chinese geographical knowledge up to date.

Can Zheng He's voyages be called an imperial venture? Their official purpose was to pursue a fugitive pretender to the Chinese throne—but that would not have required expeditions on so vast a scale to such distant places. The Chinese called the vessels treasure ships and emphasized what they called tribute gathering (in the more distant spots Zheng He's ships visited, what happened was more like an exchange). Commercial objectives may have been involved. Almost all the places Zheng He visited had long been important in Chinese trade. In part, the voyages were scientific missions: Ma Huan, Zheng He's interpreter, called his own book on the subject, *The Overall Survey of the Ocean's Shores*, and improved maps and data on the plants, animals, and peoples of the regions visited were among the expeditions' fruits. But flag showing is always, to some extent, about power or, at least, prestige. And the aggressive intervention Zheng He made in some places, together with the tone of his commemorative inscriptions, demonstrates that the extension or reinforcement of China's image and influence was part of the project.

Indeed, it is hard to see how else the huge investment the state made in his enterprise could have been justified. Zheng He's expeditions were on a crushing scale. His ships were much bigger than anything European navies could float at the time. His first fleet was said to comprise 66 junks of the largest ever built, 225 support vessels, and 27,870 men. The seventh voyage—probably the longest in reach—sailed 12,618 miles. The voyages lasted on average over two years each. Some silly claims have been made for Zheng He's voyages. Ships of his fleet did not sail beyond the limits of the Indian Ocean—much less discover America or Antarctica. His achievements, however, clearly demonstrated China's potential to become the center of a maritime empire of enormous reach.

But the Chinese naval effort could not last. Historians have debated why it was abandoned. In many ways, it was to the credit of Chinese decision makers that they pulled back from involvement in costly adventures far from home. Most powers that have undertaken such expeditions and attempted to impose their rule on distant countries have had cause to regret it. Confucian values, as we have seen, included giving priority to good government at home. "Barbarians" would submit to Chinese rule if and when they saw the benefits. Attempting to beat or coax them into submission was a waste of resources. By consolidating their landward empire, and refraining from seaborne imperialism, China's rulers ensured the longevity of

Giraffe. "The ministers and all the people gathered to gaze at it and their joy knows no end," commented Zhen-tu, the Chinese court painter who recorded the arrival of one of several giraffes at China's imperial zoo in the early fifteenth century. Imperial propaganda identified giraffes with mythical beasts of good omen.
1977–42-1. Tu, Shen. "The Tribute Giraffe with Attendant". Philadelphia Museum of Art: Gift of John T. Dorrance, 1977.

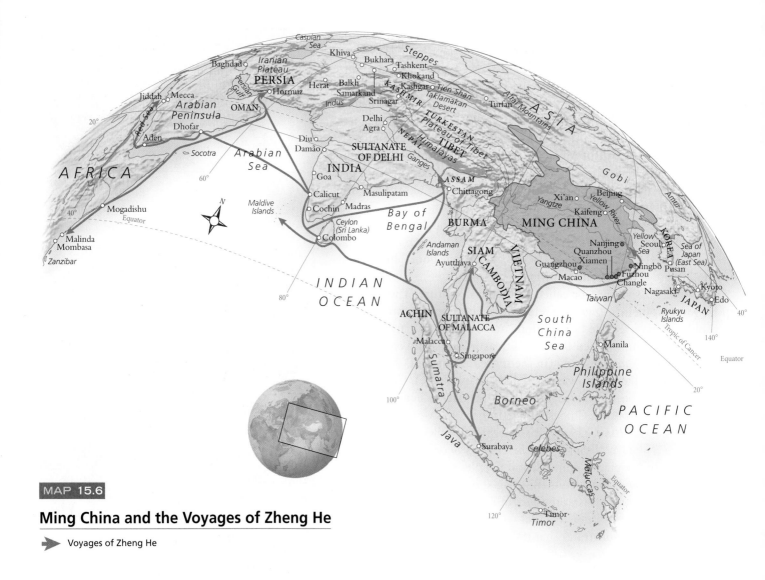

MAP 15.6

Ming China and the Voyages of Zheng He

➤ Voyages of Zheng He

their state. All the maritime empires founded in the world in the last 500 years have crumbled. China is still there.

Part, at least, of the context of the decision to abort Zheng He's missions is clear. The examination system and the gradual discontinuation of other forms of recruitment for public service had serious implications. Increasingly scholars, with their indifference to expansion, and gentlemen, with their contempt for trade, governed China. In the 1420s and 1430s, the balance of power at court shifted in the bureaucrats' favor, away from the Buddhists, eunuchs, Muslims, and merchants who had supported Zheng He. When the Hongxi (huhng-jher) emperor succeeded to the throne in 1425, one of his first acts was to cancel Zheng He's next voyage. He restored Confucian office holders, whom the Yongle emperor had dismissed, and curtailed the power of other factions. In 1429, the shipbuilding budget was cut almost to extinction. The scholar-elite hated overseas adventures, and the factions that favored them so much that they destroyed all Zheng He's records in an attempt to obliterate his memory. Moreover, China's land frontiers became insecure as Mongol power revived. China needed to turn away from the sea and toward the new threat.

By the late fifteenth century, the scholars' position seemed unshakable, and the supremacy of Confucian values could not be challenged. Zhu Zhanji, the Hongxi emperor who took the throne in 1425, aspired to Confucian perfection. He ordered the slaughter or expulsion of court magicians and exiled 1,000 Buddhist and Daoist monks. He resumed a Confucian priority: study of the penal code, which previous Ming emperors had neglected. He reintroduced the palace lectures, during which Confucian professors instructed the emperor. He endowed a library alongside the Confucian temple at the sage's birthplace in Qufu (choofoo). He patronized artists whose work radiated Confucian serenity. Wu Wei (woo way), the emperor's favorite painter, had Daoist patrons, too, but his representations of ascetics meditating in sketchy landscapes demonstrate the triumph of thought over nature and, therefore, by implication, of Confucianism over Daoism.

By the end of the fifteenth century, there was little chance the Chinese would resume a strategy of expanding the empire and no chance that they would expand by sea. For the rest of the Ming period (1368–1644), China did not cease to be a great imperial power, but frontier stability became far more important to the ruling elite than frontier expansion. The transfer of the imperial capital from the southern citty of Nanjing to the northern city of Beijing under the Yongle emperor (r. 1402–1424) symbolized this concern. The state never resumed the active patronage of overseas expansion. The growth of trade and of Chinese colonization in southeast Asia was left to the private initiative of merchants and migrants. China, the empire best equipped for maritime imperialism, opted out. Consequently, lesser powers, including those of Europe were able to exploit opportunities in seas that Chinese power vacated.

THE BEGINNINGS OF OCEANIC IMPERIALISM

Even under the Yongle emperor, China confined its seaward reach to the monsoonal seas of maritime Asia and the Indian Ocean—seas of terrible hazards and fabulous rewards. As we have seen, the Indian Ocean was relatively easy to cross but relatively hard to enter or exit. For most of history, therefore, it was the preserve of peoples whose homes bordered it or who traveled overland—like some European and Armenian traders—to become part of its world. Moreover, all the trade was internal. Merchants took no interest in venturing far beyond the monsoon system to reach other markets or supplies.

From Europe, however, access to the Indian Ocean was well worth seeking. Merchants craved a share of the richest trades and most prosperous markets in the world, especially the spices, drugs, and aromatics that were the specialities of producers in Sri Lanka, and parts of India and what is now Indonesia. These products, sold to rich buyers in China and southwest Asia, and, to a lesser extent, in Europe, were the most profitable in the world, in terms of price per unit of weight. Many Europeans sought to find out where they came from and to take part in the trades. But the journey was too long, laborious, and hazardous to

The Early Ming Dynasty

1350s	Yangtze region dissolves into small warring states
1360–1363	Zhu Yuanzhang conquers his rivals
1368	Zhu Yuanzhang founds Ming dynasty
1405	Zheng He leads first naval expedition
1425	Hongxi emperor succeeds to throne; Zheng He's voyages cancelled
1487	Zhu Youtang succeeds to throne; Confucian values ascendant

Wu Wei was one of the most original and influential artists of late-fifteenth-century China. But his values were those of his patrons, the conventional scholar-elite of the imperial court. This painting is typical. The scholar staring thoughtfully into the distance is drawn in delicate and flattering contrast to the heavy, blotchy ink used to depict the tree.

Wu Wei, "Scholar Seated Under a Tree", China. Ink & traces of colour on silk. 14.7 x 8.25. Chinese and Japanese Special Fund. Photograph © 2007 Courtesy Museum of Fine Arts, Boston

generate much profit. From the Mediterranean, merchants had either to travel up the Nile and proceed by camel caravan to a Red Sea port, or to negotiate a dangerous passage through the Ottoman Empire to the Persian Gulf. In either case, they obviously could not take ships with them. This was a potentially fatal limitation because Europeans had little to offer to people in the Indian Ocean basin except shipping services. For most of the fifteenth century, until the 1490s, there was much debate in Europe about whether it was possible to approach the Indian Ocean by sea at all.

To understand why, until the late fifteenth century, Europeans were so backward in navigation compared with Indian Ocean peoples and unable to gain direct access to Asian markets and supplies, we must look at the wind map (see Map 15.7). For most of history, winds and currents have played a huge part in conditioning, and even determining, who and what went where in the world.

Europe's only effective access by sea to the rest of the world is along its western seaboard, into the Atlantic, which has a fixed-wind system. That is, instead of changing direction seasonally, as in monsoonal systems, the prevailing winds in the Atlantic are always the same. It took a long time to develop navigation with fixed-wind systems because, until navigators explored and decoded those winds' pathways, adventurers could not get home. Navigators either sailed into the wind—which usually resulted in their being blown back without discovering any useful new lands or routes—or they sailed with the wind, never to be heard of again.

The Norse explorers of the North Atlantic in the tenth and eleventh centuries (see Chapter 11) overcame these limitations by sailing west with the currents that cross the Atlantic below the Arctic, and then picking up the westerlies, which took them home. But this route led only to relatively poor and underpopulated regions. For the Atlantic to become Europe's highway to the rest of the world, explorers had to develop ways to exploit the rest of the fixed-wind system. They had to discover the winds that led to commercially important destinations. There were, first, the northeast trade winds, which led to the resource-rich, densely populated regions of the New World, far south of the lands the Norse reached. There was also the South Atlantic wind system, which led, by way of the southeast trade winds and the westerlies of the far south, to the Indian Ocean.

The technology to exploit the Atlantic's wind systems only gradually became available during a period of long, slow development in the thirteenth, fourteenth, and fifteenth centuries. Like most technology, for most of history, it developed by trial and error. We know little about the process, because the work went undocumented. Humble craftsman labored to improve hull design and rigging—and therefore the maneuverability of ships—and to make water casks secure for the long voyages explorers had to undertake. Historians have traditionally emphasized the contribution of formal science in developing maritime charts and instruments for navigating by the stars. Now it seems that these innovations were irrelevant. No practical navigator of this period in Europe seems to have used them.

In addition to gradually developing technology, gradually improving knowledge of winds and currents prepared Europeans to explore maritime routes to the rest of the world. The European discovery of the Atlantic was launched from deep in the Mediterranean, chiefly by navigators from Genoa and the island of Majorca. They forced their way through the Strait of Gibraltar, where the strength of the adverse current seemed to stopper their sea, in the thirteenth century. From there, some turned north to the familiar European Atlantic. Others turned south into waters unsailed, as far as we know, for centuries, toward the Madeira and Canary Islands and the African Atlantic. Early efforts were long and laborious because explorers' vision was limited to the small patches of the ocean before them, with their apparently unremitting winds. Navigators were like code breakers deprived of information to work with. Moreover, the Black Death and the economic downturn of the mid–fourteenth century interrupted the effort, or at least slowed it down.

Only the long accumulation of information and experience could make a breakthrough possible. Navigators had no means to keep track of their longitude as they beat their way home against the wind. They made increasingly huge deep-sea detours to find westerlies that would take them home. Those detours led to the discovery of the Azores, a mid-ocean string of islands more than 700 miles west of Portugal. Marine charts made not later than the 1380s show all but two islands of the group. Much longer open-sea voyages now became common. From the 1430s, the Portuguese established way stations, sown with wheat or stocked with wild sheep, on the Azores.

Several attempts were made during the fifteenth century to explore Atlantic space, but most doomed themselves to failure by setting out in the belt of westerly winds. Presumably explorers chose this route because they wanted to be sure that they would be able to get home. We can still follow the tiny gains in the slowly unfolding record on rare maps and stray documents. In 1427, a Portuguese pilot called Diogo de Silves established for the first time the approximate relationship of the islands of the Azores to one another. Shortly after 1450, the westernmost islands of the Azores were reached. Over the next three decades, the Portuguese crown often commissioned voyages of exploration farther into the Atlantic, but none is known to have made any further progress. Perhaps they failed because they departed from the Azores, where the westerlies beat them back to base.

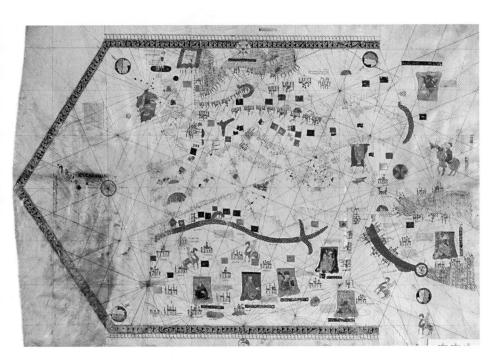

The Azores. The Atlantic voyage of Diogo de Silves of 1427 was unrecorded, except on this map, made in Majorca in 1439. The Azores, which Silves sailed around, can be seen on the extreme left, alongside the traces of a stain made when the famous French novelist, George Sand, spilled an ink pot when examining the map while on a vacation on Majorca with her lover, the composer Frédéric Chopin, in 1838–1839.

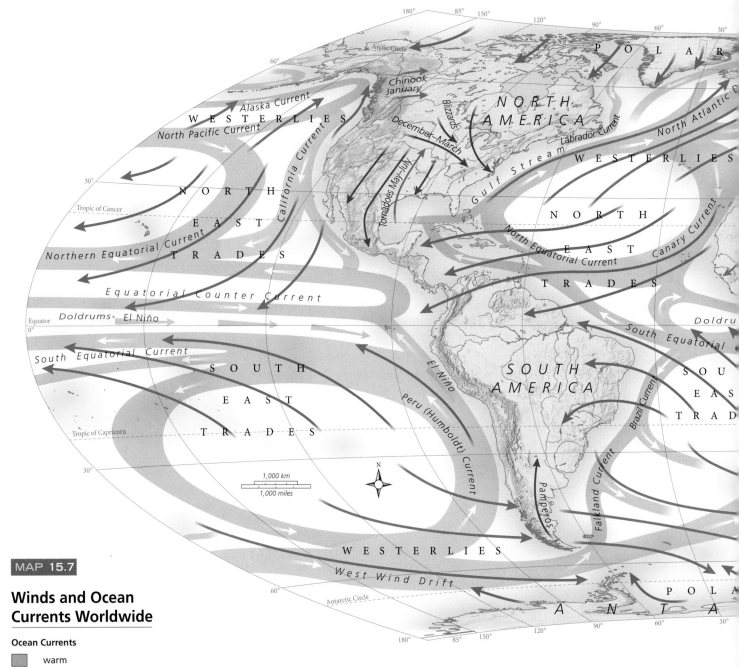

MAP 15.7

Winds and Ocean Currents Worldwide

Ocean Currents
- warm
- cold

Prevailing Winds
 warm
 cold

Local Winds
warm
 cold

MAP EXPLORATION

www.prenhall.com/armesto_maps

Not only was exploitation of the Atlantic slow, it yielded, at first, few returns. One exception was Madeira, which paid enormous taxes to the Portuguese crown thanks to sugar planting in the mid–fifteenth century. The explorers' hope of establishing direct contact with the sources of West African gold proved false, though they were able to get gold at relatively low prices through trade with West African kingdoms. This trade also produced something saleable in European markets. From 1440, Portuguese desperadoes obtained increasing numbers of slaves through trading and raiding. But markets for slaves were limited because great slave-staffed plantations, of the sort later

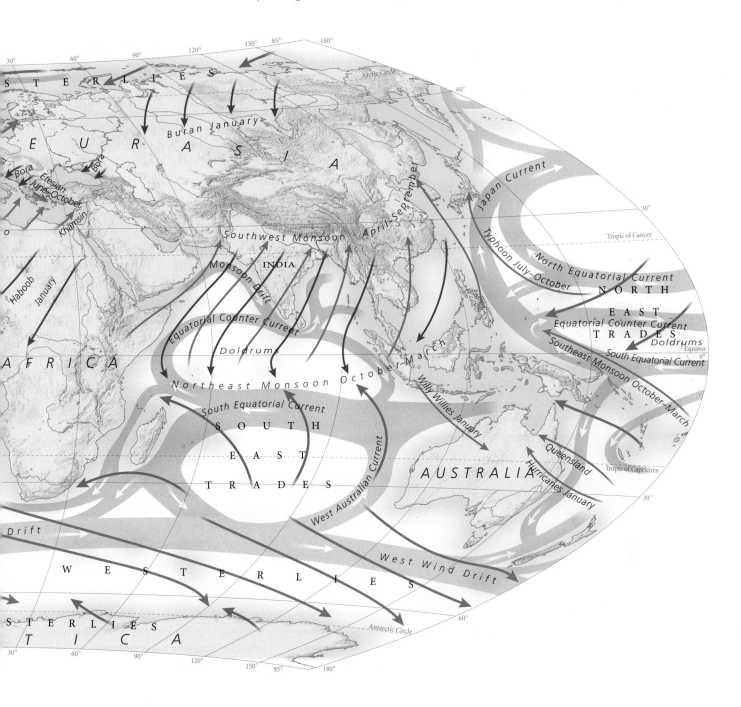

familiar in the southern United States, hardly existed in Europe, where most slaves were still in domestic service. The Canary Islands attracted investment because they produced large amounts of natural dyestuffs and seemed potentially exploitable for sugar. But their inhabitants fiercely resisted Europeans, and the conquest was long and costly.

In the 1480s, however, the situation changed, and Atlantic exploration began to pay off. In the North Atlantic, customs records of the English port of Bristol indicate that quantities of whaling products, salt fish, and walrus ivory from the ocean increased dramatically after a lull in the previous decade. In

Beginnings of European Oceanic Imperialism

Tenth and eleventh centuries	Norse explore North Atlantic
Thirteenth and fifteenth centuries	Europeans make advances in maritime technology and knowledge
1430s	Portuguese establish way stations in Azores
1440s	Portuguese begin to obtain West African slaves
1450–1480	Portuguese crown commissions voyages of exploration of the Atlantic
1482	Portuguese found trading station of Saõ Jorge da Mina on West African coast
1484	Sugar production begins in Canary Islands
1492–1493	First voyage of Christopher Columbus
1496	John Cabot discovers direct route across North Atlantic
1497–1498	Vasco da Gama rounds Cape of Good Hope
1500	Vasco da Gama reaches India

West Africa, in 1482, Portuguese traders opened a new post at São Jorge da Mina, near the mouth of the Benya River. This was close to gold fields in the Volta River valley, and large amounts of gold now began to reach European hands. In 1484, sugar production at last began in the Canary Islands. In the same decade, Portuguese made contact with the Kingdom of Kongo. Although voyages toward and around the southernmost tip of Africa encountered unremittingly adverse currents, they also showed that the far south of the Atlantic had westerly winds that might at last lead to the Indian Ocean. By the end of the decade, it was apparent that Atlantic investment could yield dividends.

As a result of gains made in the 1480s, the 1490s were a breakthrough-decade in Europe's efforts to reach out across the ocean to the rest of the world (see Map 15.8). In 1492–1493, Christopher Columbus, in voyages a group of Italian bankers financed and with backing from the Spanish `monarchs, discovered fast, reliable routes across the Atlantic that linked the Mediterranean and the Caribbean Sea. In 1496, John Cabot, another Italian adventurer, backed by merchants in Bristol and the English crown, discovered a direct route across the North Atlantic, using variable springtime winds to get across and the westerlies to get back. His route, however, was not reliable and, for over 100 years, was mainly used to reach the cod fisheries of Newfoundland.

Meanwhile, Portuguese missions sought to determine whether the Indian Ocean was genuinely landlocked. In 1497–1498, a Portuguese trading venture, commissioned by the crown and probably financed by Italian bankers, attempted to use the westerlies of the South Atlantic to reach the Indian Ocean. Its leader, Vasco da Gama, turned east too early and had to struggle around the Cape of Good Hope at the tip of Africa. But he managed to get across the Indian Ocean anyway and reach the pepper-rich port of Calicut at the tip of India. The next voyage, in 1500, managed to avoid the Cape of Good Hope and to reach India without a serious hitch.

The breakthroughs of the 1490s opened direct, long-range routes of maritime trade across the world between Europe, Asia, and Africa. Success may seem sudden, but not if we view it against the background of slow developments in European chronology and knowledge and the accelerating benefits of Atlantic exploration in the previous decade. Was there more to it than that? Was there something special about European culture that would explain why Europeans discovered the world-girdling routes, linking the Old World to the New and the Indian Ocean to the Atlantic, rather than explorers from other cultures? Some European historians have argued just that—that Europeans had something others lacked.

Such a suggestion, however, seems ill conceived. Compared to the peoples of maritime Asia, Europeans were special mainly in being slow to launch long-range voyages. The Atlantic, the ocean they bordered, really was special, however, because its wind system inhibited exploration for centuries but rewarded it spectacularly once it was launched. Moreover, the breakthrough explorations were not the work of "Europe" but of people from a few communities on the Atlantic seaboard and in the Mediterranean. What distinguishes them is not that they set off with the right kind of culture, but that they set off from the right place.

THE EUROPEAN OUTLOOK: PROBLEMS AND PROMISE

In some ways, indeed, Western Europe in the fifteenth century was beset with problems. Recovery from the disasters of the fourteenth century was slow. Though plagues were less severe than in the fourteenth century, they remained frequent. Though used to the severe climate of their little ice age, Western Europeans did not reoccupy the high ground and distant colonies that they had vacated in the fourteenth century. In most places, population increase was modest and probably did not reach levels attained before the Black Death. Food supplies were unreliable, and harvests frequently failed.

Human foes joined impersonal enemies—plague, war, and famine. In 1396, a crusade to drive the Turks from the Balkans failed. It marked the beginning of a long period of Turkish advance on the Balkan and eastern Mediterranean frontiers of Christendom. Meanwhile, in the northeast, Lithuanians, most of whom remained pagan until the late fourteenth or early fifteenth century, eroded the conquests of German knightly orders along the Baltic Sea (see Chapter 12). In the early fifteenth century, Thule Inuit raiders finally obliterated the Norse colony on Greenland (see Chapter 14).

Meanwhile, hard times created opportunities for those with the skill or luck to exploit them. High mortality opened gaps in elites, which bureaucrats could fill, thanks, in part, to a revolution in government. The use of paper made it cheap and easy to transmit rulers' commands to the farthest corners of their realms. To help legitimize the newcomers' power, Western moralists redefined nobility as the product of virtue or education rather than ancestry. "Virtue is the sole and unique nobility," declared a Venetian coat of arms. A doctrine of late fifteenth-century Italian social thought invoked Greek mythology to make its point: "Neither the wealth of Croesus [reputedly the richest man in the world] nor the antiquity of the blood of Priam [the king of Troy in Homer's epics] could rival reason as an ingredient of nobility."

New economic divisions appeared. The line of the Elbe and northern Danube Rivers and the lands between became a cultural fault line. To the west of this line, underpopulation boosted the value of labor. The effects were to liberate peasants and urban communities from landowners' control, split up landholdings, encourage tenancies, and convert cropland to pasture. In the east the opposite occurred. Landholders responded to the loss of manpower and revenue by clamping down on peasants' rights and forcing formerly free towns into submission. New definitions of nobility were rejected. East of the Bohemian forest, nobility was ancient blood or acquired "by martial discipline," and that was that.

Scored by heresies, trenched by conflicting social values, riven by economic cracks, Western Europe nevertheless showed signs of self-confidence and optimism. Scholars and artists pursued, with renewed vigor, the project of recovering the legacy of classical antiquity—the cultural achievements of ancient Greece and Rome. The movement is commonly called "**the Renaissance**" on the grounds that the civilization of classical antiquity was reborn—but "the" is a much-abused word. Scholarship has now identified renaissances in almost every century for the previous thousand years. No radically new departure occurred in the fifteenth century from what had gone before—merely an accentuation of long-accumulating tendencies. Humanist students adopted a predominantly secular curriculum: grammar, rhetoric, poetry, history, and moral philosophy, imbibed mainly from

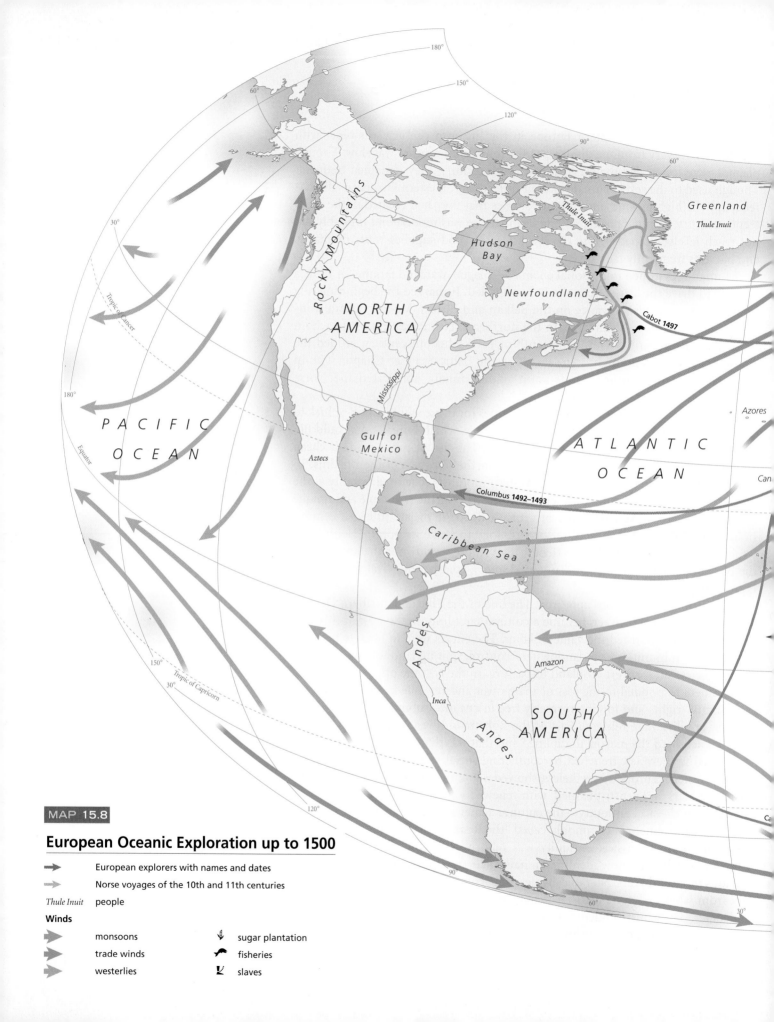

MAP 15.8

European Oceanic Exploration up to 1500

→ European explorers with names and dates

→ Norse voyages of the 10th and 11th centuries

Thule Inuit people

Winds

→ monsoons

→ trade winds

→ westerlies

↓ sugar plantation

🕊 fisheries

 L slaves

Labels on map:

Greenland
Thule Inuit
Thule Inuit
Hudson Bay
Newfoundland
Cabot **1497**
Rocky Mountains
NORTH AMERICA
Mississippi
Gulf of Mexico
Aztecs
Azores
ATLANTIC OCEAN
Can
Columbus **1492–1493**
Caribbean Sea
PACIFIC OCEAN
Andes
Amazon
Inca
SOUTH AMERICA
Andes
Ce
Tropic of Cancer
Equator
Tropic of Capricorn

NORWAY
SWEDEN
ENGLAND
Baltic Sea
LITHUANIA
Vistula
HOLY
ROMAN
EMPIRE
Elbe
POLAND
HUNGARY
Venice
Danube
ITALY
Genoa
Florence
SPAIN
Majorca
Granada
Algiers
Oran
OROCCO
Mediterranean Sea
Alexandria
Cairo
EGYPT

RUSSIA
Volga
Black Sea
Caspian Sea
OTTOMAN EMPIRE
Jerusalem
Baghdad
Hormuz

E U R A S I A

Karakorum
Beijing
Shanghai
PACIFIC
OCEAN
Macao
Manila
Tropic of Cancer

Himalayas
Ganges
Mons
BURMA
Khmer
Bay
of
Bengal
Rangoon
THAI
KINGDOM
Bangkok
Malays
South
China
Sea
Menado
Malacca

S a h a r a
Nile
Mecca
Arabian
Peninsula
Massawa
Aden
Horn of
Africa

Diu
Bombay
Goa
INDIA
Calicut

Cabral 1500–1501
de Gama 1497–1498

150°

AFRICA
Niger
Volta
Sierra Leone
São Jorge
de Mina
Congo

Mogadishu
Malinda
Kilwa
Sofala

I N D I A N

O C E A N

Tropic of Capricorn

de Gama 1497–98

Kalahari
Desert
Cape Town

30°

90°

60°

30°

0°

515

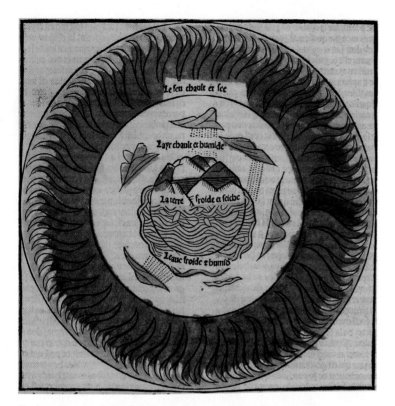

Le feu chault et fec

Layr chaule et bumide

La terre froide a feiche

Leaue froide et bumid

The four elements. In the fourth century B.C.E., Aristotle proposed that all matter is composed of four elements—earth, water, air, and fire—and exhibits different combinations of four qualities—moist, dry, hot, and cold. Over 1,800 years later, as this fifteenth-century illustration demonstrates, people in the West still believed in this theory. The artist shows the Earth as a sphere, with one large landmass emerging from an encircling ocean. Earth, "cold and dry," is surrounded by water, "cold and moist," and air, "hot and moist." The fourth element, fire, "hot and dry," forms an outer ring.

classical texts. The classics as well as—even, instead of—Christianity came to inform common ideas of morality, politics, and taste. Spreading, at first, from a few French and north Italian schools, **humanism** gradually became Europe's most prestigious form of learning. Political thinkers turned back to Greek and Roman history for instruction. Religious innovators modeled their ideas on evidence from early Christianity. Artists adopted realism and perspective from what they thought were Greek and Roman models.

Florence demonstrates humanism's power and limitations. In the fifteenth century, classical taste transformed the art and architecture of this Italian city. Comparisons with the Roman republic inspired its citizens to think of themselves as free and self-governing. Yet power gradually fell into the hands of a single family, the Medici, who patronized art in the classical tradition but who actually spent more on jewels and on gaudy, gemlike artworks that could display their wealth. When they were temporarily overthrown in 1494, after their banking business collapsed, the state that replaced them was no Roman-style republic. Rather, it was the rule of a "godly" clique, inspired by a hell-fire preacher, who preferred piety to humanism. Botticelli (1444–1510), the great artist who had painted pagan erotica for a Medici villa, turned to biblical subjects.

Still, across Europe, the rise of humanism had lasting consequences for Christian culture. Humanists painstakingly scrutinized the language of the Bible and the historical traditions of the church, exposing incorrect translations and departures from the practices of early Christianity. New styles in church architecture reflected classical taste and, more deeply, arose from the desire to create a setting for the kind of devotion that humanism inspired. Open sanctuaries, brilliantly lit and approached through wide naves and aisles allowed worshippers to see and take part in events at the altar.

Humanism also helped arouse European interest in the wider world. Some important and provocative geographical writings of classical antiquity became widely known in the West. In the early fifteenth century, the work of the ancient Greek scholar Ptolemy, originally written in Alexandria in the second century, invited intense speculation about geography, mapping the world, and the limits of exploration. The first-century B.C.E. work of Strabo, a Greek geographer who sought to reconstruct Homer's mental map of the world, prompted questions about finding previously unknown continents in the ocean. Humanists' fascination with the history of language reinforced the search for "primitive" peoples who might cast light on the question of how language originated.

Chivalry, however, was more important than humanism in stimulating overseas exploration. **Chivalry** could not, perhaps, make men good, as it was supposed to do. It could, however, win wars. In 1492, for instance, the monarchs of the Spanish kingdom of Castile extended the frontier of Christendom by conquering Granada, the last Muslim kingdom in Spain, in "a beautiful war," said

The Church of San Lorenzo. Filippo Brunelleschi, the trend-setting architect of Florence, got the commission to design the parish church of the ruling Medici family in 1418. He based his concept on laws of mathematical proportion that, he believed, ancient Greek and Roman architects had followed. He copied the ground plans of the most ancient churches he knew, and, to support the clergy's growing desire to make congregations participate actively in worship, he opened domes above the sacred spaces to fill them with light.

the Venetian ambassador. "There was not a lord present who was not enamored of some lady," who "often handed warriors their weapons . . . with a request that they show their love by their deeds." The queen of Castile died uttering prayers to the Archangel Michael as "prince of the chivalry of angels."

The typical chivalrous hero of the time took to the sea, conquered an island, married a princess, and became a ruler. Explorers—often men of humble social origins—tried to embody these fictions in real life. Adventurers in the service of the Portuguese Prince Henry (1394–1460), included former pirates and violent criminals. They indulged in chivalric rituals and gave themselves storybook names, like Lancelot and Tristram of the Island. They also colonized the Madeira Islands and parts of the Azores, and explored the coast of West Africa as far as Sierra Leone. The commercial sector that helped to back overseas adventures was looking for new opportunities—especially the Genoese, whose role in the eastern Mediterranean at this period was largely confined to high-bulk, low-profit shipping and trading. Marginal noblemen, shut out from advancement at home and imbued with chivalric ideas were willing to take amazing risks. That, plus the availability of high-risk investment, helps to explain many early forays in Atlantic exploration.

Prince Henry himself—traditionally misrepresented as a navigator motivated by scientific curiosity—imagined himself a romantic hero, destined to perform great deeds and win a kingdom of his own. The truth is that he never went exploring, and his desperate efforts to make enough money to pay his retainers

Chivalry. Most artists—including Albrecht Dürer (1471–1528) in this engraving—favored the famous moment in the story of St. Eustace, a legendary early Christian martyr, when he was converted by a vision of the cross that appeared between the antlers of a stag while he was out hunting. But it was the later episodes of the story—in which Eustace has a series of adventures at sea—that helped to inspire late-medieval European seafarers in search of fame, fortune, and sanctity.

included slave raiding and a soap monopoly. His followers included the father-in-law of Christopher Columbus, a weaver by training who reinvented himself as a "captain of cavaliers and conquests," and who took to exploration to escape the restricted social opportunities of home.

Alongside chivalry, millenarian fantasies may have influenced overseas expansion. The first king of Portugal's ruling dynasty was actually called "Messiah of Portugal." Columbus claimed that the profits of his discoveries could be used to conquer Jerusalem and help complete God's plans for a new age. Franciscan friars who supported Columbus believed that an "Age of the Holy Spirit," which would precede the end of the world, was coming soon, and some of them came to see the New World as the place where such an age might begin.

Europe's outreach into the Atlantic was probably not the result of science or strength, so much as of delusion and desperation. This was a space race where it helped to come from behind. The prosperous cultures with access to the Indian Ocean felt no need to explore remote lands and seas for new resources. For cash-strapped Europe, however, the attempt to exploit the Atlantic for new products was like the efforts of underdeveloped countries today, anxiously drilling for offshore wealth from oil or natural gas. In some ways, it paid off.

IN PERSPECTIVE: Beyond Empires

The imperial habit was spreading, and new empires were forming in environments that had never experienced imperialism before. Russia, for example, extended empire to the Eurasian far north. Mwene Mutapa introduced it in sub-Saharan East Africa. The Aztecs and Incas practiced it in the Americas on an unprecedented scale. Nonetheless, most of Africa and the Americas, as well as the whole of Australia and most of the Pacific island world, as far as we know, had still not experienced anything like empire. While some empires revived, most of the world remained in the hands of communities with modest political ambitions. These were still organized as kinship networks, chiefdoms, or small states. More remarkably, perhaps, some regions with an imperial past, or under imperialist threat, shied away. Instead, they developed systems in which independent states coexisted with varying degrees of mutual hostility. The world of the late fourteenth and fifteenth centuries had four such areas.

In North Africa, Mamluk Egypt was an immensely rich and productive state but remained confined to the Nile valley, unable to expand beyond the deserts that fringed it. A second area lay westward, along Africa's Mediterranean coast. Here numerous small states, founded on the profits of trade or piracy, flourished where Mediterranean and Saharan trade routes met. At the western end of North Africa, Morocco emerged as a kingdom on the edge of the Islamic world, holding Christendom at bay.

South and southeast Asia were a third empire-free region. In India, the sultanate of Delhi never fully recovered from the setbacks of the mid–fourteenth century. Hindu states proliferated, some warlike, specifically, toward Islam. The most militaristic, perhaps, was Vijayanagar—the name means "City of Victories"—with its 60 miles of sevenfold walls (see Map 15.9). This was the state, as we saw at the start of the chapter, that Abd-ar-Razzek, the Persian ambassador, had to cross the Indian Ocean from Iran to reach in 1417. It impressed another Muslim visitor in 1443 as "such that the eye has seen nothing like it." Chinese expansion nibbled at the edges of southeast Asia, but China's renunciation of imperialism left the native states of the region free to try one another's strength. The Thai—founders of what is now called Thailand—certainly had expansionist ambitions. In the early fifteenth century, they created the region's largest state at the expense

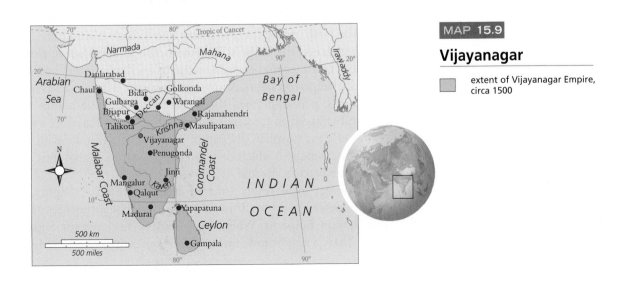

MAP 15.9

Vijayanagar

extent of Vijayanagar Empire, circa 1500

Vijayanagar. The steep, gleaming dome that dominates the ruins of Vijayanagar surmounts a shrine nearly 500 years older than the city itself, which arose in the fourteenth century as a focus of resistance against Muslim invaders from the north, on the rocky, easily defended site. By the early fifteenth century, Vijayanagar was the capital of a large state, formed by conquest and controlling much of southern India.

of their neighbors, the Burmese, Khmer, Mons, and Malays (see Map 15.8). Nonetheless, the region lacked a dominant empire and remained home to a state system in which a number of regional states contended with each other.

Finally, most of Europe continued to enclose a state system. East of the Vistula River, where geography favored the formation of large, unstable states by conquest, Russia, as we have seen, undertook a massive imperial enterprise. A brief union of the Polish and Lithuanian states in 1386 created what, on the map, at least, also looked like an empire of daunting dimensions, stretching from the Baltic to the Black Sea. Farther west, however, small states got stronger, and the dream of reuniting them and recreating the old Roman Empire faded—or began to look unrealistic.

Something like what we now call **nationalism** emerged. That is, group feeling developed where people's mutually intelligible speech and a common sense of identity defined by birth caused them to merge into a single community. In the fifteenth century, for instance, the kings of England began to use English, alongside French and Latin, as a language for official documents and correspondence. National communities adopted patron saints. At international gatherings, such as universities and church councils, people defined themselves according the nation to which they belonged and engaged in ferocious disputes over precedence. At a Council of the Church in 1415, the Castilian delegation settled such a dispute with the English by overturning the bench on which their rivals were sitting, so that the Castilians could occupy a higher place in the hall.

Second, states increasingly asserted their absolute sovereignty, rejecting any obligation to defer to such traditionally supranational authorities as the church or the Holy Roman Emperor. When, for instance, the Emperor Sigismund visited England in 1415, a knight rode into the sea to challenge him to renounce all claim to authority in England before he was allowed to disembark. Kings of France called themselves "emperors in their own realm" and those of Castile in Spain asserted "my sovereign absolute power."

Some rulers developed ideological grounds for their claims to absolute sovereignty. French kings were supposedly endowed with divine powers to heal and able to perform "miracles in your own lifetime." Richard II of England (r. 1377–1399) had himself painted in a sumptuous image, attended by angels, opening his hands to receive the body of Christ from the hands of the Virgin Mary herself.

Meanwhile, the power of the state really did increase. One reason was improved communications. As paper replaced parchment, increasing the output of documents, royal bureaucracies reached more people in more parts of the realm. Changes in the concept of law also strengthened the state. Traditionally, the law was seen as a body of wisdom handed down from the past. Now it came to be seen as a code that kings and parliaments could endlessly change and recreate. The state's power also expanded over vast new areas of public life and common welfare: labor relations, wages, prices, forms of land tenure, markets, the food supply, livestock breeding, and even, in some cases, what personal adornments people could wear.

Finally, while the state was growing more powerful, the power of the church declined. Between 1378 and 1415, rulers in Latin Christendom could not agree whom to recognize as pope. The power vacuum eroded what little unity Christendom still had. Secular states became stronger as heresies arose. Under the influence of reformers who demanded—among other changes—lay control of appointments in the church and worship in everyday language, Bohemia for a time refused to recognize papal authority. Reformers known as conciliarists argued that the church should become a kind of republic, with power transferred from Rome to bishops who would meet periodically.

How much difference did the state system make to Europe's prospects? Historians have engaged in a pointless debate on the question. On the one hand, the state system deprived Europeans of unified command, of the sort found, for instance, in the Chinese or Ottoman Empires. On the other hand, it stimulated competition among rulers, multiplying the possible sources of patronage available to innovators. For European maritime expansion, the state system was not decisive in launching most initiatives. The explorers and would-be empire builders relied on private enterprise, with little or no state backing. Columbus, for instance, got no direct financial support from the Spanish crown—the myth that

CHRONOLOGY

ca. 1325	Aztecs found city of Tenochtitlán
1368	Beginning of Ming dynasty
1370–1406	Reign of Timur
Late fourteenth century	Ethiopia expands into surrounding regions
1405	First voyage of Zheng He
1417	Voyage of Abd-ar-Razzak to Vijayanagar (India)
1430s	Portuguese establish way stations in Azores
1440s	Portuguese begin to obtain slaves from West Africa
ca. 1450	Inca begin period of expansion and conquest
1453	Ottomans capture Constantinople
1462–1505	Reign of Ivan the Great
ca. 1475	Center of power in southern Africa shifts from Zimbabwe to Mwene Mutapa
1480s	Portuguese make contact with Kingdom of Kongo
1482	Portuguese establish trading post of São Jorge da Mina on West African coast
1484	Sugar production begins in Canary Islands
1490s	First Portuguese diplomatic missions arrive in Ethiopia
1492–1493	First voyage of Christopher Columbus; Spanish kingdom of Castile captures Granada, last Muslim kingdom in Spain
1496	John Cabot discovers direct route across North Atlantic
1497	Pilgrimage of Muhammed Touray Askia, ruler of Songhay, to Mecca; first voyage of Vasco da Gama
1500	Vasco da Gama reaches India; Aztec Empire at its peak

Queen Isabella of Castile pawned her jewels for him is nonsense. Prince Henry's Atlantic enterprise was a private venture. Furthermore, as the example of southeast Asia shows, a state system was not in itself sufficient to produce overseas imperialism. For that, the stimulus of coming from behind was necessary. Asian states were at the nodes of the world's richest trades. They had no need to explore new markets or conquer new centers of production, because everything came to them anyway. Europeans, on the other hand, had to expand if they were to gain access to anything worth exploiting.

For all its hesitations and limitations, fifteenth-century expansion was new and potentially world changing. The new routes pioneered in the 1490s linked the populous central belt of Eurasia to the Americas and Africa, and Europe to Asia by sea. We can see the beginnings of a framework of an interconnected globe—a **world system** able to encompass the planet. The expanding empires of the age were reaching toward each other. Where they made contact, they became arenas of unprecedented scale for trade and for transmitting technology, ideas, sentiments, and ways of life. The consequences would transform the world of the next three centuries: worldwide encounters, commerce, conflict, contagion, and cultural and ecological exchange.

PROBLEMS AND PARALLELS

1. Why can the last half of the fifteenth century be considered an age of expansion? How did the beginnings of a world system emerge around 1500?

2. Why were African states fragile in this period?

3. What is meant by the term *ecological imperialism*? How did the Inca exploit the many different ecosystems of their empire? What was role of tributary networks in the Aztec Empire?

4. How did the Russian and Turkish worlds expand in the fourteenth and fifteenth centuries?

5. Why did the Chinese turn away from maritime expansionism in the fifteenth century? Why was frontier stability more important than expansion?

6. How do the developments discussed in this chapter demonstrate the importance of winds in world history? Why should the beginnings of European oceanic imperialism be viewed as having as much to do with geography as with culture?

7. How did the rise of nationalism and the state system drive European expansion?

DOCUMENTS IN GLOBAL HISTORY

- From the *Narrative of the Journey of Abd-ar-Razzak*
- The founding of Tenochtitlán

- From Ma Huan, *The Overall Survey of the Ocean's Shores*

Please see the Primary Source CD-ROM for additional sources related to this chapter.

READ ON

The material on Abd-er-Razzaq comes from R. H. Major, ed., *India in the Fifteenth Century* (1964). D. Ringrose, *Expansion and Global Interaction, 1200–1700* (2001) gives the background.

On Ethiopia, S. C. Munro-Hay, *Ethiopia: the Unknown Land* (2002) and R. Pankhurst, *The Ethiopians: A History* (2001) are valuable general histories. W. G. Randles, *The Empire of Monomotapa* (1975) is excellent on Mwene Mutapa. On West Africa in this period, E. W. R. Bovill, *The Golden Trade of the Moors* (1995) is a readable classic. Songhay is not well served by books in English but a useful collection of sources is J. O. Hunwick, ed., *Timbuktu and the Songhay Empire: Al-Sa'di's Ta'rîkh al-Sudan Down to 1613, and Other Contemporary Documents* (1999). Anne Hilton, *The Kingdom of Kongo* (1985) is outstanding.

Of histories of the Inca and Aztecs, J. V. Murra, *The Economic Organization of the Inca State* (1980), T.N. D'Altroy, *The Incas* (2003), and M. Smith, *The Aztecs* (2002) are particularly strong on ecological aspects.

My material on the White Sea comes from R. Cormack and D. Gaze, eds, *Art of Holy Russia* (1998). J. Martin, *Treasures of the Land of Darkness* (2004) is enthralling on the economic background to Russian expansion. I. Gray, *Ivan III and the Unification of Russia* (1972) is a businesslike introduction. Ibn Khaldun's great work is *The Muqaddimah: an Introduction to History*, tr. Franz Rosenthal (1969). B. F. Manz, *The Rise and Rule of Tamerlane* (1999) is the outstanding work on its subject.

For the Ottomans, see H. Inalcik, *The Ottoman Empire: the Classical Age* (2001). E.L. Dreyer, *Early Ming China* (1982) and *Zheng He: China and the Oceans in the Early Ming Dynasty* (2006) cover the Chinese topics of this chapter admirably. L. Levathes, *When China Ruled the Seas* (1997) is readable and reliable.

On Europe C. Allmand, ed, *The New Cambridge Medieval History, VII* (2005) is comprehensive, while M. Aston, *The Prospect of Europe* (1968) offers a short introduction. On Portuguese expansion, P.E. Russell, *Henry the Navigator* (2001) is admirable and F. Bethencourt and D. Curto, eds, *The Portuguese Empire* (1998) provides a broad survey. P.O. Kristeller, *The Cambridge Companion to Renaissance Humanism* (1996) is an unsurpassed classic on its topic and M.H. Keen, *Chivalry* (1986) is on the way to attaining the same status.

Gender and Power in a Medieval Kingdom

In 1184 an extraordinary event occurred in the Caucasus kingdom of Georgia. Tamar, a woman, ascended the throne. As we read in Chapter 13, Georgia on the eve of the Mongol invasions was flourishing. After centuries of fragmentation brought on by Arab conquest, Turkish raids, and internal strife, Georgia coalesced into a unified state when dynastic alliances brought the entire country under the rule of the Bagrati family in 1008. By the end of the reign of David II (1089–1125, known as "the Builder"), the kingdom held sway from the Black Sea to Persia, and its subjects included peoples of many cultures and faiths. Once a backwater region, Georgia had emerged as a great Christian power bridging Byzantium and the Islamic East.

● ● ● ● ●

This was the setting for the coronation of Tamar. Despite being crowned coruler with her father Giorgi III in 1178 (in keeping with Bagratid tradition), Tamar had to be crowned again after he died. Giorgi had repressed the nobility, and the aristocracy saw his death as an opportunity to reassert control. But the more important reason for its challenge to Tamar's accession had to do with her sex.

As a woman, Tamar's claim to power was shaky. Not only had no woman ever ruled the kingdom, but Georgia, though strong, was surrounded by hostile enemies—all ruled by men. A nation governed by a woman was seen as weak. Strength in battle was the chief virtue of the Georgian monarch, but Tamar's sex precluded her from fighting. She would have to validate her rule through other means.

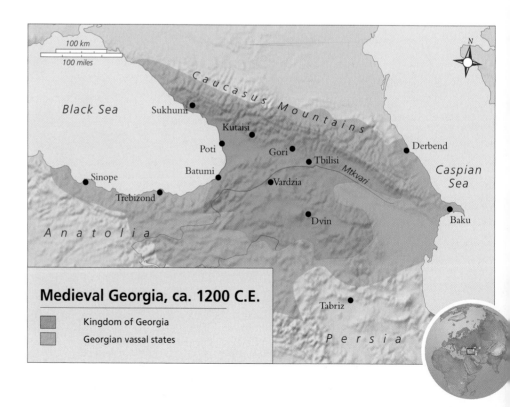

Medieval Georgia, ca. 1200 C.E.

- Kingdom of Georgia
- Georgian vassal states

Photo 1 Vardzia

The earliest surviving image of Tamar is found at Vardzia, in southwest Georgia (Photo 1), in the Church of the Dormition (Photo 2). Vardzia is a vast complex of churches and monastic living quarters hewn out of solid rock on a cliff 1000 feet above the Mtkvari River. In its heyday it housed up to 50,000 people. Begun by Giorgi, Vardzia was chosen for its impregnable location. Tamar finished its construction in 1186. Although the Georgian court constantly moved around the kingdom, Vardzia was one of the cultural centers of the country. The Church of the Dormition, the last structure to be completed, was the most important religious building in the complex. It was a place where the nobles of the kingdom would gather for feasts and celebrations.

Photo 2 Vardzia, Church of the Dormition

Photo 3 Tamar and Giorgi before the Virgin Mary

Photo 4 Tamar and Giorgi (detail)

**Photo 6
St. Katherine**

The frescoes planned for the church's interior presented a perfect opportunity to legitimize Tamar's rule. Of all the images inside the church, the most prominent is the scene of Tamar and her father standing before the Virgin Mary and the Christ child (Photo 3). Giorgi stretches his hands in supplication while Tamar, behind him, presents a model of the finished church. The Virgin accepts their offer, and an angel hovers above with a scepter, symbolizing divine approval of their rule.

The composition of the scene asks the viewer to consider Tamar and Giorgi together. Although both figures are adorned with halos to indicate their closeness to God, Tamar is placed second to show that her rule also derives its legitimacy through her father, even though he has been dead for two years. Giorgi's masculinity mediates between Tamar and the divine. Tamar, a woman, receives her power from God through him.

The similarity between Giorgi's and Tamar's dress further emphasizes the close connection between father and daughter (Photo 4). Both monarchs wear identical crowns. Their embroidered, Byzantine–style robes closely resemble each other. Except for earrings, little about Tamar's outfit suggests that she is a woman. The first impression of royal power at Vardzia excludes any consideration of Tamar's gender.

The description near her head reinforces Tamar's de-sexed status. She is described as *mepeta mepe*, or "king of kings." Though grammatically the Georgian language makes no distinction between gender, which could argue for translating *mepeta mepe* as "monarch of monarchs," the female consorts of Georgian kings were known as *dedopali*—"queen." Thus, the application of *mepeta mepe* was a conscious decision to masculinize Tamar's power. A clear message is being conveyed: Tamar, as "king" is unlike any other woman. Any other *living* woman, that is.

Near Tamar's image at Vardzia is a fresco painting of Saint Nino. As with Tamar, Vardzia is the first surviving appearance of this saint in Georgian art, lending it great symbolic importance. Nino's location on the south wall, directly opposite Tamar, forms a visual axis between the two women. Any consideration of Tamar's image must take into account its relationship with Nino.

Like Tamar, Nino had to overcome objections to her sex. As the apostolic saint who brought Christianity to the kingdom in the fourth century (see Chapter 9), Nino embodies Georgian Christianity. She is a patriotic figure, beyond the limitations of gender. Her portrait (not shown here) placed opposite Tamar's further deemphasizes Tamar's sex and strengthens Tamar's claim to rule. The ideals of nationhood that Nino represents associate themselves with Tamar, rendering Tamar's femininity irrelevant.

Although the image of Tamar, and that of Nino nearby, stress masculine and gender neutral aspects of royal power, they do not deny Tamar's femininity. Indeed, the depiction of Tamar's face embodies idealized notions of feminine beauty that prevailed in Georgia at that time (Photo 5). Her skin is pale, especially compared to her father's ruddy complexion. Most striking, however, is the smooth oval face and the distinctly oriental shape of her eyes, which are unlike those found on any figure in the church, such as the image of St. Katherine, dressed like Tamar, in Byzantine imperial costume. Katherine's angular face and broad eyes differ sharply from Tamar's (Photo 6).

Thus, in contrast to the Western Christian adornments—Byzantine robe, crown, scepter—that masculinize her power, Tamar's physical beauty derives from Eastern, non–Christian models. Her conspicuously oval face and eyes conform to Persian ideals of feminine beauty, as evidenced by a Seljuk bowl showing a queen from twelfth–century Iran (Photo 7). So, though Tamar's power as ruler is masculine (or defeminized) and Western, her role as an ideal female is Eastern. In a Christian kingdom that straddled the cultural divide between East and West, it was necessary to depict royal power in Christian terms, but it was also acceptable to portray feminine beauty in a non-Christian way. Considered together, Tamar is both king and ideal woman. The nobles who viewed the image of Tamar at Vardzia would have understood the message.

Photo 5 Tamar

Questions to Consider

1 How does the image of Tamar at Vardzia suggest that the concept of gender can be manipulated?

2 Giorgi had been an unpopular king. How does Tamar's gender shed a more positive light on his reign? In turn, how does Giorgi legitimize Tamar's right to rule?

3 How does the characterization of Byzantium as "Western" at Vardzia differ from the way the empire is typically viewed?

4 What does the representation of Persian ideals of beauty at Vardzia say about the dynamics of cultural interaction between countries?

Sources

Allen, W. E. D. A *History of the Georgian People*. London, 1932.
Eastmond, A., ed., *Eastern Approaches to Byzantium*. Aldershot, 2001.
Eastmond, A. *Royal Imagery in Medieval Georgia*. University Park, 1998.
Lordkipanidze, M. *Georgia in the Eleventh to Twelfth Centuries*. Tbilisi, 1987.
Thomson, R.W. *Rewriting Caucasian History: The Medieval Armenian Adaptation of the Georgian Chronicles: The Original Texts and the Armenian Adaptation*. Oxford, 1996.
Vivian, K. *The Georgian Chronicle: The Period of Giorgi Lasha*. Amsterdam, 1991.

Photo 7 Seljuk bowl, Persia

The Mixtec World-View of the fifteenth century, ▷
painted on deer hide. At the center of the world
the god Xiutecutli spills the life forces of fire
and blood. Trees grow toward each of four directions. At the top, a sun disc, rising over temple
steps, signifies east. In the west, where the sun
sets, the tree is uncolored.
*National Museums and Galleries on Merseyside,
Liverpool, England, U.K.*

ENVIRONMENT

since 1492
Columbian exchange

since 1513
Atlantic navigation–
Gulf Stream mastered

CULTURE

ca.1500–1600
Portuguese maritime empire

since 1565
Pacific Navigation–
Japan current mastered

since early 1600s
Dutch navigation of "roaring 40s"

since ca. 1640
Decline of steppelands

mid–16th century
Atlantic slave trade takes off

ca.1550–1650
Expansion of Asian empires

1640
Closing of Japan

1600–1700
Western Scientific Revolution

CHAPTER 16
Imperial Arenas: New Empires in the Sixteenth and Seventeeth Centuries

Portuguese, armed mainly with bows, resist the attack on Hormuz, which restored the island fortress to Persian rule, in 1622. This was the first of a long series of campaigns in which indigenous powers ejected the Portuguese from their trading outposts on the coasts of Asia and East Africa.

The letter was only one page long. But Jeronimo de Quadros put his heart into it, as he poured out his troubles to his king. In 1572, after a career spent fighting up and down the east coast of Africa and Arabia and in the Persian Gulf, he had succeeded his father as commander of a Portuguese fort on the Persian mainland, at a spot the Portuguese called Comorão, modern Kumora. Sixteen years later, he was concerned about the rewards for service he hoped to receive back home. By the end of the 1580s, those concerns were becoming urgent. All the other Portuguese garrisons in the region had fallen to native enemies. Jeronimo de Quadros's own fort was becoming indefensible. He had, he wrote, only seven Portuguese and 45 native mercenaries under his command. With these, he had to man the fort, control local marauders, and escort traders who might want to do business with Portugal. He had difficulty keeping his men supplied with arrows. Gunpowder and shot were so far beyond his reach that they were not even worth mentioning. Every year, he explained, he had to rebuild his fort after the rains "because it is made of mud." His most revealing problem was the want of sufficient opium to meet the needs of his men. Their task was so hopeless, in this remote and abandoned corner of an overextended empire, that they could only face it with the help of narcotics. Though the fate of Jeronimo de Quadros is unknown, his fort finally fell into enemy hands shortly afterward. Now, like all the Portuguese forts that once dotted the region, it lies in ruins. Quadros's predicament was typical of the sixteenth, seventeenth, and eighteenth centuries, when empires seemed to overreach the limits of the possible and to exceed the scope of the technology at their command.

● ● ● ● ●

Nowadays, *empire* has become one of the dirty words of politics. Politicians, exchanging abuse across the world, commonly call each other "imperialists." We recoil from the idea that any political community should be subject to another. It seems to go against our respect for principles we call freedom or self-determination. But from the sixteenth century to the eighteenth, when the unprecedented growth of empires was one of the most dramatic features of the history of the world, empires spread as much by collaboration as by conquest. They were not usually held together by force, because no state had enough resources for such a task. Empires' moral effects on their subjects

FOCUS questions

- HOW WERE empires the agents of change in the sixteenth and seventeenth centuries?
- WHY WERE the Dutch able to replace the Portuguese as the main European imperial power in Asia?
- HOW WERE maritime empires different from land empires in Asia during the sixteenth and seventeenth centuries?
- WHAT ROLES did war and conquest play in the Mughal and Ottoman Empires?
- WHY WERE Native Americans so important in the Spanish conquests of the Aztec and Inca Empires?
- WHY DID the global balance of trade begin to shift during the seventeenth century?

were mixed. Some communities were victimized, subjugated, exterminated, or enslaved, while enhanced economic opportunities enriched others, as markets grew and trade routes lengthened. Above all, empires were arenas of exchange—and not solely or primarily of exchange of trade. They stimulated—and sometimes enforced—human migrations on a scale never previously undertaken, over unprecedented distances, and in unprecedented directions. Technologies, religions, political ideas, artistic tastes became interchangeable across vast distances as never before.

Finally—and perhaps most importantly of all—**imperialism** helped to introduce a new era in evolution. Formerly, for hundreds of millions of years, ever since the continents of the world began to drift apart, the life-forms of landmasses divided by uncrossable oceans developed independently of one another. Each continent had its own peculiar plant and animal life. Everything tended to be different—from human types to microbes. About 500 years ago, this long history of divergence ended. As empires crossed oceans, the continents came into mutual contact. They swapped life-forms. The world we inhabit today began to take shape—in which you can find specimens of the same creatures, wherever climate permits, all over the world (see Chapter 17).

So empires offer a framework for understanding all the major long-range, long-run changes of the period. Western historians used to see the empires founded from Western Europe as the sources of the most important initiatives, and even to call the period as a whole the "Age of European Expansion." But imperialism was not a peculiarly Western vice. Asian, African, and Native American peoples created and led some of the most impressive empires of the period. And the "European" empires usually depended on non-European collaborators who saw an advantage in cooperating with the Europeans. Indeed, the numbers of Europeans involved in creating the empires and making them work were normally small compared with the numbers of native peoples or of non-European migrants from elsewhere. The influences that shaped the empires and made them different from one another, generally owed more to environmental or economic circumstances than to their home countries and the traditional allegiances of their ruling elites.

MARITIME EMPIRES: PORTUGAL, JAPAN, AND THE DUTCH

Until about 500 years ago, most empires were concerned with controlling large amounts of two resources: people and land. They may have had ideological or religious reasons for wanting to extend their territorial control; or they may have engaged in conquests out of hatred or insecurity. The economic purpose underlying empire, however, was usually to gain control of, or power over, the places and people that produced valuable goods.

Less commonly, imperial communities could enrich themselves by controlling trade as well as, or even instead of, production. By land, imperialism of this kind is hard to achieve without occupying vast amounts of territory, because traders tend to find ways to outflank imperialists. At sea, however, the opportunities are better. By seizing what is often a limited number of suitable ports, or by patrolling what are often limited routes of access that winds, currents, and straits shape, imperial-minded people can obtain a stranglehold on trade in some commodities, within some climatic or geographical zones. Or they can colonize limited amounts of coastal territory that seaborne communications link, to produce and ship commercial commodities for their own profit. As we have seen, empires of these kinds flourished—briefly and at intervals—in the ancient and medieval Mediterranean and in parts of maritime Asia.

From the sixteenth to the eighteenth centuries, opportunities multiplied to found and extend such empires. Technological improvements accompanied the new opportunities. European or European-designed ships began to rival, and even excel, those of traditional Asian construction, partly thanks to borrowings from Asian technology, such as rudders, bulkheads between the ship's interior compartments, more streamlined designs for long-range commercial vessels, and technical aids that enabled navigators to determine their position by the sun and stars. Improvements in artillery and fortifications made it ever easier to defend coastal forts and trading posts. Naval powers that mustered enough shipping and shipboard firepower could use convoys to control sea-lanes or even exclude rival ships by aggressive policing. Meanwhile, sea charts—which professional seamen traditionally despised because it was a matter of professional pride for them to navigate by memory and experience—gradually became an accepted and necessary part of nautical equipment. The expanding reach of exploration helped to improve these nautical maps. Gradually, too, longitude-finding techniques improved. In 1584, King Philip II of Spain decreed a prize for anyone who could solve the problem of determining longitude at sea. Other states initiated similar schemes. A long and fitful series of improvements followed, although no really reliable method was devised until the late eighteenth century.

Improved technology, however, was of little use without new routes where it could be deployed. As we saw in detail in Chapter 15, until the sixteenth century, the world's only really effective long-range, ocean-crossing routes were confined

◉ MAKING CONNECTIONS ◉

LAND EMPIRES AND MARITIME EMPIRES COMPARED

TYPE OF EMPIRE	CHARACTERISTICS
Maritime	• Control of international trade via strategic seizure of suitable ports, control of sea-lanes • Colonization of limited coastal territory • Production and shipment of high-value commodities • Limited military confrontation and investment in imperial colonies • Exploitation of improved maritime technology • Expanded use of sea charts for exploration, control of far-flung regions • Dependence on native collaborators
Land	• Emphasis on control of large amounts of people and land • Large military investment required to staff outposts and fund armies • Land and sea access routes vulnerable unless controlled • Massive capital investment to support imperial colonies and build infrastructure • Superior technology needed to overcome resistance from natives • Expanded social and cultural contacts with imperial subjects • Dependence on native collaborators

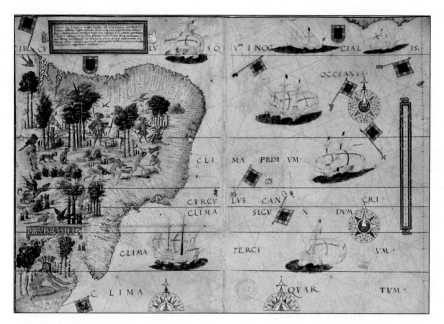

Lines of latitude. By 1519, when Lopo Homem produced this map of Brazil, the images mapmakers used to convey the nature of the country were well established: feathered Tupi Indians; valuable dyewood logged by Native American woodcutters; lush forests full of parrots and monkeys. The lines of latitude on the map separate the climatic zones first identified by geographers in ancient Greece.

to monsoonal seas. This was chiefly because **monsoons** are seasonal. They blow toward land in summer—sucked landward by warming air, rising over large land masses. In winter, the direction of the wind is reversed. Navigators therefore know that if they venture out to sea with a following wind, they will be able eventually to return home. In the **fixed wind systems** of the Atlantic and Pacific Oceans, by contrast, the direction of the prevailing winds never shifts for long. The ambitious navigator's choice is bleak: to risk a voyage with a following wind, taking you ever farther from home, with the prospect of never being able to return; or to sail against a headwind and probably never get far. In consequence, shipping crossed and recrossed the monsoonal seas of the Indian Ocean and maritime Asia for centuries, creating dynamic economies and generating enormous wealth, before the Atlantic or Pacific was developed as a major trading space. In the sixteenth century, however, the monopoly of the Indian Ocean ended. With the discovery of the Gulf Stream in 1513, the last major element of the wind and current system of the Atlantic became known to navigators. Thereafter, the principal routes of trade among Europe, Africa, and the Americas were established in the form that has remained normal, for seaborne commerce, to the present day: outward bound with the easterly trade winds, toward the Caribbean and the central zones of the Americas, then northward with the Gulf Stream to the region of westerlies that bring ships back to Europe. In the Pacific in the 1520s and 1530s, Spanish navigators explored the easterly wind corridors that link the New World to Asia, but the route back long eluded explorers. After many unsuccessful attempts to find it, an expedition of 1564–1565 solved the problem by exploiting the way the winds circulate in the northern Pacific, using the Japan Current to get back to the west coast of America from the Philippines. Finally, in the early seventeenth century, Dutch sailors began to exploit the fierce westerly winds that enable sailing ships to circle the globe around 40 degrees latitude south. This made it possible to link the commerce of the Atlantic, Pacific, and Indian Oceans with new speed and reliability. In particular, the Dutch opened a fast new route between Europe and the East Indies, sailing nonstop, if necessary—or with a stop or two at the island of St. Helena in the middle of the South Atlantic and at the Cape of Good Hope on the southern tip of Africa—all the way from Holland to Java in what is today Indonesia. The speediest method was to bypass the Indian Ocean to the south with the westerlies, then turn north with the Great Australia Current, skirting the coast of western Australia, and heading directly for the Sunda Strait toward the East Indies (see Map 15.1).

As explorers cracked the wind codes of the world's oceans, previously inconceivable interconnections became possible: directly between Europe and the Indian Ocean; between America and Asia; or among Europe, Africa, and the Americas.

The Portuguese Example

On an unprecedented scale, Europeans could now gain access to the commerce of the Indian Ocean and maritime Asia. The main motive was simple. The economies of the region were hugely richer and more productive than those of Europe. Anyone who could get ships into the region and carry some of its trade could make money here. Moreover, the region produced luxury manufactures of a quality Europeans could not produce for themselves: textiles, especially, from India and China, and increasingly, as time went on and trade developed, porcelain from China and Japan. Even more important were the foodstuffs, drugs, and spices that only grew in environments that could not be reproduced in Europe, and that were expensive because they were as much in demand in China as in Europe. Pepper dominated the spice trade because cuisine at the time in both Europe and China privileged it as a flavor and because—with other spices—it was much used in pickling processes that, along with drying and salting, were for a long time the only way to preserve food. Finally, eastern seas attracted European traders because their markets were highly exploitable. Gold was relatively cheap, in exchange for silver, in China, but relatively expensive in India. Canny traders could make fortunes out of the difference.

Portugal was well placed to take advantage, partly thanks to a position on the Atlantic edge, close to the place from which the trade winds spring. After dividing up zones of navigation by agreement with their Spanish neighbors, Portuguese began to penetrate the Indian Ocean. Portuguese venturers opened direct trade with the pepper-growing region of southern India in 1500 and founded a coastal trading post nearby at Goa in 1510. They established direct access to the trading world of the islands off southeast Asia within a few years more. They began direct contact with Thailand and China in the second decade of the sixteenth century and with Japan in the 1540s.

In some ways, the Portuguese enterprise in Asia was a classic case of maritime imperialism. They took over Malacca in modern Malaysia to try to gain an advantage in directing trade through the Strait of Malacca. They used force to compel unwilling partners to trade with them, especially in the "Spice Islands" of what is now eastern Indonesia, where low-bulk, high-value goods, such as nutmeg, cloves, mace*, and camphor[†], and aromatic woods, such as sandalwood, were grown. They attacked rival shipping to damage other people's trade. They established expensive bases at the mouth of the Red Sea, on the coast of East Africa, and in the Persian Gulf—and, eventually, even on the Persian coast—in unsuccessful efforts to divert trade into their own hands and to strangle alternative routes. In 1529, they agreed with Spain to extend to the Pacific the system they had already agreed to observe in the Atlantic, in which each guaranteed the other's monopoly over selected routes, while denying access to the shipping of other powers. In effect they divided seaborne routes to the non-European world between them. In the early seventeenth century, they tried to control by force the trade of Sri Lanka—the world's main source of cinnamon (see Map 16.1).

Still, Portuguese imperialism was, by the standards of native Asian empires of the day, a feeble and shallow affair—a minor irritant, causing only local or temporary disruption. Portugal was a small country, with only 1.5 million inhabitants and few natural resources, except large salt pans and privileged access to the sea. It was poorer and less populous even than the Netherlands, for example.

Maritime Imperialism: Technology and Sea Routes

1513	Gulf Stream discovered
1520s–1530s	Spanish navigators explore easterly wind corridors that link the New World to Asia
1564–1565	Northern Pacific route between Asia and New World discovered
1584	Philip II of Spain offers prize for solving problem of longitude at sea
Early seventeenth century	Dutch use westerlies to circumnavigate globe

---

*Mace: an aromatic spice

[†]Camphor: an aromatic compound

The main business of the Portuguese was to participate as shippers and traders in the existing commerce of Asia, along traditional routes. Direct trade with Europe was not significant for Asia, but was important for Europe; and it grew throughout the period. Three or four Portuguese ships a year carried the whole of the Indian pepper trade to Europe in the last decade of the sixteenth century. In each of the last two decades of the century, when other European trading communities had joined in the business, 400 ships left Europe for Asia, most of them destined to return with Asian goods. But direct dealing with Europe was only a secondary element in the lives of most Portuguese in Asia. Most of Asia's Portuguese, indeed, lived beyond areas of Portuguese rule, as servants, mercenaries, technicians, missionaries, or commercial agents in Asian states. They were welcome, because their trading activities and their work as shippers in established trades contributed to the further enrichment of existing economies.

Francisco Vieira da Figueiredo was a representative figure. Like many poor Portuguese soldiers in the east, he resorted to trade to make a living. He was a chameleon who moved with ease through the various colorful islands between the Indian Ocean and the South China Sea. He served in 1642 as the envoy to Cambodia of a Spanish governor of Manila. He dealt with the Dutch East India Company, even when they were at war with Portugal. He became the intimate adviser of the sultan of Makassar in what is today Indonesia, the envoy of the ruler of Golconda in India, and a commercial agent for both of them. His object, according to English competitors, was "gain of wealth." Though he often talked of returning to Portugal, he was in his element in the east, where he could affect gentlemanly rank and presume on princely friends. His life was adapted for mobility. In Makassar, like other foreigners, he was forbidden to build a permanent residence. So he lived in a bamboo shack. But his real palace was his magnificently appointed yacht. As a trader, his first interest was in textiles from Coromandel in southeast India. He then special-

Goa. Jan Van Linschoten's travels in the Portuguese trading places of the East in the late sixteenth century were an intelligence-gathering mission that helped to launch Dutch overseas expansion. The engravings that illustrated the published versions of his account of his trip were based on drawings he claimed to have made from life. This one depicts the street life of Goa in Portuguese India. Note the business being recorded at the table of the public scribe and the merchants gathering around it, the unsuccessful peddler in European dress, the madam selling a concubine on the left, and that characteristic institution of Portuguese colonial life, the alms house, on the right.

ized in aromatic woods from Indonesian islands, gold and silver from Sumatra and the Philippines, and cloves from the Molucca Islands, which were the chief item of Makassar's trade. In 1664, when the Dutch forced him out of Makassar, he went to the island of Timor and dealt in sandalwood until his death three years later.

Typically, Portuguese blended into local society as well as local politics and regional trade by marrying or living with local women, who supported their husbands' business. Schemes to promote the supply of "eligible maidens" from Europe for Europeans living in the east were frequently launched and usually failed, or they supplied women of dubious background and morals. African or Indian wives administered their Portuguese husbands' estates while the latter were away on trading voyages. According to an English male visitor, wives acquired in the Portuguese East African possession of Mozambique excelled European women for "fidelity, behaviour to their husband, good-natured dispositions and agreeable conversation, so far as their little knowledge extends." Moralists accused some Portuguese in Goa and Bassein in Burma of large-scale pimping, training dancing girls in their personal harems and selling them as Hindu-temple prostitutes. The usual pattern, however, more resembled a scene engraved on a famous ivory casket from seventeenth-century Sri Lanka in which a Portuguese merchant or soldier and his Sri Lankan wife share a luxurious table of local dishes. Such marriages could be mutually beneficial, The merchant got access to valuable commercial contacts. His bride acquired substantial rights to share the profits of his business under Portuguese law. Her family was often rewarded with offices in Portuguese firms or trading posts.

Until well into the second half of the seventeenth century, most European involvement in Asia was of the same sort, what some historians have called "trading-post empires." There were direct trades with Europe, chiefly in spices, principally pepper, conducted by aspiring monopolists. These monopolists were the Portuguese crown, and, from about the turn of the seventeenth century, English and

The *Estado da India*. The empire that the Portuguese called the *Estado da India* was actually a string of trading posts around the edges of the Indian Ocean and east Asia. The outposts depicted here were in India in 1630, shortly before Portugal began to withdraw from most of the region in the face of native hostility and Dutch competition. Note how lightly fortified most of these places are and how several of them include mosques—sometimes within, sometimes outside the walls. Like other European overseas expansion, that of Portugal depended on native people's willingness to collaborate with it and tolerate it.

Dutch companies. A similar trade with the New World, chiefly in Chinese silks and porcelain, was conveyed annually in a single Spanish galleon via Spain's colonial outpost in Manila in the Philippines. But European participation in commerce between Asian countries and in shipping ventures within Asian waters eclipsed these trades in value and extent.

Asian Examples

To understand the increased opportunities for Europeans, we need to look at the context of the enormously increased activity—as merchants, colonists, and even, occasionally, maritime imperialists—of native Asian states and communities. At either end of maritime Asia—in Japan in the east and in Oman on the coast of Arabia and the Ottoman Empire in the west—were rulers and adventurers interested in maritime imperialism (see Map 16.1).

Toyotomi Hideyoshi (hee–day–OH-shee), the warlord who took over Japan at the end of a long era of civil war in 1585, is a case in point. He sent demands for submission to the kingdoms of mainland southeast Asia and to the Spanish governor in the Philippines. He vowed to ravish China "like a maiden" and "crush it like an egg." He proclaimed himself the gods' choice for mastery of the world. It sounds insane. But it was a rational strategy in the circumstances. The civil wars had militarized Japanese society. Professional warriors needed employment. Arms industries needed markets. Warlords' energies had to be redeployed. Japanese pirates had shown how vulnerable China was, sucking wealth into Japan, raiding Chinese cities far inland, and holding them to ransom.

Hideyoshi imagined his future conquests vividly. The Koreans and Chinese would "learn Japanese customs." Kidnapped children were taught Japanese. The land of China would be split among Japanese notables, and the Japanese emperor would be invested with the mandate of heaven. At first when the Japanese invaded in 1592, Korea, enfeebled by two centuries of peace, seemed easily conquerable. But the Korean navy had long experience of conflict against pirates and was equipped with startling new technology: "turtle ships" with reinforced hulls and ship-killing cannon. In combination with the typhoon-lashed seas and in collaboration with the Chinese fleet, the Korean sailors made it impossible for the Japanese to supply and reinforce their armies in Korea. Shortly after Hideyoshi's death in September 1598, the Japanese aborted their campaigns on the mainland of Asia.

It was not, however, the end of Japanese expansion. Okinawa and the Ryukyu Islands south of Japan became, in effect, a Japanese dependency by conquest in 1609. The northern land frontier of Japan gradually expanded to fill the whole of what we now think of as the Japanese home islands, at the expense of the native Ainu people, during the rest of the seventeenth century (see Chapter 19). And in the eighteenth century, Japanese expansion met that of Russia in the northern Pacific, where the two powers disputed control of the huge but barren and fogbound island of Sakhalin. Meanwhile, although the Japanese state formally

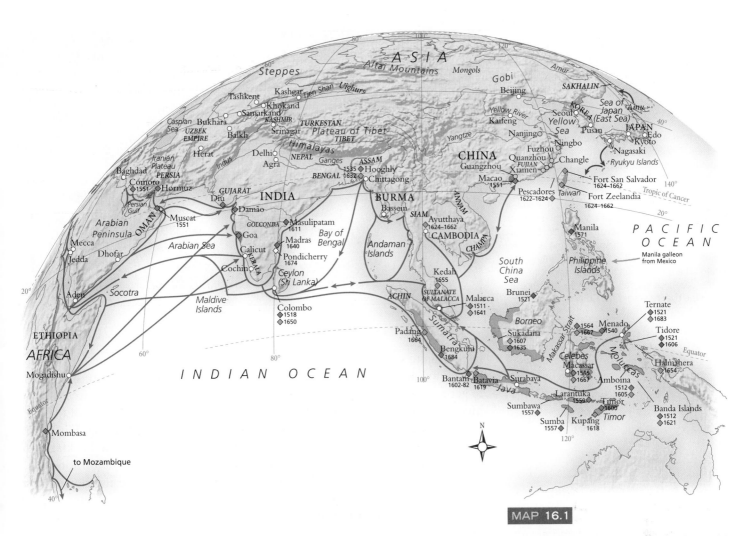

MAP 16.1

Maritime Imperialism in the Indian and Pacific Oceans, 1500–1700

◆ Portuguese territory / trading post with date

◆ Dutch territory / trading post with date

◆ Spanish territory / trading post with date

◆ English territory / trading post with date

○ major Chinese port

→ Japanese campaigns in Korea 1592–1598

➤ Japanese expansion

→ trade routes

→ Manila galleon from Mexico

MAP EXPLORATION

www.prenhall.com/armesto_maps

renounced southward expansion and, from the 1630s, practically forbade its subjects to travel overseas, illegal migrants and "pirates" continued to pour out of the country to take part in the new economic opportunities trade and colonization opened up in southeast Asia. Some were Christians, fleeing from persecution after the definitive abolition of religious tolerance in Japan in 1639, like the community whom a Portuguese missionary met in mid–seventeenth century Burma (today called Myanmar)—close-knit, hungry for the sacraments, longing to build a church. Most Japanese migration, however, was, like that of the Chinese, economically motivated. Many letters home survive, showing that the Japanese authorities were only half-hearted in suppressing the migrants' movements and content to allow them to send money home to enrich the domestic economy.

Frontiers affected cultures by changing individual lives. In the Rijksmuseum in Amsterdam, a painting of 1644 depicts the family of the rich Dutch merchant, Pieter Cnoll. His wife, Cornelia, is a beauty in an unmistakably Japanese style—daughter and fabulously wealthy heiress of one of the first officials of the Dutch East India Company and of his Japanese concubine. She called Holland "the fatherland" and corresponded with relatives in Japan. Later, she was to be a formidable businesswoman in her own right, administering her fortune after

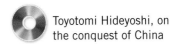

Toyotomi Hideyoshi, on the conquest of China

"Red Seal" ship. From 1592, the shogun Hideyoshi licensed foreign trading ventures by Japanese ships under the "Red Seal." Until the abolition of the trade in the 1630s, about ten voyages a year took handicrafts, copper, silver, and foodstuffs from Japan mainly to the Portuguese settlement of Macao on the coast of China, Vietnam, Thailand, and the Philippines in exchange for silk. This silk scroll of about 1630 shows Vietnamese galleys towing one of these "Red Seal ships" into a river mouth. The umbrellas indicate the market in front of the Japanese quarter. The three long houses across the river represent the Chinese quarter.

her husband's death. Then she became the tragic heroine of one of the most protracted and expensive legal cases of the seventeenth century, in her efforts to get a divorce from her grasping, tyrannical, abusive, and exploitative second husband, and to defend her fortune against him. In the background of the portrait, stealing an apple, stands her handsome Malay slave, Untung. His future would include leading a guerrilla band of runaway slaves in the backlands of Batavia, capital of the Dutch East Indies (at what is now Jakarta in Indonesia). He became king of a realm he carved out for himself in the interior of Java. Cornelia's is hardly a typical story of the overseas Japanese, but it demonstrates the fantastic range of unprecedented experiences that the empires of the time made possible.

Even greater was the outpouring of colonists from China. In many colonial outposts, in the Spanish colony of Manila, for example, though the nominal authority, the garrisons, and the guns were European—or, at least, under European officers—the real colonists, who settled the towns in large numbers and exploited the economy on a grand scale, were Chinese. Without a metropolitan government of their own committed to overseas imperialism, the migrants used Western empire builders to protect and promote their own activities.

Batavia, for example, bore the old Roman name for Holland. Its founder in 1619 was a Dutch soldier, Jan Pieterszoon Coen. Its sovereign proprietors were the directors of the Dutch East India Company, which had a government-granted monopoly on trade between Holland and Asia. But the entrepreneurs who created its economy and attracted settlers to it in its great days were Coen's two principal Chinese collaborators: Souw Beng Kong, known as Bencon—the godfather figure of the Chinese community—and the energetic labor broker whom the Dutch called Jan Con. Lanterns inscribed, "The Original Founder of the Region" flanked the entrance to Bencon's country house. In Chinese eyes, the Dutch role was subordinate. Jan Con, who arrived from China in 1619 or 1620, rose to prominence by farming coconuts and collecting the town's taxes on gambling and cattle raising. His main business was importing labor from China, hiring Chinese laborers from Fujian (foo-jee-ehn) in southern China on annual contracts to work on canals and fortifications. He diversified into the hinterland,

The Dutch merchant Pieter Cnoll painted in 1644 by Jacob Coeman. At one level, this seems an ordinary scene: a rich colonial trader with his elegant family and the trappings of his wealth. But the slave stealing an apple went on to become a famous bandit chief, while Cornelia, Cnoll's half-Japanese wife, became, after Cnoll's death, the richest business woman in the Dutch East Indies and the notorious protagonist of an agonizingly long and expensive divorce case against her second husband.

starting a sugar plantation and harvesting lumber. He opened salt pans and minted lead coins—giving Batavia a brief and rickety boom in the 1630s. But poor sugar yields and high salt-production costs ruined him—combined with English competitors' devastating policy of dumping lead coins in Batavia. He died, broke, in 1639. The Dutch never fully trusted Chinese businessmen again. But the Chinese character of the colony became even more marked after 1684, when the Chinese government relaxed controls on emigration. Thousands of Chinese residents enriched China by sending money home—like Jan Con himself, who never ceased to feel guilty for deserting his parents' home. Chinese shipping in Batavia's harbor normally outnumbered that of any other country by at least two and a half to one.

Overwhelmingly, the migrants were what we would now call economic refugees—escapees from poverty and contempt at home. In 1603, when the first of a long series of hate riots provoked a massacre of the local Chinese by native Filipinos in Manila, the emperor of China refused to intervene on the grounds that his murdered subjects were "scum, ungrateful to China, their land, their parents and ancestors for they had failed to return to China for so many years that such people were deemed to be of little worth." Yet the Chinese colony in the Philippines kept growing. By 1621, it had regained its premassacre level of 15,000, and it had more than doubled by the time of the next massacre in 1639.

Chinese and Japanese participated in empires chiefly in the seventeenth century, and, increasingly as it went on, as colonists, because their home governments, in attempts to control trade, restricted their commercial opportunities. Most merchants who operated in maritime Asia and the Indian Ocean therefore tended to come from other parts of Asia—especially from India and Armenia—and, to a limited but growing extent, from Europe. The most important single source of long-range commercial enterprise was Gujarat (goo-jah-RAHT), in northern India. Gujaratis linked maritime trade with that of the

Armenian and Indian traders dispersed throughout Central Asia and Persia. They were the biggest operators in banking as well as in commerce in the Arabian Sea. Sometimes the same individuals engaged in both types of business. Virji Vora, reputedly the richest man in the world in the early seventeenth century, was the biggest creditor of European merchants in India. He was a capitalist in the truest sense of the world, ever reinvesting his profits in commercial enterprise, so that looters who attacked his house were disappointed not to find great riches there. At times, European merchants felt oppressed by Gujarati power in key markets. In 1692, for instance, the Dutch East India Company had to sell a large cargo of nutmeg, cloves, and mace at half price to a Gujarati broker, because the company's representatives feared the power of another Gujarati—Muhammad Sahid, who was trying to control the market and was willing to undercut any competitor.

Capitalism—contrary to the traditional assumptions of Western historians—was not a European speciality. Nor—contrary to assertions still regularly made in old-fashioned history books—was it peculiar to any religious tradition. Max Weber, one of the most influential sociologists ever, first proposed the idea that religion predisposes some communities to particular kinds of economic behavior in 1904. But in most cases, the theory does not seem to work. Jains (JAH-eens), Christians, and Muslims were all prominent in Gujarat's trading community. In some places, despite the common belief that Hinduism generally regards commerce as a polluting and demeaning activity, even Hindus could engage in capitalism without losing caste. Hindus dominated the trade of Goa, although nominally this was a Portuguese-controlled city. In an auction in 1630, for instance, the local Hindu merchants numbered nearly half of the bidders and outbid their Portuguese counterparts and the government itself for about half of what was on offer. In seventeenth-century Kerala, south of Goa, most bankers were Brahmins—Hindus of the highest caste—who, according to Dutch complaints "by and large control the pepper trade."

The Dutch Connection

For over 100 years, from their arrival in the Indian Ocean in 1498, the Portuguese fitted into this Asian-dominated world, without provoking seriously disruptive conflicts. At first, Spaniards were their only European rivals, and the Portuguese came to a series of advantageous arrangements with them. Gradually, however, from roughly the 1620s, the situation changed. Asian hosts lost patience with the presence of sovereign ports and offshore trading establishments, where Portuguese religious intolerance damaged trade by discriminating against Muslim and Hindu merchants. As Asian empires expanded or grew in power, or became more assertive, they eliminated key Portuguese outposts. Even after the capture of the mainland forts of which Jeronimo de Quadros was a commander, Portuguese occupation of the offshore trading post of Hormuz was tolerated until 1622, when the Portuguese were expelled from the Persian Gulf. A series of similar expulsions followed: from Hooghly—their fort in Bengal—in 1632, from Ethiopia in 1634, and from Japan in 1639. From 1640, their own attitude to their Asian interests changed. Portugal became involved in a long and destructive war against Spain that deflected Portuguese resources from the east. Atlantic priorities took over, as Portugal's Brazilian sugar plantations became increasingly profitable and the transatlantic slave trade boomed (see Chapter 20).

Moreover, one reason why Asian communities could become more choosey about their partnerships with the Portuguese was that far more European buyers and shippers were now operating in maritime Asia. English, French, and Scandinavians all played increasing roles in the seventeenth century, but the contribution of the Dutch eclipsed them all.

The provinces of Holland and Zealand, in what is today the Netherlands, were, like Portugal, poor communities, with relatively unproductive hinterlands, on Western Europe's ocean edge. Their people had a longstanding maritime vocation as fishermen, whalers, and shippers in northern seas, particularly in the lucrative trade in timber and dried fish with the Baltic.

In the late sixteenth century, merchants from the Netherlands broke into the trading world of the Mediterranean, impelled in part by the necessities arising from their rebellion against their ruler—who, by a series of dynastic accidents, happened also to be king of Spain—and a civil war in which they were pitted against the neighboring provinces to their south in what is today Belgium. Netherlanders' initial contact with long-distance trade was the result of the fact that the Portuguese used Antwerp in the southern Netherlands as the clearing house for distributing Asian spices into northern Europe. During the war, many merchants from Antwerp migrated north to escape Spanish control. The commercial center of gravity in the Low Countries shifted with them to Holland.

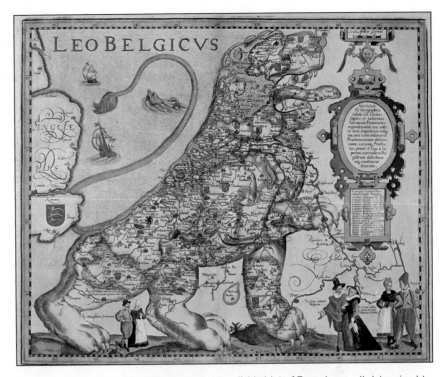

The Netherlands. Although the Netherlands were divided into 17 provinces, all determined to preserve their own separate institutions and ways of life, the inhabitants long had a sense of common identity. This map of 1550 expresses that unity by depicting the provinces as "the Belgian lion"—which was already a traditional image—strong and warlike, clawing and snapping at Germany across the Rhine, lashing the North Sea with its tail. But it also hints at the cultural differences that divided the provinces from each other by showing how the traditional dress of Holland and Belgium, shown on the right, was different from that of the province of Frisia, shown on the left. From the 1560s to 1648, religious and political conflicts heightened the differences between the northern and southern provinces of the Netherlands and shattered their sense of unity. In consequence, two separate states emerged: a Protestant-ruled republic took shape in the seven northern provinces, while the rest of the Netherlands, which eventually became modern Belgium, remained loyal to the Catholic Habsburg dynasty.

Meanwhile, in 1580, the king of Spain also succeeded by hereditary right to the throne of Portugal. This made Portuguese ships and possessions, potentially, fair game in the eyes of Dutch rebels.

In the 1590s, Jan van Linschoten, a Dutch servant of the Portuguese Archbishop of Goa, explored the prospects of extending Dutch business into the Indian Ocean. The publication of his findings ignited a craze. In 1602, after three years of hectically free competition, leading merchants of the port of Amsterdam, who largely controlled government in the province of Holland, formed a **joint-stock company** to exploit, as a monopoly, the opportunities of trade with Asia.

Historians have generally supposed that such private limited companies were more efficient than the state monopolies by which Portugal and Spain attempted to regulate long-range trade. But the English, whose system was similar to that of the Dutch, were by comparison seriously undercapitalized and could make only a modest success of it. More important for outstripping other European trading ventures was the new outward route to the East Indies, which the Dutch began to explore in the second decade of the seventeenth century.

Jan van Linschoten on Dutch business in the Indian Ocean

SOCIETAS ASIATICA.

P. Sebastianus Vieira Lusitanus, cum quing. Sociis Iaponibus Soc.IESU, triduano Scrobis tormento, et Subiecto igne pro Fide Christi necatus, in Iaponia Iendi. 6 Iunij A. 1634.
C. Screta d.   Melch: Küsell.

Christian missionaries in late sixteenth- and early seventeenth-century Japan became victims of their own success. Not only did they attract hundreds of thousands of followers, but they also established close ties to many of the daimyos, regional feudal lords whom the central authorities distrusted. The missionaries' Spanish and Portuguese allegiance also made them suspect as potential foreign agents. A series of persecutions, beginning in the 1590s, included many martyrdoms, like that of the Jesuit Sebastião Vieira, tortured to death with some of his converts in 1634 in an episode depicted here. After 1639, the only Christians allowed in Japan were a small group of Dutch Calvinist merchants, who had to trample on a crucifix in an annual ceremony, in order to prove their rejection of Christianity.

Hideyoshi, "Limitation on the Propagation of Christianity"

Even at its height, Holland's would-be monopoly of the rarer spices—cloves, nutmeg, cinnamon, and mace—was a leaky vessel. Dutch shipping never accounted for more than a seventh of the total involved in carrying the trade in these products. The Dutch never got control of pepper, which, in the seventeenth century, accounted for about 70 percent of the spice trade by value and even more by volume. Pepper demand and production grew constantly throughout the century, steadily increasing the sum of global commerce, and supplying many traditional routes and handlers.

Nevertheless, the Dutch did establish a clearly dominant position as carriers of Europe's Asian trade in the seventeenth century, effectively replacing the Portuguese while keeping well ahead of other European rivals in all theaters and—in combination with political instability in Central Asia—helping to deflect trade from the Silk Roads. Four reasons underpinned Dutch success: the speed and efficiency of their route; the problems that harassed so much of the Portuguese seaborne empire in the east as some indigenous states tranferred their favor to the Dutch; the selectively aggressive policies that, as we shall see, gradually brought the Dutch control of more—and more valuable—production of Asian communities than any European rivals; and above all, the privileged position they established in trade with Japan.

Overwhelmingly, the most valuable of the trading enterprises of maritime Asia led to Japan, because Japan was the world's leading producer of silver. Silver was relatively cheap in Japan. Merchants who took goods there, or performed services for Japanese businesses or rulers, could exchange it on favorable terms for profitable trade goods elsewhere. They used Japanese silver to buy pepper and cotton textiles in India and aromatic woods and spices from Indonesia. In China they acquired silks, porcelain, and rhubarb, which was prized as a laxative in Western medicine at this time. Increasingly they bought tea, which grew in importance as time went on and tastes spread, along with other aspects of culture, along new trade routes. Injections of Japanese silver supplied more cash for the world's markets, stimulating economic activity.

However, Japan's willingness to participate in the spreading web of economic interconnections came close to collapse in the 1630s. The main reason for this was the phenomenal success of Catholic missionaries, who had accompanied Portuguese and Spanish merchants in the country and made hundreds of thousands of converts. Fears that this alien religion would undermine traditional loyalties to the state provoked an official ban on Christianity in 1597, and the bloody martyrdom of Catholic clergy and converts until Christianity was driven underground in 1638–1639. From 1640, Dutch merchants were the only Europeans allowed in Japan—tolerated because they were willing to take part in an annual rite called "Trampling the Crucifix." Most of the Dutch merchants were Calvinists, Protestants who repudiated "graven images" such as crucifixes anyway as contrary to the Ten Commandments (see Chapter 18). The Japanese government channeled Dutch trade through an island off the port of Nagasaki and strictly monitored the merchants' contact with Japanese subjects for more than 200 years.

Yet to be able to continue to trade in Japan at all was an enormous bonus. For the rest of the century—until other Europeans began to build up their trade in other parts of Asia to levels at which they could generate comparable earnings—the Dutch dominated the handling of all the most valuable products of China and southeast Asia for European markets. The Netherlands—formerly a poor, cramped, beleaguered, divided, and marginal part of Europe—experienced a "Golden Age" of wealth, art, empire-building, and military and naval power. Dutch imperialists challenged the Spanish monarchy in parts of the New World. Taking advantage of changed Portuguese priorities, and of help from some expanding Asian powers, they drove the Portuguese out of Malacca in 1641, Sri Lanka in the 1650s, and from many places in India thereafter. They resisted Spanish and French attempts at conquest in the seventeenth century. Meanwhile, they drove the English out of the Spice Islands and defeated them in the seas around England itself. Eventually, in 1688–1699 the Dutch ruler, taking advantage of internal conflicts in Britain, invaded England and became its king by deposing his English father-in-law.

A further consequence of the growing wealth and power of the Dutch was growing ambition in empire-building in Asia. Increasingly, from the 1660s, they aimed to control not only trade in valuable commodities, but also their actual production. Refugees from Dutch aggression elsewhere poured into Makassar. Malays swelled its ships' crews. Moluccans brought their know-how in growing spices. Portuguese from Malacca introduced their long-range trading contacts. Makassar became their "second and better Malacca." According to a Dominican friar who visited in 1658, it was "one of the greatest emporia of Asia" with a ruler who collected European books and scientific instruments.

In the 1650s, the Dutch began a relentless war, first of coercion, then of conquest in the East Indies. "Do you believe," sneered the sultan of Makassar, "that God has reserved for your trade alone islands which lie so far from your homeland?" The conquest took nearly 20 years. That of Bantam, on Java, with its big pepper output, followed in the early 1680s. Southeast Asia's age of trade was ending as native Asian cultivators abandoned cash crops, which had once enriched their cultivators but now seemed only to attract foreign predators.

The Dutch policy set a fateful example, as other European trading communities also undertook more aggressive policies. Europeans began to turn from maritime imperialism, based on control of trade, to territorial imperialism, which aimed to control production. At first their efforts were modest and unsuccessful. The Portuguese expanded outward from Goa and in the 1680s conquered the passes leading toward the Deccan, acquiring a subject population of about 30,000 people. The French crown, which had opened a permanent trading establishment at Pondicherry in southeast India in 1674, contemplated taking over Thailand but had to withdraw in humiliation. The English East

The Fall of Makassar, June 12, 1660, painted by Frederik Woldemar. The capture of Makassar in what is today Indonesia was part of the Dutch campaign to build an empire in the East Indies. Makassar was an independent sultanate whose ruler was supported by the Portuguese, and the painting shows a Portuguese ship that the Dutch had already taken. While the guns in the sultan's palace exchange fire with the Dutch ships, native troops march to the sultan's aid. The neutral English trading post flies the flag of St. George. The decisive moment of the encounter came when a Dutch landing party seized the stronghold.

 Domingo Navarrete, "Of My Stay in the Kingdom of Makassar"

European Maritime Imperialism in the Indian and Pacific Oceans, 1500–1700

1500	Portuguese begin direct trade with southern India
1510	Portuguese trading post at Goa established
1571	Spanish trading post of Manila founded
1600	English East India Company established
1602	Dutch East India Company founded
1619	Dutch found trading post of Batavia (Indonesia)
1620–1640	Portuguese expelled from trading posts in Persian Gulf and Indian Ocean
1640	Dutch merchants only Europeans allowed in Japan
1674	French establish trading post at Pondicherry (India)

India Company, founded in 1600, challenged the Mughal (MOO-gahl) Empire in India to war, in an attempt to increase its share of trade, but was defeated in 1685–1688.

Gradually, however, in the eighteenth century, Europeans would take more and more production under their own direct control, building up land empires in Asia that genuinely transformed the global economy. The profits Europeans made in Asian trade in the sixteenth and seventeenth centuries had modified Europe's age-old trading deficit with Asia in Europe's favor. Now it could be reversed, as Europeans not only influenced markets, but also manipulated production.

LAND EMPIRES: RUSSIA, CHINA, MUGHAL INDIA, AND THE OTTOMANS

These European land empires in Asia were, however, all modest affairs until well into the eighteenth century—with one exception. Russian imperialism gleams from the heavily gilded surface of a remarkable painting: the "Icon of the Hosts of the Heavenly King," made in the third quarter of the sixteenth century. Led by the biblical kings Solomon and David, Russians march across a fantastic landscape of mountains and rivers, from a city of infidels, ringed by fire, toward a shrine of the Virgin Mary. Heavenly hosts, ghostly cavalry, and the Christian founder-emperors of the Russian Orthodox tradition, Vladimir and Constantine (see Chapter 9) flank the earthly army. "Although the martyrs were born on earth," reads the commentary, "they succeeded in attaining the rank of angels." Two real leaps of Russian imperialism inspired this art. First, the conquest of Kazan in 1552 gave the **czars** (ZARS)—as the Russian ruler was styled in allusion to "Caesar"—command of the entire

length of the Volga River, which was the great corridor of commerce at the western edge of Asia, and eliminated Russia's great rival for control of Siberia's fur trade. Furs summoned Russians to conquest and colonization, as gold lured Spaniards and spices captivated the Portuguese. The czars' next task was to conquer Siberia itself and control the production of furs as well as the trade in them (see Map 16.2). In 1555, Czar Ivan IV began to call himself Lord of Siberia. Three years later, he cut a deal with a big dynasty of fur dealers, the Stroganoffs, who were prepared to pay to turn that title into reality. The language of a chroniclers' account reflects the typical mind-set of European conquerors in new worlds: the assertion that pagans have no rights; that their lands are "empty"; that they are subhuman—bestial or monstrous; that financial privileges can promote colonization; and that the work is holy.

From the 1570s, the "protection" of Russian armies "against the fighting men of Siberia" was proclaimed for native peoples who submitted and paid tribute in furs. Like other European military operations on remote frontiers, the Russians ascribed their success to technology: firearms mounted on river barges, from which the waterborne conquerors exchanged bullets for bowshots with defenders on the banks. The Siberian khan was said to be dismayed to hear that "when they shoot from their bows, then there is a flash of fire and a great smoke issues and there is a loud report like thunder in the sky. . . . and it is impossible to shield oneself from them by any trappings of war."

Native peoples were subjected to tribute and controlled by oaths of traditional, pagan kinds. One Siberian people, the Ostyaks, were made to swear on a bearskin on which a knife, an axe, and a loaf were spread. The oath breaker would choke to death or be cut to pieces in battle with men or bears. The Yakuts had to swear by passing between the quarters of a dismembered dog. The first object of the conquest, however, was not to vanquish these "savages" who ranged the pine forests and tundra but to eliminate the only state able to challenge Russia in the region:

Icon of the Hosts of the Heavenly King. The "Icon of the Hosts of Heaven" is one of the most spectacular works of Russian imperial propaganda of the sixteenth century. Mounted on a warhorse, the Archangel Michael leads a Russian army from the conquest of Kazan, shown in flames on the extreme right, into the presence of the Mother of God and her son. Constantine, the first Christian emperor, and Vladimir, Russia's first Christian ruler, carry banners.

Russian Expansion Eastward

1552–1556	Russian conquest of Kazan
1555	Czar Ivan IV claims title of Lord of Siberia
ca. Late seventeenth century	Russian and Chinese expansion meet
1689	Treaty of Nerchinsk with China checks Russia's eastward expansion

the Mongol khanate of Sibir, which dominated the eastern tributaries of the Irtysh River. Thus the conquest was sold as a Crusade and depicted symbolically by representations of gospel rays spread from the eyes of Christ between colonists' cities. Russians credited Khan Kuchum with a prophetic vision in October 1581: "The skies burst open and terrifying warriors with shining wings appeared. . . . They encircled Kuchum's army and cried to him, 'Depart from this land, you infidel son of the dark demon, Muhammad, because now it belongs to the Almighty.'"[1]

China

By the late seventeenth century, Russian expansion in eastern Siberia met China's, which was preempting or pursuing Russian rivals in a war zone along the Amur River. The road that led here was kept smoother, according to a Jesuit visitor, "than Catholics in Europe keep the road on which the Sacrament is to be conveyed." The Treaty of Nerchinsk of 1689 formalized Chinese claims to vast unexplored lands of doubtful extent in northeast Asia, where some map makers imagined a huge land mass pointing to or even joining America.

Much of this territory was effectively beyond any practical frontier of settlement. Generally, however, Chinese imperialism was of an intensive kind, compared with Russia's: dedicated not merely to economic exploitation and trade, but also to colonization and to spreading Chinese ways among native peoples. Before the end of the seventeenth century, Outer Mongolia had been crudely incorporated into the Chinese Empire and more than 1.5 million settlers had been lured into Sichuan (seh-chwhan) in southern China by the promise of immunities from taxation. The Xinjiang (sheen-jeeahng) frontier in western China was peopled next, more thinly, by a mixture of enforced deportation and inducements to voluntary settlers. Two hundred thousand Chinese migrants had settled there by the end of the century. Manchuria, homeland of the ruling dynasty, the Manchus or Qing (see Chapter 21) was normally closed to settlers, but its rich soils drew them unofficially in hundreds of thousands, until the Chinese government was obliged to recognize and accept their presence. Meanwhile, the people of Manchuria were progressively converted to Chinese ways. On all fronts, the pressure of intensive new settlement provoked a cycle of conflicts and solutions ominously familiar to students of European colonialism: tribal peoples reshuffled or penned in reservations; militarized agricultural colonies growing wheat, barley, peas, and maize (which had been introduced to Asia from the Americas; see Chapter 17), while keeping the natives in check. Schools were erected to spread Chinese language and values.

The Mughal Example in India

The Russian and Chinese empires practiced large-scale colonization, with attempts at new kinds of exploitation of conquered or resettled soil. That was to be the pattern of most new imperialism from this period onward. But there were still empires of what one might call an old-fashioned kind: conquest states that tended to leave the political, social, demographic, and economic structures of their conquests largely intact and to exploit them indirectly by levying tribute. The Mughal (the name means Mongol and refers to the ruling dynasty's Afghan-Mongol origins) Empire in India was the newest and fastest-growing empire of this type in the late sixteenth and seventeenth centuries. If we can trust its founder's memoirs, it began in a mood of distraction. Babur (BAH-boor) (1483–1530) was an adventurer from Central Asia, in the mold of his ancestor, Timur (see Chapter 15). In the volatile world west of the Hindu Kush, the rugged mountains that separate India from Afghanistan, he raised war bands and exchanged kingdoms with a rapidity of turnover unattainable else-where. His dream was to rebuild Timur's empire from the city of Samarkand in Central Asia, but after he had won and lost that city twice over, he turned to India. From 1519, conquering it became his obsession. India seduced him. He rebuked Afghan followers who claimed to prefer the Afghan capital of Kabul, where he had been "the sport of harsh poverty." After 1526, when he conquered Delhi in north India and made it his capital, he never left India, though he missed the "flavor of melons and grapes" of his Afghan home (see Map 16.2).

The state Babur founded remained small and unstable until the long rule of his grandson, Akbar (AHK-bahr) (r. 1556–1605). The priorities of Akbar's empire emerge vividly from the account compiled by his friend and minister, Abul Fazl Allami, who begins by describing the emperor's jewel chest, then turns to the treasury, the coinage, the mints for gold and silver, the stupendous court cuisine with its gold-laced dishes, the emperor's writing room, his arse-nal, his elephants, horses, cows, and camels. When he turns to what he consid-ers the lesser aspects of government, he deals first with protocol, before insisting on a ruler's responsibilities for spiritual welfare; then come accounts

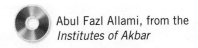

Abul Fazl Allami, from the *Institutes of Akbar*

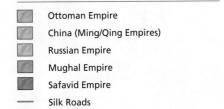

MAP 16.2

Eurasian Land Empires of the Sixteenth and Seventeenth Centuries

- Ottoman Empire
- China (Ming/Qing Empires)
- Russian Empire
- Mughal Empire
- Safavid Empire
- —— Silk Roads

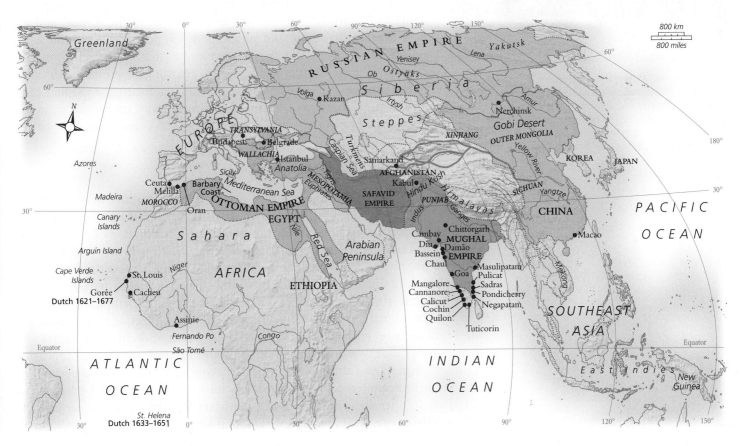

The assault on Chittorgarh. The Mughal Emperor Akbar (r. 1556-1605) commissioned artists to record his campaigns. This painting shows a notable moment in his siege of the supposedly impregnable fortress of Chittorgarh. A tunnel mined by Akbar's engineers exploded, killing hundreds of his own men. When the fort fell, most of the defenders were massacred.

of building projects, the army, revenue raising and rites (including hunting and games), lists of great nobles and court personalities.

In short, the Mughal Empire was like a business, run for profit—an investment in power and majesty, with rich returns in the form of tribute and taxes. The heartlands it ruled directly never extended much beyond the limits of Babur's conquests, in the Punjab and the Ganges valley in north India. Beyond this area, existing power structures and local rulers remained in place, supplying money and manpower for future conquests, and linked to the imperial court by every device of networking. The 800 wives Akbar assembled from the rulers who paid him tribute were, in effect, hostages and mediators of sometimes uneasy alliances. Religious tolerance was an essential ingredient of internal peace in an empire that straddled the Hindu and Muslim worlds.

The Mughal war machine was so big and costly that it was impossible to operate at a profit without the constant stream of victories that Akbar had his court artists commemorate in still ravishing, still terrifying miniature paintings. The most dramatic battle of his reign was the assault on Chittorgarh, the clifftop stronghold of a Hindu prince, in 1567–1568—recalled by a depiction of the deaths of hundreds on both sides in the accidental explosion of the mines that Akbar's engineers bored and burrowed into the cliff. Of the defending garrison of 8,000 and their 40,000 servants, 30,000 reputedly died in the last onslaught.

In some ways the Mughal Empire seems ramshackle, stumbling between victories, with no central institutions except the imperial court and army, no agreed rules of succession to the throne, and an elite divided by ethnic and religious differences and economic jealousies. The death or old age of every emperor triggered rebellion and civil war. Yet the frontier kept growing, reaching deep into south India by the time of Akbar's death in 1605, slowing during the the half century that followed. and again advancing rapidly under the emperor Aurangzeb (AW-rang-zehb) (r. 1656–1707) to cover almost the entire subcontinent.

The Ottomans

West of India were states superficially similar to the Mughals, where Muslim rulers—the Safavid (SAH-fah-vihd) dynasty in Persia and the Ottomans, based in Turkey—dominated huge territories and diverse populations by mobilizing large armies equipped with up-to-date firepower. Historians call both of them empires, but the Safavids ruled a compact state, more or less corresponding to modern Iran and—not for want of trying—never managed permanently to annex much territory farther afield. Their story belongs in Chapter 19.

The Ottomans, by contrast, were among the most effective empire builders the world had ever known. What we have already seen of them (see Chapter 15) demonstrates that. What happened in the sixteenth and seventeenth centuries would confirm it. And although the areas they conquered had all been part of big empires before, the empire the Ottomans built up had no exact precedents. The diversity literally echoed around Lady Mary Wortley Montagu, an English ambassador's wife, in 1718, who heard her servants chatter in ten different

Ankara. The artist Jean-Baptiste Vanmour, who lived in Istanbul in the early eighteenth century, and helped to make Westerners familiar with images of the city and its people, also depicted other Turkish cities of the time, including this view of Ankara in Anatolia. Vanmour emphasized the aspects of commercial, domestic, and civic life that made the Ottoman Empire seem exotic to Western eyes.

languages. "I live," she went on, "in the perpetual hearing of this medley of sounds, which produces a very extraordinary effect upon the people that are born here. They learn all these languages at the same time and without knowing any of them well enough to write or read in it."

In the Ottoman world, boundless ambitions seemed possible. The Ottomans inherited three universalist traditions: one from their steppelander ancestors, whose aim was to make the limits of their empire match those of the sky; another from Islam, whose caliphs' legacy and title the Ottoman sultans claimed; a third from ancient Rome, whose legacy they wrenched into their own grasp by conquering much former Roman imperial territory.

The Ottomans could afford to invest in strategies of conquest, because the sixteenth and seventeenth centuries were an era of prosperity in Turkey unprecedented at the time and unparalleled since. Their heartlands were in the Anatolian (an-a-TOH-lee-yahn) plateau. Beyond it, the Ottoman lands were grouped around three great waterways: the eastern Mediterranean, the Black Sea, and the twin rivers of Mesopotamia. Beyond what they called Rumelia, the westernmost of the provinces they ruled directly, lay a broad frontier zone that they controlled and that reached beyond Budapest in Hungary in Central Europe. In North Africa, beyond Egypt, the sultans enjoyed nominal allegiance, at least, from the principalities of the Barbary coast, as far west as what is now Algeria. They got control of most continental transit points between Asia and Europe: the western reaches of the Silk Roads, the Persian Gulf, the Red Sea, and the main ports of Egypt and the eastern Mediterranean seaboard. New trade routes from Europe to south and southeast Asia did not deflect existing trade from Ottoman territories. On the contrary, with improved communications and expanding demand, the total volume of the spice trade continued to grow, and more of this trade passed through Ottoman hands in the sixteenth century than ever before.

On the other hand, the Ottomans were, in some respects, disadvantageously placed. They had no outlets to the Atlantic or the Indian Ocean—or even to the western Mediterranean, except through narrow straits that enemies easily

Mughals and Ottomans

1517	Ottomans conquer Egypt
1519	Babur founds Mughal Empire
1520–1566	Reign of Ottoman sultan Suleiman the Magnificent
1526	Babur makes Delhi his capital
1529	Ottomans besiege Vienna
1656–1707	Aurangzeb extends Mughal Empire over most of Indian subcontinent

Ogier Ghiselin de Busbecq
on Suleiman the Magnificent

controlled. Wars frequently broke out on frontiers with permanently hostile neighbors—Persians in the east, Christians in the north and west. Armies shuttled back and forth across the empire in successive seasons to keep Europeans inhibited and Safavid Persians at bay. Beset, as the Ottomans were, by enemies on every side, their state needed extraordinary strength to survive. Only a state of extraordinary efficiency could expand.

Yet expand they did. They overran Egypt in 1517 and exploited it for huge annual tax surpluses that sustained campaigns elsewhere. The armies of Suleiman (soo-lay-MAHN) the Magnificent (r. 1520–1566) reached Belgrade in Serbia in the northwest Balkans in 1521 and the island of Rhodes in the Aegean in 1522. What began as a punitive expedition against Hungary in 1525 ended as the conquest of most of that country. Until Suleiman's death, the pace of conquest was enormous. He conquered Iraq from Persia and most of the shores of the Red Sea, while exerting more informal lordship over much of the rest of Arabia. Suleiman extended his rule over almost the whole southern shore of the Mediterranean, where his naval commanders, the Barbarossa (bahr-bahr-ROH-sah) brothers of Algiers, organized a seaborne empire of war galleys and pirate havens (see Map 16.2). In 1529, Suleiman was called from besieging Vienna in Austria to fight the Persians in Iraq, while a Turkish fleet raided the city of Valencia in Spain. During a single campaigning season in 1538, Ottoman forces conquered Moldavia in the northeast Balkans, besieged the Portuguese stronghold of Diu in India, and wrecked a Christian fleet off the shores of Greece. His court poet Baki (bah-KEE) hailed Suleiman as "the monarch with the crown of Alexander. . . . the earth before his gate served as prayer mat for the world."

The pace of expansion was slower under Suleiman's successors, but not because the empire was running out of energy. Rather, it was because remoter conquests brought diminishing returns. The Ottoman naval effort—it is true—faltered: outgunned in the Indian Ocean by Portugal and in the central Mediterranean by Spain. But every generation brought a net gain of territory until the last years of the seventeenth century.

The degree of imperial authority could hardly be uniform in the outlying parts of so extensive an empire, but it was felt everywhere. The younger Barbarossa, who ruled the remotest outposts on the North African coast, was loosely called a king, even in Turkish accounts. He recruited ships and men with his own resources, won his victories by his own strength—so many of them that he sold Christian captives "at an onion a head." In Islamic North Africa, the sword carved the right to rule. Yet when Suleiman summoned him to Constantinople, Barbarossa did not hesitate to obey. The khans of Crimea in what is today Ukraine negotiated terms of pay—often in the form of captive slaves—for joining the sultans' campaigns, and sometimes simply disobeyed the sultan. Turks garrisoned but did not directly rule Wallachia and Moldavia (in modern Romania). Transylvania, on the western edge of the empire, was a vassal state, with low taxes and a Christian prince whom its medieval parliament elected. In Arab lands, the sultans used religion as a source of legitimacy, but—with only sporadic displays of force to back it up—they found it hard to turn that legitimacy into effective allegiance. As we shall see in Chapter 19, even the parts of their empire that the sultans ruled directly were a patchwork of different methods and conventions of rule that were often hard to keep under close control.

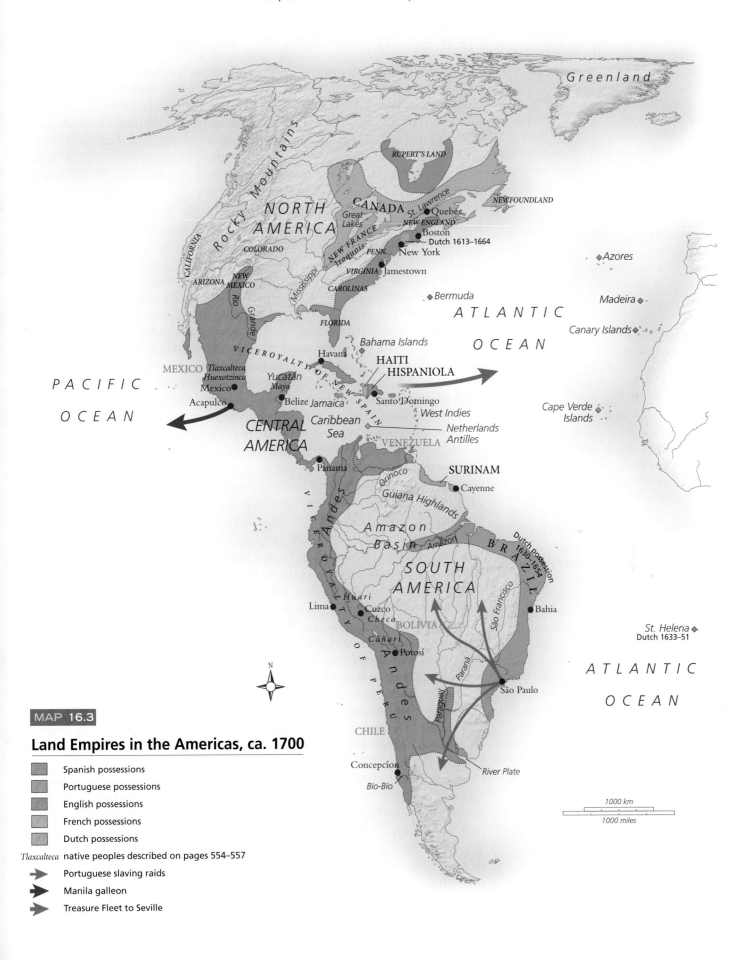

MAP 16.3

Land Empires in the Americas, ca. 1700

- Spanish possessions
- Portuguese possessions
- English possessions
- French possessions
- Dutch possessions

Tlaxcalteca native peoples described on pages 554–557

➡ Portuguese slaving raids

➡ Manila galleon

➡ Treasure Fleet to Seville

NEW LAND EMPIRES IN THE AMERICAS

Across the Atlantic, meanwhile, European imperialism led landward. Columbus (see Chapter 15) envisaged no more than a trading setup when he first saw what he thought was Japan, the Caribbean island of Hispaniola (ees-pah-nee-O-lah) (modern Haiti and the Dominican Republic) in 1492, imagining a European merchant-colony under Spanish control, trading in cotton, mastic (a resin used to make varnish), and slaves. However, none of these products was available in large quantities in the Caribbean. Columbus based his initial hopes on the illusion that the riches of Asia lay only a short way farther west. But he had grossly underestimated the size of the world. Instead, therefore, the Spaniards had to focus on exploiting the gold mines of the island. Columbus's war of conquest in Hispaniola of 1495–1496 was—albeit on a small scale—the first step toward creating a Spanish territorial empire.

The settlement of more Caribbean islands and, between 1518 and 1546, the conquests of Mexico and Peru, confirmed this trend. As a result, Spaniards found themselves obeyed over huge tracts of the most densely populated territory in the Americas. Indeed, Spain—which was a relatively poor and underpopulated country—had acquired, within the space of a few years, and in their entirety, two of the fastest-growing and most environmentally diverse empires of the age—those of the Aztecs and the Incas (see Chapter 15). This achievement was effected thousands of miles from home, with relatively primitive technology, few resources, and privately recruited bands of only a few hundred men (see Map 16.3).

How was it possible? In early colonial times, four explanations occurred to those who tried to make sense of the way the conquest had turned out. The clergy favored the view that the conquest was miraculous and providential—procured by God for his own purposes. The conquerors, or *conquistadores* as the Spanish called themselves, their heirs, and cronies explained it as the result of their own godlike prowess. But this was incredible and self-interested—an account designed to maximize rewards from a grateful crown. The Spaniards' Native American allies saw the overthrow of the Aztecs and Incas as their own work, with a little help from their Spanish friends. Illustrations in documents of the Tlaxcalteca (tlash-kahl-TEK-ah)—the most numerous and formidable of the Indian communities who joined the alliance against the Aztecs—show Native Americans in the vanguard of every attack and Spaniards, typically, bringing up the rear. Along with the Tlaxcalteca, the Huexotzinca (weh-hot-SEEN-kah), another people hostile to the Aztecs, claimed exemption from taxation in postconquest times on the grounds that the conquest had been mainly their own work.

Finally, according to early colonial analysts, the Native American empires were victims of their own shaky morale. Hernán Cortés (1485–1547), the adventurer who led the band that conquered Mexico, spread the claim that the Aztec Emperor Moctezuma II (mok-teh-ZOO-ma) (r. 1502–1520) had surrendered power into his hands in the belief that Spanish supremacy was the fulfillment of a prophesy. This claim was almost certainly false, made up to head off awkward questions churchmen and lawyers in Spain raised about whether the Spaniards had any right to rule in Mexico. In early colonial times, rumors spread that omens and signs from their gods had predisposed the Aztecs to surrender, or that they regarded the Spaniards as gods or the representatives of a departed god, destined to return as ruler. But these rumors were made up after the event, and the reported omens were borrowed from European books. The aggressive, confident, dynamic, and expanding Aztec state showed no signs of weak morale and resisted ferociously.

Bernal Diaz del Castillo, from *The True History of the Conquest of New Spain*

An Aztec account of the conquest of Mexico (*The Broken Spears*)

Yet similar stories were invoked to explain Spanish success elsewhere, too. To refer to Spaniards, the people of the Inca Empire used a term that was also the name of a god or legendary hero. So the notion that they mistook Spaniards for gods attracted people in that region, too. When the last independent Maya kingdom submitted to the Spanish monarchy in 1697, the priest who negotiated the surrender convinced himself that the Maya had yielded in supposed obedience to an ancient prophesy.

Historians have added other explanations. The technology gap is often assumed to have been instrumental in the conquests. And in some respects, Spanish war technology was important. In 1521, in the final siege of the Aztec capital Tenochtitlán, Spanish-designed, gun-carrying ships patrolled the lake that surrounded the city. Spanish steel-edged weapons were probably more effective in disabling and killing enemy warriors than the blades made from volcanic glass native armorers used. Crossbows, as long as new bolts were available, could outperform any Native American missile weapons. The importance of guns and horses, however, was probably slight. Horses are of limited value in mountain warfare and street fighting—conditions in which some of the most critical episodes of the conquests occurred. It is hard to credit claims that the defenders were awestruck by these devices or inhibited by the belief that they were magical. Such claims were always linked with efforts to mock the natives' intellectual and rational powers. In practice, Native Americans quickly adapted to European styles of warfare and used horses and firearms, where these were effective, themselves.

As we shall see in the next chapter, disease was, in the long run, of enormous importance in weakening Native American resistance to European conquerors. It is more doubtful, however, whether it was decisive in the early stages of conquest.

Native conquistadors. The conquest of Michoacán was—apart from the capture of the Aztec capital of Tenochtitlán—the toughest and bloodiest episode of the Spanish conquest of Mexico. This account by the Spaniards' native allies, the Tlaxcalteca, made in the mid–sixteenth century, emphasizes the leading role played by Native American conquistadors. The Spaniards bring up the rear, though one of their dogs takes an enthusiastic role in the vanguard.

tecçiquauhtitlá

The Native American Doña Marina rather than the Spaniard Cortés directs the battle of Tenochtitlán in the Lienzo de Tlaxcala, a mid-sixteenth-century Native American portrayal of scenes from the conquest of Mexico. The same source also always shows Doña Marina center-stage negotiating alliances. Here she commands both along the central causeway, where native warriors lead the attack against the Aztecs, and in the Spanish gunboat that native paddlers propel across Lake Texcoco.

Maladies hard to identify, made worse by malnutrition, weakened and killed many of the defenders of the Aztec capital. By the time of the conquest of Peru in the 1530s, smallpox was devastating unimmunized populations. Spanish carriers unwittingly spread it wherever they went. Yet its effects cut both ways, harming the Spaniards' allies as least as much as their enemies, while still leaving formidable numbers of foes in the field. Spaniards themselves, after all, were also operating in unfamiliar and debilitating environments.

It is worth bearing in mind that many—perhaps most—European successes were by-products of war among Native Americans themselves. Some Maya communities identified more closely with the Spaniards than with their hated neighbors, exploiting Spanish help to settle feuds sometimes centuries old. The French in Canada in the next century were drawn into wars between different Iroquois peoples. The Aztec and Inca worlds were full of conflict. Civil war wracked the Inca Empire when the Spaniards arrived. Most of its subject peoples resented Inca rule. The Huari (WAH-ree) nursed hateful memories of the Inca conquest. Only a few years before the Spaniards' arrival, the Inca had massacred thousands of recently conquered Cañari in an apparent attempt to terrorize them into obedience. Even some of the Incas' former allies had grown disenchanted. The Incas' demands for forced labor, which drove many workers hundreds of miles from their homes, were acutely resented. When the empire fell, tens of thousands of conscripted workers left their posts to return to their orignal communities.

The Aztecs' demands similarly alienated tributary peoples. The tribute system was both the strength and weakness of their state: strength, because it embodied their power to command resources from a vast area; weakness, because Tenochtitlán became dependent on tribute for basic necessities—the food and cotton the city could not produce for itself—and the luxuries from distant climates, needed to sustain the way of life of the elite: the ritual cacao and incense, the rubber for the ball game, the gold, the jade, the amber, the seashells, the exotic featherwork and ceremonial clothing. When the Spaniards' allies denied Tenochtitlan its tribute, they effectively starved the Aztec capital into submission.

The Spaniards' triumph was therefore less a battlefield victory than a diplomatic maneuver. In forming an alliance able to defy the Aztecs, the Spaniards enjoyed crucial advantages. The Aztecs at first treated the Spaniards' arrival as a diplomatic mission, rather than a hostile force, which gave the Spaniards time to make useful contacts in disaffected Native American communities. The Spaniards acquitted themselves so impressively in tests of battle that the Tlaxcalteca adopted them enthusiastically as allies and remained in alliance even after the Spaniards suffered a severe defeat at Aztec hands in 1520. The single most important ingredient in Spanish diplomatic success was probably their interpreter, whom they called Doña Marina. She was a native speaker of the main language of central Mexico and quickly learned Spanish. She was, at a crucial phase, the only person with the linguistic qualifications to mastermind negotiations. Tlaxcalan pictures of the conquest invariably show her center stage, mediating between Spaniards and Native Americans in peaceful scenes, and actually supervising military operations in depictions of war.

None of these explanations, however, really matches what happened in the Americas when Europeans arrived. For, usually, the transition to new kinds of European-led imperialism happened with little or no violence. Traditionally, historians have concentrated on conflicts between Europeans and their native "victims." Indeed, Spanish conquests in the New World have had a bloody reputation. Terror was a common tactic, not because the conquistadores were morally different from other warriors, but because they were subject to peculiarly intense strains of operating in hostile environments, often with little help of relief, surrounded by enemies whose cultures seemed savage and unintelligible. Yet considered from another aspect, the Spanish "conquest" seems remarkably peaceful. Most communities, especially within the regions previously subject to the Aztecs and Incas, offered the Spaniards little resistance or actively welcomed them, so eager were they to escape from their Native American overlords.

From Bartoleme de las Casas, *Brief Account of the Devastation of the ladies*

Even where no oppressive native empires existed, Native Americans were often surprisingly hospitable to European intruders, who usually seemed at first too few, vulnerable, and unused to local conditions to be much of a threat. Most European communities relied on native collaboration for food or allies or both. Sexual alliances with native women of elite rank, especially in areas of Spanish and Portuguese operations, helped the newcomers to get established and, according to native custom in many areas, conferred on the host communities a duty to help with labor and food. Spanish friars were amazingly successful in making themselves useful as holy men, healers, arbiters of disputes, and protectors against secular exploiters. In short, the reception of Europeans owed much to a remarkably widespread feature of Native American cultures: what we might call the **stranger effect**—the tendency some peoples have to esteem and defer to strangers, whose usefulness as arbitrators of disputes, dispensers of justice, and preservers of peace, arises from the objectivity that their foreign origins could confer on them.

Making the New Empires Work

By the end of the sixteenth century—before the French or English had established a single enduring colony anywhere in the Western Hemisphere—the Spanish monarchy in the New World effectively included all the biggest and most productive islands of the Caribbean and a continuous swathe of territory from the edge of the Colorado plateau in the north to the river Bío-Bío in southern Chile. It extended from sea to shining sea over the narrow reaches of the hemisphere, and along the Atlantic coast of what is now Venezuela, with a southerly corridor to the Atlantic, across what is now Bolivia, and along the Paraguay River and River Plate. In most areas that the Atlantic wind system made easily accessible from Europe, Spain had preempted potential rivals, except on the Brazilian coast, where, by agreement with Spain, Portugal had a series of sugar- and timber-producing colonies. The relatively late start other colonizers and would-be colonizers, in particular, the English and French monarchies, made was not the result of any inherent inferiority on their part. The best portions of the hemisphere were in other hands and only the dregs were left. It took a long time to find the will and ways to exploit them.

Unsurprisingly, therefore, in the Americas, the colonial societies of the north lived in awe of those of the south: envying their gold and silver, imitating their plantations and ranches, trying to rival their cities, coveting their territory but fearing their further expansion. English conquerors, for instance, aped those of Spain. In 1609, the first instructions to the colonists of Virginia—the first enduring English colony in North America—ordered them to maintain a pretence of divinity in dealing with the natives; and to conceal any white men's deaths to project an image of immortality. This was naive. Captain John Smith (1580–1631), the most dynamic leader of early Virginia, was a voracious reader with a storybook self-image. He claimed—in imitation of a story Columbus told about himself in Jamaica—to hold natives spellbound by his knowledge of the stars. Smith also applied methods apparently modeled on Cortés: using terror and massacre to keep natives cowed, and trying to exploit a special relationship with the natives' dominant chieftain to rule though him.

The Spanish Empire preempted European rivals in regions selected precisely because they were densely populated, with productive, established economies. In consequence Spanish policy—rarely successful in practice—was always to preserve the Native American population. This was not the case in most other parts of the Americas, where the Indians were too few, too warlike, or too unaccustomed to large-scale production to meet the colonists' labor needs. In most colonies, once reliance on native charity was no longer necessary, Native Americans seemed at best a nuisance, unless they were needed to keep trade going (as in the parts of mainland America France nominally ruled).

Throughout British America, for instance, the native peoples were a source of conflict between frontiersmen and the representatives of the crown, who wanted the protection of Indian buffer states and the benefit of a relatively dense pool of white labor, which frontier conquests would disperse. For most colonial subjects, however, the Native Americans merely got in the way of land grabbing. Genocide was the best means to deal with them. In 1637, an explicit attempt to exterminate an entire Native American people—the New England Pequots—was half finished in a massacre on Mystic River in Connecticut, where, the governor reported, the victims could be seen "frying in the fire and the streams of blood quenching the same." The tribe's very name was banned. In defiance of official policy, a settler malcontent, Nathaniel Bacon, launched war in Virginia in 1675 with the explicit aim of destroying all Native Americans, friendly and hostile alike. This was a characteristic outrage in the late seventeenth century: a period of increasing tension—which also provoked violent clashes in areas of Spanish settlement in Florida and New Mexico—between growing colonies and threatened Native Americans. In terms of the sacrifice of life on both sides, the worst such episode was King Philip's War in New England in 1676. Launched by an Native American chief, who managed to put together an uncharacteristically big Indian coalition to stem white expansion, this resistance movement threatened to reverse the direction of extermination. The white presence was, for a few months, genuinely at risk, until Native American peoples from the interior who were willing to fight for the colonists restored the balance in the white

The Pequot War. The capture of Fort Mystic in eastern Connecticut in May, 1637, was the decisive event of the war of extermination waged by New England colonists in search of security against the Pequot people. Surprised by the ferocity of Native American resistance, the settlers burned the houses in which hundreds of Indian women and children were sheltering. This illustration, made just after the war, shows the settlers' opening volleys and the routes of their two-pronged attack.

JOHN SMITH, POCAHONTAS, AND THE "STRANGER EFFECT"

The English adventurer Captain John Smith (1580–1631) liked to tell stories of how female admirers rescued him from danger. The Indian Princess Pocahontas was one of them. This engraving illustrated and advertised Smith's own self-serving account of his adventures in Virginia in the early 1600s.

Smith, who favored aggressive policies toward the Native Americans, had been captured by the Indians and condemned to death. His release probably owed more to King Powhatan's strategy of making allies of the English and using them against other Native American tribes, than to his daughter Pocahontas's supposed attraction to Smith.

King Powhatan comands C: Smith to be slayne, his daughter Pokahontas beggs his life his thankfullnes and how he subiected 39 of their kings. reade f history.

Powhatan, enthroned among his councilors by the great fire in his audience chamber, gives the command to put Smith to death.

Pocahontas, who was 14 years old at the time, is shown at successive moments of the story— first staying the executioner' hands, then pleading for Smith to be spared.

How does this illustration show the "stranger effect"?

Spanish and English Land Empires in the New World

1492	Columbus arrives in Caribbean
1495–1496	Columbus begins war of conquest in Hispaniola
1518–1546	Spanish conquests of Mexico and Peru
1609	English found colony of Virginia
1675	Bacon's rebellion (Virginia)
1676	King Philip's War (New England)

man's favor. In areas of predominantly British colonization or "Anglo" rule, preconquest population levels for Native Americans have never really revived, outside the formerly Spanish-ruled Southwest of the United States.

In some places, Native Americans were useful as slaves. On the fringes of the Amazon jungles, slaving became a major industry for Portuguese based in the port of São Paulo in southern Brazil. The early economy of the Carolinas depended on the slave trade with Native Americans, who raided neighbors as far inland as the Mississippi River valley. In this part of the North American South, there were more Native American slaves than black slaves until the destructive nature of the trade led to its abandonment in the early eighteenth century.

Generally, however, the English colonies relied on imported labor—whether enslaved or not—and so could afford to massacre their Native Americans or drive them west. They had a ready-made ideology of extermination. They were the new Israel. The Native Americas were the "uncircumcized," to be dealt with as the biblical Israel dealt with its pagan enemies: smitten hip and thigh. The English, indifferent to clerical discipline, rarely endured Spanish-style agonies of conscience about the justice of their presence in America or the morality of their wars. People who left their land under exploited or unfenced deserved to lose it. Only the line of the fence or the marks of the plow proved true tenure of land. Native Americans in British areas of expansion were too poor to exploit for tribute. It was more economical to dispossess them and replace them with white farmers or black slaves. The only colony where this reasoning was modified was early Pennsylvania. Here moral and material considerations combined to favor a policy of friendly collaboration with the Native Americans. Thanks to the founder's Quaker high morality, supposedly just prices were paid for land purchases from the Indians, who were encouraged to stay on the frontier as buffers against hostile tribes or rival European empires.

Whether expelled, exterminated, diminished by disease, or absorbed into colonial society by marrying Europeans or adopting European ways, the Native Americans retreated to the margins of colonial life wherever European colonies were founded. European involvement in the affairs of the Western Hemisphere had begun—like European penetration of Asia—as a collaborative venture in which Native American communities and states were the newcomers' essential hosts and helpers. By the late seventeenth century, however, those relationships, almost everywhere in the Americas where European and Indian cultures confronted each other, had broken down in violence or simply been transformed as the Native American population fell. Unlike Asia, the New World was not an arena in which native and European states could coexist side by side—although, as we shall see, in the eighteenth and nineteenth centuries, short-lived attempts to found native states and empires revived beyond the frontiers of European settlement.

THE GLOBAL BALANCE OF TRADE

It is not generally realized that in the colonial New World precolonial patterns of exchange often remained intact. European merchants joined existing Native American trading communities, extending the reach or increasing the volume of traffic, enhancing what Indian Ocean venturers called **country trades**, which involved local or regional exchanges that never touched Europe.

In North America, trade in deerskins and beaver pelts in colonial times extended precolonial practice. The French backwoodsmen and buckskin-clad frontiersmen slotted into an existing Native American framework that linked hunting grounds and routes of trade and tribute. The Huron, Native American farmers and traders who did not need to hunt, except for exercise and to supplement their diet, were the middlemen of the early seventeenth-century fur trade, supplying French buyers in Quebec in Canada. Spanish entrepreneurs took part in a profitable canoe-borne trade in local textiles, healing plants, and dyestuffs along the coast of Venezuela in the 1590s. Similarly, the economy that sustained the Spanish conquerors of Yucatán was no transoceanic affair of precious goods, but an extension of the age-old Maya trade with central Mexico, based largely on cacao for consumption in Mexico City.

Of course, Spanish activity was not confined to modest ventures of these kinds, along traditional grooves. The Spanish monarchy was a great inaugurator of new intra-American trade routes. New cities, founded in places never settled on a large scale before, especially on the Pacific and Atlantic coasts, became magnets to supply foodstuffs, cotton textiles, and building materials. The conquest of Peru demanded a new transcontinental route from the Caribbean to the Pacific across the Isthmus of Panama in Central America, which became, like the alternative later opened from Bolivia to the Atlantic via the River Plate, a major silver-bearing artery of the Spanish Empire. Mule-train routes that the Native American civilizations, which had no horses or mules before the arrival of the Europeans, had never required, served the new mining ventures in remote hinterlands. The conquest of much of Chile in the mid–sixteenth century stimulated the creation of a heroic new seaborne route, far into the Pacific, to overcome the Humboldt Current. Sailing ships took longer to get from Lima in Peru to Concepción in Chile than from Seville in Spain to Santo Domingo in the Caribbean.

The slow but steady spread of Spanish frontiers brought regions formerly unknown to each other into touch. The link between Mexico and Peru is the most startling case, since it seems incredible—yet true—that the Native American civilizations of those areas never had significant mutual contact until the Spaniards arrived. Although the places Spaniards occupied in New Mexico, Arizona, and Texas showed some signs of having received cultural influences from Mexico in the past (see Chapter 10), California was a genuinely new discovery, where Spanish missions in the eighteenth century first created ventures in settlement and agriculture that made the region a potential trading partner for other parts of the Spanish monarchy (see Chapter 21). Native American merchants could have navigated the Amazon and the Orinoco Rivers before the Spaniards arrived, but, as far as we know, they never did so. No one fully exploited those mighty and mysterious waterways as arteries of commerce until well into the seventeenth century.

Meanwhile, new commerce opened with the wider world. A system of convoys, the so-called **Treasure Fleets**, linked Spain to America and injected Europe's cash-starved economies with veins of gold and silver. The need for slaves led other European merchants to Spanish colonies and linked the Americas to Africa. The route of the Manila Galleon, a Spanish ship that made an annual crossing of the Pacific from

Potosí in Bolivia—the world's most productive silver mine in the late sixteenth and seventeenth centuries. The "Silver Mountain" really does have an abrupt, conical outline, but all early modern representations exaggerate that shape and emphasize its dominance over the puny dwellings and almost ant-like workers.

CHRONOLOGY

1492–1493	Columbus discovers routes to and from the New World
1500	Portuguese begin direct trade with southern India
1510	Portuguese trading post at Goa established
1513	Discovery of the Gulf Stream
1518–1546	Spanish conquest of Mexico and Peru
1519	Babur founds Mughal Empire
1519–1521	Spanish navigators complete first global navigation
1520–1566	Reign of Suleiman the Magnificent (Ottoman Empire)
1521	Spanish capture Tenochtitlán; end of Aztec Empire
1529	Spain and Portugal divide Pacific seaborne routes between themselves
1530s	Spanish conquest of Peru
1552–1556	Russian conquest of Kazan
1556–1605	Mughal expansion and centralization under Akbar
1564–1565	Northern Pacific sea route between New World and Asia discovered
1585–1598	Reign of Toyotomi Hideyoshi (Japan)
1600	East India Company founded (England)
1602	Dutch East India Company founded
Early 1600s	Dutch use westerlies to circumnavigate globe
1609	English found Virginia colony
1619	Dutch found Batavia (Indonesia)
1620–1640	Portuguese expelled from trading posts in Persian Gulf and Indian Ocean
1640	Dutch merchants only Europeans allowed in Japan
1656–1707	Mughal Empire covers most of Indian subcontinent under Aurangzeb
1674	French establish trading post at Pondicherry (India)
1676	King Philip's War (New England)
1689	Treaty of Nerchinsk with China checks Russian expansion eastward

the Philippines to Acapulco on the Pacific coast of Mexico, facilitated the direct exchange of Mexican silver for Chinese silk and porcelain. For the first time, trade girdled the world, tying the Americas, Africa, and Eurasia into a single, interconnected system.

IN PERSPECTIVE: The Impact of the Americas

Suppose Columbus had been right. Suppose the globe was small, and no Americas lay in the way of Europeans' westward approach to Asia. Europeans would still, of course, have taken part—presumably a bigger part—in Asia's carrying trades. They would have made money out of it and closed the wealth gap that separated them from the richer economies of maritime Asia. They would have contributed to recycling Japanese silver and helped to make the world's economy more liquid. They would probably have gone on to found the land empires that began to take shape in Asia in the late seventeenth century. The total volume of resources at their command would, however, have remained modest. The Americas were a huge bonanza—of land, of food and mineral resources, of opportunities for the productive deployment of labor, of new markets and manufactures. Western Europeans' privileged access to those resources made a new era in world history possible. The traditional poor relations of Eurasia—the formerly impoverished West—could now challenge previously towering economies, such as those of India and China, that had been dominant in Eurasia for thousands of years.

PROBLEMS AND PARALLELS

1. In what ways were empires agents of change in the sixteenth and seventeenth centuries?

2. How were empires created in the sixteenth and seventeenth centuries? What are the differences between land and maritime empires?

3. How did the maritime imperialism of Japan compare with Portuguese and Dutch imperial ventures?

4. What roles did native collaborators, interpreters, merchants, and middlemen play in the empires of the sixteenth and seventeenth centuries? What does the term *stranger effect* mean?

5. What are the differences and similarities among the Russian, Chinese, Ottoman, and Mughal Empires of this period?

6. How was Spain able to achieve such a vast empire in so short a time?

7. How did a global trade network emerge in the sixteenth century?

DOCUMENTS IN GLOBAL HISTORY

- Toyotomi Hideyoshi, on the Conquest of China
- Jan van Linschoten on Dutch business in the Indian Ocean
- Hideyoshi, "Limitation on the Propagation of Christianity"
- Domingo Navarrete, "Of My Stay in the Kingdom of Makassar"
- Abul Fazl Allami, from the *Institutes of Akbar*
- Ogier Ghiselin de Busbecq on Suleiman the Magnificent

- Bernal Diaz del Castillo, from *The True History of the conquest of New Spain*
- An Aztec account of the conquest of Mexico (*The Broken Spears*)
- From Bartoleme de las Casas, *Brief Account of the Devastation of the ladies*

Please see the Primary Source CD-ROM for additional sources related to this chapter.

READ ON

The best introduction to the Portuguese maritime empire is A.J. Russell-Wood, *The Portuguese Empire, 1415–1808* (1992). See now also F. Bethencourt and D. Curto, eds., *The Portuguese Empire* (2006). P.Pérez-Mallaína, *Spain's Men of the Sea: Daily Life on the Indies Fleets in the Sixteenth Century* (trans. Carla Rahn Phillips, 1998) is a superb social history of shipboard life in the age of maritime expansion. C.R. Boxer, *The Dutch Seaborne Empire: 1600–1800* (reprint, 1991) is a slightly dated but still valuable and very readable account of the rise of Dutch colonial power. Its perspective on southeast Asia should be balanced by W. Cummings, *Making Blood White: Historical Transformations in Early Modern Makasar* (2002), a sophisticated recent study of the transition from oral to literate culture in an area of increasing Dutch influence. K. So, *Japanese Piracy in Ming China During 16th Century* (1975) explores the impact of *wako* raids around the South China Sea in the sixteenth century. M. Berry, *Hideyoshi* (2001) is a superb study of that ruler. B. Walker, *The Conquest of Ainu Lands: Ecology and Culture in Japanese Expansion, 1590–1800* (2001) is important on continuing Japanese expansion.

R. L. Edmunds, *The Northern Frontier in Qing China and Tokugawa Japan: A Comparative Study of Frontier Policy* (1985) is valuable. On Qing expansion, J. Waley-Cohen, *Exile in Mid-Qing China* (1991) is important. On Batavia, L. Blusse, *Strange Company* (1986) is outstanding. J. F. Richards, *The Mughal Empire* (1996) is a fine introduction to Mughal history, while P.M. Brand and G. D. Lowry, *Akbar's India: Art from the Mughal City of Victory* (1985) explores the cultural expressions of Mughal might and ruling style. R. Murphey, *Ottoman Warfare, 1500–1700* (1999) analyzes Ottoman military power in its social, economic and geographic contexts. K. Chase, *Firearms. A Global*

History to 1700 (2003) offers an overview of the dynamics of power in Eurasia whose central thesis is simplistic but whose details on the spread of gunpowder weaponry are valuable.

My material on Russian icons comes from the Royal Academy exhibition catalog *The Art of Holy Russia: Icons from Moscow, 1440–1660* (1998). On Siberia, T. Armstrong, ed., *Yermak's Campaigns in Siberia* (1975) unites the main chronicles. J. Forsyth, *A History of the Peoples of Siberia* (1994) is the best overall study.

M. Restall, *Seven Myths of the Spanish Conquest* (2003) is essential on New World imperialism. J. H. Elliott, *Empires of the Atlantic* (2006) compares English, later British, and Spanish experience. B.E. Mundy, *The Mapping of New Spain: Indigenous Cartography and the Maps of the Relaciones Geograficas* (2000) offers an excellent scholarly analysis of the local maps and surveys collected by the Spanish government in the late sixteenth century as part of its effort to govern its new empire more effectively. A fine edition of W. Bradford, *Of Plymouth Plantation* (1999) gives a first-hand account of the creation of the Plymouth colony. E. H. Spicer, *The American Indians* (1982), is an authoritative summary of Native American history, including relations with the expanding European presence in North America.

On global trade balances in the sixteenth and seventeenth centuries, see A. Gunder-Frank, *ReORIENT: Global Economy in the Asian Age* (1998), a provocative study that argues forcefully for Asia, especially China, as the center of gravity of global trade right through to 1800. E. van Veen, *Decay or Defeat? An Enquiry into the Portuguese Decline in Asia* (2000) makes some important corrections and R. Barendse, *The Arabian Seas* (2002) is extremely helpful.

CHAPTER 17

The Ecological Revolution of the Sixteenth and Seventeenth Centuries

The flavors and colors of Italy, by way of the Americas. Tomatoes, peppers, and potatoes—as well as other, non-native fruits and vegetables—entice the shopper in a market in old Naples, 1981.

A street in Melbourne, Australia, has restaurants representing a vast range of world cuisines. Here, without turning a corner, one can experience the importance of tomatoes in the meals of Bengal in northern India and of peanuts in Malay cooking. Within a few doors' space, diners can confirm that hot chillies are prominent in the food of Thailand and Chinese Sichuan, and cassava in that of parts of West Africa. A few paces, farther on, you find how potatoes are essential at table in Ireland or northern Europe, while chocolate and vanilla are vital in French pastry. Yet before the sixteenth century, no one had ever tasted any of these ingredients in the lands that became their adopted homes. All originated in the Americas and were unknown in Europe or Asia before the sixteenth century. Indispensable items on an Italian menu are gnocchi and polenta—made from native American plants: respectively potatoes and maize (or "corn" in everyday American usage). Jerusalem artichokes originated in North America, not Jerusalem. The turkey was first recorded in Mexico, not Turkey. The pineapple was unknown in Europe until Columbus encountered and described it during his first transatlantic journey.

● ● ● ● ●

The transfer of plants and animals in the opposite direction, from the Old World to the New, transformed the food of the Americas even more deeply. Imagine an Argentine restaurant without beef steaks or a school cafeteria in North America without cow's milk, orange juice, or wheat bread, or the food of the North American Deep South without molasses or yams or pork or collard greens, or of the Caribbean without rice, coconuts, mangoes, or bananas.

These exchanges of ingredients are important because we are what we eat. Eating and cooking the food of our countries and communities are badges of loyalty and identity. To understand the way we eat now, and who we are, we have to look back at some of the profound ecological transformations that overtook the world of the sixteenth and seventeenth centuries. First, what historians now call the

FOCUS questions

- WHY WAS the Columbian Exchange so important and how did it affect nutrition in Europe and Asia?
- HOW DID the introduction of new diseases by Europeans affect population levels in the Americas?
- WHY DID the Europeans import slaves to the Americas?
- WHY DID the balance of power change between nomads and settled peoples?
- IN WHAT new ways did people around the world exploit the natural environment in the seventeenth century?
- HOW DID the European settlement in the Americas and increased contact across Eurasia redirect the course of evolution?

Columbian Exchange, the transfer of plants, animals, and microbes among the Americas, Europe, Asia, and Africa, effected transformations that, taken together, ought to be regarded as the biggest revolution that human agency ever made on Earth. A divergent pattern of evolution, hundreds of millions years old, had made the life forms of the various continents ever more different from one another from the moment the ancient continent of Pangaea split. Relatively suddenly, by the scale of the long preceding period, that pattern was reversed. About 500 years ago, travel around the globe and a mixture of conscious and unconscious transplantation of plants and creatures substituted a new, convergent pattern. People began to swap the life-forms of different continents.

Second, the human relationship with fatal pathogens underwent puzzling lurches. At one level, the period from the mid–fourteenth century to the eighteenth was an age of plagues, when lethal diseases spread over the world and ravaged populations. On the other hand, the microorganisms responsible seem, late in the period, to have retreated, with surprising and still unexplained suddenness, from their accustomed eco-niches. A worldwide population explosion began toward the mid–eighteenth century.

Third, human settlement changed both its range and its nature, invading new ecological frontiers on an unprecedented scale: farming grasslands, felling forests, climbing slopes, reclaiming bogs, penetrating game preserves and deep-sea fisheries, expanding and founding cities, turning deserts into gardens and gardens into deserts. This was part of a drive for resources and energy sources in an increasingly populous world. Hunters ransacked previously unmolested wild zones for animal furs, fats, and proteins. Much of this hunting took place at sea, in pursuit of migrating fish and wandering whales and seals. The exploration and exploitation of new frontiers created an illusion of abundance that inspired ecological overkill. Yet imperialism also had positive environmental effects, as colonialists came, in some cases, to see themselves as custodians of tropical Edens, preparing the way for a revived respect and even reverence for nature in the eighteenth-century Western World.

Finally, climate underwent global fluctuations. The little ice age (see Chapter 14) was in progress for most of the period and revived briefly at its end, though temperatures generally took an upward turn in the eighteenth century. The effects of the temperature changes, however, are hard to measure and, on the basis of present knowledge, seem surprisingly slight. They are most evident on a regional basis when they seem to explain unusually frequent and/or severe weather-induced agricultural crises. As explanations for larger trends, we have to set them aside as an unknown quantity and look at each of the other three changes in turn.

THE ECOLOGICAL EXCHANGE: PLANTS AND ANIMALS

It is tempting to pick out the well-documented introductions of life-forms as the highlights of the story, or focus on the legends of heroes who bore life-changing new foodstuffs across the oceans. Columbus is fairly credited with a lot of "firsts." From his first ocean crossing in 1492, he brought back descriptions and samples, including pineapple and cassava or manioc. On his second transatlantic voyage in

1493, he took sugarcanes to the island of Hispaniola—but let it grow wild. Pigs, sheep, cattle, chickens, and wheat made their first appearance in the New World on the same occasion. Other heroic firsts are the subjects of legends or fables. Juan Garrido, a black companion of Cortés, supposedly first planted wheat in Mexico. The story of Sir Walter Raleigh, the sixteenth-century poet, courtier, historian, and pirate, introducing potatoes to England is false but has an honored place in myth.

The real, although unwitting, heroes, however, are surely the plants and animals themselves, who survived deadly journeys and successfully adapted to new climates, sometimes—in the case of seeds—with little human help, by accident. They traveled in the cuffs or pleats of the clothing of unwitting carriers, or were caught in the fabric of cloth bales and sacks. In terms of volume and contribution to global nutrition, a few instances stand out. Out of Eurasia to new worlds in the Western and Southern Hemispheres went wheat, sugar, rice, bananas, coconuts, apples, pears, apricots, peaches, plums, cherries, olives, citrus fruits, and major meat-yielding and dairy livestock. The European grape variety *vitis vinifera* (the only grapes native to the Americas are Concord grapes) should perhaps be included, because of the importance American wines made from varieties of it have attained in the world market. Yams, okra, and collard greens were among vegetables that made the crossing from Africa (see Map 17.1).

As well as the fancy foodstuffs and flavors already mentioned the Americas supplied for Africa and Eurasia, medicinal plants crossed the ocean. Quinine, borrowed by Spanish physicians from among the medicinal plants of the peoples of Peru, had enormous long-term significance, because it can control the effects of malaria and was therefore vital for Europeans struggling to survive in the mosquito-ridden, swampy tropics. Tobacco—"with which," said a Spanish reporter in the 1540s, Native Americans "perfume their mouths"—was thought to aid digestion. But the staple products—and therefore the most important gifts of the New World to the rest, because they could feed vast populations—were maize, potatoes, and sweet potatoes.

Maize, Sweet Potatoes, and Potatoes

Maize at first revolted Old-World taste buds but fascinated Old-World plant specialists. As the Spanish botanist Juan de Cárdenas reported in one of the first scientific studies of maize in 1591, it thrives "in cold, hot, dry, or wet climates, in mountainous regions or grasslands, as a winter or summer crop, irrigated or dry-farmed," with a high yield and short land-use cycle that made Spanish wheat seem difficult to cultivate by comparison. Maize appeared in China so quickly after it emerged from America that some scholars insist that it must somehow have arrived there earlier. Two independent routes seem to have brought maize to Asia: overland from the west, maize was borne to China as a tribute plant by Turkic frontiersmen and first recorded in 1555. Meanwhile, it also came by sea to Fujian in southern China, where a visiting Spanish friar saw it cultivated in 1577. At first, it was welcomed in China as a curiosity, not a serious source of food. It rated no more than a footnote in a standard Chinese agricultural work of the early seventeenth century. But its advantages over millet and rice—it required less labor per unit of production and could grow in eco-niches where the traditional crops could not—gradually made it popular, especially in areas of new settlement. Europeans were initially even less enthusiastic than the Chinese about eating maize themselves, rather than feeding it to livestock, but it slowly

Tobacco was thought to be good for the digestive system. In this seventeenth-century Dutch illustration, Cupid carries the smoker's pipe and pouch because tobacco, like lovemaking, is a fleeting pleasure that quickly goes up in smoke.

Rice and sheep in Peru. The ecological revolution brought unfamiliar plants and animals to the New World. In the mid-eighteenth century, Baltasar Martínez sketched the economic life of Peru, including Indians using sickles to harvest rice, while a sheep grazes on a neglected clump.

Embarcadero de los Cavallos.

Transporting horses. This eighteenth-century illustration from a Spanish manual of horsemanship makes it look easy. But transporting horses by sea was a delicate, hazardous, and technically demanding business. Yet once across the ocean, a few runaway steeds could transform the Americas. In 1536, Spaniards released 12 horses on the plains of Argentina. Within a few years, the herds "looked as dense as forests."

established a place as human food in the eighteenth century in parts of the eastern and central Mediterranean, the Balkans, Ukraine, and southern Russia.

Like maize, the sweet potato had a transforming effect in parts of China. First reported in southern China near the Burmese border in the 1560s, it probably came overland from the south. Its flavor had a bad reputation with ethnic Chinese, but it was favored in hill country by immigrants and settlers who were obliged to occupy land previously thought marginal. Used, at first, only for horse fodder, sweet potatoes were rapidly adopted as human food. In 1594 a governor of Fujian supposedly recommended sweet potatoes when the conventional crops failed. The enthusiasm with which different cultures received the crop varied unpredictably. In Japan sweet potatoes never caught on, after following a south-to-north route perhaps indicated by variations in their name: they are called "Chinese potatoes" in the Ryukyu Islands, "Ryukyu potatoes" farther north in Satsuma in the southern Japanese home islands, and "Satsuma potatoes" in the rest of Japan.

Potatoes, which the Portuguese introduced to Asia in 1605, similarly failed to win popular favor in Japan, Korea, or China. They had remained a regionally restricted food in the Americas—cultivated at high altitudes in the Andes. Yet when Portuguese migrants took them to Bengal in India, they became an inescapable ingredient of Bengali meals. Potatoes conquered northern Europe, where they gradually replaced rye as the food base of a vast swathe of humankind from Ireland across Scandinavia and Germany to Poland and Russia. War spread them, for peasants favored a crop that grew concealed in the ground and so eluded seizure by plundering troops. Tried out with success in the Basque country of northern Spain and southwest France and in Ireland before the end of the sixteenth century, the potato began its war-linked career in Belgium in the 1680s under the impact of French invasion, and spread eastward with every subsequent war. Scholars and bureaucrats promoted it because of its impressive nutritional qualities. If eaten in sufficient quantities, it is the only major staple that provides all the nutrients essential to human health.

Weeds, Grasses, and Livestock

Transplantations in the opposite direction—into the New World from the Old—turned much of the Americas into farmland for food for European palates and digestions, and ranch land for European livestock. The first stage was colonization by European weeds and grasses that made parts of the New World able to support sheep, cattle, and horses instead of just bison and llamas. European plants, such as purslane and Englishman's Foot, created what Alfred Crosby, the great historian of the ecological exchange, called "empires of the dandelion." Weeds made the revolution work. They "healed raw wounds" invaders tore in the earth, bound soil together, saved it from drying out, refilled "vacated eco-niches," and fed imported livestock.

Conscious transpositions followed. Horses and cattle came first—the New World had no similar big domesticated animals. The Spanish army that invaded New Mexico in 1598 was accompanied by thousands of head of cattle, which their masters drove over mountains and deserts—including the terrible 60-mile waterless stretch known as the March of Death. To Spanish cattlemen, the South American pampa and the North American prairie were the last frontiers of an enterprise that began in the Middle Ages, when they had adopted ranching as a way to exploit the empty, conquered lands in Spain after the Muslim population had fled or been expelled.

Meanwhile, wheat arrived. The lower levels of the central valleys proved highly suitable for wheat and although most of the Indian population continued to rely on maize, wheat bread became a badge of urban sophistication. Within a few years of the Spanish conquest, the city council of Mexico City demanded a supply of "white, clean, well-cooked and seasoned bread." The valleys of Mexico supplied Spanish garrisons all over Central America and the Caribbean with wheat flour.

Not all efforts to introduce wheat in other parts of the Americas were successful, at least at first. The Spanish colonists of Florida in 1565 brought wheat seed, together with grapevine cuttings, 200 calves, 400 pigs, 400 sheep, and unspecified numbers of goats and chickens. But the crops did not "take," and the animals went wild or died for lack of fodder or were slaughtered in desperation. By 1573, "herbs, fish, and other scum and vermin" sustained the colonists when rations were short. Corn bread and fish, foodstuffs copied from the Native American diet, were their mainstays. Similarly, the first English colonists in Virginia were unable to grow food for themselves and relied on handouts from the natives to see them through their "starving time." Investors and imperialists back home blamed colonists' moral deficiencies for these failures. But the problems of the mutual adaptation of Old World farming and New World environments were formidable, especially for settlers of exposed seaboards in an era of imperial competition. Colonies sited for defense, behind marshes or swamps, in difficult climates, needed generations of investment and long periods of heartbreakingly high rates of mortality before they could be made viable. At every stage of European colonization of new worlds, the remarkable thing is not the high rate of failure but the perseverance that led to ultimate success.

Cane Sugar

Of Old World arrivals in America, cane sugar was the first transplanted product to have a major impact on world markets. It is, perhaps, the first food to have conquered unaccustomed markets by the power of supply. Instead of following the usual laws of economics, according to which demand comes first and supply responds, sugar was the first of a series of tropical products that were recommended by their availability. European taste buds became enslaved to it.

Sugar rapidly became the most important item of transoceanic trade. The first sugar refinery in the Americas opened in Hispaniola in 1513. Portuguese enterprise launched the Brazilian sugar industry. For the first 30 years of their presence in Brazil, the Portuguese exploited its coasts for nothing but logwood bought in vast quantities—perhaps 19,000 tons a year—from the natives. From the 1530s, however, they began to plant sugar around Salvador and in Pernambuco in northern Brazil. It was a difficult crop to plant, harvest, and refine, greedy of capital and demanding lots of specialized labor. And it yielded surprisingly low profits for the planters—typically only 3 percent a year.

Trading in sugar, however, was highly profitable. So it was important for planters to retain an interest in the trade after the sugar left their hands. The value of the crop doubled or even quadrupled as it crossed the Atlantic. The sugar-growing area was never extensive—parts of Brazil, some Caribbean islands, patches of coasts around the Spanish Main, and French Louisiana around New Orleans—but it was highly productive. By the 1580s, four effects

A water-driven sugar mill in Pernambuco during the Dutch occupation of northern Brazil, depicted here in a Dutch atlas of 1662. Slaves carry the mill owner, slung in a hammock under a rich awning in the foreground. The sugar cane arrives by oxcart, to be ground by the power of the mill.

were evident. First, Brazil had become the world's major producer, and the economies of the sugar islands of the eastern Atlantic—Madeira, the Azores, the Cape Verdes—(see Chapter 15) went into eclipse. Second, the need for labor in the sugar plantations and mills caused an explosion in the transatlantic slave trade. Third, the growing volume of sugar production created new American industries: refining sugar and distilling rum. In the seventeenth century, Brazilian sugar was refined locally, before export.

Finally, the competition for sugar-producing lands was becoming a major cause of imperial rivalry among European states. Dutch invaders took over the Portuguese sugar plantations in Pernambuco in 1630, then, on their expulsion nearly a quarter of a century later, concentrated on creating plantations of their own in the Caribbean and on the Guiana coast of South America, where they proclaimed a "second Brazil" in Surinam in 1667. English, French, Spaniards, Scandinavians, and even Courlanders from a duchy on the Baltic coast all set up sugar industries on Caribbean islands in the second half of the seventeenth century. Where sugar could be grown successfully, unprecedented prosperity was possible. In the 1680s, the British island of Barbados sustained a population of more than 300 people per square mile—the average figure for Western Europe at the time was 92 people per square mile. By then, the sugar trade was undergoing a further revolution that would transform it into one of the world's most popular products: the popularization of the taste for hot sugar-sweetened beverages in Europe.

Coffee, Tea, and Chocolate

For, where sugar led, coffee—and, ultimately, tea and chocolate—followed. By 1640, the coffee of Yemen (YEH-mehn) rivaled or exceeded pepper as the main trading commodity of the Arabian Sea. It continued to boom, supplying markets in Persia, where coffee consumption quadrupled to nearly a million pounds a year by the end of the century. Even larger amounts—about 17 million pounds—went to the Ottoman Empire via the Red Sea and Egypt. Coffee arrived in France in 1644 with a returning ambassador from Turkey, along with old porcelain cups of great beauty and small napkins of fine cotton muslin, embroidered in gold, silver, and silk. The coffee-drinking habit soon found patrons. In 1657, Jean de Thévenot noticed that Parisian aristocrats hired Moorish and Italian coffeemakers. Armenian importers and street brewers popularized coffee drinking in France. Within half a century, coffee became the West's favorite addictive stimulant. In his satirical domestic comedy, the "Coffee Cantata," the great German composer Johann Sebastian Bach (1685–1750) credited it with the potential to break up marriages because so many husbands stayed away from home to drink coffee in cafes.

Once the popularity of the new beverage was established, the next stage was to transplant it to new lands where Europeans could control the supply. The great coffee boom of the eighteenth and nineteenth centuries took it to Brazil, to the French islands of the Indian Ocean, and to the

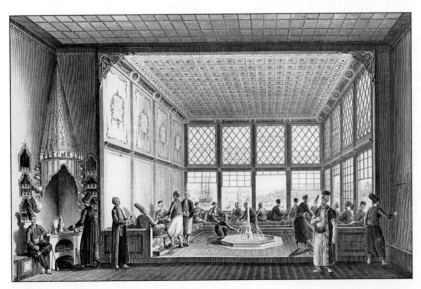

Turkish coffeehouse. In the late eighteenth and early nineteenth centuries, coffee was still a luxury item in much of the world, and coffee drinking was a social ritual for the rich, as in this coffee-house scene in Istanbul. Mass production in Java and later in Brazil, however, was already brewing coffee into a cheap drink for the West's industrial workers.

French colony of Saint-Domingue on Hispaniola, which for a while, until the black slaves there rebelled and proclaimed the Republic of Haiti in 1804, was the most productive island in the world for coffee and sugar alike. One of the most enduringly successful of the new coffee lands was Java, where the Dutch introduced the plant in the 1690s, gradually expanded production during the eighteenth century, and, in the nineteenth, fought wars to boost production on ever more marginal soils.

While coffee spread across the world from the Middle East, chocolate followed a similar path from a starting place in Mesoamerica. It took longer than coffee to penetrate European markets. In a work of 1648, credited with introducing chocolate to the English-speaking world, Thomas Gage described how colonial Mexico liked it—mixed with Old-World flavors, such as cinnamon, cloves, and almonds, as well as in the stews of bitter chocolate and chillies that were traditional Mesoamerican recipes. As the new drink became fashionable in Europe, the cacao (cah-COW) from which chocolate was made was transplanted to West Africa, where Danish plantations helped supply the growing trade in the eighteenth century. Tea also contributed to the growth of global trade, but not to the ecological exchange. China was able to supply almost the whole of world demand until the nineteenth century when the British established tea plantations in India and Sri Lanka.

Patterns of Ecological Exchange

It would be a mistake to think of the ecological exchange as merely bouncing back and forth across the oceans between the Old World and the New. Some ecological exchanges happened within the Americas. Domesticated turkeys formed no part of the first Thanksgiving meal. They were introduced to New England from Mexico later in the seventeenth century. The real maker of English economic success in Virginia was John Rolfe. He was the husband of the Indian princess Pocahontas—the forger of a kind of understanding with the natives, based on collaboration, mutual benefit, and sexual alliance that was normal in Spanish, Portuguese, and French colonies but that remained rare in English colonial practice. His vital economic contribution was to introduce "Spanish tobacco" (from the West Indies), which became Virginia's monoculture: the large-scale export crop that turned the colony from an unprofitable swamp into a field for settlers. It had to be transplanted because Europeans could not stand the taste of Virginia's native tobacco. Sweet potatoes were first recorded in Virginia in 1648, probably introduced not directly from South America, but via Europe or Africa with the slave trade.

Along the routes of transmission, gardens where plants could be adapted and bred for new climates were way stations of ecological exchange. Dutch horticulture led the way. Gardening was already a Dutch national obsession in the seventeenth century, when tulips from Turkey and chrysanthemums from Sri Lanka inspired costly "manias"—competition to grow the rarest and most spectacular varieties. Dutch plant collectors crisscrossed the world. The Dutch Prince John Maurice of Nassau grew African and Indonesian plants in his garden in Brazil and sent Chilean monkey-puzzle trees to Germany. Nicolaas Witsen, a director of the Dutch East India Company, planted the first rhubarb in

Chocolate. In this canvas of about 1640—presumably intended to adorn a dining room—the Spanish painter Juan de Zurbarán (1620–1649) exalts chocolate, raising it on a silver pedestal and placing it center stage as if he were painting its portrait. In the seventeenth century, rich Europeans consumed chocolate the way the Aztec elite had—as a luxury beverage. Zurbarán here depicts a truly global experience in conspicuous consumption: expensive chocolate imported to Spain from Mexico is to be drunk in even more costly porcelain cups imported from China.

 Thomas Gage on chocolate

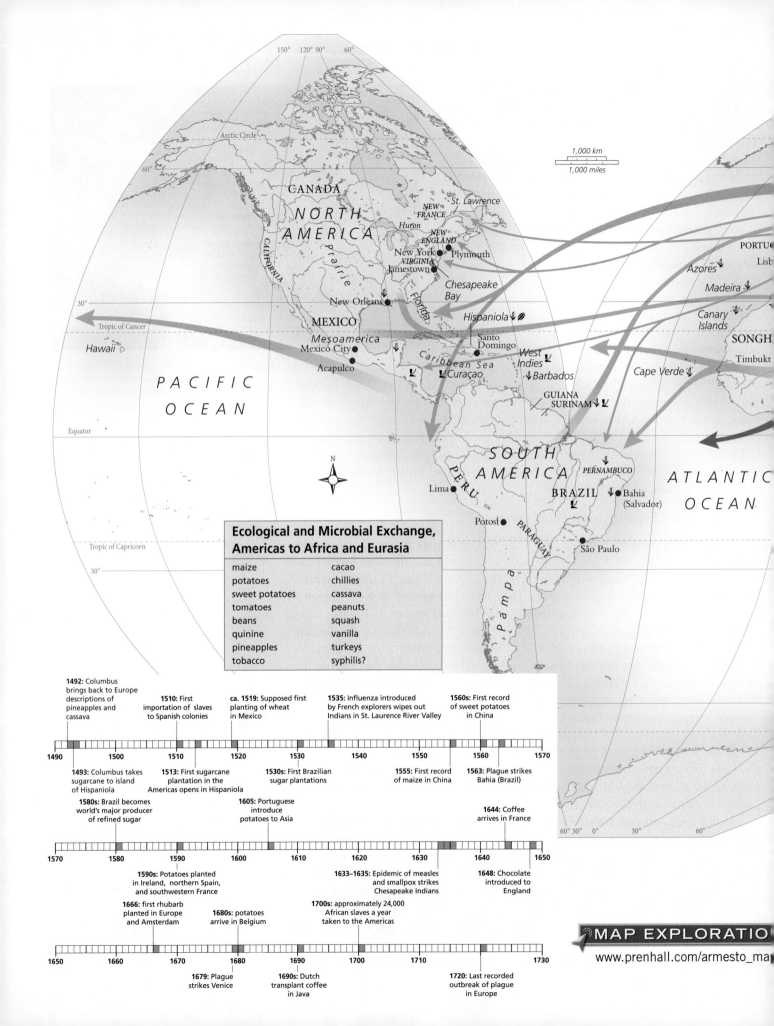

**Ecological and Microbial Exchange,
Americas to Africa and Eurasia**

maize	cacao
potatoes	chillies
sweet potatoes	cassava
tomatoes	peanuts
beans	squash
quinine	vanilla
pineapples	turkeys
tobacco	syphilis?

1492: Columbus brings back to Europe descriptions of pineapples and cassava

1510: First importation of slaves to Spanish colonies

ca. 1519: Supposed first planting of wheat in Mexico

1535: Influenza introduced by French explorers wipes out Indians in St. Laurence River Valley

1560s: First record of sweet potatoes in China

1490 — 1500 — 1510 — 1520 — 1530 — 1540 — 1550 — 1560 — 1570

1493: Columbus takes sugarcane to island of Hispaniola

1513: First sugarcane plantation in the Americas opens in Hispaniola

1530s: First Brazilian sugar plantations

1555: First record of maize in China

1563: Plague strikes Bahia (Brazil)

1580s: Brazil becomes world's major producer of refined sugar

1605: Portuguese introduce potatoes to Asia

1644: Coffee arrives in France

1570 — 1580 — 1590 — 1600 — 1610 — 1620 — 1630 — 1640 — 1650

1590s: Potatoes planted in Ireland, northern Spain, and southwestern France

1633–1635: Epidemic of measles and smallpox strikes Chesapeake Indians

1648: Chocolate introduced to England

1666: first rhubarb planted in Europe and Amsterdam

1680s: potatoes arrive in Belgium

1700s: approximately 24,000 African slaves a year taken to the Americas

1650 — 1660 — 1670 — 1680 — 1690 — 1700 — 1710 — 1720 — 1730

1679: Plague strikes Venice

1690s: Dutch transplant coffee in Java

1720: Last recorded outbreak of plague in Europe

▶ MAP EXPLORATIO

www.prenhall.com/armesto_ma

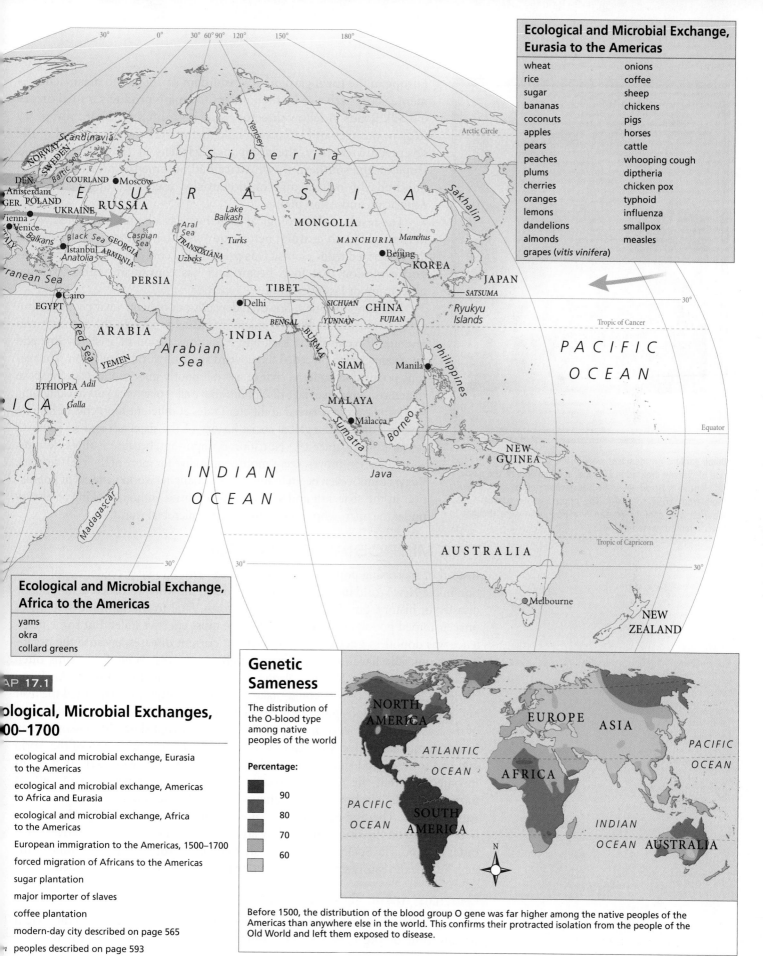

Ecological and Microbial Exchange, Eurasia to the Americas

wheat	onions
rice	coffee
sugar	sheep
bananas	chickens
coconuts	pigs
apples	horses
pears	cattle
peaches	whooping cough
plums	diptheria
cherries	chicken pox
oranges	typhoid
lemons	influenza
dandelions	smallpox
almonds	measles
grapes (*vitis vinifera*)	

Ecological and Microbial Exchange, Africa to the Americas

yams
okra
collard greens

AP 17.1

ological, Microbial Exchanges,
00–1700

ecological and microbial exchange, Eurasia
to the Americas

ecological and microbial exchange, Americas
to Africa and Eurasia

ecological and microbial exchange, Africa
to the Americas

European immigration to the Americas, 1500–1700

forced migration of Africans to the Americas

sugar plantation

major importer of slaves

coffee plantation

modern-day city described on page 565

peoples described on page 593

Genetic Sameness

The distribution of
the O-blood type
among native
peoples of the world

Percentage:

	90
	80
	70
	60

Before 1500, the distribution of the blood group O gene was far higher among the native peoples of the
Americas than anywhere else in the world. This confirms their protracted isolation from the people of the
Old World and left them exposed to disease.

Dutch garden. An idealized view of the garden that John Maurice of Nassau created in Holland, to complement the gardens he planted in Brazil, when he was governor of the Dutch colony there from 1637 to 1644. The printed verses compare John Maurice with ancient Persian emperors, who were thought to have invented gardening.

Europe in the town garden of Amsterdam in 1666—no mean achievement, as rhubarb was by then one of the main products traded on the old Silk Roads. A fellow director made it his life's work, or folly, to try to grow oranges and lemons in cold, damp Holland. By the end of the seventeenth century, the company's gardens at the Cape of Good Hope on the southern tip of Africa had become the meeting place of hundreds of ornamental or potentially useful European, African, American, and Asian plants.

The result of the ecological exchange was a better-nourished world in the eighteenth century, better equipped than before with medicinal drugs derived from plants. This presumably contributed to the population explosion that then began, and has continued, with increasing pace, more or less ever since.

Human population, however, depends not only on what people do but also on how disease-bearing microorganisms behave. In the sixteenth and seventeenth centuries, a long and hazardous period of relatively low and uncertain growth preceded the upward surge of world population. The reasons population patterns change are still poorly understood. Clearly, social structures—and marriage disciplines above all—play a big part in explaining why people seem to breed at different rates at different moments of history. (We will discuss the global social history of the sixteenth and seventeenth centuries in Chapter 19.) Nutrition is important, because it affects fertility, and, when it improves, keeps more people alive for more of their fertile years. But we cannot even begin to understand changing world patterns of population in the sixteenth and seventeenth centuries without looking at history under the microscope and examining the microbial world.

THE MICROBIAL EXCHANGE

Instead of increasing population, in accordance with known precedents, colonization in the New World in these centuries provoked the worst recorded demographic disaster in history. Smallpox, in a virulent form, fatal to the immune systems of unaccustomed populations, was probably the most effective killer. But some pestilence was doubtless unclassifiable in terms of current diseases, because the organisms responsible have evolved unrecognizably since that time. Symptoms often baffled their beholders. When a plague struck in Bahía, in 1563, José de Anchieta, the Jesuit "apostle of Brazil," could make no sense of symptoms that rotted the liver and produced a noxious pox, but he treated Indians by bleeding and peeling "parts of the legs and almost all their feet, cutting off the corrupt skin with scissors." Even if we assume that Native American societies were like those in the rest of the world and had suffered undocumented pestilence before the Europeans arrived, it seems incontestable that the diseases colonization brought were new and the effects unprecedented. "The breath of a Spaniard" was said to be enough to make a Native American die. The first Spanish navigators of the Amazon, in 1542, beheld cities built on stilts on the river banks, fed by aquaculture and the intensive cultivation of bitter manioc. The Spaniards did no more than pass through, yet by the time of the next European visitors a generation later, that populous world had vanished.

Demographic Collapse in the New World

Demographers have been unable to produce convincing figures for the extent or duration of the collapse, but even at the most optimistic estimates, the

Indian population of Hispaniola, where New World colonization began, was virtually wiped out. In the densely settled and highly exposed regions of Mesoamerica and the Andes, Indian populations typically fell by 90 percent before they began to recover—which they did only patchily and intermittently until well into the seventeenth century and in many places not until the eighteenth.

Benevolent attitudes by colonial authorities made no difference. No empire has ever legislated so persistently, or so ineffectually, for the benefit of its victims as Spain's in the New World. It is impossible to imagine a system more benevolent—in paternalist fashion—than that of the Jesuits in the vast areas of Brazil and Paraguay that the crown separated from Spain's secular dominions for an experiment in building a self-sustaining Christian community. A

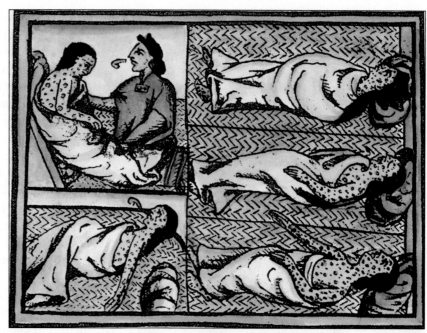

Smallpox victims. A native artist drew these victims of smallpox in sixteenth-century Mexico to illustrate a history that a Spanish friar wrote in Nahuatl—the language of the Aztecs. At top left, an Aztec physician is talking to his patient, who was almost certainly doomed. Hardly any Europeans died of smallpox at the time, but the disease killed millions of Native Americans, who had had no opportunity to develop immunity to it.

picture in a work of propaganda in praise of this enterprise, published in 1700, displays its idealistic inspiration. A jaguar lies down with a tapir, and a little child leads them. Somehow, however, this paradise had got mislaid. Baptismal records show that by 1650, of the 150,000 people the Jesuits had baptized in their missions in the four most forward frontier provinces, only 40,000 survived the raids of Portuguese slavers and the visitations of plague.

The more spacious environments of North America bred equally devastating diseases. The influenza French explorers unwittingly introduced on the St. Lawrence River valley in Canada in 1535, and the nameless plague a Spanish expedition spread in what is now the American Deep South in 1538 inaugurated a history in which every attempted European settlement infected the Native Americans. The first English settlement in Virginia spread a quick-killing disease among the Indians, "so strange that they did not know anything about it or how to cure it." The next major epidemic of 1633–1635, was recognizably of measles followed by smallpox. The Chesapeake Indians disappeared by the end of the seventeenth century. The numbers of the Huron in Canada collapsed so dramatically after contact with Europeans that one Jesuit argued desperately that it was a sign of divine favor. God was gathering his chosen to him. By the end of the seventeenth century, the Native American population in regions Europeans penetrated had fallen—according to rival estimates—by between 60 and 90 percent.

Plague and New Diseases in Eurasia

Some regions outside the Americas suffered comparable devastation. In the remoter parts of Siberia, visitors from the wider world were almost as much of a novelty as in the New World, and the unimmunized natives were equally vulnerable to unaccustomed diseases. Eighty percent of the tribespeople Russian imperialism touched east of the Yenisey River perished in the 1650s. Later, European penetration of Australia and parts of the Pacific had similar effects.

So, in a sense, the "age of plague" that started in the Old World in the late Middle Ages increased in virulence as disease-bearing microorganisms spread across the

Burial of the dead—plague-stricken or impoverished—was one of the obligations of the brethren of the religious brotherhood, or confraternity, that ran the Hospital de Caridad in Seville, Spain. The sculptures on the high altar therefore depict the entombment of Christ. This altarpiece represents a characteristically emotional baroque theme: the paradox of inhabitants of a glorious heaven sharing the miseries and suffering of earthly life.

world. Microbial evolution, meanwhile, altered the patterns of disease in Eurasia. Leprosy diminished in range, but new diseases arose or old ones mutated. Tuberculosis does not seem to have been around in Europe on a significant scale—and certainly was not a major killer—until the sixteenth century. New strains of venereal disease developed in Europe—perhaps as a result of transference from the New World.

Visitations of lethal sicknesses that Europeans continued vaguely to call plague remained a constant problem, holding down population growth in the seventeenth century in parts of southern Europe. The plague of Venice of 1679 left thousands of dead lying in a ditch, smothered in quicklime "like pickled game in a barrel" to dissolve the bodies. Plague in Spain in 1657 inspired terrifying paintings of lives stalked by death or focused on putrefaction. In a hospital in Seville, a carved altarpiece of the descent from the cross inspired a brotherhood of aristocrats who sought to atone for their sins by burying the plague dead and tending the plague sores of the poor with their own hands. China in the 1580s and 1640s endured more epidemics of greater virulence than in the more notorious plagues of the fourteenth century. A survivor of the plague in Hunan in 1657 claimed nine of ten inhabitants were smitten, with a third of them breaking out in fever at midday to "become delirious in the evening and be partly eaten by rats when found dead at sunrise."

Yet for reasons that remain ill understood, the age of plagues gradually exhausted its virulence. The last recorded outbreak of plague in Europe was in the port of Marseilles on the Mediterranean coast of France in the 1720s. The deaths of unimmunized populations left well-adapted survivors. As a result of the ecological exchange, improved nutrition fortified increasing numbers of people. Microbes shifted their targets, perhaps, or mutated for evolutionary reasons to become less deadly. After all, it is not necessarily efficient for microorganisms to kill off their hosts. Whatever the reasons for it, deadly disease receded in the late seventeenth and early eighteenth centuries from all the areas in which it had previously been most destructive.

Of course, other diseases occupied the eco-niches retreating microbes vacated, or leaped into new ones that social, economic, or environmental change opened up. Cholera and yellow fever, for instance, broke out of their tropical heartlands to attack people in some of the fast-growing, densely populated, heavily polluted cities and ports in the industrializing West (see Chapter 29). Dysentery and typhus throve in the undersanitized environments of rapidly growing towns. Dense concentrations of people helped tuberculosis to spread. Bubonic plague, in its modern form, may be another new disease of this period—or, at least, a recurrence of an old disease with new characteristics. As we have seen (see Chapter 14), historians' longstanding assumption that bubonic plague was the sole or main affliction of the "age of plague" in Europe is probably false. In China, there is no decisive evidence that any epidemic before the nineteenth century was of bubonic plague in its modern form. In Yunnan province, however, on China's southwest border, a new kind of environment, in which new kinds of disease had an opportunity to emerge, was taking shape in the late eighteenth century. In the last quarter of the century, mining towns mushroomed as 300,000 immigrants moved in from other parts of China. At the same time, strong similarities with modern bubonic plague characterized a particularly intense series of epidemics from the 1770s to the 1790s, followed by slightly less intense outbreaks until the 1820s. The most significant similarity was the presence of rats as agents of disease. Modern bubonic plague is endemic in particular kinds of rodents. It spreads to humans when rat fleas bite people and inject the bacillus into human bloodstreams. The Yunnan plague was incontestably associated with rats, according to observations made at the time, not only by physicians but also by a young poet who wrote,

> Dead rats in the East!
> Dead rats in the West!
> . . . .
> A few days following the death of the rats,
> Men pass away like falling walls!

Still, the impact of modern bubonic plague was not as severe as that of the Black Death or the other scourges of the age of plague. When plague receded from Yunnan in the 1830s, it became dormant or sporadic. The next—or, by strict standards of interpretation, the first—unquestioned major outbreak in China did not occur until 1894. In any case, the new or spreading diseases of the eighteenth and nineteenth centuries generally could no longer keep pace with growing world population or, it seems, seriously restrain its growth.

Meanwhile, however, for as long as the age of plague lasted, problems of severe regional labor shortages had to be faced. The gravest of these were in the last region to suffer devastating losses of population to disease: the New World. The solution lay in transplanting human labor. This was, in a sense, yet another kind of ecological exchange. Along with plants, animals, and germs, another life-form, another ingredient of ecosystems—human beings—was swapped and shifted across the ocean and—for the most part—ended up in the Americas.

LABOR: HUMAN TRANSPLANTATIONS

Even before native numbers thinned, the colonial Americas suffered from shortages of useful labor. The new economic activities Spaniards wished to promote were impossible without new sources of labor even in the most densely populated areas of Spanish rule. Native Americans were, with few exceptions, ill suited to the kind of work Europeans wanted done, such as plantation labor, domestic service, and specialist skills in mining and sugar refining. Most of them were—as a companion of Columbus commented when dismissing the idea that the native peoples of the Caribbean could usefully be enslaved—"not suited to hard work" as Europeans understood the term.

Europe, however, was unsatisfactory as an alternative labor source. Spanish schemes to introduce colonies of Spanish laborers failed in the sixteenth century. The Dutch encountered similar failure in the seventeenth. North America proved particularly hard to populate. Sixteenth-century attempts to found North American colonies almost all failed. Those founded in the seventeenth century took a long time to make the breakthrough into viability—renewing their populations, that is, by sustainable birth rates. They could not rely, as most of Spain's early American conquests could, on native population levels to keep them viable. There are no reliable estimates of the size of the native population of North America when the Europeans arrived—well-informed guesses range from two to seven million—but there is no doubt that the region was sparsely populated. And such people as it did have were not well suited to be a labor force for colonial empires, such as the big, densely packed native populations of Mesoamerica and the Andes provided for Spain.

Shi Daonon, "Death of Rats"

Immigration could not, at first, make up the deficit. Virginia was farmed mainly with a form of forced labor imported from England—"indentured" poor, escapees from social exclusion at home, who contracted with masters to serve for years at a time, on subsistence wages or payments in kind, with no hope of release. But there were never enough of them, and as the market for black slaves gradually opened up to the English, Africans replaced them. Again, the model of exploitation was found in the Spanish, Portuguese, and (by now) Dutch colonies to the south.

Until the second half of the seventeenth century, life expectancy in Virginia remained low. Few colonists saw the better side of 50 years old. The Virginia swampland, where the first permanent settlements were founded from 1607 onward, was so unhealthy that of the first hundred or so settlers, only 38 were still alive nine months after landing. Of the first 3,000, only a couple of hundred were still alive, after a bloody war with the Indians in 1622. The population did not begin to increase naturally until some 50 years after the first settlement. The breakthrough was accompanied by increased rates of immigration, which tripled from about 1650 to 1670.

New England's environment was less hostile: "endowed with grace and furnished with means," as a Puritan settler declared. From early in the 1630s (Plymouth, the first New England colony, was founded in 1620), the colonists could grow enough to feed themselves, and natural increase kept the population growing. Without valuable cash products, however, the region was of little appeal to immigrants. Only 21,000 came in the whole seventeenth century, and the numbers of immigrants diminished over time—only a third of that total arrived after 1640. These were problems general to northern colonies. There were only 5,000 settlers in New Netherland when the English conquered the colony, which became New York, in 1664. New France, founded in Canada in 1608, received fewer than 4,000 immigrants in the second half of the seventeenth century. France, though densely populated by European standards in early times, never persuaded many colonists to go to Canada.

In the Spanish colonies, as early as 1510, the importation of slave labor began from the only source near enough and demographically buoyant enough to provide it: Africa. By the 1570s, Spanish America was importing, on average, about 2,500 African slaves a year. The average figure over the next century and a half, during which the trade to Spanish America was fairly stable, was 3,500 a year. Brazil became a major importer of slaves from the 1570s. There were probably fewer than 15,000 black slaves in Brazil in 1600, but numbers soared thereafter with the growth of sugar plantations, and the colony was soon absorbing more slaves than the whole Spanish Empire put together.

For the first 150 years or so of the colonial era, Spanish naval supremacy and Portuguese control of many of the sources of slaves denied adequate supplies of this resource to the British, Dutch, and French colonies. But as demand for slaves grew, routes of supply diversified—through piracy and illicit trading at first, then increasingly by agreement of the Spanish and Portuguese authorities with slavers of other nationalities. In the 1640s, Dutch slavers turned the island of Curaçao, off the coast of Venezuela, into a huge slaving station, supplying Spanish colonies at first and, increasingly, their own. Scandinavian traders entered the market in the 1650s. From the late 1660s, a series of French and English com-

The Columbian Exchange: Plants, Animals, Microbes, and People

1492	Columbus arrives in the New World, beginning process of biological exchange
1500s	Horses and cattle introduced to New World
1510	Importation of slave labor in the Spanish colonies begins
1555	First record of maize cultivation in China
1570s	Brazil becomes a major importer of slaves
1580s	Brazil becomes the world's major sugar producer
ca. 1700	Native American population in regions penetrated by Europeans declines 60 to 90 percent
1700s	Coffee becomes popular in Europe and Middle East
	Coffee production begins in Brazil and Indonesia

panies tried to break into the slave trade. In the third quarter of the seventeenth century, nearly 15,000 slaves a year left Africa on average. In the final quarter, the number increased to 24,000 a year.

After experiments with other kinds of enforced labor, slavery became the universal method to develop the plantation crops, including the rice and cotton that, in preference to tobacco and sugar, suited some of the land the English seized in North America. The system was imitated from Spanish and Portuguese precedents in areas where Native Americans were reduced by disease or refused to do plantation work. Climate drove it, as is apparent from the failure of early anti-slavery laws in Georgia, which was founded in 1733 as a refuge for the British poor. Subtropical America could not be made to pay without labor from Africa. Nowhere else could supply enough workers adaptable to the climate.

WILD FRONTIERS: ENCROACHING SETTLEMENT

The slave trade was part of a bigger phenomenon: the development of new ways to exploit the soil, which, in combination with the widening of trade, hugely increased the wealth of the world. This could be called the economic dividend of imperialism: the extension of land exploited for ranching, farming, and mining, and the conversion of some land from relatively less-productive to relatively more-productive methods of exploitation.

Northern and Central Asia: The Waning of Steppeland Imperialism

In northern and Central Asia, the political background was of a shift of power, as steppeland imperialism waned and the growing strength and reach of settled empires in China, Persia, and Russia squeezed the pastoralists' domains. New attempts to galvanize the power of the steppelanders, by a succession of leaders who claimed descent from Genghis Khan or his heroic lieutenants (see Chapter 13), brought little success. Most new imperial initiatives remained penned inside the steppes. At the beginning of the sixteenth century, for instance, two new enemies locked horns in southwest Asia. The pastoralist Uzbek (OOZ-behk) Empire, under the Shaybanid (sheye-BAH-nihd) dynasty, with its heartlands in the steppes of Transoxania, between the Aral Sea and Lake Balkhash, celebrated the identity of "men of the steppe: all our wealth consists of horses; their flesh is our favorite food. . . . Houses have we none." The Safavid Empire of Persia, which was largely based on settled agriculture, was their neighbor to the south (see Chapter 19). To judge from the record of the previous 500 years, anyone tempted to bet on the outcome of a clash between these two states would back the steppelanders to win. But, during nearly a century of warfare, the Safavids repeatedly got the upper hand, until a final Persian victory in 1597 provoked the breakup of the Uzbek state into small khanates.

Meanwhile, at the eastern end of the steppes, the Mongols found it impossible to reunite their power for long enough, or in sufficient strength, to renew a lasting threat to China. The Mongols could not even, for much of the time,

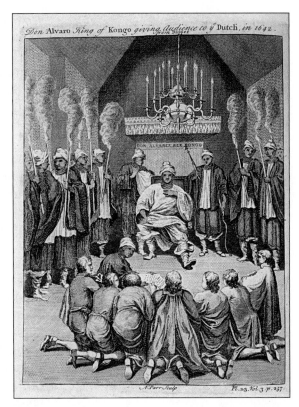

King Alvaro VI of Kongo. In the seventeenth century, wars between rivals for the crown damaged the Kingdom of Kongo, while Portuguese and Dutch envoys and traders sought to identify and back potential winners. Here Alvaro VI (r. 1636-1662) receives Dutch visitors toward the end of his reign, shortly after the Dutch had captured Portuguese slave-trading posts in neighboring Luanda. The Dutch are acting submissive because they want the king to accept the terms of a slave-trading contract.

securely dominate Tibet, which in the seventeenth century became the objective of the most ambitious Mongol chiefs.

There was, however, one uncharacteristic and perhaps deceptive instance of steppeland dynamism in the period. In the 1640s, a Manchu army, which the Chinese Empire had created to help police the Mongol frontier, intervened decisively in a Chinese civil war, conquered China (see Chapter 19), and dethroned the last Ming emperor in 1644. In some ways—in practice, more or less token ways—the Manchus imposed their own values on China. One of the first commands the new regime, which survived until 1912, issued was that Chinese should signify their submission by shaving their hair in Manchu fashion. According to Confucian notions of filial piety, hair was part of the sacred legacy children inherited from their parents and therefore should not be cut off. But the Manchu commander replied to objectors, "I spared your heads and now you want to keep your hair?" In most respects, however, the new dynasty rapidly adopted Chinese ways. Indeed, the great achievement of the Qing (cheeng)—the name the Manchu dynasty adopted in China—was to reverse the direction of empire. The Qing conquered much of the steppeland and spread Chinese culture deep into Central Asia.

Disputes over Tibet eventually provoked China into sustained war against the Mongols. In the 1690s, the Kangxi (kong-shee) emperor, himself a Manchu, campaigning in person on the Mongol front, described in letters home his days of early rising, "braving the sand and the dust" with "hands all blistered from holding the reins." By 1697, he was able to announce, with only a little exaggeration, "There is no Mongol principality that has not submitted to my rule." The historic pattern of imperialism in Central Asia was undergoing a kind of inversion. The Chinese Empire was reaching into the Mongol steppe, instead of lying at the periodic mercy of steppeland conquerors.

Why did the balance of power between settled life and pastoralism shift in favor of the former? The usual answer appeals to the so-called **military revolution** that accompanied the rise of firepower technology. Large forces of well-drilled, fire-armed infantry, with heavy artillery behind scientifically designed fortifications, made "gunpowder empires" invulnerable to steppeland cavalry. Demographic change also favored the settled peoples, whose populations grew faster than those of pastoralists. The progress of Islam and Buddhism in Central Asia supposedly eroded the ideologies of conquest that had animated earlier steppeland empires. Changes in the pattern of trade in the seventeenth century, when the role of the Silk Roads declined in relation to oceanic trade routes, cut off some of the liquid wealth that mobilized nomad war bands.

None of these explanations seems adequate. Steppelanders had adapted to new warfare technologies in the past. The Mongols, for instance, would never have been able to conquer China without incorporating infantry and siege engines into their armies (see Chapter 13). Settled neighbors had always outnumbered pastoral peoples, whose economic system, by its very nature, demands a lot of grazing land to feed relatively fewer mouths. Although many new trade routes carried more commerce than those of Central Asia, steppelanders still had plenty of wealth-creating opportunities to exploit. Chinese tribute lists and trading licenses show steppeland communities getting gradually richer, especially in horses, furs, and silks. Without definitive evidence, the best we can say is that all these changes, in combination, weakened the steppelanders relative to the empires that surrounded them. Whatever the reasons for it, the decline in the relative power of Eurasia's steppelanders was irreversible, as farmers from the Russian and Chinese Empires colonized areas of steppeland and left the pastoralists with less territory. The retreat of the steppelanders was a conspicuous element in the making of the modern world. It formed part of a broader change: an ecological revolution that extended the range and productivity of settled farming, around the world.

Pastoral Imperialism in Africa and the Americas

In some parts of the world, meanwhile, pastoralism remained or became a predominant way of life, and pastoral imperialism remained or became robust. In the African Sahel, for instance, the native tradition recovered after a challenge in the late sixteenth century from Morocco. In the 1580s, Morocco's long-cherished dreams of crossing the desert and conquering a gold-rich empire in black Africa began to look practical. The Moroccan sultan al-Mansur (ahl-mahn-SOOR) collected an army equipped with formidable firepower—2,500 marksmen and a train of camel-mounted artillery. The desert was not impassable, he argued. What merchant caravans accomplished, a well-organized army could achieve. From a Moroccan perspective, the Sahara was a sea of sand with an inviting shore. Like Spain's Atlantic, Morocco's Sahara was an obstacle course that could be crossed to a land of gold.

In 1588, al-Mansur declared war on Songhay (SOHN-geye). Nine thousand camels accompanied his task force on a march of 135 days across 1,500 miles, mostly of desert. Half the force is thought to have perished on the way, but the survivors dispersed the mounted hosts of Songhay as efficiently as Spanish conquerors had shattered the Aztecs and Incas. Morocco turned the western Sahel into a colony settled with 20,000 men. But the settler communities, often marrying locally, slipped out of Moroccan control. After an initial bonanza, the gold shipments dwindled, and by the 1630s, Morocco's gold reserves were running out. No outside power again attempted to conquer the Sahel for more than 300 years until the French arrived in the nineteenth century. The supremacy of the Sahel pastoralists remained secure.

The centuries-old process of expansion of arable farming from the Ethiopian highlands went into reverse in the sixteenth century, as pastoralist invaders from the east and south—pagan Oromo, Muslim Adil—seized lands and destroyed the monasteries that were the engines of Ethiopian frontier settlement. At the extreme southern tip of Africa, herding grew in economic importance. The region of the Cape of Good Hope had long been heavily grazed by scores of thousands of head of long-horned cattle, herded by pastoralists who called themselves Khoi and who had probably themselves been driven into the region by the expansion of Bantu farmers from the north. The total numbers of livestock doubled in the second half of the seventeenth century, when Dutch settlers introduced sheep following the establishment of a colony of the Dutch East India Company on the Cape in 1652. The Dutch followed Khoi strategies for selecting seasonal grazing and corralling their herds against predators. Although the Dutch also practiced arable farming, the extent of their ranching activities was incomparably greater.

In the Americas, of course, there had never been much pastoralism because there had never been large domesticable livestock herds, except for the llamas and

Military revolution. A late sixteenth-century view of the conquest of Szigetvár in Hungary by the Ottoman Sultan Suleiman the Magnificent (r. 1520–1566) concentrates on Turkish technology: the cannon belching fire, the pontoon bridge across the river.

their cousins in the Andes. In the sixteenth and seventeenth centuries, however, the introduction of horses and cattle made new ways of life possible, raising the prospect of empires whose economy was based on herding livestock. In some ways it is tempting to see Spanish and Portuguese imperialism in some parts of what are now Mexico and Brazil as a form of pastoral imperialism imposed on sedentary Indian peoples. Sheep and cattle, unknown before the Europeans arrived, numbered millions by the early seventeenth century and grazed hundreds of thousands of square miles of land—some of it previously unexploited, but much of it vacated by native farmers and hunters. As we shall see, in the late eighteenth and early nineteenth centuries (see Chapter 21), horse-borne Native American empire builders threatened to dominate the prairie and the pampa.

So in some parts of the world, arable farming lost acreage or yield. In others areas, methods of exploiting the soil remained limited to hunting and gathering. Although California and parts of Australia, for instance, were highly suited to arable farming, their native inhabitants were uninterested in changing methods of feeding themselves that had worked satisfactorily for thousands of years. Not until European intrusions in the eighteenth century did ranching and tillage begin fundamentally to alter their landscapes. But the main trend of the period was the extension of new forms of exploitation—especially arable farming—onto lands where it had never before been practiced. The new empires, which encouraged colonists and drove and mined for new resources, forced the pace of this change (see Map 17.2).

IMPERIALISM AND SETTLEMENT IN EUROPE AND ASIA

The Russian conquest of Kazan in the 1550s made possible the colonization of the "black earth" regions of the lower Volga River and southwest steppeland, pressing back and penning Mongol and Turkic herdsmen. By the end of the sixteenth century, a million settlers had turned a quarter of the region to grain cultivation, turning over the heavy sod with ox-drawn plows. Although the conquest of Siberia was launched for the fur trade, the ambition to see the land colonized gradually eclipsed the original vision. The foundation of frontier cities marked the progress of colonization: Tobolsk on the Irtysh River in 1587, Tomsk in 1604, Barguzinsk on Lake Baikal in 1648, Nerchinsk on the Amur River in 1654. In the mind of an eighteenth-century chronicler, Siberia had become a land of cities—22 of them, dispersed throughout the territory, depicted in an illustrative engraving as joined by rays of light to the eye of God. By then, over 300,000 peasants inhabited these settlements—outnumbering the surviving native Siberians.

Meanwhile, on a smaller scale, similar appropriations of territory by encroaching farmers displaced traditional peoples at the extremities of Eurasia, in the British Isles, and Japan. The English and lowland Scots waged wars to seize land, from Ireland to the Highlands and islands of Scotland. These were, from one point of view, culture wars that self-styled civilization waged against so-called savagery, by Protestants against Catholics, by speakers of Germanic tongues against Celtic speakers, by feudalism against tribalism. They were also economically inspired wars fought to convert pastoral land to arable. In Japan, after the Ainu War of 1669–1672, about half of Hokkaido was set aside for Japanese peasants to settle, at the expense of the displaced natives, whom the Japanese classed as primitive and savage, using language similar to that of English and Scots propaganda about the highlanders, islanders, and Gaelic Irish.

THE REMEZOV CHRONICLE

Several narrative accounts document the Russian conquest of Siberia. In the Remezov Chronicle, written about 1700, and illustrated with 154 pen and ink drawings, Russian territorial expansion is depicted as an evangelizing and civilizing mission. Shown here is the title page from the Chronicle.

"From the beginning of time, our Christian God, the All-Seer . . . decreed for the Gospels to be preached throughout Siberia to the ends of the universe and the limit of the mountains to the famous city of Tobolsk."

"And he will dwell in righteousness, and towns will arise to the Lord."

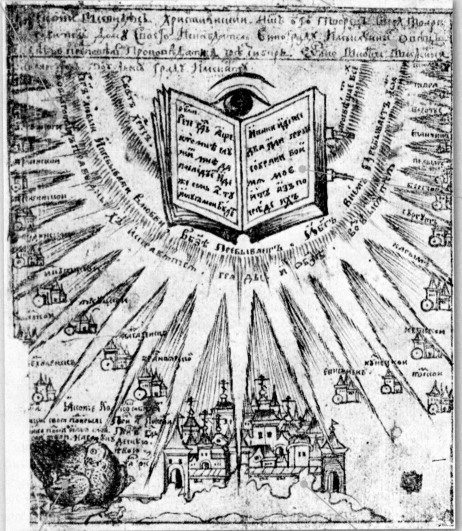

Set beneath the eye of God, the words in the open book, from the Gospels of John and Matthew, read "If any man serve me, let him follow me; and where I am there shall also my servant be. . . . where two or three are gathered together in my name, there am I in the midst of them."

The hen is a motif taken from the Gospels. The words above it, (only partly legible), read, "Just as the hen gathers its chicks under its wing, so shall I. . . . my name."

Tobolsk is flatteringly depicted, while rays from the Gospel spread to 21 other towns.

How does this illustration connect territorial expansion with the Russian state's self-proclaimed mission to spread Christianity?

Building a dike in seventeenth-century China. Peasant conscripts rig screws to drive piles into the mud to form the walls of the dike. Others use heavy wooden hammers to level the dike, or dig earth, which fellow-workers shift in baskets yoked by poles.

China

Imperial China sponsored the biggest movements of agricultural settlers in frontier regions and new conquests. Uncultivated land was wasted land. That was what late sixteenth-century Chinese officials thought, denouncing the "laziness" of gatherers of wild reeds on land that could be adapted to grow food. Manchu conquest of Sichuan in southern China was exceptionally savage, eliminating—so it was said—three-quarters of the people. Yet between 1667 and 1707, more than 1.5 million settlers arrived in Sichuan, lured by tax exemptions. Here and on the southeast frontier, the pressure of intensive new settlement provoked a cycle of conflicts. Rebellious native tribes were penned in reservations. Militarized agricultural colonies grew wheat, barley, peas, and corn while keeping the natives obedient. Schools brought Chinese language and values to the tribes.

The civil wars of the third quarter of the seventeenth century, which pitched the last Ming loyalists against the Manchu conquerors, drove Chinese peasants out of the densely populated provinces of Fujian and Guangdong (gwahng-dohng) into Guangzxi (gwahng–jshee) and the Yangtze highlands to the tea and timber industries or to cultivate sweet potatoes or maize. Celebrating his conquests against the "half-human" natives of Guizhou (gway-joh) in the mid–seventeenth century, a Manchu general described "chiseling" through the "forests that extend beyond the horizon. . . . Every day, for our imperial court, we've developed new arable lands. . . . So these far-off wastelands and tribal domains yield us menials and serving girls."

Large-scale immigration preceded the Chinese conquest of Taiwan in the 1660s. During some four decades of Dutch rule, which preceded the Chinese con-

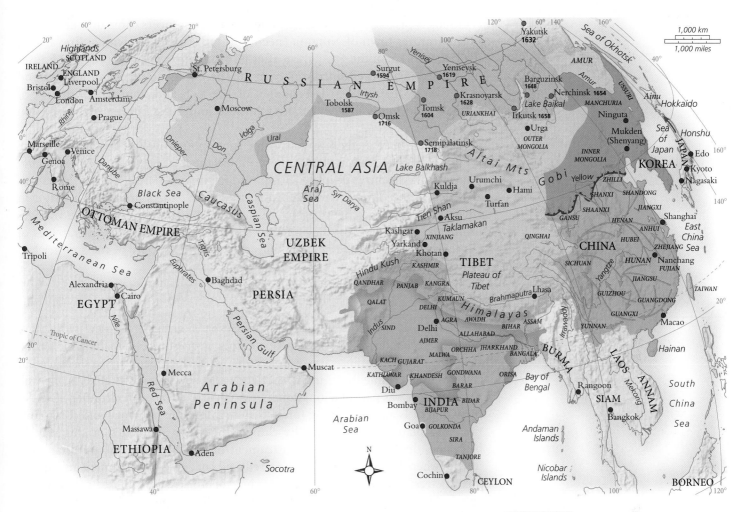

MAP 17.2

Imperialism and Settlement in Eurasia, 1600–1725

- Russian Empire ca. 1600
- Russian Empire ca. 1600–1725
- Russian cities founded 1587–1718
- Qing Empire in ca. 1644
- Qing Empire in ca. 1660
- Qing Empire by ca. 1770
- → internal migration in China in the 18th century
- Mughal Empire, ca. 1700
- Mughal Empire, ca. 1605
- → Japanese expansion northward
- *Ainu* people

quest, Dutch colonialists rewarded Chinese migrants with land concessions, cheap seed, draft animals, and tax breaks. By the time Chinese took over the government, over 35,000 settlers had brought nearly 25,000 acres under the plow, growing mainly rice and cane sugar. When the Manchu government assumed control of the island in 1684, the "raw aboriginals" enjoyed a period of official favor. The Manchus used the native deerstalkers to repress the suspect immigrant Chinese population in an offshore province where resistance to Manchu conquest had been strong. But that did not prevent the depletion of the deer herds, as Chinese peasants continued to encroach on land officially reserved for the native Taiwanese.

To the north of traditional China, in the borderlands of Mongolia and Manchuria, colonization proceeded on a different footing. The Kangxi emperor (r. 1661–1722) tried to stop the colonization of Manchuria on the grounds that he "wished to maintain the original equestrian and hunting ways and martial virtues of the Manchus and Mongols in their home territory, which should remain a recruiting ground for soldiers." In practice, however, the frontier of settlement could not be controlled. The cultivated zone of Manchuria grew by nearly 30,000 acres in the decade following Kangxi's decree.

The exploitability of illegal immigrants made them welcome. The earliest colonization had a camp-life quality of roving communities of wild ginseng diggers.

(Ginseng is prized in Chinese medicine.) Farmer pioneers came not far behind. In the frontier town of Ninguta (neen-goo-tah) (today known as Ning'an) on the river Hurka, in the generation after its foundation in 1660, only 400 households lived inside the ruined wall of mud. There was "no person of leisure" and the exiles' womenfolk—"descendants of the rich and honorable families of China"—slid barefoot down the icy hillside under the burden of water from the only well.

Yet even in this environment, some metropolitan values triumphed, while the winds of change overturned others or blew them away. Anyone with scholarly pretensions—let alone degrees—was prized in Ninguta. The deference the natives accorded to the Chinese and the prosperity of the settlers impressed a visitor in 1690. The older merchants even "greeted the military governor as a younger brother": in other words, they affected superiority over him. The hierarchies of home persisted alongside new rankings the emerging society of the frontier had evolved.

India

We can detect the same trends—imperial expansion, fostering new settlement, increasing the range of farming, and exploiting new resources—in the same period in India. Forest clearance was a policy the Mughal Emperors (see Chapter 16) embraced determinedly, in their heartlands and new conquests alike. In Bengal, deforestation was part of a longstanding struggle to advance the frontier of settlement and of Islam by granting forested areas to Muslim holy men and communities, who planted wet rice in the cleared zones. On the edges of the Mughal heartland, deforestation was an instrument of enhanced control, uprooting the jungles where bandits and rebels sheltered, and encouraging settlement and, therefore, increasing revenues for the state. The emperor received a third of every harvest. Indian peasants were generally extremely efficient, producing two crops a year almost everywhere they planted—whether of millet, rice, or wheat. Lumberjacks accompanied seventeenth-century Mughal armies. Colonists who followed them to new lands received tax concessions and cheap plows. When the Mughals conquered areas from Burma in 1665, they evicted the existing population as ruthlessly as any European imperialists and introduced hundreds of Muslim religious foundations to clear the forest and plant rice.

NEW EXPLOITATION IN THE AMERICAS

The decline of the Native American population may have led to the abandonment of vast zones that the Indians had farmed before the Europeans arrived. But colonial regimes found alternative methods to exploit the land that, in total, probably made the colonial economy as productive as the Indian system had been: mining, ranching, and plantations (see Map 17.3). The arrival of plows, which had been unknown in the Americas before the Europeans brought them, meant that heavy soils could be exploited for the first time. Horses, mules, and oxen took on burdens Native American porters formerly bore on their backs.

The Spanish Empire

The Spanish Empire in the Americas had every avenue to wealth at its disposal. Suitable environments for all the new kinds of activity were available in abundance, while traditional native economies continued to produce their time-honored crops—such as maize, beans, squash, cotton, and cacao in Mesoamerica or coca, potatoes, and sweet potatoes in the Andes—and generate tribute. The most vivid mark and measure of success were the cities of Spanish America. As soon as Columbus returned from his first voyage, and news of America began to circulate in Europe, engravers imagined what they called the Indies filled with magnificent cities. In areas of Spanish rule, the vision was quickly realized, for Spanish imperialism was uncompromisingly urban minded. It is said that when two Englishmen meet on a savage frontier they found a club. Two Spaniards in the same circumstances found a city.

Spanish colonization slotted into the existing framework of Native American civilizations. In an extraordinarily productive period of expansion in the 1520s and 1530s, while the Spanish monarchy absorbed the existing great urban centers of Mesoamerica and the Andean region through conquest or diplomacy, the biggest cities of the Americas acquired new characteristics: Spanish-speaking elites, a new Native American middle class that served Spaniards' economic needs, an African American slave class for domestic service, Spanish courts and town councils, Christian religious foundations, cathedrals, and even, in Mexico City, a university and printing press. Similar developments followed Spanish colonization in other parts of the Americas in succeeding decades. Spanish colonists founded cities wherever they went. The new cities rooted easily in areas where native cities and a strong urban tradition already existed. In other areas of mainland Spanish America—California, the frontier grasslands of North and South America—urbanization was harder, growing slowly from kernels that missions, military garrisons, and naval stations planted.

European styles in buildings smothered or supplemented the old angular look of Native American architectures with arches and domes. Some old Indian cities were flattened and rebuilt. Others were lightly adapted and recrafted. Some were abandoned, as a terrible demographic crisis unfolded with the collapse of the Native American population. New cities on new sites, like Lima (LEE-mah), Peru still perhaps the most Spanish of Spanish American cities in looks and atmosphere, replaced some Native American capitals. Parts of Old San Juan in Puerto Rico look exactly like a Spanish city of the seventeenth and eighteenth centuries, complete with walls, sea gates, courtyard gardens, and cathedral square. The civic model of life, the city-centered model of administration was extended into new areas. From the 1570s, the Spanish crown issued exact regulations to construct new cities, with their grid plan and classically inspired buildings and monumental scale, the exact placing of cathedrals, government buildings, hospitals, and schools. The archives are full of the plans of projected cities, and many of them were actually built. But in North America in the seventeenth and early eighteenth centuries, beyond the Spanish frontier,

Cuzco, home city of the Incas, never really looked like this. Built amid mountains, its monumental palaces, temples, and fortifications, constructed of huge blocks of stone, enclosed irregular spaces. But when Georg Braun and Franz Hogenberg published their views of the world's great cities in the late sixteenth century, they imagined Cuzco as a flat grid—the supposedly ideal form of Renaissance urban planning that inspired many colonial American cities.

Founding Dates for Spanish Cities in the Americas

Caribbean and North America		South America	
Santo Domingo	1496	Cajamarca	1532
San Juan (Puerto Rico)	1509	Cartagena	1532
San Cristobal (Havana)	1515	Cuzco	1533
Panama City	1519	Quito	1534
Mexico City	1521	Buenos Aires	1536
Guadalajara	1531	Lima	1535
Meridá	1542	Santiago	1541
Zacatecas	1546	La Paz	1548
San Juan Bautista	1564	Mendoza	1561
San Augustín (Florida)	1565	Caracas	1567
Santa Fé (New Mexico)	1610		

cities of English and French construction generally remained, in a sense, in the Iroquois tradition. They were largely built of wood and, though intended for permanent occupancy, had a gimcrack air of instant shabbiness.

Brazil

Other European empires in the Americas lacked the advantage of local labor sources that they could exploit on the scale of the Spanish lands. As a result, they tended at first to expand to landward on only a modest scale, so that they could increase the areas of cultivation of the crops they introduced, such as sugar in the Caribbean, West Indian tobacco in Virginia, rice in the Carolinas, and wheat almost everywhere. In Brazil, sugar was suitable only to coastal enclaves where it could be successfully grown and easily shipped to Europe. It would never, on its own, have induced planters to create a large territorial domain in Brazil's hinterland. Rivalry with Spain to control the Amazon, however, turned Portuguese thoughts toward the Brazilian interior, especially after rival Spanish and Portuguese expeditions tested the navigability of the great Amazon River system in the 1630s. Gold and diamonds, discovered in the Brazilian province of Minas Gerais (meaning "general mines") in the 1680s, proved the incentive required for Portugal to drive its Brazilian frontier inland.

British North America

Elsewhere, though explorers scoured the Americas for natural resources in the late sixteenth and seventeenth centuries, major sources of gold, silver, pearls, and precious gems remained a Spanish monopoly. The areas left for the English and French to exploit contained only fool's gold, such as the iron pyrites Martin Frobisher found in Canada in 1576, which deceived investors into ruin and lured adventurers to their deaths. Furs were the "black gold" of the far north. South of the habitat of the beaver, deerskins represented, in a more modest degree, a similar luxury product. But, like the timber and fish that also abounded in and around North America, resources of these kinds could not alone sustain permanent or populous colonies: only the French fur trappers who lived among the Indians, migrant merchants and hunters, and seasonal visitors.

Except in the Caribbean, where sugar and, later, coffee would grow on islands seized from or ignored by Spain, it was hard to find crops suitable to sustain colonial life. Tobacco was the first, introduced into Virginia in 1614. Later in the century, rice made fairly large-scale settlement practical in the coastal areas of South Carolina. Independent farmers could always cultivate smallholdings for their own subsistence, as they did with remarkable success even in the inhospitably rocky soils of New England from the 1620s. But this form of exploitation could never be the foundation of prosperity. New England only really began to reveal its potential as a great world center of

A Chinese porcelain punch-bowl, acquired in the East Indies Trade late in the eighteenth century by the Rhode Island merchant John Brown. The decoration shows the American *hong* (or "factory") in Guangzhou, as well as *hongs* for traders from other Western countries, overlooking the Pearl River.

wealth and civilized life in the eighteenth century, not because of its own resources but because so many of the inhabitants took to the sea. Like classical Greece and ancient Phoenicia (Chapter 5), New England became a maritime civilization, making up for the poverty of its home soils by trade and the exploitation of marine resources. Three trades in particular contributed to transforming New England's economy into one of the richest, per capita, in the world by the late eighteenth century: first, the slave trade, in which New England merchants worked both as shippers and dealers; second, the export of locally produced rum and manufactured goods to the slave-producing and slave-consuming markets with which the slave trade connected the New Englanders; and finally the so-called **East India trade**—mainly with China, by way of Cape Horn on the southern tip of South America—for tea and porcelain to sell at home.

From Virginia southward, English North American colonies naturally—literally, naturally—resembled those that Spanish, Dutch, and Portuguese investors were already exploiting in Mesoamerica and South America. They were hot and wet, with torrid lowlands that could be adapted to plant cash crops with the labor of imported slaves. The first English-run sugar industry in Barbados was directly copied from the Dutch enterprise in Pernambuco, with Dutch capital and know-how. The effects on settler society were predictable. Economic reliance on large-scale, capital-intensive enterprises created huge disparities of wealth. Large-scale English planters in parts of North America and the Caribbean became, in effect, the lords of huge estates, more reminiscent of the Mediterranean or Brazil, than of England or New England. In 1700, the top 5 percent of settlers by wealth owned half of one county in Virginia.

Expansion: Imperialism and Colonization in Europe, Asia, and the Americas

1520s–1530s	Absorption of Mesoamerican and Andean cities into Spanish Empire
1550s	Russian conquest of Kazan
ca. 1560–1650	Russian colonization of lower Volga and Siberia
1600s	Expansion, colonization, and intensive farming in Mughal India
	Outflow of Chinese and Japanese settlers to southeast Asia
	Export of African slaves, especially to the Americas
	British colonization of North America
ca. 1620s–1660s	Large-scale Chinese immigration to Taiwan
1667–1707	1.5 million settlers arrive in Sichuan
1680s	Discovery of gold and diamonds prompts further Portuguese expansion in Brazil
Late seventeenth century	Japanese peasants displace native inhabitants of Hokkaido
1700s	New England becomes a world center of trade

HOME FRONTS IN EUROPE AND ASIA

New wealth-creating activities were not confined to imperial frontiers. Equal efforts were under way to exploit the homelands of the empires. Governments all over the world undertook land surveys to determine the extent of production and the possibilities to increase it. In the 1570s, King Philip II of Spain ordered the most comprehensive survey of his realms that any European state had ever undertaken. It was soon extended to the New World and illustrated with maps that Native Americans made. In Japan in 1580, the shogun Hideyoshi (see Chapter 16) commanded a survey of Japan that would penetrate "the deepest caves of the mountains and the reach of oars at sea." It was to include the dimensions and soil quality of every rice field and the location of every irrigation channel. Villagers who withheld information would be crucified. Landowners who failed to cooperate would be put to the sword. Begun in 1583, driven by unpitying force, the job was finished by 1598. The Mughal regime in India was not given to such bureaucratic exertions but achieved something similar in the late sixteenth century, including a tally of average yields and market prices, field by field. In 1663, frustrated by his inability to locate undeveloped resources in France, Jean-Baptiste Colbert, the chief minister of King Louis XIV, ordered the first scrupulously accurate map of the country to be made by the latest surveying techniques. It was not fully complete until 1789 on the eve of the French Revolution.

Caribbean Sea

Santa Marta **1525**
Cumaná **1521**
Panama **1519**
Gulf of Darien
Cartagena **1532**
Maracaibo **1529**
Lake Maracaibo
Caracas **1567**
Gulf of Panama
AUDIENCIA OF SANTA FÉ 1548
Orinoco
New Amsterdam **1627**
SURINAM
Paramaribo **1613**
Santa Fé de Bogotá **1538**
VICEROYALTY OF NEW GRANADA 1739
Rio Negro
Branco
Guiana Highlands
ATLANTIC OCEAN
Quito **1534**
Equator
Belém do Pará **1616**
São Luís (Maranhão)
PRESIDENCIA OF QUITO 1563
Putumayo
Amazon
Rio Negro
Manaus **1674**
Amazon Basin
Tapajós
PARÁ 1616
MARANHÃO 1615
Ceará
PIAUÍ 1532
CEARÁ 1613
Natal **1597**
DUTCH BRAZIL 1630–1654
Tumbes **1526**
Cuenca **1557**
Marañón
Amazon
Juruá
Purus
Xingu
PARAÍBA 1532
Paraíba **1585**
Olinda
Recife ca.**1535**
Paita **1532**
MAYNAS 1638–1767
Madeira
Madre de Dios
VICEROYALTY OF BRAZIL
SOUTH AMERICA
Araguaia
Tocantins
São Francisco
PERNAMBUCO 1532
SERGIPE 1532
Fort Maurits **1637**
Sergipe del Rey
Cajamarca **1532**
Trujillo **1525**
AUDIENCIA OF LIMA 1543
Ucayali
BAHIA 1532
Bahia (Salvador) capital **1549–1763**
Callao **1537**
Lima **1535**
Huancavelica
Cuzco **1533**
MOJOS 1659–1767
MATO GROSSO 1748
Planalto de Mato Grosso
PORTO SEGURO 1532
Ilhéus **1534**
GOIÁS 1744
Minas Novas **1727**
Lake Titicaca
Vila Bela (Mato Grosso) **1752**
CHIQUITOS 1691
Goiás **1744**
Diamantina **1730**
MINAS GERAIS 1720
ESPÍRITO SANTO 1532
Arequipa **1540**
La Paz **1548**
Brazilian Highlands
Arica **1537**
Lago Poopó
La Plata **1538**
PRESIDENCIA OF CHARCAS 1559
Paraguay
Corumbá **1788**
RIO DE JANEIRO 1532
Vitória
VICEROYALTY OF PERU 1543
Potosí **1545**
Pilcomayo
Gran Chaco
Vermejo
ITATÍN 1609–1660
GUAIRÁ ca.1630–1632
SÃO PAULO 1709
São Paulo **1532**
Santos **1532**
Rio de Janeiro **1565** capital from **1763**
Tropic of Capricorn
São Vicente **1545**
Asunción **1537**
Ciudad Real **1630**
SANTA CATARINA 1532
Desterro **1640**
CHACO 1732–1767
Paraná
GUARANÍ 1630–1660
RIO GRANDE DO SUL 1777
Laguna **1654**
Coquimbo **1537**
Córdoba **1573**
Uruguay
Porto Alegre
Rio Grande **1737**
CAPTAINCY-GENERAL AND PRESIDENCIA OF CHILE 1606
Mendoza **1561**
Salado
Colónia do Sacramento Portuguese **1680–1750**
Valparaíso **1541**
Santiago **1541**
Buenos Aires **1536**
Montevideo **1726**
Concepción **1550**
Pampas
River Plate
Colorado
Valdivia **1552**
Araucanians
Rio Negro
Carmen de Patagones **1779**
San Carlos de Ancud **1763**
Patagonia
Golfo de San Jorge
Golfo de Penas
Deseado
ATLANTIC OCEAN
Bahía Grande
Islas Malv
Strait of Magellan
Cape Horn

MAP 17.3 **Land Exploitation in the Americas up to ca. 1725**

British control and settlement, ca. 1725

Spanish control and settlement before 1650

Spanish territory after 1650

Portuguese territory by 1600

Portuguese territory by 1750

French control and settlement, ca.1725

French influence

approximate western limit of French claim

Dutch control and settlement

········ fur trade routes

1682 date of foundation

Houma native people

fur-trading post

Jesuit missions

major Franciscan missions

Spanish fort

Economic Activity

hides and deerskins

copper

gold

silver mine

drugs

cocoa

diamonds

dyes

rice-growing region

sugar-growing region

major fisheries

tobacco cultivation

New Energy Sources

Efforts to explore the environment led to the discovery and release of new energy sources. Timber from deforestation made an enormous contribution, together with oil from aggressive whaling by European and Japanese seamen in previously unfrequented seas. Cottonseed oil and rapeseed oil in Japan came into use as oil-lamp fuel in the early 1600s. Extracting peat to be burned as fuel from the bogs of Holland became a major industry. In some places, people shifted to coal, mined in increasing quantities in Great Britain, Germany, and the southern Netherlands (modern Belgium; it was a territory of the Spanish monarchy at the time). Londoners in the mid–sixteenth century burned more than 20,000 tons of coal annually—a little less than a quarter of a ton per inhabitant. By 1700, coal imports to London totaled almost 400,000 tons for a population of about 600,000. In the late seventeenth century, miners in Kyushu, Japan, began to make a success of marketing coal: to peasants for fuel, to refiners of salt and sugar. The Japanese government, meanwhile, adopted policies to conserve and replant forests, reserving valuable timber for official purposes, excluding intruders from endangered forest zones, and rewarding tree planting. "Cherishing the mountains," for the local ruler of Tugaru in the 1660s, was essential to nurture life and reverse forest shrinkage so severe that loggers were invading the northernmost Japanese island of Hokkaido for timber. Coal remained abundant in China, but the market for it remained static. Wood and charcoal were still adequate to meet China's energy needs.

Shinsen Dainibon Zukan (**Revised Map of Japan**) **of 1687.** The maps of Japan that the shogun Hideyoshi commissioned have not survived, but this is one of a series based on them. Each province is marked with the name of its feudal lord or *daimyo* and the amount of his salary. The placard at the top lists each province's topographical information, including place names, temples, and shrines. The blank land to the left of it, labeled Chosenkoku, is Korea.

Land Reclamation

Land reclamation complemented the struggle to expand and settle new frontiers. In Holland, after terrible losses of lands to the encroaching sea in the sixteenth century, reclamation became a matter of survival. New windmill-pumping technology drained 57,000 acres of land in North Holland between 1610 and 1640. In all the Dutch added nearly 370,000 acres of land to the total amount available for farming during the century. A minor social revolution accompanied the transformation of the landscape, as smallholders lost access to the sea and were forced to sell out to big landowners. In England, the drainage of the fenlands, which lay just across the sea from Holland in the eastern counties, began in 1600. Enforced by military occupation, against the protests of the local inhabitants, who were dispossessed, the project brought about 480,000 acres under the plow by the early 1650s. In Japan, government-sponsored schemes drained the Yodfo River delta. The Nobi plain in northern Honshu was transformed from "a marshy plain of water birds" to an area settled with hundreds of villages. The Aka River, which once flowed through marshes, fed 12,000 acres of wet rice lands by 1650. The cultivated land area of Japan grew by 82 percent between 1600 and 1720.

FRONTIERS OF THE HUNT

Imperialism promoted more efficient—sometimes more ruthless—exploitation of the Earth. Beyond the edges of empires, we do not know enough to be sure, but improvements in the range and effectiveness of hunting, and the extension of cultivation, were happening in other parts of the world, too. When the English arrived in Virginia, they found thousand of acres under cultivation and maize stocks "of sufficient quantity to fill the holds of several ships."

The Iroquois country of northeast North America is a case in point. Toward the end of what we think of as the Middle Ages, a form of maize was developed suitable for latitudes as north as the Great Lakes. This zone, which extends just north of Lakes Ontario and Erie and along the southern shores of Lakes Huron and Michigan, had about 140 frost-free days a year. Increasingly in the sixteenth and seventeenth centuries, the new crop was planted in forest clearings between the upper Hudson River and Lake Erie, on the frontier between deciduous and evergreen trees, where ecological diversity made ambitious ways of life possible.

The very diversity of their food sources imposed a mobile way of life on the Native Americans of the region. Periodically, soil erosion and forest depletion forced them to shift the sites of their towns. Maize exhausts soil more quickly than other grains. The biggest settlement in the Great Lakes region was the Illinois town of Kaskaskia, with over 7,000 people in 1680, but villages of about 1,000 people were not unusual. To make glades for planting without hard-metal tools, Native Americans cut a ring in the trunk of a tree and set it on fire until the stump burned through. The method yielded ash for fertilizer,

Huron women. Published in 1664, the *History of Canada* by the Jesuit priest François du Creux summarized the vast output of the author's fellow missionaries on the subject and helped to spread a favorable image of the Huron among learned readers in Europe. Here the engraver shows industrious Huron women peacefully engaged in a civilized, agrarian activity—maize production, in an idealized setting, while an infant's cradle alludes to sentiments and social conventions that European readers would have found comforting and familiar.

but left a landscape strewn with stumps. Farming under these disadvantages could never entirely replace a traditional way of life based on hunting, fishing, and tapping maple trees for syrup. But, like other forest peoples of the Americas who came into contact with colonial and overseas markets, the inhabitants improved their techniques and turnover as hunters too. They adopted firearms for the kill and steel knives to skin and butcher game. Beavers, once hunted for their meat, were now more valuable for the pelts European fur traders demanded. Beavers were almost gone from southern Ontario by the mid-1630s and virtually disappeared from New England by the end of the seventeenth century. In southern parts of North America, below the beaver's natural range, deerskins for the European leather trade became an equally valuable product in the same period. They made suede breeches and book bindings and smooth yellow gloves. In the 1690s and early 1700s, Charleston, South Carolina, exported up to 85,000 deerskins a year, and the numbers increased until the deer herds were depleted in the 1770s.

CHRONOLOGY

1492	Columbus arrives in the New World, beginning process of biological exchange
1500s	Horses and cattle introduced to New World
1510	Importation of slave labor in the Spanish colonies begins
1520s and 1530s	Absorption of Mesoamerican and Andean cities into Spanish Empire
1550s	Russian conquest of Kazan
1555	First records of maize cultivation in China
ca. 1560–1650	Russian colonization of lower Volga and Siberia
1570s	Philip II of Spain orders survey of his realms
	Brazil becomes a major importer of slaves
1580s	Brazil becomes the world's major sugar producer
1580	Shogun Hideyoshi orders a survey of Japan
1600s	British colonization of North America
	Expansion, colonization, and intensive farming in Mughal India
ca. 1620s–1660s	Large-scale Chinese immigration to Taiwan
1667–1707	1.5 million settlers arrive in Sichuan
1680s	Discovery of gold and diamonds prompts further Portuguese expansion in Brazil
1690s	Charleston, South Carolina, exports up to 85,000 deerskins a year
Late seventeenth century	Japanese peasants displace native inhabitants of Hokkaido
ca. 1700	Native American population in regions penetrated by Europeans declines 60 to 90 percent
1700s	Popularity of coffee booms in Europe and Middle East and coffee production begins in Brazil and Indonesia
	New England becomes a world center of trade

IN PERSPECTIVE: Evolution Redirected

In some parts of the world, the effects of the ecological revolutions were delayed until the eighteenth or nineteenth centuries. But the decisive transformations had already occurred by the end of the seventeenth century. Across the densely populated belt of the world, from China to Mesoamerica and the Andes, a single network of communications transmitted the same varieties of plants and animals. The empires that dominated the zone responded in similar ways to the problems and opportunities of the time. New crops and animals helped the great colonizing movements of the era. They enabled farmers to penetrate new environments and exploit old ones more efficiently. The results included a huge increase in the amount of food people in affected regions could coax from the fields or cull from the wild. Evolution, meanwhile, was launched on a new course. The divergent history of life-forms, which had gone their separate ways, continent by continent, divided from each other by uncrossable seas, now gave way to a convergent trend that has produced the world we inhabit today, when the same germs, plants, and animals occur all over the world, wherever climate permits.

○ MAKING CONNECTIONS ○

NEW WAYS OF EXPLOITING THE NATURAL ENVIRONMENT

REGION/ECOLOGICAL ZONE →	NEW FORMS OF EXPLOITATION →	RESULTS
Western Hemisphere (North and South America, Caribbean)/areas with agricultural potential	Mass importation of slaves from Africa after depopulation of Native Americans due to disease	Large areas of North, Central, and South America transformed into plantations for cultivation of sugar, cotton, rice, tobacco, and indigo; creation of large African and mixed-race populations throughout Western Hemisphere
Steppeland; mountainous regions of Asia including Mongolia and Xianjang	Chinese takeover of traditional adversaries, exploitation of natural resources	Well-trained infantry, advanced artillery, well-designed fortifications end the nomadic threat; highland and steppe regions become source for raw materials
Cape of Good Hope, South Africa, Australia	Introduction of sheep and new breads of cattle, extensive farming by European settlers	Displacement of natives
North and South America/ lowlands, high plains	Farming pampas/prairies; felling forests	Creation of large-scale agricultural complexes focusing on wheat, maize, and other commodities for human and livestock consumption for domestic use and export
Mexico, South America	Development of silver and gold mines	Boost global supply of cash
Mexico, South America, and North America	Development of extensive livestock herding	Millions of square miles of lightly populated areas claimed for cattle and sheep herding
North America	Large-scale fur trade in American Midwest, West, and Canada	Beaver, deerskins, and other furs/skins become basis for gradual penetration, settlement of western and northern North America
Eurasia	Land reclamation projects; expansion of timber harvesting, mining	National leaders attempt to solidify control, expand state revenues through systematic exploitation of resources, beginning with thorough mapping and surveying projects

The ecological revolution was the essential precondition for some of the global changes of the next few centuries, fueling some of the major themes of the next two parts of this book: population growth, radical breakthroughs in exploiting the globe's resources, and the globalization of empires and trade. But such effects depended on more than the physical environment. People's mental attitudes to the world changed, too, and, like the ingredients of ecological exchange, they carried these new attitudes with them across the globe through long-range travel, trade, and empire-building. These mental revolutions are the subjects of the next chapter.

PROBLEMS AND PARALLELS

1. Why should the Columbian Exchange be regarded as one of the biggest revolutions in human history?

2. What are some of the explanations for the "age of plagues"? Why did it suddenly end in the mid–eighteenth century?

3. How did human settlement expand its range in the sixteenth and seventeenth centuries? What were the motives behind this expansion? What effect did it have on ecological frontiers? On the way colonialists viewed the natural world?

4. What are the reasons for the massive transplantation of human labor that occurred during the sixteenth and seventeenth centuries? Why did colonial America suffer from severe labor shortages?

5. Why did the balance of power between settled life and pastoralism shift in favor of the settlers in the sixteenth and seventeenth centuries? In which parts of the world did pastoralism remain a predominant way of life?

6. What factors made Spanish colonialism in the Americas more advantageous than the ventures of the English or French?

DOCUMENTS IN GLOBAL HISTORY

- Thomas Gage on chocolate

- Shi Daonon, "Death of Rats"

Please see the Primary Source CD-ROM for additional sources related to this chapter.

READ ON

The major works on the ecological exchange are A. W. Crosby, *The Columbian Exchange*, and *Ecological Imperialism.* (1986) J. F. Richards, *The Unending Frontier* (2003) is a superb, if necessarily selective, environmental history of the period. Classics on particular crops include N. Deerr, *The History of Sugar* (1949); S. Mintz, *Sweetness and Power* (1986); N. Salaman, *History and Social Influence of the Potato* (1985); and A. Warman, *Corn and Capitalism* (2003). M. Elvin, *The Retreat of the Elephants* (2004) is an inspiring general history of the Chinese environment. My book, *Near a Thousand Tables* (2002), puts the exchanges in the context of the history of food. R. Grove, *Green Imperialism* (1996) is an amazingly rich work that argues that European colonialism nurtured environmentalism.

On plague in general, see the works recommended in Chapter 14. The demographic disasters of the New World are the subject of intense controversy: see D. Henige, *Numbers from Nowhere,* (1998) and contrast W. M. Denevan, *The Native Population of the Americas in 1492* (1992). The most balanced general treatment is in D. N. Cook, *Born to Die,* (1998) though the author's argument

that demographics explain the course of "conquest" should be considered critically. On plague in China, C. Benedict, *Bubonic Plague in Nineteenth-Century China* (1996) is important.

On the Atlantic slave trade, H. Thomas, *The Slave Trade* (1999) is a lively history. R. Blackburn, *The Making of New World Slavery* (1998) is an engaging introduction. J. Thornton, *Africa and Africans in the Making of the Atlantic World* (1998) is a model of scholarship and presentation. P. D. Curtin, *The Rise and Fall of the Plantation Complex* (1998); S. W. Mintz and R. Price, *The Birth of African-American Culture* (1992), B. Solow, ed., *Slavery and the Rise of the Atlantic System* (1993); D. Eltis, *The Rise of African Slavery in the Americas* (1999) are all valuable studies of the economies and societies of slave plantations.

M. Sobel, *The World They Made Together* (1989) is important on the slave world of Virginia, and L. Ferguson, *Uncommon Ground* (1995) is full of interesting material on plantation life in the North American South generally.

C. D. Totman, *Early Modern Japan* (1995) is an account particularly strong on environmental awareness. B. Walker,

The Conquest Ainu Lands (2001) is admirable. R. L. Edmonds, *Northern Frontiers of Qing China and Tokugawa Japan* (1985) makes an admirable comparative introduction. On Chinese expansion, R. H. G. Lee, *The Manchurian Frontier in Ch'ing History* (1970), and J. Waley-Cohen, *Exile in mid-Qing China* (1991) are indispensable. Ping-ti Ho, *Studies on the Population of China* (1959) is a valuable broad survey of its subject.

D. Twitchett and J. K. Fairbank, eds., *The Cambridge History of China*, vii (1988) is an invaluable guide to China in the period. On the Manchu conquest of China, L. Struve, *Voices from the Ming-Qing Cataclysm* (1998) is a well-selected and structured collection of sources.

There is, as far as I know, no dedicated study in English, but there are some useful pages on al-Mansur's conquest of the Sahara in A. C. Hess, *The Forgotten Frontier* (1978), and J. O. Hunwick, *Timbuktu and the Songhay Empire* (2003) contains some useful documents.

On Russian Siberia, J. Forsyth, *A History of the Peoples of Siberia* (1994) is an impressive and masterful introduction. B. Dmitrishyn et al., eds., *Russia's Conquest of Siberia* (1986) is an enormous compendium of sources. The best edition of the chronicles is T. Armstrong, ed., *Yermak's Campaigns in Siberia.* (1975) J. Martin, *Treasure of the Land of Darkness* (2004) is superb on the background of the fur trade. M.

Rywkin, ed., *Russian Colonial Expansion* (1988) contains some important papers.

C. Wilson, *England's Apprenticeship* (1965) is excellent introduction to the economic history of England in the seventeenth century. For the inland see K. Lindley, *Fenland Riots and the English Revolution* (1982). J. de Vries and A. M. van der Woude, *The First Modern Economy* (1997) is the standard work on the early modern Dutch economy.

On the Mughal frontier in Bengal, R. Eaton, *The Rise of Islam and the Bengal Frontier* (1996) is of great value and importance.

On Spanish American cities V. Fraser, *The Architecture of Conquest* (1990) is a monograph (on Peru) well crafted enough to serve as an introduction.

For Brazil, J. Hemming, *Red Gold* (1978) and *Amazon Frontier* (1987) are superb and chilling accounts of the fate of the natives at the time of European conquest and colonization. S. Schwartz, ed., *Tropical Babylons* (2004) is the most up-to-date collection on the sugar colonies. G. Freyre, *The Masters and the Slaves* is a classic of such significance in Brazilian historiography that it should still be read by anyone interested in the subject. C. R. Boxer, *The Golden Age of Brazil* (1995) is almost in the same category.

B. Trigger's magnificent *A History of the Huron People*, 2 vols. (1976), is unequaled in its field.

CHAPTER 18

Mental Revolutions: Religion and Science in the Sixteenth and Seventeenth Centuries

The abrupt landscape of Peru, with its high mountains and tropically hot valleys impeded but did not deter Spanish conquerors and missionaries. Mount Huascarán, at more than 22,000 feet, was nearly twice the height of anything most Europeans had ever had an opportunity to see.

PERU

I n October 1595, a missionary rookie set out from Andamarca in the Peruvian Andes—at 13,000 feet, the highest Christian mission in the world—in search of people to convert to Christianity. With an older priest for company and guidance, Nicolás de Mastrillo (mahs-TREE-yoh) struggled on foot for many days, through tracks too steep and broken for horses. At last they reached the house of an Indian chief called Bellunti, who received them with gestures of equality, not submission—with kisses and gifts, accompanied by long and ceremonious speeches. Bellunti's fellow Indians, meanwhile, kept their bows and arrows to hand. "They would have looked better," said the missionary's letter home to Spain, "if they did not paint themselves with red pigments." Hosts and visitors sat down to dine off clay dishes of Indian food: beans, herbs, chillies, corn, and cassava. "Thus," wrote Mastrillo to his superior, "your Reverence can imagine the joy we got from seeing ourselves happily seated with some thirty Indians almost as soon as we had arrived."

A moment of tension arose when a visiting chief suddenly revealed a suspicion. "These are not fathers," he said, but spies in disguise. Evidently, the differences in behavior between lay Spaniards and missionaries were so enormous that Native Americans thought they must belong to different nations. But then the skeptical chief "looked at us again," Mastrillo reports, and "said in his language, as our interpreter repeated it to us, 'Now I believe these are fathers.'" The reason he gave for his change of mind was that the priests ate, without disdain, their hosts' food. The missionaries assured their audience that "we had come only to show them the way to heaven and that we did not intend to make them the slaves of Spaniards nor would we ask them for silver nor gold. They all seemed to cheer up at that." Next day, priests and people began to build a chapel together, and Mastrillo began to learn the local language, praying that with time and God's help he would succeed.

The letter that tells this story never reached home. Pirates captured it en route, and it ended up in an English archive. But it shows more than the precarious nature of communications across the vast distances Europeans routinely crossed in

FOCUS questions

- WHY DID European elites attempt to change Christian practice and teachings during the sixteenth century?
- HOW DID Native Americans and Africans influence Christian beliefs and worship?
- WHERE WERE Muslim and Buddhist missionaries most active in the sixteenth and seventeenth centuries?
- HOW DID the Mughal emperors deal with religious diversity?
- WHY WAS the spread of scientific thought important for the West?
- WHY WERE the Chinese so interested in astronomy?

the sixteenth century. It discloses the mind and methods of Mastrillo's mission, and the perils and promise of his work. Above all, it shows how human encounters brought cultures into contact and initiated cultural exchanges that crossed the world.

• • • • •

Westerners primarily—but by no means exclusively—initiated the contacts. Christianity, Islam, and Buddhism, all contributed to cultural exchange. The sixteenth and seventeenth centuries were an unprecedented era for the revitalization and spread of all three religions. They were also centuries of unprecedented development for Western science and secular values. Western science reached parts of the world where, previously, it had been unknown. At the same time, the ways people thought, felt, and, in some respects, behaved in the West changed as a result of encounters with non-Western cultures.

CHRISTIANITY IN CHRISTENDOM

A new sense of mission had grown in Western Christendom and, to a slightly lesser extent, in the Eastern Orthodox world in the late Middle Ages. Fervor to renew the dynamism of the early history of the Church combined with a new conviction of the obligations of the godly, which included a growing sense of the need to compel "right thinking" alongside outward conformity, and to combat heresy, unbelief, and supposedly satanic forces. People with vocations or responsibilities in the Church, or with a strong personal sense of their relationship with God, increasingly took it upon themselves to spread active, committed, Christian awareness, informed by a knowledge of dogma. Among the consequences were new religious orders, new techniques of prayer, new fashions in devotion, and increased coercion and social control (see Chapter 19). But there were still parts of society and places in the world where, so far, Christianity had hardly reached or only superficially penetrated. In the sixteenth and seventeenth centuries, the mission-minded felt the need of a new conversion strategy, addressed to people low down the social scale: the poor; the rootless masses of growing cities; the neglected country folk; the peoples of forest, bog, and mountain, who had barely entered the candle-glow of the Church; and the vast world that exploration and improved geographical learning revealed or suggested. Self-consciously godly elites set themselves the task of re-Christianizing Europe, reviving the fervor of lukewarm Christians and trying to root out pagan survivals and demonic intrusions or delusions from popular customs. Like peasants and pagans, children were part of the previously submerged world to which clerical zeal now penetrated. By the last quarter of the sixteenth century, thousands of Christian catechisms for the education of children were in print.

The countryside was Europe's pagan backyard, full of potential converts to a more intense, aware, and devout Christian life. Rural communities still lived in worlds full of spirits and demons, where natural forces were personified and placated. A miller in northern Italy in the early sixteenth century could describe a remarkably coherent universe made "of cheese and worms," from which Christian traditions about creation were entirely absent. A Jesuit priest in the city of

Bordeaux in France in 1553 was appalled to find people in the nearby countryside "who have never heard of mass nor of a single word of the faith." Another Jesuit in Spain in 1615 expressed disbelief that so many of his colleagues wanted to be missionaries in Asia or America "when we have so many people here who do not know whether they believe in God." In 1628, a member of the English parliament complained of regions of the country "where God was little better known than among the Indians." In 1693, the Swedish governor general of Livonia (in the modern Baltic States) ordered the smashing of the rocks and groves people worshipped "so that not the least memorial may be left which could be used for superstition."

Campaigns like these were part of a more general attempt by ministers of religion to enforce their claim to a monopoly over ritual. For instance, in Spain, the church hierarchy had normally been happy, in the fifteenth century, to validate lay people's claims to have experienced saintly visions. But from the early sixteenth century, the church endorsed no more such claims. The same unease was directed against the deities of local religion: the local saints and virgins, whose cults the churches swept away or replaced with the universal veneration of Christ and his mother, the Virgin Mary.

All kinds of lay competition in the clergy's proper fields became subject to attempts at control or eradication, especially such practices as fortune telling, folk healing, magic, and even fairs and festivals. The Council of Trent—a series of meetings from 1545 to 1563 of European bishops who acknowledged the pope's authority—ordered that "all superstition shall be removed" and the cults of saints and relics purged of "perversion by the people into boisterous festivities." Dancing was banned from church—and in some places forbidden altogether. Bull fighting and contests between bears and dogs were prohibited or restricted, or at least banned on holy days, not because they were torture to animals but because they were temptations for people to behave in ways of which the Church disapproved— gambling, getting drunk, or having sex.

The war on popular religion was an attempt, under the constant menace of natural disasters, to wean people away from a religion of survival in this world toward one of salvation in the next. Trials of rats and exorcisms of swarms of locusts, appeals to folk healers and wisewomen, vows to saints for worldly purposes, charms to master nature, and spells to conjure the supernatural—these were the common enemies the clergy of all Christian traditions strove to control or abolish. A German law of 1669, typical of hundreds of others, condemned such magical practices as "putting pigs' hairs in fires, binding trees on New Year's Eve, and putting St. John's wort on walls to drive out spirits, and Easter bonfires accompanied by all sorts of songs that take the name of our Lord in vain while a good deal of devilry goes on." In the seventeenth century, Catholic clergymen were prominent in reclassifying witchcraft as a psychotic delusion, but all kinds of Christian communities remained subject, with diminishing frequency, to the fear of it, and were inclined to persecute it.

Public rituals affect private lives. Formal religion now intruded as never before in Europe into the most private sphere of activity: sex. In the sixteenth and seventeenth centuries in most of Europe, successful campaigns brought under the supervision of the clergy all contracts in which men and women agreed to live with each other as man and wife. Ostensibly, for instance, the Spanish Inquisition, founded in 1478, was a tribunal of faith, originally designed to monitor the sincerity of former Muslims and Jews who had converted to

Catechism class. Balls of wool as rewards for good students, blows for the bad from the rods the schoolmaster keeps under his desk: a catechism class in progress in 1593. Thanks to printing, every student could follow the text of a lesson in a relatively cheap copy of his or her own. The illustration comes from the first catechism of the Church of England, by Alexander Nowell (ca. 1507–1602).

Witchcraft. The south German draftsman of these scenes of witchcraft turned the subject into a pretext for dark humor and social satire. Artists traditionally contrasted scenes of worldly pleasures with depictions of the pangs of hell. Here women cavort with demons in a forest clearing, where dancing hints coyly at sex, while a devil roasts meat. But the witches' executioners, stoking fires and armed with pitchforks, are almost equally demonic.

Christianity under pressure from the Spanish authorities. In practice, most of its efforts in the second half of the sixteenth century were devoted to getting lay people's sex lives under clerical control. Bigamy and fornication were among the most common crimes the Inquisition investigated. Church leaders had never completely approved of sex, but they were united in thinking it did least harm when they themselves licensed it. Charity, as well as power lust, motivated them. It seemed vital, as a saintly campaigner claimed in 1551, "to invalidate all marriages where there is no witness" because "an infinite number of maidens have been deceived and undone . . . trusting in the promise of marriage made to them; and some have left their parents' house and gone to their perdition."

The newly self-conscious godly elites did not, however, consist entirely of clergy. On the contrary, clerical demand for more responsive congregations and a more committed flock met lay demand for more access to the mysteries of religion. Indeed, the more the clergy weaned people from pre-Christian or non-Christian superstitions, the more they aroused lay appetites for a share in the experience of Christian devotion: prayer, the sacraments, scripture—all the means by which the Church claimed to deliver experience or knowledge of God. Different parts of Christendom met this lay demand in different ways, but always by finding forms of devotion that could connect lay people with God: through increased access to the sacraments of the Church, in some places; through translations of the Bible and liturgy in others; and everywhere by encouraging private prayer.

One of the most effective communicators of the Christian message to a wider public was the German theologian Martin Luther (1483–1546). He began with himself—a conviction of his own sinfulness and of his redemption by the grace that God freely offered to all humankind. In a personal mission that he began toward the end of the second decade of the sixteenth century, he looked first to his fellow priests, with patchy success. He was more successful in reaching secular rulers, whom he encouraged to take power over the Church and to confiscate its wealth to purify it and restore it to the simplicity Jesus and his apostles had practiced. Luther's greatest effect, however, was on the lay public. For he appealed to lay people over the heads of the church hierarchy, whose authority he gradually came to reject in favor—in practice—of his own reading of scripture. The printing press—a medium unavailable to earlier religious reformers—spread his message and illustrated it with pictures that even illiterate people could appreciate. He devised a style of writing vivid beyond crudity in images, for example, of the papacy as the whore of Rome copulating with the Antichrist foretold in the Bible, or the pope defecating lies. (Apologists on the other side gave as good as they got. Catholic cartoonists, for example, depicted Luther as Satan himself, complete with horns and tail.) What was more, Luther crafted his language out of various northern German dialects. Many communities could understand it, and it spread relatively easily around the trading zone of the North Sea and Baltic. Here, in Scandinavia and parts of Germany—assisted by rulers grateful for an excuse to take power over the churches of their realms and seize their property—Luther's version of Christianity became the majority religion. Patchily, it also spread, or was carried in even more radical forms by Luther's unruly disciples, into parts of Europe that major trade routes connected, along the corridors of the Rhine, Rhone, and Danube Rivers.

Within these corners and patches of Europe, Luther not only reached places and classes where Christianity had previously been superficial, but changed the lives of individuals whose Christian awareness he touched. Rumors of his death drove the great German painter, Albrecht Dürer, to despair: "who," he asked, "will expound the gospel to us with such clearness?" Hans Sachs, the poet of Nuremberg in southwest Germany, said simply, "Luther spoke—and all was light." In some provinces, the Church had anticipated his project. Cardinal Cisneros, for instance, who was head of the Spanish Inquisition from 1507 until his death in 1517, had cheap editions of devotional books published in Spanish to wean readers from the pulp fiction of the day. But Luther went further, advocating reading the Bible and conducting the liturgy of the church in languages people actually spoke instead of in Latin.

The result was a schism within Christianity that endures to this day (see Map 18.1). Some national or local churches in the affected areas—parts of Germany, France, Switzerland, Hungary, and Holland; Scandinavia; Scotland and England—seceded from obedience to the Church of Rome, calling themselves "Evangelical" or "Protestant," or "Reformed" (hence the term *Reformation* for the movement they formed). A Catholic movement that historians commonly call the Counter Reformation or the Catholic Reformation reconverted some churches to Roman obedience. Partly in reaction against Protestantism, but at a more profound level to pursue the common, underlying project to re-Christianize Europe that all Christian elites shared, new religious orders sprang up. The most significant of these for the future of world history was the Jesuits, which Ignatius Loyola (1491–1556) founded in 1540. Loyola was an ex-soldier who brought martial virtues to the movement he founded: tight discipline, comradeship, self-sacrifice, and a sense of chivalry. He was also a gifted mystic, who taught his friends and followers self-transforming techniques of prayer, and a natural intellectual, who insisted on the highest standards of learning. The Jesuits became the Roman Catholic Church's most effective missionaries and educators, both in Europe and in the wider world, and the schools they established were nurseries of science and scholarship.

Having broken the principle that the Church was indivisible and authority within the Church unique and binding on all Christians, the Protestant movements tended to split among themselves in often bitter and bloody disputes over Christian dogma and how to organize the Church. A sense of hostility among the different forms of Christianity grew up in the aftermath of the schism—leading to wars justified, if not caused, by religious cant. As a result of this climate of hostility, traditional history has exaggerated the differences between Protestant and Catholic Christianity. Few people understood or cared about the subtleties of

Martin Luther as Satan tempting Jesus (1547). Protestant propaganda during the Reformation often depicted the pope as Satan. Here Catholic propaganda turns the tables by portraying Martin Luther as the devil (note his cloven hooves and tail). Like Satan in the Bible, Luther asks Jesus to make bread out of stones, to which Jesus famously replied to Satan that human beings do not live by bread alone but according to the Word of God.
Versuchung Christi (1547), Gemalde, Bonn, Landschaftsverband Rheinland/ Rheinisches Landesmuseum Bonn. Inv. Nr. 58.3.

MAP EXPLORATION

www.prenhall.com/armesto_maps

Timeline:

1517: Martin Luther posts 95 Theses condemning abuses of Catholic church at Wittenberg

1529: At Diet of Speyer, Charles V attempts to reach compromise with Lutheran princes

1532: Henry VIII of England declares himself head of Church of England

1535: John Calvin formulates doctrine of predestination in Geneva

1545: Start of Council of Trent, which defines modern Catholicism

1555: At Peace of Augsburg; Lutheran princes win right to choose their religion

1510 — 1520 — 1530 — 1540 — 1550 — 1560

MAP 18.1

The Religious Map of Europe in 1600

- almost exclusively Catholic, with just minimal Protestant presence
- overwhelmingly Catholic, with appreciable Protestant minority
- Catholic majority, but with very strong Protestant minority
- exclusively or overwhelmingly Protestant, with only slight Catholic presence in places
- Protestant majority, with some Catholic presence
- mainly Catholic, with strong Orthodox presence
- Orthodox Christian, with significant Muslim presence in some areas of the Balkans

Lutheran locally dominant Protestant denomination

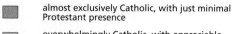

doctrine and worship that divided theologians. The doctrine most commonly said to define the Protestant reformers is that of "salvation by faith alone," according to which God imparts grace freely to anyone who professes belief in him without the sinner needing to perform pious works or obey church rules. Yet many Catholics stayed in the church while sharing Protestant views on this point, while Luther himself repeatedly insisted, in his own catechism for young Christians, "We should fear God because of his threat to those who transgress his law and love him for his promise of grace to those who keep it."

The missionary impulse within Europe produced no great revolution in spirituality. Most people remained as indifferent and shallow-minded as ever. But the language and imagery—the total communication—of the Christian faith were genuinely transformed. For Protestant clergy, services in the vernacular and the promotion of the Bible in translation were ways to help the laity become more actively involved in their faith. For Catholics, frequent communion and—to involve women in particular—the extension of the cults of the Virgin Mary and the founding of new religious orders of nuns who taught the young and nursed the sick served the same purpose.

Both traditions made God more intelligible, more accessible. "You seem to think that Christ was drunk," thundered Luther against radically subversive readings of the story of the Last Supper by rival Protestants, "and wearied his disciples with meaningless words!" This daring joke had the great virtue of treating Christ's humanity as literal and picturing him in the flesh of human weakness. In the mid–sixteenth century, the Inquisition forced the Italian painter Veronese to relabel his painting of the Last Supper as *Dinner at the House of Levi*, because it contained scenes of feasting and mirth, but by the century's end, another Italian painter, Caravaggio, could depict the *Last Supper*, without irreverence, as an episode of tavern low life. The German artist Mathias Grünewald in the 1520s had to hide his drawing of Jesus as a low-browed, warty-faced loser, but a century and a half later, the Spanish painter Murillo could revive the ancient tradition of depicting the Christ child as a naughty boy. As a result of the churches' mission to bring Christianity to the people, relevance to the lives of ordinary folk sanctified sacred subjects.

In eastern Christendom, too, reform movements led to conflicts between the Christianity of the clergy and the religion of ordinary people, and ultimately to splits in the Orthodox Church as they did in the West. A reformation parallel to those of the West began in 1621, when the Patriarch of Constantinople, Cyril Lukaris (1572–1638) renounced what he called the "bewitchment" of tradition "and took for my guide," he said, "Scripture . . . and Faith alone." The Russian priest Avvakum, "though a miserable sinner," tackled popular excesses violently. He drove mummers from his village, breaking their masks and drums, clubbing one of their dancing bears senseless, and releasing the other into the wild. In 1648, the Russian Orthodox clerical brotherhood known as the Zealots of Piety captured the czar's attention. At their insistence, the czar banished the vulgarities of popular piety from the Russian court and banned popular music as a presumed

Jesuit missionaries. The Jesuits' pride in the success of their overseas missions radiates from this eighteenth-century painting in which three of the order's sixteenth-century saints are prominently depicted. Flanked by personifications of the four continents in the foreground, the mythical giant Atlas presents the world to the Jesuits' founder, St. Ignatius Loyola. St. Francis Borja on the left-hand pedestal represents the order's preaching vocation; St. Francis Xavier, on the right, represents the ministry of the sacraments. Xavier also wears a Chinese-style vestment, a reminder of the Jesuits' long efforts to convert China. One of the leading Jesuit missionaries in China, Matteo Ricci, is in the background, among other Jesuit saints and heroes. Representatives of peoples the Jesuits converted kneel in prayer.

Exaltation of the ordinary. The Italian painter Caravaggio's "Supper at Emmaus" (1599) is famous among art historians for its innovative, dramatic use of light and shade, but it is equally extraordinary for its treatment of a sacred subject: a meeting at which Jesus revealed himself to his disciples after his Resurrection. Caravaggio depicted the disciples, not as glorious saints, but as shabby, commonplace peasants.

survival of paganism. Yet within 20 years, the clergy who had triumphed together in championing these changes fell out among themselves over a further proposed elimination of impurities: the standardization of texts and the harmonization of rituals. The leader of one party was exiled in 1666, the other burned at the stake in 1681.

CHRISTIANITY BEYOND CHRISTENDOM: THE LIMITS OF SUCCESS

Beyond Europe, the world that exploration and imperialism disclosed was a magnet for missionaries. "Come over and help us," said the Indian on the official seal of the trading company responsible, under the English crown, for colonizing Massachusetts in the early seventeenth century. On the whole, however, overseas missionizing was a rare vocation in Protestant Europe. There were a few exceptions. The conviction that the Algonquin Indians were a lost tribe of ancient Israel inspired John Eliot, who created "praying towns" in late seventeenth-century New England where native pastors led congregations in prayers, readings from the Bible, and sermons. Normally, however, only Roman Catholic religious orders had enough manpower and zeal to undertake the missions on a large scale, and outside areas of Spanish rule, their efforts were patchy.

In Asia, the contrast between the Philippines, where Spanish rule built up what is by far the biggest Christian community in Asia, and the many mission fields that proved barren or only briefly productive illustrates this. Even in the Philippines, Christian success in direct competition with Islam was limited. In the Sulu Islands, where Muslim missionaries were active within reach of protection from a strong Islamic state in Brunei, the Muslim threat could be met by force of arms, but Christian preaching could not eradicate it. In the Philippine island of Mindanao (mihn-dah-NOW), Muslim intruders arrived from the small but immeasurably spice-rich sultanate of Ternate in the 1580s. The Christian mission on Mindanao had barely begun and could not be sustained. In the late sixteenth and early seventeenth centuries, it was all Spanish garrisons could do to keep at bay Muslim hotheads who launched holy wars against the Spaniards' main base in Luzon. Yet, responding to his advisers' view that the mission was not worth the cost and effort, King Philip II of Spain (r. 1556–1598) insisted that he would rather spend all the gold in his treasury than sacrifice one church where the name of Christ was praised (see Map 18.2).

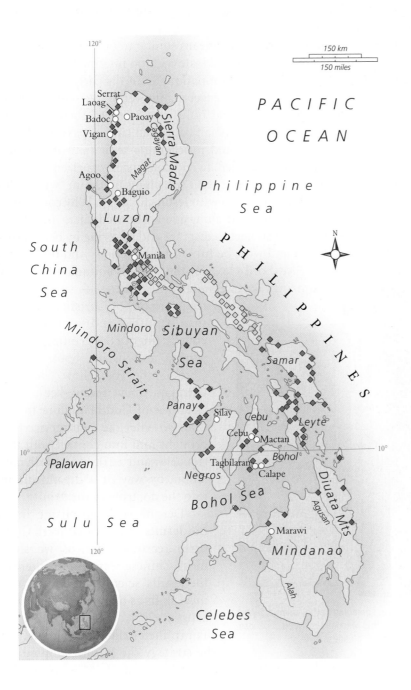

MAP 18.2

Catholic Missions in the Philippines, ca. 1700

- ◆ Augustinians
- ◆ Dominicans
- ◇ Franciscans
- ◆ Jesuits

Hideyoshi on Christian missionaries in Japan

For a while, Franciscans and Jesuits in late sixteenth- and early seventeenth-century Japan encountered amazing success by targeting lords whose conversions were catalysts for the conversions of their followers. Once the missionaries had a place to say mass and a conspicuous aristocratic patron to make Christianity respectable, they could attract potential converts by displays of devotion, such as the magnificent requiem mass sung for the local ruler's wife, Lady Gracia, at Kokura that attracted thousands of mourners in 1600. By the 1630s, more than 100,000 Japanese had been baptized. Successive central governments in Japan had treated the new religion with suspicion, as a source of subversive political ideas, foreign influence, and encouragement to local lords to usurp central authority. Sporadic persecution from the 1590s, however, had failed to halt the progress of Christianity. So from 1639, it was banned outright, and Christians who refused to renounce their faith were forced into exile or put to death.

China could not be converted by means similar to those the Jesuits followed in Japan. It was a relatively centralized state with no intermediate lords to serve as local flashpoints of Christian illumination. So in the early seventeenth century, the Jesuits concentrated their meager manpower on the scholar officials, or mandarins, who enjoyed huge social influence. Some of their converts were impressively committed: using Christian baptismal names, passing Christianity on to their friends and families, and proclaiming their faith in public. Yang Tingyun (yahng teeng yuhn) recalled a vivid conversion experience in the presence of one of the Jesuits' pictures of Jesus, which inspired him "with feelings of the presence of a great lord." Debates with Jesuits followed. Why could reverence for Buddha not be accommodated alongside acknowledgment of Jesus? How could the LORD of HEAVEN be subject to disgrace and suffering by being crucified? How could bread and wine be turned into the body and blood of Jesus? (Answer: "My Lord's love for the world is boundless.") After much agonizing, Yang repudiated his mistress—a more impressive test, perhaps, of Christian commitment than baptism—and went on to build a church, finance the printing of Christian works, and write books explaining Christianity. His fellow Christian, Xu Guangqi (shew gwang-kee), explained as an act of God his failure to pass the exam to enter the civil service that first brought him into contact with the missionaries and attributed to divine revelation, by way of a dream, his insight into the doctrine of the Trinity.

Despite such promising instances, the Jesuits failed to convert China for three reasons. First, as we shall see, most Chinese were more interested in the Jesuits' scientific learning and technical skills as mapmakers, astronomers, artists, clock makers, and designers than in their religious teaching. Second, the strategy the Jesuits adopted to con-

East meets West. This traveling altarpiece symbolizes Jesuit success in spreading Catholicism in Japan in the late sixteenth century. Imported European sacred paintings like this Madonna inspired Japanese imitators and attracted converts. The altarpiece is lacquered and gilded in Japanese style.
Photograph courtesy Peabody Essex Museum

vert China was a long-term one, and the revolutions of Chinese politics tended to interrupt it. No sooner had the Jesuits converted an empress than the Manchus overthrew the Ming dynasty in 1644 (see Chapter 17). Finally, the church lost confidence in the Jesuits' methods. This was the outcome of a conflict that began with the founder of the mission, Matteo Ricci (1552–1610). He rapidly developed a healthy respect for Chinese wisdom. Indeed, the Jesuits became mediators not only of Western culture to China but also of Chinese learning in the West. Ricci decided that the best way to proceed with Chinese converts was to permit them to continue rites of reverence for their ancestors, on the ground that it was similar to Western veneration for saints. As we have seen, this was just the sort of practice that, in the West, the clerical elite was attacking. The missionaries split over the issue, and the effectiveness of the mission suffered when Pope Clement XI ruled against the veneration of ancestors early in the eighteenth century.

In parts of south and southeast Asia, missionary strategists targeted potential converts at various social levels. In the seventeenth century in the Molucca Islands and Sulawesi (Celebes) in what is today Indonesia, Protestant and Catholic missions alike approached sultans, local notables, and village heads, with results that usually came to embrace many ordinary people but that never seem to have lasted for long. In Manado in northern Sulawesi, Franciscans launched an intensive mission in 1619. They began by obtaining permission from an assembly of village heads at the ruler's court. But these notables disclaimed power over their fellow villagers' religious allegiance. The friars preached from village to village, encountering universal hostility. The audience would shriek to drown out the preaching, urge their unwelcome guests to leave, and profess fidelity to their gods. They withheld food and shelter. The friars therefore withdrew in 1622. Their Jesuit successors made some progress by concentrating on the ruler and his family. When Franciscans returned to the villages in the 1640s, they enjoyed a much more positive reception. By the 1680s, under Dutch sponsorship, a Protestant mission in Manado made further headway by employing converted native schoolmasters to work among the children of the elite, wherever a local ruler would permit it. In Sri Lanka, Portuguese missionaries were more generally successful, but the Dutch who took over the island in 1656 were as keen to undermine Catholics as to convert Buddhists to Protestantism, and the long-term impact of Christianity proved slight.

In the New World, the bottom-up strategy of conversion was more usual. After initial contact, which, of course, often brought missionaries into touch with local leaders, ambitious programs of mass baptism and mass preaching rapidly followed. In the 1520s and 1530s, Franciscans baptized literally millions of Native Americans in the first 15 years or so of the Franciscan mission in Mexico, in an experiment typical of the time. It was an effort to re-create the actions and atmosphere of the early church, when a single example of holiness could bring thousands to baptism and altar as if by a miracle. Clearly most conversions in these circumstances cannot have been profound, life-changing experiences of the kind specified in traditional definitions of conversion.

First book printed in the New World. "In a plain style for common understanding": the first book printed in the New World was a catechism issued by Juan de Zumárraga in Mexico City in 1543. The tasseled hat signifies that the book was published under the patronage of the archbishop of Mexico. The ornamented borders were fashionable decoration for books at the time in Europe. Zumárraga was a Franciscan friar who was committed to spreading Catholic doctrine to poor and uneducated people who knew little or nothing about the faith. The church in New Spain was not just a missionary effort directed at Native Americans, but also part of a movement active throughout the Christian world, in which the clergy and the godly tried to re-express Christian doctrine in simple terms that a wide audience could understand.

The Revitalization and Spread of Christianity

1478	Spanish Inquisition founded
1500s	Spanish Christians compete with Muslims for dominance in the Philippines
Early sixteenth century	Martin Luther initiates Protestant Reformation in Europe
Sixteenth and seventeenth centuries	Elites take on task of "re-Christianizing" Europe
1520s and 1530s	Franciscans baptize millions of Native Americans
Mid–sixteenth century	Catholic Church begins Counter-Reformation
1540	Ignatius Loyola founds Jesuits
1545–1563	Council of Trent meets
Seventeenth century	Jesuits lead Christian missionary effort in China
1621	Reformation in Eastern Orthodox Church begins
1630s	Over 100,000 Japanese baptized
1639	Christianity banned in Japan

The doctrinal awareness the friars succeeded in communicating was limited. The first catechism the Franciscans used in Mexico does not even refer to the divinity of Jesus, which is a central doctrine of Christian belief. Dominican friars denounced the superficiality of Franciscan teaching, but the same problems of deficient manpower, daunting terrain, and linguistic and cultural differences hampered their own efforts.

The fear of backsliding and apostasy by new converts haunted the missions. As early as 1539, clergy in Mexico worried about the multiplication of small chapels "just like those the Indians once had for their particular gods." In central Mexico, in the mid–sixteenth century, fears that new cults disguised pagan practices convulsed the church. Doubts arose even concerning the purity of the veneration of Our Lady of Guadalupe herself—the apparition of the Virgin Mary, supposedly to an Indian shepherd boy on the site of a pre-Christian shrine, which had demonstrated the sanctity and grace of Mexican soil in the 1530s. In 1562, one of the worst recorded cases of missionary violence erupted in Yucatán, when the head of the Franciscan mission became convinced that some of his flock were harboring pagan idols. The reports that alerted him came from native informants, motivated, probably, by traditional hatred and rivalry among Indian communities, rather than by any zeal for the facts. In the subsequent persecution, 4,500 Indians were tortured, and 150 died.

In a similar case in central Peru in 1609, a parish priest was condemned for using excessive violence toward backsliders among his flock. The papers he collected include the story of a revealing trauma. Don Cristóbal Choque Casa, the son of a local Indian notable and community leader, reported that, some 30 or 40 years after a vigorous Jesuit mission had nominally converted his people, he was on his way to meet his mistress at the abandoned shrine of a tribal god, when the devil in the form of a bat attacked him. He drove out the demon by reciting the Lord's Prayer in Latin, and the following morning summoned his fellow natives to warn them not to frequent the shrine on pain of being reported to the parish priest. But that same night, he dreamed that he was irresistibly drawn to the accursed spot himself and compelled to make a silver offering to the god. The story evokes a vivid picture of the consequences of "spiritual conquest": old shrines, so neglected that they are fit only for bats and fornicators; abiding powers, so menacing that they can still haunt the dreams, even of a sinner sufficiently indoctrinated to be able to pray in Latin.

For the rest of the colonial period, the eradication of pre-Christian devotions in Peru became the work of professional "extirpators." In most of the rest of the Spanish-American world, every new generation of clergy repeated the frustrations and disillusionment of their predecessors. The Indians seemed unable to forget their old rites for appeasing nature. In the early eighteenth century, in Guatemala and Peru, priests were still making the same complaints as their predecessors a century and a half before. Indians were attached to "idols" and to their own healers and seers. They turned the saints into pagan deities. They accused each other of superstition and of working with demons. Only with extreme caution could they be trusted to revere sacred images of Jesus and the saints without idolatry.

Still, ordinary people's accessibility to the ministry of missionaries made the New World an extraordinarily rich and rewarding mission field. Aided by the tendency—exceptionally common in the Americas—of some cultures to welcome and defer to strangers, missionaries could penetrate areas otherwise untouched by any European presence, establish an honored place in their host societies, learn the languages, and guide congregations, by intimate, personal contact, into redefining themselves as Christians.

THE MISSIONARY WORLDS OF BUDDHISM AND ISLAM

Other religions paralleled Europe's mission to the infidel within.

China and Japan

In China, Zhu Hong (jew-hung) (1535–1615) and Han Shan (hahn-shahn) (1546–1623) presented Buddhism afresh as a religion people could practice "at home," eliminating the priestly character that had formerly made it seem inaccessible and unintelligible to lay followers. Lay devotees could perform the same rituals at home as monks did in a monastery. Laymen could worship Buddha, fast, adopt vegetarianism, and even don the saffron robe that signified a religious vocation. In the eighteenth century, Peng Shaosheng (pahng show-shuhng) took the same line of reform further by explaining techniques of mental prayer, unprompted by images of gods. This emphasis on direct religious experience, unmediated through a priestly class, strikingly resembled what was going on in Europe.

In seventeenth-century Japan, comparable movements, embracing both Buddhism and native religion, began with the reexamination of ancient texts, just as Christian reformers began by going back to the Bible. The monk Keichu (1640–1701) was a pioneer in recovering authentic texts of the *Manyoshu*, poetic native scriptures of the eighth century. These scriptures, along with other old myths known as the *Kojiki*, became the basis of a born-again local religion, stripped of the additions of intervening centuries and of influences from outside Japan. Among Keichu's successors in the following century, Motoori Morinaga (1730–1801) used the *Manyoshu* as Protestants used the Gospels—to reconstruct a model of purity and to denounce the degeneracy of the latter days. Meanwhile, the suppression of Christianity in Japan created an opportunity for Buddhism. Wealthy lords, merchants, and peasants endowed many new Buddhist foundations.

The Mongols

The decisive initiative in reenergizing missionary Buddhism came from within Mongolia in the 1570s. Altan Khan (1530–1583) ruled a swathe of territory along the northern loop of the Yellow River to the border of Tibet. He founded Koke Khota—the "Blue City"—to be a permanent Mongol capital near the present border of Inner and Outer Mongolia. The Chinese called it Guihua—"Return to Civilization." He was a determined pagan, who treated his gout by paddling inside the split open body of a human-sacrifice victim. But—realizing that Buddhist help would be vital to his schemes to extend his realm by conquest—he founded monasteries, sent for scriptures to Beijing, and had them translated on tablets of polished apple wood. Shrines and monasteries filled the slopes above his capital. Cultivation of Buddhism gave his khanate a distinctive profile among the client-states on China's northwest border.

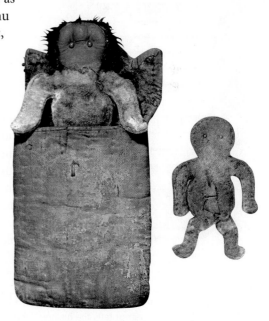

The Ongons, or Ongghot, small figures of cloth or wood kept in a box or—like these, dangling from a tent pole in a pouch—are the most conspicuous feature of Mongolian shamanism. In traditional Mongol belief, the souls of the dead "become ongghot" with the power both to help and harm living people. Using the little images, the shaman, in his ecstasy, can transmit the presence and power of these spirits into himself. In the late sixteenth and seventeenth centuries, Buddhist missionaries tried with varying success to stamp out shamanism and belief in the Ongons.

At Altan Khan's invitation, the ruler of Tibet, known as the **Dalai Lama**, visited Mongolia in 1576 and 1586. Tibet was a priestly Buddhist state, and the Dalai Lama was, by unalterable convention, the head of the Buddhist establishment. He guided reform of Mongol customs. Human sacrifices were forbidden, and blood sacrifices of all sorts stopped. The ongons—the felt images in which spirits resided, except when the rites of shamans liberated them (see Chapter 13)—were to be burned and replaced by Buddhist statues. The new religion was at first limited to the aristocracy. But over the next century, Buddhism spread down through society and outward across the Mongol dominions. The next Dalai Lama was the son of a Mongol prince. His training for his role in the 1590s took place in Mongolia, amid scholars engaged in the systematic translation of the vast body of Buddhist scriptures into Mongolian. Young noblemen joined the priesthood. Altan Khan had 100 of them ordained as priests to celebrate the Dalai Lama's first visit. Increasingly in the late sixteenth and early seventeenth centuries, the documents Mongol chiefs issued during diplomatic exchanges contain allusions to Buddhism, and when they made alliances with pagan peoples, Buddhist and pagan language and ceremonies marked the occasions.

From the 1630s, a mission Prince Neyici Toyin (1557–1653) organized took the Buddhism of Tibet beyond Mongolia into Manchuria, building the great Yellow Temple in Shenyang (shehn-yahng) to house an antique statue of Buddha. Toyin worked by "miracles" of healing that may have owed something to the superiority of Tibetan and Chinese medicine over the unscientific therapies of the shamans. Manchu political power after they conquered China in 1644 reinforced the mission. The Manchu emperors perceived Buddhist missionaries as pacifiers and potential agents of imperial policy. They appointed Tibetan lamas to instruct the Mongols, presumably in part to reconcile the Mongols to Chinese rule.

Like Catholic missions in the New World, political conquests and violence shadowed and disfigured those of Buddhists in northern Asia. Neyici Toyin burned before his tent a bonfire of ongons ten tent-frames high. Advice to Buddhist missionaries in the extreme west of Mongolia in the mid–seventeenth century was, "Whoever has worshipped ongons, burn their ongons and confiscate their cattle and sheep. From those who let the shamans and shamanesses perform fumigations, take their horses, fumigate the shamans in their turn with dog dung." In practice, the old gods did not altogether disappear, reemerging as Buddhist deities, just as in Christian America the Native American gods survived as saints and representations of the Virgin Mary. In both Mongolia and the Americas, the old gods continued to mediate between humans and nature.

Islam

The trend to what might be called low-level strategy—missionary efforts targeted on ordinary people—also seems to have affected Islamic missions (see Map 18.3). In southeast Asia (in what were to become Malaysia and Indonesia) and Africa, which were the two great arenas of Islamic expansion at the time, the means of conversion were fourfold: commerce, deliberate missionary effort, holy war, and dynastic links. As in southeast Asia, on the Islamic world's African front, the arrival of Christian Europeans hardly affected the retreat of paganism. Except in the coastal toeholds of Christendom, the same combination of merchants, missionaries, and warmongers ensured the dominance of Islam.

The Chronicles of Java. Islam in southeast Asia has often been mixed with elements from other religions. This illustrated manuscript tells the history of the island of Java in what today is Indonesia and the spread of Islam there by Sufi saints and rulers up to 1647. Written in Javanese, it seeks to give the Muslim rulers of the state of Mataram (in modern-day Indonesia) legitimacy by telling of how one of their ancestors had ties to three different religious traditions: He was blessed by a Muslim saint, practiced Hindu asceticism, and married the goddess of the southern ocean.

Merchants and missionaries spread Islam together. Trade shunted pious Muslims from city to city and installed them as port supervisors, customs officials, and agents to local rulers. Missionaries followed: scholars in search of patronage, discharging along the way the Muslim's obligation to convert unbelievers; spiritual athletes in search of exercise, anxious to challenge native shamans in contests of conspicuous austerity and supernatural power. In some areas, **Sufis** (SOO-fees)—mystics, with a feel for popular worship of natural forces, for whom, as one of them said, God was "closer than the veins of my neck"—made crucial contributions. In southeast Asia, Sufis congregated in

MAP **18.3**

The Spread of Christianity, Islam, and Buddhism in Asia by 1750

→ major Christian missions after 1500

→ Buddhist missionaries, 1650–1750

▨ predominantly under Muslim rule by 750

▨ predominantly under Muslim rule by 1500

▨ predominantly under Muslim rule by 1750

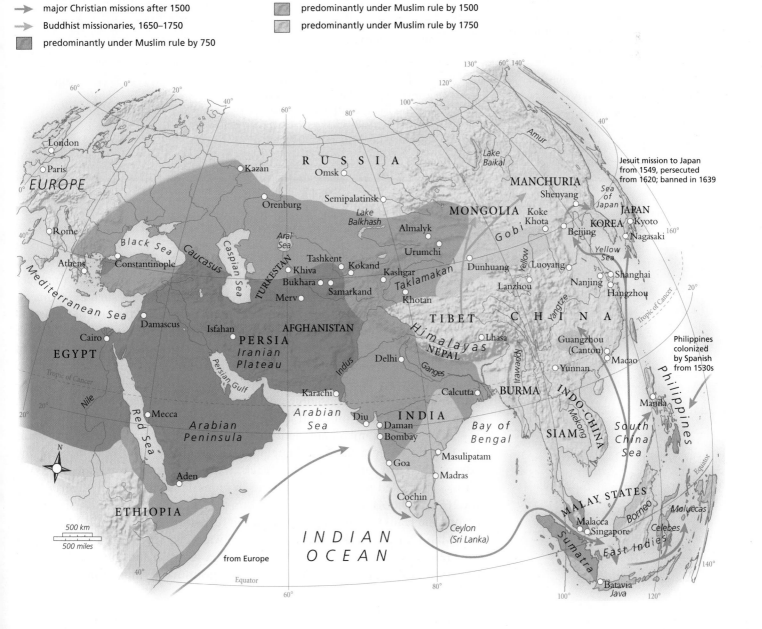

● MAKING CONNECTIONS

REVITALIZATION OF WORLD RELIGIONS

RELIGION →	REASONS FOR REVITALIZATION →	CONSEQUENCES →	NEW ADHERENTS
Christianity	• To renew dynamism of early Church • To combat heresies, paganism, witchcraft • To engage unevangelized and under-evangelized people	New religious orders; new techniques of prayer; new types of devotion; increased coercion and social control by church–state alliances; sharp restrictions on localized beliefs and rituals; emphasis on missionary efforts	Lower-class Europeans, urban and country; colonized peoples in America, Africa, Asia
Buddhism	• To popularize Buddhism in China and Japan • To adapt to native religious beliefs (China and Japan) • As a vehicle for strengthening political control (Mongolia, Manchuria)	Eliminating the need for priestly leadership; simplified rituals; emphasis on direct religious experience via meditation, ritual; creation of new systems of monasteries throughout Asia; Tibetan lamas restructured Mongol spiritual practices	Laymen, peasants, and other social classes throughout Japan, China, Central Asia
Islam	• To spread belief to southeast Asia, Africa • To adapt to native religious beliefs • To enhance Muslim spirituality	Use of merchants, Sufi missionaries, holy war (jihad), and dynastic alliances to expand Islamic influence; intermarriage as a method of advancing Islam; spread of Islamic schools increases literacy	Ordinary people, especially in southeast Asia, Africa

Melaka, and after the city fell to the Portuguese in 1511, they fanned out from there through Java and Sumatra. In the late sixteenth and seventeenth centuries, the sultanate of Aceh in northwest Sumatra in modern Indonesia was a nursery of Sufi missionaries of sometimes dubious Islamic orthodoxy, such as Shams al-Din (shahmz ahd-DEEN), who saw himself as a prophet of the end of the world and whose books were burned after his death in 1630. Even peaceful Muslim missionaries tended to see themselves as warriors of a sort, waging a "jihad of words." During the seventeenth century, perhaps under the goad of competition from Christianity, the "jihad of the sword" grew in importance, and the extension of the frontier of the Islamic world depended increasingly on the aggression of sultans, especially from central Java.

In West Africa, merchant clans or classes, like the Saharan Arabs known as Kunta, who made a habit of marrying the daughters of holy men, were the advanced guard of Islam. The black wandering scholars known as the Torokawa incited revivalism and jihad in Hausaland in modern Nigeria from the 1690s. Schools with a wide curriculum played a vital part in diffusing Islam among the Hausa, scattering pupils who in turn attracted students of their own (see Map 18.4). A sheikh who died in 1655 was able, at school in Katsina, near the present border of Niger and Nigeria, to "taste to the full the Law, the interpretation of the Quran, prophetic tradition, grammar, syntax, philology, logic, study of grammatical particles, and of the name of God, Quranic recitation, and the science of meter and rhyme." Paid by donations according to pupils' wealth, the master of such a school sat on a pile of rugs and sheepskins before his niche of books, equipped with his tray of sand for tracing letters with his finger. He might have his brazier filled with burning charcoal to warm him in

MAP 18.4

The Spread of Islam in Africa, ca. 1700

■ extent of Islam by 1700
— trade route

The Spread of Buddhism and Islam

Fifteenth and sixteenth centuries	Merchants and missionaries spread Islam
1570s	Mongol ruler Altan Khan stimulates the revival of missionary Buddhism in Mongolia
Late sixteenth century	Zhu Hong and Han Shan stress direct experience of Buddhism in China
Seventeenth century	"Jihad of the sword" takes on greater importance in spread of Islam
1630s	Missions initiated by Prince Neyici Toyin bring Buddhism to Manchuria
1690s	Torokawa scholars incite revival and jihad in Hausaland in modern Nigeria

winter and his spitoon for the husks of kola nuts that were eaten for their caffeine content. Students' manuscripts survive, smothered in annotations from the teacher's commentary, which was often in a native language instead of Arabic, the language of the Quran. At the end of this course, the student acquired a certificate, emblazoned with a long pedigree of named teachers going back to Malik ibn Anas (MA-lihk ih-bihn a-NAZ), the eighth-century codifier of Islamic law.

THE RESULTING MIX: GLOBAL RELIGIOUS DIVERSITY—AMERICAN AND INDIAN EXAMPLES

The forms of Catholic Christianity that became characteristic of Spanish America were, in their way, every bit as different from the Catholic mainstream as was the Protestantism of most of the English colonies. In part, this was because of the imperfections of the "Spiritual Conquest" of Spanish America by Catholic missionaries. Missionaries were few. Cultural and linguistic obstacles impeded communication. Pre-Christian religion was probably too deeply rooted to be destroyed. In partial consequence, Latin American Catholicism is rippled, to this day, with Native American features.

Secular scholars, and Protestant critics of Catholic missionary activities, sometimes call these Native American influences **syncretic** features or pagan survivals because Christianity and paganism seemed to fuse in a new religion that was not quite either but was a blend of both. Yet the proper comparison for colonial religion is not—or not solely—with the religion of the Native American past but with that of Europe of the same era, where clerical bafflement at the stubborn survival of popular religion was every bit as great. The Christianity of the American countryside was deficient in similar ways to that of the European countryside. Anxiety about how to survive in this world interfered with people's concern about their salvation in the next. Rites to induce rain, suppress pests, elude plague, and fend off famine drove Scripture and sacraments into neglected corners of ordinary lives. As the programs of reform unfolded in Europe, clergy and educated laity acquired ever-higher standards of doctrinal awareness, ever-deeper experiences of Christian self-consciousness. Their expectations of their flocks increased accordingly—which accounts for the continual renewal of their dissatisfaction. The more Christianized the elite became, the more Christian the clergy expected ordinary people to behave. Meanwhile, the Christianity of Indians in Spanish America had as much variety as in that of Europeans in Anglo-America.

Black America

The religion of black people in the Americas—though it varied a lot from place to place, molded into conflicting traditions by the influence of Protestantism and Catholicism respectively—always had one thing in common: it was always black—different, that is, from the religion of white people. Brazil is the best-documented area and has a characteristic profile. Here, in colonial times, black artistic vocations and religious devotion were centered on cult images that charitable associations of black Catholic laypeople often supported financially. These **confraternities**, as they are called, were vital institutions for colonial society generally, melding the culturally uprooted into a coherent community, renewing their sense of identity and belonging. They were even more important for black people, who were compulsory colonists, traumatically transferred as slaves from Africa to an alienating environment on another continent. Confraternities cushioned and comforted them in a white man's world. The confraternities were unstable organizations, "created and dissolved with extraordinary rapidity," as one of their most distinguished historians has said. Encouraged by the Church, and especially by the Jesuits and Franciscans, the black brotherhoods were hotbeds of disorder.

For the guardians of the colonial power structure, the confraternities' choice of patron saints, whose statues they paraded through the streets and elevated in shrines, was often self-assertive, sometimes defiant. St. Elesbaan, for instance, was a warrior-avenger, a black crusading emperor of Ethiopia, who led an expedition to avenge the massacre of Christians by a Jewish ruler in Yemen in 525. He was easy to reinterpret as a symbol of resistance to the many plantation owners of Portuguese–Jewish ancestry. St. Benedict of Palermo, perhaps the favorite patron of black confraternities, was born the son of Nubian slaves in Sicily in 1526. He became a hermit in his youth, to escape taunts about his blackness. Then, as a Franciscan

Shamans still burn incense on the steps of the church of Saint Thomas at Chichicastenango in the Guatemala highlands, where worshippers leave offerings of flowers and rum. The steps—a mound similar to pre-Hispanic Maya temples—seem to rival the church interior as a place of devotion. Is this paganism, Christianity, or a mixture of the two? Most local shamans now serve as officials of societies dedicated to Christian saints, and the religion of Chichicastenango may be best understood as one of the many local forms of Christianity that developed in the colonial New World.

lay brother, he rose to become guardian of his friary and work miracles after his death in 1583. The cult of St. Iphigenia, a legendary black virgin, who resisted the spells of her suitor's magicians with the help of 200 fellow virgins, embodied the triumph of faith over magic. But it had its subversive aspect, too, sanctifying virginity in a slave society where women wished sterility on themselves in order not to produce children who would become slaves. Veneration of the Mother of God was closer in spirit to the fertility religions supposedly traditional among migrants from Africa and more consistent with the interests of slave owners, who wanted their human livestock to breed. Black Catholicism was an excitant, not an opiate. Rather than playing the role commonly assigned to religion—keeping believers in their place—it inspired hopes of betterment in this world. A commonly depicted scene was of black tormentors torturing white Judas in hell.

Colonial black Catholicism really was different from that of white people. Masters excluded slaves from mass, ostensibly "on account of the smell," but really to keep them away from dangerously radical clergy. White confraternities reviled blacks people "with their guitars and drums, with their *mestizo* [mixed white and Indian] prostitutes," and with their revolutionary pretensions, "just as though they were no different from honest white people." Fugitive black slaves who set up their own backwoods communities and independent kingdoms were formally excommunicated. The church hierarchy usually refused their requests for chaplains.

Missionary activity in Brazil began in the early sixteenth century before the Counter-Reformation, when the clergy were still content with superficial levels of Christian teaching. It continued in an era of growing Catholic sensitivity to the native heritage of potential converts, who were not always called on to renounce all their culture to become Christians. The mulatto priest António da Vieira (1608–1697), who became a royal chaplain in 1641, imported "masks and rattles to show the heathen that the Christian religion was not sad." In partial consequence, Brazilian Catholicism is an umbrella term for a bewildering range of styles of devotion. Outside the Spanish and Portuguese colonies—and especially in those of the British and Dutch, where plantations were inaccessible to Catholic religious orders—the lack of missionary activity was even more marked. In consequence, African religions persisted, and syncretism happened because the slaves often learned Christianity by themselves and blended it with African religious beliefs.

White America

As for the religion of white Americans in colonial times, its great common—albeit not constant—feature was enthusiasm. Refugees from religious persecution in Europe, who took religion seriously, formed or infiltrated many colonies: Catholics and radical Protestants in British North America, Jews or so-called New Christians—descendants of Jews, whose Christianity Judaism deeply influenced—in Spanish and Portuguese colonies. Even hard-headed laymen could prove open to religious enthusiasm in the heady atmosphere of a New World where everything seemed possible and a new church might be constructed from scratch, without the corruption and distortions that had warped Christ's teaching in the Old World. Columbus and Cortés—neither of whom showed much interest in religion in their early lives—both had visions of a restored apostolic age in the lands they explored and conquered.

The most extreme form of enthusiasm is millenarianism. Millenarianism is, in some ways, the characteristic form of religious fervor of the Americas. It can be detected in pre-Christian Native American religions. In central Mexico, most peoples celebrated rites of renewal of the Earth in fire every 52 years and nourished myths of the destruction of the world in a divine furnace. But, for these and other Native American cultures we know about, time was cyclical. Every destruction was the start of a new cycle. For Native Americans, the end of time—which for Christians would be the climax of history—was strictly unimaginable.

Franciscans introduced Christian millenarianism to the New World in the sixteenth century. Most of the early missionaries came from a few Franciscan communities in southern Spain, where friars nurtured obsessions with the coming end of the world, which would be preceded by a cosmic war between good and evil leading to the Age of the Holy Spirit.

Fantasies of this kind unhinged unorthodox minds at frequent intervals. The Spanish adventurer Lope de Aguirre, during a harrowing navigation of the Amazon in the 1560s, imagined himself as the embodiment of God's wrath. His Franciscan contemporary, Francisco de la Cruz, was the self-proclaimed universal

THE CULT IMAGE OF ST. ELESBAAN

Devotion to St. Elesbaan, shown here in an early eighteenth-century statue from the Confraternity of Our Lady of the Rosary, was one of a number of politically charged, socially subversive cults that attracted black worshippers in colonial Brazil.

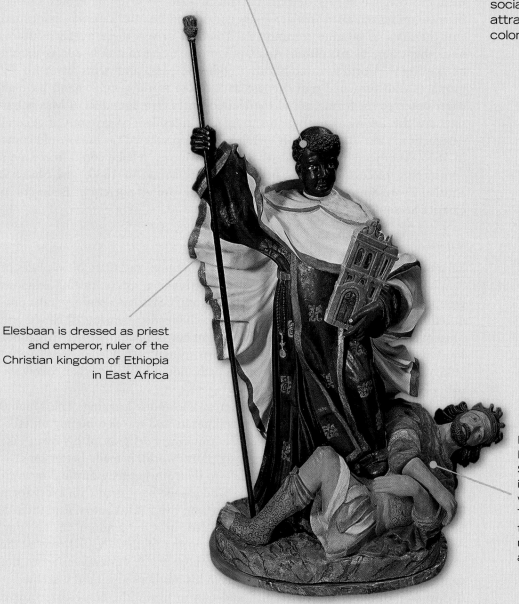

Black saints were inspiring models for the black confraternities, lay Christian brotherhoods that flourished in Brazil.

Elesbaan is dressed as priest and emperor, ruler of the Christian kingdom of Ethiopia in East Africa

Elesbaan supposedly led an Ethiopian invasion across the Red Sea to Yemen in southern Arabia in 525 to dethrone a Jewish ruler who was persecuting Christians. The many black slaves in Brazil felt persecuted by their masters, many of whom were of Jewish or allegedly Jewish ancestry.

How does this statue show the uniqueness of black Christianity in colonial Brazil?

pope and emperor of the last days. The fervor of the spiritual Franciscans mingled with whatever forms of millenariansim were inherited from Native American tradition. In Mexico in 1541, an Indian chief called Don Martín Ocelotl (oss-ehl-OT-el) proclaimed the second coming of Christ, embodied in himself. In 1579, in Paraguay, another Indian chief, Oberá the Resplendent (ob-er-AH), launched a rebellion against Spanish rule with a similar message. In Peru, so-called *Inkarrí* (een-kah-REE) movements kept legendary memories of the Inca Empire alive into modern times and fused them with expectations of the coming of a "Last World Emperor."

Meanwhile, North America inherited similar traditions and merged them with the original forms of millenarianism that grew up in Protestantism. Because millenarianism was generally considered heretical, or was associated with heresies, it became common in America, driven there by persecution, nourished there by toleration. Anabaptism (the belief that only adults should be baptized), world's-end biblical fundamentalism, and sects invented by prophets who preached that the last days of the world were at hand have all contributed to the formation of the United States. The founders of Massachusetts saw the colony as a refuge for those God intended "to save out of general destruction." The Puritan minister John Cotton predicted the end would come in 1655. Another Puritan minister, Increase Mather, felt he could hear God's "murdering pieces go off" as he watched the comet of 1680. The Shakers, another Protestant sect, called themselves "The United Society of Believers in Christ's Second Coming."

India

Religious frontiers, where rival creeds and communions meet, are often places of conflict. But they can also stimulate creative thinking, as contrasting religious groups strive to understand and live with each other. Sixteenth-century India produced an enduring new religion: **Sikhism**, which blended elements of Hindu and Muslim tradition—or, as Sikhs would say, went beyond both. Neither Hindu nor Muslim paths to God suffice, said Guru Nanak (GOO-roo NAH-nahk) (1469–1539), the Sikh founder, "so whose path should I follow? I shall follow the path of God."

Nanak was a widely traveled pilgrim of enormous learning. The Mughal emperor Akbar (r. 1556–1605), who was illiterate and traveled mainly on military campaigns, sought to outdo him by founding a religion of his own. Like Nanak he recognized that in a religiously plural world, it made better sense—and better served the peace of his realm—to look at what religions had in common rather than at what divided them. "God should be adored with every form of adoration," he said, according to a Jesuit who lived at his court. And indeed, he exhibited broad-mindedness unparalleled in Christendom in his day. Awestruck by the realism of a European painting of the Virgin Mary in the chapel he gave to the Jesuits in his palace, Akbar and his courtiers "could not contain their joy at seeing the infant Jesus in his mother's arms and it seemed as if they would like to play with him and talk to him." The emperor acquired European prints for his own painters to copy. Catholic religious imagery became part of the decor of his court.

He promoted debates between teachers of rival religions in an attempt to establish a synthesis, which he called the "Faith of God"—the Din-i-ilahi

(DEEN-eh eh-lah-HEE). In what sounds like a standard story of saintly conversion, enlightenment came to him while he was hunting, in the late 1570s. Disappointingly, but unsurprisingly, the new religion seemed like an attempt to make the Mughal state itself sacred. Akbar came to see himself as a manifestation, even an embodiment of God. Most Muslims were repelled and resolved never to try to accommodate other religions again. Later Mughal emperors felt torn between strategies of tolerance and of hostility toward non-Muslim faiths. The need to appease Hindus caused a mid–seventeenth century revival of Akbar's efforts by Dara Shukoh (DAH-rah shoo-KOH), a pretender to the Mughal throne, who proposed "the mingling of the two oceans" of Muslim and Hindu teaching. But his fanatically Muslim brother, Aurangzeb (r. 1658–1707), beat him to the throne and promoted Islam aggressively. He executed the Sikh leader, Guru Hari Rai, for blasphemy and discriminated against Hindus in distributing offices and rewards. The result was a backlash. When a Sikh prince seized the city of Jodhpur, for example, in 1707, he banned Islam and burned the mosques.

THE RENAISSANCE "DISCOVERY OF THE WORLD"

In the long run—according to traditional readings of world history—religious diversity, which arose from the splitting and mingling of religions in the sixteenth century, made the world more secular. People became less committed to their religions, because they had to live at peace with neighbors of different faiths. The mutual challenges of rival religions weakened all of them by comparison with other godless or materialistic ways of looking at the world.

But these changes, if they happened at all, took a long time to take effect. In Europe, for instance, in the sixteenth and seventeenth centuries, most of the ideas contemporaries denounced as atheism turn out, on close examination, rather to have been challenges to traditional Christian descriptions of God. Secular subjects did become more common in art, and religious subjects less so. But this may have had less to do with changing ideologies than with the economics of art. As wealth spread, so did art patronage. The Church's dominance of the art market weakened. Religions did become more mutually tolerant, in some places where they mingled, and forfeited their claims to exclusive truth. In other cases, however, the opposite occurred and, overall, on a global scale, religious warfare and persecution probably became more bitter and more widespread.

In the first half of the sixteenth century, fashions in learning, art, and letters informed by the inspiration of classical Greece and Rome, leaped from Italy, where they had originated, across Europe, in a movement traditionally called the Renaissance (see Chapter 15). During his invasion of Italy in 1515, King Francis I of France saw "all the best [art] works"; he began to collect casts of ancient sculptures and acquire the services of Italian artists, including Leonardo da Vinci (1459–1519). The sixteenth-century courts of Henry VIII of

Religious debate. The Mughal Emperor Akbar (r. 1556-1605) devised his own religion in an attempt to defuse conflicts among his subjects who were mostly Muslims and Hindus. He also presided over debates—like the one shown here from his album of paintings of the life of his court—in which Muslims, Hindus, Buddhists, Sikhs, and Christians (represented by black-robed Jesuits, whom Akbar greatly admired) were supposed to reconcile their differences. But the debates ended in bitterness and mutual antagonism.

England, the Habsburg Archduchess Mary of Hungary (who ruled the Low Countries for her nephew, the Emperor Charles V), Sigmund I and II in Poland and Lithuania, and Ferdinand I and Maximilian II in Austria and Bohemia became similar centers for spreading the Renaissance. In the 1520s, returning poets took Italian verse forms to Spain, Portugal, and England. In Spain, the great new buildings of the period—the cathedral and royal palace of Granada, the town hall of Seville, the hospital in Toledo—introduced a new look, based on classically inspired shape, harmony, proportions, space, and light. Beyond royal courts, the trade in engravings, the migrations of artists and scholars, and the taste of civic patrons, took the same classicizing tradition to the great cities of Germany and Switzerland.

Church architects tried to create spaces for the kind of devotion that study of ancient Christian texts endorsed, with open sanctuaries, brilliantly lit and approached through wide aisles and naves. Poets who scoured the reign of the Roman Emperor Augustus (r. 27 B.C.E.–14 C.E.) for models and churchmen who looked back to the time of Christ shared the same perspective. Virgil (70–19 B.C.E.), Augustus's favorite poet, was generally, if mistakenly, credited with having prophesied the birth of Jesus. Fusions of Christianity with classical philosophy became popular as never before since the fourth century, when Christianity conquered the thinking classes of the Roman Empire. Christian Platonism and Christian stoicism (see Chapter 6) were characteristic fashions of the era, and the most influential thinker of the first half of the sixteenth century, Erasmus of Rotterdam (1466–1536), made "the philosophy of Christ" a current term. The Italian sculptor Benvenuto Cellini's (1500–1571) *Crucifixion* expresses serene stoicism, rather than the searing passion earlier sculptors had represented. In a series of sculptures by Michelangelo (1475–1564), "captives" in human shape emerge from the coarse particularity of rocks. Michelangelo seems to have been trying to embody the notion that matter hides reality—which is spiritual—from our senses and that we need genius or grace to see it.

Meanwhile, the discoveries of explorers transformed the way Europeans pictured the world. They confirmed the vastness of the globe and disclosed the existence of a New World in the Western Hemisphere. In particular, the discoveries challenged European notions of what it means to be human, as encounters unfolded with a previously unsuspected range of cultures and civilizations (see Map 18.5).

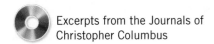
Excerpts from the Journals of Christopher Columbus

The most exciting moment of all occurred when Christopher Columbus first glimpsed what he called "naked people," on Friday, October 12, 1492, on an island he called San Salvador, which most scholars identify with Watling Island in the Bahamas. The natives were therefore probably Lucayos—a people of whom little is known, though archaeological evidence endorses Columbus's account of their material culture. His description deploys many of the categories, comparisons, and images available in his day to help Westerners understand other cultures. Many of his observations cut two ways. The natives' ignorance of warfare established their innocent credentials but also meant they would be easy to conquer. Their nakedness evoked a primitive Eden or an ideal of dependence on God, but also suggested savagery and similarity to beasts. Their lack of commercial skills showed that they were both morally uncorrupted and easily fooled. Their rational faculties made them identifiable as human and exploitable as slaves. Columbus seemed genuinely torn between conflicting ideas about the Native Americans. After all, he and his men were undergoing an experience no European had ever had before (see "Going to the Source: Columbus's Encounters in the New World," page 668–671).

Throughout his journeys to the New World, Columbus remained undecided between rival perceptions of the people—as potential Christians, as types of pagan virtue, as exploitable slaves, as savage, as civilized, as figures of fun. A long quest began to understand the diversity of humankind. Discoveries in the natural world complicated it. In the seventeenth century, as Europeans increasingly got to know the great apes of Africa and other primates, the problem of where to draw the limits of humankind grew increasingly puzzling. Discoveries about the human body kept pace with those of human cultures. Traditional ideas of human nature reeled under the impact of discoveries on every side.

Eyes adjusted slowly to the newly revealed realities. Influenced by missionaries eager to save souls among newly encountered peoples, the Church took a positive view of their natural qualities to protect them from secular exploitation and extermination. The question of whether the native peoples of the New World were fully human, endowed with rational souls, was settled—at least for Catholics—affirmatively by Pope Paul III in the 1530s, but their status needed frequent shoring up against slippage. Missionary scholars in the Americas built up files to demonstrate the social and political sophistication of native societies. A case like that of the Aztecs posed typical problems. Cannibalism and human sacrifice tarnished the record of a people who otherwise appeared highly "civil." In evidence—vividly painted by native artists at the court of the Spanish Viceroy of Mexico—compiled under missionary guidance in the 1540s, one can still see the range of qualities the clergy held up for admiration. The training of an Aztec candidate for the priesthood of the pre-Christian gods is shown in gory detail, as his teachers beat his body to bleeding. But this was evidence not of barbarism but of the similarity of Aztec values to those of their Franciscan evangelists, who also practiced devotional whipping and tortured their own flesh. The Aztec state was depicted as a well regulated pyramid, symmetrically disposed to administer justice, with an emperor at the top, counselors below him, and common pleaders at the lowest level: a mirror image of the society the missionaries had left back home. The Aztecs' sense of justice was shown to conform to the standards Europeans deemed natural. An adulterous couple, stoned to death, suggested a comparison with the ancient Jews and, therefore, openess to the milder Christian message. Justice was tempered with mercy. Though drunkenness among the Aztecs was punishable by death, the aged were depicted as enjoying exemption. Mild restraint took the place of

 Pope Paul III from *Sublimus Dei*

Michelangelo's "captives" are often described as unfinished. But they illustrate an idea of the ancient Greek philosopher Plato: Like captives from their bonds, or reality from the shadows, true forms emerge struggling from the rocks that enclose them.

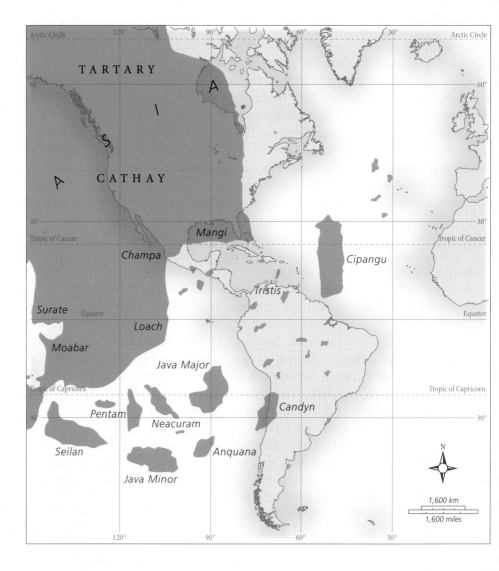

MAP 18.5

Columbus's View of the World in 1492

■ Columbus's assumptions

□ actual land area

TARTARY

A S I A

CATHAY

Mangi

Champa

Cipangu

Tristis

Surate   Equator

Loach

Moabar

Java Major

Tropic of Capricorn

Candyn

Pentam

Neacuram

Seilan

Anquana

Java Minor

1,600 km

1,600 miles

American cannibals

execution. When the Aztecs went to war, provocations on their enemies' part were shown to precede hostilities, which followed only after diplomatic efforts had been rebuffed. The natives, it seemed, practiced "just" war by traditional Christian standards—something that the Spanish monarchy strove to do with imperfect success. Missionaries could cite examples like these for every native community where they worked.

In the mid-sixteenth century, a Spanish bishop Bartolomé de Las Casas (1474–1566) was the loudest spokesman for broadening the definition of humankind to include Native Americans. He was a convert to conscience—an exploiter of Indian labor on Hispaniola, who reformed when he heard a Dominican preacher's challenge: "are the Indians not human beings, endowed with rational souls, like yourselves?" He joined the Dominicans and became the officially appointed Protector of the Indians. In effect, despite unsuccessful spells as a missionary and a frontier bishop, he was a professional lobbyist who managed, albeit briefly, to get the Spanish crown to legislate for Indian rights. Human sacrifice, according to Las Casas, should be seen rather as evidence of the misplaced piety of its practitioners, or of their pitiable state as victims of the devil, than as an infringement of natural law.

His conclusion—"All the peoples of mankind are human"—sounds self-evident, but it was a message important enough to bear repetition. It was applied patchily at first. Black people hardly felt the benefits for centuries. It made possible a new view of history, according to which all peoples were created equal, but passed through various universal stages of historic development. Broadly speaking, this model prevailed in educated European minds in the seventeenth and eighteenth centuries. Nicolás de Mastrillo himself—the young missionary with whom this chapter opened—was a glowing example. He went on to be head of the Jesuits in Peru.

THE RISE OF WESTERN SCIENCE

Partly because of privileged access to the recycled learning of classical antiquity and partly owing to the new data accumulated during the exploration of the world, Western science registered leaps in the seventeenth century that science in other parts of the world could not match.

If secularism did not displace religion to any great extent in the West, science did, in some degree, probably displace magic. Just by offering this opinion, we raise a problem: What is the difference between magic and science? Both are attempts to explain and therefore to control nature. The Western science of the sixteenth and seventeenth centuries grew, in part, out of magic. Starting with Marsiglio Ficino (1433–1499), an Italian priest and physician who worked for the Medici, the dominant family in the city of Florence, Renaissance writers argued that magic was good if it was used to heal or to accumulate knowledge of nature, and that some ancient magical texts were lawful reading for Christians.

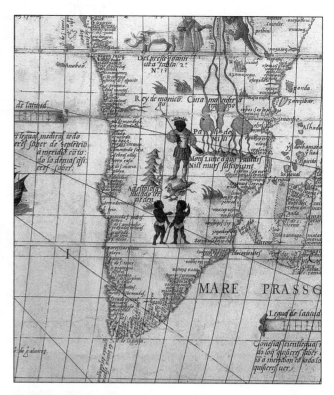

Renaissance view of Africans. The Italian navigator Sebastian Cabot's world map of the 1540s includes positive images of black Africans. The manicongo—the ruler of Kongo—appears with crown, scepter, and elegant European clothes. Pygmies, though small and poorly clad, carry sticks to prove their rational ability to use tools and "understand each other"—as the inscription on the map puts it—in civilized conversation.

The most influential text was the work supposedly written by an ancient Egyptian known as "Hermes Trismegistos" (Hermes Thrice-Blessed), but which was actually composed by an unidentified Byzantine forger. It arrived in Florence in 1460 among a consignment of books bought from the Balkans after the fall of Constantinople to the Turks in 1453 for the Medici library and caused a sensation. Renaissance scholars felt inspired to pursue "Egyptian" wisdom in search of an alternative to the austere rationalism of classical learning—a fount of older and supposedly purer knowledge than could be had from the Greeks or Romans. The distinction between magic and science as means of attempting to control nature almost vanished in the sixteenth century.

Doctor Faustus, who sold his soul to the devil in exchange for magical access to knowledge, was a fictional character, but he symbolized a real yearning. In his world, wisdom was supernatural knowledge. The Habsburg Emperor Rudolf II (r. 1576–1612), who patronized mysterious arts in his castle in Prague in what is now the Czech Republic, was hailed as the new Hermes. Here magicians gathered to probe the secrets of nature and to practice astrology, alchemy, cabbalism (the ancient mystical and magical wisdom of the Jews), and *pansophy*—the attempt to classify all knowledge and so unlock access to mastery of the universe.

None of this magic worked, but the effort to manipulate it was not wasted. Alchemy fed into chemistry, astrology into astronomy, cabbalism into mathematics,

Wonder chamber. In Europe in the late sixteenth and seventeenth centuries, art collection expanded to include the "curiosities" of nature and science. This seventeenth-century painting records the splendors of a Dutch gentleman's collection. Portraits of the owner and his wife preside over an array of objects that is modestly representative of the world: scenes from nature, the Bible, classical myth, and antique ruins—all the traditional sources of wisdom—are on the walls. A personification of the Tiber River—representing ancient Rome—is over the door. Wonders of nature—coral and shells—mingle with classical statues. On the tables, learned visitors contemplate the sphere of Earth and the heavens, and the new wonders revealed by exploration. In the center, the artist warns against religiously inspired vandals who destroyed art and learning.
Adriaen Stalbent (1589–1662) "The Sciences and the Arts." Wood, 93 x 114 cm. Inv. 1405. Museo del Prado, Madrid, Spain. Photograph © Erich Lessing, Art Resource, NY

and pansophy into the classification of nature. Would-be wizards constructed what they called "theaters of the world" in which all knowledge could be divided into compartments and displayed and "wonder chambers" where specimens of everything in nature could be gathered. The eventual outcome of this work included the methods for classifying plants, animals, and languages that we still use today. Wonder chambers developed into museums. Many of the great figures of the scientific revolution in the Western world of the sixteenth and seventeenth centuries either started with magic or maintained an interest in it. Johannes Kepler (1571–1630), who worked out the path of the planets around the Sun, was one of Emperor Rudolf's favorites. Sir Isaac Newton (1642–1727) was a part-time alchemist. The philosopher and mathematician Gottfried Wilhelm Leibniz (1646–1716) studied ancient Egyptian hieroglyphs (though he could not read them) and cabbalistic notation.

If Western science of the time owed a lot to magic, it gradually developed a direction of its own: toward empirical methods, rational explanations, and verifiable facts. One of the most conspicuous examples is the abandonment of the image of the universe centered on the Earth that appeared in the Bible and was generally accepted in the ancient world. In 1543, the Polish astronomer and churchman Nicolaus Copernicus (1473–1543) proposed reclassifying the Earth as one of several planets revolving around the Sun. His theory was formulated tentatively, advocated discreetly, and spread slowly. He received the first printing of his great book on the heavens when he was on his deathbed. It took nearly 100 years after his death to remold people's vision of the universe. In combination with the work on the mapping of orbits around the Sun published early in the seventeenth century by Johannes Kepler, the Copernican revolution expanded the limits of the observable heavens, substituted a dynamic for a static system, and wrenched the universe into a new shape around the paths of the planets, accurately represented. This shift of focus from the Earth to the Sun was a strain on eyes adjusted to an outlook that made the Earth the center of the universe. Every subsequent revelation of astronomy has reduced the relative dimensions of our dwelling place and ground its apparent significance into tinier fragments.

Scientific reasoning grew more systematic. Two particularly influential styles of thinking are illustrated—and were first fully formulated—in the work respectively of the English experimenter, Francis Bacon (1561–1626), and the French philosopher and logician, René Descartes (1596–1650). Bacon took

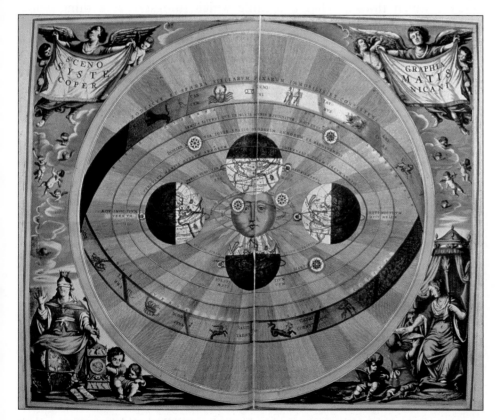

The Copernican Universe. Personifications of Justice and Learning flank a vision of the cosmos, as late seventeenth-century European scientists imagined it. A rim of stars, signified by the signs of the Zodiac, surrounds the six planets that were known at the time. The planets move around the sun in the elliptical orbits discovered by Johannes Kepler (1571–1630). The Earth, with moon attached, is no longer at the center of the universe. But as the most important planet, it is shown in detail, with emphasis on how day, night, and the seasons change as the Earth moves.

René Descartes, excerpt from
The Discourse on Method

from the Dutch scientist, J. B. van Helmont (1577–1644) the motto, "Logic is useless for making scientific discoveries." He prized observation above tradition and was said to have died a martyr to science when he caught a chill while testing the effects of low temperatures on a chicken. He devised the method by which scientists turn observations into general laws: the so-called **inductive method** by which a general inference is made from a series of uniform observations and is then tested. The result, if it works, is a scientific "law." Scientists can then use this to predict how natural phenomena will behave under similar circumstances.

Descartes, who affected laziness and detested the restless lives of active men such as Bacon (who also pursued an ambitious career in politics), made doubt the key to the only possible certainty. Striving to escape from the suspicion that all appearances are false, he reasoned that the reality of his mind was proved by its own self-doubts. His starting point was the age-old problem of **epistemology**: How do we know that we know? How do we distinguish truth from falsehood? Suppose, he said, "some evil genius has deployed all his energies in deceiving me." It might then be that "there is nothing in the world that is certain" except that "without doubt I exist [even] . . . if he deceives me, and let him deceive me as much as he will, he will never cause me to be nothing so long as I think that I am something." This left a further problem: "What then am I? A thing which thinks. What is a thing which thinks? It is a thing which doubts, understands, conceives, affirms, denies, wills, refuses, which also imagines and feels."[1]

The work of Isaac Newton typified the achievements of seventeenth-century Western science. In a bout of furious thinking and experimenting, beginning in the 1660s, he seemed to discover the underlying "secret of the universe" that had eluded the Renaissance wise men. He imagined the universe as a mechanical contrivance—like the wind-up models of the heavens in brass and gleaming wood that became popular toys for gentlemen's libraries. It was tuned by a celestial engineer and turned and stabilized by a universal force—gravity—observable in the swing of a pendulum or the fall of an apple, as well as in the motions of moons and planets.

Newton was a traditional figure: an old-fashioned humanist and an encyclopedist, obsessed by trying to determine the chronology of the Bible. He was even, in his wilder fantasies, a dabbler in magic, hunting down the secret of a systematic universe, an alchemist seeking the Philosophers' Stone, which legend said could turn base metals into gold. He was also a representative figure of a trend in the thought of his time: **empiricism**, the doctrine beloved in England and Scotland in his day, that reality is observable and verifiable through our senses. The universe consisted of events "cemented" by causation, of which Newton found a scientific description and exposed the laws. "Nature's Laws," according to the epitaph the eighteenth-century poet Alexander Pope wrote for Newton, "lay hid in Night" until "God said, 'Let Newton be!' and there was Light."

It turned out to be an act of divine self-withdrawal. Newton thought gravity was God's way of holding the universe together. Many of his followers did not agree on that point. Belief in a supreme being (though not

A vision of vision. The French philosopher Rene Descartes (1596–1650) described how we see things in his *Optics*, which was published in 1637. Light travels—in waves, Descartes guessed—between object and eye. The eye itself works like a lens, bending the light to form an impression. Science, like magic, had the power to make humans "masters and possessors of nature."

necessarily in God as Christianity describes him) throve in eighteenth-century Europe, partly because the mechanical universe could dispense with the divine "Watchmaker" after he had given it its initial winding. By the end of the eighteenth century, the French astronomer and mathematician Pierre-Simon de Laplace (1749–1827), who interpreted almost every known physical phenomenon in terms of the attraction and repulsion of atomic particles, could boast that he had reduced God to "an unnecessary hypothesis."

 Isaac Newton excerpt from *Opticks*

WESTERN SCIENCE IN THE EAST

It would be wrong, however, to speak of the rise of science at the expense of religion. There is no necessary conflict between the two, and no one in the sixteenth or seventeenth centuries, as far as we know, even suspected that there could be. Science did prove, however, in one respect, to be more powerful than any single religion. It showed more cultural flexibility, appealing more widely across the world. The spread of Christianity, Buddhism, and Islam was among the great movements of the age—but they all ran up against cultural limits. Buddhism grew mainly in Central Asia. Islam registered little appeal in Europe outside of the Turkish-controlled Balkans. Christianity was rejected in China and India and all but wiped out in Japan. The new Western science, however, had the power to penetrate everywhere. The cultural exchange that took Christianity to Asia also took Western science across Eurasia. Indeed, the same Jesuit scholars were the agents of both transfers.

In some respects, the intellectual climate in eastern Asia was unwelcoming to Western ideas. In the seventeenth century, a Confucian revival in China, Japan, and Korea impeded Western thought because it spread ancient Confucian prejudice against Western "barbarians." The Dutch, on whom, from 1639, Japan depended exclusively for information about the West, were generally regarded—said one of their few Japanese admirers—as "scarcely men, a sort of beast." According to the Korean Confucian scholar Yi T'oegye (1501–1570), "It is no exaggeration to liken [Westerners] to birds and beasts." In some ways, Japanese scholars welcomed the Western view of the world as undermining Chinese claims to cultural superiority and to China being the center of the world, but they hesitated to adopt Western ideas as uniquely true. When the Zen monk Ishin Suden (1569–1633) explained the nature of Japan as a "divine land," he used all the traditional language. In Confucian terms, Japan was "born of Earth and Heaven"; by Daoist thought, it was "grounded in the opposing principles of Yin and Yang"; and it was a "Buddha-land" for good measure.

In China, the change of dynasty of 1644 from the Ming to the Qing stimulated the Confucian revival. Because he did not want to serve rulers whom he considered to be usurpers, Wang Fuzhi (wahng foo-jih) (1619–1692) withdrew to the hills of Hunan in the distant south. There he celebrated the values of eleventh-century Confucians, and dreamed of "the order of heaven" restored on Earth. Gu Yanwu (goo yehn-woo) (1613–1682), similarly alienated from the new dynasty, returned to Confucian guidelines for life: "study all learning" and "have a sense of shame." Like any determined Renaissance scholar in Europe, he dedicated himself to "the search for antiquities." "Anything legible I copied by hand, and when I saw an inscription unseen by my predecessors I was so overjoyed that I could not sleep." He and his fellow scholars consciously guarded the spoils of time against erosion, damage, and oblivion.

This Chinese renaissance was comparable in kind with that of Europe's, but did not achieve the same effects. For the first time in recorded history, China slipped behind Europe, in some fields, in the rate of scientific achievement. On the whole, the global history of technology up to this time reflected consistent Chinese superiority. World-shaping innovations typically happened first in China. Take a few key examples. Printing and paper, the bases of modern communications until the late twentieth century, were Chinese inventions. So was paper money—without which modern capitalism would be unthinkable. So was gunpowder, the key to modern warfare. So were the rudder and the method of shipbuilding that protected the vessel against sinking by dividing the hull into separate compartments— these were vital innovations in the development of global shipping. The blast furnace, essential for modern industrialization, came from China, too. In what we think of as the late Middle Ages, however, Western technology edged ahead in two areas: clockwork and lens making (see Chapter 13). These came together in the science of astronomy.

The impact of Western astronomy in China is immediately visible in one of the world's most extraordinary books, the *Tianwen Lue* (tee-ehn-wen lehw) (*A Treatise on Astronomy*) that Manuel Dias, a young Jesuit missionary, wrote in Latin and, with native help, in Chinese in 1610—the year after the great Italian astronomer Galileo Galilei (1564–1642) first used a telescope to study the heavens. "Lately," Dias told Chinese readers, "a famous Western sage has constructed a marvelous instrument." Through the telescope, he said, "the moon appears a thousand times larger"; Saturn's rings become visible; "Jupiter appears always surrounded by moons. . . . The day this instrument arrives in China we shall give more details of its admirable use."

For a simple reason, Jesuit skill in astronomy was the most important of the many technical skills with which they impressed the Chinese. The Chinese Board of Astronomy, an official department of the Chinese imperial court, existed not for the disinterested study of the heavens but to devise a ritual calendar. The ceremonies of the imperial court were attuned to the rhythms of the stars, so that earthly order should reflect heavenly harmony. To perform the rites for movable feasts and unique occasions, the stars had to be favorable. The Chinese believed that the success of imperial enterprises, the survival of the dynasty, and the life of the empire depended on it. The environment of a star-struck court stimulated scientific knowledge. Though the Board of Astronomy was young—created in the early seventeenth century—the Chinese tradition in astronomy was ancient, and it had been practiced at court for centuries. The imperial observatory had a continuous history of some 400 years behind it, and the number and quality of recorded observations available to Chinese astronomers had been unequaled anywhere in the West until well into the sixteenth century.

Yet when the Jesuits arrived, their superiority over the Muslim personnel who then ran the observatory seemed so marked that the imperial court abandoned the entire native Chinese tradition and turned the practice of astronomy over to the newcomers. After a couple of false starts, the Jesuit Ferdinand Verbiest took over the Board of Astronomy in 1669 and systematically reformed the calendar. In 1674, at the emperor's request, the observatory was reequipped with instruments of Jesuit design. The rooftop observatory, with the instruments erected like shrines on little platforms, provided European engravers with one of their most popular Chinese pictures. The German mathematician,

Chinese armillary sphere

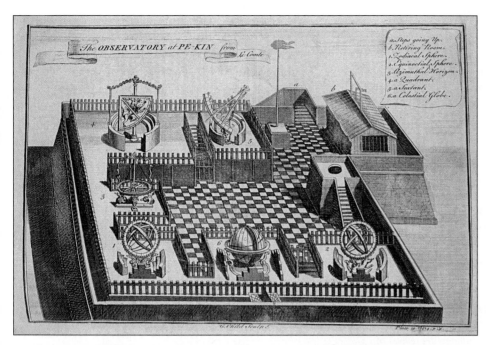

The Observatory at Beijing. In 1674, the Chinese government handed over the observatory at Beijing to the Jesuits for reorganization. Among the results was a new observatory, shown in this eighteenth-century engraving, that the Jesuits set up on the roof of the imperial palace using instruments built to European specifications. Some of these instruments have survived and have only recently been removed to a museum.

Gottfried Wilhelm Leibniz, was one of the greatest admirers of China in his day, devouring everything he could learn about the country from Jesuit writings. In 1679, he published his own book on Chinese learning. He believed that Chinese wisdom was superior to Europe's in civilized values, ethics, and politics: "I almost think," he wrote, "that Chinese missionaries should be sent to us to teach us the aims and practices of natural theology, as we send missionaries to them to instruct them in revealed religion." But he thought Europe was ahead in mathematics and what we would now call physics. The reversal in the balance of technical skill in Eurasia had begun. In succeeding centuries, similar reversals in historic patterns of power and wealth would elevate the West in other respects.

IN PERSPECTIVE: The Scales of Thought

Despite the shortcomings of the missionaries or of their congregations, the enormous extension of the frontiers of Islam, Buddhism, and Christianity remains one of the most conspicuous features of the world of the sixteenth and seventeenth centuries. Buddhism and Islam expanded into territories that bordered their existing heartlands. By overleaping the Atlantic and Pacific Oceans, Christianity registered a spectacular difference. Islam, however, had the advantage of expanding in the demographically vigorous worlds of Africa, Malaysia, and Indonesia, whereas the territories Buddhism won in northern Asia were vast but sparsely populated. As we saw in the last chapter, the millions Christianity won in the Americas quickly withered with the rapid decline of the Native American population.

CHRONOLOGY

Fifteenth century	Study of classical Greece and Rome provides foundation for the rise of Italian humanism
Fifteenth and sixteenth centuries	Merchants and missionaries spread Islam
Early sixteenth century	Martin Luther initiates Protestant Reformation in Europe
1500s	Spanish Christians compete with Muslims in the Philippines
Sixteenth and seventeenth centuries	Royal courts in northern Europe spread humanism; Contact with Native Americans challenges European notions of what it means to be human; elites take on task of "re-Christianizing" Europe
1520s and 1530s	Franciscans baptize millions of Native Americans
1540	Ignatius Loyola founds Jesuit Order
1543	Nicholas Copernicus proposes heliocentric theory
Mid–sixteenth century	Catholic Church begins Counter-Reformation
1545–1563	Council of Trent meets
1596–1650	René Descartes, French philosopher and proponent of deductive reasoning
1570s	Mongol ruler Altan Khan stimulates the revival of missionary Buddhism in Mongolia
Late sixteenth century	Mughal emperor Akbar attempts to establish the "Faith of God"
Seventeenth century	Jesuits lead Christian missionary effort in China
1621	Reformation in Eastern Orthodox Church begins
1630s	Missions initiated by Prince Neyici Toyin bring Buddhism to Manchuria
1639	Christianity banned in Japan
1669	Jesuit Ferdinand Verbiest takes over the Chinese Board of Astronomy
1687	Sir Isaac Newton publishes *Principia Mathematica*

In the long run, however, the sheer size of the New World counted for most. Because of the exclusion of Islam from the Western Hemisphere, Muslim predominance among world religions slipped in the eighteenth and nineteenth centuries, when the Americas made up and exceeded their lost population. In the balance of resources, Christendom acquired potentially vast extra weight.

Equally remarkable, and equally significant for the history of the world over the following few centuries, was the spurt of Western science and the recognition it achieved, in some respects, in China. Although China, the Islamic world, and, to some extent, India, had rich scientific traditions of their own, and although the Islamic world, like the West, had privileged access to the scientific legacy of the ancient Greeks and Romans, Westerners now caught up and pushed ahead in some respects. Of these, astronomy was of key importance in the seventeenth century because of the acceptance it won for Westerners in other cultures. And in the eighteenth century, Western superiority in military, naval, and industrial technologies would begin to be felt. The resulting shift in the world balance of power and resources is the subject we have to tackle next.

PROBLEMS AND PARALLELS

1. Why were the sixteenth and seventeenth centuries an unprecedented era in the revitalization of Buddhism, Christianity, and Islam? What role did missionaries play in this revitalization? How did the missionary strategies of these different faiths compare?

2. How successful were Christian missionaries in Asia, Africa, and the Americas? How did pre-Christian religious practices persist? What were the varieties of Christianity in the Americas? What kinds of new religious thinking emerged in India in this period?

3. How did the Renaissance "discovery of the world" impact European thinking and spirituality? How did their encounters with non-Western cultures transform the way Westerners saw the world?

4. Why were the sixteenth and seventeenth centuries significant in the development of Western science and secular values and in the transmission of Western science to other parts of the world? What was the relationship of Western science to magic? How did this relationship evolve over time?

5. How was Western science received in the East? What Western ideas were most welcome in the East and which were not? How were the Jesuits agents of cultural exchange in Asia?

DOCUMENTS IN GLOBAL HISTORY

- Hideyoshi on Christian missionaries in Japan
- Excerpts from the journals of Christopher Columbus
- Pope Paul III from *Sublimus Dei*
- American cannibals

- René Descartes, excerpt from *The Discourse on Method*
- Isaac Newton, excerpt from *Opticks*
- Chinese armillary sphere

Please see the Primary Source CD-ROM for additional sources related to this chapter.

READ ON

J. D. Tracy, *Europe's Reformations* (1999) is a reliable account but J. Bossy, *Christianity in the West* (1985) and J. Delumeau, *The Catholic Church from Luther to Voltaire* (1977) are radical and searching. My account follows F. Fernández-Armesto and D. Wilson, *Reformations* (1997). On China and Indonesia respectively, I am indebted to W. J. Peterson, 'Why Did They Become Christians?' Y. T'ing-yün, L. Chih-tsao and H. Kuang-ch'i' in J. W. O'Malley et al., eds, *The Jesuits: Cultures, Sciences and the Arts, 1540–1773* which is an important collection generally, and A. Meersman, *The Franciscans in the Indonesian Archipelago, 1300–1775* (1967). M. C. Ricklefs, *A History of Modern Indonesia: c. 1300 to the Present,* (1981) is an excellent general history that traces Islamic missionary efforts in Indonesia in the seventeenth century. On Buddhist missions, W. Heissig, *The Religions of Mongolia* (2000) is fundamental, as is M. Hodgson, *The Venture of Islam* (1977) on Islam.

R. Ricard, *The Spiritual Conquest of Mexico* (1966) is an enduring classic. P. U. Bonomi, *Under the Cope of Heaven: Religion, Society, and Politics in Colonial America* (1986) and S. Schwartz, *"A Mixed Multitude": The Struggle for Toleration in Colonial Pennsylvania* (1987) explicate the emergence of religious diversity in North America's Middle Atlantic colonies in the seventeenth century. M. Deren, *Divine Horsemen: The Living Gods of Haiti* (1985) is the best introduction to the Afro-Caribbean religion A. Métraux, *Black Peasants and their Religion* (1960) is an enduring classic.

J. Rubiés, *Travel and Ethnology in the Renaissance. South India through European Eyes, 1250–1625* (2000) is a brilliant analysis of European perceptions of religious diversity in India during the Renaissance. L. Jardine, *Worldly Goods: A New History of the Renaissance* (1998) re-examines the cultural achievements of the Renaissance in the context of the material and commercial world that produced them. L. Jardine and J. Brotton, *Global Interests: Renaissance Art between East and West* (2000) sets the global context.

S. Shapin, *The Scientific Revolution* (1998) examines how the world of seventeenth century scientists shaped their understanding of nature. A. Grayling, *Descartes* (2006) is up-to-date, readable and provocative; L. Jardine and A. Stewart, *Hostage to Fortune: the Troubled Life of Francis Bacon* (1999) is masterly. J. Waley-Cohen, "China and Western Technology in the Late Eighteenth Century." *American Historical Review* (1993) traces the reception of various western technologies, including gunpowder, in China. M. Jacob, *Scientific Culture and the Making of the Industrial West* (1997) offers a detailed analysis of how the cultural dissemination of Newtonian mechanics affected the emergence of industrial technology, especially in Britain.

CHAPTER 19

States and Societies: Political and Social Change in the Sixteenth and Seventeenth Centuries

Queen Nzinga. In 1622, before she came to the throne of Ndongo, Nzinga made a treaty with the Portuguese. This contemporary engraving shows her conducting negotiations, seated on a slave's back to avoid standing in the presence of a white man of lower rank than herself.

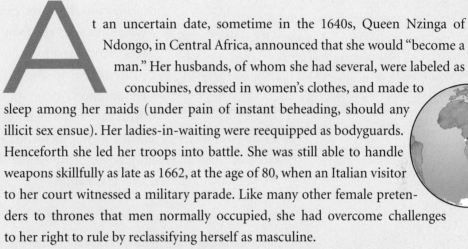

NDONGO

At an uncertain date, sometime in the 1640s, Queen Nzinga of Ndongo, in Central Africa, announced that she would "become a man." Her husbands, of whom she had several, were labeled as concubines, dressed in women's clothes, and made to sleep among her maids (under pain of instant beheading, should any illicit sex ensue). Her ladies-in-waiting were reequipped as bodyguards. Henceforth she led her troops into battle. She was still able to handle weapons skillfully as late as 1662, at the age of 80, when an Italian visitor to her court witnessed a military parade. Like many other female pretenders to thrones that men normally occupied, she had overcome challenges to her right to rule by reclassifying herself as masculine.

The decision to switch gender was not the first challenging transformation in Nzinga's life. She came to power as regent for her nephew, the rightful king according to the normal rules of succession, in 1615, but, fearful of having to surrender power, she killed him and declared herself queen. In 1622, she adopted Christianity, less—it seems—out of conviction than to secure Portuguese help against the enemies who sought to dethrone her. She used the ferocious mercenaries known as Imbalanga—private war bands that grew by kidnapping boys—to fight her battles. When they cheated her, she vowed to "become an Imbalanga" herself and lead her own war band. As this involved bloody rituals of sacrifice, cannibalism, and child killing, she had to renounce Christianity. But she returned to the faith in the 1640s to obtain more reliable help again from the Portuguese.

Hers was a surprising and bizarre career. In one respect, however, it was a representative episode of early modern politics. All Nzinga's self-transformations were strategic moves in her struggle for power in Ndongo—a hard-fought series of wars, in which she repeatedly clawed her way back from defeat and repeatedly returned victorious after being driven from her realm. That struggle was part of a longer, broader, deeper story of political change that many parts of the world echoed: the rise of strong, central monarchies, the subduing of unruly aristocracies, the shift of power from the hands of nobles into those of royal dependants.

- **HOW DID** European rulers strengthen their power in the sixteenth and seventeenth centuries?
- **WHY WERE** the Ottomans able to build such a successful and long-lasting empire?
- **WHAT ROLE** did Shiite Islam play in Safavid Persia?
- **HOW DID** Chinese society change under the Qing dynasty?
- **HOW DID** the Tokugawa shoguns govern Japan?
- **HOW DID** the "creole mentality" affect Spanish America?
- **WHAT ROLES** did African states play in the Atlantic slave trade?
- **WHAT COMMON** features affected the development of states all over the world during this period?

In the 1560s, when Portuguese explorers, slavers, and missionaries first described Ndongo, it was a loosely defined kingdom, where big landowners wielded the most power and claimed the right to elect the monarch. Over the next few decades, kings asserted their hereditary right to the throne, without the need to consult the nobility. They also used slaves as administrators, wrenching authority away from aristocrats and confiding it to their own creatures. Nzinga was the slaves' candidate for kingship. Her first rivals in the wars she fought to secure the throne were nobles. Her attachment to the hereditary principle was passionate. Twice she lost control of the burial grounds of her ancestors. Twice she defied military priorities to win them back and defend them at heavy cost. Her effort to assert the legitimacy of female rule was successful. Her nominee, her sister, Barbara, succeeded her as queen. Women occupied the throne of Ndongo for 75 of the 100 years that followed Nzinga's death.

• • • • •

Nzinga's realm was small, but fiercely contested. As we look around the world of political and social change in the sixteenth and seventeenth centuries in this chapter, first at Europe, then at parts of Asia and the Americas before returning to Africa, we see similar conflicts unfold, albeit with many differences from region to region and state to state, as monarchs searched and struggled to redistribute power to their own advantage, and new or newly empowered classes contended for a share in the growing might and resources of states.

POLITICAL CHANGE IN EUROPE

Europe already had a state system (see Chapter 11). Events of the sixteenth and seventeenth centuries enshrined the system and made the political reunification of Western Europe—which had been a dream or mirage since the fall of Rome—unthinkable for centuries. There were three principal reasons for this.

First, the ideal of Western political unity faded as the various European states solidified their political independence and exerted more control over their inhabitants. Hopes of such unity had focused in the Middle Ages on the prospect of reviving the unity of the ancient Roman Empire. The term *Roman Empire* survived in the formal name of the group of mainly German states—the Holy Roman Empire of the German Nation—that an elected emperor ruled. When King Charles of Spain was elected to be Emperor Charles V in 1519, the outlook for uniting Europe seemed favorable. Through inheritance from his Habsburg father, Charles was already ruler of the Netherlands (modern Belgium, Holland, and Luxembourg), Austria, and much of Central Europe (see Map 19.1). His propagandists speculated that Charles V or his son would be the "Last World Emperor" foretold by prophesy, whose reign would inaugurate the final age of the world before the Second Coming of Christ. Naturally, however, most other states resisted this idea, or tried to claim the role for their own rulers. Charles V's attempt to impose religious uniformity in

the form of Roman Catholicism on his empire failed, demonstrating the limits of his real power. After his abdication in 1556, no one ever again convincingly reasserted the prospect of a durable universal state in the tradition of Rome.

Second, the power of individual European states increased rulers' power against rivals to their authority and the states' power over their own citizens. In 1648, almost all European states signed the Treaty of Westphalia, which ended a long war that had devastated much of Central Europe in the name of religion. The treaty gave rulers the right to impose their religions on their subjects. Though most European states experienced civil wars in the sixteenth and seventeenth centuries, monarchs usually won them. Cities and churches surrendered most of their privileges of self-government. Aristocracies—their personnel transformed as old families died out and rulers elevated new families to noble status—became close collaborators in royal power, rather than rivals to it, as aristocrats had been so often in the past. Offices under the crown became increasingly profitable additions to the income that aristocrats earned from their inherited estates. Countries that had been difficult or impossible to rule before their civil wars became easy to govern when their violent and restless elements had been exhausted or became dependent on royal rewards and appointments. England and Scotland had been particularly hard for their monarchs to tax in the sixteenth and early seventeenth centuries. The so-called Glorious Revolution of 1688–1689, which its aristocratic leaders represented as a blow against royal tyranny, actually turned Britain into Europe's most fiscally efficient state. In place of a dynasty committed to peace, the revolution installed rulers who fought expensive wars. Taxation trebled during the reign of the monarchs the British revolutionaries crowned.

Finally, Spain, the only power capable of imposing unity on Europe, failed. Spain seems, in retrospect, an unlikely superpower. It was itself a weakly united monarchy, consisting of several distinct states, each with its own languages and laws, linked only by imperfect allegiance to a single dynasty. The biggest of these states—Castile and Aragon—permanently shared the same monarchs only from 1516. Castile acquired two other states—Granada in the south and Navarre in the north—in conquests as late as 1492 and 1511 respectively. Spain's internal resources were small compared with those of France, which probably had, at the start of the sixteenth century, a population twice as big, substantially more territory, a more favorable climate, and enormously more productive farmland. About a third of the surface of Spain is mountainous or virtually desert.

Yet Spain was unrivaled for military and naval effectiveness in Europe throughout the sixteenth century and well into the seventeenth, while also maintaining, man for man and woman for woman, Europe's best-educated population and generating some of the continent's most vibrant art and literature. Knowledge of Spanish became, like French today, a mark of education among Europe's elites.

How was Spain's strength possible? It was the result, in part, of the feebleness of its potential competitors. France spent much of the period racked by civil wars between aristocratic factions and did not fulfill its potential until the late seventeenth century, after the last of the wars was over. England, crippled by a low tax yield and split by religious dissent, failed to exploit the maritime advantages of its strategic position between the Atlantic and the North Sea. Germany was only a geographical expression, a loose collection of semi-independent states, incapable of working together. Poland, though vast in area at the time, had insecure frontiers and a powerful nobility that defied or crippled royal power. Italy was a muddle of small states that no one could unify and only Spain could dominate. As a result, smaller, less naturally favored states had moments as major powers: Sweden for much of the seventeenth century, Holland in the second half of it.

Spain had the advantage of privileged access to the silver mines of Mexico and Peru. But the importance of the silver sent back to Spain was not so much in its total value as in its predictability. While these shipments remained regular, until the second or third decade of the seventeenth century, they gave Spanish kings much better credit ratings than other rulers of the time. The total contribution silver imports made to the cost of sustaining Spanish power was small compared with the yield from taxation in the realm of Castile. Moreover, in contrast to most of the rest of Europe, where rivalry for power among monarchs, nobles, and city authorities caused frequent breakdowns and occasional wars, Castile was exceptionally united in loyalty to its monarchs. The close collaboration of crown and aristocracy began in the conquest of Granada from the Muslims, from 1480 to 1492. It was cemented in the early 1520s, when crown and aristocracy combined to suppress rebellion in some cities, and this collaboration lasted until the 1640s, when the aristocratic spirit of service to the crown collapsed—and tax revenues collapsed along with it. Moreover while religious conflicts divided other parts of Western Europe, Spain became increasingly united religiously. Almost all minority religious communities—Jews, Muslims, the few Protestants—were subjected to forcible conversion, or persecuted out of existence. Finally, Spain's opportunity resulted in part from a factor ever present in monarchical state systems: dynastic accident. Throughout the period, the ruler of Spain also ruled southern Italy and Sicily. From 1519 to 1556, Castile's king happened also to be ruler of the Holy Roman Empire. From 1504 until 1648, Spanish monarchs were nominally rulers of the Netherlands—though substantial parts of those countries were permanently in revolt from the 1570s. Between 1580 and 1640, kings of Spain were also undisputed kings of Portugal and of its vast overseas possessions in Africa, Asia, and Brazil.

There was a moment in the 1580s and 1590s when Spain seemed able to bid for the role of arbiter of Europe, or even—in the minds of some Spaniards, who fantasized about conquering Cambodia, China, and Japan—of the world (see Map 19.2).

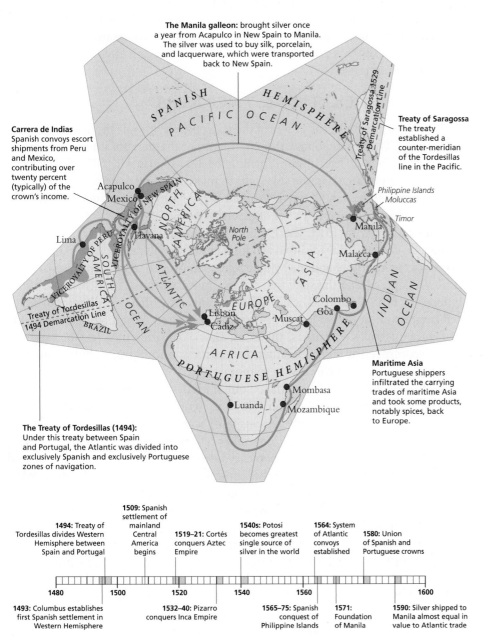

The Manila galleon: brought silver once a year from Acapulco in New Spain to Manila. The silver was used to buy silk, porcelain, and lacquerware, which were transported back to New Spain.

Carrera de Indias
Spanish convoys escort shipments from Peru and Mexico, contributing over twenty percent (typically) of the crown's income.

Treaty of Saragossa
The treaty established a counter-meridian of the Tordesillas line in the Pacific.

The Treaty of Tordesillas (1494):
Under this treaty between Spain and Portugal, the Atlantic was divided into exclusively Spanish and exclusively Portuguese zones of navigation.

Maritime Asia
Portuguese shippers infiltrated the carrying trades of maritime Asia and took some products, notably spices, back to Europe.

MAP 19.2

The Spanish Monarchy in 1600

- Dominions of the king of Spain
- Carrera de Indias
- Portuguese trade with maritime Asia

1494: Treaty of Tordesillas divides Western Hemisphere between Spain and Portugal

1493: Columbus establishes first Spanish settlement in Western Hemisphere

1509: Spanish settlement of mainland Central America begins

1519–21: Cortés conquers Aztec Empire

1532–40: Pizarro conquers Inca Empire

1540s: Potosí becomes greatest single source of silver in the world

1564: System of Atlantic convoys established

1565–75: Spanish conquest of Philippine Islands

1571: Foundation of Manila

1580: Union of Spanish and Portuguese crowns

1590: Silver shipped to Manila almost equal in value to Atlantic trade

1480 1500 1520 1540 1560 1600

Jean Bodin, from *Six Books of the Commonwealth*

Machiavelli, excerpt from *The Prince*

In 1588, Spain sent against England the first of a series of invasion fleets, the Spanish Armadas, all of which were turned back or wrecked by bad weather but which demonstrated England's vulnerability to invasion. In the early 1590s, the uniform success of Spanish armies in mainland Europe made the conquest of France and the suppression of Netherlandish rebels seem likely. And all this happened while the frontiers of the Spanish monarchy continued to advance in the Americas and Asia.

Still, the success proved unsustainable. The 1590s were a turning point, as the loyalty of Philip II's (r. 1556–1598) subordinate kingdoms showed signs of strain, state revenues ebbed, and a catastrophic decline of population, which would last for most of the seventeenth century, began. By the time Philip II died, he had already decided to leave to his heir a policy of peace. When that peace broke down in a general renewal of conflicts in Western Europe in the 1620s, the strain proved unbearable. Spanish naval supremacy in the Atlantic wavered in the late 1620s and faltered in northern Europe in the 1630s. In the following decade, Spanish armies' long unbroken record of victory collapsed with major defeats by the French.

Meanwhile, serious rebellions broke out in Naples and Catalonia, and Portugal recovered its independence in 1640. Despite an impressive recovery in the eighteenth century from this critical low point, Spain never again attempted to outclass all Europe's other powers.

WESTERN POLITICAL THOUGHT

Along with the growth of the power of the state, the way people thought about politics changed. They came to take the sovereignty of the state for granted. A French political philosopher, Jean Bodin, formulated the doctrine in 1576. Sovereignty defined the state, which had the sole right to make laws and distribute justice to its subjects. Sovereignty could not be shared. There was no portion of it for the church, or any sectional interest, or any outside power.

More radically, in 1513, the Florentine historian and office seeker, Niccolò Machiavelli, challenged traditional thinking about the purpose of the state. Political theorists of antiquity and the Middle Ages recommended various kinds of state, but they all agreed that the state must have a moral purpose: to increase virtue or happiness or both. Even the Legalist school in ancient China (see Chapter 6) advocated oppression in the wider interest of the oppressed. When Machiavelli wrote *The Prince*, his rules for rulers, the book shocked readers not just because the author recommended lying, cheating, ruthlessness, and injustice, but because he did so with no apparent concession to morality.

Machiavelli cut all references to God out of his descriptions of politics and made only mocking references to religion. The only basis for decision making was the ruler's own interest, and his only responsibility was to retain his power. He should keep faith only when it suits him. He should pretend virtue. He should also pretend to be religious. Machiavelli's other books are strongly republican in sentiment, and he may have intended *The Prince* to be ironical. Irony, however, can be the hardest form of rhetoric to detect. Later thinking borrowed two influences from *The Prince*: first, the doctrine of **realpolitik**, which says that the state is not subject to moral laws and serves only itself; second, the claim that the end justifies the means and that any excesses are permissible to ensure the survival of the state, or public safety, or national security, as some later formulations put it. Meanwhile, among moralists, *Machiavel* became a term of abuse, and the devil became known as "old Nick."

In the absence of any overriding authority or mechanism for sharing sovereignty, the European state system needed international laws. When Thomas Aquinas (see Chapter 12) summarized the previous state of thinking in the Western world in the thirteenth century, he distinguished the laws of individual states from what he called the **law of nations**, which all states must obey and which governs the relationships between them. Yet he never said what this law was or where or how it could be codified. Many jurists assumed it was just natural law or the basic, universal principles of justice—but this is also hard to identify in complex cases. The Spanish Jesuit theologian Francisco Suárez (1548–1617) solved the problem in a radical way. The law of nations "differs in an absolute sense," he said, "from natural law" and "is simply a kind of positive human law." It says whatever people agree it should say.

This made it possible to construct an international order along lines first proposed earlier in the sixteenth century by one of Suárez's predecessors at the University of Salamanca in Spain, the Dominican Francisco de Vitoria, who advocated laws "created by the authority of the whole world"—not just pacts or agreements between states. In 1625, the Dutch jurist Hugo Grotius worked out the system that prevailed until the late twentieth century. Natural law obliged states to respect each other's sovereignty. The commercial and maritime laws that they formally ratified or traditionally embraced, and the treaties they made between themselves regulated relations among them with the strength of contracts, enforceable by war. This system did not need the support of any particular ideology or religion to back it. It could embrace the world beyond Christendom. It would remain valid, Grotius said, even if God did not exist.

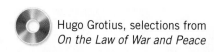
Hugo Grotius, selections from *On the Law of War and Peace*

WESTERN SOCIETY

Modern societies are divided into horizontally stacked classes that are defined according to their income or wealth—upper class, middle class, working class. But in the sixteenth and seventeenth centuries, classes intersected with other structures, in which most people were more likely to situate themselves: vertical structures—interest groups, professions, trades, the entourages and clients of powerful noblemen and officials, social orders, such as the nobility or the peasantry, religious sects, clans—whose members' sense of mutual belonging depended on the differences they felt between themselves and outsiders rather than on shared values, wealth, priorities, or education (see Figure 19.1). The elite estates or social groups, the nobility and clergy, were not classes in any sense that a modern market researcher or opinion pollster would recognize. They were communities of privilege uniting people of hugely different degrees of wealth whose tax privileges and legal advantages marked them out from the rest of society. A prince-bishop ruling a semi-independent state like Cologne in Germany or Liege in Belgium belonged to the same clerical estate as a penniless priest who wandered from parish to parish saying mass for a fee. Nobility embraced a duke with an income exceeding a king's and a rural nobleman whose only possession was a lance for hire.

Cities formed communities of a similar kind, jealous of their jurisdiction, walled against the world, and fortified in their civic identities by the enjoyment of economic "liberties"—such as the right to hold markets or fairs, or levy tolls

FIGURE 19.1   ORGANIZATION OF SOCIETY IN THE SIXTEENTH AND SEVENTEENTH CENTURIES COMPARED TO MODERN SOCIETIES

(a) Modern societies

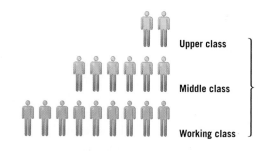

Upper class

Middle class

Working class

Classes of people differentiated by income, wealth, shared values, or education

(b) Societies in sixteenth and seventeenth centuries

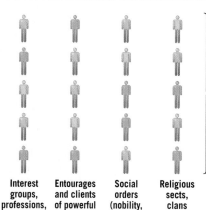

Widely varying groups whose sense of mutual belonging depends on differences between themselves and outsiders

Interest groups, professions, trades | Entourages and clients of powerful noblemen and officials | Social orders (nobility, peasantry, etc.) | Religious sects, clans

Las Meninas or ***The Maids of Honor.*** By universal acclaim, Diego Velázquez (1599–1660) was one of the most skillful painters ever, but he spent most of his time devising entertainments and designing interiors for the court of Philip IV of Spain. Service to the crown could elevate even a painter to noble rank. In one of his most famous works, Velásquez shows himself with the insignia of knighthood, painting the king and queen in the company of their daughter and her maids of honor. The intimacy and informality the royal family display in this painting were new features of court portraiture of the time.

on travelers or merchandise. In most countries, Jews formed similar communities, also distinguished by economic and legal privileges as well as disabilities. So did the Protestant minorities in France and Poland. The kinsmen and retinues of noble families had some of the same characteristics, often embracing poor and remote relations as well as retainers at every level of wealth and rank, tenants, servants, and other dependants, who gathered for festivals or accounting days and sometimes lived together in considerable numbers under a single vast roof, eating their meals in common. On a smaller scale, the "families," as they were usually called, or extended households of urban artisans, with generations of apprentices sharing their roofs, had the same characteristics.

A vast, slow process of erosion changed this way of organizing society. In most of Europe, the family was redefined as an ever-smaller knot of close kin. Between the sixteenth and eighteenth centuries, in aristocratic households, family dining rooms came to provide a privileged retreat from the communal life of the great hall of the medieval castle. This was true even for kings. Court portraits of Philip IV (r. 1621–1665) of Spain and Charles I (r. 1625–1649) of England reveal a world of nuclear families, in which the royal children and parents cluster together. In Protestantism, the family grew in importance because so many other structures of life—religious brotherhoods, guilds, and monasteries—were abolished. The glittering courts of monarchs sucked provincial aristocracies away from their estates and hereditary followings, breaking the bonds of vertical structures. "Take but degree away," as a character says in a play of William Shakespeare's, written around 1602, "untune that string and hark! What discord follows!" Everywhere that string was retuned to the clink of moneybags, as monarchs put titles up for sale. "Ducats make dukes," quipped an early seventeenth-century Spanish satirist.

Women's status was transformed. In Padua in northern Italy in the 1550s, the anatomist Gabriele Falloppio sliced open women's cadavers and found that they worked in unsuspected ways. Women were not just nature's bungled attempts to make males, as earlier medical theory claimed. In the late Middle Ages, there had been isolated and discouraging examples of women in power as regents or sovereign queens. Now women rulers appeared in unprecedented numbers in Europe. Some—like the flighty Mary, Queen of Scots (r. 1512–1567), or Catherine de' Medici (1519–1589), Regent of France—reenacted in their lives cautionary tales of the biblical Eve: submitting to lovers or favorites, manipulating menfolk. To the Scots Protestant preacher John Knox (ca. 1513–1572)—expressing a common opinion strongly—women in power were a "monstrous" aberration. But most women rulers earned praise for what Elizabeth I of England (r. 1558–1603) called her "heart and stomach of a king." In other words, men praised them for ruling like men even though they were women.

In ordinary homes, struggles between different forms of Christianity gave new importance to women's traditional domain—as the guardians of household routine. Mothers were the hearthside evangelists who transmitted simple religious faith and devotional practice from one generation to the next. Their choices ensured, in some places, the survival of Catholicism, in others the rapid progress of Protestantism. Women who married according to the clergies' new rules (see Chapter 18) could be better protected against male predators and more secure in keeping their property when their husbands died. In late seventeenth-century Massachusetts, the Puritan preacher Cotton Mather believed women were morally superior beings, because of their constant fear of death in childbirth.

There could, however, be no corresponding increase in what feminists today call women's "options." New economic opportunities on a sufficient scale were unavailable until industrialization that began in the late eighteenth century. Widowhood remained the best option for women who wanted freedom and influence. The most remarkable feature of this situation, which might have tempted wives to murder, is that so many husbands survived it. In most of sixteenth- and seventeenth-century Europe, husbands committed more detected domestic murders than wives. And women, despite their improved status, were still often victims: beaten by husbands, scolded by confessors, repressed by social rules, and cheated by the courts. "Long Meg of Westminster"—hero of an English story of 1582—proves her superiority over men in a series of fair fights, but "never let it be said," she announced when she married, "that Long Meg shall be her husband's master."

Conflicts along class lines were rare. The so-called Wars of Religion between Catholics and Protestants in sixteenth-century France resembled old-fashioned civil wars, in which aristocrats recruited private armies from their retainers, relatives, and tenants to battle each other. Other sixteenth-century rebellions were of the same character, or else were the protests of threatened minorities, such as Catholics in England and Ireland, or descendants of Moors in Spain. Or else they were assertions of provincial identity, like those of Aragonese who rioted against Spanish royal power in defense of their provincial liberties in 1590, or Netherlanders who rose up in 1568 against the foreign methods and officials of an absentee monarch, Philip II of Spain. The English Civil Wars of 1640–1653 used to be held up as a classic case of class revolution—the birth pangs of bourgeois society, struggling to emerge bloody from the womb of feudalism. But the war seems better understood as a mixture of a traditional rebellion, a provincial revolt against intrusive central government, a struggle of "ins" and "outs," and a genuine war of religion.

Patterns of social change were not uniform across Europe. From the fifteenth century, an economic divide opened in Central Europe. The fault line ran roughly along the Elbe and upper Danube Rivers. In the west, peasants could take advantage of intense demand for labor and a relative glut of exploitable land. Forms of land tenure grew more diverse. Traditional limitations on peasants' freedom to move and acquire property weakened. Similar conditions prevailed selectively in Eastern Europe. In parts of Brandenburg in Germany, for instance, the countryside had so few people in the fifteenth century that noble landlords took to the plow themselves. Generally, however, as Eastern Europe gradually took over the Mediterranean basin's former role as grain supplier to the continent, landlords increasingly restricted peasants' freedom to sell their labor.

This was a remarkable reversal of the course of history as conventionally understood. In the Middle Ages, such restrictions on peasants had not been a characteristic institution of the regions where it now began to take root. Indeed, at modest social levels, colonization beyond the Elbe had been the work of peasant escapees from a society

Queen Elizabeth I. Although it upset many men, women rulers became familiar figures in sixteenth-century Europe. Elizabeth I of England (r. 1558–1603) had her image boosted by icons like this frontispiece to a book of 1579. The inscription that appears below her throne—"her form shines to behold"; peace, "while wars fatigue neighboring peoples"; and knowledge, "while blind errors afflict the world"—sounds the themes of royal propaganda: Love embraces war, and explorers brandish scientific equipment. Yet England's real achievements at the time in science and exploration were minor, and Elizabeth, surrounded by aggressive advisors, could not keep England at peace or out of Europe's wars.

Demon barber: Czar Peter the Great (r. 1682–1725) enforces conformity to the religion of the state in Russia. The Old Believers, religious dissidents who split from the Russian Orthodox Church in the 1660s, believed that beards were part of the image of God, and that therefore it was a sacrilege to shave. Peter saw beards as signs of Russia's backwardness and of resistance to his rule, and he imposed a tax on facial hair.

of restricted opportunities and lordly oppression in the west. Now even the free towns, in Poland, eastern Germany, the Czech Republic, Slovakia, and Hungary, lost their rights of jurisdiction on a massive scale to aristocrats and rulers. In Poland, Hungary, and Bohemia, the nobility reclaimed or enforced their right to elect the king. A world of aristocratic dominance was emerging.

Traditional notions about nobility became entrenched. According to István Werbočky, Hungary's key theorist on this issue in the early sixteenth century, only the nobles were the nation. Their privileges were rights of conquest, inherited from presumed Hunnic and Scythian ancestors. Other classes descended from natural slaves or criminals. Werbočky did acknowledge that new men could join the aristocracy "by the exercise of martial discipline and other virtues and gifts of mind or body." But to him these were means to strengthen a hereditary caste—not, as most Westerners maintained, methods to open up a social group to outsiders.

Despite these growing differences between East and West, Peter the Great of Russia (r. 1682–1725) tugged and wrenched the frontier of Europe eastward by striving to make Russia more like Western Europe. It was an information revolution—a transfer of technology as well as fashion and taste from West to East. Peter's reforms redesigned his empire. He moved the capital from Moscow to the new city of St. Petersburg that he built on the Baltic, redrafted the Russian alphabet, and remodeled the aristocracy's facial hair. A popular print showed a demon barber executing Peter's command that the Russian nobility shave off their beards to make them look like "modern" European aristocrats. Preachers called Peter the sculptor and architect of Russia, remolding the country, carving the palace furniture with his own hands. He allowed women out of the home where traditional Russian practice had tried to confine them. He made two great journeys through Europe in semidisguise to learn Western ways. His role models were foreign: Dutch, German, Swedish. He aimed to be for his country both Romulus and Numa—the founder, that is, of ancient Rome and the king who supposedly crafted its laws. He appeared in engravings in Roman tradition, baton-wielding on a rearing horse, with the title "Imperator" (emperor) engraved in Roman letters. He seriously considered making Dutch the official language of his court. He became an honorary Danish admiral and a member of the French Academy of Sciences. But rebels regarded him as Antichrist or, at best, the, satanic imposter of a true czar. Western admirers saw him as Russia's modernizer, but the report of a visit to St. Petersburg illustrates the uneasy, short-term impact of his reforms. High society there, said the report, was just like those of Paris or London, except that Russian ladies still put cosmetic blacking on their teeth. Henceforth, Russia was permanently part, by wars or alliances, of European politics. Peter the Great's daughter, Elizabeth (r. 1741–1762) was the last ruler of her dynasty, the Romanovs, in the male line. Thereafter, all the czars were products of the European dynastic marriage market.

Peter's policy, and, in particular, his decision to relocate the capital of Russia on the Baltic, should be considered in a further context: the northward shift of Europe's center of gravity. The newly rising powers of the seventeenth century—the Netherlands, Sweden, England, France—were all in the north. So were some of the most spectacularly growing cities—Amsterdam, Paris, London. The Mediterranean seemed stagnant by comparison. It was in the north that the great global trading companies and banks arose. There were undeniable advantages to

○ MAKING CONNECTIONS ○

FACTORS CONTRIBUTING TO EUROPEAN STATE-BUILDING

HISTORICAL DEVELOPMENTS →	INFLUENTIAL CONTRIBUTING FACTORS →	SOCIAL AND POLITICAL CONSEQUENCES
Renaissance: development of Western political thought	• Sovereignty becomes dominant way to indentify the state • Retaining power becomes dominant political motivation • Need for international cooperation leads to commercial, maritime laws	• Machiavelli's *The Prince* becomes handbook for gaining and maintaining power • Law of nations becomes important factor in states honoring each other's sovereignty • The "ends justify the means" to ensure states' survival
Spanish dominance 1500–1600	• Access to silver mines of Mexico, Peru • Relatively unified monarchy; aristocracy ennobled by service; religious hierarchy • Developed superior military and naval forces • Dynastic connections	• First wealthy colonial superpower controls Portugal, much of Africa, Asia, Central and South America; challenges England, France; controls much of Italy, Netherlands, Germany • Economic, military decline in seventeenth century leaves opening for other European states
Social transformation of Europe	• Smaller family units become primary social unit • Intermarriage between aristocratic, royal families • Expansion of the role of women as moral exemplars	• Religious conflicts supercede class conflict • Increasing economic freedom, opportunity for urban dwellers • Traditional notions of nobility become entrenched • Western "progress" becomes a model for Peter the Great of Russia and others

being in business in northern rather than southern Europe in the sixteenth and seventeenth centuries. Inflation flowed from south to north—stimulated by new sources of gold and silver, by new forms and expanded levels of credit, and by the demand an increase of population created. This meant goods were cheaper in the north. Northerners used that price advantage to break into the Mediterranean in the late sixteenth century. Demand for their shipping helped—to bring in grain to meet food shortages and to counter losses to Turkish and North African piracy. From shipping, northerners diversified into slaving and banking, handling—and creaming off—the wealth of the cash-rich empires of Spain and Portugal, diverting the trade of Venice and the eastern Mediterranean.

THE OTTOMANS

Europe's shifting axis of wealth affected the Ottoman Empire, a partly Mediterranean power. Yet this was a state that straddled Europe and Asia and, as we saw in Chapter 16, combined diverse traditions of political thought. The nerve center of the empire was the sultan's palace in Constantinople, the Topkapi Saray (TOHP-kah-puh sah-REYE-yuh). Its layout embodies much of the way the sultans thought about their role and is a guide to how politics worked.

Early Modern Europe: Politics, Ideas, and Society

Sixteenth through eighteenth centuries	Nuclear family grows in importance
1513	Machiavelli writes *The Prince*
1519	Charles V becomes Holy Roman Emperor
Mid to late sixteenth century	French Wars of Religion
1576	Jean Bodin formulates doctrine of sovereignty
1588	Defeat of the Spanish Armada
1618–1648	Thirty Years' War
1640s	Strain of empire precipitates decline of Spanish power
r. 1682—1725	Peter the Great attempts Westernization of Russia

The throne room is a pavilion, and many apartments are scattered through the grounds, like the tents of a nomad camp. The imperial stool is big enough for a sultan of the most morbid obesity. This was an empire that sustained memories of its ancient nomadic origins through centuries of sedentarism.

The harem could accommodate 2,000 women, the stables 4,000 horses. The scale of everything in the Topkapi palace attests to the size of the empire and the effectiveness of Ottoman authority. The grounds of 7,500,000 square feet enclosed 10 mosques, 14 bathhouses, and 2 hospitals. The kitchens were equipped to serve 5,000 diners daily and 10,000 on holidays.

The Topkapi was a fortress, a sanctuary, and a shrine. The bustle of the outer courts, where the kitchen noise competed with the clatter of the guards, contrasted with the inner silence of the sacred spaces where the sultan was cocooned, close to his vast collection of relics of the prophet Muhammad. Here, according to a visitor in 1700, "even the horses seem to know where they are."

Inside the sultan's private quarters, with its lavish alleys and secret hideaways, we can sense the hidden methods of government. Here talk was of politics: pillow talk and conversation in the baths, as well as the diplomatic encounters and the sultan's meetings with his ministers. In the absence of rules of succession to the throne, women and eunuchs conspired to manipulate the transfer of power from one sultan to the next. Sultans commonly exercised their privilege to put their brothers to death as security against rebellion, or confined them in the luxurious prison quarters known as the cages. A knock on the door might be a summons to become sultan or the rap of an executioner: Sultan Ibrahim I (EE-brah-heem) (r. 1640–1648) heard both and mistook each for the other. Access to a sultan's mother or favorite concubine was an avenue of political influence. For much of the seventeenth century, the effective chief executives of the state were queen

Ogier Ghiselin de Busbecq, "Women in Ottoman Society"

The Sultan's birthday party. Members of the imperial family, officials, and dignitaries line up, one by one, in strict order of protocol, to congratulate Ottoman Sultan Selim III (r. 1789–1807) in the Topkapi Palace in Istanbul. Konstantin Kapidagli, the painter, was highly favored at the sultan's court and imitated by painters in the West.
Dagli Orti/Picture Desk, Inc./Kobal Collection

mothers who knew little of the world beyond the harem walls, but who learned much from spies and servants, and who can be seen in paintings of court life, listening, from behind elaborate screens, to audiences with ambassadors and political council meetings.

Though Western visitors all went away heady with the exotic scents of palace life, the efficiency of the Ottoman state from the fifteenth to the seventeenth centuries could rival any Western competitors, many of whose traditions it shared. Other empires of nomadic origins failed to keep up with advances in the technology of war, but the Ottomans could float a vast navy, batter the walls of Byzantium with cannons in 1453, or blow away the Safavid cavalry of Persia with muskets. The modernization of the army influenced social change. The traditional aristocracy, the mounted "protectors"—cavalrymen who served in war and were maintained by tribute—lost roles and revenues.

The direction and balance of the conquests, which, in the fifteenth and sixteenth centuries, tilted toward Europe, gave the sultans access to huge numbers of Christian subjects, who paid discriminatory taxes and supplied a quota, the **devsirme** (dehv-SHEER-meh), of their male children to serve as Muslims in the elite slave army, the **Janissaries**, or in the sultan's administration. In the seventeenth century (see Chapter 15), the Janissaries became a hereditary corps, probably at the cost of their military efficiency, and conquests on the Christian front ceased.

To Western observers, the sultan seemed a model of despotism. He made and unmade laws, both religious and secular, at will. His subjects had no rights against his anger. And unlike Christian rulers, sultans had no need of a Reformation to curb the power of clergy. Though they had to be wary of the moral vigilance of the Islamic clerical establishment, as caliphs as well as sultans, they controlled the power structure of Sunni Islam themselves. Westerners regarded Ottoman government as disturbingly alien, but in the 1570s, the Ottoman jurist Ebu us-Suud (EH-boos-SOOD) produced a justification of the ruler's power that revealed a thorough command of Roman law and was not unlike Jean Bodin's near-contemporary theory of sovereignty in France. Still, the Ottoman system was unquestionably more autocratic than anything European "absolute" monarchs could manage. Even allowing for the inefficiencies that arise when preindustrial technology transmits commands over vast distances, the dominions of Sultan Murad IV (moo-RAHD) (r. 1623–1640) were more tightly reined to the center than those of his counterparts in most of Europe. His Spanish contemporary, Philip IV, for instance, was generally regarded as the most powerful Christian king of his day. He ruled multiple kingdoms with the aid of an up-to-date bureaucracy, but without an overarching source of authority. In different places, his rule was known by different titles, legitimized by different theories, embodied in different institutions, and constrained by different laws. Not so Murad's.

In most of the Ottoman Empire, for instance, the sultan's representatives were chosen in a remarkably uniform way. It is not true, as Europeans used to say, that these men were all in a formal sense the sultan's slaves. The head of the civil service, the Grand Vizir was indeed a slave, but lesser officials and provincial governors were drawn from every class and every part of the empire. Typically, in the sixteenth century, they trained as pages in the sultan's household before taking provincial commands, where they were maintained by revenues from designated areas. They rose through the administrative ranks of the provinces to which they were assigned.

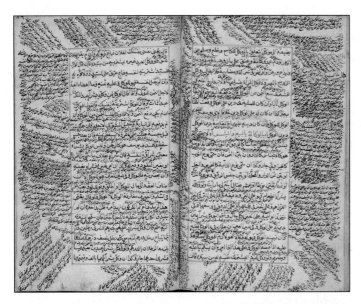

Ottoman law book. Written in Arabic in Istanbul in 1517 by Ibrahim al Halabi, the Islamic legal textbook known as *Multaqa al-Abhur (Confluence of the Currents)* remained an authoritative guide to the laws of the Ottoman Empire for 300 years. It contains rules for almost every human activity: spiritual rites, domestic relations, inheritance, commercial transactions, and crimes. The section shown here refers to buying and selling done by third parties. Various commentators made notes on this copy of the text.

Military and administrative life was incomparably the best route to wealth in the empire. Provincial governors made more out of their offices than even the richest merchants made from trade. The emphasis was not quite on plunder to the same extent as in Mughal India. Suleiman the Magnificent (r. 1520–1566; see Chapter 16) regulated the fees courts charged to litigants and practiced restraint in taxation and exploitation as part of the ideology of the state. Still, rational exploitation of subjects' wealth was the aim of the rulers of the empire. *Dirlik* (DEER-leek)—the term applied to provincial government— literally meant "wealth."

Increasingly, in the seventeenth century, the need to make the state efficient in war, in the face of the mounting costs of modern weaponry, drove changes in administrative practices. The lower ranks of the provincial administration became a career dead end, as governors came more and more from the army. The result was the rise of enormously powerful provincial governors. When some of them rebelled in 1658, the state barely mustered the resources to beat them.

Despite the central training of the ruling elite, and its close dependency on the sultan, it is easy to overrate the degree of control the empire exercised in the provinces. The system could perhaps best be characterized as centralization tempered by chaos. Rival governors, for instance, sometimes got simultaneous letters of appointment to the same place and were left to fight it out. Banditry usurped authority—fed with manpower by deserters from the army and peasants whom immoderate tax gatherers forced into outlawry. In a typical incident in 1606, Canbolado lu Ali Pasha (jahn-boh-LAHD-oh-loo AH-lee PAH-shah), a notorious bandit chief, proposed to police the eastern front on the Persian border with 16,000 men in exchange for lucrative governorships for himself and his kin. The sultan granted his request. The following year, the army overthrew him, but his success shows at once a weakness of the state and a manipulative skill sultans had to practice. Many states of the time faced problems with bandits, but most tried to deal summarily with them. The Ottomans negotiated with them and tried to manipulate them. This was typical of the Ottoman approach, which was always flexible and adaptable. There was one law, but it could always be modified to take into account local custom. The sultan derived his authority from religious principles, but these could be emphasized in different ways to suit different communities. Uniform rules, in theory, governed taxation, but in practice it was arbitrary and changeable.

Historians always tend to date "decline" too early, because they know what follows. To speak of Ottoman decline in the seventeenth century seems premature. It might be fairer to say that the Ottomans ceased to expand. In 1683, the attempt to capture the Habsburg capital Vienna failed, and in subsequent treaties, the Ottomans gave up further ambitions in Europe. If they faltered, it was not so much because of imperfections in their system of government—which, after all, had proved itself in the past—as because of an unexplained stagnancy in the population of their empire. Its growth did not match those of the populations of Europe, India, China, or Japan. And in the eighteenth century, population growth slowed, relatively speaking, even more.

MUGHAL INDIA AND SAFAVID PERSIA

Like that of the Ottomans, the empire of the Mughals in India throve on the economic success of the people they ruled. Or perhaps it would be fairer to say that the Mughals and their subjects enriched each other. The Mughals' fantastic demand for revenues stimulated economic inventiveness and forced peasants to produce for urban markets. Spectacular spending on war, buildings, and luxuries recycled wealth and restimulated an economy that high taxation might otherwise have stifled.

The Mughals' understanding of the nature of sovereignty was rooted in their conviction that they descended from Timur and ultimately from Genghis Khan (see Chapters 13 and 15). The names they gave their children and their dynasty reflect their Mongol and Islamic heritage. They ran their empire as a conquest—which, of course, it was, but it is more usual for conquerors to come to identify with the realms they rule. As we have seen (see Chapters 16 and 17), outside the relatively small, centrally administered core of the empire, Mughal methods of control relied on dividing tribute among a network of their relations, followers, clients, and allies. Like the Mongols and the Ottomans, they never established clear rules of succession to the throne. Every reign saw dynastic rebellions and wars of succession. Rivalries and alliances shifted unstably. The Mughals had always to balance the conflicting claims of rival aristocracies—the descendants of Timur, the Afghans and Persians who helped establish the dynasty in the 1520s, and the native Indian warrior chiefs on whom they relied increasingly to keep their empire together and extend it. A painting for the emperor Akbar (r. 1556–1605) captures a familiar scene. A chain gang of captured rebels—some of them clad as beasts, others stripped naked—appears at his palace, shaking their chains defiantly, while their captors exult.

The emperor Aurangzeb (r. 1658–1707) found the formula to keep the system going for a time: constant war to keep the aristocracies occupied, and continual conquests to multiply their rewards. A new generation of leaders arose, "born in the camp," as one of his ministers observed. New nobles, recruited from

Captive rebels arrive at the palace of the Mughal Emperor Akbar (r. 1556–1605) in 1573, wearing animal skins to symbolize the unnatural perversity and bestiality of the act of rebellion. The emperor is offstage to the right, because it would diminish his dignity to depict him in the company of rebels. The painting is one of a series Akbar commissioned to commemorate the great events of his reign.

Isfahan, a vital center of trade, provides unmistakable evidence of the power, wealth, and dynamism of Safavid Persia. In this illustration, from the 1725 edition of *Voyages to Moscow, Persia, and the East Indies* by the Dutch traveler Cornelis de Brun (1652–1726), a camel caravan approaches the city.

the frontier regions of the Deccan in south India as Aurangzeb's conquests grew, were promoted above old ones, getting the choicest shares of tribute. Newcomers composed nearly half the upper ranks of the aristocracy by the end of the reign. Restlessness and rebellion in the heartlands and older conquests were among the results as ambitious or disaffected nobles clashed with each other and fought with the imperial administration. Rural disruption and loss of revenues followed. In part, the Mughal Empire was a victim of its success. It expanded too fast to sustain the system of keeping nobles dependent by assigning them revenues. Still, when he died in 1707, Aurangzeb left a treasury stuffed with reserves greater than Akbar's.

Squeezed between the Ottomans and the Mughals, the Safavids of Persia (1501–1773) ran, in some respects, a similar state to both of them, with universalist rhetoric, a nominally all-powerful ruler, and flexible relationships between the ruler and subordinate sources of authority. Like the Ottomans, the Safavids benefited from the growth in trade across Eurasia: especially, in the Safavid case, in the silk trade of the lands they ruled. Like the Ottomans, they drew on ancient traditions of kingship, as well as Muslim political thought, to legitimize their rule. The first ruler of the dynasty commissioned a lavishly illustrated history of the ancient Persian kings. Their rules of succession were, like the chaotic systems that prevailed among the Ottomans and Mughals, divisive and bloodily enforced. Shah Abbas I (ah-BAS), the Great (r. 1588–1629) imprisoned his sons and exterminated his remoter relations. Isfahan (IHS-fah-hahn), his capital, resembled a great Indian or Ottoman city, full of unmistakable evidence of power, wealth, confidence, and energy. Its central plaza was seven times the size of St. Mark's Place in Venice. The goalposts installed there for games of polo were of marble. At one end, the great mosque was offset at an angle to guarantee a good view of the domes and minarets, displayed behind a gate 90 feet high. There were 273 public baths and 1,802 inns for commercial caravans.

Nevertheless, Safavid rule never relied on the kind of uniform bureaucracy the Ottomans used. Practices resembling those of the Mughals kept them in power. Except in some frontier regions, where they relied on accommodations with local rulers, the Safavids deployed a hereditary class of warrior horsemen of Turkic origin, known as the Qizilbash (KIH-zihl-bahsh), to enforce taxation and repress rebellion. As time went on, however, the Qizilbash tended to put down roots in the regions they ruled and frequently became rebels themselves. To tie elite loyalties firmly into the center, the Safavids used marriage, distributing the womenfolk of the ruling house around the provinces. Where possible, rulers exterminated troublesome Qizilbash clans or replaced them with their own personal representatives. But the dynasty rarely had the power to put these devices into practice.

The Safavids, however, practiced politics that were unique in two respects. First, they were fiercely Shiite. They contemplated neither the religious pluralism of the Mughals nor the toleration of the Ottomans. They wanted to rule an exclusively Shiite Muslim people. Shiism was the basis of their claim to legitimacy. Religious minorities were forced to convert or were persecuted toward extinction. Second, the Safavids had no nostalgia for a mythic

Excerpts from the biography of Shah Abbas I

Flagellants. Iranians shout religious slogans and beat themselves with iron chains in Tehran during the Shiite religious festival of Ashura in March 2004. Ashura marks the day when Imam al Hussein, the "leader of the martyrs" and grandson of the prophet Muhammad, was killed in Karbala in 680 C.E. in what is today Iraq.

steppelander past. On the contrary, they claimed to be enemies of the nomads, and as we saw in Chapter 17, defeated the Uzbek steppelanders (see Map 19.3).

The Safavids' religious policies are hard to understand, since—at the start of the period—most of the people they ruled were not Shiites. A desire to have a distinctive ideology, in opposition to that of the Ottomans, seems to have impelled them. Or perhaps, like Akbar in India, they wanted a religion of their own. Like so many dynasties—like Islam itself—warrior holy men, who turned tribesmen from deserts and mountains into formidable armies founded the Safavid dynasty. The first Safavid shah, Ismail I (shah ihs-mah-EEL) (r. 1501–1524), was a visionary who conversed with a vision of Muhammad's nephew Ali (see Chapter 8) and who appears, from his powerful, egocentric poetry, to have considered himself to be an incarnation of God. To a Venetian traveler, it seemed that throughout Iran "the name of God is forgotten and only that of Ismail remembered." He imposed Shiism by force. But force is never enough to change emotional allegiances. In subsequent reigns, dazzling, frightening ceremonial impressed Shiism on the people's minds. In 1641, a visiting Western observer described a typical ritual, designed to commemorate the death of one of the great martyrs of Shiism: a terrifying mock

Letter from Selim I to Shah Ismail I

MAP 19.3

The Safavid Empire, 1501–1736

- Safavid Empire, 1722
- territory under Ottoman control 1722
- Mughal Empire, 1722
- easternmost limit of area contested by Ottomans to 1736
- ➤ Uzbek invasion, 1587
- *Uzbeks* people

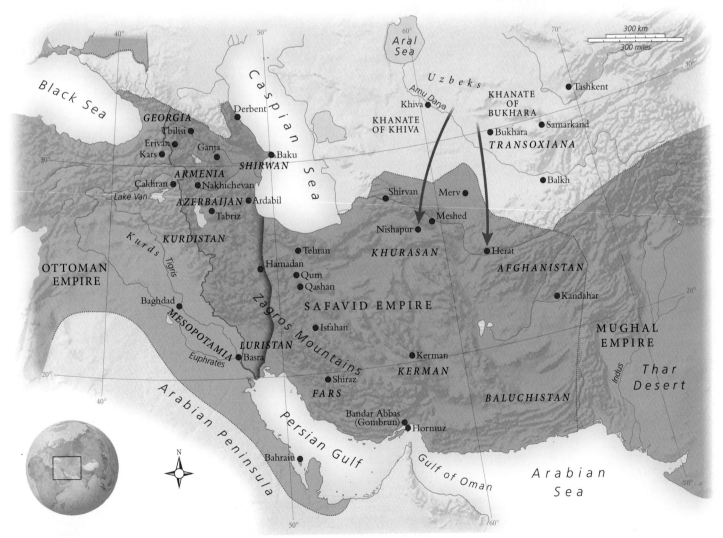

A SAFAVID BATTLE TUNIC

Talismanic shirts, designed to protect the soldiers who wore them in battle and ensure victory over enemies, were worn throughout the Muslim world from the fifteenth century onward. This Safavid battle tunic, most likely from the late sixteenth century, was designed to be worn next to the warrior's skin and is embroidered with verses from the Quran.

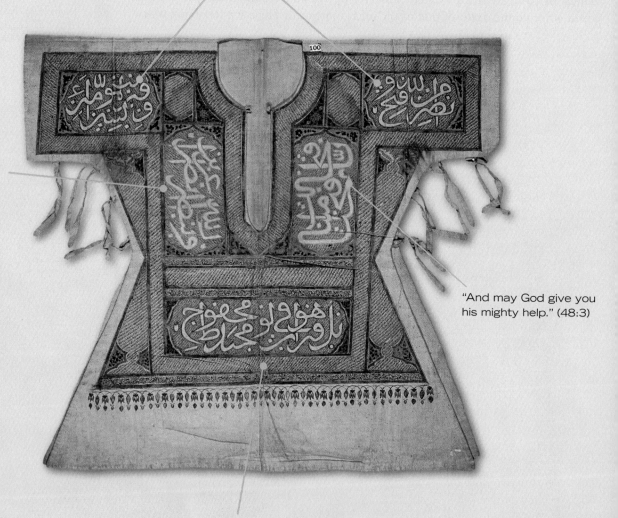

"Help is from God and speedy victory. So give the good news to the believers." (61:13)

"Truly we have given you a glorious victory." (48:1)

"And may God give you his mighty help." (48:3)

"This is the Glorious Quran, preserved in writing." (85:21–22)

Why was there a close connection between religion and war in Safavid Persia?

conflict, a melee of horses, camels—some painted black to appear more fearsome—and "naked persons who struggled and screamed as if in despair, gashed with wounds, which they beat to make them spurt blood." An accompanying parade featured mourning women, and children, dressed in hides that were pierced with arrows and smeared with blood. Throughout such ceremonies, messages of hatred were directed against the supposed heirs of the martyr's murderers—the Safavids' Sunni Ottoman neighbors.

Paradoxically, perhaps, Safavid rulers never seemed very pious—tending to exempt themselves from Islamic rules about drink and sex—until one of the last shahs of the dynasty, Husain (r. 1694–1722), who engraved Islamic law in stone, smashed the 6,000 wine bottles in the imperial cellars, forbade song, dance, coffee, games, and prostitution, and banished even respectable women from appearing in the streets. In retrospect, these commands seem like a desperate attempt to capture the allegiance of an alienated clergy.

It is remarkable not so much that the Safavids ultimately failed as that they succeeded for so long. Whereas the Ottomans and Mughals were able to renew their strength by making new conquests, the Safavids' opportunity to match that means of success were limited. Ismail I thought himself invincible. When Ottoman artillery stopped his cavalry at the Battle of Chaldiran (CHAHL-dih-rahn) in Iraq in 1514, he flew black banners inscribed with the word *revenge*. But he never achieved that revenge. Ismail withdrew into a world of drinking and womanizing. The Safavids did make some gains on the Turkish front later in the sixteenth century, and Safavid armies won impressive successes well into the seventeenth century. They raided Ottoman Baghdad twice. Scores of thousands of Georgian, Armenian, and Circassian prisoners were drafted into the slave corps that served the shahs as administrators. Portuguese intruders were turned out of the Persian Gulf. But the strength of the Ottomans to the west and of the Mughals to the east left the Safavids nowhere to expand.

Islamic Empires: The Ottomans, Safavid Persia, and Mughal India

Fifteenth and sixteenth centuries	Ottomans create an elite slave army, the Janissaries
1501–1722	Safavid dynasty in Persia
r. 1501–1524	First Safavid ruler, Shah Ismail I, imposes Shiism by force
1520s	Afghans and Persians help establish Mughal power in India
1570s	Ottoman jurist Ebu us-Suud justifies the Sultan's power
1658	Rebellion of provincial governors against Ottoman authority
1683	Ottomans fail to capture Vienna and cease conquests on the Christian front
r. 1658–1707	Emperor Aurangzeb engages in almost constant warfare in India
r. 1694–1722	Last Safavid ruler, Husain, imposes strict Islamic law
ca. Eighteenth century	Mughal power begins irreversible decline
1857	End of Mughal Empire

CHINESE POLITICS AND SOCIETY

While Europe became ever more divided among competing states, and the Ottoman, Mughal, and Safavid Empires consolidated, the unity of China survived potentially devastating threats.

Under the Ming dynasty (1368–1644), sixteenth-century China enriched its subjects. Fernão Mendes Pinto, a Portuguese window shopper in Beijing, walked around markets "as if in a daze" at the "silk, lace, canvas, clothes of cotton and linen, furs of marten, musk ox, and ermine, delicate porcelain, gold- and silver plate, seed pearls and pearls, gold dust and gold bullion." And as for the base metals, gems, ivory, spices, condiments and foods—"well, all these things were to be had in such abundance that I feel there are not enough words in the dictionary to name them all." The wealth gap between China and most of the rest of the world probably went on increasing over the next two centuries, as demand soared for newly popular goods in which China dominated world markets: porcelain, fine lacquerware, tea, ginseng, and rhubarb. By the mid–seventeenth century—before prolonged civil wars limited its growth—China probably contained about a third of the population of the world.

Chinese porcelain. Ming dynasty porcelain bowls from China, with their distinctive blue and white glazes, make superb ceiling ornaments. Two hundred sixty of them decorate a room in the Santos Palace in Lisbon, Portugal. The ceiling dates from the 1660s, but some of the bowls are more than a century and a half older.

Excerpt from Chinese Eunuchs: *The Structure of Intimate Politics*

Chinese Politics

The emperors' authority, unlimited in theory, was restricted in practice by the power of the 20,000 or so scholar **mandarins** who ran the administration. They qualified for their jobs by passing competitive examinations in knowledge of classical Confucian texts. In consequence, most of them never questioned Confucian ideas. They wanted emperors to stick to the performance of sacred rites and the administration of justice. The empire, they felt, was best left in a state of peaceful balance, without undertaking the risks of aggression against its neighbors. Traditionally, emperors had escaped the control of bureaucrats by appealing to other factions, such as the Buddhist clergy, the court eunuchs, and the army. In the sixteenth century, however, the supremacy of the mandarins appeared unshakable. The emperor was not allowed to leave the capital—ostensibly, to prevent the delegation of power into profane hands while he was away. For example, the Zhengde (jehng-duh) emperor (r. 1505–1521) moved out of the palace and surrounded himself with eunuchs and monks. In a series of incidents beginning in 1517, he insisted on going on campaign on the Mongol frontier, in defiance of the mandarins, to escape the suffocating presence of his ministers. But he was obliged to abandon the expeditions when the scholars, in effect, went on strike, crippling the administration.

The gravest crisis arose in 1587, when the Wanli (wahn-lee) emperor (r. 1572–1620) resolved to defy the mandarins. Evidence of widespread corruption in the civil service had undermined his confidence in the moral order traditional Confucianism recommended. He proposed to assert his power by altering the rules of succession, passing over his eldest son in favor of a son by his favorite concubine. Factions supporting the rivals traded accusations of witchcraft and distributed pamphlets among the people. After ten years of stalemate, in which government effectively came to a halt, the emperor backed down. Intellectual trends reflected the shift in the location of power. The philosopher Li Zhi (lee jeh) wrote a new version of Chinese history, in which emperors counted for nothing, and the heroes were mandarin ministers of state. The effectiveness of Ming government was never fully restored after this crisis.

The Ming Empire seemed unable to cope with ecological disasters—floods and famines—in the 1630s. The peasant rebellions that followed became civil wars as independent army commanders fought each other to control or even capture the throne. Meanwhile, from about 1590, the Ming delegated defense on the Mongol frontier to the northwest to Nurhaci, a chief of a pastoral war band in Manchuria (see Chapter 17). Chinese support enabled him to unite the Manchus. He began to call himself emperor and to represent himself as the spiritual heir of Manchu ancestors who had conquered northern China in the twelfth century. In 1636, Nurhaci's successor, Abahai, decreed a new ideology, which he called "Qing." The name was an allusion to "pure" water, which would quench the "bright" flame of "Ming." After intervening decisively in China's civil wars, the Manchus methodically and bloodily took over the country, proclaiming the Qing (chihng) dynasty.

It was a long drawn-out business. The last Ming claimant to the throne was executed in 1662. The last Ming loyalists were not rooted out from their nests on the island of Taiwan until the 1680s. Yet it was the partisans of the defeated dynasty who dictated ideology to the newcomers.

The shock of conquest by the Manchus made Chinese intellectuals rethink the whole basis of political legitimacy. The most startling and innovative result was the development of a doctrine of the sovereignty of the people, similar to that of Western Europe. Huang Zongxi (hwang dzohng-shee) (1610–1695) thought that a state of nature had once existed when "each man looked to himself" until benevolent individuals created the empire. Corruption set in, and "the ruler's self-interest took the place of the common good. . . . The ruler takes the very marrow from people's bones and takes daughters and sons to serve his debauchery." Lü Liuliang (loo lee-o-lee-ahng) (1629–1683) went further: "The common man and the emperor are rooted in the same nature." "It might seem as though social order was projected downwards to the common man," but, from the perspective of heaven, "the principle originates with the people and reaches up to the ruler. . . . Heaven's order and Heaven's justice are not things rulers and ministers can take and make their own."

Yet, whereas in the West, this sort of thinking helped to justify republics and generate revolutions, nothing comparable happened in China until the early twentieth century, when a great deal of Western influence had done its work. There were plenty of peasant rebellions under the Qing whose rule lasted until 1912, but, as throughout the Chinese past, these revolts aimed to renew the empire and replace the dynasty, not end the imperial system and transfer the **mandate of heaven** from a monarch to the people. Unlike the West with the memory of ancient Greece and Rome, China had no examples of republicanism or democracy to look to in its history or idealize in myth. Still, the work of Huang, Lü, and similar theorists passed into Confucian tradition. It helped to keep radical criticism of the imperial system alive and prepare Chinese minds for the later reception of Western revolutionary ideas.

Chinese Society

China experienced a sometimes violent revolution in the ownership of land. Peasant revolts in the 1640s challeged landowners' privileges. An incident from 1645 shows what was going on. A powerful clan's poor relation called Huang Tong (hwang tohng) roused tenants "for the pleasure of working off their petty grievances"—as a hostile court official put it—into attacking his rich kinsmen. He broke into the county capital and, after looting and bloodletting, tore down the walls. Over the next few decades, the government gradually abolished limitations on peasants' freedom to sell their labor. In 1681, peasants could no longer be sold along with the land they farmed but were free to "do as they please." The last restrictions on peasant freedom were swept away in the early eighteenth century. As a result, the landlord life became less attractive. Land was still valued as a source of prestige or security, but agriculture was despised as "the labor of fools," while peasant fierceness made rent collection "a task to be feared." Individuals determined to reacquire ancestral lands no longer sought to restore estates that had been broken up by dividing the property among all the heirs. China became increasingly a land of peasant smallholders. Rural investment took the form of pawnbrokering by city-dwelling loan sharks who lent money to peasants to buy seed grain. A history of hatred between city and country began that has lasted to this day.

So in China, as in Europe, economic change broke down some of the traditional structures of society. Migrations probably contributed to the effect. The clan, or extended family that persisted from one generation to another, however, was a social structure that could not be destroyed. Ancestor worship made the clan into a religion. The administrative system perpetuated its role because Chinese clans, thousands strong, combined to select the best candidates from among their members to take the exams to enter the civil service and become mandarins. The rich members of the clan would pay for the education of the children of their poorest relations, if there was a chance that some bright young boy (girls could not take the exams) would rise to an office of influence in the state and favor his kin. Men normally married women from outside their own clan, and these wives then came to support the interests of their husbands' clan. There are signs that the restriction and even oppression of women got worse in seventeenth-century China. Female foot binding literally hobbled its victims and restricted their mobility (see Chapter 12). Widow suicide, though it never attained the degree of compulsion that it did in Hindu India, was increasingly encouraged. Widows who stayed alive often prospered in business, but remarried much less often than in Europe, where the remarriage of widows and widowers was a standard way to cope with the effects of high mortality.

Elements in China's seventeenth-century experience combined to strengthen and spread the sense of Chinese identity. This may seem surprising. We might expect the disruptions caused by civil war and the Manchu conquest, the dislocations of mass migrations over vast distances, the spillage of population by immigration overseas to Taiwan and southeast Asia, or migration to the plains of Mongolia on an unprecedented scale to have weakened allegiance to the state. The vastness of the empire meant that China's new rulers had to exhibit great skill in adapting their legitimacy: as Manchus in Manchuria, as khans in Mongolia, as protectors of the Buddhist establishment in Tibet. Only on their extreme western frontier, where their subjects were Muslims, did the Qing emperors show hostility to the local culture. In the rest of the empire, however, their policy was to favor the adoption of Chinese culture. By the end of the eighteenth century, China's ethnic minorities had largely forfeited their traditional identities and had come to think of themselves as Chinese. Internal migrations helped. They induced minorities to leave their traditional homelands and encouraged a sense that everyone within the empire was Chinese. Meanwhile, the overseas Chinese found themselves thrust into communities composed of migrants from many parts of China. As a result they increasingly felt—paradoxically, perhaps—a common sense of belonging to the same community, which they projected home in their letters.

Qing strategy was to reconcile the different Chinese elites, especially the scholar-gentry, from among whom the mandarins were mostly recruited, to Manchu rule with generous rewards and with complete deference to the Confucian point of view that was deeply rooted among the Chinese elites. The Kangxi emperor (r. 1661–1722), who was the second Manchu to rule China, took lessons in the Confucian classics daily before dawn. The Qing avoided the impasse with the mandarins in which late Ming rule had been mired for three reasons. First, the scholars clung to the Qing as guarantors against disorder. Second, the dynasty and the

Ming and Qing China: Politics and Society

1368–1644	Ming dynasty
1500s	Commercial economy booms
1587	The Wanli emperor precipitates a crisis by challenging the mandarins
1630s	Ecological disasters undermine Ming power
1640s	Peasant revolts challenge landowners' privileges
1644–1912	Qing dynasty
Seventeenth and eighteenth centuries	Mandarins reconciled to Qing power
Early eighteenth century	Last restrictions on peasant freedom eliminated

bureaucracy had a common enemy in the warlords whose armies survived the civil wars that had brought down the Ming and who ruled vast areas with little input from the central government. The Kangxi emperor overthrew them in 1673. Finally, the Qing had their own power base in the Manchu warrior-elite. A twofold problem arose: how to perpetuate the martial readiness of Manchus, softened by adopting Chinese ways, and how to preserve a balance in the dynasty between Chinese and Manchu identities. Though the Qing emperors spoke and wrote Chinese, they kept up their knowledge of the Manchu language, privileged Manchus who remained loyal to their traditional culture, and founded schools of martial virtue for Manchu sons.

TOKUGAWA JAPAN

Compared with the mutiethnic, religiously and socially diverse societies that the Qing, Ottomans, or Mughals ruled, the Japanese already had a remarkably uniform set of notions about themselves. The only ethnic minority in the Japanese islands was the Ainu people of the far north, and most of them lived outside the boundary of the Japanese Empire in 1600. The Japanese treated those Ainu whom they did conquer with deep suspicion and forbade them to mix with Japanese people. In any case the number of Ainu was relatively small.

Nevertheless, in other respects, the dynamic features of the period affected Japan as sweepingly as any of the other newly or lately interconnected regions in Eurasia that we have been discussing. Historians have always regarded the seventeenth century as a period of deepening Japanese isolationism. And Japanese governments did try increasingly to exclude foreign culture—but only that of "barbarian" Westerners. Chinese and Korean arts and ideas remained welcome, and, indeed, Confucianism revived spectacularly in the Japanese elite's scale of values (see Chapter 18). Moreover, imperial expansion went on, and although the government severely controlled trade, this was not to prevent it. On the contrary, Japan's overseas trade continued to grow throughout the seventeenth and eighteenth centuries, partly through the Dutch and Chinese agents who were allowed restricted trading privileges in Japan, and partly through illegal trade that the Japanese authorities condemned as piracy but never wholly suppressed. In any case, Japan was big and booming enough to generate its own internal commercial revolution. The area under cultivation doubled in 100 years from the mid–sixteenth century. Population rose from something like 12 million in about 1550 to 30 million, according to a census of 1721.

Peasants and merchants were the big gainers from the new prosperity, as peasants switched to surplus production to feed the growing cities, and merchants exploited the expanding markets. Edo (EH-doh), the old name for Tokyo, was one of the biggest cities in the world, with at least 600,000 people in 1700. A service-industry bourgeoisie of merchants, clerks, and craftsmen throve in booming cities. Peasant prosperity eased the former cycle of famine and rebellion. In an atmosphere of social peace, governments encouraged people to concentrate on getting rich. The writer of novellas, Saikaku, was the spokesman of the age. "Heaven says nothing," announces his most famous book, *The Japanese Family Storehouse* (1688), "and the whole earth grows rich beneath its silent rule." He collected stories about money making and "placed them in a storehouse to serve each family's prosperity." Most of his stories tell of self-enrichment by hard work or intelligence. A street scavenger who picks up sticks becomes a chopstick-manufacturing millionaire.

Manchu warrior. "The bandits' heads were strung together. . . . Without even combing his horse's mane, he returned to make his report." The poem about this portrait of Zhanyinbao, of the Chinese imperial guard, in 1760, praises his prowess in law enforcement, but the artist shows him in hunting dress, armed with the bow that the Qianlong emperor, in the Manchu tradition, favored for the hunt. The realism and animation with which the subject's face is portrayed suggest that one of the Jesuit court artists painted this picture.
The Metropolitan Museum of Art, Purchase, The Dillon Fund Gift, 1986 (1986.206) Photograph © The Metropolitan Museum of Art

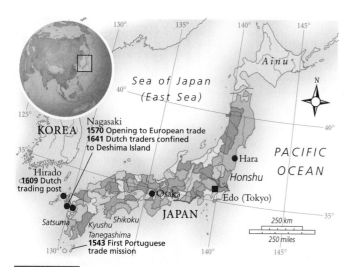

MAP 19.4

Tokugawa Japan

—— *daimyo* boundaries

—— Tokugawa domain from 1614

Ainu people

A desperate widow makes a fortune by raffling off her own house. "Now, if ever, trade is an exciting venture. So let none of you risk slipshod methods in earning your livings." The new economic climate had losers, too. Peace was bleak for the traditional warrior class, the samurai, who suffered from effects of the commercial boom: relatively low land values, high interest rates, and stagnation in the amount of rice the peasants had to provide to pay samurai pensions. Many samurai were reduced to the role of ronin—underemployed freelance soldiers, drifting between service to different lords. Lords (called **daimyo**) rarely paid samurai proper salaries. Exploitative pay was sometimes masked as "emergency reductions," sometimes as loans from the samurai that the daimyo never repaid.

Korea experienced similar problems with impoverished members of its noble class, or *yangbans*, as they were called. Traditionally, they discharged responsibilities in war and administration and, in official positions, could obtain land and wealth. But those excluded from office led lives of impoverished idleness, amid prostitutes and low-life hangers on, satirized in popular literature and art.

Clearly, however, for those who shared it, Japanese prosperity was founded on what Japanese call the Great Peace: the era of internal peace that followed the reunification of Japan in 1600 under a dynasty of chief ministers, the Tokugawa, who ruled as *shoguns* in Edo, while the emperors remained secluded figureheads, performing sacred rites in a provincial court at the old capital in Kyoto. The key to stability was management of relations between the shoguns and the 260 or so daimyo who ruled Japan's provinces (see Map 19.4). The daimyo had to be drawn from a limited number of noble families, but the shogun appointed and frequently transferred them from one domain to

○ MAKING CONNECTIONS ○

CHINA AND JAPAN: STABILITY AND CHANGE, 1500–1700

STATE AND SOURCES OF STABILITY →	CHALLENGES →	SOCIAL, CULTURAL, AND POLITICAL ADAPTATIONS
China / Confucianism; scholar mandarins run the state regardless of emperor, dynasty	• Ecological disaster—floods and famines in the 1630s • Peasant rebellions, civil wars resulting from natural disasters • Conquest by Manchus • Pressure for land reform, challenges to landowners	• Development of the docrine of sovereignty of the people • Elimination of right to sell peasants along with land • Break-up of large estates • Continuation of clan loyalty, ancestor worship amid social, economic change
Japan/ ethnic homogeneity; imperial system of rule; stable population and economic prosperity	• Christian missionaries convert many people • Disenfranchisement of traditional warrior class (samurai) • Need to maintain peace between shoguns and provincial rulers (daimyo)	• Enforced isolationism from West balanced by continuing trade with Asia • New emphasis on Confucian, Buddhist beliefs • Encouragement of commercial revolution, urbanism

another. Some daimyo, however, effectively managed to secure hereditary succession in their chosen regions. The Shimazu lords of the huge, domain of Satsuma in southern Japan, for instance, built up enough regional power to exercise effective autonomy (and, eventually, in the nineteenth century to challenge the shoguns). Normally, the Tokugawa obliged daimyo to maintain houses—and, in effect, leave hostages—at the shogun's court in Edo and reside there for part of each year. The shoguns also arranged marriages between daimyo families. In these respects, the system resembled the way many European monarchs dealt with their most powerful nobles.

A Daymo, or feudal lord, seated in an elaborate litter carried by porters. The screen at the side is rolled up so that he can observe the sights and sounds of Edo, as Tokyo was called under the Tokugawa shoguns (1600–1868). His samurai retainers march beside him.

THE NEW WORLD OF THE AMERICAS

Historians' favorite question about European overseas colonization is whether it created frontier societies–removed from models of society in the European homelands by generation gaps and pioneer radicalism—or exact duplications of home: transplanted Old Worlds. The answer of course is that the colonies were both. Molded and changed by new challenges and opportunities, settler communities usually tugged at nostalgic images of a home they aped or mirrored. An early apologist for the Spanish Empire conceived it as the colonists' obligation to rebuild New Spain in the image of the old Spain. Hence Spaniards built European-style arches in earthquake zones in the Americas, even though earth tremors could—and did—easily reduce such structures to ruin. Even Puritans, who really did consciously want to make something new of New England, went about it by fencing and planting to create English-style fields.

Yet the results nearly always did mark the beginning of something that was different from Europe. Colonies had to adapt to new environments and, in many cases, to the presence of new neighbors. Sectarian religious communities, democratic commonwealths, and plantation economies were all new, for instance, to the English experience. A bureaucratic state, with little delegation of authority to nobles and towns, was unknown in Spain. While slaves had existed in Europe in the Middle Ages, slavery on the American scale was unprecedented. Huge mixed-race populations, of the kind that filled Spanish and Portuguese America, had never before had a chance to emerge outside the Muslim world. The new colonies were products of their environments, which changed the people who lived in them.

The New World really was new. The Spanish experience there was one of the biggest surprises of history: the creation of the first great world empire of land and sea, and the only one, on a comparable scale, erected without the aid of industrial technology. A new political environment took shape. Historians have scoured sixteenth-century Europe for the origins of the "modern state," in which the authority the aristocracy exercised shrank to insignificance. The crown enforced an effective monopoly of government jurisdiction. The independence of towns withered. The church submitted to royal control. And sovereignty—formerly definable in terms of the right to pronounce justice—became increasingly identified with supreme legislative power, as laws multiplied.

States in Europe developed along those lines, but only the Spanish Empire in the New World fully matched all the criteria. Great nobles were generally absent from the Spanish colonial administration, which was staffed by professional,

 Tokugawa Shogunate, The Laws for the Military House

university-trained bureaucrats whom the crown appointed and paid. Town councils were largely composed of royal nominees. Church patronage was exclusively at the disposal of the crown. With a few exceptions, feudal tenure—combining the right to try cases at law along with land ownerhip—was banned. Though Spaniards with rights to Native American labor or tribute pretended to enjoy a sort of fantasy feudalism, speaking loosely of their Native American "vassals," they were usually denied formal legal rights to govern or administer justice to these people, and the vassals in question were subject only to the king. Meanwhile, a stream of legislation regulated—or, with varying degrees of effectiveness, was supposed to regulate—the new society in the Americas. The Spanish Empire was never efficient, because of the vast distances royal authority had to cover. Remote administrators could and did ignore royal commands. But this was a modern state because it was a bureaucratic state and a state governed by laws.

It also threw up new kinds of social effects, new microsocieties: the shipboard world of to-ing and fro-ing across the Atlantic and Pacific; the missions; the slave plantations; the little kingdoms runaway slaves called **maroons** set up; the households Spanish conquerors founded with pretensions to nobility and native wives or concubines. In Spanish colonies, **creole** (persons of at least partly European descent who were born in the colonies) consciousness arose at an early stage. In some ways it was evident in the first generation of the conquerors. Pride in mixed ancestry—or false claims to it, especially claims to be descended from Indian nobility—was one sure sign of creole self-assertion. So was the use of Native American languages alongside or instead of Spanish. In the late sixteenth and early seventeenth centuries, Fernando de Alva Ixtlilxochitl's (eesh-tleel-ZOCH-eet-el) was a typically self-conscious creole voice: a historian of his community in Texcoco (tehsh-KOH-koh) in Mexico, an interpreter of Native American language in the law courts, a government representative on municipal councils, a promoter and collector of Aztec literature. In the same period in Peru, the royal Inca blood of Garcilaso de la Vega made him highly sought after as a godparent by young families in the Spanish town where he lived.

Historians have often supposed that the trauma of conquest and the catastrophic effects of the unaccustomed diseases Europeans introduced shocked Native Americans into docility. In many ways, however, it is remarkable how much—and how long—their society survived. Sometimes it simply evaded the Europeans. The Inca state, for instance, withdrew in the 1530s to a new, lowland environment centered on the fortress city of Vilcabamba (veel-kah-BAM-bah) in Peru, until a further Spanish conquest uprooted it in 1572. Independent Native American states survived for generations and sometimes for centuries beyond the reach of Spanish power in the rain forests of Guatemala, the Mexican desert, the Florida swamps. In other cases, Native American communities survived by forming partnerships with Spanish religious orders as their protectors, or—especially in the former Aztec and Inca subject areas—by collaborating with the Spanish monarchy and simply continuing to pay to the new elite the tribute they had formerly paid to Native American imperialists.

Mixing of the races. One of the most popular subjects for painters in eighteenth-century Spanish America was the vast range of skin complexions that intermarriage among Europeans, Native Americans, and black Africans produced. Hundreds of sets like this one survive, each consisting of many portraits of couples and their children, with every imaginable gradation of skin color. No one knows exactly what these paintings were for, but Spaniards who returned to Europe brought them home as souvenirs.

In some places, the substitution of new elites, not conquest, transformed politics and society. The new elites were not just composed of Europeans but also of newly elevated Native American individuals and communities. In the Aztec world, for instance, where war and disease wiped out much of the former generation of leaders, Spaniards—especially missionaries—formed new relationships with surviving youngsters, who became committed to Christianity and new values under the influence of mission schools. In urban environments a new class of opportunistic Native American *ladinos* arose—who learned Spanish and earned Spanish trust. In Panama the Spaniards elevated new local big men, mistrustful of the ritual functions of the leaders they displaced and whom they identified as "demonic." Everywhere, the children of marriages between Spaniards and Indians assumed a potentially advantageous place in colonial society. Because people at the time were more sensitive to differences of class than of race, these *mestizos*, as the descendents of Europeans and Native Americans were called, had access to positions of power and opportunities of wealth.

Don Francisco Arove and his sons, leaders of the maroon kingdom of Esmeraldas, who submitted to the Spanish crown by treaty in 1599. A government official commissioned the painting for presentation to King Philip III. The mixed culture of this community of runaway slaves is reflected in the appearance of its leaders: their black faces, their rich clothing in the style of Spanish noblemen, the costly ear and nose ornaments borrowed from Native American tradition.

Of all the new kinds of society the global interconnections of the period created, the most novel were surely those of "the world the slaves made" in the Americas. From Virginia to Bahía (bah-HEE-ah) in Brazil, much of Atlantic-side America became, in early colonial times, a world that was more African than European. In 1553—when black people in Mexico were doing little more than domestic labor—the viceroy, the representative of the king of Spain, was afraid that they would swamp white settlers. In fact, black people rarely came to form a majority in the Spanish colonies—Cuba and Santo Domingo were two exceptions. Elsewhere, however, Africans were often the largest part of the population. By the end of the seventeenth century, England's Caribbean colonies had over 120,000 black slaves and only about 15,000 white inhabitants. The slaves practiced their own religions (see Chapter 18), maintained their own household patterns, and ate their own food. They created languages of their own to bridge the communication gaps among people from so many different parts of Europe and Africa. One of the earliest documented of these new languages is Sranan, still the main language of Surinam, the former Dutch colony in South America. Slaves invented it in an amazingly short time, under a brief period of British rule, in the 1650s and early 1660s. Despite high mortality and rapid turnover in the slave population, they stuck to it through the subsequent 300 years of Dutch rule—adopting some Dutch words, but maintaining Sranan essential structures and vocabulary.

Even in tightly controlled plantations, slave communities often created autonomous institutions. In Jamaica, the British were never able to eliminate the secret power of the *obeah-men*, whom they denounced as sorcerers, or curb the "benches" of elders, who were the self-regulating judges of the slaves. Though specialists debate the issue, the evidence from British North America suggests that slaves themselves seem to have evolved the social order of plantation life—the family structures, the regulation of relationships, the norms of behavior. Their African culture was only slowly transformed, because most owners resisted Christianizing their slaves. The Bible might give them subversive ideas about the equality of men. Clergy might interfere with owners' rights of abuse.

Sranan, Dutch, and English Compared

Sranan	Dutch	English
brada	broder	brother
buku	boek	book
datra	doctor	doctor
faya	vuur	fire
gado	god	god
ingi	Indiaan	Indian
kerki	kerk	church
masra	meneer	mister
noso	neus	nose
omeni	hoeveel	how much
skribi	schrijven	write
srudati	soldaat	soldier
trow	trouwen	marry

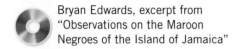

Bryan Edwards, excerpt from "Observations on the Maroon Negroes of the Island of Jamaica"

As well as African ways of life, there were African political structures in America: independent states established by runaways, sometimes in collaboration with Native Americans. Colonial authorities were forced to recognize the most successful maroon kingdoms. It was easier to establish a working relationship than run the risks of war and of inflaming slaves' grievances. The best-known case is that of the maroon kingdom of Esmeraldas in the hinterland of what is today Colombia, which signed a treaty with the Spanish crown in 1599. The Spanish viceroy commissioned a commemorative painting of the event from Alonso Sánchez Galves, the best painter in the colony at the time. It shows the maroon leader and his sons, richly attired as Spanish gentlemen, but bejeweled with ear and nose ornaments of gold in African or Native American fashion.

Beyond the reach of British colonies, too, in the seventeenth and eighteenth centuries, maroon states in South Carolina and Jamaica were protected by agreements with the colonial authorities that guaranteed their peaceful toleration in exchange for joint regulation of the fate of new fugitives from the plantations (see Map 19.5). In the backcountry of Surinam, a maroon state was established in 1663 (the year the maroons of Jamaica received the first treaty acknowledging their autonomy), with the connivance of planters who sent their slaves there to evade the head tax on them that they were required to pay to the colonial government. The best documented and longest lasting of the runaways' states was upcountry from Pernambuco (pehr-nam-BOO-koh) in Brazil, where the kingdom of Palmares (pal-MAHR-eshs) defended its independence from Portugal for almost the entire seventeenth century. At its height, under King Zumbi (ZOOM-bee), in the late seventeenth century, it had a royal guard 5,000 strong, an elaborate court life that impressed visiting Portuguese, and a black elite rich enough to have many slaves of their own.

Europeans dealing in the slave trade convinced themselves that slavery represented a civilizing process: the recovery of one of the virtues of the ancient Greek and Roman worlds, which slave energy had fueled, and the removal of slaves from the supposedly "barbarous darkness" of Africa to the "light" of Christian European civilization. In practice, it is hard to imagine anything more destructively barbarizing. Slavery nourished its own forms of lies and cant: racism, which depicted blacks as inherently inferior to whites, or claimed that they were better off enslaved than at home. It corrupted owners, by giving them power over the lives and bodies of their slaves and encouraging them to abuse it. It corrupted shippers, who overcrowded their cargoes to maximize their profits and, in verifiable incidents, tossed slaves overboard for the insurance ship owners could earn for dead "cargo." It kept black and white people in mutual fear and loathing, driving black rebels to horrific and despairing acts to find refuge or gain revenge, and trapping colonial governments in policies of inhuman rage and repression. It let loose predatory gangs of slavers and bounty hunters. It encouraged war in Africa between predator states that profited from the trade and their victims. The moral effects are important because every memory of inhumanity is precious in a world still riddled with vices of cruelty and greed.

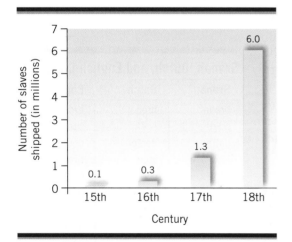

FIGURE 19.2 THE ATLANTIC SLAVE TRADE, FIFTEENTH TO EIGHTEENTH CENTURIES

From Cañizares-Esguerra, Jorge; Seeman, Eric, Atlantic in World History: 1500–2000, *© 2007. Electronically reproduced by permission of Pearson Education, Inc., Upper Saddle River, New Jersey.*

AFRICA

The social, political, and demographic effects of the slave trade in Africa are hard to measure. The slaves that crossed the Atlantic came especially from the West African bulge, the Congo basin, and Angola. The New

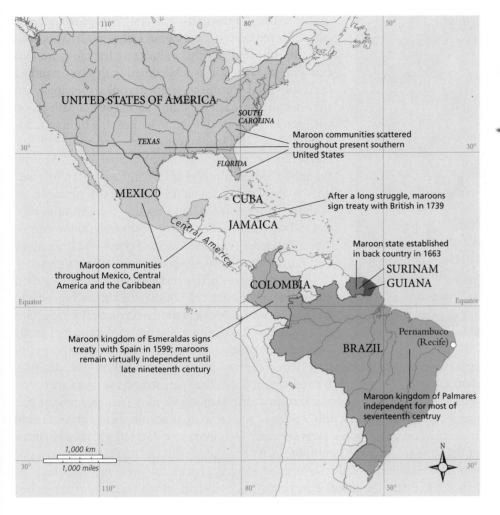

MAP 19.5

**Maroon Communities
in the Americas, 1500–1800**

MAP EXPLORATION
www.prenhall.com/armesto_maps

World needed substantial numbers of them. Outside British North America, most slave communities in the Americas did not reproduce naturally, for reasons that historians still do not fully understand. Constant new imports were therefore required just to maintain labor levels. Over one and a half million black slaves reached the New World by the end of the seventeenth century, and nearly six million more in the eighteenth (see Figure 19.2). The numbers shipped out of Africa were even larger, because many slaves died during the passage across the Atlantic. From the best available figures, almost 400,000 of those exported from Africa before 1800 never reached the Americas.

Overwhelmingly, they were obtained through black African sellers by war and raiding that reached hundreds of miles into the interior. Despite the size of the catchment area, it is hard to believe that the export of manpower on the scale demanded did not seriously affect the victim societies. For a time the Angola region of West Africa seems to have developed a marked excess of females over males because many more men than women were shipped across the Atlantic. On the fringes of African slave-trading societies, some areas may have been depopulated.

The political effects are glaring. Dahomey illustrates them—one of many slave-trading states that sprang up or grew in West Africa during the slaving era (see Map 19.6). The kingdom arose in the interior of the present state of Benin

Archibald Dalzel's *History of Dahomey* of 1793 was a slaver's defense of the slave trade, and the engravings in it reflect the author's prejudice against black Africans. The royal court of Dahomey in West Africa is presented as a contemptible blend of despotism, silliness, and immorality.

Africa, the Americas, and the Slave Trade

Late sixteenth century	Maroon kingdom of Esmeraldas
Seventeenth and eighteenth centuries	Slave states proliferate in West Africa; Maroon states in South Carolina and Jamaica
Late seventeenth century	Black slave population of British Caribbean reaches 120,000
	Maroon kingdom of Palmares reaches its height
ca. 1700	Number of slaves shipped to New World reaches 1.5 million
ca. 1800	Number of slaves shipped to New World reaches 7.5 million

in the early seventeenth century. Europeans already called the region the Slave Coast. Dahomey lived by war, and subordinated all other values to a ferocious warrior cult. Guests at the king's table dined with silver-handled forks on food European-trained cooks prepared, but they had to approach the king's palace over a path paved with skulls and were obliged to witness the human sacrifices with which Dahomeyans celebrated royal funerals and annual commemorations of former kings. Around the mid–seventeenth century, Dahomey began to accumulate muskets in exchange for slaves it obtained by raiding farther north. The 18 trading communities subject to Dahomey in the 1680s grew to over 200 within 20 years. Dahomey acquired a strip of coast—so King Agaja told European traders—to control outlets for slaves.

Yet with a productive territory in an area of varied commerce, Dahomey did not depend on slaving, which, by the best available calculations, accounted for perhaps 2.5 percent of its economy. Slaving apologists frequently pointed out that a war ethic motivated Dahomeyan aggression and that Dahomey prized captives more as potential human sacrifices than as slaves. White slave traders claimed that they performed a work of mercy by redeeming their victims from certain death. Dahomey's wars were not fought primarily for slaves. Indeed, only a third of the campaigns acquired enough victims to cover the costs. Still, some facts are clear. Dahomey rose and fell with the rhythms of the slave trade, and its cult of ferocity coincided with the market for captives of war. The economics of the slave trade obliged African suppliers to be warriors or bandits, because the prices Europeans paid, made it worth raiding for slaves but not worth raising them.

Farther west, the history of Ashanti shows that state-building on an even greater scale was possible with resources other than slaves. Gold was the basis of Ashanti's spectacular rise from the 1680s to the dimensions of a great kingdom by the mid–eighteenth century, occupying 10,000 square miles of present-day Ghana and commanding a population of 750,000. The royal chest was said to be able to hold 400,000 ounces of gold. The throne was a golden stool said to have been called down from the sky. The court sheltered under ceremonial umbrellas as big as trees. For the annual yam ceremony, when the king's tributaries gathered with their followers, the capital at Kumasi housed 100,000 people. More adaptable than Dahomey, Ashanti used firepower to defeat mounted armies from the Sahel, while coping with a variety of environments and fronts. Part of its armies' success was owed to outstanding intelligence and logistics, with fast runners operating along cleared roads. Even Ashanti, however, increasingly relied on slaving to supplement its gold during the eighteenth century.

To the east of the Gold Coast, Akwamu was another substantial slave-stealing state of a distinct character. Its ruler enslaved many of his subjects by arranging phoney denunciations for adultery—a crime many African states punished by servitude—and mobilizing gangs of "smart boys" to kidnap victims. Similarly, in the other main slave-producing region—the Congo basin and Angola—the profits of slaving

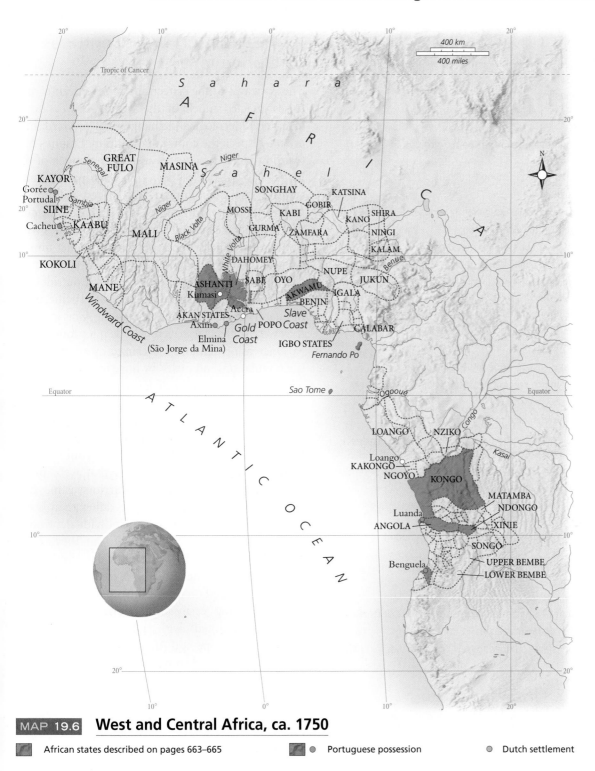

MAP 19.6 **West and Central Africa, ca. 1750**

African states described on pages 663–665   Portuguese possession   Dutch settlement

enabled ambitious monarchs to consolidate and centralize states. Kongo became a hereditary kingdom, whose rulers appointed the chiefs of subordinate states, and who succeeded, on the whole, in preventing, or at least limiting, enslavement of their own subjects. Ndongo, in the interior of what is now Angola, grew similarly rich and centralized and, as we saw, under the formidable warrior queen, Nzinga, resisted Portuguese attempts at conquest for most of the seventeenth century.

CHRONOLOGY

1368–1644	Ming dynasty
Fifteenth and sixteenth centuries	Ottomans create an elite slave army, the Janissaries
Sixteenth through eighteenth centuries	Nuclear family moves to the center of European society
1500s	Chinese commercial economy booms
1501–1722	Safavid dynasty in Persia
r. 1501–1524	First Safavid ruler, Shah Ismail I, imposes Shiism by force
1513	Machiavelli writes *The Prince*
1519	Charles V becomes Holy Roman Emperor
1520s	Afghans and Persians help establish Mughal power in India
1570s	Ottoman jurist Ebu us-Suud justifies the Ottoman Sultan's power
1576	Jean Bodin formulates doctrine of sovereignty
1603–1868	Tokugawa shogunate
1618–1648	Thirty Years' War
1630s	Ecological disasters undermine Ming power
1640s	Strain of empire precipitates decline of Spanish power
1644–1911	Qing dynasty
Seventeenth and eighteenth centuries	Mandarins reconciled to Qing power
1658	Rebellion of provincial governors against Ottoman authority
1658—1707	Emperor Aurangzeb engages in almost constant warfare
r. 1682–1725	Peter the Great attempts Westernization of Russia
1683	Ottomans fail to capture Vienna and cease conquests on the Christian front
Late seventeenth century	Maroon kingdom of Palmares reaches its height
Seventeenth and eighteenth centuries	Slave states proliferate in West Africa; Japan undergoes a "commercial revolution"
Eighteenth century	Last restrictions on freedom of Chinese peasants eliminated; Mughal power begins irreversible decline
1721	Population of Japan reaches 30 million
ca. 1800	Number of slaves shipped to New World reaches 7.5 million

IN PERSPECTIVE: Centuries of Upheaval

The upheaval of the sixteenth and seventeenth centuries affected much of the world. As we saw in Chapter 18, ecological exchanges had reversed, in a crucial respect, the course of evolution. Empires had overflowed like tidal waves and covered much of the globe. The balance of power between pastoral and settled peoples in Eurasia had shifted definitively toward the latter. Migrations and exchanges of culture crossed oceans and continents, sometimes with profoundly transforming effects. For the first time, a single—if, so far, small-scale—system of trade encircled the Earth. Some regions were still outside this system: Australia and most of the South Pacific, parts of inland Africa, the far interiors of the Americas. But they were unlikely to be left outside it for long.

Increasing demand was caused by gradually rising population, and fueled by huge increases of cash, which the silver mines of Japan and the Americas unlocked. New economic opportunities enriched new countries and new classes. A military revolution, as scholars now call it, introduced new technology to war: firearms that a peasant could handle with little training; fortifications that were proof against traditional horse-borne warriors; armies disciplined in the routines of battle rather than being trained, like knights of old, in individual combat. These changes started in Europe, but they transformed warfare in all the "gunpowder-empires" of the Old World. The military revolution loosened aristocracies' hold on one of the most basic forms of power, creating easily drilled armies of massed infantry, equipped with guns. Stronger states emerged in Europe and Africa; stronger empires in Asia; unprecedented empires in the Americas.

PROBLEMS AND PARALLELS

1. How did the power of the state grow in the sixteenth and seventeenth centuries? How did monarchs seek to redistribute power to their own advantage? Which newly empowered classes contended for a share in the growing might and resources of states?

2. Why was Spain such an unlikely superpower in the sixteenth and seventeenth centuries? What were the sources of its strength? Why did it eventually lose its preeminent position in Europe?

3. How did the way Westerners think about politics change in this period? What were the significant societal changes in Europe during this period?

4. What are the similarities and differences among the Ottoman, Mughal, and Safavid Empires during this period?

5. What economic and social changes occurred in China during the early Qing dynasty? How did these changes affect Chinese politics? How was Japan affected by the dynamic features of this period?

6. In what ways were European colonies in the Americas products of their environments? How did the colonies change the people who lived in them? In what ways was the Spanish Empire a modern state? How did slave communities in the Americas create autonomous institutions?

7. What effect did the slave trade have on African states during this period?

── DOCUMENTS IN GLOBAL HISTORY ──

- Jean Budin, from *Six Books of the Commonwealth*
- Machiavelli, excerpt from *The Prince*
- Hugo Grotius, selections from *On the Law of War and Peace*
- Ogier Ghiselin de Busbecq, "Women in Ottoman Society"
- Excerpts from the biography of Shah Abbas I

- Letter from Selim I to Shah Ismail I
- Excerpt from *Chinese Eunuchs: The Structure of Intimate Politics*
- Tokugawa Shogunate, The Laws for the Military House
- Bryan Edwards, excerpt from "Observations on the Maroon Negroes of the Island of Jamaica"

Please see the Primary Source CD-ROM for additional sources related to this chapter.

── READ ON ──

The account of Queen Nzinga is indebted to a work by J. K. Thornton *Africa and Africans in the Making of the Atlantic World* (1995). A very readable introduction to the social transformation of early modern Europe is G. Huppert, *After the Black Death: A Social History of Early Modern Europe* (2d edn, 1998). G. Parker, *The Military Revolution: Military Innovation and the Rise of the West, 1500–1800* (1988) is a vastly influential though technologically oriented statement of the connection between military and political change in Europe and globally. B. Downing, *The Military Revolution and Political Change* (1992) takes a closer, regionally differentiated look at political transformation. R. Carr, ed., *Spain: a History* (2000) is the best introduction to its subject. R. Harrison, *Hobbes, Locke, and Confusion's Masterpiece: An Examination of Seventeenth-Century Political Philosophy* (2002) is a masterful explication of seventeenth century political philosophy. O. Hufton, *The Prospect Before Her* (1996) and I. Maclean, *The Renaissance Notion of Woman* (1983) are important for understanding the role of women in the West.

I. M. Kunt, *The Sultan's Servants: The Transformation of Ottoman Provincial Government* (1983) looks at the local and bottom-up forces affecting Ottoman governance, while H. Inalcik, *The Middle East and the Balkans Under the Ottoman Empire: Essays on Economy and Society* (1993) explores the mutual impact of rulers and ruled in the most ethnically and religiously diverse area of Ottoman control. K. Barkey, *Bandits and Bureaucrats: The Ottoman Route to State Centralization* (1994) studies Ottoman state formation from the perspective of the central government.

I. Gallup-Diaz, *The Door to the Seas and the Key to the Universe. Indian Politics and Imperial Rival in Darien, 1640–1750* (2002) takes an ethno-historical perspective on Indian responses and resistance to European encroachment in this period. Peter Jackson and Lawrence Lockhart, eds., *The Cambridge History of Iran: Volume 6, The Timurid and Safavid Periods* (1986) is the standard history of Persia during this period.

R. Huang, *1587: a Year of No Significance* (1982) tells the story of the crisis of that year in China. My account of the rise of the Qing is indebted to L. Struve, *Voices from the Ming-Qing Cataclysm* (1998). F. Wakeman, Jr., *The Great Enterprise* (1985), looks at the social bases of early Qing political and military power. Pak Chi-won, *Tale Of a Yangban* (1994) ofers a story of Chinese influence in Korea. C. Totman, *Politics in the Tokugawa Bakufu* (1967) is the classic study of the political transformations of Japan after unification. S. Morillo, "Guns and Government: A Comparative Study of Europe and Japan", *Journal of World History* (1995) uses Japan as a case study in the primacy of social over military change, challenging Parker's "military revolution" thesis.

P. P. Boucher, *Cannibal Encounters. Europeans and Island Caribs, 1492–1763* (1999), traces cultural interactions in the Caribbean and demonstrates the effectiveness of Carib resistance to Europeans. J. Thornton, *Africa and Africans in the Making of the Atlantic World, 1400–1800* (1998) is an excellent study of the role of Africa and the African diaspora in developments of this period.

Columbus's Encounter with the New World

Columbus's encounter with people of the "New World" in 1492 was the beginning of a long history of contact, conflict, and contagion across the Atlantic. It was also the first account we have of Europeans and Native Americans coming face to face. Their interactions with each other would lead peoples on both sides of the ocean—Europeans, Native Americans, and eventually Africans—to think about themselves in new ways. But how—and how much—do we know about what happened at that first encounter?

The following passages are extracted from an almost day-by-day diary that Columbus probably rewrote later from notes he made during the voyage. As the extracts show, five themes underlay Columbus's account. First, he tried to describe the natives' appearance in terms that Europeans could understand. Second, he sought to emphasize the natives' natural goodness and innocence. They lived, he thought, like Adam and Eve before the Fall or in the mythical Golden Age that the ancient poets had portrayed. Third, he was alert for evidence that Europeans could easily dominate these people. Fourth, he wanted to tell King Ferdinand and Queen Isabela, his royal patrons, what he thought they wanted to hear: that he had reached the rich kingdoms of Asia, that abundant gold and spices were nearby, and that the natives could be converted to Christianity. Finally, he wanted to amaze and entertain his readers. As someone accustomed to the far-fetched tales of medieval travellers, he was quick to point out any details that Europeans would find bizarre, quaint, or picturesque (Photo 1).

Photo 1 An Illustration from *The Travels of Sir John Mandeville*, a fourteenth-century "book of wonders" which recounts the adventures of an English knight who journeys throughout the Middle East, Ethiopia, and India. Mandeville's fantastic stories tell of lands whose inhabitants had the bodies of humans but the heads of dogs, of a people the size of pygmies whose mouths were so small that they had to suck all their food through reeds, and of a race of one-eyed giants who ate only raw fish and raw meat. *The Travels* had an enormous impact on late medieval Europe and exerted great influence on Columbus's perceptions of the world. Here, a dog-headed creature spears a Knight.

Thursday, 11 October, "San Salvador"

In order… that they should feel great friendship for us, because I realised that they were people who were more likely to be delivered and converted to our holy faith by love than by force, I gave them some red bonnets and some glass beads which they hung around their necks, and many other things of little intrinsic value, with which they were highly delighted. And they ended up so much obliged to us that it was a wonder. Afterwards, they came swimming to the ships' boats where we were waiting, and they brought us parrots and cotton thread in little balls and spears and many other things, and traded them for other things which we gave them, such as small glass beads and hawks' bells.… They all go naked as their mothers bore them, and the women too. And all the men whom I saw were young, for I saw none who was more than thirty years old, very well formed, with handsome bodies and very good faces, hair that is thick, rather like the strands of a horse's tail, and short.… Some of them paint themselves black.… and some paint themselves white and some red and others with whatever pigment they find.… They carry no weapons, nor are they aware of them; for I showed them swords and they picked them up by the blade and cut themselves through ignorance. They know no iron.

All of them without exception are of goodly stature and fair of face and well proportioned. I saw some who had the marks of wounds on their bodies and I made signs to ask what these were, and they showed me how men from other islands, which lay nearby, came there and tried to capture them.… And I thought and do believe that men come here from the mainland to take them as slaves. They must make good servants.… for I see that they very smartly repeat whatever is said to them. And I believe that they will easily be made Christians, for it seemed to me that they belonged to no religion. If it please our Lord, at the time of my departure, I shall take six of them to your Highnesses so that they can learn to talk.…

Columbus's first glimpse of what he called "naked people," occurred on Friday, October 12, 1492, on an island Columbus called "San Salvador" (Holy Savior), which most scholars identify with Watling Island in the Bahamas. The natives were therefore probably Lucayos—a people of whom we know little, though archaeological evidence endorses Columbus's account of their rudimentary material culture.

Saturday, 13th October, "San Salvador"

After sunrise, there came many men to the beach, all young men as I have said, and all of good stature, very handsome folk… none of them are black, but of the colour of the Canary Islanders, nor ought one to expect otherwise, since the island is on a straight line from east to west with the island of Hierro in the Canaries.

The ancient Greeks had taught that climate determined a person's skin color and other physical characteristics. So Columbus compared these natives to the Canary Islanders, dark-skinned people whom Europeans had known about since the late 1300s. The Canary Islands are on the other side of the Atlantic off the coast of West Africa, but are on the same latitude as the Bahamas and also have a warm climate. Europeans would therefore expect the peoples of the Bahamas and the Canaries to look like each other, and Columbus said they did.

Sunday, 14th October, "San Salvador"

At dawn I... went along the coast of the island ... to see the other side....And there... the people all came to the beach calling to us and giving thanks to God. ... And one old man came aboard my boat, and others called to everyone in loud voices, 'Come and see the men who have come from heaven! Bring them food and drink!' Many came, including many women, each bringing something, giving thanks to God and flinging themselves on the ground, and they raised their hands to heaven and then called loudly to us to come ashore....

And it was in order to see all this that I set out this morning so that I should be able to give to your Highnesses an account of everything, including where to build a fortress... although this does not appear necessary to me, as these people are all very unpractised in warfare, as your Highnesses will see from seven [sic] of them whom I ordered to be seized to take them off and learn our language and then return them. But your Highnesses, when you so order, can take the whole population off to Castile, or keep them as captives on the island itself, because with a garrison of fifty men they could all be held in subjection and could be made to do whatever was required....

Columbus consistently sought to portray the natives' natural goodness. He saw them as peaceful creatures, who were uncorrupted by material greed and had some idea of natural religion. But he was also quick to point out that their ignorance of warfare meant that they could be easily conquered, exploited, or even enslaved.

Tuesday, 16th October, "Fernandina"

The people here seem to me to be somewhat more civilised, more commercially-minded and cleverer, for I have noticed that whenever they have brought cotton or some other little thing to my ship, they are better at settling the price than the others. And on the last island I even saw cotton cloth woven into wraps, and better-mannered folk, and the women wear a little slip of cotton in front of their bodies which scantily covers their private parts. ... I do not recognise any known religion here and I think the people will turn Christian very readily, for they are of a good understanding....

Columbus describes his next encounters in much the same terms, with increasing emphasis on his search for useful products, especially gold, until the entry for Tuesday, October 16, on the island he called "Fernandina," after King Ferdinand.

Friday, 19th October, "Isabela"

... like the others I have found... and share the same beliefs; and they believed that we came from heaven, and they give of whatever they possess in exchange for any truck—which is little enough, of course. And I think they would do the same with spices and gold, if they had any. I saw a fine house, not very big, with two doors, for they are all like that, and I went inside there and saw a marvellous piece of handiwork, like compartments fashioned in a way I could not describe and set into the ceiling were shells and other things. I thought it must be a temple and I called them and asked by signs if they offered prayer there. They said no. And one of them went aloft and offered me everything that was there, of which I accepted nothing.

From sign language, Columbus inferred that an island whose name he usually transcribed as "Samoete" was gold-rich and was the home of a king. In the entry dated Friday, October 19, he reported finding it and calling it "Isabela" after the queen. However, Columbus failed to make contact with the rumored king or verify his existence. The explorer's thoughts reverted to the original purpose of his voyage: "to go to the mainland [of China] ... and give your Highnesses" letters to the Great Khan [a former title of the ruler of China that was now over a century out of date] and ask for a reply and return with it' or to visit Cipangu—Marco Polo's name for Japan—which Columbus tentatively identified with the island the natives called "Cuba". But the natives of Cuba turned out to be.

Tuesday, 11th December, "Hispaniola"

And so I say again … that Caniba is none other than the people of the Great Khan, who must be very close by here. And they must have ships to carry the natives off and because they do not come back, they think they must have been eaten.

Tuesday, 18th December

…all hold [the king] in such estate and deference, although he goes about naked like the rest. When he came aboard the ship, he found that I was eating at my table under the stern-castle and hastened to sit down beside me and he would not give me a chance to come to greet him nor rise from the table, but insisted that I should continue eating…

After the meal, a squire brought a belt, made like those of Castile… which he took and gave to me, and two pieces of wrought gold, which were very fine, which made me think that they do not get much of it here, though I believe they are very close to where it comes from and is plentiful….

Columbus was now among Arawak peoples, whose material culture was more impressive, by European standards, than that of the Lucayos. Their artifacts included elaborate stonework and richly carved woodwork. The expedition was about to reach Hispaniola, where reports of Carib cannibalism multiplied. Typically, Columbus misinterpreted the name "Cariba" by which the Arawaks called their enemies, as "Caniba" meaning, he thought, "people of the Great Kha." The English words "Caribbean" and "cannibal" derive from the same root. Columbus at first did not believe in cannibalism, which was a commonplace of the wonder-tales of medieval travel books, but he did find a "king" on Hispaniola.

Columbus left a garrison on Hispaniola when he went back to Spain the following month. His evaluation of the peaceful nature of the island's inhabitants, however, proved sadly deceptive. By the time he returned to Hispaniola in November 1493, the garrison had been massacred. Eventually, Columbus felt obliged to reduce the island to obedience by a savage war in 1495-96.

The impact of Columbus's reports about the peoples of the islands he visited is shown in the woodcuts made to illustrate an account of the voyage, published in various editions and translations in 1493. One example shows naked, timid natives on Hispaniola, tentatively trading with merchants in oriental dress, whose galley lies offshore (Photo 2). This reflects Columbus's belief that he had been close to Asia, an illusion he clung to until his death in 1506.

Photo 2

Questions to Consider

1 What were Columbus's rival perceptions of the Native Americans he encountered?

2 How did Columbus's feelings about the natives develop as he traveled around the islands?

3 How did Columbus show the island peoples in a favorable way? What did he say about them that was not favorable?

4 How reliable are Columbus's assertions about the peoples he met on the islands?

5 Why did Columbus emphasize the islanders' nakedness or near-nakedness, the claims that they regarded his crews as 'men from heaven' and had no recognizable religion, and the islanders physical normality?

6 What evidence, if any, is there in these sources for the way the Native Americans perceived their visitors?

Sources

Extracts and commentary based on F. Fernández-Armesto, *Columbus on Himself* (London, 1992).

A Buddhist world map by the Japanese monk-painter Sokaku, ca. 1709. In the world-view of Buddhists and Hindus, the Earth is divided into seven island continents, each separated by an encircling sea, and each continent double the size of the preceding one. This example shows the continent of Jambudvipa, which forms the innermost circle of continents. The map incorporates European geographical knowledge, including Europe itself in the upper-left corner.

ENVIRONMENT

since ca. 1700
Global navigation and trade

since 1720s
Rise of global horticulture

CULTURE

since early 1700s
Decline of Asian empires

ca. 1720–1790
European Enlightenment

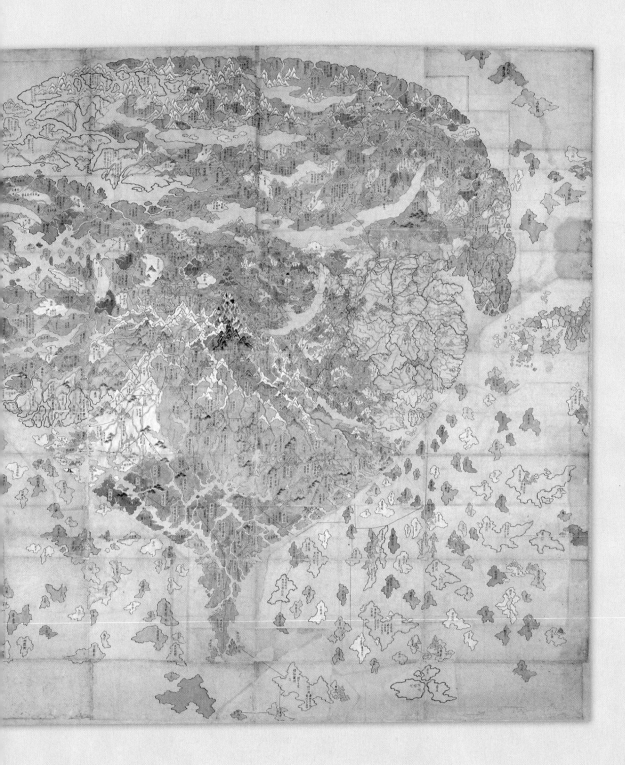

ca. 1750
Population boom starts:
Europe, China, and the Americas

since ca. 1760
British industrialization

1780–1800
● Peak of Atlantic slave trade

1756–1757
British conquest of Bengal

1776–1783
American Revolution

1789–1795
French Revolution

CHAPTER 20

Driven by Growth: The Global Economy in the Eighteenth Century

Avenging angels soar through the dust-filled sky over Lisbon, Portugal after the earthquake of 1755. The themes highlighted by the painting are echoed in the literature of the time: the revival of religion in the aftermath of horror, divine righteousness, the moral opportunity for displays of charity, the leveling effects of the disaster, which reduced the rich to the same destitution that the poor suffered.

Here is a tale of an optimist and a pessimist. Both were brilliant mathematicians, fascinated by statistics. The optimist was a French nobleman: Marie Jean Antoine Nicolas de Caritat, Marquis de Condorcet, born in 1743, who adopted with enthusiasm every radical cause that came his way. The pessimist was an English clergyman, Thomas Malthus, born in 1766, whose skepticism about human nature grew bleaker as the events of his time in Europe flung shadows and gushed blood. Condorcet believed humankind was heading for perfection. Malthus believed it was heading for extinction.

For Condorcet, in *The Progress of the Human Mind*, published shortly after his death in 1794, one of the proofs of progress was the growth of population: evidence—he thought—that people were growing happier, healthier, more fertile, longer lived, and more willing to bring children into the world. Indeed, he correctly spotted the broad global population trends of his day. In the second half of the eighteenth century, world population was booming. Between about 1750 and 1850, the population of China doubled, that of Europe nearly doubled, and that of the Americas doubled three times. The overall figures are hard to compute and mean nothing, of course, for anywhere in particular, but they expose a vivid backdrop to the events of the time. In 1700, world population was perhaps a little over 600 million. A hundred years later, it had climbed to around 900 million. The global population explosion of modern times had begun.

Among Condorcet's contemporaries, virtually no one believed there could be any such thing as overpopulation. Increased population promised more economic activity, more wealth, more manpower, more strength. But what, to Condorcet, seemed reason to rejoice, Malthus reinterpreted as the beginning of catastrophe. In his *Essay on the Principle of Population* of 1798, Malthus drew the statistical basis of his thinking from Condorcet's work but refiltered it through his own pessimistic vision. He concluded that population was rising so much faster than food production that humankind was bound for disaster. "The power of population is indefinitely greater than the power in the earth to produce subsistence for man," he wrote. "Population, when unchecked, increases in a geometrical ratio. Subsistence only increas-

FOCUS questions

- WHY DID the world's population rise in the eighteenth century?
- WHY DID rising population stimulate economic activity in parts of Europe?
- WHY WAS China's position as the world's richest economy threatened in the late eighteenth century?
- HOW DID British exploitation affect India's economy?
- HOW DID imperial expansion stimulate economic activity?

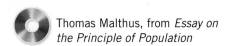

Thomas Malthus, from *Essay on the Principle of Population*

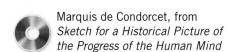

Marquis de Condorcet, from *Sketch for a Historical Picture of the Progress of the Human Mind*

es in an arithmetical ratio." Only "natural checks"—famine, plague, war, and catastrophe—could keep numbers down to a level at which people could be fed.

● ● ● ● ●

Condorcet and Malthus were in their own ways typical of their time. For the intellectual and moral climate of Europe changed abruptly in the 1790s when revolution and war undermined confidence in reason and in basic human goodness. Ironically, Condorcet was a victim of changes he was incapable of recognizing. He wrote his great work during 1792, while hiding from revolutionaries who wanted to chop off his head, and he died in prison shortly after they captured him. So his was a heroically defiant voice, insisting on the goodness of his persecutors and a future better than the present and the past. Malthus was an earnest, honest observer, peering with anxious charity into a grave new world of overpopulation tempered by disaster.

Malthus wrote so convincingly that he panicked the elites of the West into believing him. His view, according to the influential English writer William Hazlitt (1778–1830), was "a ground on which to fix the levers that may move the world." Among the disastrous consequences Malthus' book may have encouraged were the wars and imperial ventures that people's fear of running out of space and resources provoked. But Malthusian anxieties proved false. Populations rise and fall, and trends never last long. Overpopulation is rare in history. Experience suggests that people breed less when they attain prosperity. Despite the huge increase of world population since Malthus's day to over 6 billion, food production has matched or exceeded it.

Condorcet was closer to being right than Malthus was about the stimulating effects of population increase in the world of his day. We cannot fully understand anything else in the history of the eighteenth century without it: the speeding up of economic activity; the extension of settlement into new lands; the huge increases in production as empires grew in pursuit of resources; the drive of science to find new ways to understand and exploit nature; the intellectual challenges that accompanied all this ferment. On the whole, with exceptions, shifts in the balance of wealth and power also reflected demographic change. Rising regions, like Europe, China, and parts of North America and Africa were those that experienced sharp population increases, whereas areas of relatively stable population, such as the Ottoman Empire, housed stagnant or declining states (see Map 20.1).

POPULATION TRENDS

Population growth took two forms: dispersal on under-exploited frontiers, and concentration in growing cities and denser agricultural settlements. Around 1500, there were perhaps 80 million people in Europe. Modest, faltering growth in the sixteenth and seventeenth centuries raised the overall figure to about 120 million. It rose by about 50 percent to 180 million in the next hundred years.

Some areas hugely exceeded this rate. Russia's population doubled. We can see similar patterns in China and India. China had nearly 350 million people by 1800, India some 200 million. No reliable figures exist for Central and northern Asia, but the incoming colonists who arrived to turn suitable patches of steppe and forest in these areas into grassland on which their herds could graze made a significant difference in what were—in relation to their enormous size—sparsely populated regions.

Although figures are unavailable for Africa, evidence of restless migration suggests that the population was increasing there, too. In East Africa, for example, Oromo herdsmen (see Chapter 17) spread over much of Ethiopia. The cattle-rearing Masai of what is now Kenya expanded to fill all the land available for the kind of herding economy that suited them. In Central Africa, the Mongo people from equatorial Zaire in what is today the Congo colonized the lower Kasai and Sunkuru valleys and the forest fringe. In the far south, settlers of Dutch origin spread ever farther into the interior from the Cape. It is hard to see how the relentless growth of the slave trade in the seventeenth and eighteenth centuries could have been sustained without a rising population in the West African regions the slavers most frequented. East Africa, meanwhile, supplied slaves on a lesser scale to markets in Muslim Asia and to new European plantations in the Dutch East Indies and the islands of the Indian Ocean.

In the Americas, the effects of Old World diseases had penetrated most areas by the seventeenth century. Disease still had destructive work to do in previously protected places, particularly in the American West, where smallpox and measles decimated Native Americans in the early nineteenth century. On the whole, however, a population boom replaced the Americas' era of demographic decline. In Spanish America, while Indian populations showed signs of recovery, increased numbers of settlers and slaves were moving inland. By the end of the eighteenth century, Spain's American empire probably contained 14.5 million people. The population of British North America increased five-fold in the first half of the century, and nearly tenfold to 2.5 million in the second half. Numbers of white and black people rose, while the numbers of Native Americans dwindled, as they were driven from their lands or exposed to unaccustomed diseases (see Figure 20.1). Immigrants replenished and overflowed the space the Native Americans left behind. In the Caribbean, slaves accounted for most of the increase. The slave population in the British West Indies grew—mainly because so many new slaves were brought from Africa—during the eighteenth century from about 120,000 to nearly three-quarters of a million, who lived alongside about 100,000 white people.

Some parts of the world lagged behind in population growth or experienced it in different ways. Japan's demographic surge ended before the mid–eighteenth century, when it had over 30 million inhabitants. Japanese censuses of 1721 and 1804 reveal hardly any change. The population was disproportionately concentrated in a small part of the country, around and between Osaka and Ise Bays, where there was perhaps genuine pressure of overpopulation, or at least a sense that space was tight. Indeed, the census figures show outward movement from the heartland into the islands of Shikoku, Kyushu, and western Honshu. Japanese families seem to have practiced a wide variety of measures to restrain fertility, including delayed marriage, infanticide, and contraception. In Europe, the French were taking similar measures. The most populous country in Europe, France was also the first to experience a slowdown in the rate of population increase, which was already noticeable before the end of the eighteenth century. The Ottoman and Persian Empires were the other main areas exempt from spectacular population growth. They seem, for unknown reasons, to have registered only small increases. It helps to understand the fading of the Ottoman Empire, among the great powers of the world, to know that the ratio of its population relative to that of Europe as a whole dropped from perhaps about 1:6 in 1600 to about 1:10 in 1800.

Urbanization

Irrespective of the overall trends in population, urbanization—the growth of cities and towns—increased during this period over most of Eurasia and the Americas,

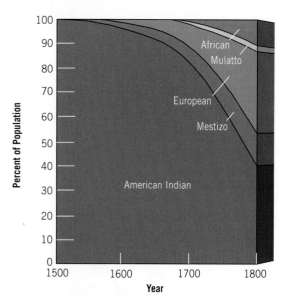

FIGURE 20.1 THE AFRICAN, NATIVE AMERICAN, EUROPEAN, AND MIXED RACE POPULATION OF THE AMERICAS, 1500–1800

Colin McEvedy and Richard Jones, Atlas of World Population History *p. 280. Reproduced with permission of Curtis Brown Group Ltd, London on behalf of the Estate of Colin McEvedy. © Copyright Colin McEvedy 1978.*

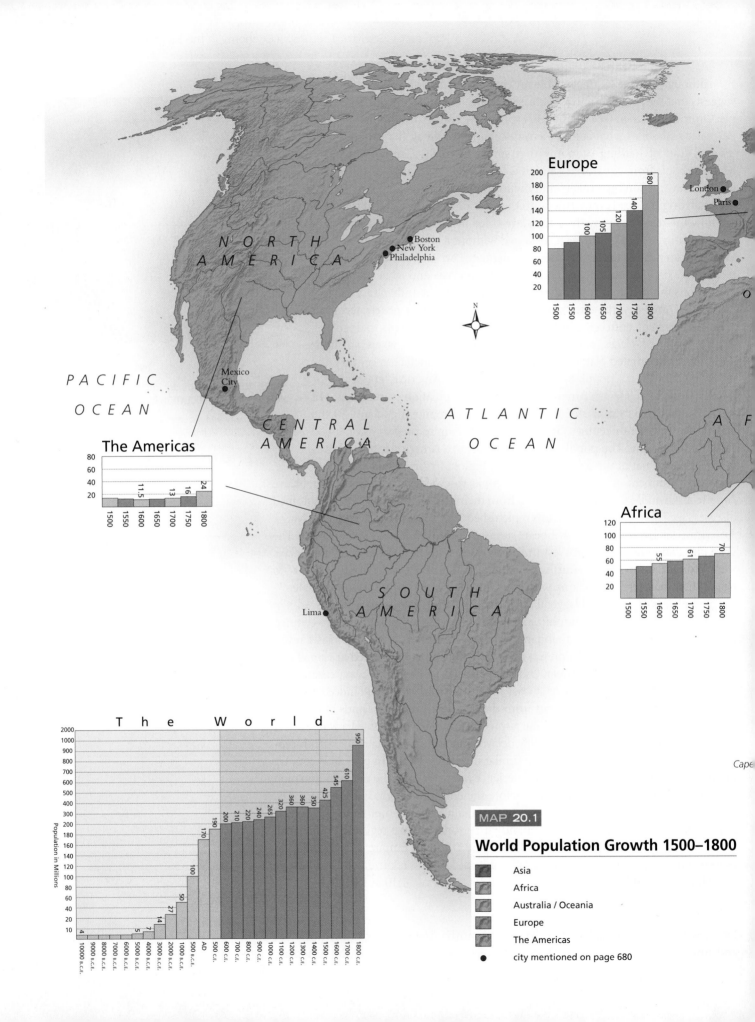

Europe

200
180
160 — 180
140 — 140
120 — 120
100 — 100   105
80
60
40
20

1500 1550 1600 1650 1700 1750 1800

London
Paris

Boston
New York
Philadelphia

NORTH
AMERICA

PACIFIC

OCEAN

Mexico
City

The Americas

80
60
40 — 24
20 — 11.5   13   16

1500 1550 1600 1650 1700 1750 1800

CENTRAL
AMERICA

ATLANTIC

OCEAN

SOUTH
AMERICA

Lima

Africa

120
100
80
70
60 — 55   61
40
20

1500 1550 1600 1650 1700 1750 1800

Cape

The   World

2000
1000 — 950
900
800
700 — 610
600 — 545
500 — 425
400 — 350   360   360   320
300 — 265   240   220   210   200
200 — 190
180
170
160
140
120
100 — 100
80
60
50
40
27
20 — 14
10 — 4   5   7

Population in Millions

10000 B.C.E. 9000 B.C.E. 8000 B.C.E. 7000 B.C.E. 6000 B.C.E. 5000 B.C.E. 4000 B.C.E. 3000 B.C.E. 2000 B.C.E. 1000 B.C.E. 500 B.C.E. AD 500 C.E. 600 C.E. 700 C.E. 800 C.E. 900 C.E. 1000 C.E. 1100 C.E. 1200 C.E. 1300 C.E. 1400 C.E. 1500 C.E. 1600 C.E. 1700 C.E. 1800 C.E.

MAP 20.1

World Population Growth 1500–1800

- Asia
- Africa
- Australia / Oceania
- Europe
- The Americas
- ● city mentioned on page 680

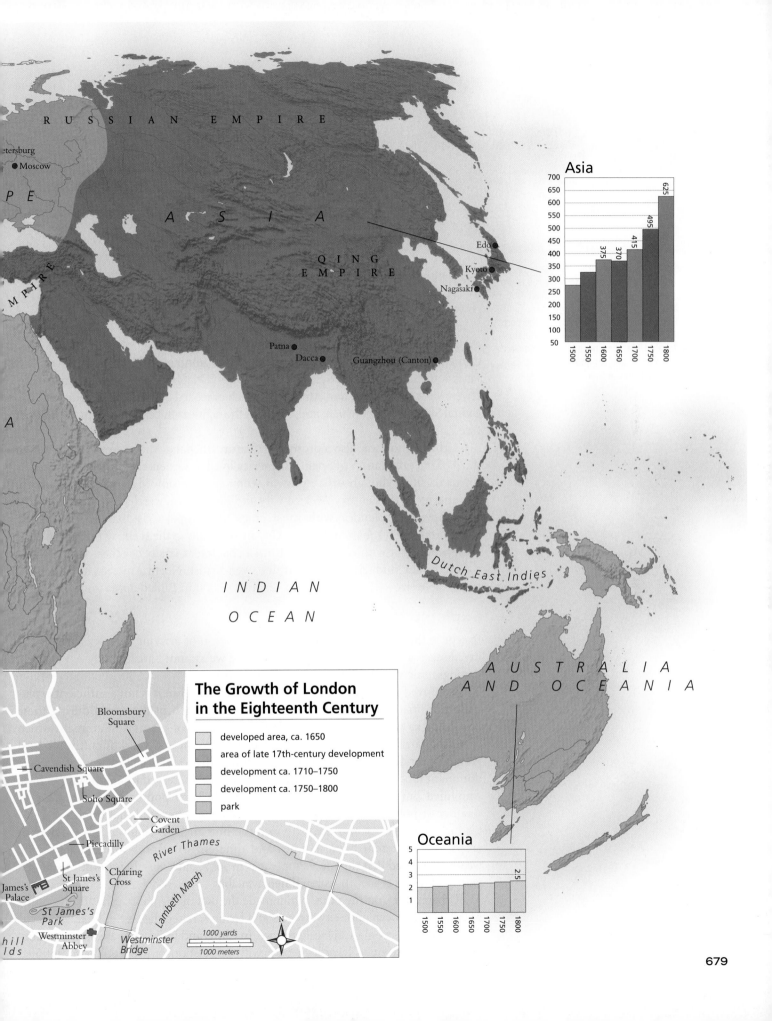

RUSSIAN EMPIRE

etersburg
● Moscow

PE

A S I A

MPIRE

A

QING
EMPIRE

Edo ●

Kyoto ●

Nagasaki ●

Patna ●
Dacca ●

Guangzhou (Canton) ●

INDIAN

OCEAN

Dutch East Indies

AUSTRALIA
AND OCEANIA

Asia

700							
650							625
600							
550							
500						495	
450							
400					415		
350			375	370			
300							

1500 1550 1600 1650 1700 1750 1800

The Growth of London in the Eighteenth Century

- ▢ developed area, ca. 1650
- ▢ area of late 17th-century development
- ▢ development ca. 1710–1750
- ▢ development ca. 1750–1800
- ▢ park

Bloomsbury Square

Cavendish Square

Soho Square

Covent Garden

Piccadilly

River Thames

James's Palace

St James's Square

Charing Cross

Lambeth Marsh

St James's Park

Westminster Abbey

Westminster Bridge

hill
lds

1000 yards
1000 meters

N

Oceania

5							
4							
3							2.5
2							
1							

1500 1550 1600 1650 1700 1750 1800

The Tokaido Highway. This scroll map depicts an aerial view of one of the most famous roads in Japan—the Tokaido Highway—as it looked from 1660 to 1736. This highway was the main land route from Edo (the old name for Tokyo) to the port of Osaka and the center of a densely populated zone. The Tokaido Highway became the route on which super-express highways and high-speed railroad lines were built in the twentieth century.

though, of course, cities large in their day were small by present-day standards. China, India, and Japan housed the most urbanized societies. The vast extended urban area of which Guangzhou (gwang-joh) in southern China was the center had as many people as all the capitals of Western Europe put together. By the best available estimates, at the end of the eighteenth century, Dacca in what is today Bangladesh, the world's greatest center of textile production, had over 200,000 people, Patna in northern India had over 300,000. In Japan, the population was, to an exceptional degree, concentrated in cities, with at least 6 percent of Japanese living in urban concentrations of over 100,000 inhabitants. The corresponding figure in Europe was only 2 percent.

But Europe also experienced intensified urbanization and, in pockets, exceeded even Japan's rate. Britain had only one big city, but it was a monster of a place. London approached a million inhabitants by the beginning of the nineteenth century. Paris at the same time had over half a million, and Naples in southern Italy not many fewer. Moscow, Vienna, and Amsterdam each exceeded 200,000, as did Russia's new capital St. Petersburg, which, at the start of the eighteenth century, did not even exist (see Chapter 19).

Urbanization was also a prominent feature of change in the Americas. Nearly a third of the population of Spanish America lived in settlements officially classed as towns or cities, though urban growth seems to have slowed in many areas in the last quarter of the century. Mexico City and Lima, Peru, were colonial capitals able to compete in splendor with most cities of Europe. Cristóbal de Villalpando painted the main square of Mexico City in 1695, lining the scene with lavish buildings, peopling it with elegantly costumed characters, costly coaches, snooty social rituals. By the mid–eighteenth century, even British North America had towns of respectable size—15,000 people in Boston, 12,000 in Philadelphia and New York.

Explanations

Except in the New World, where the combination of arriving migrants and receding disease accounts for rising population, we cannot satisfactorily explain the demographic growth of the eighteenth century.

Improved food supply played an important part, but it is not a sufficient explanation on its own. Nutrition did improve over much of the world during these years, thanks to the worldwide ecological exchange of plants and animals, which increased farmers' options and extended the amount and yield of cultivable land (see Chapter 17). Over the long term, **monocultures** (the cultivation of a single dominant food crop, such as potatoes or rice) have increased food output, but have simplified human food chains and have made large populations vulnerable to weather or political crises. The ecological exchanges reversed that trend and reintroduced complexity and diversity into the human food chain. A wider range of crops, with different harvest times and different tolerances for changes in the weather, ensured that the food supply was proof against variable conditions. If bad weather hit one crop, others remained available.

Urbanization, on the other hand, made the diet of the poor worse. It interposed middlemen between poor city dwellers and farmers, raised the cost of food, and separated consumers from fresh local produce. In China and India, increased food production does not seem to have kept pace with population growth. Still, concentrated

MEXICO CITY IN 1695

"The capital of the New World." Seventeenth-century Mexico City sought, in the words of one commentator, to be "an imperial city of great size, space, concourse and population." Cristóbal de Villalpando's painting of the city's main square in 1695 captures this vision and emphasizes order, geometry, and European-style elegance. Yet the painting also shows why critics claimed to find Mexico City chaotic and confusing. By this date, uncontrolled growth had raised its population to nearly 100,000. Native Americans, beggars, lepers, and low-life elements are scattered through the scene.

The volcano in the background is a reminder that the splendor of the city remains at the mercy of nature or God.

The native market, where vendors prepare and sell foodstuffs in their thatched stalls.

Water carriers fill their pitchers at a famous fountain, around which Native American women sit shading themselves under elegant umbrellas.

Elegant carriages and elaborate manners suggest the wealth, status, and European tastes of the city's elite.

Elegant shops in the Spanish market.

How does this painting document the size, importance, and roles of cities in the eighteenth century?

markets for anything, including food are more efficient than dispersed ones. Improved shipping, canals, and coastal trade made the distribution of bulk foods easier, notably in China, Japan, and Europe—areas that already had relatively good transport networks. Ultimately, while many people may not have eaten better food in the eighteenth century (and may even have gotten less healthy food), more people around the world did get more food, ate more regularly, and survived longer to work and reproduce.

Improved hygiene may have helped increase populations, but it is not likely to have been decisive. Urbanization bred ever more unsanitary conditions, even in the most technically ambitious and sophisticated societies, until well into the nineteenth century (see Chapter 24). An age of typhus and cholera succeeded the age of plague because bigger cities meant that more people were exposed to water contaminated by human sewage and to the lice that spread typhus. Typhus and cholera only began to disappear in the nineteenth century when European and American cities constructed sewage systems and provided clean water for their inhabitants to drink and bathe in. Typhus, typhoid, and other fevers, some of tropical origin, colonized eco-niches in growing cities and could reenact scenes reminiscent of the age of plague. A particularly deadly series of local epidemics in England in the 1720s killed 100,000 people. In Japan, however, the remarkable absence of cholera in this period may have been the result of exceptional standards of sanitation and of the use of human waste as fertilizer—which ensured that Japanese streets, unlike those in other parts of the world, were kept clean of human feces.

We can group other existing explanations for the new demographic trend under two main headings. First, there is what we might loosely call the theory of *progress*, which represents population growth as the result of successes in the struggle against death—successes that postponed early mortality and extended people's fertile lives. According to this theory, human health improved because of better medical and public health strategies. Second, environmental conditions may hold the key. The survivors of plagues and epidemics developed immunities to diseases, for instance, or—some historians have argued—the microorganisms that carried diseases fatal to humans may have evolved into less deadly forms. We can look at each of these in turn, seeing what they contributed and trying to identify possible factors that have not yet received adequate attention.

Medicine

Some improvements in health were clearly the result of improved medical science or care. But most medicine remained useless and ignorant, and nothing that was new in medicine affected the plague. In some parts of Europe, professionals—doctors and trained midwives—handled childbirth, babies were freed from tight swaddling clothes, and breast-feeding was praised. But these practices were still the exception and are unlikely to have had much effect on population statistics. In most places, a declining death rate among people in their fertile years seems to have been crucial, rather than any reduction in infant mortality.

The exchange of ideas about cures, methods for treating the sick, and medicinal plants was part of the great cultural exchange across Eurasia and between Europe and the Americas. It boosted the variety of medicinal drugs and plants of every society it touched. Eighteenth-century European medicinal drugs looked—by today's standards—increasingly effective as time went on. Such ingredients as spider's webs, unicorn horn, powdered snake flesh, and moss scraped from human skulls disappeared from medical textbooks in favor, for instance, of opium, quinine, and chemical remedies. But these expensive preparations probably did no good to most people and only a little good to a few. In the West, the humoral theory of medicine inherited from the ancient Greeks (see Chapter 6), which attributed ill health to imbalances in the body between basic juices or fluids called *humors*, gradually receded. But nothing particularly scientific replaced it. Diet and exercise—or lack of them—were still considered fundamental both to the causes and treatment of disease. Contagion was suspected as a cause, but no one had any idea how it worked. Environmental circumstances got an increasing share of blame, as medical theorists blamed *miasmas* or "corrupt air" from mists and gases from the earth as unhealthy. No one yet recognized germs or microbes as dangerous or knew anything about viruses.

Still, despite the deficiencies of medicine, two diseases were conquered or contained: scurvy (the vitamin C deficiency that particularly afflicted long-range seafarers) and smallpox. A crisis in the history of scurvy occurred in 1740–1744, when the British naval commander George Anson lost almost 1,400 out of a complement of over 1,900 men during a round-the-world voyage. Scurvy was only the worst of a plague of deficiency diseases, including beriberi, blindness, and "idiotism, lunacy, convulsions," that afflicted Anson's crews. But the terrible death toll provoked a systematic inquiry by the British navy into how to treat it. James Lind, a naval surgeon who had seen service in the West Indies, tried out a large selection of possible remedies on a sample of 12 patients at sea. "The consequence was," he recorded, "that the most sudden and visible good effects were perceived from the use of the oranges and lemons; one of those who had taken them, being at the end of six days fit for duty."

Lind had discovered a cure for scurvy, but not a preventive. Unlike with other vitamins, the human body cannot store more vitamin C than it needs in a day, and there was still no way to preserve oranges and lemons at sea for long enough to secure the health of the crews. The only effective remedy was to replenish ships with fresh supplies at every opportunity and to eat as many fruits and green vegetables as crews could find wherever a ship could land, ravaging desert islands for the barely edible weeds sailors called scurvy grass. The Spanish-sponsored voyage of Alessandro Malaspina, the most ambitious scientific expedition of the eighteenth century, from 1789 to 1794, virtually banished scurvy from the fleet with ample supplies of oranges and lemons (see Chapter 22). Other navies, however, that lacked the Spaniards' advantage of a large colonial empire with frequent ports of call, remained desperate for alternative diagnoses and easier cures. A surgeon with experience of Russian Arctic exploration advised "warm reindeer blood, raw frozen fish, exercise," and any edible greens that might come to hand. During his Pacific voyages from 1785 to 1788, the French explorer Jean-François de La Pérouse mixed quinine and extract of spruce trees in the crew's drinking water. The eighteenth-century British explorer of the Pacific, Captain James Cook, put his faith in sauerkraut. Yet despite these discoveries, official resistance to new ideas meant that the issue of citrus-juice rations to English sailors did not begin until as late as 1795. Even then, of course, although doctors knew that doses of citrus juice worked, they did not know why because vitamins had not yet been discovered.

Scurvy was not a major killer. More important, for the population statistics, was progress in containing smallpox—still a significant taker of young lives. China, India, and the Middle East had long know about inoculation as a means of prevention. Now the practice spread to Europe. In 1718, Lady Mary Wortley Montagu, wife of the British ambassador in Constantinople, volunteered her six-year-old son to be a guinea pig in an inoculation experiment by an "old Greek woman, who had practised this way for many years." After injection, the boy was covered in pustules, with swollen arms, dry mouth, and an urgent fever. Yet the experiment was a success, and when London was threatened with an epidemic in 1721, Lady Mary repeated it on her daughter. King George II (r. 1727–1760) had his daughters inoculated, and

James Lind, from
A Treatise on Scurvy

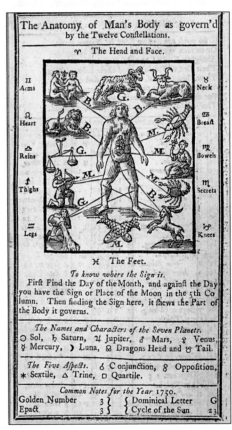

The Anatomy of Man's Body as govern'd by the Twelve Constellations. Almanacs provided a wide range of information, self-improvement advice, and wisdom—practical, religious, and scientific—to eighteenth- and nineteenth-century Americans. First published in 1732, Benjamin Franklin's *Poor Richard's Almanack* was a huge success, selling nearly 10,000 copies a year. As this woodcut from 1750 indicates, many people still clung to the ancient belief that the movement of the planets and the position of the stars influenced the well-being of the parts of the human body.

Vaccination. When Louis Léopold Boilly painted this scene of a smallpox vaccination in 1807, the procedure still seemed curious and alarming. But it had become a routine part of doctors' domestic visits across much of Europe and the Americas.

Lady Mary Wortley Montagu, from *Letters*

British high society adopted the practice. Lady Mary had achieved an ambition she conceived as a patriotic duty: "to bring this useful invention into England." Cheap, mass methods of inoculation soon followed. In 1796, Edward Jenner substituted cowpox for smallpox in the inoculation process. This was a considerable improvement, since cowpox had the same immunizing effect, but carried almost no risk of harming inoculated persons.

The Ecology of Disease

The success of this campaign against smallpox was remarkable. More remarkable still was the way the global profile of disease changed on its own without humans doing anything to affect it. Part of this was a consequence of ecological exchange. Fewer populations suffered from lack of natural immunization. Global communications meant that more and more people could contract the same diseases, just as they made the same plants and animals familiar over a vast range of the world. Still, migrations of disease-bearing organisms remained dangerous. Yellow fever crossed the Atlantic from Africa and spread beyond the tropics, hitting cities as far north as Philadelphia repeatedly in the eighteenth century. Cholera became a frequent visitor to European cities. Tropical forms of malaria were deadly to European visitors and would-be colonists. The European cocktail of diseases that despoiled the Americas of native peoples in the sixteenth and seventeenth centuries continued to wreak havoc on new discoveries. Toward the end of the eighteenth century, Hawaii suffered much as the Americas had done. Tahiti's population declined from 40,000 in 1769 to 9,000 in 1830. When European colonization began in Australia in 1788, smallpox wrought havoc there among the Aboriginal population.

Yet in terms of global population, a remarkable fact more than balanced these losses. In the eighteenth century, the age of plague ended. The last European pandemic of a disease its victims called "plague" occurred from 1661 to 1669, rolling from Turkey across Europe to Amsterdam, where it killed 34,000 people over two years in 1663–1664. In 1665, it emptied London—more people fleeing in panic than dying of plague. Ascending the Rhine River, it ended by filling mass graves in Spain and Italy. Thereafter, Europe suffered only local outbreaks. The last outbreak of a level of severity characteristic of the age of plague occurred in 1711 in eastern Germany and Austria, with over a half a million deaths. The last occurrence of any sort in Western Europe was the outbreak in the French Mediterranean port of Marseilles in 1720. Between corpse-strewn gutters and mass plague pits, the Archbishop of Marseilles strode, comforting the afflicted, with a bundle of herbs under his nose in hopes of warding off the disease, or leading the population in penitential processions and prayers to the Sacred Heart of Jesus. Eleven of his twelve companions were infected and died at his side.

After that, plague never returned to Europe. Changes in the distribution of carrier species of rats, fleas, and lice (see Chapter 14) may have played a part. But the demise of plague could be like most other forms of species extinction: a product of evolution. The microorganisms that bear disease are more volatile, more apt to evolve, than other, bigger organisms, because they are individually short lived. They go through many generations in a relatively short span of time. So species come and go much faster in the microbial world than among the great, lumbering plants and animals whose evolution we normally observe. We think of evolution as a slow-working process. Microbes experience it fast. Those that kill off their hosts are obviously not adaptively successful. They need to find new eco-niches to ensure their own survival, or they are self-condemned to disappear. For reasons we do not know—but which must be connected with their own evolutionary advantage—hostile microorganisms may sometimes switch their attention away from one set of victims to another. Historically, our improving health may owe less than we suppose to our own cleverness and more to the changing habits and nature of microbes.

ECONOMIC TRENDS: CHINA, INDIA, AND THE OTTOMAN EMPIRE

More population means more economic activity. That is not surprising. But eighteenth-century economic activity did mark a new departure from long-prevailing global patterns, as the gap in production, and therefore in wealth, began to narrow. The West began to catch up with China and India. The new rich among the world's economies began to emerge in Europe and America. By the end of the eighteenth century, India went into sharp relative decline. China maintained its supremacy, but signs suggested that its days as the world's richest society were numbered.

China

The distribution of the world's most productive and profitable industries indicates what was going on. The most intensive concentrations of industrial activity were still in east and south Asia. Take the case of the Beneficial and Beautiful whole-saling firm, founded in the seventeenth century in the city of Hangzhou (hahng-joh) on the coast of central China. According to records collected in the early nineteenth century, the firm built up its cloth sales to a million lengths a year by making bold rebates to tailors. In the early eighteenth century, the firm employed

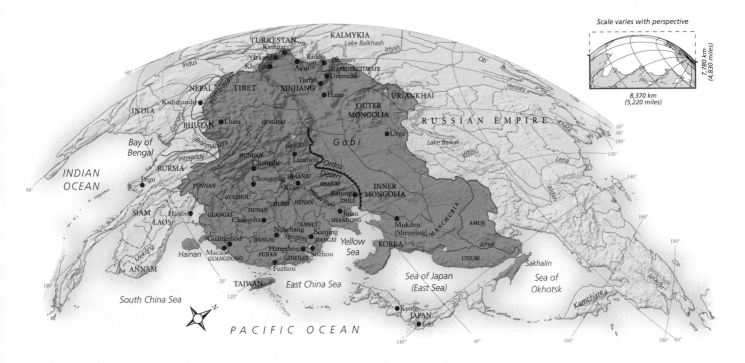

MAP 20.2

China in the Late Eighteenth Century

▨ Qing Empire by 1770

⌁ Great Wall

Scale varies with perspective

7,780 km (4,830 miles)

8,370 km (5,220 miles)

4,000 weavers and several times that number of spinners. The dyeing and finishing were concentrated in a specialized suburb of the city, where in 1730 10,900 workers were gathered under 340 contractors and, claimed the firm's publicity, "for two hundred years now there has been no place, either north or south, that has failed to consider Beneficial and Beautiful cloth to be lovely."

The tale of the Beneficial and Beautiful Company was an exceptional but not an uncharacteristic story. A porcelain center in eighteenth-century Jiangxi (jee-ahng-shee) province in southern China "made the ground shake with the noise of tens of thousands of pestles. The heavens are alight with the glare from the furnaces, so that one cannot sleep at night." Farther south were ironworks that employed 2,000 to 3,000 men, and water-driven hammers pounded incense "without any expenditure of muscular effort." In the southwest provinces, similar machines for husking rice were lined up by the hundred, while water-driven papermakers hummed "like the whirr of wings." The great cty of Nanjing had three imperial textile factories at the start of the eighteenth century, employing 2,500 artisans and 664 looms. Near what is today Shanghai, in 1723, there were about 20,000 textile workers and dyers. The imperial government appointed the entrepreneurs in state factories, and they could make fabulous private fortunes without cheating the throne. A typical example, Zaoyin, whose career was largely spent managing imperial factories, was a shy, modest man who pretended to read as he was carried in his litter to screen his eyes from the sight of the common people rising in respect as he passed. But he made a famous collection of rare art works and curiosities, "without speaking of silver, treated like mud," as his own nurse reported. "No matter what thing there is on earth, there it was piled up like mountains or the waters of the sea."

The sheer size of China's internal market guaranteed a dynamic economy (see Map 20.2). In about 1800, over 10 percent of grain production was for sale rather than eaten by the farmers who grew it, together with more than a quarter of the raw cotton produced throughout the empire, and over half the cotton cloth—amounting to 3 billion bolts of cloth a year. Nearly all the silk, tea, and salt in the empire likewise was sold on the market.

Foreign trade, against this background, was of relatively small importance to China. It was vital, however, for the economies of much of the rest of the world. In the foreign trading posts (called **factories**), of Guangzhou, the world clamored for admittance at China's barely open door. All the trade of Europeans and Americans in

Guangzhou. In 1800, Guangzhou harbor still carried more international trade than any other port in the world. European traders were not allowed anywhere else in the Chinese Empire. Their residential quarters and warehouses are the white buildings in the center foreground. A European merchant probably commissioned the painting as a souvenir of his stay in China.
Photograph courtesy Peabody Essex Museum.

search of Chinese tea, silk, rhubarb, and porcelain was funneled through this narrow opening. A privileged group of Chinese merchants controlled the trade. China's favorable trade balance, moreover, continued to expand, thanks to the growth of the European tea market. Dutch tea purchases in Guangzhou rose from about 1.5 million guilders (in Dutch currency) in 1729–1733 to nearly 16.5 million in 1785–1791. By that time, the British had taken over as the main customers, transporting nearly 300 million pounds of tea in the 20 years after Britain reduced the tea tax in 1784.

The "barbarians," as the Chinese called the Europeans, still paid almost entirely in silver. Eventually, Western merchants found a commodity they could market in China. Opium was the only foreign product Western suppliers controlled (the poppies from which opium was derived were grown in northern India under British rule) that Chinese consumers wanted, or came to want, in large quantities. As with the milder drug China exported in exchange—the tea that banished sleep or, at least, promoted wakefulness—supply seems to have led demand. When China first banned the opium trade, in 1729, imports were reckoned at 200 of what the Chinese called "chests" a year. One thousand chests were recorded in 1767. In 1773, the British East India Company imposed a monopoly on the opium trade in India. By the early nineteenth century, 10,000 chests of opium were entering China annually. This was a significant new element in global trade. Foreigners now had, for the first time in recorded history, a chance to narrow their habitual trade gap with China (see Chapter 25).

China's economic supremacy had lasted a long time, but it was vulnerable to erosion in three ways. First, foreign suppliers could exploit the opium market. Second, they could find substitutions for their imports from China—making their own porcelain and silk, growing their own rhubarb, finding alternative places, such as India and Sri Lanka, where they could plant tea. Finally, they could outstrip Chinese production by mechanizing their industries. All these changes would occur in the nineteenth century. In the long run, the last of these changes made the greatest difference. For China could not mechanize production. The empire was caught in what the historian Mark Elvin has called a "**high-level equilibrium trap**." Industries that were meeting huge demands with traditional technologies had no scope to increase output. An economy with a vast pool of labor had no means or incentive to replace human muscle with machines.

Comparison with Britain illustrates the point. Starting from a low threshold, Britain could triple cotton-cloth production between the 1740s and 1770s. A similar rise in Chinese output would have glutted the world. The entire world supply of raw cotton would have been insufficient to meet it. In about the 1770s or 1780s, a single Chinese province imported yearly, on average, six times as much raw cotton as the whole of Britain. Cheap labor is good for industrialization, but cheap capital is better. In the teeming worlds of India and China, the cost of labor relative to that of capital may have been too low for industry's good. The trap was typified by the experience of a Chinese official in 1742 who proposed to save peasants in his charge four-fifths of their labor by installing expensive copper pumps at a wellhead. Aghast at the immobilization of so much hard wealth, the peasants continued to prefer to draw water by hand. China's unwillingness to mechanize is not surprising. The frustration some of us feel today at our continued dependence on the internal combustion engine and fossil fuels shows how the inertia of inferior technologies can arrest progress.

India

The Indian economy was even more vulnerable than China's to manipulation by foreign imperialism and competition from mechanizing systems. Yet Indian industries in the eighteenth century were scarcely less impressive than those of China. In Bengal, where it seemed to a British observer that "every man, woman, or child

Dutch trading post. With its huge fluttering flag, formal grounds, spacious quarters, and splendid gates in the Mughal style, the Dutch trading post at Hoogly in northeast India looks like an outpost of empire. In fact, however, it represents how dependent European merchants of the seventeenth century were on the wealth of the East. The post opened for trade in 1635, so that the Dutch East India Company could acquire relatively cheap silk in India and exchange it at a handsome profit for silver in Japan.

in every village was employed in making cloth," each major type of textile was the specialist product of a particular subcaste. A Dutch silk factory in Bengal, with 700 or 800 workers, was modeled less on European precedents than on the official textile factories the Mughals sponsored to supply the imperial wardrobe with fine cloth. Other kinds of economic specialization concentrated vast amounts of manpower and produced goods of outstanding quality and high value. In Kurnool, a town of only 100,000 people on the Krishna River, is said to have had 30,000 to 60,000 iron ore workers. Until Benjamin Huntsman perfected the manufacture of cast steel in the 1760s, "the finest steel" in Britain "was made by the Hindoos" in India and imported at £1,000 per ton (which was more than 40 times the annual wages of a skilled British worker). By the conventional economic standards of Europe, the Mughals' tax demands—exacting perhaps 50 percent of the gross product of the empire—might seem depressing to any developing industrial spirit. But high taxation created a huge administrative class with surplus spending power (see Chapter 21). Their demand may have stimulated the concentration of production. Mughal India was almost certainly the world's most productive state in terms of manufacture for export, despite the modest technical equipment with which its industries were generally supplied (see Map 20.3).

Against this background, India's industrial collapse is astonishing. The ancient drain of Westerners' silver into India, which had been going on since pre-Roman times (see Chapter 7), was reversed in Bengal by the 1770s, In 1807, John Crawfurd reported that "kite makers, falconers, astrologers, and snake-charmers" had replaced useful trades in Bengal. A French missionary claimed, "Europe is no longer dependent on India for anything, having learned to beat the Hindus on their own ground, even in their most characteristic manufactures and industries, for which from time immemorial *we* were dependent on *them*. In fact the roles have been reversed and this revolution threatens to ruin India completely."

How did this collapse happen? Indian industry may have been caught, like China's, in an equilibrium trap. But it was more fragile in any case: less high powered, less technically advanced. The decline of Indian industry probably started with the decline of the Mughal Empire in the eighteenth century—skewered at its heart by Persian and Afghan invaders who sacked Delhi, the Mughal capital, shredded at its edges by usurping officials and rebellions. The impoverishment of the Mughal court deprived native industry of its best market. After Persian invaders looted the imperial treasury at Delhi in 1739, the nobles could no longer buy the products of Bengal. Then, with an exactness rare in history, India's industrial debacle coincided with one of the dramatic new developments of the next chapter of this book: the establishment of British rule or influence over most of India and, in particular, over its former industrial heartlands. Between the 1760s and the 1780s, in the early years of British rule in Bengal, silver imports into India virtually ceased. Instead, the British used tax revenues they extracted from the country to pay for the goods they exported to it. The British East India Company and its servants shamelessly exploited their monopoly by cutting prices to suppliers and acquiring allegedly low-quality Indian goods at confiscatory prices before reselling them to Indians and Europeans at enormous profits. Nor did the British neglect the opportunity to impose high prices for primary materials on Indian manufacturers. In 1767, for

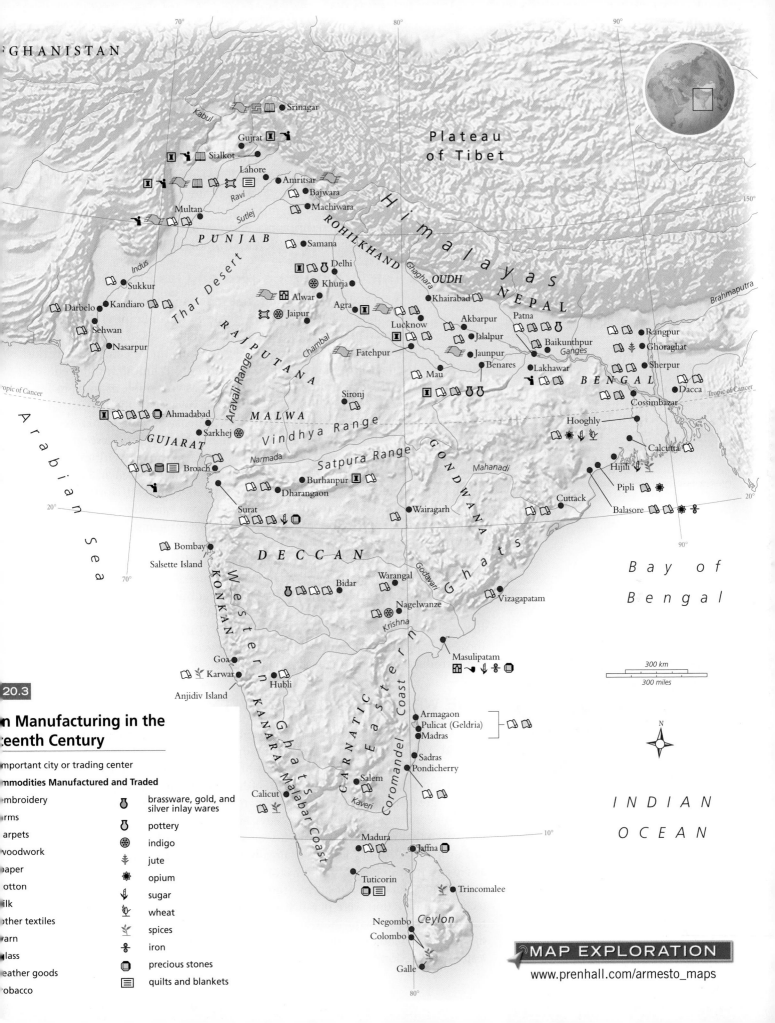

20.3

n Manufacturing in the
eenth Century

mportant city or trading center

ommodities Manufactured and Traded

mbroidery

rms

arpets

oodwork

aper

otton

ilk

ther textiles

arn

lass

eather goods

obacco

brassware, gold, and silver inlay wares

pottery

indigo

jute

opium

sugar

wheat

spices

iron

precious stones

quilts and blankets

MAP EXPLORATION

www.prenhall.com/armesto_maps

300 km

300 miles

Global Population and Economic Trends

ca. 1500	Population of Europe reaches 80 million
Eighteenth century	Urbanization increases in Europe and the Americas; most intense concentrations of industry found in east and South Asia
ca. 1750–1800	Indian industry goes into decline
1750–1850	Population of China doubles; population of the Americas increases sixfold
1784–1814	British import 300 million pounds of tea from China
Late eighteenth century	Ottoman Empire loses control of its shipping industry
1794	Condorcet's *The Progress of the Human Mind* published
1796	Edward Jenner develops improved smallpox vaccine
1798	Malthus's *Essay on Population* published
ca. 1800	Population of Europe reaches 180 million

The moon. By the time Galileo published the results of his astronomical observations through a telescope in 1610, the instrument was famous throughout Europe, and a Jesuit missionary had even written a book about it in Chinese. The telescope revealed that the moon, formerly perceived as being a perfect sphere, was in fact ridged and pitted.

instance, the company's representative sold silk yarn to weavers at double the price he paid for it.

The rapidity of the transformation of India from an economic powerhouse to a declining economy surprised contemporaries. For the Irish statesman, Edmund Burke (1729–1797), it was one of the "stupendous revolutions that have happened in our age of wonders." The dual nature of India's predicament, political and commercial, decorates the ceiling of the East India Company's headquarters in London, where Britannia, enthroned, receives the riches of the east from an abject procession led by India.

The Ottoman Empire and Its Environs

As in India, some of the same inducements and problems affected the industrial development of the Ottoman Empire. Here, too, raw materials were abundant. The vitality of the luxury market impressed every European visitor. But the selectivity of Turkish talent for industry and the lack of technical inventiveness in important trades made the empire as vulnerable as India to European competition. According to a voyager in the Persian Gulf in the mid–eighteenth century, the expensive spending habits of local notables mainly benefited French importers. In the second half of the eighteenth century, the carrying trade of the Ottoman Empire passed entirely into foreign hands—mainly French, English, and Venetian. In 1775, Tunisian shippers (Tunis in North Africa was nominally part of the Ottoman Empire) abandoned a heroic effort to compete with French shippers, whose home government supported them with tax breaks and naval protection. Persian silk, previously transmitted through Ottoman territory, and Egyptian linen disappeared from the export lists of the empire, as British, French, and Italian manufacturers produced cheaper alternatives. A critical observer of the Turks in 1807 admitted that "Europe certainly cannot surpass them in several of their manufactures"—essentially fine textiles—and that "in many of the inferior trades," Turkish workmen were equal to those of France. But he added that from laziness or lack of enterprise they "have not introduced or encouraged several useful arts of later invention."

THE WEST'S PRODUCTIVITY LEAP

The overall picture is clear. In the eighteenth-century world, economies in northern and Western Europe were becoming more developed, catching up with, and, in some respects, surpassing, the parts of Asia that had previously been enormously more productive. At first sight, **industrialization** in Europe looks like one of those great transformations of history that just happen because of impersonal forces—economic, demographic, environmental—beyond human control—necessities that mother invention. It seems to detect any idea of industrialization in Europe until the process had already begun to unfold. Yet a conspicuously active and fruitful period in the history of Western science preceded and accompanied—though it did not cause—industrialization (see Chapter 18). Science and technical innovation were parallel results from the growing curiosity about the real world and a growing interest in tinkering with things to see how they work. It makes sense to look into the realm of ideas to try to find the origins of Europe's leap in production.

The Scientific Background

The scientific revolution that occurred in the West during the seventeenth and eighteenth centuries extended the reach of human knowledge to subjects that had formerly been too remote or too difficult to understand. Galileo Galilei (1564–1642) could see the moons of Jupiter through his telescope. Anton van Leeuwenhoek (1632–1723) saw microbes through his microscope. Marin Mersenne (1588–1648) measured the speed of sound. Robert Hooke (1635–1703) could sniff what he called "nitre-air" in the acrid smell of vapor from a lighted wick, before Antoine Lavoisier (1743–1794) proved the existence of oxygen by isolating it and setting it on fire. Isaac Newton (1642–1727) could wrest the rainbow from a shaft of light or feel the force that bound the cosmos in the weight of an apple (see Chapter 17). Luigi Galvani (1737–1798) could feel the thrill of electricity in his fingertips. Friedrich Mesmer (1734–1815) thought hypnotism was a kind of detectable animal magnetism. Through life-threatening demonstrations with kite and keys, Benjamin Franklin (1706–1790) claimed to show lightning is a kind of electricity. Their triumphs made believable the cry of philosophers: "Nothing that we do not sense can be present to the mind!"

Demonstrations of the power of invisible forces in nature were domestic entertainments for rich people in eighteenth-century Europe. Intently, and with indifference to suffering, the scientist who dominates this painting of such a scene by Joseph Wright of Derby, in 1768, proves the vital necessity of air by depriving a bird of it. As the bird dies, a girl is revolted. Lovers carry on regardless. A father tries to explain science; a young man is enraptured by it.
Joseph Wright of Derby (1734–1797). "An Experiment on a Bird in the Air Pump." Oil on canvas. National Gallery, London, UK/The Bridgeman Art Library.

These discoveries accustomed Europeans to the idea that barely detectable forces can have enormous power, just as the strength of the body reposes in threadlike muscles. Nature was full of invisible powers that could replace human effort. The idea of harnessing natural energy arose unsurprisingly in the context of scientific thought. Steam, the first such power source in nature to be harnessed to replace muscles, was a fairly obvious case. You can see it and feel its heat, even though it takes imagination to believe that it can work machinery and make things move. But engineers in late eighteenth-century Britain used a discovery of "pure" science—atmospheric pressure, which is invisible and only an experiment can detect—to make steam power exploitable. Still, it is not enough to have a good idea. Conditions have to be right before good ideas get applied. The principles of the steam engine had been known in ancient Rome, and the science of the West had largely been anticipated in China. But, just as conditions in China restrained industrial output in the eighteenth century, conditions in parts of Europe promoted it. Population was rising fast enough to boost demand, without activating a high-level equilibrium trap. The global context favored economies that had privileged access to the Atlantic sea-lanes of global commerce. And, within Europe, new energy sources were being explored and released. The most conspicuous case is Britain's, where, in the second half of the eighteenth century, industrial output exhibited the most dynamic increases of any economy in the world (see Map 20.4).

The British Example

Britain was puny, in population terms, compared with the industrial giants of Asia. Britain still had fewer than 9 million people in 1800. But this was a dramatic increase from the 5.3 million recorded in 1731. To make up for the lack of manpower, Britain had unrivaled resources of untapped energy just below the surface of its soil. Coal production throughout Western Europe rose dramatically in the eighteenth century, but the biggest supplies, of the best quality, were in Britain. In the late seventeenth century, the annual output of British coal miners was less than 3 million tons.

MAP 20.4

Industrial Britain, ca. 1800

⛏	iron works
⚓	shipbuilding
●	major urban growth
♆	pottery
✗	cutlery
▢	woolens/cloth/cotton
◧	silk
▨	coalfields
═	turnpike road network, 1750

Manchester 33   journey time from London, in hours

By 1800, it had reached almost 14 million tons. Part of the increase was due to steam pumps, which enabled miners to dig deeper, below the water table, into shafts that could be drained. In turn, the pumps got people thinking about wider applications of steam-driven technology.

Britain, moreover, was an outstanding example of success in exploiting a position on the Atlantic. Britain tightly controlled the economies of its colonies in and across the Atlantic, so that their trade enriched British shippers and suppliers. British-ruled Ireland's agricultural surplus helped feed England and Scotland. Some of the profits of the slave economy of the West Indies went into agricultural improvement in Britain or investment in the infrastructure of roads, canals, and docks. The same shippers handled slave transfers and raw cotton imports, and exported the produce of the first major industrialized sector of the economy: cotton textile manufacture. By the 1770s, the Atlantic world of Africa and the Americas absorbed more of Britain's exports than Europe or Asia did and almost the entire export output of the British cotton and iron industries.

The merchant marine tripled to nearly 700,000 tons by 1776. Investment in infrastructure transformed the road network and stagecoach services. During the century, the time it took to get to London from Scotland was cut from 256 to 60 hours, and the journey from London to the city of Manchester fell by about 75 percent to 33 hours.

The cumulative effect of all these changes was a sharp increase in Britain's national product in the 1780s. For the rest of the century, annual output grew at 1.8 percent compared with 1 percent previously. Pig-iron production doubled and then doubled again. Exports, which had more than doubled in the first three-quarters of the century to over £14 million in value, reached £22 million by the century's end.

It would be exaggerated, however, to speak—as historians used to do—of an eighteenth-century Industrial Revolution. In most industries, development was piecemeal, and methods remained traditional. Huge gains in productivity resulted simply by applying traditional methods with more manpower and more capital investment to meet rising demand. In England, between 1785 and 1800, beer production rose by about a third, as did that of tallow candles. Soap manufacture rose by over 40 percent in the same period. Overwhelmingly, these industries grew without significant mechanization, and the spectacular growth of London provided their market. In the same period, sales of imported commodities, which required little processing, grew comparably or even more impressively. Tobacco sales increased by over a half; those of tea more than doubled.

The great exceptions—where transformed methods did boost production—were the textile and iron industries. Improved smelting techniques using coke, made from coal, drove changes in how the iron and steel trades were organized. By eliminating charcoal smelting and producing iron goods to replace wooden ones, these techniques doubly relieved pressure on failing timber resources. Output of iron rose from 17,350 tons in 1740 to over 125,000 tons in 1796. The first iron bridge spanned the river Severn in 1779. The first iron ship sailed in 1787. In 1767, Richard Arkwright patented a machine that enabled a single operative to spin 16 threads of yarn at once. In 1769, he adapted it to be powered by a water mill, turning—with improvements achieved over the next few years—a hundred spindles at a time. In 1779, Edmund Crompton found a way to use water or steam to power a machine to weave the yarn into cloth. In consequence, the cost of processing 100 pounds of raw cotton into cloth was cut by more than half in 20 years. The first steam-powered textile mill opened in 1785. Raw cotton imports, which amounted to under 3 million pounds weight in 1750, reached nearly 60 million pounds in 1800. A new way of working evolved in mechanized factories, with huge concentrations of workers, a pattern that would revolutionize the societies it affected in the next century.

Historians have always wondered and often asked whether there was anything special about British values or mind-sets or "spirit" that might help to explain why Britons took up the opportunities of the age with so much enthusiasm and effectiveness. Commercial values may have occupied a relatively high priority in British culture. Certainly, people thought so at the time. Napoleon—who developed intense hatred for Britain after he became ruler of France in 1799—sneered at "a nation of shopkeepers," but Britons accepted the sneer with pride. Early in the eighteenth century, the English novelist Daniel Defoe exulted in the incalculably huge number of British tradesmen. You may as well, he said, "count the stars in the sky." The agricultural writer Arthur Young (1741–1820) jokingly advised his sons to "get children" because "they are worth more than ever they were."

There was a serious theory behind Young's joke. The British economist David Ricardo (1772–1823) recognized a principle of economics—that labor adds value to a product. He went further. Value, he argued, is proportional to the labor invested in it, "labor . . . being the foundation of all value, and the relative quantity of labor . . . almost exclusively determining the relative value of commodities." In its crude form, the theory is wrong. Goods are not always exchanged at values proportionate to the labor invested in them. Capital plays a part (and is not always just stored-up labor, since raw natural assets can be sold for cash). So does the way the goods are perceived. Rarity value—which Ricardo did recognize, citing objects of art and "wines of a peculiar quality"—is the most obvious example. Advertizing and recommendation can also add value. Still, the principle is right. Ricardo drew from it a counter-intuitive conclusion. If labor makes the biggest contribution to profits, one would expect high wages to reflect this (as generally, in modern industrial societies, they do). Ricardo, however, thought that to maximize profits, capitalists would always keep wages low. "There can be no rise in the value of labor without a fall in profits." In fact, wages were static in England and rose a little in Scotland. Industrialization did not drive wages down, because the growth of population and of trade continually drove demand upward.

In broad context, however, Britain's eighteenth-century experience seems more characteristic than extraordinary—just a more pronounced case of an effort to maximize the use of resources that was happening all over western and northern Europe. By the time of the French Revolution in 1789, for instance, similar, if smaller industrial complexes were emerging in parts of France, Belgium, eastern Germany, and northern Spain. This effort was most widely generalized in the case of land—universally

The first iron bridge. The Iron Bridge spanning the River Severn at Coalbrookedale in England was the world's first cast iron bridge. Completed in 1770, it has come to be regarded as a symbol of the beginning of the Industrial Revolution. The Iron Bridge is also one of the last of its type to have survived intact. It was erected in just three months using sections made in a local foundry.

Daniel Defoe, from *The Complete English Tradesman*

David Ricardo, from *On Wages*

Agricultural improver. Thomas Coke of Norfolk (1752–1842), shown on the left, was an exemplary British agricultural improver, whose work with sheep was particularly influential. He boosted his flock from 800 to 2,500 without increasing the amount of grazing land the sheep needed, thanks in part to the scientific improvement he made in the South Down breed, depicted here, which produced highly prized mutton.

recognized, along with labor, as the most basic resource of all. In Britain, landholdings were considerably consolidated during the eighteenth century, with important consequences for efficiency. By 1790, over a quarter of the land in England was concentrated in estates of over 3,000 acres. In much of the highland zone of Scotland, landlords expelled or exterminated smallholders to make way for large sheep-grazing estates. Over most of the country, landowners adopted a common program: reducing labor costs, replacing inefficient farming with grazing, improving soils by draining and fertilizing, enhancing livestock by scientific stockbreeding, diversifying crops to maximize use of the earth, and, perhaps most importantly, by "enclosing" land—fencing off under-exploited land that had been open to anyone in the community for their own use. French agriculturalists who called themselves "physiocrats" recommended ways to improve agriculture to enrich France. Agricultural improvement societies promoted English-style changes in Spain and Spanish America. Similar approaches spread over much of Europe, as far east as Poland and as far south as northern Italy.

These European changes had parallels in east Asia beyond the reach of the equilibrium trap. In Korea and Japan, many works of popular agricultural advice were published to satisfy a passionate market for agricultural improvement. In Korea, farmers began to sow barley after the rice harvest to boost grain production. As in England, small landholdings were consolidated into huge farms for cash crops: ginseng, tobacco, and cotton. A measure of the Korean economic boom was the 1,000 new markets that sprang up in the first half of the eighteenth century. In Japan, too, agriculture became commercialized, as peasant subsistence agriculture virtually disappeared. Cotton cultivation spread from Osaka almost throughout the country. Osaka also lost its monopoly of oil lamp and soy sauce production, and Kyoto its dominance over silk output. The new crops that ecological exchange made available also played their part. In 1732, for instance, a locust plague in Kyushu destroyed the grain, but people had sweet potatoes to fall back on. Famines still occurred, but now local communities could afford social-welfare schemes to mitigate their effects. Landowners paid a wealth tax to supply emergency rice stocks, make loans to new businesses, and support the elderly. The leveling off of Japanese population levels looks like a classic case of prosperity having a restraining effect on birthrates. In Okayama, over the century as a whole, the average size of a household declined from seven persons to five.

THE EXPANSION OF RESOURCES

The effort to coax more food from the soil was only one aspect of a worldwide search for new food resources—a search in which Western Europeans occupied a privileged place.

Global Gardening

In the late eighteenth century, the botanical garden of Madrid in Spain was the nursery of a uniquely widespread empire. In the half-century after its foundation in 1756, it was one of the grand ornaments of European science, forming the last link in a chain of such gardens in Manila in the Philippines, Lima in Peru, Mexico City, and the Canary Islands off the coast of Africa. At least in theory, samples of the plant life of every climate the

Spanish monarchy occupied could be centralized in a single place of research. From Peru, for instance, in 1783, came 1,000 colored drawings and 1,500 written descriptions of plants. Perhaps the most important collections were those of Hipólito Pavón, whose expedition to Chile and Peru in 1777–1788 allowed him to indulge his personal passion—the study of the healing properties of plants—and to produce the most complete study of quinine yet attempted. Another prolific contributor was José Celestino Mutis, who presided over scientific life in one of the heroic outposts of the Spanish Empire at Bogotá, in what is today Colombia, from 1760 until his death in 1808.

At their best, empires could gather useful specimens from an astonishing diversity of climes, and make their flowers bloom together in scientific proximity. The Botanical Garden in Paris performed a comparable role. The French Jesuit missionary, Pierre Nicolas le Chéron d'Incarville, sent rare Chinese and Japanese plants there with Russian caravans across Asia. In England, the Royal Botanical Gardens at Kew, London, and the garden of the University of Oxford had similar functions, as, in the Netherlands, did the town gardens of Amsterdam and Utrecht and the University Garden of Leiden.

The plants of the world could gather in Europe and be redistributed around European empires, because only these empires were scattered widely enough around the globe, and had the environmental range, to exploit the opportunities to the full. European empires became laboratories of ecological exchange. Pierre Poivre, for instance, launched one of the most breathtaking experiments in France's Indian Ocean island colonies in 1747. Until he transformed them, the islands were economically unsuccessful—diminishing assets, wasted by deforestation and repeated attempts to introduce plantation monocultures. Poivre trained to be a Jesuit but, too young for ordination, filled in his time by traveling widely in Asia to study natural history. He smuggled 3,000 valuable spice plants out of southeast Asia and planted them in the island of Mauritius (maw-RIH-shihs) off the east coast of Africa, where they eventually became the basis of a commercially successful operation in cloves, cinnamon, and pepper. When he became governor of France's Indian Ocean colonies 20 years after his first introductions, he combined the policy of diversifying crops with a strategy to restore the islands' forests to maintain rainfall levels.

Similar transplantations occurred to and fro, as the ecological exchange became more systematic and planned. Coffee is a case in point. Southern Arabia had long enjoyed a world monopoly of coffee. But in 1707, the Dutch introduced it into Java, the main island of what is today Indonesia, as part of a system of political control in which local rulers guaranteed to deliver it at prices that exploited producers, who had to be forced to grow it. Coffee was one of the most commercially successful products of the eighteenth century. The French planted it in the island of Bourbon (modern Reunion) in the Indian Ocean and in Saint-Domingue (modern Haiti) in the Caribbean, and the Portuguese in Brazil (see Chapter 17). By midcentury, the Arabian coffee trade had ceased to grow, and the British East India Company no longer sent regular ships there. Since almost all coffee drinkers of the era took their cups heavily sweetened, the sugar and coffee trades grew together, and sugar, of course, had wider applications.

The Botanical Garden of Madrid. By establishing a series of botanical gardens on both sides of the Atlantic, the Spanish monarchs in the eighteenth century promoted the transplantation of scientifically interesting or useful plants—including species good for health or nutrition—between continents. Today, the Botanical Garden of Madrid is little more than a park, but it retains reminders of its original functions, including the eighteenth-century plant house in the background of this photograph, and the bust of the great Swedish botanist, Carolus Linnaeus (1707–1778), in the foreground.

Map of Mauritius in 1835. In the eighteenth century, French administrators introduced forest conservation to the Indian Ocean island and banned colonists there from growing what were thought to be ecologically unsuitable crops, such as cotton and wheat. The map shows the surviving forests in the center and the lower left.

The expansion of sugar lands in the seventeenth-century Atlantic was followed, in the eighteenth century, by a similar expansion around the Indian Ocean. By 1800, sugar had probably replaced pepper as southeast Asia's major export.

Even places too isolated for the global ecological exchange to affect could achieve high levels of productivity. Hawaii is a case in point, since it remained outside the range of European navigation until 1778. The earliest European accounts of Hawaii were full of praise for the native farmers. Expeditions from the late 1770s to the 1790s recorded fields outlined with irrigation ditches and stone walls, "made with a neatness approaching to elegance," planted with taro, breadfruit, sweet potato, sugarcane, and coconut, and laid out in a pattern calculated to impress readers at home as civilized. The roads "would have done credit to any European engineer." An engraving made on the basis of reports from the British navigator George Vancouver's expedition early in the 1790s shows a field system of a regularity that arouses one's suspicions that it was made up to present a picture attuned to European ideals. Yet the same array of farmers' geometry is visible today, under the surface of fields tilled no longer, in the noon sunlight on the slopes of Hualalai and the Kohala Mountains on the Big Island of Hawaii. Only in Hawaii, moreover, among Polynesian settlements, was fish farming fully developed. Into the grid of fields and pools, other constructions were slotted. Massive platforms of stone supported temples of exact symmetry, and the wall-building techniques were adaptable to the demands of fortifications two or three times the height of a man. Early European visitors could recognize not only institutions of statehood but also an islandwide empire in the making—a process completed in 1795, when the first king, Kamehameha I, defeated the last of his enemies and extended his rule over all the Hawaiian islands.

The Pacific generally was a latecomer to the great ocean-borne exchange of foodstuffs (see Map 20.5). In 1774, a Spanish expedition tried to annex Tahiti. It failed, but left Spanish hogs behind, which first improved, then replaced, the native breed of pigs. By 1788, the small, long-legged, long-snouted native pigs had disappeared. In consequence, Tahiti had an advantage in the pork trade that soon transformed the Pacific as a result of two developments. First, Captain James Cook (1728–1779) perfected a method to keep salt pork edible after a long sea voyage. Second, Australia became a British colony. In 1792, George Vancouver shipped 80 live pigs from Tahiti to Sydney in Australia to create a food source for the colonists. But it proved more economical for Australia to import pork ready salted from Tahiti than to breed its own pigs. In the first year of the trade, 1802–1803, merchants in Sydney—Australia's first middle class—handled 300,000 pounds of the meat. By the time the trade waned in the late 1820s, ten times that amount had changed hands. The muskets that paid for the pork stimulated civil war and turned Tahiti into a monarchy.

The breadfruit was an eye-catching part of the abundance that made the South Sea islands wonderful to eighteenth-century European sailors: places of restoration where the long-felt wants of seaboard life were supplied. Along with the sexual license of Tahitian life, on an island where "the only god is love," ample fresh food helped to make the South Seas seem "certainly the paradise of the world," according to a British visitor in 1787. In the lingo of modern economists, this was a world of "subsistence

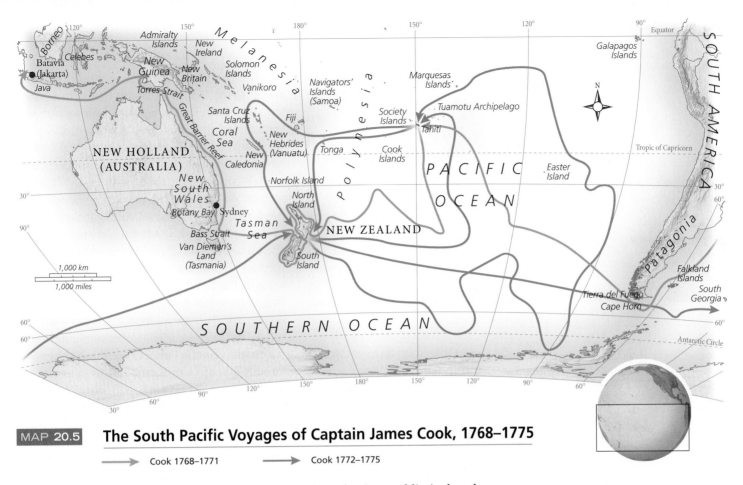

MAP 20.5 **The South Pacific Voyages of Captain James Cook, 1768–1775**

⟶ Cook 1768–1771   ⟶ Cook 1772–1775

affluence," where there was little specialization in food production and limited trade in food products, but where, in normal times, abundance was spectacular.

In most islands, yams, taro, and plantains contributed most to the basic diet, but when in season, breadfruit was the making of every feast, the starchy complement to the festive meats: pigs, turtles, dogs, chicken, fish, and some prestigious larvae, such as the grubs of the longhorn beetle, which infests coconuts. The most widely favored way to prepare breadfruit was to bake it whole in hot embers or in pits with hot stones. It was also eaten in fish stews, cooked in coconut milk. Because it is a seasonal product, and—unlike taro—rots if not harvested when it is ripe, it was also dried, fermented, and smoked. It helped to communicate an illusion of nutritional richness and became a fixture in Europeans' mental picture of the South Sea–island Eden in the eighteenth century.

The "inestimable benefit" of "a new fruit, a new farinaceous [grainlike] plant" was among the prizes that lured the French explorer, the Count de La Pérouse, to his death in the South Pacific in 1788. The same search inspired the voyage that ended with events Hollywood turned into the most famous episode of eighteenth-century naval history: the mutiny on the *Bounty*. Captain William Bligh's mission as commander of the British warship *Bounty* in 1787 was to pluck a bit of the paradise of the South Pacific in the form of breadfruit tree seedlings and transfer it to the slave hell of the Caribbean. On Jamaica, Bryan Edwards, a planter who was always on the lookout for ways to improve the slave economy, believed that breadfruit could energize slaves and turn his island into a hive of industry. So the British government sent Bligh to Tahiti.

William Hodges' vision of Tahiti, remembered from the artist's experiences as resident artist with Captain Cook's expedition of 1772: "a voluptuaries' paradise . . . a habitat for nymphs."

Sydney. Crowned by brushland, with natives in canoes in the foreground, this is what the harbor of Sydney, Australia looked like soon after the colony of New South Wales was founded in 1788. The governor's house is high on the hillside to the left, and fields are taking shape around the cove.

He brought his single-minded, demonic energy to the task. In the South Pacific, most of his men mutinied. The captain and the loyal survivors were cast adrift in midocean and saved, after terrible deprivations, only by Bligh's startling ability as a navigator. Meanwhile, some of the mutineers lived in self-condemned exile with their Tahitian women on Pitcairn, an uncharted island where predictable quarrels led to feuding in which most of them were killed. The Royal Navy hunted down and executed others. After six years' bloodshed and hardship and with a new ship, Bligh completed his mission. But these was an ironic twist—the breadfruit experiment proved disastrous. Breadfruit is not a particularly useful food. It has few nutrients. It does not keep well. The slaves would not eat it.

Other food transfers were more successful. Captain James Cook, the explorer who was responsible for so many more famous initiatives in Pacific history, was also the prophet of pigs and potatoes in New Zealand. The Dutch had discovered New Zealand in 1642, but it was then forgotten. Cook rediscovered the islands in 1769. The native inhabitants of New Zealand, the Maori, who preferred their own food, resisted his first efforts to introduce new foodstuffs (see Chapter 14). "All our endeavours for stocking this country with useful animals are likely to be frustrated by the very people we mean to serve." But Maori in the north of New Zealand were trading potatoes by 1801, and pigs became a trading item by about 1815. Other attempted introductions, such as goats, garlic, cattle, and cabbage, failed because they did not fit into traditional Maori ways of farming. Cook's shipboard scientist, Johann Reinhold Forster, suffered for his efforts to introduce sheep and goats to the islands, especially from the smell their manure produced when they were stabled in the cabin next to his to protect them from the weather. Potatoes, however, proved popular in New Zealand because they were sufficiently like the kumara or sweet potatoes that had long been familiar to the Maori. who also welcomed pigs, which could be grazed and eaten.

The same expedition succeeded in a series of other introductions. Forster reported:

> We have imported goats into Tahiti and laid the foundations of a numerous breed of animals most excellently calculated for the hills occupying the inland parts of this isle . . . and in all the isles we made presents of garden seeds and planted potatoes in Queen Charlotte's Sound with a good quantity of garlic: so that future navigators may be refreshed in these seas more than they would expect.[1]

New Zealand was an outstanding example of what Alfred Crosby called **Neo Europes** (New Europes): lands in other hemispheres where the environment resembled Europe's enough for European migrants to thrive, European plants to take root, and a European way of life to be transplanted. Even with help from the climate, however, it was not easy to catch reflections of home in such distant mirrors. The strenuous efforts the British had to apply to adapt in the Australian colony of New South Wales are vividly documented. Take, for instance, the case of James Ruse. He was a pardoned convict who had been a farmer in England. In 1789, he received a grant of 30 acres at Parramatta in Australia. The "middling soil," it seemed to him, was bound to fail for want of manure. He burned timber, dug in ash, hoed, clod molded the earth, dug in grass and weeds, and left the soil exposed to sun for sowing. He planted turnip seed "which will mellow and prepare it for next year" and mulched it with his own compost, made from straw rotted in pits. He and his wife did all the work themselves.

Success with such untried soils depended on experimentation with varied planting strategies. Early Australia was a strange sort of new Europe at first—made with yams, pumpkins, and maize. On the warm coastal lowlands where the first settlers set up, maize did better than the rye, barley, and wheat that the founding fleet shipped from England in 1788. Firs and oaks were planted, but the food trees were more exotic: oranges, lemons, and limes grew alongside indigo, coffee, ginger, and castor nut. On the outward voyage, the fleet acquired tropical specimens, including bananas, cocoa, guava, sugar cane, and tamarind. In 1802, visitors could admire "the bamboo of Asia" in the governor's garden in Melbourne, the capital of New South Wales. The most successful early livestock were introduced from Calcutta in India and the Cape of Good Hope in South Africa, which also supplied fruit trees.

In the long run, a European model did prevail, but it was primarily a Mediterranean one. Sir Joseph Banks, the British botanist who equipped the founding expedition, believed that over most of its extent the Southern Hemisphere was about ten degrees cooler at any given latitude than the Northern. He therefore expected Botany Bay in southern Australia to resemble southwest France and sent over citrus fruits, pomegranates, apricots, nectarines, and peaches. "All the vegetables of Europe" fed the colonists in the 1790s, but Mediterranean colors predominated in visitors' descriptions. The first governor had oranges in his garden, "as many fine figs as ever I tasted in Spain or Portugal," and "a thousand vines yielding three hundredweight of grapes." Watkin Tench, whose study of the soils was vital to the colony's success—his samples can still be seen, dried to powder, in a Sydney museum—commended the performance of grape "vines of every sort . . . That their juice will probably hereafter furnish an indispensable article of luxury at European tables has already been predicted in the vehemence of speculation." He also spotted the potential of oranges, lemons, and figs. By the time of a French visit in 1802, peaches were so plentiful that they were used to fatten the hogs. The French commander saw, in the governor's garden, "the Portugal orange and the Canary fig ripening beneath the shade of the French apple tree." The Mediterranean world also provided Australia with an exportable staple—wool. The first consignment of merino sheep, a Spanish breed, left for New South Wales in 1804. Only five rams and one old ewe survived the journey, but these were enough to begin the stocking of the country, which today has more sheep than people.

This Australian experience set the pattern for the colonial New Europes of the nineteenth century, where "the roots are European but the tree grows to a different pattern and design." The North American West, New Zealand, and to a lesser extent, the "cone" of South America—Uruguay, Argentina, and Chile—were all settled, displacing the native cultures with dynamic, outward-going, and relatively populous economies. All defied their original planners and developed their own distinctive characters—tricks that the alchemy of settlement worked in the crucible of new environments.

Transplanting breadfruit. Thomas Gosse, the official artist of the British expedition that took breadfruit from Tahiti to Jamaica in the 1790s, gave pride of place to the Tahitians in the pictures he painted of the voyage. He depicted the British in a marginal, subordinate, and passive role. The breadfruit was supposed to provide cheap food for Jamaica's slaves, but the slaves rejected it.

Economic Revolution in the West

Seventeenth and eighteenth centuries	Scientific revolution
Eighteenth century	Concentration of landholdings in Britain
1756	Botanical Garden of Madrid founded
1760–1808	José Celestino Mutis leads scientific study in Colombia
1769	Captain James Cook rediscovers New Zealand
1770s	The Atlantic world absorbs more British exports than Europe or Asia
1780s	Sharp increase in Britain's national product
1800	British coal production reaches 14 million tons
1805	Merino sheep introduced to Australia

IN PERSPECTIVE: New Europes, New Departures

"There was never," observed Samuel Johnson (1709–1784), the English man of letters, contemplating his own era, "from the earliest ages a time in which trade so engaged the attention of mankind, or commercial gain was sought with such general emulation." The world was encircled by a cycle that was speeding up: growing population, growing demand, growing output, growing commerce, all stimulated each other. The big gainers were economies that bordered the Atlantic, where traders and shippers could participate in the increasing opportunities worldwide. For the Atlantic led to the wind systems of the world and, by relatively easy access, to exploitable empires.

Overseas colonies were an unmixed blessing for the states that founded them. Colonies demanded heavy investment and paid modest returns. They drained manpower from home countries without always adding much to long-term demand. On the contrary, colonies tended to develop regional economies, "creole mentalities," and—as we shall see in the next chapter—independence movements. The biggest, most precocious, and, in terms of cash yield, richest of the empires—that of Spain—never stimulated much of a commercial or industrial revolution in Spain itself. Yet gradually, in less obvious ways, overseas imperialism did contribute to European world dominance.

The New Europes made the West big. A culture crammed, for most of its history, into a small, remote, and beleaguered corner of Eurasia, now had much of the Western Hemisphere and important parts of the Pacific and Africa at its disposal. Even without the technical and scientific advantages the West was beginning to build up, the growing resources available to Western economies were enough to change the world.

China and Japan were also big gainers from the economic and demographic changes of the eighteenth century. But a future in which the West would be increasingly dominant was already visible. In the late eighteenth and early nineteenth centuries, the industrialization of Britain would keep rough pace with the deindustrialization of India at British bayonet point. Domination of India acquired even greater significance in the nineteenth century when the British turned Indian land over to the production of tea and opium, which destroyed China's trade balance, and ultimately to the farming of quinine in industrial quantities, which enabled European armies to treat malaria, one of the worst hazards of tropical environments. Meanwhile, other eighteenth-century developments, which are the subjects of the next two chapters, contributed to reshaping world history: the growth, strain, instability, and—in some cases—collapse of land empires, and the increasing exchange of ideas between parts of Asia and the West.

CHRONOLOGY

ca. 1500	Population of Europe reaches 80 million
Seventeenth and eighteenth centuries	Scientific revolution in the West
ca. 1700	Population of Europe reaches 120 million
Eighteenth century	Urbanization increases in Europe and the Americas; concentration of landholdings in Britain; most intense concentrations of industry found in east and south Asia; economic boom in Korea and Japan
1721–1804	Population of Japan stabilizes
ca. 1750–1800	Indian industry goes into decline
1750–1850	Population of China doubles; population of the Americas increases sixfold
1756	Botanical Garden of Madrid founded
1769	Captain James Cook rediscovers New Zealand
1760–1808	José Celestino Mutis leads scientific study in Colombia
1770s	The Atlantic world absorbs more British exports than Europe or Asia
1777–1788	Hipólito Pavón's expedition to Chile and Peru
1780s	Sharp increase in Britain's national product
1784–1814	British import 300 million pounds of tea from China
1787	*Bounty* begins journey to South Pacific
Late eighteenth century	Ottoman Empire loses control of its shipping industry
1794	Condorcet's *The Progress of the Human Mind* published
1796	Edward Jenner develops improved smallpox vaccine
1798	Malthus's *Essay on Population* published
ca. 1800	British coal production reaches 14 million tons; population of Europe reaches 180 million; 10,000 "chests" of opium imported into China annually
1805	Merino sheep introduced to Australia

PROBLEMS AND PARALLELS

1. Why is the population increase of the eighteenth century central to understanding the history of this period? What are the various explanations for the demographic growth of the eighteenth century? What was the impact of increased urbanization and health care on the demographic trends of this period?

2. How does the economic history of the eighteenth century mark a departure from prevailing global patterns? Why did the disparity in productivity and wealth between China and India and the West begin to narrow? Why did Ottoman economic activity decline?

3. How did the demographic changes and the speeding up of economic activity affect the global balance of power? Why did

Europe's productivity leap in the eighteenth century? How did science contribute to European technical innovation in this period?

4. How did "global gardening" affect people's lives in large regions like Europe and smaller-scale societies like Hawaii? What does the term *New Europes* mean?

5. What are the social, economic, and political reasons for the rise of Britain as a world power in the eighteenth century? What factors led to its military and economic strength?

DOCUMENTS IN GLOBAL HISTORY

- Thomas Malthus, from *Essay on the Principle of Population*
- Marquis de Condorcet, from *Sketch for a Hstorical Picture of the Progress of the Human Mind*
- James Lind, from *A Treatise on Scurvy*

- Lady Mary Wortley Montagu, from *Letters*
- Daniel Defoe, from *The Complete English Tradesman*
- David Ricardo, from *On Wages*

Please see the Primary Source CD-ROM for additional sources related to this chapter.

READ ON

On the great eighteenth century thinkers about population, see William Godwin, *Progress, Poverty and Population: Re-Reading Condorcet, Godwin and Malthus* (1997). Robert Duplessis, *Transitions to Capitalism in Early Modern Europe* (1997) contains much nuanced information on European demographics and is a good overview of the run up to industrialization, distinguishing Britain from the Continent. Margaret Jacob, *Scientific Culture and the Making of the Industrial West* (1997) shows the cultural conduits through which Newtonian mechanics influenced technological progress. See also Joel Mokyr, *The Lever of Riches: Technological Creativity and Economic Progress* (1990), which is perhaps overly optimistic.

On China during the eighteenth century, Pamela Crossley, *The Manchus* (1997) is useful, as is Joanna Waley-Cohen, "China and Western Technology in the Late Eighteenth Century", *American Historical Review* (1993). But now fundamental are Kenneth Pomeranz, *The Great Divergence: China,*

Europe, and the Making of the Modern World Economy (2001) and Andre Gunder-Frank, *ReORIENT: Global Economy in the Asian Age*. For a contrasting view, see David Landes, *The Wealth and Poverty of Nations* (1998). Huri Islamoglu-Inan, *The Ottoman Empire and the World Economy* (1987), puts the Ottoman economy in perspective. Seema Alavi, ed., *The Eighteenth Century in India* (2002) collects the most significant work on the Indian economy and the impact of British commercial and political interventions.

Grove, *Green Imperialism: Colonial Expansion, Tropical Island Edens and the Origins of Environmentalism, 1600–1860* (1996) is excellent for the development of resources. *The Journals of Hipolito Ruiz: Spanish Botanist in Peru and Chile, 1777–1788*, trans. Richard Schulte et al. (1998) provides a fascinating first-hand account. Dodge, *Islands and Empires: Western Impact on the Pacific and East Asia* (1976) is useful, while Alfred Crosby, *Ecological Imperialism: The Biological Expansion of Europe, 900–1900* (1993) is a classic.

CHAPTER 21

The Age of Global Interaction: Expansion and Intersection of Eighteenth-Century Empires

Fort Jesus, Mombasa, in what is today Kenya, was one of a string of forts the Portuguese founded around the rim of the Indian Ocean. It fell to Omani attackers in 1698—one episode in Portugal's long retreat from most of its eastern outposts in the face of hostility or competition from non-European empires.

n September 1697, after 18 months of siege, all the 2,500 defenders were dead, except a few Swahili mercenaries under a local sheikh known as Bwana Daud. Fort Jesus, at Mombasa, on the east coast of Africa, in what is now Kenya, was the principal Portuguese station at the western end of the monsoon wind system of the Indian Ocean. It looked as if it was bound to fall to new rivals for the creation of a seaborne empire: the Sayid (SEYE-yihd) dynasty of Oman, in southeast Arabia.

MOMBASA

"Loyalty counted more with me than ambition or maternal love," wrote Daud later to the King of Portugal. By heroic efforts, he held out until a relief force of 200 men arrived. But the Omanis did not give up, and by December 1698, the situation was again desperate. Only ten defenders survived. They retreated into the innermost bastion of the fort and resolved to die fighting. A few hours after the last of them was cut down, a relief force from the Portuguese colony of Goa in India appeared offshore. They saw the red flag of Oman fluttering over the ramparts, turned around, and headed for home. Over the next three decades, despite periodic reversals, Sayid imperialism mopped up all the Portuguese stations on the Swahili coast of East Africa.

It was part of a deliberate Omani strategy to control westward trade along the old monsoonal routes. Oman was an unusual kind of state. It created an unusual kind of empire. The Omani brand of Islam was neither Sunni nor Shiia, but maintained that the true heir of the prophet Muhammad was whoever was the best qualified to lead the people: the **imam** (ih-MAHM), as the Omanis called him. In practice, the Sayids had established a hereditary monarchy, but they remained formally committed to the idea of the imamate. This religious principle ensured that their people rejected the ideologies of neighboring empires: the Sunni Ottomans, Shiite Persia, and the Christian Portuguese.

On the coast of East Africa, peaceful colonization by Omani merchant families had preceded armed intervention. Independent city-states had dotted the region and the islands offshore since at least the twelfth century when local rulers began to mint the earliest coins so far discovered in this region. These states had a common economic culture—commercial and maritime—a common religion in Islam, and a common language, Swahili (swah-HEE-lee). In grammar, Swahili was like the Bantu

FOCUS questions

- WHY DID China rely more on colonization than on conquest to expand its empire in the eighteenth century?
- WHAT INTERNAL problems and foreign foes did the Ottoman Empire face in the eighteenth century?
- HOW DID Britain become the dominant power in India?
- WHY WAS the slave trade so important for the economies of West Africa, Europe, and the Americas?
- WHY DID new Native American empires begin to arise during the eighteenth century?
- WHY DID the British and Spanish colonies in the New World come to resent imperial control from Europe?

languages neighboring inland peoples spoke, but influences from the sea, especially Arabic, increasingly saturated its vocabulary. Portuguese incursions in the sixteenth century had disrupted the trade of all but a handful of East African ports—Mombasa was one of the exceptions—but merchants from Arabia and, to a lesser extent, India never stopped trading in the area.

Omanis established garrisons at Mombasa, Kilwa, Zanzibar, and Pemba. At first, the imam directly appointed governors from Oman. For the native East Africans, the Omanis were as foreign as the Portuguese. Resentment and rebellions among the Swahili followed. At home in Oman, splits in the political elite were common, as some of the Sayids' subjects felt that the dominance of one dynasty was a betrayal of the spirit of the imamate. Oman could not fully exploit commercial opportunities, because it never had enough shipping to handle all the African ivory and Indian cloth that crossed the ocean, though the large East African slave trade did become concentrated in Omani hands. Political control was weak. The Omani Empire became a loose network of autonomous small states, tied by a sense of kinship among Sayid clan members, like the regional branches or offshoots of a family business.

Beyond the reach of Omani naval power, even more informal networks spread, as Omani migrants crossed the Indian Ocean. They were welcome, wherever Islam was practiced, as descendants of the Prophet and speakers of perfect Arabic. They became judges, royal advisers, and the husbands of rich women. They founded dynasties in the southeast Asian islands of Borneo and Sumatra. "They have spread everywhere throughout the Malay countries," complained a Dutch governor in Melaka in 1750, "and have revealed too much to the natives": too much, that is, about the vulnerability of European outposts.

● ● ● ● ●

In one respect, the emergence of Omani power is a typical story of the time—intelligible in a context of multiplying opportunities to accumulate wealth and multiplying temptations to invest it in empire. Yet in other ways, the Omani network seemed an old-fashioned empire in its day—concerned to control trade, not production, clinging to maritime outposts, and stringing them together into the loosest kind of web—whereas the trend was for maritime empires to turn landward, build up territorial conquests, and centralize power. On the whole, in the eighteenth century, Europeans were becoming relatively more successful in encounters with enemies in other parts of the world. Though they still did not dare to tackle China or Japan, European arms gradually established their superiority against Indian and southeast Asian foes. At the least, it could be said that European operations in Asia were no longer at the mercy of native empires, as they had been, in most areas, in the seventeenth century. These are related problems: the growth of land empires and the rise of Western power, wealth, and inventiveness.

ASIAN IMPERIALISM IN ARREST OR DECLINE: CHINA, PERSIA, AND THE OTTOMANS

Empires grew not only or even solely by conquest, but by colonization. In the eighteenth century, an era of colonization worldwide or, at least, world widespread, peopled the border lands of the expanding empires and lined political frontiers with settlers. Painstakingly recruited, thinly spread, colonists began to extend the limits of the inhabited world. At the edges of the empires to which they belonged, where they reached out to touch the outposts of other expanding peoples, they helped to mesh the world together.

China

China's was, by most standards, the world's fastest-growing empire in the eighteenth century. It engulfed Tibet in 1720, thrust deep into Central Asia, and made territorial gains along the borders with Mongolia, Russia, Burma, and Vietnam. Chinese continued to colonize recently absorbed lands in Manchuria and Taiwan (see Chapter 19). The conquest of China's "wild west" in Xinjiang was complete by 1759. When the scholar Ji Yun (chuh-ywuhn) made his journey of exile there ten years later, he felt the awe of entering "another world"—the usual sentiment of a Chinese traveler on leaving China. Yet he soon settled down on a formerly wild frontier that was being tamed with remarkable speed. The hick town of Urumqi (oo-room-chee), where he made his new home, had bookshops selling classical Chinese texts. His neighbors grew Chinese peonies and peaches. Settlers kept coming from the east. By 1788, an emancipated convict was able to make a fortune by opening a shop selling Chinese delicacies.

By the end of the century, at least 200,000 Chinese immigrants had settled in Xinjiang. Plenty of them were criminals and political undesirables, but many others were volunteers. For merchants the opportunities in Xinjiang were so profitable that they were punished for wrongdoing by being sent back home. A government that reimbursed travel costs and offered loans for seeds, livestock, and housing, with a grant of four-and-a-half acres of land per family and temporary exemption from tax sweetened the paths of legitimate migrants. Settlement was concentrated beyond the mountains on arable land where market towns mushroomed. The lead and iron mines of Urumqi produced nothing for export. The frontier's own boom absorbed everything the mines produced.

For the ruling Manchu Qing dynasty, colonization of the frontier was too important to be left to the Chinese. In a reshuffling of tribal peoples, reminiscent of the

Tribute. The Qianlong emperor of China (r. 1735–1796) loved horses, as a good Manchu should. Here, in a painting probably produced by Chinese and Jesuit painters at the emperor's court, he receives some of the famed horses of Central Asia from Mongol envoys. The background to this scene was the expansion of the Chinese Empire and the emperor's efforts to bring nomadic peoples under imperial discipline.
The Tartar envoys presenting their horses to Emperor Qianlong. 1757. 45 x 257 cm. Musee du Louvre/RMN Reunion des Musees Nationaux, France. SCALA/Art Resource, NY

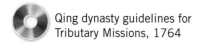

Qing dynasty guidelines for
Tributary Missions, 1764

The Qianlong emperor. When the Qianlong emperor
(r. 1736–1796) attained an advanced age, Chinese portraits generally showed him splendidly
enthroned and enveloped in gorgeous robes,
embroidered with images of power and virility.
But the artist, William Alexander, who visited
China with an ill-fated British embassy in 1793,
was free to capture this informal, intimate likeness of the emperor.

frontier defense strategies of the late Roman Empire (see Chapter 8), the Qing moved Mongol bands about like knights on a chessboard, shifting some between weak points in the borderlands, inducing others into the empire from outside. In an affecting ceremony in Beijing in 1771, the Qianlong (chee-ehn-luhng) emperor (r. 1735–1796) welcomed back into the imperial fold the Khan Uphasha of the Torghut people. China had wooed this tribe for nearly 60 years. The Torghut now abandoned Russian overlordship in the Volga valley, where they had found refuge for over a century, to return to their long-lost homeland in western Mongolia. It sounds like a happy story—but the vacancy had arisen only because the Chinese had fought the local inhabitants to extinction to clear the way for the Torghut.

Meanwhile, Chinese continued to overspill the borders of China by sea. They became miners in Malaya, and farm laborers in the Spanish-ruled Philippines. Some of them made fortunes as businessmen and brokers. In Manila, the capital of the Philippines, in 1729, the archbishop and other leading citizens complained that they had tried to obtain for a Spaniard the contract to supply the city with bread, but were unable to wrest the concession from the Chinese. Immigrants went on repeopling Chinese quarters in Manila and Batavia, the capital of the Dutch East Indies, despite the periodic massacres inflicted by native Filipinos and Javanese who feared the Chinese would "swamp" them. The migrants flowed in, in defiance of the efforts of the Chinese government to stop them—or, at least, to persecute those who returned home. A famous case was that of Zhen Yilao, who made a fortune in the Dutch East Indies and acted as "introducer" of new Chinese colonists for the Dutch after a massacre in 1740. He returned to his home province of Fujian in southern China in 1749 to, he said "fulfill his filial duty of looking after his ageing mother." His punishment was the seizure of his fortune and condemnation to exile—this time, to be spent inside the borders of the empire. Chinese traders benefited increasingly, as trade in southeast Asia slipped out of the control of states and large companies. Armenians, independent Europeans, and Bugis from Sulawesi (Celebes) in Indonesia also stepped into the breach, but the Chinese predominated. In 1732, Chinese controlled 62 percent of the shipping into Batavia from other parts of southeast Asia.

Content with profit, they rarely made bids for power. A rebellion broke out in the Chinese quarter of Batavia in 1740, not so much to seize power as for self-defense. In Batavia, according to the rebels, "so few Dutchmen and so many Chinese live, and...nevertheless the Dutch dare to treat the Chinese so harshly and oppress them so unjustly that it cannot be tolerated. The Chinese nation is forced to unite and declare war against the Dutch."[1] In Manila, the growing sense of common identity among the Chinese became so strong that it overcame the usual Chinese emphasis on clan or family lineage, especially as the Chinese became entangled in new kinship structures as a result of locally contracted marriages. A Chinese had to woo his intended bride's family and placate them with gifts. Traditionally, Filipino women remained part of their parents' families, which their husbands joined. But the Chinese were ghetto dwellers, that is they lived in exclusively Chinese neighborhoods. So mixed marriages, unlike those between two Filipinos, took a bride away from her parents' home. The structure was neither wholly Filipino nor particularly Chinese, but something new.

At some times and in some places, overseas Chinese took power for the sake of trade. For instance, after trouble with European advisers and French envoys in the late seventeenth century, Thailand underwent a revulsion against European influence. But the Thai court had a long tradition of installing foreign favorites. So from 1700, Chinese were dominant, occupying the position of royal favorite and pur-

Multicultural city. Batavia, the capital of the Dutch East Indies, was, according to Captain Cook, the unhealthiest port in the world. It was also one of the busiest. This engraving from 1764 showed the teeming shipping in the harbor and revealing scenes in the foreground of life in what was effectively a Dutch-Chinese city. From under her umbrella, a Chinese lady in grand Western dress, scowls at tipsy Dutchmen. Crocodiles share the canal with a Chinese pleasure boat and commercial barges.

chasing most of the other principal offices in the kingdom. Chinese concubines, selected by Chinese favorites, surrounded King Thaisa (r. 1709–1733). But the Chinese community was too successful for its own good. The Thai became jealous of its growing profits and afraid of its growing numbers. When a new Thai king, Borommakot, suspended the pro-Chinese policy in 1733–1734, the Chinese, who by now numbered 20,000, fell under suspicion of plotting to oust him. Expected vengeance from China did not materialize. Overseas adventures remained private initiatives, in which the Chinese state was uninterested.

Back in mainland China, the economic dynamism of the empire was evident from the tax returns. Revenues rose by about two-thirds in the eighteenth century, despite substantial tax reductions, especially the abolition of the poll tax in 1712. The increase in the revenue was the result of rising population, rising production, and rising trade. The Qianlong emperor enjoyed an annual surplus of 8 to 9 million silver dollars and left 400 million silver dollars in his treasury at his abdication in 1796—probably more than twice as much as the Mughal Empire in India amassed at its height. By the emperor's last years, however, Chinese expansion was slackening or stagnating. Territorial expansion stopped. The emperor grew old and inert. His last portraits show him wasted, wrinkled, shrunk into old age—a sad contrast with his youthful portraits as huntsman, warrior, or pilgrim to sacred shrines. The influence of the corrupt favorite, Hensho, was blamed for the state's lack of vigor. But China had reached the limits of expansion with the technology at its disposal and had little wish or will to make new conquests, adopt new technologies, or undertake new initiatives. The giant, as Napoleon noticed, had "fallen asleep."

The Asian Context

It is tempting to see this as part of an Asian general crisis of the late eighteenth century. Most of the other great Asian empires—Ottoman, Mughal, Persian, Japanese, Thai—lost impetus during the eighteenth century. The large states that had taken shape in southeast Asia stopped expanding or broke up, as kings complained that "officials and monasteries" usurped their power. Burma, which today calls itself Myanmar, first shrank, then split, then collapsed in 1752, after long civil wars between ever more-powerful provincial rulers. Partial recovery directed Burmese energies against the neighboring Thai Empire in what the Burmese represented as holy wars on behalf of Buddhism. This was a crisis for which an era of internal peace from 1709 to 1758 had left the Thai ill prepared. Burmese invaders effectively wiped out the Thai capital at Ayutthaya in 1767. The Thai Empire shattered among five small states. Vietnam also fell apart in the chaos of peasant rebellions between 1771 and 1778.

Persia and the Ottoman Empire

In southwest Asia, static population levels held back the Persian and Ottoman worlds. The Safavid Empire in Persia fell in 1722. Like Humpty Dumpty, no one seemed able to put it back together. Although Safavid shahs regained the throne at intervals until the 1770s, the dynasty had lost the allegiance of its subjects (see Chapter 19). Ironically, the Safavid emperors, who had forced their Shiite Islam on their people, found themselves condemned for their own lack of piety. Between 1719 and 1730, Persia was the playground of invading Afghan warlords. The former bandit chief, Nadir (NAH-deer) Shah, who drove them out tried to end internal strife by turning Persian ambitions outward and to discipline the Shiite clergy by privileging Sunni Islam. He sought to bring the Afghan chiefs into line by reviving the old Afghan practice of raiding India. He even sacked the Mughal court in Delhi and stole its treasure in 1739. He bought English warships to regain control of trade in the Caspian Sea and the Persian Gulf. But he could never escape from rebellions—not even when, in an attempt to secure his throne, he killed the heirs of the Safavids and had his own son blinded. After his assassination in 1747, rulers survived only by leaving the power of regional warlords intact, or playing them off against each other. State institutions were neglected. Nadir Shah's navy rotted away.

The Ottoman Empire—the Safavids' neighbor and longtime enemy—was more robust, but encountered difficulties that seemed crippling. The check to Ottoman expansion toward the end of the seventeenth century (see Chapter 19) shocked the ruling Ottoman elite, who embarked on long and inconclusive self-examination to try to understand why the empire was beginning to stagnate. The efficiency of the state declined, as hereditary officeholders gradually took over the administration. This surrender of power to men whom sultans could not easily remove or replace was precisely what the traditional Ottoman system of government was designed to avoid. The numbers of slave-bureaucrats, who tended to strengthen central control because they depended on the sultan's patronage, declined as the empire lost control of the various Christian subject-peoples in Europe and the Caucasus, from whom the administration traditionally recruited fresh intakes of slaves. Sultans had to rely increasingly on the Muslim clergy to keep the administration going. But clerics were hard to manage because, unlike the Sultan's slave-bureaucrats, they were not reliant on his patronage. As early as 1717, the wife of an English ambassador noted how the

Lady Mary Wortley Montagu, from *Letters*

clergy "engrossed all the learning and almost all the wealth of the Empire. Tis they that are the real authors, tho' the soldiers are the actors, of revolutions."

As a result of the economic changes described in Chapter 20, trade revenues fell. Trade with France, for instance—formerly the Turks' best overseas customer—accounted for only 5 percent of France's imports by the late eighteenth century, compared with about 16 percent when the century began. Imports from Turkey had accounted for 10 percent of Britain's trade in the mid–seventeenth century. The total fell to less than 1 percent by the end of the eighteenth. The end of the coffee monopoly of southern Arabia, as coffee production grew in the East Indies and West Indies, was a serious blow to the Ottoman economy.

The balance of power between the empire and its neighbors, which, for so many centuries, had favored the Ottomans, was clearly shifting. A long series of border wars with Russia led in 1774 to the Treaty of Küçük Kaynarca (koo-CHOOK kye-NAHR-jah), in which the Ottomans ceded control of the north shore of the Black Sea. Compared with the former glory of the empire (see Chapter 19), this was a serious setback, for not only did the Ottomans lose control of important trade routes, but they also conceded sovereignty over a Muslim population to a Christian power. This undermined the sultans' traditional status as protectors of Islam. Russia consolidated its gains in further campaigns that diminished the area under Ottoman rule in the Caucasus. In 1798, France invaded Egypt and Syria. The French soon withdrew to fight more urgent wars in Europe, but henceforth, Ottoman overlordship in the empire's North African provinces, which, in addition to Egypt, included Algeria, Tunisia, and Libya, existed in name only. These areas became virtually autonomous.

Meanwhile, the empire's control of other outlying areas also weakened. In the Balkans, many Christian communities dodged Ottoman control, by withdrawing into hill regions, where they planted maize on the upper slopes, beyond reach of the Turkish tax collectors. On the empire's Balkan frontier with Russia in what is today Romania, the empire conceded autonomy to the local inhabitants. The Arabian provinces—never a secure part of the Ottoman dominions—seceded in a religiously inspired rebellion. Muhammad ibn Abd al-Wahhab (moo-HA-mahd ih-bihn AHBD ahl-wah-HAB) (1703–1787) launched a religious reform movement named **Wahhabism** after him, calling for a return to Quranic purity, and rejecting the legitimacy of the Ottomans' claims to the caliphate. The Wahhabites conquered Arabia and pressed on the borders of Ottoman-controlled Iraq (see Map 21.1).

The Ottomans' difficulties can be measured in their loss of prestige. Long feared and admired in Europe, they had been loathed but never before disdained. From 1739, Austrians first, then Europeans generally, began conventionally to call the empire the "sick man of Europe" and to eye the sultans' possessions like greedy creditors around a rich man's deathbed. In reality, the empire's sickness was by no means terminal, but its relative decline

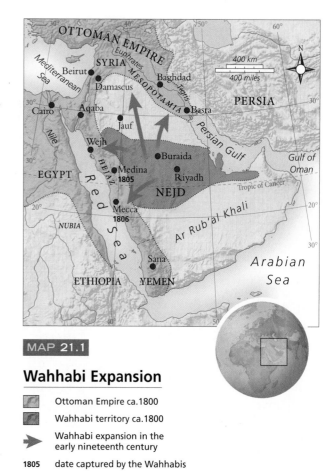

MAP 21.1

Wahhabi Expansion

- Ottoman Empire ca.1800
- Wahhabi territory ca.1800
- Wahhabi expansion in the early nineteenth century
- **1805** date captured by the Wahhabis

Trends in Asian Imperialism

Eighteenth century	China is world's fastest-growing empire; Persia and Ottoman populations static; Ottoman government goes into prolonged decline
1720	China conquers Tibet
1722	Safavid Empire collapses
1759	Chinese conquest of Xinjiang complete
1767	Burmese invasion leads to disintegration of Thailand
1771–1778	Vietnam collapses under strain of peasant rebellions
1774	Ottomans cede land to Russia in the Treaty of Küçük Kaynarca

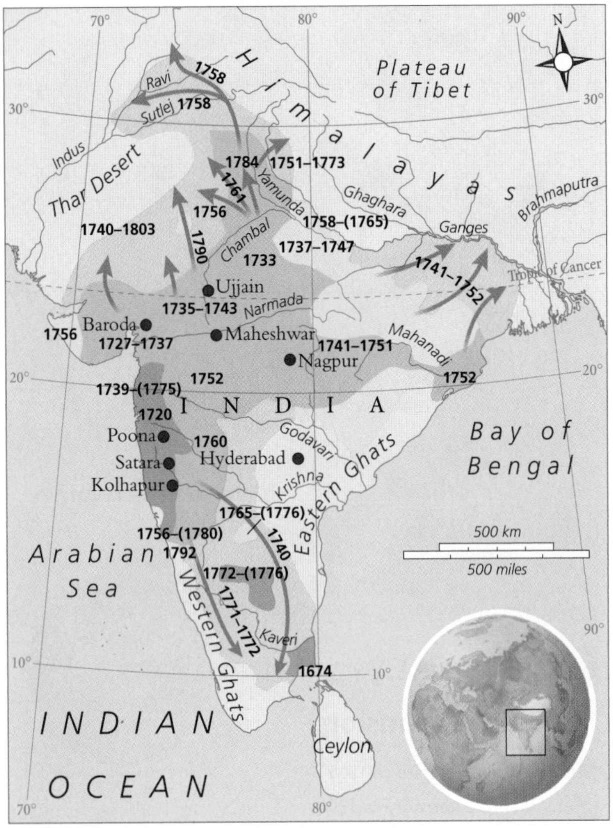

MAP 21.2

The Marathas

■	Core territories
■	Maratha's expansion, 1708–1800
□	Maratha's subject states
□	areas of irregular tribute
1739	date of acquisition by Marathas
(–75)	date of subsequent loss by Marathas to ca. 1800
→	Maratha campaigns into neighboring territory, with date

by the standards of its European neighbors was obvious. In 1807, a Spanish spy, who, like so many double agents, found it impossible to resist all sympathy with the culture of his enemy, wrote an account of the empire in his pretended character as a friendly critic. "Although I am a Muslim," he wrote,

when I see a nation without the slightest idea of public law, or of the rights of man; a nation in which scarcely one in a thousand knows how to read and write; a nation where no one enjoys security of property, and where human blood is made to flow for trivial reasons and without any just process; a nation—in short—determined to close its eyes to enlightenment and to reject the torch of civilization that shines quite clearly before it, will, for me, always seem a nation of barbarians.[2]

IMPERIAL REVERSAL IN INDIA: MUGHAL ECLIPSE AND BRITISH RISE TO POWER

The most dramatic reversal of fortune—and the one with the most profound implications for the future—happened in India. The Emperor Aurangzeb (r. 1658–1707) had driven the frontiers of the Mughal state southward with relentless energy (see Chapter 19). But after his death, expansion halted, and gradually, the empire exhibited signs of the strains that arise from success. Widened borders enclosed ever more-diverse cultures, religions, political systems, and ethnic identities. Sikhs and Hindus were hard to accommodate in the fiercely Muslim ideology that Aurangzeb had imposed. The Emperor Muhammad Shah (r. 1719–1748) exploited the opportunity to take control of the Muslim clergy by claiming the privilege of judging between rival schools of Islamic law. He appealed to the Shiite minority by calling himself "heir of Ali," the prophet Muhammad's son-in-law who had been murdered in the seventh century, and revived imperial pretensions to religious leadership by giving himself the title of "Shadow of God on Earth." But these measures only alienated him further from most religious communities in the realm.

Victories could be profitable. The Mughals had always made money out of war in the past. But empire was a capital-intensive business, subject to diminishing returns. The tax burden necessary to sustain Aurangzeb's policy provoked increasingly frequent peasant rebellions. Accommodations with conquered elites became increasingly generous—triggering the anger of the Mughal's old comrades and supporters, who resented the privileges granted to the elites in recently conquered lands. The growing importance of merchants to whom the government farmed out the collection of taxes and from whom the government borrowed large sums made this resentment worse. In the remoter parts of the empire, the Mughals, in effect, delegated power to local elites.

The danger of this policy became obvious in a dramatic sequence of events, beginning in 1719–1720. The emperor made spectacular concessions to petty Hindu princes, called the **Marathas** (mah-RAH-tahs), who ruled in Maharashtra, and whom their Muslim neighbors despised as little better than bandits. The Nizam al-Mulk (nee-ZAHM ahl-MOOLK), who governed for the Mughals on the frontier with Maharashtra, responded by defying Mughal authority. In 1725, he conquered Hyderabad in central India and established it as an effectively independent Muslim state. He paid no tribute to the Mughal emperor in Delhi. He handed out offices and parcels of tribute without reference to the emperor. He took three-quarters of the tribute due to the Mughals and left the remaining quarter to buy peace with his Hindu neighbors. The Mughal Empire still claimed "lordship of the universe" and monopolized reverence and religious rituals. Prayers for the emperor were still offered in mosques throughout India right through the eighteenth century. It was becoming clear, however, that the Mughal state was in permanent decay and that India was up for grabs (see Map 21.2).

Native princes contemplated replacing the empire or seizing control of what remained of it. Or else they simply ceased to obey the emperor. After 1761, for instance, the Marathas expressed obedience to the Mughals only in treaties. Otherwise, they largely ignored the emperor, though some continued to send formal petitions to court and issue coinage with the imperial stamp. But tradition still counted. Regional or local rulers could not challenge the empire without calling into question their own legitimacy, which emperors conferred. Traditionally, conquerors or reunifiers of India had always come from outside, as had the Mughals themselves, who originated in Afghanistan. It was easier for Indians to accept a foreign conqueror than one from inside the empire. Huns, Afghans, Mongols, Turks, and Persians had all played this role in the past. Now, because of the huge shifts of power that had overtaken the world, potential imperialists were unlikely to come from within Asia. By an unforeseeable sequence of events, the successors of the Mughals would be British.

As late as 1750, the British East India Company (EIC), which had been founded in 1600, insisted that its officials think of themselves as the "agents of merchants" rather than as a military colony. The circumstances of violent competition with French rivals in India, however, were already forcing the company's men to rethink their roles. Young Robert Clive (1725–1774), for instance, was a clerk in the southwest Indian port of Madras. His family thought him useless for any job more demanding. But he spent his leisure reading military history and when fighting broke out, he found soldiering to be his true vocation.

In 1756, Clive turned what was to have been a punitive expedition into a campaign of conquest. The province of Bengal in northeast India was by far the most important trading area in India for European commerce. In the 1730s, for instance, nearly half Holland's imports from Asia, and as much as two-thirds of all Asian exports to England, originated in Bengal. The *Nawab* (nah-WAHB), the local ruler, alienated the British by allying with France, seizing the British port of Calcutta, and allegedly allowing the mistreatment and murder of British women and children. In dealing with him, passion replaced the usual prudence of British policy, and Clive enjoyed greater freedom of action to pursue vengeance than frontier colonels were usually allowed. The French were unreliable allies for Indian rulers. During wars in Europe, the British could rely on continental allies to distract them. Bengal was full of internal dissent: Hindu resentment of Muslim rule, warlord rivalry with the Nawab, popular resentment of heavy taxation, military unrest at overdue pay.

Clive blundered into this tense arena like a typical conqueror. His barely professional army of a little over 1,000 Europeans and 2,000 Indian trainees was

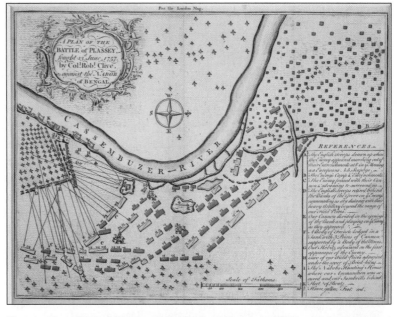

Plassey. The version of his plan of the battle of Plassey in 1757 published by Robert Clive does not conceal his poorly chosen position. His troops, with their backs to a wood and a river, were easily surrounded. He seeks to give the impression that he won the battle by maneuvering his artillery to rake the attackers' flank with fire. In reality, the outcome was decided when the enemy began to quarrel among themselves leading to what was, in effect, a battlefield rebellion among the Bengali commanders.

outnumbered in the field by over 12 to 1 and had hardly any technical advantages. The Nawab had French guns and gunners. But, like so many conquerors, Clive aimed to destroy the enemy by dividing them. He succeeded by putting together a coalition that ousted the Nawab at Plassey in 1757 by what was in effect a battlefield coup. Traditionally, historians have represented the battle as the result of British superiority, whereas in fact it showed only the superiority of some Bengali factions over others. A delightful illustration made at the time to celebrate Clive's heroism displays the propaganda image: Clive's army is drawn up in neatly ordered lines of fire. The Nawab's force is a straggly tangle. In Clive's drawing, the enemy appears to flee before a relentless British advance. What really happened is that, confronted by a conspiracy among his supposed followers, the Nawab fled after little more than exchanges of cannon and skirmisher fire.

Bengal was easily the richest of the fragments into which the Mughal Empire dissolved. Clive looted it—"astonished," he said, "at my own moderation." Booty never dulls the appetite it feeds. Clive's men almost mutinied at dissatisfaction with their share of the plunder even though it had made them all rich. Yet, well managed, Bengal was the biggest prize of any pirate since Pizarro seized Peru for Spain in the 1520s (see Chapter 16). The East India Company (EIC) raised £2 million in 1761–1764 and almost £7.5 million in 1766–1767. The riches of Bengal paid for the conquest of other Indian principalities. By 1782, the East India Company, whose motto had once been "trade, not war," was keeping an army of 115,000 men in India (see Map 21.3).

The parallel with the Spanish conquerors in the Americas is striking. The British first installed a puppet ruler in Bengal, then used the profits of confiscatory policies to conquer the Ganges River valley and the shore of the Bay of Bengal, just as the Spaniards had used the wealth and manpower of the formerly Aztec-dominated highlands of Mexico to conquer the surrounding regions. As in Mexico and Peru, the speed of the conquerors' triumph gave it the illusion of inevitability. Once the growth of a land empire had begun, it had to continue. Security always demanded control of the next frontier. The existing setup in India, in which native princes bargained with rival Western buyers and shippers, became intolerable to the British once they realized they could enforce a monopoly. With Bengal in their power, the British extended their control over the spice-rich south.

Under cover of the next European war in the 1790s, which again neutralized the French threat, Britain put together a coalition of Indian clients and mercenaries to defeat piecemeal the only regional powers capable of reversing the trend. Tipu (TEE-poo) Sultan, ruler of Mysore in south India, posed the biggest threat. His ambitions were obvious. He spurned the Mughals, took imperial trappings for himself, and looked to the distant Ottomans to legitimate his claims. In the 1780s, while the Mughal emperor swallowed his pride and sought the protection of a Maratha leader, Mahadji Scindia, Tipu confronted the British for supremacy in India. He wrote accounts of his dreams in a revealing book. Amid scenes of emeralds, tiger shoots, and white elephants, it includes visions of French troops and of the expulsion of the British. Yet Tipu was more than a dreamer. Political realism, idealized as holy war, underpinned his anti-British policy. He realized that Indians could no longer deal with the British in the traditional frameworks of commerce and politics. They had to be expelled or obeyed.

Tiger mauling a British soldier. A British officer's death in a tiger's jaws in 1792 became a symbol at the court of Tipu Sultan of Mysore of the fate he wished to inflict on the British. Tipu's very name meant "tiger," and he adopted the beast as his badge.

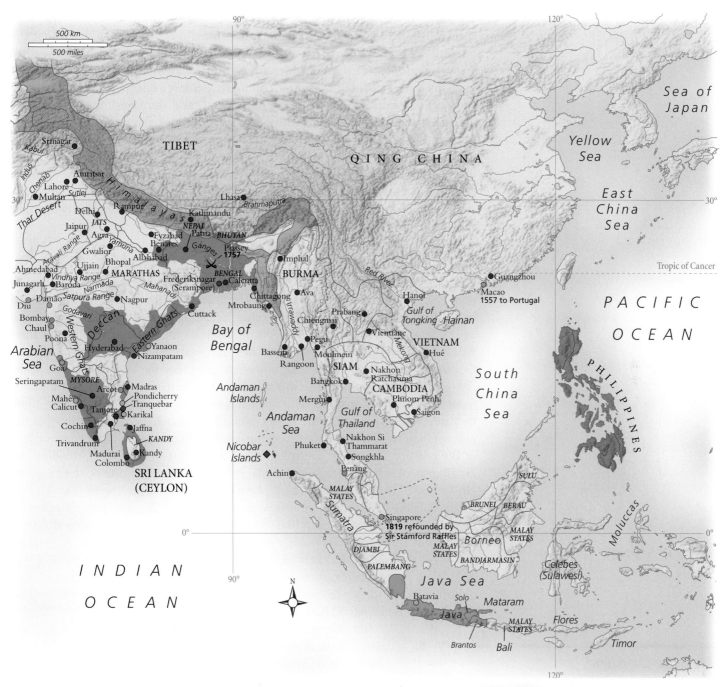

MAP 21.3

European Expansion in South and Southeast Asia, ca. 1800

- area under British rule, ca. 1800
- area under Dutch control and possessions 1765
- Spanish possessions
- French possessions
- area under Portuguese control and possessions 1765
- Danish possessions
- petty tribal polities
- other states
- frontiers ca. 1765

Their own revolution, which began in 1789 (see Chapter 22), and then the need to defend France against invaders in the 1790s distracted Tipu's French allies. His neighbors preferred to back the British rather than to support him. If they had to submit to rulers, they preferred to have them far away in London rather than dangerously close in Mysore. Hopelessly besieged in his capital at Seringapatam in 1799, Tipu died in the fighting. The Maratha states in south India accepted British overlordship after a defeat in 1806.

British supremacy was only the latest variant on an old theme of Indian history: the establishment of dominance over India by foreign military elites. But in a crucial sense, the phenomenon was new. Britain's India was the first big European empire on the mainland of Asia. The British could now seize or clear much of India to grow products that suited them. They could smother the potential competition of Indian industries, shifting the balance of the world's resources in favor of the West (see Chapter 20). Britain's Indian Empire was at once the last of the old adventurer conquests, achieved with native collaboration and without conspicuous technical advantages, and the forerunner of the new industrial conquests, by which Europeans would extend their empires in the next century. There were, as yet, no machine guns or ironclad ships or quinine pills to give Westerners technical advantages. Steam power and rifles were in their infancy. But British industry affected—if it did not effect—the conquest of India. By the 1790s, standard British artillery was so superior to the Indian product that the finely decorated cannon of Tipu Sultan were good to the British only for their value as scrap metal.

THE DUTCH EAST INDIES

Events in India vividly illustrated the way European imperialism elsewhere in Asia was also turning to territorial conquest. The Spanish, painfully slowly, continued to build up their empire in the Philippines, crushing a rebellion after the British briefly seized Manila in 1762. The Portuguese, despite being expelled from their East African outposts by the Omanis, hesitantly expanded their frontiers around Goa on the southwest Indian coast into what they called the New Conquests, pushing to control trade routes into south India, and acquiring 30,000 new Indian subjects. The Dutch, meanwhile, built up a land empire on Java in Indonesia. In 1740, they intervened to support the ruling dynasty and exacted coastal territory as the price of their help. In 1749, they took the whole of Mataram, and in the second half of the century, effectively controlled most of the rest of the island, dividing the kingship between rival Javanese clients. In 1774, the heir to one of the resulting kingdoms, Yogyakarta, composed a poem in which the Dutch were converted to Islam. Sheikhs in Mecca in Arabia accused the Dutch Muslim puppet rulers of being "the devil's kings," taunting, "Shall the Europeans be more powerful than Allah?" But Dutch rule was usually indirect, through Dutch-appointed regents on whose collaboration the Dutch relied. These were always leading members of traditional elites, but their right to rule was often—from a Javanese point of view—doubtful. So they depended on the Dutch just as the Dutch depended on them, and the relationship benefited both sides.

In the end, the landward turn did the Dutch little good. Their strength was in their shipping, and a seaborne, piratical empire suited their talents and technology. Their weakness was a shortage of manpower. Territorial acquisitions gradually overstretched and exhausted them. The Dutch could only pay for war by enforcing high prices. As they devastated rivals' lands, uprooted surplus crops, and destroyed competitors' ships, they ran the risk of ruining the entire region and being left profitless, as one of their leaders warned, "in depopulated lands and empty seas."

Yet what choice did the Dutch have? Unlike the Spaniards and Portuguese, they had little access to marketable assets, such as gold and silver mines or sources of slaves. They could finance their inroads into eastern markets in only two ways: by the profits of intra-Asian trade and shipping, or by diversifying into production by growing their own cash crops. By opting for the latter strategy, they committed themselves to seizing the spices and, in the end, the land the spices grew on, by force. They ended up with an empire,

Mughal Decline

1600	East India Company (EIC) founded
Eighteenth century	Spanish, Dutch, and Portuguese expand holdings in southeast Asia
1707	Death of Aurangzeb and the end of Mughal expansion
1725	Nazim al-Mulk conquers Hyderabad
1756–1757	Robert Clive leads EIC conquest of Bengal
Late eighteenth century	Marathas offer only nominal obedience to the Mughals
1761–1764	EIC revenues: £2 million
1766–1767	EIC revenues: £7.5 million
1806	Maratha states accept British overlordship

the Dutch East Indies (modern Indonesia), whose costs exceeded its profits. Only the conversion of much of Java to the cultivation of coffee closed the gap between costs and profits.

THE BLACK ATLANTIC: AFRICA, THE AMERICAS, AND THE SLAVE TRADE

Equaling or exceeding the vast movements of internal colonization in Asia was the shift of people across the Atlantic. Most of them were black Africans, forced into slavery and transported to the New World. In the eighteenth century, nearly 400,000 were imported into English North America, nearly 1 million into Spanish colonies, over 1 million into the Caribbean, and some 3 million into Brazil. The structures of the trade were the same as in the previous century (see Chapter 19), but its scale grew (see Map 21.4).

Our traditional image of the horrors of the Atlantic crossing comes from slave memoirs and the writings of abolitionists who sought to do away with the slave trade. Skeptics have wondered whether shippers can really have been so careless of their cargo as to tolerate—and even invite—heavy losses of life en route. Yet such evidence as the often-reproduced deck plan of the British slave-ship *Brookes* in 1783 is decisive. Slaves were stacked "like books on a shelf," in spaces little more than five feet high by four feet wide. The ship's surgeon explained that the slaves were not supposed to be able to turn round: "the slaves that are out of irons are . . . closely locked to one another, and those which do not get quickly into their places are compelled by the cat [lash]." He watched their "laborious and anxious efforts for life," which resembled those "we observe on expiring animals subjected by experiment to bad air of various kinds." In an autobiography published in 1789, Olaudah Equiano, a West African who had been enslaved as a boy, described the conditions of his own experience as an item of cargo. "The closeness of the place, and the heat of the climate, added to the number in the ship, which was so crowded that each had scarcely room to turn himself in, almost suffocated us. This produced constant perspirations, so that the air soon became unfit . . . and brought on a sickness among the slaves, of which many died, thus falling victim to the improvident avarice, as I may call it, of their purchasers." The *Brookes* lost 60 slaves out of 600 on the crossing.

Yet, strictly from the point of view of profits, the slavers knew what they were doing. Tight packing had no noticeable effect on rates of mortality, compared with such figures as are available for comparison with the more humane conditions specified—though not always observed—for Portuguese ships. In a telltale case, a captain from the British port of Liverpool in 1781 had 130 slaves thrown overboard to claim the insurance for lost cargo. It was a peculiarly horrifying instance, but it was normal to dispose of sick or mutinous slaves in the same way.

The economics of slavery are hard to understand. Forced labor, according to economic theory, is never efficient, and the difficulty of managing slaves to maximize production is one of the few conclusions on which all observers of slave plantations in the eighteenth century agreed. Yet slavery was just one form of forced labor, on which, in various forms, most eighteenth-century economies relied. Indentured workers, peasants tied to the land, unpaid apprenticeships, and convict workers all made compulsion seem normal. Traditional forms of employment generally gave employers—masters, as they were commonly called—enormous

Olaudah Equiano, excerpt from *The Interesting Narrative*

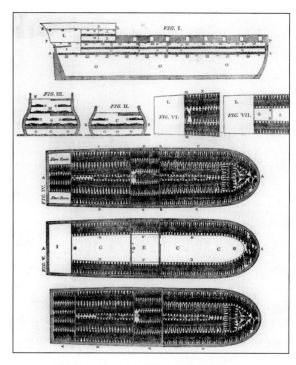

The slave ship *Brookes*. Over 600 slaves were crammed into a space on the *Brookes* designed to carry no more than 450 persons. The extent of the inhumanity and inefficiency in the slave trade is shocking.

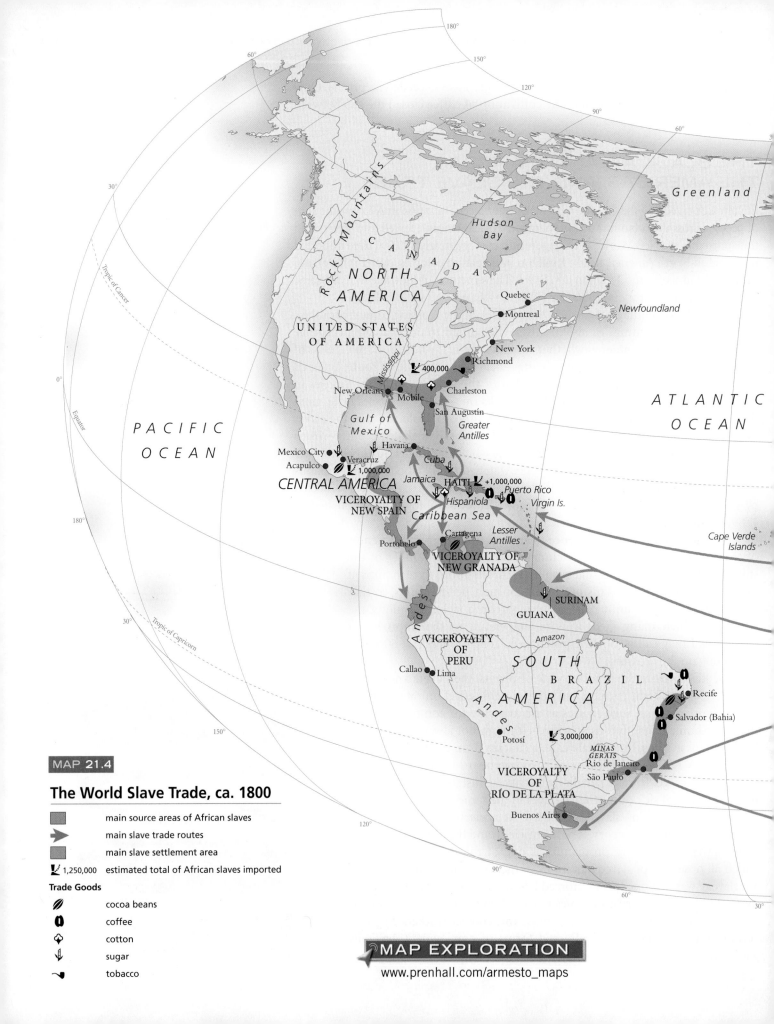

PACIFIC
OCEAN

ATLANTIC
OCEAN

Greenland

Hudson
Bay

Newfoundland

C A N A D A

NORTH
AMERICA

Rocky Mountains

Quebec
Montreal

UNITED STATES
OF AMERICA

New York
Richmond

400,000

New Orleans
Mobile
Charleston

Mississippi

San Augustín

Gulf of
Mexico

Greater
Antilles

Mexico City
Acapulco
Veracruz
1,000,000

Havana

Cuba

CENTRAL AMERICA

Jamaica
HAITI
+1,000,000
Puerto Rico

VICEROYALTY OF
NEW SPAIN

Hispaniola
Virgin Is.

Caribbean Sea

Lesser
Antilles

Cape Verde
Islands

Portobelo
Cartagena

VICEROYALTY OF
NEW GRANADA

SURINAM

GUIANA

VICEROYALTY
OF
PERU

Amazon

Andes

SOUTH
AMERICA

BRAZIL

Callao
Lima

Recife

Salvador (Bahia)

Potosí
3,000,000

MINAS
GERAIS
Rio de Janeiro
São Paulo

VICEROYALTY
OF
RÍO DE LA PLATA

Buenos Aires

MAP 21.4

The World Slave Trade, ca. 1800

main source areas of African slaves

main slave trade routes

main slave settlement area

1,250,000 estimated total of African slaves imported

Trade Goods

cocoa beans

coffee

cotton

sugar

tobacco

MAP EXPLORATION

www.prenhall.com/armesto_maps

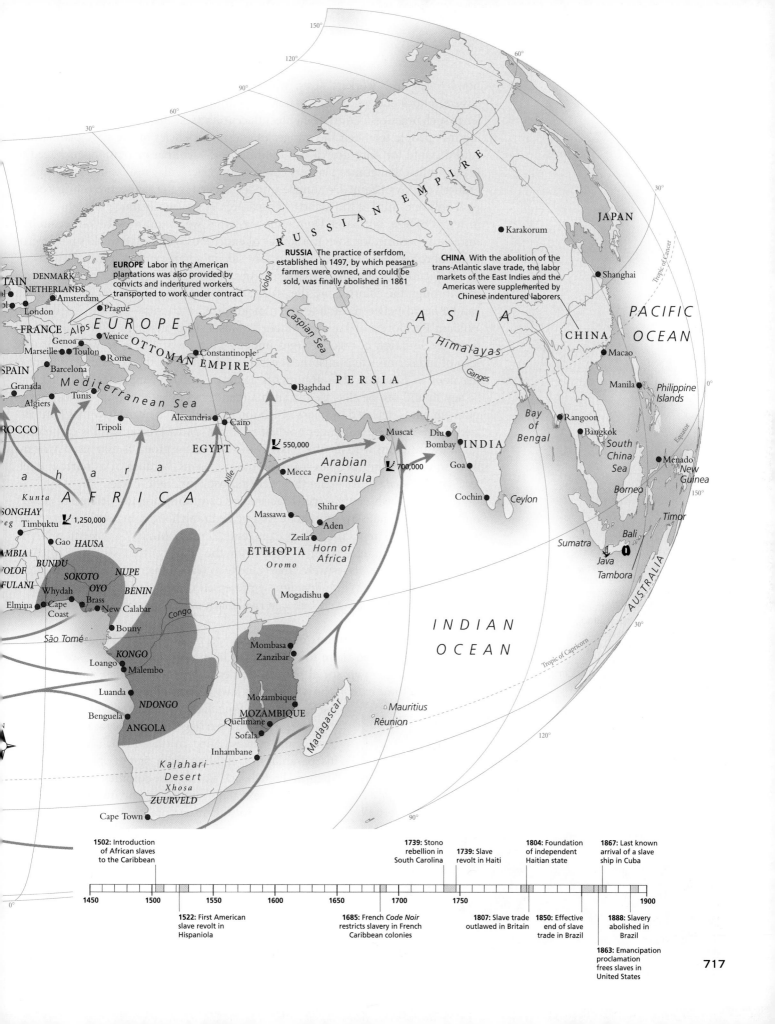

RUSSIA The practice of serfdom, established in 1497, by which peasant farmers were owned, and could be sold, was finally abolished in 1861

EUROPE Labor in the American plantations was also provided by convicts and indentured workers transported to work under contract

CHINA With the abolition of the trans-Atlantic slave trade, the labor markets of the East Indies and the Americas were supplemented by Chinese indentured laborers

RUSSIAN EMPIRE

• Karakorum

JAPAN

Tropic of Cancer

• Shanghai

PACIFIC OCEAN

DENMARK
NETHERLANDS
• Amsterdam
London
• Prague
FRANCE   Alps
EUROPE
Genoa • Venice
Marseille • Toulon
• Rome
SPAIN
Barcelona
• Granada
Mediterranean Sea
Algiers • Tunis
OCCO
Tripoli

OTTOMAN EMPIRE
• Constantinople

A S I A

CHINA

Macao

• Baghdad

PERSIA

Himalayas

Ganges

• Manila
Philippine Islands

0°

Alexandria • Cairo
EGYPT

Muscat

Diu
Bombay   INDIA

• Rangoon
• Bangkok

South China Sea

Equator

🏺 550,000

• Menado
New Guinea

150°

a   h   a   r   a
AFRICA

Kunta

SONGHAY
eg • Timbuktu   🏺 1,250,000

Gao *HAUSA*
AMBIA
BUNDU
VOLOF *SOKOTO* *NUPE*
FULANI   *OYO* *BENIN*
Whydah • Cape
Elmina • Coast Brass
  New Calabar
• Bonny

Mecca

Massawa
• Shihr
• Aden
Zeila
ETHIOPIA   *Horn of Africa*
Oromo

🏺 700,000

• Goa

Cochin   *Ceylon*

Sumatra

Bali
Java
Tambora

Timor

• Mogadishu

I N D I A N
O C E A N

AUSTRALIA

30°

Congo

KONGO
Loango
• Malembo
Luanda
NDONGO
Benguela •
ANGOLA
São Tomé

Mombasa
Zanzibar

Mozambique
MOZAMBIQUE
Quelimane
Sofala •
Inhambane

Madagascar

△ *Mauritius*
Réunion

Tropic of Capricorn

120°

Kalahari Desert
Xhosa
ZUURVELD
Cape Town •

90°

1502: Introduction of African slaves to the Caribbean

1739: Stono rebellion in South Carolina

1739: Slave revolt in Haiti

1804: Foundation of independent Haitian state

1867: Last known arrival of a slave ship in Cuba

| 1450 | 1500 | 1550 | 1600 | 1650 | 1700 | 1750 | 1800 | 1850 | 1900 |

0°

1522: First American slave revolt in Hispaniola

1685: French *Code Noir* restricts slavery in French Caribbean colonies

1807: Slave trade outlawed in Britain

1850: Effective end of slave trade in Brazil

1888: Slavery abolished in Brazil

1863: Emancipation proclamation frees slaves in United States

power over their workers' lives: where the workers lived, how they spent their leisure, whom and when they married. So until economic thought began to challenge such practices in the late eighteenth century (see Chapter 22), it is not surprising that people tolerated the savageries and inefficiencies of the slave plantations. And demand for slave-grown commodities was such that plantations managed to make profits. Sometimes planters could enjoy spectacular results in a small space. France's colony of Saint-Domingue (modern Haiti) in the eighteenth century occupied only one-third of the island of Hispaniola. It was hardly much of a land empire in terms of size, but Saint-Domingue was what we would now call an economic miracle. It became, for a while a source of enormous wealth, the world's major producer of coffee and sugar, with important sidelines in indigo and cacao.

Depictions of the life of black societies in the Americas range from the idealized through the colorful and the satirical to the horrific. But the crack of the lash can be heard between the lines even of idealized accounts—like the Englishman William Beckford's of Jamaica, where he was a slave owner in 1788. He claimed that "the situation of a good negro under a kind owner . . . is very superior (the idea of indiscriminate punishment excepted) to those of the generality of labouring poor in England." His arguments against excessive whippings included that "They should not be chastised in such a manner as to lay them up, for the end of punishment is defeated by a loss of labour," and "When a negro becomes familiarized to the whip, he no longer holds it in terror." More typical was his contemporary Edward Long, who justified slavery in 1774 on the grounds that black Africans were so unlike other peoples—among other reasons, because of a "narrow intellect" and "bestial smell"—that they were almost a different species.

In contexts where such crude racism was commonplace, the defense of slavery on the grounds that slaves might be well treated rang hollow. In South America, no area had a rosier reputation than eighteenth-century Minas Gerais (mee–NAHS jeh–REYE), a mining district in Brazil, for the "liberty" that slaves there could enjoy. Yet even here, slaves were "free" chiefly to obtain their gold quotas by extortion or prostitution. White Portuguese preserved order by techniques of selective terror, exploitation of dislike between rival black nations, and large rations of rum and tobacco.

Yet within the constraints of plantation life, black people retained a degree of initiative that allowed them to continue, as in the previous century (see Chapter 19), to craft their own social worlds, domestic practices, values, and norms of behavior. To some extent, the white men's laws reflected these values. In the 1780s, the Spanish and French crowns enacted codes guaranteeing slaves' rights to marriage, to the inseparability of husbands and wives, and, in the French case, to the inseparability of children from parents before puberty. Spanish, French, and Portuguese colonies had many local laws against sexual abuse of slaves by owners, removing slave children from their parents' care, and denying conjugal rights to married slaves. In practice, this worked against slave marriage, because owners tended to discourage or prevent their slaves from marrying to escape the consequences of the laws. As a result, neither Church nor state recognized most sexual alliances between slaves, but those unions were often stable, nonetheless.

In most of the colonies that depended on slave labor, marriage between black and white seemed to threaten the

Punishment for disobedient slaves—as for mutinous soldiers and seamen—was brutal not because the offenses merited it, but to terrorize and cow the victims. This early nineteenth-century depiction of the whipping of a slave in Brazil is based on the tradition of representing the scourging of Christ in paintings. The planter, turning casually aside to his rum and tobacco, seems contemptible. The slave woman tied to the tree looks more innocent in her nakedness than the onlookers.
Dagli Orti (A)/Picture Desk, Inc./Kobal Collection

social order. The only universally tolerable kind of sex between people of different color was between white men and black women, where the power relationship was clear. In early eighteenth-century Surinam, a Dutch colony on the northeast coast of South America, for instance, white women were flogged, branded, and banished for fornication with black men. Their male black partners were liable to the death penalty. In 1764, when Elizabeth Sanson, a rich, free, black widow, 50 years old, wanted to marry the local church organist—a white man 30 years her junior—the local governing council ruled it "repugnant and loathsome," not because of inter-racial sex, which was common enough in Surinam between white men and black women, but because it would reverse the normal relations of power. She was rich and therefore powerful even though she was black. He was poor and thus relatively powerless despite being white. It was "inevitable," the councilors wrote, "that because of the blacks' awareness of our superiority over them, we must maintain our position, we being a people of a better and nobler nature than they."

Yet there was nothing to stop a white master in Surinam from taking a black mistress, or—indeed—marrying her if he wished (although other slave-holding colonies, such as those in British North America, outlawed such interracial marriages). Hendrick Schouten, one of the leading colonists in Surinam in the mid–eighteenth century, had a black wife to whom he wrote tender poems and who features in a comic dialogue he authored, in which he appears as a henpecked husband, as she nags him over his bad moods and impatience at meal times. Clearly, in at least one household, the normal power relationship was reversed, or at least equalized. In Spanish colonies, the moral power of the church had some positive influence. Spanish clergy pressured white masters to marry slave concubines, and with some success, persuaded owners to grant dowries to female slaves on marriage. Some owners were canny enough to realize that they could save money that way. It was cheaper to get slaves to breed than to replace them by purchasing new ones. In general, however, the traditions of African societies, not the church, molded slaves' attitudes to marriage. Transportation on the same ship, or membership of the same group of runaways, or association in the same religious brotherhoods (see Chapter 19) became forms of ritual kinship, within which marriage was taboo.

Some mainland colonies—those, far from the main markets, where slaves were relatively expensive to buy—found that it made sense not to jeopardize their investments by wasteful ill use. Better conditions of life for the slaves were the key to improved security and natural increase of population. In the Chesapeake colonies of Virginia, Delaware, and Maryland, for instance, most of the slave population was born locally from about 1750. In most of the New World, however, plantation life in the eighteenth century was clearly inhumane and brutal. In and around the Caribbean, slaves rebelled frequently, ran away when they could, and—above all—refused to reproduce. Colonial authorities could usually suppress rebellions. In 1739, the British authorities in Jamaica solved the problem of runaways inventively, by negotiating a treaty with Captain Cudjoe, the ruler of the maroon state of runaway slaves in the interior of the island (see Chapter 19). In return for British recognition of his autonomy, he agreed to return future fugitive slaves to their plantations. But the slaves' most effective form of resistance was to refuse to give birth. Hard labor, harsh punishment, poor food, meager clothing, and unsanitary housing all worked against the natural increase of population. Even more significant were low birthrate and high infant mortality. It seems likely that slave women chose not to bring children into the wretched world they were forced to inhabit. The British West Indies had only 350,000 slaves in 1780, although planters had imported 1.2 million by that time.

QUARTERONA, SCHIAVA NEL SURINAM

Quadroon woman. John Stedman fought as a mercenary against rebellious black slaves in the late eighteenth century, but his sympathetic account of them helped the antislavery cause. He particularly admired the so-called "quadroon" looks typical of women, like the one shown here, who had one white and three black grandparents. Even in Surinam, where laws regulating slaves were particularly repressive, black women could achieve wealth and high status by marrying white men. *Dagli Orti (A)/Picture Desk, Inc./Kobal Collection*

 Phyllis Wheatley, "To The Right Honorable William, Earl of Dartmouth . . ."

Cudjoe making peace. The British commander, Colonel John Guthrie, extends a hand in peace to the maroon leader, Captain Cudjoe, in Jamaica in 1739. After eight years of indecisive war, the British conceded autonomy to a maroon state in the interior of the island. The maroons in turn agreed to harbor no more runaway slaves.

In the second half of the eighteenth century, slaves exported from West Africa in British ships were worth ten times the value of all other African exports put together. This disparity protected African states from European imperialism, as Europeans were not particularly interested in controlling the products of the land, or—yet—of developing plantations of their own in Africa. Disease, mainly malaria and yellow fever, was another factor. Europeans had a hard time surviving in West Africa in the eighteenth century. On the underside of the West African bulge, the slaving states established in the seventeenth century enjoyed a certain stability or at least a power of survival in the eighteenth. Oyo, Dahomey, Allada, Whydah, Ashanti were secure against all enemies except each other. European slave stations multiplied along the coast, changing hands with the rhythms of European wars. Danish enterprise in the 1780s was still adding to the numbers of slave forts begun 100 years previously along the Gold Coast. St. Louis, the chief French station on the Senegal River in the same period, had 600 French officials and soldiers. The biggest station was at Gorée, south of Cape Verde, where the chaplain in the 1780s secured the prettiest slave girls for himself on the pretext of founding a sisterhood of the Sacred Heart. At that time, Miles Barber of London had 12 establishments on the west coast of Africa, handling about 6,000 slaves a year. Near one of his stations off Conakry in modern Ghana, a remarkable independent trader dominated business at the mouth of the River Bereira: Betsy Heard was the English-educated daughter of a British trader and an African slave. The slave-trading compound on Bence Island in West Africa in mid-century was owned by a syndicate of Scots eccentrics, who built a golf course, served by black caddies in kilts woven in Glasgow—a canny example of how even small-scale imperialism stimulated home industry.

There was little pressure from white colonialism in other parts of Africa. In Kongo, the long struggle against Portuguese domination wore down the state, which crumbled in the late seventeenth century. King Pedro IV (Kongolese kings had Portuguese names—see Chapter 15) effected a brief revival. In 1706, he captured and burnt at the stake Dona Beatriz Kimpa Vita, a visionary rebel who claimed to be a virgin and mother. She decreed the use of the "Salve Regina," a Christian hymn to the Virgin Mary, in her own honor, claimed to have replaced Christianity, expelled white people, and installed a puppet king. But the wars had wasted Kongo and ruined its former agricultural prosperity. The fruitful collaboration with Portuguese missionaries and officials could not be fully restored.

Slave states as rapacious and militaristic as anything known earlier (see Chapter 19) grew up in the savanna toward the south of the Congo drainage area, from the Kwango River to Lake Tanganyika. Luanda was the greatest of these states. A bracelet of elephant sinews confirmed its kings' sacred nature. But a network of women, who strengthened the dynasty by marriage, exercised the real power. A female elder, known as the *Lukon-kashia*, played a major role in selecting the king. In Luanda, court "cities," as Europeans called them, attracted praise for their cleanliness, rational grid plans of streets, and public squares. Slavery was the basis of Luanda's domestic economy as well as of its commerce. Slaves were needed to work soil adapted for cassava and maize, New World crops that revolutionized productivity in Africa.

Meanwhile, the northern Zambezi valley experienced renewed Portuguese interest with a gold rush in the 1740s. Most of the lower valley ended up in the hands of adventurers called *prazeros*—Portuguese colonists who established personal dominance over the native populations. The once-mighty empire of Mwene Mutapa, which had defeated Portuguese attempts at conquest in the sixteenth century, had broken up. In coastal East Africa, as we saw at the beginning of this chapter, the Omanis replaced the Portuguese definitively from 1729, when the Portuguese failed to recapture Mombasa. In the long run, Omani rule benefited trade. The biggest European menace appeared in the southern tip of the continent, where the Xhosa (KOH–sah) felt increasing pressure from the Dutch expansion from the Cape. But here the black and white antagonists were evenly matched. The Dutch farmers (or "Boers") halted at the edge of the Zuurveld in wars that ended in 1795. By that time the Boers had fallen out among themselves, and the British had seized the Cape Colony from the Dutch East India Company.

The really big threats to African states came not from European imperialism but from within Africa. Ethiopia continually tried and continually failed to contain Oromo migrations. Early in the eighteenth century, the Oromo began to organize in what were recognizably states of their own and to become Muslims. Oromo became high officials and commanders inside what was left of Ethiopia and rulers of effectively independent provinces. A siege mentality took over the Ethiopian elite, with rival factions and sects squabbling over a diminishing powerbase. In the 1760s, the most powerful provincial governor, Mika'el Suhul, who built up a well-trained army, equipped with firearms, dispensed with the normal conventions of loyalty and took government into his own hands. Ethiopia's "Era of Princes" began, in which the emperor was a pawn or puppet of warlords. "How is it," wailed a chronicler of the 1780s, "that the kingdom has become contemptible to striplings and slaves? How is it that the kingdom is a laughing-stock of the uncircumcized?"

In parts of West Africa, meanwhile, the continuing expansion of the Islamic world put relentless pressure on local African states. Senegambia fell to Muslim-led revolutions that displaced native dynasties. Bundu fell in 1690 (though its kings remained pagans for over 100 years thereafter), and Futa Jallon fell in 1725. Samba Gelaajo Jeego, ruler of Futa Toro, who is still a subject of popular songs in the region, enlisted French help, but to little long-term result. Muslims conquered Futa Toro in 1776. Muslim Tuareg (too-AH-rehg) warriors and Kunta holy men proved, in combination, an irresistible force along the middle Niger River. The process gathered pace. In 1794, a holy man in the Sahel, Usuman da Fodio, had a vision in which he was "girded with the Sword of Truth, to unsheathe it against the enemies of God." The strict Islamic Wahhabite movement from Arabia inspired him. He saw himself as the "Renewer of Faith" promised by prophesies, and the forerunner of the **Mahdi** (MAH-dee), a Muslim messiah, whose coming would inaugurate a cosmic struggle, preceding the end of the world. A poet among his followers announced "a time to set the world in order."

Usuman attracted a fervent following among the Fulani, traditional herdsmen of the Sahel, who called themselves "a cloud that has settled upon God's earth, so dense that escape from it is impossible." Their empire was a combination of three traditions: another pastoralist attempt to exploit the Sahel's potential for long-range grazing of flocks; another frustrated step to unify the area politically; and another holy war inspired by Islamic militancy. By 1820, Usuman's followers had conquered an empire that stretched from Bornu to beyond the Niger, with a capital of sunbaked clay buildings at Sokoto (see Map 21.5). This really was the world's last great pastoralist empire. It lasted until British conquest in 1906.

Elmina. The Portuguese founded the fort of Elmina, on the underside of the West African bulge, near the rivers Pra and Benya, in 1482 to trade mainly for gold from the Volta valley. But, as with most European trading posts in the region, slaving rapidly became the main activity. The Dutch captured the fort and took over the trade in slaves there in 1637.

Fulani cavalrymen. The strength of the Fulani empire was its cavalry, deployed to good effect in the grasslands of the African Sahel. European firepower checked Fulani expansion in the nineteenth century and overthrew the empire in the early 1900s, but horsemanship and the use of traditional weapons remain practices of high prestige in parts of West Africa.

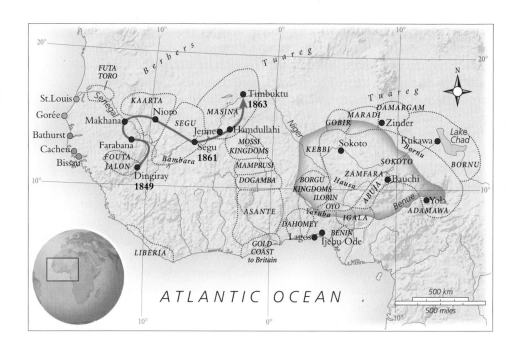

MAP 21.5

The Sokoto Fulani Kingdom, ca. 1820

Sokoto Fulani Kingdom, ca. 1820

● British possession

● French possession

● Portuguese possession

.... borders, ca. 1820

→ Jihad route of al-Hajj 'Umar Tal

Hausa people

LAND EMPIRES OF THE NEW WORLD

The case of the Fulani had parallels in the Americas. By the eighteenth century, horse-borne hunting made the South American pampa and North American prairie desirable places to live in. Intrusions of farmers and city dwellers on the edges enhanced the new economic opportunities horses, cattle, and sheep offered.

The Araucanos and the Sioux

Pastoralism and mining enabled native peoples of the pampa in what is today Argentina to open new trade with Chile and to absorb lessons in large-scale chieftaincy from the Araucanos—the impressive warriors of the South American southwest, who maintained effective independence beyond the frontiers of the Spanish Empire. By the mid–eighteenth century, chieftains on the rivers Negro and Colorado, such as Cacapol and his son Cangapol "the Wild," could turn the elective position of war chief into hereditary rule. They could organize lucrative trade in furs, assemble harems of a size to mark their status, impress a Jesuit visitor as "monarchs over all the rest," raise thousands of warriors, and threaten the city of Buenos Aires.

A similar transformation began to affect the North American prairie. Huge kills of buffalo for their hides generated a trading surplus, which in turn introduced maize to Native American hunters' diets, whiskey to their religious rites, and guns to their armories. As the horses multiplied, the plains became a source of supply for the white colonies on the edges of the region. Even before white men disputed control of them, the prairies became an arena of competition between ever-growing numbers of immigrant Native American peoples—many driven, as much as drawn, from east of the Missouri River by the pressure of white empire building. Those with agricultural traditions edged toward or into nomadism. All tended to become herders of horses as well as hunters of buffalo—which forced them into unstable contact with each other on shared trails and pastures. The Sioux were converts to nomadism. Numbering 25,000 by 1790, increasing rapidly thereafter, they were a potentially imperial or at least domineering people who became the terror of a settled Native American world still intact on the upper Missouri River.

Even when they had adopted a horse-borne way of life and an economy based on the slaughter of bison, the Sioux kept an interest in their traditional forest economy. Even when their conquests covered the plains, they extended them into new forests farther west, where deer hunting still conferred special prestige. The Black Hills in South Dakota were their "meat store," which they seized from Kiowa, Cheyenne, and Crow. Meanwhile, trade exposed the region to killer diseases of European origin. Smallpox epidemics eased the Sioux's conquest of the Arikara and Omaha peoples just as diseases had paved the way for white imperialism among unimmunized Native Americans. The Sioux adopted the values of imperial society, rewarding skill in battle above other qualities and tying social status to the possession and distribution of booty. White people did not introduce imperialism to the plains. They arrived as competitors with a Sioux Empire that was already taking shape there.

A Sioux warrior's bow made of carefully selected ash wood and strung with two buffalo sinews twisted together. Shown in its buckskin case with attached quiver.

Portugal in Brazil

East of this region, France's attempt to create an American land empire failed. The French, despite the density of their home population, were reluctant emigrants in the eighteenth century. Before France ceded it to Spain in 1763, Louisiana—a vast territory that took in most of the Mississippi valley—was little more than an outline on the map. In 1746, it had only 3,300 settlers, mostly concentrated around New Orleans at the mouth of the Mississippi River, while South Carolina alone, in a poorer region with a less congenial environment, had 20,000.

Other European empires, however, made substantial inroads in other parts of the hemisphere. The Portuguese got a second wind after their seventeenth-century troubles with the Dutch (see Chapter 17) and the Omanis, developing a vast, rich domain to landward in their previously neglected outpost of Brazil. As Portugal withdrew from or lost most of its sovereign outposts in Asia and East Africa, Brazil became, for want of anything better, the jewel in the crown of a now compact empire. Most of the Brazilian coast was less than two months' sail from Lisbon or the African slave ports on the other side of the Atlantic.

Exploitation of the Brazilian hinterland remained largely an affair of private slavers and ranchers, operating out of the southern city of São Paulo, until the 1680s, when reports of gold and diamond finds deep in the interior began to accumulate. In the "golden century" from the 1690s, gold and diamonds replaced sugar as Brazil's cash crops. We can see the effects in the depth of gilding that coats countless eighteenth-century Portuguese church walls. An era of ambitious demand for high art began in a land awash with wealth. Some cash went on British service industries and manufactured goods, stimulating industrialization in Britain. Some of it ended up in India and China, funding the West's persistent balance of payments deficit with the east. Much of it funded the creativity of sculptors and painters, like Aleijadinho, the crippled, black genius whose sculptures are among the wonders of the churches in Minas Gerais. Other black slaves produced impressive church music for wealthy Portuguese-Brazilians. Gold and silverwork were banned in Brazil in 1766 to protect Portuguese craftsmen. By then, the Portuguese had pushed Spanish outposts back roughly to the line of the present linguistic boundary between Spanish and Portuguese in South America. Although Spain's New World land empire was much bigger, Portugal's was in some ways more impressive: carved out of hostile jungle environments. Brazil had little useful Native American manpower, and most of what there was—when the Portuguese could catch them—had to be enslaved and forcibly redistributed to work the mines and plantations.

The black Brazilian sculptor Aleijadinho (ca. 1730–1804) carved this statue of the prophet Ezekiel for the church of Nosso Senhor do Bom Jesus de Matosinho, in the province of Minas Gerais. Because Aleijadinho's hands were crippled, he would not have been able to depict the animation, emotion, and decorative detail displayed here if he had not been carving in soapstone, which is soft when freshly quarried but hardens on exposure to air.

Spanish America

Eighteenth-century Spanish expansion happened more modestly, through a collaborative approach, winning over native communities that could not be conquered. The experience of the late seventeenth and early eighteenth centuries showed that the Spanish Empire could triumph by force only on exceptionally well-settled frontiers, like New Mexico, which the Spanish bloodily reconquered from Native American rebels in the 1690s. The policy of scattering frontier garrisons over a wide area often left their defenders surrounded by enemies and isolated. Instead, in the eighteenth century, Spanish strategy switched to a method that proved surprisingly successful: attracting peoples into the monarchy through prolonged negotiations, on equal terms. Communities that accepted Spanish rule moved into the supposed security and prosperity of rationally planned settlements.

In the second half of the century, the Spanish persuaded Indians to settle in 80 new towns on the Argentine and Chilean frontiers, and in many more settlements on and beyond the northern edge of effective Spanish power, in what is now the southwest United States. The triumph of the process is represented by scenes like that of the foundation of San Juan Bautista in Texas in 1754, sketched by a native artist in a report sent home to Spain. Through the neat files of the colonnaded streets, processions of Indians and Spaniards thread, with their traditional arms and dress and music, to meet the mission folk in the main square and erect celebratory crosses in each of its corners: an idealized scene, no doubt, but one that represents, at least, the way Spanish administrators wanted their empire to be. Similar means drew runaway slaves back into the empire. At San Antonio in Texas, black settlers had the right to exclude white colonists, except for a priest. By 1779, San Antonio had nearly 1,500 citizens.

In California, 21 new missions extended Spain's reach beyond its remotest garrisons in the late eighteenth century. From 1769 to his death in 1784, the Franciscan missionary Brother Junípero Serra founded a string of mission stations along the coast of upper California, where the arrival of an annual ship was the only contact with the rest of the Spanish monarchy. Here he converted the environment as well as its inhabitants, wrenching the natives out of nomadism, producing new crops—wheat, grapes, citrus, almonds, olives—from the soil. His foundations stretched from San Diego to San Francisco, to keep the wilderness, paganism, and rival empires—British and Russian—at bay. In these respects, the missions were successful. They worked economically, too. They had 427 head of cattle in 1775 and at least 95,000 by 1805. But prosperity did not help the Native Americans survive the unfamiliar diseases that contact with Europeans brought. The Indians, as a missionary observed, "fattened and sickened."

At the other end of the empire, where the Jesuits tended the southeast frontier in Paraguay until the Spanish government expelled them in 1768, dozens of mission churches, now ruined or restored, mark the boundaries. Even on Spain's most troublesome frontier, in what is now southern Chile, progress was made in the 1770s and 1780s, when the Spaniards adopted the policy of treating with native peoples on equal terms, conceding their claim to possess sover-

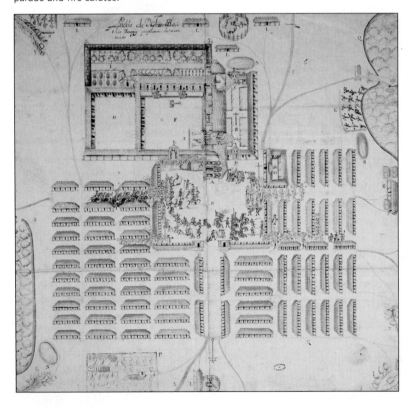

This idealized view of the main square of San Juan Bautista, Texas, in 1754 illustrates the way the Spanish monarchy eventually won over native communities it could not conquer. It shows the consecration of the main square by the erection of crosses at its corners. The mission is at the top, with its garden and magnificent church, and the town hall is to the right. Nuns, with the children from their school, emerge from the mission buildings to attend the ceremony. Parties of Indians are arriving at all the main entrances to the square, while Spanish troops and Native Americans parade and fire salutes.

eignty. Previously hostile Indian peoples joined the Spanish monarchy, and even the Mapuche, whom the Spanish could not conquer, allowed the Spaniards to build a road and a string of missions to promote trade.

Creole Mentalities

Colonies laboriously created, carefully built in the image of Europe, gradually grew away from home. Creole sentiments and values began to emerge almost as soon as colonies were established. Some settlers came to the Americas to escape their mother countries. Others, determined to remold the frontier in the image of home, were none the less seduced by the novelties of the New World, turning their backs on the ocean, striking inland, and seeking a new identity. In some ways the New World tended to drift away from the old almost as soon as the two shores were linked, slipping as if from newly tied moorings. Internal economic systems developed, followed by new loyalties, and finally by political independence.

By the eighteenth century, creolism—it might fairly be said—was a strong Spanish-American ideology. In 1747, the enlightened French naturalist, Georges-Louis, Count de Buffon, lost patience with overly idealistic depictions of the New World, which, it must be admitted, owed a lot to empires' desires to make themselves look good. He sketched out an alternative America, a grim world of harsh climates, dwarfish beasts, stunted plants, and ugly and degenerate people. His views sparked fiercely patriotic reactions in the New World. Creole science responded to European scholars' contempt for America by arguing that American nature was superior to that of the Old World—according to some claims, even the sky in the Western Hemisphere was more benign, and the influences of the stars were more favorable there. The creole elite of Peru affected Inca dress and collected Inca artifacts. In Mexico, discoveries in the late eighteenth century, including the "Maya Pompeii" (Pompeii, a Roman city in southern Italy buried by a volcanic eruption in 79 C.E., had been rediscovered in the 1730s)—the ruins of Palenque in 1773—and the uncovering of the Aztec "calendar stone" under the paving of the main square of Mexico City in 1790, boosted interest in Native American antiquities. Scholars began to describe the ruins of Xochicalco—the most complete surviving city from Aztec times—at about the same time.

These movements in Hispanic America had parallels in British colonies. Until independence in 1776, most of the leaders of the colonies that became the United States still thought of themselves as Englishmen, but the sense of being American was beginning to take shape. Gradually, elites in British North America identified with fellow colonists. In Thomas Jefferson's (1742–1826) mind, the rights of true-born Englishmen came to include the right to renounce English identity. Americans were founding a new society, independent of Britain, just as their Saxon ancestors had founded a new society when they went to Britain in the fifth century, independent of their native Germany. This was the reason behind Jefferson's frustrated efforts to have Hengist and

Aztec calendar stone. Just after European scholars had proclaimed the natural inferiority of the New World, spectacular archaeological finds in Mexico seemed to vindicate pre-Columbian America's claim to house great civilizations. This "Aztec calendar," unearthed in 1790, appeared to demonstrate mathematical proficiency, elevating the knowledge its makers had from "superstition" to "science." The glyphs on the carving surround an image of the god Tonatiuh who is crowned with a sunbeam and arrayed with images of a jaguar's head and claws, a sky serpent, a feathered shield with an emblem of the sun, and a basketful of the remains of human sacrifice.

Horsa, the supposed founders of Anglo-Saxon England, adorn the seal of the United States. At Monticello, Jefferson's estate in Virginia, his domestic museum was rich in American specimens and Native American artifacts. Painted buffalo hides hung in his hall. "Savage" carvings from Tennessee lined the atrium, rather as a Renaissance Italian palace might exhibit Roman inscriptions and statues (see Chapter 15). The portraits Jefferson collected included supposed makers of America—the explorers Christopher Columbus and Amerigo Vespucci hung alongside heroes of the American Revolution, such as George Washington and the Marquis de Lafayette. After the Revolutionary War, in the 1780s, the French traveler Michel-Guillaume Jean de Crèvecoeur, who had once believed that American freedom was an overseas version of England's "national genius," revised his opinion. Americans, he thought, were "neither Europeans nor the descendants of Europeans" but "a new race of men." Joel Barlow (1754–1812), the first epic poet of independent America, hailed, "call'd from slavish chains, a bolder race."

Toward Independence

The America that broke away from Britain in the war of 1775–1783 was in many ways a brand new society, though its origins had been laid more than 150 years before. Until the mid–eighteenth century, British settlements were sparse and scattered, clinging to the eastern rim of the continent. As a destination for migrants in the seventeenth century, the attractions of the West Indies outclassed mainland North America. After 100 years of colonization, the total white population of the mainland colonies was around 250,000. Many of the successful colonies had been conscious experiments by idealists and religious pilgrims. Economic self-betterment had been the explicit aim only of those desperate enough to sign away their liberty and labor for the term of an indenture, to buy a passage from home and a few tools and clothes with which to start an independent life when their bond was paid. In the eighteenth century, as colonial horizons broadened and the prospects of a good life in America became better defined, the mood of migrants changed. Their numbers exploded. In the 1770s, on the eve of the Revolution, the total population was probably over 2.5 million (see Figure 21.1).

This astonishing increase—by a factor of ten within three generations—had no precedent or parallel elsewhere in the New World. It was an accelerating process, most of which was crammed into the last third of the entire short period. Between the mid–eighteenth century and the outbreak of the Revolution in 1775, the number of towns founded in New England tripled each year, as—roughly—did the populations of Georgia and South Carolina. In the 1760s, the population of New York rose by nearly 40 percent and that of Virginia more than doubled.

From about 1760, a rush of settlers scaled the previously impassable wall of the Appalachian Mountains to found a new biblical "land of Canaan" between the Susquehanna and the Ohio Rivers. Crèvecoeur, whose book *What Is an American?* was to make him a founding father of American identity, imagined himself joining a mass of immigrants, heading out from Connecticut to the wilds of western Pennsylvania. There he found "a prodigious number of houses rearing up, fields cultivating, that great extent of industry opened up to a bold and indefatigable people." In 1769 on the day the land office opened at Fort Pitt on the site of what is today Pittsburgh 2,790 claims were staked. Ten thousand families were living on this frontier by 1771. The most adventurous imaginations were overstimulated by what they saw. George Washington dreamed in the 1760s of laying "with very little money the foundation of a noble estate" on the Ohio

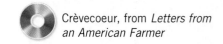

Crèvecoeur, from *Letters from an American Farmer*

River. He was disappointed and eventually had to make do with the presidency of a new republic instead.

The migrants who stimulated and swelled this growth came with alienated loyalties. Those from within England itself were almost all young. Those from within Britain were mostly from Scotland and, within Scotland, mostly from the Highlands and Islands—regions that the English and Lowland Scots establishment had only recently conquered and that were subject to vicious political and religious persecution. Many of the hearts and minds in which the Revolution was conceived were those of newcomers, gripped in a ferment of exciting possibilities. British America was a colonial region in flux, exploding with instability. Independent America was, to a great extent, a nation of latecomers.

New Englanders could never fully participate in the landward turn. Except in the Connecticut River valley and as domestic servants, slaves were largely unsuited to the climate. Nor could the New England economy pay for them. Farmer-settlers worked wonders with rocky soils—which were duly abandoned, to be replaced by mills or returned to forest, as newer, better farmland opened up farther west. Mountains and the boundaries of rival states cut the maritime colonies off from the interior. They were best equipped for a seaborne trading economy. The impoverished hinterland of New England drove work and wealth creation seaward, to the cod and whale fisheries and long-range trade.

In a sense, these were the wages of success. Early in the eighteenth century, New England's population outgrew its capacity to grow food. A trading vocation replaced the farming vocation with which the founding fathers had arrived. Yet New Englanders in their own way, by sea, drifted apart from the mother country, just as the landward-driving settlers and investors in the Ohio valley edged away by land. For the ocean led to the world. Ever-improving maritime technology was always—slowly, by small step-by-step advances, or by sudden leaps, such as the introduction of a method to determine longitude in the late eighteenth century—opening more of the globe to commerce. Gradually, during the century, it became a marked disadvantage for a trading people to be limited by the regulations of empire. New England's quarrels with Britain focused increasingly on issues of barriers to trade and the freedom of the seas, and disputes over the definition of contraband—what goods were legal to trade in and what taxes merchants and consumers had to pay on those goods. The great symbolic acts of resistance that preceded the Revolutionary War happened offshore and made these issues explicit in acts of civil disobedience: the Boston Tea Party in 1773 and the seizure of the small British warship *Gaspée* in Narragansett Bay, Rhode Island, in 1772—"God damn your blood!" screamed the respectable merchants who boarded and burned this piracy-control vessel.

Meanwhile, under the stress of war with France in the 1750s and 1760s and in the flush of victory that followed the end of France's American empire in 1763, Britain's attitude to America became more centralizing and interventionist. The British colonies had their own institutions and liberties that got in the way of some of the most crucial functions of government, especially the housing of troops and the levying of taxes. Increasingly vigorous government from Britain was designed to make the colonial administration more uniform, to exploit the colonies' growing wealth and security by taxing them, and to organize defense on modern,

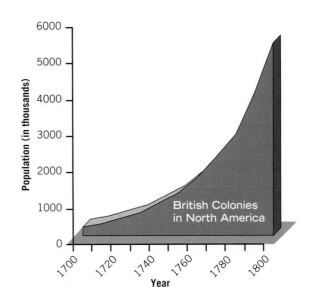

FIGURE 21.1 POPULATION GROWTH IN BRITISH NORTH AMERICA, 1700–1800

Historical Statistics of the United States *(Washington, DC: Government Printing Office, 1976), 1168.*

Long Wharf, Boston. In 1770, when Paul Revere engraved and published this view, Long Wharf still extended out further than any other wharf in colonial Boston. The view shows the arrival in September 1768 of British troops sent to quell disorders that rocked the city almost continuously from the late 1760s.

efficient, and, therefore, more centralized and expensive lines. These measures aroused the resentment of colonists anxious to retain the privileges and liberties that they had secured during the long period in which the home government had taken little interest in their affairs. The new demands of the pre-Revolutionary years came not so much from the colonists as from a Britain anxious to exact efficiency from its empire. The threat to the colonies' comfortable habits of effective self-rule and cheap government provoked confrontation.

It became increasingly obvious, moreover, in the early 1770s that British rule threatened two vital colonial interests. In 1772, a British judge declared slavery illegal on English soil, in a judgment that aroused premature anticipation among black people in America. Vermont rapidly adopted the ruling into its own laws, but it was unwelcome in the slave-dependent economies of much of British America. It seemed only a matter of time before colonial slave owners clashed with an elite in Britain that increasingly favored abolishing both the slave trade and slavery itself. Moreover, the British government was determined to keep the peace on the "Indian" frontier, and to preserve Native American buffer states between the British and Spanish Empires in the interior of North America. This was precisely where American colonists were looking to expand.

A period of increasing interventionism from Europe and increasing friction with colonial elites was broadly paralleled in the Spanish monarchy, where reformist governments in the same period took increasingly burdensome measures in a similar spirit: reasserting bureaucratic controls, reorganizing imperial defense, eliminating traditional colonial customs, maximizing the power and fiscal reach of the crown. Spanish administrators were as intrusive and troublesome in Spanish colonies as royal governors were in those of Britain. In both empires, the home governments tried to ease local bigwigs out of influential offices and replace them with creatures of the home government. In both empires, the results included growing, and potentially revolutionary, resentments. For both empires, the Americas housed some of the most remote, most difficult to govern provinces, with local populations that stubbornly sought to protect their own interests. In both empires, home governments encouraged militarization—mobilization and training for defense. These measures were a rational response to the problems of security in vast territories with ill-defined frontiers, but the effect was to create potential reservoirs of armed revolutionaries.

The Seven Years' War, which began in 1756 and ended in 1763, removed the French threat to the colonists' security with the British conquest of Canada and the French cession of Louisiana to Spain. The colonies were now free to challenge their rulers in England. By imposing high costs on imperial defense, the war encouraged Britain to seek new ways to tax America, with all the familiar consequences. It trained American fighters in the skills they would need if they were ever to challenge British forces. The experience of military collaboration between American militias and British regulars initiated or exposed cultural differences. The floggings and other brutalities of discipline that troops in the British army were subject to repelled the volunteers in the colonial militias, while the British attacked colonial resistance to stationing troops in private houses, which was the usual practice elsewhere in the British Empire, as "neglect of humanity" and "depravity of nature." The colonists saw themselves as true-born Englishmen but were shocked to find that their fellow countrymen from across the Atlantic did not share their self-perception. Mutual alienation led to violence.

Historians used to depict the uprising in 13 of the English mainland colonies in the 1770s as a peculiarly English affair—the inevitable outcome of long-standing traditions of freedom that colonists took with them as a heritage from deep in the English past. On the contrary, current scholarship tells us, it was an improvised solution to short-term problems, a typical convulsion of a colonial world that was full of rebellions in the late eighteenth century: against the British government in the north of Ireland, against Spain in Colombia and Peru. The war was in one sense an English civil war, pitting self-styled free-born Englishmen against an intrusive government, recycling the rhetoric of seventeenth-century conflicts in Britain itself in which the "commonwealth" had fought the crown. At another level, it was an American civil war, in which at least 20 percent of the white population, and most of the black people and Native Americans, sided with the British. Increasingly, it also became an international conflict. After the first three years' campaigns, when the raw American forces proved surprisingly effective, France in 1778 joined by Spain in 1779 saw the opportunity to inflict a defeat on the British. Usually, the British won eighteenth-century wars by buying the alliance of other powers on the continent of Europe. This time, no such allies were available. French intervention proved decisive, and the colonies that now began to call themselves the United States of America were the main beneficiaries.

The Spanish colonies, with their longer, stronger tradition of creole consciousness, were likely to follow the example of the northern revolutionaries. Indeed, rebellions and conspiracies multiplied in Spanish America during the 1770s and 1780s. Soon after the emergence of the independent United States, Alessandro Malaspina—one of the new breed of scientifically trained Spanish naval officers—prepared an official fact-finding voyage across the Hispanic world. In part, it was to be Spain's answer to the great Pacific voyages of

British defeat. John Trumbull (1756–1843) painted the surrender of British to American forces at Yorktown in Virginia in 1781 in symbolic fashion. American General Benjamin Lincoln accepts the surrender on a horse with a raised forepaw—a traditional symbol of triumph, under a darkening sky that suggests the shadowing power of divine providence. Only the Americans are shown victorious in the painting, whereas the war against the British was brought to this conclusion thanks to French and Spanish help. A large French army participated in the siege of Yorktown, and the French fleet forced the surrender by preventing the British from escaping by sea.
John Trumbull (American 1756-1843),The Surrender of Lord Cornwallis at Yorktown, 19 October 1781, 1787-c. 1828. Oil on canvas, 53.3 x 77.8 x 1.9 cm (21 x 30 5/8 x 3/4 in.) Yale University Art Gallery, Trumbull Collection.

the Briton Captain James Cook, and the Frenchmen Bougainville and La Pérouse (see Chapter 20): the most ambitious survey of the Americas and the Pacific ever undertaken. The results were dazzling—the product of the efforts of an enlightened government, which, as the German naturalist Baron von Humboldt (1767–1835) acknowledged, spent more on scientific research than any other monarchy of the day. Malaspina and the scholars who accompanied him gathered hundreds of thousands of samples, drawings, maps, and reports about plants, animals, native peoples, geology, climate, and the oceans.

Yet Malaspina was also responsible for reporting on the political state of the empire and the best measures of reform. Much of the background of rebellion in the English colonies was also visible in those of Spain: the emergence of distinctive political identities, the political unrest, the resentment over taxes. The eighteenth-century Mexican revolutionary, Servando de Mier, announced the political program of creolism: "America is ours, because we were born in it." He asserted the "natural right of peoples in their respective regions. God has separated us from Europe by an immense sea and our interests are distinct."

Spanish America was poised, for a moment, between two possible futures. On the one hand, as Malaspina envisioned, Spain could delegate authority into provincial hands, slash defense costs, and open trade to universal competition. On the other, the monarchy could continue to attempt to enforce an eighteenth-century model of ever more rigorous centralization, regulate trade for the benefit of Spain not the colonies, spend heavily for defense, and risk provoking the kind of revolution that had already shattered Britain's American empire. Unfortunately, Malaspina's voyage was a long affair, which outlasted the moment when the Spanish government might have embraced reform. By the time he returned to Spain in the 1790s, the French Revolution was sending shudders of horror down establishment spines. The Spanish government was in no mood to embrace reform. Malaspina was disgraced, and almost all the vast feedback of information from his scientific team was locked up, unpublished, in state archives. In America, two decades later, when war against French invaders immobilized the Spanish state, local elements, in both Spain and America, fell back on the old Spanish tradition of setting up local councils, or juntas, to handle affairs in an emergency. Once in place, most of the American juntas saw little reason to accept a return to Spanish rule, even after the French were driven from Spain in 1814, except under terms that left them in effective control.

The independence revolutions had similar causes across the Americas but, in important respects, differing outcomes. The Caribbean saw only one successful revolution: that of Haiti from 1791 to 1802 (see Chapter 19). On few other islands were there more than feeble and brief efforts to join or mimic the revolutions on the North and South American continents. Canada remained aloofly loyal to the British crown. Britain's recently acquired French Catholic subjects in Quebec evidently thought it better to be ruled from distant London than from Boston or Philadelphia. Peru and Brazil embraced independence with some reluctance. Peru's revolutionaries included elements for whom the royal government in Spain was too liberal. Independent Brazil remained a monarchy, ruled until 1889 by emperors descended from the royal house of Portugal, the former colonial power. This was understandable, since, for Brazil, the Napoleonic Wars (1799–1815) had brought the colonies closer to the mother country after the Portuguese royal family chose exile in Brazil when France overran Portugal in 1807. For the Spanish Empire, the Napoleonic invasion of Spain in 1808 was an alienating experience that exposed new quarrels between the colonial and metropolitan elites. Despite the republican

MAP 21.6

The Americas in 1828

- area gaining independence from imperial control, ca. 1783–1828
- British possession
- Russian possession
- → Sioux expansion

rhetoric that had been prominent in the rebellions, Mexico and Peru also flirted with ideas for monarchical government at intervals during their rebellions and after they won independence in 1821 and 1825 (see Map 21.6).

Brazilian independence came rapidly and almost bloodlessly in 1822 when a Portuguese prince was proclaimed Emperor Pedro I of Brazil, through destructive internal conflicts followed. In the United States, foreign help shortened the war for

Slavery and Empire in the New World

1690s	Gold and diamonds replace sugar as Brazil's main revenue source
Eighteenth century	Imports of black slaves: English North America: approx. 400,000; Spanish colonies: approx. 1 million; Caribbean: approx. 1 million; Brazil: approx. 3 million; European expansion into South American pampa and North American prairie
1756–1763	Seven Years' War
1775–1783	American colonies gain independence from Britain
Late eighteenth century	Slaves are West Africa's most valuable export
1789	Olaudah Equiano publishes his autobiography
1791–1802	Haiti gains independence from France
1822	Brazil proclaims independence from Portugal

independence, and the fighting, though traumatic and divisive, lasted barely eight years, from 1775 to 1783. The Spanish colonies had no such luck. Most of them were condemned to nearly two decades of destruction in merciless violence against Spanish armies that demonstrated surprising strength. It may be—though no research confirms it—that, because they happened a generation or two later than those of North America, Spanish America's independence wars were less restrained by the enlightened, professional etiquette of the eighteenth-century battlefield when wars tended to be short and governed by formal rules. The wars of independence, which had caused long and total interruptions of foreign trade, ruined the economies of the Spanish colonies, whereas the United States, enjoying the protection of the French and Spanish navies, actually gained new trading partners and multiplied its shipping during its struggle against the British.

IN PERSPECTIVE: The Rims of Empires

It was not only in the Americas that the rights of empires were questioned. When the French navigator Louis de Bougainville left the island of Tahiti in the South Pacific in 1768, he set up an engraved plaque with the words, "This land is ours." A French satirist, Denis Diderot, who was also one of the most influential intellectuals of the mid–eighteenth century (see Chapter 22), put a rejoinder into the mouth of a fictional Tahitian: "If a Tahitian landed one day on your shores, and scratched on one of your rocks or the bark of your trees, 'This country belongs to the people of Tahiti,' what would you think?" Diderot went further: "Every colony, whose authority rests in one country and whose obedience is in another, is in principle a vicious establishment." Much of the European elite was happy to applaud the independence of the former colonies.

There was little revulsion of feeling between the mother countries and their rebellious children. The independence of most of the Americas might have opened a new chasm in the Atlantic, splitting the Atlantic world that had grown up in the previous three centuries. On the contrary, Atlantic trade continued to grow after the independence of most of the Americas, as did migration from Europe. Conflict did not interrupt the exchange of ideas. Independence did, however, make a difference. The independent colonies had the prospect of becoming empires in their own right by expanding in their own hinterlands. For the United States, the outlook was particularly encouraging. The circumstances in which it achieved independence left the new country strong and wealthy, by comparison with other parts of the hemisphere, and the states had enormous, under-exploited resources in nearby lands.

The exploitation of colonial frontiers had hardly begun. No recorded crossing of North America from the Atlantic to the Pacific was made until 1793. Knowledge of the interior of the hemisphere was so ill recorded that patriots in Washington, D.C., in the early 1800s were unsure where the Rocky Mountains were. Scholars in Europe did not know that the Amazon and the Orinoco Rivers in South America were connected until Baron von Humboldt—one of the world's most adventurous scientists—made the journey between them in 1800. Only a beginning had been made. Yet what had been achieved did matter.

Empire-building initiatives had become—for a while—almost a European monopoly. Native Asian empires had crumbled, or their expansion had largely

CHRONOLOGY

1690s	Gold and diamonds replace sugar as Brazil's main revenue source crop
Eighteenth century	China is world's fastest-growing empire; Chinese tax revenues increase by two-thirds; Persia and Ottoman populations static; Ottoman government goes into prolonged decline; Spanish, Dutch, and Portuguese expand holdings in southeast Asia; European expansion into South American pampa and North American prairie; scale of Atlantic slave trade increases
1707	Death of Aurangzeb and the end of Mughal expansion
1720	China conquers Tibet
1722	Safavid Empire collapses
1756–1757	Robert Clive leads East India Company (EIC) conquest of Bengal
1756–1763	Seven Years' War
1759	Chinese conquest of Xinjiang complete
1761–1764	EIC revenues: £2 million
1766	Gold and silverwork banned in Brazil to protect Portuguese craftsmen
1766–1767	EIC revenues: £7.5 million
1767	Burmese invasion leads to disintegration of Thailand
1771–1778	Vietnam collapses under strain of peasant rebellions
1774	Ottomans cede land to Russia in the Treaty of Küçük Kaynarca
1775–1783	American colonies gain independence from Britain
Late eighteenth century	Marathas offer only nominal obedience to the Mughals; Slaves become West Africa's most valuable export
1780s	Spanish and French laws protect the rights of slaves
1789	Olaudah Equiano publishes his autobiography
1789	French Revolution begins
1791–1802	Haiti gains independence from France
1799	British conquer Mysore
ca. 1800	200,000 Chinese immigrants settled in Xinjiang
1806	Maratha states accept British overlordship
1822	Brazil proclaims independence from Portugal

halted. The nineteenth century saw few if any reversals comparable to those the Omanis had inflicted on the Portuguese, for instance. From now on, successful empire builders would need continually to update their war-making technology, with industrially produced guns and ships. For most of the nineteenth century, only a few powers—European, for the most part, and the United States—had effective access to such technology.

Though most of the world remained outside the rule of the empires of the age, imperialism had bridged some of the world's great chasms of communication. There were touch points of empire, at which the colonialism of rival powers met, in some of the most impenetrable places of the globe. In the late eighteenth century, Chinese and Japanese agents vied to collect tribute from native chiefs in Sakhalin Island, north of Japan, where Russia was also beginning to cast covetous looks. In the depths of Brazil, Portuguese soldiers wiped out the Jesuit missions in 1755, with Spanish permission, in a murderous rationalization of a previously vague frontier. In 1759, tiny British and French armies of 2,000 or 3,000 men settled the fate of Canada in a battle the British won under the modest church spires of Quebec City. In 1762–1763, the British occupied Spanish Manila in the Philippines, on the edge of the South China Sea, where the purely commercial maritime expansion of China had met the rival, armed imperialisms of Portugal, Holland, England, and Spain. In 1788, a French expedition anchored off Botany Bay in Australia only to find that a British colonizing venture—using convict exiles—had just beaten them to it.

In 1790, Britain and Spain almost went to war when Spanish forces seized British ships, dispatched from Sydney in Australia, at Nootka Sound, on the northwest coast of America, where British, Spanish, and Russian expansion converged. In 1796, the Spanish crown's glib Welsh agent, John Evans, persuaded the Mandan Indians of the upper Missouri to hoist the Spanish flag, defining a new frontier with the British Empire, represented by the formerly French fort of La Souris, two-weeks' march away. The hand of empire may have lain lightly on some lands, but it stretched long fingertips over the world.

PROBLEMS AND PARALLELS

1. Where were the touch points of empire in the eighteenth century? Why did land empires expand in this period?

2. How did China use colonization and settlement to expand its territory? What impact did Chinese immigration have on southeast Asia?

3. How did the Ottoman, Mughal, Persian, Japanese, and Thai Empires lose impetus in this period?

4. Why did the British gain ascendancy in India? What are the parallels between British imperialism in India and the Spanish conquest of the Americas?

5. Why did the slave trade last so long in the Americas? What was the economic rationale for slavery?

6. How did black people in the Americas craft their own social customs and norms of behavior? Why were laws enacted to prevent marriage between blacks and whites?

7. How did ecological change and the presence of Europeans strengthen certain Native American peoples in the eighteenth century?

8. How did the growth of national identity affect relations between European mother countries and their colonies? Why did conflict between empires and the colonies have little impact on trade and the exchange of ideas?

DOCUMENTS IN GLOBAL HISTORY

- Qing dynasty guidelines for Tributary Missions, 1764
- Lady Mary Wortley Montagu, from *Letters*
- Olaudah Equiano, excerpt from *The Interesting Narrative*

- Phyllis Wheatley, "To The Right Honorable William, Earl of Dartmouth . . ."
- Crèvecoeur, from *Letters from an American Farmer*

Please see the Primary Source CD-ROM for additional sources related to this chapter.

READ ON

On Mughal decline and the rise of British influence, Jos Gommans, *Mughal Warfare: Indian Frontiers and Highroads to Empire 1500–1700* (2003) provides important background, and Marshall Hodgson, *The Venture of Islam, Volume 3: The Gunpower Empires and Modern Times* (1977) is a classic that also covers the Ottoman and Persian experiences in this age. Dirk Kolff, *Naukar, Rajput, and Sepoy: The Ethnohistory of the Military Labour Market of Hindustan, 1450–1850* (2002) shows the complexity of the political and ilitary interaction between Indian and European powers. Evelyn Rawski, *The Last Emperors* (1999) covers China and the slowing of Qing imperialism.

Jorge Cañizares-Esguerra and Erik Seeman, eds., *The Atlantic in Global History: 1500–2000* (2006) is a broad-ranging introduction to the contours of Atlantic history, including the slave trade. Hugh Thomas, *The Slave Trade: The Story of the Atlantic Slave Trade, 1440–1870* (1999) is massively detailed and comprehensive. The classic first-hand account of Oludah

Equiano is readily available in *The Interesting Narrative and Other Writings* (2003).

Fascinating work is being done on the dynamics of American land empires in the late colonial period. See Jorge Canizares-Esguerra, *How to Write the History of the New World: Histories, Epistemologies, and Identities in the Eighteenth-Century Atlantic World* (2001), which is brilliant on creolism, while T. Burnard, *Creole Gentlemen: The Maryland Elite, 1691–1776* (2002) is excellent on the same phenomenon in North America. R. Price, ed., *Maroon Societies: Rebel Slave Communities in the Americas* (1996) collects important work on Atlantic slave rebellions. *The Malaspina Expedition 1789 to 1794: Journal of the Voyage by Alejandro Malaspina: Cadiz to Panama*, ed. Andrew David, Felipe Fernández-Armesto et al. (2002) provides a fascinating first-hand account of the Spanish crown's attempt to improve its knowledge of its American colonies, fix frontiers, improve scientific and geographical knowledge, and generate maps.

CHAPTER 22

The Exchange of Enlightenments: Eighteenth-Century Thought

As a portrait painter, the British artist Henry Perronet Briggs made a specialty of theatrical subjects. His study of Rajah Rammohun Roy (1774–1833) seems romantic and dramatic, giving the Indian sage a visionary stare and a strange, vaguely oriental outfit, in a setting that seems to recall the Mughal Empire.

INDIA

n the spring of 1829, an exciting rumor reached the English Bishop of Calcutta. India's most widely respected thinker, Raja Rammohan Roy, had turned to Christianity. Roy, who was born in 1774, had spent most of his life in Bengal under British rule, except for a period of study in London. He had become an admirer of Western ways, a master of Western languages, a scholar of Western science. He was only sixteen when he wrote a rejection of his ancestral religion, *A Reasoned Renunciation of the Idolatrous Religion of the Hindus*. As a teacher, he introduced his pupils to the writings of Western philosophers. He translated Western literature into Indian languages. He promoted printing and popular education as ways to spread critical new readings of ancient Hindu scriptures, and he challenged rituals that he thought contrary to right reason. He led movements to abolish female infanticide and the custom that required widows to burn themselves to death on their husband's funeral pyres. He argued for freedom for women.

In short, many observers saw Rammohan as representative of a new phase of global history: the slow but unstoppable triumph, from the late eighteenth century onward, of Western ideas, as growing Western power, and the example of Western economic and military strength, spread them around the world. Indeed, there is much truth in that image. But it does not do justice to the complexity of Rammohan's thought, or to the diversity of the traditions he inherited. He was a scholar of the Veda (VEH-dah) and of classical Persian literature long before he became a student of Western learning, and his liberal, radical, humane, and skeptical notions were confirmed, not created, by Western influence. He seems to have known about Aristotle from Arabic editions before encountering the original Greek texts. He sought not to turn India into an eastern version of the West, but to use Western help to restore what he saw as a golden age of reason, from deep in India's own past. He rejected popular superstition and social abuses, whether they were Indian or Western.

FOCUS questions

- WHAT WAS the Enlightenment and how did it influence Western social, political, and economic thinking?
- HOW DID China and Japan view Europe in the eighteenth century?
- WHY WERE the ideas of Rousseau so influential?
- WHY WAS there a reaction against the cult of reason, and what forms did it take?
- HOW DID Enlightenment ideas influence the course of the French Revolution and Napoleon's policies?
- WHAT INTELLECTUAL trends did Europe, the Americas, Islam and east Asia have in common in the eighteenth century?

He was selective, moreover, in the Western culture he admired. The authors Rammohan loved and taught were, above all, those connected with the great, innovative movement of eighteenth-century European thought that we call the **Enlightenment**—writers who elevated reason, science, and practical utility, challenged conventional religion, and sought ruthlessly to expose every kind of cant. When the bishop of Calcutta congratulated him on his supposed conversion to Christianity, Rammohan quickly denied it with the kind of irreverent wit he had picked up from European writers he admired: "My Lord, I assure you, I did not abandon one superstition merely in order to take up another." The Enlightenment, indeed, was the source of the most powerful influences that spread from Europe over the world of the nineteenth and twentieth centuries. Even before the eighteenth century was over, the Enlightenment made a home in the Americas, with some modifications, and gripped fingerholds in Asia.

• • • • •

Moreover, the Englightenment was global in its inspiration, as well as its effects. A great deal of debate among historians has focused on the problem of where the Enlightenment started. England, Scotland, France, and the Netherlands all have their partisans. In some ways, we can trace its origins all over northern and Western Europe. This debate misses the more fundamental contribution made by the interaction of Western European thought with ideas from overseas, and, in particular, from China. Like all topics in the history of thought, the Enlightenment is complex and elusive. We had better begin by admitting that and relishing the challenge it presents.

The best way to approach the Enlightenment may be by first telling a story that expresses its character better than any attempt at a dictionary-style definition. We can then look at the global exchange of influences that surrounded enlightened ideas, the key texts that encoded them in Europe, and the changes that overtook and—ultimately—transformed the Enlightenment during the eighteenth century.

THE CHARACTER OF THE ENLIGHTENMENT

To understand what the Enlightenment was like, a good place to start is Kittis in northern Finland, near the Arctic Circle, where a French scientist, Pierre Louis Moreau de Maupertuis, pitched camp in August, 1736. The light reflected and refracted among the rocks and ice made it seem, he said, "a place for fairies and spirits."

Maupertuis was engaged in the most elaborate and expensive scientific experiment ever conducted up to that time. Traditionally, Western scientists had assumed that the Earth was perfectly spherical in shape. Seventeenth-century theorists, however, led by Isaac Newton in England, argued that it must be distended at the equator and flattened at the poles, owing to centrifugal force (the thrust, that is, or sense of thrust you get on the edge of a circle in motion, which tends, for instance, to fling you off a merry-go-round). Meanwhile, mapmakers working on the survey of France for King Louis XIV (see Chapter 18) made a series of observations that sug-

Pierre Louis de Maupertuis (1698-1759), on his return from the Arctic in 1737, seems to flatten the globe in this portrait by the French artist Robert Lervac-Tournières. The hero points the way forward. A map of the area he surveyed in Finland is on the table, with the Laplanders' fur-lined cap he wore on his expedition.

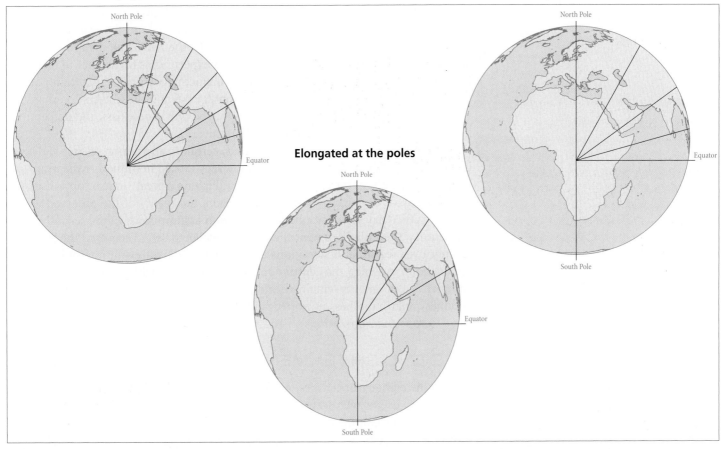

Perfectly spherical

Elongated at the poles

Distended at the equator and flattened at the poles

MAP 22.1

The Shape of the Earth

gested the contrary. The world seemed to be football shaped: elongated toward the poles. The French Royal Academy of Science decided to end the debate by sending expeditions—of which Maupertuis's was one—to measure the length of one degree along the surface of the circumference of the Earth. If measurements at the Arctic Circle matched those at the equator, the globe would be spherical. Any difference between them either way would indicate where the world bulged (see Map 22.1).

In December 1736, Maupertuis began to measure his baseline, some 12 miles long—"the longest baseline that ever was used"—on the ice of the river. The measuring rods were made of fir wood because of all available materials it was least likely to shrink from the intense cold. "Judge what it must be like," he wrote, "to walk in snow two feet deep, with heavy poles in our hands, . . . in cold so extreme that whenever we would take a little brandy, the only thing that could be kept liquid, our tongues and lips froze to the cup and came away bloody, in a cold that congealed the extremities of the body, while the rest, through excessive toil, was bathed in sweat."[1]

It should have been all but impossible to achieve total accuracy under such conditions, but Maupertuis's readings were overestimated by less than a third of one percent. They helped to convince the world that the planet was indeed shaped as Newton had predicted—squashed at the poles and bulging at the equator. On the front page of his collected works, Maupertuis appears in a fur cap and collar over a eulogy that reads, "It was his destiny to determine the shape of the world."

Like many scientific explorers seared by experience, Maupertuis eventually became disillusioned by science but inspired by nature. He set off believing that every truth was quantifiable, and that every fact could be sensed. By the time of his death in 1759, he had become something of a mystic. "You cannot chase God in the immensity of the heavens," he concluded, "or the depths of the oceans or the chasms of the Earth. Maybe it is not yet time to understand the world systematically—time only to behold it and be amazed." In the *Letters on the Progress of the Sciences*, which he published in 1752, the next experiments for science to tackle, he felt, would be on dreams and the effects of hallucinatory drugs—"certain potions of the Indies"—as the only way to learn what lay beyond the universe. Perhaps, he speculated, the perceived world is illusory. Maybe only God exists, and perceptions are only properties of a mind "alone in the universe."

Maupertuis's mental pilgrimage between certainty and doubt, science and speculation, rationalism and religious revelation reproduced in miniature the history of European thought in the eighteenth century. First, in a great surge of optimism, the perfectibility of man, the infallibility of reason, the reality of the observed world, and the sufficiency of science became common assumptions. In the second half of the century, the Enlightenment flickered as intellectuals rediscovered the power of feelings over reason and sensations over thoughts. Then revolutionary bloodshed and warfare, in which the century ended, seemed for a while to put out the torch completely. But embers remained: enduring faith that freedom can energize human goodness, that happiness is worth pursuing in this life, and that science and reason—despite their limitations—can unlock progress and enhance lives.

THE ENLIGHTENMENT IN GLOBAL CONTEXT

During the eighteenth century, despite the long reach of some European empires, China's was, as we have seen (see Chapter 21), by almost every standard, still the fastest-growing empire in the world. China also looked like the homeland of a more modern society—in key respects—than any you could find in the West. It was a better-educated society, with over a million graduates from a highly demanding educational system, and a more entrepreneurial society, with bigger businesses and bigger clusters of mercantile and industrial capital than you could find anywhere else. It was a more industrialized society, with higher levels of production in more specialized concentrations, and a more urbanized society, with denser distributions of population in most areas. China's was even—for adult males—a more egalitarian society, in which the hereditary landed gentry had social privileges similar to those of their Western counterparts, but had to defer to scholar-bureaucrats who were drawn from every level of rank and wealth in society.

The Chinese Example

Described with frank admiration by the Jesuits on whom Europeans relied for information, China was bound to excite positive interest among European thinkers who were looking to improve the societies they inhabited. One of China's greatest fans was also one of Europe's most influential thinkers. The French philosopher François-Marie Arouet (1694–1778), who wrote under the name Voltaire, was the best-connected man of the eighteenth century. He corresponded with Empress Catherine the Great of Russia (r. 1762–1794), corrected the King of Prussia's French poetry, was friends with the official mistresses of King Louis XV of France (r. 1715–1774), and influenced statesmen all over Europe. His works were read in Sicily and the Balkans, plagiarized in Vienna, and translated into Swedish. He saw China, in part, as a source of inspiration for his own art. In 1733, he adapted a Chinese play for the Parisian stage under the title, *The Orphan Boy of China*. More generally, Confucianism attracted him as a

Voltaire. When Voltaire died in 1778, the sculptor Jean-Antoine Houdon (1741–1828) used the great writer's death mask (a plaster cast of the face made just after a person died) to represent him realistically. But this sculpture remains highly charged with symbolic meaning. Voltaire is robed like an antique philosopher-sage; his hands are wrinkled with useful toil; a sardonic smile represents his use of irony and humor to challenge the institutions of church and state.

philosophical alternative to organized religion, which he detested. And he sympathized with the Chinese conviction that the universe is orderly, rational, and intelligible through observation. In the Chinese habit of political deference to scholars, he saw an endorsement of the power of the class of professional intellectuals to which he belonged. In the absolute power of the Chinese state, he saw a force for good.

Not everyone in Europe's intellectual elite, not even in his native France, shared Voltaire's opinion. Voltaire's colleague and collaborator, Denis Diderot (1713–1784), ridiculed him for believing Jesuit propaganda. In 1748, in *The Spirit of Laws*, a work that inspired constitutional reformers all over Europe, the baron de Montesquieu (1689–1755) claimed that "the cudgel governs China"—a claim Jesuit accounts of Chinese habits of harsh justice and judicial torture endorsed. He condemned China as "a despotic state, whose principle is fear." Indeed, a fundamental difference of opinion divided Montesquieu and Voltaire. Montesquieu advocated the rule of law and recommended that constitutional safeguards should limit governments. Voltaire never really trusted the people and felt that strong, well-advised governments could best judge the people's interests. Montesquieu, moreover, developed an influential theory, according to which Western political traditions were benign, and tended toward liberty, whereas those of Asian states were hopelessly despotic and concentrated power in the hands of tyrants. "This," he wrote, "is the grand reason of the weakness of Asia, and of the strength of Europe; of the liberty of Europe and of the slavery of Asia." *Oriental despotism* became a standard term of abuse in Western political writing.

François Quesnay (1694–1774), Voltaire's colleague, who echoed the idealization of China, countered that "enlightened despotism" would favor the people rather than elites. Confucianism, he argued, restrained despotism. In their day, Quesnay's ideas were even more influential than Montesquieu's. He even persuaded the heir to the French throne to imitate a Chinese imperial rite by plowing land in person as an example to agrarian improvers. *Enlightened despotism* also entered the political vocabulary, and many European rulers in the second half of the eighteenth century sought to embody it. One way or another, whether you favored China or rejected its examples, Chinese models seemed to be shaping European political thought. By the 1760s, a satirist in England could complain that busts of Confucius were replacing those of Plato and Aristotle in fashionable houses, and that instead of relying on the classics, "we take our learning from the wise Chinese." In the same decade, the leading minister of the French crown conceived a plan to develop a policy of intellectual exchange with China and arranged for two Chinese scholars to study in the French Academy of Science. The plan failed, however, because the two Chinese decided to work as Christian missionaries instead. The English dramatist Oliver Goldsmith (1728–1774) composed fictional *Letters of a Chinese Philosopher* to express disapproval of his own society.

Meanwhile, Chinese influence was changing elite taste in Europe. Until the eighteenth century, China exercised its artistic influence on the West almost entirely through porcelain, lacquers, and textiles. Now the delights of Chinese wallpaper became accessible to a rich elite, and European furniture and dishes were decorated with genuinely Chinese themes. The French painter Jean-Antoine Watteau's (1684–1721) designs for Chinese scenes to decorate

Baron de Montesquieu, from
The Spirit of the Laws

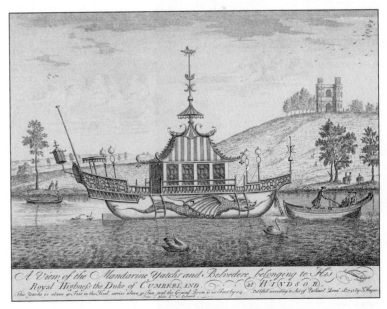

The Duke of Cumberland's "Mandarin Yacht"—a fake Chinese junk, built to sail on his large artificial lake near London. Cumberland was a son of King George II (r. 1727–1760), and the Mandarin Yacht helped to influence a fashion for things Chinese—gardens, porcelain, furniture, interior design—among the European elite in the eighteenth century.

an apartment for Louis XIV inaugurated a taste for Chinese-style schemes. It spread through all the palaces of the royal dynasty of Bourbon, which ruled France, Spain, and Naples, and was connected by marriage with many of Europe's other leading dynasties. From Bourbon courts, the Chinese look radiated through Europe. In England, the king's son, the Duke of Cumberland, sailed on a fake Chinese pleasure boat. William Halfpenny's *Chinese and Gothic Architecture* (1752) was the first of many books to treat Chinese art as equivalent to Europe's. Sir William Chambers, the most fashionable British architect of the day, designed a pagoda for Kew Gardens in London and Chinese furniture for aristocratic homes, while "Chinese" Thomas Chippendale, England's leading cabinetmaker, popularized Chinese themes for furniture. By midcentury, engravings of Chinese scenes hung even in middle-class French and Dutch homes.

Japan

Enthusiasm embraced Japan as well as China. Jesuits, of course, did not praise Japan, whose rulers had expelled them in the 1630s. Since then, Japanese governments had relentlessly persecuted Christianity. The Japanese policy of excluding foreigners kept Europe in ignorance of Japanese life. But the activities of the Dutch East India Company in Japan opened a window. Engelbert Kaempfer, a company envoy, published the most influential account of Japan in 1729. He presented Japan in an ambiguous light, as a land of heavy punishments and light taxation. His portrait of a rampant Lord High Executioner and of a people in "slavery and submission" fed into European ideas of Japan for centuries to come, but he was also frank about the peace, order, and prosperity he observed. Opinion about Japan in Europe split as it did over China. Montesquieu saw Japan as an illustration of oriental despotism. Voltaire saw it as the embodiment of "the laws of nature in the laws of a state."

India

Voltaire found an even better model in India. In 1756, he published *Dialogue Between a Brahman and a Jesuit*. The Brahman speaks with Voltaire's voice. He wants, above all, "a state in which the laws are obeyed." Voltaire's work on India was more profound than his assertions about China and Japan, because he recognized how much Western thought owed to ideas that had originated in Indian civilization. "It is probable," he averred, "that the Brahmins were the first legislators of the earth, the first philosophers, the first theologians." The study in the West of Asian languages strengthened this contention as the century went on. The Collège Royal in France introduced Chinese studies in the 1730s, but it was Jesuit work on Indian languages, especially Sanskrit, that facilitated the most remarkable disclosure. In 1786, the English scholar Sir William Jones realized that Sanskrit—the language of the Indian classics—was related to Latin and Greek and probably shared with them a common root (see "Going to the Source: 'Dutch Studies' in Japan and Sanskrit Among the British," pages 764–767). Although Western observers found little to praise or imitate in Indian science, they could not help but notice the effectiveness of the traditional methods on inoculation against smallpox. As we have already seen (see Chapter 20), inoculation was introduced to Europe thanks to the influence of Turkish practices, and Westerners needed to be reassured that this alarming new procedure was effective.

The Islamic World

Muslim Turkey and Persia, too, influenced Western minds in the eighteenth century, mainly as sources of exotic imagery, and also, in Turkey's case, as a model of good and bad practice in government. Montesquieu added objectivity and credibility to his critiques of Western society in his *Persian Letters* (1721) by pretending that they were the

Edward Wortley Montagu in Turkish dress. Turkish dress was more than an affectation for the English traveler, Edward Wortley Montagu, painted here in 1776, the year of his death. His father had been British ambassador in Constantinople. His mother, Lady Mary, had written appreciatively about Turkey, where she learned the technique of inoculation against smallpox and had it tried out on her son.

work of a Persian sage. Playwrights favored Turkish settings and characters for social satire. In 1782, Wolfgang Amadeus Mozart's *The Abduction from the Seraglio*, one of the great comic operas of the age, showed Turks outfoxing Europeans in cunning and exceeding them in generosity. In its plot, a lovelorn youth fails comically to rescue his girlfriend from the harem of an Ottoman official, who, however, generously allows the lovers to go free, together. Turkey was often cited as a model for Europe to follow in hygiene, education, charitable institutions, and generally of what a late seventeenth-century traveler praised as their "order, . . . economy and the regulation of provisions." In 1774, Simon-Nicolas-Henri Linguet pointed out that in Turkey and Persia the Quran protected political liberty by restraining the power of rulers. Well-informed observers of Turkey commended the Ottomans for religious toleration, respect for laws, customs, and property rights, and for benevolence toward minorities—the very virtues that some political philosophers of the Enlightenment thought that Europe lacked.

Nonetheless, over the century as a whole, European critics of Ottoman life and customs became increasingly strident. Features of government formerly praised as evidence of strength and wisdom—the lack of a governing aristocracy, for instance, the docility of the sultan's subjects, the vulnerability of high officeholders to the sultan's mood—came to be seen, through the lens of the Enlightenment, as arbitrary and despotic. Turkey, even more than China, became a reference point for denunciations of oriental despotism. "In such distressful regions," wrote a follower of Montesquieu, "man is seen to kiss his chains, without any certainty as to fortune and property; he adores his tyrant; and without any knowledge of humanity or reason, is reduced to have no other virtue but fear."

THE ENLIGHTENMENT'S EFFECTS IN ASIA

European interest in Asia transformed Europe, but changed Asia only a little.

The Enlightenment and China

Historians have generally regarded the Chinese attitude to European ideas at the time as arrogant, unrealistic, and restricted by outmoded traditions. In fact, it reflected the historic world balance of power. Westerners had always had more to learn from China than the other way round. Even in the eighteenth century, the inferiority of the West was only beginning to be reversed. So it is not surprising that the Chinese were still highly selective in their receptivity to Western ideas. At the beginning of the century, when Jesuits were already installed as the emperors' favorite astronomers, mapmakers, and technicians (see Chapter 18), one of them complained that the Chinese still "cannot be persuaded that anything which is not of China deserves to be regarded." The Jesuit concerned, Father Chavagnac, found it particularly distressing that some Chinese scholars still expressed skepticism when he showed them his map of the world. "They all cried out, 'So where is China?' 'It is this small spot of land,' said I. 'It seems very little,'" was their reply.

Nevertheless, the Jesuits did extend their activities at court in eighteenth-century China. "Every day," they claimed in letters home during the reign of the Kangxi emperor (r. 1661–1722), "from two hours before noon to two hours after noon, we were at the emperor's side, lecturing on Euclid's geometry, or on physics, astronomy, etc." The emperor wrote a famous poem in praise of one of his Jesuit-made clocks, and commissioned Jesuits to map inner Asia. He commanded and—according to his flatterers—supervised the translation of a collection of Western mathematical works, including Euclid's and all the texts Jesuits recommended on the calendar. The Yongzheng (yung-jheng) emperor (r. 1722–1735) restricted missionaries'

Concubine. In the eighteenth century, Chinese emperors inaugurated a fashion at the imperial court for having one's portrait painted in Western dress. Here the favorite concubine of the Qianlong emperor (r. 1735–1796) wears a Western suit of armor. The artist, Giuseppe Castiglione, was a member of the Jesuit mission in China from 1730 until 1768. He also helped design the gardens of the imperial summer palace, with their complicated series of fountains that constituted a feat of hydraulic engineering.

Chinese clock. Though the history of clock making in China dates back to the eleventh century, mechanical clocks were unknown until the Jesuit missionary Matteo Ricci arrived in the late 1500s (see Chapter 18). Western technology thereafter played a key part in diplomatic relations between the West and China. In the reign of the Kangxi emperor (1661–1722), an imperial clock and watch factory was established within the imperial palace at Beijing. The emperor himself studied mathematics and applied science, and one of his surviving poems reads, "The skill originated in the West / But, by learning, we can achieve the artifice / Wheels move and time turns round / Hands show the minutes as they change." The clock above, made in Guangzhou in about 1790, is an automated musical table clock sounded by 12 bells and 22 hammers. The exquisite design displays both Chinese and European artistic styles.

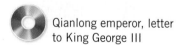

Qianlong emperor, letter to King George III

freedom to make converts but had himself painted in a Western curled wig and coat. For the Qianlong emperor (r. 1735–1796), European artists painted his favorite concubine dressed in Western armor and the horses of his stable in Western style. Other Jesuits designed his gardens and engineered its fountains and mechanical statues.

A story often told to demonstrate the Chinese attitude is that of a British embassy that arrived in China in June 1793. The mission lacked nothing that might embellish its dignity and emphasize its prestige. King George III (r. 1760–1820) had made its leader Lord Macartney an earl and equipped him with a staff of 84 attendants. The king's gifts for the Chinese court, worth over £15,000, a huge sum in the eighteenth century, included a letter to the emperor in a box made of gold and all the most new-fangled hardware of early British industrialization: a planetarium, globes, mathematical instruments, chronometers of apparently magical accuracy, a telescope, instruments for chemical and electrical experiments, plate glass, Wedgwood ware (the best pottery British factories could provide), silver-plated knives and forks, and samples of textiles woven on power looms.

The Chinese were not wholly contemptuous of these efforts. Esteem for Western technical ingenuity was high, and the Qianlong emperor had a formidable collection of Western mechanical devices. Indeed, restrainedly pleased at the arrival of this "first tributary mission" from Britain, the emperor ordered that on account of the envoys' long journey they should be given a better welcome than equivalent missions from Burma and Vietnam. He did not, however, endorse the high value the British put on themselves. He indulged, as a bit of barbarian bad manners, the ambassador's refusal to follow Chinese custom by knocking his head on the ground in deference to the throne. The British, the emperor said, were incapable of "acquiring the rudiments of our civilization." They possessed nothing China wanted. Their representatives could not be allowed to reside permanently at the imperial court. "It is your bounden duty," the emperor concluded in his reply to George III, "reverently to appreciate my feelings and to obey these instructions henceforth for all time."

Western technology made its biggest impact, perhaps, on war. In 1673, the emperor threatened to expel all Christians from China unless the Jesuits consented to design and manufacture artillery for him. The priests' designs continued in use until the mid–nineteenth century. They supervised gunnery practice, under compulsion, insisting that they were men of peace. In the mid-1780s, when news of the development of hot-air balloons in the West reached the Chinese court, the Chinese immediately inquired about its possible military applications. "Only in war," an imperial prince explained, "do we have no regard for expense, difficulty or danger. We are ready to try anything." Nonetheless, Chinese interest in adopting new technology waned for a while thereafter. Westerners still seemed just clever barbarians to the Chinese, useful in their place, dangerous when they aimed higher.

Western Science in Japan

Admiration for the West penetrated deeper—though still not very deep—in Japan. The shogun Yoshimune (r. 1716–1745) took an interest in science and technology comparable to Kangxi's. From 1720, he allowed Chinese translations of Western books to circulate in Japan. The Japanese scholar Miura Baien (1723–1789) recognized that Western astronomy had revolutionized knowledge of the universe. Like many Western philosophers of the time, he advocated practical utility and technical efficiency above traditional values. "A tiny lantern that lights humble homes," he wrote, "is worth more than gems." Iron and copper, from which goods were made that people could use, should be valued above silver and gold. Yet despite Japanese sympathy for aspects of Western thought, it was hard to find ways to promote Western knowledge. Japan's seventeenth-century experience (see Chapter 19) still made its government determined to exclude Christianity and limit foreign access to the country. Since the representatives of the Dutch East India Company were the only Europeans allowed in Japan—and even then only under tight restrictions—access to sources of scientific information was haphazard. Japanese scholars had no way to judge what information was accurate or up to date. The interpreters who negotiated with the Dutch worked exclusively in Portuguese, the traditional language of Western commerce in east Asia. Japanese scholars who wanted to read the Western books that reached Japan had to teach themselves Dutch from scratch (see "Going to the Source: 'Dutch Studies' in Japan and Sanskrit Among the British," pages 764–767).

The case of Rembert Dodens's *Cryidetboeck*, a Dutch study of plants published in 1554, is instructive. In 1659, a Dutch embassy presented an edition of 1618 to the shogun. Hidden away in the palace library, it was extracted at Yoshimune's command in 1717, in the belief that it might contain useful medical knowledge . It was handed over to a translator, who eventually produced his translation in 1750. The work was by then nearly 200 years out of date. The same translator worked on another supposed guide to plants for 24 years before realizing that it was a zoological work that had no medical information.

Something like a breakthrough came only in 1771, when the dissection of a corpse demonstrated the accuracy of European books of anatomy. A group of enthusiastic beginners in "Dutch studies" started meeting six or seven times a month to puzzle over the meaning of Western books. "After about a year," wrote one of them, "we became capable of reading as much as ten or more lines of text per day if the particular passage was not too difficult."

So China remained the dominant intellectual influence in Japan, and Confucianism remained the foundation of Japanese thought. Most new developments came not from the West but from Japanese reactions against Confucianism. Independently, Japanese thinkers discovered principles similar to those philosophical radicals in Europe and America advocated: the virtues, especially, of universal reason—*ri*, the Japanese called it—approached scientifically, through observation. Ogyu Sorai (1666–1728) advocated experience in place of speculation as the key to truth. "History," he declared, "is ultimate knowledge." Tominaga Nakamoto (1715–1746) went further, doubting the possibility of any universally valid statements because experience seemed too diverse. In a work of 1713, Kaibara Ekken argued that nature was in a constant state of flux and so could only be understood by observation, not by the grand generalizations of Confucian theory. Some radicals embraced an egalitarian theory of human nature. Ishida Baigan (1685–1744), a strong advocate of reason as the unique means to truth, was one of many teachers who opened their classes to people of modest social backgrounds, in the belief that commoners had the same mental powers as the gentry.

Korea and Southeast Asia

In Korea and Vietnam, too, national revulsions from Confucianism and Chinese cultural dominance stimulated new thinking. In Korea, the movement called "practical learning" started as a reaction against Confucianism but acquired some knowledge of Western technology by way of China. A design for a Western crane, copied from a Chinese book, helped to build a castle. Koreans began to model world maps on Western examples. In the mid–eighteenth century, Yi Ik began a systematic study of Western learning in Chinese books. In the 1780s, a group of Korean intellectuals spontaneously founded a society to introduce Catholicism into the country. In Vietnam, meanwhile, the most remarkable case of independent thinking echoing new ideas from the West appeared in the work of the poet, Ho Xuang Huong. "Down

A MEETING OF CHINA, JAPAN, AND THE WEST

Eastern and Western Enlightenments meet in this late eighteenth-century Japanese painting on silk.

The Japanese man, who seems the dominant presence, in this discussion group, is perhaps a self-portrait of the artist, Shiba Kokan, who played a big part in promoting "Dutch learning" in Japan. His position near the European suggests his admiration for Western science.

In the background, firefighting teams from Japan, China, and Holland tackle the same blaze with their respective techniques. The Dutch seem to be most effective.

The unidentified Dutchman displays a book of anatomy—one of the sciences in which the Japanese acknowledged Western superiority. The closeness of the Dutch and Japanese figures is emphasized, while the Chinese participant sits somewhat apart, listening critically.

How does this painting illustrate the global exchange of ideas in the eighteenth century?

● MAKING CONNECTIONS ●

ENLIGHTENMENT INFLUENCES IN ASIA

COUNTRY/ REGION →	EXAMPLES OF INFLUENTIAL IDEAS →	SOURCES →	SOCIAL/POLITICAL/ECONOMIC CONSEQUENCES
China	Western astronomy, mathematics, scientific methods, technology	Jesuit missionaries; European diplomats	Imperial leaders collect Western mechanical devices; use Western-designed artillery
Japan	Western astronomy, mathematics, scientific methods, technology; Japanese concepts of universal reason, scientific observation	Dutch diplomats, merchants; Japanese thinkers (Sorai, Nakamoto, Ekken)	Restrictions on trade and interaction limit exposure to Western ideas, technology; Japanese ideas spread more rapidly as reaction against Confucianism
Korea, Vietnam	Korea: "practical learning"	Korea: reaction against Confucianism and interest in Western technology, religious inspiration	Korea: development of new technology aids in construction, mapmaking; Catholicism introduced by intellectuals
	Vietnam: interest in women's rights	Vietnam: Ho Xuang Huong (writer)	Vietnam: critique of traditional marriage practices

with husband-sharing!" she exclaimed when her husband took a second wife. "One [wife] rolls in warm blankets, the other freezes. . . . I've turned into a half-servant, an unpaid maid! Had I known, I would have stayed single."

Other Asian cultures were even less hospitable to Western thought. In Thailand, an exchange of embassies with France in the 1680s stimulated, at first, enormous interest in both countries. For the French, Thailand offered a model of the exotic. For the Thai, the French presented an insight into the Western technical proficiency already admired in China. Kosa Pan, the Thai envoy to France, took home a large collection of European maps, and the French mission to Thailand established an observatory in the royal palace. The king—suitably screened from the profanity of contact with ordinary people—attended lectures that Jesuit astronomers gave. But this period of receptiveness did not last long. Western influence in Thailand receded after a palace revolution there in 1688.

The Ottomans

Inhibited by Muslim religious scruples, the Turks and Persians, too, were relatively slow to open up to the worldwide exchange of ideas. The first printing press in Turkey was only set up in 1729. When the authorities closed it down in 1742, it had produced only 17 titles. In 1798, French armies invaded Egypt and Syria, leaving—after their early withdrawal—seeds of Western-style thinking. Here, as in India, aspects of Western thought were enthusiastically embraced but only in the nineteenth century, and only after unmistakable demonstrations of Western military strength (see Chapter 25).

THE ENLIGHTENMENT IN EUROPE

Even in Europe, in some quarters, new thinking met distrust, censorship, and persecution. To understand why—and to identify the defining themes of the thought of the time—the best source is the French *Encyclopedia*, subtitled *Reasoned Dictionary of the Sciences, Arts and Trades*, which appeared in 17 volumes of texts and 11 volumes of

Camera obscura. Denis Diderot's *Encyclopedia* promoted technology and "useful" knowledge—in this case, the construction of a camera obscura, which was the forerunner of modern photography. The camera obscura captured an image by projecting rays of light from an object through a pinprick opening onto the inner wall of a chamber. Painters used this technique to ensure realism in their art.

illustrations between 1751 and 1772. By 1779, about 25,000 sets had been sold throughout Europe, in the teeth of condemnation by reactionary governments and established churches. This may not seem many, but the ideas the *Encyclopedia* contained reached the entire European elite, one way or another, and circulated in countless spinoff works. Diderot, who masterminded the entire project, wanted a comprehensive work that would "start from and return to Man," while covering every intellectual discipline along the way. The aim of the *Encyclopedia*, he announced, was "to assemble the knowledge scattered over the face of the Earth . . . that we may not die without having deserved well of mankind."

Of course, however, the book was not merely a disinterested panorama of knowledge. It had a slant. First, its values were practical. There was enormous emphasis on utility, engineering, mechanics, technology. There was, according to Diderot, "more intelligence, wisdom, and consequence in a machine for making stockings" than "in a system of metaphysics." Second, the writers of the *Encyclopedia*'s approach to knowledge advocated reason and science as means to truth, drawing heavily on the work of Scottish and English philosophers of the early part of the century. The first page depicted Reason pulling a veil from the eyes of Truth. Third, although the contributors by no means agreed among themselves on questions of political philosophy, the tone of the *Encyclopedia* was generally highly critical of the existing record of Europe's monarchies and aristocracies. Drawing on another English thinker, John Locke (1632–1704), most contributors on political questions seemed to favor constitutional guarantees of the liberty of the citizen against the state. Indeed, many contributors to the *Encyclopedia* insisted on the "natural equality" of all men. Finally, the work was uniformly hostile to organized religion.

The Belief in Progress

Underlying the whole project was a heady kind of optimism: belief in progress. Indeed, only optimists could have undertaken such an ambitious project. To make progress credible, someone had to think up a way to understand evil, and explain away all the disasters and woes of the world. This was a long-unfulfilled task of theologians, who never satisfactorily answered the atheists' challenge, "If God is good, why is there evil?" In the seventeenth century, the growth of atheism made the task seem urgent. "To justify the ways of God to man" was the objective the English poet John Milton (1608–1674) set himself in his great verse epic, *Paradise Lost*. But it is one thing to be poetically convincing, quite another to produce a reasoned argument. In 1710, the German philosopher Gottfried Wilhelm Leibniz (1646–1716) did so. He was the most wide-ranging thinker of his day, combining outstanding contributions to philosophy, theology, mathematics, linguistics, physics, and law with his role as a courtier to the ruler of the German state of Hanover. He started from a truth traditionally expressed and witnessed in everyday experience: good and evil are inseparable, because each is meaningless without the other. Freedom, for example, is good, but must include freedom to do evil. Altruism is good only if selfishness is an option. But of all logically conceivable worlds, ours has, by divine decree, the greatest possible surplus of good over evil. So—in the phrase Voltaire used to mock this theory—"All is for the best in the best of all possible worlds." "Whatever is, is right," echoed Alexander Pope (1688–1744), the most elegant English poet of the age, in his verse *Essay on Man*. Leibniz formulated his argument in an attempt to show that God's love was compatible with human suffering. It was not Leibniz's purpose to endorse progress, and his "best world" could have been interpreted as one in which nothing ever changed, in which the ideal amount of evil was inherent in human beings. But, in alliance with the conviction of human goodness, which most thinkers of the Enlightenment shared, it made the goal of a secular golden age possible, toward which people could work by using their freedom to adjust the balance, bit by bit, in favor of goodness.

Even then, the suspicion that it was merely a historical phase, enjoyed by their own times, but exceptional by the standards of history in general, inhibited believers in progress. The Marquis de Condorcet (see Chapter 21), for instance, thought he could see "the human race . . . advancing with a sure step along the path of truth, virtue, and happiness" only because political and intellectual revolutions had subverted the crippling effects of religion and tyranny. The human spirit was now at last "emancipated from its shackles" and "released from the empire of fate."

New Economic Thought

If you believe in human goodness, you believe in freedom. Thinkers pessimistic about human nature, like the Chinese Legalists, tend to favor strong, even repressive governments to keep destructive instincts in check. Optimists hope to liberate people to do good. Montesquieu and the authors of the *Encyclopedia* were particularly concerned to recommend political freedom, but economic freedom was an equally important theme in the thought of the time.

Free trade was a new doctrine. The long experience of an unfavorable trade balance with Asia had induced two obsessions in Western economic thought: bullion—gold and silver—is the basis of wealth; and to grow rich, an economy must behave like a business and sell more than it buys. According to the Spanish moralist, Tomás de Mercado, what "destroys this abundance and causes poverty is the export of money." All European governments came to believe this. In consequence, they tried to evade impoverishment by hoarding bullion, trapping cash inside the realm, limiting imports and exports, regulating prices, defying the laws of supply and demand, and founding empires to create markets for their goods that they could control.

The consequences were woeful. Overseas investment was restricted, except in imperial ventures. The protection of trade nourished inefficiency and squandered resources on policing. Competition for protected markets caused wars and, consequently, waste. Money drained out of circulation. These conditions, which clearly inhibited economic growth, were much criticized from the late seventeenth century onward. The eighteenth-century French school of economic thinkers known as the physiocrats devised the slogan **laissez-faire** to mean "leave the market to itself." The British economist David Ricardo (see Chapter 21) agreed. "Wages," he recommended, "should be left to the fair and free competition of the market, and should never be controlled by the interference of the legislature." The decisive moment in the shift toward economic freedom came in 1776, when the Scots professor of moral philosophy, Adam Smith, published *The Wealth of Nations*.

Smith had a lofty view of the importance of the law of supply and demand, believing that it affected more than the market. "The natural effort of every individual to better his own condition" was the foundation of all political, economic, and moral systems. Taxation, Smith felt, was more or less an evil. First, it was an infringement of liberty. Second, it was a distortion in the market. "There is no art which one government learns sooner than another than that of draining money from the pockets of the people." Self-interest could be left to serve the common good. "It is not from the benevolence of the butcher, the brewer or the baker that we expect our dinner, but from their regard to their own interest." "In spite of their natural selfishness and rapacity," Smith declared, the rich "are led by an invisible hand to make nearly the same distribution of the necessaries of life which would have been made, had the earth been divided into equal portions among all its inhabitants."

Olympes de Gorges, *Declaration of the Rights of Woman and the Female Citizen*

Mary Wollstonecraft, *A Vindication of the Rights of Woman*

The Wealth of Nations appeared in the same year as the Declaration of Independence and should be counted among the United States' founding documents. It encouraged the American Revolution, for Smith said that government regulations limiting the freedom of colonies to engage in manufacture or trade were "a manifest violation of the most sacred rights of mankind." The United States has remained the homeland of economic liberalism ever since.

Social Equality

Smith's arguments for freedom included the claim that freedom would deliver equality. This is not necessarily true, but it was characteristic of the time. Reason suggested that all men are naturally equal. So what about women? Montesquieu saw no reason to exclude them. The ideas we now call **feminism**—that women collectively constituted a class of society, historically oppressed and deserving of emancipation—appeared in two works of 1792, the *Declaration of the Rights of Woman and of the Female Citizen* (*Déclaration des droits de la femme et de la citoyenne*) by Marie-Olympe de Gouges and *A Vindication of the Rights of Woman* by Mary Wollstonecraft. Both authors had to struggle to earn their living. Both led irregular sex lives. Both died tragically. Wollstonecraft died in childbirth in 1797 at the age of 38. De Gouges was guillotined in 1793 during the French Revolution for defending the king and queen of France. "Women may mount the scaffold," she said, "they should also be able to ascend the bench," that is, to become judges. Both writers rejected the entire previous tradition of female championship, which praised women for their domestic and maternal virtues. Instead, they admitted women's vices and blamed male oppression.

Anticlericalism

For most of the philosophers who worked on the *Encyclopedia*, the great obstacle to progress was the Church. They catalogued the crimes of the Church—inquisitions, persecutions, clerical abuses of power. They ridiculed the doctrine of the incarnation, which said that Christ was God in human flesh. The reader of the article on cannibalism was referred to articles on the Eucharist, Communion, altar, and such. "We must show that we are better than Christians," wrote Diderot in a letter to a contributor, "and that science makes more good men than grace." In his *Persian Letters*, Montesquieu had carried the attack further, blaming Christianity and Islam alike for inhibiting sex and discouraging procreation. Voltaire erected his own temple to "the architect of the universe, the great geometrician" but regarded Christianity as an "infamous superstition to be eradicated—I do not say among the rabble, who are not worthy of being enlightened and who are apt for every yoke, but among the civilized and those who wish to think." Many people in France ceased to mention God and the saints in their last wills. Donations to religious foundations dwindled. King Louis XV abandoned the rites, traditional for French kings, of touching subjects with scrofula, a disfiguring skin disease, in the hope of a miracle cure, because he found belief in miracles embarrassing.

We can measure the progress of the Enlightenment across Europe in anticlerical acts. In 1759, Portugal

"The cult of reason was taking on the characteristics of an alternative religion." For Catholicism, reason is a gift of God and can enlighten faith, but eighteenth-century critics in France denounced the Church for smothering reason and encouraging superstition. They also hated the Church for wasting—as they thought—economic resources and supporting an oppressive political order. Many of them advocated deism—belief in God, without the supposed irrational doctrines of Christianity. In 1794, this "cult of the Supreme Being" briefly replaced Catholicism as the official religion of France, in a gaudy ceremony presided over by the head of a group of fanatics who had seized power during the Revolution. *Pierre-Antoine Demachy, Festival of the Supreme Being at the Champ de Mars on June 8, 1794. Musee de la Ville de Paris, Musee Carnavalet, Paris, France. Bridgeman-Giraudon/Art. Resource, NY*

expelled the Jesuits and confiscated their property. In 1762, Catherine the Great of Russia secularized a great portfolio of property belonging to the Orthodox Church. Between 1764 and 1773, the Jesuit Order was abolished in most of the rest of the West. In the 1780s, governments in parts of Europe confiscated church lands and forced 38,000 monks and nuns into lay life. A Spanish official proposed seizing most of the church's land. In 1790, the King of Prussia, one of the largest German states, proclaimed absolute authority over the clergy in his realm, both Protestant and Catholic. Meanwhile, among the European elite, the cult of reason was taking on the characteristics of an alternative religion. In the secret ceremonies of freemasonry, a profane hierarchy celebrated the purity of its own wisdom, brilliantly portrayed in Mozart's opera *The Magic Flute*, first performed in 1791. In 1793, revolutionary committees banned Christian worship in parts of France and erected signs proclaiming, "Death is an Eternal Sleep" over cemetery gates. In the summer of 1794, the government in Paris tried to replace Christianity with a new religion, the cult of the Supreme Being.

To some extent, the success of science encouraged mistrust of religion. From John Locke, eighteenth-century radicals inherited the conviction that it was "fiddling" to waste time thinking about what, if anything, lay beyond the scientifically observed world. The evidence of our senses was all true and—with certain exceptions about sound and color that experiments could confirm—it was all caused by the real objects our senses seemed to disclose to us. Thus, the jangling is proof of the bell, the heat of the fire, the stink of the gas. "Freethinking" atheism got a boost from the microbial world, with its apparent evidence of spontaneous generation. The very existence of God—or at least, the validity of claims about God's unique power to create life—was at stake.

THE CRISIS OF THE ENLIGHTENMENT: RELIGION AND ROMANTICISM

This attitude, however, which we would now call *scientism*, did not satisfy all its practitioners. The Scottish philosopher David Hume (1711–1776) pointed out that sensations are not really evidence of anything except themselves—that objects cause them is just an unverifiable assumption. Many scientists, like Maupertuis, drifted back from atheism toward religion, or became more interested in speculation about truths beyond the reach of science. In 1799, with the aid of a powerful microscope, Lorenzo Spallanzani observed fission—cells reproducing by splitting. He demonstrated that if heating killed bacteria—or *animalculi*, to use the term favored at the time, or germs, as he called them—they could not reappear in a sealed environment. He concluded that living organisms did not appear from nowhere. They could only germinate in an environment where they were already present. No known case of spontaneous generation of life was left in the world.

Religious Revival

The churches, moreover, knew how to defeat unbelievers. Censorship did not work. But appeals, over the intellectuals' heads, to ordinary people did. Despite the hostility of the Enlightenment, the eighteenth century was actually a time of tremendous religious revival in the West. Christianity reached a new public. In 1722, Nicolas Ludwig, Count Zinzendorff experienced an unusual sense of vocation. He built the village of Herrnhut (meaning "the Lord's keeping") on his estate in eastern Germany to be a place of refuge, where persecuted Christians could share a

Voltaire, "On Universal Toleration"

George Whitfield. Long after his death, George Whitfield (1714–1770) was remembered for the emotional effects of his preaching. In the 1770s, the artist John Wollaston recalled Whitfield's charisma. The congregation concentrate on him, yet he seems spiritually absent, as if transported by rapture, unengaged with his audience. His hands stretch out to lay people, including women, in the gesture his church—the Church of England—reserved for the rite in which bishops ordain priests. Whitfield's message was indeed that gifts of the Holy Spirit were universal, given to laypeople as well as to ordained clergy.
John Wollaston, George Whitefield, *ca. 1770. National Portrait Gallery, London.*

Sympathy with nature. Antonio de Ulloa's *Relación histórica del viaje á la América Meridional*, first published in 1752 as a result of his expedition to the equator in 1735 to measure the sphericity of the earth, provided a clear and accurate description of South American geography. The frontispiece of the work shows a figure representative of the useful sciences revealing Faith to the Indians. In the background Mount Cotopaxi erupts. With Chimborazo, Cotopaxi became a symbol of the unconquerable yearning that characterized romantic sensibilities.
© The Trustees of the British Museum

sense of the love of God. It became a center from which evangelical fervor—or "enthusiasm," as they called it at the time—radiated over the world. Zinzendorff's was only one of innumerable movements of religious revival in the eighteenth century to offer ordinary people an affective, unintellectual solution to the problems of life: proof that, in their way, feelings are stronger than reason, and that religion—for most people—is more satisfying than science. As one of the great inspirers of Christian revivalism, Jonathan Edwards (1703–1758) of Massachusetts, said, "Our people do not so much need to have their heads stored, as to have their hearts touched." His meetings, characteristically, were occasions for congregations to purge their emotions in ways intellectuals found repellent. "There was a great moaning and crying through the whole house," observed a witness to one of Edwards's sermons, "What shall I do to be saved—Oh, I am going to Hell—oh, what shall I do for Christ, etc., etc., so that the minister was obliged to desist—the shrieks and cries were piercing and amazing."

Preaching was the information technology of all these movements. Between 1740 and his death in 1758, George Whitfield (or Whitefield—he spelled it both ways) was always on the move, all over Britain and across the American colonies. Addressing a congregation composed of almost the entire population of Boston, he made the town seem "the gate of heaven. Many wept enthusiastically and cried out under the Word, like persons that were hungering and thirsting after righteousness. The Spirit of the Lord was upon them all." In 1738, with a "heart strangely warmed," John Wesley (1703–1791) began a mission to the workers of town and country in England and Wales, traveling 8,000 miles a year and preaching to congregations of thousands at a time, at open-air meetings. He communicated a mood rather than a message—a sense of how Jesus can change lives by imparting feelings of love. Catholic evangelism was equally stirring and targeted the same enemies—materialism, rationalism, apathy, and formalized religion. One observer compared Alfonso Maria Liguori's (1696–1787) mission among the poor in Naples in Italy to the preaching of a biblical prophet. In 1765, the pope authorized devotion to the Sacred Heart of Jesus—a bleeding symbol of divine love.

Music contributed to the mood. The eighteenth century was a time when God seemed to have all the best tunes—from the moving hymns that John Wesley's brother, Charles wrote, to the stirring settings of Christ's passion by the German composer Johann Sebastian Bach (1685–1750). In 1741, George Friedrich Handel wrote *Messiah*, telling the life of Jesus in music so sublime that when the first London performance approached its climax, King George II rose to his feet and heard the "Hallelujah Chorus" standing, a custom the audience at modern performances still repeats. The scriptures Handel set to music made an effective reply to skeptics: Jesus was "despised and rejected," but "I know that my Redeemer liveth, and though worms destroy this body, yet in my flesh shall I see God." Mozart's music, too, ultimately served the Church better than the Masonic movement. He died in 1791 while at work on his great *Requiem Mass*—his own triumph over death.

Cynically, the so-called enlightened despotism of some European monarchs collaborated with religious revival as a means to distract people from politics and strengthen churches as institutions of social control. King Frederick the Great of Prussia (r. 1740–1786) was a freethinker who liked the company of philosophers at dinner. He employed, for a while, both Maupertuis and Voltaire. But he favored religion for his people and his troops, founding hundreds of military chaplaincies and requiring religious teaching in schools. He was applying a principle his sometime friend, Voltaire uttered: "If God did not exist, it would be necessary to invent him."

The Cult of Nature and Romanticism

The cult of nature was something Christians and their enemies could agree on. Nature seemed both more beautiful and more terrible than any construction of the human intellect. In 1755, an earthquake centered at Lisbon, Portugal, shook even Voltaire's faith in progress. One of Europe's greatest cities, home to nearly 200,000 people, was reduced to ruins. It was the single most destructive natural disaster on record in European history. As an alternative to the return to God, radical philosophers responded to the call, "Return to Nature" which one contributor to the *Encyclopedia*, Baron d'Holbach, uttered in his *System of Nature* in 1770: "She will console you, drive out from your heart the fears that hobble you . . . the hatreds that separate you from Man, whom you ought to love." "Sensibility" became a buzz word for responsiveness to the power of feelings, which were valued even more than reason.

It is worth remembering that exploration in the eighteenth century was constantly revealing new marvels of nature. New World landscapes strongly inplemened the minds of the kind eighteenth-century people called **romantic**. Modern scholars seem unable to agree about what this term really meant. But it signified a mindset that became increasingly characteristic of Europeans in the second half of the eighteenth century, and increasingly dominant in the world thereafter. Romantic values included imagination, intuition, emotion, inspiration, and even passion, alongside—or in extreme cases, ahead of—reason and scientific knowledge as guides to truth and conduct. Romantics professed to prefer nature to works human beings created, or, at least, wanted art to demonstrate sympathy with nature. The influence of American landscapes on romantic minds began with the beautiful and exciting drawings that two young Spanish scientists, Jorge Juan and Antonio de Ulloa, made during a scientific expedition to the equator. In work published in 1752, they combined scientific diagrams with images of awestruck reverence for untamed nature. Their drawing, for instance, of the volcanic Mount Cotopaxi erupting in Ecuador, with the phenomenon, depicted in the background, of arcs of light seen in the sky on the mountain slopes, combines precision with rugged romance. The Andean settings they recorded remained the source of the most powerful romantic images of America. Cotopaxi became a favorite subject of American landscape painters.

The merging of science and romance is apparent in the work of one of the greatest scientists of the age, Baron Alexander von Humboldt (1769–1859). In the 1790s, he began a series of journeys of scientific exploration in America. His aim, he declared, was "to see Nature in all her variety of grandeur and splendour." The high point of his endeavors came in 1802, when he tried to climb Mount Chimborazo—Cotopaxi's twin peak. Chimborazo was thought to be the highest mountain in the world—the untouched summit of creation. Sickened by altitude, racked by cold, bleeding copiously from nose and lips, Humboldt had almost reached the top when he was forced to turn back. His story of suffering and frustration was just the sort of subject romantic writers were beginning to celebrate in Europe. The English poet John Keats (1795–1821) hymned the "lover who canst never have thy bliss." The German novelist Friedrich von Hardenberg (1772–1801) praised the "blue bloom" that can never be plucked. The cult of the unattainable—an unfulfillable yearning—lay at the heart of romanticism. Humboldt's engravings of the scenery he encountered inspired romantic painters in the new century.

Cult of the unattainable. Humboldt stoops to pluck a botanical specimen near the foot of Mount Chimborazo. Humboldt's account of his climb to the top of Chimborazo is a poignant litany of the cult of the unattainable so characteristic of romanticism.

This new romantic movement was not just a reaction in favor of nature against the cult of reason. It was also an adoption by educated people of the feelings and attitudes of the uneducated populace. Its poetry, said the leading English figure in the movement, William Wordsworth (1770–1850), was "the language of ordinary men." Its grandeur was that of solitudes rather than cities, mountains rather than mansions. Its religion was "enthusiasm," which was a dirty word among the intellectuals of the old regime but which drew thousands to listen to popular preachers. The music of romanticism ransacked traditional songs for melodies. Its theater and opera borrowed from the entertaining antics of street performers. Its prophet was Johann Gottfried Herder (1744–1803), who praised the moral power of the "true poetry" of "those whom we call savages." Its philosopher was Jean-Jacques Rousseau (1712–1778), who taught the superiority of natural passions over cultivated refinement. Its portrait paintings showed society ladies in peasant dress in gardens landscaped to look natural, reinvaded by romance. The German collector of folk tales, Jakob Grimm (1785–1863) devised its slogan: the People make poetry. "The people" had arrived in European history as a creative force and as a remolder of the educated elite in the people's own image.

Rousseau and the General Will

Of the thinkers who broke with the outlook of the *Encyclopedia*, Rousseau was the most influential. He was a restless super tramp with a taste for low life and gutter pleasures. He changed his formal religious allegiance twice without once appearing sincere. He betrayed all his mistresses, quarreled with all his friends, and abandoned all his children. Addiction to his own sensibilities became the guideline of his life. In 1750, in the prize-winning essay that made his name, he repudiated one of the most sacred principles of the Enlightenment—"that the Arts and Sciences have benefited Mankind." The fact that the topic could be proposed at all shows how far disillusionment with enlightened optimism had gone. Rousseau's denunciations of property and the state offered nothing in their place except an assertion of the natural goodness of humankind in its primitive state. Voltaire loathed these ideas. "One wants to walk on all fours," like an animal, he said, after reading Rousseau.

Nonetheless, Rousseau's political thinking helped shape the politics of his day and has remained influential ever since. Rousseau regarded the state as a corporation, or even a sort of organism, in which the individual identities of the citizens are submerged. At a previous, unknown stage of history, the act occurred "by which people become a people, . . . the real foundation of society." "The people becomes one single being. . . . Each of us puts his person and all his power in common under the supreme direction of the general will." Citizenship is fraternity—an organic bond, equivalent to the blood bond between brothers. The commands of the general will are perfect freedom—social or civil freedom, Rousseau called it—and anyone constrained to obey them is simply being "forced to be free." "Whoever refuses to obey the general will shall be compelled to do so by the whole body."

Rousseau was vague about the moral justification for this obviously dangerous doctrine. The German philosopher Immanuel Kant (1724–1804), however, provided one. By setting aside one's individual will or interests and exercising reason instead, one can identify objective goals of a kind whose merit everyone can see. Submission to the general will limits one's own freedom in deference to the freedom of others. In theory, the "general will" is different from unanimity or sectional interests or individual preferences. In practice, however, it just means the tyranny of the majority. Rousseau admitted that "The votes of the greatest number always bind the rest." In Rousseau's version of the way his system works, political parties are outlawed because "There should be no partial society within the state."

The same logic would forbid trade unions, religious communions, and reformist movements. Yet the passion with which Rousseau invoked freedom made it hard for many of his readers to see how illiberal his thought really was. Revolutionaries adopted the opening words of his essay of 1762: "Man is born free and everywhere he is in chains!"

Pacific Discoveries

Underlying the elevation of the common man and woman to be fit for participation in government were influences from surprising directions: the Pacific and the Americas. The Pacific in the eighteenth century stretched between myths: an unknown continent called *Terra Australis*, supposedly awaiting discovery in the south, and the rumored sea passage around America in the northwest. Investigation of those myths became the objective of the English navigator Captain James Cook (see Chapter 19). After sailing on coal carriers in Britain, he had joined the Royal Navy as an able seaman. War service in the North Atlantic drew attention to his uncanny gifts as a coastal surveyor and chart maker. In 1769, he was ordered to Tahiti in the South Pacific to observe the transit of the planet Venus and returned with a burning vocation to sail "not only farther than man has been before but as far as I think it possible for man to go."

From *Captain Cook's Journal During his First Voyage Round the World*

In three voyages of Pacific exploration, he ranged the ocean with a freedom never before attained. He crossed the 70th parallel north and the 71st south. By charting New Zealand, the west coast of Alaska, and the east coast of Australia, he defined the limits of the Pacific Ocean. He also filled in most of its remaining gaps on the map. He brought a new precision to mapmaking, using the latest technology for finding longitude—the exquisitely accurate chronometer the English inventor John Harrison (1693–1776) had developed. He exploded the myth of Terra Australis, or at least pushed its possible location into latitudes "doomed to lie forever buried under everlasting snow and ice." His achievements overflowed the map of the Pacific. By rigorous standards, for instance, of hygiene and nutrition aboard ship, he contributed to the conquest of scurvy (see Chapter 19). He suggested the colonization of Australia and New Zealand. His ships brought back sketches and specimens of plants and beasts unknown in Europe.

Cook was the spearhead of an enormous scientific invasion of the Pacific by late eighteenth- and early nineteenth-century expeditions from Britain, Spain, France, Russia, and the newly independent United States. They acquainted the European public as never before with the dimensions and diversity of the world. As with the case of the Americas in previous centuries, another "new world" became available for Western imperialism to exploit, and another treasury of natural resources was open to enrich Western economies. From the point of view of intellectual history, the most important discoveries Western explorers made in the Pacific were of its peoples.

Observers dismissed some of them as intellectually insignificant. William Dampier, author of the first description of some of the aborigines of Australia, published in 1697, found their material culture "nasty" and their appearance repellent, "having no one graceful feature in their faces." The aborigines attracted little scientific study in the eighteenth and early nineteenth centuries, but the inferior status to which Westerners assigned them seemed to require no endorsement from science. It struck those Westerners who met them as obvious. Despite the British government's pious orders to its subjects "to live in amity and kindness" with the aborigines, ruthless persecution and exploitation followed. In contrast to the practices Europeans adopted toward Native Americans or the Maoris of New Zealand, British imperialists never bothered to make treaties with Australian aborigines. Colonists hunted such people without qualms, like

Chronometer. Outwardly, it looks like other timepieces of its era, but John Harrison's marine chronometer revolutionized navigation in the eighteenth century. Three problems made clocks inaccurate at sea: moisture got into the cases, pendulums changed length with changes in temperature, and friction disturbed the moving parts. Harrison's solutions to these problems were so perfect that when the famous explorer Captain Cook tested the chronometer at sea in 1774, he found it accurate to within a few seconds over any distance in any conditions. Because differences in longitude match differences in time, navigators could now always be sure of their position and could safely judge their distance from charted dangers.

Omai—the restless young Tahitian who sailed to England with Captain Cook in the 1770s—became the darling of London society. He is shown here painted by Sir Joshua Reynolds, the most fashionable portrait painter of the day, in heroic fashion, in misplaced oriental attire, and bare feet, against a majestic backdrop. In Western eyes, Omai embodied the idea that the untutored, "natural" man could be effortlessly noble.

kangaroos. Early painters of the "black fellows" were divided in their perceptions. There are some noble-looking "savages" among their subjects. More commonly, however, the aborigines are like monkeys, crawling on the earth or scampering in the trees.

From other parts of the Pacific, however, explorers brought home fine specimens of Pacific manhood, whom admirers instantly classed as **noble savages**—exemplars, that is, of the fact that to be morally admirable you did not need to be white, or Western, or Christian, or educated in social customs or intellectual traditions that Europeans recognized as "civilized." In 1774, English society lionized Omai, who had been a restless misfit in his native Polynesia. Duchesses praised his natural graces, and Sir Joshua Reynolds, Britain's most fashionable painter, painted him as an example of calm, uncorrupted dignity. Lee Boo, from Palau in Micronesia, was equally convincing as a "prince of nature." Visitors to the Pacific found a sensual paradise. The French explorer, Louis Antoine de Bougainville (see Chapter 19) called Tahiti the island of Venus, the Roman goddess of love, and the ease with which visitors could obtain sexual favors from Tahitian women became one of the most persistent themes of literature about the place. Romantic primitivism became inseparable from sexual opportunity. Images of Tahiti as the ravishing home of inviting nymphs filled Westerners' minds and canvases. Diderot focused on sex to highlight the mutual incomprehension of a Tahitian girl and a French chaplain: "Honest stranger, do not refuse me. Make me a mother."

Wild Children

The disappointments of previous centuries had not put to rest the quest for "natural" man. On the contrary, interest in such problems as the origins of language, the origins of political and social life, and the moral effects of civilization was never so acute, and scholars' anxiety to examine specimens of primitive humanity untouched by rules of civilized society was greater than ever. "Wolf children" seemed, for a while, to be likely to supply the required raw material for analysis. Carolus Linnaeus (1707–1778)—the Swedish botanist who devised the modern method of classifying species—thought that wild children were a separate species of human beings. Plucked from whatever woods they were found in, wrenched from the wolves and foxes that suckled them, they became experiments in civilization, subjected to efforts to teach them language and manners.

Numbers of recorded cases increased in the seventeenth and eighteenth centuries. Was this because of renewed interest in wild children, stimulated by comparisons with the "savages" discovered by overseas expansion? Or was it simply a function of the explosion of population in the Europe of the day, expanding the limits of towns and cultivation, squeezing the remaining tracts of unpopulated "wilderness"? All the experiments to "civilize" these children failed. Boys, which bears supposedly raised in seventeenth-century Poland, continued to prefer the company of bears. "Peter the Wild Boy" whom rival members of the English royal family struggled to possess as a pet in the 1720s, hated clothes and beds and never learned to talk. The "savage girl" kidnapped from the woods in France in 1731 preferred raw frogs to food cooked in the kitchen and for a long time, she imitated birdsong better than she spoke French. The most famous case of all was that of another French child, the "Wild Boy of Aveyron." Abandoned in infancy in the high forest of southwest France, he survived by his own wits for years until he was kidnapped for civilization in 1798.

He learned to wear clothes and to dine elegantly, but never to speak or to like what had happened to him. His tutor described him drinking fastidiously after dinner in the window of the room, "as if in this moment of happiness this child of nature tries to unite the only two good things which have survived the loss of his liberty—a drink of limpid water and the sight of sun and country."

The Huron as Noble Savage

The most prolific and influential source of ideas about the nobility of savagery were the Native American Huron of the Great Lakes region of North America (see Chapter 19). Although missionaries who worked among the Huron were candid about the defects of their savage way of life, the secular philosophers who read them tended to accentuate the positive and eliminate the negative. Cautionary tales were filtered out of the missionary accounts, and only an idealized Huron remained. This transformation of tradition into legend became easier as real Hurons literally disappeared—first decimated, then virtually destroyed by the diseases to which European contagion exposed them.

The great secularizer of legends about the Huron was Louis-Armand de Lom de l'Arce, who called himself by the title his family had sold for cash, Sieur de Lahontan. Like many refugees from a hostile world at home, he left France for Canada in the 1680s and set himself up as an expert on its curiosities. The mouthpiece for his free-thinking anticlericalism was an invented Huron called Adario, with whom Lahontan walked in the woods, discussing the imperfections of translations of the Bible, the virtues of republicanism, and the merits of free love. Lahontan's devastating satire on the church, the French monarchy, and the pretensions and pettiness of the French elite fed directly into Voltaire's tale of the 1760s of a "natural" Huron sage in Paris.

The socially intoxicating potential of the Huron myth was distilled in a comedy of uncertain authorship, performed in Paris in 1768, which also inspired or plagiarized Voltaire's portrait. The Huron in this comedy excels in all the virtues of noble savagery as huntsman, lover, and warrior against the English. He travels around the world with an intellectual's ambition: "to see a little of how it is made." When urged to adopt French dress, he denounces imitation as fashion "among monkeys but not among men." "If he lacks enlightenment by great minds," comments an observer, "he has abundant sentiments, which I esteem more highly. And I fear that in becoming civilized he will be the poorer." Unhappy in love, the Huron urges the mob to breach the prison fortress of Paris, the Bastille, to rescue his imprisoned love. He is therefore arrested for sedition. "His crime is manifest. It is an uprising."

THE FRENCH REVOLUTION AND NAPOLEON

Believers in the nobility of the savage found it relatively easy to believe in the wisdom of the common man. The Bastille was a symbol of oppression. Copies of the *Encyclopedia* that the government had seized were kept there. Voltaire had been briefly and comfortably imprisoned there. Urban myth insisted that hundreds of prisoners of conscience suffered there. In fact, like most organs of the French state, it was rickety, and like the government's treasury, virtually empty. Rebels who broke into it in search of arms and gunpowder on July 14, 1789, found only a handful of inmates.

The Enlightenment

r. 1661–1722	Kangxi, Chinese emperor, tutored by Jesuit scholars
1680s	Louis-Armand de Lom de l'Arce leaves France for Canada
1685–1750	Johann Sebastian Bach, composer
1689–1755	Baron de Montesquieu, author of the *The Spirit of the Laws* and *Persian Letters*
1694–1778	François Marie Arouet (Voltaire), leading philosopher and admirer of China
1703–1791	John Wesley, founder of Methodism
1712–1778	Jean-Jacques Rousseau, author of the *Social Contract*
1713–1784	Denis Diderot, publisher of the *Encyclopedia*
1720	Chinese translations of Western books allowed to circulate in Japan
1736	Maupertuis's expedition to the Arctic Circle
1740–1758	Preaching career of George Whitfield, emotional preacher
1771	Japanese "Dutch studies" group begins study of Western books

The Fall of the Bastille by the French artist Jean-Pierre Houel (1735–1813). Houel's paintings contributed to the myth that the Bastille, a medieval fortress in the heart of Paris, was a terrifying, cruel, and secretive prison, in which a repressive monarchy tortured its many victims. But when a citizen army captured the castle on July 14, 1789, they found only a small, demoralized garrison and a handful of privileged inmates lodged in comfortable cells, not chained in dungeons. This did not stop Houel from romanticizing the event. Each time he painted a different version of the fall of the Bastille, he enlarged the crowds, increased the flames, and exaggerated the scale of the struggle.

The Declaration of the Rights of Man and Citizen

Background to the Revolution

To those who endured it, or experienced its consequences, the Revolution that—according to the conventional narrative—broke out in France on that day seemed so momentous that they searched the past for its causes. Historians have gone on looking deep into the history of the prerevolutionary old regime in France for explanations. In fact, however, like most political upheavals, the French Revolution arose suddenly in the particular circumstances of the time and unrolled rapidly in ways previously unforeseeable. The costs of wars—especially French participation in the American Revolutionary War, which ended in 1783 and added substantially to the French state's debts—left the monarchy desperate to increase tax yields. France was a rich country with a poor government. By summoning the Estates General, the medieval assembly of the realm, for the first time since 1614 to meet the crisis, royal ministers took a big risk. Deputies to the estates expected to be able to demand changes that would go far beyond finance. Many arrived resentful, having sat on consultative bodies whose advice the government had dismissed. Most belonged to the literate minority the Enlightenment had affected. They had strong inclinations toward constitutionalism in politics and anticlericalism in religion. All of them had read the gutter press of the day: scandal sheets about alleged sexual and financial shenanigans at court.

Local assemblies elected the deputies. "Public opinion," King Louis XVI (r. 1774–1792) once wrote in one of his schoolbooks, "is never wrong." The regulations for electing the assembly emphasized that "His Majesty wishes that everyone, from the extremities of his realm and from the most remote dwelling places, may be assured that his desires and claims will reach him." As a result, the deputies arrived charged with "books of grievances," many of them full of the complaints of peasants hungry after bad harvests, venting their rage on big landowners. Most of them demanded lower taxes and relief from traditional obligations of peasants and the traditional privileges of lords—the lords' exclusive rights to keep pigeons and hunt game, to evade taxes, to charge fees to hold markets and fairs, to mobilize forced labor. In June, the Estates General gave itself the title of National Assembly with the right to "interpret the General Will of the nation." In August, it enacted the Declaration of the Rights of Man and the Citizen. "Men are born free and remain equal in rights," this document proclaimed. Sovereignty, said the Declaration, no longer rested with the king but with the whole people. As in all revolutions, radicals exploited the mood in favor of change to organize and agitate for even more change than most people wanted.

Revolutionary Radicalism

In 1790–1791, the revolutionaries concentrated on the church, enacting a "civil constitution of the clergy" that turned priests into public servants and nationalized church property. The pope rejected it. So did the king, who had never been wholehearted in his support of radical reform. Once his opposition to continuing reform became known, the king became a virtual prisoner of the assembly. Opponents of the Revolution began to leave the country. Foreign powers feared the Revolution might be exported abroad. In March 1792, war broke out, and Austria and Prussia invaded France.

In the atmosphere of war, anything can happen, and only harsh measures can give governments control over events. In August 1792, when it was obvious that Louis XVI was in contact with the invaders, the monarchy was overthrown. In 1793, the royal family was executed. Aristocrats, priests, and government officials were massacred in urban riots and peasant rebellions. The most ruthless revolutionary factions seized power over what remained of the state, while local committees of militants and self-appointed "people's tribunals" imposed revolutionary unity by terror. In the bloodiest spell, during June and July 1794, 1,584 heads were chopped off in Paris, and thousands of peasants and workers were killed in the provinces. "It was not," admitted a member of the government, "a question of principles. It was about killing."

The idealism that had launched the Revolution became hard to sustain in the face of so many crimes committed in the name of liberty. Take the example of a leading revolutionary propagandist, the Marquis de Sade (1740–1814), who called himself Citizen Sade after the revolutionaries liberated him from the Bastille to which his family had begged the government to confine him in the 1780s. His private correspondence exposes his revolutionary enthusiasm as a sham. In contrast to the enlightened idealism he claimed to profess, he had a record of wicked behavior unsurpassed among the annals of eighteenth-century sexual athletes. He gave his name—*sadism*—to morbid forms of sexual cruelty. His offenses included ejaculating over a crucifix; torturing, imprisoning, and poisoning prostitutes; and—so he claimed—"proving that God does not exist" by inserting consecrated communion wafers in the rectums of people with whom he was going to have anal sex. His sexual antics were a distortion of liberty, his egotism a warped version of individualism, his violence and cruelty a caricature of the vicious fervor of revolutionary injustice. As if in parody of Rousseau, de Sade thought no instincts could be immoral because all are natural. And as if in parody of Pierre Laplace's elimination of God from science (see Chapter 20), he thought no passions should be condemned because all are governed by the motions of chemical forces in the body. The unresolved quest of his brief political career as a revolutionary spokesman—he ended his days in an insane asylum—was to combine the extreme individualism to which he was inclined with the social responsibility the revolution demanded.

Napoleon

When revolutions unleash chaos, people often turn to a "strong man." In 1799, a military coup brought France's best general to power as dictator. Napoleon Bonaparte (1769–1821) called himself First Consul of the Republic, then, from 1804, after more victories had increased his popularity, Emperor of the French. His military genius and the skill and strength of his armies turned Europe into a playground for his political experiments. French power extended at its height over Spain, Portugal, Italy, Belgium, the Netherlands, Switzerland, most of Germany, Poland, and parts of Austria and Croatia. French influence overshadowed Scandinavia. French armies carried revolutionary ideas into Russia, Egypt, and Syria (see Map 22.2). The wars were the nearest thing to world war that the world had yet seen, igniting contests for trade and dominion in India, where the British seized the opportunity to extend their conquests, and in the Americas, where British armies attacked Buenos Aires in Argentina and burned the White House in Washington, D.C. Colonies changed hands in the Caribbean, North America, the Indian Ocean, and South Africa, and even, in Haiti's case, achieved independence (see Chapter 21). But the major global effects arose from the new political forms and ideas generated in Europe and the way an increasingly interconnected and well-informed world took them up.

In an age of political innovations, Napoleon was one of the most inventive rationalizers of states. He imposed a uniform law code on his conquests. The **Code Napoleon** is still his most impressive legacy and forms the basis of the civil and often criminal laws of much of Europe, Latin America, and sub-Saharan Africa. He subordinated the Church to the state. He decreed the abolition of ancient monarchies and republics. He summoned new states into being, changed the boundaries of old ones, and imposed constitutional government where it had never existed before.

Napoleon. The French painter Jean Ingres's (1780–1867) portrait of Napoleon enthroned as Emperor of the French amazes the onlooker. How could so much majesty, magnificence, and power come within the reach of an outsider? Napoleon came from Corsica, a poor Mediterranean island that had only become part of France in 1768; his army service began in the artillery—a corps other soldiers despised at the time; his father though claiming aristocratic blood, had been a lawyer—a bourgeois occupation. Yet Napoleon turned France from a republic into a monarchy and crowned himself emperor in 1804. Though regal and romantic, Ingres's image also seems showy and vulgar. Napoleon's brother, Lucien, told the emperor that it was more distinguished to be head of a republic than to be an emperor.
Jean Auguste Dominique Ingres (1780–1867), Napoleon on His Imperial Throne, 1806. Oil on canvas, 259 x 162 cm. Musee des Beaux-Arts, Rennes. Photograph © Erich Lessing/Art Resource, NY

MAP 22.2

Napoleon's Empire, ca. 1799–1815

- Territories under direct French control
- states ruled by members of Napoleon's family
- other dependent states

The French Revolution

1783	End of the American Revolutionary War
1789	Convening of the Estates General
June 1789	Estates General becomes the National Assembly
July 14, 1789	Storming of the Bastille
1790–1791	Creation of the Civil Constitution of the Clergy
March 1792	Invasion of France by Austria and Prussia
January 1793	Louis XVI executed
1799	Napoleon overthrows Directorate

He substituted aristocracies at will, demoting ancient families and raising up new ones. He cultivated a romantic image of himself as "a fragment of rock hurled into space"—a meteor that changed the fate of a continent. To the poor, he was the man who fulfilled the French Revolution, and to the rich, the man who tamed it. The heirs of the Enlightenment admired him for making reason, rather than ideology, the guide of his politics. But critics charged that for Napoleon reason was a substitute for morality. In some ways, he ruled a barbarian empire, descended as much from that of Charlemagne as from Rome. Sometimes he had himself painted as a Roman emperor. Sometimes he preferred to be depicted among ancient pagan German gods. Historians have detected opportunism and lack of any general principles in his behavior. A cruel police state operated wherever he ruled.

To the disappointment of the idealists who advocated "liberty, equality, and fraternity," the French Revolution had failed to change the world. The wars the Revolution started were the real anvil of change, and Napoleon was their smith and hammer. After the shake-up of the Napoleonic Wars, which did not end until Napoleon's final defeat in 1815, no form of political legitimacy would be beyond challenge in Europe. Constitutional struggles dominated European politics and influenced those of the world, along with the conflict of new or newly effective political ideas, which we shall look at in the next part of this book: nationalism, militarism, secularism, democracy, and socialism.

Immanuel Kant defines the Enlightenment

IN PERSPECTIVE: The Afterglow of Enlightenment

The French Revolution was part of the dark side of the Enlightenment—both its creation and its destroyer. It opened with noble cries—for liberty, equality, and fraternity, the rights of man and of the citizen, the sovereignty of the people. It ended with the sickening scream that forms the last line of the "Marseillaise," the French national anthem, calling for troughs full of the "impure" blood of aristocrats, traitors, and foreigners.

In Britain, the statesman and philosopher Edmund Burke (1729–1797) was so appalled by the Revolution's excesses that he reached for the comforts of conservatism. In Spain, in the black paintings of Francisco Goya (1746–1828) and in Germany, in the private darkness of Ludwig van Beethoven's (1770–1827) late music, we can sense another response: retreat into hag-ridden disillusionment. In the *Critique of Pure Reason* of 1781, Immanuel Kant proposed a rickety, human-scale world of "crooked timber" in place of the grand ruined structures of the Age of Reason. The Enlightenment was streaked with shadows. In Paris in 1798, Etienne Robert Gaspard displayed a freak light show in which he made monstrous shapes loom at the audience from a screen or appear to flicker eerily, projected onto clouds of smoke. In other demonstrations of the wonders of electricity, the real-life forerunners of Frankenstein made corpses twitch to thrill an audience. It was not the sleep of reason that produced these monsters. They were creations of its most watchful hours—the hideous issue of scientific experimentation, the brutal images of minds tortured by revulsion at revolutionary crimes.

The Enlightenment survived in America. The United States' Constitution of 1787 embodied some of the dearest political principles of Montesquieu and the authors of the *Encyclopedia*, substituting the sovereign people for a sovereign government, switching many powers from the executive to the legislature, creating a long list of constitutional guarantees of freedom, outlawing any "establishment of religion," and expressing confidence in the people's fitness to decide their own fate. Assumptions about human equality—though they did not extend to black people, Native Americans, or women—typified American society. No formal aristocracy was acknowledged. Servants treated employers with a familiarity that shocked European visitors. Money became a more powerful indicator of social distinction than birth. To the surprise of much of the world—and that of some Americans—the United States managed to avoid becoming a military dictatorship, the fate of so many other supposedly republican and egalitarian revolutions.

Even in Europe, the idea of progress survived. In the nineteenth century, it strengthened and fed on the "march of improvement"—the history of industrialization, the multiplication of wealth and muscle power, the insecure but encouraging victories of constitutionalism against tyranny. It became possible to believe that despite human failings progress was irreversible. Evolution programmed it into nature. It took the horrors of the late nineteenth and twentieth centuries—a catalogue

An image of war. Francisco Goya's art began to desert the conventional subjects demanded by his early patrons in the 1790s. Under the dark and bloody impact of the French Revolution, he produced scenes of witchcraft and torture. It was the Spanish War of Independence against Napoleon in 1808–1814, however, that released from his imagination colossal monsters like this: an image of war wading through the land and overshadowing the wreckage of lives.

CHRONOLOGY

r. 1661–1722	Kangxi, Chinese emperor, tutored by Jesuit scholars
1680s	Louis-Armand de Lom de l'Arce leaves France for Canada
1685–1750	Johann Sebastian Bach, composer
1689–1755	Baron de Montesquieu, author of *the Spirit of the Laws* and *Persian Letters*
1694–1778	François Marie Arouet (Voltaire), leading philosopher and admirer of China
1703–1758	Jonathan Edwards, New England preacher
1703–1791	John Wesley, founder of Methodism
1712–1778	Jean-Jacques Rousseau, author of the *Social Contract*
1713–1784	Denis Diderot, publisher of the *Encyclopedia*
1720	Chinese translations of Western books allowed to circulate in Japan
1736	Maupertuis's expedition to the Arctic Circle
1740–1758	George Whitfield, emotional preacher
1771	Japanese "Dutch studies" group begins study of Western books
1752	Publication of Maupertuis's *Letters on the Progress of Science*
1776	Publication of Adam Smith's *The Wealth of Nations;* United States Declaration of Independence
1783	End of the American Revolutionary War
1789	Convening of the Estates General; Estates General becomes the National Assembly
July 14, 1789	Storming of the Bastille
1790–1791	Creation of the Civil Constitution of the Clergy
1792	Invasion of France by Austria and Prussia; publication of Mary Wollstonecraft's *A Vindication of the Rights of Women*
January 1793	Louis XVI executed
Late 1700s and early 1800s	Romantic movement
1793	Lord Macartney's mission arrives in China
1799	Napoleon comes to power in a military coup
1804	Napoleon crowns himself Emperor of the French
June 18, 1815	Napoleon suffers final defeat at Battle of Waterloo

A Muslim Indian's Reactions to the West

of famines, failures, inhumanities, and genocidal conflicts—to make most people question whether progress was inevitable or even real.

The effects of the Enlightenment rippled over the world. Europeans and the inhabitants of European colonies in the Americas felt growing confidence as a result of their sense that their societies were making scientific and technical progress. Rivals in Asia seemed stagnant by comparison. Western visitors to Turkey in the last decade of the century felt certain that the Ottomans had not only lost their lead in power and wealth—they had slipped into inferiority through neglect of science, "too stupid to comprehend," an English observer averred, "or too proud to learn." Even China seemed to have sacrificed former advantages. A Dutch envoy in 1794 declared:

that the scientific knowledge possessed by the Chinese is of very ancient date, and they obtained it long before the sciences were known in Europe. But everything has remained in its primitive state, without their even seeking, like the Europeans, to make further progress, or to bring their discoveries to perfection. . . . We have consequently so far surpassed them.

The former greatness of Asia—it was commonly alleged by the end of the century—had shifted to Europe.

During the following century, Asians increasingly shared this Western point of view. Rammohun Roy was not alone in his day in trying to appropriate the scientific learning of the Enlightenment for Indians' use. Indians joined the scientific societies that the British founded in India. Indians also founded others of their own. Bal Shastri Jambedkar, a professor of mathematics who collaborated closely with English colleagues in the scientific community in Calcutta in the 1830s, published his work in Indian languages and translated useful texts. In the same period, the work of surveying India began increasingly to rely on Indian, not British, experts. Where Western scientific impact led, the influence of Western thinking on political, economic, and philosophical subjects soon followed.

India had privileged access to Western ideas because of the vast number of Westerners, especially Britons, whom British imperialism introduced to that country. Other European empires had similar effects in areas they colonized. And, increasingly in the nineteenth century, the effects of Western intellectual movements spread beyond the reach of imperialism. French invaders spread them in Egypt and Syria. Missionaries spread them—selecting those ideas that were not anti-Christian or anticlerical—almost wherever they went. So did the many Westerners who were employed as technicians throughout the world in the nineteenth century. Jesuits were instrumental in China. Dutch merchants and ambassadors penetrated Japan. Books helped to make Western ideas accessible worldwide and communicated them to parts of the world Westerners in person could hardly hope to remold. The consequences are apparent in most of the rest of this book. Up to this point in our story, the exchanges of culture we have chronicled have been mutually influential or have tended to be dominated by influences exerted on Europe from outside. From this point onward, global history becomes increasingly a story of Western influence.

PROBLEMS AND PARALLELS

1. How was the Enlightenment global in its inspiration, as well as in its effects? How did ideas from overseas, particularly from China, influence the Enlightenment?

2. How did Asian cultures influence writers like Voltaire, Diderot, and Montesquieu? Did they view Asian cultures as models for Europe or as negative examples to be avoided?

3. What role did religion play in the development of the Enlightenment? How was preaching the "information technology" of religious revivals in the West?

4. How did Diderot's *Encyclopedia* serve as a vehicle for advancing Enlightenment thinking in eighteenth-century Europe?

5. Why was Romanticism often seen as antithetical to the Enlightenment?

6. How did influences from the Pacific and the Americas shape the elevation of the "common man"? What does the term *noble savages* mean?

7. Was Napoleon a ruler who symbolized the Enlightenment or who undermined its ideals?

DOCUMENTS IN GLOBAL HISTORY

- Baron de Montesquieu, from *The Spirit of the Laws*
- Qianlong emperor, letter to King George III
- Olympes de Gorges, Declaration of the Rights of Woman and the Female Citizen
- Mary Wollstonecraft, *A Vindication of the Rights of Woman*
- Voltaire, "On Universal Toleration"
- From *Captain Cook's Journal During his First Voyage Round the World*
- The Declaration of the Rights of Man and Citizen
- Immanuel Kant defines the Enlightenment
- A Muslim Indian's Reactions to the West

Please see the Primary Source CD-ROM for additional sources related to this chapter.

READ ON

Crawford, S. Cromwell, *Raja Rammohun Roy and Progressive Movements in India: A selection from records, 1775–1845* (1983) is useful. Maupertuis is best approached through his own writings, but there are useful studies by D. Beeson, *Maupertuis* (1992), and M. Terrall, *The Man Who Flattened the Earth* (2002).

On the Enlightenment in general, P. Gay, *The Enlightenment* (1995), is a classic which is still stimulating. J. Israel, *Radical Enlightenment: Philosophy and the Making of Modernity* (2001) is a superb study that emphasizes the Dutch contribution. O. Gunn, *First Globalization* (2003) is a useful introduction to the global context.

A. Çirakman, *From the "Terror of the World" to the "Sick Man of Europe"* (2002) traces changes in the image of the Ottomans in the West. Li Yan and Du Shiran, *Chinese Mathematics: A Concise History* (1987) is fundamental. J. Waley-Cohen, *The Sextants of Beiking* (1999) is a broad survey of Chinese science, with special attention to interchange with the West. Her 1993 article in *the American Historical Review,* "China and Western Technology in the Late Eighteenth Century" puts the Macartney mission in context. F. Wakeman,

The Great Enterprise (1986) is a good introduction to China in the period.

For the context of Dutch studies, L. Blussé, et al., *Bridging the Divide* (2001) is enthralling. J. B. Bury, *The Idea of Progress* (1982) is an unsurpassed classic.

T. Ellingson, *The Myth of the Noble Savage* (2001) is an important revisionist work. M. Newton, *Savage Girls and Wild Boys: A History of Feral Children* (2003) is a fascinating overview of its subject. A. Pagden, *European Encounters with the New World from Renaissance to Romanticism* (1994) is indispensable.

C. L. Johnson, ed., *The Cambridge Companion to Mary Wollstonecraft* (2002) is a mine of information and a valuable guide to work on early feminism.

J. C. Beaglehole's classic *The Life of Captain James Cook* (1992) is still the best biography.

S. Schama, *Citizens* (1991) tells the story of the French Revolution with vision and verve. C. Jones, *The Great Nation* (2003) is excellent on the background of eighteenth-century France. There are so many books about Napoleon: P. Geyl, *Napoleon: For and Against* (1967) is a magisterial survey of the literature.

"Dutch Studies" in Japan and the Study of Sanskrit among the British

Otsuki Gentaku was a poor Japanese scholar who wanted to write a study of unicorns. His deeper ambition was to learn Dutch—a language regarded as of modest literary and scientific value even in Europe in his day. In October 1785, when he was 29 years old, he had saved enough money to go to Nagasaki, where there were teachers of the language.

JAPAN
ENGLAND
INDIA

Meanwhile, in Krishnagar, India, an English judge, Sir William Jones, was rising before dawn every day to study the ancient Indian language, Sanskrit (which no one actually spoke). After a year's study, he considered himself "tolerably strong" in the language, and "charmed with knowing so beautiful a sister of Latin and Greek.".

• • • • •

Both these events were episodes in the global exchange of culture that accompanied and, in part, caused the Enlightenment. Yet it seems extraordinary that scholars should have made such huge sacrifices to learn languages they might have despised as alien or exotic. Writings of the time help us understand their efforts and those of others like them.

Extract I is from *Rangaku Kotohajine* (meaning "Dawn of the Study of Dutch"). This autobiographical work by Sugita Genpaku, who was Otsuki Gentaku's first tutor in Dutch, appeared in 1815. He describes how he became interested in Dutch and struggled to learn it. Extract II consists of passages from an address Sir William Jones gave to a group of English students of Indian subjects in Calcutta in 1786.

Although Sir William Jones and Sugita Genpaku have acquired heroic status in the history of Eurasian cultural exchange, neither was the first in his field. Jesuit scholars had studied Sanskrit and proclaimed its glories before Jones got around to it. Jones, however, recognized that Latin, Greek, and Sanskrit all shared a common origin. This really made Sanskrit studies "take off" in the West.

Dutch had been studied in Japan since 1745 under the shogun Yoshimune, who, like so many rulers of the time, was interested in astronomy. In the hope of improving Japanese astronomy, he encouraged interpreters to read Dutch books. Some official interpreters took up the challenge, but their work had little effect. The group of physicians who gathered around Sugita Genpaku in the 1770s was therefore responsible for a genuine breakthrough.

In Extract I, the author refers to two of his companions in Dutch studies: Hiraga Gennai, a samurai who devoted himself to botany, and the physician Maeno Ryōtaku, who had already made a start in Dutch. The book that sparked their interest, *Ontleedkundige Tafelen* (Anatomical Tables), published in 1734, was itself a Dutch translation of a German work on anatomy.

Extract I from *Rangaku Kotohajine*

Often when I met Gennai Hiraga and others, we would say to each other: "the more we become aware of Dutch learning, the more strongly we are impressed by their empirical spirit. It would be a great benefit, if we should translate their books into Japanese. It is a pity that so far no one has tried it. Really, we must somehow find a way. . . . We might get some interpreters of Nagasaki to make out the

...Continued

contents of those books. Even just one volume of them, if rendered into Japanese, would be of immense value to the nation!" Seeing, however, no prospect of the sort, we would only draw deep breaths in despair. . . .

It was, as I remember, on the night of March 3, 1771, I received a letter . . . inviting me to be present at a dissection held by a certain official doctor on the following day. The executed body to be dissected was a female criminal about 50 years old. . . .

The old man [performing the dissection] went on explaining various organs such as the heart, the liver, the gallbladder and the stomach. Further, he pointed to some other things and said: "I don't know what they are, but they have always been there in all the bodies which I have so far dissected." Checking them later with the Dutch charts, we were able to identify them to be main arteries and veins and suprarenal glands. . . .

Comparing the things we saw with the pictures in the Dutch book Ryōtaku and I had with us, we were amazed at their perfect agreement. . . . Also, the positions and the forms of the intestines and the stomach were very different from the traditional description.

After the dissection was over, we were tempted to examine the forms of the bones too, and picked up some of the sun-bleached bones scattered around the ground. We found that they were nothing like those described in the old books, but were exactly as represented in the Dutch book. We were completely amazed.

On our way home, three of us talked of what a startling revelation we had seen that day. We felt ashamed of ourselves for having come this far in our lives without being aware of our ignorance. How presumptuous on our part to have served as official doctors when we were totally without knowledge of the true make of our bodies which should be the foundation of the art of healing! Upon today's experience, suppose we should by some means, learn even the bare outline of the truth about the body, and practice our medicine according to that knowledge, we should be able to justify our claim for medical profession. Thus we talked and sighed. Ryōtaku, too, said all was very true, he was in complete agreement. I broke the spell saying, "Even this one volume of Ontleedkundige Tafelen—suppose we translate it—many facts about the body will be clarified and the art of healing will be greatly benefited. I would like, by some way or another, read this book without the aid of a Nagasaki interpreter."

Next day, we gathered at Ryōtaku's house. We talked over the experience the day before. Then we faced the book. But it was as though we were on a boat with no oar or rudder adrift on the great ocean—a vast expanse and nothing to indicate our course. We just gazed at each other in blank dismay.

After the passage of one year or so, our vocabulary was enlarged, and naturally we became informed of Dutch things in general. By and by we found ourselves capable of translating as many as ten lines a day without much trouble when the language was not very complicated.

A New Book of Anatomy.
"I considered the forms of expression in many ways, trying and trying, and in the four years I rewrote the manuscript eleven times over before handing it over to the printers." After heroic labor, Sugita Genpaku published *A New Book of Anatomy* (Katai-Shin-Sho), in the late 1770s—the culmination of years of "Dutch Studies."

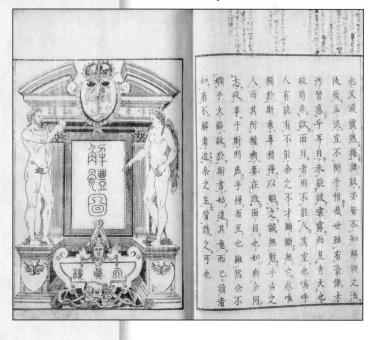

...Continued

When I first obtained that book of anatomy and ascertained its accuracy by actual observation, I was struck with admiration by the great difference between the knowledge of the West and that of the East. And I was inspired to come to the determination that I must learn and clarify the new revelation for applying it to actual healing and also for making it the seed of further discoveries among the general physicians of Japan. . . .

Extract II Address by Sir William Jones

The Sanskrit language, whatever be its antiquity, is of a wonderful structure; more perfect than the Greek, more copious than the Latin, and more exquisitely refined than either, yet bearing to both of them a stronger affinity, both in the roots of verbs and in the forms of grammar, than could possibly have been produced by accident; so strong indeed, that no philologer could examine them all three, without believing them to have sprung from some common source, which, perhaps, no longer exists.

. . . That the Hindus were in early ages a commercial people, we have many reasons to believe; and in the first of their sacred law-tracts, which they suppose to have been revealed . . . many millions of years ago, we find a curious passage on the legal interest of money, and the limited rate of it in different cases, with an exception in regard to adventures at Sea; an exception, which the sense of mankind approves, and which commerce absolutely requires, through it was not before the reign of Charles I [King of England, r. 1625–1649] that our own jurisprudence fully admitted it in respect of maritime contracts.

We were told by the Grecian writers, that the Indians were the wisest of nations; and in moral wisdom, they were certainly eminent: their Nito Sàstra, or System of Ethicks, is yet preserved. I am not disinclined to suppose, that the first moral fables, which appeared in Europe, were of Indian or Ethiopian origin.

The Hindus are said to have boasted of three inventions, all of which, indeed, are admirable, the method of instructing by apologues, the decimal scale adopted now by all civilized nations, the game of Chess, on which they have some curious treatises; but, if their numerous works on Grammar, Logick, Rhetoric, Musick, all which are extant and accessible, were explained in some language generally known, it would be found, that they had yet higher pretensions to the praise of a fertile and inventive genius.

What their astronomical and mathematical writings contain, will not, I trust, remain long a secret: they are easily procured, and their importance cannot be doubted.

Sanskrit, Latin, and English Compared		
SANSKRIT	**LATIN**	**ENGLISH**
trayas	tres	three
sapta	septem	seven
ashta	octo	eight
nava	novem	nine
sarpa	serpens	snake ("serpent")
raja	regem	king ("royal," "regent")
devas	divus	god ("deity")
pitar	pater	father

Questions to Consider

1 Why did the two writers choose, respectively, Sanskrit and Dutch?

2 Were their motives primarily scholarly?

3 What did Sugita Genpaku admire about Dutch learning and why?

4 What was Jones's view of India and Indians?

5 What did the two writers learn from their studies?

6 What new insights did their studies enable them to offer to their fellow countrymen?

Sources

Extract I Matsumoto Tomio Ogata ed., *Dawn of Western Sciences in Japan* by Sugita Genpaku (Tokyo: Hokuseido Press, 1969).

Extract II *The Works of William Jones*, (London, 1807).

The Frustrations of Progress to ca. 1900

Ottoman World Map. In 1803, the Turkish Military ▶
Engineering School published this world map—the
first Ottoman map based on Mercator's projection—in
an atlas using European geographical knowledge and
map-making techniques.

ENVIRONMENT	since 1800 Global population boom	since ca. 1800 Coal and steam power

CULTURE		1800–1880 Decline of slavery

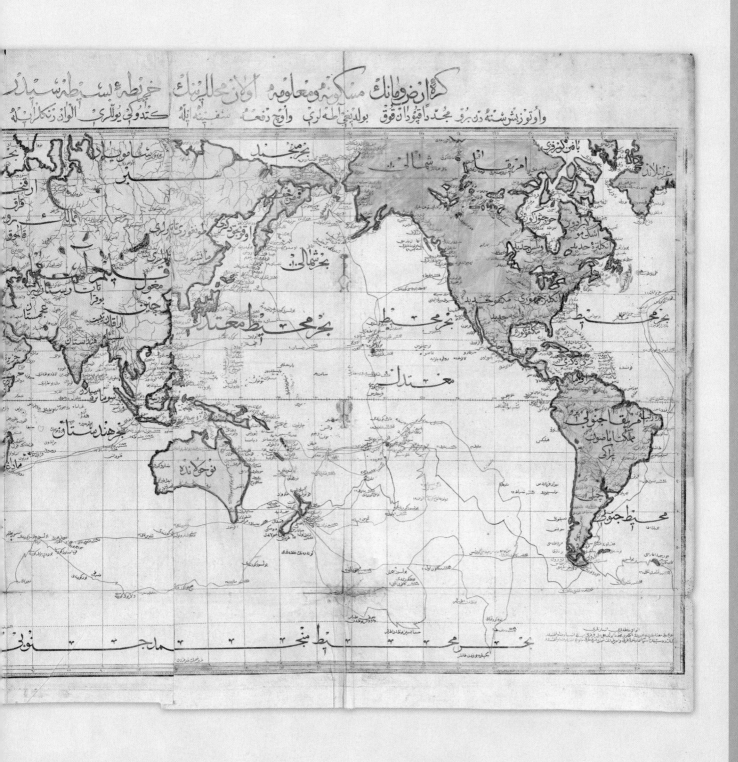

since 1850
Industrialization of food production

ca. 1850
Electricity

1870–1900
Famine and drought worldwide

1840s–1860s
Opium Wars, China

1860s–1910
Mass migrations

1870–1871
Franco-Prussian War

1885
Berlin Conference–Partition of Africa

CHAPTER 23

Replacing Muscle: The Energy Revolutions

Ambroise-Louis Garneray (1783–1857) was among the artists whose heroic whaling scenes helped to inspire Hermann Melville's novel *Moby Dick*. Garneray's depiction of whalers at work in the North Atlantic in 1836 emphasizes the solitary combat between the heroic harpooner and the great, black sea beast, and shows other dangers—the fragile boat, its frantic crew, the spurt of blood from the wounded whale, the foaming sea. In the background, the ship is calm—with fires ready to render the whale's blubber—and the icebergs are impassive.
Photograph courtesy of the Peabody Essex Museum

THE WORLD

t is a tale of monsters, but not a horror story. *Moby Dick* by the American writer Hermann Melville is one of the most gripping, moving sea sagas ever written. It is the tale of a seaman's hunt for revenge against a huge white whale that snapped off his leg: a monstrous man, a monstrous beast, a monstrous obsession. When Melville wrote it in 1851, whaling was still a close encounter between man and beast in the wild, in an open boat that the lash of a whale's tail could easily crush or smash to splinters. The harpoonists had to weary, worry, and bleed the whale to death. Then they would haul the carcass alongside their ship, dismember it, and the whole crew would kneel between decks in blood and blubber to chop and melt down the fat before it turned putrid. The fat was precious. Before the development of the fossil-oil extraction industry, whaling was the world's main source of oil. Blubber supplied lipids—fat for human food—and lubricants to grease machinery and light lamps.

The world was facing a fat crisis—a worsening shortage of both lipids and lubricants. Within a few years, however, a series of developments and innovations solved the problem. In 1856, a French experimenter won an official competition to find a cheap edible fat for the French navy. He called his mixture of beef fat and milk "margarine" because its pallid gleam was supposed to resemble the little pearls known in France as marguerites. Margarine did not increase the world's stock of fat, but it did make what was available go further. Soon after, in 1858, fossil oil emerged in the New World, skimmed out of the ground in Ontario, Canada, then pumped from the earth in Pennsylvania in 1859. People had been using fossil oil for thousands of years in small ways where it was available through natural seepage. Brick tunnels under rivers in Mesopotamia in the second millenium B.C.E., for example, used bitumen mortar derived from petroleum. Now, for the first time, extraction on a massive scale began, as a way to replace other increasingly scarce and expensive sources of fat. In 1865, the first fully industrial whaling ship was launched in Norway, with explosive harpoons and a fast steam engine that could tow dead whales into port for quick processing. Even the gigantic blue whale—which previous hunting techniques could not touch—now became whalers' prey.

FOCUS questions

- WHY DID the world's population begin to rise rapidly during the nineteenth century?
- WHY DID industrialization increase the world's food supply?
- HOW WAS industrialization related to the growth of military power?
- WHY DID the economies of the United States and Latin America develop in different ways?
- WHY DID Japan and China pursue different policies toward industrialization?
- HOW DID British imperialism affect the economic development of India and Egypt?

Meanwhile, the search was on for other sources of fat. Increasingly intensive methods to produce feed supported more livestock and therefore boosted supplies of animal fat. New grazing areas opened up in Argentina, Australia, and the American West. Demand for edible oil drove European powers into colonial ventures to produce palm, peanut, and coconut oil.

• • • • •

Fat—oil from animals, plants, and minerals—made the world of the nineteenth century work. It supplied raw energy for growing numbers of human consumers. It was used in products from soap to shoe polish. It greased the machines of industrialization. It induced new adventures in long-range empire-building. But fat was just one of many sources of energy that nineteenth-century people exploited on a scale previously never experienced in the history of the world. Oils and fats, along with muscle power, traditional fuels (wood, peat, and coal), and relatively limited exploitation of wind power and waterpower were the only means humans had to supplement the power of the Earth and the Sun and to devise ways to deliver energy that suited human activities. The fat crisis was part of a bigger picture: a revolution in the sources of energy that kept human society working. The way people responded to the crisis brought together major themes of the nineteenth century: new ways to exploit the planet's resources; new ventures to release energy and redirect it to new uses.

The main reason why people needed to multiply the sources of energy in the mid–nineteenth century is the first subject of this chapter: population explosion, which strained supplies of exploitable energy. We then turn to the response: industrialization, which, in the parts of the world where it happened, replaced muscle power with machines. The following three chapters will cover the major consequences of industrialization: new forms of imperialism and the effects of industrialization on society and politics.

GLOBAL DEMOGRAPHICS: THE WORLD'S POPULATION RISES

Population growth, and the rising demand it fueled, lay at the heart of the drive for new sources of energy. In 1800, by the best available calculations, there were about 950 million people in the world. By 1900, there were about 1.6 billion people (see Map 23.1). After centuries when .5 percent per year growth in population was hard to sustain for more than a few decades, to have more than 1 percent growth yearly for over a century was revolutionary. Around 1800, only four large areas in the world could reasonably be called densely settled—with, say, more than four people per square mile: in East Asia (China, Japan, and Korea), southeast Asia (Indochina, Malaysia, Indonesia), the Indian subcontinent, and Western Europe. By 1900, parts of Africa and the Americas, especially along the coasts, had become regions of comparable density.

In part, population increase was the result of continuing favorable trends in global disease (see Chapter 17). In some ways, it is surprising that the world stayed relatively healthy. There were good reasons to expect—as many students of population supposed at the time—that global health would get worse. As people got more crowded together, new eco-niches opened for disease. The improvements in long-range communications, with consequent huge increases in the range and rate of travel and migration, made it easier for disease to spread. The danger, which threatened throughout the century, finally struck in 1917–1919, when an influenza pandemic killed at least 30 million people worldwide. But by then, the rate of population increase was so quick that the disaster hardly made a dent in the world's population.

Meanwhile, moreover, epidemics multiplied. The growing cities of the period were ill planned and poorly equipped with drainage and sanitation. Urban plagues—especially cholera and dysentery, which are contracted through contaminated water supplies, and typhus, which is spread by body lice—arose in areas that had never experienced them before. Cholera arrived in China from India in 1820 and soon became a common problem in Europe. Populations uprooted and transferred from countryside to town often suffered nutritionally, especially in the early stages of urbanization, before the food supply was properly organized and regulated. Polluted and nutritionally inadequate food was a major problem in nineteenth-century cities. Infected milk helped to spread tuberculosis, one of the century's killer diseases in urban environments. Heating milk to make it safe only began late in the century. Manufacturers and grocers like Henry J. Heinz of Pittsburgh (see Chapter 24), who could successfully promote their wares as healthy, made fortunes. Nevertheless, the age of plague did not return, and new killer diseases were never generalized enough or lethal enough to check demographic growth.

Nor were rural populations exempt from ecological disasters. Although food production soared in global terms, its effects were unevenly distributed, and famine killed more people in the nineteenth century than at any other period in recorded history. Political neglect made the effects worse, especially in the territories of large empires under distant or indifferent rulers. In some ways, the most successful crops of the period—the most prolific, the most nutritious—were traps, because people became overreliant on them. When fungal disease ruined the potato crop, horrific famines followed in 1845–1859 in Ireland, where a million people died and a million more were driven overseas, and in Belgium and Finland in 1867–1868. People who usually ate potatoes to survive had no other crop to fall back on.

Famine killed at least 4.3 million people in India in 1876–1878, or probably more like 7 million if one allows for the caution of official British estimates. The famine that afflicted China at the same time was officially "the most terrible disaster in twenty-one dynasties." In the 1890s, droughts associated with an unusual concentration of El Niño events caused 12 million deaths in India and 20 million in China. Famines triggered plagues. In India, for instance, smallpox had killed a third of the population of the densely populated province of Bengal—almost wiping out a generation of children—after a famine in 1770. A cholera epidemic killed half the population of Guntur in eastern India, after the crops failed in 1833. Smallpox and cholera also followed the great Indian famine of 1896.

Slum life. Social reformers of the late nineteenth century listed sanitation, children's welfare, and animal abuse as some of the most pressing problems associated with urban conditions. This snapshot, taken around 1900 in New York City, captures all three issues: The ragged children play in a filthy gutter while a dead horse, presumably used to pull a cart or a trolley car, rots just a few yards away.

The Irish Potato Famine of 1845–1846 challenged English assumptions about the benefits of their rule in Ireland. George Frederick Watts (1817–1904), one of the most fashionable British painters of the day, depicted the human tragedy of the famine in this work of 1850. The grieving father stares at the onlooker with inescapable reproach.

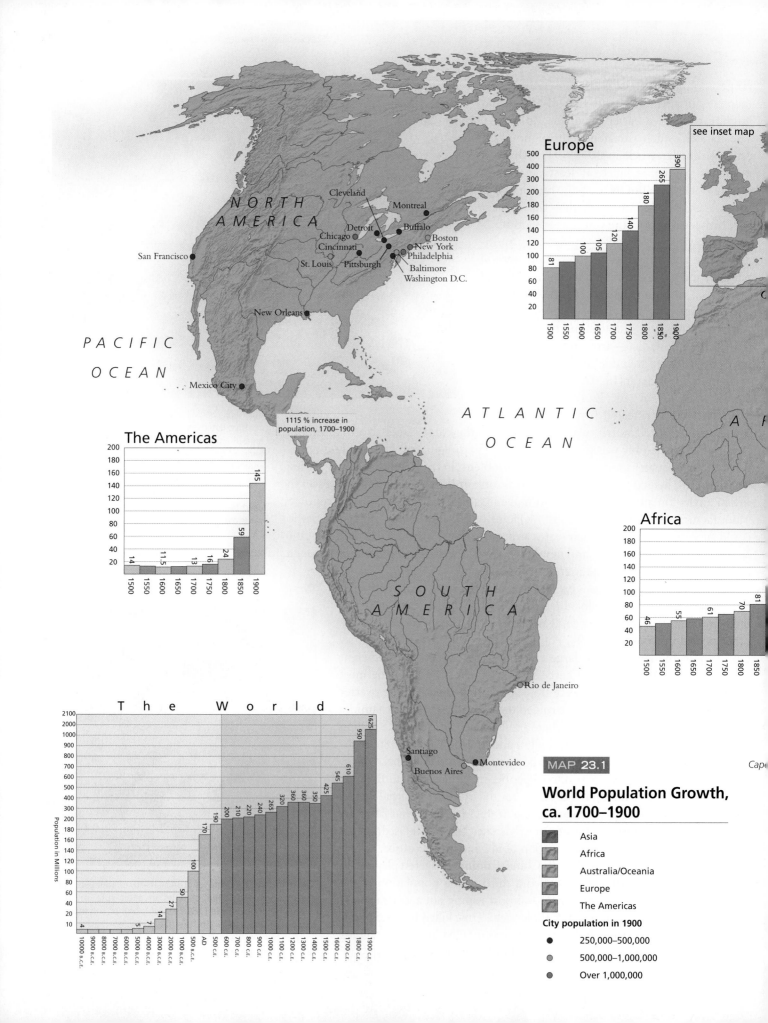

Europe

81		100	105	120	140	180	265	390
1500	1550	1600	1650	1700	1750	1800	1850	1900

see inset map

NORTH
AMERICA

Cleveland
Montreal
Detroit
Buffalo
Chicago
Boston
Cincinnati
New York
St. Louis
Pittsburgh
Philadelphia
Baltimore
Washington D.C.

San Francisco

PACIFIC
OCEAN

New Orleans

Mexico City

1115 % increase in
population, 1700–1900

ATLANTIC
OCEAN

The Americas

14	11.5		13	16	24	59	145	
1500	1550	1600	1650	1700	1750	1800	1850	1900

SOUTH
AMERICA

Rio de Janeiro

Africa

46		55	61		70	81	
1500	1550	1600	1650	1700	1750	1800	1850

The World

Population in Millions

4				5	7	14	27	50	100	170	190	200	210	220	240	265	320	360	360	350	425	545	610	950	1625
10000 B.C.E.	9000 B.C.E.	8000 B.C.E.	7000 B.C.E.	6000 B.C.E.	5000 B.C.E.	4000 B.C.E.	3000 B.C.E.	2000 B.C.E.	1000 B.C.E.	500 B.C.E.	AD	500 C.E.	600 C.E.	700 C.E.	800 C.E.	900 C.E.	1000 C.E.	1100 C.E.	1200 C.E.	1300 C.E.	1400 C.E.	1500 C.E.	1600 C.E.	1700 C.E.	1800 C.E.	1900 C.E.

Santiago
Montevideo
Buenos Aires

MAP 23.1

Cape

World Population Growth, ca. 1700–1900

- Asia
- Africa
- Australia/Oceania
- Europe
- The Americas

City population in 1900

- ● 250,000–500,000
- ● 500,000–1,000,000
- ● Over 1,000,000

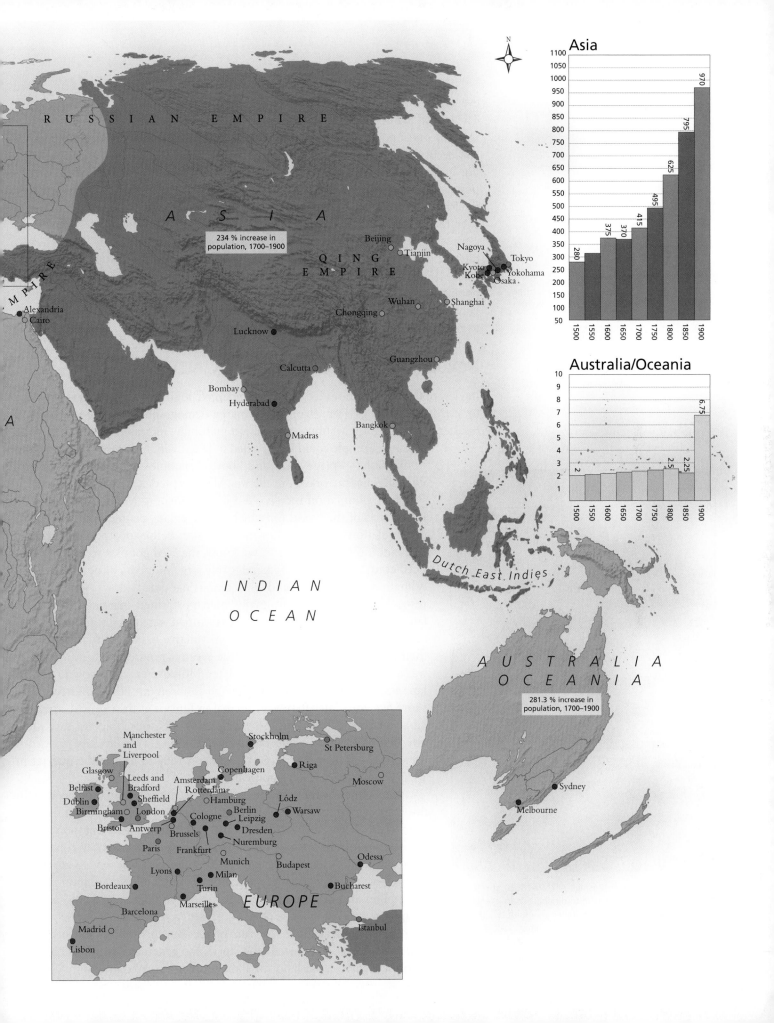

RUSSIAN EMPIRE

A S I A

234 % increase in
population, 1700–1900

QING
EMPIRE

Beijing
Tianjin
Nagoya
Tokyo
Kyoto Yokohama
Kobe
Osaka

Wuhan
Shanghai

Chongqing

Alexandria
Cairo

Lucknow

Calcutta

Guangzhou

Bombay
Hyderabad

Bangkok

Madras

INDIAN

OCEAN

Dutch East Indies

AUSTRALIA
OCEANIA

281.3 % increase in
population, 1700–1900

Sydney

Melbourne

Asia

Year	Value
1500	280
1550	375
1600	370
1650	415
1700	495
1750	625
1800	795
1850	970

Australia/Oceania

Year	Value
1500	2
1600	2.5
1800	2.25
1900	6.75

Europe (inset map)

Manchester and Liverpool
Stockholm
Glasgow
Copenhagen
St Petersburg
Riga
Belfast
Leeds and Bradford
Amsterdam
Moscow
Dublin
Sheffield
Rotterdam
Hamburg
Lódz
Birmingham
London
Berlin
Warsaw
Bristol
Antwerp
Cologne
Leipzig
Brussels
Dresden
Paris
Frankfurt
Nuremburg
Odessa
Munich
Budapest
Lyons
Milan
Bucharest
Bordeaux
Turin
Barcelona
Marseilles
Madrid
Istanbul
Lisbon

EUROPE

Nonetheless, population growth proved irrepressibly robust, recovering from every catastrophe. In the Western world, the ascent of population was uninterrupted. The United States had 76 million people by the end of the nineteenth century—making it the most populous state in the Western world. Spectacular population increases also occurred in Europe. Most European countries roughly doubled their populations during the nineteenth century. The continent, which had about a fifth of the world's population at the start of the century, had about a quarter by its end. The population of the Russian Empire, including the peoples it conquered in Asia, increased fourfold to over 130 million. Taken together, the demographic trends of the nineteenth century represented a real shift in the global balance of resources in favor of the West. The traditional pattern of global history, in which the hugely populous and productive societies of East and South Asia predominated, was ending or over. In some ways, the population figures mask an even greater shift: The extra people that Europe and the United States acquired produced hugely disproportionate increases in wealth, thanks to giant strides in the output of food and manufactures.

FOOD: TRANSITION TO ABUNDANCE

In view of the way famine and disease accompanied population growth, it is tempting to see Malthusian logic (see Chapter 20) linking demographic increase to ecological disaster. According to Malthus, population naturally increased faster than food resources. People could be expected to breed with little restraint unless and until disasters—plague, war, and, above all, famine—checked them. In reality, things never worked out the way Malthus predicted, for two reasons.

First, population increase did not conform to Malthus's prophesies. In all parts of the world for which we have data, people practiced forms of population control. In Europe, for instance, they postponed marriage. In France, uniquely as far as we know, married couples routinely practiced contraception. In India, relatively large numbers of people took up celibate ways of life, and the remarriage of widows was severely restricted. In Japan, traditionally, men postponed marriage until their late twenties or early thirties, whereas women were usually about 21 years old when they adopted one of the distinctive hairstyles that advertised their availability for marriage. As the century progressed, however. there was a clear drift toward marrying later. Moreover, for unknown reasons, Japanese women began to delay having children until their mid-twenties, some five years later than was normal in Europe at the time. Marriage in Japan became a privilege for the head of the household, so that most households had only one childbearing couple. The average size of a household fell from nearly five persons in 1800 to four and a quarter in 1870, a demographically significant drop.

Second, new ways to produce food outstripped population growth. In this respect, Malthus's critics, who expected "progress" to prevent disaster, were right. It is hard to distinguish cause and effect, but population increase and the growth of the food supply were inseparably connected. Food production soared, partly because more land was devoted to it and partly because of new, more efficient methods of exploitation. In the Philippines and in Java, for instance, where population growth had long been static, rates of increase rose to 1 percent a year, largely because women started marrying at under 20 years of age. But this was an adjustment to new conditions that boosted food stocks and generated wealth. Large-scale deforestation released land for food production. Wetlands were adapted

Rice cultivation in Japan. Hiroshige (1797–1858) specialized in painting comforting images of traditional Japan. Here bent-backed peasants labor virtuously under enriching rain in regularly patterned rice fields, surrounded by benign landscape. In the 100 years after the artist's death, enhanced efficiency enabled the Japanese to harvest more rice without extending the area under cultivation.

for rice farming. Previously marginal soil was exploited to grow coconuts, not necessarily for food but for their fiber, which was much in demand for matting, and for coconut oil, which was used in everything from cooking to making soap.

Sometimes food production rose simply because farmers applied traditional methods more systematically. This seems to have been the case in Japan, where agrarian output rose throughout the second half of the century, and well into the next, without any significant increase of the amount of land devoted to farming. In Egypt, wheat and barley production nearly doubled in the last two decades of the nineteenth century, while the acreage under cultivation increased by less than half. But in most regions for which evidence survives, numerous small increases of the grazed or cultivated area amounted to a huge total increase. More spectacularly, a few major initiatives or accidents incorporated vast, previously unexploited frontiers. Occasionally, this happened through natural growth with little or no human effort. Natural means added almost 600 square miles, for instance, to the fertile Yellow River delta in China in the second half of the century. But natural losses—to encroaching seas and deserts—always tend to offset natural increases. So human hands have to intervene to stop losses and reclaim land. In the Netherlands, for instance, 11,000 acres were reclaimed from sea and wasteland during the nineteenth century. Partly in consequence, in the second half of the century, the number of cattle doubled, and the number of pigs increased fourfold.

James Fenimore Cooper, from *The Praire*

Beyond question, the greatest extension of the frontier of food production happened in the vast open lands of Argentina, Brazil, Uruguay, Australia, and North America. The incorporation of the North American prairie to raise cattle and grow grain was the most conspicuous large-scale adaptation of the environment for human purposes ever recorded. It may therefore be regarded as one of the most important events in history. In 1827, when James Fenimore Cooper wrote his novel *The Prairie*, the region seemed a place without a future: "A vast country incapable of sustaining a dense population." People called it the Great American Desert. Almost nothing grew naturally there that human stomachs could digest. Except in a few patches, the soil was too tough to plow without industrial technology. Yet by the end of the nineteenth century, the same plains had become the world's granary, with some of the most productive farming the world has ever seen—to say nothing of the great cities that were scattered across it (see Map 23.2).

The extension of grazing was the first stage in the region's transformation. This was the common experience of previously under-exploited grasslands in the period. Much of southeast Australia and New Zealand became sheep-rearing country, though at first more for wool than for meat. The South American grasslands of the pampa, the *sertão* in Brazil, and much of Patagonia in southern Argentina bred cattle and sheep. Refrigeration on steamships enabled Argentina to become a major exporter of beef and mutton. But the scale of production possible on the North American prairie exceeded that of other areas because so many markets were close at hand there. Partly, this was a result of railway construction, which concentrated large, though temporary, labor forces in parts of the region. Driving cattle herds from grazing lands to railway construction centers was a lucrative new business of the mid–nineteenth century. When the railways were built,

Grain elevator, 1879. Farmers packed their harvested grain into burlap sacks and brought the wagonloads to country elevators like this one in Moorhead, Minnesota. Note the pile of wood on the left to power the elevator's steam engine.

the big concentrations of population in the Mississippi River valley and along the seaboards of North America became easily accessible to the products of the prairie.

Grains soon became more important than meat products. Planted by human hands, new kinds of humanly edible grass—wheat and maize above all—began to replace the native prairie grasses. But the change could not have happened without help from new industrial technologies. Steel plows turned the sod of the prairie. Railways transported the grain across what would otherwise be uneconomic distances. Houses built from precision-milled lumber and cheap nails made in Chicago spread cities in a region where most construction materials were simply unavailable. Repeating rifles destroyed the vital links in the earlier ecosystem: the buffalo herds and their human hunters, the Native Americans. Grain elevators, introduced in 1850, made it possible to store grains without vast amounts of labor. Harvesting machinery enabled a few hands to reap large harvests. Wire enclosed farmland against buffalo and cattle. Giant mills—which still stand in many Midwestern towns, where nowadays, they tend to get converted into apartments and shopping malls—processed the grain into marketable foodstuffs.

In 1861, the British novelist and postal official Anthony Trollope saw the results while touring the United States on official business: concentrations of food resources that had no precedent or parallel. Trollope was "grieved by the loose manner in which wheat was treated" in Minneapolis—"bags of it upset and left upon the ground. The labor of collecting it was more than it was worth." In Buffalo, New York, he saw some of the 60 million bushels of grain that passed through the city every year. But the transformation of the prairie was only beginning. The year after Trollope's visit, the Homestead Act made land in the West available to anyone—in practice, almost exclusively to white people—who wanted it at nominal prices. Five hundred million acres were added to the United States's farmland in the remainder of the century. In more modest degree, similar changes occurred in other parts of the American grasslands. Argentina had been a net importer of grain in the 1860s. By 1900, it exported 100 million bushels of wheat and maize a year. Canada also became a major grain exporter.

Not only did the amount of land for food production increase, fertilizers increased productivity, too. To some extent, the increase was due to the spread of age-old techniques using natural fertilizer to enhance soils. In Europe, farmers kept their fields constantly productive, alternating beets or turnips with clover or alfalfa, which renew the soil because they recycle significant amounts of nitrogen. Root crops, such as turnips, rutabagas, and potatoes, could keep cattle alive throughout the winter, generating more manure. In 1860, British farms still got 60 percent of their fertilizers from recycling their own animal waste. But the system increasingly needed supplements because the market demanded more and more meat. Turnips, moreover, demand a lot of fertilizer in most soils. The first consequence was the midcentury guano boom. The *guano* (bird dung) of Peru was rich in nitrogen: mountains of excrement on islands off the Pacific coast, where huge flocks of birds fed off the abundant fish. The normally rainless climate preserved the nitrogen from being washed away. In the 1850s, the main handler of Peruvian guano exported over 200,000 tons a year to Britain alone. Meanwhile, in 1843, new sources of guano began to be mined in southwest Africa, and the first chemical fertilizers came into production. There was "a manfactory of fertilizer in almost every town" in Britain by 1863, according to the *Farmer's Magazine*, British output of superphosphates, as the new chemical fertilizers were called, rose from 30,000 tons in 1854 to 250,000 tons in 1866. At first, manufacturers mainly enhanced the fertilizing properties of bonemeal and ash, but as time went on, mineral phosphates became increasingly important.

Anthony Trollope, from *North America*

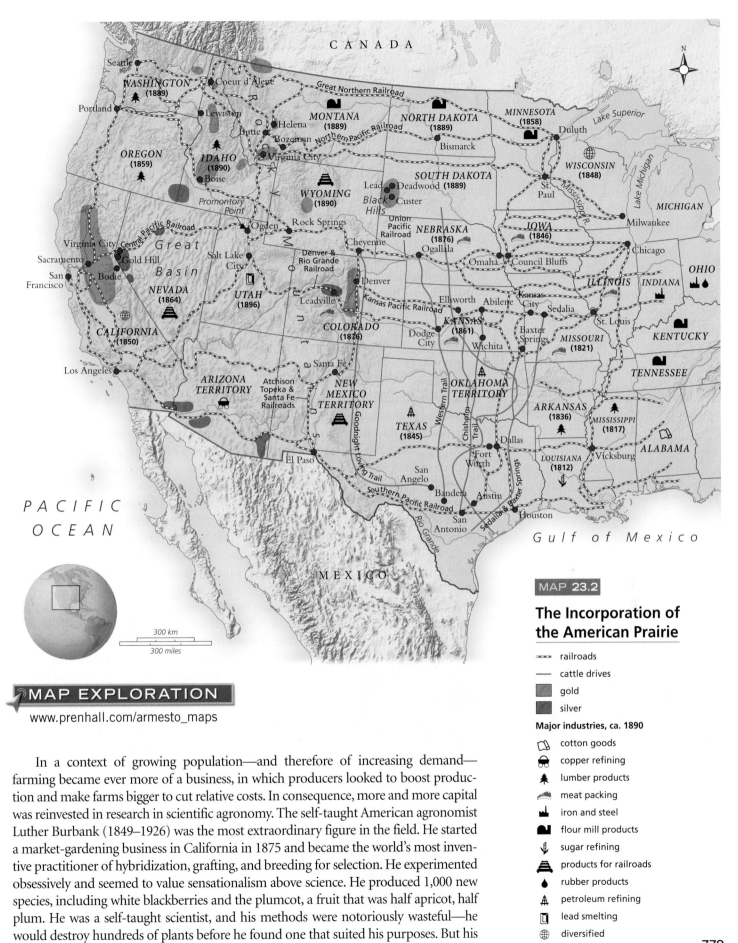

PACIFIC
OCEAN

MEXICO

MAP EXPLORATION

www.prenhall.com/armesto_maps

MAP 23.2

The Incorporation of the American Prairie

- ⌇⌇⌇ railroads
- —— cattle drives
- ▨ gold
- ▨ silver

Major industries, ca. 1890

- 📖 cotton goods
- 🫖 copper refining
- 🌲 lumber products
- ⛰ meat packing
- 🏭 iron and steel
- 🏭 flour mill products
- ⚗ sugar refining
- 🏛 products for railroads
- ● rubber products
- ⚚ petroleum refining
- 🗌 lead smelting
- 🌐 diversified

In a context of growing population—and therefore of increasing demand—farming became ever more of a business, in which producers looked to boost production and make farms bigger to cut relative costs. In consequence, more and more capital was reinvested in research in scientific agronomy. The self-taught American agronomist Luther Burbank (1849–1926) was the most extraordinary figure in the field. He started a market-gardening business in California in 1875 and became the world's most inventive practitioner of hybridization, grafting, and breeding for selection. He experimented obsessively and seemed to value sensationalism above science. He produced 1,000 new species, including white blackberries and the plumcot, a fruit that was half apricot, half plum. He was a self-taught scientist, and his methods were notoriously wasteful—he would destroy hundreds of plants before he found one that suited his purposes. But his enormous commercial success encouraged the spread of scientific techniques to improve strains and develop new plants for newly exploited environments.

Alongside the growing output of farming, industrialization revolutionized the availability of food by transforming techniques of preserving, processing, and supply. Lazaro Spallanzani's (1729–1799) observations of bacteria (see Chapter 22) revealed new possibilities. Simultaneous heating and sealing could keep food edible indefinitely. Stimulated by the demands of the large armies Europe mobilized in the early nineteenth century, huge bottling and canning operations began. When the wars were over, canned foods became widely available to civilians. By 1836, a French firm was selling 100,000 cans of sardines a year. By 1880, factories on the west coast of France were producing 50 million tins of sardines annually. Canning soon became adapted to virtually every kind of food. The results were hugely significant. Canning kept more food in the supply chain for longer. It also made it possible to transport unprecedented quantities of easily perishable food in bulk over long distances. This in turn promoted more regional specialization in the production of particular foods and more economies of scale.

In the 1870s, Australian engineers made an even more dramatic breakthrough in preservation techniques: the compressed-gas cooler. Meat from Australia, South America, or New Zealand could now be refrigerated and shipped to Europe, say, at relatively modest cost. The resulting economies of scale actually made meat processed in this way cheaper in some markets than locally produced meat. In combination with new means to ship large quantities of grain over long distances by railroad and steamship, new production and processing techniques changed the world pattern of food production (see Map 23.3). Food no longer had to be produced near to where it was eaten. In industrializing areas, agriculture declined. British agriculture virtually collapsed in the last generation of the nineteenth century. All over Western Europe, farmers abandoned wheat for other crops, such as dairy products, smoked meats, fruits, and vegetables, in the face of long-range imports.

Food itself became an industrial product, as manufacturers took on more and more processing, until they were delivering some foods, mass produced on a vast scale, in forms in which consumers could eat them without further preparation. Cookies and crackers, once artisanal products or foods baked a few dozen at a time at home, became factory-made items. In 1859, the world's three major producers, all in Britain, made 6 million pounds of cookies. By the late 1870s, the same firms were producing 37 million pounds. Other industries created new foodstuffs. In the 1840s, chocolate, formerly a luxury beverage, became a cheap food manufactured as candy bars especially in Britain, Switzerland, and Holland. In 1865, the German chemist Baron Justus von Liebig perfected cubes of beef extract, which could be made into broth by adding water. Moral crusaders sought a low-protein food that would reduce "passion" and promote chastity. They found it when the American Reverend. Sylvester Graham, inventor of the graham cracker, also invented breakfast cereals in the 1830s. These products were suitable for industrial production methods and, by the 1890s, absorbed much of the world's increased output of grain.

For all its inefficiencies—the scars of famine, the failures of distribution—the huge increase in available food had an unprecedented impact on the world.

Chicago meat packinghouse, 1892. Once cattle had been slaughtered and turned into dressed beef, the carcasses sat in immense cooling rooms before being shipped by rail across North America.

MARKET ROOM.

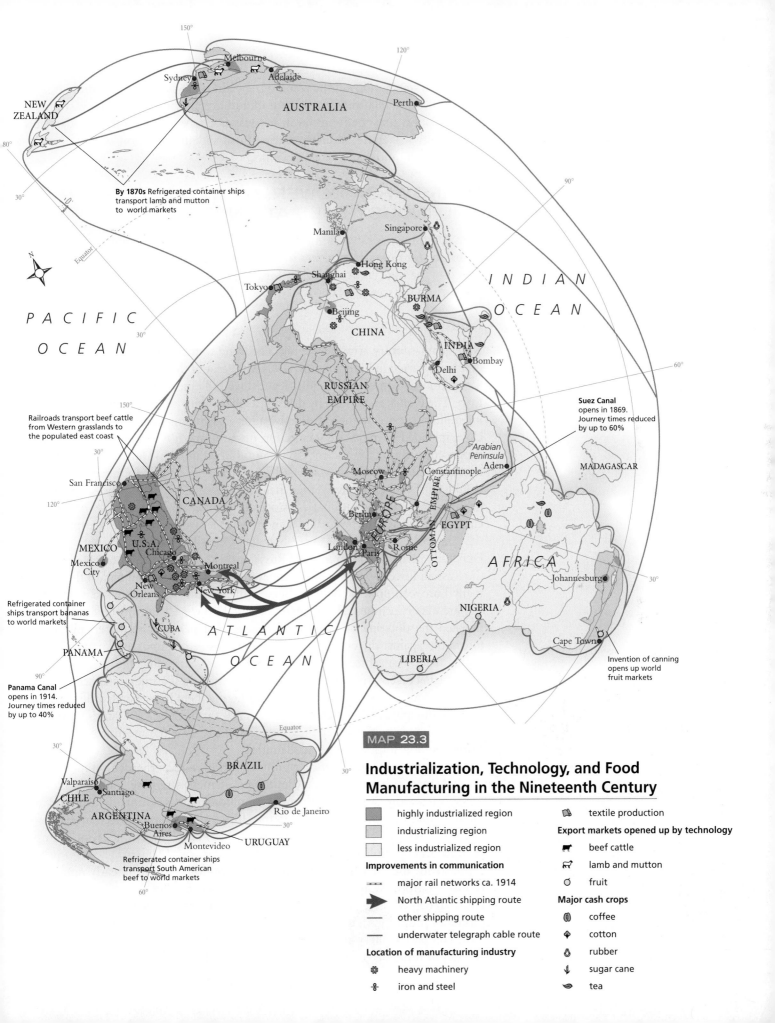

By 1870s Refrigerated container ships transport lamb and mutton to world markets

Railroads transport beef cattle from Western grasslands to the populated east coast

Refrigerated container ships transport bananas to world markets

Panama Canal
opens in 1914. Journey times reduced by up to 40%

Refrigerated container ships transport South American beef to world markets

Suez Canal
opens in 1869. Journey times reduced by up to 60%

Invention of canning opens up world fruit markets

PACIFIC OCEAN

INDIAN OCEAN

ATLANTIC OCEAN

Oceans and places

NEW ZEALAND

AUSTRALIA
Sydney · Melbourne · Adelaide · Perth

Manila · Singapore · Hong Kong · Shanghai · Tokyo · Beijing

CHINA · BURMA · INDIA · Bombay · Delhi

RUSSIAN EMPIRE · Moscow

Arabian Peninsula · Constantinople · Aden · MADAGASCAR

Berlin · EUROPE · London · Paris · Rome · OTTOMAN EMPIRE · EGYPT · AFRICA

CANADA · San Francisco · U.S.A. · Chicago · Montreal · New York · New Orleans

MEXICO · Mexico City · CUBA · PANAMA

NIGERIA · LIBERIA · Johannesburg · Cape Town

BRAZIL · Rio de Janeiro

CHILE · Valparaiso · Santiago · ARGENTINA · Buenos Aires · Montevideo · URUGUAY

Equator

MAP 23.3

Industrialization, Technology, and Food Manufacturing in the Nineteenth Century

▨ highly industrialized region	▨ textile production
▨ industrializing region	**Export markets opened up by technology**
▨ less industrialized region	🐂 beef cattle
Improvements in communication	🐑 lamb and mutton
⊶ major rail networks ca. 1914	♂ fruit
➤ North Atlantic shipping route	**Major cash crops**
— other shipping route	◉ coffee
— underwater telegraph cable route	♦ cotton
Location of manufacturing industry	♦ rubber
❋ heavy machinery	↓ sugar cane
⚵ iron and steel	🍃 tea

Because so much of it was the result of new kinds of science and technology, it was achieved with a relatively small input of additional labor. Part of the vast increase of population that the food boom fed was free to engage in other kinds of economic activity. Trade, industry, agriculture, and urbanization were linked in a mutually sustaining cycle of expansion.

ENERGY FOR POWER: MILITARIZATION AND INDUSTRIALIZATION

Even food, however, was a modest source of extra energy compared with those mobilized for militarization and industrialization. Again, these developments were linked to the midcentury fat crisis, for armies and industries put relatively intense pressure on sources of fat compared with other resources.

Militarization

Nineteenth-century armies were big. The trend to make them bigger than they had ever been started in Europe in the 1790s when fear of the French Revolution induced a coalition of conservative countries to invade France with apparently invincible force. The French responded by drafting a citizen army or "nation in arms"—imposing military service on the entire active adult male population. This was not, in principle, intended to militarize society. On the contrary, it was an old-fashioned ideal, supposedly inspired by ancient Greek and Roman models. During the Renaissance, classical scholars, such as Machiavelli (see Chapter 18), had argued that citizens would fight more effectively than paid professional warriors. The same idea lay behind American revolutionaries' insistence on the moral superiority of voluntary citizen armies over the professional and mercenary troops the British employed.

The effect, however, was to create mass armies. The Grand Army with which the French Emperor Napoleon invaded Russia in 1812 numbered over 600,000 men, and the Russian forces opposing him were even larger. In the second half of the century, many European powers could mobilize armies numbering millions. The effects on warfare were enormous. The German theorist, Karl von Clausewitz (1780–1831), formulated the doctrine of "total war"—waged not just against the enemy's armed forces, but against the entire population of a hostile country (see Chapter 26). The results made war worse—multiplying the victims, spreading the destruction, and encouraging preemptive attacks. Similarly, the era of mass armies transformed society by taking young men from their homes, gathering them in barracks, drilling them in military discipline, and teaching them loyalty to the state. "Peasants," it was said, "became Frenchmen" through their service in the army in the late nineteenth century. Armies became forges of national identities.

The economic consequences of militarization were, perhaps, even more significant. Armies concentrated huge numbers of men, straining food supplies and transport resources. Navies consumed unprecedented amounts of iron and steel for shipbuilding and of coal to keep the ships going. Every serviceman had to be nourished with efficient energy sources. We have already seen plenty of examples of how war stimulated energy-delivering industries. Margarine was invented expressly for the French navy. Canning was a response to war in early nineteenth-century Europe. Canned milk was developed in the American Civil War (1861–1865). Massive armed forces demanded unprecedented quantities of mass-produced munitions, guns with ever more rapid rates of fire, and ever bigger and more complex artillery and engineering services. Every gun and cartridge had to be greased to function. In 1857, the issue of cartridges supposedly greased with pig

Karl von Clausewitz, from *On War*

and beef fat that soldiers had to break open with their teeth sparked a major rebellion among the native troops of Britain's Indian army. To the Muslims, pigs were unclean. To the Hindus, cows were sacred. (In fact, the cartridges were greased with vegetable oil.) Wartime logistics provided models and, sometimes, generated innovations in production, supply, and communications. Huge production lines, for instance, first appeared in state bakeries that produced dry bread for navies. These bakeries inspired the factory system of production that was necessary for large-scale industrialization.

Industrialization

New energy resources—what we now call **fossil fuels**—fueled industrialization. Peat and coal were the first to be exploited. They were traditional fuel sources, now extracted from the ground on an unprecedented scale. Oil followed (and, eventually, in the twentieth century, natural gas). In effect, mining and drilling for coal and oil released buried sunlight, accumulated millions of years ago when plants

An early Union ironclad on the Mississippi River during the Civil War. Although the British and French navies already had ships built entirely of iron by 1860, U.S. naval experts were reluctant to believe that these vessels could be effective. But the Union navy put iron plates on wooden ships and began building iron-hulled vessels in 1862, in response to Confederate plans to launch similar ships and buy others from Britain.

and creatures—which store energy from the Sun in the carbons that form their bodies—were buried and crushed. Fossil fuels are therefore a form of concentrated energy. A few pounds of coal can produce as much heat as an acre of timber. So the first effect of the release of coal from the ground was to liberate land for farming that had formerly been used to produce wood for fuel, helping along the massive growth of food production. The second was to provide energy for new forms of power.

Coal-generated energy and steam power were inextricably linked. Steam powered the pumps that drained the mines. Coal fueled the furnaces that produced the steam. Iron and steel were inescapably part of the picture. They were the materials from which the machinery was made to convert coal to energy and steam to power—the rods and the pistons, the cogs and casings of the engines. Coal produced the heat that fused the ores and forged the metals. The metals in their turn enclosed the spaces in which the coal burned.

Fuel consumption and production leaped. Coal purchases accounted for over a quarter of the expenses of the world's biggest steamship company in the 1860s. Japanese coal production had always been modest, but it rose from 390,000 tons in 1860 to 5 million tons in 1900. Increases of a similar order of magnitude occurred in Belgian and Spanish coal mines over the same period. The most productive coalfield in the world was already that of South Wales in Britain. Here, in the same period, output soared from 11.4 million to 35.1 million tons a year. German coal was of problematic quality, but nineteenth-century developments made its exploitation worthwhile. Over 100 million tons were being mined annually by the end of the century.

But what was all this extra energy for? Statistics seem to dominate the story of industrialization whenever historians tell it. Understandably, economic historians, looking to quantify the subject and make it seem scientific, like to measure industrial change in terms of productivity figures. These are sometimes suggestive, sometimes spectacularly revealing. Machinery in use in Britain by the 1830s, for instance, could produce in 135 hours the same amount of cotton that took 50,000 hours to spin by hand. This certainly helps to explain the appeal of industrialization. But it also points to a paradox. In an age of increasing population, more muscle power was becoming available worldwide. So why bother to mechanize?

In part, the explanation lies in the geography of industrialization. On the whole, it happened earliest and fastest in regions where labor was relatively expensive: in areas such as Europe and Japan, where the size of the workforce was relatively modest compared with, say, China and India; or in the United States, which, despite the huge increase in its population, was still seriously under populated in the nineteenth century. Second, and perhaps more significant, industrialization was a function of demand. Population increase accounted in part for increasing demand, but so did the multiplication of sources of wealth—the new resources unlocked from the soil, the enormous expansion of financial institutions, the growth in the money supply as governments took on increasing responsibilities and minted cash to pay for them, using the gold and silver from new mines, which were particularly productive in this period in North America, southern Africa, and Russia. Figures are not available, but it seems likely that the growth in the money supply worldwide would have been hugely inflationary if production and trade had not increased proportionately and absorbed its effects. Although mechanization stripped workers of employment in traditional industries and in unindustrialized parts of the world, it generated new wealth and, therefore, new employment opportunities in other activities and other areas. Trade and capital were essential extra spokes in the cycle that linked food, population, and industry. They provided incentives to mechanize and money to invest in mechanization.

Economic circumstances alone, however, cannot explain industrialization. Indeed, it was more than an economic phenomenon. For the contemporaries who took part in it, the appeal of industry was a form of enchantment. Like magic, or like today's information technology, which seems to affect many people in the same way, it multiplied power and effected dazzling transformations. A passenger aboard the

Power to rival Nature's: Philippe-Jacques de Loutherbourg, born in France in 1740, made his career as a painter in England, where his work as a stage designer helped to add a showy, theatrical quality to his art. His painting of the great ironworks of Coalbrookdale in the English Midlands shows the rural setting typical of early industrial sites, and displays the "sublime," "picturesque," and "romantic" qualities for which he became famous. The smoke and flames from the forge are more on the scale of a volcano than of a factory.

first commercially viable locomotive train—George Stevenson's *Rocket* in Britain, which achieved a speed of 35 miles per hour in 1829—called it a "magical machine with its flying white breath and rhythmical unvarying pace. When I closed my eyes the sensation of flying was delightful." A witness of the unveiling of one of the century's most impressive technologies—Sir Henry Bessemer's process for turning iron into steel in 1856—described the event with the slack-jawed awe of a sorcerer's apprentice: "Out came a volcanic eruption of such dazzling coruscations as had never been seen before. When combustion had expended all its fury, most wonderful of all, the result was steel!"

Industrial technology represented, for its early witnesses, the triumph of imagination over nature. Admirers of mechanization saw it as romantic—a perspective we have lost today. The English artist Joseph Turner (1775–1851) painted the speed of the locomotive. The German composer Felix Mendelssohn (1809–1847) turned the noises of steam navigation into music. The British author Samuel Smiles (1812–1904), whose writings convinced the English-speaking world of the virtues of industrialization, declared, "We may justly look upon the steam engine as the noblest machine ever invented by man." Engineers became heroes. Smiles wrote their lives in the style of romances of chivalry, or even of fairy tales. A band played "Hail! The Conquering Hero Comes" when the most inventive engineer of the age, I. K. Brunel (1806–1859), appeared at the opening of a bridge he designed in England.

There were martyrs as well as heroes. One hundred workers died digging two miles of a railway tunnel Brunel designed. And, of course, industrialization had its enemies. It threatened the livelihoods of workers in traditional crafts. Moralists condemned production techniques that forced workers into soulless rhythms of work in the backbreaking, disease-breeding environments of factories and mines, and as we shall see in Chapter 24, their laments were justified. Not everyone appreciated the romance of steam. For some people, railways desecrated the countryside or damaged and stole the land. Nostalgia for the fate of the land inspired artists, novelists, and reactionary social movements (see Chapter 26) wherever industrialization occurred.

Even industrialists often seemed uncommitted to what we should now call entrepreneurial spirit. In England, "captains of industry" typically devoted their wealth to creating a rural idyll for themselves— buying country estates and building country houses, in imitation of traditional landed aristocrats. Their managers, who could not afford country estates, imitated the longed-for way of life in so-called garden suburbs, leafy oases of large houses and private parks that were built outside the big industrial cities. In France, industrialists commonly affected scorn for entrepreneurship. In 1836, a member of a great textiles dynasty of northern France went on a pilgrimage "to obtain illumination from the Holy Ghost, so that we should never undertake anything in business above our strength, lest we should be troubled by hazardous speculations." Another French industrialist, Francois Wendel, died in 1825, leaving a fortune of 4 million francs, about $80 million in today's money, from his ironworks, having become, he said, an iron master

Fanny Kemble, from *Records of a Girlhood*

The romance of steam. Joseph Mallord Turner (1775–1851)—the most defiantly original English artist of his day—made the railway seem part of nature, blurring the steam into the clouds, the rails into the landscape.

Knight of industry. Far from keeping upstarts in their place, the code of chivalry has for centuries encouraged and equipped enterprising men who have risen in Western society. The swashbuckling, self-made American tycoon Cornelius Vanderbilt (1794–1877) is depicted in this stained glass window in the most socially respectable church in Newport, Rhode Island with the armor and Christian symbols of a medieval knight.

and owner of profitable businesses "against my will." His fellow countryman, the industrial magnate Jules Siegfried engraved "To work is to act" on his cuff-links, but defied the prevailing work ethic to retire from manufacturing textiles at the age of 44. In Japan (as we shall see), entrepreneurs insisted on motives for their work that were connected with honor or patriotism rather than profit. Again, they sought to imitate the warrior aristocracy. Even in the United States, which, as a young country, was less subject to old-fashioned inhibitions, industrialists practiced similar evasions. Cornelius Vanderbilt (1794–1877), the multimillionaire owner of steamships and railroads, liked to see himself as a "knight of industry" and had himself depicted in a church window dressed in a medieval suit of armor. In the southern states, manufacturers aped planters' lifestyles. Industrialization, in short, succeeded only where people could reconcile it with traditional values.

Of course, industrialization impacted on the rest of the world—by creating global inequalities of wealth and power that are the subjects of later chapters of this book, and by linking unindustrialized regions in a grid of high-speed communications. Even parts of the world that had few or no factories or mechanized production methods, such as China, India, and South America, got railways, steamshipping, and electric telegraphs. The first successful experiment in steam locomotion was carried out in 1804, when Richard Trevithick carried ten tons of iron along nine miles of tracks in Britain. The local paper predicted "a thousand instances" of uses "not yet thought of." Trevithick's designs were too slow and cumbersome to be commercially useful, but viable railways were being built in Britain by 1830, and they spread around the world with amazing speed. Although the web of railways was densest in industrial regions, the rails also stretched across vast distances of the unindustrialized world, delivering to ports and factories ingredients for the machines to turn into saleable goods, and food and drugs to keep the workers at their tasks. By the 1840s, the United States had more rails than Britain. The first line across the American continent opened in 1869. By 1900, the United States had nearly 170,000 miles of track. Most of the network linked regions of primary products to centers of industrial processing and consumption.

Among the most intensive scenes of railway building in the mid–nineteenth century were India and Cuba—colonial lands where the ruling powers discouraged manufactures and exploited their basic products to serve industries in Britain and Spain, the "home countries." India's case is especially spectacular. Railway construction began in 1852. Fifty years later, India had nearly 42,000 miles of track—more than all the rest of Asia put together. One hundred fifty million pounds of British capital made the enterprise possible. In terms of labor, however, this was a genuinely Indian enterprise, with over 370,000 Indians a year working on the lines by the 1890s. Indian contractors, who supplied workers and, in most cases, supervised the work, made the biggest fortunes in railway construction. Jamsetji Dorabji Naegamwalla (1804–1882) was the most successful of all. He was an illiterate carpenter in a British-run dockyard when, in 1850, he realized the potential of the railways. He employed thousands of Indians and a handful of European engineers, ensuring the smooth running of the operations the government confided to him by getting to know his men and boosting their morale by his constant presence on the job. When a viaduct he built collapsed in 1855, he bullied the authorities to let him rebuild it at extra cost and waive their usual demand for cash securities in advance. Unlike most British contractors who worked on railway construction, he made money and retired in 1870 to enjoy his wealth.

The development of steam-powered shipping kept pace with that of the railways. In 1807, the first commercial steamboat, built by Robert Fulton, navigated the Hudson River, traveling 150 miles upriver from New York City to Albany in 32 hours. Twelve years later, the steamship *Savannah* crossed the Atlantic in 27 days. That voyage, however, was a failure. The *Savannah* spent only 80 hours of the crossing under steam, relying on sails for the other 568 hours. The engine was gutted, and the ship was sold as a sailing vessel. Technical improvements in propulsion and fuel consumption were needed. The first regular transatlantic steam service began in 1838. Ten or 12 days instead of 6 weeks became the normal length of an Atlantic crossing between Western Europe and North America.

Paintings collected in the Peabody Essex Museum in Salem, Massachusetts, show the advantages of the early steamers. Owners chose to have their vessels depicted in stormy seas because the regularity of all-weather sailing was an important selling point. When the English novelist Charles Dickens crossed the Atlantic in 1842, he endured the "staggering, heaving, wrestling, leaping, diving, jumping, pitching, throbbing, rolling and rocking," as the ship braved head-winds "with every pulse and artery of her huge body swollen and bursting." It was in adverse weather that the steamers demonstrated their superiority over sail. British steam tonnage at sea exceeded that under sail by 1883.

Intersecting rail and shipping lines were the scaffolding of the world, along which trade and travelers could clamber to every part of it. James Hill, the American railway millionaire and philanthropist who built the Episcopal cathedral of St. Paul, Minnesota, founded a steamship line that connected the fastest rail route across the Rockies with the Russian Trans-Siberian railway, which opened in 1900 and linked Moscow and St. Petersburg with Russia's Pacific port of Vladivostock. Steam transport linked the great food-producing and consuming belt of the world, from Vladivostock to Vancouver on Canada's Pacific coast. The railways made a startling difference. They wrenched trade in new directions. They made it possible for land-based systems of communications to carry freight on a scale previously possible only by sea. The world's great hinterlands, far from seas and ports and even navigable rivers, in the innermost parts of the continents, could be integrated into an increasingly global economy.

Indian railway. When it began to operate in 1881, the Darjeeling Railway in northwest India ran 55 miles from the port of Calcutta, mounting steep slopes to reach the tea-growing regions. This loop, photographed in the late nineteenth or early twentieth century, shows one of the devices the British engineers who built the railway used to conquer the sharp ascent. The tea the trains carried eventually went to England, supplying a cheap stimulant for the workforce of British industry.

The steamship *Brittania*. In this painting of the 1840s, the sailing vessel seems doomed to shipwreck, while the steamship braves the gale. Owners commissioned ship portraits of this sort to encourage business and build confidence in the sailing qualities of their vessels.
Photograph courtesy of the Peabody Essex Museum

Transatlantic telegraph line. An 1866 lithograph depicts the third and finally successful attempt to lay an underwater telegraph line between Europe and North America. This cable reduced the time it took messages to cross the Atlantic from the length of a sea voyage to a few minutes.

It was hard to think of a power source better than steam, but electricity—normally, like steam, generated by burning coal but also by hydroelectric power—began to rival steam power in some applications. The English physicist Michael Faraday, a self-educated amateur, conducted remarkable experiments in the 1830s and 1840s that demonstrated the possibilities of various applications, including electric lighting. The biggest contribution arose from one of his first gadgets: an electromagnetic induction machine, made in 1831. The following

⊙ MAKING CONNECTIONS

INDUSTRIALIZATION AND MILITARIZATION

INDUSTRIAL DEVELOPMENT →	MILITARY ADAPTATION →	EFFECTS
Food technology: preservation, production, innovation	To supply massive armies of nation-states: canning of food, beverages; automated production lines for baked goods; new products like margarine to supply naval personnel	Extension of ability to provision large-scale armies/navies across continents and ocean; projecting military power; ability to manage colonies more effectively
New energy sources: fossil fuels	Coal-generated energy and steam power fuel industrialized production of weapons, ammunition	Largest industrial nations (Europe, U.S.) develop massive armies, navies equipped with weapons and ammunition that are more deadly
Transportation technology	Railroads, steamships used to transport troops and supplies rapidly across oceans, continents	Tighter control of homelands, colonies through technologically advanced military forces
Electrical technology	First practical application focuses on communication—telegraphy, used by military forces to coordinate troop movements	Ability to maintain control of large-scale armies on battlefields, or across continents and oceans via telegraph messages

year, the American Samuel Morse used Faraday's discovery to transmit messages. The first long-range telegraph line linked Washington, D.C., to Baltimore, Maryland, in 1844. Submarine cables to transmit telegraph messages crossed the Atlantic in 1869, shrinking the ocean to the dimensions of a pond. An electric age was about to succeed the age of steam. The gasoline-fueled internal combustion engine, invented in the 1890s, also pointed the way to a further stage of locomotion, without rail tracks. It would have as transforming an impact on the twentieth century as the steam-powered engine had on the nineteenth.

INDUSTRIALIZING EUROPE

One way to measure the spread of industrialization is to map the distribution of steam-powered businesses. By these standards, Europe developed early and mightily. In the first half of the nineteenth century, Britain, Spain, Italy, and Belgium all doubled their steam-driven industrial capacity. France and Russia tripled theirs. In what is now the Czech Republic (but what was then part of the Austrian Empire), capacity grew fivefold, and Germany's capacity multiplied by six. So industrialization was a genuinely widespread phenomenon. It transcended traditional national boundaries. In 1830, the Englishman John Cockerill's core business was manufacturing textiles in Belgium. He set up a heavy machinery factory in the city of Liege to manufacture his own equipment. He diversified into weaving in Germany and Russian-ruled Poland and into producing cotton yarn in Spain. He went into mining in various European countries to obtain raw materials for his engineering factories and into international banking to finance his operations. He even dabbled in unrelated businesses—he had a sugar plantation in the Dutch colony of Surinam on the northeast coast of South America. His empire collapsed in 1837. He then went to build railways in Russia.

From 1815 to 1914, city growth matched and even came to exceed army growth as the motor of change in Europe. Industrialization helped shape what remains, on the map, a conspicuous feature of the modern world: a zone of densely clustered industrial cities from Belfast in Northern Ireland and Bilbao in northwest Spain to Rostov and St. Petersburg in Russia (see Map 23.4). By 1900, nine European cities had more than a million people. Most of the population of Britain and Belgium had forsaken agriculture for industry and rural life for the cities. In the rest of industrializing Europe, the same drift to the towns was evident. The Russian Empire remained an overwhelmingly peasant country, but two-thirds of the inhabitants of St. Petersburg, Russia's capital, were former peasants. The biggest factories in Europe were state undertakings in Russia. Twenty per cent of Austrians were factory workers. In 1896, factories in Hungary made the machines and equipment for the world's first electric underground railway in London.

Still, if industrialization was becoming a European phenomenon, capacity tended to be concentrated in particular areas. Only Belgium, which is small, was a fully industrialized country in the sense of having industry evenly scattered throughout its territory. Southern Britain actually lost industrial capacity, which became concentrated in northern and central England and along the river Clyde in Scotland. In France, the northeast had most of the country's industry.

Population, Food, and Energy

1780–1831	Karl von Clausewitz, developer of theory of "total war"
ca. 1800	Global population: 950 million; areas with regions in excess of four people per square mile: East Asia, southeast Asia, India, Western Europe
1804	First successful railroad locomotion
1807	First commercial steamboat
1850s	British imports of guano reach 200,000 tons per year
1850–1900	500 million acres added to U.S. farmland
1860–1900	Japanese coal production rises from 390,000 to 5 million tons; British coal production rises from 11.4 million to 35.1 million
1866	British output of chemical fertilizers reaches 250,000 tons
1869	First transcontinental railroad in United States; first telegraph messages cross the Atlantic
1870s	Australian engineers develop compressed-gas cooler
1900	German coal production reaches 100 million tons annually
ca. 1900	Argentina exports 100 million bushels of wheat per year; global population: 1.6 billion; new areas with regions in excess of four people per square mile: Americas, Africa

The Industrialization of Europe by 1914

Land use 1914

- mountainous area/wasteland
- agriculture and stock rearing
- forest
- industrial area

Resources

- coalfield
- oil
- potash

Manufacturing industry

- textiles
- iron smelting
- machinery
- shipbuilding

Population growth

- city with population over 500,000 in 1850
- city with population over 500,000 in 1914
- city with population under 500,000 in 1914
- principal railways 1914

Scale varies with perspective
6,220 km (3,870 miles)
5,980 km (3,720 miles)

Map labels

Solikamsk · Perm' · **1891 Trans-Siberian railway to Vladivostok** · Archangel · *White Sea* · *Lake Onega* · *Lake Ladoga* · *Volga* · Moscow · St. Petersburg · RUSSIAN EMPIRE · *Don* · *Caspian Sea* · Baku · FINLAND · Vasa · *Gulf of Bothnia* · SWEDEN · NORWAY · Christiania (Oslo) · *Baltic Sea* · Danzig · Warsaw · Kiev · *Dnieper* · *Dniester* · Odessa · Sebastopol · *Caucasus* · PERSIA · Copenhagen · Malmö · Rostock · DENMARK · Oder · SILESIA · *Carpathian Mountains* · ROMANIA · Bucharest · *Black Sea* · OTTOMAN EMPIRE · Hamburg · Berlin · Bremen · Leipzig · *Elbe* · Dresden · Prague · *SAXONY* · Vienna · AUSTRIA-HUNGARY · BULGARIA · SERBIA · Constantinople · *North Sea* · NETHERLANDS · Amsterdam · Antwerp · BELGIUM · GERMANY · *RUHR* · Essen · Cologne · Frankfurt · Munich · *Rhine* · Trieste · Sarajevo · Salonica · GREECE · Athens · Edinburgh · Glasgow · Manchester · Liverpool · Belfast · Birmingham · Dublin · BRITAIN · *Ireland* · Dover · London · Calais · Paris · SWITZERLAND · *Alps* · Milan · Ancona · ITALY · Naples · Rome · ALBANIA · MONTENEGRO · *Adriatic Sea* · Bristol · Cardiff · Limerick · Cork · Le Havre · *Seine* · Le Creusot · *Loire* · Lyon · Turin · Genoa · Corsica · *Sicily* · Brest · Nantes · Clermont-Ferrand · FRANCE · *Rhône* · Toulon · Marseille · *Sardinia* · *Mediterranean Sea* · Bordeaux · Toulouse · *Pyrenees* · Barcelona · Santander · Bilbao · Gijón · La Coruña · SPAIN · Madrid · Alicante · ATLANTIC OCEAN · Oporto · *Tagus* · Granada · PORTUGAL · Lisbon · Cádiz · DONBAS · *Volga*

In Switzerland, it was in the north. In Germany, most industry was located in two regions: the Ruhr in the west and in Silesia and Saxony in the east. Italy's industries were concentrated in the north in Piedmont and Lombardy and focused on the cities of Turin and Milan. In Russia, the two favored areas were in St. Petersburg and in the Donets Basin to the north of the Black Sea. In Spain, only the Basque Country and Catalonia were industrialized.

What made the difference between zones of industrialization and the unindustrialized regions that remained alongside them? Most of the key regions were favored by the availability of coal and iron deposits and access to major markets, but some places bucked this trend. Catalonia in Spain, for instance, had major metallurgical industries despite lacking iron or coal, and being ill placed to communicate with other urban areas. Except by appealing to some sort of commercial spirit that remains hard to describe or define, no one has ever really been able to explain this.

To try to understand why neighboring areas responded differently to the opportunity to industrialize, the Low Countries are a good place to look. If Britain was, as is commonly said, the first industrial nation, Belgium was the second. Yet Belgium's neighbor, the Kingdom of the Netherlands, hardly participated in industrialization until late in the nineteenth century. Belgium had the highest density of population in Europe—698 persons per square mile, but the Netherlands was also relatively thickly settled, with 487 people per square mile. Indeed, in no other region of comparable size in Europe, outside England, was population so concentrated.

As the century wore on, Belgian entrepreneurs increasingly concentrated on iron and steel production, for which their country was well supplied with raw materials. Belgium had the most efficient iron- and steel-making equipment in the world by 1870, each furnace producing on average a third more iron than those of Britain, over half as much again as those of Germany, and more than double those of France. Zinc and glass were other Belgian specialities. Belgium was also well served by railways. Its 1,800 miles of track in 1870 constituted a substantial network for such a small country.

The Netherlands, meanwhile, remained overwhelmingly agricultural. Its industrial sector was dedicated to food processing, especially to making candy, using the cane sugar from Dutch colonies in the Caribbean and the Dutch East Indies and, increasingly, the beet sugar Dutch farmers produced. (French scientists had discovered how to extract sugar from beets in the early 1800s.) Dutch milk-processing firms supplied 80 percent of the British market for condensed and powdered milk by the end of the century, and the Netherlands was Europe's biggest manufacturer of margarine. Despite the traditional importance of shipbuilding, Dutch iron and steel production only began to catch up with European averages in the 1890s.

So why were the two countries, which had similar histories and cultural profiles, so different? If anything, the Netherlands had historic advantages: a large colonial empire and a tradition of long-range trade—both of which, according to some economic theorists in the nineteenth century, should have stimulated industrial development. Dutch coal was mainly anthracite and hard to mine—but similar limitations did nothing to restrain industry in Germany. If there is such a thing as an industrial or capitalist spirit, it is unlikely that it should have been prevalent in one country and not in its neighbor. Indeed, when global conditions changed in the late nineteenth and twentieth centuries, the Netherlands did turn to industrialization.

In the nineteenth century, however, the two countries' economies were complementary: Belgium specialized in heavy industries, while the Netherlands specialized in producing and processing food for industrializing markets, including those of Belgium. The patchiness of industrialization, in short, was essential to industrialization's success. It was part of a pattern of specialization in which some regions supplied food and raw materials while others concentrated on manufacturing. If some places had comparative advantage in resources, others had comparative advantage in finance and access to markets, or a relatively disciplined or suitably educated labor force. The system was reproduced at global level, as large areas of the world became suppliers of primary produce to industrializing economies.

INDUSTRY IN THE AMERICAS

The United States was a surprising industrializer. It was a country with a long history of supplying raw materials—pelts and skins, whaling products—for other people's industries. The southern states produced raw cotton for mills in Britain, and tobacco and sugar, which contributed to the world economy mainly as mild drugs to make workers' dreary lives more bearable. The Midwest had, by the mid–nineteenth century, an obvious future as a source of food for the world. The rest of the American interior had vast stocks of lumber, agricultural land, and mineral deposits. The states' main manufacturies in the eighteenth century had specialized in the partial processing of raw products, such as turning sugar into molasses and rum.

Still, in other ways, the United States was a suitable arena for industry. High per capita incomes meant there was money for investment. A large, active merchant marine enabled the country to participate in global markets. A relatively small population meant there was a labor shortage that mechanization could make up. The fact that slavery was lawful in almost half the country until 1865 meant that a lot of labor was unproductively tied down, raising labor costs elsewhere. Nor did the abolition of slavery do much for this problem, because most former slaves remained in the South as sharecroppers or owners of small, relatively unproductive farms. On the other hand, high immigration rates from Europe (see Chapter 24) meant that enough manpower became available to make factory systems viable, and ensured growing domestic demand for the products of industry. There was plenty of coal and iron, especially after huge iron-ore deposits were discovered near the Great Lakes in 1844. The United States also had high tariffs for most of the nineteenth century, which were designed to shut out European products and foster native industry.

Andrew Carnegie (1835–1918)—a self-made millionaire and immigrant from Scotland who had risen from a child laborer in a textile factory by sacrificial saving and shrewd investing in the steel industry—called in professional chemists to make the most of technological innovations. By the end of the century, the United States was producing 10 million tons of steel a year. Productivity in Carnegie's plants was spectacular. His workers produced more than ten times as much per man as their German counterparts—the best steel at the lowest prices. "The Republic," wrote Carnegie in 1885, "thunders past with the rush of an express." By the 1890s, factories in the United States produced twice as much as those of Britain and half as much again as the whole of Europe. Railroad

The Magic of industry. An engraving of Andrew Carnegie's Pittsburgh steelworks in 1886 captures the magic-like brilliance—glittering sparks, thunderous noise, mysterious haze, dynamism, and light—of the Bessemer converter. The result is gleaming white steel. The human agents are dwarfed.

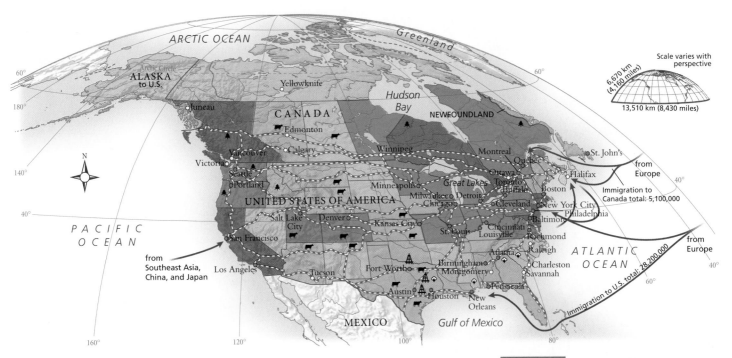

MAP 23.5

Industrialization, Urbanization and Immigration in the United States and Canada, 1860–1920

Population living in urban areas, 1920

- over 60%
- 40–60%
- 20–40%
- less than 20%

Resource-based industry

- cattle ranching
- cotton growing
- timber production
- oil production
- major industrial city
- major railroads

Immigration 1860–1920

- to the U.S.
- to Canada

expansion became faster and fuller than in Europe (see Map 23.5). As we shall see (see Chapter 24), European, especially British, investors were alert to the opportunities the United States offered.

Nothing like this industrialization happened in the rest of the Americas. Canada became an agricultural country, thanks to the domestication of its own prairie, but not an industrial one. Fewer than half a million Canadians, out of a total of some 7 million, worked in manufacturing at the beginning of the twentieth century, and a third of those manufacturing workers processed timber and food.

Most of Latin America was even less industrialized. The Latin American wars of independence were unlike that of the United States. Theirs were mostly long struggles, unaided by outside powers, leaving many of them exhausted and divided (see Chapter 22). The newly independent nations, after spending heavily on the fight against Spain, had to maintain big armies in wariness of each other and to suppress domestic discontent. They lacked the north's incentive to mechanize. Latin America had plenty of ex-slaves, Indians, and illiterate laborers. In a sense, the region never fully emerged from colonial-style exploitation. Its own elites became the exploiters of their own peasants, whereas at first, until the emancipation of the slaves, the United States hardly had any dependent peasants, and none of them lived in the areas that industrialized. In North America, small farmers were their own bosses. Big North American ranchers used the mobile labor of "cowboys."

Free trade, which most of the independent Latin American states practiced, favored industrializing economies that could produce cheap goods, and condemned Latin American economies to underdevelopment (see Map 23.6). Having fought Spanish monopolists under the banner of free trade, the new countries were unable to protect their native industries, such as they were, against European imports. They became locked into a role as producers of primary products: the ore, timber, and rubber that supplied the factories of Europe and the United States; the foods and fertilizers that fed the workforces; the tobacco and coffee that provided the the stimulants that fought workers' need for sleep; the sweets that kept their blood sugar up. The grasslands of South America

Caribbean Sea

1904–1919:
Panama canal
constructed

Santa Marta
Barranquilla
Cartagena
Maracaibo
Barquisimeto
Valencia
Caracas
VENEZUELA
⚓ **1854**
TRINIDAD
BRITISH GUIANA
Georgetown
Paramaribo
Cayenne
FRENCH GUIANA

Panama
PANAMA
Medellín
Bogotá
COLOMBIA
⚓ **1851**
Ciudad
Bolívar
SURINAM
1815:
to Netherlands

Buenaventura
Cali

Quito
Equator   Río Negro   Equator

ECUADOR
⚓ **1853**
Guayaquil
Cuenca
Tumbes
Iquitos
Putumayo
Amazon
Manaus
Santarém
Pará
(Belém)
São Luiz do Maranhão

Madeira
Tapajós
Xingu
B R A Z I L
⚓ **1888**
Pernamb
(Recife)

Trujillo
Yungay
PERU
⚓ **1854**
Maceió

Callao
Lima
Islas de Chincha
Pisco
Cuzco
*Planalto do
Mato Grosso*
Bahia
(Salvador)

Arequipa
Mollendo
Tacna
Arica
Pisagua
Iquique
Tocopilla
Antofagasta
La Paz
BOLIVIA
⚓ **1854**
Santa Cruz
Sucre
Potosí
Corumbá
Goyaz
Pirapora
Minas Novas
Diamantina
Santa Cruz
Belo Horizonte
Ouro Prêto
Victoria

Atacama Desert
Tropic of Capricorn
Jujuy
Salta
PARAGUAY
⚓ **1870**
Paraguay
Paraná
São Paulo
Rio de Janeiro
Santos
Tropic of Capricorn

MAP 23.6

**South American Economies,
ca. 1900**

Major export products

≈ bananas
🐂 beef
🌰 cacoa
☕ coffee
🔲 copper
♤ cotton
▲ guano
✳ hides
▽ nitrates
⬧ rubber
⬇ sugar
🔳 silver
🔲 tin
🌿 tobacco
🌱 wheat
▪▪ wool
⚎⚎ major railways by 1910
⚓ 1853 date slavery abolished
✳ major port

Caldera
Copiapó
CHILE
⚓ **1823**
La Serena
Viña del Mar
Valparaíso
Santiago
Talca
Concepción
Tucumán
Santiago del
Estero
Catamarca
La Rioja
Córdoba
Mendoza
San Luis
Chilecito
Corrientes
Pôrto Alegre
Rio Grande
ARGENTINA
⚓ **1853**
Rosario
URUGUAY
⚓ **1853**
Buenos
Aires
Colonia
Montevideo
La Plata
Uruguay

**BUENOS
AIRES**
Mar del Plata

Andes
Valdivia
Puerto Montt
Río Negro
Neuquén
Bahia Blanca

Patagonia
Chubut
Rawson
(Chubut)

N

Punta Arenas
Tierra del Fuego
FALKLAND ISLANDS

PACIFIC OCEAN
ATLANTIC OCEAN

500 km
500 miles

never followed the grain-rich, city-sprinkled model of the North American prairie, not even in Argentina, which had plenty of prairielike land—the pampa—that remained ranching country throughout the century. The pampa was too far from most centers of population. "The promises of the pampa, so generous, so spontaneous, many times go unfulfilled," wrote the Spanish philosopher and diplomat José Ortega y Gasset (1883–1955). "Defeats in America must surely be worse than elsewhere. A man is suddenly mutilated . . . with no treatment for his wounds." The success of the United States became a standing reproach to the economically frustrated countries to its south.

Much of Latin America became a continent of disillusioned hopes. In 1857, Carlos Barroilhet, who did more than anyone else to explain the merits of guano to the world, prophesied that Peru was destined to be "at once the richest and happiest nation on Earth," but by the 1880s, guano—much depleted by overexploitation—was considered a "curse." Competition from African guano and chemical superphosphates undermined a monopoly on which governments had staked all their economic plans. Brazil, similarly, lost its rubber monopoly when British businessmen smuggled out some plants and replanted them in Malaya. Late nineteenth-century Brazil relied more on coffee—another asset subject to increasing global competition—than rubber. Mexico lost its potentially most valuable territories—unmined gold and silver, untapped oil—in war with the United States in 1846–1848. At the century's end, Argentina seemed still—in some ways, more than ever—a land of promise. Frozen meat exports and a meat-extract processing industry made the dominance of ranching in the pampa seem like a wise strategy. According to an "oath to the flag" that educational reformers introduced in 1909, Argentina was simply "the best land in the world," which would know "no history without a triumph." But its economy remained at the mercy of foreign investment and precarious global markets, and its promise was never fulfilled.

Ankle-deep in coffee on a plantation in Brazil in the early twentieth century. The freshly harvested beans are tipped into troughs to be washed. Business imperialism continued to promote long-range ecological exchange as global trade increased, making South American coffee a major product alongside coffee from southeast Asia, and sending Brazilian rubber trees to southeast Asia.

JAPAN INDUSTRIALIZES

Commodore Perry sailed into Tokyo Bay on July 8, 1853. His mission was to persuade or oblige the Japanese to open their ports to trade with the United States. He meant business in every sense of the word. He had four heavily armed ships with him. "The universal Yankee nation," wrote the expedition's interpreter, Samuel Williams, had arrived to end Japan's "apathy and long ignorance" with the example of "a higher civilization," elevated by "the success of science and enterprise." Nevertheless, what Williams actually saw in Japan conformed only in part to the stereotype of a country consigned to backwardness by isolation. Williams noted a mixture of railroads—which dock areas already had—"and telegraph, . . . shaven pates and nightgowns, soldiers with muskets and drilling in close array, soldiers with petticoats, sandals, two swords, all in disorder." Japan's modernization had already begun in selective respects, and the country was well poised to invest in innovative technologies: rich, urban, with a long history of commercial growth and a large middle class (see Chapter 20).

JAPANESE VIEWS OF AMERICAN NAVAL TECHNOLOGY

Commodore Matthew C. Perry's expedition to Tokyo in 1853 aroused great interest among the Japanese, who closely observed the American "black ships" anchored offshore. In his diary, Perry wrote that "at early sunrise. . . . a corps of artists . . . came close to the ship's side, but made no attempt to come on board, busying themselves in taking sketches of the strange vessels." One of the purposes of the sketches was to give the shogun and his officials accurate information about the barbarians and their technology.

The paddle wheel from one of the expedition's steamers. Intended to be a technical drawing, it shows the passion with which the Japanese studied every detail of the American expedition even though they were unfamiliar with the workings of a steamship.

The care with which the artist depicts the black smoke billowing out of the ship's funnel shows that he had never seen anything like this before.

The steamship *Susquehanna*, which served as Perry's command ship. The Japanese inscription indicates that the flag at the stern of the warship had "about 30 white stars on navy blue background, said to be the number of states."

How do these sketches illustrate Japan's attitudes toward "modernization" and the adoption of Western technology in the nineteenth century? ●

At first, Japanese industrializing policies focused on the army and navy. The urgent task in the mid–nineteenth century was to close the technology gap that had opened up between Japan and the Western powers. But the slogan "Increase Production, Promote Industry" soon replaced "Prosperous Nation, Strong Military" as Japan's guiding principle. The project for the elites of late nineteenth-century Japan was to create an industrial economy like those taking shape in Europe and the United States. Japan would become the "floating wharf of the Pacific." "We need industry to attain the goal of becoming a rich nation," declared the government in 1868.

At first, unfair terms of trade held Japan back. Western powers, exploiting their temporary military advantage, imposed "unequal treaties" that allowed them to sell products in Japan cheaply and exempted their nationals from having to obey Japanese laws or be judged in Japanese courts. The trade balance remained adverse—Japan imported more than it sold abroad—until the 1880s. It was "a source of lamentation," according to a government report of 1880. In 1884, only 176 nongovernment factories employed more than 50 people, and only 72 were steam powered. By 1899, however, Japan was able to break out of the unequal relationship and revise the terms of trade with the West, while imposing terms on China after defeating that country in a war over Korea in 1895. Japan's total foreign trade increased tenfold between 1877 and 1900. The emperor presided at the opening of the first long-distance railway in 1872, but there were still only 100 miles of track in 1880. Nearly 5,000 miles were added in the next two decades. At the century's end, 50 cities had telephone exchanges, handling 45 million calls a year.

There were surprising successes. Buttons, previously unknown in Japan, became a major export by 1896. The textile-producing area of Lancashire in Britain inspired Japanese entrepreneurs to reorganize their country's cotton production. The value of the weaving output quadrupled in the 1890s. Cotton yarn production swelled more than sixfold to 250 million pounds—25 percent of Japan's total industrial output—by 1900. This was a remarkable achievement, because cotton textiles were one of the world's most competitive sectors. But to some extent, women's labor financed the enterprise by keeping costs down.

Two strategies were essential: first, expanding traditional economic activities and reinvesting the profits in new industries; and second, heavy investment by the state to kick start industrial enterprises. Exports of traditional Japanese products, especially raw silk and tea, paid for industrialization, taking up what would otherwise have been China's expanding markets. Raw silk was by far the main export, still accounting for over a third of Japan's export trade in the 1890s. By 1900, Japan exported practically as much silk as China.

Meanwhile, the strategy of involving state finance in the establishment of industry began to pay off, at the cost of huge losses for the treasury. In the 1880s, state enterprises sold off mining interests and textile centers to private companies. Shipyards, established to build warships in the 1850s and 1860s, diversified into civil engineering and the production of iron and steel for industry. The foundations of wealth were available at cut price. The Hiroshima Spinning Mill cost the state 49,000 yen to set up. It was sold to private investors for 12,000 yen. Great corporations, of the kind that still dominate Japanese economic life, such as Mitsui and Mitsubishi, were able to take advantage, thanks to connections with the government and to the wealth they had accumulated during the era of the Tokugawa shoguns (1603–1868). Powerful, dictatorial

The Tokyo terminus of the new Tokyo-Yokohama railway line, built in 1872 with the aid of foreign engineers. From a series of prints called "Famous Places on the Tokaido: A Record of the Process of Reform," it was published only seven years after the Meiji Restoration opened Japan to foreign trade and ideas in 1868.

company chairmen dominated them, but this was not a conservative style of leadership. On the contrary, it ensured that innovation for long-term success remained more important than short-term profiteering. Myths multiplied of heroic entrepreneurs, just like the heroic engineers in England whose lives Samuel Smiles romanticized. The head of Mitsui supposedly began his career as a newspaper boy, while the employee who rose to head Mitsubishi started in life by selling flowers. The theme of rags to riches was old and prominent in Japanese literature (see Chapter 19) and was probably an incentive or inspiration for capitalism. The Japanese government primed the pump with huge issues of coinage. Between 1816 and 1841, it increased the amount of money in circulation by 80 percent, and increased it by 50 percent more before it started cutting back in the 1880s.

Japan's was industrialization Japanese style—not a copy of that of the West. Japanese responded to the West by trying to adapt rather than ape, equal rather than imitate. Symbolically, the artist who drew one of Japan's first steam-powered factories in 1872, made the smoke from the factory chimneys curl in a pattern that matched the steam from the summit of Mount Fuji, the sacred volcanic mountain near Tokyo. Western theorists of the merits of private enterprise and enlightened self-interest were well known in Japan, and, indeed, some Japanese thinkers advocated them. "The government should never attempt to compete with the people in pursuing industry or commerce," wrote Matsukata Masayoshi in 1878. He claimed that self-interest made private enterprise efficient. But the Japanese preferred to see business as a form of service to the community and the state. They knew the laws of supply and demand, but preferred to regulate consumption for moral reasons. Industrialists claimed to have patriotic motives. Fukuzawa Yukichi (1835–1901) convinced samurai of the merit of trade "for profit and for Japan." His books and pamphlets sold 10 million copies in Japan in his lifetime. Eiichi Shibusawa, who spent a long time as the government minister responsible for industrial development, confessed that he began by thinking that only the military and political classes were honorable. "Then," he wrote, "I realized that the real force of progress lay in business."

These mental habits and convictions made collaboration between the state and the private sector easy. Government and business worked together. The Western division between the state and private enterprise did not apply. Industrialists collaborated with government to restrain domestic demand and prioritize strength for war. Governments responded with contracts and concessions. In part this was because some influential Japanese misunderstood Western models. Okuba Toshimichi, who visited the manufacturing cities of Birmingham and Glasgow in Britain in the 1870s, reported that there was "no instance" in Europe where "a country's productive power was increased without the patronage and encouragement of its officials." This was not a false observation, but the inference he drew was misleading. The engine of Western capitalism—unless you count Russia as Western—did not need the state to stoke it, only to keep hands off the damper.

More mattered than just profit. Japanese firms had strong corporate identities, whereas in the West, class divisions tended to prevent bosses and workers from developing close partnerships. Occasionally, Japanese investors behaved like those in other countries. The Kyoto Pottery Company collapsed in 1892 because shareholders grew impatient after five years without dividends. But investors generally seem to have preferred capital growth to quick rewards. As in the West, modern enterprises such as railways were disproportionately popular with investors. Cement manufacturers made low profits and rarely issued dividends, but they rejoiced in producing from "dirt at home" instead of spending "gold abroad." Similar attitudes prevailed in brick making, shipyards, and the gas industry.

The price was paid in more than cash. In the 1890s, the Ashio copper mines became a scandalous symbol of the costs of industrialization: rabid expansion, deforestation, flooded villages, and the poisoning of downstream waters. Nonetheless, the overall achievement of industrialization in Japan was remarkable. Compared with the beginning of the nineteenth century, Japan's national output of manufactured goods, raw materials, and agricultural products had quadrupled, and the proportion contributed by industry had at least doubled (see Map 23.7).

MAP 23.7

The Industrialization of Japan to 1918

Modernization under the Meiji

- main industrial areas by 1918
- railways built 1868–1918

Traditional industries

- ceramics
- textiles
- silk

Industries developed after 1868

- manufacturing
- machine building
- shipbuilding
- chemicals
- city of over 500,000 in 1918
- other major city

Li Hongzhang (1823–1901). The Chinese statesman and general Li Hongzhang was the chief negotiator of the treaty that ended the first Sino-Japanese War in 1895. In 1896, he also negotiated a treaty that granted Russia the right to build the Trans-Siberian railroad across northern Manchuria.

Feng Guifen on self-strengthening

CHINA AND INDUSTRIALIZATION

As so often in Chinese history, peasant rebellion, rather than foreign example, was the spur to change. Western industrialization should have alarmed Chinese officials and intellectuals in the first half of the nineteenth century. It eroded Chinese domination of the global economy and reversed the military balance of power—with effects that China painfully felt, as we shall see in the next chapter. But influential Chinese did not develop their response until 1861. They called it "**self-strengthening**."

In 1860, two events brought on a sense of crisis. First, huge areas fell into the hands of peasant revolutionaries, notably the Taipings, who mounted a serious threat to the ruling Manchu Qing dynasty from 1852 to 1864. Second, an Anglo-French army occupied Beijing, the Chinese capital. The immediate pretext for this invasion was an apparently trivial matter of diplomatic procedure: Chinese failure to comply with a promise to receive British and French ambassadors at the emperor's court in Beijing rather than in the southern city of Guangzhou. But the background included a series of incidents that convinced the Westerners that they had to humble China to secure freedom of action for Western merchants and missionaries (see Chapter 25).

While smarting under their humiliations, China's elites took comfort from the outcome. The Western barbarians clearly had no intention of trying to wrest the mandate of heaven from the Qing like earlier invaders. Their aims were commercial, and the Chinese could buy their goodwill with trade. The result was a new openness toward the barbarians whose armies the imperial government could hire to suppress the peasant rebels. Barbarian skills could perhaps be employed to strengthen China.

As an official memorandum of early 1861 put it, China had the chance "to snatch good fortune out of disaster, to transform weak to strong, this should provide China with cause of great rejoicing." Civil servants reporting to the emperor during this period insisted that the technology that gave the barbarians a present advantage was all of Chinese origin, anyway. They were largely right.

In November 1861, Wei Muting used these facts to sugar a bitter pill. China would have to relearn its old skills from the foreigners. Shipbuilding and munitions manufacture were technologies China could adopt from Europe. "Now that we know what they depend on for victory," agreed Prince Gong, the emperor's chief minister, "we should try to master it."

Because European soldiers of fortune and merchants helped the Chinese government suppress the Taiping rebellion, General Li Hongzhang could inspect Western munitions closely. "If China were to pay attention to these matters," he concluded, "she would be able to stand on her own a hundred years from now." He called for a revolution in values that would elevate technicians and engineers above scholars and writers. "Seek machines that make machines and men who make machines."

> Western machinery can produce farming, weaving, printing and pottery-making equipment for the daily use of the people. It is not solely for the purpose of making weapons. What is wondrous is that it utilizes the power of water and fire to save labor and material resources. . . . Several decades hence, among the rich peasants and prosperous merchants of China, there will inevitably be men who follow the example of Western machine manufacturing in their pursuit of profit.[1]

As in Japan, the early impact of mechanization was confined to munitions. The Jiangnan arsenal opened in 1865 to manufacture guns and ships. It also had a translation department charged with keeping up to date with Western knowledge in armaments. It was an important initiative but never managed to produce rifles as good or as cheap as imported models. Its ships cost twice as much as those available from competitors abroad. A naval yard inaugurated in 1866 built 40 ships, none of which performed well.

Zeng Guofan (dzung gwoh-fahn), the model administrator responsible for modernizing China, went on insisting that imperial rule and rites were perfect. "Propriety and righteousness" came above "expediency and ingenuity." After his death in 1872, the focus of self-strengthening switched to civilian industries, the infrastructure, and the economic basis of a strong state: civil steamships, mechanization of coal mining and textile manufacture, and the telegraph system. A railway-building boom, paid for with foreign capital, followed in the 1880s, linking coal mines and agricultural hinterlands to the ports. Yet China remained a preindustrial power. Private investment was channeled through state-run monopolies in all these fields.

In war against Japan over who would dominate Korea in 1894–1895, the difference between the belligerents showed. On paper the Chinese navy, which had cost more than Japan's, looked more formidable—bigger and more heavily armed with two ironclads of 7,000 tons each—than the Japanese navy, which had no ship bigger than 4,000 tons. But before the conflict, a Japanese officer was disgusted to see that piles of garbage littered the Chinese decks and that washing hung from the guns. The Chinese war machine was like "an overfired sword, no sharper than a rusty kitchen knife." The imperial household had diverted money for munitions to rebuild a palace outside Beijing that the British and French had burned in 1861. When battle began, the Chinese guns had only three rounds of ammunition each. Most of their ships avoided action. The Japanese captured or sank those that did fight.

China and the West were mutually blinded by perceptions of each other's barbarism. From 1840, the Opium Wars (see Chapter 25) exposed China's weakness and dispelled the Western respect for the empire and its people that had featured so prominently during the Enlightenment (see Chapter 22). In China, it was heresy to acknowledge the West as civilized. For Westerners, the Chinese were Asiatic barbarians to be treated with contempt. For most of the Chinese elite, the big problems were those of longest standing: the peasant uprisings, of which that of the Taipings was the most threatening; the unrest of Muslim minorities, whose rebellions the Qing repressed with difficulty; the erosion of state power to provincial bosses. Carefully measured deference to selective Western superiority seemed the best course. "Chinese essence, western practice" became the government's slogan after humiliating defeat in the Sino-Japanese war of 1894–1895.

In the 1880s, the tea trade shrank in the face of Indian competition. Although Chinese silk exports remained significant despite Japanese competition, new exports from China were geared to an industrializing world: primary foodstuffs intended for processing abroad, skins and straw, hog bristles and timber, coal and iron ore. Much of the trade supplied Japanese industries that were outstripping those of China. The era of dominance for China through its luxury products was largely over.

INDIA AND EGYPT

In the nineteenth century, India deindustrialized. Was this the inevitable result of the unbeatable competitiveness of mechanized textile production in Britain? Or was it a deliberate effect of empire, as the British wrecked India's industries to boost their own? It was probably a bit of both. India's traditional industries, particularly cotton textile weaving, began to collapse in the 1820s, before Britain had a systematic policy with regard to India. The disappearance of the great courts and armies of the Mughal era (see Chapter 21) left India without the motors of demand that once drove its economy. Indians had to turn back to the land.

The British made matters worse. They bureaucratized tax collection—cutting out native Indian capitalists. From an industrial giant, India became a producer of raw materials for the British Empire: tea, coffee, quinine, opium, jute, cotton. Early in the century, while the balance of trade with China was still unfavorable, Britain's trade drained cash from India's economy. Industrialization elsewhere lowered prices for Indian products. The export of labor began. Millions of Indian laborers emigrated in the second half of the century, most to work on construction projects or plantations elsewhere in the British Empire, in East Africa, the Pacific, or the Caribbean. India still had a favorable trading balance with its Asian trading partners, but not with Britain. The machinery of British cotton mills pulverized Indian manufactures. By the end of the nineteenth century, British-made textiles accounted for over a third of India's total imports. India bought two-fifths of Britain's cotton exports. The British set the tariffs to favor their own exports. British firms effectively monopolized India's shipping, insurance, and international banking. (see Map 23.8)

The British built a new economic infrastructure in India: dams, bridges, tunnels, roads, harbor installations, and, above all, as we have seen, railways. But the railways moved troops, administrators, travelers, and the primary goods the empire demanded. They did not contribute, as they did in Europe or North America, to internal industrialization.

In most of the rest of the world, industrial models of development had little appeal. Rulers wanted to get their hands on modern munitions—generally by buying them from the West—and to hire Western technicians to train their armies to use those armaments. In some places these minimal strategies achieved remarkable success. Elsewhere, rulers or elites welcomed Western investment to build railways and bridges, but rarely tried to start factories to compete with Western manufactures.

MAP 23.8

The Politics of Cotton

→ raw cotton from U.S. to Britain

→ cotton textiles to India

→ raw cotton from India to Britain

⬧ cotton-producing region

🏭 textile town

▨ major cotton-producing states

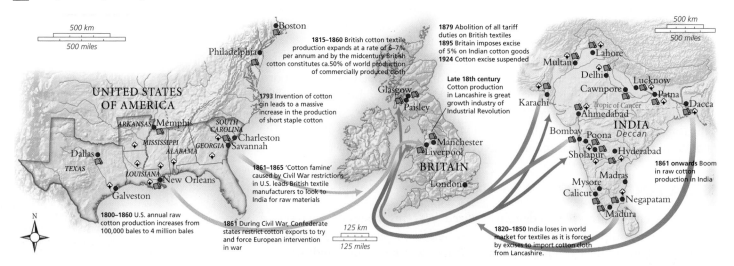

The big exception was Egypt. Its population had grown rapidly, even by nineteenth-century standards, from 2.5 million inhabitants in 1800 to 6.8 million in 1882. The passage of French Revolutionary armies through the country in 1798–1799 was an experience Egypt shared with much of Europe. While they were in Egypt, French officials saw opportunities for industrialization. They opened factories for guns, gunpowder, food, and beer. After they departed, the farsighted Mehmet Ali (MEH-meht A-lee) (1769–1849)—who, from 1805, was nominally the viceroy or khedive (heh-DEEV) for the Ottoman Empire but was, in effect, an independent monarch and the founder of a dynasty that ruled Egypt until 1953—bought in the services of Western, mostly French, experts to reproduce the activities already characteristic of industrializing Britain: cotton mills, munitions factories, steelworks, shipyards, a printing press. One of his French hired hands, Louis-Alexis Jumel, introduced a new strain of cotton that proved amazingly successful as the basis of fine textiles. In 1826, Mehmet Ali imported 500 steam-powered looms from Britain. About ten years later, Egypt was producing 1,200,000 bolts of cotton cloth a year. The industry was a state monopoly. Mehmet Ali suppressed private competitors. He found, however, that British industrialists were equally hostile to competition from him. In 1839, Britain forced Egypt to abandon protective tariffs when they blocked Mehemet Ali's attempt to overthrow the Ottoman Empire with French support. As a result, the Egyptian cotton industry dwindled, and Egypt, like the American South, became a major exporter of cash crops—sugarcane and raw cotton. Continuous irrigation was required to force the extra output, needed to support the military and government facade of a modern state, from the land. The peasants were impoverished and overburdened, and the opportunity to modernize on the Western European model slipped out of Egypt's grasp.

Egyptian intellectuals remained faithful to Western models of development. Rifaa Tahtawi (rih-FA tah-TA-wee) (1801–1871) introduced the notion of a secular state, and advocated universal education. Ali Pasha Mubarak (A-lee

The Suez Canal. The French artist Edouard Rion (1833–1900) went to Suez to record Egyptian life for the French illustrated press just before the opening of the canal. Engravings of many of his paintings—including this bustling interpretation of the inaugural procession of ships through the canal in November 1869—appeared as illustrations to the account of the canal's construction written by Ferdinand de Lesseps, the canal's promoter and chief engineer.

Industrialization in Global Context

1798–1799	French armies occupy Egypt
Nineteenth century	India deindustrializes
1800–1850	Dramatic increase in steam-driven industrial capacity in Europe
1805–1849	Rule of Mehmet Ali in Egypt, proponent of industrialization
1835–1918	Andrew Carnegie, American industrialist
1839	Britain forces Egypt to end protection of cotton industry
1846–1848	Mexican-American War
July 8, 1853	Commodore Perry sails into Tokyo Bay
Mid–nineteenth century	Japanese industrialization focuses on military technology
1860	Peasant revolutionaries take control of large parts of China
	Anglo-French army occupies Beijing
1861	China begins "self-strengthening" program
1877–1900	Japan's foreign trade increases tenfold
1890s	United States produces twice as much steel as Britain
1895	Japan defeats China in war over Korea
1900	Nine European cities have populations of more than a million

PAH-shah moo-BAH-rahk) (1824–1893) produced Western-inspired writings and public works for the government on engineering, fortifications, irrigation, mechanized agriculture. Khedive Ismail (heh-DEEV ihs-mah-EEL) (r. 1863–1879), Mehemet Ali's grandson, tried to revive his grandfather's program. Ismail proclaimed Egypt part of Europe. Borrowing money at outrageous interest from European bankers, he built docks, sugar mills, an opera house in Cairo, and a school for girls. He had the Suez Canal driven across Egyptian land using French engineers and French capital. The canal opened in 1869 and, by connecting the Mediterranean to the Red Sea, reduced the sailing time from Europe to India and the Far East from months to weeks (see Map 23.3). But his extravagances bankrupted the state. In 1875, Britain purchased Ismail's shares in the canal. In 1879, his European creditors forced Ismail to abdicate. Much of Egypt's revenue was assigned to repay foreign debts, and 1,300 foreign bureaucrats arrived to manage the country's finances and armed forces. In September 1881, the handful of native Egyptian officers still left in high ranks rebelled under the slogan "Egypt for the Egyptians."

Britain responded by occupying key parts of the country "to save," as a British official claimed, "Egypt from anarchy, and all European nations interested in Egypt from incalculable losses in blood and treasure." The intervention was probably more self-interested than the rhetoric implied. Egypt became, in effect, a British dependency with a puppet government and a large British garrison until after the Second World War.

IN PERSPECTIVE: Why the West?

In 1800, China was probably about eight times as productive as Britain. By 1900, Britain produced about three times as much as China. In 1800, Britain and Germany combined contributed less than 5 percent of global industrial production. By 1900, those two countries alone accounted for nearly a third of the output of the world's industries. China's share in the same period fell from over a third to barely 6 percent (see Figure 23.1). Industrialization had dwarfed a giant and hoisted jacks-of-all-trades to the top of the beanstalk. Why did the West beat the rest—or most of the rest, if we include Japan—to the benefits of industrialization?

The West had few of the advantages commonly alleged. Traditional Western values, which were those of the landed aristocracy and the church, were industrialization's antibodies, training elites to have contempt for trade. Factories went up in a world where, according to the English essayist William Hazlitt (1778–1830), "people were always talk-

FIGURE 23.1 SHARE OF WORLD MANUFACTURING OUTPUT, 1750–1900

Derived from B. R. Tomlinson, "Economics: The Periphery." in Andrew Porter (ed.). *The Oxford History of the British Empire: The Nineteenth Century,* Oxford 1990, p. 69 (Table 3.8).

Shares of World Manufacturing Output, 1750–1900

	1750	1800	1830	1860	1880	1900
Europe	23.1	28.0	34.1	53.6	62.0	63.0
China	32.8	33.3	29.8	19.7	12.5	6.2
India	24.5	19.7	17.6	8.6	2.8	1.7

ing of the Greeks and Romans." Nor did Europe's supposedly scientific culture breed industry. The late eighteenth-century inventors of industrial processes—coke smelting, mechanized spinning, steam pumping, and the steam-driven loom—were all heroes of what Samuel Smiles called self-help. They were self-taught artisans or entrepreneurs with little or no formal scientific training. Science had no inbuilt practical vocation until the late nineteenth century. It would be fairer to say that industry hijacked European science—bought it for useful research, diverted it to social responsibility. Nor is it enough—though it is important—to say that the distribution of coal and iron privileged some economies for industrialization. In some places outside the West and beyond Western control, coal and iron reserves were left unexploited. In others, such as New England and parts of northern Spain and Italy, determined industrializers found ways to compensate for the lack of them.

The West's real advantage was commercial. Commerce makes specialization possible. Without extensive systems of long-range trade, large concentrations of labor dedicated to manufacturing particular items or producing particular primary products are impossible. In the eighteenth and nineteenth centuries, Western Europe and North America were excellent environments for banking and what would now be called financial services industries, thanks to the climate of economic liberalism (see Chapter 22), and the commitment of states to foster commerce. Europe was not unique in this respect. Capitalism and commercial entrepreneurship were also ingrained in many communities and ruling elites in Asia. In China, however, commerce did not enjoy the same level of support from the state. Moreover, China was slow to change this attitude in the nineteenth century.

The pace of commerce is a function of the size of the market, and it is worth noting that European populations experienced exceptionally high growth rates in the nineteenth century. The population of Europe more than doubled to over 400 million in 1900, even though during the same century over 40 million Europeans migrated to other continents. Was this increase a cause or effect of industrialization? At least we can say that population growth was particularly strong in the most industrialized zones. The populations of Belgium, Britain, and Germany all rose faster than the average.

Westerners, finally, came from behind. That is where innovation usually comes from, because leaders in any field have little interest in promoting change. Economies like those of India and China, which had productive traditional industries and enormous reserves of labor, felt no call to mechanize.

CHRONOLOGY

1780–1831	Karl von Clausewitz, developer of theory of "total war"
1798–1799	French armies occupy Egypt
Nineteenth century	India deindustrializes
ca. 1800	Global population: 950 million; areas with regions in excess of four people per square mile: East Asia, southeast Asia, India, Western Europe
1800–1850	Increase in steam-driven industrial capacity: Britain, Spain, Italy, Belgium doubled; France, Russia tripled; Czech Republic increased fivefold; Germany increased sixfold
1804	First successful railroad locomotion
1805–1849	Reign of Mehmet Ali in Egypt, proponent of industrialization
1807	First commercial steamboat
1835–1918	Andrew Carnegie, American industrialist
1839	Britain forces Egypt to end protection of cotton industry
1846–1848	Mexican-American War
Mid–nineteenth century	Japanese industrialization focuses on military technology
1850–1900	500 million acres added to United States farmland
1850s	British imports of guano reach 200,000 tons per year
July 8, 1853	Commodore Perry sails into Tokyo Bay
1857	Sepoy Mutiny in India
1860	Peasant revolutionaries take control of large parts of China; Anglo-French army occupies Beijing
1860–1900	Japanese coal production rises from 390,000 to 5 million tons; British coal production in South Wales rises from 11.4 million to 35.1 million
1861–1865	American Civil War
1861	China begins "self-strengthening" program
1866	British output of chemical fertilizers reaches 250,000 tons
1869	First transcontinental railroad in United States
1870s	Australian engineers develop compressed-gas cooler; Belgium leads world in iron- and steel-making equipment
1877–1900	Japan's foreign trade increases tenfold
1890s	United States produces twice as much steel as Britain
1895	Japan defeats China in war over Korea
Late nineteenth century	Belgium and Netherlands develop increasingly complementary economies
1900	German coal production reaches 100 million tons annually; Argentina exports 100 million bushels of wheat per year; global population: 1.6 billion; nine European cities have populations of more than a million

Industrialization was disastrous for many of the people who took it up. Like the ancient adoption of farming, it had adverse consequences for nutrition, health, and what we would now call quality of life. It nourished oppression and tyranny. So why did people accept it—why, indeed, did they relish it so much that almost every community that has had the chance to industrialize over the last 200 years has opted to do so?

Industrialization had one immediately obvious benefit—it released land for food production. It was no longer necessary, for instance, to maintain forests to provide wood for fuel. Forests in England halved between 1800 and 1900. The conservation policies of eighteenth-century Japan (see Chapter 20) were abandoned. In the nineteenth century, the carefully husbanded woodlands that formerly covered much of the islands of Honshu, Kyushu, and Shikoku largely vanished as coal replaced wood as a source of fuel, and Japan devoted more land to agriculture. The opposite happened in much of New England, where the rock-ribbed soil, which had largely been under the plow in 1800, began to revert to forest as food production shifted westward in the 1820s and 1830s.

Second, as we shall see in Chapter 24, the long-term consequences of industrialization tended to spread the benefits surprisingly widely. In its early stages, mechanization hugely increased the burden of labor for the workers who operated the machines. But it was labor saving for others. And technical improvements gradually liberated even the machine workers to enjoy increased leisure.

Finally, it is worth dwelling for a moment on the example of agrarianization. As readers of earlier parts of this book know, early farming communities adopted new production methods despite adverse short-term effects. In part, this was because most people—especially those most likely to suffer, because they were poor and powerless—had no say in decision making. Industrialization, like farming, was an elite option. It appealed to people whose power it increased. It enabled the controllers of industrial wealth to join or replace existing elites, and it empowered industrialized and industrializing communities to dominate the rest of the world and extort or exploit its resources.

PROBLEMS AND PARALLELS

1. How did fat—oil from animals, plants, and minerals—make the world of the nineteenth century work? What other sources of energy were exploited in the nineteenth century?

2. How did the population explosion of the nineteenth century lead to new ways to exploit and use the Earth's resources?

3. Why did population increase not conform to Malthusian logic?

4. Why was the incorporation of the vast, open lands of Argentina, Brazil, Australia, and North America so important?

5. How did industrialization revolutionize the world's food supply?

6. How did militarization and industrialization put intense pressure on the world's energy sources in the nineteenth century?

7. What are the explanations for nineteenth-century industrialization? Why did industrialization have social consequences?

8. Why did Japan industrialize more rapidly than China?

9. How did industrialization affect India and Egypt?

DOCUMENTS IN GLOBAL HISTORY

- James Fenimore Cooper, from *The Praire*
- Anthony Trollope, from *North America*
- Karl von Clausewitz, from *On War*

- Fanny Kemble, from *Records of a Girlhood*
- Feng Guifen on self-strengthening

Please see the Primary Source CD-ROM for additional sources related to this chapter.

READ ON

C. A. Bayly, *The Birth of the Modern World* (2004) is an insuperable survey of global history in the nineteenth century. E. A. Wrigley, *Peoples, Cities and Wealth: the Transition of Traditional Society* (1989) provides an overview of some of the most conspicuous issues. P. N. Stearns, *The Industrial Revolution in World History* (1998) is an introductory essay.

On food, F. Fernández-Armesto, *Near a Thousand Tables* (2003) is a short, general history. J. Burnett, *Plenty and Want* (1988) surveys the topic for Britain. J. Goody, *Cooking, Cuisine and Class* (1982) is an ingenious, anthropologically informed work that opens up comparative perspectives. P. N. Stearns, *Fat History* (2002) studies attitudes to fat in France and the USA. On famine, M. Davis, *Late Victorian Holocausts* (2002) is important and challenging.

On the domestication of the prairie, W. Cronon, *Nature's Metropolis* (1991) is essential reading. R W. Paul, *The Far West and the Great Plains in Transition* (1998) is an excellent study. W. Cronon et al., eds., *Under an Open Sky* (1993) includes some important essays. On fertilizers W. M. Mathew, *The House of Gibbs and the Peruvian Guano Monopoly* (1981) is a most helpful monograph. On Burbank, F. W. Clampett, *Luther Burbank* (1926) provides a rather uncritical outline.

On the militarisation of society, E. Weber, *Peasants into Frenchmen* (1979) is a classic study. P. Paret, *Clausewitz and the State* (1985) is a useful study of Clausewitz's work in social and political perspective.

G. R. Taylor, *The Transportation Revolution* (1951) is an old but still authoritative study of the infrastructure of industrialization. On the industrialization of Europe, T. Kemp, *Industrialization in Nineteenth-century Europe* (1969) provides an overview. D. Landes *The Unbound Prometheus* (1969) is a classic survey. P. N. Stearns, *Lives of Labor* (1975) takes a comparative approach focussed on workers' experience.

On Britain and France, P. O'Brien and R. Quainault, eds., *The Industrial Revolution and British Society* (1993), and P. O'Brien and C. Keyder, *Economic Growth in Britain and France* (1978) are in some respects correctives of the still important classic study, P. Mathias, *The First Industrial Nation* (1969). T. Zeldin, *France 1848–1945*, 2 vols, (1973) is a wonderful book: sensitive and stimulating with an impressively original method. For Germany, T. Pierenkemper and R. Tilly, *The German Economy during the Nineteenth Century* (2005) is a good brief introduction. J. Mokyr, *Industrialization in the Low Countries* (1976) is basic. E. H. Kossmann, *The Low Countries 1798–1914* (1978), and J. C. H. Blom and E. Lamberts, eds., *History of the Low Countries* (1998) provide useful overviews. J.L. Van Zanden, *The Economic Development of the Netherlands since 1870* (1996) includes a brief history of Dutch indutrialization. J. de Vries and A. van de Woude, *The First Modern Economy* (1997) is an influential survey of pre-nineteenth century Dutch economic history. Spain is superbly covered by D. Ringrose, *Madrid and the Spanish Economy* (1983), and N. Sanchez-Albornoz, ed., *The Economic Modernization of Spain* (1987). For Italy, J. Cohen and G. Federico, *The Growth of the Italian Economy* (2001) is an efficient introduction. D. C. North, *The Economic Growth of the United States* (1966) is a venerable and reliable work. G. J. Kornblith, ed., *The Industrial Revolution in America* (1998) contains some stimulating essays. M. Girouard, *The Return to Camelot* (1981), and D. C. Lieven, *The Aristocracy in Europe 1815–1914* (1993), are helpful on the survival of an aristocratic ethos in the industrializing West.

J. Batou, ed., *Between Development and Underdevelopment* (1991) is an important collection on attempts at industrialization in the extra-Western world in the nineteenth century.

R. Bin Wong, *China Transformed: Historical Change and the Limits of European Experience* (2002) is of fundamental importance; L. Aiguo, *China and the Global Economy since 1840* (1999) is a helpful introductory work. India is covered in D. Kumar, ed., *The Cambridge Economic History of India, II* (2005), and I.J. Ker, *Building the Railways of the Raj* (1998). M.B. Jansen, ed., *The Cambridge History of Japan V* (1995), and S. Sugiyama, *Japan's Industrialization in the World Economy* (1988) deal with Japan; S. Hanley and K. Yamamura, *Economic and Demographic Change in Pre-industrial Japan* (1967) is valuable on the background and takes a critically acute approach to controversial issues in historical demography. On the Middle East, R. Owen, *Cotton and the Egyptian Economy* (1969), and *The Middle East and the World Economy* (1993). C. Issawi, ed., *The Fertile Crescent, 1800–1914* (1988) is a useful economic overview of the Middle East, with many documents. P. J. Vatikiotis, *The History of Modern Egypt* (1991) is an outstanding survey.

Debate on the reasons for the West's great leap forward is mainly conducted in K. Pomeranz, *The Great Divergence* (2001); A. Gunder Frank, *ReOrient*; D. Landes, *The Wealth and Poverty of Nations* (1999); and J. Goody, *The East in the West* (1996).

CHAPTER 24

The Social Mold: Work and Society in the Nineteenth Century

Akira Kurosawa's epic movie of 1954, *The Seven Samurai*, was set in the Japan of the sixteenth century, but it depicted the predicament of the samurai in modern times. By the nineteenth century, the samurai had become an obsolete class, whose prestige and wealth had been diminished by social, economic, and political changes. But in their own eyes, and in those of most Japanese, they still embodied timeless values of honor and courage. In the movie, the seven find work as mercenaries, defending villagers from bandits. In the process, they teach the peasants the art of war, thus rendering themselves—and by extension, all samurai—useless.

As the police closed in, four fugitives struggled in bitter March cold through the mountains south of Osaka, Japan. When the first one faltered, his companions accepted his offer to commit ritual suicide. Indeed, they helped by slicing off his head. Another one soon dropped from exhaustion and then hanged himself from a tree.

Now only Oshio Heihachiro—a former police magistrate who had led an unsuccessful rebellion—and his son were left. They doubled back to their home city, disguised as priests, and forced a former client to take them in. When the police caught up with them, Oshio's son wanted to flee, but, screaming, "Coward! Coward!" Oshio stabbed him to death, set fire to the house, stood defiantly on the threshold, slashed his own throat, and perished amid the flames on May 1, 1837. When his charred remains were carried off, the heat had so bloated and twisted his head that he looked, said onlookers, like a great toad.

In Japan, Oshio has always been regarded as a hero, despite, or perhaps because of, his horrific suicide. He was a member of the hereditary warrior caste—a samurai and proud of it—who had grown up believing that nobles' obligations to the poor were more important than their privileges over them. Early in his career, he acquired a reputation as an infallible and incorruptible detective, rooting out secret practitioners of Christianity—which still had faithful followers, 200 years after Japan banned the religion—and exposing scandals in the administration. He then retired, after a mystical vision, to meditate and found a small school.

The circumstances that drove him to rebellion were not new. But It was a new kind of revolt in Japanese history. For the first time, noble samurai made common cause with the poor and the peasants against the middle class. As had happened so often before in Japan, and as happened sooner or later in every society dependent on one staple crop, the 1830s were a decade of rice failures and famine. In 1837, as the price of rice reached unprecedented levels, Oshio saw poor people dying of starvation in the streets of Osaka. Yet the state granaries were well stocked, and the officials who ran them and got rich by driving up prices were shipping rice to the capital. Oshio petitioned local officials to open the warehouses, but they threatened him with prosecution for meddling where he had no official status.

JAPAN

FOCUS questions

- HOW DID industrialization change society and the economy?
- WHY WAS Marx wrong in predicting that industrialization would lead to violent revolution?
- WHY WERE the slave trade and slavery abolished in the nineteenth century?
- WHY WERE some aristocracies able to adapt to the changes industrialization brought?

He sold his library, bought a cannon and muskets, and hired an artillery expert to train his men in the use of firearms. He then issued a summons to revolt, promising to "visit Heaven's vengeance" on the officials and merchants, and calling on peasants to join the revolt and burn the tax records on which the authorities relied. He stressed, sincerely, that he did not aim to seize power, only to right injustice.

The modernization and industrialization of Japan (see Chapter 23) would soon destroy Oshio's world. But his type of revolt, and the kind of alliance of aristocrats and peasants he led, was repeated over and over. Not just in Japan but wherever they arose, the new kinds of wealth that commerce and, in some places, industry generated threatened to subvert traditional society by diminishing the old role of aristocracies, elevating the middle class, reducing and ruining peasants, creating an industrial working class, and eliminating traditional forms of labor such as slavery and serfdom.

● ● ● ● ●

In the nineteenth century, Oshio's call was echoed in surprising places around the world. In Bengal in India, for instance, a landlords' agent, Titu Mir, led a peasant revolt against moneylenders, tax collectors, and rent gougers in 1831. In England, at about the same time, conservative aristocrats saw workers and landowners as natural allies in a struggle to save the old economy of the land against the new economy of capital. In North America, some slave owners appealed to their slaves to fight alongside them against would-be liberators who wanted to subordinate the states to the federal government. In Latin America aristocratic rebels recruited peasant guerrillas to fight in civil wars. In France middle-class intellectuals—typified by the apologist of terrorism, Auguste Blanqui (1805–1881)—dreamed of leading the masses to progress. In the Ottoman Empire Butrus Bustani, a Western-influenced aristocrat, spoke up for rebellious peasants in Lebanon in the midcentury. In Russia the great novelist, Count Leo Tolstoy (1828–1910), renounced his wealth and adopted a peasant's way of life.

Traditional resentments—of merchants by aristocrats, of profiteers by peasants—grew with the growing wealth gaps of the age. Increasing trade generated new wealth, but little of it reached the workers who grew and mined raw materials in the unindustrialized world. And it took a long time even for industrial workers in the West to obtain a substantial share in the new prosperity. As the pace of commerce speeded up, and its reach broadened, so did the range of economic opportunities and rewards, and so did the numbers of people worldwide who were left behind or left out. Industrialization accelerated these effects. And it affected more than just the regions in which it happened, because it made global wealth gaps gape ever more widely, turning some regions and peoples into suppliers of staple products for consumers in industrial economies that were located hundreds or even thousands of miles away.

Even in unindustrialized societies, economic status rivaled age-old ways of determining people's place in society—parentage, ancestry, birthplace, learning, strength, sanctity. Where industry flourished, social change was even more convulsive. Instead of identifying with communities that embraced people at all levels of rank and prosperity—neighborhoods, cities, provinces, sects, families, clans, big households, ethnic groups—people, uprooted and regrouped in industrial centers, came to define themselves in terms of wealth or what they increasingly called class.

It was a common assumption of nineteenth-century observers in the West that the world was being redrawn on class lines. Some governments even adopted class as a way to categorize their populations. Everyone fit into the world as a noble, a bourgeois, a peasant, or a worker. In Europe, the German revolutionary philosopher Karl Marx (1818–1883) championed a new theory of history: that all change was part and product of inevitable **class struggles** that pitted the rich against those whom they exploited.

Marx's view was exaggerated, but it helps to show how people at the time perceived the often traumatic social changes that accompanied the economic changes of the nineteenth century.

This chapter is about how people fit into this changing world: the spaces they occupied, the way their work patterns altered, the shifts in the nature and location of labor, the new relationships people developed, the shaken kaleidoscope of class and rank. In the first half of the chapter, we concentrate on industrializing societies, because they exerted a disproportionate influence on everyone else. After looking at the differences that industrialization made to people's lives and experiences of work in industrializing areas, we shall turn to changes in the way labor was recruited and distributed beyond—and in the shadow of—the industrializing world, and finally to the way industrialization affected the elites, who employed or commanded that labor.

Karl Marx, from *The Communist Manifesto*

THE INDUSTRIALIZED ENVIRONMENT

Machines created unprecedented differences of power and wealth: between regions and countries, of course, but also, within industrializing regions, between classes, sexes, and generations.

Palaces of Work: The Rise of Factories

Industrialization transformed the way people worked and the places they worked in. It is easy to say that—especially now, when the age of the vast factories is over in much of the West. But at the time, industrialization was a strange experience for those caught up in changes that seemed disruptive, disturbing, and often hard to endure. Work moved from country to city, from outdoors indoors, from homes and small workshops into factories and mines, from relatively healthy to relatively unhealthy environments: deafening, psychologically straining, mentally exhausting, personally alienating, in ways that the traditional rural economy had never been. One kind of traditional workplace practically disappeared in industrializing societies. In the past, small groups of workers had shared intimate surroundings: workshops in which a few equals or near equals collaborated, or households in which a master craftsman marshaled apprentices who lived together like a large family. Now seismic social upheavals raised factories, like "smoking volcanoes" (as contemporaries said), burying the world of artisans and flattening the traditional social hierarchies.

Factories were new settings that reorganized work and reordered life. They are the best markers of the changes industrialization brought. They made startlingly different impressions on different people, but the passions they inspired—for and against— were always profound. For their admirers, factories represented a truly noble achievement: proof of progress, a seemingly magical extension of human power over the rest of nature, a romantic adventure in making a new future for humankind. In 1802–1803, for instance, the German artist, C. A. G. Goede, traveling between the industrial cities of Birmingham and Shrewsbury in England, marveled at "mountain and valley in flames" for miles around, where "fire-spitting volcanoes" turn the horizon purple, "beautifully lit by the gleaming glow of coal. One might believe oneself in Vulcan's workshop"—the forge of the ancient Roman god who supposedly stoked the world's volcanoes. Indeed, there were no precedents, except in myth, for what machines could do. The power of mechanization did make people feel godlike. The ways early nineteenth-century artists painted factories are full of echoes of volcanic imagery.

Early depictions, moreover, show factories in remarkable harmony with nature, sited in the countryside for convenient access to raw materials. The French artist Philippe-Jacques de Loutherbourg painted Coalbrookdale in England in 1801, with furnaces ablaze in a cozy pastoral setting. In 1830, Karl Schurz painted the new Lendersdorf steel works, near Cologne in Germany, in the style of a farmyard scene against a background of rolling hills. Only the smoke from the chimneys hints at the revolutionary nature of the activity under the rather rickety roof. William Ibbitt painted mid–nineteenth-century Sheffield, another English industrial center, as an ideal city, merging into the surrounding light, clean despite the smoke of the 50 factory chimneys that rose parallel with the spires of churches. On a hill in the foreground, workers relax, children play, a middle-class family surveys the city with pride.

Even as they got bigger and multiplied, factories were still remarkable creations of the imagination: spaces of a type never before conceived and, therefore, never before designed. Architects sought models from the ancient world and fiction, raising fantasy buildings, bristling with turrets, battlements, spires, and domes, to be what contemporaries called cathedrals of work or castles of industry. In a newspaper's praise of the factories of Sabadell, outside Barcelona in Spain, in 1855, we can detect all the emotions factory builders invested in their efforts. "These factories, grand and elegant . . . are sumptuous palaces that ought to inspire their owners and all the people with pride. . . . These palaces house no pharaohs, no orgies, but are a means of life for hundreds of families. These palaces are not there to inspire insanity or arrogance, but love of work and respect for effort and for merit." The words express genuine belief in the nobility of work. The language also reveals the power hunger of industrialists who based their claims to wealth and influence on merit rather than wealth. The moral tone of bosses' **paternalism** leaps from the page. More than just money inspired industrialization at its best.

Paternalism also made economic and political sense. One of the big problems for historians of industrialization is to explain why people left the land for factories and the country for the towns. Most of those who did probably had no choice. The mechanization of agriculture reduced the amount of rural work available. Landowners' own

Unthreatening industry. William Ibbitt's engraving of industrial Sheffield, in northern England, in the mid–nineteenth century, depicts the towering factories, which rival the city's churches, the outpouring smoke, and the huge sprawl of the growing city. But, nestling in nature, industry seems at ease with the environment, and traditional rural life is undisturbed in the foreground.

economies of scale concentrated more land in fewer hands. Global specialization shifted production of food and industrial raw materials out of the industrializing world, leaving some rural workforces unemployed. Yet the very success of industrialization meant that factory owners had to compete with one another for labor, as industries multiplied and businesses crowded the marketplace. Farsighted factory owners, moreover, realized that contented workers were the most productive.

Some entrepreneurs were genuinely motivated by vision or vocation, by religion and charitable sentiments. The British writer Samuel Smiles spoke of the spirit of industry as "the gospel of work." Henry J. Heinz (1844–1919) of Pittsburgh epitomized that spirit. His example can stand for hundreds. His pious Lutheran family had immigrated to Pennsylvania

Fantasy castle. Barcelona's factories made perhaps the most extravagant ensemble anywhere of "palaces of progress." The Casarramona factory was designed in 1910 by Josep Puit i Cadafalch, a figure of heroic stature in antiquarian scholarship, art patronage, and Catalan politics, as well as an architect of high repute and enormous influence. He experimented with a variety of medieval sources of inspiration and made this textile factory into a Moorish fantasy castle, with minaret-like towers.

from Germany, and his early ambition was to be a minister. Biblical quotations filled the notebooks in which, in his teens, he began to collect recipes for pickles and catsup. When he made a fortune from his canned and bottled food business, Heinz chose a famous slogan: "57 Varieties," not because there were really 57 of them—there were soon many more—but because the number came to him during a vision while he was riding an elevated railway in New York City. The vast factory he built in Pittsburgh resembled a church, with huge arches and stained-glass windows. In its workers' cafeteria, organ music entertained the diners. Heinz treated his employees as members of a religious congregation. They were expected to work hard. In 1888, entry-level employees got five cents an hour for a ten and-one-half hour day—lower wages than many other local employers paid.

But Heinz provided generous benefits, calculated for the common good of everyone in the firm. His workers, for instance, got free uniforms, medical and dental treatment, and, if they handled food, a daily manicure. There were dressing rooms with hot showers, a gymnasium, a roof garden, and a reading room. The firm organized employees' recreation. Heinz had carriages to take workers for rides in the park and hired trains for outings to local beauty spots. He provided lectures, concerts, and free courses in dressmaking, hatmaking, cooking, drawing, singing, and citizenship. There were four dances a year, at which, a worker recalled, "Mr. Heinz stayed on the balcony, waving down at us," and a Christmas party, where Mr. Heinz welcomed Santa Claus. Critics branded this style of management as paternalist and self-serving, but Heinz's methods had a strong and, in their own way, a genuinely benevolent message: capital and labor were not inevitable enemies but natural allies. Management—not exploitation and profiteering—was the key to success. Heinz's good works went beyond the factory walls and the employees' lives. His philosophy stressed the purity of his products. In a period when state controls on hygiene were in their infancy, and mass-produced food was often watered down or even polluted, Heinz delivered nutritious, safe food, and he made it pay.

 Samuel Smiles, from *Self Help*

Critics of Industrialization: Gold from the Sewers

Philanthropic industrialization was important, because it showed that industry did not only benefit people who were already rich. It could spread the benefits of prosperity widely and increase leisure for workers as well as bosses. Its reach, however, was limited. Most bosses did not share Heinz's devotion to good works. And with

PULLMAN, ILLINOIS

Pullman, Illinois, shown here in a diagram, was a town of 12,000 inhabitants at its height in the early 1890s. George Pullman built the town to house workers to produce luxury railway carriages in his enormous factory. His aim was to extract more productivity by providing a morally elevating environment for workers to live in. In practice, however, they resented living in dreary paternalism "under Mr. Pullman's thumb."

The uniform streets were designed in an imitation gothic style. Residents could be evicted at ten days' notice. When Pullman cut wages, he did not cut rents.

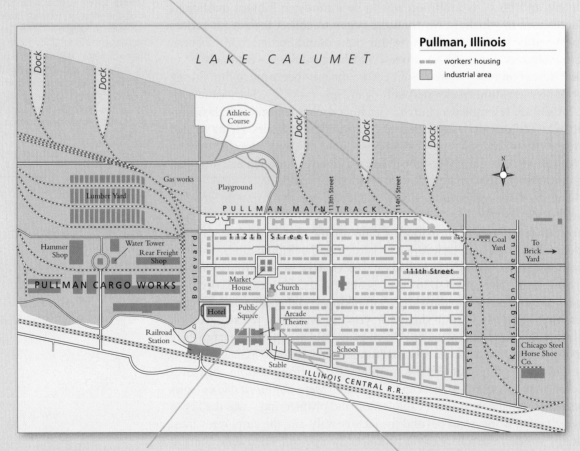

Pullman, Illinois

- - - workers' housing
industrial area

LAKE CALUMET

Dock · Dock · Dock · Dock · Dock

Athletic Course

Gas works

Lumber Yard

Playground

PULLMAN MAIN TRACK

113th Street · 114th Street

N

Hammer Shop

Water Tower Rear Freight Shop

112th Street

Coal Yard

To Brick Yard

PULLMAN CARGO WORKS

Market House

Church

111th Street

Boulevard

Hotel

Public Square

Arcade Theatre

Kensington Avenue

Railroad Station

School

115th Street

Chicago Steel Horse Shoe Co.

Stable

ILLINOIS CENTRAL R.R.

The church remained empty because no congregation could afford the rent Pullman demanded. The church, he said, was there "not for moral or spiritual welfare" but for "artistic effect."

The glass-roofed Arcade was an indoor shopping mall. The adjoining theater censored "immoral pieces." Pullman allowed no bars or liquor stores in the town.

How does the layout of Pullman embody nineteenth-century paternalism?

the rush to industrialize came unplanned evils. Outside the relatively few exemplary factories and model industrial towns, in the streets and slums that the concentration of labor created, the effort to erect a romantic environment for the industrial society was a horrible failure.

Industrialization plunged workers into misery: uprooting lives, disrupting families, imposing bleak new working conditions, throwing up hideous cities rife with filth and disease (see Map 24.1). Visiting the British city of Manchester in 1835, the French writer Alexis de Tocqueville, who was widely admired as the greatest analyst of the societies of his time, recoiled from the atmosphere of the "palaces" of industry. "These vast structures," he wrote, "keep air and light out of the human habitations which they dominate; they envelop them in perpetual fog; here is the slave, there is the master; there is the wealth of some, here the poverty of most.... Here humanity attains its most complete development and its most brutish; here civilization effects its miracles, and civilized man is turned back almost into a savage." He found "men, women and children yoked together to the machine, which knows no weariness." Yet "from this filthy sewer, pure gold flows." A popular hymn called on Englishmen to build Jerusalem among "dark satanic mills." The will to do so was certainly present, but the task was evidently overambitious.

Karl Marx foretold that industrialization would aggravate class warfare. At first, as he contemplated the industrializing world in the 1830s and 1840s, it looked as if he must be right. Industrialization increased the opportunities for people at all levels of society to indulge sociable habits—including, of course, those of riot and rebellion. Employers—despite many glowing examples of good works and kind bosses—commonly set out to exploit their workers to the limit. Workers, Marx thought, must soon discover their power, realize that their labor was the source of society's wealth, and demand their fair share of prosperity. The result would be a bloody revolution, in which the working class, or **proletariat**, would overthrow the bourgeoisie and impose its own dictatorship. "Workers of the world arise," he proclaimed in 1848, "you have nothing to lose but your chains!" Riots, if not rebellions, were commonplace in industrializing cities. Socialists, who demanded that workers should get the full economic benefits of their labor, threatened—and sometimes shattered—civil peace.

Yet, in the world's most industrialized societies, Marx's warnings that impoverishment would drive the workers to revolution went unfulfilled. In part, this was because those warnings were heeded in time. Workers soon had more than chains to lose. Increasingly, they had a genuine stake in the societies of which they formed part. In the second half of the nineteenth century, reformers responded with a new concept: "public health"—sewers and clean water provided by municipal authorities. The rise of town planning was in part the triumph of a romantic sense of the beauty of light and air, but it also showed the power of industrial capitalism to "improve." Light and air contributed to public health. The uniformity of the grid plan for city streets spoke to the depths of an ideal of social equality. Governments stepped up their services to their citizens, especially by regulating health, education, and the food supply.

Meanwhile, moral restraint, Christian good works, and "enlightened self-interest" blunted the fangs of industrial capitalism and helped to ensure, in the long run, that workers benefited from the wealth industries created. Warned, perhaps, by prophets like Marx and the social movements he helped to inspire, or driven by the energy of the market, employers raised wages and improved

MAP 24.1

The Growth of Manchester, 1840–1900

- - - - railway
▪ railway station
▪ park
▪ built-up area 1840
▫ growth of city 1840–1900

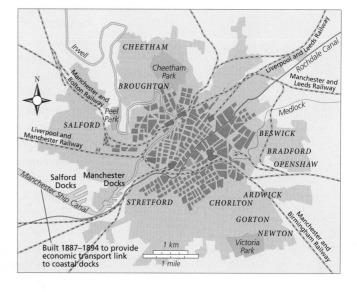

Instant metropolis. In the second half of the nineteenth century, exploitation of the North American prairie and the development of commerce on the Great Lakes turned Chicago from a small fort and trading post into a vast city. This image was made in 1892, when the city shaped its World's Fair to mark the 400th anniversary of the European discovery of the New World.
Dagli Orti (A)/Picture Desk, Inc./Kobal Collection

A Luddite pamphlet

working conditions. Cheap food, better pay, and declining disease smothered or at least diminished revolutionary inclinations. Prosperity bought out proletarian rage. As William Cobbett (1763–1835), one of the leading English reformers of the early nineteenth century, observed, "You can't agitate a man on a full stomach."

Businesses and governments were not inspired by pure benevolence. States wanted to be able to recruit large and effective armies. Employers realized that good wages and healthy workforces enhanced production and increased demand for their manufactures. In many countries, churches championed the workers, forestalling revolutionaries' appeal and making revolution unnecessary.

The case of the United States of America is the most remarkable, because Marx expected revolution to start there. Instead, socialists in America were the first to sell out to capitalism. Rather than leading the world into socialism, America led the world in revulsion from it. Industry developed so fast that it soaked up all the new labor that immigration and population rise created, so that the United States rapidly became a high-wage economy. The frontier (see Chapter 23) sucked restless and rebellious individuals out of industrializing areas. Cheap land in the West enabled even poor settlers to achieve prosperity. The American dream became a nightmare for socialists, diverting the hopes of the poor from revolution to self-enrichment.

Socialists yearned for a better future. Other critics and enemies of industrialization yearned for a lost past. Traditional workers smashed machinery to defend their jobs. In 1811–1813, the British government assigned 12,000 troops to repress machine-wrecking rioters, more soldiers, though of inferior quality, than Britain sent to fight Napoleon in 1808. Romantics deplored a world that the English priest and poet, Gerard Manley Hopkins (1844–1889), described as "seared with trade, bleared, smeared with toil, . . . wearing man's smudge." Some of them tried to escape. Ironically, the escapees from industrialization were often also its beneficiaries. G. Poldi-Pezzoli, one of the fathers of industrial Milan in northern Italy, had a medieval-style room in his house, where he would retreat among his collection of medieval art. In Barcelona, in the last decades of the century, the sublime architect Antoni Gaudi, professed to hate the machine age and created fantasy buildings in which captains of industry could feel secluded.

Cragside was the most extravagantly escapist mansion of nineteenth-century England. It was built in remote, rural Northumbria and was designed to embody the doctrines of the artists of the **Arts and Crafts** movement, who championed craftsmanship and opposed industrial uniformity. The owner and builder of the house, however, was William Armstrong (1810–1900), Britain's biggest arms manufacturer. Cragside was also the first house in England to be lit by electric light. The machine age enabled the rich to live out their romantic fantasies in comfort.

When factory workers got home, however, they would often find the misery that Philip Kay, a doctor who treated cotton workers, described in Manchester in 1832: "loathsome wretchedness" in houses "dilapidated, badly drained, damp." Or the worker might be confined to one of the cellar dwellings swilling with filth from the street and sopping with wetness from underground. Disease got trapped in the bad ventilation.

Reformers stressed the effects of an industrial environment on workers' morale. Jaume Balmes, the great ethical critic of Barcelona's industrialization, thought the workers were worse off than ancient slaves, who had at least some protection from the economic ups and downs that could turn poverty into destitution overnight. Moral criticism, of course, tended to reflect the values of the critics, and workers did not necessarily share it. Philip Kay watched the tenants of vile housing "denying themselves the comforts of life in order that they might wallow in the unrestrained licence of animal appetite." For workers, the vices he had in mind were rational survival strategies. Gambling was a form of investment for people with too little spare cash to save. Alcohol was a lubricant for lives stuck in drudgery.

One of the most effective criticisms on urban overcrowding was—in the words of a London physician in 1858—that "it almost necessarily involves such negation of all delicacy, such unclean confusion of bodies and bodily functions, such mutual exposure of animal and sexual nakedness, as is rather bestial than inhuman." Karl Marx, the middle-class theorist of communism, who slept with his maid, claimed that ruthless bosses sexually abused their workers. Popular songs—the genuine utterances of the working classes—tended to mock middle-class prudery and praise pleasures that moralists attacked, including drink, gambling, idleness, and promiscuous sex.

Bosses—according to critics of industrialization—were in moral danger, too. A Barcelona newspaper urged workers to see their masters as divine instruments for the workers' own welfare. It warned owners that "the mechanics in your factories are made of the same clay of which you are formed . . . and must not be confused with the machines you have in your workshops." This mixture of conscience tempered by common sense was typical of the Catholic response to industrialization in countries where the church molded the moral consensus. Archbishop Affré of Paris died at the barricades that workers erected in the revolution of 1848. Pope Leo XIII (r. 1878–1903) acknowledged the need to bring Catholic social teaching up to date if only to save workers from seduction by socialism. He would not undermine a social hierarchy in which the church had a strong vested interest, but he did authorize trades unions and encouraged Catholics to found their own. He could not denounce property—the church had too much of it for that—but he could remind socialists that Christians, too, were called to social responsibility. He could not endorse socialism, but he did condemn naked individualism.

URBANIZATION

Nineteenth-century urbanization was on a scale the world had never known. There had been gigantic concentrations of people before, especially in China, but never had so much population, in so many places, been gathered together in big cities.

In the industrializing world, this was hardly surprising. Some factories remained relatively isolated or attached to small towns. Overwhelmingly, however, economic considerations drove industry into cities, and people settled where the factories were. Owners needed to concentrate labor and

Cragside. The study is the most modest room at Cragside, the gigantic baronial-style mansion built in the romantic countryside in northern England, for William Armstrong (1810–1900). Armstrong made a fortune by inventing and manufacturing, among many other things, the Armstrong gun, one of the first modern forms of artillery. The house is full of gadgets—including the earliest electric lighting in any private house in Britain—although the architect, C. Norman Shaw, belonged to the Arts and Crafts movement, which favored old-fashioned artisanship.

Most Populous Cities in 1900

Name	Population
1 London, United Kingdom	6,480,000
2 New York, United States	3,437,000
3 Paris, France	3,330,000
4 Berlin, Germany	2,707,000
5 Chicago, United States	1,717,000
6 Vienna, Austria	1,698,000
7 Tokyo, Japan	1,497,000
8 St. Petersburg, Russia	1,439,000
9 Manchester, United Kingdom	1,435,000
10 Philadelphia, United States	1,418,000

United Nations; United States Census Bureau

Shanty town. Construction workers in a shanty town outside Berlin, depicted by Kurt Ekwall in 1872. Begging children implore a prosperous couple, who have come to "do good" among the poor and hungry.

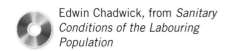

Edwin Chadwick, from *Sanitary Conditions of the Labouring Population*

communications and realized that they could make "economies of scale," saving on costs by making big investments and getting disproportionately big returns. As steam power and improved transport came on line, production could move nearer to convenient markets, making cities even bigger. As the scale and number of factories grew in any one place, so did the size of local markets, leading yet more businesses, especially those supplying food, to gather in the same places. The result was a new way to organize life around specialized production processes. The dynamics of locating production in factories turned former villages, such as Manchester and Birmingham in Britain and Essen in the German Rhineland, into great cities.

In most of the places it affected, industrialization created, at first, flimsy, ill-built cities: fearsome breeders of disease and disorder. Manchester in the 1830s and 1840s and Barcelona in the 1850s and 1860s are the best-known examples, because of the many philanthropic reformers, inquiries, and reports that exposed the horrors of the conditions in which workers lived. In the 1840s, works such as Edwin Chadwick's *Sanitary Conditions of the Labouring Population* in Manchester, or Jaume Salarich's survey of working-class health in Barcelona in the 1850s, clinically described the effects of breathing in the atmosphere of the textile mills: profuse sweat, exhaustion, gastric trouble, difficulty breathing and moving, poor circulation, mental weariness, nervous prostration, corrosion of the lungs, poisoning from machine oils and dyes. Slums clung to city centers. Shanties spread around city edges. Kurt Ekwall painted Berlin's shantytown in 1872, complete with a visiting middle-class family doling out pennies to ragged children.

Food is an even more basic index of the standard of living than hygiene and housing. Even in this connection, it took a long time for urbanization to deliver benefits, because growing towns make fresh foods relatively expensive and hard to obtain. As late as 1899, R. Seebohm Rowntree conducted pioneering investigations into the working class of the city of York in northern England. He found most

Izmir on the Mediterranean coast of Anatolia was one of the busiest ports in the Ottoman Empire in the eighteenth and nineteenth centuries. By 1829, when this view was painted, it was handling more than half the empire's exports. Izmir was also the port of entry for most of the foreign textiles, brought principally by French shippers, that the empire imported.
Photograph courtesy of the Peabody Essex Museum

VIEW OF THE TOWN AND BAY OF SMYRNA   VUE DE LA VILLE ET RADE DE SMIRNE

families were inadequately fed for the work they had to do, and many were actually sick for want of food. The normal diet of working families was monotonous, with only occasional treats of meat and fish. Unlike their rural counterparts, they could not normally grow vegetables or keep a pig. Workers saved by living almost entirely on oatmeal and water.

It was not only the industrialized world that experienced the madcap growth of cities. It also happened in parts of the world that played only a minor or marginal role in industrialization. Mining, for instance, was a way to produce raw materials that could create mushroom-growth towns, such as San Francisco in California and Kimberley and Johannesburg in South Africa. In 1871, diamonds were found on a farm at Kimberley. By the end of the century, 100,000 miners worked there. Gold turned Melbourne, on Australia's farthest Pacific edge, from a rudimentary settler village in 1837, the year Queen Victoria came to the throne, into the third largest city in the British Empire, with over 800,000 people, by the time she died in 1901. Growth during Melbourne's mining boom years from the 1850s surpassed "all human experience" in the opinion of a citizen astonished by the crowded wharves, the "scream of the engines, the hubbub of the streets" and the "swarming masses."

Global trade, meanwhile, stimulated port cities all over the world. The most conspicuous examples were in regions where industrialization was taking off. New York, for instance, experienced enormous growth—from 60,000 inhabitants at the beginning of the nineteenth century to nearly 3.5 million by 1900. But outside the industrializing world, ports from which primary produce was shipped overseas could experience, in proportion, much the same growth. Alexandria on Egypt's Mediterranean coast had only a few thousand people at the start of the nineteenth century, but it had grown to about 250,000 by the century's end, because it was a transitional port for Egyptian cotton. Lagos on the Nigerian coast boomed in the late nineteenth century because of palm oil and cocoa, Buenos Aires in Argentina grew rapidly thanks to the refrigerated meat trade. Calcutta in India, which was a small settlement when the nineteenth century began, started the twentieth century with more than 750,000 people, because of its role in exporting the dyes and coarse fibers of Bengal. In the 1850s, Shanghai became the port of choice for European merchants operating in China. It soon replaced Guangzhou as the great trading metropolis of China. Thanks in great part to its role in exporting opium, the population of Izmir on the Mediterranean coast of Turkey grew at a rate of 2 percent a year from the 1840s, to house more than 200,000 people by the 1880s.

Izmir dramatically illustrates a further feature of the new cities of the nineteenth century. It had French-built boulevards and British gas lighting. There were 5 newspapers, 17 printing houses, a public library that filled 10 houses, and one of the first theaters in the Ottoman Empire. This demonstrates how a new kind of cultural life became possible. Cities now were different from those of earlier times—fearsome, heavily policed, filled with rootless populations, and stalked by new diseases. But they gradually acquired new benefits: the facilities for recreation, education, and welfare that are only possible where many people congregate and large resources concentrate.

Opera in the jungle. The nineteenth-century rubber boom turned Manaus, in the Brazilian rain forest, into a grand, rich city, with this enormous opera house that attracted famous singers and musicians from Europe. But Manaus was ruined toward the end of the century, when rubber production shifted to the British colonies in Malaya.

Towns were remodeled or enlarged on new principles of urban planning. Paris and Vienna acquired the boulevards familiar today. Vast grids of rationally planned streets were added to Madrid and Manhattan. In Cairo and Alexandria, spectacular new quarters enveloped the chaotic old cities in networks of straight streets (see Map 24.2). Opera houses arose in places as surprisingly remote as Cairo and Manaus, the center of the rubber-producing region in the Amazon jungles of Brazil. City walls fell because modern artillery had made them obsolete. New roads, sewerage, water-supply systems, public baths, large stores, street lighting, cafes and clubs, sporting facilities, and such urban means of transport as trolleys and buses multiplied. New kinds of public spaces arose on cast-iron arches: snaking bridges and so-called crystal palaces—glass-covered markets, railway stations, greenhouses, shopping arcades. London's Crystal Palace, scene of the first great Universal Exposition of 1851—set the trend and housed, appropriately, a display of the industrial arts of the world. Madrid's main market was the most innovative example, built in 1870 and designed by an amateur (for it was beyond the imagination of most professional architects) to enclose more than 100 acres in a pyramid of glass.

New urban spaces permitted new kinds of social activity. Mass education was a remarkable development. In some places investment by the state spurred education, partly because states wanted people to be trained for soldiering. Thirty-five percent of girls—and 70 percent of boys—went to school in Japan in 1890. Compulsory universal education, introduced in many European countries and the United States during the nineteenth century was in one respect the most remarkable development

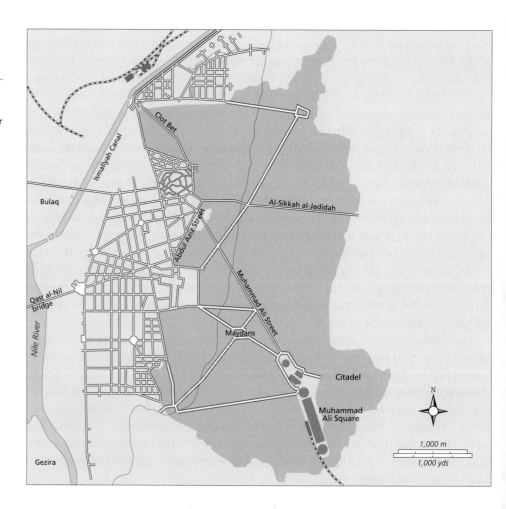

MAP 24.2

Cairo, ca. 1900

old city

new streets and neighborhoods after 1869

railways

○ MAKING CONNECTIONS ○

INDUSTRIAL TRANSFORMATIONS IN THE NINETEENTH CENTURY

ECONOMIC/POLITICAL TRANFORMATIONS →	SOCIAL CHANGES →	CHANGES IN DAILY LIFE
Development of industrial/factory-based employment	Urbanization, increased population density; increased labor specialization, formal division of work and leisure time	Work moves from country to city, outdoors to indoors; from homes and small workshops to factories and mines; large, impersonal work environments, bleak working conditions
Salary-based labor system	Shift from proprietorship to large-scale enterprises where power is concentrated in small number of factory, mine owners	Plentiful workers relatively powerless to negotiate unless organized; strict organization of daily routines
Urbanization and mixture of factory–residential districts	Proximity of work offset by increase in air and water pollution; grimy surroundings, lack of public sanitation in high-density cities	Increased exposure to epidemics of cholera, dysentery, and chronic diseases such as tuberculosis
Increased power of municipal, national governments to regulate	Development of idea of "public health" to stem disease, child mortality rates, epidemics, etc.	Increased town planning, public sanitation by 1900 lead to longer life span, increased livability of cities
Growth of global trade	Increased movement of goods and traders in port cities all over the world; generation of wealth	Foreign goods and luxury items as well as technological innovations spread rapidly in industrialized countries

of all, for it defied two cherished beliefs of the time: the doctrines of parental responsibility for children and individual freedom.

BEYOND INDUSTRY: AGRICULTURE AND MINING

The new trends rightly capture our attention, but even the spread of industry and the growth of towns left most individual lives in the nineteenth century unaffected. Urbanization seemed to skip huge areas of the globe, which remained largely a world of peasants even in the West. In those parts of Asia and Africa that fell under colonial rule, many of which like British India and French Indochina had long and ample urban traditions, the proportion of town dwellers in the population hardly grew. The rise of urban workplaces was just one of many contexts in which the role and nature of labor changed. Even in Europe, most people still lived and worked on the land in the nineteenth century.

Nonetheless, unindustrialized and deindustrialized regions lived in the shadow of industrialization and were affected by its demands and subjected to similar pressures for social change. Even in the country, the context of work in ever-larger fields, employing ever-less labor, bred different feelings and ways of life from traditional agriculture, with its communal habits, companionship, and shared rituals that marked the passage of the seasons or the festivals of local saints and gods.

The big areas of growth in agriculture were of two kinds. On one hand, prosperous, independent farmers and ranchers in the American Midwest, Australia, and Argentina could produce meat and grain with methods that involved relatively little labor. Advertisements for the harvesting machines that the McCormick Company of Chicago made in the midcentury illustrated the point vividly. Two horses and one man

Industry joins agriculture: The McCormick Company of Chicago helped transform the prairie in the late nineteenth century by supplying a mechanical reaper to make up for the shortage of farm labor. The spider's web shown here on a hand-held sickle symbolizes the demise of old methods.

Peasants from Adjara. The region of Adjara, in present-day Georgia, straddles the southeastern shore of the Black Sea and was contested by the Ottoman and Russian empires throughout the nineteenth century, with Russia gaining the upper hand in 1878. Soon thereafter, the port of Batumi was developed into a major seaport and rail terminus and commercial agriculture quickly transformed the lives of the peasantry. Farmers, like the ones shown here on their way to market, produced crops, such as tea, for consumption throughout the Russian Empire, and crops, such as corn, for both local markets and export abroad.

were all that were needed—the poster seemed to say—for vast fields that stretch toward distant mountains. The company produced 1,500 reapers a year in the 1850s—and nearly 15,000 in the 1870s. Ranching remained unmechanized but required only a small and specialized workforce—cowboys or, in Argentina and Uruguay, *gauchos*, who tended to be freelancers, cultivating and celebrating their personal independence.

On the other hand, farmed products, such as palm oil and cocoa from West Africa, cotton from Egypt and India, and opium from India and Turkey were labor intensive. To satisfy the market, peasants had to be mobilized—induced or compelled—into growing these crops, along with other, lesser but still important items of growing demand, such as rubber, coffee, and easily transportable foodstuffs like bananas and citrus.

The pressures or promise of the market made peasants switch from subsistence agriculture or farming only to supply local outlets to export crops. *Max Havelaar* is the best-known Dutch novel—indeed, virtually the only Dutch novel widely known outside the Netherlands. It is a fearless condemnation of colonialism and, in particular, of the system by which the Dutch, in collaboration with native elites, forced peasants in the Dutch East Indies to grow coffee, because it was a cash crop, whether their land was suitable for it or not. In the late nineteenth century, the Dutch forced about half the population of Java to take part in this system. Elsewhere in the Dutch East Indies in the 1870s, people seem to have had more children to meet the colonial government's demands for forced labor. In Egypt, too, world demand for primary materials forced peasants to grow a product—cotton—they could not eat and could sell only at prices they were unable to influence. Peasant landholdings tended to split under the strain. By the end of the century, Egypt had some 2 million landless peasants, who were subject to forced labor in the irrigation works and conscription into the army.

So agriculture, like industry, became increasingly a specialized activity, with particular crops concentrated in favored regions and large domains. Revolutions in tenure arose as the brokers or middlemen who sold peasants' crops to merchants began to invest in land themselves, using their control of credit to obtain holdings cheaply.

The Ottoman Empire, for instance, became a net exporter of crops for the first time in history, thanks to the grapes and opium of western Anatolia, where exports increased by more than 500 percent between 1845 and 1876. Private owners took over state landholdings, while much land passed from the hands of peasants into those of tribal or local chiefs, city merchants, moneylenders, and officials. Sixty percent of the soil of Ottoman Syria—once a peasant land—was officially reclassified as large estates in the early twentieth century. The estate owners included some local families, but many were outsiders—especially Armenians, Greeks, and Jews.

In West Africa, palm-oil production, formerly the work of gatherers of wild plants, became, from the 1840s, a focus of increasingly systematic farming. Harvesting palm fruits, pounding the nuts to extract the oil, and getting the product to market demanded plenty of labor. Typically, a group of independent farmers would combine under an elected leader. In some areas, especially in what is now Nigeria, families could operate small, independent palm-oil farms. Alternatively—and more insistently as time went on—merchants would grab land and start slave-operated plantations. Much of the profit went into private armies, maintained to fight for power or to seize more slaves. Labor was wrenched out of food production to keep up the flow of oil. Transporting and marketing the oil enriched a growing commercial class.

In southern Bengal, indigo planting was the big new opportunity. But it required capital investment, which forced peasants to borrow. Getting a loan—said a magistrate in 1830—was a "misfortune" that reduced the borrower to "little better than a bond slave to the factory." In the second half of the century, jute—a cheap fiber good for making rope and bags—became dominant. Small cultivators could grow jute economically with little capital on plots of an acre or two. Peasants abandoned rice to grow it. But reliance on a single exportable crop left producers at the mercy of the market and led to high levels of debt, incurred to tide them over hard times or meet high rents. The peasant class survived, but the rising standards of commercial and industrial activity elsewhere in the world left them impoverished. A poet of the early twentieth century summed up the effects:

> The Westerners came and took control.
> Now look how much money they have made.
> They can now be disdainful of the Bengalis. . . .
> Look, the Bengali race is ruined.

The **caste system** gripped India more tightly than ever, as the British imposed burdens and forms of discrimination that were supposedly traditional because they were enshrined in ancient texts, but that people had not formerly practiced much. In southern India, especially, British policy favored the concentration of the best agricultural land in the hands of a few dominant families, reducing many peasants to abject poverty and to social and economic dependency.

In some places, where Western immigrants themselves took to the land, they could also end up joining the ranks of the losers in the global marketplace. In the mid–nineteenth century, the Portuguese government began settling poor white farmers in Angola, in southwest Africa, as a way to extend and perpetuate Portuguese control of the native Africans. Most of these settlers never made a success of their ventures, renouncing the opportunities to grow export crops, turning instead to subsistence farming to feed their own families, living in hovels, and dressing in rags. The plight of black peasants in Angola was even worse. Before the

The face of Africa, scarred and pitted by colonial exploitation: open-cast diamond mining in the "blue earth" at Kimberley, South Africa in 1872. At that early stage—not much more than a year after the first diamond was discovered on the De Beers's farm—the diggings were checkered with the square plots of individual prospectors. The inability to dig deep enough to find diamonds on small plots led to the consolidation of these shallow digs into bigger holdings and to the formation of the De Beers Mining Company in 1874. By 1914, the Kimberley pit had become the largest man-made crater ever dug.

1870s, having their land seized and being enslaved were their usual fate. Late in that decade, when Portugal officially abolished slavery, their status hardly improved in practice. Not until the early twentieth century did the authorities make serious or sustained efforts to stop the illegal export of slaves.

The erosion of independence and of local prosperity was a common—but not universal—consequence of the specializations the global market encouraged. In the second half of the century, Thailand, formerly a self-sufficient country, began to specialize in a few exportable commodities: rice—which accounted, on average, for 60 to 70 percent of total exports—tin, and teak. The emphasis on rice ensured that some traditional ways of life continued. The Thai stayed on the land, increasing output almost entirely by extending the amount of land under cultivation. They resisted the lure of high wages or returns from activities outside agriculture and left commerce to Chinese immigrants. The amount of capital investment required for growing rice was modest, and, among foreigners, Chinese supplied most of it. Thailand therefore never succumbed to foreign "business imperialists" (see Chapter 25). Relative to other staple foods, rice earned good profits for the people who grew it. Only about 50 percent of the export price went to the middleman, miller, and shipper.

As well as the fruits of increasingly specialized agriculture, the unindustrialized world also supplied the industrializing world with raw minerals in ever-larger quantities (see Map 24.3). Where mines were located, the impact was often intense. The Kimberley diamond mines in South Africa were a good example. "Every foot of the blue ground," said Cecil Rhodes (1853–1902), one of the big early investors in the enterprise and a champion of the British Empire in Africa, "means so much power." Mines meant power to their owners. To workers, they signified the destruction of traditional life. As soon as diamonds were discovered, black African workers

MAP **24.3**

Major Mineral Finds of the Late Nineteenth Century

- cobalt
- copper
- diamonds
- iron ore
- gold
- manganese
- silver
- tin

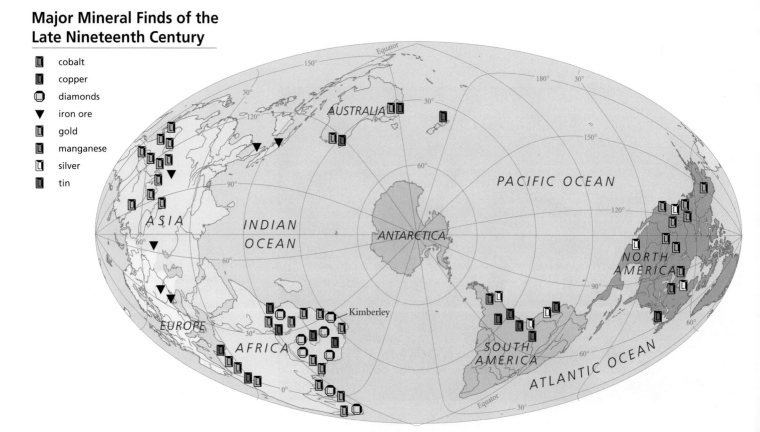

wrenched from agrarian and pastoral communities poured in, struggling to re-create the layouts and routines of their characteristic home villages in the squalid, lawless vicinity of the mines. Black mine workers were forbidden to acquire licenses to establish their own diggings. Though nominally not slaves, they could be fined or flogged for desertion of employment, and their wages were never more than a fifth of what white miners earned for similar work.

Although miners in Europe and North America were better treated, it was not necessary to go far beyond the frontiers of the industrializing world to see mines wreak comparable havoc. The Río Tinto copper mines in Spain recruited thousands of workers from all over Spain and Portugal in the 1870s and 1880s. The company aimed to practice the sort of productive benevolence associated with the best factories at the time. But decent housing and modest health care and schooling did little to ease the feelings of alienation understandable in uprooted communities, or the impatience workers felt at the company's paternalism. Living conditions were always overcrowded, because the building program could not keep up with the demand for labor. The environment was literally poisonous, as sulphurous fumes hung over the area whenever the wind fell. Most of the British staff—the management and most of the top technicians were Britons—were housed apart in what would now be called a gated community, where ordinary workers and local people were forbidden to enter.

CHANGING LABOR REGIMES

The virtual disappearance of slavery—and the total disappearance of plantation slavery in the Americas—was perhaps the most surprising episode of the nineteenth century. Almost every preindustrial society we know about has considered slavery a normal and legitimate relationship—a suitable status for supposedly inferior people, for captives, or for those unable to survive except as a master's chattel. Nineteenth-century Western science produced new justifications for slavery, stronger than any previously advanced: certain races were inescapably inferior to others. Black people were, according to schemes of classification that some anthropologists proposed, more like apes than Europeans.

Slavery and the Slave Trade

On the other hand, slavery repelled believers in three doctrines of growing appeal in the world, and especially in parts of the West: evangelical Christianity, egalitarianism (the idea that all human beings are equal to each other), and economic liberalism. According to evangelical Christians, Jesus' message of universal love outlawed slavery. According to egalitarians, all people were equal, and it was nonsense for anyone to be born into slavery. For economic liberals, and especially for those who believed in free trade, slavery was irrational, because people worked better when they did so freely and for wages.

Impeccable in theory, the free-trade doctrine did not seem to be borne out in reality. On the contrary, the world economy relied, as it had relied for centuries, on compulsion to work. In much of Africa, according to early nineteenth-century observers, slaves were both a vital labor force and a major export product. In the tropical and subtropical latitudes of the Atlantic-side New World, slavery was the

Industrialization, Mechanization, and Urbanization

Nineteenth century	Factories in the United States and Western Europe reorganize work and reorder workers' lives
1811–1813	British use 12,000 troops to repress machine-wrecking rioters
1842	Poor living conditions in Manchester detailed in Edwin Chadwick's *The Sanitary Condition of the Labouring Population*
1844–1919	Henry J. Heinz, industrialist and proponent of paternalist management
1845–1876	Ottoman agricultural exports increase fivefold
1848	Publication of Marx's and Engels's *The Communist Manifesto*
1851	London's Universal Exposition held at Crystal Palace
1867	Publication of Marx's *Capital*
1870	New central market built in Madrid
ca. 1875	McCormick Company of Chicago produces 15,000 reapers per year
r. 1878–1903	Pope Leo XIII, advocate of social reform
Late nineteenth century	Arts and Crafts movement
ca. 1900	Cotton cultivation in Egypt contributes to the creation of 2 million landless peasants
	Population: Izmir, 200,000; Alexandria, 250,000; Calcutta, more than 750,000; Melbourne, 800,000; New York, 3.4 million, London, 6.5 million

only labor force available. It was not only the plantation economies of the Americas that depended on slavery. The trade in slaves sustained shipping in Europe and America and many states in Africa. In Liverpool, Britain's leading port, a quarter of the ships were engaged in the slave trade at the start of the nineteenth century. Without slavery, cotton manufacture in Europe, the rum industry of New England, and the arms trade to Africa would all be jeopardized. In the long run, mechanization might make slavery out of date. But no one could foresee this in the early nineteenth century. On the contrary, the kind of plantation environment in which slavery was entrenched seemed unsuitable for mechanization. In any case, in slave-owning societies, slavery was part of culture and tradition. People practiced it not because it was profitable but because it was part of the fabric of life. So it was not just economics that eliminated slavery. The rise of a new morality changed cultural assumptions. Reformers dismantled the system despite the dictates of tradition, ideology, economics, and what passed for science.

They started with the slave trade. This was an easier target than slavery, because it did not involve problems of how to compensate slave owners or dispose of liberated slaves. In the 1790s, in Europe and America, a tremendous wave of sentiment against the trade broke against the fears and obstacles that vested interests raised. But in 1803, Denmark outlawed the trade. Britain and the United States followed. The abolition of the slave trade became a sort of British national crusade, in which the navies of other European and American countries joined. The crusade transferred to the African mainland. Indeed, it became a way to justify British imperialism and inspired destructive wars, in which thousands of native slave-traders and their families, who thought they were simply engaged in a traditional and lawful activity, died. Meanwhile, Britain paid rulers in parts of Africa and the Indian Ocean to stop dealing in slaves.

Reformers expected the abolition of the slave trade to lead to the disappearance of slavery. Demographic trends suggested this possibility. As we have seen, plantation slave populations in the eighteenth century normally had high death rates and low birth rates (see Chapter 20). But abolition had two unforeseen effects that combined to frustrate the abolitionists' predictions.

First, abolition made slaves more expensive and therefore gave new life to the slave trade. The total number of slaves shipped across the Atlantic from Africa to the Americas in the nineteenth century was about 3.3 million. Slavers made great fortunes, charging premiums for the risks they faced in running the gauntlet of the British Navy's patrols. By the 1830s, Pedro Blanco of Cadiz in Spain became known as the "Rothschild of slavery"—an allusion to the world's richest banking family at the time. He reckoned that if he could save one vessel in three from capture he could make a profit. At his slave-holding camp on a group of islands in the mouth of the Gallinas River in West Africa, he could keep 5,000 slaves at a time, guarded by lookout posts 100 feet high equipped with telescopes to warn of approaching British patrols. He permanently employed a lawyer, 5 accountants, 2 cashiers, 10 copyists, and a harem of 50 beautiful African slave girls.

Second, abolition of the slave trade made slave owners more careful of their slaves. As a result, in some areas formerly destructive of the fertility of slave women, such as the Caribbean islands, the number of slaves began to grow, or at least to stay steady, through natural reproduction. When

Anti-slavery Society. Thomas Clarkson, veteran campaigner against slavery, was 80 years old, "grey and bent...feeble and tottering" and weak-voiced when he addressed the international Anti-slavery Society Convention in London in 1840. But here the painter, Benjamin Haydon, presents a rejuvenated and vigorous Clarkson. Though several women were allowed to attend the meeting, they were not permitted to speak on the grounds that such exhibitionism would be unseemly for ladies.

Spain joined the movement to end the slave trade in 1818, its government allowed owners a period of grace during which they could import slave women of fertile years, so that "by propagating the species, the abolition of the commerce in slaves should be less noticeable in future." Meanwhile, in the southern United States, the number of slaves multiplied from under 1 million at the start of the century to almost 4 million by 1860. The upward trend was unstoppable. Even when federal law banned the trade after 1808, world demand for cotton continued to drive the rise of slavery in the South.

Slaves played surprisingly little part in their own liberation. Though rebellions were frequent—and frequently bloody—most plantation societies learned to live with them, absorbing the costs of suppression or confining the runaways to roles that were troublesome rather than fatal to planter control. The big exception was Haiti, the French colony called Saint-Domingue where rebellious slaves seized power in the 1790s. The French Revolution, igniting expectations about "the rights of man" (see Chapter 22), provided Haitian slaves with a basic ideology of liberation. Yet controversy in Haiti during the early years of the Revolution focused not on whether slavery was right or wrong but on whether free black and mixed-race people should have the right to vote. The slave revolt that began in 1791 seems to have started outside enlightened and revolutionary circles—with rumors that the king of France had freed the slaves, with voodoo ceremonies, and with a slave leadership barely connected with free black people, some of whom rebelled against white rule at the same time.

In 1792, a new phase began, when Léger-Félicité Southonax arrived as the representative of the French Republic with orders to pacify the colony. The following year, impelled in part by revolutionary fervor and in part by concern at the worsening security situation, with the British poised to invade, he freed the slaves of the northern province—creating at a stroke, he said, "200,000 new soldiers for the republic." He befriended and promoted the most talented officer among the freed slaves, Toussaint L'Ouverture (1746–1803), who, in effect, seized power in 1797. A visiting Englishman admired the "perfect system of equality" he observed under the new regime, with black and white people of different social ranks eating together.

After the French captured L'Ouverture in 1802, Haitian resistance became desperate, and the rule of former slaves much harsher. In 1804, L'Ouverture's successor as leader of the revolt, Jean-Jacques Dessalines, proclaimed "Independence or Death." In a remarkable reversal of the white man's usual rhetoric, he denounced the French as barbarians:

> What have we in common with that bloody-minded people? Their cruelties compared to our moderation—their color to ours—the extension of seas that separate us—our avenging climate—all plainly tell us they are not our brethren. . . . Let them shudder . . . at the terrible resolution we are going to make—to do to death any native of France who shall defile, with his sacrilegious footstep, this land of liberty.

The Haitians officially won their liberty in 1825 at the cost of agreeing to pay a crippling indemnity to compensate French property owners. But by excluding white colonists, the Haitians deprived their country of much-needed capital investment and technical expertise. They also sent tremors of fear through the planter societies of other parts of the Americas. In 1823, Thomas Clarkson, who was the British representative of the Haitian state, came close to threatening planters elsewhere with the same fate those in Haiti had suffered.

Slavery in the Nineteenth Century

1790s	Abolitionist sentiment on the rise in Britain and the United States
1791–1803	Haitian Revolution
1800	1 million slaves in the United States
1800–1900	3.3 million slaves shipped from Africa to the Americas
1803	Denmark outlaws slave trade
1807	Britain outlaws slave trade
1809	Importation of slaves outlawed in United States
1823	Spain outlaws slavery
1825	Haiti wins official independence
1834	Slavery abolished in the British Empire
1848	France outlaws slavery
1860	4 million slaves in the United States
1863	Emancipation Proclamation (United States)
1869	Paraguay outlaws slavery
1885	Egypt outlaws slavery
1886	Cuba outlaws slavery
1888	Brazil outlaws slavery

Even without the Haitian example, emancipation of slaves was likely to follow the abolition of the slave trade. Otherwise, the work of the abolitionists would have been largely fruitless. In the 1820s and 1830s, some Spanish-American republics led the way, not because they were peculiarly virtuous, but because slavery played a relatively small part in their economies. Paraguay, where most of the slaves were Native Americans, was exceptional in delaying emancipation until 1869. Although slavery had been unlawful in England itself since the 1770s, the British Empire as a whole did not ban it until 1834. It took the Civil War (1861–1865) to free the slaves of the Southern states of the United States—and even then the federal government's Emancipation Proclamation in 1863 was more a practical response to war conditions than an act of morality. After various false starts, Spain freed its slaves—but not those of its colonies—in 1823. France decreed emancipation in 1848, and the Netherlands in 1863. The Spanish colony of Cuba held out until 1886 and the Empire of Brazil until 1888.

Slavery survived longer in Africa and what we think of as the Middle East, but thanks in part to British insistence, its scope gradually diminished, as did the numbers of slaves. Persia signed an antislave trade treaty with Britain in 1882 but never enforced its terms. Egypt made slavery illegal in1885. Formal laws against the slave trade were proclaimed in the Ottoman Empire in 1889 and in Zanzibar in 1897—which, as part of an Omani trading empire that had ousted the Portuguese from much of East Africa (see Chapter 21), throve as a slave-trading center. In practice, state bans were hard to enforce in Islamic society, where religious law licenced slavery, and where many Islamic authorities regarded antislavery legislation as contrary to Islam (just as many Christian planters cited the Bible to justify their support for slavery). There were still, by the most widely accepted estimate, 100,000 black slaves in the Sahel in sub-Saharan Africa at the end of the nineteenth century.

Slavery was not the only form of forced labor to dwindle in the nineteenth century. There was also serfdom in which peasants were tied to the land they worked and could be sold along with, but not apart from, it. When the century began, the hereditary rule of lords limited the freedom of the peasant serfs of Eastern Europe to move, trade, and marry. The wars that arose early in the century in the aftermath of the French Revolution shifted the frontiers of serfdom eastward, forcing the emancipation of the peasants of Prussia in central and eastern Germany. In the Habsburg Empire, serfdom vanished bit by bit—often at the insistence of lords who thought free peasants would be more economically efficient. After peasant revolts, the Habsburg monarchy finally granted all former serfs freedom and land in 1853–1854. The Habsburg government made this concession to win peasant loyalty and free up labor for railway construction. In Thailand, almost the entire male population was bound by forced labor laws, which the Thai government abolished bit by bit throughout the century.

Even Russia, where most people were still serfs, joined the trend. In 1847, an influential German travel writer, Baron von Haxthausen, claimed that Russian society would never come to resemble that of the rest of Europe. Some Russians were proud of their country's distinctive reputation and wanted to keep it as different as possible. The ruling elite, however, found it embarrassing that Western Europe considered Russia backward. They postponed the liberation of the peasants only because of prudent fear of possible unforeseen consequences. However, increasing peasant violence in the 1840s, and, in 1855, the shock of defeat in the Crimean War by Turkey, France, and Britain helped to concentrate minds in favor of reform. The Czar proclaimed emancipation of the serfs in 1861. In the background, Russia felt the irresistible pressure of a European model of economic change: recognition that Russia had to enter the railway age and that the empire had to reorganize its manpower for industrialization.

Tippu Tip, "the biggest slaver of them all," whose activities on behalf of Sultan Barghash of Zanzibar (see Chapter 25) almost succeeded in preempting European imperialism, before he became a collaborator in the empire-building efforts of King Leopold II of the Belgians. In the opinion of Jerome Becker, one of Leopold's agents in the Congo in the 1880s, "From his [Tippu's] immense plantations, cultivated by thousands of slaves, all blindly devoted to their master, and from his ivory trade, of which he has the monopoly, he has in his duplex character of conqueror and trader, succeeded in creating for himself in the heart of Africa a veritable empire."

TIPPOO TIB

In Japan, meanwhile, peasants became participants in an enlarged marketplace as communications improved, and cities grew and multiplied. Individual farms tended to replace the traditional village collectives in which all the village families had worked the land in common and shared the harvests. There were crosscurrents. New regulations favored landowners, especially by limiting traditional tenants' rights in common land. But the peasants' lot generally improved. In 1868, the government promised, "the common people, no less than the civil and military officials, shall be allowed to pursue their own individual callings so that there may be no discontent." In the 1870s, government decree freed the dependent peasants and workers of Japan. In 1877, when disaffected samurai attempted a rebellion of the type Oshio Heicharo had tried to launch in 1837, the peasants were on the other side, drafted into the government's army, armed with guns, and drilled in obedience.

In some parts of the world, convicts became a substitute for slave labor. "Hard labor" became a way to exploit criminals' potential for work and to exact retribution from them on behalf of society.

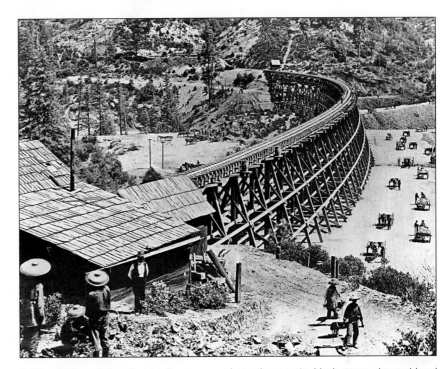

Coolies. Picks and shovels, wheelbarrows, one-horse dump carts, black gunpowder, and hand drills were the meager tools and materials with which coolies hired by the Central Pacific Railroad dug and hacked their way over the towering Sierra Nevada Mountains of California. Because white workers were scarce in the American West in the late nineteenth century, the railroad brought in thousands of Chinese to do the most backbreaking labor.

In Japan, criminals worked in the notorious Ashio copper mine (see Chapter 23). Governments in Europe deported convicts in their hundreds of thousands—often for minor crimes—to remote, previously uncultivated lands. Australia alone, for instance, absorbed over 150,000 convicts from Britain between 1788 and 1868. Some Pacific Islands, Siberia, former slave-holding states in the United States after the Civil War, and French Guiana in northwest South America relied on convict labor to sustain their economies.

The slaves' main successors worldwide, however, were millions of **coolies**: laborers, mainly from poor communities in India and China, conned or coerced at miserable wages as contracted or indentured workers for some of the era's most demanding work on sugar plantations, tropical mines, and colonial railway-building projects (see Map 24.4). Technically, the Chinese government required that every recruit from Chinese jurisdiction should enter "freely and voluntarily" into his agreement with his employers and shippers. In practice, officials connived in what were effectively deportations or abductions. In the 1860s and 1870s, French recruiters shipped some 50,000 laborers from India to the Caribbean, where, Indian government officials complained, the French "tried everything they could to keep Indians in perpetual servitude." A British report of 1871 characterized the condition of Chinese and Indian laborers in British Guiana in South America as the new slavery. A Chinese government inquiry in 1873 found that "the lawless method by which the Chinese were—in most cases—introduced into Cuba, the contempt there shown for them, the disregard of contracts, the indifference about working conditions, and the unrestrained infliction of wrong, constitute a treatment which is that of a slave, not of a man who has consented to be bound by a contract." After Spain abolished slavery in Cuba in 1886, slave catchers stayed in business—now hunting down runaway Chinese workers. There were perhaps 25,000 Chinese in California in the 1850s.

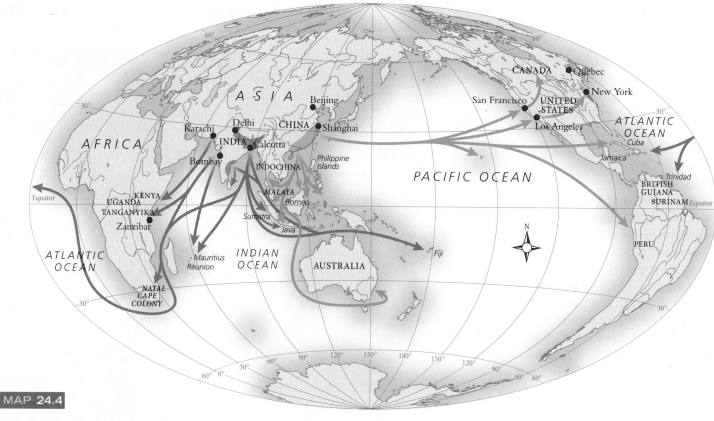

MAP 24.4

The Movement of Indentured Labor in the Late Nineteenth Century

- ■ core area of Indian migration
- ■ core area of Chinese migration
- → Indian migrants
- → Chinese migrants

Tea picker. Tea was an imperial beverage in the nineteenth century. First, Britain encouraged mass production of tea in India to undermine Chinese exports. Then the British introduced the crop to Sri Lanka, where this harvester is shown at work in a photograph from the 1890s. This "Ceylon tea" is now prized, but it was originally a cheap, inferior beverage to help keep British industrial workers alert.

The Central Pacific Railroad employed 10,000 of them. From 1868, by agreement with China, 16,000 arrived annually. Many went to factories in San Francisco, where "Little China" had nearly 50,000 residents by 1875. Violence and immigration controls followed. When the British writer Rudyard Kipling visited California in 1889, he could see "how deep down in the earth the pigtail [which all Chinese men had to wear under the Qing dynasty] has taken root."[1]

From 1834, when the British Empire abolished slavery, until the eve of the First World War in 1914, 4 million workers, mainly from India and China, kept the empire supplied with cheap labor. France conquered Indochina from the 1850s to the 1880s in part to solve the problems of a labor shortage elsewhere in the French Empire.

Female and Child Labor

So although slavery was abolished in most places and formal serfdom disappeared from Europe, other forms of forced and dependent labor survived and spread. In industrializing economies, it is doubtful how far wage labor was morally superior to slavery. Unlike the masters of slaves, factory owners did not have the legal right to sell their workers or, at least in theory, sexually abuse them. But work in the factories and mines of the West and its colonies was highly disciplined, unless and until governments allowed workers to organize in trade unions and bargain collectively for their wages. Women and children joined the workforce. Child labor was, of course, entirely forced labor, as was much of the work that women did. Both categories made a substantial contribution to the success of industrialization. In Germany in 1895, nearly 700,000 workers were under 16 years of age. In France in the 1890s, 32 percent of the manufacturing workforce were women. Well over half the industrial workforce in late nineteenth-century Japan were women, mostly from rural backgrounds, living in supervised dormitories and sending most of their meager pay back home to their village relatives. The biggest source of employment for women was the result of other social and economic changes. Urbanization increased demand for domestic servants and for retail staff in shops and markets.

Trends similar to those of the West were visible in patches wherever industrialization—on however small a scale—occurred. In Ottoman-ruled Syria and Lebanon, for instance, 85 percent of the workforce in silk reeling, which was the only steam-powered industry in the area, was female on the eve of the First World War. Women were dragged into new forms of work in the unindustrialized or deindustrialized worlds, too. Indian tea plantations relied on female labor to pick the tea leaves, partly because women were supposedly nimble fingered, partly because they were cheap to hire and relatively easy to exploit. In northern Bengal, stripping jute and plucking tea leaves joined the dehusking of rice as women's work. Most families came to depend on women's wages. In West Africa, men

Cautionary tale. The artist hides the adultress's face from the onlooker in this morality painting by the British artist Augustus Egg (1816–1863). The emphasis is on the injured husband, who clenches his fist and crumples the incriminating evidence, and on the violated innocence of the children. The painting is one of a series of three. In the others Egg depicted the woman's just deserts: expulsion from the family home and death in squalor and poverty.

took over much of the work of pounding the palm nuts to extract their oil, which was traditionally women's work. But women were diverted into selling oil and food. Their menfolk benefited. As in the industrializing world, the new economic opportunities of the era led men to assert claims to women's labor and to the proceeds that labor earned.

Although some women turned to jobs outside the home to escape the domination of parents or husbands, it is hard to resist the impression that women were—as usual— employed where men could best exploit their labor. In a German factory, a survey in 1900 revealed that half the women employed claimed that they worked because their husbands could not earn enough to support their families. The problems of balancing factory work and family life were formidable—especially since factory workers married relatively young, typically in their early twenties in highly industrialized countries, such as Britain and Germany, in the late nineteenth century. Even women who stayed at home worked harder, as factories and mines sucked in their men folk and deprived wives of their husbands' help at home. In the growing cities, prostitution boomed, often employing, in effect, enslaved women.

In the long run, industrialization led Westerners to reevaluate womanhood and childhood. By comparison with men, women and children were, somewhat contradictorily, perceived as ideal for certain industrial tasks but were also treated as marginally efficient workers. Gradually, mechanization took them out of the labor market. Society rationalized the process by representing it as a form of liberation and even of elevating the status of women and children. Womanhood was placed on a pedestal. Children were treated as a distinct rank of society—almost a subspecies of humankind—whereas formerly they had often been seen as little adults, or as "enemies" who needed discipline, or simply as negligible, even expendable, given the high rates of child mortality.

These were uniquely Western cults, barely intelligible in cultures where women and children were still men's partners in production (see "Going to the Source: U. S. and Egyptian Feminism before World War I," pages 910–913). The status looked enviable in artists' and advertisers' images of delicate femininity or angelic childhood. But there were disadvantages. Societies that freed children from the workplace tried to pen them inside schools. For many children, and for parents who needed their children's wages, compulsory education was a form of tyranny.

New Labor Patterns

1788–1868	150,000 convicts shipped from Britain to Australia
1850s	25,000 Chinese live and work in California
1853–1854	Serfs in Habsburg Empire emancipated
1860s and 1870s	French ship 50,000 Indian laborers to the Caribbean
1861	Serfs in Russia emancipated
1870s	Japanese workers and peasants freed by official decree
1880s	5.25 million immigrants arrive in the United States
1890s	32 percent of French work force is female; 1 million settlers move to Siberia; 14 million people emigrate from China
1890–1920	Migration adds 18.2 million people to U.S. population
1895	700,000 German workers under 16 years of age
1914	30 percent of the population of Argentina is foreign born

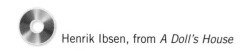

Henrik Ibsen, from *A Doll's House*

In 1863, the English novelist Charles Kingsley wrote a popular and sentimental story about boy chimney sweeps, a dirty and dangerous form of child labor, who changed magically into spirits or "water babies." This sort of transformation, however, did not occur naturally. The romantic ideal of childhood was more often forced than coaxed into being. Schools were repressive and designed to mold pupils according to adult agendas.

Women liberated from work were assigned a role and rights that resembled, in some respects, those of children. In the early nineteenth century, Montreal in Canada was the only place in the world where, owing to a constitutional quirk, women could assert the right to vote. But the suffrage for women was withdrawn in 1834 after a single election, "to protect their modesty." Stiflingly male-dominated, middle-class homes confined women. The Norwegian dramatist Henrik Ibsen (1828–1906) brilliantly captured the atmosphere in 1879 in his most famous play, *A Doll's House,* which depicts the married household as an oppressive pen from which a woman must struggle to escape. For middle-class women, the fall from the pedestal could be bruising. In 1858, the British artist Augustus Egg painted an adulteress in three terrible stages of decline and destitution. Great composers devoted operas to sexually promiscuous heroines who invariably came to a bad or a sad end—Giuseppe Verdi's *La Traviata* (1851), Georges Bizet's *Carmen* (1875), Giacomo Puccini's *Manon Lascaut* (1891) and *La Bohème* (1896). The fallen woman became the favorite villain or victim of the age.

Even for peoples formerly enslaved, only a modified form of freedom emerged. Even in Haiti, the army kept slaves at work. In areas of previously slave-staffed plantations, a labor crisis followed emancipation. It was met, in different degrees in different places, by enforcing new sources of labor, but also, in general, by going back to an older pattern of tenure with peasants, renting the land and sharecropping, forced to give landlords a percentage of their harvests. Liberated slaves were too numerous to command much power in a free labor market. In the British West Indies, they made up 80 percent of the population. In the French and Dutch Caribbean, the proportions were 60 and 70 percent respectively. Poor European immigrants supplied the labor industry needed in the United States, while Indian and Chinese coolies in the Caribbean kept labor there relatively cheap. For most black people in the United States, part of the consequence of emancipation was economic misery and subjection to "color bars:" In many states white people excluded them not just from the right to vote and equal opportunities in employment, but from supposedly public spaces and services. Black Americans were subjected to the petty humiliations, enforced by violence if necessary, of exclusion from white churches, schools, restaurants, hotels, athletic and recreational facilities, hospitals, and even streetcars, railroad cars, drinking fountains, cemeteries, and park benches.

Free Migrants

Massive migration of free labor was the final feature that helped to reshape the world's labor force. Population increase—so great as to overspill from some areas—combined with improved, cheap, long-range communications to make unprecedented migration rates possible.

Russian and Chinese migration into northern Asia—Siberia and Manchuria—illustrates this well. Russia's population exceeded 167 million in 1900—an increase of nearly 20 million in the last two decades of the nineteenth century. Siberia relied on convict labor until the 1870s, but by the end of the century, almost all the migrants there were free. Nearly 1 million settlers entered Siberia during the 1890s while the Trans-Siberian Railway was under construction (see Chapter 23). About 5 million followed in the first decade or so of the twentieth century, when the railway was complete. Chinese colonization of Manchuria increased after 1860 when the Qing relaxed the rules restricting it. China, indeed, was still the world's most prolific source of long-range colonists. The age-old Chinese diaspora in southeast Asia gathered pace, rising to a total of almost 14 million in the 1890s, and leaping further in the years before the First World War.

Meanwhile, the steamship trade, which also facilitated coolie migration, helped to populate under-exploited frontiers in the Southern Hemisphere and the North American West, and to provide labor for North American industrialization. Europe, because of its exceptional rise in population, was the main source of free migrants. "New Europes," areas with similar climates and environments to those the migrants left behind, were the most attractive destinations. There were areas of this kind in North America, the southern cone of the Americas—Brazil, Argentina, Chile, and Uruguay—Australia, New Zealand, and South Africa. Transatlantic routes were the most popular and carried the most traffic, chiefly because of the economic opportunities that North American expansion created.

Italian immigrants. The photographs Lewis Hine (1874–1940) took of immigrants arriving at Ellis Island in New York City in 1904-1905 launched his career as one of the most socially influential photographers in U.S. history. This shot of an Italian mother and her children, which Hine hand colored, typifies his talent for capturing the dignity and promise of the poor and oppressed.

Most transatlantic migrants headed for the United States, which gained more than 128,000 migrants in the 1820s, and over 500,000 in the 1830s. Numbers trebled in the next decade. Until then, most migrants came from Germany, Britain, and Ireland. A further leap in the 1880s brought the total to over 5.25 million, from all over Europe and especially from Scandinavia, Italy, Central Europe, and the Russian Empire. This was the manpower that fueled continental expansion and industrialization. In 1884, the Statue of Liberty arrived in New York City from France in 214 crates to welcome the wretched of the Earth into America. The cost of erecting it ($100,000, around $5 million in today's money) almost prevented it from being unpacked.

From 1890 to 1920, migration brought a net gain of 18.2 million people to the United States—more than in the entire previous history of the country (see Map 24.5). In combination with industrialization, this turned the United States into a major world power. After 1892, the United States enforced new rules. Immigrants were subject to strict quotas and questioned for suitability. Political undesirables and the morally suspect, including prostitutes and polygamists, were excluded as were those suffering from infectious diseases, such as syphilis and tuberculosis. Canada and the South American countries of the River Plate region, especially Argentina, also made huge gains. By 1914, when 13 percent of the population of the United States was foreign born, the corresponding figure in Argentina was 30 percent. Nearly half Argentina's immigrants came from Italy and nearly a third from Spain. Most of the rest were Eastern Europeans.

HUNTERS AND PASTORALISTS

When the pattern of world population settled after the shake-up, some former parts of it had vanished or shrunk. After slaves, the numbers of pastoral and foraging peoples diminished the most. In some places, the advance of mechanized agriculture simply wiped them out or penned them in reservations where they were doomed to decline. In others, they were converted to settled ways of life. Alternatively, the unfamiliar diseases that contact with outsiders introduced diminished or destroyed them. They survived only in environments too unappealing for better-armed peoples to contest, such as the harsh Kalahari, where San hunters of southern Africa fled to elude their black and white persecutors, or in the vast but merciless Australian interior, where aboriginals retreated from white settlers, or in the North American and

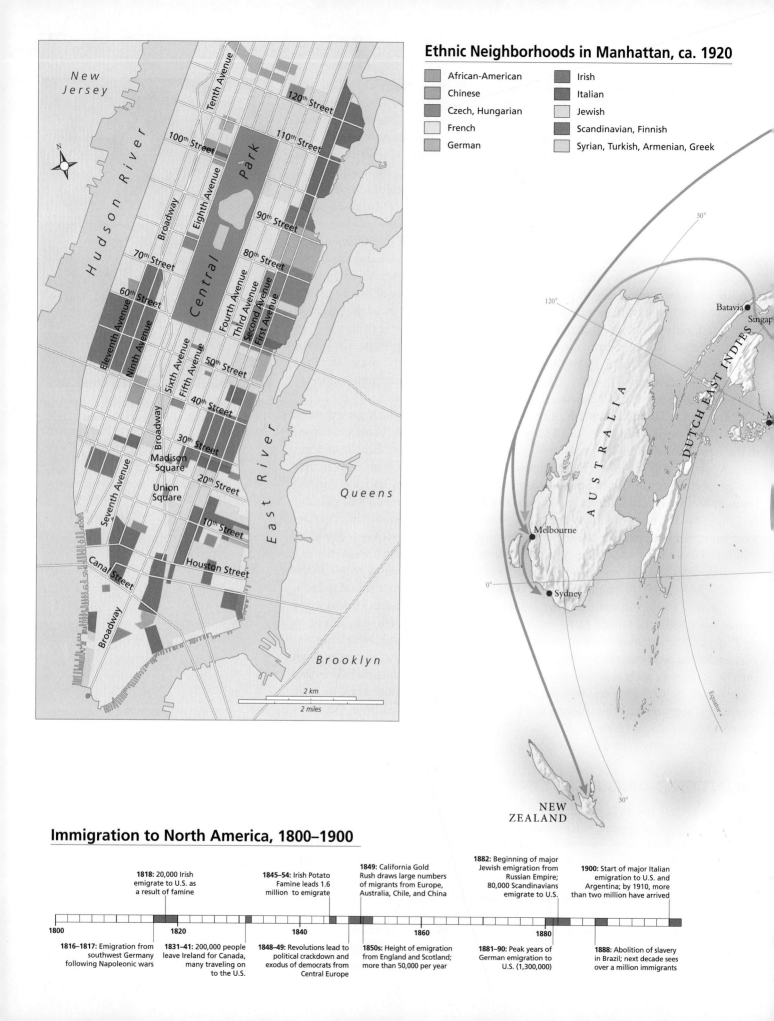

Ethnic Neighborhoods in Manhattan, ca. 1920

- African-American
- Chinese
- Czech, Hungarian
- French
- German
- Irish
- Italian
- Jewish
- Scandinavian, Finnish
- Syrian, Turkish, Armenian, Greek

New Jersey

Hudson River

Tenth Avenue
120th Street
100th Street
110th Street
Broadway
Eighth Avenue
Central Park
90th Street
70th Street
80th Street
Fourth Avenue
Third Avenue
Second Avenue
First Avenue
60th Street
Eleventh Avenue
Ninth Avenue
Sixth Avenue
Fifth Avenue
50th Street
40th Street
Broadway
30th Street
Madison Square
20th Street
Union Square
Seventh Avenue
10th Street
Canal Street
Houston Street
Broadway

East River

Queens

Brooklyn

2 km
2 miles

30°
120°

Batavia
Singap

DUTCH EAST INDIES

AUSTRALIA

Melbourne

0°

Sydney

Equator

30°

NEW ZEALAND

Immigration to North America, 1800–1900

1818: 20,000 Irish emigrate to U.S. as a result of famine

1845–54: Irish Potato Famine leads 1.6 million to emigrate

1849: California Gold Rush draws large numbers of migrants from Europe, Australia, Chile, and China

1882: Beginning of major Jewish emigration from Russian Empire; 80,000 Scandinavians emigrate to U.S.

1900: Start of major Italian emigration to U.S. and Argentina; by 1910, more than two million have arrived

1800 — 1820 — 1840 — 1860 — 1880

1816–1817: Emigration from southwest Germany following Napoleonic wars

1831–41: 200,000 people leave Ireland for Canada, many traveling on to the U.S.

1848–49: Revolutions lead to political crackdown and exodus of democrats from Central Europe

1850s: Height of emigration from England and Scotland; more than 50,000 per year

1881–90: Peak years of German emigration to U.S. (1,300,000)

1888: Abolition of slavery in Brazil; next decade sees over a million immigrants

MAP 24.5

World Migration, ca. 1860–1920

Transatlantic migration

→ to North America

→ to South America and the Caribbean

→ to Europe from the Americas

Other European migration

→ to Australia and New Zealand

→ to North Africa

Asian migration

→ to the Americas and Australia

→ Russian migration into Siberia

→ Indian migration within British Empire

⋯ transcontinental railroad

▢ major exporters of people

▢ major importers of people

ARCTIC OCEAN

ATLANTIC OCEAN

OCEAN

MADAGASCAR

SOUTH AFRICA

Cape Town

Lake Nyasa

Lake Victoria

Lake Tanganyika

A F R I C A

Congo

Nile

Niger

Lagos

Dakar

Mombasa

Mogadishu

YLON

Bombay

INDIA

Calcutta

IA

Tashkent

Baku

OTTOMAN EMPIRE

Constantinople

Odesa

AUSTRIA-HUNGARY

Naples

ITALY

Genoa

Marseille

Suez Canal 1869

Euphrates

Tigris

angtze

CHINA

A S I A

Novosibirsk

Beijing

Trans-Siberian Railway

4 million

6 million

Ob

Yenisei

Moscow

EUROPE

St. Petersburg

GERMANY

Hamburg

Amsterdam

Antwerp

Southampton

Liverpool

BRITAIN

IRELAND

SPAIN

PORTUGAL

RUSSIAN EMPIRE

3 million (2.5 million British)

7 million returnees

8 million

24.1 million

ARCTIC OCEAN

CANADA

Halifax

Quebec

Boston

New York

see inset map

Canadian Pacific

Northern Pacific

Central Pacific

Vancouver

San Francisco

Los Angeles

UNITED STATES

NORTH AMERICA

New Orleans

CUBA

JAMAICA

Panama Canal 1914

PUERTO RICO

MEXICO

Mexico City

OCEAN

Belém

BRAZIL

Rio de Janeiro

Amazon

SOUTH AMERICA

URUGUAY

Montevideo

Buenos Aires

PERU

Lima

Valparaíso

CHILE

ARGENTINA

Equator

835

An Auracano chief in native dress with the Andes behind him, painted in 1853. The native peoples of the extreme southern cone of the Americas fought off Spanish conquistadores and resisted the Chilean and Argentine republics, until industrially produced machine guns defeated them in the late nineteenth century.

Eurasian Arctic. Occasionally, the hesitations of potential enemies saved them: inhibitions that were sometimes romantic, sometimes practical, sometimes a bit of both. In 1884, for instance, when the Swedish government was considering the fate of the Sami—the reindeer herders of the far north—some theorists argued that the pastoralists were relics of an inferior race, whom the laws of nature doomed to extinction. Opponents countered that Sami culture was "the only one suited to expansive regions of the country." The "small peoples of the north," as Russians called them, benefited from the perceptions of romantics who saw them as embodiments of the ideal of the noble savage (see Chapter 22), and of Russian and Finnish sympathizers, who saw them as survivors from an earlier phase of their own peoples' past.

Most pastoralists and foragers, however, lacked such protectors. Railways carved up the lands of the surviving hunter peoples of the North American West. Reservations broke up their communities. Phoney treaties shifted them onto marginal lands where survival was hard. Exemplary massacres harassed them into submission. Thanks to rifles and machine guns, frontier generals could plan to exterminate native peoples "like maniacs or wild beasts." Free rations of cattle bought off the survivors of wars. In 1872, an American army officer reported of the Shoshone of the Great Plains: "Their hunting grounds have been spoiled, their favorite valleys are occupied by settlers and they are compelled to scatter in small bands to obtain subsistence." He described the same depths of demoralization and beggary to which other Native American peoples of the mid- and far west had plunged.

Similar ruthlessness solved the problem of what to do with foragers in the grasslands of South America. In the 1840s, an Argentine president decided that white competition doomed his country's Indians "to disappear from the face of the Earth." In the 1880s, machine guns fulfilled his prophesy. In that decade, the discovery of gold in the far south of Argentina in Tierra del Fuego turned the remotest limits of the American hemisphere into contested territory. Professional man hunters arrived to wipe out the native foragers, charging around five dollars for every Indian they killed. At the opposite end of the hemisphere, in the Aleutian Islands off the coast of Alaska, missionaries and bureaucrats saved the native fishing communities from extermination by Russian conquerors, but could not mitigate the effects of diseases to which the inhabitants had no resistance. An epidemic in 1838–1839 wiped out half the population, by official estimates. When Russia sold Alaska to the United States in 1867, another wave of casual looters arrived, with another alien culture, imposed by force.

Less dramatically, but equally effectively, governments in the Old World induced nomads to change their way of life. Mehmet Ali, the khedive of Egypt (see Chapter 23), turned nomadic Arab tribal leaders into landowners, mobilized the desert warriors, and seized their horses. The former nomads shifted to the towns or became "lost among the peasants." Russian governments in the same period forced Muslim Khazaks and Kirgiz nomads in Central Asia into agriculture by confining them to land grants too small for them to sustain themselves by grazing their flocks.

ELITES TRANSFORMED

Industrialization created proletariats. The dwindling of slavery, serfdom, and foraging transformed rural lives and work patterns. Migration and new forms of social control shook up the role and distribution of the world's labor. At the top end of society, the changes of the period were almost as traumatic for those they touched. While peasantries and working classes suffered, the era of industrialization transformed aristocracies or, at least, severely tested them. They survived by diversifying from an emphasis on landed estates into new economic activities. When they failed to adapt, they perished.

In Japan, the government abolished samurai privileges in the 1870s. A military draft for all able-bodied men in 1873 effectively eliminated the main legal distinction—the right to bear arms—between samurai and commoners. Japan now had no warrior caste. Many samurai benefited from the abolition of distinctions within their own class. Lower samurai were now free to accumulate wealth and honor. Professions that had formerly been considered socially beneath them, such as merchants and civil servants, opened up to the gentry, and many of them became dependents of the government. They also served as officials and as officers in the new European-trained army and navy, or invested in new industries. Others declined into poverty and merged into the ranks of the commoners.

Traditionally, in China merit had been the means to attain high social rank. But families with inherited wealth had an advantage because they could afford good schooling for their sons and tended increasingly to monopolize access to the scholar elite in the nineteenth century. "The gentry are at the head of the common people," said imperial instructions to magistrates, "and to them the villagers look up." The impoverished landowners of China shook off the ties of extended kin and the traditional social obligations of their status. Thanks to their efforts to find new sources of wealth, by engaging in trade, or by exploiting the labor of poor neighbors and tenants on their land, they found themselves demonized as "evil gentry."

The British aristocracy survived the collapse of land prices by diversifying into commerce, by marrying American heiresses, and by absorbing into its ranks the "beerage"—the new class of wealthy entrepreneurs, such as those who owned the massive, mechanized breweries that supplied the workers' beer. Reversals of traditional class relationships were the favorite theme of comic writers. W. S. Gilbert and Sir Arthur Sullivan, whose works dominated musical theater in late nineteenth-century Britain, devoted much of their satire to merciless jokes about egalitarianism and most of their plots to reversals of rank in topsy-turvy worlds, in which noblemen become working-class apprentices, common seamen, and gondoliers, while an attorney's clerk rises to be Lord High Admiral and an ex-convict becomes Lord High Executioner.

The **new rich** were among the most satirized villains and clowns of the age. In Charles Dickens's novel *Our Mutual Friend* (1864–1865), the middle-class Mr. Veneering suddenly emerges with a mansion, an aristocrat's coat of arms, and the ambition to win a seat in parliament. The type was familiar in real life. Sir William Cunliffe Brooks (1819–1900) was a British banker, but so "common"—in the opinion of an aristocratic friend—that even his housekeeper made fun of his lower-class accent. He bought a castle in 1888 and turned the old kitchen of his hunting lodge into a chapel, decorated with hunting trophies. "The effect," said a visitor, "was that you were in a baronial hall, or the comfortable private chapel of an old baron."

The sons of the new rich acquired the habits, friends, and tastes of gentlemen at the numerous new and expensive schools—called "public" in Britain only because they sought to be of public importance—and the growing universities. Old blood allied with new money. Industrialization shifted the balance of power and wealth away from landed estates and into cities. But landowners could also benefit, by mining coal and iron ore on their estates or by leasing or selling the land on which to build towns and docks. The third Marquess of Bute (1847–1901) did

Elite uniforms. The Freemason's Lodge of Freetown, in Sierra Leone in West Africa, presents an address to the Duke of Connaught, a son of Queen Victoria, on December 15, 1910. The white ladies, in their tea dresses under the canopy, and the top brass with ceremonial swords and pith helmets, look positively informal by the standards of the black dignitaries, who wear what appears to be full evening dress in the heat of the tropical day. It would be hard to find a more telling image of determination to defy the environment.

all these things and left an estate worth nearly $10 million, equivalent to several hundred million today. As early as the 1840s, about a sixth of England's landed gentry earned a significant part of their wealth in business, mainly through manufacturing, banking, and railways. Aristocracies were becoming middle class while the middle class was adopting aristocratic tastes.

Every industrializing economy had its new rich and its declining aristocracies. In Spain, the vulgar tycoon, the Marquis de Salamanca, who made a fortune out of Madrid real estate, typified new money, with his shady deals and showy ways. The novelist Pérez Galdós satirized the decline of old money in one of his best novels, *Mercy* (1897), about hard times for an aristocratic family, who were maintained by their maid's talents as a beggar. In Russia, Anton Chekhov's play *The Cherry Orchard* (1904) features an old landed family compelled to sell its estate, and the upwardly mobile local entrepreneur who buys them out, after enduring years of their exploitation and contempt.

In the United States, "old" money, which was in truth not very old, was more vulnerable to intrusion by the new rich because the country had no landed aristocracy and no titled nobility. Nonetheless, in a book entitled *Our Benevolent Feudalism* in 1902, W. J. Ghent argued that American millionaires were developing into an hereditary nobility. In 1899, Thorstein Veblen proposed in *The Theory of the Leisure Class* that America had acquired an elite whom inherited wealth exempted from having to worry about money. In the 1870s and 1880s, Samuel Ward McAllister attempted to create high society, based on the admission of supposedly suitable people to entertainments given by socially exclusive hostesses in New York City—exclusive, that is, according to McAllister himself. "We want the money power," he explained in 1872, "but not to be controlled by it." In effect he was admitting that the American aristocracy was open to new money, and indeed, merchants and railroad men's sons and daughters got into McAllister's list of America's "First Four Hundred." Old money did occasionally resist. At Newport on the Rhode Island coast, Southern planters and New York tycoons built palatial summer "cottages" of marble and gilt. But the coal merchant's wife who built the breathtaking mansion of Rosecliff there found herself alone at her house's inaugural ball. Her neighbors boycotted her party. Snobbery was indissoluble, even in champagne.

Outside the West, too, the rise of the new rich was probably the biggest change in the composition of the elite. As we have seen, most purchasers of land came from outside the peasantry or aristocracy. Westernization made the rise of a new class easier, by spreading values and tastes distinct from those of traditional aristocracies. In the 1870s, one Angolan chief looted his own people to build a medieval-looking castle and collect violins. In the 1890s, another hired an ex-slave who had worked for the Portuguese as a maid to teach him European etiquette. Almost everywhere, Western dress became the uniform of the world's elite—at least for men. Formal suits with top hats, ties, stiff collars, and striped pants were the uniform of male power, whether affected by the well-to-do of Freetown in Sierra Leone in West Africa, or the Maori chiefs of New Zealand. The self-reinvented samurai who staffed the Japanese government chopped off the topknots from their hair and clamped shiny top hats to their heads. Among the relics of José Rizal, the leader of Filipino nationalism in the last years of the nineteenth century, are his yellowing stiff collars, lovingly preserved at the fort of Santiago in Manila (see Chapter 26).

Thorstein Veblen, from *The Theory of the Leisure Class*

IN PERSPECTIVE: Cultural Exchange—Enhanced Pace, New Directions

Despite differences of pace, texture, and density in the spread of railways and mechanized production, and despite the complexity and perplexities of social change, the common experience of industrialization restored a kind of uniformity to Western society. A gap opened between the developed and underdeveloped worlds. The technology gap became a wealth gap between the regions that supplied commodities and those that turned them into manufactured goods. These worldwide inequalities were hugely bigger, and would prove more enduring for the future, than the internal class differences that divided industrializing societies.

Meanwhile, exchanges of culture crossed the world with greater intensity and speed than ever before. No example is more eye catching or more obviously attuned to the pace of industrialization than the standardization of time. Until the nineteenth century, every place determined its own time of day according to the sun and set its clocks accordingly. But the railway made it impossible to maintain this "natural" time. People could move too fast. The railway schedules became too complex. In 1852, an electric telegraph system was set up to transmit the time at the Royal Observatory in Greenwich across Britain. In 1880, Greenwich time became by law the official standard time for the whole country. At the International Meridian Conference, held in Washington, D.C., in 1884, the same standard became the basis for a sequence of time zones covering the entire globe (see Map 24.6).

Cultural exchange got faster and more complicated than ever. In part, this was because people—who in every age have been the most effective agents of cultural change—could travel farther and more frequently than formerly. The world's first travel agent, Thomas

Cultural exchange. The fashion for Japanese art and taste in the late nineteenth-century West extended to women's clothing. Paintings of Westerners in Japanese kimonos—like these American women painted in San Francisco around 1880—demonstrate the fashionable appeal of Japan. Note the view of Mount Fuji in the background on the left-hand panel. *Photograph courtesy of the Peabody Essex Museum*

MAP 24.6 **Time Zones of the World**

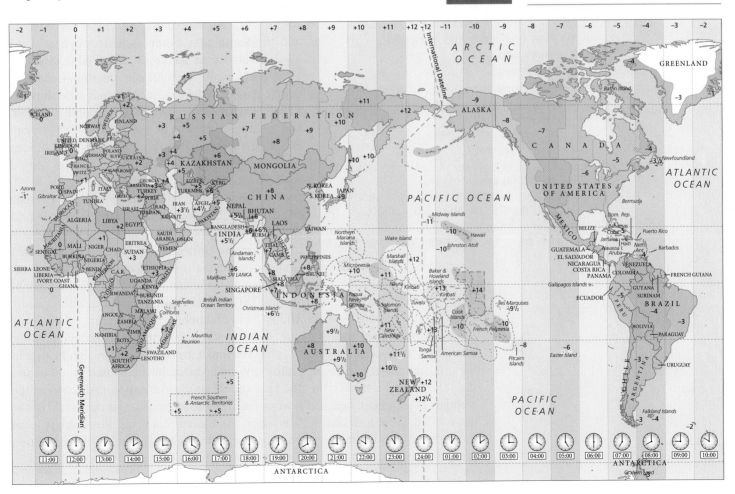

CHRONOLOGY

1791–1803	Haitian Revolution
1800	1 million slaves in the United States
1800–1900	3.3. million slaves shipped from Africa to the Americas
1807	Britain outlaws slave trade
1809	United States outlaws importation of slaves
1825	Haiti wins official independence
1834	Slavery abolished in the British Empire
1838–1839	Epidemic wipes out half of the native population of the Aleutian Islands
1842	Edwin Chadwick's *The Sanitary Condition of the Labouring Population*
1845–1876	Ottoman agricultural exports increase fivefold
1848	France outlaws slavery; publication of Marx's and Engels's *The Communist Manifesto*
1850s	25,000 Chinese live and work in California
1853–1854	Serfs in Habsburg Empire emancipated
1860s and 1870s	French ship 50,000 Indian laborers to the Caribbean
1861	Serfs in Russia emancipated
1863	Emancipation Proclamation (United States)
1867	Publication of Marx's *Capital*
1870s	Japanese workers and peasants freed by official decree; samurai privileges abolished
ca. 1875	McCormick Company of Chicago produces 15,000 reapers per year
1880s	5.25 million immigrants arrive in the United States; bounty offered for killing Indians in Argentina
1885	Egypt outlaws slavery
1886	Cuba outlaws slavery
1888	Brazil outlaws slavery
1890s	32 percent of French work force is female; 14 million people migrate from China
1890–1920	Immigration adds 18.2 million people to U.S. population
Late nineteenth century	Arts and Crafts movement
ca. 1900	Cotton cultivation in Egypt contributes to the creation of 2 million landless peasants
	Population: Izmir, 200,000; Alexandria, 250,000; Calcutta, more than 750,00; Melbourne, 800,000; New York, 3.4 million; London, 6.5 million
1914	30 percent of the population of Argentina is foreign born

Cook and Company, founded in Britain in 1841, began by organizing a local trip for a temperance society in England. By 1900, Cook's was selling 3 million travel packages a year. Most of the trips the firm organized were still within Britain and were sold to working- and middle-class tourists. But Cook's also took luxury travelers, big-game hunters, business people, and even high officials of the British Empire across the world.

Cultural exchange, however, was not one-way Westernization. What Europeans considered exotic style became fashionable in the West. The Japanese-inspired style that Western designers called "Japonisme" was the most striking case. The French painter Claude Monet (1860–1926) portrayed his wife in a kimono. Camille Pissarro (1830–1903) copied Japanese prints—notably in his famous painting of umbrellas in Paris. Giacomo Puccini, the leading operatic composer at the turn of the century, borrowed from what little he knew of Japanese, Chinese, and even Native American music and put it in his operas. These exchanges took in wider influences, too. In the 1890s, the Czech Anton Dvorák was among the first European composers to draw on African-American music. European painters and sculptors began to discover the wonders of what they called primitive art from Africa and the South Seas. Some exchanges bypassed the West altogether. In the 1890s, Chief Mataka of the Yao—deep in the East African interior—made his people don Arab dress, launched Arab-style ships on Lake Nyasa, planted coconut groves and mangoes, and rebuilt his palace in the mixed Arab–African Swahili style that had long dominated the East African coast (see Chapter 21). "Ah!" he exclaimed, "now I have changed Yao to be like the coast!"

Although cultural transmissions increasingly crisscrossed the world, one route was new and would become dominant. The big new influences came from the United States, heralding trends that would dominate the twentieth century. This was surprising at the time. North America had previously followed European and, to some extent, Latin American cultural leadership. In politics, as we shall see, the United States launched, nurtured, or revised some ideas of enormous and growing influence in the world—including, notably, democracy and socialism—but it is hard to find a movement of any significance in the arts, literature, science, or philosophy that started in the United States before the 1890s. Then, however, the flood began, as European composers discovered the wonders of American ragtime. It was a small beginning, but it was the herald of the dawn of an "American century" in which the United States was increasingly to be the source of worldwide trends in popular culture, entertainment, the arts, taste, food, and, ultimately, the major source of new technology and ideas.

PROBLEMS AND PARALLELS

1. What were the advantages and disadvantages of modernization and industrialization in Japan and Europe in the nineteenth century? Who were the winners and losers from this process?

2. How did industrialization change daily life for the average urban dweller? Did these changes improve life or make it more difficult?

3. What does the term *paternalism* mean? Why did Karl Marx's prediction of a workers' revolution not come to pass?

4. How did large-scale urbanization transform social, economic, political, and cultural life in the nineteenth century? What types of organizational structures, architecture, and municipal systems developed to cope with highly concentrated populations? How did machines change the way people viewed the environment?

5. What forms of labor replaced slavery in the nineteenth century?

6. How did industrialization change women's and children's lives?

7. How did massive migration of free labor reshape the world's labor force?

DOCUMENTS IN GLOBAL HISTORY

- Karl Marx from *The Communist Manifesto*
- Samuel Smiles, from *Self Help*
- A Luddite pamphlet

- Edwin Chadwick, from *Sanitary Conditions of the Labouring Population*
- Henrik Ibsen, from *A Doll's House*
- Thorstein Veblen, from *The Theory of the Leisure Class*

Please see the Primary Source CD-ROM for additional sources related to this chapter.

READ ON

My version of the story of Oshio Heicharo is based on I. Morris, *The Nobility of Failure* (1988). The best general survey of the nineteenth-century world is C. A. Bayly, *The Birth of the Modern World* (2003).

T. Hunt, *Building Jerusalem*, (2004) and A. Briggs, *Victorian Cities* (1993) deal with urbanization in the British state and empire. J. Merriman, ed., *French Cities in the Nineteenth Century* (1981) is a good survey of France; C. Chant and D. Goodman, et al., eds., *European Cities and Technology: industrial to post-industrial city* (1999) is a valuable six-volume collection of essays and documents. Peter Hall, *Cities in Civilisation* (1998) is particularly good on urban culture. On the effects on health, D. Brunton, *Health, Disease, and Society in Europe* (2004) is a highly useful collection of documents. R. J. Evans, *Death in Hamburg* (1987) is an impressive case study.

On working conditions in the industrializing world, P. Stearns, *Lives of Labor* (1975) is particularly good. J. Burnett, ed., *Useful Toil* (1994) is a valuable collection of English working-class autobiographical materials. A. Kelly, *The German Worker* (1987) does a similar job for Germany. R. C. Alberts, *The Good Provider* (1973) is a lively biography of Heinz. G. Marks and S. M. Lipset, *It Didn't Happen Here* (2000) is a useful attempt to explain the failure of socialism in the U.S.A.

M. Lynch, *Mining in World History* (2004) is a magisterial survey, with emphasis on technological aspects. S. Kanfer, *The Last Empire* (1995) is an enjoyable history of De Beers.

D. Avery, *Not on Queen Victoria's Birthday* (1974) studies the Río Tinto case.

On rural conditions in the unindustrializing world, S. Bose, *Peasant Labour and Colonial Capital* (1993) is an outstanding study of Bengal; for Thailand, J. C. Ingram, *Economic Change in Thailand* (1971) is excellent. On Africa, M. Lynn, *Commerce and Economic Change in West Africa* (2002), and W. G. Clarence-Smith, *Slaves, Peasants, and Capitalists in Southern Angola* (1979) are important. J. McCann, *Green Land, Brown Land, Black Land* (1999) surveys sub-Saharan Africa with emphasis on the ecological effects of economic development. C. Issawi has published a series of invaluable works, rich in documents, on the Middle East, notably *The Economic History of the Middle East* (1966) and *An Economic History of Turkey* (1980), which can be supplemented with R. Kasaba, *The Ottoman Empire and the World Economy*; P. Richardson, *Economic Change in China* (1999) is a good introductory survey on that country.

For changes in labor regimes, H. Thomas, *The Slave Trade*, (1999) and D. Northrup, *Indentured Labor in the Age of Imperialism* (1995) are fundamental. The eight volumes of P. J. Kitson and D. Lee et al., eds., *Slavery, Abolition, and Emancipation* (1999) make an invaluable collection of mainly literary and theoretical source materials. S. Miers and R. Roberts, eds., *The End of Slavery in Africa* (1988) and P. C. Emmer and M. Morner, eds., *European Expansion and Migration* (1992) are useful collections. P. Kolchin, *Unfree Labor* (1990) compares America and Russia.

Western Dominance in the Nineteenth Century: The Westward Shift of Power and the Rise of Global Empires

Unequal combat in the Opium Wars. The British ironclad, *Nemesis*, blows Chinese war junks to smithereens with impunity, on January 17, 1841, off Guangzhou. The print was circulated at the British shipbuilders' and arms-makers' expense, partly to advertise their wares.

O n February 10, 1842—Chinese New Year's Day—General Yijing (yee-jing) consulted the oracles in the Temple of the War God. China was at war with Britain. Yijing was the commander of a force sent to root the invaders from Ningbo (nihng-boh), a key port on the coast of central China for controlling the Yangtze River system. He could succeed, the oracle warned, only if "you are hailed by humans with the heads of tigers." A few days later, a band of aboriginal recruits arrived dressed in tiger-skin caps. The general was delighted and distributed similar caps throughout the army. Following ancient Chinese war magic, he ordered his forces to attack at the hour designated as that of the tiger on the day of the tiger in the month of the tiger.

CHINA

Yijing also tried other ways to secure victory, some magical, some original, but all with a touch of desperation about them. He flung a tiger's skull into the Dragon's Pool to arouse the dragon to attack the foreigners. He contemplated attacking the British ships with monkeys strapped with firecrackers to their backs. But the plan proved impracticable, and the monkeys died of starvation.

The campaign was chaotic. Chinese troops mistook and fought their own men. The supply department failed, inflicting unendurable hunger on the army. Thousands of porters who carried the army's baggage died or deserted. Commanders received rewards for writing reports on nonexistent victories. Embezzlers raided the war chest. Only a fraction of the army arrived in time for the battle. Misunderstanding their orders, troops attacked the main city gate armed only with knives.

They faced, moreover, a new kind of "barbarian." The British forces had state-of-the-art munitions—products of the early phases of industrialization—and steam-powered gunboats. They could recruit large numbers of men—"black devils," as the Chinese called them—from India, where Britain was building up an empire of its own. The Chinese proved powerless to stop the invasion. The aggressors could go where they liked and do what they liked.

At first glance, the outcome of the campaign looks like a triumph for modernity. Ancient methods and magic failed in the face of professional, disciplined forces equipped with industrially produced guns and ships. The dynamic out-thrust of a go-ahead Western nation shattered an inward-looking, self-satisfied empire.

FOCUS questions

- WHY DID China cease to be the world's richest nation in the nineteenth century?
- WHY WAS the West able to subjugate so much of the world?
- HOW DID African states resist Western imperialism?
- WHAT WAS business imperialism?
- WHERE WERE the "New Europes"?
- WAS THE United States an empire in the nineteenth century?
- HOW DID social Darwinism justify imperial rule?

Such conclusions would be unfair or at least exaggerated. Chinese respect for ancient rituals, such as omen taking and the invocation of dragons, did not usually cloud rational judgment or get in the way of military efficiency. The deficiencies of organization and generalship in Yijing's command were not unique to, or typical of, Chinese warfare. The Chinese government was actually negotiating with France at the time to buy the latest military and naval technology from the West, but the war broke out before the Chinese could acquire the much-needed equipment.

Nevertheless, the conflict revealed how much the balance of power in the world had shifted during the early stages of industrialization. For most of recorded history—for most of this book—China had been the source of most world-shaping technological innovations. In partial consequence, China had also been the world's greatest power, secure in its people's conviction of China's unique status as the "central country," with the strength to influence and sometimes dictate politics far from its own borders and shores. Britain, by contrast, had spent most of history on the edge of Eurasia—literally, a marginal part of the world—absorbing influences from outside rather than radiating its own influence to the rest of the world. Now the positions were reversed. Thanks in part to the substitution of machine power for manpower, a small country like Britain could easily defeat a giant, such as China. Thanks to the exploration of the wind systems of the world and the development of technologies of long-range communications, a position on the edge of the West had turned from a disadvantage into an advantage. From the shores of the Atlantic, powers in Western Europe and North America could reach out across the world, using seaborne communications to mesh together increasingly ambitious, increasingly vast territorial domains. The broader context of General Yijing's failures reveals a further vast shift in global history: an economic shift—upheaval in the traditional balance of wealth and reversal in the traditional structures of trade.

● ● ● ● ●

THE OPIUM WARS

A trade dispute, indeed, had provoked the war of which Yijing's campaign formed part. At the center of the dispute was opium. The British wanted to sell opium in China. The Chinese authorities wanted to stop them. As we have seen (see Chapter 21), British merchants in the eighteenth century found that there was growing demand in China for opium, a product they could ship from India at large profit. The opium trade represented an important breakthrough into a market in which, previously, most foreigners had virtually nothing to sell. To buy the products of China, to meet booming demand, above all, for tea in Europe and North America, Westerners had to pay cash. To earn that cash, they had to work hard, trading and shipping products between Asian markets or exploiting resources in other parts of the world. In the early nineteenth century, the trade in opium expanded sharply. The annual value of the opium that reached China rose fivefold in the 20 years preceding the mid-1830s. As the trade increased, so did the alarm it caused in China, much as today's global traffic in heroin and cocaine alarms the West. Because narcotics are addictive, they create their own captive markets and command high prices. This makes them ideal commodities for relatively poor producer economies seeking outlets in rich economies.

Chinese statesmen and intellectuals were united in blaming opium addiction for demoralizing, enfeebling, and impoverishing increasingly large numbers of Chinese. They were also aware that the drain of revenues threatened one of China's great historic sources of strength: its favorable balance of trade with the rest of the world. The situation became acute in the 1830s, because Britain abolished trading monopolies among its own subjects and opened free trade with China. In 1839, therefore, the Chinese emperor appointed Commissioner Lin to find ways to end the opium trade.

In February of that year, Lin drafted a letter for the British monarch Queen Victoria. The letter was never sent, but it is an admirable summary of Chinese thinking. The draft begins by declaring that human nature is the same in all peoples and climes and that all peoples have the same capacity to distinguish evil from good. The document stresses the benevolence of the Chinese Empire in allowing commerce with foreigners: "Rhubarb, tea, and silk are all valuable products of ours, without which foreigners could not live."

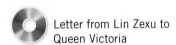

Letter from Lin Zexu to Queen Victoria

> "But there is a class of evil foreigner," the draft went on, "that makes opium and brings it for sale, tempting fools to destroy themselves, merely in order to reap profit. Formerly the number of opium smokers was small; but now the vice has spread far and wide. . . . Our great, unified Manchu Empire regards itself as responsible for the habits and morals of its people and cannot rest content to see any of them become victims to a deadly poison. For this reason we have decided to inflict very severe penalties on opium dealers and opium smokers. . . . What it is here forbidden to consume, your dependencies must be forbidden to manufacture, and what has already been manufactured Your Majesty must immediately search out and throw into the sea, and never again allow such a poison to exist in Heaven or on Earth. When that is done, not only will the Chinese be rid of this evil, but your people too will be safe. For so long as your subjects make opium, who knows but they will not sooner or later take to smoking it?" The draft added an appeal to something the British understood: commercial considerations. "The laws against the consumption of opium are now so strict in China that if you continue to make it, you will find that no one buys it and no more fortunes will be made. Rather than waste your efforts on a hopeless endeavour, would it not be better to devise some other form of trade?"

The British—those of them in charge of trade and government, at least—were unresponsive to appeals grounded in morality. Nor were they disposed to suspend opium production while the trade remained profitable. Commissioner Lin was wrong to think that the threat of suspending commerce in rhubarb or tea would force Britain to agree with Chinese wishes. Rhubarb sold in relatively small quantities, and the British had huge stockpiles of tea. It was no good hoping for British cooperation. If China wanted to stop the opium from reaching its people, China had to act on its own.

In the spring and summer of 1839, Lin confiscated all the opium he could find and flushed it into the sea—writing a poem of apology to the Spirit of the Sea for this act of pollution. He was unable, however, to secure promises from the British merchants that they would withdraw from the trade, and in January 1840, the imperial court suspended trade with Britain. The British acknowledged that China could punish its own subjects for smoking opium. But to ban the trade itself was unlawful interference in the freedom of commerce, and to confiscate the chests of opium from British merchants was an outrage against private property.

Destroying opium. Commissioner Lin destroyed the opium he confiscated from Western—chiefly British—merchants at Guangzhou in 1839 by mixing it with lime and flushing it into the sea or, in the example here, setting it on fire.

The Treaty of Nanjing

Britain responded to Chinese provocations with obviously disproportionate counter demands: for compensation and indemnities for the confiscated opium, for territorial concessions, and for the liberalization of trade. In the summer of 1840, a British expeditionary force blockaded China's ports, occupying the Guangzhou (Canton) waterfront and reopening trade by force. The following year, after the Chinese refused Britain's terms, British warships, with opium vessels in their wake, sacked China's coastal and river towns. The British hardly noticed General Yijing's counterattack of 1842.

In the Treaty of Nanjing, which ended the war, China ceded Hong Kong to Britain, opened five other ports to British trade, and paid a colossal indemnity of 21 million silver dollars (equivalent in purchasing power today to around $2 billion). Henceforth, British officials, not Chinese, would have the right to settle disputes between British and Chinese subjects. Britain would have what we now call "most favored nation" rights in China. British subjects would automatically enjoy any privileges and immunities that China conceded in future to other foreigners. The United States, France, and Sweden soon persuaded or forced the Chinese to grant them similar treaties.

To the Westerners' surprise, the subsequent growth of trade still favored the Chinese, at least until the late 1850s. Tea was a more valuable drug in the West than opium was in China, and the market for it was bigger and faster growing. Britain's official deficit with China rose from under $20 million in the year of the Treaty of Nanjing to nearly $55 million in 1857. It took a further series of British incursions and invasions from 1856 onward to wrest from China terms of trade weighted in Westerners' favor. In 1860, the Taiping rebellion virtually paralyzed the Chinese state. A French and British task force found it easy to march to Beijing, burn the imperial summer palace, and exact the terms the Westerners wanted from the Chinese government (see Chapter 23).

Henceforth, foreigners dominated China's trade and bought up the best real estate in the major trading centers (see Map 25.1). In 1880, for instance, two British steamship companies handled between them 80 percent of China's shipping business. The effects of the wars partly account for this relatively sudden leap to Western ascendancy. In the background, other influences piled up. First, industrialization in the West compensated for China's size and enabled Western economies to overtake China's in wealth. Meanwhile, Western imperialism in other parts of the world increased the resources available to Western powers.

The rise of the West to economic superiority over China—and, indeed, of some Western powers to economic dominance within China—was one of the major reversals of history. Since then, the world has experienced an abnormal situation, in which—until the last few years, at least—China has been stagnant and, by the technical standards of Western powers, backward or under developed, while historical initiative—the capacity for some groups in the world to influence others—has been concentrated in the West. Whereas for centuries China had been the only country to occupy the position of a *superpower*—a state exceeding in strength that of all rivals combined—Western states have been the main contenders for that role. Britain exercised it briefly in the nineteenth century, and the United States has enjoyed it—briefly again, so far—in the late twentieth and early twenty-first centuries.

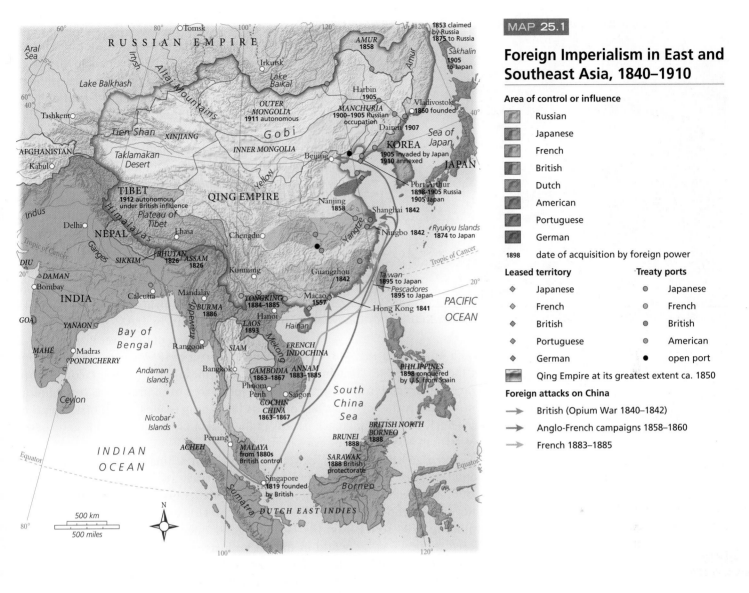

MAP 25.1

Foreign Imperialism in East and Southeast Asia, 1840–1910

Area of control or influence

- Russian
- Japanese
- French
- British
- Dutch
- American
- Portuguese
- German

1898   date of acquisition by foreign power

Leased territory

- ◇ Japanese
- ◇ French
- ◇ British
- ◇ Portuguese
- ◇ German

Treaty ports

- ○ Japanese
- ○ French
- ○ British
- ○ American
- ● open port

Qing Empire at its greatest extent ca. 1850

Foreign attacks on China

- → British (Opium War 1840–1842)
- → Anglo-French campaigns 1858–1860
- → French 1883–1885

THE WHITE EMPIRES: RISE AND RESISTANCE

The change occurred in the context of a new feature of global history in the nineteenth century: the rise—beginning, like industrialization, in Western Europe and rapidly coming to include Russia, the United States, and Japan—of enormous empires that spread across the globe and virtually carved up the world among them. Previously, most of the really big empire-building initiatives in the world had originated in Asia, and the empires expanded by land into territories that bordered on those of the conquerors. Such was the nature of the empires of the Persians, Arabs, Chinese, Indians, and steppelanders such as the Mongols—the empires whose stories have dominated much of this book. Even at the height of their predominance, Chinese rulers had never sent fleets beyond the Indian Ocean, or armies beyond Central Asia (see Chapter 15).

Alongside the great empires, smaller imperial ventures had also set out to control trade rather than production, to dominate sea-lanes and harbors rather than large stretches of land. Most European imperialism had been of this character. Until the eighteenth century, as we have seen (see Chapter 21), no empire except Spain's had really been able to combine these roles on a large scale. Europeans overseas had generally depended on the goodwill of local collaborators in existing economic systems.

An allegory of the British Empire, by the Scottish painter William Dyce, decorated the favorite residence of Queen Victoria (r. 1837–1901). Britannia's lion signifies empire, and her trident stands for Britain's rule of the sea. The gods of wisdom, science, and industry attend her with personifications of liberty, work, and war. Other figures representing beauty and commerce humbly reach for the hem of her garment, hoping to be saved from storms and sea monsters.

Now their relationship with the world they had entered changed, as they exploited the advantages of industrially equipped armies and navies to control the production of the key commodities of global trade. The combination of land and sea empires became commonplace.

As in industrialization, Britain established an early lead in imperialism. The first world war—different, of course, from the First World War of 1914–1918—began during the French Revolution in the 1790s (see Chapter 22) and ended with the final defeat of Napoleon in 1815. The British government had already begun to think globally, locating colonies in strategic positions along the world's trade routes. While continental European powers fought and distracted each other, British governments pushed global thinking to new extremes. In 1807, they launched an unsuccessful invasion of the River Plate region of South America. In 1812–1814, Britain fought the War of 1812 to check the ambitions of the United States. Britain took advantage of these wars to wrest colonies from France, Spain, and Holland and to seize useful stations to control global communications by sea, including Malta and other Mediterranean islands, South Africa, parts of the Dutch East Indies, French islands in the Indian Ocean, and islands and coastal positions in and around the Caribbean.

Other governments had, as yet, no such vision. China was still self-absorbed, confident of its role as the central country and barely aware of events in the wider world. Japan was still proudly ignorant of global events—content to rely on Dutch informants, who managed to keep the fall of Holland to French revolutionary armies in 1794 secret from the Japanese government for years. Even the French closed windows to the world in the early nineteenth century, although they had invaded Egypt and Syria in the late 1790s, with the ultimate aim of establishing an empire in the east, where, as Napoleon said, "great reputations are made." First, France withdrew from Egypt, then abandoned the effort to reconquer Haiti from rebellious slaves, then, in 1803, sold to the United States its claims to the vast territory in North America known as Louisiana. The British could consolidate the conquests they had already made, thanks to a long period of peace with other European countries that lasted for almost 40 years after the fall of Napoleon in 1815.

For other powers, the empire-building process really took off in the second half of the century, when the world experienced a tremendous increase in imperialism (see Map 25.2). For European powers, Africa was the biggest arena. African resistance and tropical disease had deterred or defeated earlier would-be conquerors from Europe, who seized patches of coast but never got far inland. Now, however, in a notorious scramble for territory, in the last two decades of the nineteenth century, seven European powers seized 10 million square miles of Africa. The Pacific was sliced up in similar fashion. In southeast Asia, in the same period, only Thailand eluded European, Japanese, or American imperialism. Even in parts of the world largely exempt from the rule of these empires, in most of continental Latin America, and east and southwest Asia, local governments had to accept economic domination—a form of exploitation that has come to be known as **business imperialism**—and political interference in both their internal and foreign affairs.

Existing empires enlarged. The extent of land under French rule doubled between 1878 and 1913. The total territory of all European empires more than doubled to more than 20 million square miles over the same period, while the total population of their empires increased from a little over 300 million to over 550 million people (see FIgure 25.1). New empires emerged: those of Germany, Italy, and Belgium (or rather, strictly speaking, of King Leopold II of the Belgians, for his empire in the Congo was, at first, a so-called free state under the king's personal rule). These were new countries, outcomes of European rebellions and wars: Belgium only came into being in 1830, while Italy and Germany were forged by the unification of many smaller states in the 1860s. Italy's was a particularly significant empire, because it was built up by a state with no direct access to the Atlantic. Italy used the Mediterranean as a route to expand into North Africa and the Levant, and the new Suez Canal, which opened in 1869, as a means of access to imperial conquests in East Africa. Portugal acquired a "third" African empire in Angola and Mozambique to replace those it had lost in the Indian Ocean and Brazil. The Netherlands withdrew from West Africa to concentrate on building up a huge empire in Indonesia. Some parts of Europe took little part: the Scandinavian powers and Spain engaged in the outreach of this period only to a modest extent, while the Habsburg Empire, centered in Austria and Hungary, with limited access to the sea, showed no interest in overseas expansion. Russia's vast land empire left it little scope and energy for maritime adventures (see Chapter 21). With these exceptions, however, it is fair to speak generally of "European" global imperialism.

In part, we need to understand European expansion against the background of demographic change. Europe's population soared. At the beginning of the nineteenth century, most of Malthus's fellow intellectuals (see Chapter 20) believed that what they called "progress" could sustain population growth and, in particular, that agricultural improvement could enhance nutrition in Europe and generate enough surplus food to feed many mouths. Broadly speaking, they were right. During the nineteenth century, most European countries roughly doubled their populations. Russia's increased four times over. At the same time, Europe generated enough surplus population to populate "New Europes" in the temperate parts of the Americas, Australia, New Zealand, Algeria, and South Africa. Over the eighteenth and nineteenth centuries as a whole, despite big rises in population in some parts of Asia, Europe's share of world population rose from around a fifth to over a quarter.

In places that European outreach targeted, native populations declined as a proportion of the global whole. In some places they declined in absolute terms. Africa illustrates the role of demography. The figures are glaring. From rough parity with Europe's population in the seventeenth century, Africa's share of world population dropped to little more than 8 percent by 1850. The reasons for this are unknown. It seems, however, that while plague (see Chapter 14) receded from Europe, sub-Saharan Africa's killer diseases—malaria, sleeping sickness, yellow fever—remained rampant, and in North Africa plague lingered. Although we lack the data to make comparisons with earlier periods, the incidence of recorded plagues in North Africa grew in the eighteenth century—in the

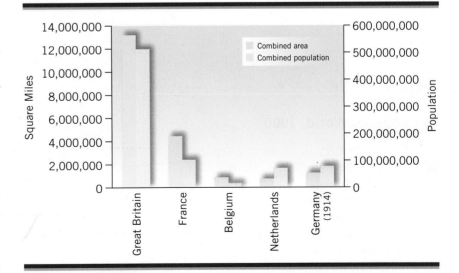

FIGURE 25.1 EUROPEAN EMPIRES: AREA AND POPULATION, ca. 1939

Niall Ferguson, Empire: The Rise and Demise of the British World Order and the Lessons for Global Power, *New York: Basic Books, 2003, p. 242.*

Greenland

ICELAND

ALASKA

Rocky Mountains

C A N A D A

Great Lakes

St. Lawrence

NEWFOUNDLAND

Missouri

St. Pierre and Miquelon

Chicago

UNITED STATES OF AMERICA

New York
Washington DC

Mississippi

Los Angeles

Rio Grande

BRITAIN
London

DENM

NETH.
BELGIUM
Paris
FRANCE

SPAIN

PORTUGAL
Lisbon
Madrid

GIBRALTAR
Ceuta
Melilla

Azores

Madeira

MOROCCO
IFNI

ALGERIA

RIO DE ORO

Sahar

ATLANTIC
OCEAN

Bermuda

MEXICO

Havana
CUBA
U.S. occupation

Mexico City

Jamaica

Bahamas

DOMINICAN REPUBLIC
Puerto Rico
Virgin Islands
St. Martin
HAITI
LEEWARD ISLANDS
Guadeloupe
West Indies
Martinique

Canary Islands

CAPE VERDE
ISLANDS

Senegal

Sahel

WE

BRITISH HONDURAS
HONDURAS

GUATEMALA
SALVADOR
NICARAGUA
Curaçao

COSTA RICA

BARBADOS
WINDWARD ISLANDS
TRINIDAD AND TOBAGO

GAMBIA
PORTUGUESE
GUINEA

GOLD
COAST

NIG

SIERRA LEONE

LIBERIA

Niger

P A C I F I C

O C E A N

VENEZUELA
Orinoco

COLOMBIA

Guiana Highlands

BRITISH GUIANA
DUTCH GUIANA
FRENCH GUIANA

TOGO
Fernando
Po
SAO TOME
AND
PRINCIPE

RIC
MUN

Galapagos Islands
to Ecuador

ECUADOR

Amazon
Basin

Amazon

Ascension

Marquesas Islands

PERU

Lima

B R A Z I L

São Francisco

ST. HELENA

Tuamotu Islands

BOLIVIA

Andes

Rio de Janeiro
São Paulo

WALVI
to Cape

Pitcairn Island

CHILE

ARGENTINA

PARAGUAY

Paraná

Paraguay

Santiago

URUGUAY
Buenos
Aires

Patagonia

FALKLAND
ISLANDS

MAP 25.2

The Imperial World, 1900

- Ottoman Empire
- ◆ Britain and possessions
- ◆ France and possessions
- Denmark and possessions
- ◆ Spain and possessions
- ◆ Portugal and possessions
- ◆ Netherlands and possessions
- ◆ German Empire and possessions
- ○ Russian Empire and possessions
- Japan and possessions
- Italy and possessions
- ◆ United States and possessions

N

RUSSIAN EMPIRE
Siberia

AUSTRO-HUNGARIAN EMPIRE

Gobi

QING
EMPIRE

KOREA
Beijing
Port Arthur
Jiaozhou

JAPAN
Tokyo

EMPIRE

PERSIA
Tehran

AFGHANISTAN

Nanjing
Shanghai

NEPAL

BHUTAN

KUWAIT
BAHRAIN

Delhi
Ganges

Himalayas

Yangtze

Suez
Canal

INDIA

Chandernagore

Burma

Macao
Hong Kong
Taiwan

OMAN

Arabian
Peninsula

Diu
Damão
Bombay

Guangzhouwan

Yanaon

SIAM

Bangkok

Manila

Mariana
Islands

Guam

ANGLO-
EGYPTIAN
SUDAN

ERITREA
HADHRAMAUT

Goa

Mahé

Madras
Pondicherry
Karikal

FRENCH
INDOCHINA

Saigon

PHILIPPINE
ISLANDS

Marshall
Islands

Addis
Ababa

Aden
FRENCH SOMALILAND
BRITISH
SOMALILAND

CEYLON

BRITISH
NORTH BORNEO

Caroline
Islands

ETHIOPIA

ITALIAN
SOMALILAND

MALDIVE
ISLANDS

BRUNEI

MALAYA
SARAWAK

PACIFIC OCEAN

BRITISH
EAST
AFRICA

Singapore
Borneo

KAISER WILHELM'S
LAND

Gilbert
Islands

GERMAN
EAST
AFRICA

Zanzibar

Seychelles

Chagos Islands

DUTCH EAST INDIES

New
Guinea

BISMARCK
ARCHIPELAGO

EASTERN
RHODESIA

Batavia
Java

PAPUA

Solomon
Islands

Ellice
Islands

BRITISH
CENTRAL
AFRICA

Amirante Islands

Comoro Islands

Cocos Islands

Christmas
Island

PORTUGUESE
TIMOR

Santa Cruz
Islands

ZAMBEZI

SOUTHERN
RHODESIA

PORTUGUESE
EAST
AFRICA

MADAGASCAR

Mauritius
Réunion

INDIAN
OCEAN

Fiji

SOUTH AFRICAN
REPUBLIC

New
Caledonia

ORANGE FREE STATE

NATAL

BASUTOLAND

AUSTRALIAN
COLONIES

Lord Howe
Island

Darling

Sydney

NEW
ZEALAND

**Percentage of Earth's Land Surface
Controlled by Colonial Empires in 1914**

Independent: 29.8%

Chinese: 6%

Ottoman: 1.5%

Russian: 15%

Portuguese: 1%

French: 7.7%

Spanish: 1%

Belgian: 1.6%

Italian: 1.8%

German: 1.6%

British: 21.5%

Japanese: 0.4%

Dutch: 1.4%

United States: 7.6%

Danish: 1.5%

The Battle of Omdurman. "Whatever happens, we have got the Maxim gun and they have not," wrote a cynical British poet about combat between modern Western armies, armed with machine guns, repeating rifles, and heavy artillery, and their non-Western foes who still fought with spears, swords, and shields. This contemporary commemorative panorama of the British victory over the Sudanese at the Battle of Omdurman revels in the slaughter wrought by irresistible technical superiority. Almost 11,000 Sudanese were killed, and at least 16,000 wounded in this battle, at a cost of 48 British lives—half of which were lost when a British colonel insisted on fighting one anachronism with another by launching a cavalry charge.

very period when plague disappeared from Europe. The last outbreaks in the Maghrib, as far as we know, were in 1818–1820 and in Egypt in 1835. The decrease of population in Africa altered the continent's role in the world. For European intruders, it came to make more sense to take over African soil and exploit its products and potential directly, instead of milking the continent for slave labor.

Even so, demographic changes alone cannot account for the ascent of Europe to global hegemony. Europe still did not have enough manpower to dominate the world. Industrial technology, however, made up much of the shortfall. Europe's advantage became visible in the late eighteenth century. In the 1770s, the chronometer solved the problem of how to find longitude at sea. This hugely increased the security of long-range navigation because it enabled sailors to know when they were approaching dangerous coasts. New steel-making technology (see Chapter 23) enhanced guns of European manufacture. Rifled guns and breach-loading artillery improved in the same period, as did techniques for making tropical-weight clothing. Gradually, medicines good enough to keep European armies alive in the tropics came into use—especially, in the second half of the century, quinine pills and powders from plantations in India and Java. Quinine could stave off the effects of malaria, the biggest tropical killer disease. Steam power, meanwhile, made the labor of European workers more productive and improved the precision, adaptability, and reliability of European armies in hostile environments. Victim-peoples of Western imperialism found it hard to resist invaders borne on steamboats, fortified by quinine, and armed with steel guns.

In the last quarter of the century, machine guns, especially the Maxim gun, patented in 1884, made a huge difference because unlike heavy artillery, they could be easily transported to almost any destination. In 1880, General Roca machine-gunned his way through the Native American defenders of the pampa in central and southern Argentina. The following year, a similar campaign of extermination began against the Yaqui Indians in northwest Mexico. The government expropriated their lands, giving 1 million acres to a frontier rancher and over 1.2 million acres to a United States construction company. In 1884, French guns silenced opposition to their takeover of Indochina. British gunships blasted the southeast Asian kingdom of Burma out of existence in 1885. In 1893, white settlers in what is now Zimbabwe in southern Africa shot the spear-armed Ndebele warriors to pieces. In a typical gesture of despair in 1895, Ngoni priests in Mozambique in East Africa threw away their bone oracles after defeat by invincibly well-armed Portuguese. In 1898, the classic case occurred: the battle of Omdurman, where the British mowed down the previously invincible forces of a Sudanese leader. The Sudanese losses were 11,000 dead and 16,000 wounded. British losses are usually put at 48 killed, 382 wounded. "Whatever happens we got/The Maxim gun and they have not," wrote a cynical British versifier. Like all technological advantages, the West's military superiority could not be permanent, but it was vital while it lasted.

Still, it would be a mistake to attribute the empires' dominance to technology alone, any more than to demographics alone. Despite medical advances, disease could still defeat white armies in tropical climes throughout the century. In South Africa in 1879, it killed twice as many British soldiers as were lost in combat to the Zulus. In Cuba in 1898, during the Spanish-American War, three times as many Americans fell to disease as to enemy action. Partly because of the ravages of disease, it took France 13 years of brutal warfare, from 1882, to conquer Vietnam (known to the French as Tonkin China), even with an army of 35,000 men. "Tonkin cholera, Tonkin misery, Tonkin famine, Tonkin cemetery" became a grim joke in Paris. Nor did Western armies always have things all their own way on the battlefield. Their supremacy was patchy at first, for technological advantages were slow to mature. During wars against the Sikhs of northwest India in the 1840s, the British found that the defenders could almost match their firepower. In 1876, an alliance of Sioux and Cheyenne almost annihilated a force of United States' cavalry at the Battle of the Little Bighorn. In 1879, a Zulu army surprised a British force at Isandlhwana in South Africa. Of 1,800 British troops, only about 350 escaped alive.

After all these defeats, the white man took effective revenge, but as well as waging and winning conventional battles in wars of resistance, underequipped native defenders on colonial frontiers could prolong the wars with guerrilla tactics. Such tactics kept the British out of Afghanistan in the 1840s and 1870s and harassed the French in in the interior of Algeria, where native fighters never ceased to resist the colonizers after the French occupied the city of Algiers in 1830. In the 1870s, the French logged 2,380 guerrilla incursions in Algeria. In the East Indies, the Dutch lost 15,000 men subduing resistance in Java in the 1820s. It later took them 30 years, from 1873, to bring the sultanate of Aceh in northern Sumatra under control, thanks to the deadly combination of fierce native guerrillas and killer diseases.

Two cases illustrate the possibilities of successful native resistance in conventional warfare. The Maori wars in New Zealand lasted a long time: from 1845 to 1872, on and off. British forces only reported victories against Maoris, but British propaganda masks a remarkable fact. Maoris repeatedly got the better of the British by devising effective tactical and technical responses to the invaders' superior firepower. The Maori quickly became masters of musket warfare, copying the volley-firing discipline of European troops. Indeed, the Maori were among the most effective users of muskets. In the 1830s, in a frightening imitation of European methods, musket-armed Maori conquered the Chatham Islands, southeast of New Zealand, dispossessing and slaughtering the native fisher folk. In 1862, a British missionary thought that the Maori were "apparently equal to an English regiment as regards order and discipline."

Moreover, the Maori developed an ingenious method of defense, digging underground bunkers of the kind Western armies later adopted in fighting each other, while posting snipers to break up British attacks. In consequence, they sometimes won offensive battles—at least in the early phases of the wars, before the British had the advantages of newer rifles—while in defensive engagements, the Maori were virtually unbeatable, despite being habitually outnumbered. They also made cunning use of strategic withdrawals. Frequently, British artillery expended a fortune's worth of shells against Maori defenses, only to find they were unoccupied. When the Maori finally ceased to resist, it was partly because their own ranks were divided—the British had seduced some to their side. Partly, too, the inequality of numbers between settlers and Maori had become too great. The Maori were outnumbered by more than three to one in a land that by the end of the century had nearly 750,000 white settlers. Even after the conclusion of the wars in 1870, an independent Maori zone remained

Dutch attempts to conquer Aceh began in 1873 and raged on and off for 30 years. Aceh had been an independent sultanate for centuries, and it was still imperfectly subdued when the Dutch conceded Indonesian independence in 1949. The photograph shows one of the small units the Dutch organized in response to the guerrilla methods of the Acehenese, with three Dutch officers for only sixteen native riflemen.

unconquered, gradually integrating, by peaceful accommodation, into the emerging New Zealand state (see Chapter 26). The Maori also proved adept at European business and technology, developing their own sawmills and European-style shipping.

Ethiopia proved to be even more robust. Emperor Menelik II (r. 1889–1913) beat the European imperialists at their own game. He came to the throne as a passionate modernizer with a love of gadgets—the sort of man, said one of his European aides, who "would build an escalator to the moon." He used improved revenues from expanding trade to buy Western military technology. By the mid-1890s, he had 100,000 modern rifles. He also reformed the army's supply services, while upholding the traditional methods of recruiting soldiers, via the warrior aristocracy and local chiefs, and the traditional ideology of crusade. He proved that an African state could compete with European empires on equal terms in the scramble for Africa.

While respecting areas of European control, Menelik conquered an empire of his own as far as Lake Turkana in the south and the swamplands of the upper Nile to the west. Campaigns began with traditional chants of self-praise from the troops and ended in "terrible butchery," as a European observer reported, "by soldiers drunk with blood." Menelik scattered garrisons in conquered territory, imposed Christianity on pagan communities, and introduced the customs and dress of his native province of Shoa. In 1896, Italy attempted to take over his empire. At the battle of Adowa, the Italian army crumbled in the face of Ethiopian firepower. The Italians lost a third of their 18,000 men killed, plus a further 1,500 wounded and 1,800 captured. Ethiopia emerged from the scramble for Africa as the only enlarged native African state.

Ethiopia is a reminder that even in the nineteenth century imperial expansion was not a white privilege. Other native African states tried it, but all succumbed, sooner or later, to conquest by Europeans. Khedive Ismail of Egypt (r. 1863–1879), for instance, was, for a time, one of Africa's most successful native imperialists. He proclaimed his ambitions openly. The opera he commissioned for the opening of the Cairo Opera House in 1871 was Giuseppe Verdi's *Aida,* a celebration, in Ismail's eyes if not in those of Verdi, who was an empire-hating liberal, of ancient Egyptian wars of conquest southward. In 1878, Ismail announced that he would present, at the Universal Exposition of that year in Paris, a map showing Egypt's borders resting on Lake Chad in Central Africa, with a project to open a route to the Atlantic.

Ismail realized that steam power could open up the potential of the African interior. He believed that he could exploit Western sympathies to help him create an empire for Egypt among the remotest reaches of the Blue and White Niles. Posing as the policeman of slave-trading routes, he would raise finance for empire-building among antislavery philanthropists in Britain and France. He employed Europeans to lead armies and administrators into what he called the "province of Equatoria," on the Nile in Central Africa, in a world of great lakes and waterfalls that were only beginning to find their way onto maps in Europe. But the difficult environment and vast distances defeated him. His armies were overwhelmed or isolated. Along the Red Sea and Blue Nile, he encountered invincible resistance from the native states. Meanwhile, his ambitions bankrupted Egypt, and his westernizing ways helped provoke a nationalist rebellion. In 1882, Britain took control of the Egyptian government (see

A European view of the battle of Adowa. In contrast to the Ethiopian version of the battle depicted on the Closer Look on page 855, the European press managed to invest the Italian defeat with the heroic quality of a last stand against overwhelming odds. In this typical example from a British newspaper, *The Graphic,* the light is falling on the Italians' gleaming uniforms, which convey an impression of civilization and almost of sanctity, in contrast to the demonic savagery of their Ethiopian attackers. The Italian troops are surrounded by spent cartridge cases. The kneeling soldier on the right, with his transfixed look and prayerful posture, is trying to reload despite a mortal wound. Outlined against the gunsmoke, on a rearing horse, General Baratieri, the Italian commander, who was killed in the battle, raises his helmet in a last salute to rally his doomed troops.

A CLOSER LOOK:
AN ETHIOPIAN VIEW OF THE
BATTLE OF ADOWA

In the Battle of Adowa in 1896, the Ethiopians under the command of Emperor Menelik II (r. 1889–1913) annihilated an invading Italian army. An Ethiopian painting from early in the twentieth century shows the victors in a more positive light than in the European version of the same battle on page 854.

Menelik calmly directs his troops. He is dressed in imperial regalia and accompanied by officials and holy men who survey the action from underneath umbrellas that signify their rank. The umbrellas are dark colored as a sign of mourning that Christian blood was being shed by both sides.

Astride a white horse, and protected by a halo painted in the national colors of Ethiopia, St. George leads Menelik's army.

Ethiopian firepower includes cannon, machine guns, and repeating rifles.

Legendary Ethiopian heroes, clad in traditional dress, slash the Italian infantry with swords.

With his horse facing backward, the Italian commander, General Baratieri, appears ready to order a retreat.

How does this painting provide a different perspective on nineteenth-century imperialism from the version that most Westerners believed in at the time?

Chapter 23). What remained of Ismail's conquests eventually became the Anglo-Egyptian Sudan—in effect, an unruly part of the British Empire.

In northwest Africa, meanwhile, the sultan of Morocco, Mulay Hassan (moo-LAY HAH-sahn) (r. 1873–1894) tried to preempt European imperialism by claiming dominion over the Sahara, as ruler of "all the tribes not subject to another sovereign" and of "the land of all the tribes who mention the sultan in their prayers." These were unrealistic pretensions. The desert peoples acknowledged "no other chief than Allah and Muhammad." Religious leaders commanded respect and sometimes organized resistance to imperialism from whatever quarter it came. In the 1890s, the holy man Ma el Ainin (ma ehl-eyein-NEEN), whose breath supposedly made sand miraculous, fought off French and Spanish invaders in the western Sahara, without even paying lip service to the sultan. His stronghold at Smara still stands in the desert. After Mulay Hassan's death, rebellious sheikhs and jealous European powers weakened his empire until, in 1904, France and Spain partitioned Morocco between them.

The sort of empire Mulay Hassan imagined in North Africa, Said Barghash (r. 1870–1888), sultan of the island of Zanzibar in East Africa, dreamed of in the heart of the continent. "Chosen," he claimed "by Providence to found a great African kingdom which will extend from the coast to the great lakes and beyond to the west," he realized that he needed to conciliate European powers. He therefore posed as a foe of the slave trade—but, along with ivory, slaves were the wealth of the region he claimed. Instead of relying, like Khedive Ismail, on European officers, Barghash employed African and Arab agents to represent him in the African interior. They were often deeply implicated in slaving, which was a provocation to the Europeans. In the early 1880s, Barghash's governor in Ugogo, Mwinyi Mtwana, gave Germany an excuse to intervene by charging outrageous tolls on caravan traffic. The Germans put him to death and took over his territory. Barghash's system was doomed. By the time of his death, Britain and Germany had dismembered and shared out his territories. Zanzibar became a British protectorate in 1890.

METHODS OF IMPERIAL RULE

If white imperialism was not imposed by weight of numbers, or solely by force of superior technology, it must have relied—indeed, it did rely almost everywhere—on native collaborators. Thanks to historians' work in the last 50 years or so, we know much more about how people in territories that received European imperialism reacted to it. Far from being passive playthings of white superiority, we can now see that native Asian, African, and Pacific states were participants in the process and that native peoples were its exploiters and manipulators, as well as its victims. Without the consent of native communities, empire was expensive. Even at its best, empire was probably only marginally profitable in most places. Without native help in policing and administration, the Western colonial empires could never have functioned.

India, for instance, had fewer than 1,000 British administrators in the 1890s in a country of 300 million people. European observers considered Java, with 300 Dutch administrators for 30 million people "over-governed." British troops in India never numbered more than 90,000 men—0.03 percent of the population. The rest of the Indian army, more than 200,000 men, was made up of Indian troops under British officers. Though empires sometimes shipped large armies to their colonies for conquests or to repress rebellions, they could never afford to keep such forces in place for long.

The most common device for harnessing native cooperation was what the British called **indirect rule** (or *dual role* as the Dutch called it, or *association* to use the term the French applied in Indochina). "The keynote of British colonial method, said Frederick Lugard (1858–1945), the official largely responsible for developing the system of indi-

○ MAKING CONNECTIONS ○

TECHNOLOGY AND IMPERIALISM

TOOLS AND TECHNOLOGY →	REGION OF DEVELOPMENT/DATE OF INVENTION →	EFFECTS
Invention of chronometer	Britain / 1770s	Allowed for precise location of longitude, increasing security of long-range navigation; effective planning of voyages
Steelmaking technology	Britain and Western Europe / 1730s–1800s	Increased productivity in steelmaking creates more products; more effective small arms and artillery
Rifles and breach-loading artillery	Britain and Western Europe / 1840s–1900	Combined with better materials (see above) to improve weaponry
Tropical-weight clothing	Britain and Western Europe / 1850s–1900	Allowed more mobility, comfort in tropical zones for colonial military and officials
Quinine pills, powders, and other medicines	Europe (1750); large-scale use by 1850	Used to stave off effects of malaria; helped increase mobility of European colonial officials and soldiers in Africa/Asia
Steam power	England / 1769–1900 (continuously improved)	Powering ships, railroads, vastly increased speed over wind-propelled sails or horsepower on land
Machine guns	Europe / 1860s–1900 (continuously improved)	Allowed for annihilation of native resisters of colonialism in Latin America, Central America, Indochina, Africa, and Burma

rect rule in Africa, was "to rule through and by the natives." As a British parliamentary committee recommended in 1898, "Adopt the native government already existing; be content with controlling their excesses and maintaining peace between them."

Lugard exaggerated in claiming that this was a uniquely British method, which "has made us welcomed by tribes and peoples in Africa." On the contrary, it was how most successful empires succeed and have succeeded throughout history. Europeans were welcome in many places that became regions of indirect rule because of the *stranger effect* (see Chapter 16). Some cultures are disposed to grant what to us seem surprising degrees of power to outsiders—sometimes because of the high esteem accorded to the exotic and strange, such as we show for rarities and curiosities from distant shores, and sometimes because of a shrewd calculation. The foreigner is a useful arbitrator in disputes, because outsiders can be—or appear to be—objective. So, as long as they retained local power, many native elites in colonial lands were willing to grant the topmost level of authority to European intruders and pay them to exercise it.

Indirect rule worked particularly well in British colonies because British administrators, even though they were usually middle class, had an aristocratic outlook and education and came from an old monarchy. They could sympathize with traditional elites and aristocracies and could even sense that they had more in common with them than with many of their fellow Britons. In 1897, the aristocratic wife of a British governor in Fiji in the Pacific made the point in her diary: "How can I make it clear to Nanny," she wrote, that the "native ladies," as she called the wives of local chiefs, "are my equals?" whereas "Nanny," who was a working-class English woman, was emphatically

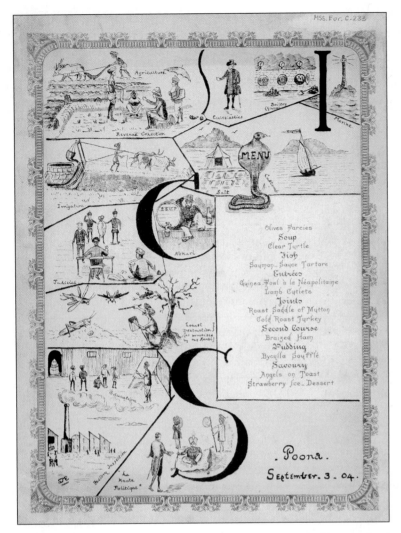

White Man's Burden. The Indian Civil Service (ICS) was the highly paid, professional bureaucracy that governed Britain's Indian Empire. Until the 1920s, its members were overwhelmingly British. This dinner menu for members of the ICS in 1904 looks lavish and self-indulgent at first but reveals much about the difficulties of governing distant empires: the range of activities for which the civil servants felt responsible; the differences in development in the largely rural India of the day; nostalgia for the tastes of home; and the self-mocking humor that helped English administrators cope with their jobs.
© The Trustees of the British Museum

not. Especially after 1877, when Queen Victoria of Britain officially took the title of Empress of India, British administrators sought to link the traditional Indian elite to the crown with aristocratic trinkets: coats of arms, lavish ceremonies, knighthoods, and other titles. Indirect rule was more than a charade, however. Local, regional, and subordinate native rulers retained real power. More than one third of India was divided among states ruled by Indian princes, and native sultans ruled virtually the whole of Malaya. Friendly native chiefs administered parts of German East Africa (modern Namibia). Regents, as the Dutch called traditional local rulers, and autonomous sultanates, survived in the Dutch East Indies. Even the French, whose republican principles should have made them hostile to the idea of working with the traditional hereditary elites of their colonies, accepted the necessity of indirect rule. Morocco and Tunisia were French *protectorates* under the formal rule of figurehead Arab monarchs, for instance, whereas most of Algeria was considered part of France, run by the same system of provincial administration as was France itself. In their tropical African possessions, the French delegated awkward jobs, such as tax collecting, to native chiefs. They also ruled through native monarchs in Cambodia, Laos, and Vietnam. In practice, European powers could exercise jurisdiction at their discretion, even in territories classed as protectorates or nominally shared, like the Anglo-Egyptian Sudan, with native corulers. When they thought it necessary, they could change the personnel or nature of local and regional government in their colonies. But the trouble and expense of direct rule were always best avoided if possible. Everywhere, local collaborators kept the European empires going. A local chief named Ngailema settled the boundary between French and Belgian spheres on the lower Congo River, extorting rich gifts from both sides.

Still, even in areas of indirect rule, European imperialism could have transforming effects on methods of government and ways of life. Changes in legal systems are a good way to measure the impact of empire. In Malaya, in the second half of the century, the court of the Sultan of Kedah closely imitated European practices, while the Sultan of Johor, Abu Bakr, who ruled for most of the second half of the nineteenth century, struck English visitors as "a perfect English gentleman." The sultans' subjects still regarded the ruler's power as supernatural and revered the symbols of royalty as sacred, but trial by jury replaced magical ordeals and appeals to oracles. The state enforced its exclusive right to violence. Cases traditionally settled by private vengeance became matters of public law. Male adulterers—formerly fair game for injured husbands—now paid steep fines. Such transformations, however, remained dependent on local sympathies. In 1892, a French administrator in Senegal in West Africa proposed that the ordeal of the hot blade (which supposedly would not burn the mouth of an innocent man) be discontinued, together with the practice of punishing not just the offender, but his entire family. The suggestions struck local chiefs as so radical that they had to be shelved.

The British far preferred to rely on traditional aristocracies rather than on the "educated natives" whom the French favored. But educated natives were indispensable. Interpreters were vital. "The commanders come and go," ran a French saying in West Africa, "but the interpreters are always there." Even though most colonial regimes privileged some particular set of laws—usually those of their own mother country—in practice many competing systems of traditional and customary law inevitably applied in vast territories inhabited by many different historic communities. Locals, who knew their way around the native cultures, were vital guides. Four thousand of them served in the administration of the British-ruled parts of India in the late 1860s. Twenty years later, Indians occupied nearly two-thirds of the jobs. Bankimcandra Chattopadhyaya, whom Bengalis regard as one of their greatest writers, showed the contradictions of this class of *babus*, as the British called their Indian helpers. Bankim accepted office under the British as a deputy magistrate. He earned British admiration and won British rewards, including a medal, which, in one of his own short stories, features as a payoff for a corrupt magistrate. The hero of his novel, *Anandamath*, of 1882, warns his fellow countrymen, "There is no hope of the revival of true faith if the English do not become rulers. . . . Our knowledge of ourselves cannot grow without knowledge of the world. The English are well versed in knowledge of the world and they are great teachers too. Therefore we shall make them kings." On the other hand, his work has terrifying passages of revolutionary bloodshed directed against the British. His attitude toward Indian independence in the late nineteenth century was like St. Augustine's toward chastity in the late fourth century. He wanted it, but not yet.

An alternative strategy to indirect rule or reliance on native administrators was to ship collaborators in from far away. When Frederick Lugard marched into Uganda in East Africa in 1890, his forces included many African Muslims: a Somali chief porter, Sudanese soldiers, and sharpshooters from Zanzibar. When Henry Morton Stanley claimed the lower Congo in Central Africa for King Leopold II of the Belgians in 1880, he found a French outpost commanded by a black Senegalese sergeant, dressed "in dirty African rags," who declared "in all seriousness that, being the only White man there, he was glad to see others arrive to keep him company." In Sierra Leone in West Africa, Britain established a black colony of freed slaves from the Caribbean, who created an imitation of England in their capital at Freetown, with garden parties, lecture circuits, concerts, and a temperance union to combat alcoholism. Sawyer's bookshop in Freetown sold such English middle-class manuals of behavior as *The Ballroom Guide* and *Etiquette and the Perfect Lady*.

In other places, local allies enabled the Europeans to rule. The British fought the Zulus with the help of other peoples of South Africa, and recruited Hausa gunners from what is today Nigeria to keep order in West Africa. The French conquerors of Tukolor on the Niger River in West Africa in 1889 incorporated thousands of other Africans into their army. Then, when their native soldiers rebelled, the French enlisted the conquered Tukoloros against them. In the 1890s, the British Empire nurtured the Kingdom of Lozi in southern Africa while pulverizing the neighboring Ndebele people into submission. The Lozi king acquired a portrait of Queen Victoria, visited London to great acclaim, and became a satisfied client of white imperialism.

Indirect rule. Snapped in late 1920, the French ambassador to Cambodia takes center-stage, in a posture of rigid authority, as the nominal ruler of the country, King Sisowath Monivong, (r. 1904–1927), stands to his right, in French uniform and a subordinate role. Like other imperial powers elsewhere, the French in Indochina preferred to mask the reality of their power behind the facade that native monarchs and elites retained control of their own countries.

Female bravery. Legend has it that a young Scots woman was first to hear the bagpipes of the relief force that on March 5, 1858 raised the siege of Lucknow. Some 3,000 British and Indian troops and civilians had been besieged at Lucknow since July 1, 1857 during the rebellion against British rule in 1857–1858 that the British called the Indian Mutiny. Balladeers celebrated the incident and the fashionable English artist, Frederick Goodall (1822–1904), painted it.

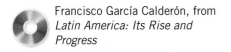

Francisco García Calderón, from *Latin America: Its Rise and Progress*

In getting and keeping the empires going, women were among the most important native collaborators. "White" women were in short supply in the European colonial territories in the first half of the nineteenth century, but relations between European men and native women could be advantageous to both parties, opening useful local links for the colonizers and, for local groups, exploitable channels of communication with the incoming elite. The future British field marshall Sir Garnet Wolseley (1833–1913) wrote as a young officer to his mother from India that with a native concubine he could supply "all the purposes of a wife without any of the bother." Concubinage, however, virtually ceased in India after a rebellion among native soldiers against British rule in 1857, which panicked the British into distancing themselves further from native society. Female emigration from Europe stepped up in the late nineteenth century. In the Dutch East Indies, less than a quarter of the European settler population was female in 1860. The proportion had risen to well over a third by the end of the century. India saw a similar rise in the numbers of British women. In former times, the children of sexual alliances between natives and newcomers had often played important roles in cementing the alliances on which empires relied. In the nineteenth century, that became ever harder, because racism classed "half breeds" as inferior and kept them on the margins of the communities from which they sprang.

BUSINESS IMPERIALISM

The most indirect form of imperial rule was economic control—business imperialism, which left government in local hands but bought up resources, skimmed off wealth, introduced foreign business elites, reduced economies to dependency, and diverted wealth and political influence abroad. Again, industrialization made business imperialism possible. The world was increasingly divided between primary producers and industrial manufacturers. This division made interregional trade vital as never before. It opened a wealth gap between the primary and secondary producers and gave the rich of the industrialized countries surplus capital with which to buy up the productive capacity of much of the rest of the world. Though the evidence is insufficient, scholars debate whether large-scale foreign enterprises blocked development of smaller and more local initiatives, frustrating economic growth and industrialization in regions where business imperialism was rife.

Latin America registered the most obvious effects. In a sense, colonialism never really ended in Latin America. Native communities, or "indios," as they were called, constituted most of the population in most of the region, but they never exercised a fair share of power or acquired a fair share of wealth. Instead, they became the quasicolonial victims, the exploited human "resources" of their countries' own elites. These elites, though they drove out the representatives of the Portuguese and Spanish crowns, continued themselves to represent European culture—to speak the languages and maintain the customs and privileges of the European conquerors.

Moreover, in the second half of the nineteenth century, foreign investors became a powerful extra elite tier in much of Latin America. A new form of colonial-type dependency arose, this time on international big business. Overwhelmingly, the investors were Europeans, from the major imperial powers of the day—Britain, Germany, and France—and from the United States. In the **Monroe Doctrine** of 1823, the United States had unilaterally decreed a ban on European colonialism in the New World. Thanks in large part to European agreement, the ban worked, and European powers stayed out of most of mainland Latin America for most of the time. Now European capital found a way around the ban. Indeed, business imperialism almost became the forerunner of reimposed European rule. In 1864, the French government installed a puppet ruler in Mexico, on the pretext of securing Mexican debts owed to European creditors. The adventure proved a fiasco. Popular rebellion, the need for troops in Europe, and United States' diplomacy drove the French away in 1867, but the involvement of foreign business in the Latin American economy kept growing.

British investments in Latin America rose from $425 million in 1870 to $3.785 million by 1913. This added up to two-thirds of the total foreign investment in the region. British companies controlled over half the shipping in Argentina and Brazil and most of South America's railways. By 1884, Europeans owned two-thirds of Chile's nitrates—the valuable new fertilizers of the period (see Chapter 23). Argentina's foreign trade almost trebled in the last three decades of the century. Foreign capital led the boom. Similar developments occurred in other parts of Latin America. Like other forms of imperialism, business imperialism was a collaborative project between locals and strangers: local elites and foreign capitalists. In 1870, a British firm opened for business in Rosario, Argentina's second city, to provide water and drainage. The local authorities demanded high levels of investment and a high share of the yield for themselves. In Brazil, British power in the coffee market aroused many complaints, but Brazilians owned or acquired most plantations, and the government accepted underdevelopment and economic inferiority to foreigners as inevitable.

Hostility to foreigners was more normal, though rarely effective. In 1860, the president of Peru, Ramón Castilla, restive under foreign control of the trade in natural fertilizers, voiced what became the standard complaint: "On many occasions we have been treated with grave lack of respect, as if for the great international potentates there did not exist a common law of nations." The Argentine epic poem of 1872, *Martín Fierro*, by José Hernández, celebrated a gaucho of expansive tastes, for whom the land could never be big enough. It recalled a golden age before bosses, "gringos," and Englishmen, demonic and effeminate, who were "good only to give work." In the last years of the century, nationalists who resented business imperialism adopted the text as a call to independence.

A pattern emerged: local interests attracted foreign investment. This led to foreign control of key technologies for the production and transportation of primary commodities. The consequence was dependence on foreign markets and financiers and, often, political control by foreign businessmen. In 1870, for instance, the government of Costa Rica contracted out its railway-building program to an engineer from the United States. A few years later, his nephew began using the railway to ship bananas to North America. His firm eventually grew into the United Fruit Company—a conglomerate so rich and monopolistic that it became more powerful in the early twentieth century than any government in Central America.

The United States itself, meanwhile, was an important arena for European businessmen, who plowed massive investments into industrial

Business imperialism. Even countries that "business imperialism" condemned to produce primary products for the industrialized world could experience industrialization of their own. Some cotton-growing countries, for example, sought to become textile manufacturers. This early twentieth-century photograph of a factory in Ecuador shows automated spinning under way on the right, and cylinders full of carded cotton on the left.

Exploitation. Carefully posed in the self-conscious style favored by photographers at the time, this scene of ivory-bearers in French Congo in 1890 served as a postcard. Part of the message that the person who sent it wrote is on the largest tusk and in the margin at the right.

The New European Imperialism: Africa and Asia

Nineteenth century	European population explosion fuels economy and creates surplus population for global migration; Africa's population declines
ca. 1815–1835	Value of opium exported to China increases fivefold
1820s	Dutch lose 15,000 men in conquest of Java
Summer 1840	British blockade Chinese ports in response to Chinese suspension of trade
1842	Treaty of Nanjing ends Opium War
1850–1859	Value of world trade increases by 80 percent
1857	End of Mughal rule in India
1860–1861	Anglo-French force occupies Beijing
1863–1879	Khedive Ismail attempts to build an Egyptian Empire
1869	Suez Canal opens
1870–1900	World industrial production quadruples; world shipping doubles; world trade doubles in volume
1870s	French face increased guerrilla warfare in Algeria
1877	Queen Victoria takes title of Empress of India
1878–1913	Total territory of European empires doubles to 20 million square miles; total population of European empires expands from 300 million to 550 million
1880–1914	Most of Africa brought under European control
1884	Maxim machine gun patented
r. 1889–1913	Emperor Menelik modernizes Ethiopian army and expands empire in Africa
1890s	300 Dutch administrators oversee the government of 30 million Indonesians
1896	Battle of Adowa
1898	Battle of Omdurman

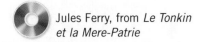

Jules Ferry, from *Le Tonkin et la Mere-Patrie*

outlets and construction projects. The British novelists Anthony Trollope and Charles Dickens made fun of European investors who sank their money in towns that were never built and railways that went nowhere in the Americas. But there were plenty of genuine and profitable opportunities.

The scale and success of business imperialism raise a further question: Was all imperialism really economic? Imperialism was the result of capitalism and industry: a drive for markets. Between 1850 and 1859, the value of world trade increased by 80 percent. During the last quarter of the century, world trade roughly doubled in volume and increased in value by a third. Between 1870 and 1900, world industrial production roughly quadrupled. World shipping nearly doubled to about 30 millions tons.

There were some cases of clearly profitable imperialism. Between 1831 and 1877, revenues from the Dutch East Indies covered a quarter of Dutch state expenditure. Phosphates in Morocco, diamonds in South Africa, and gems, ivory, and rubber in the Congo enriched, respectively, France, Britain, and the king of the Belgians. It used to be thought that the Portuguese Empire in Africa was a silly extravagance for such a poor country, but in fact it seems to have been acquired as an act of economic calculation. Russia's expansion into Central Asia was—in part at least—directed toward lands that could grow cotton for Russia's fledgling textile industries. France, as we have seen (see Chapter 24), embarked on the conquest of Indochina in the 1880s partly to solve its labor problems. Indochina also yielded coal, zinc, and tin for French industry.

Few parts of Africa with exploitable resources were left out of the global economy. Traditional traders were exterminated or became extinct. Some suffered because they were slavers, others because they got in the way of armed greed. King Leopold II proclaimed war on slave traders in the Congo. But his real aim was to cloak his ruthless ivory and rubber grabbing in moral rhetoric. The native palm-oil traders of the Niger delta in West Africa were innocent of slaving, but British merchants cheated and impoverished them. Driven into rebellion in 1895, the natives apologized for their attack on the representatives of the British Niger Company, "particularly in the killing and eating of parts of its employees. . . . We now throw ourselves entirely at the mercy of the good old Queen [Victoria], knowing her to be a most kind, tenderhearted and sympathetic old mother." The face of Africa was scarred and pitted with roads, railways, and mines, or scratched and scrubbed for plantations and new crops. The scramble for Africa was, in part, a scramble for resources (see Map 25.3).

In view of the strength of economic imperialism, it is tempting to see greed as the spur to empire-building. But there was more to it than that. Purely political competition among the powers drove imperialism, too, and patriotic pride and the pursuit of glory inspired imperialists who were indifferent to economics. Like other external wars, imperial adventures were ways to export unrest. In Britain, the empire rewarded otherwise potentially rebellious groups. The Scots and Irish, who tended to resent English rule, were disproportionately represented in the ranks of British colonial officials and merchants. The empire gratified the working class, and popular culture celebrated it. Nationalist rhetoric encouraged

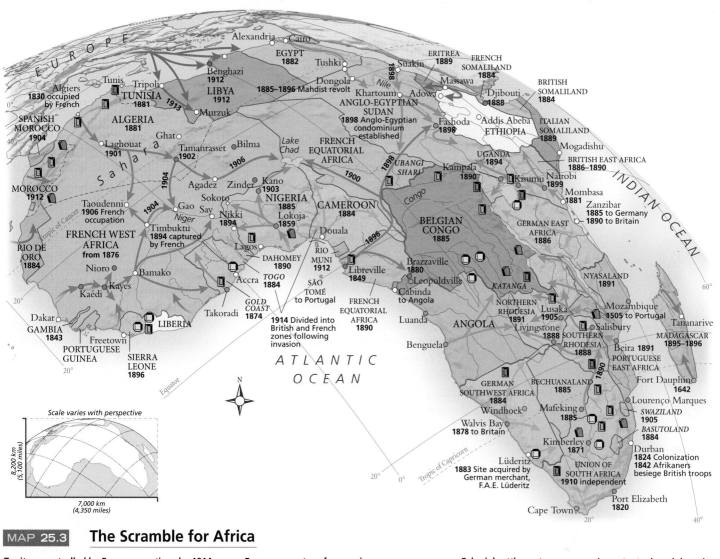

MAP 25.3 The Scramble for Africa

Territory controlled by European nations by 1914
- Belgium
- Britain
- France
- Germany
- Italy
- Portugal
- Spain

1883 date of taking control

—— borders in 1914

European routes of expansion
- → Belgian
- → British
- → French
- → German
- → Italian
- → Portuguese
- → Spanish

1888 foundation date of colonial settlement

Colonial settlements
- ◉ Belgian
- ◦ Boer
- ◦ British
- ◦ French
- ◦ German
- ● Italian
- ◦ Portuguese
- ◦ other settlement

Important mineral deposits
- ◆ coal
- ▯ copper
- ◈ diamonds
- ▮ gold

imperialism and spread pride in empire throughout society. "C is for colonies," trumpeted *An ABC for Baby Patriots*, "Rightly we boast/ That of all great countries/ Great Britain has the most." The "Great Game"—Anglo-Russian rivalry for power and prestige in Central Asia—drew Russia deeper into Asia to forestall the expansion of British India. It is true, too, that the scramble for Africa was prompted by rivalries among European powers—initially, over control of access to the natural riches of the Congo basin.

In some ways, however, competition among the great powers did more to frustrate empires than promote them. Iran (Persia) and Afghanistan stayed independent, partly by playing off the British against the Russians. Thailand staved off colonialism by balancing French and British power. China was so weakened by the end of the century that the country seemed ripe for partition among European powers and Japan, but they could not agree on how to divide the spoils.

IMPERIALISM IN THE "NEW EUROPES"

Some lands were subjected to empire not primarily because of their potential contribution to global trade but because they were "New Europes"—regions similar in climate to much of Europe and therefore exploitable for European colonization. By a combination of accidents, most of these regions—in South Africa, New Zealand, and Australia—belonged to the British Empire, or, like Chile and Argentina, were deeply influenced by British business imperialism.

South Africa had already become a New Europe. In some ways, it was less oppressive than those elsewhere in the world, for here, at least, the European settlers allowed the native peoples to survive, so that they could exploit their labor. In most other regions of similar climate—in the South American cone of Argentina, Chile, and Uruguay, the North American West, Australia, and, with less success, in New Zealand—white settlers waged wars of extermination against the native inhabitants. Australia and New Zealand were exploited at first mainly for sheep raising. This was a marginal activity from the perspective of the global economy, though Australian wool, in particular, was an exportable commodity. But toward the end of the century, refrigeration enabled both countries to export meat and dairy products to Britain. Gold rushes, meanwhile, attracted huge investment and coaxed large cities into being in Australia, California, and South Africa.

Canada was exemplary among the New Europes. In some ways, Canada's nineteenth century seems unspectacular. During the century that followed the end of the War of 1812, in which the Canadian colonies repelled attacks from the United States, the population grew—modestly by the standards of other parts of the Americas—tenfold to about 8 million people. The vast territorial expansion across the continent to the Pacific—which mirrored and matched that of the United States—included much unproductive territory. The Canadian prairies did produce grain, but never as much as those of the United States. A railway crossed the continent on Canadian territory, but it carried less freight and fewer passengers than the parallel railways in the United States. Yet merely to survive, alongside a United States that frequently seemed to be threatening to annex it, was an achievement for Canada. Even though the Atlantic-side Canadian provinces, with their English-speaking inhabitants, had little in common, commercially or culturally, with the mainly French settlements in Quebec, all of them managed to combine in 1867 in a confederation that the British largely put together. Thanks in part to the dynamic vision of the man the British chose to be the first Canadian prime minister, Sir John A. Macdonald (1815–1891), the confederation took responsibility for the whole of British North America, incorporated British Columbia on the Pacific coast in 1871, drove rails across the continent, and created a state with the potential Canada subsequently came to exhibit, as a country remarkable for social welfare, cultural pluralism, constitutional flexibility, prosperity, and peace. The main casualties of the process of creating a Canadian nation in the nineteenth century were the native peoples—ignored in the making of the constitution, brushed aside in the westward drive. By the

Vancouver, British Columbia, on the Pacific coast of Canada. The crammed houses, bravely flying their flapping laundry, trapped amid telegraph wires, and dwarfed by warehouses seem to imply that space was at a premium. In fact, Canada was thinly populated, and a vast expanse of wilderness and small, isolated prairie settlements separated Vancouver in the early twentieth century from eastern Canada.

early twentieth century, they had declined at a rate similar to that of most Native Americans of the United States, to a total of around 100,000 people.

The system Britain had established in Canada was really a variant of indirect rule, with elected colonial leaders exercising direct power instead of native chiefs and traditional aristocracies. Demographics, combined with improved communications, made this possible. Toward the end of the nineteenth century, Britain's other colonies of white settlers in Australia and New Zealand were approaching population thresholds—about 4 million and about 750,000, respectively—that enabled them to have the same status as Canada in the British Empire. South Africa, the last of Britain's New Europes, was more of a problem. Unlike the other colonies, it still had its native population. Indeed, black people made up a majority in South Africa. It had even more mineral wealth than Australia—by the end of the century, South Africa was the world's main supplier of gold and dia-

Sydney. New Europes rapidly came to look like old Europe. George Street, Sydney, Australia, photographed in 1899, looks like a commercial street in a prosperous English provincial city of the same era.

monds. It also had a sizable community called *Boers*, white citizens, mainly of Dutch ancestry who spoke not English but *Afrikaans*, their own dialect of Dutch, whose attitude to the British Empire was, at best, wary, and who had to be forced into collaboration in a series of wars, ending only in 1902. Effectively, Britain bought the Afrikaaners' loyalty by giving them power over black South Africans. As one of the Afrikaaner leaders wrote, rejecting British desire to grant civil liberties to "every civilized man" regardless of color, "I sympathize profoundly with the Native races of South Africa, whose land it was long before we came here to force a policy of dispossession on them. . . . But I don't believe in politics for them. . . . When I consider the political future of the Natives in South Africa I must say that I look into shadows and darkness; and . . . feel inclined to shift the intolerable burden of solving the . . . problem to the ampler shoulders and stronger brains of the future."

French imperial planners imagined Algeria in North Africa as a New Europe, too, or a sort of Old World America, where France could encourage American levels of input and achievement among the colonists, while penning the native races—Arabs and Berbers—in doomed desert reservations. Algeria was a "promised land," to be farmed "with gun in hand," as the French writer Alexis de Tocqueville (1805–1859) put it. The Algerian city of Philippeville looked American to him; distorted into wild West ugliness by an economic boom. The city of Algiers would become like a town in the American Midwest—"Cincinnati in Africa." Tocqueville believed that Algeria, with its narrow but rich coastlands along the Mediterranean, its vast inland plains, its great open spaces, and its untapped resources would play a crucial role in the future of France. Thomas Bugeaud, the French general charged with the conquest of the Algerian interior in 1837 thought that "conquest will be fruitless without colonization. . . . Agriculture and colonization are the same thing." Tocqueville was convinced that native races, whether in Africa or America, were incapable of civilization. The best the natives could hope for was to be joined with their conquerors and absorbed by them. In 1850, 130,000 Europeans lived in Algeria. There were more than 500,000 by 1900. The more extravagant schemes to make colonization prosper included flooding the Sahara to make a navigable inland lake.

Where they worked, New Europes really did reproduce much of the look and feel of old Europe. In 1850, Jorge Mármol, one of the first of Argentina's long line of great novelists, described the lives of the elite of the capital Buenos Aires, surrounded by embossed wallpapers, Italian carpets, Spanish paintings, and French scent. To this day, New Zealand has the English-style municipal gardens colonists planted in the spent craters of volcanoes to remind them of home. The University of Dunedin, founded in 1869, near New Zealand's most remote, southernmost point, is modeled on that of Glasgow in Scotland. In 1885, an English historian visiting Australia found "English life all over again."

EMPIRES ELSEWHERE: JAPAN, RUSSIA, AND THE UNITED STATES

Japan, Russia, and the United States, lagged only slightly behind Western Europe, in imperialism, as in industrialization.

Japanese intellectuals began to envy Europeans their empires in the late eighteenth century, when Honda Toshiaki, one of the leading Japanese scholars of Western literature, argued that Japan needed long-range shipping, munitions, and an empire of its own. Colonies could be stripped of resources and their populations exploited for labor, while "the ruler father" could "direct and educate the natives in such a manner that there will not be a single one of them who spends even one unproductive day." Japanese rule extended into the islands that lay north of Japan. Overseas empires were like unified nationhood, parliamentary constitutions, codified laws, industrial economies, trousers, and bow ties: signs of modernization, qualifications for admission to the circle of the great powers.

The era of Japanese adventures overseas coincided almost exactly with the great age of Western imperialism. A sense of urgency drove Japan to compete for the diminishing living-space that rival empires claimed. Japan's long period of demographic stability ended in the late nineteenth century when its population began to grow. Soldiers and businessmen allied to advocate empire. For samurai who had lost their social privileges (see Chapter 24), external wars were a means of discipline, a purifying ritual for a society polluted by change at home. Victory in the war of 1894–1895 against China (see Chapter 24) equipped Japan with the foundations of an empire: possession of Taiwan and the Pescadores Islands, semicontrol of Korea, and a springboard for further expansion at Russian and Chinese expense (see Map 25.4).

In Siberia, Russians, of course, already had an empire in territory that bordered their own. They continued to build up their land empire in Europe itself on their western and southern frontiers. Russian imperialism took a huge leap in the Napoleonic Wars (1799–1815), with the annexation of Finland from Sweden in 1809 and the consolidation of Russia's hold on Poland and the Baltic states. The colonization of "New Russia"—southern Ukraine—followed. The port of Odessa on the Black Sea had 30,000 people in 1823, and 630,000 in 1914. In 1853–1856, in the Crimean War, Britain and France intervened to halt the Russian advance into the Balkans at Ottoman expense. So Russian efforts turned to Central Asia. A huge domain there was converted to cotton cultivation to supply industries in Russia's heartlands. A long struggle to overcome the Chechens in the Caucasus Mountains extended from the 1830s to the

The first satirical Muslim journal in the Russian Empire, was published from 1905 to 1917 in Tbilisi, Georgia, the administrative capital of Russian Transcaucasia. Although the Russian Empire had many Muslim subjects, they were divided into competing and often mutually hostile national groups. This journal targeted educated Azerbaijani readers, many of whom had more in common with Shiite Iran than with the Sunni Islam practiced by other Muslims in the Caucasus. The cover page of the November 22, 1909, issue shows the Russian bear growling menacingly while the symbol of Turkish wisdom, the legendary popular philosopher Mullah Nasreddin, sleeps unaware.

NORWAY
SWEDEN

ARCTIC OCEAN

Alaska
1867 Russia sells
to U.S. for $7.2M
Wrangel Island

Severnaya Zemlya

Barents Sea

Novaya Zemlya

New Siberian Islands

St. Petersburg

Moscow

Ural Mountains

Ob

Yenisey

YAKUTSK

KAMCHATKA
1697–1732

Uralsk Kazan Perm
Samara
Volga
Yekaterinburg
Orenburg
1730
Ural
Surgut

TOBOLSK

RUSSIAN EMPIRE

Yakutsk
Lena

Okhotsk

Petropavlovsk

YENISEYSK

Chechens
Astrakhan
Caspian Sea
1734
Tobol'sk
Omsk
Tomsk
Yeniseysk
IRKUTSK

NORTHERN SAKHALIN
1853 claimed
1875 secured
Sakhalin

Kurile Islands
1854–1875

Tbilisi
Caucasus
URAL'SK
TURGAY
AKMOLINSK
Semipalatinsk
Krasnoyarsk
Lake Baikal
Chita
Nerchinsk
1918–1922
occupied
by Japan
AMUR
1858

SOUTHERN SAKHALIN
1875 to Russia
1905 to Japan

Baku
Aral Sea
Syr Darya
1873
SEMIPALATINSK
1864
TOMSK
Irkutsk
URYANKHAI
1912–1921
Russian protectorate
1918–1920
occupied
by Japan
Khabarovsk

KHIVA
1873
TRANSCASPIAN
1873
Khiva
SAMARKAND
1864
Irtysh
Lake Balkhash
SEMIRECH'YE
1871
MANCHURIA
1900–05: occupied by Russia
Hokkaido

Tehran
Ashkhabad
Bukhara
1868–1870
Tashkent
1871–1881 temporarily
held by Russia
KWANTUNG
1905 leased
territory
Harbin
1905
Vladivostok
1860
Hunchun **1905**

PACIFIC OCEAN

BUKHARA
1868
TURKESTAN
FERGHANA
1895
Tien Shan
MONGOLIA
Changchun
KOREA
1910: to Japan
Sea of Japan (East Sea)
JAPAN

PERSIA
Pamirs
Port Arthur
1898–1905 leased
from China
Seoul
Honshu
Tokyo

AFGHANISTAN
Kabul
Hindu Kush
Taklamakan Desert
XINJIANG
Beijing
Darien
Qingdao
Shikoku
Kyushu

INDIA
Himalayas
TIBET
QING EMPIRE
CHINA
Suzhou
1914–1922
occupied
by Japan
Bonin Islands
1875

Hangzhou
Ryukyu Islands
1879

Changsha
FUJIAN Fuzhou
TAIWAN (Formosa)
1895
Xiamen
(Amoy)
Pescadores
1895

600 km
600 miles

MAP 25.4 **Russian and Japanese Expansion, 1868–1918**

	Russian Empire, ca. 1855	**1868**	date of foundation or acquisition	⟶	Japanese attacks in Sino-Japanese War, 1894–1895
	acquisitions 1856–1876		Trans-Siberian Railway, built 1891–1917	⟶	Japanese attacks in Russo-Japanese War, 1904–1905
	acquisitions 1877–1914		Japanese Empire, 1870	—	borders 1914
	temporary acquisition, with dates		Japanese, 1874–1895	*Chechens*	people described on page 866
	Russian sphere of influence, 1914		Japanese, 1905–1910		

1860s. Meanwhile, the fantasy of a seaborne empire on the Pacific, reaching to the Antarctic, haunted Russian naval planners' imaginations. Not much came of it. In 1867, Russia sold Alaska to the United States and withdrew from the North American mainland. But the Aleutian Islands off the coast of Alaska remained a maritime frontier, divided between Russia and the United States (see Map 25.4).

Retreat from Alaska made Russia focus even more on Central Asia. In 1868, the Russian Empire declared the native aristocracy of Transoxania dispossessed. Sparing only a few places, which were left to particularly powerful or particularly obedient native dynasties, Russian armies enforced a new system of direct rule

Manifest Destiny: The spirit of "American Progress," depicted by John Gast in 1872, hovers over the westward march of white settlers. She trails a telegraph wire, as the land behind her is turned into fertile fields. Symbols of technological advance race across the plains. Rather than leading the march, the Native Americans on the left flee, casting frightened glances at their pursuers. By the 1890s, Native Americans had either been wiped out or confined to reservations by the U.S. army.

and direct taxation. In 1891, a new law limited landholding in the steppes of what is now Kazakstan to 40 acres per person—far less than a nomad needed to survive. Russia, meanwhile, ruled Chechnya by terror, on the grounds, as a Russian viceroy in the Caucasus put it, that "One execution saved hundreds of Russians from destruction and thousands of Muslims from treason." As the Russian novelist Fyodor Dostoevsky (1821–1881) said, "In Europe we were hangers-on and slaves, whereas in Asia we shall go as masters." Finally, in the 1890s, Russian imperialism concentrated on the Far East, where it met Japanese empire-building, with grave consequences for the future.

The United States was also an empire. Most nineteenth-century Americans were perfectly frank about it and proud of expanding their territory at other people's expense. They called this America's "manifest destiny." The United States absorbed Mexicans, Canadians, and Native Americans by force or the threat of it. Canada was driven back on the borders of Minnesota in 1818, Maine in 1842, and what are now the states of Oregon and Washington in 1846. The United States' great leap across the continent began in earnest in the 1830s, with attempts to sweep all the native peoples of the Midwest and southeast into a small, resource-poor Indian territory in what is today the state of Oklahoma. It was a genocidal act that the Cherokees called the Trail of Tears, in which thousands died from disease, exposure, and starvation. Many United States planners hoped that it would kill off most Native Americans. Indeed, by 1900, the total Native American population of the United States was recorded as 237,196—a decline of probably 50 percent during the nineteenth century. Only in some parts of the Southwest did Indians escape eclipse. In the last quarter of the nineteenth century, the United States launched a war of extermination against the remaining Native American peoples in its territory. Meanwhile, in the 1840s, conquests gobbled up Mexican territory north of the Rio Grande, adding most of what is now the Southwest and California to the growing empire.

In 1896, the United States government officially declared the land frontier closed. The country was now settled from coast to coast. Almost immediately, American imperialism spilled into the oceans. In the Pacific, the Hawaiian kings had fended off European predators for years and sustained a clever diplomatic balance to keep potential conquerors at bay. But the numbers of foreign immigrants to Hawaii increased, and the economic power of traders from the United States became dominant. The game Hawaii's native rulers played therefore got harder, until white settlers overthrew the Hawaiian monarchy in 1893 with American military and diplomatic support. Annexation to the United States followed in 1898. Meanwhile, the United States also annexed American Samoa in the South Pacific and seized the Philippines, Guam, and Puerto Rico, after defeating Spain in 1898. Spain's former colony Cuba, which was nominally independent after 1901, became a virtual United States' protectorate, and the United States took permanent possession of a naval base there at Guantanamo Bay. It also acquired the Canal Zone from Panama in 1904 after enabling Panama to secede from Colombia. The whole American hemisphere became a United States sphere of influence and "Uncle Sam's backyard."

The Imperial Ambitions of Japan, Russia, and the United States

1803	Louisiana Purchase transfers vast territory from France to the United States
1809	Russia annexes Finland
1823	United States issues the Monroe Doctrine
1830–1860	Russians struggle to conquer Chechens
1867	Purchase of Alaska from Russia by the United States
1890s	Russian imperialism focuses on the Far East
1894–1895	Japan defeats China, takes Taiwan
1896	Land frontier of the United States declared closed
1898	U.S. annexes Hawaii, seizes Philippines, Guam, and Puerto Rico after defeating Spain
1904	U.S. acquires Panama Canal

RATIONALES OF EMPIRE

How did imperialists justify their activities? Two rationales were overwhelmingly popular: what imperialists called their **civilizing mission**, and the doctrine that they were inherently, naturally superior. These two justifications overlapped and shaded into each other.

Doctrines of Superiority

The most influential doctrine originated in a different context: in the search for a scientific way to explain the tremendous diversity of nature, and in the development of a theory of change that, originally conceived to apply to biology, got wrenched out of its original background and applied to society.

In 1800, the "Creation Oratorio" of the Austrian composer Joseph Haydn proclaimed in ravishing music the traditional, biblical account of how the planet got filled with so many different plants and creatures. God had created the world and everything in it in six days. It was a metaphor—a poetic myth, designed to reveal more than literal truth. Most people who thought about it already knew that the planet was immensely old—fossils discovered in the eighteenth century had proved that—and that life developed slowly, growing in complexity, from simple, primitive forms. What remained unknown—the "mystery of mysteries," as the young English scientist, Charles Darwin, remarked in the 1830s—was how those life-forms changed, or how God changed them, into the amazing variety visible in the natural world.

Darwin's earliest scientific interests were in sponges and beetles—indications of his interest in life-forms regarded as primitive. In 1839, he got a chance to extend his observations, when he accepted a post as the only resident scientist on a small round-the-world mission by the British navy. Two stops on the expedition's route inspired new thinking. First, in Tierra del Fuego at the southern tip of South America, he was shocked to see how little the natives had, at least in European eyes, of material culture or intellectual or spiritual lives. "Man in his natural state," Darwin reported, was "so beastly, so vile, a foul, naked, snuffling thing." He was particularly surprised that the local Indians could endure the ferocious, freezing climate in a state of virtual nakedness and guessed that their bodies must have adapted to the environment in which they lived. He began to see humans for what they are—well-adapted animals.

Later in the voyage, further revelations occurred to him off the northwest coast of South America, in the Galápagos Islands, where the diversity of species, and the differences among species from island to island, seemed so great as to be almost inexplicable. "I never dreamed," he wrote, "that islands would be so differently tenanted. Temples filled with the varied productions of God and Nature . . . filled me with wonder." Clearly, by some means, the different conditions from island to island must have encouraged life-forms to develop in different ways. When Darwin got home, two circumstances made his thinking crystalize.

First, he devoted himself to the study of how species change under the influence of domestication: how farmers, stockbreeders, and pigeon fanciers, for instance, select for breeding or hybridization to ensure that the offspring of their animals will inherit favored characteristics. Maybe nature functioned in the same way, favoring characteristics most suitable to particular environments. Ill-adapted specimens of plants or animals would be unlikely to pass on their characteristics to subsequent generations. They would tend to die earlier and have a shorter fertile life span than more successful specimens. Or, in the case of breeding species,

A Fuegian on the frontispiece of Robert Fitzroy's *Narrative of the Surveying Voyage of HMS Adventure and Beagle* (1839). "Nothing," wrote Darwin in his *Beagle* journal, "is more likely to create astonishment than the first sight in his native state of a barbarian—of man in his lowest and most savage state. One's mind hurries back over past centuries, and asks, could our progenitors have been men like these, men who do not appear to boast of human reason. I do not believe it is possible to describe or paint the difference between savage and civilized man. . . . It is greater than between a wild and domesticated animal." The remarkable environmental adaptation that made the Native American inhabitants of Tierra del Fuego, at the tip of South America, able to withstand the cold was one of the observations that influenced Darwin's thinking about a theory of evolution.

"Scientific" racism. The British anatomist Charles White (1728–1813) believed that "various species of men were originally created and separated by marks sufficiently discriminative" to enable a scientist to rank them in a hierarchy of nature. The skeletons of white people showed that they were "most removed from brute creation," while the bodies and, especially, the skulls of black people "differed from the European and approached to the ape."

Charles Darwin, from *The Origin of the Species*

they might find it harder to attract mates. Conversely, the fittest would survive longest and breed most.

Second, Darwin's personal circumstances affected his theories. He had married his cousin, and, to their distress, the couple had produced sick children who struggled to survive. When his favorite daughter died, it became "impossible," he said, "for me ever to feel joy again." He found himself secretly beginning to hate God. Indeed, in his later years, he ceased to go to church, subscribed anonymously to an atheist organization, and, to his wife's disappointment, treated the local clergyman with contempt, while avoiding former friends whose religious faith was undisturbed. More important for the world, however, than Darwin's personal agonies and religious doubts was his growing conviction that his own family demonstrated the truth of the theory that was forming in his mind. Nature was "clumsy, wasteful, blundering, low, and horribly cruel," or rather, indifferent to sentiment. Nature would allow only strong, well-adapted specimens to survive and pass on their characteristics to their offspring. He held the struggle for life in awe, partly because his own children were victims of it. "From the war of nature, from famine and death," he wrote, "the production of higher animals directly follows."

Darwin published that opinion in *The Origin of Species by Means of Natural Selection* in 1859. As his theory became accepted, other thinkers proposed terrible refinements that came to be known as **Social Darwinism**. Nature decreed "the survival of the fittest" and the extinction of the weak. Conflict is natural, therefore good. The elimination of weak specimens serves society. Inferior races are justly exterminated in favor of master races. The feeble or stupid should not be allowed to breed. Nature decrees the rule of more evolved races and individuals over those less evolved. "Degenerate" people—what we would now call the underclass—represented throwbacks to some more primitive stage of evolution. It would be unfair to blame Darwin for these consequences. He advocated the unity of creation and so, implicitly, defended the unity of humankind. He was the enemy of self-styled anthropologists of the day, who claimed that different races belonged to different species. Darwin was an unfailing opponent of slavery.

Nevertheless, no clear line divided social Darwinism from scientific Darwinism. Darwin was the father of both. As early as 1839, he claimed that "When two races of men meet, they act precisely like two species of animals. They fight, eat each other. . . . But then comes the more deadly struggle, namely: which have the best fitted organization or instincts (i.e., intellect in man) to gain the day?" Black people, Darwin speculated, would have evolved into a distinct species had European imperialism not ended their isolation. He even admitted that a scientist of nature confronted with examples of black and white people "without any further information" would undoubtedly classify them as separate species. As it was, he thought, black people were doomed to extinction in competition with white people. Unsurprisingly, many people saw Darwin's theories as justifying the inequalities of their day: a world sliced by the sword and stacked in order of race.

A French anthropologist, the Comte de Gobineau, who died in 1882, the same year as Charles Darwin, arrayed humankind in order of excellence, with white people at the top, black people at the bottom, and others in between. Craniologists measured skulls and proved to their own satisfaction that the skulls of black people resembled those of apes. The French and Belgians said that black Africans who adopted European culture had evolved into a higher state of being human. "No full-blooded Negro," stated the *Encyclopedia Britannica* in 1884, "has ever been distinguished as a man of science, a poet, or an artist, and the fundamental equality claimed for him by ignorant philanthropists is belied by the whole history of the race." The governor of the Dutch East Indies in 1850 thought "the right of rule" was "a characteristic of the pure white race" to which "the black man bows down humbly." Some black people and Eskimos in Europe were actually displayed in zoos.

The Civilizing Mission

Alternatively, imperialists appealed to what they called their moral superiority. "The basic legitimization of conquest over native peoples," a French administrator insisted, "is the conviction of our superiority, not merely our mechanical, economic, and military superiority, but our moral superiority." Sir Francis Younghusband, who led a British military expedition to Tibet in 1902, claimed to have witnessed evidence of European superiority over Asian and African peoples—"not due to mere sharpness of intellect, but to that higher moral nature to which we have attained."

Moral may seem an odd word for the kind of superiority that enabled some people to kill, dispossess, and exploit others. A British administrator in South Africa was surely right when he observed "how thin is the crust that keeps our Christian civilization from the old-fashioned savagery—machine guns and modern rifles against knob sticks and assegais [short spears] are heavy odds and do not add much to the glory of the superior races." But in part moral superiority signified what we should now call superior morale. Europeans, white North Americans, and Japanese certainly seemed more determined in the late nineteenth century than their counterparts in other parts of the world to seize other people's lands and wealth. To some extent, this seems to have been a reaction to historic positions of inferiority—Europe's with respect to Asia, Japan's with respect to China and Korea, that of the United States to most of the rest of the Americas and, indeed, to most of the rest of the world. In part, too, it is worth remembering that in the nineteenth century, ancient ideas of virtue were still current in classically educated minds. For nineteenth-century Europeans and white North Americans, virtue still included personal strength—physical and, therefore, military strength—as it had for the ancient Greeks and Romans.

The civilizing mission seemed inapplicable to much of the colonial world, and especially to India, whose civilization was older and, arguably, richer than that of Europe. But the British managed to think themselves into what they saw as a civilizing role even in India. In 1835, the British historian and legislator Thomas Babington Macaulay dismissed Indian civilization as "absurd history, absurd metaphysics, absurd physics,

Rudyard Kipling, *The White Man's Burden*

The civilizing mission, New Guinea, 1919. The British missionary stands in a position of authority, on the right. The white women are relaxed and wear hats. The New Guineans are presumably receiving instruction, but it might as well be orders. Almost everything in the scene is mysterious. Is a class or a religious service taking place? Why do only females, not males, hold books? Why is the lady in the black hat seated facing the back of her chair?

absurd theology." A single shelf of a good European library, he claimed, "is worth the whole native literature of India and Arabia." The English, he predicted, would be to the Indians as the Romans, in their day, had been to the ancient Britons. English would be the new Latin. "Indians in blood and color" would become "English in tastes, in opinions, in morals and in intellect."

Civilization was also undeniably a property of Chinese and Japanese societies. Western admiration for China never died out entirely, though the Opium Wars did much to subvert it. Thereafter, China's backwardness was widely acknowledged in the West, but most commentators realized that it was a temporary trick of history and would soon be reversed. Japan's potential to catch up was obvious from the 1870s onward (see Chapter 24). For Westerners, therefore, China and Japan were potential rivals, who could be recruited or resisted. Many Europeans adopted a defensive attitude to what they called "the Yellow Peril." The German Emperor, Wilhelm II (r. 1888–1918), was among the loudest such voices (as was his contemporary, the United States president Theodore Roosevelt). In 1900, Wilhelm exhorted German members of an international task force sent to Beijing to rescue European residents from Chinese rebels, the so-called Boxers, who had killed the German ambassador and murdered European missionaries and their Chinese Christian converts: "You should give the name of German such a cause to be remembered in China that for a thousand years no Chinaman shall dare look a German in the face."

On the whole, it is hard to assess the imperialists' claims to have governed for the benefit of their victims. Under the grasping rule of King Leopold II of the Belgians, 10 million people in the Congo died in massacres or from stunningly callous neglect. Native peoples who perished to make room for white empires in the Americas and Australia had no opportunity to count blessings. The British Empire can claim to its credit to have spent much blood and treasure in suppressing the slave trade (see Chapter 24). But even this was not an exclusively benign business. In 1879, in southern Sudan, General Charles Gordon, who was in charge of anti-slaving operations there, was sickened by the skulls and skeletons his men's work left: slavers' womenfolk slaughtered to stop them breeding, thousands of slaves abandoned to starve when caravans were disrupted or destroyed.

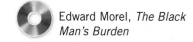 Edward Morel, *The Black Man's Burden*

For those who suffered from it, imperialism was often a path to hell, paved with the good intentions of white people who stumbled under the burdens of their self-imposed and self-proclaimed imperial responsibilities. Outside Europe, North America, and a few other lucky locations, the last three decades of the nineteenth century were an age of famine, exceeding all others up to that time for mortality and perhaps for every other kind of measurable severity (see Map 25.5). Equally adverse conditions, including a worldwide drought, associated with a series of El Niño events, returned toward the end of the 1880s and in the second half of the 1890s. Lake Chad in Central Africa shrank by half. Nile flood levels fell by 35 percent. Thirty million people may have died in India and an equal number in China. In some respects, imperialism helped people find food for survival. Cheap iron from Europe increased food production enormously in West Africa when it was turned into plows. Before the arrival of European imports there, a hoe blade cost a cow. It is hard, however, to exempt European imperialism from some of the blame for the consequences of famine. "Europeans," a missionary in India heard, "track famine like a sky full of vultures." Cteshwayo, the Zulu king who tried to defeat the British Empire in South Africa in 1879, thought "the English chiefs have stopped the rain." If they did not engineer famine, white imperialists at least mismanaged it. Humanitarian sentiment, like food, was plentiful in their countries, but they found no way to turn their surplus of either to practical use.

Earlier, native states had handled famine relatively well. China coped with protracted crop failure in 1743–1744. In India in 1661, to the admiration of European observers, the Mughal emperor Aurangzeb (see Chapter 21) "opened his treasury" and saved millions of lives. Western countries—with the exception of the Russian Empire, where crop failures killed millions around the middle Volga and in Ukraine in 1878–1881—seemed able to save people from famine in the late nineteenth century if they so wished. The American Midwest suffered as badly as almost any other part of the world from the drought of 1889–1890, but relief was well organized, and deaths were few.

IN PERSPECTIVE: The Reach of Empires

At the start of the nineteenth century, the English poet and artist William Blake could still draw Europe as one of the Graces among equals in the dance of the continents. But over the century as a whole, unprecedented demographic, industrial, and technological strides transformed Europe's place in the world. The result was a period of European world dominance. By 1900, European powers directly ruled much of the world, and European political influence and business imperialism combined to guide or control much of the rest.

It was, by the standards of world history, a brief phenomenon. By the end of the nineteenth century, Japan and the United States had overtaken many European countries in industrial strength and in their capacity for war. In the twentieth century, European empires would collapse as spectacularly and as quickly as they had arisen (see Chapter 28). Meanwhile, even under imperialism, people continued to make their own history, thanks to systems of indirect rule and the empires' reliance on collaborators. Still, the nineteenth remains a century of a "European miracle": the sudden, startling climax of long, faltering commercial out thrust, imperial initiatives, and scientific progress.

Despite their defects, the empires were of immense importance in global history as arenas of cultural exchange. As we saw in Chapter 23, imperial commerce followed the lines laid down by the effects of industrialization, dividing the world

Imperial game. Soccer and cricket originated in expensive English boarding schools but spread around the world and to all classes. Soccer rapidly became popular almost everywhere in the world, outside the United States and Canada. Cricket, however, caught on only—with few exceptions—in lands subject to the British Empire. Here boys improvise a game with makeshift equipment, against the tropical background of St. Kitt's in the British West Indies.

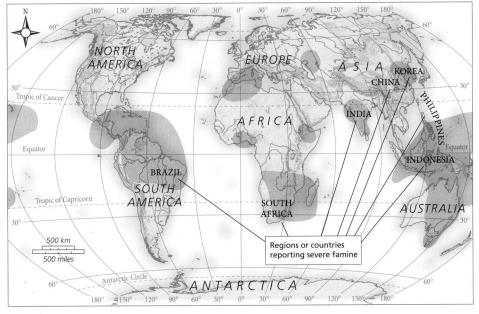

MAP 25.5

The Global Drought of 1876–1878

▨ dry regions

CHRONOLOGY

Nineteenth century	European population explosion fuels economy and creates surplus population for global migration; Africa's population declines
1803	Louisiana Purchase transfers vast territory from France to the United States
1807	British launch unsuccessful invasion of River Plate region of South America
1809	Russia annexes Finland
1812–1814	War of 1812
1823	United States issues the Monroe Doctrine
1830s–1860s	Russians struggle to conquer Chechens
1839	Charles Darwin begins around-the-world expedition
1842	Treaty of Nanjing ends Opium War
1845–1872	Maori Wars in New Zealand
1850	130,000 Europeans live in Algeria
1850–1859	Value of world trade increases by 80 percent
1857	End of Mughal rule in India
1863–1879	Khedive Ismail attempts to build an Egyptian Empire
1867	Purchase of Alaska from Russia by the United States; Canadian Confederation is formed
1869	Suez Canal opens
1870–1900	World industrial production quadruples; world shipping doubles; world trade doubles in volume
1870s	French face guerrilla warfare in Algeria
1875	Indian Act defines the status of indigenous peoples in Canada
1877	Queen Victoria takes title of Empress of India
1878–1913	Total territory of European empires doubles to 20 million square miles; total population of European empires expands from 300 million to 550 million
1880–1914	Most of Africa brought under European control
1884	Maxim machine gun patented
1889–1913	Emperor Menelik modernizes Ethiopian army and expands empire in Africa
1890s	Russian imperialism focuses on the Far East
1894–1895	Japan defeats China
1896	Land frontier of the United States declared closed
1898	Battle of Omdurman; U.S. annexes Hawaii and seizes Philippines, Guam, and Puerto Rico from Spain
1899–1902	Boer War
1900	500,000 Europeans live in Algeria, 4 million live in Australia, 1 million live in New Zealand
1904	U.S. acquires Panama Canal

into specialized areas of primary production and manufacturing, encircling the Earth with steamship routes and railroads. As Chapter 24 made clear, these arteries carried culture as well as commerce. Empires intensified the process of exchange. Like distorting mirrors, the colonies reflected imperfect images of Europe around the world.

Cultural exchange happened despite climate and distance. Indian thinkers and writers gave a discriminating welcome to Western influence. The first great Indian advocate of Western ideas, Raja Rammohan Roy (1772–1833), was a child of the Enlightenment (see Chapter 22). Yet the roots of his rationalism and liberalism predated his introduction to Western literature. They came from Islamic and Persian traditions. The next great figure in Roy's tradition, Isvarcandra Vidyasagar (1820–1891), did not learn English until he was on the verge of middle age. When he argued for the remarriage of widows or against polygamy, or when he advocated relaxing caste discrimination in the schools, he found ancient Indian texts to support his arguments. But he dismissed the claims of pious Brahmans who insisted that every Western idea had an Indian origin. He resigned as secretary of the Sanskrit College of Calcutta in 1846 because of opposition to his program to include "the science and civilization of the West" in its curriculum. "If the students be made familiar with English literature," he claimed, "they will prove the best and ablest contributors to an enlightened Bengali renaissance." And, indeed, vernacular Indian writers did inject Western influences into their work, with revitalizing effect. The British in India were like many foreign, "barbarian" conquerors before them, adding a layer of culture to the long-accumulated sediments of the subcontinent's past.

Today, what were once British colonies still have legislatures and law courts modeled on those of England, universities copied from Scotland, and sports that colonists from England's public schools spread (see Chapter 24). The French Empire spread French culture, Parisian cuisine, and the Code Napoleon (see Chapter 22). Africa became the great growth land of Christianity, thanks to the missionaries who followed or, in some cases, carried the flags of European empires. European empires spread their languages everywhere. In much of the ex-colonial world, European tongues—English, Spanish, Portuguese, French, Russian—remain the language of first choice. The colonial worlds reciprocated the exchange. Mughal-style adorned nineteenth-century British buildings. The industrialists of Paisley in Scotland copied Indian patterns for their textiles. Curry from India has become virtually an English national dish, as has Indonesian rijstafel in Holland and North African couscous in France. From the end of the nineteenth century, images and works of art looted from empires affected European imaginations and gave artists new models to follow. Despite the barriers to understanding that pseudoscientific racism erected, far frontiers kept increasing the white world's stock of examples of noble savagery (see Chapter 22). In the twentieth century, as we shall see, social scientists found, among the subject peoples of empire, disturbing new perceptions: new ways to see not only the "primitives" and "savages," but also themselves and the nature of human societies.

PROBLEMS AND PARALLELS

1. Why did the British and other foreign powers gain significant control of the Chinese economy by the late nineteenth century?

2. How do the Opium Wars illustrate a shift in global history?

3. Why were European powers able to control so much of Asia, Africa, the Pacific, and the Middle East in the nineteenth century?

4. How did the Maori and Emperor Menelik of Ethiopia resist European imperialism?

5. What methods did Europeans use to govern native peoples in their colonial possessions? What does the term "business imperialism" mean?

6. How did Europeans justify imperialism?

7. What were the imperial ambitions of Japan, Russia, and the United States in the nineteenth century?

DOCUMENTS IN GLOBAL HISTORY

- Letter from Lin Zexu to Queen Victoria
- The Treaty of Nanjing
- Francisco García Calderón, from *Latin America: Its Rise and Progress*

- Jules Ferry, from *Le Tonkin et la Mere-Patrie*
- Charles Darwin, from *The Origin of the Species*
- Rudyard Kipling, *The White Man's Burden*
- Edward Morel, *The Black Man's Burden*

Please see the Primary Source CD-ROM or additional sources related to this chapter.

READ ON

On the Opium War, A. Waley, *The Opium War Through Chinese Eyes* (1979) is a lively collection of sources. J. Y. Wong, *Deadly Dreams: Opium, Imperialism, and the Arrow War (1856–1860) in China* (1998) is excellent on the consequences and on the second Opium War.

H. L. Wesseling, ed., *Expansion and Reaction* (1978) contains ground-breaking papers on imperialism. H. L. Wesseling, *The European Colonial Empires* (2004) is the best overall survey. The same author's *Divide and Rule: The Partition of Africa*, (1996) and T. Pakenham, *The Scramble for Africa* (1991) are outstanding in different ways—the first for impeccable judgement, the second for thrilling vividity. On Britain, W. R. Louis, ed., *The Oxford History of the British Empire*, vol. iii (2001), ed. by A. Porter, is sweeping in its coverage. D. R. Headrick, *Tools of Empire* (1981) is important on the technology of imperialism. A. Knight, *The Mexican Revolution*, vol. i (1990) is a model work, from which I drew the details on the Yaqui. J. Belich, *The New Zealand War* (1998) is a brilliant work which reset the agenda of the study of colonial warfare.

On Africa, *The UNESCO History of Africa*, vol. vii (1990) and *The Cambridge History of Africa*, vol. vi (1985) offers expert general surveys. G. Prins, *The Hidden Hippopotamus* (1980) is a sensitive, anthropologically informed study of Lozi history. N. R. Bennett, *Arab Versus European: Diplomacy and War in Nineteenth-Century Central Africa* (1986) is useful, especially on Zanzibar. The details on Ma el-Ainin come from J. Mercer, *Spanish Sahara* (1976).

On Johor, J. Gullick, *Malay Society in the Late Nineteenth Century* (1987) is invaluable. Many novels of Bankimcandra Chattopadhyaya are available in English, as are those of Jorge Mármol. On business imperialism, D. C. M. Platt, *Business Imperialism* (1977) is the indispensable introduction. A. de Tocqueville, *Writings on Slavery* is the source of the material on that writer. On the Russian Empire, D. Lieven, *Empire*, is the best survey.

On Darwin, the best books are the provocative A. Desmond and J. Moore, *Darwin* (1994), and E. J. Brown, *Charles Darwin* (1996) of which two volumes have appeared so far. M. Bates and P. S. Humphrey, eds., *The Darwin Reader*, (1956) is a good introduction to Darwin's writings.

CHAPTER 26

The Changing State: Political Developments in the Nineteenth Century

Nene, leader of Maori in Hokianga in northern New Zealand, took the name Tamati Waka after Thomas Walker, his British godfather, whe he was baptized a Christian in 1839. Nene sought to befriend and, if possible, exploit the British. He sided with them in the Maori wars of the 1840s, achieving fame as the Maori "who did more than any other to establish the queen's (meaning Queen Victoria of England) authority".

I n 1882, a British visitor wandered into an ill-mapped area in the northern heart of New Zealand's North Island. James Kerry-Nicholls called himself an explorer, but he was really engaged in what we might now call adventure tourism. He thought he was still in the British Empire. Instead, he found an "extensive region ruled over by the Maori king" that was, to all intents and purposes, a sovereign state, "inhabited exclusively by a race of warlike savages, ruled over by an absolute monarch, who defied our laws, ignored our institutions, and in whose territory the rebel, the murderer, and the outcast took refuge with impunity."

NEW ZEALAND

Kerry-Nicholls was in an independent Maori state in what is still known as the King Country. In the early 1880s, it occupied over a fifth of the territory of the North Island and had a population, by contemporary estimates, of some 7,000. The truth about it hardly justified Kerry-Nicholls' indignation. The Maoris reserved the right to imprison or kill outsiders who entered their territory without a visa, but they were not warlike savages. In the King Country, they had given up war and practiced peaceful resistance to the British—simply ignoring British orders. Invited to parley with the British in the year of Kerry-Nicholls's visit, King Tawhiao, "habited in European attire," bejewelled with a polished greenstone in one ear and a shark's tooth in the other, listened patiently to their proposal to give up his independence in exchange for land. "I approve," said the King, referring to the boundary of his kingdom,

> of you administering affairs on that side—the European side. . . . My only reason for going on that side is to hear—to listen. . . . I will remain in the place where my ancestors and my fathers trod. . . . What I have said to you is good: it has been said in the daylight, while the sun is shining. . . . You can remain on your side, and administer affairs, and I will remain on my side.

The King Country was the last stronghold of a movement that had originated in the 1850s to unify the Maori into a single state to confront British aggression and stop individual chiefs from ceding Maori land. Twenty-six Maori tribal groups had come together in 1858, numbering in all perhaps 25,000 or 30,000 souls, to elect a king by agreement among the chiefs. The groups had no ties of kinship or traditional alliances with each other. "Do not be concerned for your own village," said one native prophet to his people. "No, be concerned for the whole land." "I and my

FOCUS questions

- WHY WAS Westernization often equated with modernization in the nineteenth century?
- WHY WAS nationalism so potentially disruptive?
- WHY DID some African and Asian states succeed in resisting Western imperialism?
- HOW DID the growth of armies and bureaucracies increase the power of states?
- WHAT ROLES did nineteenth-century socialists want government to play?
- WHY DID organized religion and the state come into conflict in the nineteenth century?

people," said a chief, "will march to show sympathy for the island." In 1861–1863, the British tried to destroy this new state, sending in armies up to 14,000 strong, with mortars, cannon, and a gun that fired 110-pound shells. But after defeats and inconclusive engagements (see Chapter 25), they simply gave up. The King Country gradually settled into uneasy coexistence with the British Empire.

Presumably, the Maori got the idea of a unitary state, ruled by a "king," by imitation from the British. Their purpose, as one Maori leader explained, was "that they should become united, to assemble together and become one, like the Pakehas," as they called the white men. Presumably, too, had the Maori not faced a common enemy, they would have continued their long-standing methods of political organization in mutually warring chiefdoms. The idea of switching from armed to peaceful resistance was attributed to native prophets, but perhaps it owes something to the influence of Christian missionaries and the model of Jesus' kingdom (which was, as the Bible says, "not of this world"), or maybe even to the secular notion of civil disobedience that some Western intellectuals at the time advocated to effect peaceful change.

• • • • •

The political inventiveness of the Maori happened on a small scale, but it illustrates general features of the way nineteenth-century states grew and changed. New states emerged out of disunited traditional groupings, such as chiefdoms and tribes. Old states made themselves more systematic by eliminating political anomalies, devising constitutions, codifying laws, rationalizing institutions, breaking the power of rival sources of authority (such as clergies, aristocracies, city councils, or heads of tribes or clans), and imposing centralization or, at least, increasingly consistent methods of administration, on their subjects. *Modernization* is, strictly speaking, a meaningless word, since every era produces its own modernity, but we can follow tradition in using it as a label for these processes, because they produced states similar to those that prevail in today's world.

Some models of state development or refashioning began in Europe and North America and spread through the world in the course of the "white man's" outreach—by example, or by the power of imperialism. The process certainly did not end where white rule ended, and some instances, at least, probably happened independently of any white initiative. Examples we have already met illustrate this: the reforging of Japan and Egypt in response to European industrialization and imperialism, the success of Ethiopia in the scramble for Africa, or the Sioux's efforts to create an empire in the North American prairie. As we shall see in this chapter, some states modernized far from the frontiers of European empires or the reach of European influence.

Nevertheless, the story of state modernization, and the study of the problem of how and why it happened, must begin in the West, partly because some features of modern states emerged there first. For much of the world, modernization really was *Westernization*, the conscious imitation of the world's most powerful and most prosperous states: Britain, France, Germany, and the United States. While the scope and power of states grew in many parts of the world, the strongest and most enduring influences of the period came from the West. Here models of state development unfolded and were imitated around the world. Here theories about politics and society were formulated that achieved global importance and, often, global impact. From this point in the story of the world, Westernization is one of the most conspicuous global themes.

We will look at its clearest manifestations: nationalism, constitutionalism, militarization, centralization, and bureaucratization before turning at the end of the chapter to some of the other influential but, for the time being, frustrated political movements of the period: religiously inspired utopianisms, democracy, and other new or developing forms of political radicalism that radiated from the West.

NATIONALISM

Nationalists claimed that a people who shared the same language, historic experience, and sense of identity made up a nation, an indissoluble unit, linked (to quote a Finnish nationalist) by "ties of mind and soul mightier and firmer than every external bond." Nationalists believed that everyone must belong to a nation of this kind, and that every nation had to assert its identity, pursue its destiny, and defend its rights. "The voice of God" told Giuseppe Mazzini (1805–1872)—the republican fighter for Italian unification—that the nation was the essential framework in which individuals could achieve moral perfection.

Odd as this notion seems, many people believed it. In the nineteenth century, most people in Europe came to believe it. Nationalism triumphed in the West, stimulated by the American and French Revolutions and the Napoleonic Wars, and encouraged by belligerents who wanted to inspire their people to fight. It spread from the West to touch or transform much of the world by the end of the century.

Nationalism in Europe

Almost all European states contained more than one nation (see Map 26.1). Many European nations straddled the borders of states. **Nationalism** was therefore a potentially disruptive doctrine. German nationalism yearned to unite all German-speaking people in a single state. French nationalists wanted to meld France's historic communities into a unified force and secure what they claimed to be France's natural frontiers—by incorporating all the land west of the river Rhine and north of the Alps. Spain remained, as a British visitor observed, a "bundle" of nations—including, notably, Castilians, Catalans, Basques, and Galicians— unsure whether they wished to become a single Spanish nation. British statesmen kept talking about England, forgetting that the English, Irish, Scots, and Welsh were all supposed to have combined in a new British nation. Italian nationalists wanted to convert their peninsula from a "geographical expression" into a state. In Central Europe the Habsburg monarchy juggled minorities that often quarreled with each other, privileging Germans, Hungarians, and, to some extent, Poles in areas where they predominated, acknowledging in various ways other groups that had more or less distinct homelands, such as the Slovenes, Croats, and Czechs. Even more than that of the Habsburgs, the Ottoman Empire in southeast Europe had uncontainably conflicting nations within its borders. "Judge what would happen," wrote the Ottoman foreign minister in 1862, "if free scope were given to all the different national aspirations. . . . It would need a century and torrents of blood to establish even a fairly stable state of affairs." The Greeks achieved independence from the Ottomans in 1830, Romania and Serbia did so by 1878. Bulgaria, though still technically subject to Turkey until 1908, functioned effectively as a sovereign state hostile to the Ottoman Empire from the 1880s.

 Fustel de Coulanges on nationalism

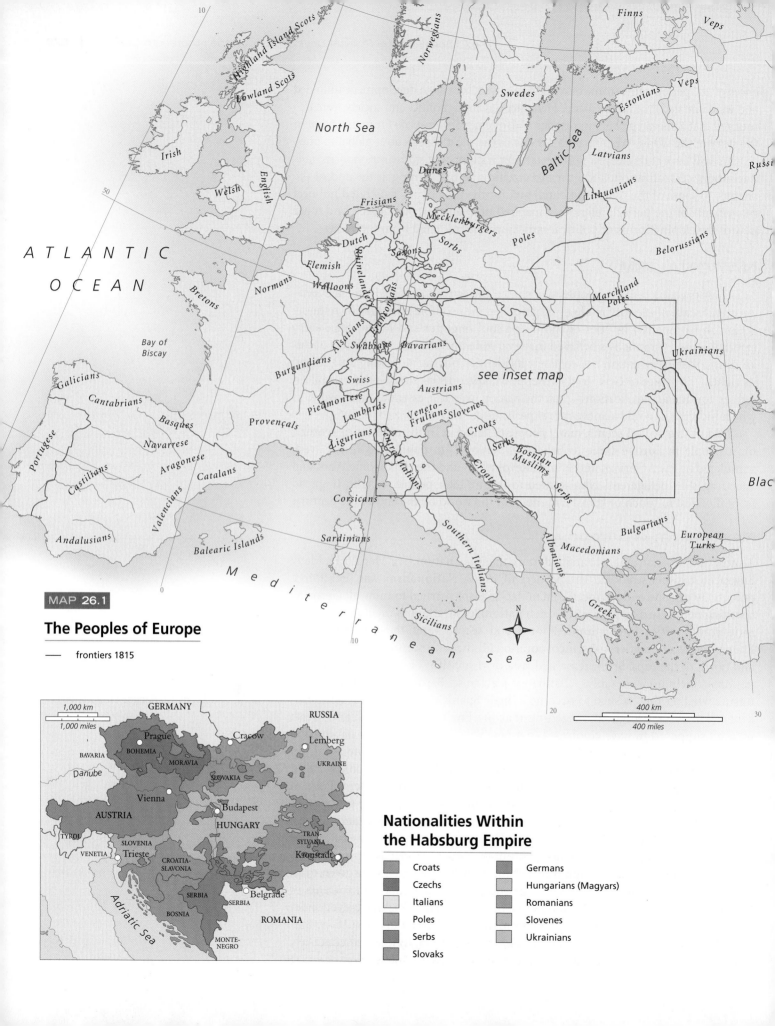

ATLANTIC
OCEAN

North Sea

Baltic Sea

Mediterranean Sea

Bay of
Biscay

Irish

Welsh

English

Highland Island Scots

Lowland Scots

Norwegians

Swedes

Finns

Veps

Danes

Estonians

Veps

Latvians

Russi

Lithuanians

Poles

Belorussians

Frisians

Mecklenburgers

Sorbs

Dutch

Saxons

Flemish

Rhinelanders

Walloons

Normans

Bretons

Galicians

Cantabrians

Portugese

Castilians

Navarrese

Basques

Aragonese

Catalans

Valencians

Andalusians

Provençals

Balearic Islands

Sardinians

Corsicans

Sicilians

Piedmontese

Ligurians

Lombards

Swiss

Burgundians

Alsatians

Swabians

Bavarians

Franconians

Austrians

Central Italians

Veneto-Friulians

Slovenes

Croats

Serbs

Croats

Bosnian Muslims

Serbs

Marchland Poles

Ukrainians

Southern Italians

Albanians

Macedonians

Bulgarians

European Turks

Greeks

Blac

see inset map

N

MAP 26.1

The Peoples of Europe

—— frontiers 1815

400 km

400 miles

1,000 km

1,000 miles

GERMANY

RUSSIA

BAVARIA

Danube

BOHEMIA

Prague

MORAVIA

Cracow

Lemberg

UKRAINE

SLOVAKIA

Vienna

AUSTRIA

Budapest

HUNGARY

TYROL

SLOVENIA

VENETIA

Trieste

CROATIA-SLAVONIA

TRAN-SYLVANIA

Kronstadt

SERBIA

SERBIA

Belgrade

BOSNIA

ROMANIA

Adriatic Sea

MONTE-NEGRO

Nationalities Within the Habsburg Empire

■ Croats		■ Germans	
■ Czechs		□ Hungarians (Magyars)	
□ Italians		■ Romanians	
■ Poles		■ Slovenes	
■ Serbs		□ Ukrainians	
■ Slovaks			

Some large states that enclosed many nations tried to stir themselves into consistency, usually by oppressing minorities. Government campaigns of "Russification" in the Russian Empire or "Magyarization" in Hungary meant, in practice, suppressing historic languages and, sometimes persecuting minority religions. In Britain, the Highlanders of Scotland—a nation with its own language and religious traditions and ways of life—were expelled from their land and sent into exile in a vicious campaign that was euphemistically called "clearances." Governments in London proposed to deal with the problem of the cultural and religious distinctiveness of the Irish by implanting an "agent of civilization"—an English Protestant clergyman—in every Irish parish. In effect, this was a failed attempt to wean the Irish from Catholicism.

Without bringing fulfillment to big communities, nationalism threatened minorities with destruction or repression. Some of them, like Finns and Poles in the Russian Empire or Slavs and Romanians in the Habsburg Empire, could respond with counter-nationalisms of their own. The Jews were not so lucky.

The year 1848 was one of largely failed constitutionalist revolutions in Europe. One of several women among the leaders of the Romanians who rebelled against Russian and Turkish domination was Ana Ipatescu, who had scandalized society by leaving her first husband and mobilizing revolutionary sentiment. Here, having proclaimed a provisional government, she leads a rather inauspicious band of followers. Onlookers seem to anticipate the inevitable defeat.

The Case of the Jews

The Jews had no national homeland. Their rising population—with a rate of increase remarkable even by European standards—seemed to provoke or aggravate **anti-Semitism**. So did changes in Jewish society and its relationship to the world around it. The triumph of enlightened principles in the French Revolution and their spread in the Napoleonic Wars extended the "rights of man" to the Jews. Except in Spain and Portugal and in the Russian Empire, governments relaxed official legal and financial disabilities against Jews. Many European Jews discarded the traditional exclusiveness of the ghetto in favor of assimilation into secular society. Heinrich Heine (1797–1856), a German Jew, filled his poetry with Jewish self-awareness but regarded Christian baptism as "a ticket into European culture." Part of Jewish self-emancipation was to adopt the dress and manners of host societies and conform to their way of life. From 1810, a reform movement that started in Germany brought these new ways into the synagogues, introducing organ music, singing in melodic unison, and sermons. The very success of Jews in blending into gentile society seemed to excite anti-Semitism. This growing and increasingly conspicuous community, anti-Semites claimed, might take over the wealth and power of the world.

When the world's biggest synagogue opened in Berlin in 1866, the chief rabbi preached in German about his hopes of a "common Messiah" to unite all nations in brotherhood. This seemed an overoptimistic program. There were two alternatives. The first was for Jews to espouse Jewish nationalism—which some did with increasing desperation as anti-Semitism grew. They turned to the search for a homeland, perhaps somewhere in Africa, or perhaps in Palestine (an idea first suggested by a Balkan rabbi in the 1840s). The second possibility, which most Jews embraced, was to

The era of Jewish emancipation allowed European Jews more freedom and a wider recognition of their faith and culture. This painting by G. E. Opitz portrays the dedication of a new synagogue in Alsace in eastern France in 1820.
George Emanuel Opitz (1775–1841), Dedication of a Synagogue in Alsace, ca. 1820. The Jewish Museum/Art Resource, NY.

join in the nationalism of the country in which they lived. Joseph Moses Levy (1812–1888), owner of England's biggest newspaper, sought, in a rival journalist's sneer, "to be numbered among the Anglo-Saxon race." The young Walter Rathenau (1867–1922), whose family owned the largest electricity-producing firm in Germany, believed that German Jews could help Germany achieve world supremacy.

Assimilation, however, was always risky for unconverted Jews, unless they were immensely rich. In the prayer book of French Jews in the 1890s, France was praised as the country "preferred by God," and the French, according to the country's chief rabbi in 1891, were "the chosen race of modern times." None of this prevented French anti-Semitism, as became all too clear in the case of a Jewish officer in the French army accused of spying for the Germans in 1893. Captain Alfred Dreyfus was obviously innocent, but the French gutter press bayed for his blood, in effect because he was Jewish. He was led into exile and imprisonment crying, "Long live France!" and later, after his innocence was proved, he won medals fighting in the French army. In Romania, in 1875, the press threatened a prominent British Jew, Sir Moses Montefiore (1784–1885) with lynching when he went there to plead for the rights of Jews. Yet a Jew wrote the period's most heartfelt celebration of Romanian nationhood in Yiddish, a language only Jews spoke.

Nationalism Beyond Europe

Beyond Europe, nineteenth-century nationalism is hard to distinguish from patriotic resistance against European imperialism (see Map 26.2). It seems clear, however, that by the end of the century, many independence movements in European empires overseas had adopted nationalism as their own ideology. Rebels proclaimed as "nations" countries, such as "the Philippines," "Indonesia," "Algeria," and "India," that had never existed before, and that housed many different historic nations.

This phenomenon started in the Americas. Propagandists in the United States popularized the idea of an "American nation" during their Revolutionary War. Before it, residents of the thirteen North American colonies that rebelled against Britain had all considered themselves "true-born Englishmen." In Latin America, similar sentiments developed during the wars of independence fought against Spanish rule between 1810 and the 1820s. The success of the idea of nationalism was even more surprising in Latin America than in the United States. Though the Creole elites shared a common identity as "Americans," their desire to exercise power in states of their own creation exceeded their willingness to remain united. Spanish-American unity was a Humpty Dumpty, smashed by its fall. Paraguay and Uruguay fought to stay apart from Argentina and Brazil. Bolivia and Ecuador rejected union with Peru. In the 1830s, large states that had emerged from the independence wars dissolved into small ones. Gran Colombia split into Colombia and Venezuela. Venezuela, like Uruguay, was a country seemingly invented on the spur of the moment. It had no identity as an administratively or socially distinct unit in colonial times. The United Provinces of Central America crumbled into Guatemala, Honduras, Nicaragua,

Costa Rica, and El Salvador. The fissures continued to spread, detaching Texas and California from Mexico, and almost detaching Yucatán as well in the 1840s.

Brazil, meanwhile, like the United States, emerged formally united but, unlike the United States, was highly fragile in the short term (see Chapter 21). Offshore currents in the South Atlantic divided coastal Brazil into two zones, between which it was hard to communicate. The ranch-rich São Paulo region in the south had always been a law unto itself. In the interior, there was a wild west of mining, slaving, and logging with its own boss class. Northern Brazil was the domain of rich coffee and sugar planters. Unity survived destructive civil wars in the 1830s only because the regions were incapable of collaborating in revolt and because the emperor supplied a powerful symbol of legitimacy for the new country. Ethnic diversity added to the complexity of regional divisions. Brazil had more black people than other Latin American states—an inheritance of the importance of slavery in the sugar plantations in the colonial economy. As slave labor became ever harder to obtain, the country needed more and more free immigrants of diverse origins.

MAP 26.2

Resistance to European and United States Imperialism, 1880–1920

Anti colonial uprisings and incidents

- anti-British
- anti-Dutch
- anti-French
- anti-German
- anti-Italian
- anti-Portugese
- anti-Russian
- anti-Spanish
- anti-American
- — boundary at 1914

MAP EXPLORATION

www.prenhall.com/armesto_maps

An Argentine gaucho. The painter Eduardo Morales specialized in romantic landscapes of his native Cuba. Here he portrays an Argentine cowboy, a gaucho, and the landscape of Argentina itself in a similar romantic style. The man's horse, however, seems groomed for a formal riding contest, with forepaw raised in a tradition more appropriate for depicting rulers and warriors than cowboys.

Yet the new states of the nineteenth-century Americas rapidly bred a sense of nationhood in at least some of their citizens. When the United States seized California from Mexico in 1846, one youngster there was appalled "because I am a *Californio* who loves his country and a Mexican on all four sides." In 1843, a Bolivian intellectual found his country's constitution excessively nationalistic, because it "declares from the start . . . that the Bolivian nation comprises all Bolivians. Beyond Bolivians, no other elements of the nation exist." In consequence, Bolivia had become a narrow-minded country, dedicated to "independence and isolation, without limit, without quarter."

In the second half of the century, nationalist sentiment in the individual Latin American states increased, partly in detestation of interference from the United States, and the countries fought each other. In Argentina, nationalism tended to get distracted by romantic identification with the *gauchos*—the rugged cattle drovers of the pampa. In Brazil and Paraguay, the romantic sympathy took the form of yearning for an idealized "Indian" world, though poetry written in praise of the Indians excited little political activity on Native Americans' behalf. The first fully independent Mexican state in 1822 based the official symbol of the nationhood it claimed—an eagle devouring a snake atop a prickly pear cactus—on an Aztec carving. In Colombia, Ecuador, and Venezuela it was the landscape that inspired nationalist poetry and art.

In sub-Saharan Africa, too, the nationalist idea was implanted, at least in part, from the United States. It started in Liberia, a colony of ex-slaves founded in 1821 as a private venture by philanthropists, with help from racists who wanted to rid the United States of black people. Liberia proclaimed its independence in 1847, with a constitution based on that of the United States, but more radical in its insistence on "national rights and the blessings of life." One of the earliest Liberian presidents, Stephen A. Benson, perceived "the makings of a great nation" in the colony in 1856. In 1872, Edward Blyden, an outstanding black intellectual who had settled in Liberia, where he taught Latin and Greek, proclaimed "Africa for the African."

West African missionaries helped to spread nationalism, imagining national churches similar to those that Protestants maintained in Europe. Black intellectuals saw the political potential of this model. James Africanus Horton, for instance, a black doctor from the colony of ex-slaves that the British established alongside Liberia in Sierra Leone, pointed out in 1868 that "We have seen European nations who in long years past were themselves as barbarous and unenlightened as the negro Africans are at present, and who have exhibited wonderful improvement within the last century. This should urge the Africans to increased exertions, so that their race may, in course of time, take its proper stand in the world's history." Talk of nationalism began to have real political effects in West Africa. In 1871, Fanti chiefs in what is now Ghana met to found a confederation "to advance the interest of the whole Fanti nation."[1]

North of the Sahara, meanwhile, nationalism emerged among communities forced into self-definition as the Ottoman Empire retreated and European imperialism threatened. In the second half of the nineteenth century, Egyptian intellectuals began to give the Arabic word *watan*—which originally just meant something like "birthplace"—the sense of the European term *nation*, with the same romantic associations. One of the most influential of them was Ali Mubarak Pasha (see Chapter 23), who published a nationalist novel in 1882, the very year when opponents of British and French influence rose up with the cry, "Egypt for the Egyptians!" Mubarak wrote in the preface to his book:

> One of the strongest things, we feel indebted to, and on which we, being steeped in its sacred rites, make demands, is the nation. ... For at every moment enlarges us, ... enriches us, just as it has done to our ... ancestors and will do to our sons and grandsons who follow us. We are thus obliged to give it our boundless duty, as it deserves.

To some extent, Western empires deliberately encouraged nationalism around the world, regarding its spread as evidence of successful Westernization and of the fulfillment of Westerners' supposedly civilizing mission. In the early 1850s, a British statesman, Lord Grey, believed that by bringing the chiefs of the Gold Coast (modern Ghana) together, Britain had turned "barbarous tribes . . . into a nation." British administrators in Canada assumed that nation making was an obligation of empire. Even without official collaboration, Western empires tended to have this effect. In colonial settings, budding nationalists could read and learn about what was going on in Europe. Many of them went to Europe to study or at least attended European-style schools at home. To them, nationalism seemed an alternative form of political legitimacy with which to confront traditional elites allied with or controlled by outsiders.

José Rizal (1861–1896), for instance, the great spokesman of Filipino nationalism in the late nineteenth century, was the best student in Greek at Madrid University in Spain in his day. He was also competent or excellent in Latin, French, English, German, Italian, Dutch, Swedish, and Portuguese, as well as his native Malay and Chinese. He dressed and conversed like a typical upper-class Spaniard. La Solidaridad—one of the cells from which the nationalist movement in the Philippines was formed—was founded in Barcelona in Spain among Filipino students in 1888. Rizal crammed his writings with allusions to classical, Spanish, English, and German literature, but he also searched for inspiration in the poetic traditions of his homeland. He was a hybrid of Europe and Asia—a misfit wherever he went, known in Hong Kong as "the Spanish doctor" and labeled in the Philippines as a "Chinese half-breed." Spanish observers noticed Rizal's patriotic poetry as early as 1879 and identified him as "a man who bears watching, a rare and new kind of man . . . for whom the mother country is the Philippines, not Spain." He spent his last years in exile, charged with conspiring with other nationalists to make the Philippines independent. The experience only deepened his sense of rootedness in his own country. When he returned to Manila and was shot by the Spaniards as a rebel, he struck out the words "Chinese half-breed" on his death warrant and wrote "pure native" instead.

Rizal's subversive novels—especially *El Filibusterismo*, which, he said, is about "patriots waiting to be hanged"—showed how literature could help forge nationalism in colonial environments. Equally powerful were the novels that another culturally ambiguous figure whom we met in the last chapter, Bankimcandra Chattopadhyaya in India, wrote. Bankim wrote Western-style fiction, but often chose politically inflammatory themes. His most overtly nationalist novel, *Anandamath* (1882), is about a guerrilla leader

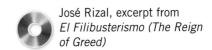

José Rizal, excerpt from *El Filibusterismo (The Reign of Greed)*

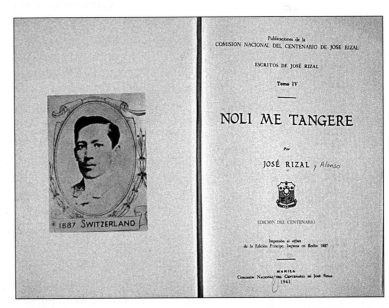

José Rizal. In 1887, José Rizal published, in the form of a novel, what he called "the first impartial and bold account" of the Filipino independence movement and the injustice that inspired it. "Felicity" Rizal wrote, "is proportional to liberty." He compared Spanish rule to a wooden bridge—vulnerable to wind and rot.

inspired by visions to shed British blood. *Anandamath* and *El Filibusterismo* both became handbooks of their respective countries' nationalist movements.

In a further level of ambiguity, Bankim himself served the British as a deputy magistrate. This was typical of the nationalists who formed the first enduring all-Indian political organization, the Indian National Congress, in 1885. Most of the founder members and early recruits belonged to the civil service or the legal profession. Most of the leading figures were graduates of the British-style universities founded in 1857 in Calcutta, Bombay, and Madras.

Western models promoted the growth of nationalism worldwide (see Map 26.2). Nevertheless, other influences were also at work. Toward the end of the century, Japan became a model for Asian nationalists because its success demonstrated that Asian nations could rival or even surpass Western powers. Vietnamese nationalism, meanwhile, fed on memories of age-old resistance to the Chinese as well as on opposition to the French in the nineteenth century. To some extent, nationalism happened independently wherever big empires provoked subject-peoples to react or rebel. The Russian, Habsburg, Chinese, and Ottoman Empires all faced similar problems. Chinese nationalism was itself an expression against the ruling Qing dynasty, even though the emperors' Manchu origins were now a long way in the past (see Chapter 21). Opponents of the regime appealed to Chinese "purity." The first rebellion of the movement that called itself "nationalist," in Guangzhou in 1895, was an attempt to found a Chinese state free of Manchu domination.

CONSTITUTIONALISM

The rise of nationalism becomes intelligible against the background of rapid shifts of power: revolutions, conquests and counter-conquests, and the rise of imperialism dethroned old regimes, reshaped states, and challenged long-established forms of political legitimacy. Nationalism was one way to justify the new structures of power or challenge old ones. **Constitutionalism**—the doctrine that the state is founded on rules that rulers and citizens make together and are bound to respect—was another.

Constitutionalism was not confined to Europe, but Europe was its great battleground. After the French Revolutionary Wars, most European states tried to prevent another such explosion by sanctifying existing frontiers and outlawing or restricting constitutional reforms. By mutual agreement, they intervened to repress each other's revolutions. The system worked well, and revolutionaries achieved freedom to act only in the relatively short periods when the major European powers fell out among themselves. The nineteenth century was therefore a great age for monarchies. All the new European states of the period—Belgium, Greece, Romania, Serbia, Bulgaria—were kingdoms or principalities. Republics that fell during the Napoleonic Wars—in Venice, Genoa, and the Netherlands—were not restored. Even in Latin America, some states toyed with plans for monarchical systems. Mexico and Haiti had monarchs for a time. Brazil's monarchy survived until a military coup in 1889.

Most European monarchies, however, eventually felt compelled to compromise their authority by granting or accepting constitutions, or passing laws to enlarge the numbers and nature of those of their subjects admitted to the political process. Constitutionalism not only redistributed power; it also changed the way people thought about the state—no longer the domain of the ruler, but of the rule of law, to which the monarch and government were themselves subject. Constitutionalism did not necessarily embody the idea that the people were sovereign, but it at least implied that more than one person and more than one class shared sovereignty. In Britain, for instance, though no written constitution was ever granted, or even formally sought, a series of Reform Acts turned parliament from an enclave of the aristocracy and gentry into an assembly that was still heavily aristocratic but also representative of the middle class and even, from 1867, of the more prosperous workers.

On the fringes of Europe, the Ottoman and Russian Empires staved off constitutionalism with difficulty. In 1864, the Russian monarchy permitted district assemblies with representatives from all classes to meet, while judges became at least nominally independent of the government. The Ottoman court convened an assembly of provincial representatives in 1845, explicitly limited to "those who are respected and trusted." The sultan quickly abandoned this experiment in constitutionalism, but in 1876, a constitutional revolt proclaimed "respect for the national will" and made the executive responsible to the legislature. "All Ottoman subjects," the new constitution decreed, "regardless of whether they possess property or fortune, shall have the right to vote." Religious liberty and equality before the law were enshrined. The constitution lasted only a few months before the sultan reimposed his authority, but resentment festered among the educated classes of the empire.

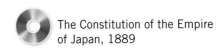

The Constitution of the Empire of Japan, 1889

Constitutionalism spread, along with other Western ways, to Japan, where experiments with various kinds of legislatures began in 1868. In 1882, the decision to draw up a constitution was based on the results of a fact-finding mission to Berlin, Vienna, Paris, and London. Because Japan was now an industrializing economy, thought the framers of the constitution, the middle class would be sure to rise to power. The constitution, introduced by decree of the emperor in 1889, had to provide a framework in which this change could occur peacefully, without jeopardizing the powers of the throne or the interests of other classes, such as the landlords, peasants, and industrial workers. Sovereignty remained the prerogative of the "sacred and inviolable" emperor, The ruler would govern "with the consent" of a representative assembly, elected by a franchise restricted to those rich enough to pay property taxes, and an upper house, modeled on Britain's House of Lords, composed of hereditary nobles and distinguished men whom the emperor appointed for life. The assembly could initiate new laws and veto the budget. The constitution also enshrined what we now call civil and human rights—including rights to hold and transfer property, to speak and associate freely, to practice religion without hindrance, and to be tried under the law, as well as the right of all men to compete for office under the state without discrimination as to birth or creed. The emperor, however, could suspend these rights in emergencies. Political parties were recognized as playing a role in running the assembly, but not the country. Because it was considered vital for the emperor to remain "above politics," he appointed ministers, on the advice of senior statesmen, without reference to party. Prussia, one of the more authoritarian states in Germany, provided the closest Western model to Japan's constitution.

In other parts of the world, constitutionalism was rarely more than a series of movements that never achieved power, or a dream of intellectuals who were largely without influence until the twentieth century. As we have seen, copycat constitutions accompanied the independence of all the new Latin American states of the nineteenth century, but they were usually mere formalities that disguised the rule of military strongmen, dictators, and oligarchies. The same can be said of Liberia's constitution. Nonetheless, there were impressive attempts to create effective constitutions. In the North American southeast, under the influence of German missionaries who began work in 1817, and the inspiration of their charismatic chief, Sequoia (1770–1843), the Cherokee people established their own republic alongside the United States, with representative institutions and laws codified in a written version of their own language. The Cherokee state flourished until the United States crushed it, seized its land, and expelled its peoples in the 1830s. The Fanti

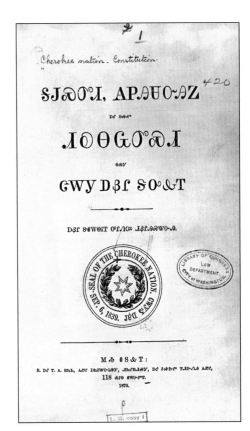

Constitution of the Cherokee Nation. Sequoia (ca. 1770–1843) developed a writing system for the Cherokee language in 1809, in which each of 85 symbols stands for a syllable. In 1839, a Cherokee assembly used it to write the Constitution of the Cherokee Nation, which provided for all land to be common property and for a chieftain, legislature, and judiciary to be elected by all males over 25 years old, descended from "Cherokee men by free women." Black people and Cherokee men who were part black, however, were explicitly denied a vote.

confederacy in West Africa, as James Africanus Horton described it, was "the pivot of national unity, headed by intelligent men, to whom a great deal of the powers of the kings and chiefs are delegated. . . . Through it the whole of the Fantee race, numbering some 400,000 souls, can . . . boast of a national assembly." The chiefs between them elected a king-president. Education and road maintenance were among the responsibilities of the government.

Although constitutionalism was Western inspired, traditional societies often had similar systems or conceptions of government of their own that limited rulers' power or subjected them to control or scrutiny by aristocratic or (less often) popular assemblies. When, for instance, the war leader Atiba reconstructed the collapsed Kingdom of Oyo in what is now central Nigeria in the 1850s, he looked back to his people's traditions, restoring the rites of ancient gods, founding temples for guardian deities, instituting worship of royal ancestors, even though he and most of his people were nominally Muslims. He enjoyed such grandiose titles as Owner of the World and of Life, Owner of the Land, and Companion of the Gods. In practice, however, the king could not act without the support of the council composed of representatives of noble families, who nominated officials and had the right, rarely exercised, to demand his self-sacrifice by ritual suicide. In what is now Ghana, the king of the Asante was known as "He Who Speaks Last" because, although he made policy decisions, he listened first to the views of the rest of the chiefs.

CENTRALIZATION, MILITARIZATION, AND BUREAUCRATIZATION

Whether monarchical or republican, constitutional or absolutist, nineteenth-century states tended to become more centralized. Industrialization and militarization boosted the power of governments. It became possible, as never before, to enforce unity and exact obedience from areas remote from a country's capital. We have already seen what a powerful source of industrial and social change militarization was (see Chapter 23). It is not surprising, therefore, that it should also have had enormous political consequences. Because armies consumed large amounts of taxes and conscripts, their growth was an important—though not a necessary—condition for centralization and bureaucratization.

In and Around the Industrializing World

In the Ottoman Empire, for instance, Sultan Mahmud II (r. 1808–1839) reorganized the army on European lines in 1826 and used his new troops to wipe out the Janissaries, the old, politically unreliable, hereditary military corps. He introduced European officers, training methods, and manuals. The army became the spearhead of movements of political reform and the self-appointed guardian of what increasingly—as the multinational empire shrank—felt like a Turkish nation-state. Under the next sultan, a new bureaucracy took over tax collecting, which the state had formerly farmed out to local agents. To some extent, these Ottoman reforms were inspired not directly by European examples, but by those of Muhammad Ali in Egypt (see Chapter 23). He had launched a similar program as early as 1820, conscripting peasants into an army he called the New Order. To recruit and pay for the army, he radically overhauled the administration, dividing Egypt into 24 provinces and creating layers of bureaucracy that reached from the capital into every village. To a lesser extent, rulers in Libya, Tunisia, and Morocco imitated the Ottoman reforms and created bureaucracies that, however, remained largely confined to the cities and functioned elsewhere, if at all, alongside traditional local and tribal authorities.

OTTOMAN MILITARY OFFICERS OF THE LATE NINETEENTH CENTURY

Westernization and modernization in the Ottoman Empire in the nineteenth century often focused on the armed forces. Foreign officers, especially from Germany and Britain, helped to train and reorganize Ottoman forces, and many Ottoman officers studied at military academies in Western Europe. A Parisian illustrated paper from 1895 showed officers of the sultan's household in uniforms modeled—except for the fezzes—on those worn in Western armies.

Cavalry Major Riza Bey, the sultan's aide-de-camp.

Colonel Sadik Bey, a prominent enthusiast for Western technology and an accomplished amateur photographer.

Lieutenant Colonel Chefket Bey wears the more practical field uniform of an artillery officer.

ARMÉE OTTOMANE

SADIK-BEY
Colonel d'infanterie, aide de camp de
S. M. I. le Sultan.

RIZA-BEY
Commandant de cavalerie, aide de camp
de S. M. I. le Sultan.

CHEFKET-BEY
Lieutenant-colonel d'artillerie.

How do the uniforms of these officers show the impact of Westernization in the nineteenth century?

In the industrializing world, the most spectacular cases of restructured state power were those of Germany, Italy, the United States, and Japan. In the 1860s, all of these countries experienced wars that were broadly similar in two respects. First, the wars unified countries that were either fragmented or in danger of fragmentation. Germany and Italy had long been disunited—"geographical expressions" divided among many different states. Japan had a long history as a unitary state, but power over remote provinces had slipped out of the central government's control. The United States was still a new state, but its own constitution had never really settled a crucial issue: whether the separate states had permanently and irrevocably renounced their sovereignty in favor of the federal government. When some of the slave-holding states exercised what they claimed was their right to secede from the Union, the federal government contested it.

Second, the civil wars in all four places pitted relatively industrializing or industrialized regions against one another. In Japan, the regions of Choshu and Satsuma in the south supplied most of the manpower and equipment on the victorious side. These were areas where the local rulers had invested most in modernizing their armed forces and producing munitions on a massive scale. In Italy, the armies that conquered the rest of the peninsula came mainly from the kingdom of Piedmont in the northwest, where most Italian industry was concentrated. In Germany and the United States, the stories of the wars were similar: broadly speaking, industrializing regions overcame unindustrialized ones, though in Germany the divisions were less clear-cut than in the American case.

China also underwent a "restoration" after troubles in the 1860s, but they were troubles of a different order from those experienced in Germany, Italy, Japan, and the United States. China endured old-fashioned rebellions—Muslim risings on the edges of the empire, peasant revolutions at its heart—and the invasions by Britain and France recounted in the last chapter (see Map 26.3). The restoration, moreover, did not involve the radical recrafting that circumstances really required. In some ways decentralization continued, in defiance of the trend in the industrializing world. The Chinese government sold offices—effectively wrecking the virtues of the ancient examination system as a method for filling high positions under the state by merit. The number of magistrates who bought their jobs doubled in the second half of the nineteenth century. Partly to maximize sales, the government appointed magistrates for unhelpfully short terms, so the local administration of

Samurai rebellion. In 1877, the revered hero of the Meiji Restoration, Saigo Takamori (1827–1877) rebelled against the government that he had helped to establish, but the government's modern conscript army eventually defeated his force of samurai. Here an idealized Takamori (he was, in fact, obese) rallies his troops against a naval attack.

justice tended to fall into the hands of petty officials who, once appointed as magistrates' underlings, remained in their jobs indefinitely.

Centralization did not always or even primarily mean extending the power of central institutions. It was also a matter of sentiment—overcoming traditional provincial, regional, and communal loyalties with a common sense of allegiance to the state. Governments increasingly used universal military service (see Chapter 24) to create a statewide sense of political community, usually in combination with efforts to cultivate nationalism and spread nationalist feelings. Japan's army, typically, became a nursery for reeducating young men in a new version of samurai values, focused on the notions of obedience to the emperor and self-sacrifice for the state. "I wish the army," declared the emperor in 1875, "to be the entire nation." "We are your supreme commander in chief," stated the emperor's instructions to soldiers in 1882, "Our relations with you will be most intimate when we rely on you as our limbs and you look up to us as your head."

MAP 26.3

Revolts in the Qing Empire, 1850–1901

- Qing Empire
- ☙ tribal risings
- ☙ Muslim revolts
- area of Northwestern Muslim rising 1863–1873
- area controlled by Taiping rebels 1853–1863
- → Taiping rebellion
- area of Boxer uprising 1900–1901
- Guizhou Muslim uprising 1854–1872
- ➜ opium trade

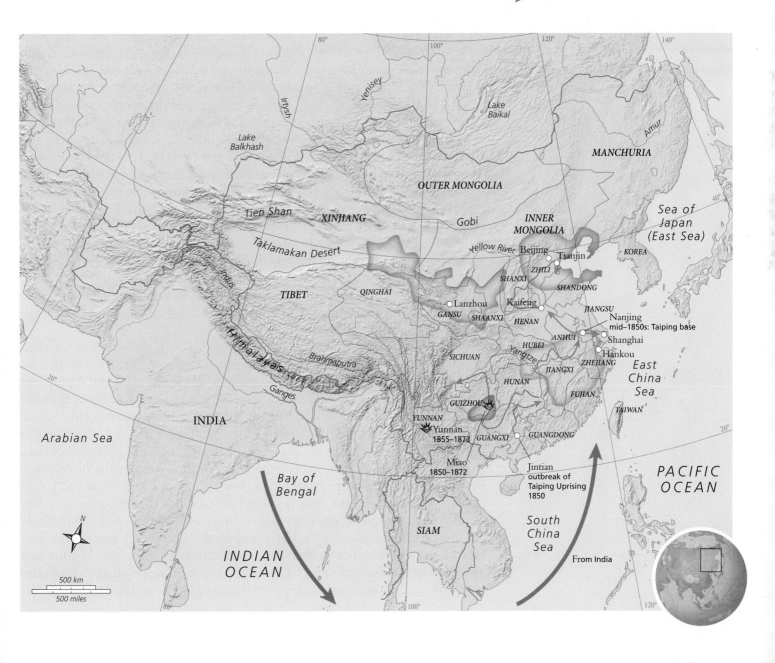

"Honored dead." The reality of the field of Gettysburg was litter-strewn and squalid, with gaping, crumpled corpses. Photography helped to take romance out of depictions of war.

The Japanese army, in consequence, felt no loyalty to the civil government and remained, in effect, outside and above the constitution. A similar pattern can be discerned in Spain and in the Latin American states, where the wars of the early nineteenth century armed and militarized huge proportions of the populations. Armies became the agents of independence and in some cases of modernization, the guardians of the state, and, therefore, the arbiters of constitutional conflicts. To some extent, all countries that used their armed forces to mobilize the entire society ran the same risk of suffering or actually did suffer similar consequences: militarized societies produced politicized armies. The United States was fortunate that by the time of its Civil War (1861–1865) the country had developed civil institutions and traditions strong enough to survive the trauma. Civil conflict in the United States never led, as it has done in most countries, to military dictatorship. Britain, too, escaped the danger by keeping its army small and avoiding conscription until 1916 during the First World War.

As well as bringing armies into politics, militarization made wars worse. The Prussian military theorist Carl von Clausewitz (1780–1831) assumed that wars were inevitable and that they were bound to involve the entire populations of the warring powers. Everyone was an enemy. The only rational way to wage war, he thought, was "to the utmost. . . . He who uses force unsparingly, without reference to the bloodshed involved, must obtain a superiority." He advocated attrition and general destruction to "wear down" the enemy. The ultimate objective was to leave the enemy permanently disarmed. This encouraged belligerents to fight for unconditional surrender when they were winning, to resist it obstinately when they were losing, and to impose harsh terms in victory. Clausewitz's ideas eventually influenced the entire military and political establishment of Europe and America.

In combination, the improved technology of war, the doctrines of militarism, and the transformation of society into a battleground all made the horrors of war worse. The disasters of the Crimean War in the 1850s and the carnage of the American Civil War also set the stage for what followed. Many of the most gruesome aspects of World War I in Europe were foreshadowed by trench and scorched-earth warfare in the United States. Photographers and chroniclers of the American Civil War and the Franco-Prussian War of 1870–1871 introduced a chilling new awareness of war's consequences. The photographs of Matthew Brady (1823–1896) showed fields full of dead and dying Confederate and Union soldiers. The novels of the French writer Emile Zola (1840–1902) depicted foul hospital scenes, decaying dead, gangrenous wounded, and frenzied amputations. His most vivid material, supplied by a field surgeon, brought a new kind of brutal realism to fiction. But neither the new doctrines of militarism nor the new awareness of its effects eliminated the old way of looking at war as a chivalrous, romantic, and glorious adventure full of dashing heroes, waving flags, and colorful uniforms. So wars went on. Peace Congresses were for cranks. Alfred Nobel (1831–1896), the guilt-racked, lonely Swedish weapons magnate who invented dynamite, took refuge in extravagant projects for world peace. War would "stop short instantly," he promised in 1890, if it were made "as death-dealing to the civilian population at home as to the troops at the front." The best hope he could see for peace was the invention of a method of germ warfare or a weapon of mass destruction.

Beyond the Industrializing World

It is tempting to suppose that similar effects on the state could not happen outside the industrializing world. But major new military technologies always affect political and social organization and, as we have seen many times before in this book, relatively simple innovations in war could have big consequences in preindustrial societies. This did not cease to be the case in the nineteenth century. In southeast Africa, for instance, King Shaka reorganized the Zulus into a unified kingdom capable of putting an army of 50,000 men into the field. Shaka invented or adapted a heavy-bladed thrusting spear and developed intensive drills to accustom infantry to use it. The parallel with the effects of firearms drill on Western armies is irresistible. When he claimed his kingdom in 1816, his clan had perhaps 350 warriors. By the time family conspirators murdered him in 1828—a common hazard of kingship in Shaka's part of the world— he was ruler of perhaps 250,000 subjects.

In any case, as the arms trade spread industrially produced weaponry around the world, militarization accompanied it. The Zulus began to rearm with firearms after encountering them in the hands of Boer enemies in 1838. Baskore of Maradi (r. 1854–1875) in what is now northern Nigeria, developed the existing bureaucratic traditions of the region of Katsina, where his realm was centered, to keep an effective army mobilized to gather booty and tribute.

In the first half of the century, the most remarkable case in sub-Saharan Africa was that of the kings of Asante (ah-SHAN-tee) in West Africa. Before the kingdom's conquest by the British in the late nineteenth century, the Asante kings imposed the rule of their own dependants in the provinces, burdened rich rivals with punitive taxes, and employed what historians have not hesitated to call a bureaucracy to systemize the tax system. Held together even after the British abolished the slave trade, the Asante kingdom at its height covered 150,000 square miles and had 3 million to 5 million inhabitants. Beyond a core area around the capital, Kumasi, where the ruler's war companions ruled their own followers without much interference from the court, a central treasury that also ran the kings' own commercial transactions— mining, slave trading, and hunting for ivory—regulated tribute, poll taxes, inheritance taxes, and tolls. Early in the century, the kings adopted Arabic as a language of record keeping, which thereafter was done on paper instead of in the old form of piles of shells and coins, used as tokens and counters. The Asante usually did not displace traditional rulers of conquered peoples but redesignated them as captains of the Asante king and placed resident agents alongside them to keep them in order. Bureaucrats were at the disposal of the king. "We are willing to prove to your majesty," ran the declaration of office of the highest treasury official, "our devotion to your person by receiving your foot on our necks, and taking the sacred oath that we will perform all your commands. Our gold, our slaves and our lives are yours, and are ready to be delivered up to your command."

Remarkable as the Asante case was, it never made the kingdom invulnerable to European conquest. By that standard, Ethiopia was the most successful

King Shaka. Struggling to make a living, the black South African painter Gerard Bengu (1910–1990) worked as an illustrator for children's textbooks on Zulu history. His historical works have all the vices of these kinds of books in any country, as this overidealized and romanticized vision of King Shaka (ca. 1787–1828) shows. Yet in his private work, Bengu painted the lives of his people with moving realism.

⦾ MAKING CONNECTIONS ⦾

STATE MODERNIZATION IN THE NINETEENTH CENTURY

TYPE OF DEVELOPMENT/IDEOLOGY →	CORE IDEA/PURPOSE →	SCOPE AND RESULTS
Nationalism	Uniting people who shared same language, historic experience, and sense of identity into a cohesive state	Worldwide; positive effects include increased self-government, popular sovereignty; negative effects include repression of minorities (ethnic, religious, racial) within larger states; promotion of assimilation
Constitutionalism	Belief that state is founded on rules that rulers and citizens create and are bound to obey within a legal framework	Worldwide; beginning in Britain, United States, and Europe; vigorously opposed because the implication that sovereignty was shared by more than one person/one class; threatened divine right of monarchy and aristocracy; eventual spread to Middle East and Asia
Centralization	Overcoming traditional provincial, regional, communal loyalties by fostering of allegiance to the state; often extending power of central institutions	Worldwide, especially in quickly developing regions; often propelled by civil wars (United States, Japan, Germany, Italy) and in areas threatened with fragmentation
Militarization	Use of armed forces to mobilize populations; boosts power of governments to tax and spend on a large scale	Worldwide, especially in industrializing regions and colonial territories; use of larger armies, advanced technology expands warfare to civilian population, increases military and civilian casualties; arms race for improved technologies
Bureaucratization	Systemizing tax collecting, census taking, and regulation; often relying on regional governors to exercise local authority	Worldwide, in old empires (Ottoman), new industrial states (United States, Germany, Britain) and regions with progressive rulers (Ethiopia, Thailand, Asante kingdom); improved ability to harness economic systems to government goals

case of political modernization in sub-Saharan Africa. In the third quarter of the century, Ethiopia emerged from a long period of internal war and weak leadership. The emperors never enjoyed uncontested legitimacy or universal obedience, but at least they had credible programs of reunification. The system of government had to be loosely federal, with regional rulers exercising authority without reference to the center, except for paying tribute and defending the country from external enemies. Even the most powerful of the warlords, Menelik of Showa, who subsequently rebelled and captured the throne for himself, paid dazzling tributes. In 1880, for instance, he sent the emperor 600 horses and mules with saddles and bridles trimmed in gold and silver, $80,000 worth of cotton goods, and $50,000 in cash. Provincial rulers could assemble treasure on this scale only by conquering more territory. So expansion and the enrichment of the emperor's treasury went on simultaneously, and as resources built up at the center, Ethiopia began to show potential for transformation into a centralized state.

Asante King. Reminiscences of the greatness of the Asante kings persisted after defeat by the British in the late nineteenth century. In this photograph of the 1890s, King Agyeman Prempeh I, borne by slaves, sits on his litter under the royal umbrella, surrounded by drummers and praise singers. Shortly after the photograph was taken, the British arrested and exiled him and provoked a further—and, for the Asante, disastrous—war by demanding custody of the Asante's sacred golden stool.

In the 1870s, as a result of victories against Egyptian invaders, Emperor Yohannes IV began to build up a huge supply of captured modern weapons and to reorganize the army so that it had a professional core. When Menelik became emperor in 1889, he concentrated on creating a militarily efficient state, armed with the best guns he could buy from Europe. He established garrisons in remote parts of the empire, dominating the country, stimulating markets, and spreading Christianity. Local farmers had to keep the soldiers supplied. Intermarriage between soldiers and provincials generally eased the potential conflicts the system risked and turned the garrisons into effective agents of the central authority. Huge provinces remained effectively autonomous under their traditional chiefs, but Ethiopia looked increasingly like a modern state, acquiring, by the end of the first decade of the twentieth century, extensive postal, telegraph, and telephone services, and a rail link to the outside world through the French colony of Djibouti on the Red Sea. The emperors were architects of Ethiopia's modernization, but they imported technical know-how from Europe. Alred Ilg, a young Swiss engineer, was Menelik's chief aide, attending to everything from the palace plumbing to foreign policy. Menelik also made much use of Italian technical advice and arms shipments before the outbreak of conflict with Italy in 1896. As a result of all these changes, Ethiopia played a unique role among native African states in the late nineteenth century. As we have seen, Ethiopia not only repulsed European invasion but participated in imperial expansion on its own account alongside European powers (see Chapter 24).

The case of Ethiopia calls to mind that of Thailand (Siam), a southeast Asian state that modernized even more thoroughly than Ethiopia and also achieved the distinction, unique in its region, of avoiding European conquest. In the 1830s, Prince Mongkut, who already had a reputation as an outstanding Buddhist scholar and reformer, came into contact with French Catholics and Protestant missionaries from the United States, and immediately appreciated that Thailand had a lot of catching up to do if it were to survive in a Western-dominated future. He studied Latin, Greek, and Western science and mathematics, and read British newspapers from Hong Kong and Singapore to keep in touch with Western news. When he became king in 1851, he began cautious reforms, inaugurating a government newspaper, printing laws, and—in a break with a tradition formerly thought sacred—allowing his face to be seen in public. He permitted his subjects to petition him, gave women rights to choose marriage partners, and educated his successor, Chulalongkorn, in a Western as well as a traditional curriculum.

Chulalongkorn (r. 1868–1910) inherited an enormous empire—bigger than any that southeast Asia had ever seen. But it was highly decentralized and variegated: a tributary empire at its edges, with hundreds of traditional communities in every kind of dependence, all with their own peculiar relationships to the throne. When Chulalongkorn came of age in 1873, he immediately created a Privy Council and Council of State with advisory and legislative powers. He abolished the slave trade. He established a palace school and placed royal princes in charge of departments of government, bypassing the old customs by which ministers succeeded by hereditary right or by choice of hereditary patrons. In the 1870s and 1880s, royal commissioners brought outlying autonomous regions of the Thai Empire under control and subject to the central administration. From 1888 onward, after a royal prince had visited England to report on British methods of government, a cabinet system of decision making was gradually introduced, with ministries inspired by the British example. In 1897, the king went to Europe and professed himself "convinced that there exists no incompatibility" between the acquisition of Western know-how "and the maintenance of our individuality as an independent Asiatic nation." Although Western examples obviously inspired his reforms, he presented them as triumphs of Buddhist morality.

Examples of various degrees of bureaucratic centralization could be multiplied in every continent. Until the British invasions of the 1840s, the Sikh state in the Punjab in northern India was developing by creating a bureaucracy, taking a census, surveying the territory it occupied, and introducing a consistent scheme of taxation, with the help of foreign—including British—experts. In the Central African highlands, King Mutesa (r. 1857–1884) of Buganda in what is now Uganda imported European weapons to equip his own servants and clients and Christian missionaries to strengthen his bureaucracy. He was able to dismiss local chiefs at will and concentrate unprecedented power in his own hands. In West Africa, the empire of Sokoto survived throughout the nineteenth century, in part because it created a bureaucracy to replace the local power of chiefs. The kingdoms of Fouta Toro and Fouta Jalon became elective monarchies, relying on Muslim clergy as servants of the state in the localities (see Map 26.4). Tawhiao, the proud Maori who impressed and alarmed James Kerry-Nicholls in New Zealand, had counterparts in state creation all over the world.

Nationalism, Constitutionalism, Militarization, Centralization, and Bureaucratization in the Nineteenth Century

1783–1830	Simon Bolívar, leader in the fight for Latin American independence
ca. 1800–1850	Asante kings centralize and bureaucratize their kingdom
1805–1872	Giuseppe Mazzini, Italian nationalist
1810	Beginning of Jewish reform movement
ca. 1810–1830	Wars of independence from Spain fought in Latin America
1820	King Shaka controls most of southeast Africa
1821	Founding of Liberia
1822	First fully independent Mexican state
1829	Greece gains independence from Ottoman Empire
1830s	Large Latin American states dissolve into smaller ones
1832	Great Reform Act becomes law in Britain
1839	Constitution of the Cherokee Nation
1845	Ottoman sultan convenes an assembly of provincial representatives
1873–1901	British conquest of Kingdom of Asante
1861–1896	José Rizal, Filipino nationalist
1864	Creation of district assemblies in Russia
1867	Second Reform Act becomes law in Britain
1870s–1880s	King Chulalongkorn of Thailand (Siam) modernizes his state
1878	Romania and Serbia gain independence from Ottoman Empire
1889	Japanese constitution created by imperial decree
1893	French Captain Alfred Dreyfus accused of spying for the Germans
1895	Nationalist rebellion in Guangzhou region of China
Late nineteenth century	Ethiopia undergoes political modernization

RELIGION AND POLITICS

State power mopped up traditional rivals. Nationalism, militarization, and centralization eclipsed other traditional allegiances. Aristocracies, as we have seen, were on the wane anyway in most places (see Chapter 24). Religion, however, was more problematic. Religions often had their own powerful institutional structures and rich clergies. They also had the moral authority to challenge governments. States often needed religion for support or to uphold claims to political legitimacy. In the nineteenth century, morality, family life, and the spaces in which social relationships were forged—the household, educational institutions, and the workplace—became arenas fiercely contested between religious institutions and states. In the West, civil marriage was, perhaps, the state's most important intrusion on what in the previous few centuries had become a precinct of religion. Most countries with codified law made at least some provision for it. Education was another battleground, usually resolved by compromise, because clergy were too cheap and too valuable as teachers to eliminate from schools. States that had not already done so, in some cases, even took over existing religions, funding them and appointing clerics. Japan's ancient popular religion, Shintoism, which had always been a chaotic mix of local nature and ancestor cults, became a national organization under imperial leadership with the emperor as chief priest, largely because nineteenth-century intellectuals in Japan perceived state control of religion to be one of the strengths of Western powers.

Europe and the Americas became arenas of state-Church competition–what in Germany after 1873 came to be called a ***Kulturkampf***, "a conflict of cultures" between the state and the Roman Catholic Church. Church-affiliated and secularist political parties engaged in constitutional struggles over the degree to which constitutions should embody religious traditions and reflect religious values. Secularists used the word *liberal* to denote a program of religion-free politics. In this, as in so many respects, the United States provided a model. Its Constitution had insisted from the first that the federal government shall "make no establishment of religion." This was not, however, because Americans were irreligious or because the state was jealous of religion. Rather it was to protect religious freedom. Secularism in Europe, by contrast, was a program to increase state power, and it therefore aroused much opposition. In Latin America, too, the conflict was fierce. A story about Simón Bolívar (1783–1830), the principal leader and spokesman of the successful independence movements of the early nineteenth century, illustrates this. In 1812, he was in Caracas, the main city of Venezuela, when an earthquake struck. Monks took to the streets to bless the dying and denounce the rebels against Spain. Bolívar dragged a monk from the pulpit of a church, threatened him with the sword, and said, "If nature opposes us, we will fight against it and make it obey us." But politicians

Modernization personified. The clothes suggest an upper-class Englishman of the era and an expensively educated English schoolboy. But the faces are those of Chulalongkorn, the king of Thailand, and his son, photographed in about 1890. Westerners' image of Thailand at the time has been distorted, thanks to the much-loved Hollywood and Broadway musical *The King and I*, which depicts an exotic court, presided over by an unbending patriarch king. In fact, however, King Chulalongkorn (r. 1868–1910), was Westernized in his sentiments as well as in his outlook and policies.

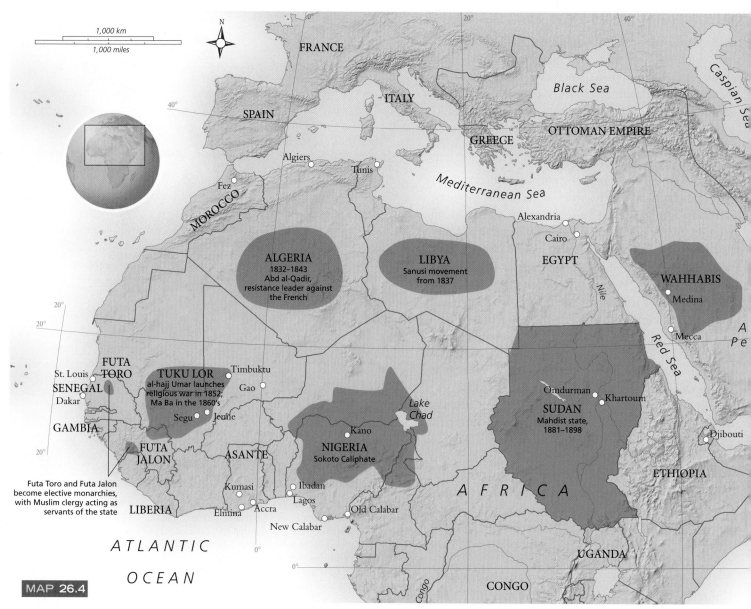

MAP 26.4

Muslim Reform Movements in Africa and Arabia in the Nineteenth Century

■ Islamic reform movement

could not change nature, and religious sentiment was too deeply rooted in human nature and communities to be defied. Churches continued to be able to mobilize people for political action.

In Europe, the Catholic Church fought back with surprising success. Pope Pius IX (r. 1846–1878) responded to challenges to church authority and Christian belief with defiance. He refused to submit to force or defer to change. He condemned almost every social and political innovation of his day. When Italy occupied Rome in 1870 he retreated into virtual seclusion in the Vatican. For a godly vocation undiluted by compromise, his fellow bishops rewarded him by proclaiming papal infallibility in religious doctrine and morals in 1870. His successor, Leo XIII (r. 1878–1903) turned the church into a reforming institution, a privileged critic of abuses of secular power. But after Leo's death, the political fashion changed in Rome, and the church became much more conservative. There were always clergy in every faith who were prepared to collaborate with repression and authoritarianism on the political right.

Meanwhile, religion resisted a deeper challenge from atheism that science claimed to validate. Charles Darwin's theory of evolution (see Chapter 25) suggested, to some of its advocates, a new God-free explanation for life. Impersonal evolution threatened to replace divine Providence as the motor of change. If science could explain a problem as "mysterious"—to use Darwin's word—as the diversity of species, it might yet be able to explain everything else. Religious doubts multiplied among European and American elites. From the 1870s, groups calling themselves "humane" or "ethical" societies aimed to base moral conduct on humane values rather than on the fear of God or the dogmas of religious institutions. Christianity was stirred in response, rather than shaken. Evangelizing movements spread Christian awareness in the new industrialized, urban workforces of the period. In 1867, the English poet, Matthew Arnold, stood on Dover Beach and heard in his mind the "melancholy, long, withdrawing roar" of the "the Sea of Faith." But in 1896, the Austrian composer Anton Bruckner died while writing his great "Ninth Symphony"—a dark document of religious doubts smothered in a glorious finale of resurgent faith.

Among many instances of the continuing vitality of Islam as a source of political inspiration in the nineteenth century, none was more spectacular than the movement the self-taught prophet, Muhammad Ahmad (moo-HA-mahd AH-mahd), proclaimed in the Sudan in 1881. Calling on followers to "put aside everything that resembles the customs of Turks and infidels," he came to see himself as the *Mahdi*—the successor of the Prophet Muhammad, the restorer of the faith, whose coming would herald the end of time. His support grew. He organized his followers into a war machine on Quranic principles—the Quran was the only text he knew. He claimed to speak with the Prophet. He condemned as infidels all who opposed him. His domain on the upper Nile was impregnable— "a desolation of desolations, an infernal region, a howling waste of weed, mosquitoes, flies and fever, backed by a groaning waste of thorns and stones—waterless and waterlogged," as a European described it. His typical follower was, as the British admitted (in lines by the great poet of the British Empire, Rudyard Kipling [1865–1936]) "a pore benighted 'eathen, but a first-class fightin' man." The Mahdi himself had a different explanation for his success: "Every intelligent person must know that Allah rules, and his authority cannot be shared by muskets, cannons, or bombs. . . . He who surrenders shall be saved, but if . . . you persist in denying my divine calling, . . . you are to be killed." The Egyptian and British governments sent armies that failed to suppress the movement until 1898, when a crushingly well-armed British force slaughtered the Mahdists at the Battle of Omdurman (see Chapter 25).

The Mahdi was only one of many founders of Islamic states or disturbers of secular ones (see Map 26.4). In 1852, al-Hajj Umar (ahl-HAHJ OO-mahr), leader of an austere Muslim sect known as the Tijjaniya, launched religious war in the western Sudan, creating a revolutionary state. Ma Ba did the same, probably in imitation, in

Church-State Conflict. The struggle between the Imperial German government and the Catholic Church was one of the most intense cultural conflicts of the late nineteenth century. In this cartoon from the 1870s, Pope Pius IX and Otto von Bismarck, the German chancellor, play a game of political chess. Each piece on the chessboard represents a German church leader whom Bismarck sought to remove from public life. Bismarck is clearly winning the game, while the Pope considers his next move.

Senegambia in West Africa about a decade later. Before attacking a city, he would pray in public amid a crowd of chanting holy men and distribute written charms to his warriors. "You are my equals and my brothers before Muhammad. . . . I am a man of little value, but one who calls you to God and his prophet." In 1860, also in West Africa, the King of Sine told the French that they wanted to do with subject-peoples "as we have always done. These people are my slaves. . . . I will take their property, their children and their millet." But Muslim holy men summoned them to revolt, which the French only repressed with difficulty.

In other regions, too, religion remained a revolutionary force in the world, generating movements of popular rebellion that always failed but that kept cropping up. A few examples illustrate this fact. In 1847, a conflict known as the Caste War broke out in Yucatán in southeast Mexico. Maya rebels threatened to kill all white people. Government supporters retorted with threats to exterminate the Maya. The rebels' rallying point was the so-called Talking Cross of the shrine of Chan Santa Cruz—an oracle proclaiming divine sanction and success for the rebel cause. In the 1850s, in the South African Transkei, the Xhosa people were powerless to rebel against the British, because their cattle were dying from a new kind of lung sickness. A woman prophet urged them to a gesture of despair as an alternative to rebellion: sacrificing their surviving livestock to persuade the gods to get rid of the British.

In Ethiopia, when a new emperor seized the throne in 1855, he called himeslf Tewodros II to appeal to peasants who expected the resurrection of a fifteenth-century emperor of the same name who had befriended the peasantry. This movement transcended religious boundaries. Tewodros II was a Messiah for Christians and a Mahdi for Muslims. He behaved in this respect, as in so many others, like a modernizer in the Western mold, secularizing much church property.

In Japan in the 1860s, samurai reactionaries were the most menacing opponents of Westernization, but a woman who claimed to be a divine incarnation inspired thousands of peasant followers to rebel. She preached equality and peasant solidarity. In China at around the same time, a failed examination candidate and local school teacher, who came to see himself as a "brother of Jesus," led a rebellion that, as we have seen, paralyzed China and almost overthrew the Qing Empire (see Chapter 25). In 1866, a woman who called herself the Virgin of the Rosary led a rebellion in Bolivia. In the North American plains, meanwhile, the Ghost Dance was a traditional—or, at least, fairly old—Native American ritual to bring the dead back to life. In the 1880s, prophets associated it first with a project to bring on the end of the world, then with a plan to invoke divine help against the whites. Most Ghost Dancers never intended violent resistance, but alarmed settlers called in the United States' cavalry. Shortly after the cavalry massacred Sioux Ghost Dancers at Wounded Knee in 1890, Native American rebels in northern Mexico adopted a local woman prophet as the figurehead of their revolt against a modernizing regime in Mexico City.

On the whole, despite the continuing vigor of religiously inspired politics, religion lost out

Ghost dance. The American artist Frederick Remington (1861–1909) was the most famous and popular illustrator of the life of the "Wild West". He painted this version of the Sioux Ghost dancers for *Harper's Weekly*, allegedly from sketches made by members of the South Dakota Home Guard, who suppressed the movement, massacring and scalping 75 Sioux, in December 1890. As the painting suggests, Remington had no personal sympathy for Native Americans. *Ogallala Sioux performing the Ghost Dance at the Pine Ridge Indian Agency, South Dakota. Illustration by Frederic Remington, 1890. The Granger Collection.*

in its conflicts with secular states. The charms religious zealots such as the Mahdi issued did not work against the machine gun. Sacred notions of political authority succumbed to new kinds of legitimacy that nationalists, constitutionalists, and bureaucrats advocated.

NEW FORMS OF POLITICAL RADICALISM

In principle, there was nothing new about popular revolutionary movements of religious inspiration. We have met them many times before in this book. Meanwhile, however, even more radical challenges—even more subversive ways of thinking about the state and forms of political behavior—were building up strength for the future.

Steps Toward Democracy

In the West, enthusiasm for democracy began to mobilize popular movements and became a major force for change independent of any sect. Increasingly, in the nineteenth-century West, citizens sought to take the constitutional changes of the era further and create states in which the political process was open to all. But where did the idea of democracy come from? The two usual—but not necessarily mutually exclusive—answers are from ancient Greece and primitive Christianity. Greek examples provided models of states in which all citizens shared decision making, even though Greek citizenship was restricted to free adult males who usually also had to own property to participate in political life. The Christianity of the apostolic age enshrined the notion of the equality of all members of the group.

However that may be, the United States—perhaps because men steeped in reverence for both the classics and Christianity founded it—was the effective laboratory of democracy for the nineteenth-century world. Democracy as we usually understand it today—with a representative legislature, elected on a wide suffrage, and political parties—was, in effect, an American invention. Although the American executive is not formally subordinate to Congress, all major officeholders under the president have to submit to confirmation by the Senate, and all, including the president, report to Congress, which has—and sometimes indulges in—a right to impeach them. Despite major imperfections—slaves, Native Americans, and women were excluded from political rights—democracy developed early in the history of the new republic. Some of the states were more generous than others in enlarging the franchise, but by the early 1840s, almost all adult, white, and free males could vote in all the states of the United States.

From the perspective of Europe, however, democracy seemed at first to be one of America's "peculiar institutions," like slavery, that it would be best to avoid. It appeared to be foolish for elites to share power with poorly educated masses who tended to vote for populists, demagogues, and charlatans. The bloodshed of the French Revolution seemed to show that the "common man" was an untrustworthy political partner. In consequence, the first half of the nineteenth century was a time of democratic retreat in most of Europe, as rulers withdrew or diluted constitutions that they had conceded to enlarge political nations in the crises of the Napoleonic Wars. The new constitutions that did emerge in Europe at this time were designed to create alliances among monarchs, aristocrats, churches, and the middle classes and thus to defend traditional privileges by enlarging support for them. Whenever possible, the birth of working-class organizations was aborted, radical presses censored, demonstrators shot. In Britain, the Reform Act of 1832, often hailed as a first step toward democratic progress, actually disenfranchised working-class voters.

Nevertheless, the model of the United States became increasingly attractive as the young country proved itself. European radicals who visited America returned enthused. The first influential apologist for American democracy was a German,

Karl Postl, who in 1828 recommended a "system which unites the population for the common good." In 1831, Alexis de Tocqueville, one of the most influential voices of the nineteenth century (see Chapter 24), followed Postl. Tocqueville was a French aristocrat, not previously noted for liberalism, keen to see equality in action—much as one might decide to visit a fairground freak. Between 1835 and 1840, he published *Democracy in America*. His aristocratic self-confidence in the face of popular sovereignty helped reconcile Europeans to democratic change. Tocqueville was not an uncritical admirer of the United States. On the contrary, he noted grave faults: the costliness and inefficiency of government; the corruption and ignorance among public officials; the political bombast; the conformism that offset individualism; the intellectually feeble popular religion; the tension between crass materialism and religious enthusiasm; the "tyranny of the majority"; the threat of rule by and for the rich. But he predicted an American-style future for the world. While most Europeans of his class felt the terror and menace of the revolutionary mob, Tocqueville saw "the same democracy . . . advancing rapidly toward power in Europe." Properly managed, the result would be "a society which all men, regarding the law as their work, would acknowledge without demur." Where rights were guaranteed, he wrote, democracy would "shelter the state" from tyranny, on the one hand, and lawlessness, on the other.

With all its shortcomings, the America Tocqueville described seemed exemplary. Its bottom line was expressed in dollars and cents—the prosperity America delivered for Americans—and in military clout—the success in war the United States demonstrated against Mexico in the 1840s. "Democracy," announced a Hungarian revolutionary after a visit to America, "is the spirit of our age." Democracy became the first American cultural product to conquer Europe—even before jazz, rock music, casual manners, fast food, and tight jeans. The decisive moment came in the 1880s, when James Bryce, a future British ambassador to the United States, revisited the subject of democracy in *The American Commonwealth*. The book provided a blueprint for constitutional change around the world. Bryce recommended

Alexis de Tocqueville, from
Democracy in America

Stump Speaking. George Caleb Bingham (1811–1879) chronicled the life of the Missouri valley in the mid-nineteenth century in his accomplished, well-observed paintings. He was also active in politics on behalf of Andrew Jackson, which gives his political scenes an edge of personal commitment. Typically, as here in *Stump Speaking* (1853–1854), a politician's passion contrasts with the attitudes of his audiences—variously cool, critical, idly curious, sneering, bored, or depraved.
George Caleb Bingham (American, 1811–1879), Stump Speaking, *1853-54. Oil on canvas, 42 1/2 x 58 in. The Saint Louis Art Museum, Gift of Bank of America. Photo © The Saint Louis Art Museum.*

a wide suffrage, but with some property qualifications, since for the poor, he thought, "a vote is a means to mischief." He advised against salaried politicians, who were likely to accept bribes and be overly influenced by money. He felt the American system was too prone to be dominated by the rich. (This was, perhaps, unfair. In Bryce's Britain, members of Parliament were unpaid, and only the rich or their protégés could normally afford to run for office.) But on the whole, Bryce approved of America. Democracy was like a "lamp, whose light helps those who come after it."

The efforts of Tocqueville, Bryce, and their like changed the way European elites perceived democracy. In the last two decades or so of the nineteenth century, most European countries modified their constitutions in a democratic direction and, in particular, enlarged the franchise. New states of the early years of the new century—Norway, Australia, New Zealand, and Iceland (which was under the Danish crown but autonomous)—had even more determinedly democratic constitutions than the United States. Norway and New Zealand even allowed the vote to women and to formerly despised ethnic minorities, the Sami in Norway and the Maori in New Zealand. It is rarely appreciated that in Europe, though France, Switzerland, and—with less consistency—Spain were beacons of universal male suffrage, the most conspicuous concentration of states with democratic franchises was in the former Ottoman dominions in the Balkans. In Greece, Bulgaria, Serbia, and Romania, the right to vote was more widely shared than in Britain or Scandinavia. In this respect, the dawn of European democracy—it is fair to say—came up in the east. This was understandable. The newest states, repudiating the empires that preceded them, had the least historic baggage to discard in adopting democracy.

There was, however, no uniform march of progress toward practical democracy in most of Europe. On the contrary, democracy remained marginal throughout the century. For effective democracy is not just a matter of how many people have the right to vote. Everywhere, small groups tried to manipulate mass electorates. In Romania, the constitution was often suspended or ignored. In Britain, the biggest single extension of the franchise—in 1884–1885—was accompanied by a redistribution of parliamentary seats to preserve the existing parties' shares of power. Constitutional reform in Europe never completely pried open the half-closed world of the dominant political caste and its adopted recruits. The aristocracy retained formal power. Parliamentary dictatorship in Greece subverted the democratic constitution by patronage and intimidation. Greek governments regularly hired thugs to frighten voters at election times. When Germany introduced universal male suffrage in 1871, it was limited to elections for one chamber of the national legislature, the Reichstag, whose power was limited.

The Expansion of the Public Sphere

Even where there was little or no democracy, more people got involved in what historians and sociologists now like to call the **public sphere**: in clubs, institutions, and associations outside the home, in arenas of debate in cafes and bars, and in places of worship. Newspapers brought affairs of state home to everyone who was literate. To some extent, public readings of newspapers made even illiterate people politically informed. In Cuba, this was the normal entertainment for workers in factories while they rolled cigars. In Barcelona in Spain in 1852, a young monk visited a factory at lunchtime to find the workers all listening to young children reading aloud from "highly colored political journals which generally spread subversive doctrines, mocked holy things . . . spoke ill of the proprietors and government, and preached socialism and communism." Catholic clergy provided reading material for factories to deflect workers from hearing too much inflammatory or revolutionary propaganda.

The public sphere was widest and most developed in North America and parts of Europe. That is why democracy got a foothold in those regions. But there were outposts and echoes in other parts of the world. Although the number of people who took part in political life in Latin America was relatively small, compared with the United States, they contested power with great commitment, and sustained ferocious debates in the press. In Brazil, the proliferation of political clubs, newspapers, and rallies preceded the abolition of slavery in 1888 and the proclamation of the republic in 1889. In Cuban cigar factories, lectors employed to read to the workers spread radical political messages. In the last two decades of the nineteenth century, most Argentinian intellectuals generally and genuinely regarded their country as a democracy: that was the message of the leading newspaper, *La Nación*, and its founder, the former president, Bartolomé Mitre.

In Japan the spread of education (see Chapter 24) was bound to enlarge the public sphere. The way the state recruited officials moved into new arenas, as examinations replaced samurai privileges as a means to recruit staff. Even in China, the political class expanded, thanks in part to the creation of hundreds of new provincial academies to train officials. On the whole, the Qing rulers responded to crisis by resisting social or political change and clinging to the notion that the inherited order of society was sacred. The terms of public debate, however, were enlarged. The work of Feng Guifen (fung gway-fun) (1809–1874), director of one of the largest provincial academies, included radical proposals, based on study of Western politics. At the height of the crisis caused by rebellion and Anglo-French invasion in the 1860s, he advocated the professionalization of the civil service and popular election of village headmen to provide the lowest level of the judiciary. The government, however, shelved his proposals.

WESTERN SOCIAL THOUGHT

The clash of political visions in the nineteenth-century West was the echo of a mightier clash of rival philosophies: part of a worldwide tension between secularism and religiosity in everyday conceptions of life and the world. Were men apes or angels? Were they images of God or heirs of Adam? Would the goodness inside them emerge in freedom or was it corroded with evil that had to be controlled? Just after the Napoleonic Wars, in 1816, the English writer Thomas Love Peacock, gathered fictional philosophers in the setting of his comic novel, *Headlong Hall*. "Mr. Forster, the perfectibilian," expected "gradual advancement towards a state of unlimited perfection," while "Mr. Escot, the deteriorationist," foresaw, with gloomy satisfaction, "that the whole species must at length be exterminated by its own imbecility and violence." These extremes of optimism and pessimism echoed real debates. In France, for instance, Louis Blanc (1811–1882) believed that the state could eliminate all human wickedness, while his contemporary, Alphonse Karr, looked for no improvement in society and thought that attempted reforms only made things worse. The politics of fear and hope collided in conflicts that pitted rival kinds of radicalism—reformist philosophies that claimed to get to the root of the world's problems—against each other.

Socialism was an extreme form of optimism. Socialists believed in the ideals of equality and fraternity that those thinkers in the Enlightenment who believed in the perfect ability of human nature had proclaimed (see Chapter 22). Early socialist communities in Europe and America practiced sharing and cooperating. Charles Fourier (1772–1837) planned a settlement called Harmony, where even sexual orgies would be organized on egalitarian principles. In Texas in 1849, Étienne Cabet (1788–1856) founded a town he called Icaria, where abolishing property and forbidding rivalry would prevent envy, crime, anger, and lust. Clothes, according to Cabet, ought to be made of elastic to make the principle of equality "suit people of different sizes."

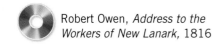 Robert Owen, *Address to the Workers of New Lanark*, 1816

These experiments, and others like them, failed, but the idea of reforming society as a whole on socialist lines appealed enormously to people unrewarded or outraged by the unequal distribution of wealth in the industrializing world. Economic theorists maintained that since workers' labor added the greater part of the value of most commodities (see Chapter 24), the workers should get the lions' share of the profits—or so some socialists inferred. This was a capitalist's kind of socialism, in which ideals carried a price tag. Louis Blanc convinced most socialists that the state could impose their ideals on society. John Ruskin (1819–1900) echoed these arguments in England. For him "the first duty of a state is to see that every child born therein shall be well housed, clothed, fed and educated," and he relished the prospect of increased state power to accomplish it.

Meanwhile, Karl Marx (1818–1883) predicted the inevitability of socialism's triumph through a cycle of class conflicts. As economic power passed from capital to labor, so workers—degraded and inflamed by exploitative employers—would seize power in the state. "Not only," he announced, "has the bourgeoisie forged the weapons that bring death to itself. It has also called into existence the men who are to wield those weapons—the modern working class, the proletarians." The transition, he believed, would inevitably be violent. The ruling class would try to hold on to power, while the rising class struggled to gain it. So he tended to agree with the thinkers of his day who saw violence as good and conducive to progress. In part, the effect was to help inspire revolutionary violence, which sometimes succeeded in changing society, but never seemed to bring the communist utopia into being or even into sight. All Marx's predictions, so far, have proved false. Yet the brilliance of his analysis of history ensured that he would have millions of readers and millions of followers.

While mainstream socialists put their faith in a strong, regulatory state to realize revolutionary ambitions, or sought to capture the state by mobilizing the masses, visions of revolutionary violence sidetracked others. Some of these "anarchists," as they called themselves, turned increasingly to the bloodstained ravings of Johann Most (1846–1896), the first great ideologue of terror. The entire elite—including their families, servants, and all who did business with them—was, for Most, legitimate targets of armed struggle, to be killed at every opportunity. Anyone caught in the crossfire was a sacrifice in a good cause. Most devised the phrase "propaganda of the deed" as a euphemism for murder. In 1884, he published a handbook on how to explode bombs in churches, ballrooms, and public places, where the "reptile brood" of aristocrats, priests, and capitalists might gather. He also advocated exterminating policemen on the grounds that these "pigs" were not fully human. The bombs of terrorism exploded in elite ears. The propaganda of the deed captured the world's press. Social outcasts and the chronically disaffected formed solemn pacts to assassinate rulers, provoke revolutions, fight wars of resistance against the state, and defy the repressive realities of politics and economics.

In most European countries in the late nineteenth century, socialists built up mass organizations for political and industrial action. They believed their triumph was determined by history. The questions that divided them were whether that triumph should be triggered violently, pursued democratically, or engineered by industrial action. In Milan in northern Italy, in 1899, Giuseppe

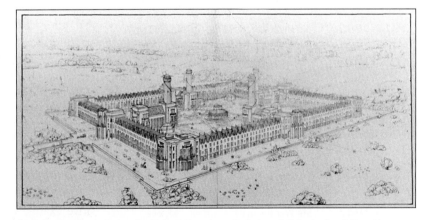

Socialist utopia. A design for Robert Owen's projected socialist utopia of New Harmony, Indiana. Owen's socialism had Christian origins, though the minaret-like towers and central pavilion make this view of New Harmony resemble Mecca. The symmetry recalls classical models of an ordered life. The grandeur and fantasy are typical of the "progress-palace" tradition of nineteenth-century factory architecture.

Pelizza, a convert to socialism from a guilt-ridden middle-class background, began a vast symbolic painting. He depicted a crowd of workers, advancing, "like a torrent, overthrowing every obstacle in its path, thirsty for justice." Except for a Madonna-like woman in the foreground—who seems bent on a personal project, appealing to one of the rugged leaders at the head of the march—the workers are individually characterless, moving like parts of a giant machine, with a mechanical rhythm, slow and pounding. No work of art could better express the grandeur and grind at the heart of socialism: noble humanity, mobilized by dreary determinism.

Opponents of socialism included philosophical pessimists, who believed humans could not be reformed, and that only law and order could redeem their wickedness. Between extreme optimism and extreme pessimism, centrist political thinking developed. In the nineteenth century, the English philosopher Jeremy Bentham (1748–1832) devised the most influential form of centrist thinking, called **utilitarianism**. Bentham proposed a new way to evaluate social institutions without reference or deference to their antiquity or authority or past record of success. He thought good could be defined as a surplus of happiness over unhappiness and that the aim of the state was "the greatest happiness of the greatest number." For Bentham, social utility was more important than individual liberty. His doctrine was thoroughly secular. Bentham's standard of happiness was pleasure, and his index of evil was pain. His views therefore appealed to the irreligious. Today, he is treated like a secular saint. His body is exhibited at University College, London, to encourage students. Bentham and his friends also attempted austerely rational and scientific thinking about how to run society. But the greatest happiness of the greatest number means sacrifices for some. It is strictly incompatible with human rights, because the interest of the "greatest number" will always tend to leave some individuals without benefits.

Modifying, then rejecting utilitarianism, Bentham's disciple, John Stuart Mill (1806–1873), came to adopt a scale of values with freedom at the top. Liberty, he thought, is absolute, except where it interferes with others. "The only purpose," he wrote, "for which power can be rightfully exercised over any member of a civilised community, against his will, is to prevent harm to others"—not to make him happier. For Bentham's "greatest number," Mill substituted the individual. "Over himself, over his own body and mind, the individual is sovereign." Mill's individualism, however, never excluded social priorities. "For the protection of society," the citizen "owes a return for the benefit." He can be made to respect others' rights and to contribute a reasonable share of taxes and services to the state. Freedom and social priorities, however, did not commend themselves to everybody. Philosophical opponents of liberalism—the most eloquent of whom was the German Friedrich Nietzsche (1844–1900)—favored "heroes" and "supermen" to solve social problems. Dictators in the next century would adopt these ideas.

Meanwhile, Benthamism was amazingly influential. The British state was reorganized along lines Bentham recommended. The penal code was reformed to minimize unhelpful pain. The government bureaucracy was restaffed with administrators who had passed competitive exams. Capitalist and libertarian prejudices could never quite exclude public interest from legislators' priorities, even under nominally right-wing governments. Benthamism made social welfare seem like the job of the state. In promoting social welfare, Germany led the way, introducing pensions, health services, and education for all in the 1880s.

John Stuart Mill, from *On Liberty*

Religion, Utopianism, Democracy, and Political Radicalism in the Nineteenth Century

1748–1832	Jeremy Bentham, proponent of utilitarianism
1772–1837	Charles Fourier, created planned community of New Harmony based on egalitarian ideals
1788–1856	Étienne Cabet, founded utopian community of Icaria
1806–1873	John Stuart Mill, combined individualism with social reform
1811–1882	Louis Blanc, argued that the state could eliminate human wickedness
1818–1883	Karl Marx, predicted socialism's inevitable triumph
1835–1840	Publication of Alexis de Tocqueville's *Democracy in America*
ca. 1840	Almost all adult white males can vote in the United States
1844–1900	Friedrich Nietzsche, rejected liberalism and religion
r. 1846–1878	Pope Pius IX, opponent of social and political innovation
1847	Caste War begins in southeast Mexico
1873	*Kulturkampf* launched by Bismarck
1881	Muhammad Ahmad calls on Muslims in the Sudan to join his reform movement

The German policy is often seen as an attempt to preempt the appeal of socialism—as indeed it was. But it was also the outcome of a trend, begun during the Enlightenment, of philosophical respect for the common man. Australia and New Zealand copied German initiatives in an attempt to create a common identity for settlers—an identity, moreover, distinct from those of the snobbish and class-ridden society that migrants from Britain had left behind. A worldwide consensus in favor of a socially responsible state gradually emerged. The main disagreements, which would be bloodily fought out in the following century, were over how far that responsibility extended.

IN PERSPECTIVE: Global State-Building

All the transformations of nineteenth-century states need to be understood against a common background: the declining credibility of traditional forms of authority, as conflicts overthrew old supremacies and economic change enriched new aspirants to power. During the changes that followed, the sphere of the state unquestionably enlarged. States had still not penetrated vast areas of the globe, but these regions were now clearly the exception—underpopulated and relatively inaccessible environments. In most of the rest of the world, the state had arrived: imposed from outside by imperialist invasions, or created from within by monarchs or elites, usually in imitation of Western powers. In parts of the world with long experience of states, such as Japan, Egypt, and Thailand, governments had extended their reach. States took on new responsibilities as their power increased. Education, as we have seen, received a boost from militarization. States interfered more and more in religion and family life. It even became increasingly accepted that the state was responsible for the total well-being of its citizens.

After all the wars, reforms, constitutional conflicts, radical thinking, and administrative tinkering, how strong were the states and empires that covered most of the world at the century's end? Had they reformed for survival? Or were they, as socialists thought, doomed to disappear? Age-old rivals of the state—religious institutions and

Noble workers. Giuseppe Pelizza's painting *Il Quarto Stato*, completed between 1899 and 1901. Pelizza was convinced that artists were workers who had a social responsibility to educate, elevate, and inspire other workers. Although he himself was born into a well-off, middle-class Italian family, he believed that only a person who was born, bred, and lived among the working class could undertake this duty.
G. Pellizza da Volpedo The Fourth Estate. *Milano, Galleria Civica D'Arte Moderna. © Canali Photobank.*

allegiances—had proved remarkably strong. And although local, regional, and tribal loyalties were in retreat, they had only been checked, not destroyed. As we shall see, they would often reemerge in the twentieth and twenty-first centuries. At the end of the nineteenth century, it looked as if some states, such as Japan, the United States, and the British Empire, had met the challenges of the century successfully and recast themselves in lasting form. Others, such as the Ottoman Empire and China, looked inadequately reformed and vulnerable. In between were superficially strong states, such as the German and Russian Empires, and that of the Habsburgs, which were to prove surprisingly fragile when tested in the twentieth century. While white empires continued to grow, there were signs that the days of their supremacy were numbered. Their power was founded on technological superiority, which was a wasting asset. Nonwhite powers in Asia and Africa had already demonstrated that they could copy the trick, either by buying European technology with which to fight back against the empires, as Ethiopia had or, like Japan, launching their own industrialization programs.

To maintain its power in the world, Europe needed peace at home. Only brief wars broke that peace in the nineteenth century. For almost 40 years after the defeat of Napoleon in 1815, no major war flared on Europe's home ground. The wars of the midcentury to 1870 were short and did not overstrain the belligerents. After 1870, short-term military service became the universal fashion in the West—with the major exceptions of Britain and the United States but including almost all of Latin America—and Japan, as states sought to give more male citizens experience of military service. Armies therefore had to make up in technology what they lacked in professional ability, because most recruits did not serve long enough to become skilled soldiers. Ever more efficient means of mobilizing armies were called on, as railways linked front lines to barracks and bases all over Europe. Ever more accurate and long-range weapons were required to compensate for soldiers' lack of expertise in firing them. The result was an arms race that made peace precarious, and an atmosphere of anxiety among the powers to mobilize rapidly should a new war threaten: a recipe, in short, for rupturing peace. Still, until the end of the nineteenth century, enough powers were sufficiently evenly matched to keep the peace for most of the time.

By then, however, the fear of revolution had so diminished, and the habit of short wars had become so familiar, that neither the fragility of peace nor the fear of war excited much alarm in Europe. The balance of power, on which peace depended, was beginning to tilt toward war, because of the uneven distribution of heavy industry. By 1900, Germany produced vastly more coal, iron, and steel than all the other European powers combined. The Russian Empire, with its huge population, was beginning to show signs of being able to catch up. This fact—little

CHRONOLOGY

1748–1832	Jeremy Bentham, proponent of utilitarianism
1772–1837	Charles Fourier, created planned community of New Harmony based on egalitarian ideals
ca. 1800–1850	Asante kings centralize and bureaucratize their kingdom
1805–1872	Giuseppe Mazzini, Italian nationalist
1806–1873	John Stuart Mill, combined individualism with social reform
ca. 1810–1830	Wars of Independence from Spain fought in Latin America
1811–1882	Louis Blanc, argued that the state could eliminate human wickedness
1818–1883	Karl Marx, predicted socialism's inevitable triumph
1820	King Shaka gains control of most of southeast Africa
1821	Founding of Liberia
1822	First fully independent Mexican state
1829	Greece gains independence from Ottoman Empire
1830s	Large Latin American states dissolve into smaller ones
1832	Great Reform Act becomes law in Britain
1835–1840	Publication of Alexis de Tocqueville's *Democracy in America*
1844–1900	Friedrich Nietzsche, rejected liberalism and religion
1845	Ottoman sultan convenes an assembly of provincial representatives
1846–1848	Mexican-American War
r. 1846–1878	Pope Pius IX, opponent of social and political innovation
1847	Caste War begins in southeast Mexico
1861–1896	José Rizal, Filipino nationalist
1867	Second Reform Act becomes law in Britain
1870s–1880s	King Chulalongkorn of Thiland modernizes his state
1871	German unification
1873–1901	British conquest of Kingdom of Asante
1873	*Kulturkampf* launched by Bismarck
1878	Romania and Serbia gain independence from Ottoman Empire
1881	Muhammad Ahmad calls on Muslims in the Sudan to join his reform movement
1889	Japanese constitution created by imperial decree
1893	French Captain Alfred Dreyfus accused of spying for the Germans
1896	Battle of Adowa
1895	Nationalist rebellion in Guangzhou region of China
Late nineteenth century	Ethiopia undergoes political modernization

noticed outside Germany—made a trial of strength seem urgent. In the arena of Europe, the sand that the changes of the nineteenth-century kicked up was raked into new patterns of alliance, made with war in mind rather than to contain change or maintain the balance of power. The arena was ready for the gladiators.

PROBLEMS AND PARALLELS

1. How did new states emerge in the nineteenth century? What roles did nationalism, constitutionalism, militarization, and bureaucratization play in state development?

2. What were the differences between European nationalism and nationalist movements outside Europe? What was the relationship between constitutionalism and modernization in the nineteenth century?

3. Why did many nineteenth-century states emphasize centralization? Who benefited from centralization? Which groups lost power?

4. Why did religion and politics clash in the nineteenth century? Why did the clergy oppose the theory of revolution?

5. Why was religion a "revolutionary force in the world" during the nineteenth century?

6. How did democracy become more widespread in the nineteenth century? What does the term the *public sphere* mean? Why did new forms of political radicalism emerge in the nineteenth century?

DOCUMENTS IN GLOBAL HISTORY

- Fustel de Coulanges on nationalism
- José Rizal, excerpt from *El Filibusterismo (The Reign of Greed)*
- The Constitution of the Empire of Japan, 1889

- Alexis de Tocqueville, from *Democracy in America*
- Robert Owen, *Address to the Workers of New Lanark,* 1816
- John Stuart Mill, from *On Liberty*

Please see the Primary Source CD-ROM for additional sources related to this chapter.

READ ON

The opening story comes from J. H. Kerry-Nicholls, *The King Country* (1974), J. Belich, *The New Zealand Wars* (1988), and *Making Peoples* (1996) are gripping revisionist studies of New Zealand. B. Anderson, *Imagined Communities: Reflections on the Origin and Spread of Nationalism* (1991) is the fundamental starting point for contemporary thinking about nationalism. G. Wawro, *Warfare and Society in Europe, 1792–1914* (2000) is a solid introduction to the impact of militarization on European states and society. Lord Durham's *Report on the Affairs of British North America*, ed. by C. Lucas (1970), shows the thinking that went into the emerging political structure of the British Empire.

Nationalism and state building beyond Europe is beginning to receive more attention in the literature. Among the many books by B. Lewis *The Middle East* (1997) is a good introduction to the politics of the Arab world. F. R. Hunter, *Egypt Under the Khedives, 1805–1879: From Household Government to Modern Bureaucracy* (1984) is the foundational work on the emergence of the modern Egyptian state. H. S. Wilson, *Origins of West African Nationalism* (1969) analyses the impact of colonial rule on the emergence of African nationalisms, while *West African Kingdoms in the Nineteenth Century*, ed. by D. Forde and P.M. Karberry (1967), studies the range of successes in indigenous African state building. B. Farwell, *Prisoners Of the Mahdi* (1967), recounts the story of three

western prisoners of the Mahdi in the Sudan and lived to tell the story, and explores this religiously inspired revolt against colonial encroachment. M. A. Klein, *Islam and Imperialism in Senegal, 1847–1914* (1968) provides a more analytical account of the interaction of religion and imperial pressure. *José Rizal and the Asian Renaissance* (1996), sets a very broad context. His novels and many of Bankim's are available in English translations.

C. A. Bayly, *The Birth of the Modern World. 1780–1914* (2004) is indispensable for understanding the nineteenth-century state in global dimension. D. Ralston, *Importing the European Army: The Introduction of European Military Techniques and Institutions in the Extra-European World, 1600–1914* (1996) studies several key examples of non-European states attempting to the new world of militarized centralization. D. Wyatt, *A Short History of Thailand* (1984), explores one of the few cases of successful Asian resistance to imperial pressures. R. Scheina, *Latin American Wars: Volume I, The Age of Caudillos, 1791–1899* (2003) gives a detailed military narrative that reveals the reasons behind the failures of Latin American state building. K. Pomeranz, *The Great Divergence: China, Europe, and the Making of the Modern World Economy* (2001) is excellent on the different paths taken by Britain and China after 1800, linking political regimes to economic development in unexpected ways.

Egyptian and U.S. Feminism Before the First World War

Egypt in the 1890s and early 1900s was under-industrialized, predominantly Muslim, and under British rule. The United States was one of the most prosperous and powerful countries in the world, with a "modern" economy, a democratic constitution, and a cultural heritage indebted to the European Enlightenment. We might expect that women in the U.S. fared better than their Egyptian counterparts: enjoying more access to education, paid work, and public life, with more political and social rights, including freedom to marry and divorce. Indeed, some Egyptian feminists held up the model of American womanhood as an example to work toward. But what issues did feminists in the two countries care about? And how much did they really differ from each other?

UNITED STATES

EGYPT

• • • • •

Malaka Hifni Nasif (1886–1918), wrote under the pen name Bahithat al-Badiya ("Seeker in the Desert"). She was a graduate of, and later a professor at, the first woman's teacher training school in Egypt. Extract I is from a speech she gave to an all-female audience in 1909.

She was an educated, professional, independent woman. However, she contracted a polygamous marriage with a Bedouin chief and lived with him in the desert. Her role in public life was strictly as an advocate for education, health, and charities—not for women's social emancipation or political rights. She opposed female suffrage. Readers of her work are bound to ask whether her concern for the education of women was mainly focused on making them attractive to men. Egyptians who sought brides abroad were the most consistent targets of her criticism.

Another Egyptian, Qasim Amin (1863–1908), was a male champion of women's right to education and participation in public life—in equality with men, in most respects. Extract II is from *The Liberation of Women* (1899), his first book on the subject. In it, he argued that women's rights were consistent with Muslim teachings—especially in connection with the cases against polygamy, arbitrary divorce, arranged marriages, and the veiling and seclusion of women. The extract shows how he was more radical than Malaka. It also shows how his feminism fit into a broader political and social program of liberal and democratic modernization.

Extract III is from a speech of 1894 to a Senate committee by Elizabeth Cady Stanton (1815–1903), one of the most prominent U.S. feminists of the late nineteenth and early twentieth centuries. She devoted a lifetime to campaigning for women to have the same access to education and political participation as men.

Extract IV is by Rena Rietveld Verduin, a 25-year-old farmer's wife from Illinois who had never got beyond fifth grade and spent most of her life doing household chores and bringing up children. The occasion of her speech in 1926 was one of the regular debates on major issues held by a local culture club. Arenas like this, where ordinary women could take part in the public sphere, were simply unavailable in the Egypt of Malaka Hifni Nasif.

EXTRACT I (MALAKA HIFNI NASIF)

If we pursue everything Western we shall destroy our own civilization, and a nation that has lost its civilization grows weak and vanishes. Our youth claim that they bring European women home because they find them more sophisticated than Egyptian women. . . .

...Continued

I am the first to admire the activities of the Western woman, and her courage, and I am the first to respect those among them who deserve respect, but respect for others should not make us overlook the good of the nation. . . .

Our beliefs and actions have been a great cause of the lesser respect that men accord us. How can a sensible man respect a woman who believes in magic, super-stition, and the blessing of the dead, and who allows women peddlers and washer-women, or even devils, to have authority over her? . . . Good upbringing and sound education would elevate us in the eyes of men. . . .

If had the right to legislate, I would decree:
1. *Teaching girls the Quran and the correct sunna [practice of the Prophet].*
2. *Providing primary and secondary school education for girls, and compulsory preparatory school education for all.*
3. *Instructing girls to the theory and practice of home economies, health, first aid, and childcare.*
4. *Setting a quota for females in medicine and education so they can serve the women of Egypt.*
5. *Allowing women to study any other advanced subjects they wish without restriction.*
6. *Bringing up girls from infancy stressing patience, honesty, work, and other virtues.*
7. *Adhering to the sharia [Islamic law] concerning betrothal and marriage, and not permitting any woman and man to marry without first meeting each other in the presence of the father or male relative of the bride.*
8. *Adopting the veil and outdoor dress of the Turkish women of Istanbul.*
9. *Maintaining the best interests of the country and dispensing with foreign goods and people as much as possible.*
10. *Making it incumbent upon our brothers, the men of Egypt, to implement this program.*

EXTRACT II (QASIM AMIN)

History demonstrates that the status of women is inseparably tied to the status of a nation. When the status of a nation is low reflecting an uncivilized condition for that nation the status of women is also low. . . . On the other hand, we find that women in nations with a more advanced civilization have gradually advanced from the low sta-tus to which they have been relegated, and have started to overcome the gap that has separated them from men. One woman is crawling while the other is running. . . . The American woman is in the forefront, followed by the British, the German, the French, the Austrian, the Italian, and the Russian woman, and so on. . . .

Westerners, who like to associate all good things with their religion, believe that the Western woman has advanced because her Christian religion helped her achieve freedom. This belief, however, is inaccurate. Christianity did not set up a system which guarantees the freedom of women; it does not guarantee her rights through either specific or general rules; and it does not prescribe any guiding principles on this topic. . . .

Muslim women praying.
In keeping with Muslim practice, Egyptian women pray apart from their male counterparts at the Amr Ibn Al As mosque in Cairo toward the middle of the twentieth century. Though Egyptian women gained the right to vote in 1956, their educational and professional opportunities remain more limited compared to women in the West.

...Continued

[In contrast,] the Islamic legal system, the shari'a, stipulated the equality of women and men before any other legal system. Islam declared women's freedom and emancipation, and granted women all human rights during a time when women occupied the lowest status in all societies. . . .

Within the shari'a, the tendency to equate men's and women's rights is obvious, even in the context of divorce. Islam had created for women mechanisms worthy of consideration and contrary to what westerners and some Muslims imagine or believe . . . nothing in the laws of Islam or in its intentions can account for the low status of Muslim women. The existing situation is contrary to the law, because originally women in Islam were granted an equal place in human society. Unacceptable customs, traditions, and superstitions inherited from the countries in which Islam spread have been allowed to permeate this beautiful religion.

The most significant factor that accounts for the perpetuation of these traditions, however, is the succession over us of despotic governments. . . . When despotism prevails in a country, its impact is not limited to individual cases only, since it is central to the ideology of the supreme ruler. . . . A despot spits his spirit into every powerful person, who whenever possible, dominates a weaker one. . . . These despotic systems have also influenced the relationships between men and women—man in his superiority began to despise woman in her weakness. . . .

I do not exaggerate when I say this has been the status of women in Egypt until the past few years, when we have witnessed a decrease in the power of men. This change is a consequence of the increased intellectual development of men, and the moderation of their rulers. We have observed that women at present have more freedom to look after their own affairs. . . . Likewise, many men have given women a special status within the family structure. This has occurred among men who are confident in their women and have no worries regarding their trustworthiness. This is a new kind of respect for women.

EXTRACT III (ELIZABETH CADY STANTON)

The isolation of every human soul and the necessity of self-dependence must give each individual the right to choose his own surroundings. The strongest reason for giving woman all the opportunities for higher education, for the full development of her faculties, for forces of mind and body; for giving her the most enlarged freedom of thought and action; a complete emancipation from all forms of bondage, of custom, dependence, superstition; from all the crippling influence of fear—is the solitude and personal responsibility of her own individual life. The strongest reason why we ask for woman a voice in the government under which she lives; in the religion she is asked to believe; equality in social life, where she is the chief factor; a place in the trades and professions, where she may earn her bread, is because of her birthright to self-sovereignty; because, as an individual, she must rely on herself. . . .

Nothing strengthens the judgment and quickens the conscience like individual responsibility. Nothing adds such dignity to character as the recognition of one's self-sovereignty; the right to an equal place, everywhere conceded – a place earned by personal merit, not an artificial attainment by inheritance, wealth, family
...Continued

and position. Conceding then that the responsibilities of life rest equally on man and woman, that their destiny is the same, they need the same preparation for time and eternity. The talk of sheltering woman from the fierce storms of life is the sheerest mockery, for they beat on her from every point of the compass, just as they do on man, and with more fatal results, for he has been trained to protect himself, to resist, to conquer. . . .

EXTRACT IV (RENA RIETVELD VERDUIN)

The question, as you have heard, to be discussed tonight is: Resolved that women should not enter higher education. I will try and convince the audience that women should enter higher education. . . .

Through an education girls are enabled to become self-supporting and acquainted with the ways of the world. Through an education girls learn to earn a livelihood and are not so liable to throw themselves away in marriage on some worthless man. . . . Why, men seem to think that the women have no business on the face of the earth except to work and slave for them. . . . Women are treated something like this: After a woman is married, that good master of hers takes her, builds four walls around her and tells her, "Now little woman you just mind your business in here, and see to it that everything is kept in good order and that the meals are prepared just as I want them, and that nothing is prepared that I don't like. And if you need any money, come to your Master for it. And never you mind what's going on outside of those walls; that's none of your business. We can do very well without you." And he expects the woman to bow her poor head and say amen to all this. . . . Girls, get an education and escape slavery.

Elizabeth Cady Stanton and Susan B. Anthony. Two of the great pioneers of U.S. feminism (and founders of the National Woman Suffrage Association in 1869) Elizabeth Cady Stanton and Susan B. Anthony plot strategy, circa 1881.

Questions to Consider

1 What criticisms did Malaka Hifni Nasif make of her fellow women?

2 Is there any evidence of her limited political aspirations for women?

3 How do Qasim Amin's priorities for women compare to those of Malaka?

4 How does he appeal to Islamic law and why?

5 What other justifications does he find for female emancipation?

6 Why do Stanton and Verduin emphasize education, and how do their aspirations for women's education compare with those of the Egyptian feminists?

7 What criticisms do the Americans make or imply of men, and how do these compare with what the arguments the Egyptians make?

Sources

Extract I M. Badran and M. Cooke, eds., *Opening the Gates: A Century of Arab Feminist Writing* (Bloomington: Indiana University Press, 1990).

Extract II Qasim Amin, *The Liberation of Women* (Cairo, 1899).

Extracts III and IV Gerda Lerner, ed., *The Female Experience: An American Documentary* (London and New York: Macmillan, 1992).

Cyberspace. This map of the Internet looks a lot like the Milky Way. But each of the wispy strands represents millions of computer networks that criss-cross the planet like a lattice. The reddish wisps indicate networks in East Asia and the Pacific. Europe, Africa, the Middle East, and Central and South Asia are green. North America's heavily wired landscape is evident in the predominance of blue, while the relatively few yellow fibers suggest the scarcity of connections in Latin America and the Caribbean. Sectors of the Internet that have yet to be mapped shimmer in white like distant galaxies.

ENVIRONMENT

since 1905, 1918, 1930
Relativity—Quantum mechanics

CULTURE

1914–1918
World War I

1929–1939
Great Depression

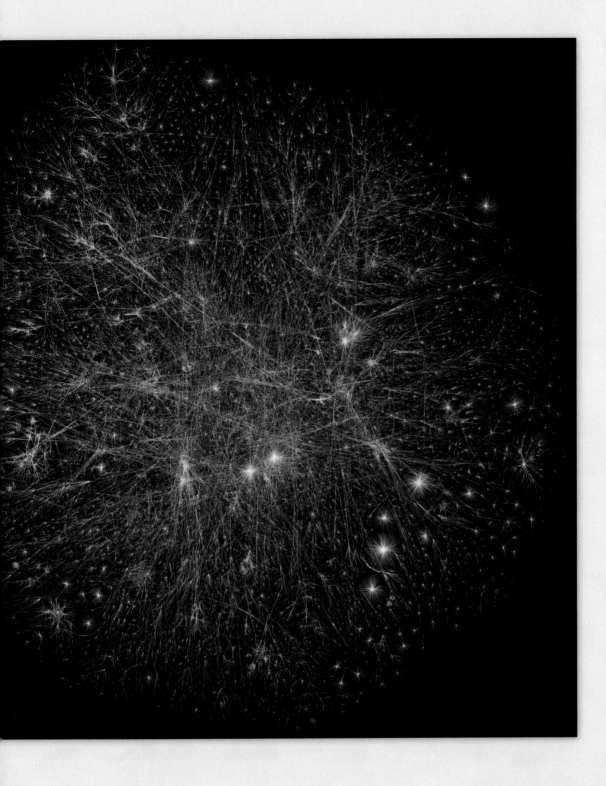

since 1950s
Global warming

since 1960s
Intensive deforestation

since mid–1980s
AIDS epidemic

since 1990s
Genetically modified crops

1936–1945
World War II

1945–1989
Cold War

since early 1950s
Television

since mid–1990s
Internet

CHAPTER 27

The Twentieth-Century Mind: Western Science and the World

Dr. Edward H. Hume taking a patient's pulse at the Yale-Hunan Clinic. Dr. Hume founded the clinic in the city of Changsha, in Hunan, China in 1914 and was its dean until 1927. The presence of guards shows that this photograph was taken after the clinic began to attract socially elevated patients.

Edward H. Hume's heart sank when he saw the gateway to the city where he was to begin his new life. After researching bubonic plague in India, he arrived in China in 1905 as part of a team from Yale University. His aim was to start a clinic, and his ambition, if possible, was to found a medical school. His destination was Changsha, in remote Hunan province, where the Chinese government allowed foreigners to settle as part of its policy to develop the interior. The city gate stared back at him, blindly and defiantly—symbolically bricked-up against him at the orders of the local gentry, who resented having foreign barbarians stationed in their midst. The local officials did their best to obstruct him. The notables of the town shunned him. For the poor, however, Hume's services were attractive. With the backing of Yale alumni, he could afford to treat them for nominal sums. So they frequented his clinic, as well as visiting the shops of his Chinese rivals—an astrologer, a fortune-teller, a physiognomist who diagnosed illnesses by scrutinizing the faces of the sick, and an old soldier who had retrained as a folk pediatrician. Some members of the merchant class favored Hume, too, because he carefully kept corpses off his premises, shipping hopeless cases away before they died. Observers therefore judged his methods to be superior to those of traditional Chinese medicine. A notorious bandit, who had a bullet in his leg, was one of the first patients at Changsha's Yale Clinic.

For nearly three years, Hume had no patients from among the mandarins, the scholar-elite who monopolized positions of authority in China. Then one morning he heard harsh voices outside his clinic. "Carefully! Set the chair down! . . . Stand aside, you brats! This is a mandarin's chair!" The newly arrived visitor expected to jump the waiting line of patients, but Hume's doorman insisted on the rules. "Yes, Great One," the doorman explained, "I know you are an official; but this foreign doctor would dismiss me in an instant if I admitted you out of turn. . . . I am not worthy, Great One, to stand opposite you."

A few minutes later, Hume welcomed into his surgery his first mandarin patient. The newcomer seemed apprehensive, but appeared reassured when the foreign doctor began to check his pulse. The mandarin even complimented the physician on his mastery of a technique long practiced in China. But when Hume

FOCUS questions

- **WHY DID** Western science dominate the world during the first half of the twentieth century?
- **WHAT FORMER** certainties about the cosmos and human nature did science undermine during the twentieth century?
- **WHY DID** many people turn away from science in the late twentieth century?
- **HOW DID** styles in the arts mirror developments in science?
- **WHY HAVE** many people in the West come to rely on non-Western forms of medical treatment?

dropped his patient's wrist and shoved a thermometer into his mouth, the mandarin exploded with rage. "Why," he said to the attendant who accompanied him, "did you let this foreigner put this strange, hard thing inside my mouth? Can't you see that he knows nothing of medicine?" Only subsequently did Hume learn how he had offended his patient. He had read his pulse by taking his left wrist; but Chinese tradition dictated that a doctor must also check a series of pulse points on the right arm. By proceeding straight to taking the patient's temperature, Hume had exposed himself, in his patient's eyes, as an ignoramus.

It was a disappointing episode for the young physician. He realized that the authorities had sent the mandarin to report on the foreigner's practices. He hoped to make a favorable impression since he knew that official approval would expand and enrich his practice. His failure was an episode in a long, slow, and sometimes fitful story of the assimilation of Western medicine in China—which was itself a strand in a larger fabric of history: the spread of Western science—led by Western medicine and military technology, but extending to every kind of science and to scientific habits of thought—across the world. In no area was the rise of the West to world dominance more apparent than in the worldwide appeal of Western science. Hume played his own modest part in the story with increasing success. Gradually, painstakingly, he won Chinese confidence, building up support not only by successfully treating many difficult cases, but also by using the accumulated goodwill of the school for boys and girls that the Yale mission maintained alongside the clinic. Hume's experience, in microcosm, echoed that of Western influence generally.

• • • • •

In the twentieth century, science came to set the agenda for the world. Whereas previously scientists had tended to respond to the demands of society, now science drove other kinds of change. The pace of scientific discovery—with the dazzling revelations scientists disclosed about the cosmos, nature, and humankind—commanded admiration and radiated prestige. In Europe and the Americas, the period was convulsively innovative. A scientific counterrevolution exploded certainties inherited from seventeenth- and eighteenth-century science. Revolutions in psychology and social anthropology made people rethink cultural values and social relationships. A new philosophical climate eroded confidence in traditional ideas about language, reality, and the links between them. Ever larger and costlier scientific establishments in universities and research institutes served their paymasters—governments and big business—or gained enough wealth and independence to set their own objectives and pursue their own programs. New theories shocked people into revising their image of the world and their place in it.

The lessons of Western science proved equivocal. New technologies raised as many problems as they solved: moral questions, as science expanded human power over life and death; practical questions, as technologies multiplied for exploiting the Earth's resources of energy. Increasingly in the twentieth century, ordinary people and nonscientific intellectuals lost confidence in science. Uncertainty corroded the hard facts with which science was formerly associated. Faith that science could solve the world's problems and reveal the secrets of the cosmos evaporated.

In part, this was the result of practical failures. Though science achieved wonders for the world, especially in medicine and communications, consumers never seemed satisfied. There was no progress without problems. Every advance unleashed side effects. Technological advances seemed to privilege machines that fought wars and destroyed or degraded environments. Science seemed best at devising engines of destruction, but could only make people happy in modest ways, and did nothing at all to make them good. Even medical improvements brought equivocal effects. The costs of treatment sometimes exceeded the benefits. Health became a purchasable commodity. Medical provision buckled, in prosperous countries, under the weight of public expectations and the intensity of public demand.

As the power of science grew, more and more people came to fear and resent it and react against it. Despite its stunning successes, science proved strangely self-undermining. It stoked disillusionment, even as it spread. It disclosed a chaotic cosmos, in which effects were hard to predict, and interventions regularly went wrong. A century dominated by Western science ended with the recovery of alternative traditions that Western influence had displaced or eclipsed.

The stories of these changes fill this chapter—starting with the global diffusion of Western science, then turning back to the West to see how science changed from within, and how art mirrored the changes. In the remaining chapters, we can look at the effects of the changes on politics, culture generally, and the environment.

WESTERN SCIENCE ASCENDANT

The early twentieth-century world seethed with discontent at Western hegemony and sparkled with visions of a brighter future that political leaders, religious enthusiasts, and secular intellectuals promised or called for. Yet the allure of Western science proved irresistible (see Map 27.1). Its global appeal was twofold. First, it worked. Western military technology won wars. Western industrial technology multiplied food and wealth. Information systems devised in the West revolutionized communications, business, leisure, education, and methods of social and political control. Western medical science saved lives. Paradoxically, the only way for the rest of the world to beat the West, or catch up with it, was to "modernize"—code for imitating the West in science and technology. Second, Western science offered the promise of infallibility: of knowledge that was certain because it matched observation, fulfilled predictions, and withstood tests. Chinese revolutionaries actually called science a faith and represented "scientism" as an alternative to Confucianism.

China

The Chinese reception of Western science began in a continuous and systematic fashion in the 1860s, at the start of the "self-strengthening" movement (see Chapter 23). In 1866, Beijing's Foreign Language Institute opened a "mathematics" department. In fact, it was a Department of Science and Technology, with the aim of emulating the West or, as its first director said, "for the use of logical reasoning, methods of manufacturing and being practical," as well as mathematics strictly understood. "If we can concentrate on being practical," the director added, "and learn all the essentials, then this is the path to strengthening China." It was a promising beginning, but, as we have already seen, Chinese self-strengthening was patchy in the nineteenth century, and the absorption of Western ideas was always slow and subject to the restraining effects of mistrust of foreigners, whom Chinese continued to see, all too often, as barbaric or demonic.

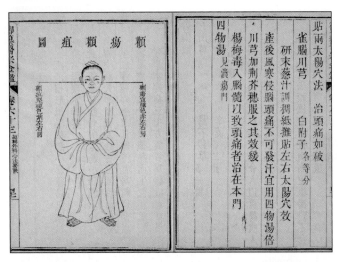

Chinese Herbal Medicine. In 1869, the emperor of China, Tongzhi, presented the United States government with 933 volumes of materials on Chinese herbal medicine and ancient Chinese agricultural techniques. This illustrated volume from the *Complete Survey of Medical Knowledge* demonstrates the proper usage of pertinent Chinese herbal medicine for illness.

Nor was the pace of change uniform in all the sciences. At first, medicine lagged behind mathematics and military and industrial technology. In 1876, for instance, a comparative study of Chinese and Western medicine by Chinese physicians upheld the superiority of ancient Chinese methods. In 1883, however, the Beijing School of Medicine launched a Western-style curriculum. Chinese students began to go abroad to study medicine. In 1900, the United States' government received an indemnity from China for the losses caused to American business interests by the chaos and bloodshed of a rebellion in China that Western forces helped to suppress. The government used the money to finance scholarships for Chinese students in America. By 1906 there were 15,000 Chinese students studying science abroad—13,000 of them in Japan, where the Western scientific curriculum was already triumphant. European and American doctors, meanwhile, acquired Chinese assistants and, in some cases, took advantage of growing Chinese interest in Western methods to move to China to practice. Dr. Hume was one of about 100 Western physicians in China in his day. In 1903, the University of Beijing acquired a medical department. Meanwhile, in essays published from 1895 onward, the scientific translator Yan Fu (yen foo) introduced Darwin's theory of evolution to China (see Chapter 25), and 20 or 30 Western scientific books were being translated into Chinese each year, with dozens more reaching China via Japan.

The revolution of 1911 that overthrew the Qing dynasty and made China a republic stimulated the pace of change, bringing to positions of power and authority intellectuals indebted to the West for many of their political ideas. They proclaimed what they called New Culture, in which science would play a prominent part, to modernize and "save" the country from Western and Japanese competition. After the revolution, syllabus reforms replaced ancient Chinese mathematics—apart from the use of the abacus—with a Western-style mathematical curriculum. Translations of Western science textbooks helped in a vital part of the process: developing a modern scientific vocabulary in Chinese. Until the term *kexue* (keh-shweh-jahng) became current from 1915, no Chinese word expressed everything the word *science* meant in English. New journals applied scientific methods and principles to social and personal problems.

Chinese who studied abroad continued to infuse China with Western intellectual influences. In 1914, Chinese students at American universities met at Cornell University in New York State to found the Science Society of China. When they returned home, it became one of the most influential organizations in the country, dedicated to popularizing Western-style science and promoting scientific education. The society succeeded. Science as Westerners understood it became part of the general curriculum, as well as the core of professional training. By 1947, for instance, China had 34,600 medical practitioners trained according to Western methods. The numbers more than doubled over the next ten years. By the end of the twentieth century, all Chinese physicians had at least some Western-style training.

In China, Western science had to rely chiefly on its inherent appeal to make headway. While the Qing had ceded a few, relatively small urban areas to foreign custody or control, in most of the country Western power was exercised only indirectly. Westerners had to buy or bribe their way into positions of influence. Yet Western science still exercised an irresistible fascination, even where it could not be forced on people. It is not surprising, therefore, that in parts of the world under the direct rule of Western empires, the uptake was even greater, for European empires acted as agents for the spread of Western science. India is the best example to concentrate on. It had a colonial government committed to promoting science and a native intelligentsia anxious to learn.

India

In 1899, the British viceroy of India, Lord Curzon, declared that the British had come to India to bring the benefits of their law, religion, literature, and science. The value of the first three for India might be debatable, but the benefits of "pure, irrefutable science" and, in particular, of medical science were indisputable. Science also served, incidentally, the aims of British policy, breaking through traditional barriers of caste and community, serving "rich and poor, Hindu and Mohammedan, woman and man." Curzon made the colonial government invest heavily in scientific education and the employment of Western scientists, and he induced the native princes who still ruled much of India to do the same. By 1906, India had research institutes devoted to veterinary science, agriculture, and forestry. The central government employed its own scientific research teams. By 1914, these existed for medicine, meteorology, veterinary science, botany, agriculture, forestry, and geology. In 1913, the Indian *Journal of Medical Research* was launched. These efforts were paralleled in neighboring parts of the British Empire. In Malaya, for instance, where the native elite had begun to accept Western schooling in the 1890s, the Sultan Idris Training College for Medicine opened its doors to students in 1920.

In the first couple of decades of the century, European personnel, of course, hugely predominated in the new scientific institutions. To achieve Indianization—training Indians in scientific work—the government had to overcome ingrained racial prejudice, typified in 1880 by the British Superintendent of the Geological Survey of India, who declared Indians "utterly incapable of any original work in natural science." Outstanding Indian scientists, trained in England, had to struggle for recognition, accept lower pay than their British counterparts, or take service with native princes. But their achievements gradually began to speak for themselves. In 1897, the viceroy—not without opposition from prejudiced individuals—awarded a research grant to Jagadis Chandra Bose, as "the first explorer and inventor in the electrical sciences that India has yet produced." The numbers of native scientists multiplied, thanks in part to Western-inspired educational institutions—especially the Jesuits' schools and the Indian universities the British had founded—and, in part, to the networks of education and exchange of ideas that Indian intellectuals established for themselves.

Prafulla Chandra Ray was at the heart of these networks, establishing an international reputation in chemical research and founding his own successful pharmaceutical business in Bengal. By 1920, he and his students and colleagues had published over 100 research papers, many in British and American journals. "Our age," he announced at the Indian Science Congress that year, "is preeminently an age of science. The fate of a nation will depend henceforth more upon the achievements of its students of science than upon the skill of its generals or the adroitness of its diplomatists and statesmen." In the 1920s, when the government proposed to add a chemistry department to the teams of scientists it maintained, Indian scientists opposed the idea because the teams were led by British bureaucrats, while Indian experts were better qualified for the work. In 1930, Chandrasekhara Venkata Raman, a pupil of Jagadis Chandra Bose, won the Nobel Prize in physics for work on the diffusion of light in liquids–the first non-Westerner to be so honored.

Sir Jagadis C. Bose, Indian physicist and botanist, in 1896. Bose was a professor at Calcutta and studied the polarization and reflection of electric waves. He also worked on experiments that demonstrated the sensitivity and growth rates of plants.

MAP 27.1

Spread of Western Scientific Learning, 1866–1961

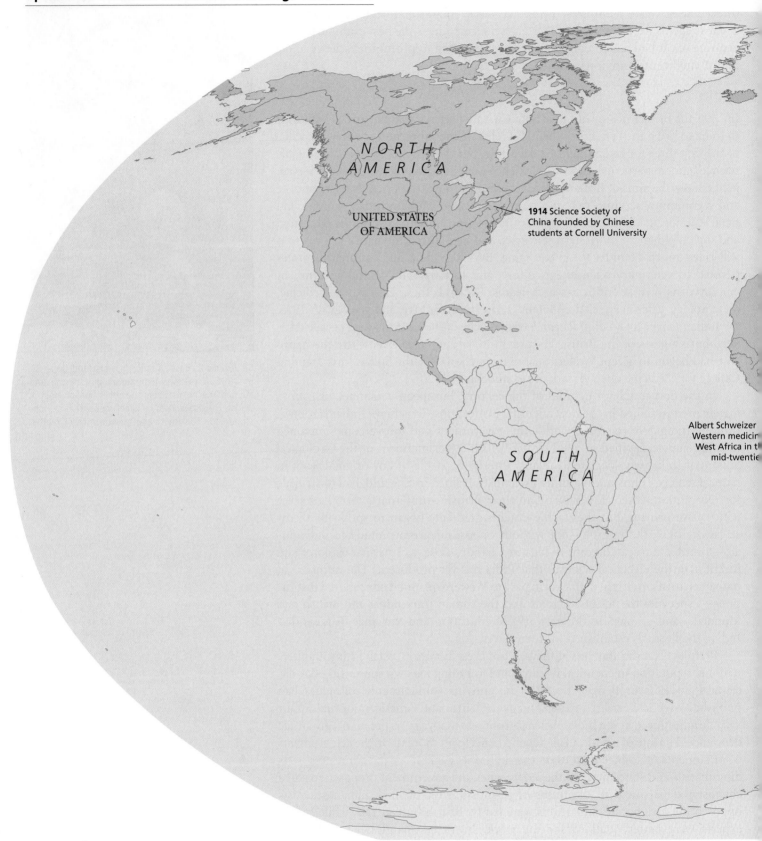

NORTH AMERICA

UNITED STATES OF AMERICA

1914 Science Society of China founded by Chinese students at Cornell University

SOUTH AMERICA

Albert Schweizer Western medicin West Africa in t mid-twentie

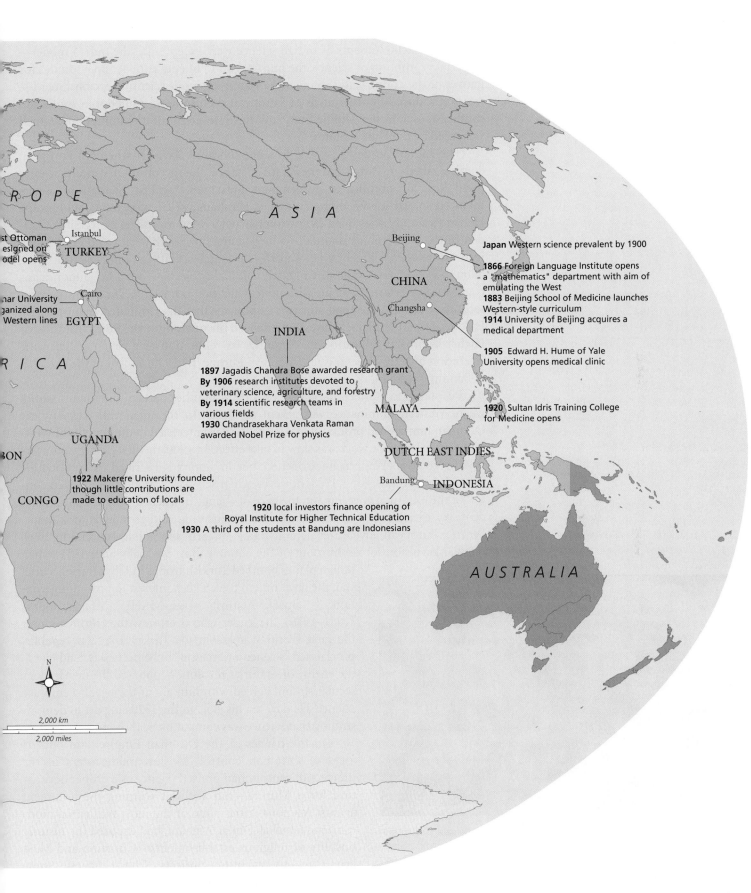

ROPE

Istanbul

st Ottoman
esigned on
odel opens

TURKEY

nar University
ganized along
Western lines

EGYPT

Cairo

RICA

UGANDA

BON

CONGO

1922 Makerere University founded,
though little contributions are
made to education of locals

A S I A

Beijing

CHINA

Changsha

INDIA

1897 Jagadis Chandra Bose awarded research grant
By 1906 research institutes devoted to
veterinary science, agriculture, and forestry
By 1914 scientific research teams in
various fields
1930 Chandrasekhara Venkata Raman
awarded Nobel Prize for physics

MALAYA

DUTCH EAST INDIES

Bandung

INDONESIA

1920 local investors finance opening of
Royal Institute for Higher Technical Education
1930 A third of the students at Bandung are Indonesians

Japan Western science prevalent by 1900

1866 Foreign Language Institute opens
a "mathematics" department with aim of
emulating the West
1883 Beijing School of Medicine launches
Western-style curriculum
1914 University of Beijing acquires a
medical department

1905 Edward H. Hume of Yale
University opens medical clinic

1920 Sultan Idris Training College
for Medicine opens

AUSTRALIA

N

2,000 km

2,000 miles

The Wider World

Though the achievements of Indian science were exceptional, the Indian model—imperial promotion of science, the multiplication of educational opportunities for natives of the country, the emergence of an indigenous scientific establishment—were reproduced in other areas of European dominion or influence in south and southeast Asia, in the Middle East, and, to some extent, in the Philippines, which was ruled by the United States.

The Indian model, however, was not followed slavishly wherever European empires ruled. In Dutch Indonesia, for instance, the reception of Western science owed little or nothing to government initiatives. Wealthy plantation owners financed an astronomical observatory at Lembang, where stargazers could escape Holland's cloudy skies in an effort to construct a reputation. The University of Leiden in the Netherlands maintained field centers in South Africa and Java. These institutions served largely as laboratories for Dutch scientists. Some scientific initiation, however, was available to Dutch colonial subjects. From 1913, Indonesians could study Western medicine without leaving their homeland. The following year, secondary schools dropped admissions policies that discriminated against native Indonesians. In 1920, local investors financed the opening of the Royal Institute for Higher Technical Education in Bandung. Its reputation as a center of scientific education quickly came to rival schools in Europe. By 1930, a third of the students at Bandung were Indonesians.

Resistance to Western science was strongest in other parts of the Islamic world, where Western dominance was absent or shaky. In the nineteenth century, the Ottoman Empire had produced many intellectuals interested in the benefits of Western science, but their work was slow to take effect. In 1900, the first Ottoman university designed on Western lines opened, but its library subscribed to no scientific research periodicals. After 1908, however, when self-styled modernizers seized control of the Ottoman government, the pace of change quickened. Learned societies in dentistry, agriculture, veterinary medicine, engineering, and geography took shape. When a European adventurer demonstrated an early airplane in Istanbul in 1909, popular revulsion forced him out of the country. But, especially after 1911, when Italian planes bombed Turkish troops in Libya during a brief war, the government took a keen interest in promoting aviation. Kemal Ataturk (keh-MAHL AH-tah-toork) (1881–1938), the leader who overthrew the Ottomans after the First World War and made Turkey a secular republic, proclaimed "science and reason" to be his legacy. Said Nursi, the enemy of Ataturk's revolution, opposed the new leader's secularism but agreed with him about the need to embrace science. He devoted his exile in the 1920s in part to demonstrating that science was compatible with Islam.

On the fringes of the Ottoman Empire, and outside areas of Ottoman control, Muslim modernizers of the nineteenth century had praised science as a proper occupation for a Muslim—but without winning the argument against religious critics. One of the most influential modernizers, Jamal al-Din al-Afghani, had exposed the historic hostility of religious establishments—Christian and Muslim alike—to scientific projects. The Lebanese Shiite scholar, Husayn al-Jisr, who died in 1909, was the first great apologist for Darwin in the Islamic world. The Egyptian

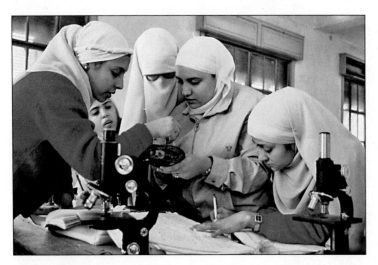

Muslim nursing students. Cairo University in Egypt, where female Muslim students wear *hijab* (headscarves). Some women students cover their faces completely. Many aspects of Western culture, including science, spread in part because they adapt easily to a variety of cultural environments. Western science has eastern roots—Islamic and Chinese influences—that many non-Westerners who study it can recognize.

Ismail Mazhir (1891–1962) continued his work in a series of translations of Darwin, beginning in the 1920s but incomplete until 1961. His great project to demonstrate that Darwin's theories were consistent with Quranic accounts of creation was still in progress at the end of the twentieth century, when the Pakistani intellectual, Ziauddin Sardar, championed it. Scientific interpretation of the Quran was, at that time, one of the most popular types of literature in the Muslim world.

Meanwhile, other forms of Western science seeped into and soaked the educational systems of much of the Muslim Middle East. Science was a foreign implant there. A survey of scientific research in the Middle East, conducted during the Second World War (1939–1945), found only a handful of Muslim scientists to consult. In 1952, a survey in Egypt counted 1,392 individual practitioners of science. At that stage, more than 70 percent of them had at least one degree from a university abroad—most from British and American institutions. By 1957, the total number of Egyptian scientists had risen to 3,600. By 1973, there were 10,655. In 1961, the great Muslim educational center of Cairo, known as al-Azhar, was reorganized along the lines of a Western university. Similar changes were under way throughout the Arab world. Over the following two decades, at least 6 million Arabs studied Western-style science at universities.

In sub-Saharan Africa, meanwhile, Western science spread more slowly and selectively. While European empires lasted, racist assumptions inhibited the colonial authorities from training native African scientific elites. Britain founded some research institutes in its East African colonies, notably Makerere University in Uganda, but their scientific staffs were recruited in England, and they educated few Africans. French research institutes had many African field centers, but these, too, were unconnected to indigenous communities. Belgian scientific work in the Congo was locally financed, but otherwise uninvolved with native Congolese. For most of the first half of the century, therefore, black Africans were the passive recipients of Western science, especially of medicine. Albert Schweizer (1875–1965), a Swiss theologian who retrained as a doctor and devoted himself to the care of the sick in

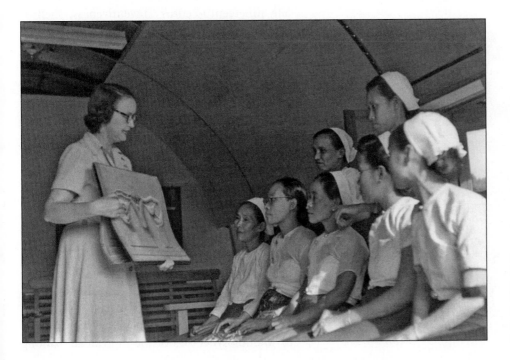

Colonial science. A British midwife instructs Burmese nurses in midwifery in the 1950s. The picture is posed to suggest Western superiority. The students—some older and presumably wiser than their teacher—are in Western-style uniforms, submissively listening to a lesson reinforced by simple diagrams.

Gabon in French West Africa for nearly 30 years, typified the spirit of the medical missionary, transforming the life expectancy of his patients not so much by his medical skill, which was never advanced, as by his efficient hospital buildings, his emphasis on hygiene, and his ability to dispense Western medicine. Thousands of idealistic young Western volunteers followed similar vocations. From the 1930s until the 1980s, as Western medicine increasingly relied on medication with new pharmaceuticals, which were invented at a dizzying pace, the power of Westerners to save African lives slashed death rates and helped bring a population explosion to Africa.

Medicine everywhere was the banner bearer of Western science, partly because that of the West probably was more effective than any other tradition, and partly because it attracted official support around the world. Missionaries valued and practiced it as an antidote to what they called superstition and magic. Western administrators saw it as a means to gain favor from indigenous elites and power over native populations who became dependent on Western medicines.

THE TRANSFORMATION OF WESTERN SCIENCE

Even while it achieved enormous influence and registered enormous effects across the world, Western science was changing from within. The very qualities that made it attractive—its benign inventions, its power to increase knowledge, its promise to disclose truths you could trust—crumbled. The inventions proved equivocal, the knowledge elusive, the certainties unattainable.

With hindsight, we can also detect the origins of the conflicts that beset science in the early twentieth century. On the one hand, they were years of impressive progress. Conventionally, historians represent the first decade or so of the new century as a spell of inertia, a golden afterglow of the romantic age that the real agent of change, the First World War, would turn blood red. But even before the war broke out in 1914, the worlds of thought and feeling were already alive with new colors. Technology hurtled into a new phase. The twentieth century would be an electric age, much as the nineteenth had been an age of steam. In 1901, Guglielmo Marconi broadcast by wireless radio across the Atlantic. In 1903, the Wright brothers took flight in North Carolina. Plastic was invented in 1907. The curiosities of late nineteenth-century inventiveness, such as the telephone, the car, and the typewriter, all became commonplace. Other essentials of technologically fulfilled twentieth-century lives—the atom smasher, the steel–concrete skyscraper frame, even the hamburger and Coca Cola™—were all in place before the First World War.

On the other hand, when the century opened, the scientific world was in a state of self-questioning, confused by rogue results. In the 1890s, X-rays and electrons were discovered or posited, while puzzling anomalies became observable in the behavior of light. In 1902, a young French mathematician, Henri Poincaré, questioned what had previously been the basic assumption of scientific method: the link between hypothesis and evidence. Any number of hypotheses, he said, could fit the results of experiments. Scientists chose among them by convention—or even according to "the idiosyncrasies of the individual." Among

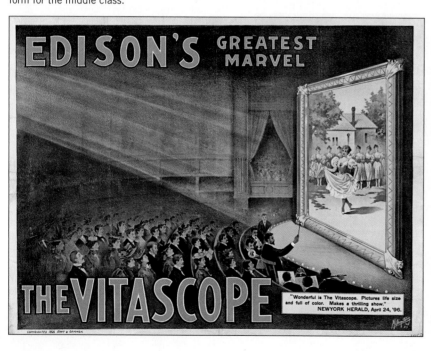

The Vitascope was an early device for projecting cinematic images, displayed here showing the ballet *Giselle* in an advertisement of 1896. The gilt frame, prominent orchestra, and choice of theme all evoke the marketing context: a tasteful art-form for the middle class.

EDISON'S GREATEST MARVEL

THE VITASCOPE

"Wonderful is The Vitascope. Pictures life size and full of color. Makes a thrilling show."
NEWYORK HERALD, April 24, '96.

examples he cited were Newton's laws (see Chapter 19) and the traditional notions of space and time. He provided reasons to doubt everything formerly regarded as demonstrable. He compared the physicist to "an embarrassed theologian, . . . chained" to contradictory propositions. His books sold in the thousands. He became an international celebrity, whose views were widely sought and reported.

Science usually affects society less by what it does or says, than by how it is misunderstood. This was particularly so for most of the twentieth century, when all academic disciplines became highly professionalized and specialized, with their own jargons and long training programs designed to exclude outsiders and amateurs. Practitioners of other kinds of learning tended to treat science as a benchmark discipline, whose objectivity they wish to emulate, but whose language and findings they could barely comprehend. Readers misinterpreted Poincaré to mean that "Scientific fact was created by the scientist," and that "Science consists only of conventions. . . . Science therefore can teach us nothing of the truth; it can only serve us as a rule of action."

Physics

Poincaré claimed that he had never intended to say or imply such things. But he set the tone for at least 100 years of struggle between science and skepticism—skepticism about our ability to know anything for certain. "The nature of our epoch is multiplicity and indeterminacy," announced the Austrian poet, Hugo von Hofmannsthal (1874–1929). "Foundations that other generations believed to be firm are really only sliding." Science seemed a laboratory transformed by the magic of a sorcerer's apprentice.

The result of this skepticism was that science, for all its achievements, could never replace ideology. It could not command ordinary people's allegiance the way that religious or political systems could. Science strode ahead, proposing solutions to theoretical problems about the nature of the universe and practical problems in every field. Its admirers and many of its practitioners came to believe in its unique virtue and even in its potential power to supplant other guides to life, such as religion, reason, instinct, and common sense. But there were always people who sneered at it, or snubbed it, or doubted its claims, or feared its consequences.

Thanks to the way Poincaré shook up perceptions of the nature of science, people became more willing to listen to radical theories from unlikely people, such as Albert Einstein (1879–1955), a minor official in the Swiss Patent Office, whose academic vocation had become frustrated because his teachers undervalued the originality of his mind. In 1905, he emerged from obscurity, like a burrower from a mine, to detonate a terrible explosion. His theory of relativity exploded traditional physics and reshaped most educated people's image of the cosmos. The impact of the explosion registered only gradually, as, up to 1915, Einstein worked out the implications of his thinking and knowledge of it spread.

According to traditional physics, and to commonplace observation and intuition, the speed of a body ought to affect the speed of the light it reflects or projects, rather as a ball gains speed from the vigor with which it is thrown. Yet experimental data, which accumulated in the 1890s, seemed to show that the speed of light never varied. Most people assumed an error in the measurements. Einstein proposed, instead, that the invariability of the speed of light was a scientific law. He resolved the contradiction by proposing that the apparent effects of motion on speed were illusions. Rather, time and space change with motion. Mass increases with velocity, whereas time slows down.

Einstein's work broke on the world with the shock of genius: the jarring sensation of seeing something obvious that no one had ever noticed before. The implications of a cosmos in which time was unfixed took a lot of getting used to.

Major Inventions—1850–1914

1852	Gyroscope
1853	Passenger elevator
1856	Celluloid
	Bessemer converter
	Bunsen burner
1858	Refrigerator
	Washing machine
1859	Internal combustion engine
1862	Rapid-fire gun
1866	Dynamite
1876	Telephone
1877	Phonograph
1879	Incandescent lamp
1885	Motorcycle
	Electric transformer
	Vacuum flask
1887	Motorcar engine
1888	Pneumatic tire
	Kodak camera
1895	Wireless radio
	X-rays
1897	Diesel engine
1902	Radio-telephone
1903	Airplane
1911	Combine harvester

Theoretical physicist Albert Einstein writes an equation on a blackboard while turning to his audience at the California Institute of Technology, ca. 1931. Einstein's distinctive looks—the ever-alert eyes, the deliberately disordered hair—became the universal image of a "typical," perhaps ideal, scientist.

In Einstein's universe, every appearance deceived. Mass and energy could be changed into each other. Twins aged at different rates. Parallel lines met. The curvature of the trajectory of light literally warped the universe. Intuitive notions vanished as if down a rabbit hole to Alice's Wonderland. Scientists hungered for an explanation that would resolve the apparent contradictions. Nonscientists were confused. Beyond doubt, however, experiment confirmed that, broadly speaking, Einstein was right. "The spirit of unrest," the *New York Times* said in 1919, "invaded science."

While Einstein proposed a restructured universe, other scientists repictured the tiniest particles, or *quanta* of which the universe is composed. Ernest Rutherford's work in Britain in 1911 proved a conjecture first discussed in the 1890s: that atoms consist of masses and electric charges, including a *nucleus* surrounded by *electrons*. The basic structure of matter, it seemed, was being laid bare. But it kept dodging and slipping out of the experimenters' grasp. For the rest of the century, ever smaller particles, ever more elusive charges continued to come to light. Between 1911 and 1913, work on atomic structures revealed that electrons appear to slide erratically between orbits around a nucleus. Findings that followed from the attempt to track the untrappable particles of subatomic matter were expressed in a new field of study called **quantum mechanics**.

The terms of this new science were paradoxical—like those employed by the Danish Nobel Prizewinner, Niels Bohr (1885–1962), who described light as consisting, simultaneously, of both waves and particles. By the mid-1920s, more contradictions piled up. When the motion of subatomic particles was plotted, their positions seemed irreconcilable with their momentum. They seemed to move at rates different from their measurable speed and to end up where it was impossible for them to be. Working in collaborative tension, Bohr and his German colleague, Werner Heisenberg (1901–1976), proposed a principle they called uncertainty or indeterminacy. Their debate provoked a revolution in thought. Interpreters made a reasonable inference—observers are part of every observation, and there is no level of inspection at which their findings are objective.

This was of enormous importance because practitioners of other disciplines at the time—historians, anthropologists, sociologists, linguists, and even students of literature—were seeking to class their own work as scientific, precisely because they wanted to escape from subjectivity. It turned out that what they had in common with scientists, strictly so-called, was the opposite of what they had hoped—they were all implicated in their own findings.

Maybe it was still possible to pick a way back to certainty by following mathematics and logic. These systems, at least, seemed infallible, and they guaranteed each other. Mathematics was reliable because it was logical and logical because it was mathematical—or so people thought, until 1931, when the Czech logician, Kurt Gödel, severed mathematics from logic and showed that both systems, ultimately, must yield contradictory results.

Gödel, inspired an unintended effect. He thought, like many earlier philosophers, that we can reliably grasp numbers, but he helped make others doubt it. He believed that numbers really exist, objectively, independently of thought, but he provided encouragement to skeptics who dismissed them as merely conventional. The effect of Gödel's demonstrations on the way the world thinks was comparable to that of termites in a wooden ship that the passengers had thought was watertight. If mathematics and logic leaked, science would sink. "Logics die" was the comment of the Irish poet, Brendan Behan (1923–1964).

Of course, the implications of the discoveries of Bohr, Heisenberg, and Gödel took a long time to change minds. Only gradually, through percolation within the scientific community and vulgarization in the press and popular science books, could they modify how ordinary people thought about the world. In the light of the theoretical contributions of quantum science and revolutionary logic and mathematics, however, the world was beginning to look increasingly disorderly. Meanwhile, practical discoveries and empirical observations jarred, even more uncomfortably, the equilibrium of the old picture of the cosmos.

In 1929, thanks to a powerful new telescope operated at Mount Wilson, near Los Angeles, by Edwin Hubble, the universe was found to be expanding. It seemed so strange a finding that some physicists sought to explain away the evidence for 50 years. By the 1970s, however, most cosmologists took the view that expansion started with a **big bang**, an explosion of almost infinitesimally compressed matter, which is still going on. For some interpreters, notably Pope John XXIII (r. 1958–1963), this was evidence of divine creation, or, at least, a description of how God did it. For others, it was a naturalistic explanation of change in the universe that made divine intervention an unnecessary hypothesis.

Contributions later in the century only seemed to put more space between science and certainty. In 1960, in one of the most challenging works a philosopher ever wrote about science, Thomas Kuhn argued that scientific revolutions were the result not of new discoveries about reality but of what he called paradigm shifts, changing ways of looking at the world, and new ways of expressing them. Most people drew an inference Kuhn repudiated—that the findings of science depended not on the objective facts but on the mindset of the inquirer.

In the 1980s, **chaos theory** cast doubt on one of the blessings science still promised for the world. Science specialized in inferring laws from experience and using those laws to make predictions about the future. Chaos theory made the world seem unpredictable. The idea emerged in meteorology, as a result of the dawning awareness that weather systems are so complex that, ultimately, causes and effects are untraceable. A butterfly flapping its wings, according to an image that became the most popular way to sum up the theory, can work up a storm. There is still, according to this way of thinking, some deep order in nature, some chain of cause and effect in which the whole of experience is linked—but we cannot see it whole.

Throughout these shake-ups, workers in theoretical physics never abandoned the search for a comprehensive way to explain the cosmos—a "theory of everything" that would resolve the contradictions of relativity theory and quantum mechanics. The way matter behaves—at least, the way it behaves when we observe it—is riddled with paradoxes that subtle thinking has to reconcile. By the end of the century, cosmologists were proposing terms for understanding the universe that described nothing anyone had ever experienced or could easily imagine: infinite dimensions, superstrings, supersymmetry, supergravity. No experiment validated any of these models of how the universe is structured.

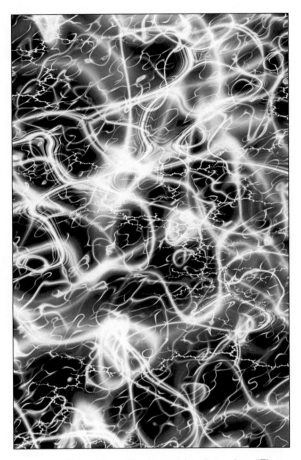

Superstrings. The superstring theory is a "Theory of Everything" (or "Grand Unification Theory") that seeks to unite gravity as a force along with the other fundamental forces (electromagnetism and nuclear forces). The theory states that fundamental particles such as quarks and electrons are not points of energy or matter, but result instead from the vibrations of "string-like" entities that are much smaller.

Human Sciences

In some respects science did deliver measurable progress. Two fields of study transformed human biology. Beginning in 1908, T. H. Morgan at Columbia University in New York initiated experiments in animal breeding that ultimately demonstrated how some characteristics are inherited by means of the transmission of genes. This led, in the second half of the century, to a new form of medicine in which doctors could manipulate people's genes to treat disease. Meanwhile, neuroscience made

Evolution on trial. People gather at an open air book-stall during the Scopes "Monkey Trial" in Dayton, Tennessee in 1925 to examine the antievolution offerings. Books by William Jennings Bryan, the former presidential candidate who led the struggle to ban evolution from the public school curriculum, are prominently advertised.

enormous progress in mapping the brain, demonstrating the distribution of mental functions, and recording how electrical impulses and releases of proteins occur, as different kinds of thinking, feeling, memorizing, and imagining take place.

Partly as a result of progress in human biology, practical medicine registered spectacular advances. Doctors could control diseases ever more effectively by imitating the body's natural hormones and adjusting their balance. That story began in 1922 with the isolation of insulin, which controls diabetes. In 1931, penicillin was discovered. It was the first *antibiotic*—a killer of microorganisms that cause disease inside the body. Preventive medicine made even bigger strides, as inoculation programs and health education became—gradually, during the century—available almost everywhere.

Many of the fiercest battles concerned biology, where advances challenged people to rethink human nature. In 1925, in a notorious case in Tennessee, an American court upheld the right of school boards to ban Darwin from the curriculum, on the supposed grounds that the theory of evolution was incompatible with the Bible. Belief in creation and belief in evolution are not necessarily contradictory. Evolution, which is the most convincing description we have of how and why species change, could, to a religious mind, be part of God's creation and Providence's plan. But simplistic-minded people on both sides of the debate kept picking fights with one another. Cases over whether schools could or should be compelled to teach evolution are still cropping up in courts in Europe and America, affecting Muslim as well as Christian schools. In some ways, evolution became more controversial as its proponents' claims became more strident. Some late twentieth-century Darwinians claimed to have found an evolutionary explanation for morality, for instance, and even to be able to explain cultural change in evolutionary terms. These claims got headlines but left most people unconvinced.

While disputes about evolution rumbled, the new science of genetics posed even more searching problems. In 1944, the Austrian physicist, Erwin Schrödinger, predicted that a gene would resemble a chain of basic units, connected like the elements of a code. His speculations invigorated the search for "the basic building-blocks" of life. A few years later, scientists in England, built up the picture of what DNA (deoxyribonucleic acid) was really like. Genes in individual genetic codes—it soon emerged—were responsible for some diseases, and perhaps for many kinds of behavior that changing the code could regulate. The codes of other species could be modified to obtain results that suit humans: producing bigger plant foods, for instance, or animals designed to be more beneficial, more palatable, or easier to transform into human food.

This discovery shed painfully strong new light on an old controversy—the **nature versus nurture** debate. On one side of the conflict were those who believed that character and capability were largely inherited and therefore could not be changed by "social engineering." Ranged against them were those who believed that experience—nurture—produced these qualities, and that social change can therefore improve our moral qualities and collective achievements. Genetic research seemed to confirm that we inherit more of our makeup than we have traditionally supposed. Meanwhile, sociobiology, a new synthesis devised by the ingenious Harvard entomologist, Edward O. Wilson, rapidly created a scientific constituency for the theory that evolutionary necessities determine differences between societies and that we can rank societies accordingly. Two fundamental convictions survived in most people's minds: that individuals make themselves, and that society is worth improving. Nevertheless, genes seemed to limit our freedom to equalize the differences between individuals and societies. Genetic and sociobiological claims inhibited reform and encouraged a mood we shall examine in the next two chapters: the prevailing conservatism of the late twentieth and early twenty-first centuries.

By the 1990s, genetically modified plants promised to solve the world's food-supply problems. The potentially adverse economic and ecological consequences, as we shall see in Chapter 30, evoked a chorus of protest. Modification of human genes presented more profound problems and provoked more profound unease. On the one hand, it promised a brighter future—eliminating genetically transmitted disease and enabling infertile couples to have children. On the other, it posed terrifying moral questions, best illustrated by the controversy over therapeutic cloning of human embryos, which was developed in the 1990s. This meant breeding or "farming," as people said, human embryos to extract useful cells from them. A woman could produce as many embryos as she might wish and pick the healthiest or most perfect specimens, or those she most preferred. The rest could be stored but, at some stage, would have to be discarded. In effect, this meant destroying human beings, since embryos, whatever their status in other respects, are unquestionably human. In the early twenty-first century, "designer babies" were already being produced where the process could prevent genetically transmitted diseases.

Research into less morally troubling methods of treatment would soon replace therapeutic cloning for infertile couples and to treat inherited disease. But the prospect of designer babies selected for particular features of character or appearance was even more troubling. It might lead to people capriciously cloning and discarding embryos to engineer children for themselves with fashionable looks or exploitable talents. The prospect arose that some societies would want to engineer human beings along the lines once prescribed by eugenics—improving the human species through controlled breeding. Governments could legislate supposedly undesirable personality genes out of existence. States could enforce normality at the expense, for instance, of genes supposed to dispose people to be criminal, or homosexual or just plain uncooperative. Morally dubious visionaries foresaw societies without disease or deviancy. In a world recrafted, as if by Frankenstein, humans now had the power to make their biggest intervention in evolution yet: selecting unnaturally not according to what is best adapted to the environment, but according to what best matches what humans happen to want at a particular moment. In 1995, a coalition of self-styled religious leaders in the United States signed a declaration opposing the patenting of genes on the grounds that they were the property of their real creator: God. The World Health Organization, UNESCO, and the European Parliament all condemned human cloning as unethical. Many countries banned it.

Subtle nightmare: the fear that human cloning could suppress individuality and eliminate diversity is cleverly aroused in this seemingly charming and innocent scene. But these are not real babies: On close examination the computer-generated images look disturbingly identical.

Meanwhile, the genetic revolution profoundly affected human self-perceptions, nudging people toward a materialist understanding of human nature. It became increasingly hard to find room in human nature for nonmaterial ingredients, such as mind and soul. "The soul has vanished," announced Francis Crick, a leading pioneer of genetic research. Cognitive scientists subjected the human brain to ever more searching analysis. Neurological research showed that thought is an electrochemical process in which synapses fire and proteins are released. These results made it possible, at least, to claim that everything traditionally classed as a function of mind might take place within the brain.

Artificial intelligence (AI) research reinforced this claim—or tried to—with a new version of an old hope or fear: that minds may not even be organic but merely mechanical. Pablo Picasso (1881–1973) painted a machine in love in 1917. Robots became the antiheroes of science fiction—the imaginary next stage of evolution, who would inherit the Earth from humankind. In the second half of the century, computers proved so dextrous, first in making calculations, then in responding to their environments, that they seemed capable of settling the debate over whether mind was different from brain. The debate was unsatisfactory because people on either side were really talking about different things. Proponents of artificial intelligence were not particularly concerned with building machines with creative, artistic imaginations, or with intuitive properties, or with the ability to feel love or hatred—qualities that opponents of AI valued as indicators of a truly human mind. Only working on ever more sophisticated robotics and seeing whether robots with highly complex circuitry developed the cognitive properties humans have could resolve these kinds of questions.

Meanwhile, two areas of scientific research previously thought to be of purely academic interest posed a further challenge to human self-perception: primatology (the study of apes, monkeys, and their ancestor-species) and paleoanthropology (the study of prehistoric humans and their ancestors). Paleoanthropologists discovered, among remains of humans' nonhuman ancestors and related primates, features formerly thought unique to our own species, *Homo sapiens*. The most challenging discoveries came from Neanderthal burials, which demonstrated that Neanderthals, who belonged to a species different from ours, had ritual lives and moral practices, including care of the elderly and reverence for the dead. Skeptics displayed apelike agility in challenging these facts—explaining them away as the result of accident or fraud. But there was too much evidence to discount altogether. It proved, in combination, that nonhuman species have existed who were morally indistinguishable from human beings. The question was important because, as we shall see in Chapter 29, it emerged at a time when the notion of **human rights** became current—a notion based in part on the assumption that being human constitutes a meaningful moral category that excludes nonhuman creatures.

Animal rights movements challenged that assumption. Improved knowledge of surviving species of nonhuman primates tended to support them. First, scientists working with macaque monkeys in Japan realized that these creatures, though modestly endowed with brains, have culture. They can learn and transmit what they learn across generations. The breakthrough discovery came in 1952, when a monkey called Ima was observed teaching her community how to wash the dirt off sweet potatoes. The tribe took up the technique. The monkeys continued to practice it, even when supplied with ready-washed potatoes, showing that washing had become a cultural rite, not a practical measure.

In subsequent decades, led by a brilliant field-worker, Jane Goodall, primatologists came to realize that chimpanzees have, albeit to a much smaller extent than human beings, all the features of culture that were formerly thought to be

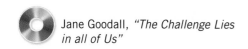
Jane Goodall, *"The Challenge Lies in all of Us"*

The Electronic Numerical Integrator and Computer— one of the first electronic digital computers in the United States—was commissioned by the U.S. Army and installed, at first, at the University of Pennsylvania in Philadelphia. The choice of female programmers was presumably dictated by the public relations objectives of this photograph.

peculiarly human, including toolmaking, language, war, rules for distributing food, and political habits. Further studies of other social animals—beginning with other great apes, such as gorillas and orangutans, and, by early in the twenty-first century, including whales, dolphins, elephants, and even rats— seemed to show disturbingly similar results, suggesting that culture is uniquely human only as a matter of degree. Meanwhile, many observations and experiments cast doubt on the belief that humans have unique cognitive properties. Nonhuman apes, for example, proved to be self-aware and showed sensibilities hard to distinguish in practice from the senses of morality and transcendence formerly thought to be human peculiarities. By the end of the twentieth century, some ethicists were campaigning for animal rights or for the redefinition of the moral community to embrace great apes.

The discoveries of primatologists and comparative zoologists belonged in a broader context of scientific change: the rise of ecology, the study of the interconnectedness of all life and its interdependence with aspects of the physical environment. The development of ecology—ecologists' exposure of a vast range of new practical problems arising from human overexploitation of the environment— became a major source of influence on changes in the late twentieth-century world. Chapter 30 is devoted to discussing them.

Anthropology and Psychology

In anthropology, as in science, the opening decade of the twentieth century was decisive. Among the supposedly scientific certainties the late nineteenth-century West treasured was that some peoples and societies were evolutionarily superior to others: an image of the world sliced and stacked in order of race. This picture suited Western imperialists, who treated it as justification of their rule over other peoples (see Chapter 25). But it was upset in the first decade of this century, largely thanks to an undersung hero: Franz Boas (1858–1942). He showed that no race was superior to any other in brainpower. He made untenable the notion that societies could be ranked in terms of a developmental model of thought. People, he

Franz Boas, from *The Mind of Primitive Man*

concluded, think differently in different cultures not because some have superior mental equipment but because all thought reflects the traditions to which it is heir, the society that surrounds it, and the environment in which it exists.

At the end of the first decade of the century, he summarized his findings: "The mental attitude of individuals who . . . develop the beliefs of a tribe is exactly that of the civilized philosopher."

> There may be other civilizations, based perhaps on different traditions and on a different equilibrium of emotion and reason, which are of no less value than ours, although it may be impossible for us to appreciate their values without having grown up under their influence. The general theory of valuation of human activities, as developed by anthropological research, teaches us a higher tolerance than the one we now profess.[1]

As well as a teacher, who dominated anthropology in the United States, Boas was a field-worker in his youth and a museum keeper in maturity—in touch with the people and artifacts he sought to understand. His pupils had Native American peoples to study little more than a railway ride away. The habit of fieldwork piled up enormous quantities of data to bury the crude hierarchical schemes of the nineteenth century. The new anthropology took a long time to spread beyond Boas's students. But it was already influencing British methods in the first decade of the twentieth century, and the other major centers of anthropological research in France and Germany gradually accepted it.

The result was **cultural relativism**: the doctrine that we cannot rank cultures in order of merit but must judge each on its own terms. As we shall see in Chapter 30, this proved problematic. Should cannibals be judged on their own terms? Or cultures that licensed slavery or the subjection of women? Or those that practiced infanticide or head-hunting or other abominations? Or even those that condoned relatively milder offenses against values the West cherished—offenses such as the mutilation or torture of criminals or female circumcision? Cultural relativism had to have limits, but anthropology compelled educated people everywhere to examine their prejudices, to see merit in cultures they formerly despised, and to question their own convictions of superiority.

The noble savage (see Chapter 22) reemerged from the eighteenth-century Enlightenment. Perhaps the most influential anthropological book of all time was Margaret Mead's *Coming of Age in Samoa*, published in 1928. Mead worked with pubescent girls in a sexually permissive society. She claimed to find a world liberated from the inhibitions, hang-ups, anxieties, and neuroses that psychology was busily uncovering in Western cities and suburbs. In the long run, as she rose to the top of her profession, to academic eminence, and social influence, her work helped to feed fashionable educational ideas: uncompetitive schooling, rod-sparing discipline, cheap contraception.

Western educators could learn from Samoan adolescents in a world without barbarians and savages, where the language of comparison between societies had to be value free. What had once been called "primitive cultures" and "advanced civilizations" came to be labeled "elementary structures" and "complex structures." The longstanding justification for Western imperialism—the civilizing mission—lapsed, because no group of conquerors could any longer feel enough self-confidence to impose their own standards of civilization on their victims.

Psychology was even more subversive than anthropology, because its discoveries or claims reached beyond the relationships between societies to challenge the notions individuals had about themselves. In particular, the claim, first advanced by

Margaret Mead. "I lived like a visiting young village princess. I could summon informants to teach me everything I wanted to know: as a return courtesy, I danced every night." The photograph shows the celebrated anthropologist Margaret Mead (1901–1978) in Samoan dress with her collaborator Fa'amotu. Fieldwork seems to have been a liberating experience for Mead.

an Austrian psychiatrist, Sigmund Freud (1856–1939), that much human motivation is subconscious, challenged traditional notions about responsibility, identity, personality, conscience, and mentality. In an experiment Freud conducted on himself in 1896, he exposed his own *Oedipus Complex*, as he called it: a supposed, suppressed desire—that he believed to be subconsciously present in all male children—to supplant his father. In succeeding years he developed a technique he called **psychoanalysis**, designed to make patients aware of their subconscious desires. Hypnosis or, as Freud preferred, free association, could retrieve repressed feelings and ease nervous symptoms. Many patients who rose from his couch walked more freely than before.

Freud seemed able, from the evidence of a few of his patients, to illuminate the human condition. Every child—he claimed to show—experienced before puberty the same phases of sexual development. Every adult repressed similar fantasies or experiences. Women who only a few years previously would have been dismissed as hysterical malingerers became, in Freud's work, case studies from whose example almost everyone could learn. This made an important indirect contribution to the reevaluation of the role of women in society (see Chapter 29). Freud's science, however, failed to pass the most rigorous tests. When the philosopher Karl Popper asked how to distinguish someone who did not have an Oedipus complex from someone who did, the psychoanalytic fraternity had no answer. Nevertheless, for some patients, psychoanalysis worked.

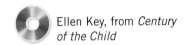

Ellen Key, from *Century of the Child*

Returnees from the horrors of twentieth-century wars became patients of psychiatry. The nightmares of trench survivors in the First World War (see Chapter 28) were too hideous to share with loved ones, their experiences unimaginable to people back home. The guilt of those who missed the war echoed the shellshock of those who fought it. Introspection—formerly regarded as self-indulgence—became routine in the modern West. Repression became the modern demon and the analyst an exorcist. The "feel-good society," which bans guilt, shame, self-doubt, and self-reproach, was among the results. So was the twentieth- and twenty-first century habit of sexual candor. So was the fashion—prevalent for much of the twentieth century—to treat metabolic or chemical imbalances in the brain as if they were deep-rooted mental disorders. The good and evil that flowed from Freud's theory are nicely balanced and objectively incalculable. Psychoanalysis and other, sub-Freudian schools of therapy helped millions and tortured millions—releasing some people from repressions and condemning others to illusions or futile treatments.

The most profound influence psychology exercised was not, however, on the treatment of mental disorder but on the way children were raised. In 1909, the Swedish feminist Ellen Key proclaimed the rediscovery of childhood. Children were different from adults. This was, in effect, a summary of the state of the idea of childhood as it had developed in the nineteenth-century West (see Chapter 24). It was, perhaps, a valid observation. But it had questionable consequences for the way children were brought up. Children who were not treated as adults in childhood "never grew up," like the tragic hero of J. M. Barrie's classic play of 1911, *Peter Pan*, who withdrew into Neverland and whose childhood sweetheart outgrew him. Generations raised on the assumption that they could not face adult realities found themselves deprived of truths about their own lives and became fodder for the new therapies of psychiatry. Generational "hang-ups" became a new curse for Western children. People outside the West, where the new image of childhood arrived patchily and late, had fewer such troubles.

In the West, better treatment for childhood disease enabled more children to lead longer lives. So children became more suitable objects in whom to invest time and emotion and, of course, study. Working on Freud's insights, educational psychologists in the West built up a picture of mental development in predictable, universal stages, as people grow up. School curricula changed in the 1950s and

Sigmund Freud on holiday in 1913 with his daughter Anna, who herself became a distinguished psychoanalyst. It was a momentous year for Freud. His most brilliant disciple, Carl Jung, broke with the master, and Freud published *Totem and Taboo*, which he later privately repudiated as "a scientific myth," full of inaccuracies. Feeling defensive about the reputation of his work he wrote *The Claims of Psychoanalysis to Scientific Interest* in the same year.

1960s to match the supposed patterns of childhood development. Generations of schoolchildren were deprived of challenging tasks because child psychology said they were incapable of them. While formal education got longer and longer, most children emerged from it with no experience of traditional elements of the curriculum that were now thought unsuitably difficult, such as calculus, foreign and classical languages, sophisticated vocabulary, ancient authors, even grammar. Other developments, which belong in Chapter 29, stimulated this trend, including, notably, the economic changes that made vocational qualifications seem disproportionately important in education, and the social pressures that made for "dumbing down."

Philosophy and Linguistics

To scientific uncertainty and cultural relativism, the opening decade of the century added potentially devastating philosophical unease. In combination with Einstein's disquieting revelations about the nature of time, the theories of the French philosopher Henri Bergson (1859–1941) proved both unsettling and inspiring. He formulated a concept he called "duration"—the new sense of time we get when consciousness "abstains from establishing a separation between present states and the preceding states." This seemingly difficult idea helped to fortify educated people's faith in free will. Time is not a constraint that nature imposes on us, but a concept that we impose on nature. Bergson coined the term *élan vital* to express the freedom we retain to make a future different from the one that science predicts—a spiritual force with the power to reorder matter. Time, the way Bergson saw it, became not a sequence of atomized events, but a product of memory, which is different from perception and therefore "a power independent of matter."

Bergson's thinking infuriated scientists and inspired artists. Novels written in the **stream of consciousness** were among the results. He argued that the theory of evolution needed rethinking. Evolution was not a scientific law but an expression of the creative will of living entities, which change because they want to change. Critics accused Bergson of irrationalism on the grounds that he was attacking science and representing objective realities as purely mental concepts. Indeed, consistent with his principles, he never tried to demonstrate the validity of his ideas by logical exposition or scientific evidence. This did not diminish their attractiveness or their effectiveness in liberating people who felt limited or inhibited by all the supposedly scientific determinism of the early twentieth century. Bergson reassured those who doubted whether, for example, history really led inevitably to the revolutions Marx predicted, or to the white supremacy "scientific" racism preached, or to the destruction the laws of thermodynamics predicted. Nature was unorganized. The chaos that made scientific minds despair offered hope to Bergson's readers.

Bergson's followers hailed him as the philosopher for the twentieth century. His first great rival for that status was an American, William James (1842–1910). The start of James's tragedy was his family's prosperity—he felt guilty when he was not earning his own living. Inside the philosopher, a capitalist was always striving to get out. James wanted a distinctively American philosophy, reflecting the values of business and hustle. He joined patriotic organizations, resisted attempts to Europeanize him, and always scampered back thankfully to America from trips abroad.

Seeking reasons to make other people share his belief in God, he argued that "if the hypothesis of God works satisfactorily in the widest sense of the word, it is true." He called this doctrine **pragmatism**. The work in which he popularized it in 1907 was hailed as the philosophy of the future. But what one individual or group finds useful, another may find useless. James's claim that truth is not what is real, but is whatever serves a particular purpose was one of the most subversive claims a philosopher ever made. James had set out as an apologist for Christianity, but by relativizing truth, he undermined it.

Linguistics produced similarly subversive developments—doubts about the reality of truth and whether language could express it. Ferdinand de Saussure, a teacher at the University of Geneva in Switzerland, is usually credited with decisive influence in this respect. But, like Einstein's, his influence was slow to affect the wider intellectual community. He began his lectures in 1907, but they were not published until after his death in 1913, in a form his pupils perfected or distorted. Mostly, they seemed revolutionary only to other students of language. But they contained a revolutionary idea: the distinction between social speech, the *parole* addressed to others, and subjective language, the *langue* known only to thought. As most students and readers interpreted it, Saussure seemed to say of language what Poincaré seemed to say of science—any language we use refers only to itself and cannot disclose remoter realities.

Mainstream philosophers were reluctant at first to pursue the implications of this idea. The dominant philosophy of the 1920s and 1930s, the years between the First and Second World Wars, was *positivism*, which asserted that what the human senses perceived was real and that reason could prove that what our senses perceive is true. But, as we have seen, developments in science and logic were making it impossible to feel such confidence. The most significant boost to the tradition Saussure inaugurated came in 1953 with the publication of *Philosophical Investigations*, by the English-trained Austrian philosopher, Ludwig Wittgenstein. The printed pages retained the flavor of lecture notes, full of anticipated questions from the audience. Wittgenstein's argument was that we understand language not because it corresponds to reality but because it obeys rules of usage. Therefore, we do not necessarily know what language refers to, except its own terms. Wittgenstein imagined a student asking, "So you are saying that human agreement decides what is true and what is false?" And again, "Aren't you at bottom really saying that everything except human behavior is a fiction?" Wittgenstein tried to distance himself from such devastating skepticism. The impact of a writer's work, however, often exceeds his intentions.

Equally disturbing, because of what it implied about human nature, was the work a linguist at the Massachusetts Institute of Technology, Noam Chomsky, published in 1957. Chomsky was impressed at how quickly and easily children learn speech. They can, in particular, combine words in ways they have never actually heard. He also found it remarkable that the differences between languages appear superficial compared with the "deep structures"—the parts of speech, the relationships between terms that we call *grammar* and *syntax*—that are common to all of them. Chomsky suggested a link between the structures of language and the brain. We learn languages fast because their structure is already part of the way we think. This was a revolutionary suggestion. Experience and heredity, nurture and nature, it implied, do not make us the whole of what we are. Part of our nature is hardwired and unchangeable. As Chomsky saw it, at least at first, this "language instinct" or "language faculty" was untouchable—and therefore perhaps not produced—by evolution. Chomsky's views remained theoretical and were, perhaps, beyond proof. But they resonated in minds worried about the problems of using language and science to access reality. He rapidly became the most-quoted figure in academic literature.

FINAL PASSAGE FROM *ULYSSES* (1922) BY JAMES JOYCE, perhaps the most famous stream of consciousness novel in the twentieth century.

James Joyce, Ulysses

. . . serene with his lamp and O that awful deepdown torrent O and the sea the sea crimson sometimes like fire and the glorious sunsets and the figtrees in the Alameda gardens yes and all the queer little streets and pink and blue and yellow houses and the rosegardens and the jessamine and geraniums and cactuses and Gibraltar as a girl where I was a Flower of the mountain yes when I put the rose in my hair like the Andalusian girls used or shall I wear a red yes and how he kissed me under the Moorish wall and I thought well as well him as another and then I asked him with my eyes to ask again yes and then he asked me would I yes to say yes my mountain flower and first I put my arms around him yes and drew him down to me so he could feel my breasts all perfume yes and his heart was going like mad and yes I said yes I will Yes.

Even more fundamentally, Chomsky argued that our language prowess, on which we tend to congratulate ourselves as a species—and which some people even claim is a uniquely human achievement—is like the special skills of other species: that of cheetahs in speed, for instance, or cows in ruminating. "It is the richness and specificity of instinct of animals," Chomsky said in a work of the mid-1980s, "that accounts for their remarkable achievements in some domains and lack of ability in others, so the argument runs, whereas humans, lacking such . . . instinctual structure, are free to think, speak and discover. . . . Both the logic of the problem and what we are now coming to understand suggest that this is not the correct way to identify the position of humans in the world." This chimed in with the disarming discoveries of primatology and paleoanthropology.[2]

By the time Chomsky entered the academic arena, unease and pessimism were rampant, especially in Europe and parts of Asia, where the material destruction and moral horror of the Second World War had been most keenly felt. The most widely accepted response to the war had emerged from a group of philosophers in Germany known as the Frankfurt School. Their great project was to find alternatives to Marxism and capitalism. They defined what they called alienation as the central problem of modern society. Economic rivalries and short-sighted materialism divided individuals and wrecked common pursuits. People felt dissatisfied and rootless. Martin Heidegger proposed a strategy to cope with this. We should accept our existence between conception and death as the only unchangeable thing about us and tackle life as a project of self-realization, of "becoming"—who we are changes as the project unfolds. This **existentialism** represented the retreat of intellectuals into the security of self-contemplation, in revulsion from an ugly world.

Existentialists. Jean-Paul Sartre (1905–1980) and Simone de Beauvoir (1908–1986), became icons of radicalism—she for her feminist classic, *The Second Sex*, he for the influence of his philosophy on postwar Western youth. At home in Paris, however, they seem like a model middle-class couple, stiffly sharing a newspaper in their under-decorated apartment.

Heidegger was discredited because he collaborated with the Nazis, a vicious German regime that provoked world war and massacred millions of people. In France in 1945, however, Jean-Paul Sartre (1905–1980) relaunched existentialism as a new creed for the post-war era. "Man," he said, "is . . . nothing else but what he makes of himself." For Sartre, self-modeling was more than an individual responsibility. Every individual action is an exemplary act, a statement about humankind, about the sort of species you want to belong to. Yet there is no objective way to put meaning into such a statement. God does not exist. Everything is permissible, and "as a result man is forlorn, without anything to cling to." "There is," he wrote, "no explaining things away by reference to a fixed . . . human nature. In other words, there is no determinism, man is free, man is freedom."

Sartre's version of existentialism fed the common assumptions about life of educated young Westerners in the 1950s and 1960s. Critics who denounced it as a philosophy of decadence were not far wrong in practice because it was used to justify every form of self-indulgence. Sexual promiscuity, revolutionary violence, indifference to manners, defiance of the law, drug abuse could all be part of becoming oneself. The social changes of the 1960s, to which we shall return in Chapter 29, would have been unthinkable without existentialism: beat culture and permissiveness—ways of life millions adopted or imitated—as well, perhaps, as the late twentieth-century's libertarian reaction against social planning. Existentialism was, briefly, the philosophical consensus of the West. But it never caught on in the rest of the world; and even in the West, people who saw more urgent problems than shaping one's personal future detested it. By the 1970s, a reaction was in the making: conservative in politics, mistrustful of materialism, inclined to religion, anxious to recover tradition and rebuild social solidarity—especially through the family. This was a global reaction. It was particularly strong in the Americas, while in Asia and Africa revulsion from Western-dominated thinking strengthened the trend.

THE MIRROR OF SCIENCE: ART

The twentieth century was a graveyard and a cradle: a graveyard of certainties, the cradle of a civilization of crumbling confidence, in which it would be hard to be sure of anything. We can see the effect of this unsettling period—literally, see it—in the work of painters. Never more than in the twentieth century, painters tended to paint not the world as they saw it directly, but as science and philosophy displayed it for their inspection. The revolutions of twentieth-century art, the chronologies of artists' changing perceptions, exactly match the jolts and shocks science and philosophy administered.

In 1909, the Italian Emilio Filippo Marinetti (1876–1944) published a manifesto for fellow artists, proclaiming what he called **futurism**. At the time, most artists professed modernism: the doctrine that the new was superior to the old. Marinetti wanted to go further. He believed that what was traditional had not only to be surpassed but repudiated and wrecked. He rejected coherence, harmony, freedom, conventional morals, and conventional language—even conventional grammar—because they were familiar. Comfort was artistically sterile. Instead, futurism glorified war, power, chaos, and destruction, which

The Diffusion and Transformation of Western Science

1842–1910	William James, American philosopher, developed the doctrine of pragmatism
1856–1939	Sigmund Freud, developer of psychoanalysis
1860s	China's "self-strengthening" program begins
1875–1965	Albert Schweizer, medical missionary to Africa
1879–1955	Albert Einstein, developer of the theory of relativity
1881–1938	Kemal Ataturk, founder of modern Turkey and proponent of secularism and Western science
1883	Western-style curriculum at Beijing School of Medicine
1885–1962	Niels Bohr, won Nobel Prize in 1922 for work on the structure of the atom
1891–1962	Ismail Mazhir, translator of Charles Darwin's work into Arabic
1897	Jagadis Chandra Bose awarded scientific research grant by the British viceroy
1901–1976	Werner Heisenberg, developed uncertainty principle
1902	Henry Poincaré questions the link between hypothesis and evidence
1903	Powered flight
1905–1980	Jean-Paul Sartre, French philosopher associated with existentialism
1907	Plastic invented
1912	Overthrow of the Qing dynasty increases pace of Westernization in China
1913	Indian *Journal of Medical Research* launched
1914	Science Society of China founded by Chinese students at Cornell University
1920	Royal Institute for Higher Technical Education founded in Indonesia
1928	Margaret Mead's *Coming of Age in Samoa* published
1931	Penicillin discovered
1944	Erwin Schrödinger predicts structure of the gene
1953	Ludwig Wittgenstein's *Philosophical Investigations* and Simone de Beauvoir's *The Second Sex* published

⦿ MAKING CONNECTIONS

TRANSFORMATIONS OF WESTERN SCIENCE AND THOUGHT

DISCIPLINE →	NEW THEORIES →	EFFECTS ON SOCIETY
Physics/Mathematics	Henry Poincaré: notes the elastic connection between hypothesis and evidence and how multiple hypotheses can fit results of experiments Albert Einstein: proposes and proves speed of light is a constant and time and space change with motion (theory of relativity) Earnest Rutherford: establishes basis of subatomic world Niels Bohr: light described as both waves and particles; links to Heisenberg's indeterminacy principle (uncertainty principle)	By mid–twentieth century, physics helped unleash the power of charged subatomic particles in practical technology including weapons (atomic bombs), communications (transistors, microprocessors, integrated circuits) The "new physics" also revolutionizes astronomy, chemistry, other physical sciences
Astronomy	Edwin Hubble: with large-scale telescopes, discovers that universe is expanding Development of radio telescopes, infrared and other means of examining distant stars	Combined with the "new physics" and jet propulsion, astronomical findings set the stage for exploration of solar system; they also challenge or confirm religious beliefs depending on religious standpoint; also raise new possibilities of extraterrestrial life
Biology	T. H. Morgan: demonstrates that genetic transmission influences physical characteristics Neuroscience demonstrates how mental functions operate within the brain	Advances in human biology lead to medical developments: controlling infections through use of antibiotics; controlling diabetes and developing large-scale preventive medical programs (inoculations, health education)

would shove humankind into novelty. Marinetti, with the followers he soon acquired, celebrated the beauty of machines, the morals of might, and the syntax of babble. Sensitivity, kindness, and fragility he dismissed as the mawkish values of old-fashioned art, created by the followers of the styles called romantic and aesthetic. Futurists preferred ruthlessness, candor, strength.

Marinetti's machine-age imagery appealed to a wide public and found echoes in the work of many artists, not all of whom accepted his brutal, radical program. Painters inspired by Marinetti's lectures painted "lines of force"—symbols of coercion. The excitement of speed—attained by the new-fangled internal combustion engine—represented for Marinetti the spirit of the age, speeding away from the past. The movement he founded united adherents of the most radical politics of the twentieth century: fascists, for whom the state should serve the strong, and communists, who hoped to incinerate tradition in revolution. The fascists and communists hated each other and relished the battles they fought with each other, first in the streets and later, when they took over states, in wars bigger and more terrible than any the world had ever seen. But they agreed that the function of progress was to destroy the past.

In retrospect, Marinetti seems uncannily prophetic. The deepening destructiveness of wars and the quickening speed and power of machines did indeed dominate the future. The speeding machines turned the world into a global village where every place

Emilio Filippo Marinetti, *"Futuristic Manifesto"*

DISCIPLINE →	NEW THEORIES →	EFFECTS ON SOCIETY
Genetics	Search for genetic codes begins in 1944, to establish basic building blocks of life—by 1950s, DNA is discovered and belief that genetic codes could help solve medical problems	Fifty years of study leads to ability to manipulate genes of plants and animals to produce more beneficial results; more controversial is the focus on cloning and genetic engineering to develop most desirable humans
Primatology and paleoanthropology	Primatology: discovery that animals also have shared culture, language, toolmaking skills Paleoanthropology: discovery of features originally thought uniquely human (rituals, morality) among nonhuman ancestors	Widened research efforts in both disciplines; reinforced connection between all humans and led to deeper understanding of ecology, the study of interconnectedness of all life
Anthropology	Franz Boas: comparative study of societies shows that no race is superior to any other in brainpower, development of thought Margaret Meade: so-called primitive cultures free of neuroses and anxieties that plague Western society	New doctrine of cultural relativism focuses on studying communities in context of their traditions; widened appreciation for non-Western, native cultures (Native American, Samoan, etc.)
Psychology	Sigmund Freud: uncovered role of human subconscious in motivating actions; developed psychoanalysis to expose subconscious feelings, thoughts Development of new theories on child raising and education by Sigmund Freud and Ellen Key emphasizing childhood as a separate phase of life	Transformation of school curricula, child raising to conform with ideas of stages of child development; belief in subconscious strata of human mind leads to widespread interest in popular psychology including psychoanalysis and dream analysis
Philosophy and Linguistics	Henri Bergson and others reconceptualize time and causation as part of human-determined memory and experience F. de Saussure and others deconstruct language as human-constructed medium that cannot convey objective reality	New understandings of deep structures of language furthered by experiments of Noam Chomsky showing that language, speech, grammar, and syntax are linked to the brain, and are hardwired

was within, at most, a few hours' travel of every other place, and where information was accessible everywhere, instantly. The machines also achieved dazzling power to destroy. Toward midcentury, people devised massive gas chambers and incinerators that put millions to death and disposed of their bodies economically and efficiently. Bombs obliterated tens of thousands at a time, and spread deadly, corrosive radiation capable of killing millions more. Marinetti claimed, "The future has begun." It sounds like nonsense or, if not nonsense, a platitude, but, in a way, he was right. He had devised a telling metaphor for the pace of the changes that he and his contemporaries experienced. It was an exhilarating time, but it was also full of terror and foreboding.

Ultimately, Marinetti's future also failed, because tradition could never quite be outstripped. It always clung to the coattails of the speeding world. But the world had to pass through the flames of war and the furnace of tyranny before settling for mere instability and insecurity. By the end of the century, power seemed to have passed outside the realm of conventional politics. The programs of scien-

Man as machine, speeding and striding into the future. The Italian artist Umberto Boccioni (1882–1916) captured the spirit of futurism in this sculpture of 1913. "Our straight line will be alive and palpitating", he wrote, aiming to "embed" the math and geometry of machines "in the muscular lines of a body".
Umberto Boccioni, Unique Form of Continuity in Space. 1913 (cast 1931). Bronze, 43 7/8" x 34 7/8" x 15 3/4" (111.4 x 88.6 x 40 cm). Acquired through the Lillie P. Bliss Bequest. The Museum of Modern Art/Licensed by Scala-Art Resource, NY.

Marcel Duchamp's painting, *Nude Descending a Staircase* (1912) was shockingly avant garde when first exhibited, but in retrospect, it seems representative of the most prominent trends in its day: dehumanizing, mechanistic, informed by science and technology, and subversive of tradition.

Marcel Duchamp (American, born France, 1887–1968) "Nude Descending a Staircase, No. 2" 1912, oil on canvas, 58 x 35 in. Philadelphia Museum of Art: The Louise and Walter Arensberg Collection. Color transparency by Graydon Wood, 1994. © 1998 Artists Rights Society (ARS), New York/ADAGP, Paris/Estate of Marcel Duchamp.

tists and technologists mattered more than those of politicians. Over people's lives, big business wielded more influence than voters exercised. Institutions of security, defense, and justice tended to slip not just out of democratic control, but even out of the control of governments. The power Marinetti praised—the power of science, the power of states—could not bring the world to order or order to the world.

Other artists, meanwhile, turned in disgust from the ideal of a machine-like universe and an engineered society, preferring a vision that atomic theory suggested—of an elusive, ill-ordered, uncontrollable world. In 1907, an artistic style called **cubism** began to hold up to the world images of itself reflected as if in a distorting mirror, shivered into fragments. Pablo Picasso and Georges Braque (1882–1963), the originators of the movement, denied they had ever heard of Einstein. But scientific vulgarizations, especially, of course, of the work of Poincaré, reached them through the press. As painters of an elusive reality from many different perspectives, they were reflecting the science and philosophy of their decade. Even Piet Mondrian (1872–1944)—the Dutch artist whose work so perfectly captured the sharp angles of modern taste that he represented the rhythms of boogie-woogie music as a rectilinear grid and Broadway in Manhattan as a straight line—had a shivered-mirror phase in the early years of the second decade of the century. Formerly, he loved to paint the trees along the river Geyn in his native Holland with romantic fidelity. Now he splayed and atomized them.

The French artist Marcel Duchamp (1887–1968) denounced his own expertise in science as mere smattering. But he, too, tried to represent Einstein's world. He called his painting, *Nude Descending a Staircase* of 1912, an expression of "time and space through the abstract presentation of motion." His notes on his baffling masterpiece of sculpture, *Large Glass*, revealed how closely he had studied relativity. Meanwhile, in 1911, the Russian artist Vasily Kandinsky had read Rutherford's description of the atom. "The discovery hit me with frightful force, as if the end of the world had come. All things become transparent, without strength or certainty." After that, he painted the world as he now saw it, suppressing every reminder of real objects. The tradition he launched, of entirely "abstract" art, which depicted objects unrecognizably or not at all, became dominant for the rest of the century. The new rhythmic beat of jazz and the noises of atonal music—developed in Vienna by Arnold Schoenberg from 1908 onward—subverted the harmonies of the past as surely as quantum mechanics began to challenge its ideas of order.

In art, the effects of the new anthropology were even clearer than those of the new physics. Picasso, Braque, and members of Kandinsky's circle (known as the Blue Rider School) copied "primitive" sculptures from museums of natural history, with the indigenous arts of the Pacific and Africa dominant at first. The range of influences broadened, as Western artists in the Americas and Australia rediscovered the art of native peoples. As in science and philosophy, Asian traditions made a big impact in the West in the last four decades of the century, especially in music, architecture, and stage design. The vogue for primitivism ensured that craftsmen outside Europe had a market for their traditional arts. Yet whenever innovations occurred in art, as in science, Western initiatives predominated globally throughout the century.

As in so many areas of modernization, Japanese artists led the way in assimilating Western influences. Outstanding painters, such as Kuroda Seiki and Wada Eisaku, were already studying in Europe in the 1890s and the early 1900s. In China, influence radiated chiefly from Russia, especially from the late 1940s, as Russian-inspired

Communists became first prominent, then all-powerful. Their characteristic subjects were stocky, heroic peasants and workers in poster-art style. This still dominated the art of Wang Guangyi (wahng gwang-yee) in the last years of the twentieth century. Meanwhile, however, China had opened up to every kind of Western influence. The outstanding young artist of the 1990s, Zhou Chunya (joe chwun-yah), was reported as saying, "Even though Western art dominates my painting style, I would say I am a Chinese painter … because I maintain a Chinese lifestyle within myself." For painters working in the shadow of Western influence, his was a typical sentiment.

Among artists who resisted or selectively filtered Western influences, those from India were most conspicuous. To a great extent, this was thanks to Abindranath Tagore, who, at the end of the nineteenth century, rejected his Western-style training as a painter to find inspiration in Mughal art (Chapter 19). His followers and successors—notably Nandalal Bose (1882–1966)—made anticolonialism part of the message of their work. At the end of the century, many artists around the world turned to folk art to supply new styles. But, even painters who were most vocal in their rejection of the West were unable to escape altogether the magnetism of Western techniques, materials, and models.

The novel, modeled on the Western tradition rather than the independently developed Japanese form, became a universal genre. Cinema, a new medium of Western origin, rapidly became the most popular art form in the world, and, although different cultures evolved their own schools of cinema, the American style, known as "Hollywood" from the Los Angeles suburb where most of the film studios had their headquarters, dominated the global market. New initiatives in sculpture and architecture, and some interesting new genres, such as video art and computer-generated art, depended on technologies that the West invented.

Paradoxically, it was in the West that the influence of Western art declined as the century wore on, but it took a long time for this to become apparent. Though governments patronized conventional artists, the characteristic art of the First World War and its aftermath was **dada**—externalized disillusionment, deliberately brutal, ugly, and meaningless. The "Dada Manifesto" of 1918 celebrated World War I, as the "great work of destruction." In Germany, Kurt Schwitters (1887–1948) scraped collages together from bits of smashed machines and ruined buildings. Max Ernst (1891–1976) exposed post-war nightmares, often using hostile materials—barbed wire, rough planks of wood. The artists who called themselves surrealists continued this trend in the 1920s and 1930s, reflecting psychology by creating paintings and films in which they aimed to externalize subconscious neuroses and desires. To some extent, their project overlapped with a school that established a more enduring tradition: expressionists, most of whom were more concerned with color and sometimes texture than with form, reached inside themselves and their subjects to represent emotion and mood.

After that, art seemed to lose some of its power to make people see the world afresh. **Surrealism** and expressionism were the last great global movements to start in the art world and overspill into ordinary people's perceptions. Plenty of great artists, challenged onlookers'

Chinese and Western traditions. Born in 1955, Zhou Chunya has been able to marry Western and Chinese traditions in his art, thanks in part to his having studied in Germany. In many ways, his art recalls traditional Chinese painting, but the figures in his *Red Man* (2001) show the influence of classical Western sculpture, and its theme—humanity's apelike nature—is indebted to Western science and figures prominently in Western art.

Bollywood. Few aspects of Indian life demonstrate the appropriation of Western culture so deeply as the Bombay (Mumbai) film industry, which has created its own imagery and values from a distant Hollywood model.

world picture, but none succeeded in changing it. Why was this? In part, it was because propaganda seduced art, especially the most powerful new art of the twentieth century, cinema. Most of the great movie directors and music composers of the 1930s and 1940s in Europe, America, and Russia got caught up in the ideological conflicts of the time. The Russian dictator, Joseph Stalin (1879–1953), wrote music criticism anonymously, dictated style for the Soviet Union, and insisted on "socialist realism" in all the arts as the only school worthy of state patronage and the only style in which it was safe for artists to paint, compose, or write. The German dictator Adolf Hitler (1889–1945) fancied himself a painter and architect and banned artists, writers, and composers whom he regarded as Jewish or "decadent." Even after the Second World War, and into the 1950s, American movie makers had to answer questions from Congress about how much "anticommunist" cinema they produced, and actors, directors, and screenwriters were banned if they were seen as being or even having once been procommunist.

More treacherously, art, like so much else in the twentieth-century West, became fodder for consumerism, commercialism, celebrity, and fashion. Artists escaped from political control by appealing to the mass market and to rich collectors. Salvador Dalí (1904–1989) was probably the most accomplished painter of the age in a technical sense. No one excelled him in mastery of his materials. His paintings, film–set designs, and the marketing of his images in poster form communicated the spirit of surrealism to a worldwide public. But many of his fellow artists hated him for his dedication to self-promotion and vulgar exhibitionism to boost the prices of his works. The great theorist of surrealism, André Breton (1896–1966), expelled Dalí from the movement and coined an anagram of his name: Avida Dollars. Picasso, the most prolific artist of the century, also became the richest by exhibiting uncanny business sense, and by becoming a celebrity, famous for being famous almost as much as for his art.

Art lost influence, too, because taste splintered. The pace of change quickened in art as in everything else. From the 1930s onward, the market lurched rapidly among fashions. Every school of artists had to repudiate every other school to attract buyers. Technology multiplied media exponentially from the 1960s onward, and the market responded by huddling in niches. Fans of one kind of music might know nothing of

THE PERSISTENCE OF MEMORY

Salvador Dalí painted *The Persistence of Memory* in 1931 to "systematize confusion and discredit reality." Time melts like soft cheese. Dimensions are distorted. Gold glows with decay. Color exceeds reality, as if in a psychotic vision. At another level, the painting showcased Dali's matchless technical skill.

Except for the livid color, the cliffs add a contrasting touch of realism. Elements of the landscape of his home in northeast Spain are common in Dalí's work.

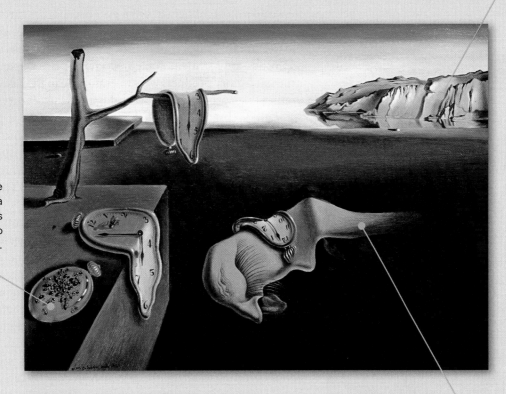

Ants feast on the gold case of a watch that seems to have turned into corrupt flesh.

Salvador Dalí (1904–1989), The Persistence of Memory 1931, oil on canvas, 9 1/2 x 13 in. (24.1 x 33 cm). Digital Image © The Museum of Modern Art/Licensed by SCALA/Art Resource, NY. (162.1934). Given anonymously. ©2005 Kingdom of Spain. ©2005 Salvador Dalí, Gala-Salvador Dali Foundation / Artists Rights Society (ARS), New York.

A human face collapses and melts, transformed into a repellent but fascinating creature that recalls the demons in the medieval and sixteenth-century paintings of hell that haunted Dalí's imagination.

How does this painting serve as a symbol of the twentieth-century mind?

any other kind. Theatergoers might avoid films and film buffs never go to plays. The two groups might never communicate with each other, despite the obvious opportunities for cross-fertilization between their arts. To a large extent, intellectual and economic differences determined the niches of taste, as some artists, seduced by theory or lured into a price-range accessible only to the super rich, lost interest in communicating with people of modest means or ordinary education. This became especially the case from the 1960s, when artists influenced by the new theories in philosophy and linguistics lost belief in the power of symbols generally. Images, some of them came to feel, like words, have no direct relationship to reality.

Painting and sculpture yielded popularity to film and to mass entertainment industries. Arts suited to the new media—cinema, radio, photography, and the gramophone at first, television in the second half of the twentieth century, computers and video toward the century's end—spread secondhand experiences, received wisdom, and hand-me-down values. The artists who really touched people were cartoonists. Walt Disney (1901–1966)—a film studio chief who specialized in anthropomorphic characters and adaptations of famous fairy tales for the screen—became, perhaps, the world's most influential artist ever because his cartoon movies depicted the most commonplace emotions, morals, and character types in ways that people of all ages in all cultures could immediately grasp. Musical theater, sacrificing sophistication for memorable melody, displaced opera. Pop music was to art what factory products were to crafts: cheap to make and capable of generating huge profits. In the second half of the century, when—for reasons we shall discuss in the next chapter—vast masses of young people in the West acquired unprecedented spending power, the record industry became the home of the most socially revolutionary and subversive arts, a role writers had once filled. Now it was rock bands who issued messages of political protest and sexual liberation to the masses. These messages proved less saleable, in the long run, than escapism.

By the end of the twentieth century, the most commercially successful genre was fantasy—the depiction of worlds that magic regulated or transformed, which suited computer-generated imagery. It seemed an ironic end to a century dominated by science, but it was symptomatic of the impatience with or revulsion from science that came to characterize popular responses. Meanwhile, the art form that attracted the most investment, and therefore attained the highest technical standards, was television advertising. Advertising jingles and images became the common artistic culture of the time—the only things you could rely on just about everyone to recognize. Sport, especially soccer, was the only rival—largely because it was telegenic and broadcast brilliantly all over the world.

Architecture ought to be the most popular art of all because people who never enter an art gallery live in some form of architecture and see buildings on their way to work. Indeed, after the Second World War, architecture replaced painting and rivaled cinema as the most socially powerful of the arts. The world had to be rebuilt, after the destruction of the war and the neglect of colonialism. However, doctrines that proved hostile to most people: functionalism and rationalism, which favored machinelike buildings, fashioned by necessity, stripped to their most elementary forms, angular in appearance, and unrelated to human scale, dominated the architecture of the period. So much had to be built so quickly that officialdom decided what and how to build, without giving much time or thought to the needs and feelings of the people who had to live in the huge apartment blocks, work in the offices, fac-

The Hobbit. The stories of the British writer J.R.R. Tolkien (1892-1973) launched a new type of literature: the fantasy novel, in which authors combined myths from different cultures to create imaginary worlds—located sometimes in the past, sometimes in space, sometimes in a "parallel universe"—where events could unfold without the limitations imposed by reason or reality. Science could not displace magic from people's minds and tastes. In some cases, the fantasy novel even became the basis of new kinds of religion.

tories, and schools of the era, and recover or die in the hospitals. Only in the 1970s did architects and urban planners begin to turn back to popular demands, tear down some of the worst excesses of functionalism, and start again on a smaller scale and along more traditional lines.

THE TURN OF THE WORLD

In the second half of the twentieth century, a reaction set in. The West rediscovered "Eastern wisdom," alternative medicine, and the traditional science of non-Western peoples. Other cultures renewed their confidence in their own traditions. One of the first signs was Niels Bohr's decision in 1947 to adopt a Daoist symbol on his coat of arms when the Danish government ennobled him. He saw the wavelike double curve, interpenetrated by dots, as a description of the universe that prefigured that of the quantum physics of which he was the leading practitioner. "Opposites," according to the motto on his coat of arms, "are complementary." In the same period, J. Robert Oppenheimer, the American physicist who led the research team that developed the A-bomb, was one of many Western scientists who turned to the ancient Indian texts, the Upanishads (oo-PAH-nee-shahdz), for consolation and insights, in a West disillusioned by the horrors of war (see Chapter 28).

Then in 1956, Joseph Needham, who had served as director of scientific cooperation between the British and their Chinese allies during the Second World War, began to publish, in the first of many volumes, one of the momentous books of the twentieth century, *Science and Civilisation in China*, in which he showed that, despite the poor reputation of Chinese science in modern times, China had a scientific tradition of its own, from which the West had learned the basis of most of its progress in technology until the seventeenth century. Indian scientists, meanwhile, had made similar claims for the antiquity—if not the global influence—of scientific thinking in their own country. In the 1960s, India became a favored destination for young Western tourists and pilgrims in search of values

"Modern" Art

1866–1944	Vasily Kandinsky, Russian artist, launched tradition of entirely abstract art
1872–1944	Piet Mondrian, Dutch abstract artist
1876–1944	Emilio Filippo Marinetti, proponent of futurism
1881–1973	Pablo Picasso, cofounder of cubism
1882–1966	Nandalal Bose, Indian artist, incorporated anticolonialism in his work
1887–1968	Marcel Duchamp, French artist influenced by Einstein's theory of relativity
Early twentieth century	Karoda Seiki and Wada Eisaku, Japanese painters, create works that assimilated Western influences
1918	Proclamation of the "Dada Manifesto"
1920s and 1930s	Emergence of surrealist and expressionist movements

The Beatles in India. Maharishi Mahesi Yogi, who claimed to be able to levitate and to procure world peace through meditation, was the most commercially successful of the Indian gurus who became fashionable in the West in the 1960s. Here members of the star rock band, the Beatles, sit at his feet. They incorporated some Indian influences into their music, and George Harrison (center, right) remained a devotee of the Maharishi's techniques.

different from those of their own cultures (Chapter 29). By the 1980s, some Western scientists, dissatisfied with the terms at their disposal for describing the complexities of the cosmos that their work revealed, turned to Asian philosophies. Zen Buddhism (Chapter 14) and Daoist descriptions of nature provided some Westerners with models to interpret the universe that seemed to match scientific discoveries.

Even in medicine, the showpiece science of Western supremacy in the early twentieth century, non-Western traditions gained ground. Westerners with experience of the world often came to respect and learn from the healers they met far afield. Edward Hume himself commented favorably on the work of traditional Chinese herbalists, from whom he had learned much during his years at the Yale Clinic in Changsha. But it took a long time for such respect to become general in the West. In the 1980s, the World Health Organization began to realize the value of traditional healers in delivering health care to disadvantaged people in Africa. In 1985, for instance, Nigeria introduced alternative medicine to hospitals and health-care centers. South Africa and other African countries set up similar programs.

Meanwhile, in the West, traditional healing arts of non-Western peoples attracted big followings. Ethnobotany became fashionable, as medical practitioners discovered the healing plants of Amazonian forest dwellers, Chinese peasants, and Himalayan shamans. Scientists—led by anthropologists impressed by the knowledge of medicinal plants that the peoples they encountered in their work had—began to appreciate that so-called primitive peoples had a cornucopia of useful drugs unknown to Western medicine. Traditional medicine had never died out in India and China. In a remarkable reversal of the direction of influence in the late twentieth century, Western patients seeking alternative medicines turned to Indian herbalism and Chinese acupuncture, along with other forms of traditional medicine in both countries. Westerners began to travel to China and India to study herbal treatments, just as at the beginning of the century, Asian students had headed to the West for the medical learning fashionable in their day. Western demand for alternative medicine became an economic opportunity for Chinese and Indian physicians in the West. The world had come full circle since Edward Hume's day.

African healing cult. In Cape Town, South Africa, a ritual of initiation into Ngoma—a shamanistic cult widespread in Africa. Practitioners use music and dance to attain a trance-like state in which they communicate with spirits, usually to access powers of healing.

IN PERSPECTIVE: Science, Challenging and Challenged

In the first half of the twentieth century, the intellectual hegemony of science was linked, unchallengeably, with the global dominance of the West. All the major new scientific initiatives came from Europe and America. The rest of the world could only endure this supremacy or attempt to imitate it. In the 1960s, however, the pattern began to shift significantly. Western scientists began to turn to non-Western, and especially to Asian, traditions of thought to help interpret some of the conflicting data their observations accumulated. These contradictions seemed, especially to nonscientists, to expose the imperfections of science as a system of knowledge that could explain the universe. Non-Western countries, especially in east and south Asia, imitated Western technologies so well that they began to build up enough wealth to invest in their own scientific institutions.

Meanwhile, revulsion from science increased prestige for what came to be known as alternative methods. Some people, especially professional scientists, remained convinced of the all-sufficiency of science and scorned these trends. Their critics called them scientistic. Toward the end of the century, divisions—sometimes called culture wars—opened between apologists of science and advocates of alternatives.

The search for the underlying or overarching order of the cosmos seemed only to lead to chaos. "Life is scientific," says Piggy, the doomed hero of William Golding's novel of 1959, *Lord of the Flies*. The rest of the characters prove him wrong by killing him and reverting to instinct and savagery. Golding died in 1993, hailed as one of the great storytellers of the century, largely because of the impact of this one novel, which seemed to be an allegory of its times. Science—in most people's judgment—soared and failed. It sought to penetrate the heavens and ended by contaminating the Earth. Among its most influential inventions, the effects of which are among the subjects of our remaining chapters, were bombs and pollutants. The expansion of knowledge added nothing to wisdom. Science did not make people better. Rather it increased their ability to behave worse than ever before. Instead of a universal benefit to humanity, science was a symptom or cause of disproportionate Western power. Under the influence of these feelings, and in response to the undermining of science by skepticism, an antiscientific reaction set in the late twentieth century. It generated conflict between those who stuck to Piggy's opinion and the vast global majority who—as we shall see in Chapter 29—turned back to religion or even magic to help them cope with the bewildering world of rapid change and elusive understanding.

The revival of unscientific ways to picture reality surprised most observers. But by making the cosmos rationally unintelligible to most people, science actually stimulated religious revival. Quantum science encouraged a revival of mysticism—a "reenchantment" of science, according to a phrase the British theologian David Griffin coined. Quantum experiments accustomed people to reliable observations that no one has been able to check objectively and to valid experiments that no one can repeat. Motions we cannot measure, events we cannot track, causes we cannot trace, and effects we cannot predict all became familiar and seemed to license metaphysical and even supernatural

William Golding's *Lord of the Flies* in the movie version directed by Peter Brook (1963). The story of the British choirboy-castaways who turn to tyranny and savagery when cut off from the disciplines of adult control is not just an antidote to the idealization of childhood but also a reminder of the fragility of civilization. In this scene the gang turns on their companion, Piggy, who maintains a touching faith that "Life is scientific."

explanations. Modern Japan is a land of high-tech Shinto, where spirits infest computers and where an office tower of steel and plate glass can be topped off with a shrine to Inari, the fox-god. Some medical practitioners collaborate with faith healers. Even religious fundamentalism—one of the most powerful movements in the late twentieth-century world—owed something to science.

The last wave of revulsion from science—or, at least, from scientism—in the twentieth century was a form of humanism: a reaction in favor of humane values. Science seemed to blur the boundaries between humans and other animals, or even between humans and machines. It seemed to take the soul out of people and substitute genes for it. It seemed to make freedom impossible and reduce moral choices to evolutionary accidents or genetically determined options. It turned human beings into subjects of experimentation. Ruthless regimes abused biology to justify racism and psychiatry to imprison dissidents. Extreme scientism denied all nonscientific values and became, in its own way, as dogmatic as any religion. The "new humanism" was much more, however, than an antiscientistic reaction. It tended to blame religion—or, at least, religious conflicts—as much as science for the failures of history, and its thinkers and practitioners sought a morality based on universal or potentially universal values. More than either science or religion, the barbarities of the violent, conflictive political history of the twentieth century stimulated the new humanism.

For the story of politics in the twentieth century matched that of science. In politics, too, the new century opened with new departures. The world's first full democracies—full in the sense that women had equal political rights with men—took shape in Norway and New Zealand. In 1904–1905, Japanese victories in a war with Russia foreshadowed the end of white supremacy. Encouraged by Japan's example, independence movements sprang into action in Europe's overseas empires. In 1911, the first great "rebellions of the masses" began. Contrary to the expectations of Karl Marx, these were not launched by urban workers, but by peasant revolutionaries in Mexico and a combination of underemployed intellectuals and disaffected soldiers in China. In Mexico, the effect was to end the power of the two elements of society that had been dominant since colonial times: the church and the big landowners. In China, the Qing dynasty, which had reigned since 1644, was overthrown, the mandate of heaven abolished, and a republic proclaimed. This was an extraordinary reversal for a system that had survived so many convulsions for more than 2,200 years, and a sign that no form of political stability, however longstanding, could now be taken for granted. Both revolutions soured, turning into civil wars, breeding dictators. This too was an omen of the future. Most of the many violent regime changes of the twentieth century had similar consequences.

CHRONOLOGY

1856–1939	Sigmund Freud, developer of psychoanalysis
1858–1942	Franz Boas, anthropologist, proved that races are of equal intelligence
1860s	China's "self-strengthening" program begins
1866–1944	Vasily Kandinsky, Russian artist, launched tradition of entirely abstract art
1883	Western-style curriculum at Beijing School of Medicine
1871–1937	Ernest Rutherford, postulated concept of the atomic nucleus
1875–1965	Albert Schweizer, medical missionary to Africa
1876–1944	Emilio Filippo Marinetti, proponent of futurism
1879–1955	Albert Einstein, developer of the theory of relativity
1881–1938	Kemal Ataturk, founder of modern Turkey and proponent of secularism and Western science
1881–1973	Pablo Picasso, cofounder of cubism
1882–1966	Nandalal Bose, Indian artist, incorporated anticolonialism in his work
1885–1962	Niels Bohr, won Nobel Prize in 1922 for work on the structure of the atom
1891–1962	Ismail Mazhir, translator of Charles Darwin's work into Arabic
1897	Jagadis Chandra Bose awarded scientific research grant by the British viceroy
1901–1976	Werner Heisenberg, developed uncertainty principle
1902	Henry Poincaré questions the link between hypothesis and evidence
1903	Powered flight
1905–1980	Jean-Paul Sartre, French philosopher associated with existentialism
1906	15,000 Chinese study science abroad
1907	Plastic invented
1913	Indian Journal of Medical Research launched
1914	Science Society of China founded by Chinese students at Cornell University
1920s and 1930s	Emergence of surrealist and expressionist movements
1920	Royal Institute for Higher Technical Education founded in Indonesia
1925	Scopes "Monkey" Trial
1928	Margaret Mead's Coming of Age in Samoa published
1931	Penicillin discovered
1944	Erwin Schödinger predicts structure of the gene
1953	Ludwig Wittgenstein's Philosophical Investigations published
1956	Publication of Joseph Needham's Science and Civilisation in China

The future that the radicals of the nineteenth century imagined never happened. Ordinary people never really got power over their own lives or over the societies they formed—even in states founded in revolutions or regulated by democratic institutions. The progress people hoped for in the early years of the twentieth century dissolved in the bloodiest wars ever experienced. And just as Western science receded in the second half of the century, so did Western empires. To those stories we must now turn.

PROBLEMS AND PARALLELS

1. How did science come to set the agenda for the world in the twentieth century? How did Western empires affect the spread of Western science? How was Western science received in China, India, and the Islamic world?

2. How was Western science transformed in the twentieth century? What effects did uncertainty have on human self-perception and religious values?

3. Why is twentieth-century Western art a mirror of twentieth-century science? How did the revolutions in twentieth-century art match the jolts and shocks of science and philosophy?

4. Why did a reaction against Western science take hold in the second half of the twentieth century?

DOCUMENTS IN GLOBAL HISTORY

Jane Goodall, *"The Challenge Lies in all of Us"*
Franz Boas, from *The Mind of Primitive Man*

Ellen Key, from *Century of the Child*
Emilio Filippo Marinetti, *"Futuristic Manifesto"*

Please see the Primary Source CD-ROM or additional sources related to this chapter.

READ ON

T. Dantzig, *Henri Poincaré, Critic of Crisis: Reflections on His Universe of Discourse* (1954) is still the fundamental study of the thought of one of the founders of modern science, whose own philosophy of science is available in Henri Poincaré, *The Foundations of Science* (1946). Also valuable for the emergence of modern physics, and more recent, is G. J. Holton, *Einstein and the Cultural Roots of Modern Science* (1997).

On the history of psychology, see the very readable book by C. P. Bankart, *Talking Cures: A History of Western and Eastern Psychotherapies* (1996), which sets the different traditions in their cultural contexts. A good study of one of the founders of modern psychology is R. B. Perry, *Thought and Character of William James* (1935). The key work by a founder of modern anthropology is F. Boas, *Mind of Primitive Man* (1911), while a foundational work of modern linguistics is availble as *Saussure's First Course of Lectures on General Linguistics (1907): From the Notebooks of Albert Riedlinger*, ed. E. Komatsu and G. Wolf (1996). For those willing to tackle one of the hardest of twentieth century philosophers, L. Wittgenstein, *Philosophical Investigations*, translated by G. E. M. Anscombe (1953) is accessible.

On the influence of Western science beyond the West, a number of fine works are available. E. H. Hume, *Doctors East, Doctors West: An American Physician's Life in China* (1949) is a first-hand account of the meeting of medical cultures, from which the story that opens the chapter comes. Li Yan and Du Shiran, *Chinese Mathematics: A Concise History* (1987), trans. by J. N. Crossley and A. W. C. Lun, and L. A. Orleans, ed., *Science in Contemporary China* (1980) both illuminate the influence of Western science in China, while J. Reardon-Anderson, *The Study of Change: Chemistry in China 1840–1949* (1991) examines the crucial transitional period of Chinese contact with Western learning. D. Arnold, *Science, Technology, and Medicine in Colonial India* (2000) does the same for the subcontinent, as does L. Pyenson, *Empire of Reason: Exact Science in Indonesia, 1840–1940* (1997) for southeast Asia. E. Ihsanoglu, *Science, Technology and Learning in the Ottoman Empire: Western Influence, Local Institutions, and the Transfer of Knowledge* (2004) traces in detail the routes and methods of the transmission of Western science into the Ottoman world. A. B. Zahlan, *Science and Science Policy in the Arab World* (1980) brings elements of that story into recent times. *The Political Economy of Health in Africa* (1991) ed. by T. Falola and D. Ityavyar, brings us into sub-Saharan Africa and back to medicine as a crucial vector of the spread of Western science globally.

P. Conrad, *Modern Times Modern Places* (1999) is a sophisticated analysis of modern art globally as a reflection of changing social and cultural trends. The iconoclastic J. Waller, *Fabulous Science* (2002) debunks many scientific myths. W. Hung, ed, *Chinese Art at the Crossroads* (1991), examines the challenges posed by modernity to historical artistic traditions with specific attention to China.

CHAPTER 28
World Order and Disorder: Global Politics in the Twentieth Century

1931: News of the Manchurian Incident flashes around the globe, as imagined by the brilliant Belgian cartoonist, Hergé. The Japanese propaganda version of the incident was false. Rogue Japanese agents, not Chinese "bandits" had blown up the railway track, and there were no casualties. The cartoon strip's boy hero, Tintin, discovers the truth and becomes entangled in the Japanese invasion of China for which the incident was a pretext.
© Hergé/Moulinsart 2006.

In the Manchuria of the 1920s and 1930s, the brothels in the city of Harbin were not merely, or even primarily, places of vice, but resembled clubs, where the regular clients became friends and met each other. The Russian journalist Aleksandr Pernikoff frequented Tayama's, which was Japanese owned and flew the Japanese flag. At the time, Manchuria was part of the sovereign territory of China, but Tayama's displayed signs of the gradually increasing level of Japanese infiltration. The Chinese government—run by the nationalist, republican party known as the Guomindang (gwoh-meen-dohng)—rightly suspected Japan of plotting to seize Manchuria, detach it from China, and turn it into part of the Japanese Empire.

MANCHURIA

On September 19, 1931, Pernikoff arrived at Tayama's as usual, crossing the seven-foot high fence of rough boards that screened the windows of the brothel from the street. The door was opened not by the regular attendant but by a clean-shaven, scholarly looking Japanese man with gold-rimmed glasses. As he shook hands with his friends, Pernikoff became aware of the tension in the atmosphere:

> "What's all this about?" Pernikoff asked in a whisper.
> "Didn't you hear?" replied one of the men. During the night, he explained, the Japanese had invaded, seized the Manchurian capital of Shenyang, and "exterminated the Guomindang vermin," on the alleged grounds that the Chinese "tried to blow up a Japanese train near Shenyang."
> "Did they blow it up?" asked Pernikoff.
> "No," answered the man, with a crooked half-smile. "The mine went off after the train had passed. But the Japanese troops were ready and waiting—they occupied the town within thirty minutes after the explosion."
> "How did they know it was going to happen?"
> "You're a fool! The mine was set wrong. . . . The Japanese expected it to wreck the train and create a proper turmoil. That's why there wasn't a single Jap on the train. Clean work," he added with admiration.

A Japanese member of the brothel's clientele, who—Pernikoff now realized for the first time—was really a secret agent, gathering intelligence on his fellow clients, rose to read out the official Japanese report of the incident. "Chinese bandits" had tried to blow up the train. Fortunately, a Japanese officer, who happened to be nearby, "being a samurai, knelt in the direction of Japan and humbly invoked the help of Amaterasu, the Sun Goddess, the divine ancestress of all Japanese." Miraculously, "by divine intervention," although thrust "up into the air" with the force of the explosion, the train descended back onto the rails, resumed its journey, and reached its

FOCUS questions

- HOW DID the world wars weaken Europe's global dominance?
- WHY WERE totalitarian and authoritarian regimes so numerous and widespread for so much of the twentieth century?
- HOW DID the United States become the world's only superpower?
- WHY DID the Cold War lead to the collapse of the Soviet Union?
- HOW DID decolonization affect Asia and Africa?
- WHY DID democracy spread around the world in the late twentieth century?
- ARE THE European Union and China likely to become superpowers in the twenty-first century?

destination without loss. "All of us in the room," wrote Pernikoff, "felt uneasy at hearing this childish account."

"What will happen now?" he asked.

"War."[1]

This episode, known to historians as the **Manchurian Incident**, was the first in a series of crises that Japanese militants manufactured over the next six years—not always with the knowledge or approval of their own government. Usually, rogue elements in the army, who conspired to force militaristic and expansionist policies on the rulers in Tokyo, contrived the incidents and began the violence that always followed them. The first results of this were to sever Manchuria from China and convert it into a Japanese puppet monarchy. Then, in 1937, followed full-scale war and the beginning of a long and tenacious Japanese attempt to conquer China and rule it as a subject territory.

● ● ● ● ●

It was a titanic conflict between states that history seemed to have earmarked to be contenders for global power. China was still by far the world's most populous country, needing only good government and a modernized economy to resume its traditional role as a superpower. Japan at the time had Asia's only industrial economy and was the only Asian state that European and American diplomats classed as a great power. Japanese motivation was simple. War was a preemptive strike, before China became too strong and outclassed all rivals.

The war in China dragged on until 1945. The Japanese occupied much of the country but could never eradicate resistance. The conflict escalated, merged with other struggles, and became part of a world war in which all the world's potential superpowers—Japan, China, the United States, Russia, and Germany—were locked, together with the British, French, and Dutch Empires and most of the other sovereign states that then existed.

The war was part of a long series of global conflicts. Catastrophically violent and destructive warfare punctuated the first half of the century. A **Cold War** between ideologically opposed antagonists dominated most of the second half, waged in local or regional outbreaks and in economic, diplomatic, and ideological competition.

We can follow the story of politics in the twentieth century along a path picked between these conflicts. To make space for the enduringly important cultural and environmental history of the century, we need to try to tell the political story briefly, rather than dwelling, as textbooks usually do, on all the many twists and turns, and all the forgettable statesmen and generals whose effects on their times were slight, and whose legacy—mercifully, in most cases—has not lasted. In the pages that follow, we divide the century roughly into three periods: first, that of the world wars, which ended in 1945; then, the so-called Cold War era of superpower confrontation that began as world war ended, continued for most of the rest of the century, and entered a new phase, dominated by the global breakup of European empires, in the 1960s. Finally, toward the end of the century, a "new world order" arose, as the United States outstripped, outgunned, or outlasted rivals.

The story foreshadows, but does not include, the end of Western world hegemony. Western initiatives—influences that originated in Europe and the United States—continued to dominate global history throughout the conflicts of the century. When the Sino-Japanese War began, China seemed, to people in Europe, a minor theater of conflict. The British writers W. H. Auden and Christopher Isherwood abandoned their journalistic assignments to cover war in China in 1939, as soon as they received news of the deteriorating situation in Europe. They emigrated to the United States, shifting their focus amid an impending conflict that seemed more relevant to them and more vital to the world.

THE WORLD WAR ERA, 1914–1945

One way to understand Japan's conflict with China in the twentieth century is as a sort of civil war within a single civilization, between peoples who shared many values and had overlapping legacies of thought, religion, and art. That, indeed, was how Japanese usually represented the conflict to themselves—as a decisive struggle to determine which country would be the "big brother" and which the "little brother" in a future common empire, or, as Japanese propagandists said, the Great East Asia Coprosperity Sphere.

The European conflicts that merged with this intra-Asian war, and that overspilled Europe itself to become a global war, had similar characteristics. At first, in the episode known as the First World War, from 1914 to 1918, national and imperial rivalries triggered hostilities. The European powers disagreed about little except how to distribute power and territory among themselves. Ideological differences only took over after the war had begun. To the great question of which country would dominate Europe, another, greater question was added: which ideology would dominate Europe? Would the common culture of European peoples in the future be religious or secular, liberal or authoritarian, capitalist or socialist, individual or collective? And which particular forms of those choices would prevail, as fascist, communist, and democratic states fought one another?

The First World War

When the struggles began, all the belligerent states had more or less the same ideology. Except for France, they were all monarchies. They were all nationalistic and imperialistic. Although most were not democratic, they all aspired to mobilize the allegiance of their peoples. They all used the same rhetoric of chivalry, idealism, and crusade.

Yet for each of the countries involved in it, the conflict embodied Clausewitz's statement (see Chapter 26)—that war was a "continuation of politics by other means." For Germany, it was an attempt to resolve two obsessions: first, to strike a preemptive blow against Russia, before industrialization turned that country into a superpower; second, to break out of maritime containment by Britain, for Germany had no access to the ocean highways except through narrow seas easily policed by British naval power. For France, the war was an attempt to wreak revenge on Germany for humiliation in their last war in 1870–1871. For Britain, it was an exercise in traditional British grand strategy: pinning down a world-imperial rival—Germany—in a continental war.

A trench with wounded and dead, June 1915, on the Western Front in northen France during World War I. The apparently unposed photograph is shocking because of the standing soldiers' apathetic acceptance of the plight of their wounded comrade in the foul, brutalizing environment of the trenches.

For the old, multinational, Habsburg Empire of Austria-Hungary, striving to contain restless and violent national minorities, war was a desperate act of impatience with Serbian subversion, which threatened to detach the empire's southern, Slavic provinces. "Better an end with terror than terror without end" became a common saying in Vienna, the Habsburg capital, in the last years before the war. For Italy, the objective was frontier snatching at Austria's expense. For the Ottoman Empire, fearing Russian expansion, it was a miscalculated gamble to risk its survival on an alliance with Germany. For the Russian czar, war in defense of fellow Slavs in the Balkans was an obligation of honor. "For Serbia," he said, "we shall do anything." His ministers also feared that Germany had "a gigantic plan of world domination" that it was vital to preempt.

For all the major belligerents, the war went wrong. On Germany's western front in northern France and Belgium, the rival armies—French, British, and Belgians on one side, Germans on the other—got stuck in the mud in long trenches that stretched from the English Channel to the Alps and that could neither be outflanked nor penetrated. In the east, Germans, Austrians, and Turks collided blunderingly with Russians in the vastness of the terrain. In the Alps, Italians hurled themselves futilely against Austrians who occupied the higher ground. In the Balkans, Germany and Austria overran Serbia and Romania, but those conquests had little effect on the outcome of the war. The elites who had started the war could not control its course or its costs.

Russia dropped out in revolution and disorder toward the end of 1917—the first of the major belligerents to collapse under the strain. Germany could therefore switch its main effort to the western front. The balance of forces, however, was already shifting decisively against the Germans, for in April 1917, the United States joined the fray.

This was a surprising development. If the war was essentially a European dispute, it was—many, perhaps most, Americans felt—no business of America's. It made sense for Americans to stick to peace and take the profits it offered. This policy, known as **isolationism**, was, however, gradually becoming impractical in the years leading up to the First World War. By the end of the nineteenth century, Western Europe and North America were growing increasingly like each other. Britain, Spain, France, Austria, and Norway were all roughly as democratic, at least in terms of their franchise, as the United States, or more so, considering the racist laws that prevented black people and other minorities from voting in large parts of the United States. Meanwhile, the United States and, to a lesser extent, Canada, while remaining big producers of raw materials, had copied the manufacturing and industrial economies of Western Europe. With the official closing of the American frontier in 1893, America lost the appearance of a pioneer country. "Uncle Sam," in the slang of the British press, had become "Brother Jonathan, a power among the powers."

America might have favored the Germans. There was a big German lobby as well as millions of German immigrants inside the United States. The British Empire was a rival that Americans viewed with traditional distaste—and many Irish-Americans detested—and had no particular reason to help. But Britain was America's biggest creditor and trading partner. Germany, meanwhile, offended against two of America's pet values: peaceful problem solving and freedom of the seas. Faced with British superiority in warships, for instance, Germany had forced the pace of the arms race in the years leading up to the war by building an enormous navy. Squeezed between

France and Russia, the Germans practiced militarism partly as a survival technique. In consequence, rightly or wrongly, Americans tended to see Germany as the greater threat and the more alien society. Once war in Europe broke out, Britain continued to command the Atlantic and to place huge orders for war material with American industry, while Germany had to resort to submarine warfare—which, being sneaky and secretive, offended American sensibilities—to unblock access to its own ports and damage British commerce. Since 1915, German submarines had occasionally sunk American merchant ships that traded with Britain. But the Germans had always backed down in the face of American protests. In 1917, however, Germany announced that its submarines would engage in unrestricted sinking of ships sailing in British waters. By then, the United States was already looking for a pretext to join the war against Germany. Its intervention was decisive, because no other belligerent could match America's power. By 1914, American industrial output was equal to that of the whole of Europe combined.

The United States did not enter the war to serve its allies. Indeed, it refused to become a formal ally and instead called itself an associated power. It went to war to meet an American agenda: to crush militarism, free the seas, weaken European empires, lift American debts, consolidate America's growing superiority in wealth, liberate the Eastern European homelands of million of American citizens, and make the world safe for democracy. But the war was a unifying experience for the powers that faced each other across the Atlantic. Three million Americans had the transforming experience of serving in Europe. "How ya gonna keep 'em down on the farm," a popular song inquired, "now that they've seen Par-ee?" Three of the world's most powerful, resourceful, and predatory states—the United States, Britain, and France—were now in partnership. The rest of the world faced a source of cultural influence of peculiar force.

America had a chance to reshape the politics of the world. The First World War was a crucible, in which the world seemed to dissolve, awaiting an alchemist to reforge it in a better form. It destroyed states, elites, empires, and traditional ways of life. Almost ten million men died in action. There were 25 million casualties in all.

Total Casualties in the First World War

Country	Dead	Wounded	Total Killed as a Percentage of Population
France	1,398,000	2,000,000	3.4
Belgium	38,000	44,700	0.5
Italy	578,000	947,000	1.6
British Empire	921,000	2,090,000	1.7
Romania	250,000	120,000	3.3
Serbia	278,000	133,000	5.7
Greece	26,000	21,000	0.5
Russia	1,811,000	1,450,000	1.1
Bulgaria	88,000	152,000	1.9
Germany	2,037,000	4,207,000	3.0
Austria-Hungary	1,100,000	3,620,000	1.9
Turkey	804,000	400,000	3.7
United States	114,000	206,000	0.1

Niall Ferguson, The Pity of War (New York: Basic Books, 1998).

MAP 28.1

Europe, the Middle East, and North Africa in 1914 and 1923

Europe, the Middle East, and North Africa, 1914

Europe, the Middle East, and North Africa, 1923

Nine million tons of shipping sank. But the statistics concealed the real depths of the destruction. The war wiped out a generation of the natural leaders of Europe. That in itself ensured disruption and discontinuity in European history. The war ended by provoking political revolution or transformation wherever its armies marched. Twelve new sovereign, or virtually sovereign, states emerged in Europe or on its borders (see Map 28.1). Superstates were demolished, frontiers reshuffled, overseas colonies swiveled and swapped. The Russian, German, Austro-Hungarian, and Ottoman Empires were felled at a stroke. Even the United Kingdom lost a limb, when revolution and civil war broke out in Ireland and ended with, in effect, independence for most of the island. Huge migrations redistributed peoples. After the war, more than 1 million Turks and Greeks shunted to safety across the newly drawn borders of their mutually hostile states.

President Woodrow Wilson (1856–1924) appreciated the opportunity and rose to the challenge. He rejected imperialism for the United States (except in the Western Hemisphere where the United States continued to intervene whenever and wherever it felt its interests were threatened). His country made its last permanent acquisitions of territory (three of the Virgin Islands in the Caribbean) shortly before entering the war by buying them from Denmark. Wilson also did his best to discourage the imperialism of his allies, though France and Britain took little notice, carving up captured German and Turkish territories between themselves. Wilson further insisted, within Europe, on "self-determination" for the peoples of the collapsed empires of Russia, Germany, Austria, and Turkey. New nations sprang into being or reemerged at the rhythm of a State Department typewriter: first, what Wilson called "Czecho-slovakia," then "Jugo-slavia," Poland, Finland, Estonia, Latvia, and Lithuania.

On the other hand, the claims of Ukraine, Georgia, Armenia, Belarus, the Kurds, and the Muslim peoples of the Russian Empire were ignored. In Africa, the belligerents swapped colonies, with no thought for self-determination. The aspirations of the Arab subjects of the Ottoman Empire were patchily treated. A leader of anti-Ottoman resistance in Arabia, Sharif Husayn (shah-REEF hoo-SAYIN) (1856–1931), proclaimed himself King of the Arabs in 1917, with popular support, but the British and French divided much of his territory between them. They left only what are now Jordan and Iraq to his heirs, and allowed a disaffected Islamist chieftain, Ibn Saud (ihb-ihn SAH-ood) (1880–1953), to conquer what is now Saudi Arabia in 1924–1925. Meanwhile, in what is now Libya, rebels against the Italians who had seized the country from the Ottomans in 1911–1912 proclaimed an Arab republic in 1918, but Italy suppressed them shortly afterward. From 1917, moreover, the British outraged Arabs by following—albeit halfheartedly—the policy of setting aside formerly Arab land in Palestine as what they called a "national homeland" for the persecuted Jews of Europe.

For Turkey itself, the loss of empire seemed a relief. The new, secular Turkish republic, founded by the war-hero Mustafa Kemal in 1923 (he later took the surname Atatürk, meaning "Father of the Turks"), had universal male suffrage in 1924 and women's right to vote from 1934. Atatürk uprooted the capital from Istanbul to new ground at Ankara in the middle of Anatolia. He made Friday, the Muslim Sabbath, a workday, imposed the Roman alphabet on a language formerly written in Arabic characters, and founded an opera, a university, and a symphony orchestra. That Turkey remained overwhelmingly Muslim still made it seem exotic to Western outsiders, but Atatürk's success inspired secular nationalists in other parts of the Muslim world. In neighboring Iran, for instance, an army strongman, Riza Khan (REH-zah hahn), seized power in 1925, proclaimed himself shah, and imitated, on a more modest scale, Atatürk's secularizing policies, abolishing the veil for women and banning Islamic religious schools.

Arab delegates. When the Ottoman Empire entered World War I on the side of Germany, the Allies determined to carve it up. As part of that effort, they promoted Arab efforts to secure independence. Delegates to the Paris Peace Conference of 1919–1920, which ratified the dismemberment of the Ottoman Empire, included British Colonel T. E. Lawrence ("Lawrence of Arabia"), who helped lead the Arab rebellion, and representatives from the Mideast. Prince Faisal, whom the British were to make king of Iraq in 1921, stands in the foreground. Lawrence is second from the right in the middle row, demonstrating his Arab credentials by wearing traditional Bedouin headgear.

 Sir Henry McMahon, letter to Sharif Husayn, 1915

Gassed. Poison gas was ineffective on the battle-field during World War I, but it symbolized the nature of technologically "advanced" weaponry: inhuman and undiscriminating. Except in the U.S. cinema, wartime artists almost entirely abandoned heroic images in favor of scenes of horror. Blindness and blundering—as here in John Singer Sargent's painting *Gassed*—became metaphors for the misconduct and incompetence of political and military leaders.

Erich Maria Remarque, from
All Quiet on the Western Front

Finally, as a result of the First World War, the balance of power, which had failed to guarantee peace, would give way to a new order of international cooperation that a global institution, the **League of Nations**, would regulate. President Wilson proposed the League as a forum to resolve international disputes peacefully. Taken together, these initiatives promised a reformed world, which, had it worked, would have been better—more peaceful, more stable, more just—than the world the First World War destroyed. But the United States Senate rejected Wilson's vision. Americans had no taste for world leadership. The costs of the Great War, in blood and treasure, had been enough for them (even though, compared to the losses European armies suffered, relatively few Americans had been killed in the war, and the United States emerged from it the richest nation in the world). When America refused to take part in the League of Nations and retreated into isolation, the new world order was doomed.

Or perhaps it was doomed anyway. The treaties the allies imposed left too many dissatisfied states. German resentment was massive and unyielding. Germany had been barely defeated, but, after it sued for peace in November 1918, the victors treated it with contempt: subject to massive reparations, loss of territory, and partial occupation by French armies, with humiliating restrictions on the right to rearm. It was also forced to accept sole guilt for causing the war. Italy remained discontented with its own modest territorial gains. Japan, meanwhile, which had joined the Allies in 1914 expecting a free hand in East Asia, felt let down by them. Russia, stripped of its traditional influence over Eastern Europe, was excluded from any real say in the postwar settlement and looked for ways to unpick it. Most of the newly erected nation states were raggedly hemmed with irrational borders that included large, resentful national minorities that caused conflict among neighbors. For example, besides Czechs and Slovaks, Czechoslovakia included Germans, Hungarians, Ukrainians, and Poles, none of whom were happy to be in the new state. Even with American participation, it is doubtful whether the League of Nations could have sorted out this mass of mutual resentments. As it was, the League was useless, its representatives—in the words of an English comedian—turning up for meetings "in taxis that were empty."

In the long run, perhaps, the big effects of the postwar settlement were on morale and changed expectations for the future. For those who took part in it, the war was an experience of unmatched horror. The men who marched away expected another war like those of nineteenth-century Europe: short, with opportunities for heroism. What they got was more than four years of suffering of an intensity never known before. Soldiers on the western front spent weeks or months on end in filthy trenches, contending with rats, lice, mud, and poison gas. While they cowered underground, artillery more powerful than any the world had ever seen pounded their dugouts. When they went over the top of the trenches to attack, they faced machine guns and died, or watched their comrades die, in the millions. Experiences too terrible to confide to loved ones back home became secret neuroses. Shell shock was the characteristic mental disease among the demobilized soldiery of the postwar years. The battlefield became soulless, desolate, a blasted, blackened, barbed-wired Golgotha. Tanks displaced cavalry. Machines crushed life out of the landscape and chivalry out of war. The soldiers' feelings of alienation were foreseen and captured in the awesomely strident music of the British composer, Gustav Holst (1874–1934). The war destroyed "even the survivors" of battle, said the German writer Erich-Maria Remarque (1898–1970) in *All Quiet on the Western Front*, the most influential of all the war-born novels and memoirs.

Gandhi as he wished to be seen. He squats in a traditional position for Indian mystics, working calmly in a scholarly, reflective manner. His gaunt body, modest loincloth, and simply furnished home proclaim his selflessness and asceticism. He adopted a spinning wheel as the symbol of his movement for Indian independence to signify tradition, patience, constructiveness, self-sufficiency, and peace.

Postwar Disillusionment

Optimism, however, survived in other places—especially where people resented the power of European empire. The war was a collective humiliation for Europe in the eyes of the world, for only American intervention had seemed to be able to end the bloody stalemate. The United States was revealed as unquestionably the world's leading power. Japan emerged more dominant than ever in East Asia and the western Pacific, where it mopped up formerly German-owned islands and bases in China. Almost before the gun smoke had cleared, nationalist movements, directed against European imperialists, got under way in India, Indonesia, Egypt, Indochina, and parts of sub-Saharan Africa. In Dutch-controlled Indonesia in 1916, the group known as Sarekat Islam mobilized a mass movement for self-government. At its 1919 congress, it claimed to have 2 million members. The Pan-African Congress, which claimed to represent all black Africans under European colonial rule, met for the first time in 1919 to demand that Africans play a part in governing their own countries "as soon as their development permits." In the same year, the Egyptian Wafd or Nationalist Party was founded to pressure the British into leaving.

In India in the same year, amid riots against the continuation of strict wartime police measures, the British authorities effectively suspended civil liberties. Mohandas K. Gandhi (1869–1948), who had made a reputation before the war in South Africa as a spokesman for the rights of oppressed black Africans and Indian migrants there, emerged as leader of the protests. He launched a movement he called **satyagraha**—literally, "the force of truth"—relying not on violence but on "passive disobedience": strikes, fasts, boycotts, and demonstrations against British rule. Other protesters derailed trains, clashed with police, and cut telegraph wires. The British responded nervously. In Amritsar in northern India, troops fired on demonstrators "to teach," their commander said, "a moral lesson": 379 unarmed people were killed and 1,200 wounded. Britain's hold—such as it was—on popular sentiment in India deteriorated rapidly after that. Gandhi's optimism was only briefly dented. "Just wait for the next European war," cried a character in the 1924 novel, *A Passage to India*, by the scholarly English liberal, E. M. Forster, who had been to India and knew the mood there. Much of the Indian intelligentsia was indeed looking forward to dismantling Western hegemony and dismembering Western empires.

Mohandas K. Gandhi, from *Hind Swaraj*

Okies. The family automobile, in a scene from the 1940 film *The Grapes of Wrath*. John Steinbeck's story of an Oklahoma farm family, forced to migrate to California by poverty and ecological disaster, focused on the difficulties of keeping brutality at bay and decent values alive in capitalist society when the economy fails.

In the euphoria of peace, even some Western politicians were free with optimistic rhetoric. The war would "end all wars." Its survivors would return to "homes fit for heroes." The year after the war ended, the architect Walther Gropius (1883–1969) founded an art school in Weimar, where Germany's new republican constitution had been written in 1919, to create built environments that would be both works of art and "would arise toward heaven from the hands of a million workers." The West would climb back out of its dugout. Progress would resume. The British writer H. G. Wells published his *Outline of History* in praise of progress in 1920. The destruction pleased, at least, those formerly excluded from the prewar order: the poor, the previously suppressed nations, men—and women—who had been denied the right to vote, the political radicals and extremists. As we have seen (see Chapter 27), some artists reveled in the wreckage of the battlefield. President Wilson also spoke with the voice of optimism. Almost as soon as the war ended, he went to Manchester in Britain to foretell an age "not perhaps golden, but brightening."

In America, where no fighting took place, this story was believable, at first. But war-scarred Europe found it hard to match this mood. Europeans were already becoming convinced of the imminent "decline of the West"—the title of the German historian Oswald Spengler's postwar blockbuster. For those who could afford it, the 1920s in Europe were an age of desperate pleasure seeking—what England's wittiest songwriter, Noel Coward, called "twentieth-century blues." For the rest, it was a time to try to salvage something from disillusionment. The results included labor unrest, extremist politics, welfare efforts crippled by economic failures, and impoverishing inflation.

Disillusionment hit America later. The war made the United States economy boom. After short-term dislocations of the peace, Americans enjoyed "seven fat years" from 1922 to 1929. Millionaire "colossi" of business and industry bestrode corporate "pyramids" of millions of share owners. A spiraling stock market seemed to promise literally universal riches. In 1924, 282 million shares of stock changed hands on Wall Street. In 1929, that figure rose to 1.824 billion. That same year, the crash came. In three weeks, beginning on October 24, American stocks fell in value by $30 billion (almost $400 billion in today's money)—equivalent almost to the entire cost of America's war effort. The effects ricocheted off the rich, bounced the economy into recession, bounded across the Atlantic, and set off a string of bank failures. Meanwhile, ecological disaster—part of the subject of Chapter 30—struck farms in the American West. "Brother, can you spare a dime?" sang crooners in the character of a war hero down on his luck. Economic depression was hard to take in communities that had become used to the accumulating prosperity of economic growth. Hollywood did wonders for Americans' morale, spinning celluloid stories of riches to rags, rags to riches.

Disillusionment afflicted parts of Latin America particularly deeply, because expectations there were so enormous. Argentina, Chile, Uruguay, Mexico, and Brazil were all self-styled lands of promise. For a while in the early twentieth century, Argentina was the world's most desired destination for migrants. In 1914, nearly a third of its population was of foreign birth. The oath of allegiance schoolchildren uttered proclaimed Argentina "the finest country on Earth." But Latin America's economies, after booming in the First World War, went into dramatic reversal after the war when European and United States demand for the raw materials Latin America produced plummeted. Violent changes of government ensued. In 1930, in Argentina, Peru, and Brazil, army officers ousted elected politicians and seized power or installed "emergency" governments with dictatorial powers. Guatemala, the Dominican Republic, and El Salvador followed suit over the next couple of years.

The economic disasters of Europe and the Americas in the 1920s and 1930s seemed to show that the West was wormwood. The rot went deeper than the corrosive international politics that caused wars and blighted peace. It was an age of fault finding with Western civilization. Some of the things people blamed were so fantastic as to be rationally incredible—yet impoverished and miserable millions were ready to believe the rabble-rousers' claims and were susceptible to the appeal of "noisy little men" proposing easy and even "final" solutions. Anti-Semites, for instance, blamed Jews, who, they claimed to believe, controlled the world's economies and exploited gentiles for their own enrichment. Advocates of eugenics claimed that unscientific breeding weakened society by encouraging inferior classes and races and feeble or mentally defective individuals to multiply and have children who would be as weak and useless as their parents.

According to the most widespread analysis, the fault lay with what people called "the system." Capitalism did not work. Marx's predictions seemed to be coming true. The poor were getting poorer. The failures of capitalism would drive them to revolution. Democracy was a disaster. Only authoritarian governments could force people to collaborate for the common good. Perhaps only totalitarian governments, extending their responsibility over every department of life, including the production and distribution of goods, could deliver justice.

Broadly speaking, there were three types of approach to the problems. First, people who still believed in democracy and capitalism thought the system could be reformed from within. The English economist, J. M. Keynes (1883–1946), advocated the most persuasive program. Governments could tweak the distribution of wealth through taxation and public spending, without seriously weakening enterprise or infringing freedom. Well-judged interventions of this sort would stimulate the economy without over-stoking inflation (see Chapter 29). Britain, France, and Scandinavia successfully adopted this kind of solution to economic depression. So did President Franklin D. Roosevelt (1887–1945) in the United States. Federal debt nearly doubled to over $40 billion in the six years of his peacetime administration (1933–1939).

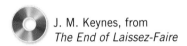

J. M. Keynes, from
The End of Laissez-Faire

The Shift to Ideological Conflicts

The two alternatives were authoritarian or totalitarian. The right-wing or *corporatist* solution was to allow private enterprise to continue to contribute to the economy, but only on the understanding that individual rights, freedoms, and property were not to be allowed to exist for their own sake, but were at the service and disposal of the state. The state would force all citizens to collaborate in the collective effort and coerce or, in extreme versions of the doctrine, exterminate any groups thought to resist the common pursuit. Left-wing versions proposed to collectivize virtually all economic activity, seizing most private property and, if necessary, eliminating "class enemies." This would end exploitation and have a morally, as well as economically, improving effect. The other main difference between Right and Left was that the Right was unashamedly nationalist, whereas the Left proclaimed internationalism, at least in its rhetoric. The Left was divided between those—usually called *anarchists*—who wanted collectives of workers to run economic activities, and *communists*, who wanted the state to own and control all production, distribution, and exchange.

Long-accumulating class hatreds underlay ideological differences. In the years before the war, European elites talked themselves into expecting a showdown with

Workers' demonstration. The Spanish painter Ramon Casas (1866-1932) specialized in meticulously painted scenes of bourgeois life of his native Barcelona, but he could also play the role of a social commentator. In 1902 he exhibited this scene of police dispersing a crowd of striking workers against a backdrop of gaunt factories. In the sky, there is gold beyond the industrial smog and perhaps a patch of hope.

Lenin on the Bolshevik seizure of power

the working class. Workers' demonstrations kindled fear and provoked massacres, painted in the early twentieth century in Barcelona in Spain by Ramon Casas, and in Russia by Ilya Repin The elation of middle-class onlookers, in feather-trimmed hats, fur muffs, and stiff collars, echoed the screams of peaceful petitioners shot by Russian troops. On the eve of war in August 1914, the British Foreign Secretary Sir Edward Grey predicted, "There will be socialist governments everywhere after this."

Such predictions were exaggerated. The first and, for a long time, the only successful revolution was hardly a workers' triumph. The Bolshevik uprising in Russia of October (or November, by the Western calendar) 1917 was a well-planned coup, which elevated a party—the Communist Party—to the role of an aristocracy, and charismatic dictators—first Vladimir Ilyich Lenin (1870–1924), then Joseph Stalin (1879–1953)—to the power of atheist czars, indeed to greater power than the czars had ever enjoyed. The country formerly known as the Russian Empire became the Soviet Union, after the Russian term for a workers' collective, although in practice the party and the state exercised control or tyranny in workplaces. Over the next few years, attempts to launch copycat revolutions were defeated in Finland, Germany, Hungary, Bulgaria, and Italy. Socialists made compromises with bourgeois rulers, often submitting to domestication and political collaboration as the price of a share of power. But left-wing militancy kept up the struggle. Moscow encouraged and eventually financed international communism. Communists often attached more importance to suppressing anarchists and other left-wing splinter groups than to overthrowing capitalist regimes. "Aren't we all socialists?" asked the bewildered English writer and freedom fighter, George Orwell (1903–1950), during a firefight between communists and anarchists in Barcelona in 1938. It was like asking, "Aren't we all Christians?" at the Massacre of St. Bartholomew's Day in 1572 when French Catholics had killed French Protestants in Paris. It may seem odd that leftists fought each other under the guns of their common enemies, but it is worth remembering that most of them accepted the Marxist dogma that revolution was inevitable. For the communists it was more important to ensure their own leadership of the revolution than to provoke it prematurely (see Map 28.2).

Even in some places beyond Europe, in the 1920s and 1930s, conflicts over power were increasingly seen as clashes of classes or ideological showdowns. In

China, for instance, the main contending parties called themselves Nationalist and Communist. Their conflict escalated in the 1930s, despite the menace Japanese invasion posed to both of them. In Peru in the same period, rival would-be dictators adopted the language of socialism and fascism respectively. But the "socialist," Raúl Haya de la Torre, was really an old-fashioned rouser of peasant millenarians, while his opponents were equally old-fashioned Catholic oligarchs. In parts of the British, French, and Dutch Empires, rebels and malcontents identified with socialism. They saw a similarity between the plight of their own peoples, oppressed by

MAP 28.2

The Growth of Political Extremism in Europe, 1922–1939

Indonesian communists. In 1925, when this photograph was taken in Batavia (now Jakarta), the Indonesian communist party had just launched a new policy of armed insurrection, after a series of unsuccessful strikes and a growing sense of desperation, as the Dutch authorities expelled its leaders. The three languages of the placard tell a story. Chinese immigrants were prominent in the movement. Malay—written here in Arabic script rather than the Roman alphabet currently preferred—was the language of the masses. The elite who ran the party, however, used Dutch. The rebellion launched the following year was another failure.

imperialism, and the worker-victims of capitalism, many of whom they got to know when they worked or studied in the metropolitan centers of the empires to which they, unwillingly, belonged. Ho Chih Minh (1890–1969), for instance, who later led a communist revolution in Vietnam, worked as a waiter in Paris after the First World War. Tan Malaka, leader of Indonesian communists, learned communism in the Netherlands after the Dutch colonial authorities expelled him from his homeland as an agitator for independence in 1922. Leopold Senghor (1906–2001), later founder of the Senegalese Socialist Party and first president of his West African country, felt drawn to socialism as a schoolteacher in France in the mid-1930s. Thus the West exported the semblance, if not the substance, of its ideological conflicts, along with so many other aspects of its culture, around the world.

Whether **fascism**—an extreme and extremely violent corporatist movement—was another splinter ideology of socialism has been passionately debated. Fascism could as well be classified as an independently evolved doctrine or as a state of mind in search of a doctrine. Or it could be merely a slick name for unprincipled opportunism: an agile insect, never still for long enough to swat. Stubbornly undefinable, its symbols best expressed its nature. In ancient Rome, the *fascis* was a bundle of rods with an axe through the middle of it, carried before magistrates as an emblem of their power to scourge or behead wrongdoers. Italian fascists adopted these bloodstained images of law enforcement as what we would now call their logo. They proclaimed the welts of the rod and the gash of the axe. They appealed to a system of values that put the group before the individual, cohesion before diversity, revenge before reconciliation, retribution before compassion, the supremacy of the strong before the defense of the weak. They justified the enforcement of order by violence, and the obstruction or obliteration of misfits, subversives, deviants, and dissenters.

When they took power, communists tended to be as ruthless as fascists. Communists persecuted and massacred class enemies. Fascists victimized or exterminated "inferior" communities and races. The Nazis in a conscious program of genocide, put more than 6 million people to death simply because they were Jews or Gypsies. In the Soviet Union, Stalin's campaign of extermination of small rural landowners and troublesome ethnic minorities claimed even more lives. Fascists and communists alike empowered the state at the expense of individuals and sacrificed liberty to social cohesion. Both sets of extremists shared belief in the omnipotence of the state, and built similar monuments—crushingly heavy, jarringly angular. Fascism had, perhaps, wider appeal. Advocating policies that could be summarized as socialism without the abolition of private property, fascists could mobilize small property owners from among the inflation-impoverished bourgeoisie. The cults of violence were equally characteristic of the militants of both Left and Right. Both extremes recruited their street armies from the same cohorts of unemployed, demobilized victims of economic slump and recession and social dislocation. The same ideals of fraternal community kept parties at both extremes together.

The politics of the twentieth century were horseshoe shaped, and the fanatics at each end seemed, in key respects, close enough to touch each other. Individuals moved between fascism and militant socialism as if through connecting doors. Benito Mussolini (1883–1945), who, as leader of the first successful Fascist Party—indeed, he coined the word *fascist*—seized power in Italy in 1922, began his political life as a socialist. The German Nazi Party—whose program was essentially fascist, with a particularly strong anti-Semitic driving force—was officially called the National Socialist German Workers' Party and campaigned for "Work and Bread." Britain's failed "man of destiny," Sir Oswald Mosley (1896–1980), was a socialist cabinet minister before he took to the streets as the leader of what he called the British Union of Fascists. Colonel Juan Perón (1895–1974), who took over Argentina in 1946 and founded a movement that still remains influential there, seemed closer to fascism than socialism. He promised employers that with "workers organized by the state, revolutionary currents endangering capitalist society can be neutralized." But he was also free with socialist demagoguery, a hero to trade unionists. His wife Eva (1919–1952), a former radio diva, became, in government propaganda, a proletarian goddess, "the faithful voice of the shirtless masses."

By 1933, when the Nazis took power in Germany, it was clear that in European politics, ideological defiance now transcended national hatreds. But the conflicts that followed were not straightforward struggles of Left and Right. Old hatreds crisscrossed the killing grounds. In some cases, liberals hunted clericalists; in others, local and regional majorities stalked racial or ethnic victims. Nationalists and imperialists gunned for liberals and separatists. Neighboring peoples indulged traditional feuds. Between 1936 and 1939, for instance, civil war in Spain seemed to project to the rest of the world images of a dress rehearsal for a global struggle of Left against Right. In reality, however, the fighting was between broad coalitions pursuing domestic Spanish agendas. The right-wing coalition partnered virtual fascists with awkward allies: traditional Catholics, who were defending the church against the seizure of its property; old-fashioned liberal centralists, who were equally numerous on the other side; romantic reactionaries who yearned to reinstate a long-excluded branch of the royal house; constitutional monarchists, who wanted to return to the cozy, corrupt, profitable parliamentary system of the previous generation; worshippers of "the sacred unity of Spain," who thought they were fighting to hold the country together. On the other side, along with all the mutually warring sects of the Left, were conservative republicans, liberal anticlericals, admirers of French and British democratic standards, and right-wing regionalists, who, recognizing the nationalists as the greater threat, supported the republicans as the lesser evil.

Ideology, in any case, could still be sacrificed to national interest. The Nazi dictator, Adolf Hitler (1889–1945), regarded Jews and communists as his main enemies, but one of his chief aims, which he made no attempt to conceal, was to crush Russia and conquer an empire of "living-space" and slave labor for Germany in Eastern Europe. He never compromised with Jews, but in 1939, he made a nonaggression pact with his communist counterpart in Russia, Joseph Stalin. For both dictators, the pact was a temporary expedient. Hitler wanted to clear the ground for a knock-out war against France and Britain to free himself to deal with Russia in the future. Stalin wanted to get his hands on the resources of Finland, Romania, the Baltic states, and eastern Poland to fortify his country against enemies farther west and re-create as much of the czarist Russian Empire as he could.

The pact was a disaster for the peace of the world. By neutralizing Germany's main foe, it wrecked the Western democracies' strategy for containing Hitler. Britain and France had attempted to buy time for their own rearmament by conceding a series of demands Hitler made and ignoring a series of his provocations. Beginning in 1934, Hitler disregarded agreed restrictions on the size of German armed forces, built

Argentine President Juan Perón salutes in military garb as wife Eva waves in a fur coat from the back of a convertible on a street in Buenos Aires, Argentina in June, 1952, with the Ritz Hotel in the background. Despite their showiness and wealth, and the policies they championed that were candidly designed to protect capitalism from revolution, the Peróns managed to convince Argentina's "shirtless masses" that they were on their side.

 Excerpts from the speeches of Juan Perón

 Adolf Hitler, excerpt from *Mein Kampf*

Peace in our time. British Prime Minister Neville Chamberlain (1869–1940) holding aloft the Munich Pact, which he signed, along with Adolf Hitler, on his return from Germany in October 1938. Chamberlain claimed the pact guaranteed "Peace in our time," but Hitler had no intention of keeping his word. The outbreak of World War II was less than a year away.

up a massive military regime, and reoccupied demilitarized parts of Germany. Then he forced German-Austrian unification, and seized most of Czechoslovakia after trumping up a border dispute over that country's German minority. The French and British hoped that fear of Russia would keep him in check, or, perhaps, that a war between Germany and Russia would exhaust both dictatorships. Many people in France and Britain also preferred to make almost any concession rather than risk the slaughter of another European war. The pact between Hitler and Stalin crushed those hopes and made war inevitable. The French and British had gambled that they could restrain Hitler by guaranteeing the integrity of his next target, Poland, even though geography made it impossible for them to offer Poland any effective assistance. The German invasion of Poland, launched in September 1939, plunged them into a war that they had never wanted to fight and for which, as events were to prove, their armed forces were not ready.

The Second World War

In Europe, the Second World War (1939–1945) reran aspects of the First. This time, however, France crumbled, not Russia, and it was on their eastern front, rather than in the west, that the Germans became stuck. Hitler overplayed his hand, turning against Russia prematurely in June 1941, without first knocking Britain out of the war. Aided by those traditional allies, "Generals January and February," and by Hitler's strategic blunders, Russia proved unconquerable. The decisive element was again American intervention—again procured against the grain of American isolationism and public unwillingness to get involved in policing the world. President Roosevelt wanted to save Europe from Hitler. Hollywood chimed in with wonderful propaganda films on behalf of the war. *Mrs. Miniver* showed plucky little Britain resisting Nazi aggression. *Casablanca*—still one of the world's favorite films—showed a wisecracking but glamorous Humphrey Bogart as an American exile in French Morocco sacrificing love for the allied cause. In the end, Hitler made America's decision himself, declaring war in December 1941 in support of his own ally, Japan.

Japanese society, already highly militarized, had become consecrated to war in the struggle to conquer China. The conflict escalated, as Japan realized that it would have to procure the energy resources it needed to subdue China by conquering Dutch and British colonies in southeast Asia. Such a vast extension of the Japanese Empire at other powers' expense was bound to become a global conflict. If Japan were to succeed, the United States would have to be neutralized or intimidated into standing aside. In December 1941, Japan launched a preemptive strike against the American Pacific Fleet at Pearl Harbor in Hawaii, gambling on being able to do a deal with the Americans later when Japan was in a position of strength after having overrun southeast Asia. The attack was a

Hiroshima, Japan after the explosion of the atomic bomb. In August 1945, Japan's defeat was already manifest, but rather than negotiate a conditional surrender or sacrifice thousands of American lives by invading the Japanese islands, President Truman (1884–1972) decided on a terrible alternative: the incineration of the Japanese cities of Hiroshima and Nagasaki with atom bombs.

startling success, but the strategy was miscalculated. The Americans were knocked out for long enough for Japanese forces to occupy French Indochina, overrun Dutch Indonesia and British Hong Kong, Malaya, and Burma, drive the United States from the Philippines and Guam, and fan out over the western Pacific. But America was enraged, Japanese forces were overstretched, and a terrible war of attrition began, in which the Americans, with help from Britain, Australia, and New Zealand and from the Chinese refusal to give up, gradually thrust the Japanese back (see Map 28.3).

America and Britain constructed a vast coalition—known informally as the Allies and officially as the United Nations—to fight or, at least, to legitimate the war. But most members of this global alliance could contribute little—in many cases because Germany or Japan occupied their national territories. In 1940, Italy joined Germany in what became known as the Axis. Mussolini gambled recklessly on German victory, but his help proved more of a drag on German resources than an asset. Italians felt little solidarity with Mussolini's regime and even less enthusiasm for war. German troops became overcommitted pursuing Italian adventures in North Africa, where the British forces triumphed in 1943, and the Balkans, where fierce resistance in Yugoslavia and Greece tied the Germans down. Meanwhile, the German campaign in Russia—Hitler's enemy of choice for ideological reasons—relentlessly ground down the German armies. Once American troops became available for the European front in large numbers in the Italian campaign in 1943 and, above all, with the invasion and liberation of France that began in June 1944, Allied victory in Europe became irreversible. But Hitler fought on—partly out of a fanatical refusal to surrender, partly out of hope that secret weapons would emerge from his research laboratories, and partly out the sheer lust for destruction that was fundamental to Nazi ideology. Indeed, the Germans were able to launch terrifying new rocket bombs, the V-1s and V-2s, against Britain toward the end of the war, but these weapons made little difference. Germany was gradually crushed between Russians from the east and the allied forces that pressed from the west. By the time Hitler killed himself on April 30, 1945, relentless aerial bombing had pulverized German industry, infrastructure, and communications; Germany's armed forces were collapsing, and the Russians were in Berlin.

On the Japanese front, there was never any real likelihood of long-term Japanese victory. Japanese leaders were aware of this. In 1941, their naval command compared war with the United States to a risky operation that would either save the life of a critically ill patient or kill him. The need for oil and gasoline for the machines of war obliged the Japanese to drive ahead rapidly to gain control of the oilfields of southeast Asia. They ended up with too many enemies and overextended lines. Once Germany was out of the war and the Allies were able to turn their full strength against Japan, the outcome was inevitable. Even so, Japan fought on, improvising weapons and refusing to surrender, which, in Japanese culture, was labeled as shame. The end came only because the war stimulated research into the devastating new technology of the atom bomb, which forced the Japanese, who had no such bombs, to surrender to the Americans, who did. In August 1945, American planes dropped atom bombs on two Japanese cities, Hiroshima and Nagasaki, virtually obliterating them, killing over 120,000 people, and poisoning the survivors with radiation.

The World War Era, 1914–1945

1914	United States industrial production equal to whole of Europe combined
August 1914	World War I begins
1915	Mohandas K. Gandhi, leader of Indian independence movement, returns to India from South Africa
1916	Sarekat Islam mobilizes mass movement for independence of Indonesia
1917	Russian Revolution begins; United States enters World War I
November 1918	World War I ends
1919	First meeting of Pan-African Congress
1919–1920	Paris peace conference
1922	Benito Mussolini's Fascist Party seizes power in Italy
1923	Turkish Republic founded
1924	Vladimir Lenin, leader of Russian Revolution dies; Joseph Stalin emerges as new Soviet leader
1929	U.S. stock market crash
1930–1931	Army officers seize power in Argentina, Peru, Brazil, Guatemala, El Salvador, and the Dominican Republic
1931	Japan invades Manchuria
1933	Nazis take power in Germany
1936–1939	Spanish Civil War
1939–1945	Nazis carry out genocide of Europe's Jews
1939	Germany invades Poland; World War II begins
1941	Germany invades Soviet Union; Japan attacks Pearl Harbor
June 1944	Allied liberation of France begins
August 1945	United States drops atomic bombs on Hiroshima and Nagasaki; World War II ends

MAP 28.3

World War II

— maximum extent of Axis
  powers in Europe and Africa

— maximum extent of Japanese
  expansion in Asia/Pacific

Movement of troops

Axis

→ German

→ Japanese

Allies

→ British

→ British Commonwealth

→ American

→ Soviet

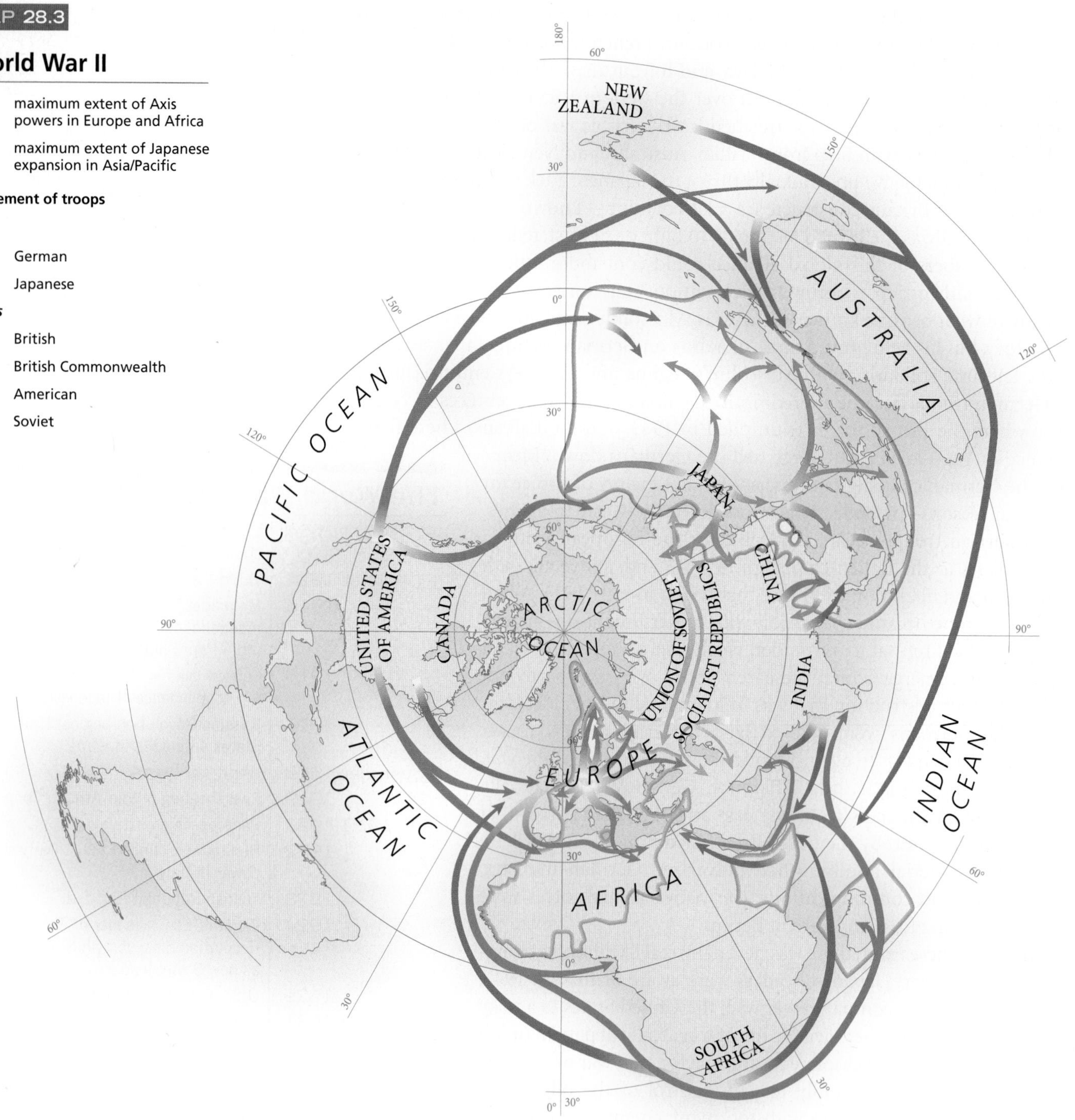

THE COLD WAR ERA, 1945–1991

Foreign involvement is a smooth-sided pit, and America found it impossible to get out. The peace was harder to win than the war. Roosevelt, like Wilson before him, had a vision of a new world order, in which the United States, Britain, Russia, and China would, in effect, divide the world among them and collaborate to police peace. But protracted conflict threatened from three sources: civil wars in "liberated" countries, the ambitions of international communism, and Russia's desire for security or power along its borders. Stalin seized or garrisoned much of Eastern

○ MAKING CONNECTIONS ○

THE WORLD WAR ERA, 1914–1945

BELLIGERENTS→	CONFLICT→	CAUSES→	OUTCOMES
Germany, Austria-Hungary, Ottoman Empire, versus Great Britain, France, Russia, Italy, other European powers	World War I, 1914–1918	Imperial and national rivalries	Defeat of Germany: dismantling of Austro-Hungary and Ottoman Empires; Bolshevik Revolution in Russia; Britain and France victorious but empires weakened and discredited; United States emerges as richest nation in the world; League of Nations formed; postwar disillusionment pervades Europe
Japan versus China	Second Sino-Japanese War, 1937–1945	Various incidents instigated by Japan lead to full-scale war in 1937 in an attempt to turn China into a subject territory	Japanese invade China and turn Manchuria into a puppet state (Manchukuo); conflict merges with World War II
Allies (Great Britain, United States, Soviet Union, other powers) versus Axis (Germany, Italy, Japan, other powers)	World War II, 1939–1945	Clash between different ideologies and forms of government (fascism, communism, democracy), and national/imperial interests	Germany, Italy, and Japan defeated; Eastern Europe falls under Soviet domination; Germany divided; Holocaust and forced migrations transform European society; Japanese Empire dismantled; European powers begin to decolonize; formation of United Nations; United States and Soviet Union emerge as nuclear superpowers

Europe. In March 1946, Winston Churchill (1874–1965), who had led the British government for most of the war years, announced the descent of an "Iron Curtain" from the Baltic to the Adriatic Seas dividing Soviet-dominated Eastern Europe from the West.

Winston Churchill, the "Iron Curtain" speech

Super-Power Confrontation

In 1947, America tried one of the most generous foreign aid programs ever, the **Marshall Plan** (named after Secretary of State George C. Marshall [1880–1959]), to try to seduce former enemies into dependence on the United States and "create the social and political conditions in which free institutions can exist." American taxpayers cheerfully surrendered the money for European reconstruction, and Western Europe rapidly began to recover. But it was too late for the east. Reparations debts tied most of Eastern Europe to the Soviet market. By choice, Russian occupation, or communist seizure of power, almost all the states east of the Iron Curtain—Poland, Czechoslovakia, Romania, Hungary, Bulgaria, Albania, the Soviet-occupied part of Germany—became Soviet satellites. At Stalin's orders, they turned down Marshall aid. Europe's civil wars had resulted in partition between armed camps. A ring of American client states, of varying degrees of obedience to Washington, faced a heavily fenced-in Soviet Empire.

George C. Marshall, "The Marshall Plan," 1947

So another opportunity had arisen to reconstruct world order—and again, the opportunity had been lost. In one respect, however, the American vision worked. Democracy took root in countries American forces occupied. Japan was the most conspicuous success, thoroughly transformed into a demilitarized, democratic state, and a staunch American ally. Italy also democratized without difficulty, though it had too large a Communist Party for American taste and was prone to

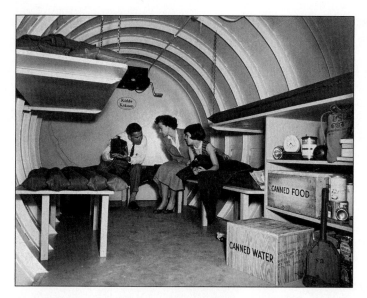

Bomb shelter. A U.S. public-information campaign photograph of the 1950s makes the "shadow of the bomb" seem almost comfortable with a family posed earnestly together around a radio in their well-stocked bomb shelter. But this reassuring propaganda was a sham. Only the elite had shelters, and if their shelters had survived an atomic bomb, these people would have emerged into a deadly, poisoned environment.

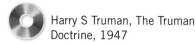

Harry S Truman, The Truman Doctrine, 1947

chronic changes of government. Germany had to be partitioned into two zones. The Soviet zone in the east became a rigid communist dictatorship, but the American-, British-, and French-occupied zones in the West were combined to form another model democracy, the Federal Republic of Germany.

The world shivered uneasily under a nuclear cloud. British experimenters had noted the explosive properties of nuclear fission as early as 1911. H. G. Wells popularized the prospect with a novel about the emergence of a utopian world from the ashes of civilization, incinerated by an atomic war. In 1935, the French researcher, Frédéric Joliot, in his speech receiving the Nobel Prize for work on nuclear energy, warned that an atomic chain reaction could destroy the world. By 1939, European scientists had nearly overcome the technical obstacles to the manufacture of the imagined bomb, but war, which ought logically to have speeded research, actually stymied it. The more immediate demands of the war effort distracted British researchers. Nazi conquest dispersed Joliot's team in France. In Germany, Werner Heisenberg (see Chapter 27) led a team equipped with essential ingredients: German uranium and Norwegian-made deuterium oxide, or heavy water, which helps control the flow of neutrons in a nuclear reaction. But Heisenberg was unwilling or unable to put a bomb in Hitler's hands.

So the first bombs were made in America. J. Robert Oppenheimer (1904–1967), a left-wing mystic with a genius for scientific administration, led the team. Had the United States kept its monopoly of the weapon, the country would have been permanently secure in the role of world arbiter for which its size and wealth equipped it. But the government felt obliged to share the secret with Britain, whose collaboration had been vital in making the bomb. Partly as a result of treason by Soviet sympathizers in the British foreign service, Russia's research team produced its own "A-bomb" in 1949.

Nevertheless, since Russia's main strength was in manpower, the new technology did not favor it. Outside the Soviet sphere of influence, Western Europe, under the nuclear shadow, could enjoy a security unthinkable without such protection, because the bomb cancelled Soviet superiority in non-nuclear military prowess. On the other hand, nuclear equivalency with the United States guaranteed Russia's free hand in territories it had already conquered or coerced. Yugoslavia broke free of Russian hegemony in 1947–1948 before the completion of the Soviet bomb. Afterwards, other East European satellite states tried to do the same and failed. Within a few years, technical improvements in the nuclear arsenal brought Russian and American firepower to the level of "mutually assured destruction." The balance of terror kept the peace between them.

Soviet and Western blocs confronted one another in a cold war that never quite reached boiling point. In ideological terms, the story of the Cold War was of resistance to international communism by liberals and democracies, or of resistance to capitalism and imperialism by self-designated representatives of inevitable progress. In international terms, it was a confrontation between the United States and the Soviet Union for world domination or, at least, for global influence. Each side looked threatening to the other. The Western allies ringed the Soviet world with treaty organizations: alliances of anticommunist states in Europe, the Middle East, and Asia. The Soviet Union turned the flank of the West by nurturing revolutionary allies among the poor and developing countries of the world (see Map 28.4).

Depending on one's point of view, the conquests of international communism were battering rams pointing at Western Europe and the rest of the world,

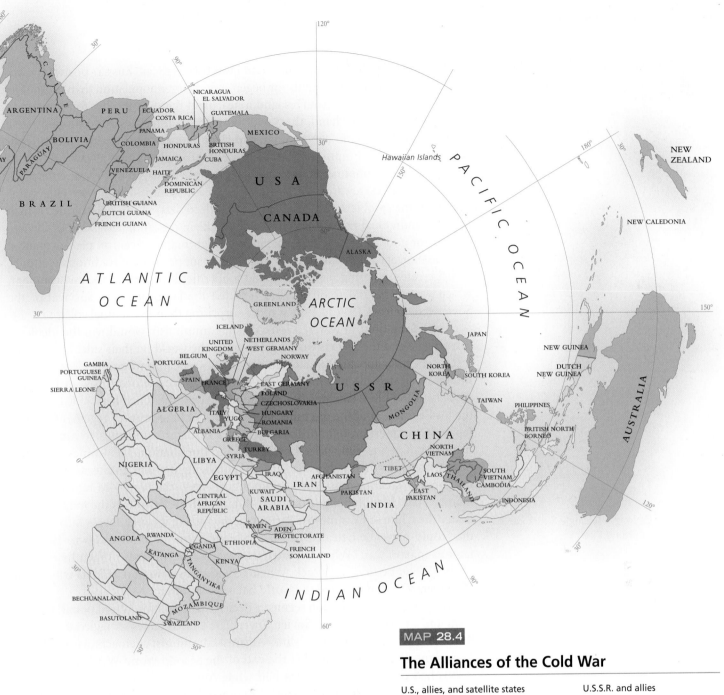

ARGENTINA
CHILE
PERU
ECUADOR
COSTA RICA
PANAMA
COLOMBIA
BOLIVIA
PARAGUAY
GUAY
VENEZUELA
HAITI
JAMAICA
HONDURAS
BRITISH HONDURAS
CUBA
DOMINICAN REPUBLIC
NICARAGUA
EL SALVADOR
GUATEMALA
MEXICO

USA
CANADA
ALASKA

Hawaiian Islands

BRAZIL
BRITISH GUIANA
DUTCH GUIANA
FRENCH GUIANA

ATLANTIC OCEAN

GREENLAND

ARCTIC OCEAN

PACIFIC OCEAN

NEW ZEALAND

NEW CALEDONIA

ICELAND
UNITED KINGDOM
NETHERLANDS
BELGIUM
WEST GERMANY
NORWAY
PORTUGAL
SPAIN
FRANCE
EAST GERMANY
POLAND
CZECHOSLOVAKIA
HUNGARY
ROMANIA
BULGARIA
YUGO.
ITALY
ALBANIA
GREECE
TURKEY
SYRIA

USSR

JAPAN

NORTH KOREA
SOUTH KOREA

MONGOLIA

TAIWAN

PHILIPPINES

BRITISH NORTH BORNEO

NEW GUINEA
DUTCH NEW GUINEA

AUSTRALIA

GAMBIA
PORTUGUESE GUINEA
SIERRA LEONE

ALGERIA

NIGERIA
LIBYA
EGYPT

KUWAIT
IRAQ
SAUDI ARABIA
IRAN
AFGHANISTAN
PAKISTAN
TIBET
EAST PAKISTAN
INDIA
LAOS
NORTH VIETNAM
SOUTH VIETNAM
CAMBODIA
THAILAND
INDONESIA

CHINA

CENTRAL AFRICAN REPUBLIC
YEMEN
ADEN PROTECTORATE
FRENCH SOMALILAND
ETHIOPIA

ANGOLA
RWANDA
KATANGA
UGANDA
KENYA
TANGANYIKA

BECHUANALAND
MOZAMBIQUE
BASUTOLAND
SWAZILAND

INDIAN OCEAN

MAP 28.4

The Alliances of the Cold War

U.S., allies, and satellite states

- U.S. and original NATO 1949
- later NATO
- NATO dependencies 1960
- other nations allied to the Western bloc by treaty

U.S.S.R. and allies

- U.S.S.R.
- Warsaw Pact 1955
- Communist satellite states
- China

or giant buffers projecting the natural caution of a Russia that had barely escaped destruction in the Second World War. Russian leaders' own rhetoric wavered between defensive anxiety and aggressive bravado, reflecting struggles for supremacy within the Soviet elite. Contenders for power drew attention to themselves by loud language. Stalin's eventual successor, Nikita Khrushchev (1894–1971), hammered loudly on the table at international conferences to distract attention from his weakness, and practiced "brinkmanship"—periodically scaring the world with the threat of nuclear war—to deter the West from aggression. One of these crises—in 1962, over the housing of Soviet missiles in Cuba—nearly did lead to nuclear conflict. But both sides backed down. The Russians removed their missiles from Cuba, the Americans theirs from Turkey. This showed that both powers recognized the need for what they called coexistence, at least between themselves.

Nikita Krushchev, Speech to the Twenty–Second Congress of the Communist Party, 1962

In retrospect, the Soviet phenomenon was bound to fail. Russia's postwar power reflected its natural endowments for hegemony: a larger population than most of its neighbors, vast natural resources, and a heartland that was too big for enemies to conquer. On the other hand, the Soviet Empire was ramshackle, no more capable than that of the czars in containing the ancient national and religious identities of its subject-peoples. Empires of the Eastern European plains have always been short lived. State-run economies tend to fall behind those managed by private enterprise, which guarantees rewards for those who create wealth. The Soviet elite compounded the problem by bad policies: collectivization of agriculture, which deprived individual peasant farmers of any stake in the land; repression of the free market for goods and services, which led to nightmares of central planning and a chronic shortage of even basic consumer goods; suppression of traditional cultures, which created festering resentment; and a horrific disregard for the environment, which wasted natural resources and polluted the landscape. The survival of the Soviet system from 1917 to 1991 is more surprising than its eventual collapse.

For a long time, however, it looked as if communism would win the ideological struggle and the Soviets would get most of the world on their side. In 1949, for instance, China appeared to have joined the Soviet camp when the Chinese communists defeated the nationalists in a civil war. Since the overthrow of the Qing dynasty in 1911 (see Chapter 29), no Chinese government had been able to replace the lost legitimacy of the old imperial order or hold the country together for long. Japanese conquest brought order, or at least a suspension of chaos, to much of the country but at a terrible price in violence and humiliation. The Chinese communists succeeded where others had failed: mobilizing popular enthusiasm, unifying the country, creating a new, uniform political elite—the Party—to replace the old mandarinate. Mao Zedong (mao dzeh-dohng) (1893–1976) was the most effective leader the Chinese Communist Party had, organizing its weak forces into an army that could never be defeated because it could never be pinned down. His most famous maxim was: "When the enemy advances, we withdraw. When he rests, we harass. When he tires, we attack. When he withdraws, we pursue." His triumph in 1949 seemed to have altered the world balance of power.

Mao Zedong, "A Single Spark can Start a Prairie Fire"

At first China's revolution seemed a decisive triumph for international communism and a great addition to Soviet power. The United States struggled to hold the line—or what was perceived as a line—against communist encroachments in Korea. The country had been divided at the end of the Second World War because Soviet troops had occupied its northern half while American forces had garrisoned the south. Supposedly, North and South Korea would be reunited after elections, but the rulers Russia installed in the north and those the United States backed in the south never allowed the elections to take place. In June 1950, the north invaded the south. America stepped in, with the authorization of the United Nations and strong military support from Britain and Australia. Despite Chinese intervention on the other side, the Americans and their allies were just about able to drive the invaders back to the north. Thereafter, Korea remained, and still remains, divided.

In Vietnam, however, a similar situation led to a disaster for the United States. In the 1950s, after French imperialism in Indochina collapsed, a partition of Vietnam between communist and anticommunist regimes led to civil war. American troops poured into South Vietnam in increasing numbers from 1961. The war of containment the Americans tried to fight proved impracticable against guerrilla incursions from communist North Vietnam. The United States got trapped in what was called *escalation:* rising costs, mounting casualties, plunging morale. Public opinion at home would neither approve perseverance nor admit defeat. America entered a 12-year agony that dominated the world's media. No war had ever before been so ruthlessly exposed on television and in the newspapers. Nightly images of dead and wounded young soldiers, atrocities, and ineptitude disturbed domestic audiences. In the morning, photojournalism splattered the previous day's bloodshed over America's breakfast tables.

Peace movements arose in response and spread beyond America across the Western world. Cults of "flower power" celebrated "love, not war." Increasing numbers of young men sought to evade serving in the military. Western youths now had a cause for their generational habits of rebellion or indifference. Protesters recoiled from the establishment decision makers. In 1968, massive street demonstrations across Europe and America toppled some governments and disturbed others. The would-be revolutionaries mostly talked themselves into inertia or grew out of rebelliousness. Protest ebbed with the war. But the effects of Vietnam seemed cataclysmic for one side in the cold war. Defeat when it came with the complete collapse of South Vietnam in 1975 diminished American prestige. The horrors of the war undermined America's moral authority. The insurgents' success encouraged America's enemies on other fronts. The American people recoiled from the exercise of responsibility for other people's liberty. The newly independent countries of the era were disinclined to take America's side. Communist takeover in Cambodia and Laos in the 1970s made the American rout seem worse. Cambodia's regime was one of the most brutal in a savage century, but its communism proved unique and demented. Its leader, Pol Pot (1926–1998), conceived a return to a purely agrarian state, such as had supposedly prevailed in Cambodia's medieval golden age. He proposed to restore it by massacring the bourgeoisie and the educated, wrecking industry, and depopulating the cities.

As if these political setbacks were not enough, the West also seemed to be losing in the economic and scientific stakes against the Soviet system. In 1957, Russia launched the first successful spacecraft, *Sputnik I*, and in 1961 put the first man in space. Space exploration was expensive and brought virtually no useful economic or scientific returns. But America, in danger of forfeiting world prestige, was forced to play catch-up, which it did, putting the first man on the moon in 1969. Meanwhile the world had the impression that Russia was ahead in the struggle to forge what a British prime minister in the early 1960s called the "white heat" of technology. Russian technical prowess seemed to do credit to Russia's economic system. Its surplus production, especially of oil and natural gas, subsidized its satellite states without impoverishing its own economy.

Gradually, however, evidence mounted that the Soviet economy was not as strong as it appeared, or as propaganda painted it. "Socialism is management," Lenin once said. But no Russian government managed the economy well. In 1954, for instance, Khrushchev launched

Atrocity. This 1973 Pulitzer-Prize winning photo shows South Vietnamese forces casually walking behind terrified children, including Kim Phuc, center, as they head down a highway after a plane dropped napalm on suspected communist guerrilla hiding places. The terrified girl had ripped off her burning clothes while fleeing.

a disastrous economic initiative known as the Virgin Lands scheme. He intended to turn vast areas of steppe into farmland—the way the great ecological revolution of the nineteenth century had transformed the North American prairie (see Chapter 23). In this case, however, the result was large-scale desertification and a food crisis in Russia. Intensive farming soon exhausted the soil of the grasslands the Russians plowed up. In all, an area greater than that of the entire farmland of Canada was lost.

In most respects, however, the era of Soviet economic success lasted until the world oil crisis of 1973, when oil-exporting countries, combining to hike the price of fuel, triggered massive global inflation. The economies of Russia's satellite regimes in Eastern Europe slipped out of economic dependence on Moscow, which could not afford to go on subsidizing them as lavishly as before, and into heavy indebtedness to Western bankers who loaned them vast sums. Then, in the 1980s, after sending troops into Afghanistan to replace a strongman ruler who was showing signs of becoming too independent with a more pro-Moscow puppet government, Russia found itself embroiled in a hopeless war against fanatical Islamic guerrillas who were financed by conservative Arab regimes and armed by the United States. The costs in blood and cash were greater than Russians were willing to bear. The American president, Ronald Reagan (1911–2004), saw the opportunity and stepped up the arms race, outstripping Russia's paying power. The Chicago economists (see Chapter 29) on whom Reagan relied for policy advice helped to convince the world that private enterprise made for prosperity and that economics was too important to be left to the state. The thinker who inspired them, the Austrian social scientist, F. A. von Hayek (1899–1992), became the source of the era's fashionable idea: order in the service of freedom.

The pope played a part in dissolving Soviet power. In 1978, a Polish cardinal, Karel Wojtyla (d. 2005), became Pope John Paul II, the first non-Italian pontiff in over 400 years. He had witnessed persecution of the Church by Nazis and communists alike. He used his wide range of acquaintances among Catholics in Eastern Europe to build up movements of resistance to Soviet domination. The first and most effective of these was the Polish trade union, Solidarność (Solidarity), which launched a series of strikes and demonstrations from 1980 onward, first against economic mismanagement by Poland's communist regime and then against the regime itself.

From 1985, the Soviet Union floated off the shoals and into the wake of the West, under a leadership that had ceased to believe in traditional socialist rhetoric. Mikhail Gorbachev (b. 1931) dismantled the command economy, freed the market, introduced accountable government, and, in the end, submitted to demands for democracy and

"Each day of labor—a step toward communism!" Russian communists adopted the hammer and sickle emblem to symbolize the alliance of peasants and workers. In practice, however, landowning peasants remained hard to convince. Joseph Stalin had millions of them massacred and exiled in the 1920s and 1930s for refusing to join collective farms. As late as 1968, however, propaganda still featured images of steel and grain—the privileged products of Soviet economic planning.

for self-determination by the Soviet Union's ethnic minorities. Moscow manipulated or permitted similar revolutions in the satellite states—the last act of a dying supremacy. Dissidents were on hand to take over revolutions they had not started but long wished for. Satellite states zoomed out of the Soviet orbit. The two European communist supranational states—the Soviet Union and the Yugoslav federation—cracked and splintered. Europe seemed to go straight from the world of Marx to the world of the Marx brothers, a popular Hollywood slapstick comedy act, with bewildering new states—Macedonia, Bosnia, Azerbaijan, Belarus, Moldava, Slovenia—bubbling over the map like *Duck Soup* in the brothers' chaotic movie of that name (see Map 28.5).

China, meanwhile, had become an enemy to both sides in the Cold War. Mao Zedong disappointed Moscow almost from the moment he took power. He was better read in Chinese pulp fiction than in Marxist theory. He admired the bandit heroes of Chinese romance more than he did Lenin or Stalin. He was a peasant by birth and developed his own theory of peasant revolution. "He doesn't understand the most elementary Marxist truths," said Stalin, who disliked and feared Mao. In any case, Mao was determined to go his own way. Under his rule, China remained as resolutely aloof from the Soviet Union as from the West and joined in the global game to offset American and Russian power. Mao denounced America for imperialism and the Russians for what he called "bourgeois deviationism"—turning the Communist Party into a new kind of middle class. He competed with both for the friendship of the successor states of dismantled empires, while pursuing an aggressive policy toward neighboring states. China overran Tibet, intervened in the Korean War, provoked confrontations on the Indian, Vietnamese, and Russian borders, and encouraged insurgents in Nepal (see Map 28.6).

Mao's domestic policies arrested China's development. He throve on crises and created his own when circumstances failed to provide them. He caused famine by

MAP 28.5

The Collapse of Communism in Eastern Europe

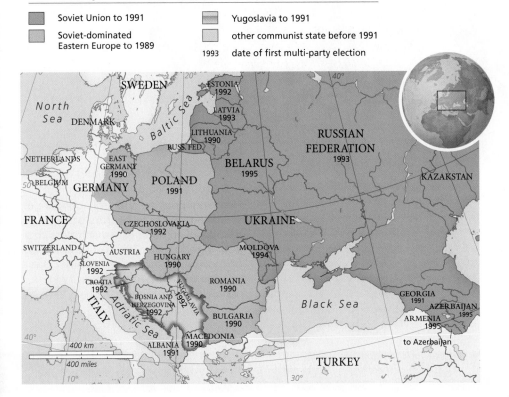

REPORTING OUR HARVEST TO CHAIRMAN MAO

Mao Zedong's "Great Cultural Revolution" was meant to remake society by forcing the privileged to share the lives of peasants and workers. But by victimizing the educated and the enterprising, Mao wrecked the economy and impoverished China. Propaganda strove to conceal the truth—not least from Mao himself.

The bystanders and the little girl nestled protectively in Mao's arm represent peasants and youth—the groups Mao tried to mobilize against professionals and intellectuals, whom he saw as enemies.

Mao, godlike in stature and simple in dress, recites his "Thoughts" to implausibly smiling adorers.

The girl on the left wears the badge of the communist party on her peasant's wide straw hat. Under Mao, the party became the country's only permitted elite.

Peasants bring agricultural abundance to Mao—like tribute-bearers to a traditional emperor or worshippers to a god. In reality, there was no abundance of food or anything else in China. Mao's policies undermined productivity in agriculture as well as industry.

How does this painting differ from what we know about China under Mao?

communalizing agriculture and environmental disaster by overhasty and absurdly impracticable schemes of industrialization. He launched campaigns of mass destruction from time to time against a sequence of irrationally selected enemies: dogs, sparrows, rightists, leftists—even, at one point, grass and flowers. He outlawed romantic love as bourgeois and, proclaiming that vice was hereditary, reduced the descendants of ancient elites—scholars, landowners, officials—to the ranks of an underclass. In 1966, his regime proclaimed a **Cultural Revolution**. In practice, this meant victimizing professionals—including teachers, scientists, doctors, and technicians, on whom the country relied—and forcing them into manual labor or degrading them with humiliating punishments. For more than three years, intellectuals were brutalized, antiquities smashed, books burned, beauty despised, study subverted, work stopped. China's economy reverted to chaos.

The long-term outcome of Mao's moral and economic failures was the reconversion of China to capitalist economics. Between 1969 and 1972, United States President Richard Nixon (1913–1994) reversed America's traditional policy of hostility, accepting China into the United Nations and opening American trade with it. It was an attempt to wedge Russia and China further apart, while mopping up some of the spoilage from America's failure in the Vietnam War. Still, Nixon's strategy worked, especially after Mao's death.

Mao's successor, Deng Xiaoping (1904–1997), recommended Chinese "to get rich"—not an objective either Mao or Confucius would ever have approved. After making remarkably liberal trade agreements with America and Japan, Deng freed up the Chinese economy, gradually returning more and more production and finance to the private sector. In 1986, Vietnam, too, adopted a policy of market liberalization. By the 1990s, China's was the fastest-growing economy in the world, at nearly 10 percent a year on average in output. Early in the new century, Chinese demand was driving up the prices of energy and commodities worldwide. North Korea was the only state in the region, in the world, really, that remained inward looking, isolated, and hostile to economic freedoms.

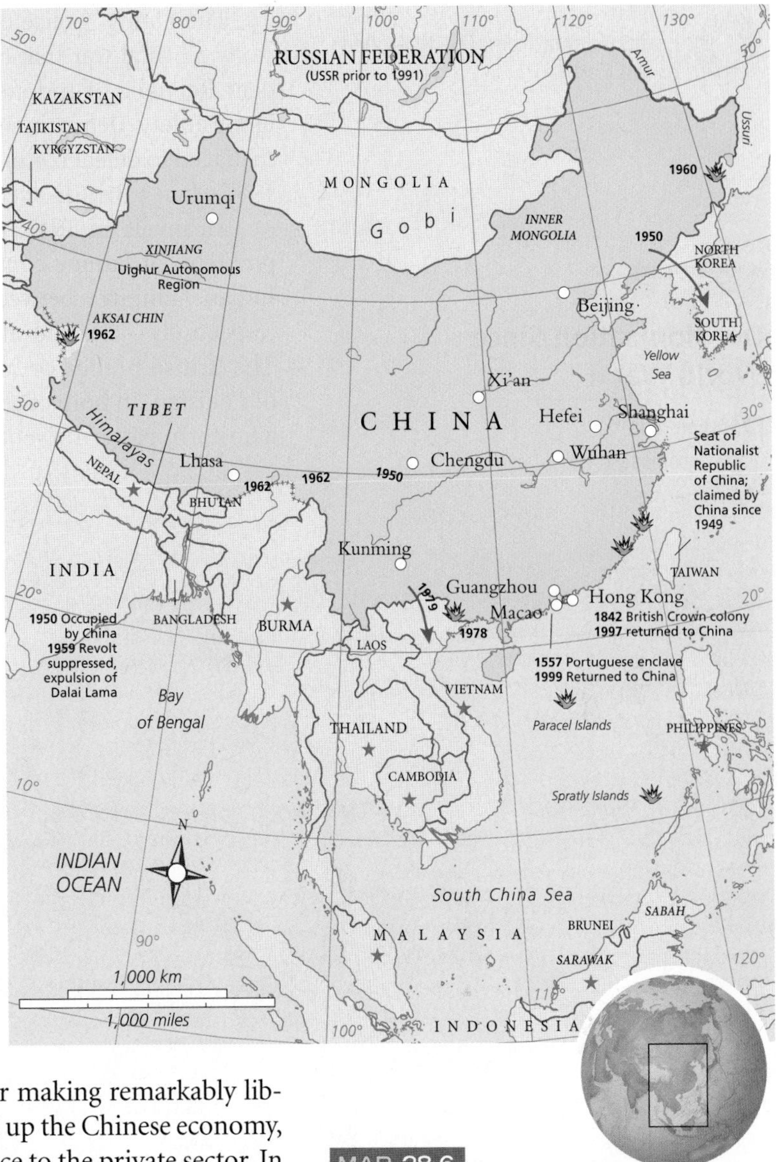

MAP 28.6

Chinese Expansion Since 1949

- Territorial/border dispute
- → Chinese invasion
- ★ Chinese support for communist insurgents

DECOLONIZATION

Before the Cold War could end, the world had to endure the agonies of decolonization—the breakup of the old European empires in Asia and Africa (see Map 28.7). The moral bankruptcy of imperialism was apparent in agonizing resistance struggles and wars of attempted reconquest. Between 1941 and 1945, self-interested Japanese aggression drove white rulers out of southeast Asia. The United States responded, after the war, by granting independence to the Philippines. In other parts of the region, the colonialists returned, only to be forced into surrendering power by fierce nationalist resistance.

 Deng Xiaoping on capitalism

Frantz Fanon, from *The Wretched of the Earth*

The Dutch "police operation" in the Netherlands East Indies (1945–1949) was really a brutal war that ended in Dutch retreat and the foundation of the independent Republic of Indonesia in a spirit of mutual resentment. The French suffered ignominious defeat in Indochina in 1954. By pouring in 40,000 men, the British managed to defeat communist insurgents in Malaya, but colonial rule ended there in 1957 when a British-selected Malay government took over.

Meanville in 1947, the British pulled out of India in haste, escaping horrific problems of famine control and ethnic and religious conflict. Partition of Britain's Indian Empire between Hindu and Muslim states—India and Pakistan, respectively—claimed at least half a million lives before borders were stabilized. The British bullied or blackmailed rulers of native states into joining either India or Pakistan. In both countries, the old patchwork of princely states was resewn into a uniform pattern. Eventually the maharajahs were stripped of their powers.

MAP 28.7

Decolonization Since World War II

- **before 1950**
- **1950–1956**
- **after 1956**

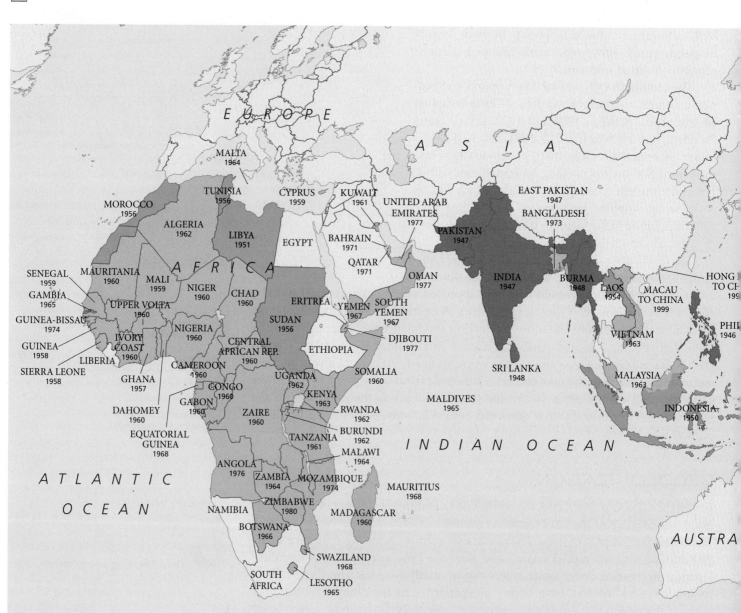

This was typical of European decolonization, which dismantled more than empire. In many places, colonial powers abandoned or sidelined the old elites—both European settlers and traditional native aristocracies—in favor of the newly anointed: upstart leaders, who came from the rising native middle classes. Usually the newcomers had been educated in Europe, or sometimes in isolated mission schools at home. Generally, the retreating colonialists felt forced to favor them. Once the colonial armies left, the new men, who commanded popular support, or revolutionary armies, or help from abroad, stepped into leading roles from backgrounds of violent resistance, cutting out traditional elites or reducing the old aristocracies and monarchies to purely ceremonial functions. Usually this policy ensured instability and tyranny in decolonized regions. In India, which became the world's most populous democracy, it worked exceptionally well. Pakistan was a less successful case. After about a generation of independence, the country was defeated in two wars against India, partitioned to accommodate secessionists in what became known as East Bengal or Bangladesh, and subjected to long periods of military rule.

Guerrilas, not rebels. In line with U.S. policy, which favored Indonesian independence and the end of Dutch colonialism in southeast Asia, the caption for this Associated Press photograph, in July, 1947, identified these fighters not as rebels against Dutch colonialism, but as "non-uniformed combat guerrillas" of "supporting units to the regular military forces" of the "Republic of Indonesia." After bitter fighting, the Dutch finally ceded Indonesian independence in 1949.

Most Westerners assumed that Africa would take much longer to decolonize than Asia but, the winds of change quickly blew up a storm in that continent, too. Because sub-Saharan Africa largely escaped the Second World War, some forms of production— especially of rubber and food—were relocated there. As a result, an ambitious African middle class developed. Meanwhile, the benefits of modern medicine produced a population boom. Uncontrollable growth in the numbers of needy people made empires obviously unprofitable. Rather than shoulder unmanageably escalating costs, it became cheaper for European powers to grant independence and foreign aid.

The role the Japanese played in Asia—uncovering the weakness of European empires and hastening their downfall—had an African counterpart. In Africa, Egypt led the way. Britain and France, the two main colonial powers, were humiliated in a showdown with Gamal Abdel Nasser (ga-MAL AB-dehl NA-suhr) (1918–1970), an Egyptian nationalist whom an officers' coup elevated to power. When he seized the Suez Canal Company in 1956, Britain and France, joined opportunistically by Israel, sent in troops hoping to topple his regime. Liberal British opinion thought "Nasser was right"—in the words of a character in Evelyn Waugh's great antiwar novel, *Unconditional Surrender*. For reasons of its own, the United States repudiated the Franco-British operation and, in effect, forced its allies to accept Egypt's case. A flight of colonial powers from Africa followed.

The cracks spread outward from Egypt. In the year of Suez, Britain evacuated Sudan, and France left Tunisia and Morocco—"protected" territories under European control but not formal European sovereignty. Algeria was a more problematic case. Although the vast interior of the country was a French colony, the parts of Algeria on the Mediterranean were considered an integral part of France itself, and their inhabitants elected members to the parliament in Paris. By the 1950s, these areas had over 1 million European settlers, many of whom were prepared to fight France, if necessary, to remain French and secure what they considered a European way of life. A savage war that broke out in 1954 between the French army and Muslim rebels

Kname Nkumah, from *I Speak of Freedom: A Statement of African Ideology*

Jomo Kenyatta, from *Facing Mt. Kenya*

settled the question in favor of independence by 1962, but not before mutinous generals and enraged settlers threatened to topple the government of France itself. Meanwhile, in 1957, Ghana in West Africa became the first sub-Saharan African state to gain its independence. After that, the skirts of empire were lifted with indecent haste. In 1960, fourteen new states came into being in Africa, including a vast tract of continuous territory from the southern Sahara to the river Congo or Zaire. Again, newcomers to the power game, schooled in resistance, replaced old elites. In Ghana, for instance, the independence leader Kwame Nkrumah (1909–1972) had "PG" for prison graduate embroidered on his cap. In Kenya, the first president, Jomo Kenyatta (1889–1978) was generally—and probably correctly—assumed to be the secret leader of the terrorists who had developed a fearsome reputation for the slaughter of white settlers and African loyalists under British colonial rule in the 1950s.

Postcolonial rulers in Africa adopted or affected secular programs, usually heavily influenced by socialism, and flirted with Moscow or Beijing, either out of ideological conviction, or to try to play off rivals to maximize their freedom of maneuver and opportunities for graft or aid. The ease with which many of them slid into despotic habits, and reduced their countries to dictatorships and destitution, dismayed Western liberals who had hoped that decolonization would bring freedom and prosperity.

Leader cults filled the gaps that the extinction or subversion of traditional loyalties left open. Some cases were truly shocking, especially in Africa. Nkrumah, who called himself the Redeemer, became prey to messianic delusions, as his troops sang, "Nkrumah never dies." Jean-Bedel Bokassa (1921–1996) declared the Central African Republic an "empire" and crowned himself its emperor, in imitation of Napoleon. He later massacred school children and was accused, not without evidence, of cannibalism. Idi Amin (1925–2003) in Uganda in East Africa, who, like Bokassa, rose by

another new method, through the ranks of the army, used terror as a method of government and plunged his country into chaos by murdering thousands of opponents and victimizing minorities. In Sierra Leone in West Africa, Siaka Stevens (1905–1988) became preoccupied with a mission to justify polygamy. In Congo, Joseph Mobutu (1930–1997) milked the economy of billions of dollars and gave himself a nickname that meant "the rooster that leaves no hen unmated." Even Félix Houphouet-Boigny (1905–1993) of Ivory Coast, long admired as a model for Africa because of his friendliness toward the former French colonists, gave way to self-indulgence, building himself a grandiose mausoleum, guarded by golden rams and sacred crocodiles, inflicting the world's biggest Roman Catholic cathedral on his home village, and banking billions in tax-proof Swiss bank accounts. Francisco Macías Nguema in Equatorial Guinea—executed by his own nephew after a coup in 1979—and Robert Mugabe (b. 1924) in Zimbabwe impoverished their countries and deployed armed gangs to tyrannize and murder opponents and intimidate electors.

In fairness, it must be said that decolonization left decolonized lands staggering under terrible burdens. Their populations were normally growing at an unprecedented pace, for which the colonial regimes had not prepared them. They were usually encumbered with

Leader cult. When colonial powers rushed ill prepared to disengage from Africa in the 1960s, they left dysfunctional states behind, prey to ruthless dictators, sprung from the new elites that Europeans promoted to offset the power of traditional leaders. Idi Amin, for instance, of Uganda, who seized power there in 1971, had been a sergeant under the British. This photograph from 1975 captures an incident of his increasingly unbalanced behavior as ruler of his country, when he forced white subjects and employees into taking bizarre and humiliating oaths of allegiance to him, drafting them into the armed services, so that they would be under military discipline, and exacting vows to fight against the white-dominated South African regime.

Hamas supporters. A series of wars from 1948 to 1974 left Israelis in occupation of lands with a large and resentful Palestinian population, many of whom, rejecting the very existence of the State of Israel, resorted to resistance by terrorism. Even peaceful demonstrations—like this one in 2005 by supporters of the radical party, Hamas—became exercises in martial discipline. Disputes over the distribution of land, water, jobs, and financial aid, and the exclusion by Israel of some Palestinian refugees from their former homes, inflamed the situation. Hamas won democratic elections—against rivals who favored accommodation with the Israel—in 2006.

irrational, indefensible, and unsustainable borders that the departing colonialists had hastily outlined. The principle of national self-determination, which had guided, however imperfectly, the dismantling of imperialism inside Europe after the First World War, was ignored in the wider world. Colonial regimes adopted three exit strategies: they crammed historically hostile communities into single states, or forced reluctant partner communities and nations into unstable "federal" superstates, or imposed borders between newly independent states that neither side found acceptable. International law treated postcolonial borders as inviolable, even where they were oppressive or unworkable.

As a result, civil wars commonly accompanied or followed decolonization, and disputes over the divisions of territory often remained unresolved into the twenty-first century: between new states, such as India and Pakistan; or between Catholics and Protestants in Ireland; Jews and Arabs in Israel and Palestine; Turks and Greeks in Cyprus; Christians and Muslims in Nigeria, Sudan, Ivory Coast, and the Philippines; Tamils and Singhalese in Sri Lanka; centralists and secessionists in Congo, western Sahara, and Uganda; rivals for resources in Angola and Mozambique; and traditional elites and historically underprivileged groups in Liberia, Sierra Leone, Rwanda, Burundi, and many other new countries in Africa and Asia.

All the ensuing wars multiplied the sufferings of the people who endured them, but the Palestinian conflict had the worst long-term effects on global history. In 1948, the British, who had occupied the country since the collapse of the Ottoman Empire in 1918, packed up and left in the face of murderous conflict between Jews and Arabs. What swiftly emerged was a division of Palestine into a Jewish state and Arab enclaves. The Jews, who called the state they founded Israel, were victorious in a series of subsequent wars that left them in control not only of territory the British and the United Nations had assigned to the Arabs of Palestine, but also land that neighboring Arab states had previously occupied. In the early twenty-first century, despite intermittent signs of progress, the resulting problems remained unresolved. Israel agreed in principle to recognize a Palestinian Arab state, but its boundaries and nature remained undetermined, while guarantees for Israeli security remained unsatisfactory. By choosing in effect to be the guarantor of Israel's survival, the United States, despite

 Palestinian Declaration of Independence, 1988

periodic attempts to act as an honest broker between the two sides, stoked Arab rage and alienated international opinion, especially in the Muslim world.

Meanwhile, the economic problems of decolonized lands mounted. In the 1970s and 1980s, the value of many primary products on the world market collapsed. This was the result of two so-called revolutions: the first, known as the green revolution oversolved the problems of famine by glutting the world with cheap grains (see Chapter 30). Simultaneously, an information revolution replaced many traditional industries and bore the West into a postindustrial age, in which services and information replaced manufacture as the main source of employment. An abyss opened where before there had merely been a gap in wealth between the ex-imperialists and their former subjects. Business imperialism was not easily thrown off. Even after colonies achieved political independence, their economic dependence often continued, sometimes on former colonial powers, more often on the Soviet Union or the United States—the cold war contenders whom newly independent governments sought to play off against one another. Cuba—never formally an American colony but always smarting under the economic control of United States businesses—played the game with some success after 1959, when idealistic revolutionaries, under Fidel Castro (b. 1927), threw out a corrupt dictatorship that had enjoyed Washington's support. Castro banned foreigners from owning Cuban land, nationalized many businesses—especially those Americans owned—and established an egalitarian welfare system. The United States took both offense and fright, and Castro more or less willingly became a client of the Soviet Union, while imposing increasingly authoritarian controls on Cuba. He even served the Russians as a surrogate force, sending troops in professed solidarity to African countries where the Soviets wanted to shore up regimes that favored them. At the end of the century, his system and his personal rule were still in place. The collapse of his Soviet ally in 1991, and the changing conditions of global trade obliged Castro to relax economic controls, but Cuba remained the best—perhaps the only—example of sustained socialism in the world.

THE NEW WORLD ORDER

At the end of the Cold War, America had another opportunity to reshape the world. President Wilson's after World War I had failed; so had President Roosevelt's after World War II. Now the omens were better in some respects. The United States had no rival and so far exceeded other countries in power and wealth that it could set the world's agenda. America's "soft power"—the example set by the success of its democratic institutions and capitalist economy, and the appeal of American popular culture, including movies, music, clothes, and fast food—disposed much of the rest of the world to accept American leadership and guidance.

Most of the world willingly adopted the democratic principles long associated with America, which American policy had sought to spread for most of the century. Strictly speaking, if one measures democracy by the extent of the suffrage, the only democracy in the world when the twentieth century began was New Zealand, which had had universal adult suffrage since 1893. In 1974, only 36 states could reasonably be called democracies, where the votes of the people genuinely chose and removed governments. By the end of the century, measured by the same standard, 139 states were democracies. By a tougher standard, including respect for the rule of law and for the civil rights of citizens in conflict with their governments, there were 86 democracies. Democratic rhetoric, at least, triumphed everywhere. Even dictatorships used it. Democracy was the only political ideology universally praised, even if governments often only honored its principles by paying them lip service (see Map 28.8).

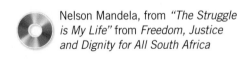
Nelson Mandela, from *"The Struggle is My Life"* from *Freedom, Justice and Dignity for All South Africa*

MAP 28.8

Freedom and Democracy, 2005

- Free*
- Partly Free
- Not Free

*Countries that are free offer open political competition, respect for civil liberties, independent civic life, and independent media. Countries that are partly free or unfree do not meet some or all of these criteria.

Global Trends in Freedom

Not Free
45 Countries
(25%)

Partly Free
53 Countries
(29%)

MAP EXPLORATION

www.prenhall.com/armesto_maps

Notable landmarks in the spread of democracy were the extinction of authoritarian government in southern Europe. Between 1974 and 1978, Greece, Portugal, and Spain all made the transition to democracy. In much of Latin America, military dictatorships seized power in the 1970s, often with the connivance of United States administrations worried about the Americas "going communist." By the 1990s, however, democracy was restored—albeit in some countries rather shakily—in almost the whole of the continent. The Philippines experienced an enduring democratic revolution in 1986, Thailand in 1992. In 1994, not long after the dissolution of the Soviet Empire, South Africa embraced democracy. This was a remarkable step by a racially privileged elite and occurred with little violence. The white parliament dissolved itself, and the outgoing elite respected the results of the first democratic elections, which brought Nelson Mandela (b. 1918) to the presidency. As he received the loyal support of the armed forces commanders, he said, "I was not unmindful of the fact that not so many years before they would not have saluted but arrested me" (see Chapter 29).

While much of the world democratized, most countries adopted what were called **human rights** into their laws. These rights included guarantees of life, personal liberty, and dignity; freedom of expression, of religion, of education, and of equality under the law; and minimal standards of nourishment, health, and housing. The Helsinki agreement of 1975, which pledged its signers to respect human rights, was particularly significant, because the Soviet Union signed it, along with most other European

"Freedom for Bush." Graffiti in Baghdad in June 2004 satirize President George W. Bush's claim to have made war in Iraq to promote freedom. One graffito clothes the Statue of Liberty in the garb of violent U.S. racists; the other shows a tortured Iraqi. American soldiers had been caught photographing each other torturing and sexually humiliating Iraqi prisoners, including innocent non-combatants. Soon after, the U.S. government admitted that it had authorized other instances of torture beyond the jurisdiction of U.S. courts.

United Nations Declaration of Human Rights, 1948

countries, Canada, and the United States. Dissident groups throughout the communist world were enormously encouraged. It was easier, however, to get assent in principle to the concept of human rights than to implement them, case by case, in communities of widely differing culture. In practice, particular states, even after encoding such rights in their own laws, ignored them whenever they wished. Even the United States—which had been loud in its advocacy of human rights in other countries, and, for a while, exemplary in respecting these rights at home—found ways around its obligations in dealing with people accused of terrorist acts or of collaboration with the enemy during wars in Afghanistan and Iraq in the early years of the twenty-first century. Some detainees captured in these wars were interned in the American naval base at Guantanamo Bay in Cuba, in an attempt to put them outside the protection of United States laws. Others, imprisoned in Iraq and Afghanistan, were subjected to torture by executive dispensation in defiance of the law. United States authorities handed still others over to governments, such as those in Syria, Egypt, and Saudi Arabia, that routinely tortured and abused prisoners.

Democratization remained imperfect. It made little impact in some states—especially in Africa and parts of the Muslim world. Some post-Soviet republics fell into the hands of authoritarian leaders. Under Vladimir Putin, who became president in 1999, Russia itself attracted fears that democracy might be in jeopardy. In South Asia, India and Sri Lanka preserved democracy pretty constantly, despite a prolonged secessionist war by the Tamil ethnic and religious minority in Sri Lanka, while Pakistan and Bangladesh were often under military rule. In southeast Asia, a fault line divided nondemocratic Myanmar, Laos, and Vietnam from the more or less democratic states that made up the rest of the region.

In Latin America, even after the military dictatorships were dismantled, Cuba remained a dictatorship, while some new democracies seemed worryingly fragile. Elected presidents of authoritarian inclinations—Alberto Fujimori (b. 1938) in Peru, for instance, and Hugo Chávez (b. 1954) in Venezuela—showed scant respect for democratic institutions. Most disturbingly, China continued to repress democratic opposition. By the early twenty-first century, however, there were signs that China might not be able to resist democracy indefinitely. The economic liberalization Deng Xiaoping launched created a new bourgeoisie, whom the government could not exclude forever from the political arena and who were not always, or even usually, members of the Communist Party. In 1997, the British colony of Hong Kong was reincorporated into the Chinese state, with its own unfettered capitalist institutions and a measure of local democracy, under a scheme announced as "one country, two systems." Meanwhile, unrest deepened in China's outer provinces, where Tibetans and large Muslim populations remained unassimilated, unwilling to think of themselves as Chinese, and resentful of Chinese rule. China, in short, was beginning to exhibit problems that the leadership might be tempted to solve by democratization.

If there was an opportunity to fashion a more democratic, more just, and more peaceful world, the United States did not take it. American leaders from the 1980s onward lacked what President George H. W. Bush (b. 1924) called "the vision thing." They made no attempt to renew efforts of the kind Wilson and Roosevelt had launched to create international institutions to preserve world peace. They dropped out of important initiatives in human rights, declining to accept the jurisdiction of an International Criminal Court. They kept aloof from efforts to establish a global environmental policy. They bypassed the United Nations when it suited them to do so. They launched military interventions and bombing raids on their own say-so against foreign targets. They exhibited what much of the world condemned as bias in their policy toward the Middle East.

The United States often felt obliged, in pursuit of its own national interests, to sponsor antidemocratic regimes, especially in the Arab world. Nor were America's own democratic credentials perfect. Two presidents—John F. Kennedy in 1960 and George W. Bush in 2000—almost certainly came to power as a result of electoral malpractice. In 1974, republican President Richard M. Nixon had to resign after revelations that he had been implicated in attempts to obstruct justice by subverting investigations into a break-in in 1972 at Democratic Party headquarters at the Watergate complex in Washington. The language Nixon used in discussing the matter with his subordinates exposed his contempt for democracy. Campaign funding became, toward the end of the century, more significant than policy in influencing the outcome of elections. About half the electorate ceased to take part in the national electoral process. Presidential elections were bought with millions of dollars and abandoned by millions of voters.

There is no question—despite the ill effects of many decisions by presidents and their advisors—that most Americans wanted America to be a benevolent superpower, and believed in the United States' traditional democratic ideals. Effectively, however, the United States had cast itself in the role of world policeman, and the American taxpayer was having to pick up the tab. This situation pleased no one. But American governments proved unwilling or unable to find ways to spread the burden, share power, or provide for a future in which America would no longer have the resources to take care of the world.

The European Union

China was the most likely successor to the United States in the role of global hegemon. Although leaders had talked of Pan-Arab or Pan-African unity, nothing meaningful had ever come of the talk or seemed likely to do so in a foreseeable future. But a chance to build loyalties across European frontiers arose from the ruins of the Second World War. The devastation of 1945 was a vast warning against conflict and a summons to collaboration. The collapse of European world empires threw the European states back on each other. The crisis gave institutional backbone to Europe's sagging identity. Six countries—France, West Germany, Italy, Belgium, the Netherlands, and Luxembourg—combined in the European Coal and Steel Community in 1952. The Messina Declaration in June 1955 proclaimed the goal of " . . . a united Europe, through the development of common institutions, the progressive fusion of national economies, the creation of a common market, and the gradual harmonization of social policies." This was a new departure in history. Never before had a group of states that had often been enemies peacefully set out to construct a common future.

Decolonization and the Post-Cold War World

1941–1945	Japanese occupation sets stage for postwar decolonization of southeast Asia
1947	Indian independence and partition into India and Pakistan
1948	State of Israel established
1950s and 1960s	Decolonization of most of Africa
1956	Suez Crisis
1959	Fidel Castro takes power in Cuba
1970s	Military dictatorships take power in much of Latin America
1970s and 1980s	Value of many commodities on world market collapses
1974	36 states have a democratic franchise
1975	Helsinki Agreement
1986	Democratic revolution in the Philippines
1990s	Under Deng Xiaoping China becomes world's fastest-growing economy
1994	Nelson Mandela becomes president of South Africa
1997	Hong Kong returns to Chinese control
1999	Vladimir Putin becomes president of Russia
2000	139 states are classifiable as democracies
2004	European Union enlarged to include 25 states

François Mitterand, "The Reconciliation of France and Germany," 1990

At every step toward those goals, Europeans dragged their feet, partly because governments were jealous of their sovereignty and partly because peoples were protective of their national cultures and identities. The Council of Ministers that effectively ran the **European Union** was deliberately an international rather than a supranational body. Entrenched forms of protection, especially over agriculture, limited the freedom of the common market.

The economic success of the European Union complicated the problems, as the community enlarged: from the 6 original member states to 12 in 1986, 15 in 1995, and 25 in 2004 (see Map 28.9). With each enlargement, consensus became harder to achieve. Some countries opted out of key initiatives, including the abolition of internal border controls and the single European currency, the Euro, introduced in 2002. Fundamental divisions opened between countries, typified by Britain, that wanted what the French president Charles de Gaulle (1890–1970) called "a Europe of National Fatherlands," and those that wanted a Europe "of regions" in which nation-states would wither away in favor of natural regional groupings, or a centralized European superstate.

To some extent, the adoption in the 1990s of the principle known as *subsidiarity* eased the difficulties. Borrowed from Catholic political thought, this doctrine held that decisions should always be taken at the level closest to the people whom the decisions most affected. But how many decision-making levels were needed among the local, the regional, and the Pan-European? Would the traditional nation states

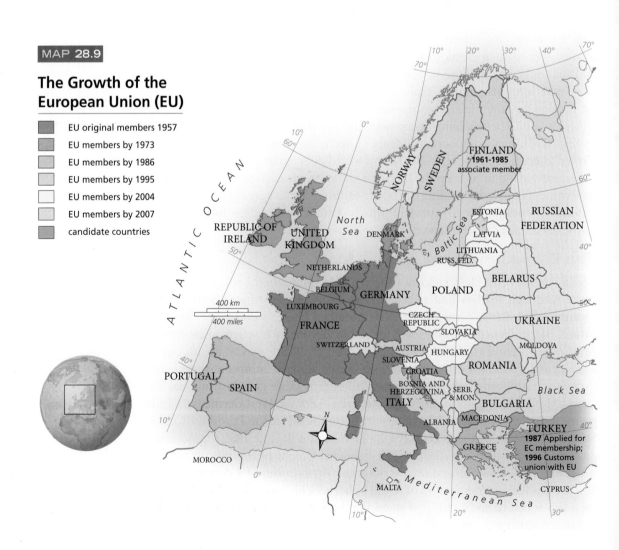

MAP 28.9

The Growth of the European Union (EU)

- EU original members 1957
- EU members by 1973
- EU members by 1986
- EU members by 1995
- EU members by 2004
- EU members by 2007
- candidate countries

retain a role, and, if so, would it be subordinate to pan-European decision making? And how large should the European Union be? Reluctance to admit Muslim states—Turkey and Bosnia—was obvious. Yet Europe needed to show that the Union could accommodate Muslims, if only because, as we shall see in the next chapter, Muslim minorities grew rapidly in the closing decades of the century, throughout Western Europe.

The big question was whether the evolving European partnership could become the "ever-closer Union" its top brass envisioned. A proposed European constitution, which represented an attempt to reconcile the conflicts between the Union and member states, was tested in a series of national referendums and parliamentary votes in 2004–2005. Each country had to endorse it for it to come into effect. Although nine countries approved the constitution, voters in France and the Netherlands rejected it by substantial margins in June 2005.

IN PERSPECTIVE: The Anvil of War

War dominated and can almost be said to have determined global politics in the twentieth century. War strained the empires that Europeans had constructed so laboriously in the nineteenth century. In the first half of the twentieth century, those empires barely endured, and in the second half, they all collapsed. Decolonization was usually violent and economically disruptive. Much of the decolonized world, especially in Africa, was left impoverished and racked by political instability. The United States was the only country that emerged from global conflict richer and stronger.

Meanwhile, war stimulated the development of new military technologies that, by the middle of the century, had become so destructive that the world readily agreed with the judgment uttered by President John F. Kennedy in 1961. "Mankind must put an end to war, or war will put an end to mankind."

At one level, contending superpowers dominated the story of global politics in the twentieth century. At another, it was a tale of ideological conflicts, in which democracy contended with rival kinds of authoritarianism and totalitarianism.

If the great wars of the first half of the century were civil wars of Western and Eastern civilizations, the Cold War was the conflict of an increasingly globalized world—a struggle to decide what the common culture of the world would be—its shared assumptions about politics and economics. The end of the Cold War was part of a more general climax that devoured authoritarian systems and spread democracy and capitalism in their wake. Yet efforts to establish a peaceful world order failed. By the end of the century, the world depended on the only remaining superpower, the United States, to act as a global policeman. No one—especially the American taxpayer, who had to pay the check—would find this satisfactory for long. The chances increased that rivals would again contest superpower status, as the European Union began to function and as China recovered momentum, after a long period of unfulfilled potential. The prospect revived that global history would again unfold from the east as the era of Chinese disintegration and weakness—which Aleksandr Persikoff had glimpsed from his brothel in Harbin at the beginnings of the Sino-Japanese War in the 1930s—came to an end.

In retrospect, the long-term significance of the war whose opening Persikoff witnessed was boundless. Dominance in East Asia and the Pacific was at stake; and over the twentieth century as a whole, this seems to have been the strategic area of greatest importance. For, as we shall see in the next chapters, during the twentieth century,

CHRONOLOGY

1914–1918	World War I
1917	Russian Revolution begins
April 1917	United States enters World War I
1919–1920	Paris peace conference
1922	Benito Mussolini's Fascist Party seizes power in Italy
1929	United States stock market crash
1930–1931	Army officers seize power across Latin America
1931	Japan invades Manchuria
1933	Nazis take power in Germany
1936–1939	Spanish Civil War
1939–1945	Nazis carry out genocide of Europe's Jews; World War II
1941	Germany invades Soviet Union; Japan attacks Pearl Harbor
August 1945	United States drops atomic bombs on Hiroshima and Nagasaki
1947	Indian independence and partition
1948	State of Israel established; Soviet blockade of Berlin begins
1948	Marshall Plan initiated
1949	North Atlantic Treaty Organization (NATO) formed; Soviet Union produces atomic bomb; communists take power in China
1950s and 1960s	Decolonization of most of Africa
1950–1953	Korean War
1955	Warsaw Pact formed
1959	Fidel Castro takes power in Cuba
1961–1973	United States involvement in Vietnam War
1966	Mao launches Cultural Revolution in China
1970s	Military dictatorships in much of Latin America
1973	World oil crisis triggers global inflation
1974	36 states have democratic franchises
1985	Mikhail Gorbachev takes power in Soviet Union
1989–1991	Collapse of Soviet control of Eastern Europe and of the Soviet Union itself
1990s	Under Deng Xiaoping China becomes world's fastest growing economy
1994	Nelson Mandela becomes president of South Africa
2000	139 states are classifiable as democracies

the great shift of the balance of population, wealth, and power westward from Asia into European and North American hands—the dominant trend of global history in the nineteenth century—began to ease. East Asian communities began to catch up economically with Europe and even, to some extent, with America. The Pacific replaced the Atlantic as the world's foremost arena of long-range trade.

Americans, meanwhile, may have relished their country's role but did not choose it. They suffered resentment and even hatred in return. In part, this was because the United States governments' exercise of global responsibilities seemed to many people to be unreasonable and unjust. On the one hand, the importance of the role of the United States for the peace of the world was well illustrated in 1990, when Iraq launched a self-interested invasion of Kuwait, and American-led forces restored the status quo. Some arenas of intervention, on the other hand, seemed poorly chosen. Under President Bill Clinton (1993–2001), military action or bombing raids in Somalia, Sudan, and Serbia seemed weakly justified and ill targeted. In 2002 and 2003, President George W. Bush launched invasions of Afghanistan and Iraq that appeared, to most of the rest of the world, to have little justification in the Afghan case and no reasonable pretext at all in that of Iraq. Both adventures were costly, and in both cases, America became committed to long-term political and military interventions, with no clear exit strategies. American power alone was evidently not enough to preserve the peace of the world indefinitely. American administrations did little to build international institutions to share the burdens or take over the task.

It was not however, solely, or even principally, American might and muscle that made the twentieth century "the American century." The magnetism of the United States was more a matter of what political scientists came to call *soft power:* cultural influence, and the appeal of American institutions and ways of life. Nor was it only American power that made many people resent America. For every admirer of American culture, others detested or despised it. To understand the context of these reactions, we have to turn to the social and cultural history of the twentieth-century world.

PROBLEMS AND PARALLELS

1. Why can Japan's conflicts with China in the first half of the twentieth century and the European conflict of World War I be viewed as civil wars?

2. Why did the non-Western world view World War I as an opportunity to challenge European colonial control?

3. How did the United States emerge as the world's leading power after World War I? What effect did post-war disillusionment have on European society?

4. Why did conflicts over power in the 1920s and 1930s come increasingly to be seen as ideological conflicts?

5. What effect did nuclear armaments have on world politics? How did the Cold War dominate world affairs from the late 1940s to the late 1980s?

6. What were the effects of colonization on decolonized lands? On former empires?

7. What are the respective strengths and weaknesses of the United States, the European Union, and China at the beginning of the twenty-first century?

DOCUMENTS IN GLOBAL HISTORY

- Sir Henry McMahon, letter to Sharif Husayn, 1915
- Erich Maria Remarque, from *All Quiet on the Western Front*
- Mohandas K. Gandhi, from *Hind Swaraj*
- J. M. Keynes, from *The End of Laissez-Faire*
- Lenin on the Bolshevik seizure of power
- Excerpts from the speeches of Juan Perón
- Adolf Hitler, excerpt from *Mein Kampf*
- George C. Marshall, "The Marshall Plan," 1947
- Winston Churchill, the "Iron Curtain" speech
- Harry S Truman, The Truman Doctrine, 1947
- Nikita Krushchev, Speech to the Twenty–Second Congress of the Communist Party, 1962

- Mao Zedong, "A Single Spark can Start a Praire Fire"
- Deng Xiaoping on capitalism
- Frantz Fanon, from *The Wretched of the Earth*
- Jomo Kenyatta, from *Facing Mt. Kenya*
- Kname Nkumah, from *I Speak of Freedom*
- Palestinian Declaration of Independence, 1988
- Nelson Mandela, from "The Struggle is My Life" from *Freedom, Justice and Dignity for All South Africa*
- United Nations Delaration of Human Rights, 1948
- François Mitterand, The Reconciliation of France and Germany," 1990

Please see the Primary Source CD-ROM or additional sources related to this chapter.

READ ON

The opening story comes from O. A. J. Pennikoff, *Bushido: The Anatomy of Terror* (1973). There are a vast numbers of books available on the first and second world wars. Good starting points for World War I include I. Beckett, *The Great War 1914–1918.* (2001), an overview of the military, political, social, economic and cultural aspects of the conflict; M. Gilbert, *First World War* (1996); N. Ferguson, *The Pity of War: Explaining World War I* (2000), a controversial revisionist account of the war; and P. Fussell, *The Great War and Modern Memory* (2000), a cultural history of the western reaction to the struggle and to its legacy. Probably the best introduction to World War II is W. Murray and A. R. Millet, *A War to be Won: Fighting the Second World War, 1937–1945* (2000). Also solid is G. Weinberg, *A World at Arms: A Global History of World War II* (1995).

I drew on F. L. Allen's *The Lords of Creation* (1996) for the background to the Depression. S. L. Engermann and R. E. Gallman, eds., *The Cambridge Economic History of the United States*, vol. III (1996) is searching and comprehensive.

The historiography of the Cold War has not surprisingly proven ideologically contentious. J. L. Gaddis, *The Cold War: A New History* (2005) is a reasonably balanced and well-written overview that emphasizes the relationship between the superpowers, the US and the USSR. O. A. Westad, *The Global Cold War : Third World Interventions and the Making of Our Times* (2005), focuses instead on the global and Third World dimensions of the conflict and their complicated connections to decolonization. I found H. Thomas, *Armed Truce* (1986) helpful. A convenient introduction decolonization itself is D. Rothermund, *The Routledge Companion to Decolonization* (2006), which presents both a detailed chronology and narrative, and thematic analysis. P. Duara, *Decolonization (Rewriting Histories)* (2004) provides significant excerpts from the writings of major leaders of decolonization movements and presents the process from the perspective of the colonized.

Books on "The New World Order" tend to range from the partisan to the paranoid, but A. Slaughter, *A New World Order* (2005) is an original if dense reconceptualization. On the EU, see J. McCormick, *Understanding the European Union: A Concise Introduction* (third edition, 2005). For a broad examination of the role of war and military power in shaping world orders, see J. Black, *War and the World: Military Power and the Fate of Continents, 1450–2000* (2000).

CHAPTER 29

The Pursuit of Utopia: Civil Society in the Twentieth Century

In war, atrocities breed atrocities. Chinese nationalist soldiers execute fellow countrymen accused of collaboration with the Japanese after the "Rape of Nanjing" in 1937.

A few days before Christmas, 1937, John Rabe found women and children, "their eyes big with terror" huddled on the grass of his garden in Nanjing. "Their one hope is that I, 'the foreign devil,' will drive the evil spirits away." Outside, rotting corpses were piling up in the streets—girls savagely raped before being shredded with bayonets or shot in the back while fleeing, babies skewered, men and women torched or hacked to death, with a ferocity Rabe found impossible to understand. The victims of the atrocities could not believe their assailants were fellow human beings. But the perpetrators were not evil spirits. They were Japanese soldiers.

CHINA

Rabe was the director of the headquarters in China of the German engineering firm, Siemens. He was also a member of the Nazi Party and an admirer of Adolf Hitler, whom he mistook for a savior of his country and a leader of moral integrity. By Christmas Eve, 650 refugees were crammed into Rabe's house and grounds. When he walked by they fell to their knees, in thanks and entreaty. Within a few weeks, more than 250,000 fugitives filled the International Safety Zone that Rabe and a few of his European friends—missionaries and businessmen—had set up to protect noncombatants from torture, rape, assault, and murder. He had to be constantly vigilant to save their lives. Japanese soldiers continually raided the zone. The Japanese authorities, while nominally respecting the zone, were "content," Rabe wrote, "to let the refugees starve to death."

In March, when the atrocities had ebbed, Rabe returned to Germany and wrote to Hitler, "fulfilling a promise made to my friends in China that I would inform you of the sufferings of the Chinese people." A few days later, the Nazi secret police arrested him. The Japanese were Germany's allies, and Hitler would not hear a word against them.

If scholars' calculations are correct, 250,000 people died at Nanjing in the six to eight weeks from December 13, when Japanese soldiers received orders to kill all prisoners of war. Rabe had witnessed one of the most intense massacres in history. Japanese soldiers who took part in the slaughter—such as Nagatomi Hakudo, who remembered "smiling proudly as I . . . began killing people"—subsequently found their own behavior impossible to understand. But although the **Rape of Nanjing**, as the episode came to be called, was a particularly conspicuous orgy of atrocities, it was by no means unusual. The most terrifying paradox of the twentieth century was that all the advances of the era—in science, in technology, in the spread of education and knowledge, in the increased availability of information, and in progress toward worldwide material prosperity—did nothing to avert moral catastrophe.

The paradox does, however, make a kind of hideous, warped sense. For people who experienced the unprecedented rate of progress in the twentieth century, **utopia** seemed attainable. A world improved or perfected seemed within reach. Massacre was just one way to get there: recreating a world without enemies. The new power of technology at the disposal of governments constituted an opportunity to reforge society for the better. The social history of the twentieth century is largely a story of utopian projects that failed, as chaos undid plans and overpowered progress. If there is a global theme in the social history of the twentieth century, this is it. Utopian ambitions inherited from the past seemed briefly realizable, before disillusionment or realism set in.

• • • • •

THE CONTEXT OF ATROCITIES

The twentieth century was a century of atrocities, partly because it was a century of war. War is morally brutalizing. Wartime censorship, which portrays atrocities as excesses of the other side, often conceals that fact from the public. Propaganda, ably supplemented by filmmakers, concentrates on the ennobling effects of combat—the incidents of heroism and self-sacrifice, the growth of camaraderie. The corrupting effects of war on character—the corrosion of decency, the demonizing of the foe—are omitted from the picture.

War stimulates massacres because it blinds people to their enemies' humanity. As we have seen (see Chapter 28), when the Sino-Japanese War started in 1931, the belligerent peoples were inclined to be prejudiced in each other's favor—to see themselves as fraternally linked. But by the time of the Nanjing outrages, Chinese called the Japanese "evil spirits," while Japanese called the Chinese "insects" or "pigs" or—in the case of women enslaved for military brothels—"public urinals." When they engaged in "killing practice," Japanese soldiers, according to their own later accounts, were taught to regard a Chinese victim as "something of rather less value than a dog or a cat."

Along with war, ideological and intercommunal hatreds stimulated horrifyingly inhuman behavior, which war conditions commonly made worse. During the Second World War, the Nazi regime consciously set out to exterminate groups the Nazis blamed for the ills of society: Gypsies, homosexuals, and, above all, Jews. The murder of millions of Jews, which historians have termed the **Holocaust**, was the most chilling example, because of the scale of the **genocide**, the systematic way in which people were killed, and the cold-blooded industrialization of the killing process. Once they had perfected the method, the killers herded Jews into death camps and drove them into sealed rooms where they gassed them to death. Pointless cruelty accompanied the Holocaust: millions enslaved, starved, and tortured in so-called scientific experiments. The weak and helpless were not spared. On the contrary, the

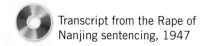

Transcript from the Rape of Nanjing sentencing, 1947

Nazi vision of utopia demanded a world from which the weak had been gutted out and discarded.

No case of genocide quite matched the Nazi campaign against the Jews, but that was not for want of other attempts. After the Second World War, German minorities were on the receiving end of campaigns of annihilation: expelled from Czechoslovakia and Poland, massacred or exiled by the Soviet Union. Massacres motivated by the desire to exterminate entire communities occurred, at intervals across the century, in Turkish Armenia, in Crimea and Chechnya in the former Soviet Union, in Iraqi Kurdistan, in Rwanda and Burundi in Central Africa, in Bosnia-Herzegovina and Kosovo in the former Yugoslavia, in southern and western Sudan, in Amazonian Brazil, in Burma, Congo, Nigeria, and other flashpoints of ethnic tension shown on Map 29.1. Other projects for purging the world of unwanted groups included the attempted extermination of political and economic communities. We can recall the ideologically driven massacres perpetrated by the dictatorships of Stalin in Russia and Mao Zedong in China, which equaled or excelled in scale anything the Nazis did, and the comparable efforts in the 1970s of Pol Pot's Khmer Rouge in Cambodia (see Chapter 28).

The history of twentieth-century atrocities showed that no level of civilization, education, or military discipline immunized people against barbarism, whenever war or fear ignited hatred and numbed compassion. During the Second World War, for instance, thousands of normally decent citizens of the German Reich, who prided themselves on their civilized attainments—including artists and intellectuals, who loved classical music and frequented museums—took part in massacres of Jews and other alleged enemies, "deviants," and "subversives" without apparently realizing that they were doing anything wrong. Scientists and physicians in Germany and Japan experimented on human guinea pigs to discover more efficient methods of killing. On a lesser scale, atrocities accompanied wars, including those fought by soldiers who were raised in democracies and relatively well educated in humane values. In the Vietnam War, for instance, in March 1968, nice, homey American boys, who loved Mom and apple pie, massacred more than 300 noncombatant peasants, women, and children in the village of Mai Lai, under the influence of fear-induced adrenalin. During war in Iraq in 2004, pictures of American soldiers of both sexes amusing themselves by torturing and sexually abusing Iraqi prisoners, many of whom proved to be innocent noncombatants, shocked the world. The perpetrators of these outrages did not even have the excuse of being depraved by combat. They were prison guards. Like some of the Japanese in Nanjing, they actually posed for souvenir photographs, smiling as they performed vicious and degrading acts.

The Holocaust. At the Nordhausen concentration camp, the Nazis spent nothing to build and operate the gas chambers they used in other camps. The inmates at Nordhausen—cataloged as too weak or ill to be useful as slave labor—were left to starve to death. In an attempt, apparently, to leave no witnesses, guards massacred the survivors when U.S. troops approached the camp in April, 1945. This photograph shows some of the more than 3,000 corpses the Americans found, but a few of the inmates were still alive.
Art Archive/Picture Desk, Inc./Kobal Collection.

 Eyewitness account of genocide in Armenia, 1915

THE ENCROACHING STATE

For most of the century, states seemed to be the most likely agents of utopia, because they controlled most resources and exercised most power—more power and more resources than ever before in history. States did not forfeit citizens' trust, even when they abused it. For the first three-quarters or so of the century, there seemed no alternative to the state as the shaper of society. Even in the liberal West, which had inherited from the Enlightenment the doctrine of social and economic

MAP 29.1

Genocides and Atrocities, 1900–Present*

☠ location and date with approximate
number of people killed

— political borders, 2006

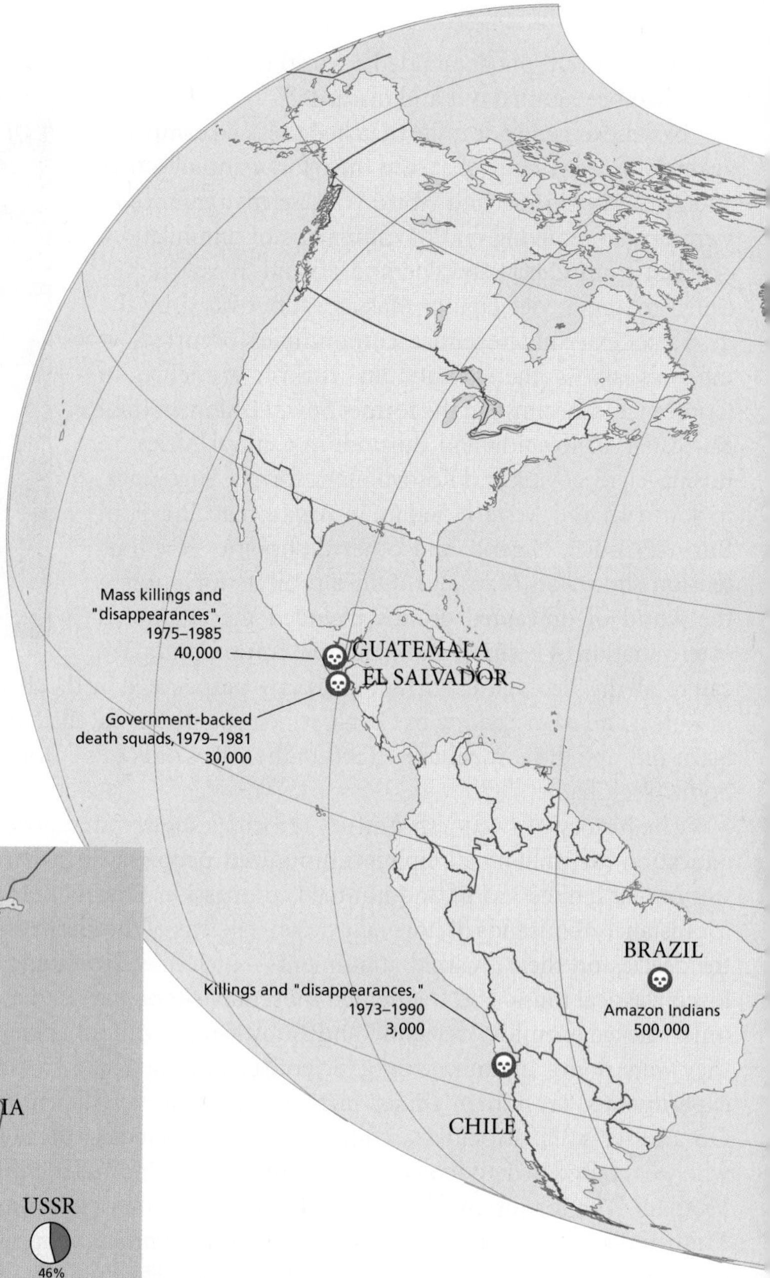

The Holocaust

■ extent of German Reich, 1942

□ under German occupation, 1942

▼ concentration camp

60,000 estimated number of Jews murdered in Holocaust

◐ percentage of total population of Jews
murdered in Holocaust

— political borders, 1939

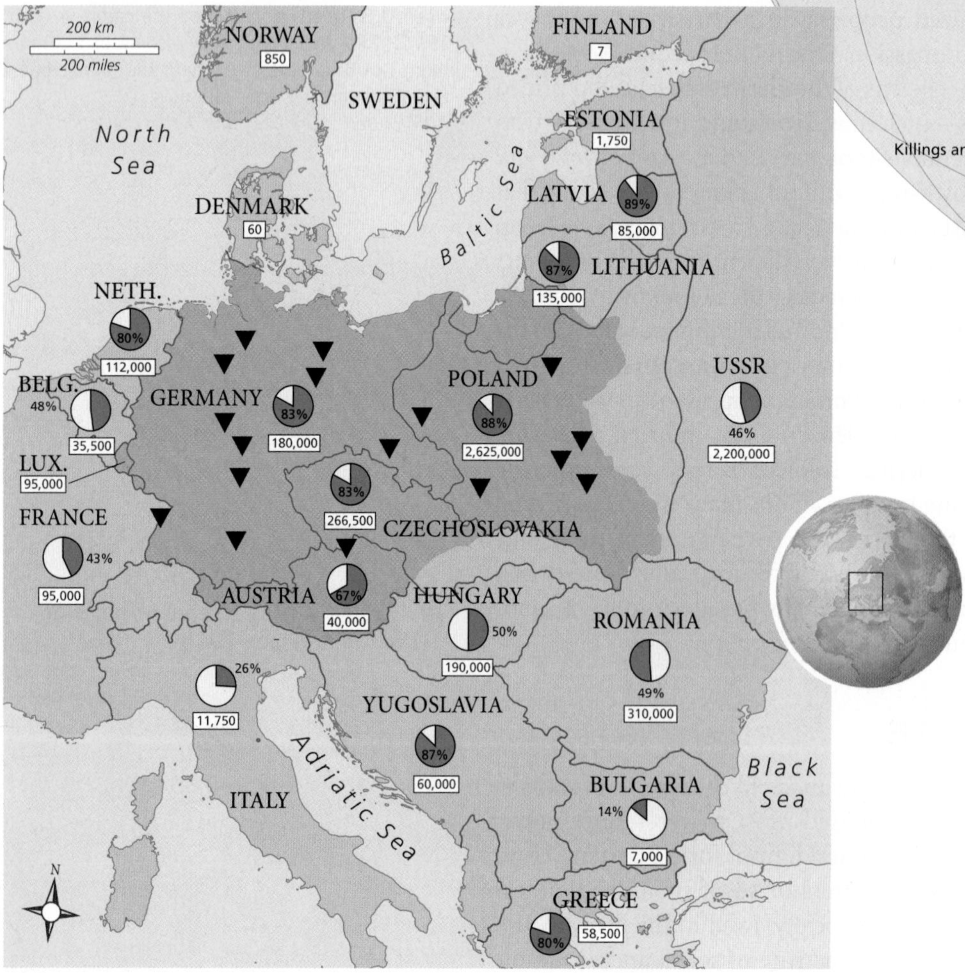

Mass killings and
"disappearances",
1975–1985
40,000

GUATEMALA
EL SALVADOR

Government-backed
death squads,1979–1981
30,000

BRAZIL ☠

Killings and "disappearances,"
1973–1990
3,000

Amazon Indians
500,000

CHILE

200 km
200 miles

NORWAY
850

FINLAND
7

SWEDEN

ESTONIA
1,750

North
Sea

Baltic Sea

LATVIA
89%
85,000

DENMARK
60

87%
135,000
LITHUANIA

NETH.
80%
112,000

BELG.
48%
35,500

GERMANY
83%
180,000

POLAND
88%
2,625,000

USSR
46%
2,200,000

LUX.
95,000

FRANCE
43%
95,000

83%
266,500
CZECHOSLOVAKIA

AUSTRIA
67%
40,000

HUNGARY
50%
190,000

ROMANIA
49%
310,000

Black
Sea

26%
11,750

YUGOSLAVIA
87%
60,000

Adriatic Sea

ITALY

BULGARIA
14%
7,000

GREECE
80%
58,500

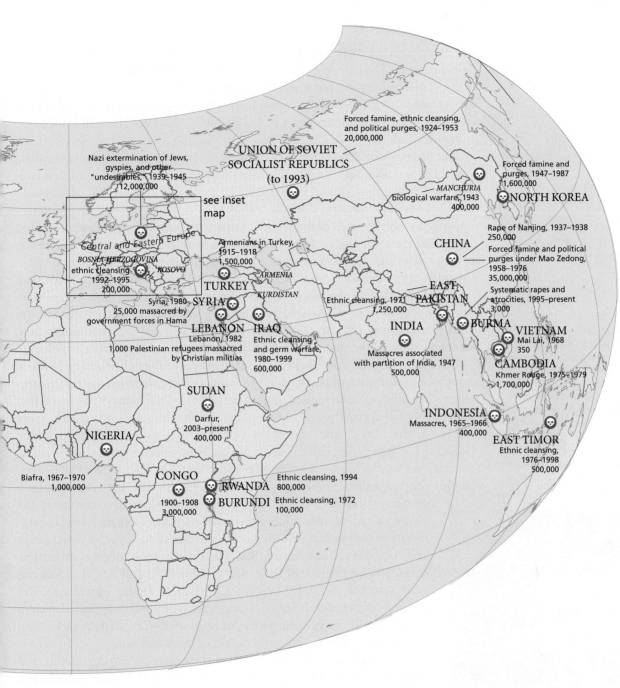

Nazi extermination of Jews, gyspies, and other "undesirables," 1939–1945 12,000,000

see inset map

Central and Eastern Europe

BOSNIA-HERZEGOVINA ethnic cleansing 1992–1995 200,000

KOSOVO

UNION OF SOVIET SOCIALIST REPUBLICS (to 1993)

Forced famine, ethnic cleansing, and political purges, 1924–1953 20,000,000

MANCHURIA biological warfare, 1943 400,000

Forced famine and purges, 1947–1987 1,600,000

NORTH KOREA

Armenians in Turkey, 1915–1918 1,500,000

ARMENIA

TURKEY

KURDISTAN

CHINA

Rape of Nanjing, 1937–1938 250,000

Forced famine and political purges under Mao Zedong, 1958–1976 35,000,000

Syria, 1980 25,000 massacred by government forces in Hama

SYRIA

LEBANON   IRAQ

Lebanon, 1982 1,000 Palestinian refugees massacred by Christian militias

Ethnic cleansing and germ warfare, 1980–1999 600,000

Ethnic cleansing, 1971 1,250,000

EAST PAKISTAN

INDIA

Massacres associated with partition of India, 1947 500,000

Systematic rapes and atrocities, 1995–present 3,000

BURMA   VIETNAM

Mai Lai, 1968 350

CAMBODIA

Khmer Rouge, 1975–1979 1,700,000

SUDAN

Darfur, 2003–present 400,000

NIGERIA

Biafra, 1967–1970 1,000,000

CONGO

1900–1908 3,000,000

RWANDA

BURUNDI

Ethnic cleansing, 1994 800,000

Ethnic cleansing, 1972 100,000

INDONESIA

Massacres, 1965–1966 400,000

EAST TIMOR

Ethnic cleansing, 1976–1998 500,000

*This map does not purport to be comprehensive, but to convey the global nature of genocides and other atrocities in the twentieth century.

laissez-faire (see Chapter 22), the state took on ever more responsibility, for education, health, and welfare. National insurance schemes and public education systems became symbols of modernity. They consumed huge proportions of national budgets, because their costs were uncontrollable. National insurance, which aimed to pay for sickness and retirement by state management of compulsory contributions, never succeeded in paying for itself, and, wherever it was tried, new schemes sooner or later replaced it. Increasingly, taxation paid for health care and pensions.

Social policy had to balance a growing demand for freedom with the need to regulate increasingly complex and unwieldy societies. Planning—which meant, in effect, a huge surrender of individual liberty to public power and an extension of

James Cook, from *Captain Cook's Journal During his First Voyage Round the World.*

When anti-smoking campaigns began in the West in the 1970s, they were often privately funded and directed against the tobacco industry's own messages. Increasingly, as evidence accumulated that smoking undermined health, governments took over, combating smoking first with taxation and public health campaigns, then with outright prohibitions on smoking in public. In the mid-twentieth century, smoking was an almost universal indulgence. By the early twenty-first century in the United States, Canada, and parts of Western Europe, smokers had become a persecuted minority, forced to practice their habit furtively and in shame.

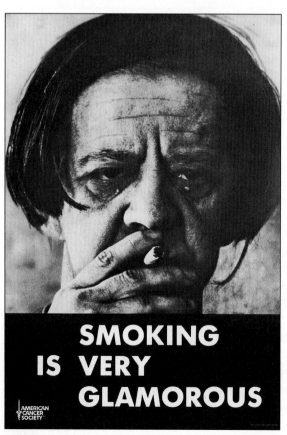

SMOKING IS VERY GLAMOROUS

state interference into the nooks and crannies of private life—seemed an irresistible cure-all. The example of the United States, where federal initiatives helped to dispel the misery of the Great Depression of the 1930s, was encouraging. The influence of the economic thought of John Maynard Keynes (1883–1946), who argued for years for the "end of laissez-faire," was important and, for some governments, decisive (see Chapter 28).

The Second World War (1939–1945) also encouraged regimentation and collectivism. The war accustomed citizens to take orders, produce by command, and consume under rationing. President Franklin D. Roosevelt (1882–1945) was able to control American industry. Canada and Britain acquired command economies almost as heavily regulated as those under fascism and communism. Peace eased but did not end these conditions. In some European countries and Japan, rationing was actually stricter after the war than during it. Emergency repairs after the Second World War renewed government power. Everyone took it for granted that governments, with the help of agencies the victorious Allies established, would get devastated economies back to work. In most of Europe, governments nationalized major industries on which the economic infrastructure depended, such as transport, communications, and energy supply. Even states that did not adopt communism applied such measures.

Medicine and schooling illustrate best the effects of the politicization of social issues. Wherever states got involved in providing health care, the results were spectacular. Compulsory, state-funded immunization ended the rapacious diseases that had regularly killed children, including polio, measles, mumps, and rubella. As we shall see in the next chapter, many major killing and maiming diseases, which affected all age groups, were controlled and even eliminated, not only in rich countries, but across the world. Health education, combined with fiscal measures, changed people's habits. Smoking—a universal relaxation in the early twentieth century—became a pariah activity in many Western countries by the century's end. Many addictive stimulants and narcotics increased in popularity as they became relatively cheap—including, especially, marijuana and coca-derived substances. But governments took tough countermeasures. Toward the end of the century, publicly funded health campaigns even targeted alcoholic beverages and fatty foods, which adversely affected only a minority of consumers. Such campaigns appeared even in countries with no historic problems associated with these kinds of food and drink, including Chile and Canada, China and India.

Above all, the state got increasingly involved in paying doctors and running hospitals. Except for the United States, all rich countries acquired huge public health establishments. The results again were positive in one way. Millions of poor people were liberated from the fear of neglect. Life, for the seriously sick, ceased to be a privilege confined only to those who could pay for treatment. On the other hand, the costs of medical care spiraled out of control, and states struggled to pay the bills. Britain's National Health Service, for instance, established on a lavish scale after the Second World War, and widely regarded as a model to follow, absorbed the biggest slice of the country's budget by the 1980s. No country was too poor to have a public health policy and at least some public funding for medical care.

Meanwhile, under the growing influence of the state, the nature of education changed. Governments' priorities for schools were concerned with solid citizenship and economic efficiency. Like democracy, education was the cure-all of a former age—a means to a dreary sort of utopia. It would transform dangerous masses into easily influenced, collaborative patriots.

It would guarantee stability and sustain progress. Theorists and a few practitioners in elite institutions pursued grander projects—such as enhancing the pleasure students take in life, acquainting them with their cultural heritage, and stimulating their critical responses. For most children, these remained postponed ideals. In the twentieth century, coarser values replaced them. The noblest aims to which governments aspired were curbing unemployment, manning the technology of the future, and keeping young criminals off the streets. More people got more education at greater cost than ever, yet almost everywhere parents and employers complained about the quality of the results. In practice, out-of-school education took up the slack: universities, in-work training, and continuing-education programs that enabled people to return to college at intervals during a working life.

No part of the world was exempt from the growth of "big government," but the United States experienced the phenomenon far less than most other countries. The reasons are clear. The world wars left American territory unscarred. The American economy never suffered from the restraints on development inflicted by the division of the world into primary and secondary producers. The United States always managed to perform both functions in a big way. Americans took seriously their perception of their country as the land of the free. Although eventually, in the 1960s, the federal government began to encourage public welfare programs, especially during Democratic presidencies, and although public budgets and bureaucracies continued to grow in the United States just as they grew everywhere in the world, America remained relatively less governed than other big countries. This fact was important in "the American century" in a world that looked increasingly to the United States for models to follow.

For a while in the third quarter of the century, however, the Scandinavian countries—Sweden, Denmark, Norway, Finland, and Iceland—were more widely admired, and the system they more-or-less shared looked like becoming the model for the world. Scandinavians favored liberal law-and-order policies with a welfare state and a mixed economy, heavily regulated and centrally planned. But the defects of the model soon became apparent. It created "Scandisclerosis" and "suicidal utopias." The former term referred to the way state regulation restrained business efficiency, while public ownership sapped the vigor of industry. The latter referred to the high suicide rates in "nanny states," where bureaucracy seemed to stifle individual initiative, and welfare provision cut the risk and zest out of life. Social engineering, however benevolent, could not deliver personal happiness. In the tawdry utopias modern architecture created (see Chapter 27), citizens recoiled from the dreariness of overplanned societies. People felt let down by progress and deceived by their leaders. By the 1980s, they began to lose faith in the viability of economic public sectors, as it became apparent to people all over the world that America's relatively underregulated economy was better at delivering prosperity.

Planning failed, not only because human beings instinctively love liberty but also because planners' assumptions were naïve. Societies and economies are chaotic systems, where unpredictable effects disrupt planners' expectations. So the four- and five-year plans that were produced almost everywhere at some time up to the 1970s were almost everywhere discarded. In the 1980s and 1990s, governments—even those nominally socialist—raced to shed nationalized industries and to make peace with market forces. The perfectly planned urban projects of the 1960s, which represented the fulfillment of the ideals of rationalist architects—creating functional, egalitarian, technically proficient environments—proved practically uninhabitable.

Failed planning. As this photograph of a street in Bucharest, the capital of Romania, illustrates, the collapse of communism in eastern Europe in 1989–1990 left grim legacies. The incompetence and rapacity of Nicolae Ceaucescu (1918–1989), Romania's communist dictator for more than 22 years, impoverished the country. Ceaucescu tore down much of Bucharest in a supposedly revolutionary program of urban planning. Unlike most of the other communist leaders in eastern Europe, he refused to yield power peacefully. Instead, he was overthrown and executed after a brief, but bloody, civil war in December, 1989. The debris from that struggle took years to clean up.

After a generation or so, they had to be demolished. At about the same time, the mixed economies and command economies favored in the postwar period were dismantled, deregulated, and restored to private enterprise. By the mid-1990s, private enterprise was responsible for more than 50 percent of output in Europe, even in formerly communist states. This was a change that swept the world. By the end of the century, only North Korea remained implacably hostile to the private sector.

This did not mean that bureaucracies ceased to grow. The balance between the public and private sector seemed impossible to get right. Whenever governments shifted responsibilities to the private sector, some communities and groups got left out of the benefits. Poverty gaps widened. Underclasses grew. Socially excluded and underprivileged communities bred crime and rebellion. More government spending had to help pay for the consequences. More state welfare agencies appeared to try to remedy the effects. Toward the end of the century, most governments faced rising crime rates and the threat of terrorism. Western governments exploited the threat by exaggerating it. Terrorism did represent a special kind of menace, for if terrorists were to get hold of nuclear, chemical, or biological weapons, they could wreak havoc. This became one of Hollywood's favorite plots and a scenario that Western governments abused to persuade citizens to forfeit liberties. In the early twenty-first century, terrorist-induced alarmism attained new heights, thanks to an entirely exceptional terrorist success that demolished the World Trade Center towers in New York and damaged the Pentagon in Washington, D.C. This was an unrepeatable attack, achieved with minimal weaponry—using razor blades to hijack aircraft that the terrorists used, in effect, as missiles. Meanwhile, terrorism took its place alongside the hazards of modern life that demanded to be policed at the expense and inconvenience of the public—along with crime, public drunkenness, drug addiction, and other antisocial behavior.

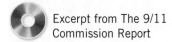
Excerpt from The 9/11 Commission Report

○ MAKING CONNECTIONS ○

THE ENCROACHING STATE

AREA OF CONCERN →	STATE ACTIONS →	CONSEQUENCES
Medicine	Compulsory state-funded immunization programs; health education; public-health campaigns focusing on smoking, food, drugs; establishment of hospitals, medical care paid for by government	Control and elimination of once virulent diseases (polio, measles, mumps, rubella, etc.); decline of smoking; increase in life expectancy; health care becomes available to poor, elderly, and previously neglected groups
Education	Public funding of education through high school and new emphasis on college education and continuing education through grants, funding	Higher rates of literacy, increased science and technology education leads to innovations, social transformations; unemployment declines as education increases
Welfare	Assistance for children and poor via direct payments, education, and health programs	Increased life expectancy, educational achievement, and employment rates among poor; improved standard of living
National Insurance	Financing of retirement by compulsory contributions from employers, employees	Improved standard of living for elderly; drastic drop in poverty levels compared to pre-1940 era, better health care through specialized medical programs for elderly (e.g., Medicare in United States)

In consequence, even after the cold war had ended, defense and internal security demanded more funds and more personnel. Public spending accounted for 25 percent of gross domestic product (GDP) in the world's seven richest countries in 1965, and 37 percent by 2000. The encroaching state, moreover, continued to press upon civil liberties, as policemen multiplied and surveillance became more intrusive. Nor could governments shed welfare responsibilities, once they had undertaken them, without alienating voters and leaving vulnerable citizens' health or welfare exposed. Britain's costly National Health Service, for instance, became a sacred cow. Public education authorities could not discard the schools they maintained. Their only remedy for criticisms of the education system was higher spending. State-funded workers' pensions became a barely affordable burden for many countries, because, as we shall see in the next chapter, life expectancy rose sharply in the late twentieth-century. But somehow, governments had to find ways to pay.

Terror alert. Secretary of Homeland Security Tom Ridge unveils a color-coded terrorism warning system on March 12, 2002, in Washington, D.C. Ridge said the nation was on yellow alert. The five-level system was in response to public complaints that broad terror alerts issued by the government since the September 11, 2001 attacks raised alarm without providing useful guidance. The vague categories—menacing without being informative—and the scary, angular graphics were part of the United States government's proclaimed "War on Terror," which justified the president in assuming, for an indefinite period, exceptional wartime powers of detention and surveillance that violated American traditions of civil liberties.

UNPLANNING UTOPIA: THE TURN TOWARD INDIVIDUALISM

Nonetheless, it is undeniable that in the last quarter or so of the century, the world turned away from social and economic planning, first toward a rival kind of utopianism, represented by confidence in **individualism** and freedom, then—when that seemed to fail, too—toward a search for a third way that would deliver both prosperity and social solidarity.

Marxists' explanations for the shift are worth hearing with respect, because Marxists have a profound need to explain the forms of radicalism with which they are out of sympathy. For them, the shift was economically determined. Like all revolutions, it accompanied a transition from one means of production to another: from industrial to postindustrial economies, from the energy age to the information age. It is true that the rise of information technology (see Chapter 28) created a major new source of wealth and empowered a new class of business people, distinguished by a distinctive mindset, numerate and imaginative. Equally, at about the same time, growing prosperity increased demand for service industries, which displaced manufacturing as the big money spinners in the global economy, and especially in the richest countries and communities. Individualism, therefore, according to the Marxist argument, re-arose as the ideology of a new "knowledge class," which now ran the world: the manipulators of information, who had replaced the puppeteers of production and the manipulators of the state. Or perhaps the demise of the industrial economy changed society because it also changed collective psychology. Because life seemed without purpose, no ideology seemed useful. Everyone could live for what they could get out of it—nothing more, nothing less. Frederic Jameson, the great exponent of this point of view, put it this way:

> As a service economy, we are . . . so far removed from the realities of production and work that we inhabit a dream world of artificial stimuli and televised experience: never in any previous civilization have the great metaphysical preoccupations, the fundamental questions of being and of the meaning of life, seemed so utterly pointless.[1]

Hippies. May Day in Vermont, 1971. One of the paradoxes of the behavior of so-called Hippies is that they venerated nature—even to the extent of celebrating ancient pagan traditions of nature worship such as May Day—but took chemical drugs to help them perceive nature's beauties. This group, snapped by hippy photographer Peter Simon, displays some characteristic features: spaced-out, empty looks, touchy-feely intimacy, and loose-fitting clothes in bright colors reminiscent of the lurid mental images some drugs induced.

The global turn toward conservatism may also have been connected with another weighty economic factor: inflation. From the perspective of economic history, inflation was the most marked feature of the twentieth century. At times, it galloped uncontrollably, attaining rates of several thousand percent a year in Germany in 1923, for example, when the central bank deliberately printed as much money as people seemed to want. But, at historically unprecedented levels, it was a constant feature of life wherever money circulated. This fact is inseparable from the huge expansion of both resources and demand, which is part of the subject of the next chapter. If, however, one single influence drove prices upward more than anything else, it was governments' spendthrift habits with the money supply. As the number of governments grew, thanks to decolonization, and utopian projects gobbled up cash, global money supply got out of control. The situation became intolerable in the 1970s. In October 1973, after another episode of warfare between Israel and its Arab neighbors (see Chapter 28), Islamic oil-exporting countries attempted to influence American support for Israel by raising their prices. This triggered worldwide inflation on an unprecedented scale. Governments only succeeded in controlling it by curtailing their ambitions, cutting expenditure, reducing borrowing, and reining in the money supply.

Deeper, longer-term influences were also at work. In part, the shift away from planning was a generational effect in the West. As the demographic consequences of the postwar baby boom began to grow, the tastes of a failed generation could be repudiated. Wartime solidarity was an emergency response for most of the societies that experienced it. It was bound to disappear into the generation gap that opened up in the 1950s and 1960s. As young people grew up without shared memories of wartime, they turned to libertarianism, existentialism, or mere self-indulgence. Youth could afford to defy parents because postwar economic recovery created plenty of well-paid work. Prosperous youth spent money in ways calculated to offend its elders and express its independence: on fashions, for instance, that were first extrovert, then psychedelic. The growth of the generation gap was measurable in the 1960s. Pop bands discarded their uniforms and grew their hair. Health statistics began to register the effects of sexual permissiveness, with epidemics of sexually transmitted disease and cervical cancer. The contribution or response of the Catholic Church—the world's biggest and most influential Christian communion—is not often acknowledged. But in the Second Vatican Council, which convened at intervals in the 1960s, the church relaxed its rules in favor of freedom. The council licensed liturgical pluralism, showed unprecedented deference to other religions, and compromised its structures of centralized authority by elevating the role of bishops to be closer to that of the pope and the role of the laity to be closer to that of the priesthood. There could be no clearer indication that individualism was reawakening. If the Church could not resist it, the state would not be able to either.

In extreme cases—and there were plenty of them in the 1960s and 1970s in the West—young rebels, alienated from the values of their elders, turned to violence. Urban guerrilla movements were never numerically strong but did wreak real havoc. They hoped that bombing, kidnapping, and shooting would spread terror, incite repression, and excite revolution. In Europe, they mounted spectacular operations against politicians, celebrities, businessmen, policemen, and servicepersonnel, without provoking the intended reactions. They were most successful in parts of Latin America. In Argentina in the 1970s, they provoked the authorities into horrifying countermeasures, involving the disappearance of at least 15,000 victims of abduction, torture, and murder by the army and police. In Brazil, from 1969 to 1973, the government waged war against a movement that specialized in kidnapping foreign diplomats. Uruguay's almost unbroken democratic tradition was suspended while the army broke the urban guerrillas. Even in these countries, however, outraged youth only succeeded in provoking reaction, never in launching revolution.

Remarkably, the generation gap opened almost as wide in communist countries as in the West. The failed revolutions that marked the coming-of-age of postwar youth in 1968 came nearest to success in Paris and Prague. Student revolutionaries on one side of the Iron Curtain denounced the crisis of capitalism, while those on the other called for a postcommunist "spring" or "thaw." In China, the ruling clique deflected youth rage into the Cultural Revolution (see Chapter 28). The revolutionaries' failures were part of a series of disillusioning experiences. In Russia, China, and other countries that communists had taken over, no relief followed for the sufferings of ordinary people, no end to the tyranny of small elites. In the rest of the world, capitalism was working: spreading prosperity, fomenting democracy, winning the approval of working-class voters. The Left switched to soft targets: sexism, racism, elitism, the remnants of colonialism, traditional morality.

The trends of the next generation, when voters swung Right, hair got shorter, fashion rebuttoned, and "moral majorities" found voice, were widely perceived as a reaction against "60s permissiveness." In reality, they represented the continuation in maturity of the projects of the young of the previous decade. Demands for personal freedom, sexual liberation, and existential self-fulfillment when one is young transform themselves naturally, when one acquires economic responsibility and family obligations, into policies of economic laissez-faire and less government. To "roll back the frontiers of the state" became the common project of those who rose to power in the West in the 1980s. Individual gratification—or, to use a widely favored euphemism, *fulfillment*—replaced broader codes of conduct and dominated many people's decision making: over whether to marry, for instance, whether to divorce, whether to procreate, how to occupy one's time.

The triumph of liberation became inseparable from sex in Western minds. The development of reliable methods of contraception, and of fairly reliable methods of protection against sexually transmitted diseases, equipped people—those who felt so inclined, at any rate—to lead undisciplined sex lives. Freedom to choose and change sexual partners proved incompatible, however, with the instinctive human tendency to feel sexual jealousy. Permissive sex subverted some of the collective loyalties on which Western society traditionally relied. Families periodically scrambled by sexual betrayal or boredom became typical of almost every Western society. Even in the small nuclear families characteristic of Western society, individualism had a dissolving effect, as family activities diminished, and family members began to eat separately and scatter for entertainment to personal video monitors, computer screens, or friendships outside the household. In the United States, fewer than one child in five was born outside wedlock in 1980. Only

Cultural Revolution. Chinese citizens march in formation through the streets of Beijing while displaying a large portrait of Communist Party Chairman Mao Zedong (1893–1976), during the Cultural Revolution in the 1960s. The photograph is ludicrously posed, with a carefully contrived balance of workers' and peasants' costumes that seems to come straight out of a theatrical wardrobe.

Warped Westernization? Brides and grooms standing in lines as the Unification Church weds 790 couples in a single mass ceremony in the 1970s in Seoul, South Korea. The sect, founded by Sun Myung Moon, and popularly called "the Moonies," was among the most successful new religious cults of the day. Its Christian roots were, at best, remote. Moon, not Jesus, was its messiah, and his followers believed him to be divine. The Unification Church exploited the appeal of Western fashion but suppressed individualism.

20 years later, the number had risen to a third. By the end of the century, two-fifths of American marriages ended in divorce. What had once been normal—parents and children sharing the same household—became exceptional. Less than a quarter of households in the United States conformed to this pattern by the end of the century.

In the rapidly urbanizing environments of the world, family stability could not thrive as it had done in the rural communities from which the new town dwellers came. Street children crowded the streets of the developing world, becoming fodder for journalism and films, and the recruits of criminal gangs, warlords' armies, insurgents, guerrillas, and terrorists. The influence of Western lifestyles that movies, music, and broadcasting spread around the world created generation gaps everywhere. In Japan, commentators called the rootless young "new humans"—so profound was their rejection of traditional values and behavior. But the same sort of phenomenon could be observed everywhere. In the Muslim world, the young expected more freedom to choose marriage partners and careers. In Korea and parts of Africa and the Americas, millions joined new religions and cults. Of course, every change set off reactions and, while gaps opened between generations, chasms opened within them.

COUNTER-COLONIZATION AND SOCIAL CHANGE

The world shrank. Ever-cheaper, ever-faster transport technologies meant that almost anyone could go almost anywhere. Long-range migration became possible for many of the poor of the world. The huge and growing disparities in wealth between the West and the rest drew migrants. Wars, tyrannies, and political instability drove them. In the second half of the twentieth century, the population boom in colonial and ex-colonial territories reversed one of the long-standing demographic trends of the past. The long flow of migration out of Europe into other parts of the world ended. Instead, **counter-colonization** began. Birth rates in the former imperial "mother countries" declined. Labor from the rest of the world filled the gap.

It happened quickly, in step with decolonization (see Chapter 28). In 1948, the first black Jamaicans to arrive in Britain were astonished to see white men doing menial work. Immigrants to Britain from the West Indies numbered tens of thousands by 1954. Those from India reached the same number the following year, and those from Pakistan two years later. By the end of the century, Britain had more than 2 million Muslims, and France had more than 4 million. The Netherlands, with a total population of only 18 million, had nearly 1 million immigrants from its colonies and former colonies in Indonesia and the Caribbean.

The exchange of population was most intense, at first, between former colonies and their European mother countries, but it soon became more general, as migrants shifted from relatively poor, overpopulated parts of the world to relatively rich, underpopulated regions (see Map 29.2). Migrants from Latin America and Puerto Rico became the largest minority in the United States—over 36-million strong by the early twenty-first century. This was a form of counter-colonization, since the United States had seized the territories most affected, California and the Southwest, from Mexico during its empire-building in the nineteenth century (see Chapter 25) and had exercised informal empire over much of Latin America for most of the twentieth century. In other places, the link between imperialist pasts and present immigration patterns was barely discernible. In Italy, Spain, and Scandinavia, most of the immigrants came from outside the old imperial territories. In the Netherlands, the numbers of Moroccans and Turks equaled or exceeded those of immigrants from former Dutch colonies. In Germany, whose overseas empire had disappeared in 1918, and Switzerland, which had never had an empire, Turks formed the biggest category of guest workers. The Philippines had been an American colony, but came to supply labor—much of it illegal—for many European countries.

Intercommunal tensions took on a new form, as communities of widely differing culture adapted to life alongside each other. One of the most remarkable changes of the late twentieth century was the way racism became socially and politically unacceptable in the West. In part, perhaps, this was another outcome of the Second World War. The Nazis had been racists, who regarded black people and Jews, in particular, as among the "subhuman" groups suitable for exploitation or extermination. The defeat of Nazism was therefore a victory for intercommunal pluralism and coexistence. The black and Asian soldiers who fought for Britain, France, and the United States demonstrated their credentials for equality. In part, too, the decline of racism was an inevitable consequence of scientific progress. The pseudoscience that justified the racism of the nineteenth century was discredited in the twentieth.

Nevertheless, it took a long time to dismantle the legacy of racism and to convince prejudiced people to accept and respect new circumstances and new science. The United States was the critical battleground, partly because America came to lead the world in just about everything, and partly because the United States, with its huge black minority, typified the problems. Some states of the Union had a history of exploiting and persecuting black people, and, in the mid–twentieth century, antiblack prejudice was still widespread in white society. Beginning in the 1940s, African Americans fought a long series of legal cases, backed by political movements that organized demonstrations—especially those led by the Rev. Martin Luther King (1929–1968)—and influenced voters, to enshrine the principal of equality in the law. Only in the 1960s, thanks to unremitting pressure from the federal courts and the administrations of Presidents John F. Kennedy (1917–1963) and Lyndon B. Johnson (1908–1973), did major breakthroughs take place. The federal government forced reluctant and resisting states to desegregate schools, outlaw whites-only privileges and facilities, and dismantle devices to stop black people's access to the right to vote. By the end of the century, it was still not clear that efforts to redress racial inequalities had gone far enough. Urban ghettoes and pockets of rural poverty remained. So, in consequence, did inequalities in education, because in America public education was locally funded.

Abolition in 1961 of the "white Australia" policy, which had restricted immigration to Australia to persons of European descent, was another landmark. Migration to the country became open to people of every hue. Racial discrimination was outlawed in all European countries by the end of the century. South Africa, however, was a sticking point. Its ruling class was white, and most white South Africans, isolated from the intellectual changes that had discredited racism in most of the

Immigrant community. A woman leaves a Turkish clothing shop in Berlin's Kreuzberg district, which has been called "little Istanbul." In 1961, the governments of West Germany and Turkey signed an agreement that allowed Turks to come to Germany as guest laborers. Many put down roots and never left. Today, Germany's Turkish community numbers over 2.5 million—the biggest minority group in the country.

 Martin Luther King, Jr., *Letter from Birmingham Jail*

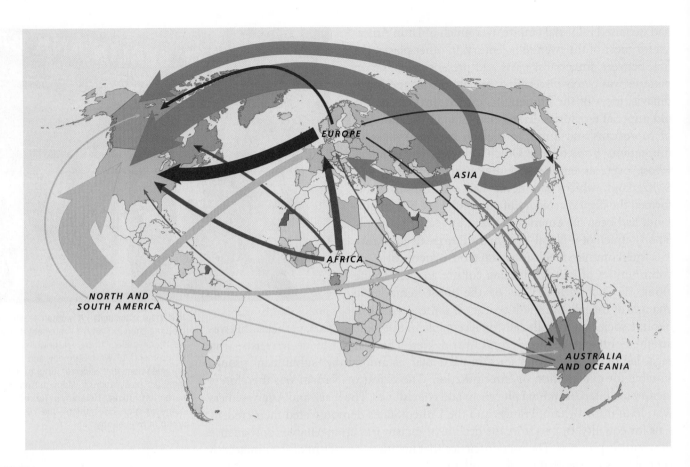

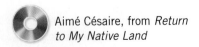

MAP 29.2

Percentage of Noncitizen Population, ca. 2005

- greater than 40%
- 18%–40%
- 8%–17%
- 2%–7%
- less than 2%

International migration trend since 1990 (arrow width reflects number of migrants)

→ North and South American immigration
→ European immigration
→ Asian immigration
→ African immigration
→ Australia and Oceania immigration

Aimé Césaire, from *Return to My Native Land*

rest of the world, clung to an outdated conviction that black and white people should be consigned to exclusive spheres of *separate development*, a system that in practice supported white privilege. Increasingly, however, it became apparent that it was wiser for white South Africans to conserve their wealth and sacrifice their political power, rather than risk both in a protracted conflict and potentially catastrophic revolution. In the early 1990s, South Africa abandoned the policy of separate development. Black people were admitted to equality of rights, and a largely black political party assumed power peacefully, without either victimizing white South Africans or causing serious economic dislocation.

In response to unresolved tensions, people fell back on a reworked sense of their own identity. New forms of black identity were, perhaps, the most conspicuous example. Early in the twentieth century, Afro-Cuban scholars in newly independent Cuba began to treat black languages, literature, art, and religion on terms of equality with white culture. Coincidentally, white musicians discovered jazz, and white primitivist artists began to esteem and imitate African "tribal" art. In 1916, in the United States, the Jamaican immigrant Marcus Garvey launched the slogan, "Africa for the black peoples of the world." The idea that black culture embodied values superior to those of white culture was the next phase. It emerged during the 1920s in the work of a Cuban generation, of whom the critic Juan Marinello and the poet Nicolás Guillén were perhaps the most influential. The idea became a movement, spreading wherever black people lived—and, on its way, transforming the self-consciousness of those who were still under colonial rule or suffering under social inequalities. In French West Africa in the 1930s, Aimé Césaire and Léon Damas became brilliant spokesmen for the black self-pride they called **Négritude**.

African independence movements gained strength in consequence; so did civil rights movements in countries like South Africa and the United States, where black people were still denied equality under the law. In the late twentieth century, when those battles had been more-or-less won, the struggle continued against racial prejudice and remaining forms of social discrimination against black people in predominantly white countries. The black consciousness movement in the United States was a case in point, encouraging the rediscovery of African roots and even of African allegiances. "Philosophically and culturally," said the Black Muslim leader who called himself Malcolm X in 1964, "we Afro-Americans need to 'return' to Africa." Rastafarianism, a movement that identified Ethiopia as the spiritual homeland of black Americans, became popular in the same period—often to the puzzlement of the Ethiopians themselves.

There was still no "master narrative" of history to rival the old, white-devised, "Eurocentric" account that almost every school curriculum taught. Black scholars had made attempts to create one, but never convincingly. Most attempts were based on obvious myths, such as the claim that black people were a lost tribe of Israel or "Nation of Islam." A more elaborate black version of global history followed, according to which Western civilization also originated in Africa and was transmitted via Egypt to ancient Greece. This seems, at best, an overstatement and oversimplification, but it is a sign of the vigor of the *Africanist* critique of our traditional picture of the world. Meanwhile, the scholarly world has come to accept that *Homo sapiens*, the species to which all of us belong, originated in Africa and that we all have a common African ancestor. These ideas have helped to justify, as well as reflect, the beginnings of a shift in the distribution of world power toward a more equitable balance, after the white, Western hegemony of the last couple of centuries (See "Going to the Source: Rival Black Voices in the Twentieth Century," pages 1056–1060).

The broader cultural impact of counter-colonization was enormous. Along with the effects of accelerated economic exchange and of increased opportunities for long-range travel by Westerners, migration changed the prevailing direction of cultural exchange. By the 1990s, in Leicester—the midmost city in England—people could listen to 40 hours a week of broadcasts in Gujerati, an Indian language. In Australia, the public broadcasting services operated in 78 languages. Vietnamese and North African restaurants abounded in Paris. Indian and Indonesian dishes had joined the national cuisines of Britain and Holland respectively.

But the spread of Asian influences in Westerners' tastes and thoughts also owed a lot to Western self-reevaluations. Under the weight of guilt about imperialism, postcolonial Westerners felt their own need for liberation from the legacy of the past. In the 1960s, travel to India became a compulsive fashion for Western intellectuals, along with Indian philosophy, mystical practices, music, and food. Political protesters in European and American streets in the same decade brandished copies of "little red books" containing selected thoughts of Mao Zedong. These fads waned, but Japanese, Chinese, and Indian art and thought became more important in the West for the rest of the century. Just as Western physicists looked to Daoism for help in understanding quantum mechanics (see Chapter 27), Western poets adopted the Japanese haiku form of verse. Zen became a widely revered, widely practiced intellectual tradition in the West. Buddhism, which had never attained the breadth of appeal of Christianity and Islam, began to attract converts in every clime. Black music and art, which had begun to influence the cultural

Négritude. Aaron Douglas (1900–1979) was one of the black painters of the Harlem Renaissance of the 1920s who sought to "hurdle several generations of experience at a leap." His work is full of reminiscences of slavery, torn between pride and resentment. *Building More Stately Mansions* reminds viewers of how slaves built monuments of civilization, from ancient Egypt to modern America.

Keith B. Richburg, from *Out of Africa: A Black Man Confronts Africa*

Fusion religion. Students' prayers at the Nizhoni school in New Mexico are supposed to contribute to "global consciousness" and world peace by "gathering knowing from within the self." The language in which the founder expresses her views draws on Zen Buddhism, traditional Navajo spirituality, and modern Western psychology.

National Organization of Women, Statement of Purpose, 1966

mainstream in America and Europe in the earliest years of the century, captured the admiration of the white world.

The prevailing values of the late twentieth century were appropriate to a postcolonial, multicultural, pluralistic era. The fragility of life in a crowded, shrinking world and a global village encouraged or demanded multiple perspectives, as neighbors adopted or sampled each other's points of view. Hierarchies of value had to be avoided, not because they are false but because they led to conflict. Relativism—the doctrine that each culture, and even individual, can choose appropriate norms, and therefore that no single set of norms is universally applicable (see Chapter 27)—displaced Westerners' confidence in the superiority of their own culture.

This doctrine, however, brought problems of its own. It made it hard to argue for the universality of human rights. It caused tension between cultural relativism and social norms. Festivals associated with majority religions had to be downplayed or modified to avoid offending minorities. Conflicts arose when migrants brought with them cultural practices and values that conflicted with the laws of their new homelands. In Islamic countries increasingly influenced by Sharia, or Islamic law, for instance, Westerners found that they could be prosecuted for using alcohol, or for not respecting traditional codes of modesty in dress and comportment for women. In the West, immigrants could not be allowed to continue some traditional practices, such as female circumcision among some African communities, or polygamy, or the marriage of minors. "Asian values" became a slogan to justify the use of the criminal law in, for example, Malaysia and Singapore, against practices the West tolerated, such as homosexuality and the recreational consumption of some drugs.

The idea that the law should treat everyone equally was so ingrained in the Western legal and philosophical tradition that it would have been unthinkable to allow people of different cultural backgrounds to be treated separately in the courts, or to be assigned separate jurisdictions, as had been usual, for instance, in the Middle Ages or under the Ottoman Empire. Most countries legislated for everyone to share the same civil rights, regardless of cultural background. Yet in practice, there were always cases of discrimination.

The status of women provoked some of the deepest difficulties. At the start of the century, no one expected uniformity in the way different cultures treated women. In the West, attention was riveted on the right to vote. In Islam, controversy centered on the rights of women in the home: to choose their husbands, for instance, or to equality with men under marriage law and in property rights. The First World War (1914–1918), however, launched a profound revolution in the role of women in Western society. In practice, women were left to take command of their lives while so many men were fighting at the front. French law created the fiction of "tacit consent" to sanction women having affairs when their husbands were absent. The dead of the First World War left gaps that societies were refashioned to fill. The young or old replaced the dead. Meritocracies replaced hereditary aristocracies in power. Women replaced men in the workplace. Before the war, only a few marginal countries gave women the vote. After it, Russia, Germany, and the United States rapidly enfranchised women. So did Britain and most other Western countries, albeit with qualifications. So did Japan and Turkey.

Women had to want to break out of domesticity, but it was not necessarily in their interests to do so. Many of those who competed with men suffered for it. They had to fight discrimination. To succeed, they had either to be *superwomen*—the term became current in the 1980s for a professional or working woman who managed her life so well that she could work outside the home and also discharge the traditional roles of wife and mother within it—or accept subordination. Although legislation to equalize opportunities became normal in the West in the last quarter of the century, it was never fully effective. Many women accepted lower wages or worse contractual terms than men in corresponding jobs, so that they could move in and out of work as their family responsibilities demanded. Some workplaces, especially in traditional male preserves, such as the armed forces, the police, the construction industry, and boardrooms in the industrial and financial sectors, had boyish or jock cultures, in which it was hard for women to fit and hard for men to adapt to their presence. Nevertheless, the cause of equality for women became one to which all governments and most people in the West committed, at least in theory.

In the second half of the century, Westerners expected people in other cultures to reevaluate women's roles in the same way. This did not seem an unattainable expectation. In some places outside the West, women led their countries: Israel, India, Sri Lanka, the Philippines, Nicaragua, Dominica, Argentina, and even Muslim countries—Pakistan, Turkey, Indonesia, Bangladesh—all had female heads of state or prime ministers between 1960 and 2000. But these were exceptional cases, and restraints on women's freedom or status remained in much of the world. China did not allow women to marry until they were 20 years old, and the growing preponderance of male over female children in China suggests that more infant girls than boys were killed or aborted. It is hard to imagine a fiercer form of discrimination than that. Opponents in Morocco and Iran interpreted government programs to establish female equality of employment and rights of freedom of marriage as infringements of parental rights and threats to the stability of home life. Female circumcision, a tradition respected in many African cultures, offended Western sensibilities. Women's educational opportunities remained restricted in much of the world outside the West, especially in rural areas. In India 87 percent of rural women were classed as illiterate at the end of the century. The corresponding figure for Bangladesh was 97 percent.

Problems associated with the status of women became acute with the ever more thorough mingling of cultures that accompanied the globe-crossing migrations of the late twentieth century. Conflicts arose over the legitimacy of arranged marriages and over the rights of divorcees. In disputes over the custody of children, for example, Western courts tended to favor mothers, Islamic courts fathers. The disputes that best illustrate the difficulty of resolving conflicts between normative laws and cultural diversity concerned the issue of appropriate dress for women and girls. In some Muslim cultures, traditions of modesty enjoined garments for women that, in various traditions, concealed most of the body and, in the most marked traditions, the whole of the face, from male eyes. To some Westerners, these rules seemed to be male-imposed infringements on female liberty—although many women freely supported them. The potential for conflict with Western laws arose in schools, where these traditional Muslim dress codes conflicted with school uniform regulations. In France, in the early twenty-first century, an apparently petty dispute divided society. The courts banned Muslim girls from wearing headscarves over their heads, on the rather unconvincing grounds that such scarves were religious symbols, incompatible with the hard-won secular nature of the French Republic.

Such disputes raised fundamental questions about the future of the world. The new multiracial societies that were taking shape in the West posed unprecedented problems. Existing populations became prey to alarmism about the adulteration of their identities or their cultures. Debate raged over whether integration in the host

The first woman to be elected an African head of state, President Ellen Johnston-Sirleaf of Liberia, photographed in November, 2005 just after her victory. Johnston gave a new twist to feminist arguments in favor of political empowerment for women by suggesting that women had special nurturing and peacemaking talents that made them more suited to leadership in the modern world than men.

Timeline of Women's Suffrage

New Zealand	1893
Australia	1902
Finland	1906
Norway	1913
Denmark, Iceland	1915
Soviet Union	1917
Canada	1918
Germany, Austria, Poland, Czechoslovakia	1919
United States, Hungary	1920
Mongolia	1924
United Kingdom	1928
Turkey	1930
Spain	1931
Brazil	1932
Indonesia	1941
France	1944
Italy	1945
China, India	1949
Mexico	1953
Kenya	1963
Switzerland	1971
South Africa	1994
Kuwait	2005

http://www.nzhistory.net.nz/politics/suffrage-worldtimeline

A 1950s DESIGNER KITCHEN

This stylish 1950s kitchen owes its sleek lines, sharp angles, and functional values to 1930s design. But the table is set for a new, postwar era. The family is small, and this room is their domain. The servants who once would have been part of this scene now have better jobs to go to.

Even the lighting is recessed for easy cleaning in a home without servants.

The refrigerator dominates—austerity has given way to abundance.

Formica™ was the era's wonder material for easily cleaned worktops.

Featureless fixed seating shows the continuing influence of designs from the 1930s.

How does the design of this kitchen comment on the changing status of Western families in the postwar period?

society—adopting its values, language, dress, manners, food, and even, perhaps, religion—best served newly arrived immigrants; or whether **multiculturalism** could work, in which people of divergent cultures agreed on a few core values, such as allegiance to the state and deference to democracy. Both responses had their disadvantages. Integration imposed on people's freedom. Multiculturalism, according to its opponents, created ghettoes and opened dangerous gaps in mutual understanding between neighboring communities. As the numbers of migrants began to reach critical thresholds, most governments in the West abandoned the language of multiculturalism and began to encourage integration. Everywhere, immigration controls tightened as governments lost confidence that multiculturalism could keep the peace. The Netherlands, where people had always prided themselves on hospitality toward immigrants, introduced stringent requirements that immigrants learn Dutch and submit to citizenship tests. Britain introduced allegiance tests. By the beginning of the twenty-first century, multiculturalism was beginning to look like another utopian dream, in danger of being discarded.

Confrontation. Pim Fortuyn (1948–2002) confronts protestors in Rotterdam during elections for the Dutch parliament. Fortuyn's Livable Netherlands Party had a distinctly anti-immigration agenda. Fortuyn was assassinated by a white Dutch environmentalist in May 2002, shortly after this photo was taken. The slogan, "Stop the Dutch Haider," alludes to Jurgen Haider of Austria, another populist politician who successfully campaigned for tough immigration controls. The way Fortuyn caresses the demonstrator was part of his public image. He was a homosexual who appeared on campaign with Moroccan boys as evidence that his opposition to immigration was not based on racial discrimination.

GLOBALIZATION AND THE WORLD ECONOMY

Not only were cultures getting more intermingled, so were economies. To a large degree, **globalization** meant the diffusion of elements of Western, and especially American, culture throughout the world, which is a subject for the next chapter. In a more generally accepted sense, it meant the increasing economic interdependence of a world of growing trade (see Map 29.3). In the last quarter of the century, in line with the worldwide withdrawal of the state from economic regulation and control, and the relaxation of controls on cross-border trade, businesses were able to drive a growing global economy by operating internationally with greater freedom than ever before.

This globalization might have been universally welcome. More trade and more intercommunication promoted peace, increased prosperity, and stimulated cultural exchange. The benefits of globalization, however, were unevenly distributed. A relatively few vast business corporations, most of them centered in the United States, handled a disproportionate amount of the world's economic activity. Shunting their assets around the world, those businesses evaded regulation by individual governments. Powerful countries—the United States above all—were able to demand free trade where it suited them but retain protective tariffs or subsidies for businesses they favored. To some extent, globalization perpetuated the old colonial pattern of the world economy—peasants and sweated labor in poor countries supplied rich ones with cheap goods, twisting the poverty gap into a poverty spiral.

Such defects, however, could probably be fixed. Some countries in East and southeast Asia demonstrated that they could exploit the opportunities of the global economy, that well-run communities could break out of underdevelopment into prosperity, and that globalization—if properly managed—could make them as rich as the West.

Japan's was the exemplary case. After its defeat in 1945, Japan was ready for a makeover. No other country endured the A-bomb. But the Japanese, who live on typhoon-lashed coasts and with seismic faults, are used to rebuilding after disaster. The psychological problems were harder to cope with. Japanese felt the shame of defeat more deeply than people of other cultures. Never before had their country surrendered or submitted to occupation. The emperor renounced his divinity. The people disclaimed superiority over other races and meekly accepted an American formula to remake their country into a democracy.

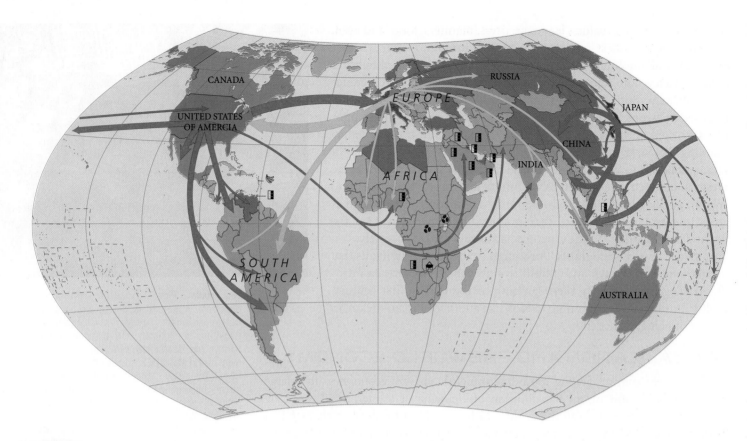

MAP 29.3

International Trade Flows, ca. 2004

Direct investment
(arrow width reflects level of investment)

→ from USA

→ from Europe

→ from Japan

Examples of countries reliant on a single export

🍌 bananas

☕ coffee

🛢 oil/petroleum

⛏ copper

Balance of trade (millions US$)

	over 30,000
	10,000–29,000 **Surplus**
	1000–9999
	0-999
	0–999
	1000-9999
	10,000–29,999 **Deficit**
	over 30,000
	data unavailable

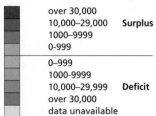

MAP EXPLORATION

www.prenhall.com/armesto_maps

The abandonment of militarism helped conserve investment for industry. In the 1950s, Japan's defense expenditure was less than 2 percent of its gross domestic product. Japan could now compete in trade for markets it had been unable to conquer in war. Even so, economic recovery was slow. The big corporations—which the Americans had abolished—returned in the 1950s and 1960s. Workers, imbedded in their firms, sacrificed an independent social life and became infused with corporate loyalty. This was not Western-style capitalism. But it worked. In 1960, a prime minister promised that incomes would double in ten years. He underestimated. Japan exceeded that target in 1967. In 1969, Japan overtook Germany to become the world's second biggest national economy. In the 1970s, despite the high price of oil, Japan caught up with the average European gross national product per capita. In 1985, Japan became the world's biggest foreign investor. Growth faltered toward the end of the century, but Japan remained in the premier league of world economic powers, with the highest per capita income in the world. The outreach of the Japanese economy—building components for European manufactures, assembling complex products from parts imported from all over the world, investing in just about every country, buying banks in the United States, founding industrial plants in Europe and Africa—was typical of the time.

Other economies in Asia followed Japan toward European or North American levels of prosperity. In South Korea in the 1960s, collaboration between governments and huge corporations launched spectacular economic growth: 9 percent a year, on average, over the following three decades. The country became one of the world's major manufacturers of cars and electronic gadgets. South Koreans completed their industrialization with the highest per capita debt burden in Asia, but they demonstrated that a country could industrialize itself out of poverty. By the end of the century, Japan and South Korea together—countries with only 3 percent of the world's population—accounted for 15 percent of its income and 10 percent of its trade.

Other "tiger" economies leaped in the same direction. The mid-to late 1960s and early 1970s were bonanza years in southeast Asia because American military involvement in Vietnam created a huge demand for supplies, leisure facilities for troops, and all the infrastructure of a wartime baseline. Not everyone benefited. Cambodia, on Vietnam's flank, got sucked into the conflict and began a long, bloody, and destructive civil war. But other neighbors were drenched in American investment. The biggest gainers were the already industrialized or industrializing economies of Japan, South Korea, Hong Kong, and Taiwan. In the mid-1960s, Singapore followed the same path. The accelerating trade of these tiger economies generated potential for investment all around the world. Most of their surplus money, however, went on projects around the shores of the Pacific. By 1987, the United States had an annual trade deficit of $60 billion with Japan. By then, the Pacific had displaced the Atlantic as the world's major arena of commerce. Communities and investments moved around the Pacific's shores with increasing ease and freedom.

Meanwhile, Latin American countries struggled to play catch-up with the rest of the West. The game began after the global economic crisis of the 1930s, when governments in Mexico, Argentina, and Brazil saw selective industrialization as a solution to the collapse of markets for their primary produce. As these policies spread through the continent, their effects proved mixed. Native industries continued to rely on machinery imported from North America and Europe. The falling prices of basic commodities made it hard for Latin American economies to accumulate capital to reinvest in industry. Mechanization made unemployment worse. In the 1960s and 1970s, partly in response to these problems, authoritarian regimes took over most of the region. In most cases, authoritarian rule only protracted the economic disappointments, straining some countries' relations with trading partners elsewhere in the world, subjecting others to new forms of dependency on United States and European corporate allies and creditors. The military junta that took over Argentina in 1976, for instance, proclaimed Argentina's commitment to "the Western and Christian world" but alienated allies by brutal repression at home and military adventurism abroad. For most Latin Americans, the period was impoverishing. Between 1980 and 1987, average personal income fell in 22 countries in the region. In Peru and Argentina, people were poorer on average in 1986 than they had been in 1970. Even Mexico, which stayed ostensibly democratic and avoided the worst of the region's economic problems, only survived by incurring massive debts—and defaulting on them in 1982.

Still, the more enmeshed the global economy got, the more opportunities multiplied. More countries, more people were able to squeeze a share of the benefits. China's was the most spectacular case. The Chinese economy registered annual growth rates of nearly 10 percent in the 1990s and the early years of the twenty-first century—enough, if those rates could be sustained, to enable China's economy to overtake that of the United States as the world's biggest by 2020. By 2004, more than 400 of the world's 500 biggest companies had branches or subsidiaries in China, overwhelmingly concentrated in regions bordering the

Shanghai in the early twenty-first century emblemized China's promise and perils. Skyscrapers symbolized the stunning growth rates that enabled China to aim for superpower status and potentially resume its normal place as the world's richest country. The price was pollution and gaping disparities in wealth.

Pacific. In the last two decades of the century, India became a leading player in high-tech industries, where many multinational companies chose to locate centers of computer manufacture and telecommunications services. In the Punjab, Maharashtra, and Tamil Nadhu, India's economic growth rates toward the end of the century were comparable to China's. In the 1980s, a dose of Chicago-style economics—the doctrine, loudly advocated by economists at the University of Chicago, that low taxes and light regulation could unleash economic success—turned the Chile of the ruthless military dictator, Augusto Pinochet, into a prosperous country with a large middle class. Integration in the global economy shored up South Africa's delicate new democracy in the 1990s and helped to provide a capital-starved economy with the wealth the country needed to make a start—at least—at rebuilding after centuries of injustice. Between 1993 and 1996, U.S. investment there increased by about 50 percent, and more than 200 American firms employed some 45,000 South Africans. Brazil, meanwhile, which had already graduated from being a producer of primary products for richer economies to being a major manufacturing economy with a lively high-tech sector, achieved, in the early twenty-first century, levels of growth not far short of China's. Even some economies that remained tied to primary production generated huge profits that their governments could invest in global markets. These were oil-exporting countries with large reserves and small domestic populations to spend them on. The countries on the Arabian shore of the Persian Gulf became major players in the global economy, with investments in the industries of every continent.

Even economists who acknowledged the benefits of globalization were prey to doubts about its stability. Some systems theorists argued that the more complex the world economy grew, the more fragile it would become, because, in an interdependent system, a local failure could cause widespread disruption. In fact the opposite happened. Early in the twentieth century, as we have seen (see Chapter 28), a local economic failure, such as the U.S. stock-market crash of 1929, could plunge much of the world into depression. In the 1980s and 1990s, markets prone to panic reacted nervously to similar collapses: of major stock markets in 1987, of the British currency in 1992, of the banking system in Argentina in 1999, of the oil-pricing system and major commodity markets at irregular intervals. But none of these disasters had uncontrollable repercussions. Perhaps the greatest panic of all ensued in 2001, when terrorists destroyed the World Trade Center in New York. The economic consequences were surprisingly slight. Even the firms worst hit by the attack were back at work within days. In practice, the globalized economy could endure terrible dislocations. Complexity made the system more robust, because multiple interconnections made it possible to bypass failures.

CULTURE AND GLOBALIZATION

Information traveled globally with even more freedom than trade. In 1971, the world's first microprocessor appeared. Together with the fiber-optic cable, this made possible the transmission of billions of units of information along a single fiber every second. In combination with radio transmission, these developments made virtually every item of information from every part of the world universally accessible. There were over 2.5 billion telephones in the world by the end of the century and over 500 million computers (see figure 29.1).

The way people handled information changed. Miniaturization boosted individualism and enabled the like-minded to form cyberspace communities that included

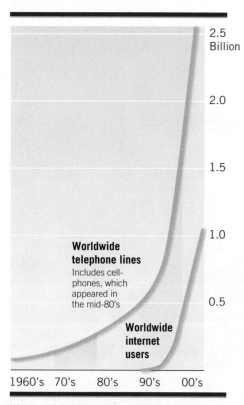

FIGURE 29.1 TELEPHONE LINES AND INTERNET USERS WORLDWIDE CA. 1960–2000

2.5 Billion
2.0
1.5
1.0
0.5

Worldwide telephone lines
Includes cell-phones, which appeared in the mid-80's

Worldwide internet users

1960's 70's 80's 90's 00's

Worldwatch Institute, www.worldwatch.org

individuals from all over the world. The trend was unstoppable. China, for instance, tried to control Internet access, especially after demonstrators coordinated their activities by computer in what almost turned into a revolution in 1989. But China had 30 million Internet users by 2000. Worldwide censorship became difficult—at least for a while. But in the early twenty-first century, major servers began to impose filters, at first to black out pornography.

People could easily drop out of the global information revolution if they wished. The surfeit of data drove some consumers into narrow-minded retreat. Some cyber communities became cyber ghettoes, in which people spent their time with minds closed to the rest of the Web. Increasing information did not necessarily increase knowledge. Wider literacy helped. By the end of the century, just about everyone in the world was familiar with writing, and probably about 85 percent of them could make at least some use of it. But most consumers used the new technology for trivial entertainments rather than self-education. Even professional intellectuals succumbed to specialization, partly in response to the proliferation of information. Students became reliant on data culled from the internet, which changed constantly and was beyond verification. Cutting and pasting became a new form of literary activity, in which no text was stable and no work genuinely original. The ready availability of data exempted people from learning anything. **Virtual reality** excited new fears. It would spawn a generation of "nerds"—introverted sociopaths who communed only with their computers. In 2004, Susan Greenfield, one of the world's leading neuroscientists, predicted a future in which technology would erode individuality, by replacing memory and making all experience second hand, in a "state of sensory oblivion."

Still, the Internet promoted globalization in the strongest sense of the world: the global spread of uniform culture. In reality, in a plural world, this was not a threat to cultural diversity, though people often perceived it as such. Cultural exchange crisscrossed in many directions. If there ever were to be a global culture, it would probably not replace diversity, but supplement it. What people really feared was not globalization but one particular form of it: global Americanization, the triumph of American popular culture, commonly called "McDonaldization" and "Coca Cola–colonialism" after two of the most prevalent products of American industry. Hamburgers and sodas symbolized American cultural influence, because the world associated American lifestyles with what became the nearest thing to a common culture the world possessed: consumerism.

Consumerism is best defined as a system of values that puts the consumption and possession of consumer goods at or near the top of social values—as high as or higher than social obligations, spiritual fulfillment, or moral qualities. Prosperity made its rise possible for the rich. Envy excited its appeal among the poor. The best index of the growing importance of consumerism in the twentieth century is the sheer scale of the growth of per capita consumption, which is among the subjects of the next chapter. As we shall see, the late twentieth-century world was a battleground of consumerism against environmentalism. Consumerism nearly always won the battles. The best evidence that consumerism was particularly strong in the United States is that Americans, on average, greatly outstripped everyone else in the world in the rate at which they consumed resources. Products that best help us measure the importance of

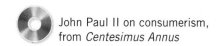

John Paul II on consumerism, from *Centesimus Annus*

Selling dreams. Garish signs of Western economic takeover and cultural invasion deface a traditional building on a prime commercial site in New Delhi, while child workers hope to make a few pennies by selling balloons to kids rich enough to feast on the fatty carbohydrates associated (in India) with U.S. fastfood businesses.

Globalization

1945	International Monetary Fund (IMF) created
1950s	Japan spends 2 percent of GDP on defense
1950s and 60s	Big corporations return to Japanese economy
1960–1967	Japanese incomes double
1960s	Asian "tigers" (Japan, South Korea, Hong Kong, and Singapore) begin rapid economic ascent
1971	World's first microprocessor
1980–1987	Incomes fall in most Latin American nations
1982	Mexico defaults on national debt
1985	Japan becomes world's biggest foreign investor
1989	Tiananmen Square protests in China
1990s	China's economy grows at annual rate of almost 10 percent
Late 1990s	Economies of India and Brazil grow at rapid rate
1995	World Trade Organization (WTO) created
2000	30 million Internet users in China
2001	Terrorist attack on World Trade Center and Pentagon

consumerism in people's values are those that can fairly be described as a waste of money—those that only provide short-term gratification, or are actually harmful. Consumption of tobacco, alcohol, and more addictive drugs makes the case. First on grounds of morality, then—as the century wore on and morality became unfashionable—on grounds of health, governments struggled to contain these extreme forms of consumerism. Nonetheless, by 2000, the alcohol industry worldwide turned over $252 billion annually, tobacco $204 billion. The term *drugs* is harder to define, and the statistics fuzzier because the trade was illegal in most of the world. But by the most widely respected estimates, the drug trade was worth about $150 billion by the end of the century, of which drugs worth about $60 billion were consumed in the United States.

Even those who condemned American cultural influence as trivial, trashy, and corrosive of traditional cultures found it hard to resist its appeal. Because American businesses dominated the major new media that controlled the worldwide transmission of culture—cinema, television, and the Internet—American images proliferated before the eyes of onlookers around the world (although by the end of the century, the Indian film industry was beginning to shape up as a potential rival). Often, those onlookers became admirers. The magnetism of American higher education was an important ingredient of America's soft power (Chapter 28). American institutions educated a disproportionate number of the world's elites.

The most pervasive index of the global appeal of American culture was the adoption of English, in the form in which Americans speak that language, as a universal code of business, politics, science, and study. This was a major reversal in the history of culture. Languages had been diverging and multiplying for perhaps as much as 50,000 years—probably longer than any other ingredients of culture. There had been convergent episodes. The spread of imperial or sacred or trading languages had sometimes displaced or extinguished other tongues. Never before, however, had a single language achieved the role of a global common tongue. Mandarin Chinese, Spanish, and Portuguese also showed some potential. The extinction of minority languages became a conservation problem (see figure 29–2).

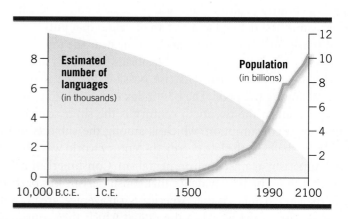

FIGURE 29–2 NUMBER OF LANGUAGES WORLDWIDE 10,000 B.C.E. TO 2100 C.E. (PROJECTED)
The United Nations Educational, Scientific, and Cultural Organization

SECULARISM AND THE RELIGIOUS REVIVAL

Most of the really powerful utopian visions of the twentieth century were secular—irreligious, even antireligious. Utopians who put their faith in the state often did so in conscious revulsion from religious establishments, which had clearly failed, after what seemed a long enough period of trying, to enhance virtue or spread welfare or justice. Communists usually regarded atheism as part of their own creed and dismissed religion as "the opiate of the masses." Nazis wanted to sweep away the Church, which they saw as an enfeebling influence that weakened the nation's martial virtues. Social planning relied for its appeal on a scientist notion: that human agency alone could change societies like chemicals in a lab, and achieve predictable results, with no need for appeals to Providence or to grace. The world—from all these perspectives—would be better off without religion, which had caused wars, retarded science, and stifled reason with dogma. One of the most popular songs of the British rock singer, John Lennon (1940–1980), was "Imagine," in which he called on the world to reject religion in order to live in peace "for today." Religion was one of the first casualties of the skepticism that, as we saw in Chapter 27, was a major twentieth-century theme.

For most of the century, the demise of religion was widely forecast. The decline of churchgoing in the West, which lasted in America until the 1960s and still prevailed in Western Europe and Canada in the early twenty-first century, seemed to suggest that prosperity would erode faith—that Mammon would tempt worshippers away from God. Religion had to face serious challenges and sometimes ferocious persecution from hostile political ideologies.

In response to secularism, however, many people with religious identities felt them more fiercely. In Egypt, for instance, the number of mosques increased nearly twice as fast as the population under the broadly secular-minded rulers of the second half of the twentieth century. The most striking case occurred in Iran, where the Shah, Mohammad Reza Pahlavi (r. 1941–1979), imposed secularization on a reluctant country in the 1960s. He claimed to be ruling people who "resembled Americans" in the "France of Asia." He ignored the Muslim clergy. He appealed to Persia's pagan past, spending—reputedly—$100 million on ceremonies recreating the glories of the Persepolis of Darius the Great (r. 521–486 B.C.E.). He seized religious endowments without compensation to redistribute the land among peasants. He also made himself unpopular in other ways—especially by outrageously disproportionate spending on the armed services rather than on social welfare—but it was by alienating religious sensibilities that he lost his throne.

A Shiite cleric, Ayatollah Ruhollah Khomeini (1900–1989) gradually emerged as the voice of outraged Islam. Broadcasting from exile, this brilliant propagandist attracted millions of followers by his obvious incorruptibility and his unshakable self-righteousness. The Shah's regime was, he proclaimed, literally the work of the devil and must be destroyed. Khomeini (hoh-MAY-nee) called for an Islamic republic—a welfare state that would enrich all its faithful and in which all the necessities of life would be free. In 1979, he inspired a revolution. His followers filled the streets, deserted the army, and paralyzed the government by striking. The Shah went into exile. An Islamic republic dominated by Shiite clergy replaced the ancient Iranian monarchy. The success of the Iranian experiment, which followed an Islamist experiment in Pakistan in 1977, encouraged similar movements all over the Islamic world.

Religion did decline in Western Europe. But in much of the rest of the world, faith's hold on people's hearts and minds seemed to increase—at least, to judge from attendance statistics at acts of worship. Traditional religion proved

Revolution's patron saint. After his death in 1989 Ayatollah Ruhollah Khomeini continued to influence Iranian politics. His shrine outside Tehran became a place of pilgrimage for followers who wanted to perpetuate Islamic revolution, like the women photographed here in 2001 on the twelfth anniversary of his death. His cult helped to mobilize voters for his unusual combination of agendas—communitarian, religious, populist, nationalist—and helped slow down and, at times, halt Iran's hesitant return to secular priorities and normal relations with the rest of the world.

ineradicable, surviving, strengthened by persecution, after all the hostile ideologies collapsed. Far from outbidding religion, prosperity nurtured it by providing relief from materialism. That is perhaps the main reason the United States, the world's richest country, became so hospitable to religion in the late twentieth century. Yet religion never lost its appeal to the victims of poverty, for whom rewards in the next world compensated for being underprivileged here and now. That may largely explain why Christian and, to a lesser extent, Muslim propagandists found huge audiences in sub-Saharan Africa.

Traditional religions, especially Roman Catholicism, Islam, radical forms of Christianity, and Lamaist Buddhism self-reformed successfully to confront secularism and widen their global appeal. The main challenge to traditional religions came not from atheism or secularism but from new kinds of religions. Most of these could be characterized as cults or folksy superstitions, or as personal religions concocted by individuals who did not see themselves as belonging in any particular communion but who picked and mixed from various traditions to create a menu of their own choice, like an Internet-surfing student plagiarizing a paper with the cut-and-paste facility.

Twentieth-century conditions favored cults in cities full of rootless, spiritually uneducated constituencies with excited expectations. Some fashions in belief were frankly weird. Astrology was the starting-point of the New Age movement, which, beginning in the 1960s, proclaimed the "dawning of the Age of Aquarius"—the doctrine that the astral prominence of the constellation Pisces is gradually being replaced, after about 2,000 years, with world-transforming effects. It is hard to believe that anyone could have taken such a doctrine seriously—but its success indicated how uneasy people felt at the time. Toward the end of the century, sects predicting the end of the world achieved a brief vogue—even though the year 2000 had no particular significance, since our system of numbering years is purely arbitrary. Surprisingly, skepticism favored the proliferation of weird beliefs because, as the English writer G. K. Chesterton (1874–1936) reputedly said, "When people cease to believe in something, they do not believe in nothing; they believe in anything."

The biggest growth point was the kind of religion called **fundamentalist**. It started in a Protestant theology school in Princeton, New Jersey, in the early twentieth century in reaction to critical readings of the Bible. The idea was that the text of the Bible contains fundamental truths that cannot be questioned, either by critical inquiry or by scientific evidence. The name "fundamentalism" has been applied retrospectively to a similar doctrine, traditional in Islam, about the Quran. It can—and sometimes does—arise in the context of any religion that has a founding text or holy scripture. Karen Armstrong—one of the foremost authorities on the subject—sees fundamentalism as modern: scientific or pseudoscientific because it treats religion as reducible to matters of undeniable fact. Apart from the bleakness of modernity, fundamentalism's other parent is fear: fear that the end of the world is imminent, fear of *Great Satans* (Iranian clerics' term for the United States and the West in general), fear of chaos, and. above all, fear of the unfamiliar. To fundamentalists, all difference is subversive. These facts help to explain why fundamentalism arose and thrived in the modern world and has never lost its appeal. In the late twentieth century, fundamentalisms in Islam and Christianity, taken together, constituted the biggest movement in the world.

All the movements we call fundamentalist are different but can be identified by the features they share: militancy, hostility to pluralism, and a determination to confuse politics with religion. Fundamentalists are self-cast as warriors against secularism. Yet, in practice, most fundamentalists are pleasant, ordinary people, who make their compromises with the wicked world and leave their religion—as most people do—at the door of their church or mosque. The militant minorities among them, meanwhile, cause trouble by declaring war on society. Some sects, with their crushing effects on individual identity, their ethic of obedience, their paranoid habits, and their campaigns of hatred or violence against the rest of the world, behaved in frightening ways like the early fascist cells.

If and when they got power, fundamentalists tended to treat people of other traditions with hostility. Bahais (bah-HAIS), Christians, Sunni Muslims, and Jews all suffered discrimination and persecution in Khomeini's rigidly Shiite Iran. In Afghanistan in the 1990s, the strict Islamic Taliban regime vandalized Buddhist monuments, smashed ancient art in the country's museums, suppressed Christian worship, ordered women out of school, and slaughtered homosexuals—of whom there were many since homosexual practice was a longstanding tradition in the country. Saudi Arabia has "religious police" who impose a rigid and uncompromising form of Islamic law even on non-Muslims. When a Christian fundamentalist general took power in Guatemala in 1982, the army persecuted Catholic churchmen and women for supposedly helping Native American rebels. Where Islamic fundamentalists took power nationally or locally, they usually imposed interpretations of Islamic law that often had dire consequences for women, whose freedoms were restricted, and for people who led supposedly irregular sex lives, who were liable to be put to death. Christian fundamentalists in the United States advocated laws to ban practices they considered objectionable on religious grounds, including homosexuality, the teaching of evolution, sex education in public schools, contraception, and abortion. Religious fundamentalism rarely managed to retain power for long, or to remain unseduced by the need for political compromise, but it continued to grow as a social movement, even when its political aspirations were frustrated or diluted.

Fundamentalism was one form of the religious response to secularism. Another was to imitate the secularists—to beat them at their own game. Traditional religions could do this by showing that they could make a difference to lives in the here and now, as well as in the hereafter, by organizing social services for worshippers and aid programs for the poor of the world. New religions could try an alternative strategy. In developed countries, a lot of the new religion of the late twentieth century looked suspiciously like secularism—or even consumerism—in disguise. In South Korea, the Full Gospel Church promised its followers health and prosperity: bounding riches and bouncing bodies. In Japan, Soka Gakkai was a Buddhist form of prosperity cult that founded its own political party and spread to other consumerist societies in Europe and America. In the United States, the "next church" movement offered car-repair ministry and classes in "discovering divorce dynamics." Instead of imitating heaven, American churches increased their congregations by imitating the familiar world of trivial, middle-class lives, with coffee parties, muzak, casual clothes, and undemanding moral prescriptions. In Orange County, California, worshippers in the Crystal Cathedral of the Reverend Robert Schuller believed that business success was a mark of divine election.

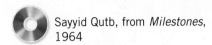

Sayyid Qutb, from *Milestones*, 1964

Liberation Theology. A Catholic priest holds hands with members of the Base Christian Community in Panama. Believers in liberation theology typically aligned themselves with left-wing, revolutionary movements, putting them in conflict with established Catholic authorities and political leaders in Latin America.

Vaclav Havel, "The Need for Transcendence in the Postmodern World"

Some new religions were essentially healing ministries—offering a form of alternative therapy for a health-obsessed age in which, in the absence of shared moral values, health was the only commonly acknowledged good. Other new religious movements of the period were more political than pontifical—striving for kingdoms of this world, of the kind Jesus disavowed. The supposedly Buddhist Aum Shinrikyo cult in Japan waged war on the rest of society. A patchily fashionable cult known as Scientology, which called itself a church, was instead classed as a political organization or as a business in many of the countries in which it operated. The **Liberation Theology** movement in Latin America was concerned with justice for the poor and oppressed, arguing that sin was not just individual moral failure but a structural feature of capitalist society. By the end of the twentieth century, it was not clear how the culture wars of religions against secularism would end.

IN PERSPECTIVE: The Century of Paradox

Traditions had to struggle to survive the quickening pace of change, which made social and political relationships unrecognizable to successive generations and bewildering to those whose lives spanned the transformations. Science drove change, inspiring new technology, reforging the way people saw the world. The relentless growth of global population, which wars did not interrupt, increased the pressure on the world's resources. But, even more than population growth, spiraling desire—consumerism, as it came to be called, lust for abundance, impatience to enjoy the rewards of economic growth—made people exploit the planet with increasing ruthlessness.

Most of history had favored unitary states, with one religion, ethnicity, and identity. Large empires have always been multicultural, but they have usually had a dominant culture, alongside which others are, at best, tolerated. In the twentieth century, this would no longer do. The aftermath of the era of global empires, the range and intensity of migrations, the progress of ideas of racial equality, the multiplication of religions, the large-scale redrawing of state boundaries made the toleration of diversity essential to the peace of most states. Those states that rejected toleration faced traumatic periods of "ethnic cleansing." Meanwhile, democracies could only contain the intense competition of rival ideologies by embracing political pluralism—that is, the admission to the lawful political arena, on equal terms, of parties representing potentially irreconcilable views.

What was true of individual states was true of the entire world. "Shrinkage" brought peoples and cultures into unprecedented proximity. The peace and future prosperity of the world at the end of the century demanded a new global consensus in favor of pluralism, and an effort to accommodate plurality of cultures—religions, languages, ethnicities, communal identities, versions of history, value systems—on terms of equality in a single global community. The British philosopher Isaiah Berlin (1909–1997) explained how such a consensus and such an effort are possible: "There is a plurality of values which men can and do seek. . . . And the difference it makes is that if a man pursues one of these values, I, who do not, am able to understand why he pursues it or what it would be like, in his circumstances, for me to be induced to pursue it. Hence the possibility of human understanding." This differs from cultural relativism. It does not say, for instance, that all cultures can be accommodated. One might exclude Nazism, say, or cannibalism. It leaves open the possibility of peaceful argument about which culture, if any, is best. It claims, in Berlin's words, "that the multiple values are objective, part of the essence of humanity rather than arbitrary creations of men's subjective fancies."[2] In a world where globalization made most historic communities defensive about their own cultures, it has been difficult to persuade them to coexist peacefully with the contrasting cultures of their neighbors. Still, pluralism is obviously the only practical future for a diverse world. Paradoxically, perhaps, it is the only truly uniform interest that all the world's peoples have in common.

Human rights provided the key test of whether universal values could thrive in a plural world. As we have seen, what was a universal right in theory could vary in practice from culture to culture, especially in connection with the treatment under the law of women, children, homosexuals, criminals, and drug users. Even in the United States, where public advocacy of human rights was as strong as anywhere, presidents seemed willing to ignore or circumvent their nominal commitment to human rights when it suited them. In 1999, the Senate acquitted President Bill Clinton of charges of attempting to subvert justice. Most of the charges against him were trivial or politically motivated. But there was little doubt that he had abused his position to prevent a fair hearing of a case of sexual harassment and discrimination that a former employee had brought against him. The most flagrant instance occurred in 2003, when the administration of George W. Bush licensed the torture of interrogation subjects during America's military interventions in Afghanistan and Iraq, and interned terrorism suspects in an offshore jail, to prevent them from having access to legal representation and the normal conditions of a fair trial.

The problems went even deeper. The experiences of the century made human rights a lively issue, but did not by any means dispel moral confusion about the value of life. Dilemmas like those John Rabe faced—the humane Nazi who tried to save massacre victims—continued to recur. Even the most basic human rights proved impossible to guarantee universally in practice. Almost everyone, for instance, by the end of the twentieth century, paid lip service to the rights to life and to equality of respect, but these values were more honored in theory than in practice. Many countries outlawed capital punishment. But this did not mean that they treated human life as inviolable. In some places, the lives of some criminals continued to be regarded as dispensable, even in most states of the United States. Many jurisdictions exempted unborn babies from the principle of inviolability of human life. The decriminalization of abortion in most of the West in the last three decades of the century served humane ends: freeing women who felt obliged to have abortions, and those who helped them, from prosecution under the law. But the effects were morally questionable. In 2004, the woman who had brought *Roe v. Wade*, the proabortion case, to the United States Supreme Court more than 30 years earlier, appealed to have the decision reversed. She had become a fervent Christian, appalled by the mass extinction of fetuses. Euthanasia became another focus of concern over the limits of human rights. Did the moribund and the vegetative have them? Did the incurably dying have a moral

An execution by guillotine in France in 1929. Revolutionary France began executing people by guillotine in 1792. The guillotine was supposed to be an efficient and humane death-machine because it killed quickly with a single blow, without torture. But during the Revolution, it made a horrible spectacle of mass executions and became a symbol not of the Enlightenment but of barbarity. France continued to guillotine condemned criminals until 1977. Today, the laws of France, like those of almost every Western country, acknowledge that even criminals have basic human rights, of which the most fundamental is the right to live.

CHRONOLOGY

1933–1935	Restrictions placed on German Jews
1936	Publication of John Maynard Keynes' *General Theory of Employment, Interest, and Money*
December 1937	Rape of Nanjing
1939–1945	World War II
1939–1945	Holocaust
1945	International Monetary Fund (IMF) created
1950s	Japans spends 2 percent of GDP on defense
1950s and 1960s	Big corporations return to Japanese economy; generation gap emerges; civil rights movement in the United States
1960s	Second Vatican Council; Asian "tigers" (Japan, South Korea, Hong Kong, and Singapore) begin rapid economic ascent
1960–1967	Japanese incomes double
1961–1973	U.S. involvement in Vietnam War
1965	Public spending accounts for 25 percent of GDP of world's seven wealthiest nations
March 1968	Mai Lai massacre in Vietnam
1968	Prague Spring
1971	World's first microprocessor
1975–1979	Khmer Rouge rule in Cambodia
1979	Islamic revolution in Iran
1980s and 1990s	Governments around the world move away from nationalized economies
1980–1987	Incomes fall in most Latin American nations
1982	Mexico defaults on national debt
1985	Japan becomes world's biggest foreign investor
1989	Tiananmen Square protests in China
1990s	China's economy grows at annual rate of almost 10 percent
Late 1990s	Economies of Brazil and India grow at rapid rate
1995	World Trade Organization (WTO) created
Late twentieth century	Christian and Islamic fundamentalism on the rise; 30 million Internet users in China; public spending accounts for 37 percent of GDP of world's seven wealthiest nations; Muslim population: Britain, 2 million; France, 4 million; migrants from Latin America largest minority group in the United States
2001	Terrorist attack on United States

right to choose to end their sufferings by physician-assisted suicide?

By the end of the century, the world seemed to have tried everything. The "final solutions" and "inevitable" revolutions that extremists of Right and Left proposed had failed. Social planning went wrong. But the return to individualism was also disappointing. It failed to restrain the growth of government, and, rather than produce universal prosperity and social peace, it widened the poverty gap and bred terrorism and crime. Every utopia turned to ashes. The world was left looking for what some political philosophers called a "third way" between capitalism and socialism, in which freedom and order would coexist, governments would make society more equal without choking differences, and individual enterprise would thrive at the service of a wider community. These objectives were easier to state than to deliver.

It is tempting to characterize the twentieth century as a century of paradox. Frustrated hopes coincided with unprecedented progress. Uncontrolled change left much of the world mired in stagnancy. Utopias nourished moral sickness, suicide, and crime. The century of democracy was the century of dictators. The century of war was also the century of pacifism. Youth achieved more wealth and influence than ever before, but the world emerged with a vast cohort of the elderly to care for. Rule by the aged survived the empowerment of the young. Globalization broke down some states and communities but encouraged others to recover historic identities. The rise of science and secularism revived faith. Finally, as we shall see in the final chapter, the twentieth century could also be called the century of ecology. But it was peculiarly destructive of nature.

⸺⸱ PROBLEMS AND PARALLELS ⸱⸺

1. Why did science, technology, education, and increased prosperity fail to avert moral catastrophies in the twentieth century?

2. The nation-state was the central actor in reorganizing societies after the economic disasters and wars of the twentieth century. Nation-states, however, were also the most efficient killers of tens of millions of people through war and misguided policies. What are the reasons for this paradox?

3. How did individualism manifest itself in both conservative and counter-conservative ways?

4. How did the demands for personal freedom, sexual liberation, and existential self-fulfillment affect Western societies? Family structures? The status of women?

5. How did globalization affect economies and cultures in the late twentieth and early twenty-first centuries?

6. What does the term *counter-colonization* mean? How did peoples redefine the sense of their own identities in the twentieth century? Why did it take so long to dismantle the legacy of racism?

7. How did traditional as well as new religions respond to secularism? What features do fundamentalist movements have in common around the world?

DOCUMENTS IN GLOBAL HISTORY

- Transcript from the Rape of Nanjing sentencing, 1947
- Eyewitness account of genocide in Armenia, 1915
- James Cook, from *Captain Cook's Journal During his First Voyage Round the World*
- Excerpt from The 9/11 Commission Report
- Martin Luther King, Jr., *Letter from Birmingham Jail*
- Aimé Césaire, from *Return to My Native Land*

- Keith B. Richburg, from *Out of Africa: A Black Man Confronts Africa*
- National Organization of Women, Statement of Purpose, 1966
- John Paul II on consumerism, from *Centesimus Annus*
- Sayyid Qutb, from *Milestones*, 1964
- Vaclav Havel, "The Need for Transcendence in the Postmodern World"

Please see the Primary Source CD-ROM or additional sources related to this chapter.

READ ON

The study of wartime atrocities is ably represented by I. Chang, *The Rape of Nanking: The Forgotten Holocaust of World War II* (1997), which shows how Nanking served as a training ground for further Japanese slaughter of civilians. *Good Man of Nanking: The Diaries of J. Rabe*, ed. by E. Wickert, translated from the German by J. E. Woods (1998) offers a first-hand account of the massacre by a German businessman who organized refuge for Chinese civilians.

D. Bell, *The Coming of Post-Industrial Society* (1976), predicted the coming of the Information Age and the social and cultural transformations it has wrought. It should be read in conjunction with F. Jameson, *Postmodernism or the Cultural Logic of Late Capitalism* (1991), a densely written but very sophisticated analysis of post-modernism as the artistic expression of its material milieu. The same author's *Marxism and Form* (1971) remains the basic manifesto of modern Marxist cultural analysis. J. Tomlinson,

Globalization and Culture (1999) explores similar themes from a different perspective.

A. Musallam, *From Secularism to Jihad : Sayyid Qutb and the Foundations of Radical Islamism* (2005) is an insightful examination of the founder of modern Islamic political fundamentalism. T. Madan, *Modern Myths, Locked Minds : Secularism and Fundamentalism in India* (1997) looks at the intersection of secularism, religion and politics for India's major faiths. S. Jacoby, *Freethinkers : A History of American Secularism* (2004) examines the paradox of the secular foundations of the U.S.'s very religiously tinged democratic culture.

N. Woods, ed., *The Political Economy of Globalization* (2000), explores key economic and political problems associated with globalization. R. Compton, *East Asian Democratization: Impact of Globalization, Culture, and Economy* (2000) uses detailed case studies of various East Asian countries to compare the political and cultural impact of globalizing economies.

CHAPTER 30

The Embattled Biosphere:
The Twentieth-Century
Environment

The World Health Organization has checked the spread of river blindness in Burkina Faso, but the problems of soil degradation and the ruin of villages continue.

"**W**hy do you travel such a long distance with this load of wood and your baby on your back?" the environmental worker asked.

"What a question!" said the woman, whose name was Rasmata. The conversation, reported in 1991, began after a long period of drought in the central African country of Burkina Faso, just south of the Sahara, on the road to the capital, Ouagadougou (wog-ah-DOO-goo). "My baby is ill. I nursed her with traditional medicine but the illness went on. . . . There is no clinic in our village—and, as we don't have any cash, I brought some wood, which I am going to sell. With the takings from the wood, I will be able to buy the modern medicine the nurse will prescribe."

BURKINA FASO

"Don't you know that it is the excessive culling of trees that is causing the advance of the desert into our country?"

"What can we do? When I was a girl, there were many fruits to be gathered. We kept a third for ourselves to eat, and sold the remainder in town. . . . Now these trees are rare and you have to go a long way to find them. We used to collect firewood from trees that had died naturally. Now there aren't any. We have to go a long way, to cut living shrub and leave it to dry out for days or weeks before we can use it for our fires. It is for lack of other produce that I sell wood. . . ."

Some of Burkina Faso's problems are natural—part of the inescapable geography of the region. The Sahara has been drying and growing for thousands of years. The prevailing northeast winds powder the land beyond the desert with infertile soil. Most of the country has, on average, only a little over two inches of rain in a good year. In the last three decades of the twentieth century, droughts became routine.

Scientific interventions have improved life in some respects. For instance, in parts of the country that have rivers and fertile land, 10 percent of the population used to suffer from river blindness—sight-destroying lesions, caused by a tiny, threadlike worm that gets into the skin when black fly bite. The people could cope only by abandoning their valleys, when the disease struck, and moving to areas with poor, arid soils, until food shortages forced them to return. The internationally funded program that checked the disease in the 1980s cost less than a dollar for each person it helped.

But Burkina Faso, like neighboring countries on the desert edge suffers from some of the most characteristic human-made environmental problems of the twentieth-century world. Thanks, in part, to the "modern medicine" and medical technology in which Rasmata had so much faith, the population of Burkina Faso doubled to 10 million in the 20 years from 1975. It was a medical triumph, but it put terrible strains on the country's resources, forcing people in some areas to farm so intensively that the soil became enfeebled, or in other areas, to increase their herds of livestock. By the end of the century, the number of cattle in Burkina Faso was growing at a rate of 2 percent a year, and those of sheep and goats at 3 percent a year. Overgrazing is as bad for soil as overcropping. What is more, the herdsmen occupied ever more land, spreading, ahead of the advancing desert, from the north of the country into the west and center. Between 1980 and 1993, a combination of drought and overexploitation of the kind Rasmata mentioned destroyed more than 3 million acres of forest in Burkina Faso.

Well-intentioned interventions in the environment by governments and international agencies often made the problems worse. To help combat river blindness, for instance, in the mid-1970s, foreign agencies insisted on a huge resettlement program, affecting 10 percent of farmers in affected areas. By the late 1980s, it was becoming impossible to sustain many of the new settlements. To feed the increased population, farmers ceased to leave fields fallow. As a result, soils could not recover their natural fertility. The rising costs of fertilizer and insecticides hugely exceeded the increase in the value of the farmers' cotton. Families moved in ways the planners had not been able to foresee—many, for instance, in search of irrigation water, flocking to Burkina Faso's extreme southeast, where a new hydroelectric dam was being built.

Fluctuations in government policy and economic fashion could have devastating effects. New projects and development strategies came and went with bewildering speed. International agencies suspended aid if projects failed to produce quick results—three- or five-year terms were normal for funding reviews in the late twentieth century. In 1983, a military coup in Burkina Faso brought in a government the West denounced as communist. Peasants were promised the right to use any land they cleared, with terrible consequences for the remaining forests. In 2000, the government began to encourage big, supposedly efficient farms. This was contrary to the traditions of a country of small family enterprises, typically of 7 to 15 acres.

Meanwhile, international market conditions tended to impoverish these peasants, obliging them to grow cheap cash crops—mainly cotton and peanuts—for rich consumer countries, on the 20 percent or so of the land they could spare from growing their own food. From the 1980s, there was a world glut of the cheap grains the farmers were encouraged to grow to feed themselves. So they had no chance to sell the produce of 80 percent of their cultivated land.

We can trace the combination of natural and man-made effects in the dust to which so much of the soil of Burkina Faso turned. In 1988, more than half the land in the country was officially classed as biologically degraded. By the end of the century, over two-thirds of the soil of the northern, central, and eastern provinces was seriously affected. All the soil in the province of Gnagna in the east had been degraded. Food economists now think that Burkina Faso can no longer support the people who live there.

Though Burkina Faso is particularly badly off, the problems it suffers from are global problems, intelligible and containable—if at all—only in a global context. Take, for example, the impact of growing numbers of people. In 1900, the population of the world was 1,630 million. In 2000, it was 6.1 billion. Global population doubled in the last 40 years of the century (the previous doubling took twice as long; the doubling before that took well over two centuries). This was not as fast as the growth rate in Burkina Faso—but it was still hard to cope with. Even before we take other factors into account, population explosion has put unprecedented pressure on the world's resources of energy, stressing and stretching our means of providing enough food and fuel to keep humankind going (see Map 30.1.)

Demand for resources, moreover, has hugely outstripped population growth. Not only are there more people in the world than ever before, but they also demand, on average, vastly more food and goods and consume vastly more energy than ever before. If the population-growth figures seem astonishing by the standards of earlier periods, the output figures are even more startlingly disproportionate. Between 1900 and 1950, global output—the total value of the goods people produced—rose, at 2003 prices, from two to five trillion dollars. Between 1950 and 2000, the total soared to $39 trillion. In other words, while the population of the world less than quadrupled, output rose more than nineteenfold. In three years during the 1990s, according to a much-quoted calculation, the growth in output exceeded that of the previous 10,000 years combined.

Why did the consumption of resources leap ahead of the rise in population? It is hard to separate cause and effect. New technologies enabled twentieth-century industries to unlock new energy resources, with a consequent rise in prosperity. In the twentieth century, the world economy grew, on average, by about 1.5 percent a year—about two and a half times as fast as in the nineteenth century, when growth

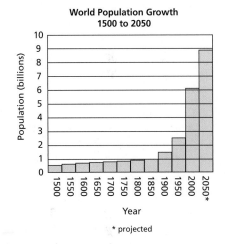

MAP 30.1

World Population, 2003

Country Area Roughly Proportional to Population

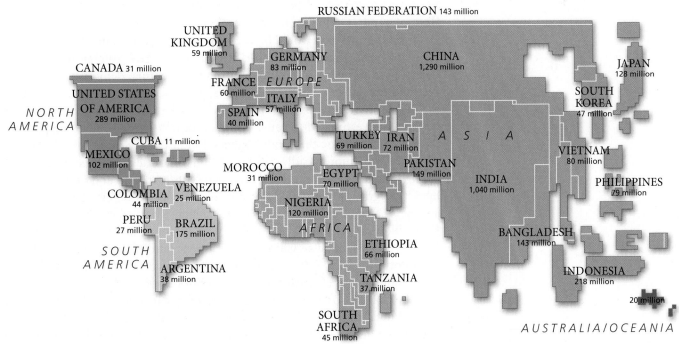

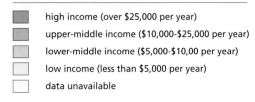

Comparative World Wealth, ca. 2004

- high income (over $25,000 per year)
- upper-middle income ($10,000-$25,000 per year)
- lower-middle income ($5,000-$10,00 per year)
- low income (less than $5,000 per year)
- data unavailable

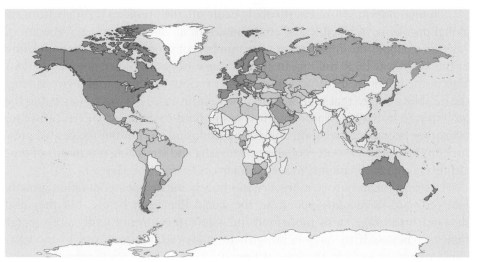

rates seemed dazzlingly high to those who experienced them. When prosperity leaps, people's expectations explode. Demand and supply feed off each other. The twentieth-century world got hooked on prosperity, locked into dependence on economic growth (see Map 30.2). Electorates wanted more food, more goods, more energy. So governments encouraged, or at least allowed, environmental overexploitation.

The distribution of consumption suggests that overconsumption is a function of prosperity, in the same way that eating stimulates the appetite. Greed grows from growth. In 1991, an average American used up between 30 and 50 times as much copper, tin, and aluminium as a citizen of India, 43 times as much petroleum, and 184 times as much natural gas. By comparison with an average inhabitant of sub-Saharan Africa, the consumption rates of Americans or Western Europeans were several times greater even than that. Facts of these kinds are usually—and validly—cited as evidence of morally deplorable inequalities. If, however, the Indian or African were to consume as much as the Westerner, it would redress the equality but not redeem the immorality. On the contrary, it would be an extension of bad habits.

Indeed, the effects would be worse because fast economic development always outstrips environmental restraints. China, where real average incomes virtually quadrupled in the last quarter of the twentieth century, demonstrates the possibilities and the dangers. By the mid-1990s, of the ten cities with the most acute air-pollution problems in the world, five were in China, where pollution-related diseases were estimated to cause 1 million deaths a year—including poisoning by fluorides and arsenic that underregulated industries released into the food chain. China emitted more deadly sulphur dioxide into the atmosphere than any other country, causing acid rain to fall on much of its own land and on that of its neighbors. Overgrazing is turning the northern steppe to desert. The Gobi Desert is advancing from Central Asia toward the Yellow River valley. And desert dust from China blows across the Pacific, mixed with sulphur dioxide, over Japan and western North America. The Chinese government hardly began to tackle these problems until the late 1990s, when it tried to reduce sulphur dioxide emissions to "only" double those United Nations guidelines considered safe.

The global disparities in consumption suggest a further, more worrying conclusion: Abundance is there to be exhausted. Given the chance, people gorge until, in effect, they burst or until they empty the pantry. Why people consume so much more than they need and why they have done so with unprecedented abandon in recent times are among the great, unsolved problems of human science, and the great formative facts of human history. Anthropologists and philosophers have identified "spiraling desire"—an instinct, or maybe a pathology, that makes people want whatever is available, or envy whatever others have. If such a thing does exist, it could well have operated cumulatively in the twentieth century, under the impact of growing, spreading prosperity.

We can understand the problems better, though maybe not solve them—if we look first at the way humans treated energy resources (food and fuel) in the twentieth century, and then at how this is connected to changes in urban and other habitats, before turning to the century's deeper environmental dangers, which are beyond human agency or human control.

The Benxi Steelworks in northern China. Satellites have identified Benxi, one of China's biggest steel production towns, as the most polluted place on earth. Smoke billows up from smokestacks as the sun attempts to penetrate the smog.

FUEL RESOURCES

Just as steam power transformed the nineteenth-century world, so electricity and the internal combustion engine transformed the twentieth century. Electricity replaced gas for lighting and replaced steam as the power source of choice for most purposes. Fossil fuels—coal, oil, natural gas—came to be seen as the means of generating electricity rather than as direct sources of heat and light in themselves. The battery and the local generator, which was usually oil fueled, meant that the potentialities of electric power could be harnessed way beyond the industrial world. Electricity facilitated new methods of long-range communication and seemingly infinite means of managing information. In 1901, Guglielmo Marconi transmitted the first wireless telegraph message across the Atlantic. Radio waves soon linked every part of the world, communicating messages at the speed of light. In the 1960s, it became possible to engrave battery-operated computers on silicon microchips no bigger than .0394 of an inch in diameter. These were the most spectacular applications of electricity, but they required relatively little power. More pervasive and more effective in changing the world were the ways in which electricity penetrated everyday life: powering factories and farms, driving domestic machinery, lighting streets and interiors, propelling the engines of locomotion and transport.

The internal combustion engine came puffing and rumbling into the world in the 1890s. It could drive almost any kind of contraption from farm tractors to lawn mowers. Most commonly, however, it powered the motor car. Cars were rich people's toys at first, but gradually got cheaper as they became articles of mass production. By the end of the twentieth century, the world had over 600 million cars. They were socially liberating—more so, perhaps than any constitutional freedoms—because they enabled people who owned them to go where they liked, when they liked, as never before. But they also had lamentable effects: aggressive drivers, ugly roads, noxious fumes, raucous noise, and a huge new source of pressure on the planet's stocks of fossil fuels. Partly thanks to the internal combustion engine, and partly because of oil's relative abundance, oil gradually replaced coal as the world's major source of energy, except in China. By the end of the twentieth century, oil supplied 40 percent of the world's energy, with coal and natural gas accounting in equal measure for most of the rest. Reliance on fossil fuels to supply the world's daunting energy requirements carried two major disadvantages.

First, fossil fuels are a limited resource. Exploration kept pace with demand for oil throughout the twentieth century, but people kept feeling the nagging

Hymn to progress. In 1937, a Parisian electricity company commissioned the chic, technically innovative painter, Raoul Dufy, to decorate a gigantic canvas in celebration of the wonders of electricity. More than 180 feet long, it is still the world's largest painting. It is a hymn to progress, portraying a succession of scientists from ancient Greece onward, in a sequence of inventiveness that climaxes in electricity, symbolized as a flying spirit, zooming through the world, spreading illumination.

 Kyoto Protocol, Article 2

worry that stocks would eventually run out. Competition for oil caused or exacerbated wars. Countries with major oil fields in their territories or offshore waters combined to control the price of fuel. In 1973, for instance, the Organization of Petroleum Exporting Countries (OPEC), an alliance of major oil producers, hiked the price and plunged the world into crisis. After a brief spell of energy rationing in the industrialized world and endangered revenues for the oil producers, a new era of cooperation between producers and consumers began in the 1980s. Exploitation of alternative energy sources, especially natural gas, diluted oil producers' power in the marketplace, while the producers themselves realized that they would sell a lot more oil if they stopped trying to restrain global economic growth. When price stability resumed, so did high levels of production and consumption.

The second big disadvantage of fossil fuels is that they release carbon gases into the atmosphere. In the Ice Age that began about 150,000 years ago, there were 200 parts of carbon dioxide per million in the air around the Earth. In the 1800s, the level rose to 280. Today, there are 350 parts per million. Most of this increase is the result of human agency: the recirculation of carbon formerly locked in forests or buried underground for millions of years in the form of coal, oil, and gas. In the late twentieth century, the problem got worse because of carbon-charged gases used in refrigerators, air conditioners, and aerosol sprays—from perhaps 20,000 tons annually in 1950 to some 1.3 billion tons in 1990, when international controls at last began to take effect (see Figure 30.1).

During the late twentieth century, observers grew increasingly anxious about the effects of these emissions on climate. Carbon in the atmosphere intensifies the effects of the rays of the sun, boosting temperatures, killing the plankton on which marine life depends for food, melting the edges of the icecaps, raising sea levels, and—if sustained for long enough—modifying the flow of ocean currents and the pattern of the world's winds. Popular science calls this phenomenon the **greenhouse effect**. We simply do not know what the consequences would be if the world's wind and current system were to change permanently, but the periodic disasters caused by the temporary oscillations observable at intervals and recorded earlier in this book (Chapter 14) are alarming.

In view of the problems fossil fuels posed, energy consumers in the late twentieth century invested heavily in alternative sources of power. The idea of hydroelectricity was simple. As water cascades from a higher to a lower level, it can be used to turn turbines that would generate electricity. But the idea never worked

FIGURE 30.1 GLOBAL CO$_2$ EMISSIONS, IN BILLIONS OF METRIC TONS

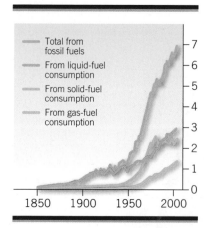

© *Time Inc. Reprinted by permission.*

in a fully satisfactory way. Hydroelectricity was available only where the right conditions of terrain and water supply favored it. It needed big rivers that could be dammed to concentrate and regulate the flow of water. Moreover, as we shall see, dams nearly always harmed agriculture.

Nor was nuclear power a fully satisfactory answer. It was the most cost-efficient form of power generation ever devised, but it, too, used an exhaustible resource: uranium, some types of which are constructed of atoms that release tremendous amounts of energy when split. Moreover, nuclear power left lethal waste products that radiated deadly agents. Apart from burying these contaminants in the ground, at the immediate cost of the space they take up and the future risk of their getting disturbed or seeping into the water table, there was no way to dispose safely of radioactive wastes.

In theory, hydrogen—the most common element on the planet—was the most promising energy source. As early as 1874, the great French master of science fiction, Jules Verne (1828–1905), imagined a hydrogen-powered world. In the 1960s, rockets were launched into outer space with motors powered by hydrogen electrons. In the early twenty-first century, the giant American automobile corporation General Motors claimed to have spent $1 billion on research into a hydrogen-driven alternative to the internal combustion engine. But hydrogen motors need frequent refueling, and business has no economic incentive to create an infrastructure of hydrogen service stations before there are hydrogen cars that will need them. It is partly a chicken-and-egg problem. There will be no mass switch to hydrogen cars until the service stations are in place, and no network of service stations will be in place until drivers have hydrogen cars.

Toward the end of the twentieth century, the search for fossil-fuel substitutes switched to what people called **renewable energy**, culled from the wind, the sun, the tides, even—potentially—the power of magnetism and the motion of the planet or even of the entire expanding universe. These remedies all posed their own problems. The sun is unreliable, and its rays are unevenly distributed around the globe. It is hard to devise turbines to harness the tides. Wind power, as exploited in the late twentieth and early twenty-first centuries, required vast numbers of ugly and intrusive windmills to generate relatively modest output. Technology to harness magnetism on a large scale has eluded researchers. Planetary and cosmic forces are, so far, beyond our grasp. Nevertheless, enough had been accomplished by the end of the century to demonstrate the viability of renewable solutions and to encourage further work.

FOOD OUTPUT

Population growth meant the world needed not only more fuel but also more food—hugely more than ever before. At the same time, dwellings, cities, and industries have taken up space that might otherwise be used to grow food. Meanwhile, the spread of deserts—*desertification*—has put more pressure on existing land. Most of this is not the result of human agency. The spread of the Sahara in Africa, for instance, has been one of the most continuous, relentless processes observable on our planet since the last Ice Age ended 20,000 years ago. People, however, have made the problem of the loss of cultivable land much worse.

In some places, for instance, in the twentieth century, as so often before—only now on a bigger scale—overexploitation wasted soils and exhausted irrigation resources. In 1932, unrestrained overcropping helped to turn much of Oklahoma and other parts of the North American west into a "Dust Bowl." In the *Grapes of Wrath*, the Nobel Prize–winning novelist, John Steinbeck (1902–1968), described the odyssey of a family of poor farmers driven from their land and forced into oppression

Gasoline shortage, United States, 1973. A line of parked cars ends with an ominous sign about the lack of fuel. A pedestrian bends down to the driver of one vehicle, perhaps asking if any filling stations nearby have a supply of the precious commodity. As petroleum supplies dwindle and competition for them increases, scenes like this may soon be repeated across the world.

Winds of change. Even renewable energy sources have ecological costs. Wind exploitation demands the concentrations of thousands of turbines that disfigure landscapes—as here, in the California desert—and demand maintenance.

and misery as they struggled to reach a new life in California. Marginal land all over the world became ever less productive as the result of a vicious circle of cause and effect. Farmers, like those in Burkina Faso, had to force more food from less land, while the spreading deserts edged into their fields. The result was overexploitation. Farmers had to sow fields that needed to be left fallow to recover their fertility with new crops. So soils became more exhausted, and food supplies became more precarious. Much of the world is still trapped in this cycle, especially in parts of Africa and Asia. Population growth raises food needs. Farmers resort to overcropping to meet them. The land is impoverished in consequence. Food output falls, and hunger—or nowadays, more commonly, dependence on foreign aid—spreads.

Two traditional responses to the problem of trying to get more output from less soil are irrigation and fertilization. In the twentieth century, these remedies often proved worse than the problem they were designed to cure. Take irrigation first. In the second half of the twentieth century, the proliferation of huge dams—usually combining irrigation schemes with efforts to generate hydroelectric power—made desertification worse. Dams usually have to be backed by reservoirs, which increase the extent of the surface-area of water, exposing more water to the sun, which speeds up evaporation. Meanwhile, the reservoirs absorb the water from the smaller streams and tributaries in the vicinity. This increases the salt content of the soil, because freely flowing streams no longer dilute the salt. So the dams actually leach fertility from the soil.

Yet from the 1930s, when the world's first great dams blocked the Volga River in Russia and the Colorado River in the American West, until the late 1960s, when the adverse effects of excessive damming became intolerable, dams were prestige monuments. Beloved by governments, they were showpiece projects, like the temples and pyramids of antiquity. Indeed, leaders who commissioned them often proudly compared the dams to just such ancient structures. A classic example occurred in Egypt. Built with Soviet aid during the cold war, the Aswan Dam stretched across the Nile in the 1960s. It generated massive amounts of electricity and made it possible to regulate irrigation in Egypt with great precision. But it also trapped the silt that the Nile had carried since time immemorial to enrich Egypt's fields, shrinking the Nile delta, raising salt levels in the lower river, and choking off the flow of nutrients on which much

Aswan High Dam. Four monstrous, cavernous hydraulic tunnels lie under the unfinished Aswan High Dam during the dam's construction in Egypt in 1964. The dam came to symbolize the ecological irresponsibility of high-cost, high-prestige hydraulic projects. It displaced population, swamped precious archaeological sites, exposed valuable water to evaporation, impoverished soils, and sped pollutants down the Nile, extinguishing much marine life in the eastern Mediterranean.

Mediterranean marine life had formerly depended. Perhaps the single most disastrous project was the diversion in the 1950s of the two great rivers of Central Asia—the Oxus and Jaxartes (or Amu Darya and Syr Darya)—in what was then the southern Soviet Union. Soviet planners hoped to irrigate a vast plain for cotton production. Instead, they dried up the Aral, a huge inland sea, wrecked its fishing industry, and exposed deadly salt flats, from which the salt blew over the landscape, turning it barren. Though the fashion for dams declined, some monster projects continued, like dinosaurs escaping extinction. Between 1975 and 1991, Brazil and Paraguay collaborated to build a series of dams nearly five miles long across the river Paraná. The system generates more electricity than any other development in the world. In 2003, China opened an even bigger dam across the Yangtze—one of Mao Zedong's pet projects, at last brought to completion after nearly half a century of planning, debate, and construction. This Three Gorges Dam will eventually flood so much space that 2 million people will have to be resettled. At the time of its inauguration, more than two-thirds of the river waters of the world passed through dams, and China continued to plan and in some cases start work on more massive hydroelectric projects (see Figure 30.2).

In the second half of the twentieth century, the amount of land under irrigation increased from under 247 million acres to almost 644 million acres. By the century's end, 40 percent of the world's food was grown on irrigated land. Most irrigation water is pumped from below ground, where huge lakes and freshwater seas lie. But even this water is an exhaustible resource. The Ogallala Aquifer—a vast body of water—underlies the North American prairie. But 150,000 pumps are sucking it dry. In 1970, farmers in Kansas were told there was enough water left for a 300 years' supply. By the 1990s, the estimate had been revised to perhaps 20 or 30 years. The water table under the Sahara—where a vast inland, freshwater sea lies—falls measurably year by year. Unchecked consumption of irrigation resources in California, the Indian Punjab, the Murray-Darling river system in Australia, and the Cochabamba valley in Bolivia has had similar effects on the water table.

Fertilization, meanwhile, proved as mixed in its effects as irrigation. As we have seen (see Chapter 23), nineteenth-century agriculture relied on natural fertilizers, especially bird dung or guano. Chemical fertilizers supplied a relatively small market and seem to have had few or no ecological side effects. That changed in 1909 when Fritz Haber, a German chemist, discovered how to extract nitrogen from the atmosphere and use it to manufacture commercial fertilizer. It was like plucking food from the air. No other single invention did more to feed the growing population of the world in the second half of the century. In 1940, the world used some 4 million tons of artificial fertilizer. By 1990, it was using about 150 million tons. Phosphate mining provided another source of fertilizers. Agrochemicals manufacturers found ways to double-dose the soil with chemicals to stimulate crops and kill weeds.

The practice had a startling effect on the ecosystems it touched. Many kinds of insects lost their weedy habitats. The birds, reptiles, and small mammals that fed off the insects lost their food supply. By the 1960s, the effects were so marked that Rachel Carson, a former United States' government agronomist, published her immensely influential book, *Silent Spring*, in which she predicted an America without birdsong. An ecological movement sprang up and mobilized millions of people, especially in Europe and America, to defend the environment against pollution and overexploitation. "Pollution, pollution," sang the satirist Tom Lehrer, warning listeners to beware of two things: "don't drink the water and don't breathe the air." Norman E. Borlaug, the Nobel Prize–winning agronomist who helped to develop fertilizer-friendly crops, denounced "vicious, hysterical propaganda" against agrochemicals by "scientific halfwits," but he could not stem the tide of environmentalism at a popular level. Only the resistance of governments and big business could check it.

In any case, the arguments were not as decisively imbalanced as Rachel Carson and her followers claimed. Despite the environmentalists' protests, humankind at that moment needed agrochemicals. Population growth was outstripping farmers' capacity to feed the world. Even when used together, irrigation and fertilization could not meet the growing demand for food.

In theory, the world could have got by in other ways. Farmers could cut down on production of less nutritious foods and increase more efficient forms of output. Beef, for instance, has tended to attract inefficient methods of production in recent times, because it commands relatively high prices. Farmers, especially in the United States, therefore tend to produce it by feeding grain to cattle. It takes on average seven units by weight of grain to fatten about one unit of beef. Humans could get ten times as many calories from eating the grain themselves as they would get from eating the beef that ate the grain. Though beef is particularly wasteful, all livestock raising is a relatively inefficient way to use edible grain. Yet more than 70 percent of

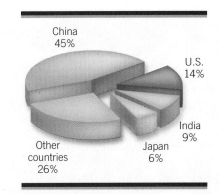

FIGURE 30.2 THE SHARE OF THE WORLD'S DAMS

© 2005 Pacific Institute for Studies in Development, Environment, and Security. www.pacinst.org

Earth Day. The American collage artist Robert Rauschenberg claims for artists a role in "determining the fate of the Earth." His poster, *Earth Day* (1970) advertises a propaganda device of the ecological movement—an annual day of awareness of the dangers of pollution and overexploitation. But the dangers are present 365 days a year. Designating a single day may be distracting or trivializing. So Rauschenberg's poster seems parochially American, with its symbolic eagle and U.S. doomscapes. *Robert Rauschenberg (American, b. 1925-) Earth Day 1970, color lithograph, 52 1/2 × 37 1/2 inches - 133.4 × 95.3 cm. Los Angeles County Museum of Art, gift of The Sidney and Diana Avery Trust. Photograph copyright © 2000 Museum Associates/LACMA. © Robert Rauschenberg and Gemini G.E.L./Licensed by VAGA, New York, NY*

the grain grown in the United States at the end of the twentieth century, and some 40 percent of the world's grain, was devoted to animal feed.

Even more nutrition could be wrested from even less land if people were willing to live on diets of soybeans, high-lysine maize, insects, plankton, algae, and compacted edible bacteria. But by and large they are not, and in the global food market, the hungry are in any case powerless. Taste and culture are more powerful than hunger because they command more funds. Even the hungry cannot adapt to food they find tastes bad or strange, or that they cannot digest, as aid agencies have found when they have tried to make people drink milk in cultures unfamiliar with that product. Globally, the food market is geared to profit, not production. Farmers are not going to switch from more profitable to less profitable markets. Nor can they afford to do so.

As fears of global food shortages became acute early in the second half of the twentieth century, there was therefore only one way out: make plant foods more productive. Agronomists had to develop fast-growing, high-yielding, disease-resistant varieties of nutritious staples for a range of different environments. In the 1950s, research concentrated on some of the traditionally most successful and most adaptable grains, especially wheat, rice, and maize. The big breakthrough came with the adaptation of dwarf varieties of wheat from Japan and of rice from Taiwan and Indonesia. These crops were stunted in stature and so could be sprayed with fertilizers without toppling them over. Experiments in Mexico and Washington State produced amazingly successful hybrids. By 1980, the world's average wheat yield per acre was double that of 1950. Under experimental conditions, the most successful new varieties yielded ten times as much again as older ones. The new crops covered three-quarters of the world's grain-growing areas by the early 1990s. Meanwhile, in 1970, the UN Food and Agriculture Organization reversed its predictions of widespread famine and estimated that the world could grow enough food to feed 157 billion people.

The **green revolution**—as people called it at the time—saved millions of lives. Even with the huge increase in global food output, failures of distribution contributed to many famines in the third quarter of the century. Without the new varieties the green revolution nurtured, the death toll would surely have been much higher. Nevertheless, the agronomists' successes came at a price. The new varieties were heavily dependent on chemical fertilizers and pesticides. So, as the green revolution spread, the world was—in effect—doused with poisons and pollutants. By 1985, according to the World Health Organization, pesticides had caused 1 million deaths, mostly among agricultural workers. Meanwhile, the new wonder crops crowded out traditional, local staples. The result was that peasant farmers in poor, economically deprived regions of the world produced ever-increasing quantities of cheap grains for survival and had little or no produce that they could sell at fair prices to rich consumers. Global poverty was becoming institutionalized.

Toward the end of the twentieth century, some scientists proposed to remedy the problems of the green revolution by switching to **genetically modified (GM) crops.** It became possible to modify the genes of food crops to make them resistant to insects, for example, without needing insecticides, or to deliver high yields with relatively little irrigation. The GM strategy, however, was rather like buying a rattlesnake to kill a rat—the proposed solution might be worse than the problem it was supposed to address. The new strategy might have undesirable ecological side effects of its own. Outside the United States, most governments were reluctant to encourage it, in case GM crops displaced or cross-pollinated with existing varieties and caused further losses of biodiversity (see Figure 30.3). Nor would GM crops liberate farmers from reliance on chemical fertilizers.

Moreover, GM technology demanded high investment in the form of development capital. A few companies that had the power to control it dominated the market for GM seeds. With the United States government's blessing, the big bankrollers patented genes, excluded competition, and produced seed that would not reproduce naturally—in effect, compelling farmers to buy new seed every year. If widely adopted, GM would perhaps guarantee cheap food for the world for the future. But this would not necessarily be a good thing. It would condemn food producers, including most of the world's peasants, to poverty as part of a system of overproduction, depriving them—should they become dependent on GM crops—of the opportunity to specialize in the supply of rare and expensive food to rich markets. In short, GM would make the poor poorer by forcing them to buy seed to produce goods they could not sell.

Cheap food was a by-product of the success of the green revolution. At the start of the twentieth century, an average American family spent about 35 percent of its income on food. By the end of the century, the corresponding figure had fallen to less than 15 percent—and that money bought a lot more to eat. Abundance of choice grew with abundance of quantity. Big multinational companies made the most of the situation. Cheap, mass-produced foods, with low unit profits, could make fantastic fortunes for the companies that sold them if they marketed them on a large enough scale. The American hamburger firm McDonald's became a globally recognizable example of this sort of strategy. It began as a local no-frills drive-in restaurant in San Bernardino, California, in 1937. By the end of the twentieth century, McDonald's had tens of thousands of outlets in 120 countries. Global urbanization favored the trend. In booming cities, migrants from the countryside were cut off from the sort of food they formerly ate: painstakingly grown plant foods, freshly harvested and locally prepared. A massive switch to mass-produced food occurred in just about every major urbanizing environment in the world—not just in the industrialized West. Paradoxically, while prosperity grew and food became abundant, many people's diets deteriorated.

At the same time, the science of dietetics failed. In the last 40 years of the twentieth century, on dieticians' advice, Western governments promoted massive health campaigns in favor of high-carbohydrate diets, recommending bread products, potatoes, pasta, rice. Cheap foods, laden with carbohydrates, especially in the form of sugar, glutted the market. In combination with the problems of distribution that urbanization created, the result was a pandemic of obesity. It started in the West, especially in the United States. In 1950, 5 percent of Americans were classified as clinically obese. By the end of the century, the figure rose to over 20 percent. It then jumped to 26 per cent in 2001. Particularly alarming was the rate of increase among the young. Well over a third of under-19-year-olds qualified as obese according to the standard definition. Though the United States weighed in at the top of the fat stakes, the same trend was detectable throughout the Western world. By the end of the century, it was beginning to be noticeable in much of the rest of the globe, even in countries where obesity was virtually unknown—including China, India, and even Japan, which, starting from a low statistical base, registered the world's steepest increase in clinical obesity in the 1990s.

Remarkably, late twentieth-century obesity was particularly a problem of the poor. This was a stunning reversal of what had been, almost universally, the pattern of the history of the world up to this time. In just about every previous period, in most societies, the rich were fat and the poor were thin. Now, it was the other way

DDT. In the 1950s, DDT (dichloro-diphenyl-trichloroethane) was a "wonder-insecticide" credited with controlling the mosquitoes that transmit malaria. "U.S. monoplanes daily swoop over Korea's capital," proclaimed the proud caption to this U.S. propaganda photo, "in the battle against disease and insects," spraying the city with DDT. In 1962, in the revolutionary environmentalist manifesto, *Silent Spring*, Rachel Carson denounced DDT for causing cancer and killing birds and other animals.

FIGURE 30.3 COUNTRIES LEADING IN GENETICALLY MODIFIED (GM) AGRICULTURE.

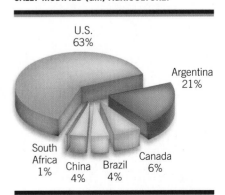

U.S. 63%

Argentina 21%

South Africa 1%

China 4%

Brazil 4%

Canada 6%

The Food and Agricultural Organization of the United Nations

Basic Resources: Fuel and Food

1890s	Development of internal combustion engines
1930s	World's first great dams constructed
1932	Dust Bowl emerges in central and western United States
1940–1990	Use of artificial fertilizer increases from 4 to 150 million tons
1950–1980	Wheat yields per acre double
1950–2000	Land under irrigation increases from 247 to 644 million acres
1965	Organization of Petroleum Exporting Countries (OPEC) formed
1962	Publication of Rachel Carson's *Silent Spring*
1973	OPEC oil embargo against the United States, Western Europe, and Japan
Late twentieth century	Acceleration of use of genetically modified crops; search for alternative fuels intensifies
ca. 2000	600 million cars worldwide; fossil fuels account for most of world's energy consumption; carbon dioxide levels in the atmosphere reach 350 parts per million
2003	Gates of the Three Gorges Dam over the Yangtze River closed

round. Formerly, abundance was a luxury. Only the rich could afford to be fat. When cheap food became abundantly available to the poor, the rich—at least, those of them who were fashion conscious—fled from fatness into dieting. In the twentieth-century West, wealth could buy you a thin physique by way of expensive "health foods," plastic surgery, personal trainers, and gymnasium fees. The world became one in which "You can never be too rich or too thin," as Wallis Simpson (1896–1986) had said. She was a waif-thin, almost wafer-thin, socialite, whom King Edward VIII of Britain renounced his throne in 1936 to marry. Meanwhile, the poor consoled themselves with calories in quantities they could never before afford.

The rise of obesity drove health agencies into panic. Yet one of the most remarkable facts about late twentieth-century obesity is how little harm it did. Most obese people managed to stay healthy and even to stay alive until a ripe old age. Nonetheless, the dramatically deadly new diseases of the period included two major killers to which the corpulent are particularly prone: heart diseases and type-II diabetes. More than 60 percent of type-II diabetes cases in America, according to a study done at Harvard University in 2001, were directly attributed to excessive weight. For the many people prone to the effect, fat in the bloodstream coated and clotted their arteries, inducing high blood pressure and causing strokes and heart attacks. A recent article in the *New England Journal of Medicine* estimates that if not reversed obesity will lower life expectancies for American children from diabetes, heart disease, and high blood pressure. If this is right, children may grow up to have shorter lives than their parents had. Life expectancy, in other words, will fall for the first time in American history. In short, twentieth-century food strategies succeeded in fighting famine and feeding the world. But they failed in just about every other important respect: overproducing abundance, increasing poverty, diminishing biodiversity, and undermining health.

URBANIZATION

In a world in which agriculture was getting more uniform and was becoming, under the pressure of economies of scale, a vast business that huge corporations ran, it got increasingly hard to be a peasant. A few rich countries, such as Germany and France, subsidized their small farmers. In most of the rest of the world, peasants abandoned the land and followed the new roads and railway lines toward cities and a promise of prosperity that often remained unfulfilled. This was one of the most dramatic new departures ever in the way people live. For 10,000 years, most people had lived in agricultural settlements. Now centers of industrial manufacturing and services took over. Towns and cities became the normal environments for people to live in. By the end of the century, half the world lived in settlements with populations of 20,000 or more (see Map 30.4). Cities grew even in countries where agriculture remained the economically dominant way of life. In Nigeria, typically for regions struggling to escape from a role as primary producers for other people's industries, a fifth of the population lived in towns in 1963. By 1991, the proportion had shot up to a third.

Urbanization came at a high short-term cost in terms of living standards. The world hardly seemed to have learned from the degradation of urban life in the industrializing cities of the nineteenth century (see Chapter 24). Now, as urbanization spread to new regions, the same problems recurred on a greater scale. Towns grew like fungus: profusely and unhealthily. The Brazilian town of Cubatão, which

Obesity in China. Patients, all of them young, perform aerobics at the Aimi Fat Reduction Hospital in Tianjin, China in March 2005. The hospital, which attracts obese people from several Asian countries, uses acupuncture, diet, and intensive exercise to help patients shed weight.

sprang suddenly from the mangrove swamps at the foot of the Serra do Mar mountains in the 1960s, typifies the horrors. Within 20 years, Cubatão became Brazil's major center for producing steel and fertilizers. In 1980, when 35 percent of infants there died before their first birthday, people who breathed toxic smog under acid rain called their home town the "valley of death."

Cleanups eased these problems in Cubatão by the end of the century, but the pattern kept being repeated elsewhere. In 1980, half the world's city dwellers had no access to treated water. In effect, they had to drink untreated sewage or pay a premium for bottled water. Over the twentieth century as a whole, air pollution probably killed as many people as war. Decent housing provision could not keep up with the surge of formerly rural populations to big towns (see Map 30.3). Shanties enveloped many of the great or growing cities of the world. In India in the 1990s, 1.5 million people lived on the streets of the cities, not out of poverty but simply because of the lack of housing. And though civic authorities tried to keep urban pollution under control, some effects of urbanization surprised the world and defied solutions. Nonrecyclable waste piled up. "Food deserts" emerged in towns where, with no means to grow food or store it in ways traditional in rural environments, newcomers to city life found themselves at the mercy of suppliers of the cheap, high-energy fast foods that were filling and satisfying but rarely nutritious. This is why mass obesity rapidly outgrew its origins as a disease of the newly affluent in North America and Europe, and became a worldwide urban scourge. The social consequences, meanwhile, of rapid urbanization proved hard to control. Rootless populations with unanchored loyalties, bred criminal organizations and gangs and even helped to produce the private armies for the civil wars that disturbed parts of Africa, southeast Asia, and Latin America.

By the century's end, however, there were signs that urbanization was easing. São Paulo in Brazil and Mexico City—overgrown giants with populations approaching 20 million each by some counts—began to shrink. The rise of markets for rare, traditional, artisanal, and exotic foods promised to restore the rural economy in parts of the world.

The reality of pell-mell urbanization. Lagos, Nigeria, is the biggest city in sub-Saharan Africa, growing at a rate of 5 to 6 percent a year. Its population is estimated to be between 10 and 15.5 million. The photograph shows some of the results: overcrowding, gerry-building, a transport system that barely functions, unregulated trading, accumulating litter.

Population in Urban Areas, ca. 2005

(percent of total population)

■	75 and above
■	50–74
■	25–49
□	0–24

Urban Areas with more than 5 Million People

● 2000

○ 2015 (projected)

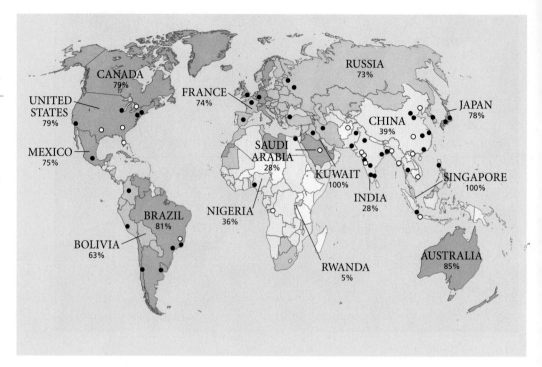

Cities would certainly remain humans' main habitat. But the trend suggested that concentrations of 100,000 to 1 million people would be normal, and that megacities of over 10 million people would shrink.

THE CRISIS OF CONSERVATION

In the twentieth century, the human domain expanded. People took up more space and depleted more resources than ever before. One result was predictable—other species could not compete. As well as crowding out some life-forms, humans blasted others into oblivion, hunting them to extinction, exterminating them with pest controls, or depriving them of their habitats or foods. By swapping plants and animals around the world—releasing invading species into unfamiliar habitats—humans condemned some native animals in affected zones to death by predation. In the 1960s, venomous Pacific snakes that had hitchhiked in the wheels of American army planes invaded Guam where they had no natural enemies and ate almost all the birds on the island within 15 years. Meanwhile, in the eastern Mediterranean, where the salt levels in the discharge from the Nile altered the ecology, new predators invaded from the Red Sea and wiped out unique local species.

At the start of the twenty-first century, the world faced the loss of more species than at any time since the end of the last Ice Age. One percent of recorded species of birds and mammals has disappeared in the previous 100 years. Because of pesticides, invertebrate species, which are less well documented, are likely to have suffered far more. According to the warnings of one of the most eminent authorities, 20 percent of all invertebrate species were in imminent danger of extinction as the twentieth century drew to a close. The extinction of a species is not an isolated event. Every species is a part of the ecosystem and a link in the food chain. Every extinction threatens other species.

But how much of the disaster was really the fault of humans? Some human communities have long considered themselves to be lords or stewards of creation, or in some sense to have special responsibility for other species. So, in the twentieth century, people who became aware of the appalling rate of species extinction tended to blame humans for it. Yet in the remote past, without our aid, nature has repeatedly turned over species—eliminating some, evolving others. The Ice Age of 245 million years ago, when the Earth became a "snowball," almost wiped out all life. Sixty-five million years ago, the dinosaurs vanished. As we have seen, the extinction of many kinds of large animals followed the end of the last Ice Age, when overexploitation by human hunters may have played a part in it. To some extent, current alarm may be a trick of the evidence. We are better informed than ever before about the state of preservation of species in the wild. We are aware of more extinctions, so we suppose more extinctions are underway. To some extent, too, the current situation is unfolding independently of human agency. Species extinction is a routine event in nature. Nonetheless, human activity undoubtedly speeded up the turnover of species during the twentieth century.

The amount of resources humans consumed left less for other species. The vigor with which farmers used pesticides and weed killers not only eliminated the species whose habitats were suppressed, but also others that fed on them. The pressure rising populations exerted on living space has probably edged many species out of existence. Half the deforestation of history happened in the twentieth century—almost all of it in tropical and wooded regions (see Map 30.4). In the last 40 years of the century, the Amazonian forests of Brazil shrank by 10 percent. In southeast Asia, those of Thailand, Malaysia, and Borneo in Indonesia disappeared on a similar scale. By the end of the century, Africa had lost half its tropical forests, Latin America nearly a third. The traditional human inhabitants of these environments—foragers and seasonal farmers—survived, but their habitats shrank, and their situation grew ever more precarious. So did that of the creatures who shared their traditional homes.

On the other hand, the twentieth century was remarkable for the recovery of forests in temperate zones, especially in Japan and North America, and for the flowering of many movements to conserve species and habitats. People launched projects to save endangered species, or to reintroduce into particular localities species that had already disappeared from them. If more species were lost through human action than ever before, more were also saved. And if human settlement eradicated some habitats, it created others in which wildlife throve. Every late twentieth-century town or suburban dweller has stories of possums under the couch, or racoons in the garbage, or foxes or coyotes in the shrubbery, or rabbits colonizing airports, or deer following the railway lines into the hearts of the cities or snacking on gardens.

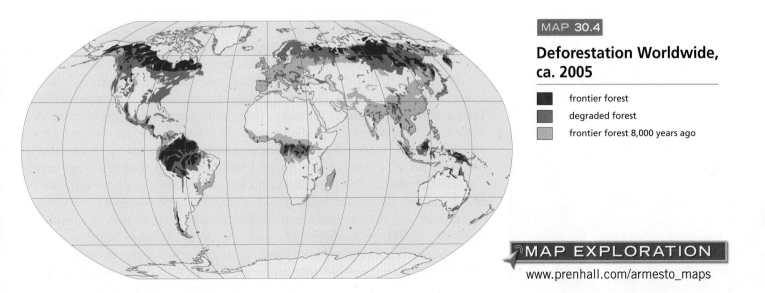

MAP 30.4

Deforestation Worldwide, ca. 2005

- frontier forest
- degraded forest
- frontier forest 8,000 years ago

MAP EXPLORATION

www.prenhall.com/armesto_maps

These successes, such as they were, happened on land. The bleakest story of environmental change and species depletion is a sea story. In the twentieth century, fish as a foodstuff leaped in popularity, like a salmon jumping the rapids. Historians debate why. In the second half of the twentieth century, after the beneficial health effects of fish oils became known (they boost nutrition, reduce cholesterol, and help prevent heart attacks), health concerns may have played a part. It is tempting to suspect that a romantic longing for wild, unfarmed food may have been influential, too. Fish is still largely a product of the hunt. Though industrial trawlers now make the catch, they still have to track the fish in the wild.

Whatever the reasons, the amount of fish that fisheries handled worldwide grew fortyfold in the twentieth century. Over that period, according to historian John McNeill, the world consumed 3 billion tons of fish. If McNeill's calculations are right, that exceeds the whole catch landed during the entire previous history of the world. Some varieties were fished to near extinction (see Map 30.5). At the end of the century, Atlantic cod stocks stood, according to common calculations, at only 10 percent of their historic average. California sardines became rarities. North Sea herrings—once a staple food in much of Europe—are now a costly treat. The Japanese sardine fishery was the most abundant in the world in the 1930s but had virtually collapsed by the mid-1990s. Off Namibia in southern Africa, fishermen caught millions of tons of sardines in the 1960s. By 1980, none were left. At the end of the century, the predicament of the Chilean sea bass, which has become a trendy dish in the United States and Western Europe, precipitated a crisis. Profit-conscious Chilean fishermen pleaded with clients to go on eating the species, while ecological enthusiasts tried to persuade restaurateurs to ban it.

If fish stocks are permanently lost, the results will be catastrophic. The use of fishmeal in fertilizers and animal feeds makes fish a vital food source for the world, way beyond the tonnage humans directly consume. But was the apparent depletion of the world's fishing stocks in the twentieth century an irreversible disaster or a temporary blip? Fish migration patterns change, and the fact that we have lost sight of traditional stocks of some species in the vastness of the ocean does not necessarily mean that they have disappeared forever. Some extraordinary cases of recuperation have been recorded. The supply of Maine lobsters, for instance, waxed and waned almost regularly during the twentieth century. Some oyster beds, once thought to have been exhausted, are now plentiful again. In the late twentieth and early twenty-first centuries, the recovery of populations of whales and harbor seals showed that marine conservation programs could work. In 2005, successful conservation policies attracted blame for an increase in the incidence of shark attacks on people in Australian waters. Fish conservation methods seem to be working for Atlantic cod and haddock. Roughly, fishermen now concentrate on each species in turn, allowing the other to recover.

Still, by the end of the twentieth century, many authorities concluded that the future lay with fish farming. Fish farms produced 5 million tons of food worldwide in 1980, and 25 million tons by the end of the century. China accounted for more than half the total. Fish farming is an effective method of food production. Farmed salmon yield fifteen times more nutrition per acre than beef cattle. The sea bass grows twice as fast under farmed conditions as in the wild. In the wild, it takes a million eggs to produce a fish. By the early twenty-first century, farmers were regularly turning 60 percent of eggs into fish. Meanwhile, techniques of fish farming improved. What was formerly a freshwater and coast-bound activity began to be possible in the deep ocean. So, despite the losses from overfishing, the world's stocks of edible fish probably were and are secure for the foreseeable future. Again, of course, we will to pay an environmental cost. Fish farms are eco-niches for new marine plagues. Farmed species will inevitably escape into the wild and crowd out others by infection and crossbreeding.

Salvation or disaster? Fish farming is likely to supply increasing amounts of the world's protein and solve the problem of overfishing. But it creates new eco-niches for disease and threatens biodiversity. The photograph shows a fish farm in China, where aquaculture programs are among the most developed in the world.

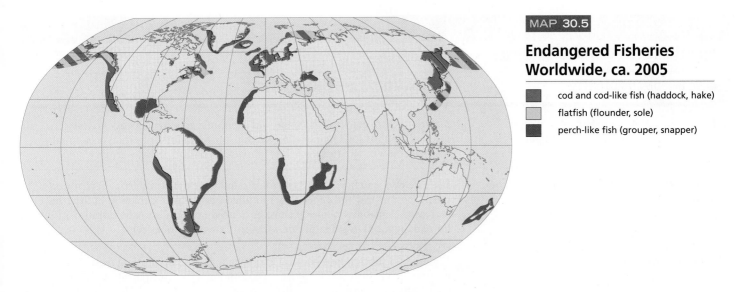

MAP 30.5

Endangered Fisheries Worldwide, ca. 2005

- ■ cod and cod-like fish (haddock, hake)
- ▢ flatfish (flounder, sole)
- ■ perch-like fish (grouper, snapper)

THE UNMANAGEABLE ENVIRONMENT: CLIMATE AND DISEASE

Ecological alarmism has become a trend of our times—a modern, secular form of millenarianism. We scare ourselves into expecting the apocalypse, the end of the world, or at least the end of civilization as we know it. Our fears could well come true. Civilizations have collapsed because they failed to get their relationship with the environment right. Overexploitation is a constant temptation. We still succumb to it. No period can match our own for the sheer wasteful carelessness with which we pollute our planet and consume its resources. But the ecological problems of our times do not start or stop with our self-inflicted difficulties. Bigger dangers are worrying precisely because they are not of our making. If we caused them, we could control them. But we do not cause them. They are beyond our control.

The Earth is still in its infancy. The planet has, at a reasonable guess, several billion years to go before it sizzles or freezes into lifelessness. By supposing that we could destroy our planet, we are guilty of a kind of arrogance. The Earth is hugely bigger than anything we have power to wreck. Nature will surely outlast our species. Trees that were here before humans existed will go on growing after humans have gone. So will microbes and—probably—insects, reptiles, birds, and marine species vastly older than humankind. When the planet perishes, it will be nothing to do with us. It will happen long after we are gone. And the cause will rest with cosmic forces that we are aware of but have no power to influence.

These considerations are worth bearing in mind, because if we kid ourselves into thinking that all ecological problems are our own fault, we shall be deluded into supposing that we can fix them all. It is worth remembering that we have hardly scratched the surface of the planet we inhabit. Our deepest oil wells are only thousands of feet deep. Most species have never been cataloged and are perhaps unknown. The oceans, a habitat we have not yet begun to colonize and have still done little to exploit, make up 90 percent of the planet.

So despite our self-inflicted disasters, a lot of nature still threatens us without being threatened in return. In 2005, a hurricane devastated and drowned New Orleans, provoking President George W. Bush to acknowledge that Nature was "the world's greatest superpower." Some of the dangers prophets invoke are close to the edges of science fiction. Asteroid bombardment, for instance, is unlikely to happen, but the threat of it demonstrates the perplexities we face in confronting natural

● MAKING CONNECTIONS

GLOBAL ENVIRONMENTAL CHALLENGES

AREA OF HUMAN ACTIVITY →	ENVIRONMENTAL AND SOCIAL EFFECTS
Fuel resources: human dependence on electricity, internal combustion engine, and fossil fuels	Electricity permeates everyday life and economic activity; dependence on internal combustion engine to power transport and link suburban residential districts; oil wars; increased carbon-dioxide levels and global warming
Food resources: need to supply over 6 billion humans	Increased dependence on agrochemicals and large dams and irrigation projects; reliance on hybrid and genetically modified staple crops; depletion of fisheries, increased availability of cheap, mass-produced food leads to deterioration of human diets and overreliance on carbohydrates, fats (obesity)
Housing: increased urbanization/ suburbanization	Widespread substandard housing and urban air, water pollution; increased nonrecyclable waste; dependence on automobiles for transportation; favorable environment for criminal organizations; gangs
Swapping plants and animals around the world to increase yields	Displacement of indigenous plant/animal species from native environments; disappearance of thousands of species of plants/animals, adding to decline in biodiversity

The power of nature. The center of Hurricane Katrina's rotation at 9:15 A.M. EST on August 29, 2005 over southeast Louisiana. Winds over 135 mph and accompanying floods effectively destroyed much of the city of New Orleans and emptied all but the highest ground of population, causing billions of dollars of damage, costing many lives, and provoking a crisis of conscience in the United States Despite long-standing predictions of disaster, many parts of New Orleans and surrounding communities had been left without adequate defenses or relief.

forces outside human control. The United States government is popularly supposed to have plans to deflect or explode an approaching asteroid with nuclear missiles, but such a defense would have unpredictable and incalculable consequences.

We face more immediate dangers. Two of the most powerful sources in nature remain barely understood and beyond our power to manage: disease-bearing microorganisms and climate. Either or both could destroy humankind with no help from us. Take climate first. For all our accumulated cunning, we cannot control climate change or reverse its effects. At best, we seem able only to edge it in directions in which we do not want it to go: speeding up global warming, reducing rainfall, intensifying desertification. As we have seen, for most of the period this book covers, from the waning of the last great Ice Age some 20,000 years ago, the world has been experiencing a protracted warming phase. From about the fourteenth century C.E. to about the eighteenth, warming went into a temporary eclipse. Allowing for many ups and downs, temperatures declined slightly but significantly over much of the world (see Chapter 14). Around the mid–nineteenth century, however, warming seems to have intensified. Despite a wavering in the third quarter of the twentieth century, when falling temperatures excited prophesies of a new Ice Age, global temperatures by the turn of the millennium recovered or exceeded levels last reached some 800 years ago (see Figure 30.4). If this phase continues, rising sea levels could swamp much of the world. Crops vulnerable to heat could become uncultivable. Areas, for instance, devoted now to cool-temperature varieties of rice will have to switch to some other, currently unknown staple, or be abandoned.

We do not yet know how to cope with global warming if the planet continues to heat up. Some of our efforts to deflect it seem feeble: cutting the rates of increase of carbon emissions, often by relying on trivial measures, such as recycling refrigerators (which are cooled by carbon-based gases) and banning aerosol sprays. On the other hand, a new Ice Age may occur. We do not at present know how to prepare for it. The future, it seems, will be fire or ice.

Or disease will dominate it—a recurrent age of plagues (see Chapter 14). Despite the stunning achievements of medical science, humans still do not control—or even adequately understand—the microbial world in which much disease originates. The spectacular victories of the twentieth century include the defeat of some of the most terrible killing and maiming diseases doctors faced: polio, smallpox, and a whole range of illnesses formerly responsible for heartbreaking levels of infant mortality. For a time, new treatments almost eliminated tuberculosis, though it revived in the late twentieth century. New remedies spared the lives of diabetics, though the disease is acquiring increasing numbers of victims. Improved surgery made organ transplants possible. Kidneys could be swapped beginning in the early 1950s, hearts transplanted starting in 1967 (though the use of surgical devices to regulate the heart prolonged more lives among those who suffered from heart disease.) Medicine made a big contribution to the rising life-expectancy figures. Sanitation and public health care probably made an even more spectacular difference. But, in privileged places, the effects were impressive. In much of Western Europe, Canada, Australia, New Zealand, and the United States, average life expectancy at the end of the century was in the mid-seventies for men and the low eighties for women. Fears multiplied of a future in which the workforce would be too small to support an increasingly elderly population and the rising costs of caring for the health of the aged. In Japan, the trend was similar, with 16 percent of the population aged over 65 in 1998. Japan, faced with the world's biggest increase of over-70-year-olds in the population, began to subsidize old people to resettle overseas. In China, at the end of the century, most people could expect to live into their late 60s. In India, life expectancy rose to an average of 63 years of age.

The massive increase of world population in the late twentieth century was, above all, a triumph of what we might call death control. The great population growth of the eighteenth century was probably the result of adjustments in the microbial world (see Chapter 20). That of the twentieth, by contrast, arose from human agency: medical remedies, and the preventive measures of public health policy.

But scientific self-congratulation over these successes masked worrying, persistent problems. Medical advances were unfairly distributed. Life expectancy in the African countries of Benin, Burkina Faso, Burundi, and Angola, at the end of the twentieth century, remained stuck at an average in the mid-40s. In Guinea-Bissau the figure in 1998 was 42 for men and 45 for women. In Uganda, Rwanda, and Malawi, the average for both sexes was 42 or under. In much of the rest of sub-Saharan Africa, the situation was little better. At 112 deaths per thousand in Nigeria and 90 in Ivory Coast, sub-Saharan infant mortality rates were three or four times worse than those of most of East and southeast Asia, and immeasurably worse than those of Western Europe (see Map 30.6).

Moreover, and inseparably, medical advances were costly. Health-care costs in America left many of the poor out of the loop. In Europe, where state-run national health services ensured a fairer distribution of benefits, taxpayers struggled to keep pace with the costs. In Britain, for instance, the National Health Service cost £400 million to run in 1951, about £32 billion a half-century later. The cost more

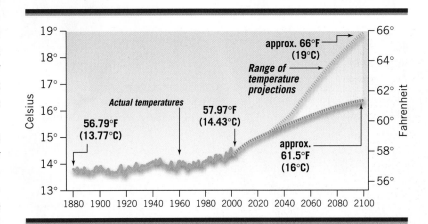

FIGURE 30.4 GLOBAL ANNUAL AVERAGE TEMPERATURES AND PROJECTIONS, 1880–2100
© Time Inc. Reprinted by permission.

Poliomyelitis was one of the horrific new killer-diseases of the twentieth century that science managed to contain. Sanitation created an eco-niche for polio to develop. Before the twentieth century, mildly unsanitary drinking water contained tiny amounts of the virus so people acquired immunity naturally. But after the 1920s, the disease became rampant. It paralyzed Franklin D. Roosevelt, the future U.S. president, in 1921. Most victims died through paralysis of the brain. This 1955 photograph shows mothers and children in London waiting in line with affected cheerfulness and real fear for the newly developed vaccine.

than doubled over the following two years, while inflation generally rose at less than 2 percent a year. By that time, it was absorbing 6.6 percent of the nation's income. The leap in life expectancy made health-care costs worse. People lived longer, contributed less to national wealth as they got older, and consumed more of that wealth in health care. By the early 1990s, health care costs absorbed between 7 and 10 percent of the gross domestic product of most developed countries, and over 14 percent in the United States.

Furthermore, although medicine eliminated old diseases, new ones—or new forms of old ones—arose to torment humanity. The effects of pollution, drug abuse, undiscriminating sex habits, and affluence—which condemned the unwary to overindulgence and inertia—were major killers. Far more lethal, however, was the rapid evolution of viruses. Some killers, such as Ebola, Lassa fever, and the immune-destroying virus known as HIV, leaped from the eco-niches in which they had formerly been contained and began to attack humans. New forms of influenza appeared regularly, though none attained the virulence of the pandemic of 1918–1919, which claimed an estimated 30 million lives worldwide. A new strain of tuberculosis, which emerged in the late twentieth century, resists every known drug and kills half the people it infects. Bubonic plague has returned to India. New strains of cholera and malaria have emerged. Malaria cases in India rose a hundred fold to 10 million between 1965 and 1977. In sub-Saharan Africa, malaria kills 1 million children a year. Yellow fever—which had almost been eradicated by the midcentury—killed 200,000 people a year in Africa in the 1990s. Measles, a disease that immunization was expected to eradicate, was still killing 1 million people a year at the end of the century. New viruses can defeat antibiotics and other drugs, which decline in effectiveness as a result of overuse.

Other new diseases arose in man-made eco-niches: Legionnaire's disease, which breeds in the dampness of air-conditioning systems, was the prime example. Intensive farming created breeding conditions for salmonella in chickens and accumulated toxins in the food chain. Human-variant CJD, or "Mad Cow disease," is a brain-killing dis-

Life Expectancy, ca. 2005

(years)

	70 and above
	60–69
	50–59
	40–49
	less than 40

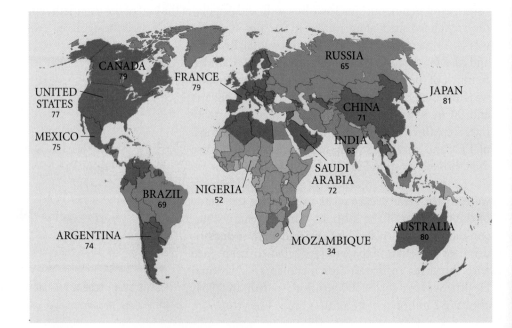

ease, apparently caused by intensive cattle-farming methods—recycling dead sheep and cattle as fodder—and was transmitted to at least some of its victims in tainted food. Twentieth-century interventions in the environment opened many new eco-niches for disease: in overfertilized soil, stripped of much insect life; in polluted waterways; and in the disturbed depths of the sea, where bacteria multiply in searing hot vents that humans have only lately begun to penetrate. In an increasingly interconnected world, human carriers took diseases way beyond accustomed environments. Toward the end of the century, West Nile virus from Africa turned up in New York City. A variant form of influenza from China caused widespread deaths, especially in Canada. Dengue fever from Asia has become endemic in parts of the Caribbean.

Broadly speaking, infectious diseases ceased to be major killers, though old ones constantly threatened to reemerge and new ones to develop. Chronic diseases, meanwhile, arose to replace infections as the major menace. Cancer and heart diseases grew spectacularly, especially in rich countries, without anyone knowing why. By the 1980s in the United States, one death in every four was blamed on cancer. In Britain, one death in three was ascribed to heart disease, which caused 10 million deaths a year worldwide by the end of the century. Some forms of cancer were "lifestyle diseases." Cervical cancer, for instance, was thought to be connected to sexual promiscuity or adolescent sexual intercourse, while smoking, according to most authorities, caused lung, throat, and mouth cancers and contributed to heart disease and stroke. Obesity and its related disorders, as discussed earlier, owed their prevalence, in part, to bad eating habits. In the second half of the twentieth century, evidence began to accumulate that some medical treatments were actually contributing to the disease environment. Doctors prescribed drugs so widely that people were becoming dependent on them, while many viruses and strains of bacteria were developing immunity to them. Even where physical health improved, mental health seemed to get worse. The highly competitive capitalist societies of the developed West became prey to various neurotic disorders collectively known as stress. Worriers "medicalized" their anxieties and feelings of malaise, classifying them in their own minds as medical problems and taking them to the doctor. Medical services, already hard-pressed, became overburdened.

Two new diseases demonstrated the microbial world's destructive potential. The first was the influenza of 1918–1919, the second, the scourge of AIDS, which lashed into prominence in the 1980s. AIDS started in Africa as a sexually communicated syndrome between men and women. It then broke out in the West, where, at first, it was particularly virulent among homosexuals. Eventually it spread around the world as a result of the transfusion of infected blood or the transmission—usually through sex—of other bodily fluids. By the beginning of the new millennium, the virus generally held to be responsible for AIDS, a condition in which the patient's immunity to all kinds of disease is progressively destroyed, had killed 27 million people and infected perhaps as many as 80 million worldwide. Although the disease seemed to be under control in most of Europe and the Americas, it was rampant in Africa and much of Asia, where, for a mixture of cultural and economic reasons, governments were less committed to fighting it. Toward the end of the century, doctors in South Africa reckoned that AIDS accounted for 40 percent of deaths among sexually active people (see Map 30.7). A new, more virulent, and perhaps untreatable strain seemed to be emer0ging in the United States early in the twenty-first century.

Bird flu. In 2005, bird flu became one in a long series of new diseases feared as the potential "next plague." Health workers culled tens of millions of poultry wherever the infection appeared. The photograph shows such an operation in progress in Turkey. Farmers lost livelihoods. Governments spent fortunes. Fear of bird flu has thus far proved exaggerated. The disease has not spread easily to humans. But mounting health scares showed growing awareness of the world's vulnerability to unfamiliar viruses.

 Nelson Mandela, Closing Address to the Thirteenth International AIDS conference, 2000

IN PERSPECTIVE: The Environmental Dilemma

We can monitor the environmental transformations of the twentieth century on the map. The surface of the Earth has become a gridwork of routes laid out by human hands. Instead of the physical features—rivers, mountains, forests, deserts—that used to be the markers travelers relied on, roads, rails, air routes, and shipping lanes now connect or, in their absence, isolate locations.

The results were not evenly spread across the world. On the contrary, a development gap widened between regions of growing prosperity, which produced and consumed immeasurably more than other regions, and underdeveloped parts of the world, where most people got little chance to share in the increased wealth. At the century's end, the average income of people in the poorer half of the world was less than 5 percent of that of citizens of the top 20 richest countries.

In the late twentieth-century world, prosperity seemed to be the best contraceptive. In rich, industrialized communities, population growth slowed or went into reverse. Where poverty reigned, children were too valuable a resource to forego. As a result, the world's wealth gaps widened. Growing populations strained resources in the regions that could least afford to feed and care for large numbers of people, while the relative wealth of the developed world multiplied. This should not surprise anyone. Human reproduction resembles, in some respects, the production of commodities. It operates according to laws of supply and demand. Birthrates fall as income rises, because in mechanizing societies, manpower loses value and people therefore produce fewer babies. Economic progress promotes a further kind of change that also holds down population. Women's "liberation" encourages women to switch from having children to other kinds of productive activities.

Migration from poor, overpopulated areas, in Africa and parts of Asia and Latin America, into rich areas that have a shortage of labor was an inevitable consequence, with huge social, political, and cultural effects (see Chapter 29). Industrialized nations invited guest workers in, while struggling to regulate their numbers. It then proved hard to prevent the erosion of traditional cultures or the outbreak of intercommunal violence.

By the end of the century, however, there were signs that the various regions of the world were on a convergent course. In most of Latin America and Asia, population growth slowed down. Demographers began to predict that world population would peak in the early twenty-first century, and then begin to fall, probably between 2020 and 2050.

On the far side of that peak in population, the world will look different. A big shift has occurred across the world in the demographic balance between old and young, north and south, east and west. While population continued to soar in Africa and the Americas, Europe was demographically stagnant by the end of the century. The population of much of Eastern Europe—especially of Russia, Latvia, and Ukraine—fell in the 1990s. Political and economic dislocation (see Chapter 28) contributed to the effect. In parts of Western Europe—

MAP 30.7

HIV in Africa

HIV Prevalance Rates in African Adults
(15-49 Years of Age) as of the End of 2003

- 0.0%–1.9%
- 2%–4.9%
- 5%–9.9%
- 10%–19.9%
- 20% or greater
- no data

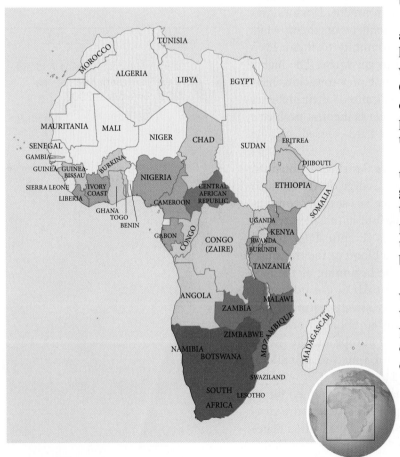

Spain, Italy, and Germany—the overall population levels would also have fallen if immigrants had not helped keep the numbers up. Declining birth rates and declining male fertility—the causes of which are unknown—combined with increased life expectancy to boost the relative numbers of the elderly and inactive and reduce those of the young.

China suffered from a similar problem because the regime, alarmed at the pace of population growth, began to penalize families who chose to have more than one child. The Chinese government imposed compulsory abortions, sterilization, and punitive fines on offenders. The result is that in the early twenty-first century China faces a population imbalance comparable to that of Europe, with a large aging population and a relative dearth of young labor. India experimented with birth control programs under government encouragement, but never imposed policies as severe as those of China. India's growth rate fell to about 2 percent a year by the end of the millennium, but it was still vigorous enough to ensure that the size of its population would continue to rank second in the world—and might even overtake China's. By the end of the century, birth rates in Thailand, Indonesia, the Indian Ocean island of Mauritius, and much of Latin America were not much higher than in Europe. The pattern for the future looked increasingly like one of stabilizing population worldwide.

Meanwhile, in Africa and most of the Islamic world, especially the Muslim countries on the edges of the Indian subcontinent, populations were increasing rapidly. In these regions, and in parts of Latin America that are still in the early stages of a transition to European- or Japanese-style demographics, the ratios of old and young are reversed (see Figure 30.5). There are huge numbers of young people, not enough for them to do, and, typically, not enough locally produced food for them to eat.

The twentieth century was a period of intense and frequently violent competition between ideologies. Adherents of different kinds of political totalitarianisms fought wars against each other and against democracy. Religions conflicted with atheism and secularism as well as with each other. Battle lines formed around incompatible understandings of human rights and responsibilities. Economic systems collided. Whole civilizations—according to some predictions—threatened to clash. It seems surprising, on the face of it, that amid all this friction and frenzy environmentalism should

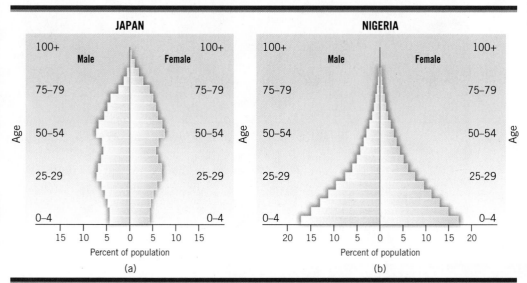

FIGURE 30.5 THE POPULATIONS OF JAPAN AND NIGERIA COMPARED

Reprinted with permission of the Population Reference Bureau.

THE EARTH AT NIGHT

Darkness can often be more revealing than the light. Composite satellite imagery, taken over a one-year period early in the twenty-first century, shows the impact of humans on the planet.

Rich, developed regions like the U.S., Europe, and Japan pulsate with light. Lights also fan out along major arteries—such as the Nile River in Egypt or the Trans-Siberian railway in Russia.

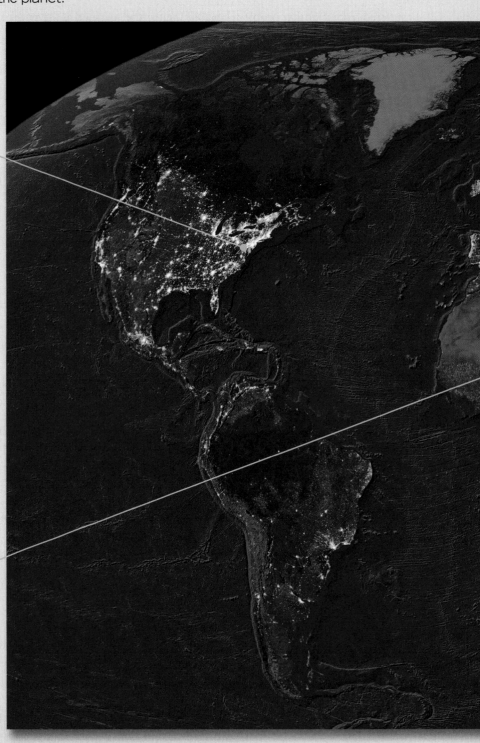

Natural gas burn-off is a by-product of petroleum extraction that leads to atmospheric pollution. Billions of gallons of gas go up in smoke each year.

Does this photograph suggest a hopeful or a pessimistic assessment of the future?

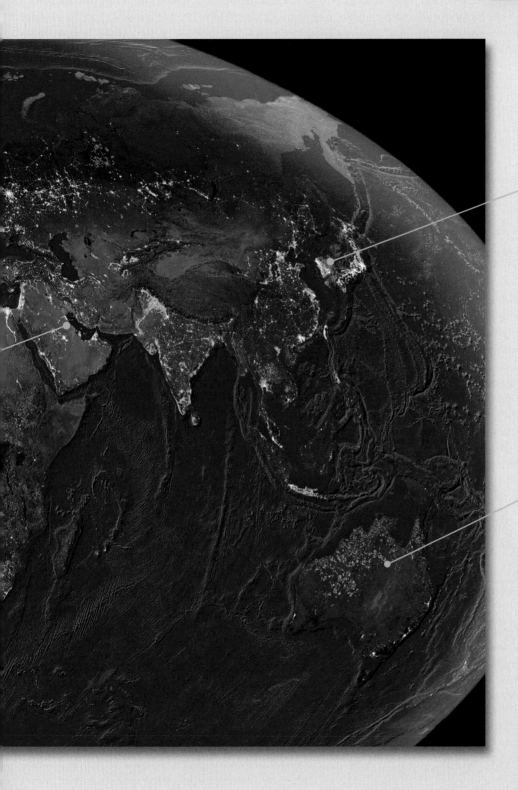

Night fishing off the coasts of Japan and Argentina, where scores of boats use bright lights to attract squid to the surface.

Fires burn, either from slash-and-burn agriculture in Africa and South America, or in the case of Australia, set off by lightning and other natural causes.

have found the space to express itself and emerge, by the end of the century, as a contender to be the world's most widely shared consensus. One way to measure this is to count the increase in the number of international environmental organizations. There were 20 when the Second World War started in 1939, and about 40 in the late 1940s. By 1990, there were 340. Such an increase would have been impossible had the century not also witnessed unprecedented human impact on our planet. As the century wore on, the changes humans wrought—and the damage they inflicted—became glaringly visible and measurable, provoking the movement that we now usually call environmentalism: a deepening and spreading conviction that humans are part of the web of the natural world; that our relationship with our environment is the inescapable framework for everything we do; and that, in consequence, care of the environment is our essential priority, whether as a self-interested strategy, or as a moral or religious duty that we owe to other forms of life.

In the early twenty-first century, much of the world is experiencing growth fatigue—the feeling people have in some rich communities that we do not want a world winding into the stratosphere of spiraling desire, at ever more irresponsible levels of consumption, production, and resource depletion. Rationally, we do not need to grow richer. Instead, those of us who enjoy the privilege of relative prosperity in an unequal world need to safeguard our riches by redistributing them more fairly. The opposite argument says that capitalism works—at least, it works less badly than any other economic system ever devised in the entire course of human history, because it is attuned to human nature. People are always going to want to better themselves economically. We can no more renounce the pursuit of material "happiness" than stop the world in its orbit. So it is best to try to make a virtue of this trait and find environmentally sustainable ways to increase the world's wealth and free markets to distribute it more evenly.

We can best understand the eco-history of recent times in the context of changing notions about the place of humankind in nature—the results of the new science described in Chapter 27. We know too much about our common ancestry with other animals, the limits of our peculiarities compared with other social and cultural creatures, the moral overlap between *Homo sapiens* and other species, and our ties to a complex, interconnected ecosystem, to go on thinking of humans as apart or distinct from the rest of nature. The future of our relationship with the rest of nature is best considered in the light of evidence dispersed throughout this book. Many of the failed civilizations of the past weakened or wrecked themselves by overexploiting their environments. What are we going to do with our world? It is, so far, the only one we have to live in.

CHRONOLOGY

1890s	Development of internal combustion engines
1900–2000	1 percent of recorded bird and mammal species go extinct; amount of fish handled by world's fisheries increases 40-fold
1918–1919	Worldwide influenza epidemic
1930s	World's first great dams constructed
1932	Dust Bowl emerges in central and western United States
1940–1990	Use of artificial fertilizer increases from 4 to 150 million tons
1950	Global population 2.5 billion
1950–1980	Wheat yields per acre double
1950–2000	Land under irrigation increases from 247 to 644 million acres
1962	Publication of Rachel Carson's *Silent Spring*
1965	Organization of Petroleum Exporting Countries (OPEC) formed
1970	Global population 3.7 billion
1973	OPEC oil embargo against the United States, Western Europe, and Japan
1978	First known cases of AIDS
1980	50 percent of world's urban population has no access to treated drinking water
1980–2000	Fish-farm production increases from 5 to 25 million tons
1990	Global population 5.3 billion
Early 1990s	Health-care costs absorb 14 percent of GDP in the United States
Late twentieth century	Acceleration of use of genetically modified crops; search for alternative fuels intensifies
ca. 2000	50 percent of world's population lives in settlements larger than 20,000 people; world's four largest cities: Tokyo, 28 million; Mexico City, 18 million; Mumbai (Bombay), 18 million; São Paulo, 17 million
ca. 2000	600 million cars worldwide; fossil fuels account for most of world's energy consumption; carbon-dioxide levels in the atmosphere reach 350 parts per million
March 28, 2001	United States pulls out of Kyoto Protocol
2003	Gates of the Three Gorges Dam over the Yangtze River closed
August 29, 2005	Hurricane Katrina destroys coast of southeastern United States
2010	Global population 6.9 billion (est.)
2020	Global population 7.6 billion (est.)

PROBLEMS AND PARALLELS

1. How has population explosion put unprecedented pressure on the world's energy resources and food supply? Why do people consume more food, goods, and energy than ever before?

2. What are the drawbacks of fossil fuels? How do they contribute to the greenhouse effect? What are the advantages and disadvantages of alternate sources of power?

3. Why did the increased use of fertilization and irrigation in the twentieth century have such harmful effects on the environment? What costs were associated with the green revolution? What are the drawbacks of genetically modified crops?

4. Why did obesity increase in countries such as China, India, and Japan where it had previously been rare?

5. How did twentieth-century urbanization affect human societies? What pressures do megacities put on the environment?

6. How significant is the "crisis of conservation"? Is the outlook bleak?

7. What threats do disease and climate pose to humans in the early twenty-first century?

DOCUMENTS IN GLOBAL HISTORY

- Kyoto Protocol, Article 2

- Nelson Mandela, Closing Address to the Thirteenth International AIDS conference, 2000

Please see the Primary Source CD-ROM or additional sources related to this chapter.

READ ON

The story of Rasmata comes from O. Bennett, ed., *Greenwar: Environment and Conflict* (1991). On Burkina Faso, D. E. McMillan, *Sahel Visions: Planned Settlement and River Blindness Control in Burkina Faso* (1995) is a fascinating, personally engaged anthropologist's account of one development project. There is little else of book-length available in English, but important pamphlets include B. Paaru-Laarsen, *The Concept of Drought and Local Social and Economic Strategies in the Northern Burkina Faso*, and M. Ou draogo, *Land Tenure and Rural Development in Burkina Faso* (2002). The context is covered in M. Mortimore, *Roots in the African Dust: Sustaining the Sub-Saharan Drylands* (1998).

J. E. McNeill, *Something New Under the Sun* (2001) is a superb global history of the twentieth-century environment. D. Worster, *Nature's Economy* (1985), and A. Bramwell, *Ecology in the Twentieth Century* (1989) are excellent surveys of environmentalism with contrasting arguments. F. Harris, ed., *Global Environmental Issues* (2004) is a useful and comprehensive overview. On the idea of spiraling desire, M. Girard, *Violence and the Sacred* (1979) is fundamental. D. Worster, *Dust Bowl* (1982) is an outstanding case study of degradation.

On energy, J. Twidell and T. Weir, *Renewable Energy Resources* (2005) is a good introduction to renewables. D. Yergin, *The Prize* (1993) is the classic account of oil. M. Klare, *Blood and Oil* (2004) is both scholarly and shocking. J. Rifkin, *The Hydrogen Economy* (2003) sketches the possible hydrogen-dependent future. On China, V. Smil, *China's Environmental Crisis* (1993) is perhaps the best study.

On biodiversity, K. J. Gaston and I. J. Spicer is *Biodiversity* (2004) is a sober introduction. R. Leakey and R. Lewin, *The Sixth Extinction* (1996) is vigorous, challenging, and controversial.

T. M. Swanson, ed., *The Economics and Ecology of Biodiversity Decline* (1998) is a helpful collection, which demonstrates the difficulties clearly. W. D. Ean, *With Broadax and Firebrand* (1997) narrates the destruction of the Amazonian forest. L. Lear, *Rachel Carson* (1998) is a useful life of the great environmentalist.

On food, K. Blaxter and N. Robertson, *From Dearth to Plenty* (1995) sets the context well. D. Goodman and M. J. Watts, eds., *Globalising Food* (1997) is important and wide-ranging. E. Sclosser, *Fast Food Nation* (2001) is an influential study of U. S. excess. G. Critser, *Fat Land* (2004) is journalistic and sensationalist but full of data. H. Levenstein, *Revolution at the Table* (2003) takes a longer-term view of changes in the American diet. M. Goran, *The Story of Fritz Haber* (1967) is a good biography of the pioneer of modern fertilizers.

J. Hardoy, D. Mitlin and D. Satterthwaite, *Environmental Problems in an Urbanizing World* (2001) is a good introduction to twentieth-century urbanization.

L. D. D. Harvey, *Global Warming: The Hard Science* (1999) is clear and minatory about climate. L. Garrett, *The Coming Plague* (1994) is a page-turner on disease, though much criticized for exaggerating the problems. S. Levy, *The Antibiotic Paradox* (2002) is useful for understanding the limitations of some twentieth-century therapies. A. Macfarlane, *The Savage Wars of Peace* (2003) is a wonderful study of the impact of public health policies, with special reference to Britain and Japan. I. Illich, *Limits to Medicine: The Expropriation of Health* (1999) is a classic study of the modern social history of health issues, on which L. Payer, *Medicine and Culture* (1996), and P. Starr, *The Social Transformation of American Medicine* (1984) are also important.

Rival Black Voices in the Twentieth Century

In the early twentieth century, thanks initially to ragtime and jazz from the American Deep South and European artists' discovery of the art of sub-Saharan Africa, the world was awakening to a new respect for black artists. In parts of the United States and Latin America, and in some European colonies in Africa, educational and economic openings for black people were improving, despite racial prejudice and segragation.

For black people, this meant opportunities but also posed intellectual problems. Should they aspire to be "American" or "French," or whatever, or should they insist on a special "black" (or, as they usually said at the time Negro or Black) identity? If so what would that identity be? Did all black people share an essential blackness? Were those who thought that way racists? How did black identity relate to Africa? How black did you have to be to feel black? The extracts below from the United States, the Caribbean, and French West Africa represent some of the answers black people gave to these questions in the early twentieth century.

CARIBBEAN

WEST AFRICA

UNITED STATES

• • • • •

PART ONE: THE UNITED STATES

During the nineteenth century, black Americans had felt Africa call to them. But the notion of returning "home" to Africa was out of favor by 1900. The senior black spokesman of the time, Booker T. Washington (1856–1915), opposed it. W. E. B. Dubois (1868–1963), his successor, as the most influential black intellectual in the U.S., as was more radical. He was not content for black people simply to accept their lot and rely on education and economic improvement to raise them toward equality. He demanded social reforms. His major book, *The Souls of Black Folk*, was full of references to Africa. Dubois was convinced that a common history connected black people throughout the world, but that history was now in the past. Black Americans had to be "both a Negro and an American."

W.E.B. DuBois. The distinguished and thoughtful scholar around 1900, just a few years before the publication of *The Souls of Black Folk.*
Courtesy of the Schomburg Center for Research in Black Culture.

EXTRACT 1A (FROM *THE SOULS OF BLACK FOLK*)

It is a peculiar sensation, this double-consciousness, this sense of always looking at one's self through the eyes of others, of measuring one's soul by the tape of a world that looks on in amused contempt and pity. One ever feels his two-ness—an American, a Negro; two souls, two thoughts, two unreconciled strivings; two warring ideals in one dark body, whose dogged strength alone keeps it from being torn asunder.

The history of the American Negro is the history of this strife—this longing to attain self-conscious manhood, to merge his double self into a better and truer self. In this merging he wishes neither of the older selves to be lost. He would not Africanize America, for America has too much to teach the world and Africa. He would not bleach his Negro soul in a flood of white Americanism, for he knows that Negro blood has a message for the world. He simply wishes to make it possible for a man to be both a Negro and an African, without being cursed and spit upon by his fellows, without having the doors of Opportunity closed roughly in his face.

Perhaps the most eloquent and impassioned of those who disagreed with Dubois was Marcus Garvey (1887–1940), the Jamaican-born leader of the "Back to Africa" movement. The Declaration of Rights of the Negro Peoples of the World was drafted and adopted at a convention in New York in 1920, over which Garvey presided, and at which he was elected provisional president of Africa.

EXTRACT 1B (FROM THE DECLARATION OF RIGHTS OF THE NEGRO PEOPLES)

In order to encourage our race all over the world . . . we demand and insist on the following Declaration of Rights:

1. *Be it known to all men that whereas, all men are created equal and entitled to the rights of life, liberty and the pursuit of happiness, and because of this we, the duly elected representatives of the Negro peoples of the world, invoking the aid of the just and Almighty God do declare all men, women, children of our blood throughout the world free citizens, and do claim them as free citizens as Africa, the Motherland of all Negroes.*

2. *That we believe in the supreme authority given to man as a common possession; that there should be an equitable distribution and appointment of all such things, and in consideration of the fact that as a race we are now deprived of those things that are morally and legally ours, we believe it right that all such things should be acquired and held by whatsoever means possible.*

3. *That we believe the Negro, like any other race, should be governed by the ethics of civilization, and therefore, should not be deprived of any of those rights or privileges common to other human beings.*

4. *We declare that Negroes wheresoever they form a community among themselves, should be given the right to elect their own representatives to represent them: legislatures, courts of law, or such institutions as may exercise control over that particular community.*

13. *We believe in the freedom of Africa for the Negro people of the world, and by the principle of Europe for the Europeans and Asia for the Asiatics; we also demand Africa for the Africans at home and abroad.*

PART TWO: THE CARIBBEAN

In 1906, Fernando Ortiz was interviewing black inmates in a Cuban jail. He had, as far as is known, no black ancestry himself. He was working on a thesis on the connections between race and crime. What impressed him, however, was the way the black inmates retained elements of culture—music, language, food, religion—that originated in Africa. Ortiz became an advocate of the African input to Cuba's heritage and an enthusiast for the work of black artists. Partly, thanks to his success, white advocates and imitators of black speech, music, prose, and imagery became numerous. It was relatively easy for black Cubans to feel thoroughly Cuban, especially since most people in the country had at least some black family connections. The poetry of Nicolas Guillen (1902–1989), one of the twentieth century's greatest poets, expresses this attitude. In the late 1920s, he became a leading exponent of *negrismo*—the assimilation of black influences in literature, especially his masterful use of the rhythms of black music and the street talk of black Cubans. In the prologue to a collection of poems published in 1913 he wrote:

Extract 2a (Prologue...)

I daresay my poems share the same ingredients as Cuba's population, where all of us are a little bit tar-brushed. Does it hurt? I don't think so. Still, this is worth saying before we put it to one side: The African input into the country is so profound...that for us, no poetry could be native if it forgot to be black. Blacks, I think, bring really solid, vital ingredients to the Cuban mix. And the two races that overflow this island, at equal depths, who look different on the surface, are linked below it by a sort of drag-hook, like those submerged land bridges that join continents. For now, and for the foreseeable future, the spirit of Cuba is mestizo [mixed race]. And our final, definitive color will rise to the surface of our skin from deep in our spirit. One day we shall speak of 'Cuban color.' These poems aim to bring that day closer.

—prologue to **Songoro Cosongo** *(1931),* **Obra poética,** *(1974)*

In the same period, the leading writer of Haiti was Jacques Roumain (1907–1944), who founded the Haitian communist party. Haiti was a largely black country, and Africa occupied a mythic place in Haitian folklore, as the destination of departed souls. Roumain played on this idea in his poem, *Sur le chemin de Guineé* (On the Road to Guinea, 1927):

Jacques Roumain in the 1930s. His writings still influence Haitian culture and the pan-African world.

Extract 2b (*Sur le chemin de Guineé*)

It is a long road to Guineé;
Here are the branches, the trees, the forest:
Listen to the sound of the wind in its long hair
of eternal night.
It is a long road to Guineé
Your fathers impatiently await you
along the road; they're muttering.
They await you.
Here's where the streams rustle together
like rosaries of bones.
It is a long road to Guineé
Your welcome won't be a luminous one
in that country of black men:
under that smoky sky broken by the cry of the birds,
around the eye of the mango
the trees lash open upon the spoliation of clarity
By the banks of the water there awaits you a
peaceful village and the house of your fathers
and the hard family stone upon which to rest your head.

PART THREE:
LÉOPOLD SENGHOR AND WEST AFRICA

By the 1930s, all art expressive of black identities tended to be classed under the term "negritude," invented by the poet Aimé Césaire (b. 1913), from the French Caribbean island of Martinique (See Chapter 29). He defined negritude as "the affirmation that one is black and proud of it . . . that there is a solidarity between blacks . . ." A tougher definition was that of Césaire's literary collaborator, the poet Léopold Senghor (1906–2001), who later became President of Sénegal in West Africa. "Negritude," he wrote, "is the consciousness of being black, the simple recognition of fact, implying acceptance and responsibility for one's destiny as a black man, one's history and one's culture. It is the refusal to assimilate, to see oneself in the 'Other.' Rejection of the Other is affirmation of the self."

Where Césaire saw black fellow feeling as a temporary response to colonialism and racism, and wanted to expand this sentiment to include other oppressed peoples, Senghor believed in the unity of black people, no matter what their history and culture were. This idea was present in his earliest work on the subject:

EXTRACT 3A

I propose this definition [of civilization]: a racial response by humans to their environment. Race is a reality. I do not mean "racial purity." There is difference, which is not to say that there is inferiority or antagonism. . . . There is no civilization without literature that expresses and illustrates its values, like a jeweler fitting germs into a crown. . . . But how can we conceive a black literature except in a black language? Black literature in French does seem possible; Haiti has proved it and other black literatures have arisen by borrowing a language from Europe: black American, black Spanish, black Portuguese. . . . But in the end literature of that kind would never be able to express our entire soul. There is a flavor, an odor, an accent, a black timbre that European instruments can never attain.

—speech in Dakar, Senegal, September 10, 1937

Black consciousness. In November 1970, four "Bush Negro" chiefs from Surinam—direct descendants of maroon communities established in South America in the sixteenth and seventeenth centuries (see Chapter 19)—toured West Africa to great acclaim. Here they are being received as dignitaries by Chief Apétor II of Togo. "The same wind that drove us against our will from Africa," one Bush Negro chief observed during the trip, "has now helped us to find the way back."

EXTRACT 3B

Do Negroes exist—pure Negroes, black Negroes? Science says, No. I know that there is, there has been a Negro culture . . . a single, unitary culture, a civilization, rather: a culture, that is, born of the interaction of race, tradition, and environment. And when it migrated to the Americas, its style stayed intact. . .

It is a fact often noticed that the Negro feels words and ideas, even that he is peculiarly responsive to the sensible—I might even say "sensual"—qualities of words, and to the spiritual, not intellectual, properties of ideas. . . . Emotion is Negro, just as reason is Greek. . . . The very way the Negro feels explains the way he perceives objects, sees their essence with a directness that is almost violent, loses himself in them, needs them, communes with them, even identifies with them.

—from Négritude et Humanisme (Negritude and Humanism)

Questions to Consider

1 How did Dubois and Garvey differ? Why was Africa so important in the search for black identity?

2 Compare the extracts from Nicolas Guillen (Cuba) and Jacques Roumain (Haiti) with each other and with those from the U.S. How did differences of history and culture affect the way writers understood what it meant to be black?

3 How does Leopold Senghor's notion of negritude resemble those of earlier explorers of black identity? Does it make sense to generalize as broadly as Senghor does about "the Negro"? What are the consequences of doing so?

Sources

Extract 1a W. E. B. DuBois, *Souls of Black Folk* (Chicago: A. C. McClurg, 1903).

Extract 1b M. Garvey, Declaration of the Rights of the Negro Peoples, 1920.

Extract 2a N. Guillen, Prologue to "Songoro Cosongo" (1931).

Extract 2b J. Roumain, "On the Road to Guinea" (1927), excerpted from *Voices of Negritude*, Julio Finn, ed. (London/New York: Quartet Books, 1988).

Extract 3a L. Senghor, speech given in Dakar, Senegal on September 10, 1937.

Extract 3b L. Senghor, *Négritude et Humanisme* (1964) pp. 11–35.

Abolitionism Belief that slavery and the slave trade are immoral and should be abolished.

Aborigine A member of the indigenous or earliest-known population of a region.

Aborigines Indigenous people of Australia.

Afrikaans An official language of South Africa, spoken mostly by the Boers. It is derived from seventeenth-century Dutch.

Age of Plague Term for the spread of lethal diseases from the fourteenth through the eighteenth centuries.

Ahriman The chief spirit of darkness and evil in Zoroastrianism, the enemy of Ahura Mazda.

Ahura Mazda The chief deity of Zoroastrianism, the creator of the world, the source of light, and the embodiment of good.

Al-Andalus Arabic name for the Iberian Peninsula (Spain and Portugal).

Alluvial plains Flat lands where mud from rivers or lakes renews the topsoil. If people can control the flooding that is common in such conditions, alluvial plains are excellent for settled agriculture.

Almoravids Muslim dynasty of Berber warriors that flourished from 1049 to 1145 and that established political dominance over northwest Africa and Spain.

Alternative energy Energy sources that usually produce less pollution than does the burning of fossil fuels, and are renewable in some cases.

Alternative medicine Medicines, treatments, and techniques not advocated by the mainstream medical establishment in the West.

Americanization The process by which other cultures, to a greater or lesser degree, adopt American fashions, culture, and ways of life.

Anarchists Believers in the theory that all forms of government are oppressive and undesirable and should be opposed and abolished.

Animal rights Movement that asserts that animals have fundamental rights that human beings have a moral obligation to respect.

Anti-Semitism Hostility or prejudice against Jews or Judaism.

Arthasastra Ancient Indian study of economics and politics that influenced the Emperor Asoka. The *Arthasastra* expresses an ideology of universal rule and emphasizes the supremacy of "the king's law" and the importance of uniform justice.

Artificial intelligence The creation of a machine or computer program that exhibits the characteristics of human intelligence.

Arts and Crafts Movement Nineteenth-century artists and intellectuals who argued that the products produced by individual craftsmen were more attractive than and morally superior to the mass, uniform goods produced by industry.

Assassins A secret order of Muslims in what is today Syria and Lebanon who terrorized and killed its opponents, both Christian and Muslim. The Assassins were active from the eleventh to the thirteenth centuries.

Atlantic Slave Trade Trade in African slaves who were bought, primarily in West Africa, by Europeans and white Americans and transported across the Atlantic, usually in horrific conditions, to satisfy the demand for labor in the plantations and mines of the Americas.

Atomic theory The theory that matter is not a continuous whole, but is composed of tiny, discrete particles.

Australopithecine (Trans.) "Southern ape-like creatures." Term used to describe prehuman species that existed before those classed under the genus *Homo*.

Axial Age A pivotal age in the history of world civilization, lasting for roughly 500 years up to the beginning of the Christian era, in which critical intellectual and cultural ideas arose in and were transmitted across the Mediterranean world, India, Iran, and East Asia.

Axial zone The densely populated central belt of world population, communication, and cultural exchange in Eurasia that stretches from Japan and China to Western Europe and North Africa.

Aztecs People of central Mexico whose civilization and empire were at their height at the time of the Spanish conquest in the early sixteenth century.

Balance of trade The relative value of goods traded between two or more nations or states. Each trading partner strives to have a favorable balance of trade, that is, to sell more to its trading partners than it buys from them.

Bantu African people sharing a common linguistic ancestry who originated in West Africa and whose early agriculture centered on the cultivation of yams and oil palms in swamplands.

Big bang theory Theory that the universe began with an explosion of almost infinitesimally compressed matter, the effects of which are still going on.

Black Death Term for a lethal disease or diseases that struck large parts of Eurasia and North Africa in the 1300s and killed millions of people.

Boers Dutch settlers and their descendents in southern Africa, The first Boers arrived in South Africa in the seventeenth century.

Bon Religion that was Buddhism's main rival in Tibet for several centuries in the late first millennium C.E.

Brahman A member of the highest, priestly caste of traditional Indian society.

British East India Company British trading company founded in 1600 that played a key role in the colonization of India. It ruled much of the subcontinent until 1857.

Bureaucratization The process by which government increasingly operates through a body of trained officials who follow a set of regular rules and procedures.

Business Imperialism Economic domination and exploitation of poorer and weaker countries by richer and stronger states.

Byzantine Empire Term for the Greek-speaking, eastern portion of the former Roman Empire, centered on Constantinople. It lasted until 1453, when it was conquered by the Ottoman Turks.

Cahokia Most spectacular existent site of Mississippi Valley Native American civilization, located near modern St. Louis.

Caliph The supreme Islamic political and religious authority, literally, the "successor" of the Prophet Muhammad.

Canyon cultures Indigenous peoples of the North American Southwest. The canyon cultures flourished beween about 850 and 1250 C.E.

Capitalism An economic system in which the means of production and distribution are privately or corporately owned.

Caste system A social system in which people's places in society, how they live and work, and with whom they can marry are determined by heredity. The Indian caste system has been intertwined with India's religious and economic systems.

Centralization The concentration of power in the hands of a central government.

Chaos theory Theory that some systems are so complex that their causes and effects are untraceable.

Chicago economics The economic theory associated with economists who taught at the University of Chicago that holds that low taxes and light government regulation will lead to economic prosperity.

Chimú Civilization centered on the Pacific coast of Peru that was conquered by the Inca in the fifteenth century.

Chinese Board of Astronomy Official department of the Chinese imperial court created in the early seventeenth century that was responsible for devising the ritual calendar.

Chinese diaspora The migration of Chinese immigrants around the world between the seventeenth and nineteenth centuries.

Chivalry The qualities idealized by the medieval European aristocracy and associated with knighthood, such as bravery, courtesy, honor, and gallantry.

Chola Expansive kingdom in southern India that had important connections with merchant communities on the coast. Chola reached its height around 1050 C.E.

Christendom Term referring to the European states in which Christianity was the dominant or only religion.

Cistercians Christian monastic order that built monasteries in places where habitation was sparse and nature hostile. Cistercians practiced a more ascetic and rigorous form of the Benedictine rule.

Citizen army The mass army the French created during the Revolution by imposing mandatory military service on the entire active adult male population. The army was created in response to the threat of invasion by an alliance of anti-Revolutionary countries in the early 1790s.

Civilizing mission The belief that imperialism and colonialism are justified because imperial powers have a duty to bring the benefits of "civilization" to, or impose them on, the "backward" people they ruled or conquered.

Clan A social group made up of a number of families that claim descent from a common ancestor and follow a hereditary chieftain.

Class struggle Conflict between competing social classes that, in Karl Marx's view, was responsible for all important historical change.

Climacteric A period of critical change in a society that is poised between different possible outcomes.

Code Napoleon Civil code promulgated by Napoleon in 1804 and spread by his armies across Europe. It still forms the basis for the legal code for many European, Latin American, and African countries.

Cold war Post–World War II rivalry between the United States and its allies and the Soviet Union and its allies. The cold war ended in 1990–1991 with the end of the Soviet Empire in Eastern Europe and the collapse of the Soviet Union itself.

Columbian Exchange Biological exchange of plants, animals, microbes, and human beings between the Americas and the rest of the world.

Commune Collective name for the citizen body of a medieval and Renaissance Italian town.

Communism A system of government in which the state plans and controls the economy, and private property and class distinctions are abolished.

Confraternities Lay Catholic charitable brotherhoods.

Confucianism Chinese doctrine founded by Confucius emphasizing learning and the fulfillment of obligations among family members, citizens, and the state.

Constitutionalism The doctrine that the state is founded on a set of fundamental laws that rulers and citizens make together and are bound to respect.

Consumerism A system of values that exalts the consumption and possession of consumer goods as both a social good and as an end in themselves.

Coolies Poor laborers from China and India who left their homelands to do hard manual and agricultural work in other parts of the world in the nineteenth and early twentieth centuries.

Copernican revolution Development of a heliocentric model of the solar system begun in 1543 by Nicholas Copernicus, a Polish churchman and astronomer.

Council of Trent A series of meetings from 1545 to 1563 to direct the response of the Roman Catholic Church to Protestantism. The council defined Catholic dogma and reformed church discipline.

Counter Reformation The Catholic effort to combat the spread of Protestantism in the sixteenth and seventeenth centuries.

Countercolonization The flow of immigrants out of former colonies to the "home countries" that used to rule them.

Country trades Commerce involving local or regional exchanges of goods from one Asian destination to another that, while often handled by European merchants, never touched Europe.

Covenant In the Bible, God's promise to the human race.

Creoles People of at least part-European descent born in the West Indies, French Louisiana, or Spanish America.

Crusades Any of the military expeditions undertaken by European Christians from the late eleventh to the thirteenth centuries to recover the Holy Land from the Muslims.

Cubism Artistic style developed by Pablo Picasso and Georges Braque in the early twentieth century, characterized by the reduction and fragmentation of natural forms into abstract, often geometric structures.

Cultural relativism The doctrine that cultures cannot be ranked in any order of merit. No culture is superior to another, and each culture must be judged on its own terms.

Cultural Revolution Campaign launched by Mao Zedong in 1965–1966 against the bureaucrats of the Chinese Communist Party. In lasted until 1976 and involved widespread disorder, violence, killings, and the persecution of intellectuals and the educated elite.

Culture Socially transmitted behavior, beliefs, institutions, and technologies that a given group of people or peoples share.

Cuneiform Mesopotamian writing system that was inscribed on clay tablets with wedge-shaped markers.

Czars (Trans.) "Caesar." Title of the emperors who ruled Russia until the revolution of 1917.

Dada An early twentieth-century European artistic and literary movement that flouted conventional and traditional aesthetic and cultural values by producing works marked by nonsense, travesty, and incongruity.

Dahomey West African slave-trading state that began to be prominent in the sixteenth century.

Daimyo Japanese feudal lord who ruled a province and was subject to the shoguns.

Daoism Chinese doctrine founded by Laozi that identified detachment from the world with the pursuit of immortality.

"Declaration of the Rights of Man and Citizen" Declaration of basic principles adopted by the French National Assembly in August 1789, at the start of the French Revolution.

Decolonization The process by which the nineteenth-century colonial empires in Asia, Africa, the Caribbean, and the Pacific were dismantled after World War II.

Deforestation The process by which trees are eliminated from an ecosystem.

Democracy Government by the people, exercised either directly or through elected representatives.

Devsirme Quota of male children supplied by Christian subjects as tribute to the Ottoman Sultan. Many of the boys were drafted into the janissaries.

Dharma In the teachings of Buddha, moral law or duty.

Diffusion The spread of a practice, belief, culture, or technology within a community or between communities.

Dirlik (Trans.) "Wealth." The term applied to provincial government in the Ottoman Empire.

Divine love God's ongoing love for and interest in human beings.

Dominicans Order of preaching friars established in 1216 by Saint Dominic.

Druze Lebanese sect that regards the caliph al-Hakim as a manifestation of God. Other Muslims regard the Druze as heretics.

Dualism Perception of the world as an arena of conflict between opposing principles of good and evil.

Dutch East India Company Dutch company founded in 1602 that enjoyed a government-granted monopoly on trade between Holland and Asia. The company eventually established a territorial empire in what is today Indonesia.

Dutch East Indies Dutch colonies in Asia centered on present-day Indonesia.

East India Trade Maritime trade between Western Europe and New England and Asia (predominantly India and China) between 1600 and 1800. Westerners paid cash for items from Asia, such as porcelain, tea, silk, cotton textiles, and spices.

Easterlies Winds coming from the east.

Ecological exchange The exchange of plants and animals between ecosystems.

Ecological imperialism Term historians use for the sweeping environmental changes European and other imperialists introduced in regions they colonized.

Ecology of civilization The interaction of people with their environment.

Economic liberalism Belief that government interference in and regulation of the economy should be kept to a minimum.

Edo Former name of Tokyo when it was the center of government for the Tokugawa shoguns.

El Niño A periodic reversal of the normal flow of Pacific currents that alters weather patterns and affects the number and location of fish in the ocean.

Elan vital The "vital force" hypothesized by the French philosopher Henri Bergson as a source of efficient causation and evolution in nature.

Empiricism The view that experience, especially of the senses, is the only source of knowledge.

Emporium trading Commerce that takes place in fixed market places or trading posts.

Enlightened despotism Reforms instituted by powerful monarchs in eighteenth-century Europe who were inspired by the principles of the Enlightenment.

Enlightenment Movement of eighteenth-century European thought championed by the *philosophes*, thinkers who held that change and reform were desirable and could be achieved by the application of reason and science. Most Enlightenment thinkers were hostile to conventional religion.

Enthusiasm "Religion" of English romantics who believed that emotion and passion were positive qualities.

Epistemology The branch of philosophy that studies the nature of knowledge.

Eugenics The theory that the human race can be improved mentally and physically by controlled selective breeding and that the state and society have a duty to encourage "superior" persons to have offspring and prevent "inferior" persons from reproducing.

Eunuchs Castrated male servants valued because they could not produce heirs or have sexual relations with women. In Byzantium, China, and the Islamic world, eunuchs could rise to high office in the state and the military.

European Union (EU) Loose economic and political federation that succeeded the European Economic Community (EEC) in 1993. It has expanded to include most of the states in Western and Eastern Europe.

Evolution Change in the genetic composition of a population over successive generations, as a result of natural selection acting on the genetic variation among individuals.

Examination system System for selecting Chinese officials and bureaucrats according to merit through a series of competitive, written examinations that, in theory, any Chinese young man could take. Success in the exams required years of intense study in classical Chinese literature. The examination system was not abolished until the early twentieth century.

Existentialism Philosophy that regards human existence as unexplainable, and stresses freedom of choice and accepting responsibility for the consequences of one's acts.

Factories Foreign trading posts in China and other parts of Asia. The chief representative of a factory was known as a "factor." Though the earliest trading posts were established by the Portuguese in the sixteenth century, the number of factories grew rapidly in the eighteenth and nineteenth centuries, with European and American merchants trading for silk, rhubarb, tea, and porcelain.

Fascism A system of government marked by centralization of authority under a dictator, stringent socioeconomic controls, and suppression of the opposition through terror and censorship.

Fatimids Muslim dynasty that ruled parts of North Africa and Egypt (909–1171).

Feminism The belief that women collectively constitute a class of society that has been historically oppressed and deserves to be set free.

Final Solution Nazi plan to murder all European Jews.

Fixed-wind systems Wind system in which the prevailing winds do not change direction for long periods of time.

Fossil fuels Fuels including peat, coal, natural gas, and oil.

Franciscans Religious order founded by Francis of Assisi in 1209 and dedicated to the virtues of humility, poverty, and charitable work among the poor.

Free trade The notion that maximum economic efficiency is achieved when barriers to trade, especially taxes on imports and exports, are eliminated.

French Revolution Political, intellectual, and social upheaval that began in France in 1789. It resulted in the overthrow of the monarchy and the establishment of a republic.

Fulani Traditional herdsmen of the Sahel in West Africa.

Fundamentalism The idea that a sacred text or texts contains fundamental truths that cannot be questioned, either by critical inquiry or by scientific evidence.

Futurism Artistic vision articulated by Emilio Filippo Marinetti in 1909. He believed that all traditional art and ideas should be repudiated, destroyed, and replaced by the new. Futurists glorified speed, technology, progress, and violence.

Gauchos Argentine cowboys.

General will Jean-Jacques Rousseau's concept of the collective will of the population. He believed that the purpose of government was to express the general will.

Genetic revolution Revolution in the understanding of human biology produced by advances in genetic research.

Genocide The systematic and planned extermination of an entire national, racial, political, or ethnic group.

Ghana A medieval West African kingdom in what are now eastern Senegal, southwest Mali, and southern Mauritania.

Global gardening The collecting in botanical gardens of plants from around the world for cultivation and study.

Globalization The process through which uniform or similar ways of life are spread across the planet.

Glyph A form of writing that uses symbolic figures that are usually engraved or incised, such as Egyptian hieroglyphics.

GM Crops that have been *genetically modified* to produce certain desired characteristics.

Golden Horde Term for Mongols who ruled much of Russia from the steppes of the lower Volga River from the thirteenth to the fifteenth centuries.

Grand Vizier The chief minister of state in the Ottoman Empire.

Greater East Asia Co-Prosperity Sphere Bloc of Asian nations under Japanese economic and political control during World War II.

Green revolution Improvements in twentieth-century agriculture that substantially increased food production by developing new strains of crops and agricultural techniques.

Greenhouse effect The increase in temperature caused by the trapping of carbon in the Earth's atmosphere.

Guardians Self-elected class of philosopher-rulers found in Plato's *Republic*.

Guomindang (GMD) Nationalist Chinese political party founded in 1912 by Sun Yat-Sen. The Guomindang took power in China in 1928 but was defeated by the Chinese Communists in 1949.

Habsburgs An Austro-German imperial family that reached the height of their power in the sixteenth century under Charles V of Spain when the Habsburgs ruled much of Europe and the Americas. The Habsburgs continued to rule a multinational empire based in Vienna until 1918.

Haj The pilgrimage to Mecca that all faithful Muslims are required to complete at least once in their lifetime if they able.

Han Dynasty that ruled China from ca. 206 B.C.E. to ca. 220 C.E. This was the period when the fundamental identity and culture of China were formed. Chinese people still refer to themselves as "Han."

Hanseatic League Founded in 1356, the Hanseatic League was a powerful network of allied ports along the North Sea and Baltic coasts that collaborated to promote trade.

Harem The quarters reserved for the female members of a Muslim household.

Herders Agriculturalists who emphasize the raising of animals, rather than plants, for food and products, such as wool and hides.

High-level equilibrium trap A situation in which an economy that is meeting high levels of demand with traditional technology finds that it has little scope to increase its output.

Hinduism Indian polytheistic religion that developed out of Brahmanism and in response to Buddhism. It remains the majority religion in India today.

Hispaniola Modern Haiti and the Dominican Republic.

Hohokam People Native American culture that flourished from about the third century B.C.E. to the mid–fifteenth century C.E. in south-central Arizona.

Holocaust Term for the murder of millions of Jews by the Nazi regime during World War II.

Holy Roman Empire A loose federation of states under an elected emperor that consisted primarily of Germany and northern Italy. It endured in various forms from 800 to 1806.

Homo erectus (Trans.) "Standing upright." Humanlike tool-using species that lived about 1.5 million years ago. At one time, Homo erectus was thought to be the first "human."

Homo ergaster (Trans.) "Workman." Humanlike species that lived 800,000 years ago and stacked the bones of its dead.

Homo habilis (Trans.) "Handy." Humanlike species that lived about 2.5 million years ago and made stone hand axes.

Homo sapiens (Trans.) "Wise." The species to which contemporary humans belong.

Human rights Notion of inherent rights that all human beings share. Based in part on the assumption that being human constitutes in itself a meaningful moral category that excludes nonhuman creatures.

Humanism Cultural and intellectual movement of the Renaissance centered on the study of the literature, art, and civilization of ancient Greece and Rome.

Hurons A Native American confederacy of eastern Canada. The Huron flourished immediately prior to contact with Europeans, but declined rapidly as a result of European diseases such as smallpox. They were allied with the French in wars against the British, the Dutch, and other Native Americans.

Husbandry The practice of cultivating crops and breeding and raising livestock; agriculture.

Ice-Age affluence Relative prosperity of Ice-Age society as the result of abundant game and wild, edible plants.

Icon A representation or picture of a Christian saint or sacred event. Icons have been traditionally venerated in the Eastern, or Orthodox Church.

Il-Khanate A branch of the Mongol Empire, centered in present-day Iran. Its rulers, the Il-Khans, converted to Islam and adopted Persian culture.

Imam A Muslim religious teacher. Also the title of Muslim political and religious rulers in Yemen and Oman.

Imperator A Latin term that originally meant an army commander under the Roman Republic and evolved into the term *emperor*.

Imperialism The policy of extending a nation's authority and influence by conquest or by establishing economic and political hegemony over other nations.

Incas Peoples of highland Peru who established an empire from northern Ecuador to central Chile before the Spanish conquest in the 1530s.

Indian National Congress Political organization created in 1885 that played a leading role in the Indian independence movement.

Indirect rule Rule by a colonial power through local elites.

Individualism Belief in the primary importance of the individual and in the virtues of self-reliance and personal independence.

Indo-European languages Language family that originated in Asia and from which most of Europe's present languages evolved.

Inductive method Method by which scientists turn individual observations and experiments into general laws.

Industrial Revolution The complex set of economic, demographic, and technological events that began in Western Europe and resulted in the advent of an industrial economy.

Industrialization The process by which an industrial economy is developed.

Information technology Technology, such as printing presses and computers, that facilitates the spread of information.

Inquisition A tribunal of the Roman Catholic Church that was charged with suppressing heresy and immorality.

Iroquois Native American confederacy based in northern New York State, originally composed of the Mohawk, Oneida, Onondaga, Cayuga, and Seneca peoples, known as the Five Nations. The confederacy created a constitution sometime between the mid-1400s and the early 1600s.

Isolationism Belief that, unless directly challenged, a country should concentrate on domestic issues and avoid foreign conflicts or active participation in foreign affairs.

Jainism A way of life that arose in India designed to free the soul from evil by ascetic practices: chastity, detachment, truth, selflessness, and strict vegetarianism.

Janissaries Soldiers in an elite Ottoman infantry formation that was first organized in the fourteenth century. Originally drafted from among the sons of the sultan's Christian subjects, the janissaries had become a hereditary and militarily obsolete caste by the early nineteenth century.

Jesuits Order of regular clergy strongly committed to education, scholarship, and missionary work. Founded by Ignatius of Loyola in 1534.

Jihad Arabic word meaning "striving." Muhammad used the word to refer to the inner struggle all Muslims must wage against evil, and the real wars fought against the enemies of Islam.

Joint-stock company A business whose capital is held in transferable shares of stock by its joint owners. The Dutch East India Company, founded in 1602, was the first joint-stock company.

Kaaba The holiest place in Islam. Formerly a pagan shrine, the Kaaba is a massive cube-shaped structure in Mecca toward which Muslims turn to pray.

Keynesianism Economic policy advocated by J. M. Keynes, based on the premise that governments could adjust the distribution of wealth and regulate the functioning of the economy through taxation and public spending, without seriously weakening free enterprise or infringing freedom.

Khan A ruler of a Mongol, Tartar, or Turkish tribe.

Khedive Title held by the hereditary viceroys of Egypt in the nineteenth century. Although nominally subject to the Ottoman sultans, the khedives were, in effect, sovereign princes.

Khmer Agrarian kingdom of Cambodia, built on the wealth produced by enormous rice surpluses.

Kongo Kingdom located in west central Africa along the Congo River, founded in the fourteenth century. The Portuguese converted its rulers and elite to Catholicism in the fifteenth century.

Kulturkampf (Trans.) "The struggle for culture." Name given to the conflict between the Roman Catholic Church and the imperial German government under Chancellor Otto von Bismarck in the 1870s.

Laissez-faire An economic policy that emphasizes the minimization of government regulation and involvement in the economy.

Latin Church Dominant Christian church in Western Europe.

Latitude The angular distance north or south of the Earth's equator, measured in degrees along a meridian.

League of Nations International political organization created after World War I to resolve disputes between states peacefully and create a more just international order.

Legalism Chinese school of thought that emerged in the fourth century B.C.E. Legalists believed that morality was meaningless and that obedience to the state was the supreme good. The state thus had the right to enforce its laws under threat of the harshest penalties.

Levant The countries bordering on the eastern Mediterranean from Turkey to Egypt.

Liberation theology Religious movement in Latin America, primarily among Roman Catholics, concerned with justice for the poor and oppressed. Its adherents argue that sin is the result not just of individual moral failure but of the oppressive and exploitative way in which capitalist society is organized and functions.

Little Ice Age Protracted period of relative cold from the fourteenth to the early nineteenth centuries.

Logograms A system of writing in which stylized pictures represent a word or phrase.

Longitude An imaginary great circle on the surface of the Earth passing through the north and south poles at right angles to the equator.

Lotus Sutra The most famous of Buddhist scriptures.

Low Countries A region of northwest Europe comprising what is today Belgium, the Netherlands, and Luxembourg.

Magyars Steppeland people who invaded Eastern Europe in the tenth century and were eventually converted to Catholic Christianity. The Magyars are the majority ethnic group in present-day Hungary.

Mahayana One of the major schools of Buddhism. It emphasizes the Buddha's infinite compassion for all human beings, social concern, and universal salvation. It is the dominant branch of Buddhism in East Asia.

Mahdi A Muslim messiah, whose coming would inaugurate a cosmic struggle, preceding the end of the world.

Maize The grain that modern Americans call "corn." It was first cultivated in ancient Mesoamerica.

Mali Powerful West African state that flourished in the fourteenth century.

Malthusian Ideas inspired by Thomas Malthus's theory that population growth would always outpace growth in food supply.

Mamluks Egyptian Muslim slave army. The mamluks provided Egypt's rulers from 1390 to 1517.

Mana According to the Polynesians, a supernatural force that regulates everything in the world. For example, the mana of a net makes it catch a fish, and the mana of an herb gives it its healing powers.

Manchurian Incident Japanese invasion of Manchuria in 1931, justified by the alleged effort of the Chinese to blow up a Japanese train. In fact, Japanese agents deliberately triggered the explosion to provide a pretext for war.

Manchus A people native to Manchuria who ruled China during the Qing dynasty.

Mandarins High public officials in the Chinese Empire, usually chosen by merit after competitive written exams.

Mandate of Heaven The source of divine legitimacy for Chinese emperors. According to the mandate of heaven, emperors were chosen by the gods and retained their favor as long as the emperors acted in righteous ways. Emperors and dynasties that lost the mandate of heaven could be deposed or overthrown.

Manichaeanism A dualistic philosophy dividing the world between the two opposed principles of good and evil.

Manifest destiny Nineteenth-century belief that the United States was destined to expand across all of North America from the Atlantic to the Pacific, including Canada and Mexico.

Manila Galleons Spanish galleons that sailed each year between the Philippines and Mexico with a cargo of silk, porcelain, and other Asian luxury goods that were paid for with Mexican silver.

Maori Indigenous Polynesian people of New Zealand.

Marathas Petty Hindu princes who ruled in Maharashtra in southern India in the eighteenth century.

Maritime empires Empires based on trade and naval power that flourished in the sixteenth and seventeenth centuries.

Maroons Runaway slaves in the Americas who formed autonomous communities, and even states, between 1500 and 1800.

Marshall Plan Foreign-aid program for Western Europe after World War II, named after U.S. Secretary of State George C. Marshall.

Marxism The political and economic philosophy of Karl Marx and Friedrich Engels in which the concept of class struggle is the determining principle in social and historical change.

Material culture Concrete objects that people create.

Matrilineal A society that traces ancestry through the maternal line.

Maya Major civilization of Mesoamerica. The earliest evidence connected to Maya civilization dates from about 1000 B.C.E. Maya civilization reached its peak between 250 and 900 C.E. Maya cultural and political practices were a major influence on other Mesoamericans.

Mercantilism An economic theory that emphasized close government control of the economy to maximize a country's exports and to earn as much bullion as possible.

Mesoamerica A region stretching from central Mexico to Central America. Mesoamerica was home to the Olmec, the Maya, the Aztecs, and other Native American peoples.

Messiah The anticipated savior of the Jews. Christians identified Jesus as the Messiah.

Mestizos The descendents of Europeans and Native Americans.

Microbial exchange The exchange of microbes between ecosystems.

Militarization The trend toward larger and more powerful armed forces and the organization of society and the economy to achieve that goal.

Military revolution Change in warfare in the sixteenth and seventeenth centuries that accompanied the rise of fire-power technology.

Millenarianism Belief that the end of the world is about to occur, as foretold in the biblical Book of Revelation.

Minas Gerais (Trans.) "General Mines." Region of Brazil rich in mineral resources that experienced a gold rush in the early eighteenth century.

Ming Dynasty Chinese dynasty (1368–1644) noted for its flourishing foreign trade and achievements in scholarship and the arts.

Mongols Nomadic people whose homeland was in Mongolia. In the twelfth and thirteenth centuries, they conquered most of Eurasia from China to Eastern Europe.

Monocultures The cultivation of a single dominant food crop, such as potatoes or rice. Societies that practiced monoculture were vulnerable to famine if bad weather or disease caused their single food crop to fail.

Monroe Doctrine The policy enunciated by President James Monroe in 1823 that the United States would oppose further European colonization in the Americas.

Monsoons A wind from the southwest or south that brings heavy rainfall each summer to southern Asia.

Mound agriculture Form of agriculture found in pre-Columbian North America.

Mughals Muslim dynasty founded by Babur that ruled India, at least nominally, from the mid–1500s until 1857.

Multiculturalism The belief that different cultures can coexist peacefully and equitably in a single country.

Napoleonic Wars Wars waged between France under Napoleon and its European enemies from 1799 to 1815. The fighting spilled over into the Middle East and sparked conflicts in North America and India and independence movements in the Spanish and Portuguese colonies in the Americas.

Nationalism Belief that a people who share the same language, historic experience, and sense of identity make up a nation and that every nation has the right to assert its identity, pursue its destiny, defend its rights, and be the primary focus of its people's loyalty.

Natural selection The process by which only the organisms best adapted to their environment pass on their genetic material to subsequent generations.

Nature versus nurture Debate over the relative importance of inherited characterizes and environmental factors in determining human development.

Nazis Members of the National Socialist German Workers' Party, founded in Germany in 1919 and brought to power in 1933 under Adolf Hitler.

Neanderthal (Trans.) "Neander Valley." Humanlike species, evidence for whose existence was found in the Neander River valley in northern Germany in the mid–nineteenth century. Neanderthals disappeared from the evolutionary record about 30,000 years ago.

Negritude The affirmation of the distinctive nature, quality, and validity of black culture.

Nestorianism The Christian theological doctrine that within Jesus are two distinct and separate persons, divine and human, rather than a single divine person. Orthodox Christians classed Nestorianism as a heresy, but it spread across Central Asia along the Silk Roads.

New Europes Lands in other hemispheres where the environment resembled that of Europe and where immigrants could successfully transplant a European way of life and European culture.

New Rich Rich people whose wealth was acquired in the recent past, often in industry or commerce.

New World Term Europeans applied to the Americas.

Nirvana The spiritual goal of Buddhism, when a person ends the cycle of birth and rebirth and achieves enlightenment and freedom from any attachment to material things.

Noble savage Idealized vision that some people in the West held about certain non-Europeans, especially some Native Americans and Polynesians. It was based on the notions that civilization was a corrupting force and that these peoples lived lives more in tune with nature.

Northwest Passage Water route from the Atlantic to the Pacific through the Arctic archipelago of northern Canada and along the northern coast of Alaska. For centuries, Europeans sought in vain for a more accessible route to the Pacific farther south in North America.

Obsidian Volcanic glass used to make tools, weapons, and mirrors.

Old regime Term for the social, economic, and political institutions that existed in France and the rest of Europe before the French Revolution.

Old World Term for the regions of the world—Europe, parts of Africa and Asia—that were known to Europeans before the discovery of the Americas.

Ongons Tibetan images in which spirits are thought to reside. Shamans claimed to communicate with the ongons.

OPEC The Organization of Petroleum Exporting Countries, an alliance of the world's major oil producers.

Oracle A person or group that claims to be able to have access to knowledge of the future by consulting a god. Ancient rulers often consulted oracles.

Oriental despotism Arbitrary and corrupt rule. Eighteenth-century Europeans saw it as characteristic of Asian or Islamic rulers.

Orthodox Church Dominant Christian church in the Byzantine Empire, the Balkans, and Russia.

Ottoman Empire Islamic empire based in present-day Turkey, with its capital at Istanbul. At its height in the sixteenth century, the Ottoman Empire stretched from Iraq across North Africa to the borders of Morocco and included almost all the Balkans and most of Hungary. The empire gradually declined, but endured until it was dismembered after World War I.

Pampas A vast plain of south-central South America that supports huge herds of cattle and other livestock.

Pan-African Congress A series of five meetings held between 1919 and 1945 that claimed to represent all black Africans and demanded an end to colonial rule.

Pangaea A hypothetical prehistoric supercontinent that included all the landmasses of the Earth.

Partition of India The division in 1947 along ethnic and religious lines of the British Indian Empire into two independent states: India, which was largely Hindu, and Pakistan, which was largely Muslim. The division involved widespread violence in which at least 500,000 people were killed.

Paternalism A social or economic relationship that resembles the dependency that exists between a father and his child.

Patrilineal A society that traces ancestry through the paternal line.

Philosopher's stone A substance that was believed to have the power to change base metals into gold.

Physiocrats Eighteenth-century French political economists who argued that agriculture was the foundation of any country's wealth and recommended agricultural improvements.

Plantation system System of commercial agriculture based on large landholdings, often worked by forced labor.

Polestar Bright star used for navigation.

Positivism Doctrine that asserts the undeniability of human sense perception and the power of reason to prove that what our senses perceive is true.

Pragmatism Philosophy advocated by William James that holds that the standard for evaluating the truth or validity of a theory or concept depends on how well it works and on the results that arise from holding it.

Proletariat The working class, which according to Karl Marx, would overthrow the bourgeoisie.

Protectorate A country or region that, although nominally independent and not a colony, is in fact controlled militarily, politically, and economically by a more powerful foreign state.

Protestantism The theological system of any of the churches of Western Christendom that separated from the Roman Catholic Church during the Reformation. The advent of Protestantism is usually associated with Martin Luther's break from the Catholic Church in the 1520s.

Psychoanalysis Technique developed by Sigmund Freud to treat patients suffering from emotional or psychological disorders by making them aware of their subconscious conflicts, motivations, and desires.

Public sphere Sites for the public discussion of political, social, economic, and cultural issues.

Qing dynasty Last imperial Chinese dynasty (1644–1912), founded when the Manchus, a steppeland people from Manchuria, conquered China. It was succeeded by a republic.

Quantum mechanics Mechanics based on the principle that matter and energy have the properties of both particles and waves.

Quran The sacred text of Islam dictated from God to the Prophet Muhammad by the Archangel Gabriel. Considered by Muslims to contain the final revelations of God to humanity.

Rape of Nanjing Atrocities committed by the Japanese during their occupation of the city of Nanjing, China, in 1937.

Rastafarianism A religious and political movement that began among black people in Jamaica in the 1930s. Its adherents believe that former Emperor Haile Selassie of Ethiopia (r. 1930–1974) was divine and the Messiah whose coming was foretold in the Bible.

Rationalism The doctrine that reason by itself can determine truth and solve the world's problems.

Realpolitik Political doctrine that says that the state is not subject to moral laws and has the right to do whatever safeguards it and advances its interests.

Reformation The Protestant break from the Roman Catholic Church in the sixteenth century.

Renaissance Humanistic revival of classical art, architecture, literature, and learning that originated in Italy in the fourteenth century and spread throughout Europe.

Renewable energy Energy that is not derived from a finite resource such as oil or coal.

Rig Veda A collection of hymns and poems created by a sedentary people living in the area north of the Indus valley where northern India and Pakistan meet. The Rig Veda provides evidence for the theory that invaders destroyed Harappan civilization.

Romanticism Intellectual and artistic movement that arose in reaction to the Enlightenment's emphasis on reason. Romantics had a heightened interest in nature and religion, and emphasized emotion and imagination.

Rus A Slavic-Scandinavian people who created the first Russian state and converted to Orthodox Christianity.

Safavids Shiite dynasty that ruled Persia between 1501 and 1722.

Sahel A semiarid region of north Central Africa south of the Sahara Desert.

Saint Domingue A French colony on Hispaniola that flourished in the eighteenth century by cultivating sugar and coffee with slave labor. It became the modern republic of Haiti after a protracted struggle that began in the 1790s.

Samurai The hereditary Japanese feudal-military aristocracy.

Sati In Hinduism, the burning of a widow on her husband's funeral pyre.

Satyagraha (Trans.) "The force of truth." Nonviolent movement launched by Mohandas K. Gandhi, with the goal of achieving Indian independence.

Savanna A flat grassland of tropical or subtropical regions.

Scientific revolution The sweeping change in the investigation of nature and the view of the universe that took place in Europe in the sixteenth and seventeenth centuries.

Scientism The belief that science and the scientific method can explain everything in the universe and that no other form of inquiry is valid.

Scramble for Africa Late nineteenth-century competition among European powers to acquire colonies in Africa.

Sea Peoples Unknown seafaring people that contributed to the instability of the eastern Mediterranean in the twelfth century B.C.E., attacking Egypt, Palestine, Mesopotamia, Anatolia, and Syria.

Second Vatican Council Council of the Roman Catholic Church that convened at intervals in the 1960s and led to major changes in church liturgy and discipline.

Secularism Belief that religious considerations should be excluded from civil affairs or public education.

Self-determination Principle that a given people or nationality has the right to determine their own political status.

Self-strengthening Mid–nineteenth-century Chinese reform movement initiated in response to Western incursions.

Seljuks A Turkish dynasty ruling in Central and western Asia from the eleventh to the thirteenth centuries.

Serf Agricultural laborer attached to the land owned by a lord and required to perform labor in return for certain legal or customary rights. Unlike slaves, serfs could not usually be sold away from the land.

Shaman A person who acts as an intermediary between humans and spirits or gods. Such a person functions as the medium though which spirits talk to humans.

Sharia Islamic law. The word *sharia* derives from the verb *shara'a*, which is connected to the concepts of "spiritual law" and "system of divine law."

Shiites Members of the most important minority tradition in the Islamic world. Shiites believe that the caliphate is the prerogative of Muhammad's nephew, Ali, and his heirs. Shiism has been the state religion in Iran since the sixteenth century.

Shinto A religion native to Japan, characterized by veneration of nature spirits and ancestors and by a lack of formal dogma.

Shogun A hereditary military ruler of Japan who exercised real power in the name of the emperor, who was usually powerless and relegated to purely ceremonial roles. The last shogun was removed from office in 1868.

Sikhism Indian religion founded by Nanak Guru in the early sixteenth century that blends elements of the Hindu and Muslim traditions.

Silk Roads Key overland trade routes that connected eastern and western Eurasia. The route first began to function in the aftermath of Alexander the Great's expansion into Central Asia at the end of the fourth century B.C.E.

Sioux A nomadic Native American people of central North America who, with the benefit of horses introduced to the Americas by the Spanish, formed a pastoralist empire in the late eighteenth and mid–nineteenth centuries.

Social Darwinism The misapplication of Darwin's biological theories to human societies, often to justify claims of racial superiority and rule by the strong over the weak.

Socialism Any of various theories or systems in which the means of producing and distributing goods is owned collectively or by a centralized government.

Socialist realism An artistic doctrine embraced by many communist and leftist regimes that the sole legitimate purpose of the arts was to glorify the ideals of the state by portraying workers, peasants, and the masses in a strictly representational, nonabstract style.

Sociobiology The study of the biological determinants of social behavior.

Solidarity Polish trade union founded in 1980 that played a key role in bringing down Poland's communist regime.

Solomids Dynasty that seized power in Ethiopia in 1270 C.E. and claimed descent from the Biblical King Solomon.

Song dynasty Dynasty (960–1279) under which China achieved one of its highest levels of culture and prosperity.

Songhay An ancient empire of West Africa in the present-day country of Mali. It reached the height of its power around 1500 C.E.

Soninke West African kingdom on the upper Niger River.

Soviet Russian term for a workers' collective.

State system Organization of early modern Europe into competing nation-states.

Steppe A vast semiarid, grass-covered plain, extending across northern Eurasia and central North America.

Stoicism Philosophy founded on the belief that nature is morally neutral and that the wise person, therefore, achieves happiness by accepting misfortune and practicing self-control.

Stranger effect The tendency some peoples have to esteem and defer to strangers.

Stream of consciousness A literary technique that presents the thoughts and feelings of a character in a novel or story as they arise in the character's mind.

Subsidiarity Doctrine that decisions should always be made at the level closest to the people whom the decisions most affect.

Suez Canal Canal linking the Mediterranean and the Red Sea. It was built by French engineers with European capital and opened in 1869.

Sufis Members of Islamic groups that cultivate mystical beliefs and practices. Sufis have often been instrumental in spreading Islam, but Muslim authorities have often distrusted them.

Sundiata Legendary hero said to have founded the kingdom of Mali in West Africa.

Sunnis Members of the dominant tradition in the Islamic world. Sunnis believe that any member of Muhammad's tribe could be designated caliph.

Surrealism Literary and artistic movement that attempts to express the workings of the subconscious.

Syllogisms A form of argument in which we can infer a necessary conclusion from two premises that prior demonstration or agreement has established to be true.

Syncretic Characterized by the reconciliation or fusion of differing systems of belief.

Taiping Rebellion Rebellion (1852–1864) against the Qing Empire that resulted in tens of millions of deaths and widespread destruction in southern China.

Tang dynasty Chinese dynasty (618–907) famous for its wealth and encouragement of the arts and literature.

Tengri "Ruler of the sky." The supreme deity of the Mongols and other steppeland peoples.

The *Encyclopedia* Twenty-eight volume compendium of Enlightenment thought published in French and edited by Denis Diderot. The first volume appeared in 1751.

The Mongol Peace Era in the thirteenth and fourteenth centuries when Mongol rule created order and stability in Central Asia and enabled goods and ideas to flow along the Silk Roads.

Theory of value The theory that the value of goods is not inherent, but rather determined by supply and demand.

Theravada A conservative branch of Buddhism that adheres to the nontheistic ideal of self-purification to nirvana. Theravada Buddhism emphasizes the monastic ideal and is dominant in present-day Sri Lanka and southeast Asia.

Third Rome Term Russians used for Moscow and Russian Orthodox Christianity. It expressed the belief that the Russian czars were the divinely chosen heirs of the Roman and Byzantine emperors.

Thule Inuit Indigenous Native American people who crossed the Arctic and arrived in Greenland around 1000 C.E.

Tillers Agriculturalists who emphasize the cultivation of plants for food and products, such as timber and cotton.

Tokugawa A family of shoguns that ruled Japan in the name of the emperors from 1603 to 1868.

Trading-post empires Term for the networks of imperial forts and trading posts that Europeans established in Asia in the seventeenth century.

Treasure Fleets Spanish fleets that sailed from the Caribbean each year to bring gold and silver from mines in the Americas back to Europe.

Tundra A treeless area between the ice cap and the tree line of Arctic regions.

Turks A member of any of the Turkic-speaking, nomadic peoples who originated in Central Asia. The Turks eventually converted to Islam and dominated the Middle East.

Uncertainty principle Niels Bohr and Werner Heisenberg's theory that because observers are part of every observation their findings can never be objective.

United Nations International political organization created after World War II to prevent armed conflict, settle international disputes peacefully, and provide cultural, economic, and technological aid. It was the successor to the League of Nations, which had proved to be ineffectual.

Universal love Love between all people, regardless of status, nationality, or family ties.

Upanishads The theoretical sections of the Veda (the literature of the sages of the Ganges civilization). The Upanishads were written down as early as 800 B.C.E.

Urbanization The process by which urban areas develop and expand.

Utilitarianism System of thought devised by Jeremy Bentham, based on the notion that the goal of the state was to create the greatest happiness for the greatest number of people.

Utopianism Belief in a system or ideology aimed at producing a perfect or ideal society.

Vaccination Inoculation with a vaccine to produce immunity to a particular disease.

Vernacular languages The languages that people actually spoke—as opposed to Latin—which was the language used by the Roman Catholic Church and was, for a long time, the language of scholarship, the law, and diplomacy in much of Europe.

Virtual reality A computer simulation of a real or imaginary system.

Wahhabbism Muslim sect founded by Abdul Wahhab (1703–1792), known for its strict observance of the Quran. It is the dominant form of Islam in Saudi Arabia.

Westerlies Winds coming from the west.

Westernization The process by which other cultures adopt Western styles or ways of life.

World system The system of interconnections among the world's population.

World War I Global war (1914–1918) sparked by the assassination of Archduke Francis Ferdinand of Austria by a Serb terrorist in June 1914.

World War II Global conflict that lasted from 1939 to 1945 and ended with the defeat and occupation of Fascist Italy, Nazi Germany, and Japan.

Zen A school of Mahayana Buddhism that asserts that a person can attain enlightenment through meditation, self-contemplation, and intuition.

Ziggurat A tall, tapering Mesopotamian temple. Ziggurats were the physical and cultural centers of Mesopotamian cities.

Zimbabwes Stone-built administrative centers for rulers and the elite in southern Africa. The zimbabwes flourished in the fifteenth century.

Zoroastrianism Iranian religious system founded by Zoroaster that posited a universal struggle between the forces of light (the good) and of darkness (evil).

M

aps use a unique visual language to convey a great deal of information in a relatively simple form. The maps in this book use a variety of different projections—techniques used to show the Earth's curved surface on a flat map—to trace the history of humans from about 150,000 years ago to the present. This brief guide explains the different features on the maps in *The World* and how to interpret the different layers of information embedded in them.

Projection A map projection is used to portray all or part of the round Earth on a flat surface, which cannot be done without some distortion. The projections in *The World* show the Earth at global, continental, country, and city scale and vary with each map. The map shown here uses a Robinson projection, which uses curvature to provide a good balance between the size and shape of the lands being depicted. As any number of projections could have been selected for each map in *The World*, great care was shown in choosing projections that best serve the goals of the author.

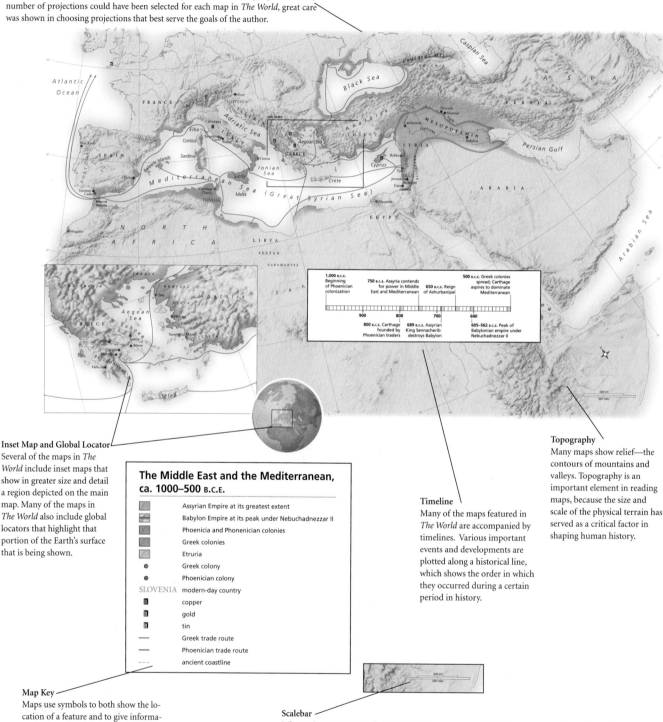

The Middle East and the Mediterranean, ca. 1000–500 B.C.E.

- Assyrian Empire at its greatest extent
- Babylon Empire at its peak under Nebuchadnezzar II
- Phoenicia and Phoenician colonies
- Greek colonies
- Etruria
- Greek colony
- Phoenician colony
- SLOVENIA modern-day country
- copper
- gold
- tin
- Greek trade route
- Phoenician trade route
- ancient coastline

Inset Map and Global Locator
Several of the maps in *The World* include inset maps that show in greater size and detail a region depicted on the main map. Many of the maps in *The World* also include global locators that highlight that portion of the Earth's surface that is being shown.

Map Key
Maps use symbols to both show the location of a feature and to give information about that feature. The symbols are explained in the key that accompanies each map.

Scalebar
When using a map to work out what distances are in reality, it is necessary to refer to the scale of that particular map. Many of the maps in *The World* (such as the one shown here) use a linear scale. This only works on equal-area maps, where distances are true. On maps with projections that are heavily curved, a special "perspective-scale graphic" is used to show distance.

Timeline
Many of the maps featured in *The World* are accompanied by timelines. Various important events and developments are plotted along a historical line, which shows the order in which they occurred during a certain period in history.

Topography
Many maps show relief—the contours of mountains and valleys. Topography is an important element in reading maps, because the size and scale of the physical terrain has served as a critical factor in shaping human history.

KEY TO MAP FEATURES IN *THE WORLD*

PHYSICAL FEATURES

- —— coastline
- ----- ancient coastline
- —— river
- ········ ancient river course
- —— canal

- glacier
- ancient lake
- marshland
- ice cap / sheet
- ice shelf

- △ elevation above sea level (mountain height)
- ⋏ volcano
- ⋊ pass

LATITUDE/LONGITUDE

- —— equator
- —— lines of latitude / longitude
- ----- tropics / polar circles
- 45° degrees of longitude / latitude

BORDERS

- —— international border
- ········ undefined border
- ------ maritime border
- —— internal border
- ········ disputed border

COMMUNICATIONS

- —— major road
- —— minor road
- ▬▬▬ major railway

SETTLEMENT / POSSESSION

- ○ settlement symbol
- ◇ colonial possession

TYPOGRAPHIC KEY

REGIONS

state / political region..... LAOS

administrative region within a state..................... *HENAN*

cultural / undefined region / group.................... *FERGHANA*

MISCELLANEOUS

tropics / polar circles.......... Antarctic Circle

people / cultural group..... *Samoyeds*

annotation........................... **1914** British protectorate

PHYSICAL FEATURES

continent / ocean..... AFRICA

INDIAN OCEAN

landscape features.....*Mekong*

Lake Rudolf

Tien Shan

Sahara

SETTLEMENTS

settlement / symbol location / definition...... Farnham

Major land borders are shown using a solid line.

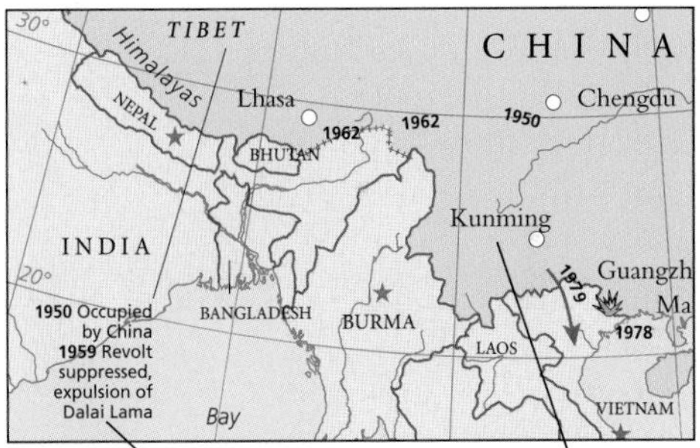

Annotations provide additional explanatory information.

Political control is identified by color.

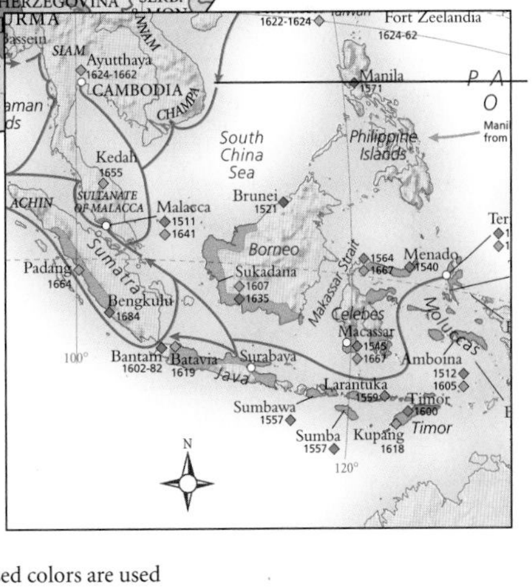

Broad arrows indicate general movement or spread of ideas, crops, or goods.

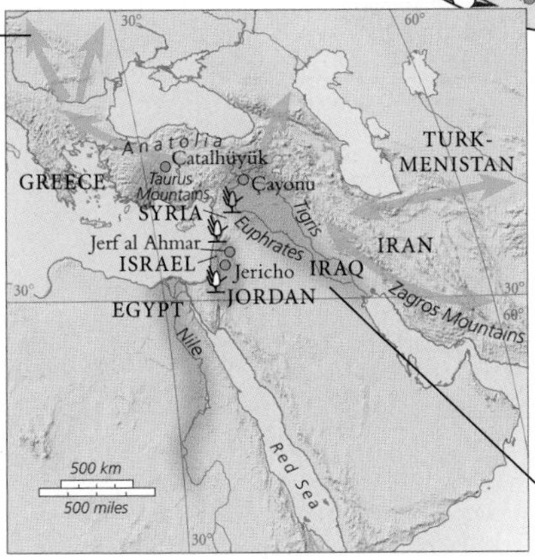

Thin arrows indicate journeys, trade routes, or campaigns.

Diffused colors are used to show a general region.

A NOTE ON DATES AND SPELLINGS

In keeping with common practice among historians of global history, we have used B.C.E. (before the common era) and C.E. (common era) to date events. For developments deep in the past, we have employed the phrase "years ago" to convey to the reader a clear sense of time. Specific dates are only given when necessary and when doing so improves the context of the narrative.

Recognizing that almost every non-English word can be transliterated in any number of ways, we have adopted the most widely used and simplest systems for spelling names and terms. The *pinyin* system of Chinese spelling is used for all Chinese words with the exception of *Yangtze*, which is still widely referred to in its Wade-Giles form. Following common usage, we have avoided using apostrophes in the spelling of Arabic and Persian words, as well as words from other languages—thus, *Quran* and *Kaaba* instead of *Qu'ran* and *Ka'ba*, and *Tbilisi* instead of *T'bilisi*. Diacritical marks, accents, and other specialized symbols are used only if the most common variant of a name or term employs such devices (such as *Çatalhüyük*), if they are part of a personal noun (such as *Nicolás*), or if the inclusion of such markings in the spelling of a word makes pronouncing it easier (*Teotihuacán*).

Throughout the text the first appearance of important non-English words whose pronunciation may be unclear for the reader are followed by phonetic spellings in parentheses, with the syllable that is stressed spelled in capital letters. So, for example *Ugarit* is spelled phonetically as "OO-gah-riht." Chinese words are not stressed, so each syllable is spelled in lowercase letters. Thus, the city of Hangzhou in China is rendered phonetically as "hahng-joh." For monosyllabic words, the phonetic spelling is in lowercase letters. So *Rus* is spelled as "roos." The table below provides a guide for how the vowel sounds in *The World* are represented phonetically.

a	as in *cat, bat*
ah	as in *car, father*
aw	as in *law, paw*
ay	as in *fate, same*
eh	as in *bet, met*
ee	as in *beet, ease*
eye	as in *dine, mine*
ih	as in *if, sniff*
o	as in *more, door*
oh	as in *row, slow*
oo	as in *loop, moo*
ow	as in *cow, mouse*
uh	as in *but, rut*

CHAPTER 1

1. L. van der Post, *The Lost World of the Kalahari* (NY: Morrow, 1958), pp. 252–261.

CHAPTER 2

1. J. L. Harlan, *Crops and Man* (1992), p. 27.

2. Charles Darwin, *The Variation of Plants and Animals under Domestication*, 2 vols (1868), i, pp. 309–310.

CHAPTER 11

1. G. Coédès, *Angor: An Introduction* (1963), pp 104–105.

2. G. Coédès, *Angor: An Introduction* p. 96.

3. Patrologia Latina, cli, col. 0572; William of Malmesbury, *Chronicle of the Kings of England*, 68 IV, ch. 2 (ed. J. A. Giles [1857], p. 360).

CHAPTER 12

1. J. T. C. Liu, *Reform in Sung China: Wang An-Shih and His New Policies* (Cambridge, MA: Harvard University Press, 1957), p. 54.

CHAPTER 13

1. P. Jackson, ed., *The Travels of Friar Willam of Rubruck* (London, 1981), pp. 113–114.

2. R. Latham, ed., *The Travels of Marco Polo* (Harmondsworth, 1972), p. 85.

3. R. L. Davis, *Wind Against the Mountain: The Crisis of Politics and Culture in Thirteenth-Century China* (Cambridge, MA: Harvard University Asia Center, 1996), p. 62.

4. J. Fennell, *The Crisis of Medieval Russia* (Longman Publishing Group, 1983), p. 88.

CHAPTER 14

1. R. Horrox, *The Black Death* (Manchester University Press, 1994), p. 16.

2. N. Cantor, *In the Wake of the Plague* (New York: Perennial/Harper Collins, 2002), p. 199.

3. D. Hall in *Cambridge History of Southeast Asia*, ed. N. Tarling (Cambridge University Press, 1992), i. 218.

4. F. Rosenthal ed. *The Muqaddimah*, 3 vols. (New York: Pantheon Books, 1958), i, 64–65.

CHAPTER 16

1. T. Armstrong, ed., *Yermak's Campaign in Siberia* (London, 1975), pp. 38–50, 59–69, 108, 163; B. Bobrick, *East of the Sun: The Epic Conquest and Tragic History of Siberia* (London, 1993), p. 43.

CHAPTER 18

1. *Principes de la philosophie* Bk I, 8,7; Discours sur la méthode, ch 4.

CHAPTER 20

1. M.E. Itoare, ed., *The Resolution Journal of John Reinhold Forster*, 4 vols. (London, 1982), ii, 409.

CHAPTER 21

1. L. Blussé, *Strange Company* (Leiden, 1986), p. 95.

2. D. Badia, *Viajes de Ali Bey* (Madrid, 2001), p. 514.

CHAPTER 22

1. *The Figure of the Earth* (London, 1738), pp. 38–40, 77–78.

CHAPTER 23

1. J. K. Fairbank, ed., *The Cambridge History of China*, x, part I (Cambridge, 1978), p. 499.

CHAPTER 24

1. D. Northrup, ed., *Indentured Labor in the Age of Imperialism* (New York, 1995), p. 247

CHAPTER 26

1. H. S. Wilson, *Origins of West Africa Nationalism* (London, 1969), p. 167.

CHAPTER 27

1. F. Boas, *The Mind of Primitive Man* (New York, 1913), p. 113.

2. N. Chomsky, *Knowledge of Language* (Wesport, CT: 1986), p. 14.

CHAPTER 28

1. D. A. J. Pernikoff, *Bushido: The Anatomy of Terror* (1943).

CHAPTER 29

1. F. Jameson, *Marxism and Form* (Princeton, 1971), p. XVIII.

2. I. Berlin "My Intellectual Path", *New York Review of Books*, 14 May (1998); The Power of Ideas, ed. H. Hardy (Princeton, 2002), p.12.

item is reproduced by permission of The Huntington Library, San Marino, California; **p. 559** Getty Images Inc.-Hulton Archive Photos; **p. 561** The Hispanic Society of America/Hispanic Society of America.

Chapter 17: p. 564 © Jonathan Blair/CORBIS All Rights Reserved; **p. 567** Koninklijke Bibliothek, The Hague, The Netherlands; **p. 568 top** Instituto Amatller de Arte Hispanico, Barcelona, Spain; **p. 568 bottom** Courtesy of the Bancroft Library, University of California, Berkeley; **p. 569** Courtesy of the John Carter Brown Library at Brown University; **p. 570** Bibliotheque Nationale de France; **p. 571** Musee des Beaux-Arts et d'Archeologie, Besancon, France/Lauros/Giraudon/The Bridgeman Art Library; **p. 574** Victoria&Albert Museum, London, UK/The Bridgeman Art Library; **p. 575** The Granger Collection, New York; **p. 576** Instituto Amatller de Arte Hispanico, Barcelona, Spain; **p. 579** Courtesy of the Library of Congress; **p. 581** Library of the Topkapi Palace Museum; **p. 583**; **p. 584** Picture Desk, Inc./Kobal Collection/The Art Archive/Musée Guimet Paris; **p. 587** Courtesy of the Library of Congress; **p. 588** Courtesy The Rhode Island Historical Society; **p. 592** Kobe City Museum/DNP Archives; **p. 593** Source: Library and Archives of Canada website, www.collectionscanada.ca.

Chapter 18: p. 598 © Richard List/CORBIS All Rights Reserved; **p. 601** By permission of the Folger Shakespeare Library; **p. 602** Bildarchiv Preubischer Kulturbesitz; **p. 605** Courtesy of the Library of Congress; **p. 605** Bodleian Library, Oxford, U.K. Copyright, **p. 606** © National Gallery, London; **p. 609** Courtesy of the Library of Congress; **p. 611** © The National Museum oF Denmark, Ethnographic Collection; **p. 612** Courtesy of the Library of Congress; **p. 617**; **p. 619** Jerry Hardman-Jones/Art Quarterly; **p. 621** The Chester Beatty Library/© The Trustees of the Chester Beatty Library, Dublin; **p. 623** The Bridgeman Art Library International; **p. 625** Bibliotheque Nationale de France; **p. 627** British Library, London, UK/Bridgeman Art Library; **p. 628** Courtesy of the Library of Congress; **p. 631** Courtesy of the Library of Congress.

Chapter 19: p. 634 By permission of The British Library; **p. 642** Derechos reservados © Museo Nacional Del Prado – Madrid; **p. 643** Courtesy of the Library of Congress. Rare Book and Special Collections Divisoin; **p. 644** Archiv fur Kunst und Geschichte, Berlin; **p. 648** Courtesy of the Library of Congress; **p. 649** V&A Picture Library; **p. 649** Courtesy of the Library of Congres; **p. 650** © DAMIR SAGOLJ/Reuters/Corbis; **p. 652** Courtesy of the Library of Congress; **p. 654** Octavio Diaz-Berrio/Diaz-Berrio Photography; **p. 659** Albert Craig; **p. 660** Braemore House, Hampshire, England; **p. 661** Museo De America; **p. 664** ©Historical Picture Archive/CORBIS; **p. 670** Courtesy of the Library of Congress.

Chapter 20: p. 673 Kobe City Museum/DNP Archives; **p. 674** The Art Archive/Museo de Arte Antiga Lisbon/Dagli Orti; **p. 680** Courtesy of the Library of Congress; **p. 681** The Bridgeman Art Library International/Corsham Court, Wiltshire/The Bridgeman Art Library; **p. 683** Courtesy of the Library of Congress; **p. 684** Private Collection/Agnew's, London, UK/The Bridgeman Art Library; **p. 688** The Bridgeman Art Library International/Rijksmuseum, Amsterdam; **p. 688** Courtesy of the Library of Congress; **p. 690** Courtesy of the Library of Congress; **p. 693** Martin Bond/Photo Researchers, Inc; **p. 694** COPYRIGHT © THE BRIDGEMAN ART LIBRARY; **p. 695** Peter Wilson © Dorling Kindersley; **p. 696** The Master and Fellows of Cambridge University Library; **p. 697** The National Trust Photographic Library; **p. 698** © The Natural History Museum, London; **p. 699** National Library of Australia, Canberra, Australia/The Bridgeman Art Library.

Chapter 21: p. 702 © Wolfgang Kaehler/CORBIS All Rights Reserved; **p. 707** Atlas van Stolk, Museum het Schielandhuis; **p. 708** © HIP/Art Resource; **p. 711** By permission of The British Library; **p. 712** V&A Images, Victoria and Albert Museum; **p. 715** Library of Congress; **p. 720** National Library of Scotland; **p. 721 top** Douglas Waugh/Peter Arnold, Inc.; **p. 721 bottom** Henning Christoph/DAS FOTOARCHIV/Peter Arnold, Inc.; **p. 723 top** Neg./Transparency no. 3273(3). (Photo by Lee Boltin). Courtesy Dept. of Library Services, American Museum of Natural History; **p. 723 bottom** Robertstock/Classicstock-.com/Robertstock/Classicstock; **p. 724** Foto Casho; **p. 725** Andy Crawford © Dorling Kindersley, Courtesy of the University Museum of Archaeology and Anthropology, Cambridge; **p. 728** The Boston Athenaeum; **p. 733** Private Collection/The Bridgeman Art Library.

Chapter 22: p. 736 Bristol City Museum and Art Gallery, UK/The Bridgeman Art Library; **p. 738** Musees De Saint-Malo; **p. 740** Musee Lambinet, Versailles/Giraudon/Art Resource, N.Y.; **p. 741** © National Maritime Museum Picture Library, London, England; **p. 742** National Portrait Gallery, London; **p. 743** The National Palace Museum/Collection of the national Palace Museum. Taiwan, Republic of China; **p. 744** Christie's Images, LTD; **p. 746** Ruth and Sherman Lee Institute for Japanese Art at the Clark Center, Hanford. CA; **p. 748** Courtesy of the Library of Congress; **p. 754** Royal Geographical Society, London, UK/The Bridgeman Art Library; **p. 755** © National Maritime Museum Picture Library, London, England; **p. 756** Sotheby's Picture Library/London; **p. 758** Gianni Dagli Orti/Corbis/Bettmann; **p. 761** Prado, Madrid, Spain/The Bridgeman Art Library; **p. 765** U.S. National Library of Medicine.

Chapter 23: p. 769 National Library of Australia; **p. 773 top** Courtesy of the Library of Congress; **p. 773 bottom** © Trustees of the Watts Gallery, Compton, Surrey, UK/The Bridgeman Art Library; **p. 776** The Art Archive/Oriental Art Museum Genoa/Dagli Orti (A); **p. 777**; **p. 780** Chicago Historical Society; **p. 783** © Judith Miller/Dorling Kindersley/Cowan's Historic Americana Auctions; **p. 784** Science Museum London/Bridgeman Art Library; **p. 785** Joseph Mallord William Turner, 1775-1851, "Rain, Steam, and Speed-The Great Western Railway." Oil on canvas, 90.8 x 121.9. © The National Gallery, London; **p. 786** John W. Corbett/John W. Corbett; **p. 787** top © British Empire and Commonwealth Museum, Bristol, UK/Bridgeman Art Library; **p. 788** Science&Society Picture Library; **p. 792** The Granger Collection, New York; **p. 795** Courtesy of the Library of Congress; **p. 798** Asian Art&Archaeology, Ic./Corbis; **p. 800** © CORBIS All Rights Reserved; **p. 803** Riou/Image Works/Mary Evans Picture Library Ltd.

Chapter 24: p. 808 Toho/The Kobal Collection; **p. 812** Sheffield Galleries&Museum Trust; **p. 813** Instituto Amatller de Arte Hispanico, Barcelona, Spain; **p. 817** NTPL/Nadia Mackenzie; **p. 818 top** AKG-Images; **p. 819** © Wolfgang Kaehler/CORBIS All Rights Reserved; **p. 820** Corbis/Bettmann; **p. 822** Courtesy of the Library of Congress; **p. 823** National Archives of South Africa; **p. 826** National Portrait Gallery, London; **p. 828** Image Works/Mary Evans Picture Library Ltd.; **p. 829** ©Bettmann/CORBIS; **p. 830** Courtesy of the Library of Congress; **p. 831** Tate; **p. 833** Corbis/Bettmann; **p. 836** Courtesy of the Library of Congress; **p. 837** The Master and Fellows of Cambridge University Library.

Chapter 25: p. 842 The Art Archive/Eileen Tweedy; **p. 846** Courtesy of the Library of Congress; **p. 848** © English Heritage/PhotoLibrary; Chapter Opener **p. 848** The Art Archive/Eileen Tweedy; **p. 852** Picture Desk, Inc./Kobal Collection; **p. 853** KIT Koninklijk Instituut voor de Tropen/Royal Tropical Institute, Amsterdam; **p. 854** Mary Evans Picture Library; **p. 855** Private Collection/Archives Charmet/The Bridgeman Art Library; **p. 859** © Roger-Viollet/The Image Works; **p. 860** © Sheffield Galleries and Museums Trust, UK/Bridgeman Art Library; **p. 861** top Courtesy of the Library of Congress; **p. 864** City of Vancouver Archives; **p. 865** Courtesy of the Library of Congress; **p. 866** Courtesy of the Library of Congress; **p. 868** Corbis/Bettman; **p. 869** Picture Desk, Inc./Kobal Collection; **p. 870** Wellcome Library, London; **p. 871** Library of Congress; **p. 873** © Kit Kittle/CORBIS All Rights Reserved.

Chapter 26: p. 876 Auckland City Art Gallery, New Zealand/Bridgeman Art Library; **p. 881** The Art Archive/Picture Desk, Inc./Kobal Collection; **p. 884** © Judith Miller/Dorling Kindersley/Sloan's; **p. 885** Courtesy of the Library of Congress; **p. 887** Courtesy of the Library of Congress; **p. 889** Bibliotheque des Arts Decoratifs, Paris, France/The Bridgeman Art Library; **p. 890** © Asian Art&Archaeology, Inc./Corbis; **p. 892** © CORBIS; **p. 893** Sonia Halliday Photographs; **p. 895** Private Collection/Michael Graham-Stewart/The Bridgeman Art Library; **p. 897** Photo by W.&D. Downey/Getty Images; **p. 899**; **p. 905** © CORBIS All Rights Reserved; **p. 912** JOANNA B. PINNEO/Aurora&Quanta Productions Inc.; **p. 913** Culver Pictures, Inc.

Chapter 27: p. 915 Barret Lyon/Barrett Lyon; **p. 916** Manuscripts and Archives, Yale University Library; **p. 921** © SSPL/The Image Works; **p. 924** Abbas/Magnum Photos, Inc.; **p. 925** Courtesy of the Library of Congress; **p. 926** Courtesy of the Library of Congress; **p. 928** ALBERT EINSTEIN and related rights TM/© of The Hebrew University of Jerusalem, used under license. Represented exclusively by Corbis Corporation; **p. 929** Mehau Kulyk/Photo Researchers, Inc.; **p. 930** Corbis/Bettmann; **p. 931** Bluestone/Photo Researchers, Inc.; **p. 933** © CORBIS; **p. 934** Courtesy of the Library of Congress; **p. 935** Photo by Max Halberstatt, Mary Evans Picture Library. Freud Copyrights courtesy of W. E. Freud; **p. 938** Gisele Freund/Photo Researchers, Inc.; **p. 943** The Red Mansion Foundation; **p. 944** Robert Holmes/Corbis/Bettmann; **p. 946** © Judith Miller/Dorling Kindersley/Biblion; **p. 946** © Judith Miller/Dorling Kindersley/Biblion; **p. 947** © Paul Saltzman (Contact Press Images); **p. 948** J.M. Janzen/Art Quarterly; **p. 949** TWO ARTS/CD/THE KOBAL COLLECTION.

Chapter 28: p. 952 © Herge'/Moulinsart 2006; **p. 956** Private Collection/The Bridgeman Art Library; **p. 959** Corbis/Bettmann; **p. 960** Imperial War Museum, London; **p. 961** Margaret Bourke-White/Getty Images/Time Life Pictures; **p. 962** Photofest; **p. 964** Museo Nacional Centro de Arte Reina Sofia; **p. 966** © Topham/The Image Works; **p. 967** Corbis/Bettmann; **p. 968** top Getty Images Inc.-Hulton Archive Photos; **p. 968** bottom Corbis/Bettmann; **p. 971** Robert Hardy/Picture Post/Getty Images; **p. 972** Courtesy of the Library of Congress; **p. 975** Nick Ut/AP Wide World Photos; **p. 976** © Swim Ink 2, LLC/CORBIS; **p. 978** Private Collection/The Bridgeman Art Library; **p. 981** Courtesy of the Library of Congress; **p. 982** © Ali Ali/CORBIS All Rights Reserved; **p. 983** © Bettmann/CORBIS All Rights Reserved; **p. 986** AP Wide World Photos.

Chapter 29: p. 992 Courtesy of the Library of Congress; **p. 998** Reprinted by the permission of the American Cancer Society, Inc.; **p. 999** © Philippe Caron/CORBIS All Rights Reserved; **p. 1001** AP Wide World Photos; **p. 1002** © Peter Simon; **p. 1003** Getty Images Inc.-Hulton Archive Photos; **p. 1004** Corbis/Bettmann; **p. 1005** ©Reuters NewMedia Inc./CORBIS; **p. 1007** "Building More Stately Mansions" Aaron Douglas (1944) Oil on canvas 58 x 42, Carl Van Vechten Gallery of Fine Arts, Fisk University Galleries, Nashville, Tennessee; **p. 1008** © Gueorgui Pinkhassov/Magnum P; **p. 1009** © (Photographer)/CORBIS All Rights Reserved; **p. 1010** Courtesy of the Library of Congress; **p. 1011** © Robert Vos/ANP/epa/Corbis; **p. 1012** © Liu Liqun/CORBIS All Rights Reserved; **p. 1015** MARK EDWARDS/Peter Arnold, Inc.; **p. 1018** © Reuters/CORBIS; **p. 1020** Carlos Reyes-Manzo/Andes Press Agency; **p. 1021** Courtesy of the Library of Congress.

Chapter 30: p. 1029 Peter/Georgina Bowater/Creative Eye/MIRA.com; **p. 1030** Musee d'Art Moderne de la Ville de Paris, Paris, France/The Bridgeman Art Library; **p. 1031 top** Tony Korody/Sygma; **p. 1031 bottom** Simon Harris/Robert Harding World Imagery; **p. 1032** Getty Images Inc.-Hulton Archive Photos; p. 1035 Courtesy of the Library of Congress; **p. 1037 top** © Mark Ralston/Reuters/Corbis; **p. 1037 bottom** © Daniel Laine/CORBIS All Rights Reserved; **p. 1040** UNEP/Peter Arnold, Inc; **p. 1042** National Oceanic and Atmospheric Administration NOAA; **p. 1044** Getty Images Inc.-Hulton Archive Photos; **p. 1045** AP Wide World Photos; **p. 1048** National Geographic Image Collection/NG Maps/National Geographic Image Collection; **p. 1054** Cidihca; **p. 1055** Dr. Silvia W. de Groot.

CONTENTS

PRIMARY SOURCE: DOCUMENTS IN GLOBAL HISTORY

Excerpt from the *Novgorod Chronicle*
Roger Bacon on experimental science
St. Francis of Assisi, Selection from *Admonitions*
St. Thomas Aquinas, from *Summa Theologica*, "Of Human Law"

Visual Sources
Mongol Yurt
Illustration from *The Life of Christ*
Illustration from *Die Proprietatibus Rerum*
Medieval European Worldview
Medieval European Medical Illustrations
Tamar, "King" of Georgia

14 The Revenge of Nature: Plague, Cold, and the Limits of Disaster in the Fourteenth Century

Text Sources
Marchione di Coppo Stefani, *"Concerning a Mortality in the City of Florence"*
University of Paris Medical Faculty, Writings on the Plague
John Ball Sermon
Ibn Battuta, Selections from the *Rihla*
Ibn Battuta, from *The Travels of Ibn Battuta*
Al Umari Describes Mansa Musa of Mali
Selections from the *Nagara-Kertagama*

Visual Sources
The Black Death
The First Horseman of the Apocalypse
The Wheel of Fortune
European Medieval depiction of Adam and Eve
Ozette Whale Fin

15 Expanding Worlds: Recovery in the Late Fourteenth and Fifteenth Centuries

Text Sources
From the *Narrative of the Journey of Abd-ar-Razzak*
Ma Huan, *The Overall Survey of the Ocean's Shores*
An Essay Question from the Chinese Imperial Examination System
Anonymous Descriptions of the Cities of Zanj
Excerpts from the Journal of Vasco da Gama

Visual Sources
Map of the Yellow River
Illustrations from the *Shanamah* (the *Book of Kings*)
Great Zimbabwe
The Founding of Tenochtitlán
French Customary Laws
God the Creator, from the *Nuremberg Chronicle*
Ptolemaic World Map
Illustration from *The Properties of Things*
Sketches by Leonardo da Vinci
Woodcut by Albrecht Durer Showing Perspective
Cupola of Santa Maria Fiore Church, Florence
First Printed Medical Text with Illustrations
Illustration from *The Travels of Sir John of Mandeville*

PART 7 Convergence and Divergence to ca. 1700

16 Imperial Arenas: New Empires in the Sixteenth and Seventeenth Centuries

Text Sources
Toyotomi Hideyoshi on the Conquest of China
Toyotomi: Hideyoshi on the expulsion of Christian Missionaries
Abul Fazl Allami, from the *Ain-i-Akbari*
Excerpts from the Biography of Emperor Akbar
Ogier Ghiselin de Busbecq, "Suleiman the Lawgiver"
Domingo Navarrete, "Of My Stay in the Kingdom of Makassar"
Jan van Linschoten on Dutch Business in the Indian Ocean

Duarte Barbosa, accounts of his journeys to Africa and India
Hans Mayr, Account of Francisco d'Almeida's Attack on Kilwa and Mombasa
Excerpts from the Journal of Gaspar Correa
Bernal Diaz del Castillo, from *The True History of the Conquest of New Spain*
Bartoleme de las Casas, from *Brief Account of the Devastation of the Indies*
Aztec Accounts of the Conquest of Mexico (from *The Broken Spears*)

Visual Sources
Chinese Map of Central Asia
Russian Views of "Peoples of the Empire"
Ottoman Naval Attack on the Island of Gerbi
View of Kilwa
View of Hormuz
Illustration from Bernadino de Sahagun's *Historia*
View of Tenochtitlán
Illustration from Columbus's account of the discovery of the Indies
Vespucci's landing in America
Francis Drake and Indians
Portuguese Map of the Caribbean and South America
Sixteenth-Century Portolan
Sixteenth-Century Map of the Atlantic
World Map by Battista Agnese
1630 Portuguese Map of the Indian Ocean
A view of Seventeenth-Century Portuguese trading posts
Jesuit Martyrs in Japan
Pocahontas, Powhatan, and John Smith

17 The Ecological Revolution of Sixteenth and Seventeenth Centuries

Text Sources
Thomas Gage, writings on Chocolate
Shi Daonon, "Death of Rats"
Thomas Dudley, Letter to Lady Bridget, Countess of Lincoln

Visual Sources
Don Alvaro of Kongo
View of Loango
Map of Kongo
Gold Coast dress
Sugar Plantation, Brazil
The Fur Trade in New York
Cod Fishing
Map of Greenland
Samuel de Champlain's map of Eastern North America
Map of Virginia
King Philip's War
View of Cuzco
Illustrations from *Voyages and Travels*
Illustrations from Jacques le Moyne and Theodore de Bry of Native Americans
First Dutch National Atlas

18 Mental Revolutions: Religion and Science in the Sixteenth and Seventeenth Centuries

Text Sources
Excerpts from Hideyoshi on Christian missionaries in Japan (see ch. 17)
Selections from the journals of Matteo Ricci
Saint Francis Xavier on the Conversion of India
Pope Paul III, *Sublimus Dei*, "On the Enslavement and Evangelization of Indians in the New World"
William Bradford, Excerpt from *Of Plymouth Plantation*
Excerpts from the Journal of Christopher Columbus
Nicolaus Copernicus, excerpt from *On the Revolutions of the Heavenly Spheres*
Francis Bacon, excerpt from *Novum Organum*
René Descartes, from *The Discourse on Method and Metaphysical Meditations*
Isaac Newton, excerpt from *Opticks*

29 The Pursuit of Utopia: Civil Society in the Twentieth Century

30 The Embattled Biosphere: The Twentieth-Century Environment

Text Sources

Visual Sources

SINGLE PC LICENSE AGREEMENT AND LIMITED WARRANTY

READ THIS LICENSE CAREFULLY BEFORE OPENING THIS PACKAGE. BY OPENING THIS PACKAGE, YOU ARE AGREEING TO THE TERMS AND CONDITIONS OF THIS LICENSE. IF YOU DO NOT AGREE, DO NOT OPEN THE PACKAGE. PROMPTLY RETURN THE UNOPENED PACKAGE AND ALL ACCOMPANYING ITEMS TO THE PLACE YOU OBTAINED THEM.

1. GRANT OF LICENSE AND OWNERSHIP: THE ENCLOSED COMPUTER PROGRAMS <<AND DATA>> ("SOFTWARE") ARE LICENSED, NOT SOLD, TO YOU BY PEARSON EDUCATION, INC. PUBLISHING AS PEARSON PRENTICE HALL ("WE" OR THE "COMPANY") AND IN CONSIDERATION OF YOUR PURCHASE OR ADOPTION OF THE ACCOMPANYING COMPANY TEXTBOOKS AND/OR OTHER MATERIALS, AND YOUR AGREEMENT TO THESE TERMS. WE RESERVE ANY RIGHTS NOT GRANTED TO YOU. YOU OWN ONLY THE DISK(S) BUT WE AND/OR OUR LICENSORS OWN THE SOFTWARE ITSELF. THIS LICENSE ALLOWS YOU TO USE AND DISPLAY YOUR COPY OF THE SOFTWARE ON A SINGLE COMPUTER (I.E., WITH A SINGLE CPU) AT A SINGLE LOCATION FOR ACADEMIC USE ONLY, SO LONG AS YOU COMPLY WITH THE TERMS OF THIS AGREEMENT. YOU MAY MAKE ONE COPY FOR BACK UP, OR TRANSFER YOUR COPY TO ANOTHER CPU, PROVIDED THAT THE SOFTWARE IS USABLE ON ONLY ONE COMPUTER.

2. RESTRICTIONS: YOU MAY NOT TRANSFER OR DISTRIBUTE THE SOFTWARE OR DOCUMENTATION TO ANYONE ELSE. EXCEPT FOR BACKUP, YOU MAY NOT COPY THE DOCUMENTATION OR THE SOFTWARE. YOU MAY NOT NETWORK THE SOFTWARE OR OTHERWISE USE IT ON MORE THAN ONE COMPUTER OR COMPUTER TERMINAL AT THE SAME TIME. YOU MAY NOT REVERSE ENGINEER, DISASSEMBLE, DECOMPILE, MODIFY, ADAPT, TRANSLATE, OR CREATE DERIVATIVE WORKS BASED ON THE SOFTWARE OR THE DOCUMENTATION. YOU MAY BE HELD LEGALLY RESPONSIBLE FOR ANY COPYING OR COPYRIGHT INFRINGEMENT THAT IS CAUSED BY YOUR FAILURE TO ABIDE BY THE TERMS OF THESE RESTRICTIONS.

3. TERMINATION: THIS LICENSE IS EFFECTIVE UNTIL TERMINATED. THIS LICENSE WILL TERMINATE AUTOMATICALLY WITHOUT NOTICE FROM THE COMPANY IF YOU FAIL TO COMPLY WITH ANY PROVISIONS OR LIMITATIONS OF THIS LICENSE. UPON TERMINATION, YOU SHALL DESTROY THE DOCUMENTATION AND ALL COPIES OF THE SOFTWARE. ALL PROVISIONS OF THIS AGREEMENT AS TO LIMITATION AND DISCLAIMER OF WARRANTIES, LIMITATION OF LIABILITY, REMEDIES OR DAMAGES, AND OUR OWNERSHIP RIGHTS SHALL SURVIVE TERMINATION.

4. LIMITED WARRANTY AND DISCLAIMER OF WARRANTY: COMPANY WARRANTS THAT FOR A PERIOD OF 60 DAYS FROM THE DATE YOU PURCHASE THIS SOFTWARE (OR PURCHASE OR ADOPT THE ACCOMPANYING TEXTBOOK), THE SOFTWARE, WHEN PROPERLY INSTALLED AND USED IN ACCORDANCE WITH THE DOCUMENTATION, WILL OPERATE IN SUBSTANTIAL CONFORMITY WITH THE DESCRIPTION OF THE SOFTWARE SET FORTH IN THE DOCUMENTATION, AND THAT FOR A PERIOD OF 30 DAYS THE DISK(S) ON WHICH THE SOFTWARE IS DELIVERED SHALL BE FREE FROM DEFECTS IN MATERIALS AND WORKMANSHIP UNDER NORMAL USE. THE COMPANY DOES NOT WARRANT THAT THE SOFTWARE WILL MEET YOUR REQUIREMENTS OR THAT THE OPERATION OF THE SOFTWARE WILL BE UNINTERRUPTED OR ERRORFREE. YOUR ONLY REMEDY AND THE COMPANY'S ONLY OBLIGATION UNDER THESE LIMITED WARRANTIES IS, AT THE COMPANY'S OPTION, RETURN OF THE DISK FOR A REFUND OF ANY AMOUNTS PAID FOR IT BY YOU OR REPLACEMENT OF THE DISK. THIS LIMITED WARRANTY IS THE ONLY WARRANTY PROVIDED BY THE COMPANY AND ITS LICENSORS, AND THE COMPANY AND ITS LICENSORS DISCLAIM ALL OTHER WARRANTIES, EXPRESS OR IMPLIED, INCLUDING WITHOUT LIMITATION, THE IMPLIED WARRANTIES OF MERCHANTABILITY AND FITNESS FOR A PARTICULAR PURPOSE. THE COMPANY DOES NOT WARRANT, GUARANTEE OR MAKE ANY REPRESENTATION REGARDING THE ACCURACY, RELIABILITY, CURRENTNESS, USE, OR RESULTS OF USE, OF THE SOFTWARE.

5. LIMITATION OF REMEDIES AND DAMAGES: IN NO EVENT, SHALL THE COMPANY OR ITS EMPLOYEES, AGENTS, LICENSORS, OR CONTRACTORS BE LIABLE FOR ANY INCIDENTAL, INDIRECT, SPECIAL, OR CONSEQUENTIAL DAMAGES ARISING OUT OF OR IN CONNECTION WITH THIS LICENSE OR THE SOFTWARE, INCLUDING FOR LOSS OF USE, LOSS OF DATA, LOSS OF INCOME OR PROFIT, OR OTHER LOSSES, SUSTAINED AS A RESULT OF INJURY TO ANY PERSON, OR LOSS OF OR DAMAGE TO PROPERTY, OR CLAIMS OF THIRD PARTIES, EVEN IF THE COMPANY OR AN AUTHORIZED REPRESENTATIVE OF THE COMPANY HAS BEEN ADVISED OF THE POSSIBILITY OF SUCH DAMAGES. IN NO EVENT SHALL THE LIABILITY OF THE COMPANY FOR DAMAGES WITH RESPECT TO THE SOFTWARE EXCEED THE AMOUNTS ACTUALLY PAID BY YOU, IF ANY, FOR THE SOFTWARE OR THE ACCOMPANYING TEXTBOOK. BECAUSE SOME JURISDICTIONS DO NOT ALLOW THE LIMITATION OF LIABILITY IN CERTAIN CIRCUMSTANCES, THE ABOVE LIMITATIONS MAY NOT ALWAYS APPLY TO YOU.

6. GENERAL: THIS AGREEMENT SHALL BE CONSTRUED IN ACCORDANCE WITH THE LAWS OF THE UNITED STATES OF AMERICA AND THE STATE OF NEW YORK, APPLICABLE TO CONTRACTS MADE IN NEW YORK, EXCLUDING THE STATE'S LAWS AND POLICIES ON CONFLICTS OF LAW, AND SHALL BENEFIT THE COMPANY, ITS AFFILIATES AND ASSIGNEES. THIS AGREEMENT IS THE COMPLETE AND EXCLUSIVE STATEMENT OF THE AGREEMENT BETWEEN YOU AND THE COMPANY AND SUPERSEDES ALL PROPOSALS OR PRIOR AGREEMENTS, ORAL, OR WRITTEN, AND ANY OTHER COMMUNICATIONS BETWEEN YOU AND THE COMPANY OR ANY REPRESENTATIVE OF THE COMPANY RELATING TO THE SUBJECT MATTER OF THIS AGREEMENT. IF YOU ARE A U.S. GOVERNMENT USER, THIS SOFTWARE IS LICENSED WITH "RESTRICTED RIGHTS" AS SET FORTH IN SUBPARAGRAPHS (A)-(D) OF THE COMMERCIAL COMPUTER-RESTRICTED RIGHTS CLAUSE AT FAR 52.227-19 OR IN SUBPARAGRAPHS (C)(1)(II) OF THE RIGHTS IN TECHNICAL DATA AND COMPUTER SOFTWARE CLAUSE AT DFARS 252.227-7013, AND SIMILAR CLAUSES, AS APPLICABLE.

SHOULD YOU HAVE ANY QUESTIONS CONCERNING THIS AGREEMENT OR IF YOU WISH TO CONTACT THE COMPANY FOR ANY REASON, PLEASE CONTACT IN WRITING: LEGAL DEPARTMENT, PRENTICE HALL, 1 LAKE STREET, UPPER SADDLE RIVER, NJ 07450 OR CALL PEARSON EDUCATION PRODUCT SUPPORT AT 1-800-677-6337.

The Political World

ARCTIC OCEAN

Arctic Circle

USA (Alaska)

Great Bear Lake

Great Slave Lake

Baffin Bay

Greenland (to Denmark)

Bering Sea

Aleutian Is (to US)

CANADA

Hudson Bay

ICELAND

Faer (to

RI OF I

Cha

PACIFIC OCEAN

Lake Winnipeg

Lake Superior

Lake Michigan

Lake Huron

Lake Ontario

Lake Erie

St Pierre & Miquelon (to France)

ATLANTIC OCEAN

Azores (to Portugal)

Gibraltar (to
Ceuta (to S
Melilla (to S

UNITED STATES OF AMERICA

Bermuda (to UK)

Madeira (to Portugal)

Casab

Midway Islands (to US)

Tropic of Cancer

Guadalupe (to Mexico)

Gulf of Mexico

BAHAMAS

Canary Islands (to Spain)

Hawaii (to US)

MEXICO

CUBA

Turks & Caicos Is (to UK)

Puerto Rico (to US)

WESTERN SAHARA (occupied by Morocco)

MAURI

Johnston Atoll (to US)

Revillagigedo Islands (to Mexico)

Cayman Is (to UK)

JAMAICA HAITI

DOM. REP.

Virgin Is (to US)

British Virgin Is (to UK)
Anguilla (to UK)

ANTIGUA & BARBUDA

Guadeloupe (to France)

CAPE VERDE

SENEGAL

Kingman Reef (to US)

Palmyra Atoll (to US)

Clipperton Island (to French Polynesia)

BELIZE

Navassa I. (to US)

ST KITTS & NEVIS

Montserrat (to UK)

DOMINICA

Martinique (to France)

GUINEA

GUATEMALA

HONDURAS

Netherlands Antilles (to Neth.)

ST LUCIA

ST VINCENT & THE GRENADINES

BARBADOS

GAMBIA

GUINEA-BISSAU

EL SALVADOR

NICARAGUA

Caribbean Sea

GRENADA

SIERRA LEONE

Baker & Howland Is (to US)

Equator

Jarvis I. (to US)

Aruba (to Neth.)

COSTA RICA

PANAMA

VENEZUELA

TRINIDAD & TOBAGO

LIBERI

KIRIBATI

Galapagos Is (to Ecuador)

COLOMBIA

SURINAM

GUYANA

French Guiana (to France)

ECUADOR

Fernando de Noronha (to Brazil)

Tokelau (to NZ)

PERU

B R A Z I L

Asc (to S

SAMOA

Wallis & Futuna (to France)

American Samoa (to US)

Cook Islands (to NZ)

French Polynesia (to France)

Lake Titicaca

ATLANT OCEAN

TONGA

Niue (to NZ)

BOLIVIA

Trindade (to Brazil)

Tropic of Capricorn

PACIFIC OCEAN

PARAGUAY

Pitcairn Islands (to UK)

San Felix Island (to Chile)

San Ambrosio Island (to Chile)

Kermadec Islands (to NZ)

Easter Island (to Chile)

Sala y Gomez (to Chile)

C H I L E

A R G E N T I N A

Tristan da (to St Hel

Juan Fernandez Islands (to Chile)

URUGUAY

Gou (to Trist

Chatham Islands (to NZ)

Falkland Islands (to UK)

South Georgia & South Sandwich Islands (to UK)

South Shetland Islands

South Orkney Islands

S O U T H E R

Antarctic Circle

Peter I Island (to Norway)

Ronne Ice Shelf

Ross Ice Shelf